# TECHNOLOGY in Action

# Premium Media Site Access Code

**Improve your grade with hands-on tools and resources!**

- Master key terms and vocabulary
- Assess your knowledge with fun Crossword Puzzles and Jeopardy games
- Prepare for exams by taking practice quizzes

And for even more tools, you can access the following Premium Resources using your Access Code. Register now to get the most out of ***Technology in Action!***

- Practice what you learn with interactive Active Helpdesk Calls*
- Use the Sound Byte lessons to practice your skills*
- Experience real-world computer situations with Simulations*
- *Check Your Understanding* section
- *Replay* videos from the authors provide a video review of each chapter Part in an easy-to-use format you can use on your phones, tablets, or computers!*

*Access code required for these premium resources

**Your Access Code is:**

Note: If there is no silver foil covering the access code, it may already have been redeemed, and therefore may no longer be valid. In that case, you can purchase online access using a major credit card or PayPal account. To do so, go to **www.pearsonhighered.com/techinaction**, select your book cover, click on "Buy Access" and follow the on-screen instructions.

**To Register:**

- To Start you will need a valid email address and this access code.
- Go to **www.pearsonhighered.com/techinaction** and scroll to find your text book.
- Once you've selected your text, on the Home Page, click the link to access the Student Premium Content.
- Click the Register button and follow the on-screen instructions.
- After you register, you can sign in any time via the log-in area on the same screen.

**System Requirements**

Windows 7 Ultimate Edition; IE 8
Windows Vista Ultimate Edition SP1; IE 8
Windows XP Professional SP3; IE 7
Windows XP Professional SP3; Firefox 3.6.4
Mac OS 10.5.7; Firefox 3.6.4
Mac OS 10.6; Safari 5

**Technical Support**

http://247pearsoned.custhelp.com

Photo credits: Goodluz/wrangler/Elena Elisseeva/Shutterstock

# Technology in Action

## COMPLETE

**11TH EDITION**

# Technology in Action

## COMPLETE

**11TH EDITION**

Alan Evans | Kendall Martin | Mary Anne Poatsy

PEARSON

Boston Columbus Indianapolis New York San Francisco Upper Saddle River
Amsterdam Cape Town Dubai London Madrid Milan Munich Paris Montréal Toronto
Delhi Mexico City Sâo Paulo Sydney Hong Kong Seoul Singapore Taipei Tokyo

**Editor in Chief:** Michael Payne
**Executive Acquisitions Editor:** Jenifer Niles
**Production Team Lead:** Laura Burgess
**Program Team Lead:** Scott DiSanno
**Project Manager:** Rhonda Aversa
**Editorial Assistant:** Melissa Davis
**Development Editor:** Shannon LeMay-Finn
**Director of Marketing:** Maggie Moylan Leen
**Marketing Coordinator:** Susan Osterlitz
**Marketing Assistant:** Jeremiah Drozd
**Operations Specialist:** Maura Zaldivar-Garcia
**Director of Digital Development:** Taylor Ragan
**Editor, Digital Learning & Assessment:** Eric Hakanson
**Media Project Manager, Production:** John Cassar
**Art Director:** Jonathan Boylan
**Cover Design:** Jonathan Boylan
**Cover Art:** © pixelparticle /Shutterstock
**Full-Service Project Management:** PreMediaGlobal
**Composition:** PreMediaGlobal
**Printer/Binder:** Courier/Kendallville
**Cover Printer:** Lehigh-Phoenix Color/Hagerstown
**Text Font:** 9/11 Helvetica Neue LT Std

Credits and acknowledgments borrowed from other sources and reproduced, with permission, in this textbook appear on the appropriate page within the text.



Library of Congress Control Number: 2014930365

10 9 8 7 6 5 4 3
V011

ISBN 10: 0-13-380296-5
ISBN 13: 978-0-13-380296-2

# Contents at a Glance

# Contents

## Chapter 1



## Chapter 2

## Chapter 3

# Chapter 5

## Chapter 6



## Chapter 7

## Chapter 9

# Chapter 10

# Chapter 12

## Chapter 13

# Dedication

For my wife, Patricia, whose patience, understanding, and support continue to make this work possible . . . especially when I stay up past midnight writing! And to my parents, Jackie and Dean, who taught me the best way to achieve your goals is to constantly strive to improve yourself through education.

**Alan Evans**

For all the teachers, mentors, and gurus who have popped in and out of my life.

**Kendall Martin**

For my husband, Ted, who unselfishly continues to take on more than his fair share to support me throughout this process, and for my children, Laura, Carolyn, and Teddy, whose encouragement and love have been inspiring.

**Mary Anne Poatsy**

# What's New
## Technology in Action, 11th Edition

We are delighted for you to explore the Eleventh Edition of *Technology in Action*!

*Explore, discover, and experience technology with the immersive and adaptive* ***Technology in Action****—the book that uses technology to teach technology!*

*Technology in Action* is a learning system that pushes the envelope of what is possible in technology, and what is helpful in teaching. It is a system that fits the way students are learning today and uses rich companion media to engage students in and out of the classroom while providing essential training on computer concepts.

### What's New

- All content has been updated as needed to ensure coverage of the most current technology and end-of-chapter exercises have been updated throughout the book.

**COMPLETELY UPDATED AND ENHANCED media offerings including:**

- **Sound Bytes:** These multimedia lessons help demystify computer concepts with audio and video presentations. All of the Sound Bytes have been updated to provide timely and accurate information.
- **Active Helpdesk Calls:** These highly interactive, engaging activities provide students with a realistic experience of how help is delivered via phone, live chat, FAQ searches, and so on. Students play the role of the staff answering technology questions using these various approaches.
  - A virtual supervisor provides support to the student throughout calls.
  - Assessment questions after each call provide instructors with a tool to gauge and track students' progress.
- MyITLab **Enhanced eBook:** The Enhanced eBook in MyITLab provides a continuous digital learning in a completely interactive environment that allows students to use technology as they learn. They don't have to stop reading to go find the activities such as Helpdesks, Sound Bytes, and Replay Videos—they just click on them and immediately experience the activity.
- MyITLab **TechTown**: This fully interactive scenario-based simulation game lets students create their own avatar and interact in a series of knowledge and puzzle-based scenarios. As they work and play, they explore the core topics of computer concepts—from what a computer is to software, hardware, networking, the Internet, social media, and more!
- MyITLab **NEW! Adaptive Dynamic Study Modules**, created specifically for *Technology in Action,* 11th Edition, provide students with personalized review based on their strengths and weaknesses.
- **UPDATED! *Replay* videos:** The *Replay* videos provide an author-narrated video review of each *Chapter Part* in an easy-to-use format students can view on their phones, tablets, or computers!
- ***With Tech Bytes Weekly, every week is new!*** This weekly newsfeed provides two timely articles to save instructors the prep time required for adding interesting and relevant news items to their weekly lectures. Tech Bytes Weekly also features valuable links and other resources, including discussion questions and course activities.
- **Jeopardy! Game and Crossword Puzzles:** These assets give students a fun way to challenge their knowledge.

In addition to these changes, all chapters have been updated with new images, current topics, and state-of-the art technology coverage. Some of the chapter changes are listed here:

**Chapter 1: Using Technology to Change the World**

- Throughout the chapter, text, figures, and photos have been updated.

**Chapter 2: Looking at Computers: Understanding the Parts**

- Throughout the chapter, text, figures, and photos have been updated.
- Gesture technology is now covered in the "How Cool Is This?" feature.

- The Keyboard section has been redesigned to reflect the shift from physical keyboards to touch screens.
- Enhanced coverage of transparent OLED displays has been added.
- Coverage of cloud storage solutions has been augmented to reflect student needs and trends.
- The "Try This: What's Inside My Computer?" activity has been updated to reflect Windows 8.1 changes.

**Chapter 3: Using the Internet: Making the Most of the Web's Resources**

- Throughout the chapter, text, figures, and photos have been updated.
- NEW "How Cool Is This?" feature has been added on the Screenleap.com screen sharing app.
- NEW Bits & Bytes on HTML5 vs Flash, Maxthon, and Outlook.com.
- Streaming audio and streaming video have been condensed to discuss streaming media in general.

**Technology in Focus: The History of the PC**

- This Tech in Focus has been updated throughout.

**Chapter 4: Application Software: Programs That Let You Work and Play**

- Throughout the chapter, text, figures, and photos have been updated.
- NEW "How Cool Is This?" feature has been added on eye-tracking software.
- "Trends in IT: Mobile Commerce: What Have You Bought with Your Phone Lately?" has been updated.
- All screen images of Microsoft Office applications have been updated to Office 2013; and discussion of new features of Office 2013 have been included in the text.
- "Bits & Bytes: Alternatives to PowerPoint" has been revised to include additional alternatives.
- NEW "Bits & Bytes: Mirror, Mirror . . ." has been added, replacing PDF Bits & Bytes on video file formats for portable media players from the previous edition.
- Media Management Software has been removed, with important pieces of the information mentioned in other places in the chapter.

**Chapter 5: System Software: The Operating System, Utility Programs, and File Management**

- Throughout the chapter, text, figures, and photos have been updated.
- Content throughout has been updated to include coverage of Windows 8.1 and OS X Mavericks.
- NEW "How Cool Is This?" feature has been added on Google Chrome syncing.
- NEW Ethics in IT feature has been added—"The Great Debate: Is Mac OS X Safer than Windows?"
- NEW "Try This: Organizing Tiles on the Start Screen in Windows 8" activity has been added.
- "The Windows Interface" section has been revised and updated to reflect changes in Windows 8.1.
- NEW "Bits & Bytes: Save Files to the Cloud Right from Your Apps" has been added.

**Technology in Focus: Information Technology Ethics**

- This Tech in Focus has been updated throughout.
- The "Using Computers to Support Ethical Conduct" section has been updated to cover Google Crisis Response.

**Chapter 6: Understanding and Assessing Hardware: Evaluating Your System**

- Throughout the chapter, text has been updated to match current hardware standards, and figures and photos have been updated.
- NEW "How Cool Is This?" feature has been added on the Arduino microcontroller project.
- NEW "Bits & Bytes: The Haswell Boost" has been added replacing the "Bits and Bytes: Not Much Power at All."
- All references to operating system utilities have been updated to reflect changes in Windows 8.1.
- Summary table figures have been redesigned for increased clarity.
- Emphasis has been shifted from desktop computers toward mobile devices.

**Chapter 7: Networking: Connecting Computing Devices**

- Throughout the chapter, text, figures, and photos have been updated.
- NEW "How Cool Is This?" feature has been added on Karma WiFi.
- A new "Bits & Bytes: Mesh Networks—An Emerging Alternative" has been added, replacing "Wake Up Your Mac Remotely."
- NEW Bits & Bytes: "Connecting to Wireless Networks on the Road? Beware of 'Evil Twins'!" moved to this

chapter from Chapter 9, and replaces "Blazingly Fast Wireless Connections on the Horizon."

- The content from the removed "Bits & Bytes: Blazingly Fast Wireless Connections on the Horizon" has been incorporated into the chapter content.

**Technology in Focus: Under the Hood**

- This Tech in Focus has been updated throughout, with many new photos.
- The "Bits and Bytes: Today's Supercomputers: The Fastest of the Fast" has been updated to reflect the newest supercomputers.
- NEW "Bits and Bytes: Forget CPUs: SoC Is the Future for Mobile Devices!" has been added.

**Chapter 8: Digital Devices and Media: Managing a Digital Lifestyle**

- Throughout the chapter, text, figures, and photos have been updated.
- NEW "How Cool Is This?" feature has been added on 3D printing.
- NEW "Bits & Bytes: Talking to Yourself" has been added.
- NEW "Bits & Bytes: Want to Read That Voicemail?" has been added, replacing Bits & Bytes on Billshrink.
- NEW "Bits & Bytes: The Fabulous Phablet" has been added.

**Chapter 9: Securing Your System: Protecting Your Digital Data and Devices**

- Throughout the chapter, text, figures, and photos have been updated.
- Screenshots throughout have been updated to reflect Windows 8.1.
- NEW "Bits & Bytes: I Received a Data Breach Letter . . . Now What?" has been added.
- The Biometric Authentication Devices section has been updated for the new iPhone 5 features.
- NEW "Bits & Bytes: Can't Remember Passwords? Try a Passphrase Instead!" has been added.

**Technology in Focus: Careers in IT**

- This Tech in Focus has been updated throughout.

**Chapter 10: Behind the Scenes: Software Programming**

- Throughout the chapter, text, figures, and photos have been updated.
- NEW "How Cool Is This?" feature has been added on the Open Data initiatives of major cities.
- NEW "Bits and Bytes: Competitive Coding" detailing collegiate and civic hackathons has been added, replacing "Bits and Bytes: My Algorithm Can Beat Your Algorithm."
- NEW "Bits & Bytes: Coding for Zombies" has been added, featuring Rails for Zombies from Code Academy.
- NEW "Bits & Bytes: The Best Résumé" has been added, replacing "Bits & Bytes: Want to Learn? Work for Free," and details the use of gitHub as a resume component.

**Chapter 11: Behind the Scenes: Databases and Information Systems**

- Throughout the chapter, text has been updated, and figures, screenshots, and photos have been updated to reflect changes in Microsoft Access 2013.
- NEW "How Cool Is This?" feature has been added on the DrawAFriend app.
- "Ethics in IT: Data, Data Everywhere—But Is It Protected?" section has been updated with a new example.

**Chapter 12: Behind the Scenes: Networking and Security in the Business World**

- Throughout the chapter, text, figures, and photos have been updated.
- NEW "How Cool Is This?" feature has been added on secure social collaboration tools.
- NEW "Bits & Bytes: Go Green with Mobile Apps" has been added.
- NEW "Bits & Bytes: US Military Brings Its Own Network . . . By Plane!" has been added.

**Chapter 13: Behind the Scenes: How the Internet Works**

- Throughout the chapter, text, figures, and photos have been updated.
- NEW "Bits & Bytes: Server in the Cloud" has been added, highlighting Google App Engine.
- The "Bits & Bytes: Gmail Features You Should Know About" has been updated.
- NEW "How Cool Is This?" feature on MOOC courses for learning has been added.

# About the Authors

## Alan Evans, MS, CPA

**aevans@mc3.edu**


Alan is currently a faculty member at Moore College of Art and Design and Montgomery County Community College, teaching a variety of computer science and business courses. He holds a BS in accounting from Rider University and an MS in information systems from Drexel University, and he is a certified public accountant. After a successful career in business, Alan finally realized that his true calling is education. He has been teaching at the college level since 2000. Alan enjoys giving presentations at technical conferences and meets regularly with faculty and administrators from other colleges to discuss curriculum development and new methods of engaging students.

## Kendall Martin, PhD

**kmartin@mc3.edu**


Kendall is an Associate Professor at Montgomery County Community College with teaching experience at both the undergraduate and graduate levels at a number of institutions, including Villanova University, DeSales University, Ursinus College, and Arcadia University.

Kendall's education includes a BS in electrical engineering from the University of Rochester and an MS and a PhD in engineering from the University of Pennsylvania. She has industrial experience in research and development environments (AT&T Bell Laboratories), as well as experience with several start-up technology firms.

## Mary Anne Poatsy, MBA

**mpoatsy@mc3.edu**


Mary Anne is a senior faculty member at Montgomery County Community College, teaching various computer application and concepts courses in face-to-face and online environments. She enjoys speaking at various professional conferences about innovative classroom strategies. She holds a BA in psychology and education from Mount Holyoke College and an MBA in finance from Northwestern University's Kellogg Graduate School of Management.

Mary Anne has been in teaching since 1997, ranging from elementary and secondary education to Montgomery County Community College, Gwynedd-Mercy College, Muhlenberg College, and Bucks County Community College, as well as training in the professional environment. Before teaching, she was a vice president at Shearson Lehman Hutton in the Municipal Bond Investment Banking Department.

# Acknowledgments

*First, we would like to thank our students. We constantly learn from them while teaching, and they are a continual source of inspiration and new ideas.*

We could not have written this book without the loving support of our families. Our spouses and children made sacrifices (mostly in time not spent with us) to permit us to make this dream into a reality.

Although working with the entire team at Pearson has been a truly enjoyable experience, a few individuals deserve special mention. The constant support and encouragement we receive from Jenifer Niles, Executive Acquisitions Editor, and Michael Payne, Editor in Chief, continually make this book grow and change. Our heartfelt thanks go to Shannon LeMay-Finn, our Developmental Editor. Her creativity, drive, and management skills helped make this book a reality. We also would like to extend our appreciation to Rhonda Aversa, our Editorial and Production Project Manager, who works tirelessly to ensure that our book is published on time and looks fabulous. The timelines are always short, the art is complex, and there are many people with whom she has to coordinate tasks. But she makes it look easy! We'd like to extend our thanks to the media and MyITlab team: Eric Hakanson, Taylor Ragan, Jaimie Noy, and Jessica Brandi for all of their hard work and dedication.

There are many people whom we do not meet in person at Pearson and elsewhere who make significant contributions by designing the book, illustrating, composing the pages, producing multimedia, and securing permissions. We thank them all. We would also like to thank the supplement authors for this edition: Wanda Gibson, Julie Boyles, Terri Holly, Stephanie Emrich, Doug Courter, Lori Damanti, Tony Nowakowski, Sara Buscaino, Sharon Behrens, Sue McCrory, Linda Pogue, and Stacy Everly.

And finally, we would like to thank the reviewers and the many others who contribute their time, ideas, and talents to this project. We appreciate their time and energy, as their comments help us turn out a better product each edition.

eleventh
EDITION 11

# 11th Edition Reviewers

**Pearson and the authors would like to thank the following people for their help and time in making this book what it is. We couldn't publish this book without their contributions.**

**A.C. Chapin** Harford Community College
**Adeleye Bamkole** Passaic County Community College
**Adnan Atshan** Passaic County Community College
**Afi Chamlou** NOVA Alexandria
**Afrand Agah** West Chester
**Alexis Stull** Fairmont State University
**Ali Soleymani** NOVA Alexandria
**Allyson Kinney** Gateway Community College
**Amy Roche** Northampton Community College
**Amy Rutledge** Oakland University
**Andrew Hobbs** Delaware State University
**Anita Girton** PA College of Technology
**Ann-Marie Smith** Delaware City Community College
**Annette Kerwin** College of DuPage
**Ann Ford Tyson (coordinator)** Florida State University
**Ann Taff** Tulsa Community College
**Barb Garrell** Delaware City Community College
**Barbara Fogle, Stuhr** Trident Tech
**Barbara Garrell** Delaware County Community College
**Barbara Hotta** Leeward Community College
**Barry Andrews** Mt. SAC
**Becky Curtain** William Rainer Harper College
**Ben Martz** Northern KY
**Ben Stonebraker** Ivy Tech
**Benjamin Marrero** Ivy Tech
**Betsy Jenaway** Macomb Community College
**Beverly Fite** Amarillo
**Bill Barnes** Catawba Valley Community College
**Billie Williams** San Diego City
**Blanca Polo** Leeward Community College
**Blankenstein** Nashua Community College
**Bobbie Hyndman** Amarillo
**Bob Lingvall** Southwestern
**Brenda Nielsen** Mesa Community College
**Brent Hussin** Wisconsin-Green Bay
**Brian Powell** West Virginia University
**Bunny Howard** SJRCC (St. John's River)
**Burton Borlongan** Mesa Community College
**Carol Fletcher** Louisiana Delta College
**Carolyn Barren** Macomb Community College
**Carolyn Borne** Louisiana State University
**Casey Wilhelm** North Idaho College
**Cathy Glod** Mohawk Valley Cmty College
**Charles Dessasure** Tarrant SE
**Charles R. Whealton** Delaware Technical and Community College
**Charles Whealton** Del Tech & Community College-Dover
**Cheryl Sypniewski** Macomb Community College
**ChongWoo Park** Georgia Gwinnett College
**Chris Belcher** CCAC-South
**Christie Jahn Hovey** Lincoln Land Community College
**Clarence Kennedy** Louisiana Delta College
**Cliff Sherrill** Yavapai College
**Cynthia Collings** Central AZ
**Cynthia Wagner** McLennan
**Dale Craig** Fullerton College
**Darrell Lindsey** SJRCC (St. John's River)
**Darrell Riddell** Ivy Tech
**Dave Burgett** McLennan
**Dave Surma** IU South Bend
**David Kerven** Georgia Gwinnett College
**David Lange** Grand Valley
**David R. Surma** Indiana University South Bend
**Debbie Christenberry** Randolph Community College
**Debbie Holt** KCTCS-Bluegrass-Cooper-CIT 105
**Deb Fells** Mesa Community College
**Debra Grande** Community College of Rhode Island
**Deena White** Grayson
**Deidre Grafel** Chandler-Gilbert Community College
**Denise Nearing** Indian River State College
**Denise Sullivan** Westchester Community College
**Dennis Stewart** NOVA Alexandria
**Desmond Chun** Chabot College
**Diane Bittle** HACC
**Diane Puopolo** Bunker Hill Community College
**Dick Schwartz** Macomb Community College
**Diedre Grafel** Chandler Gilbert Community College
**Donald Humphrey** Columbia Basin College
**Don Dershem** Mt View
**Don Holcomb** KCTCS-Bluegrass-Cooper-CIT 105
**Don Lafond** SJRCC (St. John's River)
**Donald Riggs** Schenectady County Community College
**Donna Earhart** Genesee Community College
**Don Riggs** Schenectady County Community College
**Doreen Nicholls** Mohawk Valley Cmty College
**Dottie Sunio** Leeward Community College
**Doug Medin** Western New Mexico University
**Dr. Kate LeGrand** Broward College
**Duane Johnson** Ivy Tech
**Duane Lintner** Amarillo
**Earl Latiolas** Delgado Cmty Clg
**Ed Bushman** Yavapai College
**Ed Delean** NOVA Alexandria
**Ed Eill** Delaware City Community College
**Elise Bell** CCSF

| | |
|---|---|
| **Ellen Glazer** | Broward Community College, South |
| **Ellen Kessler** | HACC-Wildwood |
| **Emily Shepard** | Central Carolina Community College |
| **Enoch Damson** | Akron |
| **Eric Cameron** | Passaic County Community College |
| **Ernest Proctor** | LA Trade |
| **Ernie Gines** | Tarrant SE |
| **Faye Tippey** | Ivy Tech |
| **Francis Seidel** | Frederick Cmty College |
| **Fred Hills** | McLennan |
| **Gabriel Viera** | South TX College |
| **Garland Berry** | Columbia College |
| **Gene Carbonara** | Long Beach Community College |
| **Gene Carbonaro** | Long Beach City College |
| **Gerald Burgess** | Western New Mexico University |
| **Gina Bowers-Miller** | HACC-Wildwood |
| **Gina Jerry** | Santa Monica College |
| **Glendora Mays** | SJRCC (St. John's River) |
| **Glen Grimes** | Collin Cty |
| **Glenn Carter** | Sonoma State |
| **Greg Hanson** | Ivy Tech |
| **Gretchen Douglas** | SUNY at Cortland |
| **Guarav Bansal** | Wisconsin-Green Bay |
| **Hal Broxmeyer** | IUPUI |
| **Helen Ortmann** | CCAC-South |
| **Helen Sheran** | East LA |
| **Hillary Miller** | Kingwood |
| **Holly Gould** | Ivy Tech |
| **Hon-Chung Kwok** | CCSF |
| **Ian Gibbons** | Hillsborough Community College-Ybor |
| **Jack Alanen** | CSU-Northridge |
| **Jaime Hicks** | Ivy Tech |
| **James Dang** | Tarrant SE |
| **James Fabrey** | West Chester |
| **James McBride** | Eastern AZ |
| **James R. Anthos** | South University-Columbia |
| **James Taggart** | Atlantic Cape Community College |
| **Janet Gelb** | Grossmont Community College |
| **Janet Laubenstein** | Northampton Cmty Coll |
| **Janine Tiffany** | Reading Area Comm College |
| **Jean-Claude Ngatchou** | New Jersey City Univ. |
| **Jeanette Dix** | Ivy Tech |
| **Jeff Bowker** | Montco |
| **Jennifer Ivey** | Central Carolina Community College |
| **Jennifer Pickle** | Amarillo |
| **Jenny Maurer** | PA College of Technology |
| **Jerry Gonnella** | Northern KY |
| **Jessica Helberg** | Northern Virginia Community College |
| **Jessie Saldana** | Cypress |
| **Jill Canine** | Ivy Tech |
| **Jim Hughes** | Northern KY |
| **Jim Poole** | Honolulu Community College |
| **Joan Heise** | Ivy Tech |
| **John Carlisle** | Nashua Community College |
| **John Dawson** | IUPUI |
| **John Enomoto** | East LA |
| **John Mayhorne** | Harford Community College |
| **John Messer** | PA College of Technology |
| **Joni Catanzaro** | Louisiana State University |
| **Jo Stephens** | University of AR Community College @ Batesville |
| **Joyce Thompson** | Lehigh Carbon Community College |
| **Judy Duff** | Louisiana Delta College |
| **Judy Scheeren** | Duquesne |
| **Juliana Cypert** | Tarrant County College |
| **Juliana.P. Cypert** | Tarrant County College-NE |
| **Julie Bell** | Delgado Cmty Clg |
| **Kae Cooper** | BCTC/KCTCS |
| **Kam Kong** | Delaware State University |
| **Karen Allen** | Community College of Rhode Island |
| **Karen Weil** | McLennan |
| **Kari Meck** | HACC |
| **Kari Walters** | Louisiana State University |
| **Kate LeGrand** | Broward Community College, South |
| **Kathie Richer** | Edmonds Community College |
| **Kathy Kelly** | Montco |
| **Kathy Olson** | Ivy Tech |
| **Kay Johnson** | Community College of Rhode Island |
| **Keith Noe** | Ivy Tech |
| **Kemit Grafton** | Oklahoma State University–Oklahoma City |
| **Ken Schroeder** | Ivy Tech |
| **Kevin Cleary** | SUNY at Buffalo |
| **Kevin Gentry** | Ivy Tech |
| **Kourosh Behzadnoori** | Tarrant SE |
| **Krista Lawrence** | Delgado Cmty Clg |
| **Kristen Hockman** | Univ of Missouri-Columbia |
| **Laura Hunt** | Tulsa Community College |
| **Laurene Hutchinson** | Louisiana State University |
| **Laurie Wallmark** | Raritan Valley Community College |
| **Leasa Richards** | Columbia College |
| **Lili Shashaani** | Duquesne |
| **Linda Arnold** | HACC |
| **Linda Moulton** | Montco |
| **Lisa Hawkins** | Frederick Community College |
| **Lisa Jackson** | Phoenix College |
| **Lisa Simpson-Kyle** | Yavapai College |
| **Lois Scheidt** | Ivy Tech |
| **Lori Laudenbach** | St. Cloud State |
| **Lorraine Sauchin** | Duquesne |
| **Lou Ann Stroup** | Ivy Tech |
| **Lucy Parker** | CSU-Northridge |
| **Lydia Macaulay** | Tarrant SE |
| **Lydia Mata** | Eastern AZ |
| **Lynne Lyon** | Durham College |
| **Lynne Stuhr** | Trident Tech |
| **Marcia Schlafmitz** | New Jersey City Univ. |
| **Marcus Butler** | West LA |
| **Marie Harlein** | Montco |
| **Marjorie Feroe** | Delaware City Community College |
| **Mark Connell** | SUNY at Cortland |
| **Marvin Daugherty** | Ivy Tech |
| **Mary Ann Zlotow** | College of DuPage |

| | |
|---|---|
| **Mary Dermody** | Chabot College |
| **Mary Johnson** | Kingwood |
| **Mary Zegarski** | NorthHampton Community College |
| **Matthew Trotter** | South TX College |
| **Meg Kletke** | Oklahoma State University |
| **Melanie Williamson** | KCTCS-Bluegrass–Cooper–CIT 105 |
| **Mel Tarnowski** | Macomb Community College |
| **Meng Has** | Burlington County College |
| **Meshack Osiro** | Ivy Tech |
| **Michael Swafford** | Tulsa Community College |
| **Michele Smolnik** | Columbia College |
| **Michelle Beets** | Iowa Central Community College |
| **Michelle Reznick** | Oakton Community College |
| **Mike Kelly** | Community College of Rhode Island |
| **Mike Puopolo** | Bunker Hill Community College |
| **NAME** | SCHOOL |
| **Nancy Evans** | Indiana University-Purdue University Indianapolis |
| **Nancy Grant** | CCAC-South |
| **Natalia Grigoriants** | Pierce College |
| **Neale Adams** | Iowa Central Community College |
| **Neal Stenlund** | Northern Virginia Community College |
| **Nelmy Vasquez** | Broward Community College, South |
| **Noah Singer** | Tulsa Community College |
| **Norma Marler** | Catawba Valley Community College |
| **Pam Ellis** | PA College of Technology |
| **Pam Uhlenkamp** | Iowa Central Community College |
| **Pat Fenton** | West Valley |
| **Pat Rahmlow** | Montco |
| **Patricia Casey** | Trident Tech |
| **Pat Vacca** | El Camino College |
| **Paul Addison** | Ivy Tech |
| **Paul Dadosky** | Ivy Tech |
| **Paul Koester** | Tarrant County College, Northwest |
| **Peggy Anderson** | SUNY at Cortland |
| **Peter Ross** | Univ. of Albany |
| **Pete Vetere** | Montco |
| **Phil Moorhead** | Ivy Tech |
| **Phil Whitney** | Bakersfield College |
| **Rachel Pena** | South TX College |
| **Randy Gibson** | Indian River State College |
| **Rebecca Giorcelli** | Fairmont State University |
| **REBECCA KIRK** | Augusta State University |
| **Rich Geglein** | Ivy Tech |
| **Ricky Barnes** | Catawba Valley Community College |
| **Robert Benavides** | Collin Cty |
| **Robert Chirwa** | KCTCS-Bluegrass-Cooper-CIT 105 |
| **Robert Deadman** | IUPUI |
| **Rob Murray** | Ivy Tech |
| **Rod Waller** | Indian River State College |
| **Roger Young** | Ivy Tech |
| **Ronald Kizior** | Loyola University Chicago |
| **Ron Enz** | Chattahoochee Tech |
| **Rose LaMuraglia** | San Diego City |
| **Rosie Inwang** | Olive Harvey |
| **Sabum Anyangwe** | Harford Community College |
| **Saeed Molki** | South TX College |
| **Sally Dixon** | Skagit Valley Community College |
| **Scott Rosen** | Santa Rosa Junior College |
| **Scott Russell** | Eastern AZ |
| **Sharon Karonias** | Northampton Cmty Coll |
| **Shelly Ota** | Leeward Community College |
| **Sherri Clark** | Ivy Tech |
| **Stacia Dutton** | SUNY Canton |
| **Stacy Johnson** | Iowa Central Community College |
| **Stacy Ward** | Grafton High School |
| **Steve Carver** | Ivy Tech |
| **Steve Hustedde** | South Mountain |
| **Steven Battilana** | West Chester |
| **Steve Singer** | Kapiolani Community College |
| **Steve St. John** | Tulsa Community College |
| **Steve Stepanek** | CSU-Northridge |
| **Sue Heistand** | Iowa Central Community College |
| **Susan Barkalow** | St. Cloud State |
| **Susan Fry** | Boise State University |
| **Susan Hoggard** | Tulsa Community College |
| **Susan LaBrie** | Northampton Community College |
| **Susie Viars-Thomas** | Grayson |
| **Sylvia Emerson** | Rock Valley College |
| **Tammy Jolley** | University of AR Community College @ Batesville |
| **Ted Allen Reasoner** | IUPUI |
| **Terri Helfand** | Chaffey Community College |
| **Terry Holleman** | Catawba Valley Community College |
| **Terry Rigsby** | Hill College |
| **Tiffany Johnson** | Tulsa Community College |
| **Thomas Liu** | New Jersey City Univ. |
| **Thomas Yip** | Passaic County Community College |
| **Timothy Hinz** | Genesee Community College |
| **Toby Gustafson** | UCR |
| **Todd Schultz** | Augusta State University |
| **Tom Foster** | Chandler Gilbert Community College |
| **Tom Ryan** | SJRCC (St. John's River) |
| **Tony Basilico** | Community College of Rhode Island |
| **Valerie Golay** | Ivy Tech |
| **Vicki Brooks** | Columbia College |
| **Virginia Huegel** | Western New Mexico University |
| **Wade Graves** | Grayson |
| **Wayne Phillips** | Chabot College |
| **Wei Liu** | Georgia Gwinnett College |
| **Will Smith** | Tulsa Community College |
| **Xin Xu** | Georgia Gwinnett College |
| **Yi Li Zhuang** | Macomb Community College |

# Letter from the Authors

## Our 11th Edition—A Letter from the Authors

### Why We Wrote This Book

The pace of technological change is ever increasing. In education, we have seen this impact us more than ever in the past year—MOOCs, touch-screen mobile delivery, and Hangouts are now fixed parts of our environment.

Even the most agile of learners and educators need support in keeping up with this pace of change. In the 11th edition of *Technology in Action*, we have responded with mobile device media, interactive ebook technology, and updated video supports. We continue to strive to make *Technology in Action* a learning system that pushes the envelope of what is possible in technology, and what is helpful in teaching. In short: we have worked hard to build a text that fits the way students are learning now.

Our combined almost 50 years of teaching computer concepts have coincided with sweeping innovations in computing technology that have affected every facet of society. From iPads to Web 2.0, computers are more than ever a fixture of our daily lives—and the lives of our students. But although today's students have a much greater comfort level with their digital environment than previous generations, their knowledge of the machines they use every day is still limited.

Part of the student-centered focus of our book has to do with making the material truly engaging to students. From the beginning, we have written *Technology in Action* to focus on what matters most to today's student. Instead of a history lesson on the microchip, we focus on tasks students can accomplish with their computing devices and skills they can apply immediately in the workplace, the classroom, and at home.

We strive to keep the text as current as publishing timelines allow, and we are constantly looking for the next technology trend or gadget. We have augmented the text with weekly technology updates to help you keep your classroom on top of the latest breaking developments and continue to include a number of multimedia components to enrich the classroom and student learning experience. The result is a learning system that sparks student interest by focusing on the material they want to learn (such as how to integrate computing devices into a home network) while teaching the material they need to learn (such as how networks work). The sequence of topics is carefully set up to mirror the typical student learning experience.

As they read through this text, your students will progress through stages of increasing difficulty:

1. Thinking about how technology offers them the power to change their society and their world
2. Examining why it's important to be computer fluent
3. Understanding the basic components of computing devices
4. Connecting to and exploring the Internet
5. Exploring software
6. Learning the operating system and personalizing their computer

7. Evaluating and upgrading computing devices
8. Understanding home networking options and keeping computing devices safe from hackers
9. Going mobile with smartphones, netbooks, tablets, and laptops
10. Going behind the scenes, looking at technology in greater detail

We continue to structure the book in a "spiraling" manner, intentionally introducing on a basic level in the earlier chapters concepts that students traditionally have trouble with and then later expanding on those concepts in more detail when students have become more comfortable with them. Thus, the focus of the early chapters is on practical uses for the computer, with real-world examples to help the students place computing in a familiar context.

For example, we introduce basic hardware components in Chapter 2, and then we go into increasingly greater detail on some hardware components in Chapter 6 and in the "Under the Hood" Technology in Focus feature. The Behind the Scenes chapters venture deeper into the realm of computing through in-depth explanations of how programming, networks, the Internet, and databases work. They are specifically designed to keep more experienced students engaged and to challenge them with interesting research assignments.

Throughout the years we have also developed a comprehensive multimedia program to reinforce the material taught in the text and to support both classroom lectures and distance learning:

- The **Helpdesk training content**, created specifically for *Technology in Action*, enables students to take on the role of a helpdesk operator and work through common questions asked by computer users. These have been updated this edition to reflect the way in which users access help today.
- Exciting **Sound Byte multimedia**—fully updated and integrated with the text—expand student mastery of complex topics.
- The **Tech Bytes Weekly updates** deliver the latest technology news stories to you for use in your classroom. Each is accompanied by specific discussion topics and activities to expand on what is within the textbook materials.

This book is designed to reach the students of the twenty-first century and prepare them for the role they can take in their own community and the world. It has been an honor to work with you over the past 11 years to present and explain new technologies to students, and to show them the rapidly growing importance of technology in our world.

# Visual Walk-Through

## Topic Sequence

Concepts are covered in a progressive manner between chapters to mirror the typical student learning experience.

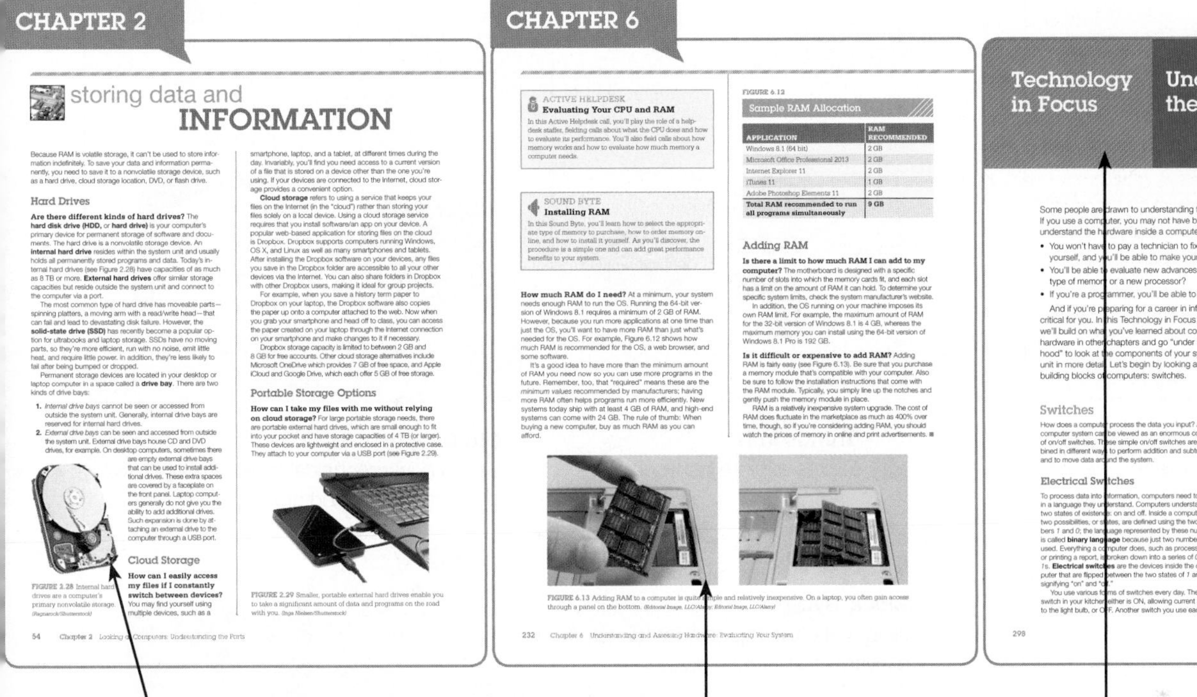

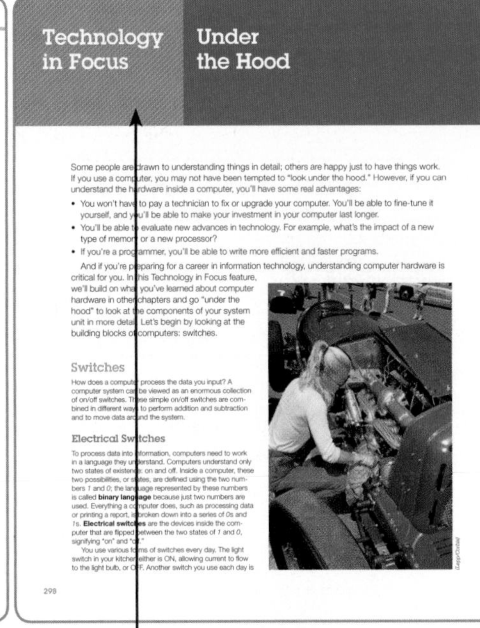

**Hardware First Introduced**
Chapter 2 is the first time students read about introductory hardware. It's covered at the beginning level because this is students' experience level at this point of the book.

**Hardware Taught in More Depth in Additional Chapters**
In later chapters, students read about hardware in greater depth because they're more experienced and comfortable working with their computers.

**Technology in Focus**
Four special features that teach key uses of technology today.

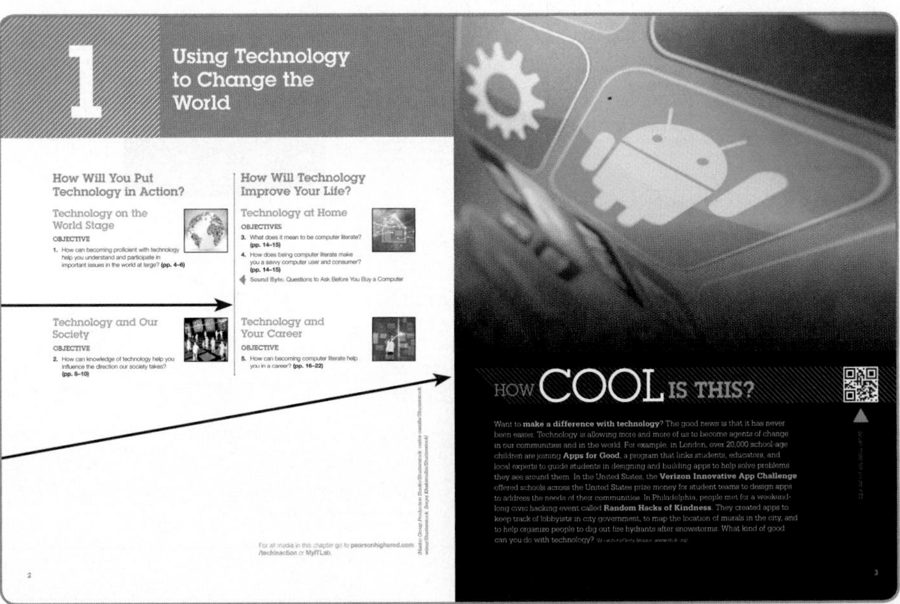

**Multimedia Cues**
Visual integration of multimedia.

**How Cool Is This?**
Highlights the latest and greatest websites, gadgets, and multimedia.

EDITION eleventh 11

# Student Textbook

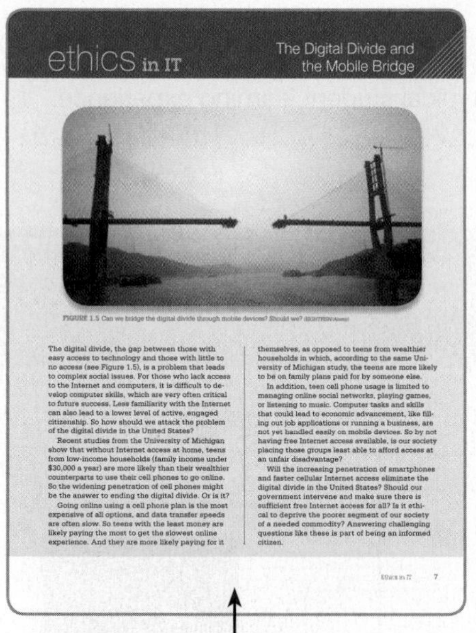


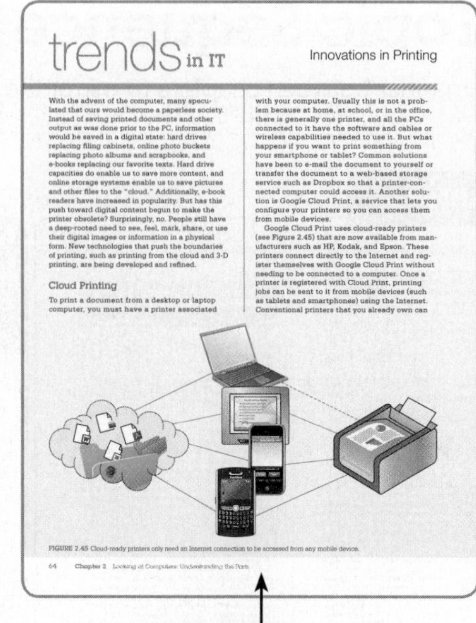


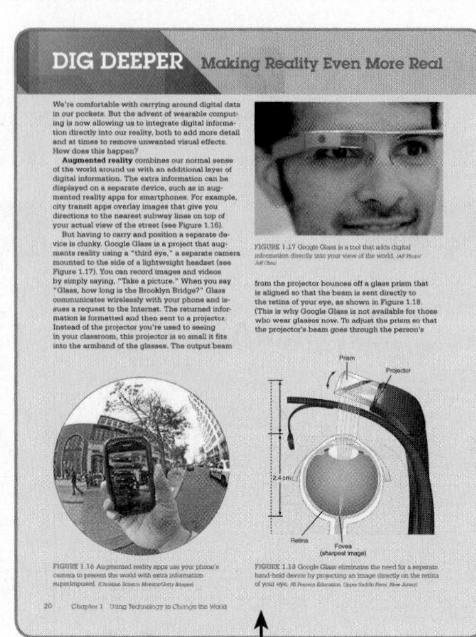

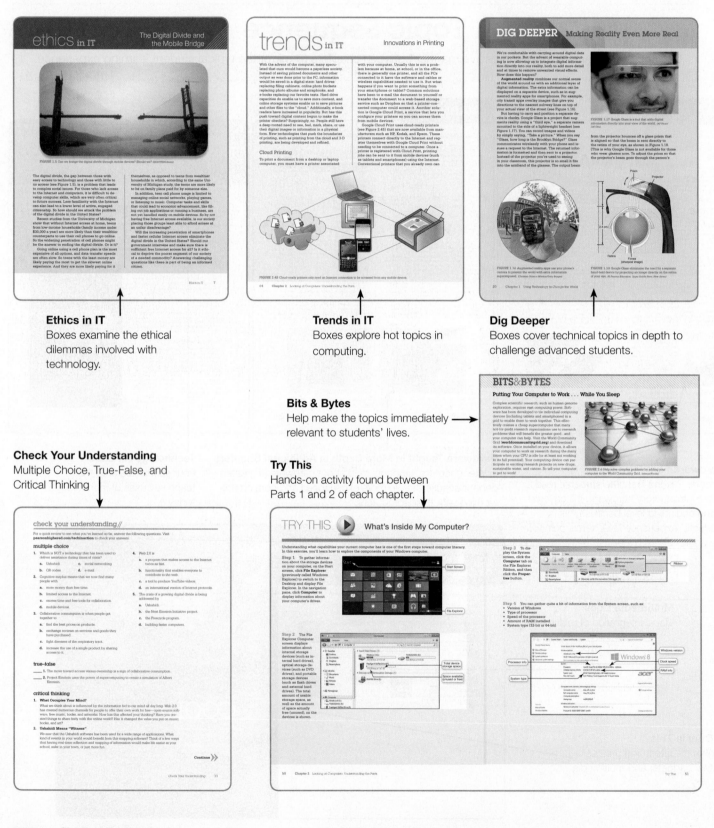

**Ethics in IT**
Boxes examine the ethical dilemmas involved with technology.

**Trends in IT**
Boxes explore hot topics in computing.

**Dig Deeper**
Boxes cover technical topics in depth to challenge advanced students.

**Bits & Bytes**
Help make the topics immediately relevant to students' lives.

**Check Your Understanding**
Multiple Choice, True-False, and Critical Thinking

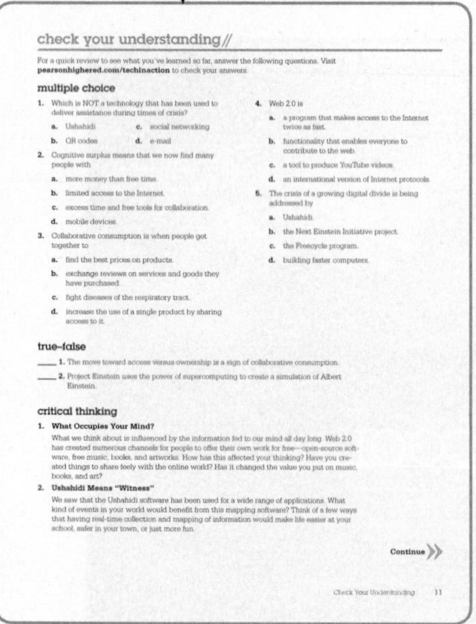


**Try This**
Hands-on activity found between Parts 1 and 2 of each chapter.

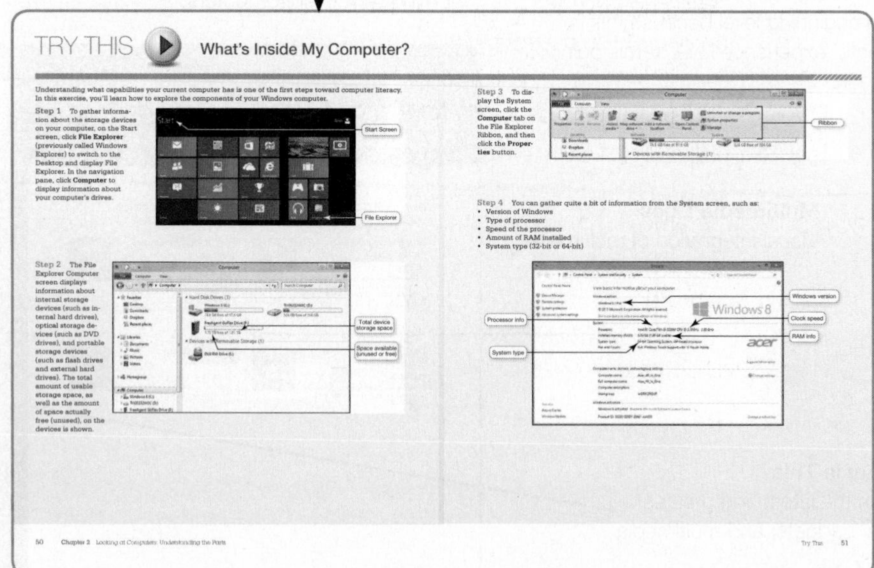

# MyITLab and Companion Media

**MyITLab** for *Technology in Action* with the Enhanced eBook personalizes learning to help your students better prepare and learn—resulting in more dynamic experiences in the classroom and improved performance in the course. Specific features include:

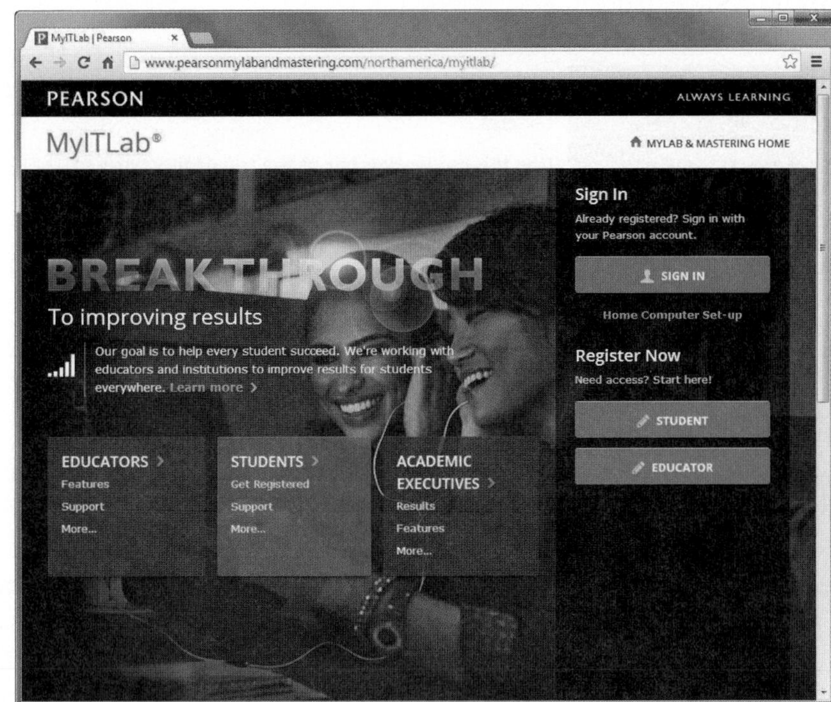


- **Adaptive Learning:** *A way to enable personalized learning at scale.* Not every student learns the same way and at the same rate. MyITLab with Adaptive Learning continuously assesses student performance and activity in real time, and, using data and analytics, personalizes content to reinforce concepts that target each student's strengths and weaknesses.
    - **NEW! Adaptive Dynamic Study Modules**, created specifically for *Technology in Action,* 11th Edition, provide students with personalized review based on their strengths and weaknesses.
- **A powerful homework and test manager:** MyITLab lets you create, import, and manage online homework assignments, quizzes, and tests that are automatically graded. The bottom line: MyITLab means less time grading and more time teaching.
- **Comprehensive online course content:** Filled with a wealth of content that is tightly integrated with your textbook, MyITLab lets you easily add, remove, or modify existing instructional material. You can also add your own course materials to suit the needs of your students or department. In short, MyITLab lets you teach exactly as you'd like.
- **Robust Gradebook tracking:** The online Gradebook automatically tracks your students' results on tests, homework, and practice exercises and gives you control over managing results and calculating grades. And, it lets you measure and document your students' learning outcomes.
- **Easily scalable and shareable content:** MyITLab enables you to manage multiple class sections, and lets other instructors copy your settings so a standardized syllabus can be maintained across your department.

**Companion Website**
Includes an interactive study guide, online end-of-chapter material, additional Internet exercises, and much more.

Use the navigation bar at the top of this page to access the student resources for each chapter.

Tech Support
Browser Tuneup

pearsonhighered.com/techinaction

The following media is available in MyITLab, and selected items are also on the companion website.

Note: To access the premium content, including Helpdesks, Sound Bytes, and Replay Videos from the companion site, students need to use the access code printed on the card in the front of the book.

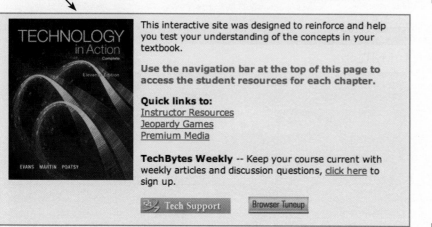

- MyITLab • **Enhanced eBook:** The Enhanced eBook in MyITLab provides a continuous digital learning in a completely interactive environment that allows students to use technology as they learn. They don't have to sto p reading to go find the activities such as Helpdesks, Sound Bytes, and Replay Videos—they just click on them and immediately experience the activity.
- MyITLab • **TechTown**: This fully interactive scenario-based, simulation game lets students create their own avatar and interact in a series of knowledge and puzzle-based scenarios. As they work and play, they explore the core topics of computer concepts—from what a computer is to software, hardware, networking, the Internet, social media, and more!
- MyITLab • **NEW! Adaptive Dynamic Study Modules**, created specifically for *Technology in Action,* 11th Edition, provide students with personalized review based on their strengths and weaknesses.
  - **Sound Bytes:** These multimedia lessons help demystify computer concepts with audio and video presentations. All of the Sound Bytes have been updated to provide timely and accurate information.
  - **COMPLETELY UPDATED AND ENHANCED! Active Helpdesk Calls:** These highly interactive, engaging activities now provide students with a realistic experience of how help is delivered via phone, live chat, FAQ searches, and so on. Students play the role of the staff answering technology questions using these various approaches.
    - A virtual supervisor provides support to the student throughout calls.
    - Assessment questions after each call provide instructors with a tool to gauge and track students' progress.
- **UPDATED! *Replay* videos:** The *Replay* videos provide an author-narrated video review of each *Chapter Part* in an easy-to-use format students can view on their phones, tablets, or computers!
- ***With Tech Bytes Weekly, every week is new!*** This weekly newsfeed provides two timely articles to save instructors the prep time required for adding interesting and relevant news items to their weekly lectures. Tech Bytes Weekly also features valuable links and other resources, including discussion questions and course activities.
- **Jeopardy! Game and Crossword Puzzles:** These assets give students a fun way to challenge their knowledge.

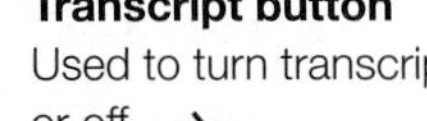

**Transcript button**
Used to turn transcript on or off

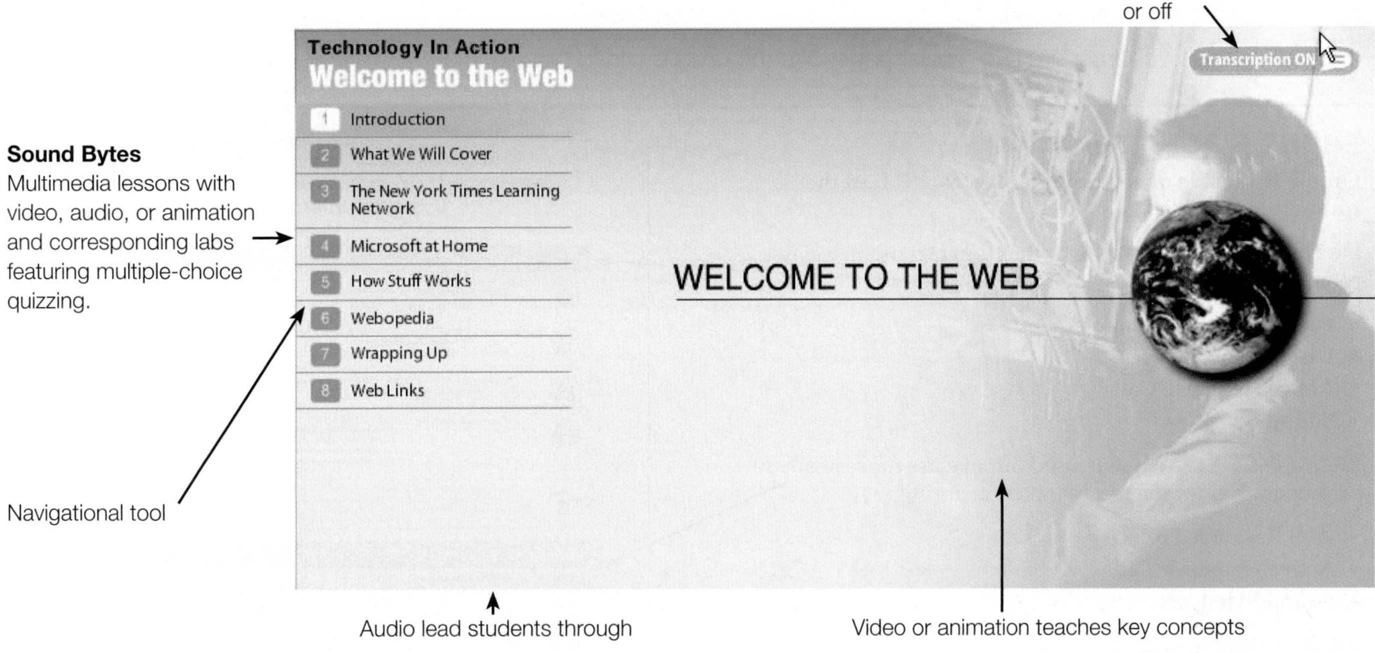


**Sound Bytes**
Multimedia lessons with video, audio, or animation and corresponding labs featuring multiple-choice quizzing.

Navigational tool

Audio lead students through

Video or animation teaches key concepts

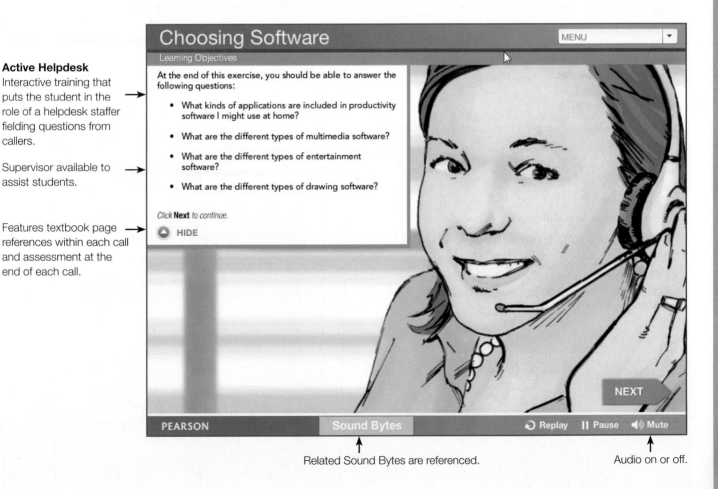

**Active Helpdesk**
Interactive training that puts the student in the role of a helpdesk staffer fielding questions from callers.

Supervisor available to assist students.

Features textbook page references within each call and assessment at the end of each call.

Related Sound Bytes are referenced.

Audio on or off.

eleventh
EDITION 11

# Annotated Instructor Edition

Provided with each chapter are two divider pages like the ones outlined below.

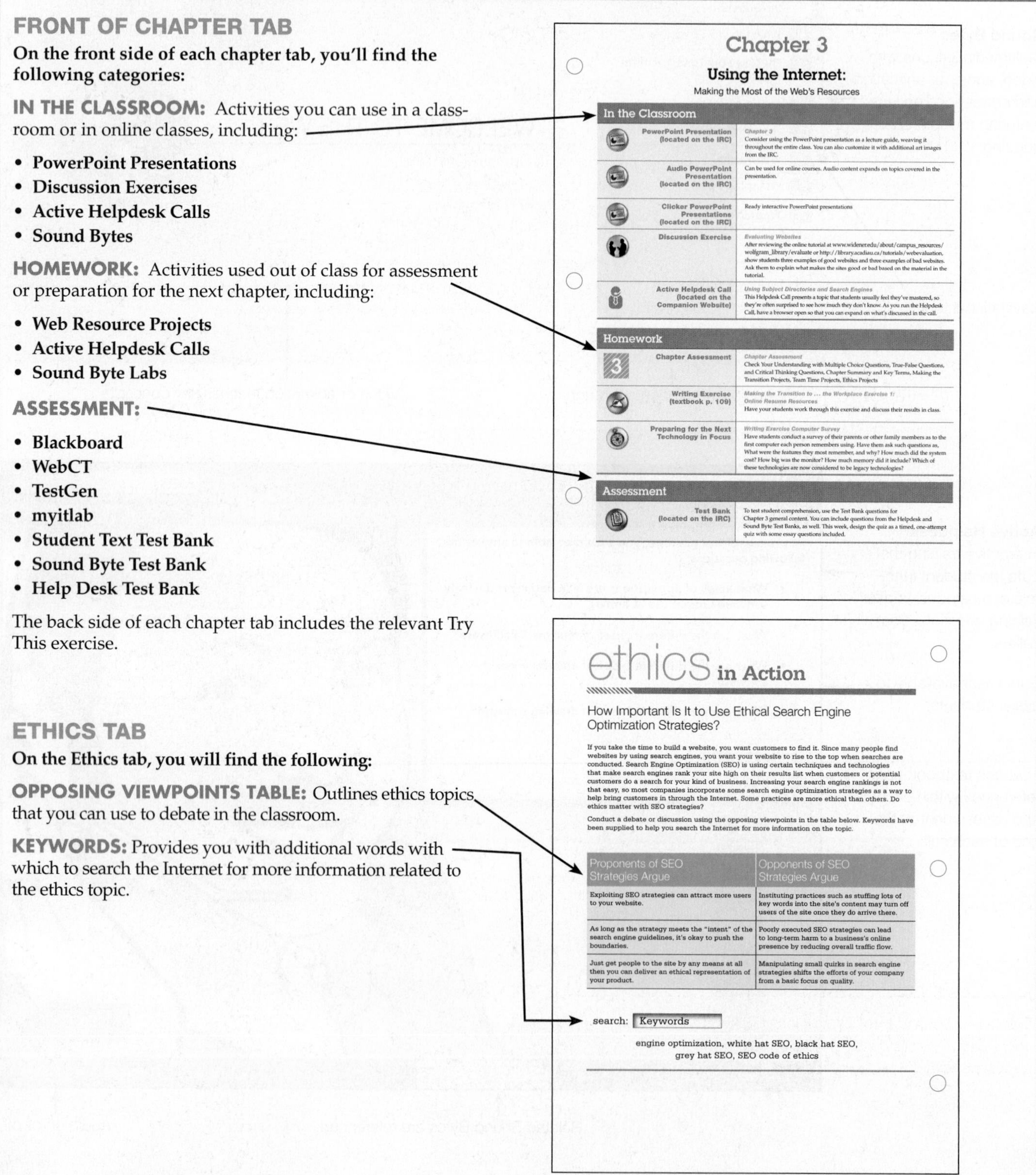

## FRONT OF CHAPTER TAB

**On the front side of each chapter tab, you'll find the following categories:**

**IN THE CLASSROOM:** Activities you can use in a classroom or in online classes, including:

- **PowerPoint Presentations**
- **Discussion Exercises**
- **Active Helpdesk Calls**
- **Sound Bytes**

**HOMEWORK:** Activities used out of class for assessment or preparation for the next chapter, including:

- **Web Resource Projects**
- **Active Helpdesk Calls**
- **Sound Byte Labs**

**ASSESSMENT:**

- **Blackboard**
- **WebCT**
- **TestGen**
- **myitlab**
- **Student Text Test Bank**
- **Sound Byte Test Bank**
- **Help Desk Test Bank**

The back side of each chapter tab includes the relevant Try This exercise.

## ETHICS TAB

**On the Ethics tab, you will find the following:**

**OPPOSING VIEWPOINTS TABLE:** Outlines ethics topics that you can use to debate in the classroom.

**KEYWORDS:** Provides you with additional words with which to search the Internet for more information related to the ethics topic.

### Chapter 3

**Using the Internet:**

Making the Most of the Web's Resources

| In the Classroom | |
|---|---|
| PowerPoint Presentation (located on the IRC) | *Chapter 3* Consider using the PowerPoint presentation as a lecture guide, weaving it throughout the entire class. You can also customize it with additional art images from the IRC. |
| Audio PowerPoint Presentation (located on the IRC) | Can be used for online courses. Audio content expands on topics covered in the presentation. |
| Clicker PowerPoint Presentations (located on the IRC) | Ready interactive PowerPoint presentations |
| Discussion Exercise | *Evaluating Websites* After reviewing the online tutorial at www.widener.edu/about/campus_resources/wolfgram_library/evaluate or http://library.acadiau.ca/tutorials/webevaluation, show students three examples of good websites and three examples of bad websites. Ask them to explain what makes the sites good or bad based on the material in the tutorial. |
| Active Helpdesk Call (located on the Companion Website) | *Using Subject Directories and Search Engines* This Helpdesk Call presents a topic that students usually feel they've mastered, so they're often surprised to see how much they don't know. As you run the Helpdesk Call, have a browser open so that you can expand on what's discussed in the call. |

| Homework | |
|---|---|
| Chapter Assessment | *Chapter Assessment* Check Your Understanding with Multiple Choice Questions, True-False Questions, and Critical Thinking Questions, Chapter Summary and Key Terms, Making the Transition Projects, Team Time Projects, Ethics Projects |
| Writing Exercise (textbook p. 109) | *Making the Transition to … the Workplace Exercise 1: Online Resume Resources* Have your students work through this exercise and discuss their results in class. |
| Preparing for the Next Technology in Focus | *Writing Exercise Computer Survey* Have students conduct a survey of their parents or other family members as to the first computer each person remembers using. Have them ask such questions as, What were the features they most remember, and why? How much did the system cost? How big was the monitor? How much memory did it include? Which of these technologies are now considered to be legacy technologies? |

| Assessment | |
|---|---|
| Test Bank (located on the IRC) | To test student comprehension, use the Test Bank questions for Chapter 3 general content. You can include questions from the Helpdesk and Sound Byte Test Banks, as well. This week, design the quiz as a timed, one-attempt quiz with some essay questions included. |

### ethics in Action

How Important Is It to Use Ethical Search Engine Optimization Strategies?

If you take the time to build a website, you want customers to find it. Since many people find websites by using search engines, you want your website to rise to the top when searches are conducted. Search Engine Optimization (SEO) is using certain techniques and technologies that make search engines rank your site high on their results list when customers or potential customers do a search for your kind of business. Increasing your search engine rankings is not that easy, so most companies incorporate some search engine optimization strategies as a way to help bring customers in through the Internet. Some practices are more ethical than others. Do ethics matter with SEO strategies?

Conduct a debate or discussion using the opposing viewpoints in the table below. Keywords have been supplied to help you search the Internet for more information on the topic.

| Proponents of SEO Strategies Argue | Opponents of SEO Strategies Argue |
|---|---|
| Exploiting SEO strategies can attract more users to your website. | Instituting practices such as stuffing lots of key words into the site's content may turn off users of the site once they do arrive there. |
| As long as the strategy meets the "intent" of the search engine guidelines, it's okay to push the boundaries. | Poorly executed SEO strategies can lead to long-term harm to a business's online presence by reducing overall traffic flow. |
| Just get people to the site by any means at all then you can deliver an ethical representation of your product. | Manipulating small quirks in search engine strategies shifts the efforts of your company from a basic focus on quality. |

search: Keywords

engine optimization, white hat SEO, black hat SEO, grey hat SEO, SEO code of ethics

# Instructor Resources

### Instructor Resources

Online Instructor Resources Include:

- PowerPoint Presentations
- New Interactive Clicker PowerPoints*
- Student Text Test Bank
- Sound Byte Test Bank
- Help Desk Test Bank
- End of Chapter Answer Keys
- Rubrics
- Web Resources
- Image Library
- Sample Syllabi
- Additional Web Projects
- What's New in 11e
- Transition Guide
- TestGen

*NEW! Interactive, clicker PowerPoints allow faculty to obtain real-time responses to open-ended or critical thinking questions, determine which areas require further explanation, and then automatically group students for further discussion and problem solving.

**Technology In Action Complete, 11/E**
**Alan Evans**
**Kendall Martin**
**Mary Anne Poatsy**

ISBN-10: 0133802965
ISBN-13: 9780133802962

Contact your local Pearson sales rep to learn more about the *Technology in Action* instructional system.

# 1 Using Technology to Change the World

## How Will You Put Technology in Action?

### Technology on the World Stage

**OBJECTIVE**

1. How can becoming proficient with technology help you understand and participate in important issues in the world at large? **(pp. 4–6)**

### Technology and Our Society

**OBJECTIVE**

2. How can knowledge of technology help you influence the direction our society takes? **(pp. 8–10)**

## How Will Technology Improve Your Life?

### Technology at Home

**OBJECTIVES**

3. What does it mean to be computer literate? **(pp. 14–15)**
4. How does being computer literate make you a savvy computer user and consumer? **(pp. 14–15)**

**Sound Byte:** Questions to Ask Before You Buy a Computer

### Technology and Your Career

**OBJECTIVE**

5. How can becoming computer literate help you in a career? **(pp. 16–22)**

For all media in this chapter go to **pearsonhighered.com /techinaction** or **MyITLab**.

*(Hasloo Group Production Studio/Shutterstock; carlos castilla/Shutterstock; winui/Shutterstock; Sergej Khakimullin/Shutterstock)*

# HOW COOL IS THIS?

Scan here for more info

Want to **make a difference with technology**? The good news is that it has never been easier. Technology is allowing more and more of us to become agents of change in our communities and in the world. For example, in London, over 20,000 school-age children are joining **Apps for Good**, a program that links students, educators, and local experts to guide students in designing and building apps to help solve problems they see around them. In the United States, the **Verizon Innovative App Challenge** offered schools across the United States prize money for student teams to design apps to address the needs of their communities. In Philadelphia, people met for a weekend-long civic hacking event called **Random Hacks of Kindness**. They created apps to keep track of lobbyists in city government, to map the location of murals in the city, and to help organize people to dig out fire hydrants after snowstorms. What kind of good can you do with technology? *(Bloomberg/Getty Images; www.rhok.org)*

# How Will You Put Technology in Action?

Ask yourself: Why are you in this class? Maybe it's a requirement for your degree, or maybe you want to improve your computer skills. But let's step back and look at the bigger picture.

Technology today is not just a means for career advancement or merely a skill set needed to survive in society. It's a tool that enables us all to make an impact beyond our own lives. We've all seen the movies that dangle the dream in front of us of being the girl or guy who saves the world—and gets to drive a nice car while doing it! Whether it's *Transformers* or *Spider-Man,* we are drawn to heroes because we want our work and our lives to mean something and to benefit others.

Technology can be your ticket to doing just that, to influencing and participating in projects that will change the world. We'd like to ask you to think about how your talents and skills in technology will let you contribute on a larger scale, beyond the benefits they will bring to you personally.

## technology on the WORLD STAGE

Recent political and global issues are showing that technology is accelerating change around the world and galvanizing groups of people in new ways. Let's look at a few examples.

### Political Issues

**Social Networking Tools.** At the end of 2010, a series of revolutions took place across the Arab and North African regions fueled by social networking tools like Facebook and Twitter. The "Arab Spring" highlighted how **social networking** tools enable the gathering of groups of people to connect and exchange ideas, and they brought together people facing repression and censorship in many countries in the region.

In fact, politicians worldwide have begun to incorporate social networking as part of their political strategy (see Figure 1.1). In the United States, politicians like Barack Obama have Twitter and Facebook accounts that they use to communicate with their constituents. In Italy, Beppe Grillo drew the largest vote in a recent election for a single party using mainly Facebook and Twitter in place of television and newspaper ads. In India, the finance minister took his public discussion about budget not to the airwaves but to a Google+ Hangout session. Yatterbox, a British social media website, follows the social media activities of members of the House of Commons, the Scottish Parliament, and the Northern Ireland Assembly. UK politicians post over two million social media updates a year.

An advantage of social media is that others can immediately connect and engage in a two-way conversation. During the debate in the British Parliament on the legalization of gay marriage, for example, lawmakers were leaving chambers to tweet updates. The public had a chance to try to influence how the vote went through real-time feedback using social media. Social networking tools are therefore providing a level of instant connection and information distribution that is reshaping the world. What can you do with social networking tools that will change the future of your community?

**FIGURE 1.1** German Chancellor Angela Merkel is one of many politicians using a Google+ Hangout to reach out to her constituents. Has technology ushered in a new, more participatory style of democracy? *(Steffen Kugler/picture-alliance/dpa/AP Images)*

**Crisis-Mapping Tool.** Another example of the interaction of technology and society is the software tool Ushahidi. Following a disputed election in Kenya, violence broke out all over the country. Nairobi lawyer Ory Okolloh tried to get word of the violence out to the world through her blog, but she couldn't keep up with the volume of reports. But two programmers saw her request for help and in a few days created Ushahidi (Swahili for "testimony"). It is a **crisis-mapping tool** that collects information from e-mails, text messages, blog posts, and Twitter tweets and then maps them, instantly making the information publicly available. The developers then made Ushahidi a free platform anyone in the world can use (see Figure 1.2). So when earthquakes rocked Haiti, Ushahidi instantly told rescuers where injured people were located. When a tsunami brought Japan to the brink of a nuclear catastrophe, Ushahidi let anyone with a mobile phone find locations with clean water and food.

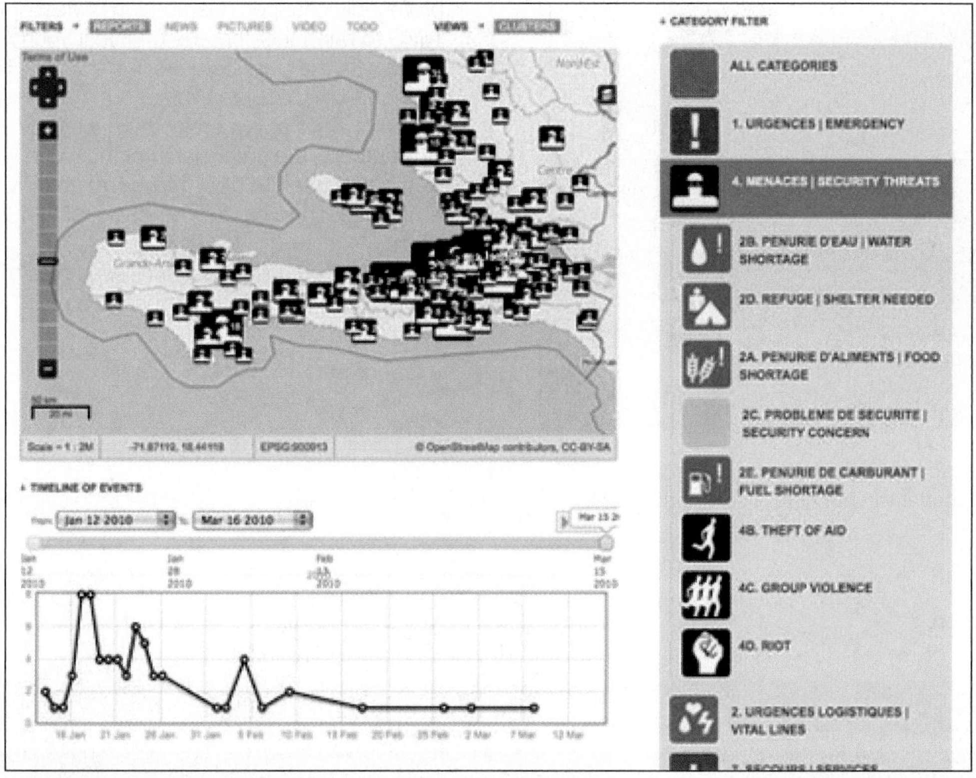

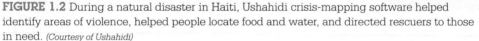

**FIGURE 1.2** During a natural disaster in Haiti, Ushahidi crisis-mapping software helped identify areas of violence, helped people locate food and water, and directed rescuers to those in need. *(Courtesy of Ushahidi)*

Chile, Palestine, Somalia, and the Democratic Republic of Congo have all used this crisis-mapping software to save lives in times of political upheaval. In what other ways could technology help us face times of crisis?

## Other Global Issues

Political crises are not the only arena in which technology is enabling global change.

**Health Care.** Infectious diseases account for about one-fifth of all deaths worldwide. Researchers say the odds of a flu pandemic occurring in the next century are nearly 100%. Could technology help us develop and deliver vaccines in a way that saves lives? With newer scientific visualization tools, scientists are developing antibodies for flu viruses and even HIV, viruses that are difficult to target because they continually change shape. Computationally intense modeling software is helping researchers increase the pace of vaccine production, saving lives.

Retinal prosthetics are another example of global health concerns being addressed with technology. Macular degeneration and retinitis pigmentosa are two diseases that destroy the retina; they account for the majority of blindness in developing nations. Sheila Nirenberg of Cornell University is working on a microchip that can replace the function of the retina, translating incoming light into the electrical pulses the brain needs for vision. These biomedical chips could restore quality vision to the blind.

**The Environment.** What if every cell phone in the world had built-in atmospheric sensors? Then millions of points of air and water quality data from around the world could be constantly acquired. Tagged with geographical information, the data could alert scientists to new trends in our environment. And what if phone sensors could monitor for flu viruses? We could protect ourselves from pandemics by identifying outbreaks very early. Ideas like these are being explored by University of California—Los Angeles researcher Dr. Deborah Estrin, the director at the Center for Embedded Networked Sensing. Can you think of other ways you could use your cell phone to improve society?

**The Digital Divide.** There is a great gap in the levels of Internet access and the availability of technical tools in different regions of the world. The term coined for this difference in ease of access to technology is the **digital divide**. One danger of a digital divide is that it prevents us from using all the minds on the planet to solve the planet's problems. But this challenge created by technology is also being answered by technology.

The Next Einstein Initiative (NEI) is a plan to focus resources on the talented mathematical minds of Africa (see Figure 1.3). By expanding the African Institute for Mathematical Sciences (AIMS) across the continent, the future of Africa can be

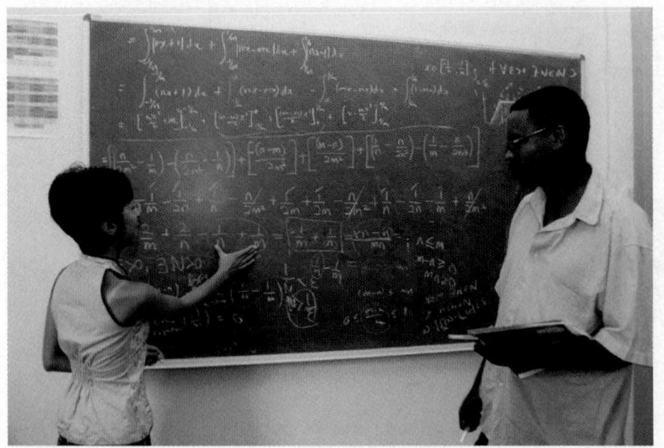

FIGURE 1.3 The Next Einstein Initiative is rallying the support of the world to identify mathematical genius. *(AIMS – Next Einstein Initiative)*

profoundly changed. Cambridge professor Neil Turok founded AIMS to bring together the brightest young minds across Africa with the best lecturers in the world. The NEI has won funding from Google's Project $10^{100}$, an initiative to award $10 million to a set of five projects selected by open public voting. By capturing the enthusiasm of the world with presentations distributed through TED (**ted.com**) and Project $10^{100}$, there is now a push to create 15 additional AIMS centers across Africa.

Figure 1.4 shows additional examples of people putting technology into action to impact the world. How will you join them? ■

FIGURE 1.4

## Technology in Action: Taking on Global Problems

| PERSON/ ORGANIZATION | GLOBAL PROBLEM | TECHNOLOGY USED | ACTION | FIND OUT MORE . . . |
|---|---|---|---|---|
| **Peter Gabriel/ The Witness Project** | Human rights abuses | Video cameras | Provides video documentation of human rights abuses; the project contributed to the arrest of warlords in the Democratic Republic of Congo for the recruitment of child soldiers | The Witness Project: **witness.org** |
| **Johnny Lee/Google** | The digital divide prevents many from taking advantage of modern learning devices like smartboards | Nintendo Wii remote and open source software | Enables users to create a smartboard for $50; the smartboard can record and store lecture content and is touch sensitive | Johnny Lee's blog: **procrastineering .blogspot.com** |
| **United Nations World Food Programme (WFP)** | One in seven people in the world do not get enough food to eat | GIS (geographical information systems) and mobile devices | The WFP can analyze the location and need for food, positioning food where it will help the most | World Food Programme: **wfp.org** |
| **Hod Lipson and Evan Malone/The Fab@Home Project** | Cost and access barriers prevent people from having basic devices, gears, and parts | 3-D printers and open source software | Printers enable users to fabricate 3-D objects such as electrical parts | Fab@Home: **fabathome.org** |
| **Massachusetts Institute of Technology (MIT) Center for Future Civic Media** | Disposal of so many display devices into landfills | Software that allows multiple displays to connect and be reused | The software enables users to create one huge display device from a set of smaller units, thereby keeping monitors out of landfills | Junkyard Jumbotron: **jumbotron.media .mit.edu** |

# ethics in IT The Digital Divide and the Mobile Bridge

**FIGURE 1.5** Can we bridge the digital divide through mobile devices? Should we? *(EIGHTFISH/Alamy)*

The digital divide, the gap between those with easy access to technology and those with little to no access (see Figure 1.5), is a problem that leads to complex social issues. For those who lack access to the Internet and computers, it is difficult to develop computer skills, which are very often critical to future success. Less familiarity with the Internet can also lead to a lower level of active, engaged citizenship. So how should we attack the problem of the digital divide in the United States?

Recent studies from the University of Michigan show that without Internet access at home, teens from low-income households (family income under $30,000 a year) are more likely than their wealthier counterparts to use their cell phones to go online. So the widening penetration of cell phones might be the answer to ending the digital divide. Or is it?

Going online using a cell phone plan is the most expensive of all options, and data transfer speeds are often slow. So teens with the least money are likely paying the most to get the slowest online experience. And they are more likely paying for it themselves, as opposed to teens from wealthier households in which, according to the same University of Michigan study, the teens are more likely to be on family plans paid for by someone else.

In addition, teen cell phone usage is limited to managing online social networks, playing games, or listening to music. Computer tasks and skills that could lead to economic advancement, like filling out job applications or running a business, are not yet handled easily on mobile devices. So by not having free Internet access available, is our society placing those groups least able to afford access at an unfair disadvantage?

Will the increasing penetration of smartphones and faster cellular Internet access eliminate the digital divide in the United States? Should our government intervene and make sure there is sufficient free Internet access for all? Is it ethical to deprive the poorer segment of our society of a needed commodity? Answering challenging questions like these is part of being an informed citizen.

# technology and OUR SOCIETY

Technology is also allowing us to redefine very fundamental parts of our social makeup—how we think, how we connect with each other, and how we purchase and consume products.

## Technology Impacts How We Think

**What We Think About.** What do you think about in your free time? In the late twentieth century, a common trend was to think about what to buy next—or perhaps what to watch or listen to next. Information and products were being served up at an amazing rate, and the pattern of consumption became a habit. As more and more web applications began to appear that allowed each individual to become a "creator" of the web, a new kind of Internet came into being. It was nicknamed **Web 2.0**, and it had a set of new features and functionality that allowed users to contribute content easily and to be easily connected to each other. Now everyone could collaborate internationally at the click of a mouse.

Web 2.0 has fostered a dramatic shift across the world from simply consuming to having the ability to volunteer and collaborate on projects. In his book *Cognitive Surplus: Creativity and Generosity in a Connected Age*, author Clay Shirky created the term **cognitive surplus** to mean the combination of leisure time and the tools to be creative. The world's population has an estimated one trillion hours a year of free time. When coupled with the available media tools and the easy connectivity of Web 2.0, and with generosity and a need to share, projects like Ushahidi and the Witness Project (see Figure 1.4) emerge.

But why would anyone bother to work on projects like these in their free time? Modern theories of motivation show that what pushes people to apply their free time in altruistic causes, for no money, is the excitement of autonomy, mastery, and purpose (see Figure 1.6):

- **Autonomy:** the freedom to work without constant direction and control.
- **Mastery:** the feeling of confidence and excitement from seeing your own skills progress.
- **Purpose:** the understanding that you are working for something larger than yourself.

Together, these three factors play into how we are fundamentally wired and can produce incredibly motivated behavior. The combination of motivation, technology, and a cognitive surplus is leading to powerful projects that are changing the world.

## Technology Impacts How We Connect

**Connecting Through Music.** In many societies, people connect intimately in gatherings and local celebrations through shared experiences. Technology like classical composer and conductor Eric Whitacre's Virtual Choir has added breadth to this aspect of our lives. Whitacre began the idea of a virtual choir by posting to YouTube a video of himself conducting one of his works, "Lux Aurumque." The idea was that listeners would follow his lead and, as they heard the piano track, each would record their part of the piece as either a soprano, an alto, a tenor, or a bass. The submitted videos were edited together, the audio was aligned, and the first piece from the Virtual Choir was released, with 50 recorded voices. A blog connects the members of the choir and builds a real sense of community between members. A glance at the Virtual Choir Map (**ericwhitacre.com/the-virtual-choir/map**) shows the physical location of each voice (see Figure 1.7).

**Connecting Through Business.** One of the most profound ways we can connect with each other is to support other people's dreams.

FIGURE 1.6 Our understanding of human motivation can play a role in our use of technology to impact society.

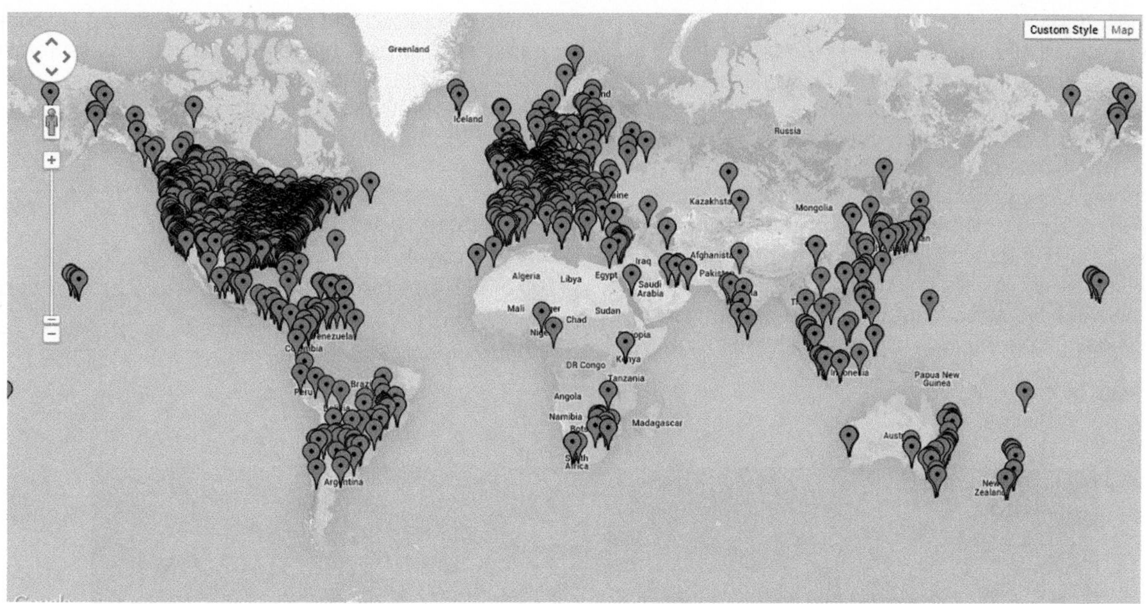


**FIGURE 1.7** The Virtual Choir 4 performance of "Fly to Paradise" included over 5,900 singers from 101 countries. *(Eric Whitcare's Virtual Choir 4 - Fly to Paradise. Courtesy of Music Productions, Ltd.)*

Kickstarter (**kickstarter.com**) helps us connect in this way by allowing people to post their ideas for community projects, games, and inventions and to ask for funding directly. Donors are given rewards for different levels of pledges, such as a signed edition of a book or a special color of a product. This style of generating capital to start a business is known as **crowdfunding**, asking for small donations from a large number of people, often using the Internet.

## Technology Impacts How We Consume

Technology is changing all aspects of how we purchase and consume goods—from strategies for convincing you to purchase a certain product to the mechanics of how you buy and own things.

**Marketing.** New strategies in marketing are counting on the fact that most people have a cell phone with a camera and Internet access. A technology called **QR (quick response) codes** lets any piece of print host a link to online information and video content. From your smartphone, simply run your QR app and hold the phone near the QR image anywhere you see it—like the one you see here and on page 3 page of this chapter. Your phone scans the QR image and then takes you to a website, video, schedule, or Facebook page for more information about the product.

Studies show 82% of shoppers go to the Internet on their cell phone before they make a purchase. They are often using so-called location-aware price comparison tools. Apps like ShopSavvy and RedLaser scan the bar code of the item and then compare prices with those of nearby stores and with the best prices available online. Techy shoppers can then get "mobile coupons" (or *mobicoupons*) delivered to their cell phones thanks to sites like Zavers and Cellfire. The future promises specialized coupons created just for you based on your location and past buying preferences.

Marketers also have to be aware of the phenomenon of **crowdsourcing**—checking in with the voice of the crowd. Consumers are using apps like MobileVoice to check people's verdicts on the quality of items. Forward-thinking companies are using this input to improve their products and services. AT&T, for example, has an app that lets customers report locations of coverage gaps.

**Access Versus Ownership.** Even the idea of ownership is evolving thanks to new technologies. Items like cars and bikes can become "subscriptions" instead of large one-time purchases. For example, Zipcar allows hundreds of thousands of people to use shared cars, and Call a Bike is a popular bike-renting program in Germany. With Zipcar, a phone call or online reservation activates your personal Zipcard. This card allows you to automatically open the door of the car you have reserved, and away you drive. GPS technology is used to track where the car is, whether it has been dropped off at the right location, and how far it has been driven. In Germany, racks of Call a Bikes are located at major street corners in large cities. Simply call the phone number printed on the bike and it texts you a code to unlock the bike. When you're done riding the bike, simply relock it and you're billed automatically. The New York City version of this program, Citi Bike, saw riders cover over 700,000 miles in the first three weeks of the program (see Figure 1.8).

These subscription-style business models are spreading now to smaller goods. Swap.com helps people trade books, clothes, and DVDs with one another using the power of peer-to-peer connections—for example, to find the best set of matches for used roller blades in exchange for a baby crib.

Rachel Botsman and Roo Rogers make the case in their book *What's Mine Is Yours: The Rise of Collaborative Consumption* that the real fuel beneath these services is a shift in our acceptance of sharing. **Collaborative consumption** implies that we are joining together as a group to use a specific product more efficiently. We are so constantly connected with each other that we have again found the power of community. There are increasing opportunities to redistribute the things we have purchased and to share the services a product provides instead of owning it outright. Add in the pressure of mounting environmental concerns and a global financial crisis, and we are migrating toward collaborative consumption. ■

**Before moving on to Part 2:**

- **Watch Replay Video 1.1** .
- Then check your understanding of what you've learned so far.

**FIGURE 1.8** New York City's Citi Bike program uses digital technology to change our lifestyle from one of ownership to one of subscription. The program delivered 250,000 rides in the first three weeks. *(Tim Clayton/TIM C LAYTON/Corbis / APImages)*

# check your understanding//

For a quick review to see what you've learned so far, answer the following questions. Visit **pearsonhighered.com/techinaction** to check your answers.

## multiple choice

**1.** Which is NOT a technology that has been used to deliver assistance during times of crisis?

- **a.** Ushahidi
- **b.** QR codes
- **c.** social networking
- **d.** e-mail

**2.** Cognitive surplus means that we now find many people with

- **a.** more money than free time.
- **b.** limited access to the Internet.
- **c.** excess time and free tools for collaboration.
- **d.** mobile devices.

**3.** Collaborative consumption is when people get together to

- **a.** find the best prices on products.
- **b.** exchange reviews on services and goods they have purchased.
- **c.** fight diseases of the respiratory tract.
- **d.** increase the use of a single product by sharing access to it.

**4.** Web 2.0 is

- **a.** a program that makes access to the Internet twice as fast.
- **b.** functionality that enables everyone to contribute to the web.
- **c.** a tool to produce YouTube videos.
- **d.** an international version of Internet protocols.

**5.** The crisis of a growing digital divide is being addressed by

- **a.** Ushahidi.
- **b.** the Next Einstein Initiative project.
- **c.** the Freecycle program.
- **d.** building faster computers.

## true–false

_____ **1.** The move toward access versus ownership is a sign of collaborative consumption.

_____ **2.** Project Einstein uses the power of supercomputing to create a simulation of Albert Einstein.

## critical thinking

**1. What Occupies Your Mind?**

What we think about is influenced by the information fed to our mind all day long. Web 2.0 has created numerous channels for people to offer their own work for free—open-source software, free music, books, and artworks. How has this affected your thinking? Have you created things to share feely with the online world? Has it changed the value you put on music, books, and art?

**2. Ushahidi Means "Witness"**

We saw that the Ushahidi software has been used for a wide range of applications. What kind of events in your world would benefit from this mapping software? Think of a few ways that having real-time collection and mapping of information would make life easier at your school, safer in your town, or just more fun.

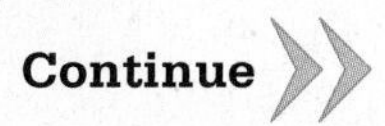

TRY THIS 

# Skyping Around the World

Understanding what your computer can do to improve your life is one of the benefits of being computer literate. In this exercise, we'll show you how to make a free phone call over the Internet using Skype, a popular Voice over Internet Protocol (VoIP) service.

## What You Need

| Wired Internet Connection or WiFi Signal | A Device (computer, smartphone, tablet, Skype-ready television) | A Friend |
|---|---|---|

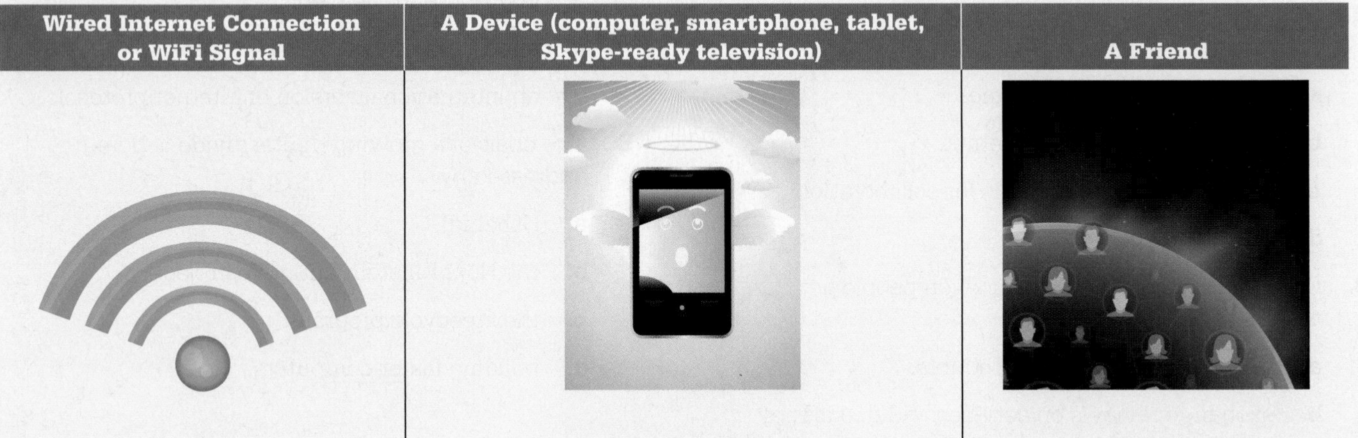

(gst/Shutterstock; Dvougao/Getty Images; filo/Getty Images; © incamerastock / Alamy)

**Step 1** **Set Up an Account.** Go to Skype (**skype.com**) and click on the **Join Us** tab. Download the proper version for your device and install. Fill out the information required to set up a free account. You'll be able to call anyone with Skype and talk with just audio, with audio and video, or with free instant messaging.

**Step 2** **Build Your Contact List.** To build your list of contacts, you can add friends one at a time by clicking **Contacts**, then **Add Contact** and **Search Skype Directory** (as shown below left). You can search for people using their name, their Skype name, or their e-mail.

(You only need to add a phone number if you plan on using Skype to call people on their *phone*, which, unlike computer-to-computer calls, is not a free service.)

For people you call frequently, drag their contact up into the Favorites section.

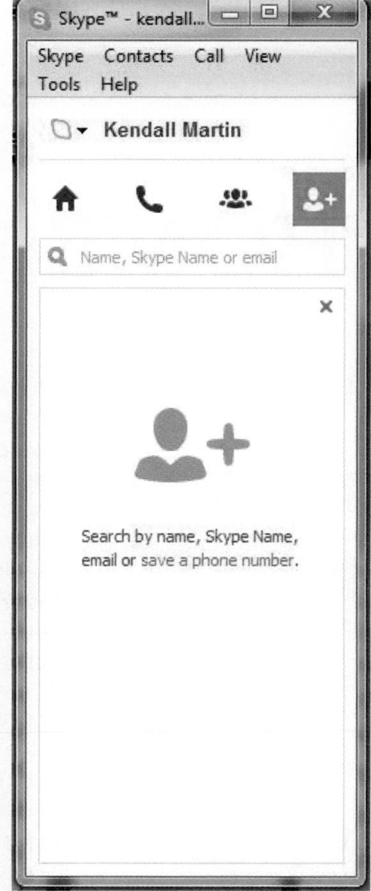


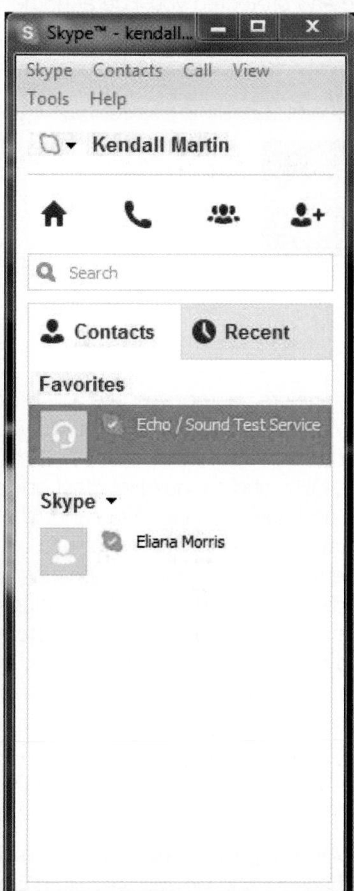


**Step 3** **Make a Call.** Now we're ready to call someone! Let's start by calling the people at Skype and making sure everything is hooked up properly. Under your Contacts list, click the **Echo/Sound Test Service**. Then call in by clicking the green **Call** button. The Skype service will answer your call, record a short message from you, and play it back to you. You'll know everything is set to go, and you can begin calling the world for free!

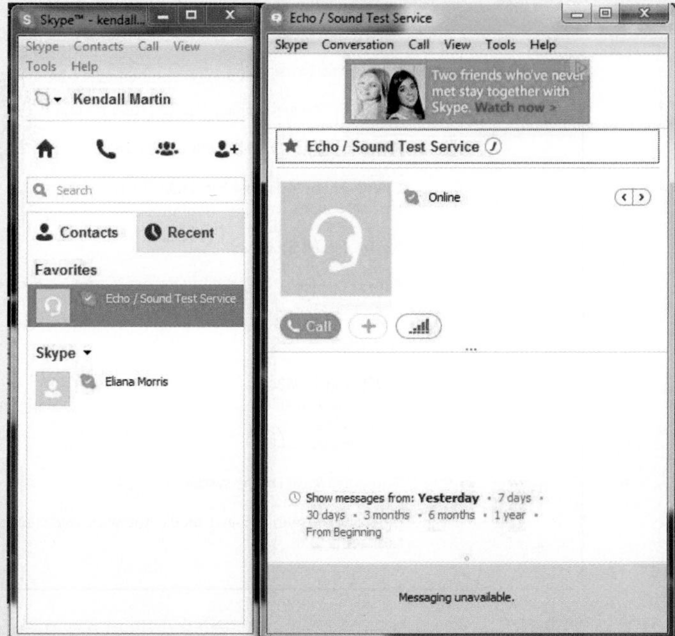

# How Will Technology Improve Your Life?

Technology is creating huge changes in the world as well as in how we behave socially, but it is also important to you on a more personal level. Being **computer literate** means being familiar enough with computers that you understand their capabilities and limitations and that you know how to use them safely and efficiently. As we discuss here, the more you understand technology, the more productive and protected you'll be at home, and the better prepared you'll be for any career.

## technology at HOME

Everywhere you go, you see ads like the one in Figure 1.9 for computers and other devices. Do you know what all the words in the ad mean? What is RAM? What is a CPU? What are MB, GB, GHz, and cache? How fast do you need your computer to be, and how much memory should it have? If you're computer literate, you'll be a more informed consumer when it comes time to buy computers, peripherals, and technology services. Understanding computer terminology and keeping current with technology will help you better determine which computers and devices you need.

Let's look at a few more examples of what else it means to be a savvy computer user and consumer—in other words, computer literate (see Figure 1.10). If you're not a savvy user now, don't worry—the following topics and more are covered in detail in the remaining chapters.

- **Avoiding hackers and viruses.** Do you know what hackers and viruses are? Both can threaten a computer's security. Being aware of how hackers and viruses operate and knowing the damage they can do to your computer can help you avoid falling prey to them.
- **Protecting your privacy.** You've probably heard of identity theft—you see and hear news stories all the time about people whose "identities" are stolen and whose credit ratings are ruined by "identity thieves." But do you know how to protect yourself from identity theft when you're online?
- **Understanding the real risks.** Part of being computer literate means being able to separate the real privacy and security risks from things you don't have to worry about. For example, do you know what a *cookie* is? Do you know whether it poses a privacy risk for you when you're on the Internet? What about a *firewall*? Do you know what one is? Do you really need a firewall to protect your computer?
- **Using the web wisely.** Anyone who has ever searched the web can attest that finding information and finding *good* information are two different things. People who are

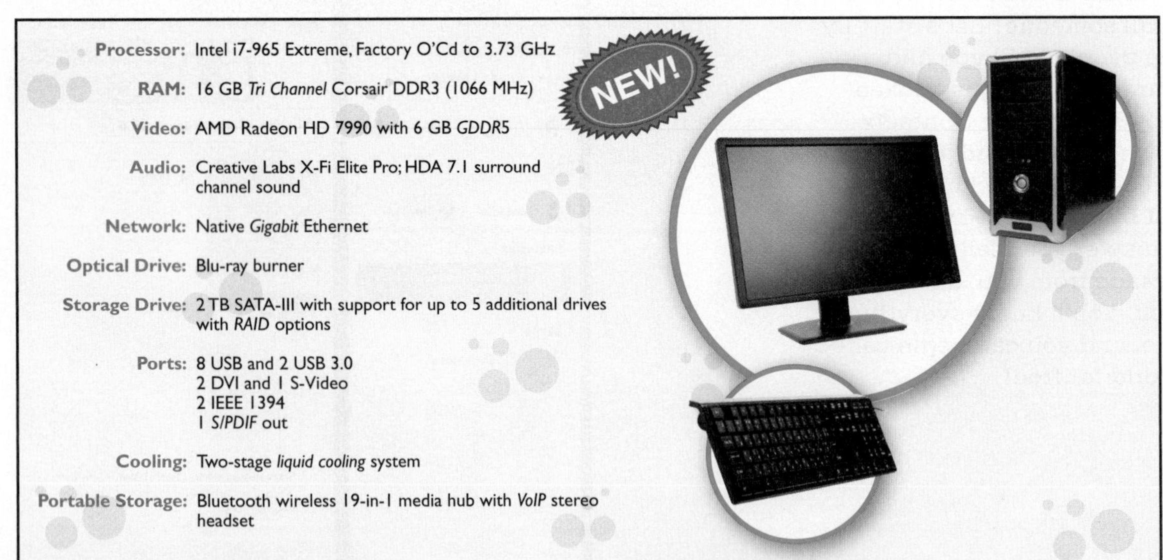

Processor: Intel i7-965 Extreme, Factory O'Cd to 3.73 GHz
RAM: 16 GB *Tri Channel* Corsair DDR3 (1066 MHz)
Video: AMD Radeon HD 7990 with 6 GB *GDDR5*
Audio: Creative Labs X-Fi Elite Pro; HDA 7.1 surround channel sound
Network: Native *Gigabit* Ethernet
Optical Drive: Blu-ray burner
Storage Drive: 2 TB SATA-III with support for up to 5 additional drives with *RAID* options
Ports: 8 USB and 2 USB 3.0
2 DVI and 1 S-Video
2 IEEE 1394
1 *S/PDIF* out
Cooling: Two-stage *liquid cooling* system
Portable Storage: Bluetooth wireless 19-in-1 media hub with *VoIP* stereo headset
NEW!


**FIGURE 1.9** Do you know what all the words in a computer ad mean? Can you tell whether the ad includes all the information necessary to make a purchasing decision? *(Akova/Fotolia; Dmytro Shevchenko/Fotolia; Norman Chan/Fotolia)*

computer literate know how to find the information they want effectively. How effective are your searches?

- **Avoiding online annoyances.** If you have an e-mail account, chances are you've received electronic junk mail, or **spam**. How can you avoid spam? What about adware and spyware—do you know what they are? Do you know the difference between those and viruses, worms, and Trojan horses? Do you know which **software** programs, the instructions that tell the computer what to do, you should install on your computer to avoid online annoyances?
- **Being able to maintain, upgrade, and troubleshoot your computer.** Learning how to care for and maintain your computer and knowing how to diagnose and fix certain problems can save you a lot of time and hassle. Do you know how to upgrade your computer if you want more memory, for example? Do you know which software and computer settings can keep your computer in top shape?

Finally, becoming computer literate means knowing which technologies are on the horizon and how to integrate them into your own life. Can you connect your television to your wireless network? What is Bluetooth, and does your computer need it? Can a USB 3.0 flash drive be plugged into an old USB 1.0 port? Knowing the answers to these and other questions will help you make better purchasing decisions.

This book and course will help you become computer literate. In Chapter 3, you'll find out how to get the most from the web while staying free from the spam and clutter Internet surfing can leave behind on your computer. Chapter 6 shows you how to determine if your hardware is limiting your computer's performance and how to upgrade or shop for a new system. Chapter 9 covers how to keep your computer and your digital life secure. You'll be able to save money, time, and endless frustration by understanding the basics of how computers and computer systems operate. ■

SOUND BYTE

**Questions to Ask Before You Buy a Computer**

This Sound Byte will help you consider important questions to ask before you buy a computer, such as whether you should buy a new computer or a used or refurbished one.

FIGURE 1.10

## What Does It Mean to Be Computer Literate?

You can **avoid falling prey to hackers and viruses** because you are aware of how they operate.

You know how to **protect yourself from identity theft**.

You can **separate the real privacy and security risks from things you don't have to worry about**.

You know how to find information and **use the web effectively**.

You can **avoid being overwhelmed by spam, adware, and spyware**.

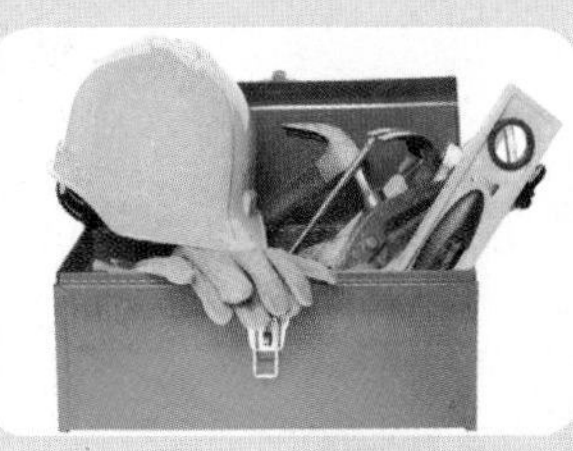

You know how to **diagnose and fix problems** with your hardware and software.

*(pn_photo/Fotolia; Danil Melekhin/Getty Images; Zakai/iStockphoto.com; Sergej Khakimullin/Shutterstock; D. Hurst/Alamy; ivanastar/iStockphoto.com)*

# technology and YOUR CAREER

**Information technology (IT)** is a field of study focused on the management and processing of information and the automatic retrieval of information. IT careers include working with computers, telecommunications, and software deployment. Career opportunities in IT are on the rise, but no matter what career you choose, new technology in the workplace is creating a demand for new skill levels in technology from employees. A study from the National Research Council concludes that by the year 2030, computers will displace humans in 60% of current occupations. Having advanced skills is becoming more critical every year.

One of the benefits of being computer literate is that you will undoubtedly be able to perform your job more effectively. It also will make you more desirable as an employee and more likely to earn more and to advance in your career. In fact, your understanding of key concepts in technology can "future-proof" you, letting you easily and quickly react to the next round of new technologies.

Before we begin looking at a computer's parts and how a computer operates in Chapter 2, let's look at a whole range of industries and examine how computers are a part of getting work done.

## Retail: Working in a Data Mine

Businesses accumulate a lot of data, but how do employees make sense of it all? They use a technique known as **data mining**, the process of searching huge amounts of data with the hope of finding a pattern (see Figure 1.11). For example, retailers often study the data gathered from register terminals to determine which products are selling on a given day and in a specific location. In addition to inventory control systems, which help managers figure out how much merchandise they need to order to replace stock that is sold, managers can use mined data to determine that if they want a certain product to sell well, they must lower its price—especially if they cut the price at one store and see sales increase, for example. Data mining thus allows retailers to respond to consumer buying patterns.

Have you ever wondered how Amazon or Netflix suggest items that fit your taste? Or how such websites automatically display lists of items people bought after they ordered the camera you just picked out? Data mining can keep track of the purchases customers make, along with their geographic data, past buying history, and lists of items they looked at but did not purchase. This data can be translated into marketing that is customized to your shopping. This is the motivation behind the discount cards grocery stores and drugstores offer. In exchange for tracking your buying habits, they offer you special pricing. In the age of data mining, you may be using its capabilities in a number of careers.

## Arts: Ink, Paints, and a Laptop?

Some design students think that because they're studying art, there's no reason for them to study computers. Of course, not all artwork is created using traditional materials such as paint and canvas. Many artists today work exclusively with computers. Mastery of software such as Adobe Illustrator, Adobe Photoshop, and Corel Painter is

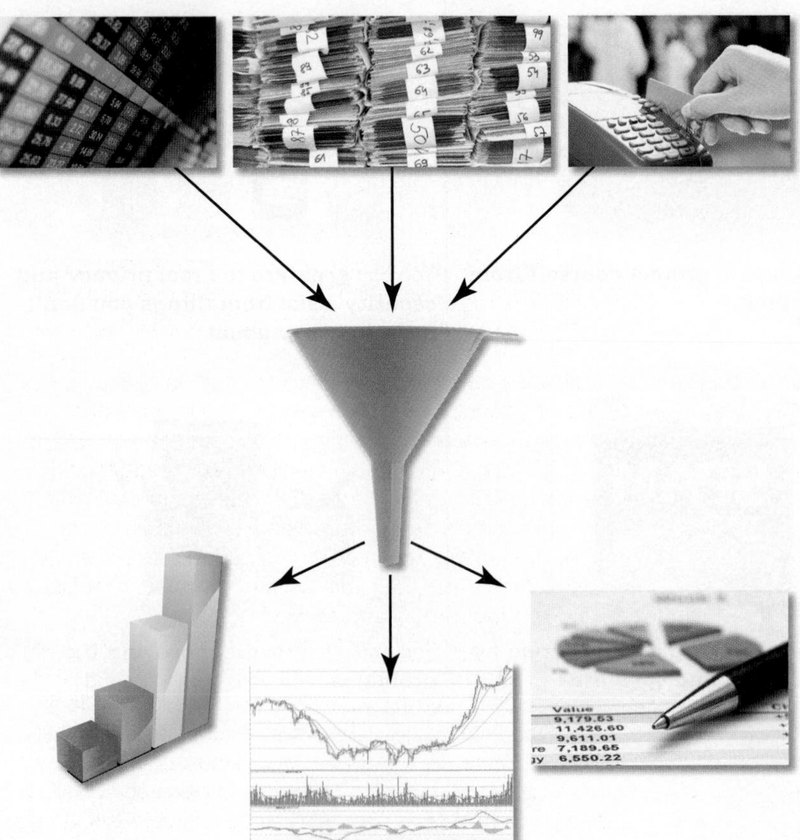

**FIGURE 1.11** Data mining is the art of translating huge volumes of raw data into presentations like charts and graphs that provide managers with information, such as buying trends, that enable them to make better decisions. *(Mclek/Shutterstock; Richard Peterson/Shutterstock; Pressmaster/Shutterstock; Simon Krzic/Shutterstock; Saleeee/Shutterstock; yuyangc/Shutterstock; Shutterstock)*

essential to creating digital art. Eventually you'll want to sell your work, and you'll need to showcase your designs and artistic creations to employers and customers. Wouldn't it be helpful if you knew how to create and manage a website?

Using computers in the arts and entertainment fields goes far beyond just producing web pages, though. Dance and music programs like the ones at the Atlanta Ballet and the Juilliard School use computers to create new performances for audiences. A live dancer can be wired with sensors connected to a computer that captures the dancer's movements. Based on the data it collects, the computer generates a virtual dancer on a screen. The computer operator can easily manipulate this virtual dancer, as well as change the dancer's costume and other aspects of the dancer's appearance, with the click of a mouse. This allows artists to create new experiences for the audience.

And what if you see yourself working in an art museum? Today, museums are using technology to enhance visitors' experiences (see Figure 1.12). New York's Museum of Modern Art (MoMA), for example, offers a full range of options for tech-savvy visitors: old-fashioned museum audio guides, podcasts that visitors can listen to with their smartphones, and multimedia tours that visitors download through MoMA WiFi (**moma.org**) to their own mobile device. These multimedia guides even enable visitors to listen to music the artist listened to when he or she was creating a particular work or to look at other works that reflect similar techniques or themes as those they're viewing. Developing these solutions for museums is a great career for someone with an artistic education and knowledge of technology.

**FIGURE 1.12** Multimedia tours using mobile devices and wireless technology are commonplace in museums and galleries. *(ZUMA Press, Inc. / Alamy)*

## BITS&BYTES

### NASA Wants You . . . to Learn

As you read this chapter, hundreds of satellites are orbiting the globe and taking detailed pictures of Earth. Until recently, these photos weren't available to the public. However, thanks to NASA and some savvy software developers, an application called World Wind is making some 10 trillion bytes of imagery available to you. Need a picture of Mount Fuji for your science project or an aerial picture of your house for your PowerPoint presentation? Just download the software from **www.nasa.gov/offices/education/programs/national/ltp/opportunities**, and you're ready to go. You'll find several learning applications at this site as well. For example, Virtual Lab lets you pretend you have your own scanning electron microscope, and Moonbase Alpha is a game that simulates life on a space settlement, complete with 3-D graphics, team play, and chatting features. With a few clicks, you can have interactive learning resources that open the world to you.

## Education: Teaching and Learning

The education industry uses computer technology in numerous ways. Courses are designed around course management software such as Blackboard or Moodle so that students can communicate outside of class, take quizzes online, and find their class materials easily. The Internet has obvious advantages in the classroom as a research tool for students, and effective use of the Internet allows teachers to expose students to places students otherwise couldn't access. There are simulations and instructional software programs on the web that are incredible learning tools. For example, teachers can employ these products to give students a taste of running a global business (see Figure 1.13) or the experience of the Interactive Body (**bbc.co.uk/science/humanbody**).

Want to take your students to a museum in another state or country? There's no need to board a plane—many museums offer virtual tours on their websites that allow students to examine the museum collections. Another resource, the Art Project, is a collaboration of several museums that allows online visitors to explore over a thousand pieces of art using the same technology employed in Google Street View. A custom viewer allows visitors to zoom in on the artwork itself at

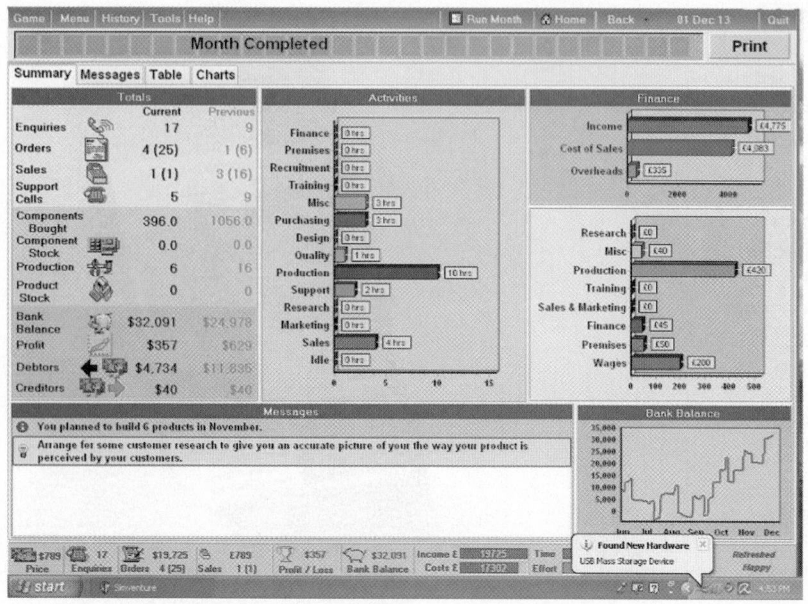


**FIGURE 1.13** Internet applications have become sophisticated learning resources. For example, SimVenture (**simventure.co.uk**) allows students to compete online for domination of a global market while giving instructors the chance to introduce many business concepts. *(Reprinted by permission of Venture Simulations, Ltd.)*

incredibly high resolution (see Figure 1.14). The information panel takes you to related videos and other related websites. So, even if you teach in Topeka, Kansas, you can take your students on a virtual tour of the Tate Britain in London.

Computerized education in the classroom may prove to be the tool that helps teachers reach greater success, despite increasing class sizes and tightening financial constraints. The Khan Academy (**khanacademy.org**) is a terrific example of a technological tool for education. Salman Khan was an investment analyst in Boston in 2006 when he began to post videos to YouTube so that he could teach algebra to his young cousins in New Orleans. Today, his nonprofit Khan Academy contains over 3,000 videos, and several million students a month use the site.

A classroom teacher can also follow what is happening in the classroom by using the *dashboard*, a screen that shows which topics each student has mastered, which they are making progress with, and which have them spinning their wheels. Now a teacher can approach a student already knowing exactly what is frustrating them and can avoid the dreaded question, "Oh, what don't you understand?"

**FIGURE 1.14** The Art Project presents an interactive tour through several museums. Thousands of works of art are displayed in high resolution with a pullout information panel (**googleartproject.com**). *(REUTERS/Stefan Wermuth)*

**FIGURE 1.15** Tissue-rendering programs add layers of muscles, fat, and skin to recovered skulls to create faces that can be used to identify victims. *(Science Photo Library/Glow Images)*

As an educator, being computer literate will help you constructively integrate computer technologies like those discussed here into lesson plans and interactions for your students.

## Law Enforcement: Put Down That Mouse—You're Under Arrest!

Today, wearing out shoe leather to solve crimes is far from the only method available to you if you want to pursue a career in law enforcement. Computers are being used in police cars and crime labs to solve an increasing number of crimes. For example, facial reconstruction systems like the one shown in Figure 1.15 can turn a skull into a finished digital image of a face, allowing investigators to proceed far more quickly with identification than before.

One technique used by modern detectives to solve crimes uses computers to search the vast number of databases on the Internet. Proprietary law enforcement databases such as the National Center for the Analysis of Violent Crime database enable detectives to analyze a wealth of information for similarities between crimes in an attempt to detect patterns that may reveal serial crimes. In fact, a law enforcement specialty called computer forensics is growing in importance in order to fight modern crime. **Computer forensics** analyzes computer systems with specific techniques to gather potential legal evidence. For example, Steven Zirko was recently convicted for two Chicago-area murders based on computer forensics work. Computer forensics examiners trained by the FBI scoured Zirko's computer and located searches for terms like *hire a hitman* and *GHB*, the date-rape drug. Zirko had also used his computer to find the daily schedule for one of his victim's two school-aged children and to get directions to her home. In many cases, files, videos, and conversations conducted using a computer can be recovered by forensics specialists and can be used as evidence of criminal activity.

## Medicine: The Chip Within

A career in medicine will connect you to new ways of using technology to better people's lives. Earlier we mentioned how biomedical chips may one day restore sight to the blind. Indeed, the goals of modern biomedical chip research are to provide technological solutions to physical problems and a means for identifying individuals.

One type of chip is already being implanted in humans as a means of verifying a person's identity. Called VeriMed, this personal identification chip is about the size of a grain of rice and is implanted under the skin. When exposed to radio waves from a scanning device, the chip transmits its serial number to the scanner. The scanner then connects to a database that contains the name, address, and medical conditions of the person in whom the chip has been implanted. In the course of a nursing career, you may be using VeriMed to help keep Alzheimer's patients safe, for example.

Currently, nonimplant versions of identity chips are used in hospitals. When chips are attached with bands to newborn infants, the hospital staff can instantly monitor the location of any baby. Elevators and doors are designed to allow only certain people to enter with a specific baby, even if hospital power is interrupted. Although the use of implantable tags is becoming more commonplace, it remains to be seen whether people will decide that the advantages of having their medical data quickly available justifies having chips implanted in their bodies. As a doctor, would you advise your patients to use an implantable chip?

# DIG DEEPER Making Reality Even More Real

We're comfortable with carrying around digital data in our pockets. But the advent of wearable computing is now allowing us to integrate digital information directly into our reality, both to add more detail and at times to remove unwanted visual effects. How does this happen?

**Augmented reality** combines our normal sense of the world around us with an additional layer of digital information. The extra information can be displayed on a separate device, such as in augmented reality apps for smartphones. For example, city transit apps overlay images that give you directions to the nearest subway lines on top of your actual view of the street (see Figure 1.16).

But having to carry and position a separate device is clunky. Google Glass is a project that augments reality using a "third eye," a separate camera mounted to the side of a lightweight headset (see Figure 1.17). You can record images and videos by simply saying, "Take a picture." When you say "Glass, how long is the Brooklyn Bridge?" Glass communicates wirelessly with your phone and issues a request to the Internet. The returned information is formatted and then sent to a projector. Instead of the projector you're used to seeing in your classroom, this projector is so small it fits into the armband of the glasses. The output beam from the projector bounces off a glass prism that is aligned so that the beam is sent directly to the retina of your eye, as shown in Figure 1.18. (This is why Google Glass is not available for those who wear glasses now. To adjust the prism so that the projector's beam goes through the person's

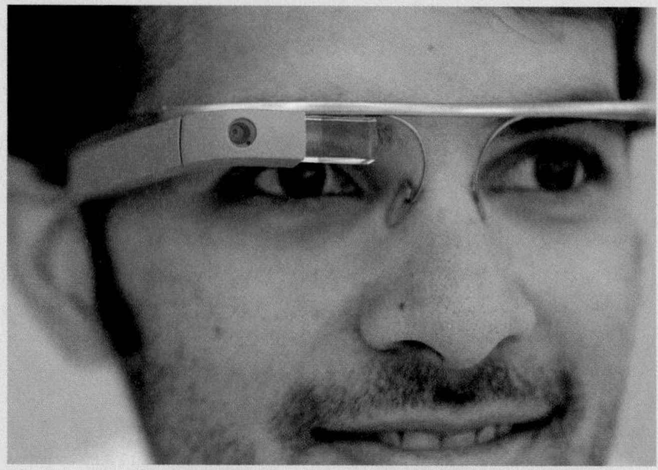

**FIGURE 1.17** Google Glass is a tool that adds digital information directly into your view of the world. *(AP Photo/Jeff Chiu)*

**FIGURE 1.16** Augmented reality apps use your phone's camera to present the world with extra information superimposed. *(Christian Science Monitor/Getty Images)*

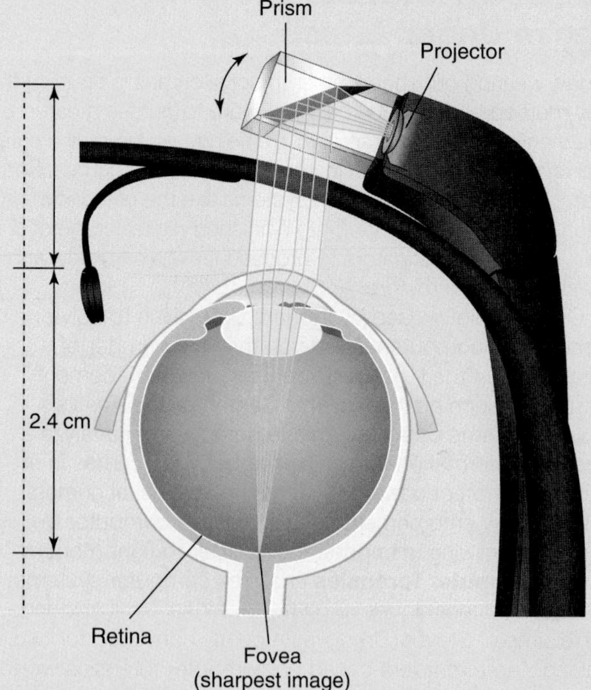


**FIGURE 1.18** Google Glass eliminates the need for a separate hand-held device by projecting an image directly on the retina of your eye. *(© Pearson Education, Upper Saddle River, New Jersey)*

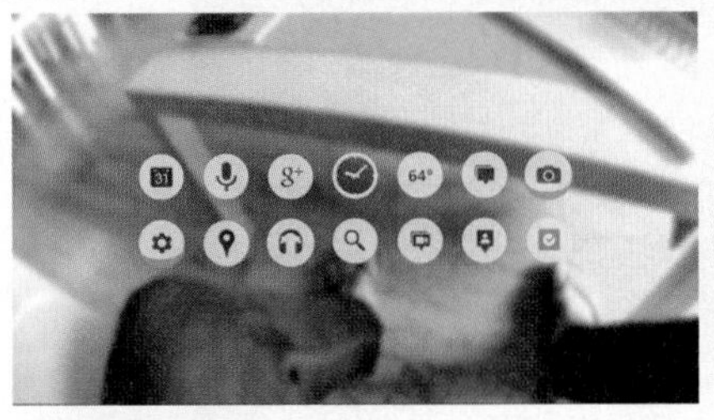

**FIGURE 1.19** Google Glass displays additional information so that it hovers in front of your eyes. *(AP Photo/Google)*

eyeglasses and then hits the retina would require individual adjustment to the prism.) When you're wearing Google Glass, the additional information hovers in space in front of you (Figure 1.19).

Meanwhile, researchers like Stephen Mann at the University of Toronto are working with wearable computers that use "point of eye" (PoE) cameras. A PoE camera is designed so that the camera is positioned directly in front of the eye itself. The ultimate PoE camera would be one that is implanted within the eye or eye socket. Mann's research group is exploring this as a way to assist partially sighted or blind people.

Digital medication has arrived with the FDA approval of digestible microchips (see Figure 1.20). Looking like regular pills, these medications have embedded sensors that transmit information to the doctor. The sensor itself is the size of a grain of sand. As it is digested, a small voltage is generated and detected by a patch worn on the patient's skin. The patch then transmits to the physician that the pill was taken; it also monitors the patient's heart rate, respiration, and temperature.

## Science: Simulating Reality

Thanks to a partnership between the National Severe Storms Lab and the National Center for Supercomputing Applications, tornado forecasting is becoming increasingly accurate.

**FIGURE 1.20** Digital medications are able to report back to physicians information about how the patient is responding to the medicine. *(magebroker.net/Superstock)*

Scientists have been able to create a model so detailed that it takes nine days for a supercomputer to generate it, even though the computer is executing four trillion operations a second. Simulations also can model the structure of solar magnetic flares, which can interfere with broadcasts on Earth. With a career in meteorology, you will be studying the data produced by these simulations, hoping to improve predictions about weather phenomena.

Other technological applications in the sciences are being used on some of the oldest sites on Earth. For example, the Galassi Tomb, located in the ancient Italian city of Caere, was originally designed in 650 B.C. and was rich with ornament and jewelry. These treasures were taken to the Vatican State collection in the 1800s when the tomb was discovered. Today, scientists are using 3-D scanners and imaging software to re-create the experience of seeing the tomb and the artifacts together as they once were (see Figure 1.21). This virtual re-creation is so lifelike that archaeologists can study the ruins on-screen instead of at the actual site. Will you be using these tools someday to make records of other decaying sites?

## Psychology: Computerized Coach

Fear of speaking in public is common, but for people with autism spectrum disorders, making proper eye contact and reacting to social cues is so difficult it can severely limit their opportunities for jobs and relationships. Researchers at the MIT Media Lab have developed a system to help improve interpersonal skills for people who have autism.

MACH (My Automated Conversation Coach) is a computer system that generates an on-screen person that can, for example, conduct a job interview or appear ready for a first date.

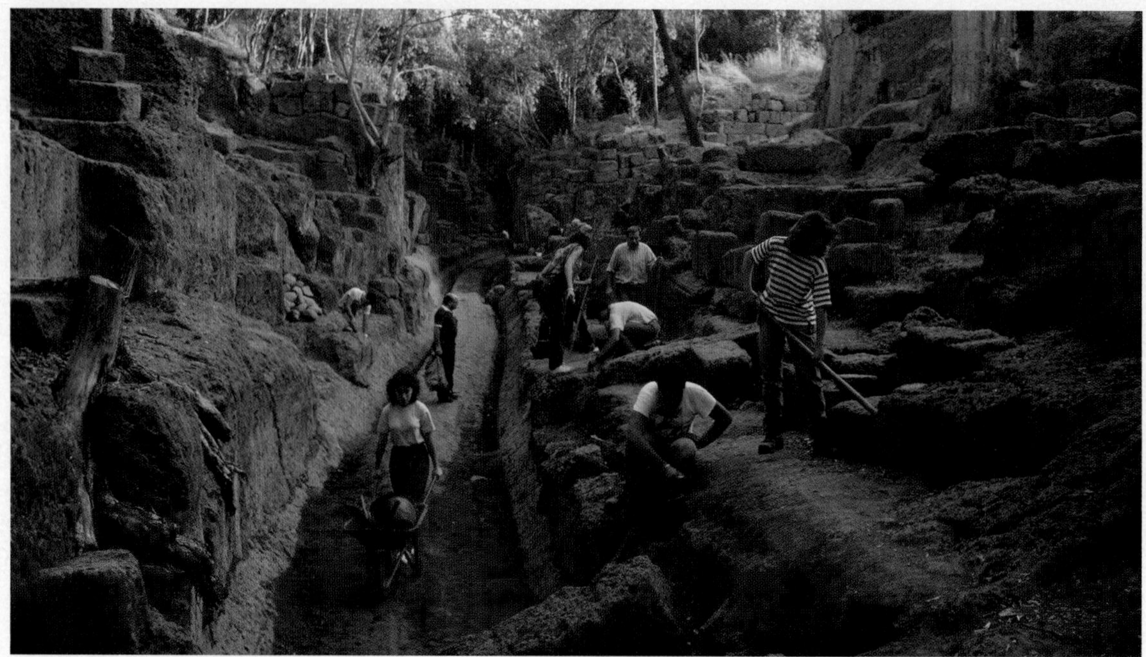

**FIGURE 1.21** These archeologists can work directly at the site, but the Etruscanning system creates a 3-D experience that simulates this experience for others. *(National Geographic/Getty Images)*

The computerized person (see Figure 1.22) nods and smiles in response to the user's speech and movement. This is an example of **affective computing**, developing systems that can

**FIGURE 1.22** My Automated Conversation Coach (MACH) generates an on-screen interviewer you can practice with over and over. *(Cultura Limited/Superstock)*

recognize and simulate human emotions. MACH users can practice as many times as they wish in a safe environment. They receive an analysis that shows how well they modulated their voices, maintained eye contact, smiled, and how often they lapsed into "umms" and "uhhhs." The software runs on an ordinary laptop, using a webcam and microphone.

While engineers work to create computers that can process data faster and faster, psychologists and computer scientists are also working to evolve systems toward a more complete understanding of human behavior. With a career that blends computer science and psychology, you could find yourself at the heart of developing a new kind of relationship between man and machine. ■

**Before moving on to the Chapter Review:**

- **Watch Replay Video 1.2** .
- Then check your understanding of what you've learned so far.

# check your understanding//

For a quick review to see what you've learned so far, answer the following questions. Visit **pearsonhighered.com/techinaction** to check your answers.

## multiple choice

**1.** Computers have limitations and cannot yet

- **a.** respond to human facial cues.
- **b.** re-create environments from hundreds of years ago.
- **c.** suggest plot endings for a story.
- **d.** transmit information from inside the human body.

**2.** The MACH project shows that

- **a.** there is a digital divide limiting access to computer systems.
- **b.** sports performance can be recorded and analyzed by software.
- **c.** there are some things computers cannot teach.
- **d.** computers can help people with interpersonal skills development.

**3.** Which of the following allows retailers to respond to consumer buying patterns?

- **a.** outsourcing
- **b.** data mining
- **c.** smart labels
- **d.** Bluetooth technology

**4.** Computer forensics uses computer systems and technology to

- **a.** simulate a person's anatomical system.
- **b.** train law enforcement officers to be more effective.
- **c.** create a crisis map.
- **d.** gather potential legal evidence.

**5.** IT is the abbreviation for

- **a.** information training.
- **b.** Internet training.
- **c.** Internet technology.
- **d.** information technology.

## true–false

_____ **1.** QR codes can store a website URL.

_____ **2.** Criminal investigators may find evidence on a computer, but that evidence cannot be used in court.

## critical thinking

**1. Working 9 to 5**

This chapter lists many ways in which becoming computer literate is beneficial. Think about what your life will be like once you're started in your career. What areas of computing will be most important for you to understand? How would an understanding of computer hardware and software help you in working from home, working with groups in other countries, and contributing your talents?

**2. Computerized Assessment**

As more and more computer-based training and testing is available, there is pressure to move toward a different educational model. Should introductory courses be run in a new style, heavily based on computer training modules to develop and assess skills? What is the role of the instructor in this model? What key factors need to be available to you to succeed in learning?

**Continue**

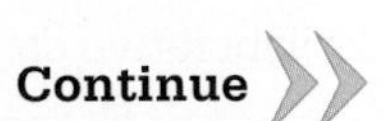

# Chapter Review

## summary//

### Technology on the World Stage

**1. How can becoming proficient with technology help you understand and participate in important issues in the world at large?**

- Whether it's political issues, environmental issues, or questions addressing the global digital divide, it's important that you become proficient with technology to be able to participate.
- Technology can be the means by which you find your voice in the world and impact others in meaningful ways.

### Technology and Our Society

**2. How can knowledge of technology help you influence the direction our society takes?**

- Technology is changing how we think, how we connect with each other, and how we purchase and consume products and services.
- By using current technology, you can become a creator of new pieces of music, connect with people from around the world, and collaborate to create or consume.

### Technology at Home

**3. What does it mean to be computer literate?**

- Computer literacy goes beyond knowing how to use a mouse and send e-mail. If you're computer literate, you understand the capabilities and limitations of computers and know how to use them wisely.
- Being computer literate also enables you to make informed purchasing decisions, use computers in your career, and understand the many ethical, legal, and societal implications of technology today. Anyone can become computer literate.

**4. How does being computer literate make you a savvy computer user and consumer?**

- By understanding how a computer is constructed and how its various parts function, you'll be able to get the most out of your computer.
- Among other things, you'll be able to avoid hackers, viruses, and Internet headaches; protect your privacy; and separate the real risks of privacy and security from those you don't have to worry about.
- You'll also be better able to maintain, upgrade, and troubleshoot your computer; make good purchasing decisions; and incorporate the latest technologies into your existing equipment.

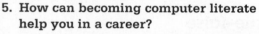

### Technology and Your Career

**5. How can becoming computer literate help you in a career?**

- As computers increasingly become part of our daily lives, it is difficult to imagine any career that does not use computers in some fashion.
- Understanding how to use computers effectively will help you be a more productive and valuable employee, no matter which profession you choose.

Be sure to check out the companion website or MyITLab for additional materials to help you review and learn—**pearsonhighered.com/techinaction**. And don't forget the Replay Videos.

## key terms//

affective computing **22**
augmented reality **20**
cognitive surplus **8**
collaborative consumption **10**
computer forensics **19**
computer literate **14**
crisis-mapping tool **4**
crowdfunding **9**
crowdsourcing **9**
data mining **16**
digital divide **5**
information technology (IT) **16**
QR (quick response) codes **9**
social networking **4**
software **15**
spam **15**
Web 2.0 **8**

## making the transition to . . . next semester//

1. **Drive**

   Researchers are finding that the critical quality that predicts whether a student will complete a course or an entire program is "grit"—his or her determination to continue toward a very long-term goal despite adversity. How does your determination change as you are given more autonomy in a course? As you feel your skills are growing? If you have a sense that the work you do matters to more people than just yourself?

2. **The Mind of the Mob**

   Crowdsourcing is the gathering of data in real time, as an event happens, from a growing crowd of people. Because of the large number of students who now own phones with Internet access, crowdsourcing on campus could start to be useful. In what settings would making decisions based on information from a gathering crowd on campus be valuable? How would you react to your professor using a form of crowdsourcing to determine your grade on an essay?

3. **Recycle, Repair, Redistribute**

   The Microsoft-authorized refurbisher program and TechSoup both help provide resources to people in need to reduce the barrier of the digital divide. These organizations recycle hardware and supply software inexpensively to needy families. How could a program be set up at your school to make people aware of these options? Could students donate materials or retrofit systems as part of their coursework? As part of a club activity? How could you make these programs work for your community?

## making the transition to . . . the workplace//

1. **Patients and Medical Computing**

   As more hospitals and doctors' offices begin to use electronic medical records (EMRs), the flow of information among the doctors and care facilities a patient uses could become much more reliable. In their training and work, doctors and nurses rely on computers. What about patients? Examine Microsoft Health Vault at **healthvault.com** for an example of an electronic medical history. How does this migration from a traditional paper records system impact the skills required for medical office workers? New ethical questions also often arise when technology changes. How would a medical facility now protect and verify its data records? What risks are there with a product like the Microsoft Health Vault?

2. **Social Media Careers**

   With the explosion of users on social media sites, businesses need to establish their presence on social media sites. Just search for "Vans" or "Starbucks" on Facebook for examples of company sites. To manage their interaction with customers (and fans), companies need to hire social media managers. Using a job site such as **Monster.com**, search for "social media manager" and review the job postings. What are the educational requirements for social media managers? What technical skills do these jobs require? Given your major, what companies would you do well for as a social media manager? What steps should you take while in school to prepare yourself for a career as a social media manager?

3. **Edges of Literacy**

   Employers always seek to hire computer-literate workers. Is the boundary of what is computer literate changing? Is it enough to just know how to use the most popular computer programs, or is writing programs important? Is it enough to know how to use Google, or are there other techniques of finding information employers expect? Is it enough to be able to install a mobile app, or do employers want you to be able to create one? How could you document for your employer your ability to learn, adapt quickly to changes in technology, and acquire new skills?

## team time//

# A Culture of Sharing

## Problem

As more and more peer-to-peer music-sharing services appeared, like BitTorrent and LimeWire, many felt a culture of theft was developing. Some argued there was a mindset that property rights for intellectual works need not be respected and that people should be able to download, for free, any music, movies, or other digital content they wanted.

But there is another view of the phenomenon. Some are suggesting that the amount of constant access to other people—through texting, e-mail, blogging, and the easy exchange of digital content—has created a culture of trust and sharing. This Team Time will explore both sides of this debate as it affects three different parts of our lives—finance, travel, and consumerism.

## Task

Each of three groups will select a different area to examine—finance, travel, or consumerism. The groups will find evidence to support or refute the idea that a culture of sharing is developing. The finance group will want to explore projects like Kickstarter (**kickstarter.com**) and Kiva (**kiva.org**). The travel group should examine what is happening with CouchSurfing (**couchsurfing.org**) to start their research. The team investigating consumerism will want to look at goods-exchange programs like Freecycle (**freecycle.org**).

## Process

1. Divide the class into three teams.
2. Discuss the different views of a "culture of sharing." With the other members of your team, use the Internet to research up-and-coming technologies and projects that would support your position. People use social media tools to connect into groups to exchange ideas. Does that promote trust? Does easy access to digital content promote theft, or has the value of content changed? Are there other forces like the economy and the environmental state of the world that play a role in promoting a culture of sharing? What evidence can you find to support your ideas?
3. Present your group's findings to the class for debate and discussion.
4. Write a strategy paper that summarizes your position and outlines your predictions for the future. Will the pace of technology promote a change in the future from the position you are describing?

## Conclusion

The future of technology is unknown, but we do know that it will impact the way our society progresses. To be part of the developments that technology will bring will take good planning and attention, no matter what area of the culture you're examining. Begin now—learn how to stay on top of technology.

## ethics project//

# Should Information Be Free?

In this exercise, you'll research and role-play a complicated ethical situation. The role you play might not match your personal beliefs; regardless, your research and use of logic should enable you to represent the view assigned. An arbitrator will watch and comment on both sides of the arguments, and together team members will agree on an ethical solution.

## Problem

The crisis-mapping tool Ushahidi has been used to collect and present information in times of unrest. This allows everyone to be involved in gathering the actual facts about what is happening and to help address the needs of people who are lost and hurt.

WikiLeaks is another example of a tool that gathers information and "frees" it by presenting it to the public. Whistleblowers and secret and classified media have been exposed to the world community through publication via WikiLeaks. However, some people feel that WikiLeaks has endangered people by revealing information that should have been kept confidential.

What is the nature of information? Should it be "free"—available without censure or government controls? Is there a limit—should only certain information be free, whereas other information should be kept away from the public for the greater good?

## Research Topics to Consider

- Electronic Frontier Foundation
- Government 2.0

## Process

1. Divide the class into teams. Each team will select a web-based tool that allows access to information.
2. Team members should each think of a situation where a person would benefit from the easy access to information and a situation where it might be undesirable.
3. Team members should arrange a mutually convenient time to meet for the exchange, using a virtual meeting tool or by meeting in person. Select the most powerful and best-constructed arguments and develop a summary conclusion.
4. Team members should present their findings to the class or submit a PowerPoint presentation for review by the rest of the class, along with the summary conclusion they developed.

## Conclusion

As technology becomes ever more prevalent and integrated into our lives, ethical dilemmas will present themselves to an increasing extent. Being able to understand and evaluate both sides of the argument, while responding in a personally or socially ethical manner, will be an important skill.

# 2 Looking at Computers: Understanding the Parts

## Understanding Digital Components

### Understanding Your Computer

**OBJECTIVES**

1. What exactly is a computer, and what are its four main functions? **(p. 30)**
2. What is the difference between data and information? **(p. 30)**
3. What are bits and bytes, and how are they measured? **(pp. 30–34)**

**Sound Byte:** Binary Numbers

**Active Helpdesk:** Understanding Bits and Bytes

### Input Devices and Output Devices

**OBJECTIVES**

4. What devices can I use to get data into the computer? **(pp. 35–41)**
5. What devices can I use to get information out of the computer? **(pp. 42–49)**

**Active Helpdesk:** Using Output Devices

## Processing, Storage, and Connectivity

### Processing, Memory, and Storage

**OBJECTIVES**

6. What's on the motherboard? **(pp. 52–53)**
7. Where are information and programs stored? **(pp. 54–56)**

**Sound Byte:** Virtual Computer Tour

### Ports and Power Controls

**OBJECTIVES**

8. How are devices connected to the computer? **(pp. 57–58)**
9. What's the best way to turn my computer on and off, and when should it be done? **(pp. 59–60)**

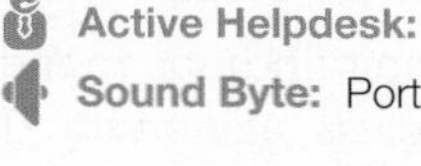

**Active Helpdesk:** Exploring Storage Devices and Ports

**Sound Byte:** Port Tour: How Do I Hook It Up?

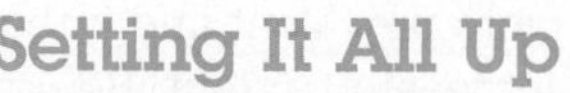

### Setting It All Up

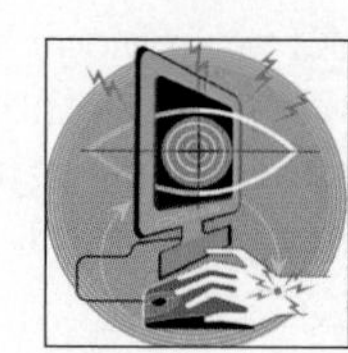

**OBJECTIVE**

10. How do I set up my computer to avoid strain and injury? **(pp. 61–63)**

**Sound Byte:** Healthy Computing

The information in this text is written for Windows 8.1. If you are still running Windows 8, your screens and task instructions may vary slightly.

For all media in this chapter go to **pearsonhighered.com/techinaction** or **MyITLab**.

*(Login/Shutterstock; Zadorozhnyi Viktor/Shutterstock; rukanoga/Fotolia; Lola & Bek/ImageZoo/Alamy)*

# HOW COOL IS THIS?

Scan here for more info

The **touch experience** is pretty common on computing devices now, making the mouse appear almost passé. But what about manipulating your computer like Tony Stark did in *Iron Man 3* by **waving your hands** in the air? Leap Motion has released a controller that senses how you move your hands to allow you to control your computing device **using just gestures**…no touching the screen needed! The inventors of this device were inspired by the **Holodeck technology** as envisioned in *Star Trek*. Although current apps aren't designed to make optimal use of this technology, many experts agree that **gesture interfaces** are the wave of the future. And you won't need to clean your fingerprints off your screens any longer! *(Leap Motion, Inc.; Courtesy of Leap Motion, Inc.)*

# Understanding Digital Components

After reading Chapter 1, you can see why becoming computer literate is important. But where do you start? You've no doubt gleaned some knowledge about computers just from being a member of society. However, even if you have used a computer before, do you really understand how it works, what all its parts are, and what those parts do?

## understanding your COMPUTER

Let's start our look at computers by discussing what a computer does and how its functions make it such a useful machine.

### Computers Are Data Processing Devices

Strictly defined, a **computer** is a data processing device that performs four major functions:

1. **Input:** It gathers data, or allows users to enter data.
2. **Process:** It manipulates, calculates, or organizes that data into information.
3. **Output:** It displays data and information in a form suitable for the user.
4. **Storage:** It saves data and information for later use.

**What's the difference between data and information?** People often use the terms *data* and *information* interchangeably. Although they may mean the same thing in a simple conversation, the distinction between data and information is an important one.

In computer terms, **data** is a representation of a fact, a figure, or an idea. Data can be a number, a word, a picture, or even a recording of sound. For example, the number 7135553297 and the names Zoe and Richardson are pieces of data. Alone, these pieces of data probably mean little to you. **Information** is data that has been organized or presented in a meaningful fashion. When your computer provides you with a contact listing that indicates that Zoe Richardson can be reached at (713) 555-3297, the data becomes useful—that is, it becomes information.

**How do computers interact with data and information?** Computers are excellent at **processing** (manipulating, calculating, or organizing) data into information. When you first arrived on campus, you probably were directed to a place where you could get an ID card. You most likely provided a clerk with personal data that was entered into a computer. The clerk then took your picture with a digital camera (collecting more data). All of the data was then processed appropriately so that it could be printed on your ID card (see Figure 2.1). This organized output of data on your ID card is useful information.

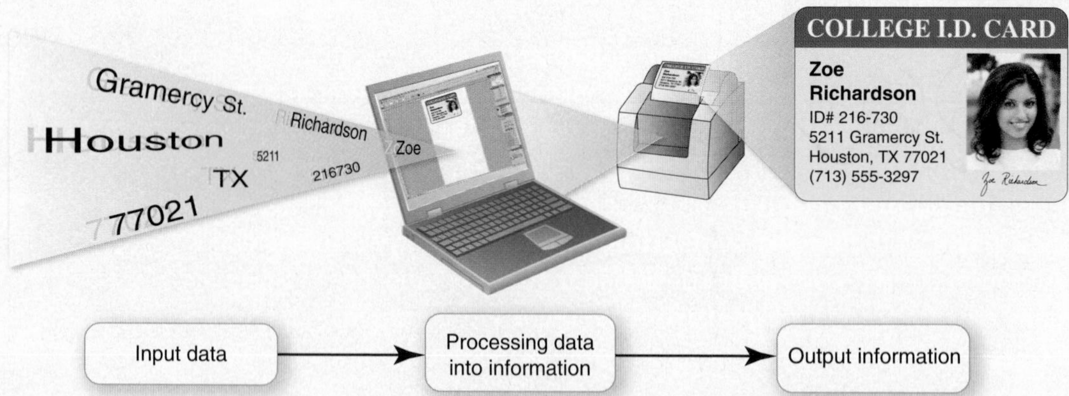


**FIGURE 2.1** Computers process data into information. *(Michaeljung/Shutterstock)*

SOUND BYTE
**Binary Numbers**

This Sound Byte helps remove the mystery surrounding binary numbers. You'll learn about base conversion between decimal, binary, and hexadecimal numbers using colors, sounds, and images.

## Bits and Bytes: The Language of Computers

**How do computers process data into information?** Unlike humans, computers work exclusively with numbers (not words). To process data into information, computers need to work in a language they understand. This language, called **binary language**, consists of just two digits: 0 and 1. Everything a computer does, such as processing data, printing a report, or editing a photo, is broken down into a series of 0s and 1s. Each 0 and 1 is a **binary digit**, or **bit** for short. Eight binary digits (or bits) combine to create one **byte**. In computers, each letter of the alphabet, each number, and each special character (such as @, pronounced "at") consists of a unique combination of eight bits, or a string of eight 0s and 1s. So, for example, in binary language, the letter *K* is represented as 01001011. This is eight bits, or one byte.

**What else can bits and bytes be used for?** Bits and bytes not only are used as the language that tells the computer what to do, they are also used to represent the *quantity* of data and information that the computer inputs and outputs. Word processing files, digital pictures, and even software are represented inside computing devices as a series of bits and bytes. These files and applications can be quite large, containing thousands or millions of bytes.

To make it easier to measure the size of such files, we need units of measure larger than a byte. Kilobytes, megabytes, and gigabytes are therefore simply larger amounts of bytes. As shown in Figure 2.2, a **kilobyte (KB)** is approximately 1,000 bytes, a **megabyte (MB)** is about 1 million bytes, and a **gigabyte (GB)** is around 1 billion bytes. Today, personal computers are capable of storing **terabytes (TB)** of data (around 1 trillion bytes), and many business computers can store up to a **petabyte (PB)** (1,000 terabytes) of data. The Google search engine processes more than 1 PB of user-generated data per *hour*!

**How does your computer process bits and bytes?** Your computer uses hardware and software to process data into information that lets you complete tasks such as writing a letter or playing a game. **Hardware** is any part of the computer you can physically touch. However, a computer needs more than just hardware to work. **Software** is the set of computer programs that enables the hardware to perform different tasks.

There are two broad categories of software: *application software* and *system software*. **Application software** is the set of programs you use on a computer to help you carry out tasks such as writing a research paper. If you've ever typed a document, created a spreadsheet, or edited a digital photo, for example, you've used application software.

**System software** is the set of programs that enables your computer's hardware devices and application software to work together. The most common type of system software is the **operating system (OS)**—the program that controls how your computer system functions. It manages the hardware, such as the monitor and printer, and provides a means by which users can interact with the computer. Most likely, the computer you own or use at school runs a version of Windows as the system software. However, if you're working on an Apple computer, you're probably running OS X.

ACTIVE HELPDESK
**Understanding Bits and Bytes**

In this Active Helpdesk call, you'll play the role of a helpdesk staffer, fielding calls about the difference between data and information, what bits and bytes are, and how bytes are measured.

## Types of Computers

**What types of computers are popular for personal use?** There are two basic designs of computers: portable and stationary. For portable computers, a number of options exist:

- In 2010, Apple introduced the iPad, which created a new class of portable computers. A **tablet computer**, such as the iPad or Samsung Galaxy Tab, is a portable computer integrated into a flat multitouch-sensitive screen. It uses an onscreen virtual keyboard, but you can connect separate keyboards to it via Bluetooth or wires.
- A **laptop** or **notebook computer** is a portable computer that has a keyboard, monitor, and other devices integrated into a single compact case.
- A **netbook** is a small, lightweight laptop computer that is generally 7 to 10 inches wide and has a longer battery life than a laptop. These have been losing market share to tablet devices.
- An **ultrabook** is a full-featured but lightweight laptop computer designed to compete with the MacBook Air. Ultrabooks feature low-power processors and solid-state drives and try to reduce their size and weight to extend battery life without sacrificing performance.
- A **tablet (**or **convertible) PC** is similar to a laptop computer, but the monitor swivels and folds flat (see Figure 2.3a). This allows it to function both as a conventional laptop and as a tablet computer using its touchscreen.

A **desktop computer** is intended for use at a single location, so it's stationary. Most desktop computers consist of a separate case or tower (called the **system unit**) that

FIGURE 2.2

## How Much Is a Byte?

| NAME | NUMBER OF BYTES | RELATIVE SIZE |
|---|---|---|
| **Byte (B)** | 1 byte | One character of data (8 bits, or binary digits) |
| **Kilobyte (KB)** | 1,024 bytes ($2^{10}$ bytes) | 1,024 characters, or about 1 page of plain text |
| **Megabyte (MB)** | 1,048,576 bytes ($2^{20}$ bytes) |  About 4 books (200 pages, 240,000 characters) |
| **Gigabyte (GB)** | 1,073,741,824 bytes ($2^{30}$ bytes) |  About 4,500 books, or over twice the size of Sir Isaac Newton's library (considered very large for the time) |
| **Terabyte (TB)** | 1,099,511,627,776 bytes ($2^{40}$ bytes) | About 4.6 million books, or about the number of volumes in the Rutgers University Library |
| **Petabyte (PB)** | 1,125,899,906,842,624 bytes ($2^{50}$ bytes) |  About 4.7 billion books, which would fill the Library of Congress (the United States' largest library) 140 times! |
| **Exabyte (EB)** | 1,152,921,504,606,846,976 bytes ($2^{60}$ bytes) | About 4.8 trillion books, which, if stored as they are in the Library of Congress, would occupy about 11,000 square miles, or an area almost the size of the state of Maryland |
| **Zettabyte (ZB)** | 1,180,591,620,717,411,303,424 bytes ($2^{70}$ bytes) |  The library required to house the 4.9 quadrillion books equal to a ZB of data would occupy about 11.3 million square miles, or an area about 1 million square miles larger than all of North America |

(Ninice64/Fotolia; Georgios Kollidas/Fotolia; D.aniel/Fotolia; Flavijus Piliponis/Fotolia)

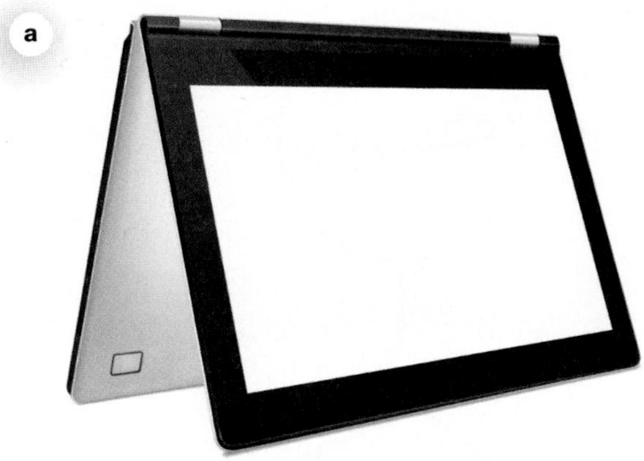

FIGURE 2.3 (a) A convertible PC has a monitor that swivels to become a touch-sensitive input device; (b) an all-in-one computer does not need a separate tower. *(© JeKh – Fotolia.com; PRNewsFoto/Apple/AP Images)*

houses the main components of the computer plus peripheral devices. A **peripheral device** is a component, such as a monitor or keyboard, that connects to the computer. An **all-in-one computer**, such as the Apple iMac (Figure 2.3b) or HP TouchSmart, eliminates the need for a separate tower because these computers house the computer's processor and memory in the monitor. Many all-in-one models, such as the TouchSmart, also incorporate touch-screen technology.

**Are there other types of computers?** Although you may never come into direct contact with the following types of computers, they are still very important and do a lot of work behind the scenes of daily life:

- A **mainframe** is a large, expensive computer that supports many users simultaneously. Mainframes are often used in businesses that manage large amounts of data, such as insurance companies, where many people are working at the same time on similar operations, such as claims processing. Mainframes excel at executing many computer programs at the same time.
- A **supercomputer** is a specially designed computer that can perform complex calculations extremely rapidly. Supercomputers are used when complex models requiring intensive mathematical calculations are needed (such as weather forecasting or atomic energy research). Supercomputers are designed to execute a few programs as quickly as possible, whereas mainframes are designed to handle many programs running at the same time but at a slower pace.
- An **embedded computer** is a specially designed computer chip that resides in another device, such as your car or the electronic thermostat in your home. Embedded computers are self-contained computer devices that have their own programming and that typically don't receive input from you or interact with other systems (see Figure 2.4).

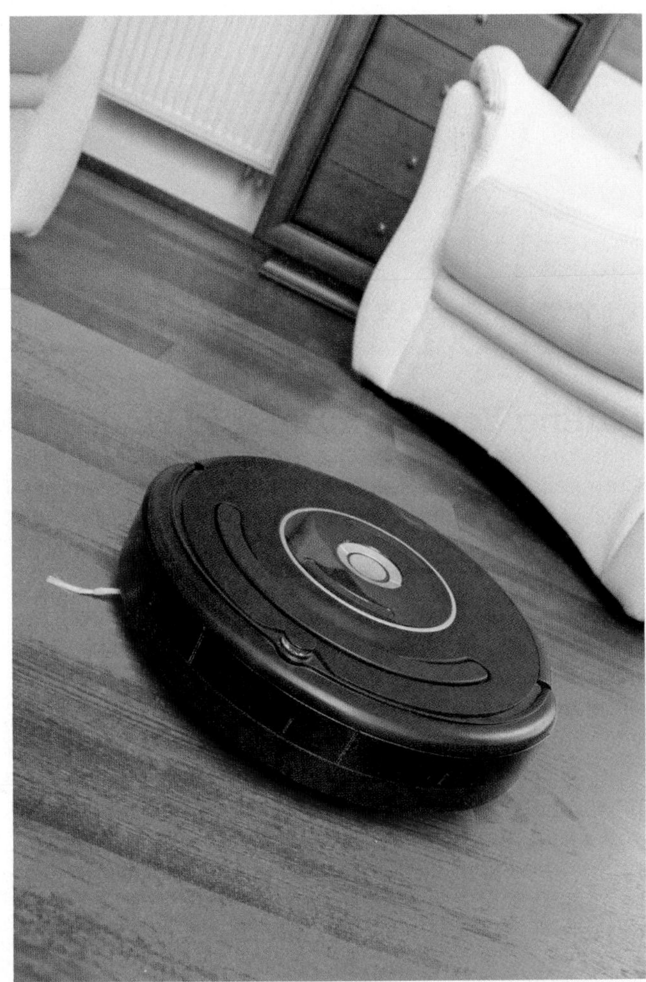

FIGURE 2.4 This robot vacuum includes an embedded computer. *(Jirsak/Shutterstock)*

Even your smartphone is a computer. Today's **smartphones** offer many features you probably use day to day, including a wide assortment of apps, media players, high-quality cameras, and web connectivity. And just like your laptop computer, your smartphone has a CPU, memory, and storage. Examples of smartphones include the iPhone and the HTC One.

Each part of your computer has a specific purpose that coordinates with one of the functions of the computer—input, processing, output, or storage (see Figure 2.5). Additional devices, such as modems and routers, help a computer communicate with the Internet and other computers to facilitate the sharing of documents and other resources. Let's begin our exploration of hardware by looking at your computer's input devices. ■

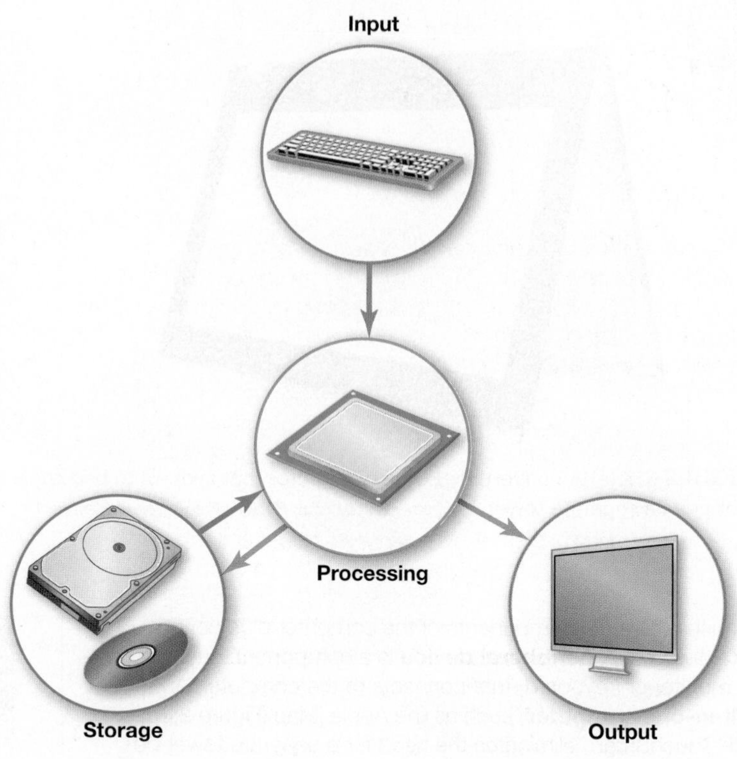


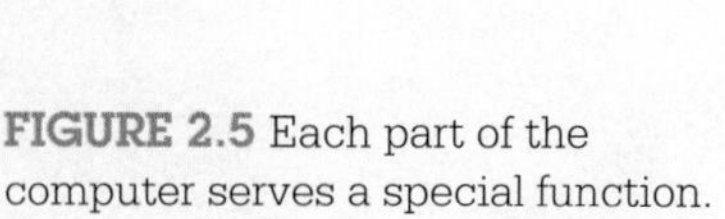

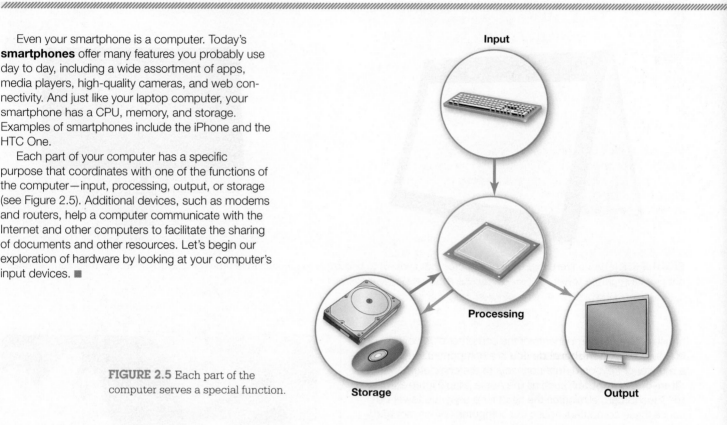

FIGURE 2.5 Each part of the computer serves a special function.

# BITS&BYTES

## Putting Your Computer to Work . . . While You Sleep

Complex scientific research, such as human genome exploration, requires vast computing power. Software has been developed to tie individual computing devices (including tablets and smartphones) in a grid to enable them to work together. This effectively creates a cheap supercomputer that many not-for-profit research organizations use to research problems that will benefit the greater good...and your computer can help. Visit the World Community Grid (**worldcommunitygrid.org**) and download its software. Once installed on your device, it allows your computer to work on research during the many times when your CPU is idle (or at least not working to its full potential). Your computing device can participate in exciting research projects on new drugs, sustainable water, and cancer. So tell your computer to get to work!

FIGURE 2.6 Help solve complex problems by adding your computer to the World Community Grid. *(adimas/Fotolia)*

# input DEVICES

An **input device** lets you enter data (text, images, and sounds) and instructions (user responses and commands) into your computer. A **keyboard** is an input device you use to enter typed data and commands, and a **mouse** is used to enter user responses and commands.

There are other input devices as well. Microphones input sounds, scanners input nondigital data (such as magazine articles and old photographs) by turning it into a digital form, and digital cameras input digital images. A **stylus** is an input device that looks like a pen, which you use to tap commands or draw on a screen. We'll explore these and other input devices next.

## Keyboards

**What is the most common way to input data and commands?** Most computing devices, such as smartphones and tablets, now respond to touch. **Touch screens** are display screens that respond to commands initiated by touching them with your finger or a stylus. Touch-screen devices use a virtual keyboard (see Figure 2.7) that displays on screen when text input is required. These keyboards show basic keyboard configurations and use special keys to switch to numeric, punctuation, and other special keys.

**Are all keyboards the same?** Whether onscreen touch keyboards or physical keyboards, the most common keyboard layout is a standard **QWERTY keyboard**. This keyboard layout gets its name from the first six letters in the top-left row of alphabetic keys and is the standard English-language keyboard layout. The QWERTY layout was originally designed for typewriters and was meant to slow typists down and prevent typewriter keys from jamming. Although the QWERTY layout is considered inefficient because it slows typing speeds, efforts to change to more efficient layouts, such as that of the Dvorak keyboard (see the Bits and Bytes on the next page), have not been met with much public interest.

**What alternatives are there to an onscreen touch keyboard?** Touchscreen keyboards are not always convenient when a great deal of typing is required. Most computing devices can accept physical keyboards as an add-on accessory. Wired keyboards plug into a data port on the computing device. Wireless keyboards send data to the computer using a form of wireless technology that uses *radio frequency (RF)*. A radio transmitter in the keyboard sends out signals that are received either by a receiving device plugged into a port on the device or by a Bluetooth receiving device located in the device. You've probably heard of **Bluetooth technology** if you use a headset or earpiece with your cell phone. Bluetooth is a wireless transmission standard that lets you connect devices such as smartphones, tablets, and laptops to peripheral devices such as keyboards and headsets. Often, wireless keyboards for tablets are integrated with a case to protect your tablet (see Figure 2.8a).

FIGURE 2.7 Virtual keyboards are found on tablets and other touch-screen devices. *(PhotoNonStop/Glow Images)*

a

b

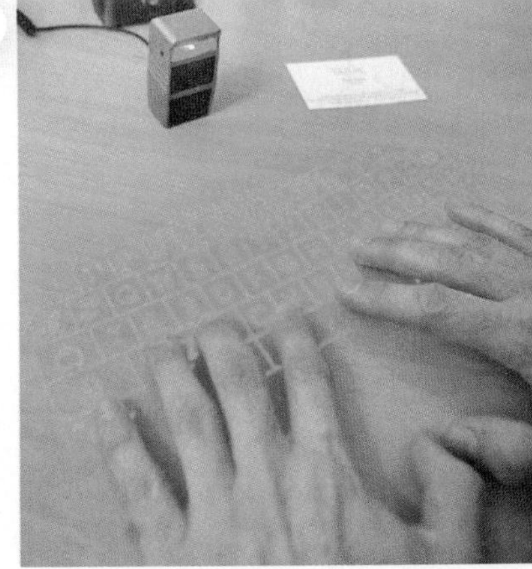

FIGURE 2.8 (a) Cases with integrated physical keyboards make tablets more typing-friendly. (b) The virtual laser keyboard projects the image of a QWERTY keyboard on any surface. Sensors detect typing motions, and data is transmitted to a computing device via Bluetooth technology. *(Logitech; Martin Meissner/AP Images)*

# BITS&BYTES

## Switching Your Keyboard Layout

The Dvorak keyboard is an alternative keyboard layout that puts the most commonly used letters in the English language on "home keys"—the keys in the middle row of the keyboard. The Dvorak keyboard's design reduces the distance your fingers travel for most keystrokes, increasing typing speed.

But did you know that you can change your keyboard from the QWERTY layout to the Dvorak layout without buying a new keyboard? You can use the Windows operating system to customize the keyboard by changing the keyboard layout. The keyboard layout then controls which characters appear on the screen when you press the keys on your keyboard. If you suffer from a repetitive strain injury such as carpal tunnel syndrome, you may find it useful to switch to the Dvorak keyboard layout. You can also switch layouts to conform to different foreign languages. Instructions for changing keyboard layouts are shown in Figure 2.9.

You might also find it useful to cover the keys on the keyboard with stickers of the corresponding characters of the newly configured layout so that the characters on your keyboard match up to the new layout.

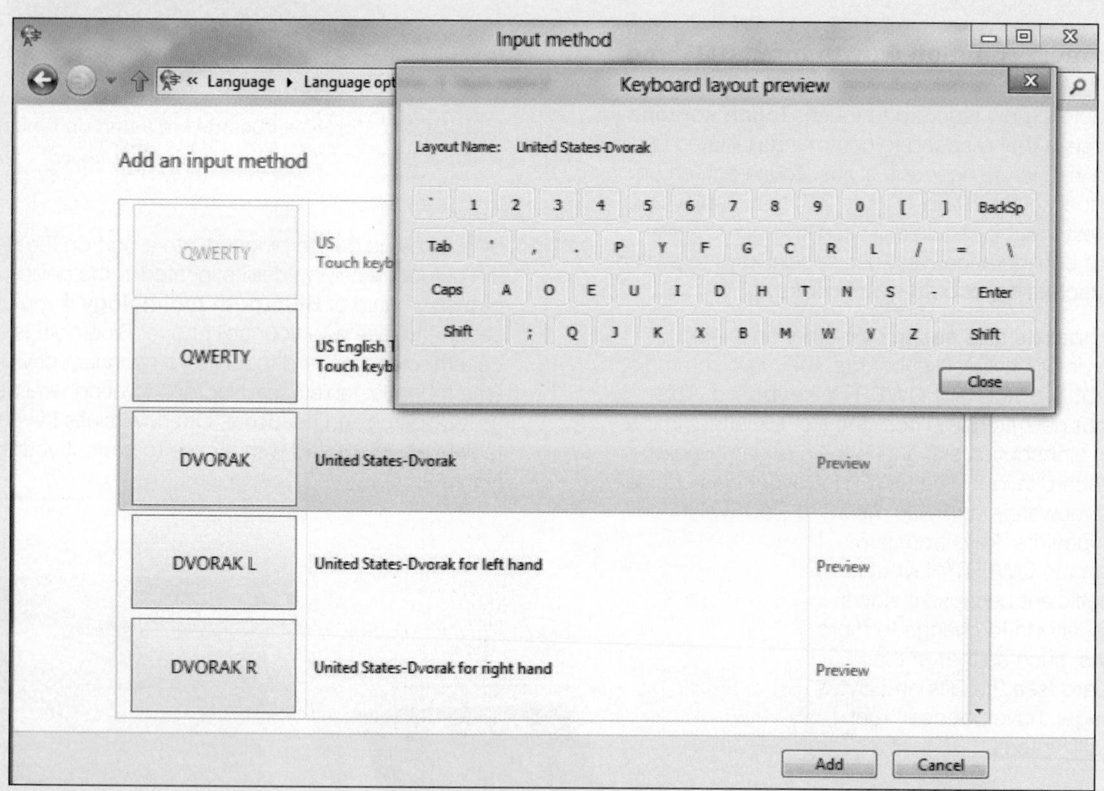


**FIGURE 2.9** You can customize the layout of your keyboard using the Windows operating system.

*>To change the keyboard layout in Windows 8.1, open Control Panel, click* **Change input methods** *in the Clock, Language, and Region section. Click the* **Options link**. *Click the* **Add an input method** *link. Scroll to find the appropriate keyboard and click the* **Preview link** *to view it. Then left-click the keyboard, and click* **Add**.

*Flexible keyboards* are a terrific alternative if you want a full-sized keyboard for your laptop, netbook, or tablet. You can roll one up, fit it in your backpack, and plug it into a USB port when you need it. Another compact keyboard alternative is the Magic Cube *virtual laser keyboard* (see Figure 2.8b) from Cellulon, which is about the size of a cell phone. It projects an image of a keyboard onto any flat surface, and sensors detect the motion of your fingers as you "type." Data is transmitted to the device via Bluetooth. The keyboard works with the latest iPhones, iPads, and Android devices.

**How can I use my keyboard most efficiently?** All keyboards have the standard set of alphabetic and numeric keys that you regularly use when typing. As shown in Figure 2.10, many keyboards for laptop and desktop computers have additional keys that perform special functions. Knowing how to use the special keys shown in Figure 2.10 will help you improve your efficiency.

## Mice and Other Pointing Devices

**What kinds of mice are there?** The mouse type you're probably most familiar with is the **optical mouse**. An optical mouse uses an internal sensor or laser to detect the mouse's movement. The sensor sends signals to the computer, telling it where to move the pointer on the screen. Optical mice don't require a mouse pad, though you can use one to enhance the movement of the mouse on an uneven surface or to protect your work surface from being scratched.

If you have special ergonomic needs or want to customize the functionality of your mouse, there are plenty of options. Most mice have two or three buttons that let you execute commands and open shortcut menus. (Mice for Macs sometimes have only one button.) As shown in Figure 2.11, many mice, such as the Cyborg R.A.T. 9 Gaming Mouse, have additional programmable buttons and wheels that let you quickly maneuver through web pages or games. In addition, the R.A.T. 9 is customizable to fit any size hand and grip style by allowing for length and width adjustments. Aside from gamers, many people use customizable mice to reduce susceptibility to repetitive strain injuries.

**How do wireless mice work?** Wireless mice usually connect the same way that wireless keyboards do—either through Bluetooth or a receiver that plugs into a USB port. Wireless mice have receivers that often clip into the bottom of the mouse for easy storage when not in use.

**Why would I want to use a mouse with a touch-screen device?** If you're using a conventional keyboard with your touch-screen device, it's often easier to perform actions with a mouse rather than taking your hands off the keyboard and reaching to touch the screen. In addition, there are new kinds of mice that are designed with touch-screen computers

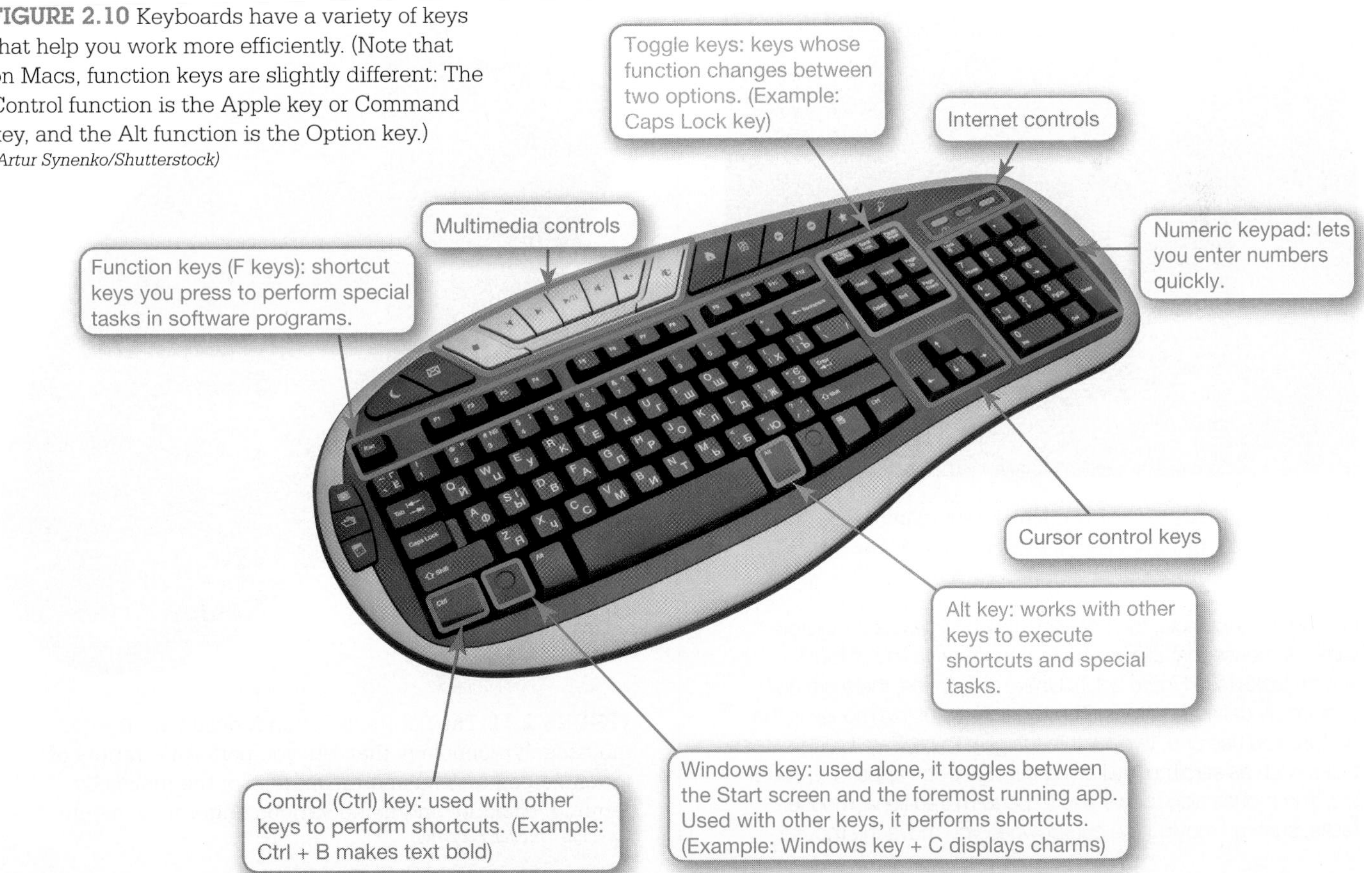
Toggle keys: keys whose function changes between two options. (Example: Caps Lock key)
Internet controls
Multimedia controls
Function keys (F keys): shortcut keys you press to perform special tasks in software programs.
Numeric keypad: lets you enter numbers quickly.
Cursor control keys
Alt key: works with other keys to execute shortcuts and special tasks.
Windows key: used alone, it toggles between the Start screen and the foremost running app. Used with other keys, it performs shortcuts. (Example: Windows key + C displays charms)
Control (Ctrl) key: used with other keys to perform shortcuts. (Example: Ctrl + B makes text bold)

**FIGURE 2.10** Keyboards have a variety of keys that help you work more efficiently. (Note that on Macs, function keys are slightly different: The Control function is the Apple key or Command key, and the Alt function is the Option key.)
*(Artur Synenko/Shutterstock)*

# BITS&BYTES

## Keystroke Shortcuts

Did you know that you can combine certain keystrokes to take shortcuts within an application, such as Microsoft Word, or within the operating system itself? The following are a few of the most helpful Windows-based shortcuts. For more, visit **support.microsoft.com**. For a list of shortcuts for Macs, see **apple.com/support**.

| TEXT FORMATTING | FILE MANAGEMENT | CUT/COPY/PASTE | WINDOWS CONTROLS |
|---|---|---|---|
| **Ctrl+B** applies (or removes) **bold** formatting to/from selected text. | **Ctrl+O** opens the Open dialog box. | **Ctrl+X** cuts (removes) selected text and stores it in the Clipboard. | **Alt+F4** closes the current window. |
| **Ctrl+I** applies (or removes) *italic* formatting to/from selected text. | **Ctrl+N** opens a new document. | **Ctrl+C** copies selected text to the Clipboard. | **Windows Key+Tab** displays open Windows 8 apps. |
| **Ctrl+U** applies (or removes) underlining to/from selected text. | **Ctrl+S** saves a document. | **Ctrl+V** pastes selected text (previously cut or copied) from the Clipboard. | **Windows Key+L** locks the computer. |
| | **Ctrl+P** opens the Print dialog box. | | **Windows Key+F** opens the Search bar in Files mode. |

**FIGURE 2.11** Customizable mice offer programmable buttons and adjustable fittings to meet most any need. *(Cyborg)*

in mind. For example, the Logitech Touch Mouse is a multitouch wireless mouse that allows you to perform a variety of touch-screen tasks (see Figure 2.12). Unlike older mice, there are no specifically defined buttons. The top surface of this mouse is the button. You use one, two, or three fingers to perform touch-screen tasks such as scrolling, switching through open apps, and zooming. The mouse also allows you to perform traditional mouse tasks, such as moving the cursor when you move the mouse.

**FIGURE 2.12** The Logitech Touch Mouse features multitouch technology that lets you perform a variety of touch-screen tasks using the surface of the mouse by tapping, clicking, and using various finger movements. *(© Hugh Threlfall / Alamy)*

**Are touch pads considered mice?** Most laptops have an integrated pointing device, such as a **touch pad (**or **trackpad)**, a small, touch-sensitive area at the base of the keyboard. Mac laptops include multitouch trackpads, which don't have buttons but are controlled by various one-, two-, three-, and four-finger actions. For example, scrolling is controlled by brushing two fingers along the trackpad in any direction. Most touch pads are sensitive to taps, interpreting them as mouse clicks. Most laptops also have buttons under or near the pad to record mouse clicks.

**What input devices are used with games?** Game controllers such as joysticks, game pads, and steering wheels are also considered input devices because they send data to the computer. Game controllers, which are similar to the devices used on gaming consoles such as the Xbox One and the PlayStation, are also available for use with computers. They have buttons and miniature pointing devices that provide input to the computer. Most game controllers, such as those for Rock Band and the Wii system, are wireless to provide extra mobility.

## Image Input

**What are popular input devices for images?** Digital cameras, camcorders, and cell phones are common devices for capturing pictures and video and are all considered input devices. These devices can connect to your computer with a cable, transmit data wirelessly, or transfer data automatically through the Internet. **Scanners** can also input images. They work similarly to a photocopy machine; however, instead of generating the image on paper, they create a digital image, which you can then print, save, or e-mail.

**How do I capture live video from my computing device?** A **webcam** is a small camera that sits on top of your computer monitor (connected to your computer by a cable) or is built into a laptop, tablet, or smartphone. Although webcams are able to capture still images, they're used mostly for capturing and transmitting live video. Videoconferencing technology lets a person using a device equipped with a webcam and a microphone transmit video and audio across the Internet. Video call sites such as Skype (see the Try This in Chapter 1, pages 12–13) and ooVoo (see Figure 2.13) make it easy to videoconference with as many as 12 people. You can also exchange files, swap control of computers, and text message during the call. There is also a mobile application to make it easy to conference on the go.

**FIGURE 2.13** Videoconferencing is simplified with software from **ooVoo.com**.
*(Courtesy of ooVoo, LLC.)*

# DIG DEEPER How Touch Screens Work

Touch-screen technology was developed in 1971 and used primarily with ATMs and fast-food order displays. The technology for monitors and other displays was made popular by the iPod Touch in 2007 and is now in many smartphones, tablets, and laptop and desktop monitors. Windows 8 finally brought the touch-screen interface to Windows users. But how do touch-screen monitors know where you're touching? How do they know what you want them to do?

The basic idea behind touch screens is pretty straightforward—when you place your finger or stylus on a screen, it changes the physical state of the screen and registers your touch. The location of your touch is then translated into a command. Three basic systems are used to recognize a person's touch: *resistive, capacitive,* and *surface acoustic wave*. All of these systems require the basic components of a touch-responsive glass panel, controller, and software driver, combined with a display and computer processor.

The *resistive system* maps the exact location of the pressure point created when a user touches the screen. The *capacitive system* (see Figure 2.14) uses the change in the electrical charge on the glass panel of the monitor, which is created by the user's touch, to generate a location. The third technology, *surface acoustic wave system,* uses two transducers (electrical devices that convert energy from one form to another) that are placed along the *x* and *y* axes of the monitor's glass plate. Reflectors, which are also placed on the glass, are used to reflect an electric signal sent from the sending transducer to the receiving transducer. The receiving transducer determines whether the signal has been disturbed by a touch event and locates the touch instantly. With all three systems, the display's software driver then translates the touch into something the operating system can understand, similar to how a mouse driver translates a mouse's movements into a click or drag.

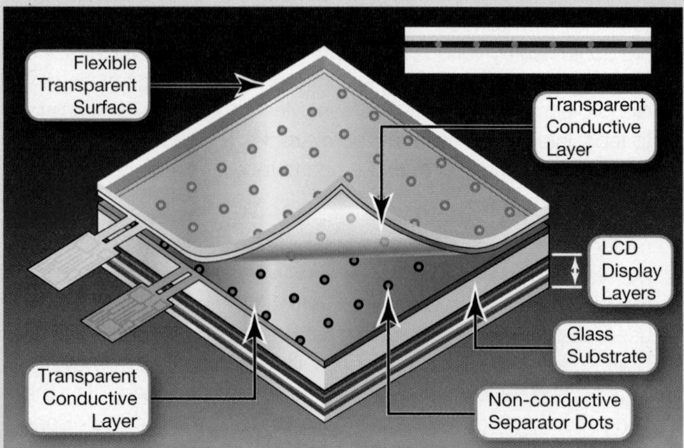


**FIGURE 2.14** Some basic touch screens use a capacitive system to detect touches and translate them into meaningful commands that are understood by the computer's operating system.

## Sound Input

**How do my computing devices benefit from accepting sound input?** In addition to letting others hear you in a videoconference, equipping your device to accept sound input opens up a variety of possibilities. You can conduct audio conferences with work colleagues, chat with friends or family over the Internet, record podcasts, and more. Inputting sound to your computer requires using a **microphone** (or **mic**), a device that lets you capture sound waves (such as your voice) and transfer them to digital format on your computer. Most laptop and tablet computers come with built-in microphones.

**What types of add-on microphones are available?** For specialized situations, built-in microphones don't always provide the best performance. You may want to consider adding other types of microphones, such as those shown in Figure 2.16, to your system for the best results. ■

Because the resistive system uses pressure to register a touch, it doesn't matter if the touch is created by a finger or another device. On the other hand, a capacitive system must have conductive input, so generally a finger is required. The surface acoustic wave system allows touches by any object.

The iPhone introduced another complexity to the touch-screen system—a multitouch user interface. In addition to just pressing the screen in one location, multitouch technology can process multiple simultaneous touches on the screen. For example, pinching or spreading out your thumb and finger together makes the display zoom out and in, respectively. The features of each touch, such as size, shape, and location, are also determined.

A touch-sensitive screen, like the one used with the iPhone and iPad and with many other smartphones and tablets, arranges the capacitors in a coordinate system so the circuitry can sense changes at each point along the grid (see Figure 2.15). Consequently, every point on the grid generates its own signal when touched, and can do so even as another signal is being generated simultaneously. The signals are then relayed to the device's processor. This allows the device to determine the location and movement of simultaneous touches in multiple locations.

After detecting the position and type of touch occurring on the display, the device's processor combines this information with the information it has about the application in use and what was being done in the application when the touch occurred. The processor relays that information to the program in use, and the command is executed. All this happens seemingly instantaneously.

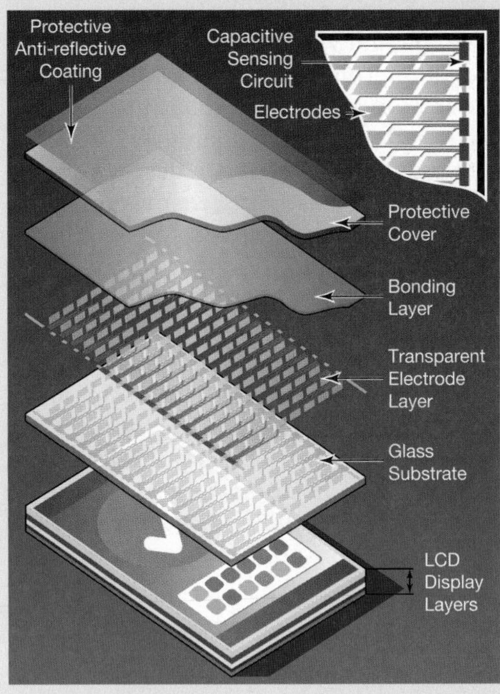


**FIGURE 2.15** Multitouch screens use a coordinate-based grid to arrange the capacitors so the circuitry can detect and respond to multiple touches occurring at the same time.

**FIGURE 2.16**

## Types of Microphones

| MICROPHONE TYPE | ATTRIBUTES | BEST USED FOR |
|---|---|---|
| **Close Talk** | • Attached to a headset (allows for listening)<br>• Leaves hands free | • Video conferencing<br>• Phone calls<br>• Speech recognition software |
| **Omnidirectional** | • Picks up sounds equally well from all directions | • Conference calls in meeting rooms |
| **Unidirectional** | • Picks up sounds from only one direction | • Recordings with one voice (podcasts) |
| **Clip-on (Lavalier)** | • Clips to clothing<br>• Available as wireless | • Presentations requiring freedom of movement<br>• Leaves hands free for writing on whiteboards |

(Yuri Arcurs/Fotolia; Blue Microphones; Sumnersgraphicsinc/Fotolia; Feliks Gurevich/Shutterstock)

# ethics in IT What Is Ethical Computing?

You've probably heard news stories about people using computers to unleash viruses or commit identity theft. You may also have read about students who were prosecuted for illegally sharing copyrighted material, such as songs and videos. These are both examples of *unethical* behavior while using a computer. However, what constitutes *ethical* behavior while using a computer?

Loosely defined, *ethics* is a system of moral principles, rules, and accepted standards of conduct (see Figure 2.17). So what are the accepted standards of conduct when using computers? The Computer Ethics Institute has developed the Ten Commandments of Computer Ethics, which is widely cited as a benchmark for companies developing computer usage and compliance policies for employees. These guidelines are applicable for schools and students, as well. The ethical computing guidelines listed below are based on the Computer Ethics Institute's work:

**FIGURE 2.17** Strive to take the "high road" and behave ethically by not claiming others' work as your own intellectual output. *(Andy Dean Photography/Shutterstock)*

## Ethical Computing Guidelines

1. Avoid causing harm to others when using computers.
2. Do not interfere with other people's efforts at accomplishing work with computers.
3. Resist the temptation to snoop in other people's computer files.
4. Do not use computers to commit theft.
5. Agree not to use computers to promote lies.
6. Do not use software (or make illegal copies for others) without paying the creator for it.
7. Avoid using other people's computer resources without appropriate authorization or proper compensation.
8. Do not claim other people's intellectual output as your own.
9. Consider the social consequences of the products of your computer labor.
10. Only use computers in ways that show consideration and respect for others.

The United States has enacted laws that support some of these guidelines, such as Guideline 6, the breaking of which would violate copyright laws, and Guideline 4, which is enforceable under numerous federal and state larceny laws. Other guidelines, however, require more subtle interpretation as to what behavior is unethical because there are no laws designed to enforce them.

Consider Guideline 7, which covers unauthorized use of resources. The school you attend probably provides computer resources for you to use for coursework. But if your school gives you access to computers and the Internet, is it ethical for you to use those resources to run an online business on the weekends? Although it might not be technically illegal, you're tying up computer resources that other students could use for their intended purpose: learning and completing coursework. (This behavior also violates Guidelines 2 and 10.)

Throughout the chapters in this book, we touch on many topics related to these guidelines. So keep them in mind as you study, and think about how they relate to the actions you take as you use computers in your life.

# output DEVICES

An **output device** lets you send processed data out of your computer in the form of text, pictures (graphics), sounds (audio), or video. The most common output device is a **monitor** (sometimes referred to as a **display screen**), which displays text, graphics, and video as soft copies (copies you can see only on screen). Another common output device is the **printer**, which creates hard copies (copies you can touch) of text and graphics. Speakers and earphones (or earbuds) are the output devices for sound.

## Monitors

**What are the different types of monitors?** The most common type of monitor is a **liquid crystal display (LCD)**. An LCD monitor, also called a flat-panel monitor, is light and energy efficient. Some newer monitors use **light-emitting diode (LED)** technology, which is more energy efficient and may have better color accuracy and thinner panels than LCD monitors. LCD flat-panel monitors have replaced cathode ray tube (CRT) monitors. CRT monitors are considered **legacy technology**, or computing devices that use techniques, parts, and methods that are no longer popular. Although legacy technology may still be functional, it has been replaced by newer technological advances.

**Organic light-emitting diode (OLED) displays** use organic compounds that produce light when exposed to an electric current. Unlike LCDs and LEDs, OLEDs do not require a backlight to function and therefore draw less power and have a much thinner display, sometimes as thin as 3 mm. They are also brighter and more environmentally friendly than LCDs. Because of their lower power needs, OLED displays run longer on a single battery charge than do LEDs, which is why OLED technology is probably the technology used in your cell phone, iPod, and digital camera.

Companies like Samsung are now working on transparent OLED display screens (see Figure 2.18). These screens allow you to see what is behind the screen while still being able to display information on the screen. These types of screens present interesting possibilities for augmented reality. *Augmented reality (AR)* is a view of a real-world environment whose elements are *augmented* (or supplemented) by some type of computer-generated sensory input such as video, graphics, or GPS data (see Chapter 1, pages 20–21). For instance, if you had a transparent screen on your smartphone and held it up to view street signs that were in English, you could possibly have your phone display the signs in another language. Currently, applications like this exist but require the use of a camera as well as your screen. But transparent screens will eliminate the need for the camera.

**FIGURE 2.18** Because they don't need a backlight, OLED displays can be made transparent. *(PhotoAlto/Milena Boniek/ Getty Images)*

**How do LCD monitors work?** Monitor screens are grids made up of millions of tiny dots, called **pixels**. When these pixels are illuminated by the light waves generated by a fluorescent panel at the back of your screen, they create the images you see on the screen or monitor. Each pixel is actually made up of three red, blue, and green subpixels; some newer LCD TVs on the market have even added a fourth color: yellow. LCD monitors are made of two or more sheets of material filled with a liquid crystal solution (see Figure 2.19). A fluorescent panel at the back of the LCD monitor generates light waves. When electric current passes through the liquid crystal solution, the crystals move around and either block the fluorescent light or let the light shine through. This blocking or passing of light by the crystals causes images to form on the screen. The various combinations of red, blue, and green make up the components of color we see on our monitors.

**What factors affect the quality of an LCD monitor?** When choosing an LCD monitor, the most important factors to consider are aspect ratio and resolution. The **aspect ratio** is the width-to-height proportion of a monitor. Traditionally, aspect ratios have been 4:3, but newer monitors are available with an aspect ratio of 16:9 to accommodate HD format video. The screen **resolution**, or the clearness or sharpness of the image, reflects the number of pixels on the screen. An LCD monitor may have a native (or maximum) resolution of 1600 × 1200, meaning it contains 1,600 vertical columns with 1,200 pixels

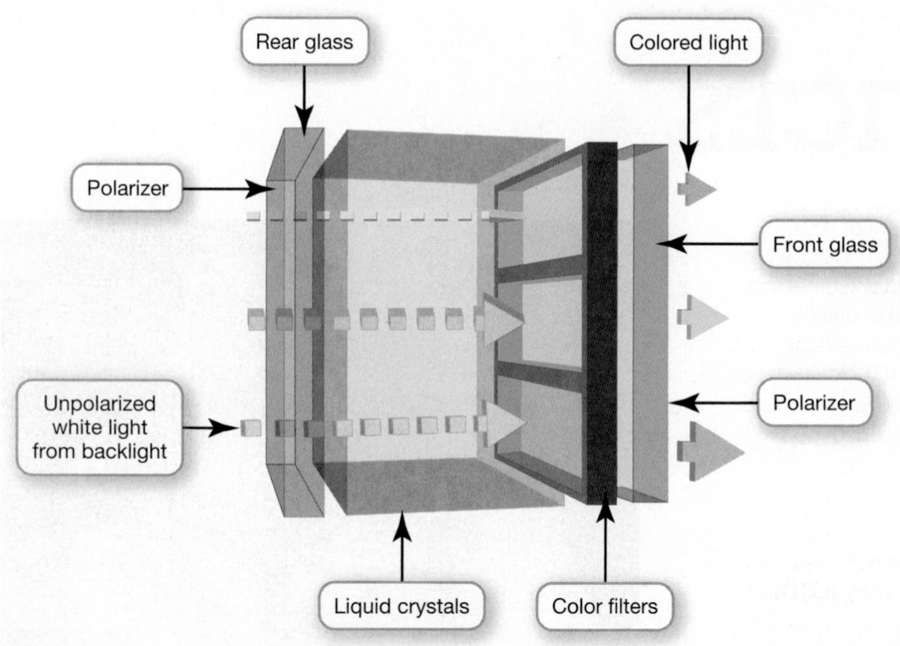


**FIGURE 2.19** A magnification of a single pixel in an LCD monitor.

in each column. The higher the resolution, the sharper and clearer the image will be, but generally, the resolution of an LCD monitor is dictated by the screen size and aspect ratio. Although you can change the resolution of an LCD monitor beyond its native resolution, the images will become distorted. Generally, you should buy a monitor with the highest resolution available for the screen size (measured in inches). Figure 2.20 lists these and other factors to consider when judging the quality of an LCD monitor.

**Is a bigger screen size always better?** The bigger the monitor, the more you can display, and depending on what you want to display, size may matter. In general, the larger the panel, the larger number of pixels it can display. For example, a 27-inch monitor can display 2560 × 1440 pixels, whereas a 21.5-inch monitor may only be able to display 1680 × 1050 pixels. However, most new monitors have at least the 1920 × 1080 resolution required to display Blu-ray movies.

Larger screens can also allow you to view multiple documents or web pages at the same time, creating the effect of using two separate monitors side by side. Buying two smaller monitors might be cheaper than buying one large monitor. For either option—a big screen or two separate screens—check that your computer has the appropriate video hardware to support these display devices.

**What other features should I look for in an LCD monitor?** Some monitors, especially those on laptop

**FIGURE 2.20**

## Factors to Consider When Shopping for a Monitor

| FACTOR | POSSIBLE PROBLEMS | LOOK FOR |
|---|---|---|
| **Aspect ratio:** Width-to-height proportion of a screen | • An odd aspect ratio may make images look distorted | • Ratios of 4:3 or 16:9 (HDTV) |
| **Screen resolution:** Number of pixels displayed on the screen | • Low screen resolution = unclear image<br>• High resolution on a small size monitor results in image being too small | • Highest resolution monitor is capable of displaying (make sure you are comfortable viewing that size image) |
| **Contrast ratio:** Difference in light intensity between brightest white and darkest black a monitor can produce | • Ratio too low results in colors fading when adjusting brightness | • Ratios between 400:1 and 1,000:1 |
| **Viewing angle:** Distance in degrees from which you can move to the side of (or above or below) a monitor before the image degrades | • Angle too low means people not sitting directly in front of the monitor will see a poor image | • 150 degrees or more is preferable |
| **Brightness:** Greatest amount of light showing when the monitor is displaying pure white (measured in candelas per square meter [cd/m$^2$] or *nits*) | • Image will be hard to see in bright rooms if brightness level is too low | • 300 cd/m$^2$ or greater |
| **Response time:** Time it takes for a pixel to change color (in milliseconds) | • High response time results in images appearing jerky | • Seek lowest possible response time if viewing live action sports |

## BITS&BYTES

### Testing and Calibrating Your PC Monitor

Most new PC monitors don't need color or tint adjustments, but some can benefit from a few tweaks that will ultimately enhance your video experience. This might be especially important if you're a web designer, digital photographer, or graphics professional. In those professions especially, you want to make sure the colors are displayed on the monitor as accurately as possible. Before you start the calibration process, check that your monitor is set to the "native" resolution (usually the recommended setting). Some monitors have their own calibration program; otherwise, you can work through the adjustments manually or use the display utility in your operating system.

If you're running Windows, you can use the Display Color Calibration utility found by displaying the Control Panel and then clicking Appearance and Personalization. Click Display, and then in the Navigation Pane, click Calibrate color. The Display Color Calibration utility will check the gamma, brightness, contrast, and color balance settings. Gamma describes the relationship between the varying levels of brightness a monitor can display. Brightness determines how dark colors appear on your display. When brightness is set too high, dark colors appear washed out. Contrast determines how white and light colors display. (Note that most laptop computers don't have controls to adjust contrast.) Color balance makes adjustments to the red, blue, and green controls.

computers, come with built-in features such as speakers, webcams, and microphones. A built-in multiformat memory card reader is convenient for displaying images directly on the monitor or for downloading pictures quickly from a camera memory card to your PC. Another nice feature to look for in a desktop LCD monitor is a built-in USB port. This feature lets you connect extra peripherals easily without reaching around the back of the PC.

**How do I show output to a large group of people?** A **projector** lets you project images from your computing device onto a wall or viewing screen. Projectors are commonly used in business and education settings such as conference rooms and classrooms. Many projectors are small and lightweight, and some, such as the 3M MPro 150 (see Figure 2.21), are small enough to fit in the palm of your hand. These portable projectors are ideal for businesspeople who have to make presentations at client locations. ***Entertainment projectors,*** such as the Discovery Expedition, include stereo speakers and an array of multimedia connectors, making them a good option for use in the home to display TV programs, DVDs, digital images, or video games in a large format. If your computing device is equipped with an HDMI port, you can also choose to connect your computer directly to an HDTV.

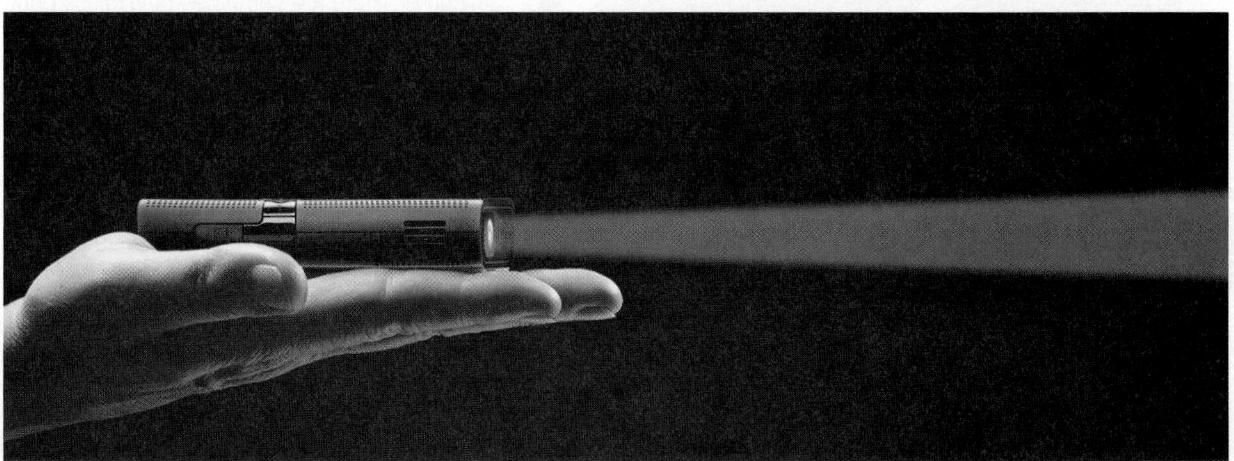

**FIGURE 2.21** Inexpensive projectors are showing up more frequently in business and the home to provide large images for movie viewing and gaming. *(3M)*

## Printers

**What are the different types of printers?** There are two primary categories of printers: inkjet and laser, both of which are considered nonimpact printers. A **nonimpact printer** such as an inkjet printer sprays ink or uses laser beams to transfer marks onto the paper. An **impact printer** has tiny hammer-like keys that strike the paper through an inked ribbon to make marks on the paper. For most users, impact printers are legacy technology.

**What are the advantages of inkjet printers?** An **inkjet printer** (see Figure 2.22) is the type of printer found in many homes. These printers are popular because they're affordable and produce high-quality printouts quickly and quietly. Inkjet printers work by spraying tiny drops of ink onto paper and are great for printing black-and-white text as well as color images. In fact, when loaded with the right paper, higher-end inkjet printers can print images that look like professional-quality photos. One thing to consider when buying an inkjet printer is the type and cost of the ink cartridges the printer needs. Some printers use two cartridges: black and color. Others use four or more cartridges: typically, black, magenta, cyan, and yellow.

**Why would I want a laser printer?** A **laser printer** uses laser beams and static electricity to deliver toner (similar to ink) onto the correct areas of the page (see Figure 2.23). Heat is used to fuse the toner to the page, making the image permanent. Laser printers are often used in office or classroom settings because they print faster than inkjet printers and produce higher-quality printouts. Black-and-white laser printers have also been common in homes for a decade. Over the past few years, the price of color laser printers has fallen dramatically, making them price competitive with high-end inkjet printers. Thus, color laser printers are a viable option for the home. If you print a high volume of pages, consider a laser printer. When you include the price of ink or toner in the overall cost, color laser printers can be more economical than inkjets.

FIGURE 2.23 Laser printers print quickly and offer high-quality printouts. *(Courtesy of Xerox Corporation)*

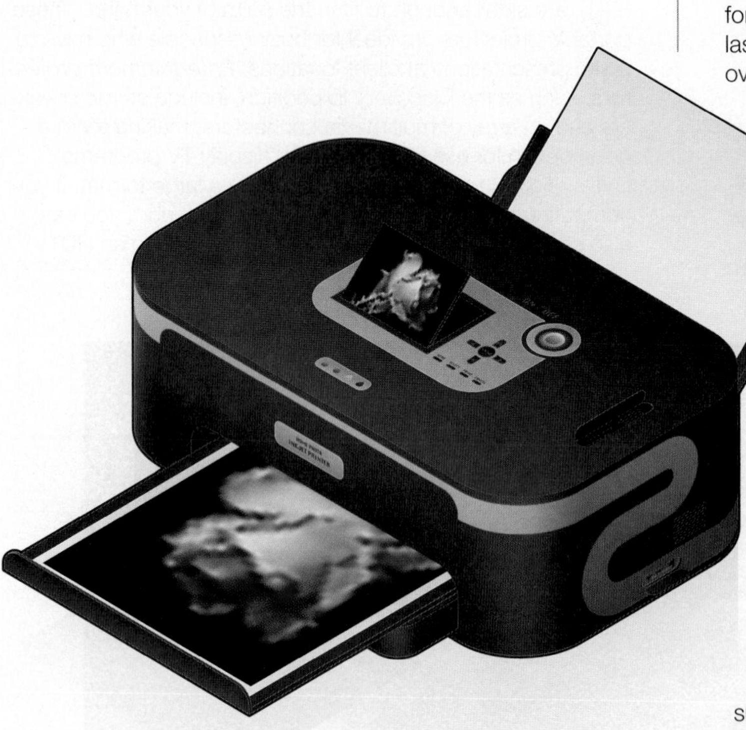

FIGURE 2.22 Inkjet printers are popular among home users, especially with the rise of digital photography. Many inkjet printers are optimized for printing photos from digital cameras. *(The Vectorminator/Shutterstock)*

**What's the best way to print from portable devices such as tablets and smartphones?** Wireless printers are a good option for home networks as they let several people print to the same printer from different devices and any location in the home. There are two types of wireless printers: WiFi and Bluetooth. Both WiFi and Bluetooth printers have a range of up to approximately 300 feet. WiFi, however, sends data more quickly than Bluetooth.

Wireless printers are also great for printing from portable devices. If you're using a device running Apple's iOS (such as an iPhone), AirPrint makes printing easy. AirPrint is a feature of iOS that facilitates printing to AirPrint-compatible wireless printers, and many printers produced today are AirPrint compatible.

For non-Apple mobile devices (or if your printer isn't compatible with AirPrint), you should try other solutions, such as Presto by Collobos Software and ThinPrint Cloud Printer by Cortado. Once you install one of these apps on your portable device, you can send documents to printers that are connected to PCs and Macs on your home network. It makes printing from mobile devices as simple as hitting print on your laptop.

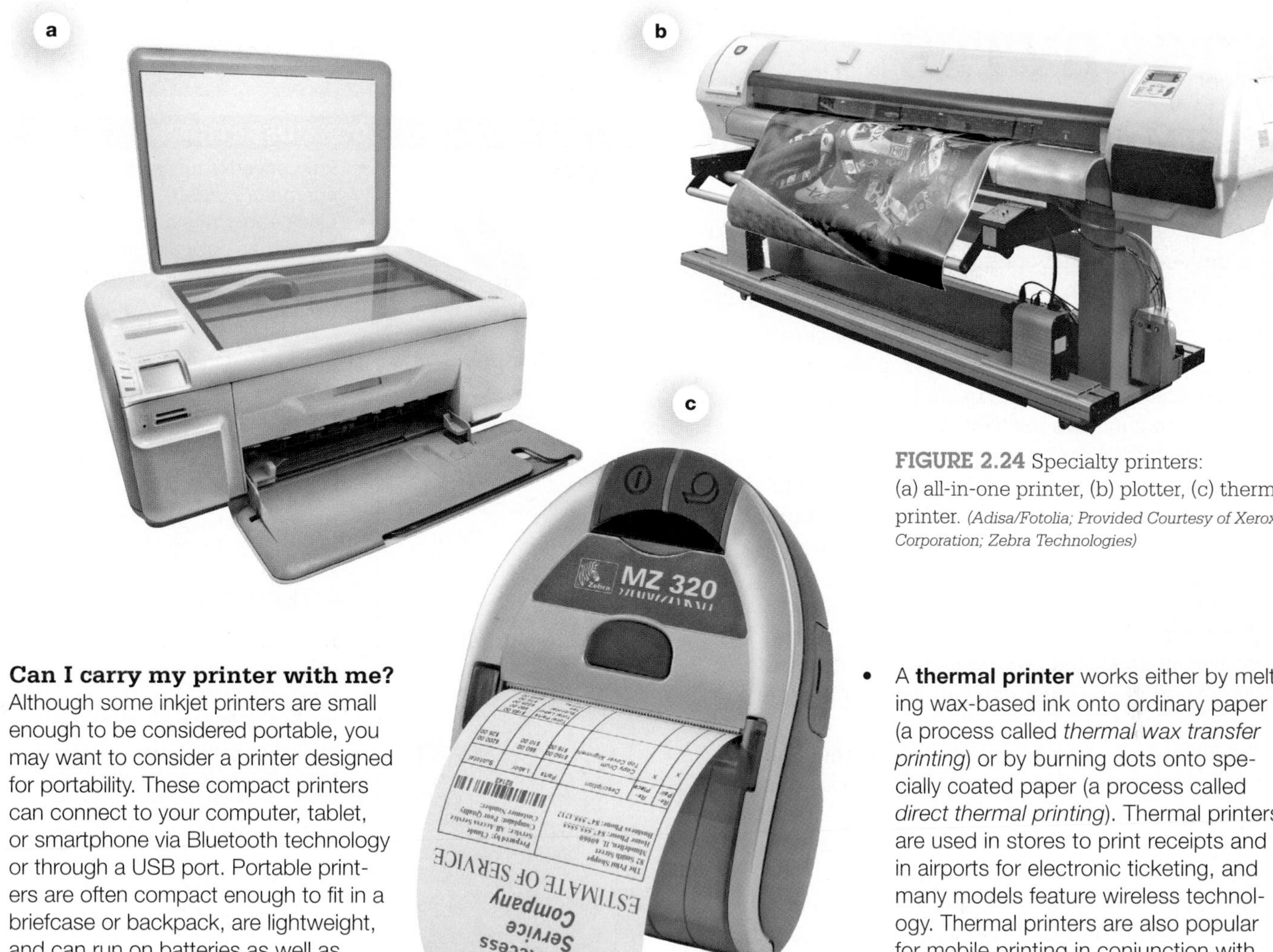


FIGURE 2.24 Specialty printers: (a) all-in-one printer, (b) plotter, (c) thermal printer. *(Adisa/Fotolia; Provided Courtesy of Xerox Corporation; Zebra Technologies)*

**Can I carry my printer with me?** Although some inkjet printers are small enough to be considered portable, you may want to consider a printer designed for portability. These compact printers can connect to your computer, tablet, or smartphone via Bluetooth technology or through a USB port. Portable printers are often compact enough to fit in a briefcase or backpack, are lightweight, and can run on batteries as well as AC power.

**Are there any other types of specialty printers?** Although you'll probably use laser or inkjet printers most often, you might also encounter several other types of printers (shown in Figure 2.24):

- An **all-in-one printer** combines the functions of a printer, scanner, copier, and fax into one machine. Popular for their space-saving convenience, all-in-one printers may use either inkjet or laser technology.
- A **plotter** prints oversize pictures that require the drawing of precise and continuous lines, such as maps and architectural plans. Plotters use a computer-controlled pen that provides a greater level of precision than the series of dots that laser or inkjet printers make.
- A **thermal printer** works either by melting wax-based ink onto ordinary paper (a process called *thermal wax transfer printing*) or by burning dots onto specially coated paper (a process called *direct thermal printing*). Thermal printers are used in stores to print receipts and in airports for electronic ticketing, and many models feature wireless technology. Thermal printers are also popular for mobile printing in conjunction with smartphones and tablets.

**ACTIVE HELPDESK**
**Using Output Devices**

In this Active Helpdesk call, you'll play the role of a helpdesk staffer, fielding calls about different output devices.

**How do I choose the best printer?** Your first step is to decide what your primary printing need is. If you're planning to print color photos and graphics, an inkjet printer or color laser printer is a must, even though the cost per page will be higher. If you'll be printing mostly black-and-white, text-based documents or will be sharing your printer with others, a black-and-white laser printer is best because of its speed and overall economy for volume printing. It's also important to determine whether you want just a printer or a device that prints and scans, copies, or faxes (an all-in-one). In addition, you should decide whether you need to print from mobile devices.

Once you have narrowed down the *type* of printer you want, you can use the criteria listed in Figure 2.25 to help you determine the best model to meet your needs.

## Sound Output

**What are the output devices for sound?** Most computers include inexpensive **speakers**, which are the output devices for sound. These speakers are sufficient to play the standard audio clips you find on the web and usually for letting you participate in videoconferencing or phone

# BITS&BYTES

## Does It Matter What Paper I Print On?

The quality of your printer is only part of what controls the quality of a printed image. The paper you use and the printer settings that control the amount of ink used are equally important.

- If you're printing text-only documents for personal use, using low-cost paper is fine. You also may want to consider selecting draft mode in your printer settings to conserve ink. However, if you're printing more formal documents, such as business correspondence, you may want to choose a higher-quality paper (determined by the paper's weight, whiteness, and brightness) and adjust your print setting to "normal" or "best."
- The weight of paper is measured in pounds, with 20 pounds being standard. A heavier paper may be best for projects such as brochures, but be sure to check that your printer can handle the added thickness of the paper.
- The degree of paper whiteness is a matter of personal preference. Generally, the whiter the paper, the brighter the printed color. However, for documents that are more formal, you may want to use a creamier color.
- The brightness of paper usually varies from 85 to 94. The higher the number, the brighter the paper, and the easier it is to read printed text.
- Opacity, or the "show through" of ink from one side of the paper to the other, is especially important if you're printing on both sides of the paper.

If you're printing photos, paper quality can have a big impact on your results. Photo paper is more expensive than regular paper and comes in a variety of textures ranging from matte to high gloss. For a photo-lab look, high-gloss paper is the best choice. Semigloss (often referred to as satin) is good for formal portraits, while a matte surface is often used for black-and-white photo printing.

calls over the Internet. However, if you plan to digitally edit audio files or are particular about how your music sounds, you may want a more sophisticated speaker system, such as one that includes subwoofers (special speakers that produce only low bass sounds) and surround-sound speakers. A **surround-sound speaker** is a system of speakers and audio processing that envelops the listener in a 360-degree field of sound. In addition, wireless speaker systems are available to help you avoid cluttering up your rooms with speaker wires.

**FIGURE 2.25**

**Major Printer Attributes**

| ATTRIBUTE | CONSIDERATIONS |
|---|---|
| **Speed**  | • Print speed is measured in *pages per minute (PPM)*.<br>• Black-and-white documents print faster than color documents.<br>• Laser printers often print faster than inkjets. |
| **Resolution**  | • Resolution refers to a printer's image clarity.<br>• Resolution is measured in *dots per inch (dpi)*.<br>• Higher dpi = greater level of detail and clarity.<br>• Recommended dpi:<br>  • Black-and-white text: 300<br>  • General purpose images: 1200<br>  • Photos: 4800 |
| **Color Output**  | • Printers with separate cartridges for each color produce the best quality output.<br>• Inkjet and laser color printers generally have four cartridges (black, cyan, magenta, and yellow).<br>• Higher-quality printers have six cartridges (the four above plus light cyan and light magenta).<br>• With separate cartridges, you only need to replace the empty one. |
| **Cost of Consumables**  | • Consumables are printer cartridges and paper.<br>• Printer cartridges can exceed the cost of some printers.<br>• Consumer magazines such as *Consumer Reports* can help you research costs. |

*(Freshidea/Fotolia; Michael Nivelet/Fotolia; ThomasAmby/Fotolia; Tomislav Forgo/Fotolia)*

If you work in close proximity to other employees or travel with a laptop, you may need to use headphones or earbuds to avoid distracting other people. Both devices plug into the same jack on the computing device to which speakers connect. Studies of users of portable media players have shown that hearing might be damaged by excessive volume, especially when using earbuds because they fit into the ear canals. Exercise caution when using these devices. ■

**Before moving on to Part 2:**
- **Watch Replay Video 2.1.**
- Then check your understanding of what you've learned so far.

# check your understanding//

For a quick review to see what you've learned so far, answer the following questions. Visit **pearsonhighered.com/techinaction** to check your answers.

## multiple choice

1. Which of the following is NOT one of the four major functions of a computer?
   - **a.** input
   - **b.** processing
   - **c.** storage
   - **d.** indexing
2. A large, expensive computer that supports many users simultaneously and that businesses use to manage large amounts of data is
   - **a.** a mainframe computer.
   - **b.** a supercomputer.
   - **c.** an embedded computer.
   - **d.** none of the above.
3. Which of the following is both an input device and an output device?
   - **a.** a touch-screen monitor
   - **b.** an optical mouse
   - **c.** speakers
   - **d.** a laser printer
4. What printer produces the highest-resolution images?
   - **a.** inkjet
   - **b.** thermal
   - **c.** laser
   - **d.** impact
5. Which is NOT important to consider when buying a monitor?
   - **a.** screen resolution
   - **b.** viewing angle
   - **c.** color depth
   - **d.** aspect ratio

## true–false

_____ **1.** Data is information that has been organized.

_____ **2.** A gigabyte is around 1 billion bytes.

## critical thinking

1. **Computer of the Future**

   Think about how mobile our computing devices have become and the convergence of different devices such as cameras, phones, and computers. What do you think the computer of the future will be like? What capabilities will it have that computers currently don't have? Do you see desktop or laptop computers becoming obsolete in the near future?

2. **Integrating Tablets into the Workplace**

   Currently, laptop and desktop computer dominate most workplaces while tablet computers are relegated mostly to personal use. What types of businesses do you think are ready for a broader use of tablet computers for their employees? What changes in current tablets do you think are required to make them more functional in the workplace?

3. **Ethics Violations**

   Review the Ethics in IT section in this chapter. Which of the Ten Ethical Computing Guidelines do you think students violate most often? Why do you think these violations occur, and what do you think could be done to reduce or eliminate such unethical behaviors?

**Continue**

# TRY THIS  What's Inside My Computer?

Understanding what capabilities your current computer has is one of the first steps toward computer literacy. In this exercise, you'll learn how to explore the components of your Windows computer.

**Step 1** To gather information about the storage devices on your computer, on the Start screen, click **File Explorer** (previously called Windows Explorer) to switch to the Desktop and display File Explorer. In the navigation pane, click **Computer** to display information about your computer's drives.

**Step 2** The File Explorer Computer screen displays information about internal storage devices (such as internal hard drives), optical storage devices (such as DVD drives), and portable storage devices (such as flash drives and external hard drives). The total amount of usable storage space, as well as the amount of space actually free (unused), on the devices is shown.

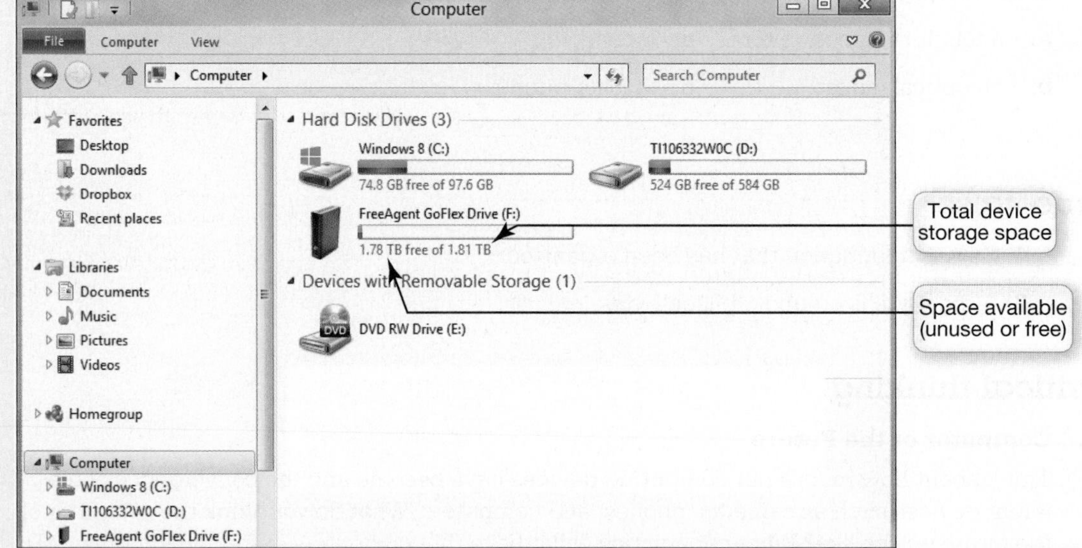

**Step 3** To display the System screen, click the **Computer** tab on the File Explorer Ribbon, and then click the **Properties** button.

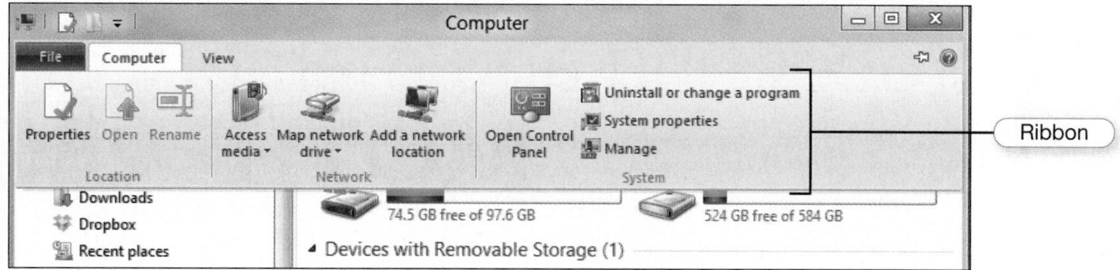


**Step 4** You can gather quite a bit of information from the System screen, such as:

- Version of Windows
- Type of processor
- Speed of the processor
- Amount of RAM installed
- System type (32-bit or 64-bit)

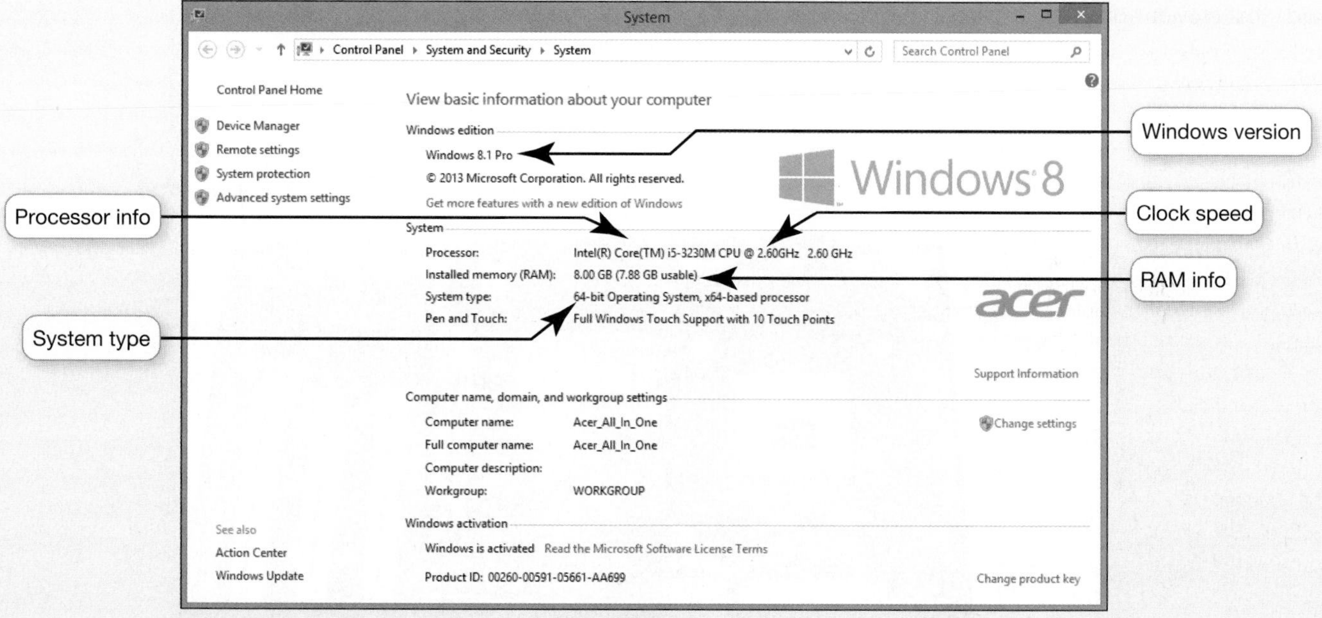

# Processing, Storage, and Connectivity

So far, we have explored the components of your computer that you use to input and output data. But where does the processing take place, and where is the data stored? And how does your computer connect with peripherals and other computers?

## processing and memory on the MOTHERBOARD

The **motherboard** is the main circuit board that contains the central electronic components of the computer, including the computer's processor (CPU), its memory, and the many circuit boards that help the computer function (see Figure 2.26). On a desktop, the motherboard is located inside the system unit, the metal or plastic case that also houses the power source and all the storage devices (CD/DVD drive and hard drive). In a laptop or all-in-one computer, the system unit is combined with the monitor and the keyboard into a single package.

**What's on the motherboard besides the CPU and memory?** The motherboard also includes slots for **expansion cards** (or **adapter cards**), which are circuit boards that provide additional functionality. Typical expansion cards found in the system unit are sound and video cards. A **sound card** provides a connection for the speakers and microphone, whereas a **video card** provides a connection for the monitor. Laptops and tablets have video and sound capabilities integrated into their motherboards. High-end desktops use expansion cards to provide video and sound capabilities.

Other expansion cards provide a means for network and Internet connections. A **network interface card (NIC)**, which enables your computer to connect with other computers or to a cable modem to facilitate a high-speed Internet connection, is often integrated into the motherboard. Lastly, some expansion cards provide additional USB and FireWire ports.

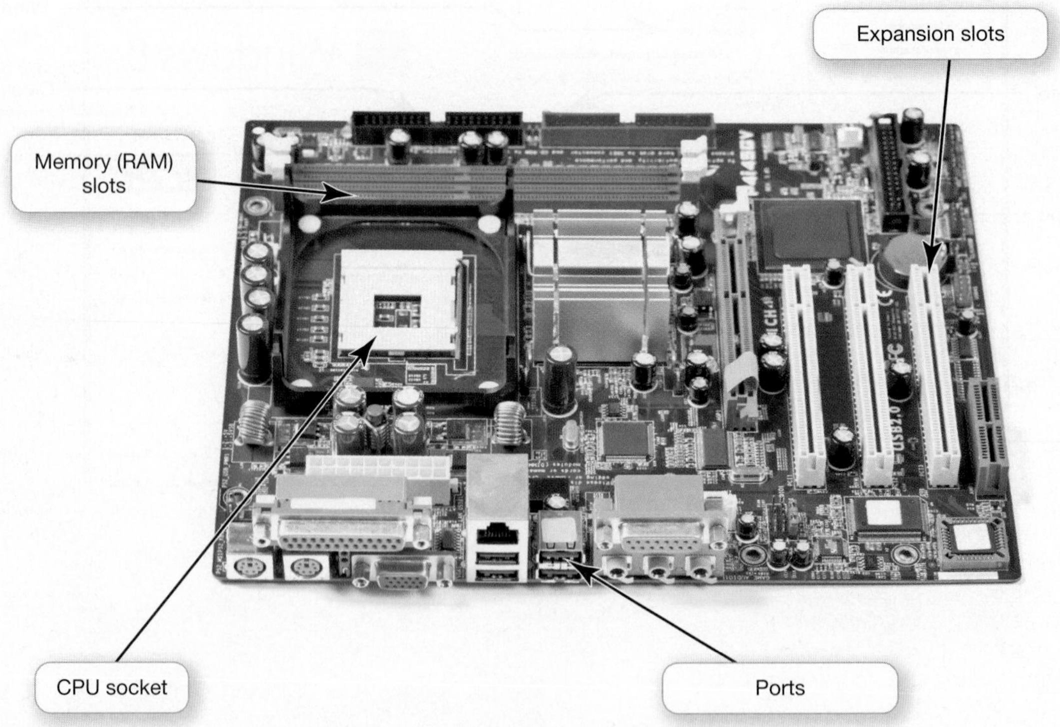


**FIGURE 2.26** A motherboard contains the socket for the computer's processor (CPU), the memory (RAM) modules, ports, and slots for expansion cards. *(S.Dashkevych/Shutterstock)*

## Memory

**What exactly is RAM? Random access memory (RAM)** is the place in a computer where the programs and data the computer is currently using are stored. RAM is much faster to read from and write to than the hard drive and other forms of storage. The processor can request the RAM's contents, which can be located, opened, and delivered to the CPU for processing in a few nanoseconds (billionths of a second). If you look at a motherboard, you'll see RAM as a series of small cards (called *memory cards* or *memory modules*) plugged into slots on the motherboard (see Figure 2.26).

Because the entire contents of RAM are erased when you turn off the computer, RAM is a temporary or **volatile storage** location. To save data permanently, you need to save it to your hard drive or to another permanent storage device such as a CD or flash drive.

**Does the motherboard contain any other kinds of memory besides RAM?** In addition to RAM, the motherboard contains a form of memory called **read-only memory (ROM)**. ROM holds all the instructions the computer needs to start up when it's powered on. Unlike data stored in RAM, which is volatile storage, the instructions stored in ROM are permanent, making ROM a **nonvolatile storage** location, which means the data isn't erased when the power is turned off.

## Processing

**What is the CPU?** The **central processing unit (CPU,** or **processor)** is sometimes referred to as the "brains" of the computer because it controls all the functions performed by the computer's other components and processes all the commands issued to it by software instructions. Modern CPUs can perform as many as tens of billions of tasks per second without error, making them extremely powerful components.

**How is processor speed measured?** Processor speed is measured in units of hertz (Hz). Hertz is a measurement of machine cycles per second. A machine cycle is the process of the CPU getting the data or instructions from RAM and decoding the instructions into something the computer can understand. Once the CPU has decoded the instructions, it executes them and stores the result back in system memory. Current systems run at speeds measured in **gigahertz (GHz)**, or billions of machine cycles per second. Therefore, a 3.8 GHz processor performs work at a rate of 3.8 billion machine cycles per second. It's important to realize, however, that CPU processor speed alone doesn't determine the performance of the CPU.

**What else determines processor performance?** Although speed is an important consideration when determining processor performance, CPU performance is also affected by other factors. One factor is the number of *cores,* or processing paths, a processor has. Initially, processors could handle only one instruction at a time. Now, processors have been designed so that they can have two, four, or even eight different paths, allowing them to process more than one instruction at a time (see Figure 2.27). Applications such as virus protection software and the operating system, which are always running behind the scenes, can have their own processor paths, freeing up the other paths to run other applications such as a web browser, Word, or iTunes more efficiently.

**Besides the number of cores, what other factors determine processing power?** The "best" processor will depend on your particular needs and is not always the processor with the highest processor speed and the greatest number of cores. Intel, one of the leading manufacturers of computer processor chips, has created a pictorial rating system for CPU chips. Intel uses one to five stars to illustrate the relative computing power of each type of CPU within the Intel line of processors. ■

SOUND BYTE

**Virtual Computer Tour**

In this Sound Byte, you'll take a video tour of the inside of a desktop system unit. From opening the cover to locating the power supply, CPU, and memory, you'll become more familiar with what's inside your computer.

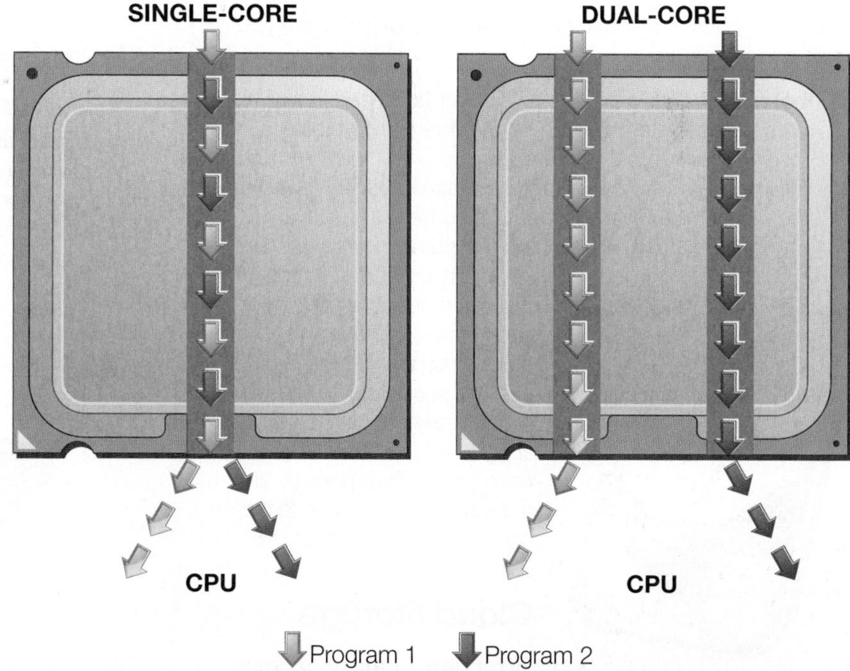


FIGURE 2.27 With multi-core processors, CPUs can work in parallel, processing two or more separate programs at the same time instead of switching back and forth between them.

# storing data and INFORMATION

Because RAM is volatile storage, it can't be used to store information indefinitely. To save your data and information permanently, you need to save it to a nonvolatile storage device, such as a hard drive, cloud storage location, DVD, or flash drive.

## Hard Drives

**Are there different kinds of hard drives?** The **hard disk drive (HDD,** or **hard drive)** is your computer's primary device for permanent storage of software and documents. The hard drive is a nonvolatile storage device. An **internal hard drive** resides within the system unit and usually holds all permanently stored programs and data. Today's internal hard drives (see Figure 2.28) have capacities of as much as 8 TB or more. **External hard drives** offer similar storage capacities but reside outside the system unit and connect to the computer via a port.

The most common type of hard drive has moveable parts—spinning platters, a moving arm with a read/write head—that can fail and lead to devastating disk failure. However, the **solid-state drive (SSD)** has recently become a popular option for ultrabooks and laptop storage. SSDs have no moving parts, so they're more efficient, run with no noise, emit little heat, and require little power. In addition, they're less likely to fail after being bumped or dropped.

Permanent storage devices are located in your desktop or laptop computer in a space called a **drive bay**. There are two kinds of drive bays:

1. *Internal drive bays* cannot be seen or accessed from outside the system unit. Generally, internal drive bays are reserved for internal hard drives.
2. *External drive bays* can be seen and accessed from outside the system unit. External drive bays house CD and DVD drives, for example. On desktop computers, sometimes there are empty external drive bays that can be used to install additional drives. These extra spaces are covered by a faceplate on the front panel. Laptop computers generally do not give you the ability to add additional drives. Such expansion is done by attaching an external drive to the computer through a USB port.

**FIGURE 2.28** Internal hard drives are a computer's primary nonvolatile storage. *(Ragnarock/Shutterstock)*

## Cloud Storage

**How can I easily access my files if I constantly switch between devices?** You may find yourself using multiple devices, such as a smartphone, laptop, and a tablet, at different times during the day. Invariably, you'll find you need access to a current version of a file that is stored on a device other than the one you're using. If your devices are connected to the Internet, cloud storage provides a convenient option.

**Cloud storage** refers to using a service that keeps your files on the Internet (in the "cloud") rather than storing your files solely on a local device. Using a cloud storage service requires that you install software/an app on your device. A popular web-based application for storing files on the cloud is Dropbox. Dropbox supports computers running Windows, OS X, and Linux as well as many smartphones and tablets. After installing the Dropbox software on your devices, any files you save in the Dropbox folder are accessible to all your other devices via the Internet. You can also share folders in Dropbox with other Dropbox users, making it ideal for group projects.

For example, when you save a history term paper to Dropbox on your laptop, the Dropbox software also copies the paper up onto a computer attached to the web. Now when you grab your smartphone and head off to class, you can access the paper created on your laptop through the Internet connection on your smartphone and make changes to it if necessary.

Dropbox storage capacity is limited to between 2 GB and 8 GB for free accounts. Other cloud storage alternatives include Microsoft OneDrive which provides 7 GB of free space, and Apple iCloud and Google Drive, which each offer 5 GB of free storage.

## Portable Storage Options

**How can I take my files with me without relying on cloud storage?** For large portable storage needs, there are portable external hard drives, which are small enough to fit into your pocket and have storage capacities of 4 TB (or larger). These devices are lightweight and enclosed in a protective case. They attach to your computer via a USB port (see Figure 2.29).

**FIGURE 2.29** Smaller, portable external hard drives enable you to take a significant amount of data and programs on the road with you. *(Inga Nielsen/Shutterstock)*

## BITS&BYTES

### Taking Care of Flash Drives

Although they're fairly rugged and can withstand much abuse, flash drives can fail. Therefore, it's important to know how to care for your flash drive to extend its life and keep your data safe.

1. Don't expose your flash drive to moisture or extreme temperatures.
2. Keep the end covered or closed when not in use. This prevents dust and other particles from interfering with the connections.
3. Never "defragment" a flash drive, as doing so can reduce its life expectancy.
4. A flash drive has a limited amount of writes in its lifetime. Depending on the device, it could be 10,000 or 100,000, which seems like a lot. However, over years of extensive use, the number of writes will add up. It's best to make edits to documents on the computer and then transfer the finished document to your flash drive.
5. Remove the flash drive correctly. All files and folders must be closed, with no active documents running, before the device is removed. To properly eject the device, use the "Safely remove hardware" feature in the taskbar, or select Eject from Windows Explorer (called File Explorer in Windows 8). (Mac users should select Eject from the Finder menu.) If you find that you can't eject the flash drive using these methods, power down the computer before removing the drive.

A **flash drive** (sometimes referred to as a **jump drive**, **USB drive**, or **thumb drive**) uses solid-state flash memory, storing information on an internal memory chip. When you plug a flash drive into your computer's USB port, it appears in the operating system as another disk drive. You can write data to it or read data from it as you would a hard drive. Because a flash drive contains no moving parts, it's quite durable. It's also tiny enough to fit in your pocket. Despite their size, flash drives can have significant storage capacity—currently as much as 256 GB. Often, flash drives are combined with other devices such as pens or pocketknives (see Figure 2.30) for added convenience.

New wireless flash drives, like the SanDisk Connect, are also appearing on the market to make transferring files from portable devices easier. Although they look like normal flash drives, these wireless drives can connect to your portable devices via WiFi after installing the appropriate app. Up to eight devices can be connected to the flash drive at once, and the drive can even stream media to three devices simultaneously. So your friend could be watching a movie stored on the flash drive while you're uploading pictures from your phone.

Another convenient means of portable storage is a **flash memory card**, such as an SD card. Like the flash drive, memory cards use solid-state flash memory. Most desktops and laptops include slots for flash memory cards, but if your computer is not equipped, there are memory card readers that you can plug into a USB port. Flash memory cards let you transfer digital data between your computer and devices such as digital cameras, smartphones, tablets, video cameras, and printers. Although incredibly small—some are even smaller than the size of a postage stamp—these memory cards have capacities that exceed the capacity of a DVD. Figure 2.31 compares the storage capacities of hard drives and flash drives.

**FIGURE 2.30** Flash drives are a convenient means of portable storage and come in many different shapes and sizes. *(ekler/Shutterstock)*

FIGURE 2.31

## Hard Drive and Flash Drive Storage Capacity

| DRIVE TYPE | IMAGE | TYPICAL CAPACITY |
|---|---|---|
| Solid-state drive (SSD) |  | 5 TB or more |
| External portable hard drive | 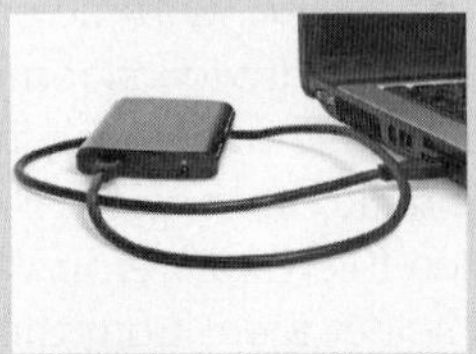 | 4 TB or more |
| Mechanical internal hard drive |  | As much as 8 TB or more |
| Flash drive | 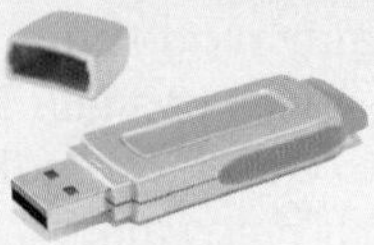 | 256 GB or more |
| Flash memory card |  | 128 GB |

(Oleksiy Mark/Shutterstock; Julia Ivantsova/Shutterstock; D. Hurst/ Alamy; Cphoto/Fotolia; © Gene Blevins/ZUMAPRESS.com)

## Optical Storage

**What other kinds of storage devices are available?** Most desktop and laptop computers come with at least one **optical drive** that can read from and maybe even write to CDs, DVDs, or Blu-ray discs. Data is saved to such discs as tiny pits that are burned into the disc by a high-speed laser. **Compact discs (CDs)** were initially created to store audio files. **Digital video (or versatile) discs (DVDs)** are the same size and shape as CDs but can store up to 14 times more data than CDs.

What if you want even more storage capacity? Blu-ray is the latest incarnation of optical storage to hit the market. **Blu-ray discs (BDs)**, which are similar in size and shape to CDs and DVDs, can hold as much as 50 GB of data—enough to hold approximately 4.5 hours of movies in high-definition (HD) digital format. Many systems are now available with BD-ROM drives and even Blu-ray burners. External BD drives are another inexpensive way to add HD storage capacity to your system. Figure 2.32 shows the storage capacities of the various optical storage media. ■

FIGURE 2.32

## Optical Storage Media Capacities

| MEDIUM TYPE | TYPICAL CAPACITY |
|---|---|
| Blu-ray (dual layer) | 50 GB |
| Blu-ray | 25 GB |
| DVD DL (dual layer) | 8.5 GB |
| DVD | 4.7 GB |
| CD | 700 MB |

# connecting peripherals to the COMPUTER

Throughout this chapter, we have discussed peripheral devices that input, store, and output data and information. A **port** is a place through which a peripheral device attaches to the computer so that data can be exchanged between it and the operating system. Although peripherals may connect to devices wirelessly, ports are still often used for connections.

## High-Speed and Data Transfer Ports

**What is the fastest data transfer port available on today's computing devices?** Thunderbolt is the newest input/output technology on the market. It was developed by Intel using fiber optic technology and can achieve blazingly fast transfer speeds of up to 10 Gb/s. **Thunderbolt ports** (see Figure 2.33) are very useful for laptops and ultrabooks because one Thunderbolt port can allow you to connect up to six different peripherals to your computer. Apple was the first computer maker to integrate the ports into their hardware although other manufacturers are now following suit.

**What is the most common port on digital devices?** A **universal serial bus (USB) port** is the port type most commonly used to connect input and output devices to the computer. This is mainly because of the ready availability of USB-compatible peripherals. USB ports can connect a wide variety of peripherals, including keyboards, printers, mice, smartphones, external hard drives, flash drives, and digital cameras, to computing devices. The current USB 3.0 standard provides transfer speeds of 4.8 Gbps and charges devices faster than previous USB ports. USB ports come in three different configurations (see Figure 2.34), which allows them to be integrated into all different sizes of devices.

**What other types of data transfer ports are there?** You may also see other ports, such as **FireWire 800**, especially on Apple computers. The current standard, FireWire 800, provides a fast transfer rate of 800 Mbps. Devices such as external hard drives and digital video cameras benefit from the speedy data transfer capabilities of FireWire. As more peripherals are released with Thunderbolt capabilities, we should see FireWire declining in popularity.

**FIGURE 2.33** Thunderbolt ports are slim and speedy, making them popular on today's ultrabooks and laptops. *(David Paul Morris/Bloomberg via Getty Images)*

**FIGURE 2.34** USB connector types (from left to right): standard, micro and mini. *(© Nikita Buida – Fotolia.com; © de_marco – Fotolia.com)*

## Connectivity and Multimedia Ports

**Which ports help me connect with other computers and the Internet?** Another set of ports on your computer helps you communicate with other computers. A **connectivity port** can give you access to networks and the Internet. To find a connectivity port, look for a port that resembles a standard phone jack but is slightly larger. This port is called an **Ethernet port**. Ethernet ports transfer data at speeds up to 10,000 Mbps. You can use an Ethernet port to connect your computer to a cable modem, or to a network.

**How do I connect monitors and multimedia devices?** Other ports on the back and sides of the computer include audio and video ports. Audio ports are where you connect headphones, microphones, and speakers to the computer. Whether you're attaching a monitor to a desktop computer, or adding a second, larger display to a laptop computer, you'll use a video port. HDMI ports are now the most common video port on computing devices.

A **high-definition multimedia interface (HDMI) port** is a compact audio–video interface that allows both HD video and uncompressed digital audio to be carried on one cable. Because HDMI can transmit uncompressed audio and video, there's no need to convert the signal, which could ultimately reduce the quality of the sound or picture. All currently available monitors, DVD players, televisions, and game consoles have at least one HDMI port (see Figure 2.35).

ACTIVE HELPDESK

**Exploring Storage Devices and Ports**

In this Active Helpdesk call, you'll play the role of a helpdesk staffer, fielding calls about the computer's main storage devices and how to connect various peripheral devices to the computer.

FIGURE 2.35 HDMI is the latest digital connector type for HD monitors, televisions, and home theater equipment. *(Feng Yu/Shutterstock)*

**What ports might I encounter on older computers and peripherals?** The **video graphics array (VGA) port** and the **digital video interface (DVI) port** are two ports to which older LCD monitors and televisions connect (see Figure 2.36). Some Apple computers still feature a Mini DisplayPort for connection of video peripherals. Adapters are available for the Mini DisplayPort that allow the connection of older DVI and VGA devices.

## Adding Ports: Expansion Cards and Hubs

**What if I don't have all the ports I need?** If you're looking to add the newest ports to an older desktop computer or to expand the number of ports on it, you can install special expansion cards (Figure 2.37) into an open expansion slot on the motherboard to provide additional ports.

Another alternative is adding an expansion hub (shown in Figure 2.38). An expansion hub is a device that connects to one port, such as a USB port, to provide additional ports. It works like the multiplug extension cords used with electrical appliances. ■

FIGURE 2.36 DVI (left) and VGA (right) cables are used to connect older LCD monitors and televisions to computing devices. (Marek Kosmal/Fotolia)

FIGURE 2.37 Expansion cards fit into slots on the motherboard in a desktop computer. *(Andrew Kitching/Alamy)*

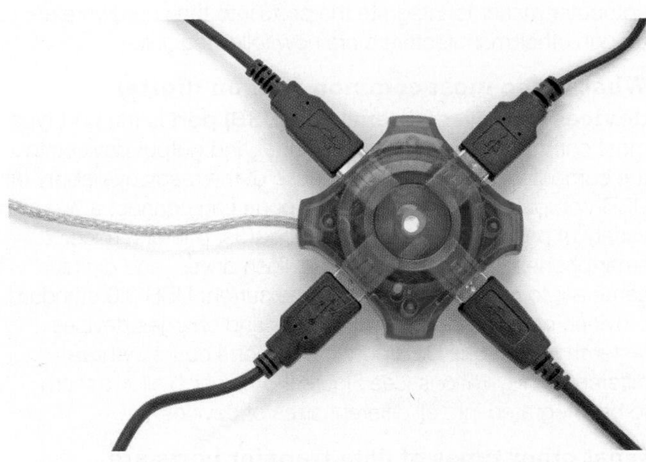

FIGURE 2.38 If you don't have enough USB ports to support your USB devices, consider getting an expansion hub, which can add four or more USB ports to your system. *(Norman Chan/Fotolia)*

SOUND BYTE

**Port Tour: How Do I Hook It Up?**

In this Sound Byte, you'll take a tour of both a desktop system and a laptop system to compare the number and variety of available ports. You'll also learn about the different types of ports and compare their speed and expandability.

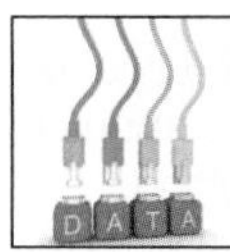

# power CONTROLS

**What's the best way to turn my computer on and off?** The **power supply**, which is housed inside the system unit, transforms the wall voltage to the voltages required by computer chips. Powering on your computer from a completely turned off state, such as when you start your computer in the morning, is called a **cold boot**. In Windows 8, you can turn your computer off by pressing the computer's power button or by using the Shut Down option from the power icon found under Settings on the Charms bar.

**Should I turn off my computer every time I'm done using it?** Some people say you should leave your computer on at all times. They argue that turning your computer on and off throughout the day subjects its components to stress because the heating and cooling process forces the components to expand and contract repeatedly. Other people say you should shut down your computer when you're not using it. They claim that it's not as environmentally friendly and that you'll end up wasting money on electricity from the computer running all the time.

Modern operating systems include power-management settings that allow the most power-hungry components of the system (the hard drive and monitor) to shut down after a short idle period. With the power-management options of Windows 8, for example, you only need to shut down your computer completely when you need to repair or install hardware in the system unit or move it to another location. However, if you use your computer only for a little while each day, it would be best to power it off completely after each daily use.

**Can I "rest" my computer without turning it off completely?** In Windows 8, the main method of power management is Sleep. When your computer enters **Sleep mode**, all of the documents, applications, and data you were using remain in RAM (memory), where they're quickly accessible when you restart your computer.

In Sleep mode, the computer enters a state of greatly reduced power consumption, which saves energy. To put your computer into Sleep mode in Windows 8, display the Charms bar, click (or touch) the Settings option, then click the Power option and select the Sleep option. To wake up your computer, press a key or the power button. In a few seconds, the computer will resume with exactly the same programs running and documents displayed as when you put it to sleep.

If you don't ever want to completely turn off your computer, you can change what happens when you press the power button or close the lid on your laptop. By accessing the Power Options System Settings window (see Figure 2.39), you can decide if you want your computer to Sleep, Hibernate, or Shut

Define power buttons and turn on password protection

Choose the power settings that you want for your computer. The changes you make to the settings on this page apply to all of your power plans.

Change settings that are currently unavailable

Power button and lid settings

| | On battery | Plugged in |
|---|---|---|
| When I press the power button: | Hibernate | Sleep |
| When I close the lid: | Sleep | Sleep |

Do nothing
Sleep
Hibernate
Shut down

Password protection on wakeup

Require a password (recommended)
When your computer wakes from sleep, no one can access your data without entering the correct password to unlock the computer. Create or change your user account password

Don't require a password
When your computer wakes from sleep, anyone can access your data because the computer isn't locked.

**FIGURE 2.39** You can determine what happens when you click the power button on your computer or close the lid through the Power Options System Settings screen.

*>To access Power Options System Settings, display the Control Panel, click* **Hardware and Sound,** *and then select* **Change what the power buttons do** *under Power Options.*

Down when you press the power button. The **Hibernate** option is similar to Sleep except that your data is stored on your hard drive instead of in RAM and your computer is powered off. This uses much less battery power than Sleep and is a good choice if you won't be using your laptop for a long time and won't have the opportunity to charge it. However, Sleep is still a good option to choose if you just won't be using your computer for a short time. You may want to set your computer so it sleeps when you close the lid but hibernates when you press the power button, giving you quick access to either option.

**What's the Restart option in Windows for?** If you're using Windows 8, you have the option to restart the computer when you display the Charms bar, click (or touch) Settings, then click the Power button (see Figure 2.40). Restarting the system while it's powered on is called a **warm boot**. You might need to perform a warm boot if the operating system or other software application stops responding or if you've installed new programs. It takes less time to perform a warm boot than to power down completely and then restart all your hardware. ■

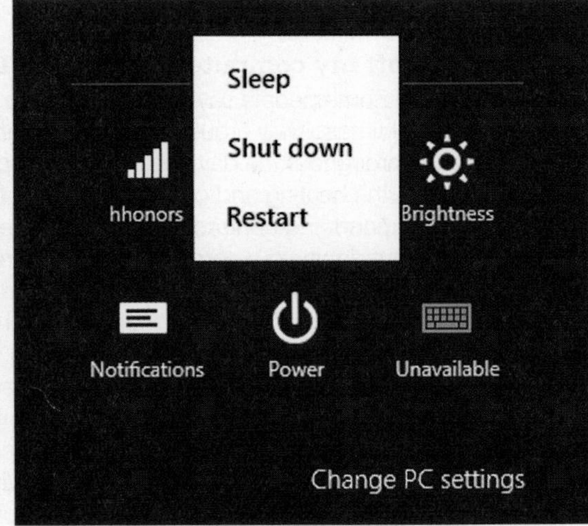


**FIGURE 2.40** The Settings panel in Windows 8 presents several power options. For a warm boot, choose **Restart**. To power down the computer completely, choose **Shut down**. To put your computer into a lower power mode, select **Sleep**.

>*To select a particular power option, display the Charms bar, click* **Settings**, *then click the* **Power** *button.*

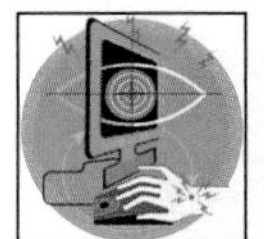

# setting it ALL UP

It's important that you understand not only your computer's components and how they work together but also how to set up these components safely. **Ergonomics** is the science that deals with the design and location of machines and furniture so that the people using them aren't subjected to an uncomfortable or unsafe experience. In terms of computing, ergonomics refers to how you set up your computer and other equipment to minimize your risk of injury or discomfort.

**Why is ergonomics important?** Studies suggest that teenagers, on average, spend 31 hours online each week. When you factor in other computer uses such as typing school reports and playing video games, there is great potential for injury. The repetitive nature of long-term computer activities can place too much stress on joints and pull at the tendons and muscles, causing repetitive stress injuries such as carpal tunnel syndrome and tendonitis. These injuries can take months or years to develop to a point where they become painful, and by the time you notice the symptoms, the damage has already taken place. If you take precautionary measures now, you may prevent years of unnecessary pain later.

**How can I avoid injuries when I'm working at my computer?** As Figure 2.41 illustrates, it's important to arrange your monitor, chair, body, and keyboard in ways that will help you avoid injury, discomfort, and eyestrain. The following additional guidelines can help keep you comfortable and productive:

- **Position your monitor correctly.** Studies suggest it's best to place your monitor at least 25 inches from your eyes. Experts recommend that you position your monitor either at eye level or at an angle 15 to 20 degrees below your line of sight.
- **Purchase an adjustable chair.** Adjust the height of your chair so that your feet touch the floor (or use a footrest to get the right position). The back support needs to be adjustable

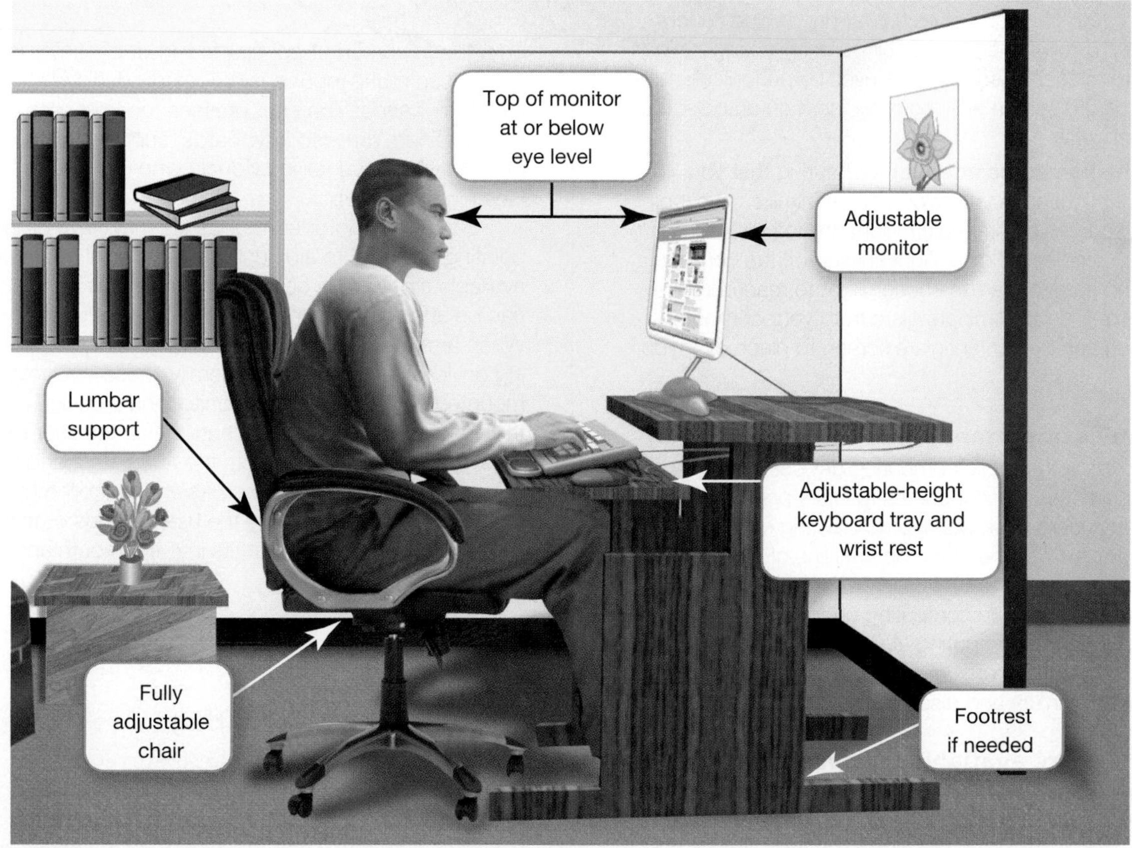


**FIGURE 2.41** Using proper equipment that is adjusted correctly helps prevent repetitive strain injuries while working at a computer.

so that you can position it to support your lumbar (lower back) region. You should also be able to move the seat or adjust the back so that you can sit without exerting pressure on your knees. If your chair doesn't adjust, place a pillow behind your back to provide support.

- **Assume a proper position while typing.** Improperly positioned keyboards are one of the leading causes of repetitive stress injuries in computer users. Your wrists should be flat (not bent) with respect to the keyboard, and your forearms should be parallel to the floor. Additionally, your wrists should not be resting on the keyboard while typing. You can adjust the height of your chair or install a height-adjustable keyboard tray to ensure a proper position. Specially designed ergonomic keyboards such as the one shown in Figure 2.42 can help you achieve the proper wrist position.
- **Take breaks.** Remaining in the same position for long periods of time increases stress on your body. Shift your position in your chair and stretch your hands and fingers periodically. Likewise, staring at the screen for long periods can lead to eyestrain, so rest your eyes by periodically taking them off the screen and focusing them on an object at least 8 feet away.
- **Ensure the lighting is adequate.** Ensuring that you have proper lighting in your work area minimizes eyestrain. Eliminate sources of direct glare (light shining directly into your eyes) or reflected glare (light shining off the computer screen) and ensure there is enough light to read comfortably. If you still can't eliminate glare from your computer screen, you can buy an antiglare screen to place over your monitor.

**FIGURE 2.42** Ergonomic keyboards, like the Truly Ergonomic Mechanical Keyboard shown here, which help users type with straight wrists and contain built-in wrist rests, facilitate proper hand position and minimize wrist strain. *(Truly Ergonomic Ltd.)*

**Is ergonomics important when using mobile devices?** Working with mobile computing devices presents interesting challenges when it comes to injury prevention. For example, many users work with laptops resting on their laps, placing the monitor outside of the optimal line of sight and thereby increasing neck strain. Figure 2.43 provides guidelines on preventing injuries when computing on the go.

So, whether you're computing at your desk or on the road, consider the ergonomics of your work environment. Doing so will help you avoid injury and discomfort.

**What devices are available for people with disabilities?** People who have physical challenges sometimes need special devices to access computers. For visually impaired users, voice recognition is an input option. For those users whose visual limitations are less severe, keyboards with larger keys are available. Keyboards that display on a touch screen or specialized input consoles (see Figure 2.44a) can make input easier for individuals who can't type with their hands: The user presses the keys with a pointing device. There are also keyboards, such as those made by Maltron, designed for individuals who can use only one hand (see Figure 2.44b).

People with motor control issues may have difficulty with pointing devices. To aid such users, special trackballs are available that can be easily manipulated with one finger and can be attached to almost any surface, including a wheelchair. When arm motion is severely restrained, head-mounted pointing devices can be used. Generally, these involve a camera mounted on the computer monitor and a device attached to the head (often installed in a hat). When the user moves his or her head, the camera detects the movement and moves the cursor. In this case, mouse clicks are controlled by a switch that can be manipulated by the user's hands or feet or even by using an instrument that fits into the mouth and senses the user blowing into it. ■

SOUND BYTE

**Healthy Computing**

In this Sound Byte, you'll see how to set up your workspace in an ergonomically correct way. You'll learn the proper location of the monitor, keyboard, and mouse, as well as ergonomic features to look for when choosing the most appropriate chair.

FIGURE 2.43

## Preventing Injuries While on the Go

| | SMARTPHONE REPETITIVE STRAIN INJURIES | PORTABLE MEDIA PLAYER HEARING DAMAGE | SMALL-SCREEN VISION ISSUES | LAP INJURIES | TABLET REPETITIVE STRAIN INJURIES |
|---|---|---|---|---|---|
| **Malady** | Repetitive strain injuries (such as DeQuervain's tendonitis) from constant typing of instant messages | Hearing loss from high-decibel sound levels in earbuds | Blurriness and dryness caused by squinting to view tiny screens on mobile devices | Burns on legs from heat generated by laptop | Pain caused from using tablets for prolonged periods in uncomfortable positions |
| **Preventative measures** | Restrict length and frequency of messages, take breaks, and perform other motions with your thumbs and fingers during breaks to relieve tension. | Turn down volume (you should be able to hear external noises, such as people talking), use software that limits sound levels (not to exceed 60 decibels), and use external, over-ear style headphones instead of earbuds. | Blink frequently or use eye drops to maintain moisture in eyes, after 10 minutes take a break and focus on something at least 8 feet away for 5 minutes, use adequate amount of light, and increase the size of fonts. | Place a book, magazine, or laptop cooling pad between your legs and laptop. | Restrict the length of time you work at a tablet, especially typing or gaming. Use the same ergonomic position you would use for a laptop when using a tablet. |

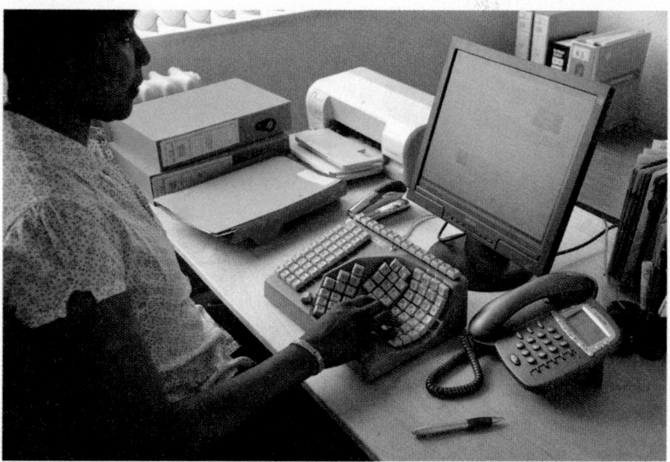

**FIGURE 2.44** (a) Input consoles for people who can't type with their hands and (b) keyboards designed for one-handed use make computer interaction easier for individuals with disabilities. *(Maltron; Maltron)*

# trends in IT

## Innovations in Printing

With the advent of the computer, many speculated that ours would become a paperless society. Instead of saving printed documents and other output as was done prior to the PC, information would be saved in a digital state: hard drives replacing filing cabinets, online photo buckets replacing photo albums and scrapbooks, and e-books replacing our favorite texts. Hard drive capacities do enable us to save more content, and online storage systems enable us to save pictures and other files to the "cloud." Additionally, e-book readers have increased in popularity. But has this push toward digital content begun to make the printer obsolete? Surprisingly, no. People still have a deep-rooted need to see, feel, mark, share, or use their digital images or information in a physical form. New technologies that push the boundaries of printing, such as printing from the cloud and 3-D printing, are being developed and refined.

### Cloud Printing

To print a document from a desktop or laptop computer, you must have a printer associated with your computer. Usually this is not a problem because at home, at school, or in the office, there is generally one printer, and all the PCs connected to it have the software and cables or wireless capabilities needed to use it. But what happens if you want to print something from your smartphone or tablet? Common solutions have been to e-mail the document to yourself or transfer the document to a web-based storage service such as Dropbox so that a printer-connected computer could access it. Another solution is Google Cloud Print, a service that lets you configure your printers so you can access them from mobile devices.

Google Cloud Print uses cloud-ready printers (see Figure 2.45) that are now available from manufacturers such as HP, Kodak, and Epson. These printers connect directly to the Internet and register themselves with Google Cloud Print without needing to be connected to a computer. Once a printer is registered with Cloud Print, printing jobs can be sent to it from mobile devices (such as tablets and smartphones) using the Internet. Conventional printers that you already own can

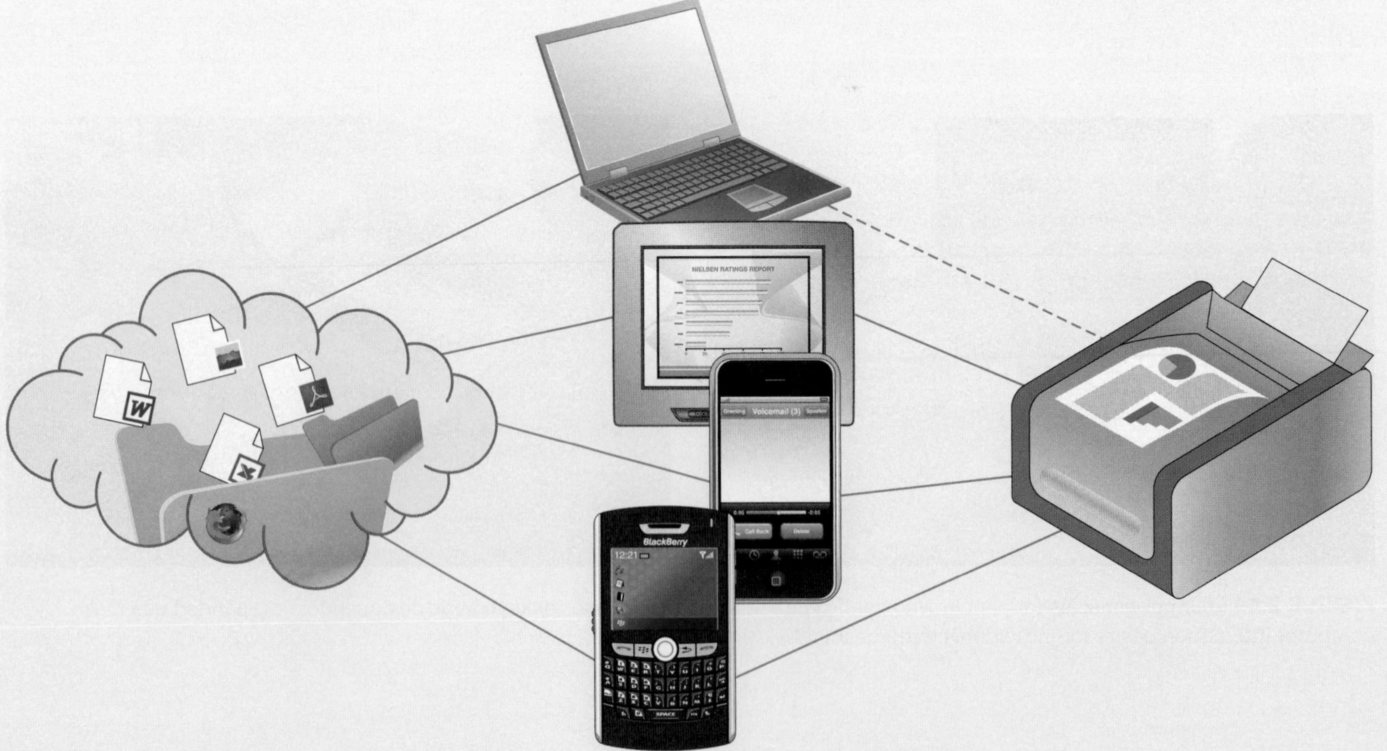

**FIGURE 2.45** Cloud-ready printers only need an Internet connection to be accessed from any mobile device.

also be registered with Cloud Print, although they require connection to the Internet through a computer.

## 3-D Printing

Printing a 3-D model of a proposed building or new prototype is common for architects and engineers. The process builds a model one layer at a time from the bottom up. The procedure begins by spreading a layer of powder on a platform. Then, depending on the technology, the printer uses nozzles similar to those in an inkjet printer to spray tiny drops of glue at specific places to solidify the powder, or the powder is solidified through a melting process. The printer repeats solidifying layers of powder until the model is built to specifications. This technology has spurred the manufacturing of a variety of consumer goods, from toys to clothing (see Figure 2.46). Shapeways (**shapeways.com**) uses 3-D printing to enable anyone to turn his or her 3-D designs into real physical models. Then, those models can be personalized, bought, or sold through Shapeways's online community.

3-D printing is being used in the medical community as well. Bespoke Innovations (**bespokeinnovations.com**) is using 3-D printing to create prosthetic limbs with more lifelike form and textures as well as to give the recipient the ability to further personalize the prosthetic to include tattoos! And researchers at Wake Forest Institute for Regenerative Medicine have developed a way to use similar inkjet technologies to build heart, bone, and blood vessel tissues in the lab. They have also developed a way to "print" restorative cells directly into a soldier's wound at the site where the injury occurred, thus significantly improving the soldier's chances of survival.

Taking traditional technologies, such as inkjet printing, and applying them to solve current human struggles is a long and tedious process, but without these pioneers experimenting with different applications, society would advance a lot more slowly.

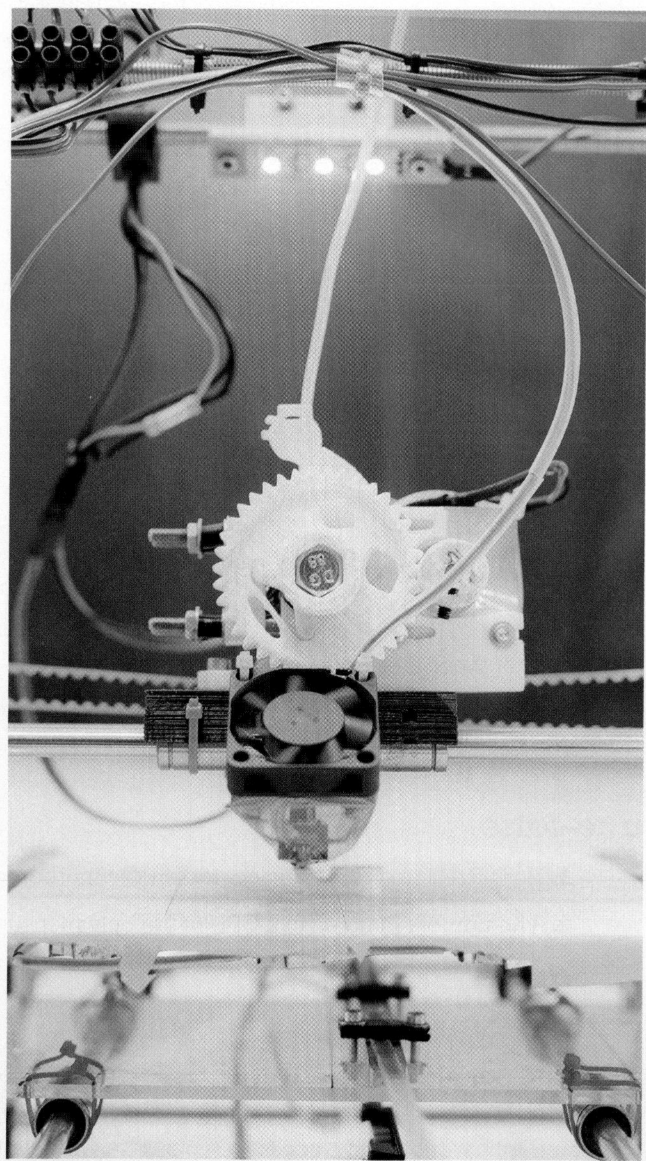

**FIGURE 2.46** 3-D printing is being used to fabricate parts for machines on demand. *(Tomas Mikula/Shutterstock)*

**Before moving on to the Chapter Review:**

- **Watch Replay Video 2.2** .
- Then check your understanding of what you've learned so far.

# check your understanding//

For a quick review to see what you've learned so far, answer the following questions. Visit **pearsonhighered.com/techinaction** to check your answers.

## multiple choice

**1.** Which is the fastest data transfer port available today?

**a.** USB
**b.** Thunderbolt
**c.** FireWire
**d.** VGA

**2.** Which optical storage media can hold the most data?

**a.** DVD
**b.** CD
**c.** Blu-ray
**d.** a flash memory card

**3.** Which of these are considered volatile storage?

**a.** flash drive
**b.** ROM
**c.** RAM
**d.** hard drive

**4.** Which of these is NOT a storage device?

**a.** flash drive
**b.** solid-state drive
**c.** internal hard drive
**d.** Thunderbolt drive

**5.** Proper ergonomics helps prevent repetitive strain injuries

**a.** only when using tablet computers.
**b.** only when using desktop computers.
**c.** in all types of computing devices.
**d.** except when using mobile computing devices.

## true–false

_____ **1.** Both RAM and ROM are located on the motherboard.

_____ **2.** The number of cores in a CPU is the only measure of a processor's expected performance.

## critical thinking

**1. Cloud Storage Alternatives**

Hard drives are great for storing data on your computer, but there are many reasons why you might want to have access to your data wherever you go. Research various types of available cloud storage (such as Dropbox and OneDrive). Which service do you think is most appropriate for students (and why)? What service would you recommend to a small business that has three physical locations and 50 employees (and why)?

**2. iPad**

The Apple iPad has been enthusiastically accepted because of its multitouch screen; useful apps; two cameras; and small, light frame. If the CEO of Apple asked you for your advice as to what to include in the next version of the iPad, what would you suggest? What features would make tablets even more appealing to students?

**Continue** 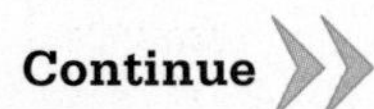

# Chapter Review

## summary//

### Understanding Your Computer

**1. What exactly is a computer, and what are its four main functions?**

- Computers are devices that process data. They help organize, sort, and categorize data to turn it into information.
- The computer's four major functions are: (1) input: gather data, or allow users to enter data; (2) process: manipulate, calculate, or organize that data; (3) output: display data and information in a form suitable for the user; and (4) storage: save data and information for later use.

**2. What is the difference between data and information?**

- Data is a representation of a fact or idea. The number 3 and the words *televisions* and *Sony* are pieces of data.
- Information is data that has been organized or presented in a meaningful fashion. An inventory list that indicates that "three Sony televisions" are in stock is processed information. It allows a retail clerk to answer a customer query about the availability of merchandise. Information is more powerful than raw data.

**3. What are bits and bytes, and how are they measured?**

- To process data into information, computers need to work in a language they understand. This language, called *binary language*, consists of two numbers: 0 and 1.
- Each 0 and each 1 is a binary digit, or bit. Eight bits create one byte.
- In computers, each letter of the alphabet, each number, and each special character consists of a unique combination of eight bits (one byte)—a string of eight 0s and 1s.
- For describing large amounts of storage capacity, the terms *megabyte* (approximately 1 million bytes), *gigabyte* (approximately 1 billion bytes), *terabyte* (approximately 1 trillion bytes), and *petabyte* (1,000 terabytes) are used.

### Input Devices and Output Devices

**4. What devices can I use to get data into the computer?**

- An input device enables you to enter data (text, images, and sounds) and instructions (user responses and commands) into a computer.
- You use keyboards to enter typed data and commands, whereas you use the mouse to enter user responses and commands.
- Touch screens are display screens that respond to commands initiated by a touch with a finger or a stylus.
- Images are input into the computer with scanners, digital cameras, camcorders, and smartphones.
- Live video is captured with webcams and digital video recorders.
- Microphones capture sounds. There are many different types of microphones, including desktop, headset, and clip-on models.

**5. What devices can I use to get information out of the computer?**

- Output devices enable you to send processed data out of your computer. It can take the form of text, pictures, sounds, or video.
- Monitors display soft copies of text, graphics, and video, whereas printers create hard copies of text and graphics.
- There are two primary categories of printers: inkjet and laser. Specialty printers are also available. These include all-in-one printers, plotters, and thermal printers. When choosing a printer, you should be aware of factors such as speed, resolution, color output, and cost.
- Speakers are the output devices for sound. Most computers include speakers; more-sophisticated systems include subwoofers and surround sound.

### Processing, Memory, and Storage

**6. What's on the motherboard?**

- The motherboard, the main circuit board of the system, contains a computer's CPU, which coordinates the functions of all other devices on the computer. The performance of a CPU is affected by the speed of the processor (measured in GHz), the amount of cache memory, and the number of processing cores.

- RAM, the computer's volatile memory, is also located on the motherboard. RAM is where all the data and instructions are held while the computer is running.
- ROM, a permanent type of memory, is responsible for housing instructions to help start up a computer.
- The motherboard also houses slots for expansion cards, which have specific functions that augment the computer's basic functions. Typical expansion cards are sound and video cards.

**7. Where are information and programs stored?**

- To save programs and information permanently, you need to save them to the hard drive or to another permanent storage device such as a DVD or flash drive, or to the cloud.
- The hard drive is your computer's primary device for permanent storage of software and files. The hard drive is a nonvolatile storage device, meaning it holds the data and instructions your computer needs permanently, even after the computer is turned off.
- Mechanical hard drives have spinning platters on which data is saved, whereas newer solid-state drives (SSDs) use solid-state memory, similar to that used with flash drives.
- External hard drives are essentially internal hard drives that have been made portable by enclosing them in a protective case and making them small and lightweight.
- Cloud storage refers to nonvolatile storage locations that are maintained on the Internet (in the "cloud") by companies such as Dropbox. Storing your data in the cloud allows you to access it from almost any computing device that is connected to the Internet.
- Optical drives that can read from and write to CD, DVD, or Blu-ray discs are another means of permanent, portable storage. Data is saved to CDs, DVDs, and Blu-ray discs as pits that are burned into the disc by a laser.
- Flash drives are another portable means of storing data. Flash drives plug into USB ports.
- Flash memory cards let you transfer digital data between your computer and devices such as digital cameras, smartphones, video cameras, and printers.

## Ports and Power Controls

**8. How are devices connected to the computer?**

- There is a wide variety of ports that allow you to hook up peripheral devices (such as your monitor and keyboard) to your system.
- The fastest type of port used to connect devices to a computer is the Thunderbolt port.
- The most common type of port used to connect devices to a computer is the USB port.
- FireWire ports provide additional options for data transfer.
- Connectivity ports, such as Ethernet ports, give you access to networks and the Internet.
- HDMI ports are the most common multimedia port. They are used to connect monitors, TVs, and gaming consoles to computing devices and handle both audio and video data.
- Audio ports are where you connect headphones, microphones, and speakers to computing devices.

**9. What's the best way to turn my computer on and off, and when should it be done?**

- Power on your computer from a completely turned-off state. In Windows 8, you can turn your computer off by pressing the computer's power button or by using the Shut Down option from the power icon found under Settings on the Charms bar.
- With the power-management options of Windows 8, for example, you only need to shut down your computer completely when you need to repair or install hardware in the system unit or move it to another location. However, if you use your computer only for a little while each day, it would be best to power it off completely after each daily use.

## Setting It All Up

**10. How do I set up my computer to avoid strain and injury?**

- *Ergonomics* refers to how you arrange your computer and equipment to minimize your risk of injury or discomfort.
- Ergonomics includes positioning your monitor correctly, buying an adjustable chair, assuming a proper position while typing, making sure the lighting is adequate, and not looking at the screen for long periods. Other good practices include taking frequent breaks and using specially designed equipment such as ergonomic keyboards.
- Ergonomics is also important to consider when using mobile devices.

Be sure to check out the companion website for additional materials to help you review and learn, including a Tech Bytes Weekly newsletter—**pearsonhighered.com/techinaction.**
And don't forget the Replay Videos .

# key terms//

all-in-one computer **33**
all-in-one printer **47**
application software **31**
aspect ratio **43**
binary digit (bit) **31**
binary language **31**
Bluetooth technology **35**
Blu-ray disc (BD) **56**
byte **31**
central processing unit (CPU, or processor) **53**
cloud storage **54**
cold boot **59**
compact disc (CD) **56**
computer **30**
connectivity port **57**
data **30**
desktop computer **31**
digital video (or versatile) disc (DVD) **56**
digital video interface (DVI) port **58**
drive bay **54**
embedded computer **33**
ergonomics **61**
Ethernet port **57**
expansion cards (or adapter cards) **52**
external hard drive **54**
FireWire 800 **57**
flash drive (jump drive, USB drive, or thumb drive) **55**
flash memory card **55**
gigabyte (GB) **31**
gigahertz (GHz) **53**
hard disk drive (HDD, or hard drive) **54**
hardware **31**
Hibernate **60**
high-definition multimedia interface (HDMI) port **57**
impact printer **46**
information **30**
inkjet printer **46**
input device **35**
internal hard drive **54**
keyboard **35**
kilobyte (KB) **31**
laptop (or notebook) computer **31**
laser printer **46**
legacy technology **43**
light-emitting diode (LED) **43**
liquid crystal display (LCD) **43**
mainframe **33**
megabyte (MB) **31**
microphone (mic) **40**
monitor (display screen) **43**
motherboard **52**
mouse **35**
netbook **31**
network interface card (NIC) **52**
nonimpact printer **46**
nonvolatile storage **53**
operating system (OS) **31**
optical drive **56**
optical mouse **37**
organic light-emitting diode (OLED) displays **43**
output device **43**
petabyte **31**
peripheral device **33**
pixel **43**
plotter **47**
port **57**
power supply **59**
printer **43**
processing **30**
projector **45**
QWERTY keyboard **35**
random access memory (RAM) **53**
read-only memory (ROM) **53**
resolution **43**
scanner **39**
Sleep mode **59**
smartphone **34**
software **31**
solid-state drive (SSD) **54**
sound card **52**
speakers **47**
stylus **35**
supercomputer **33**
surround-sound speaker **48**
system software **31**
system unit **31**
tablet computer **31**
tablet (or convertible) PC **31**
terabyte (TB) **31**
thermal printer **47**
Thunderbolt port **57**
touch pad (trackpad) **39**
touch screen **35**
ultrabook **31**
universal serial bus (USB) port **57**
video card **52**
video graphics array (VGA) port **58**
volatile storage **53**
warm boot **60**
webcam **39**

## making the transition to . . . next semester//

1. **Watching Device Demos**

   YouTube is a great resource for product demonstrations. Open your browser, navigate to YouTube (**youtube.com**), and search on any type of computer peripheral discussed in this chapter to see if you can find a demonstration of a cool product.

   How helpful are these demonstrations? Make a video demonstration of a computing device you have and post it to your course management system or present it to your classmates (as specified by your instructor).

2. **Communicating with the Computer**

   You're involved in many group projects at school. Between your work, your classes, and other outside responsibilities, you're finding it difficult to meet in person. Investigate the devices you would need to be able to have virtual group meetings.

3. **Ultrabook or Tablet**

   You need a new computing device for school. Consider the following:

   a. Explain the differences between a tablet and an ultrabook.
   b. What advantages would an ultrabook provide you for your academic career?
   c. What advantages would a tablet (such as an iPad) provide to you in the classroom? At home?
   d. Which device do you think is better suited to your needs? Explain fully.

## making the transition to . . . the workplace//

1. **Backing Up Your Work**

   You've embarked on a position as a freelance editor. You'll be using your own computer. Until now, you haven't worried too much about backing up your data. Now, however, it's extremely important that you back up all your work frequently. Research the various backup options available, including cloud backup services, external hard drives, and portable flash storage. What are the size limitations of each? What are the initial and ongoing costs of each? How frequently do the options allow you to perform backups? Which option would you choose, and why?

2. **What Hardware Will You Use?**

   When you arrive at a new position for a company, your employer will most likely provide you with a computer. Based on the career you're in now or are planning to pursue, answer the following questions:

   **a.** What kind of computer system would the company mostly likely provide to you—desktop, laptop, tablet PC, or something else? How does that compare with the type of system with which you prefer to work?

   **b.** If you were required to use a type of computer you'd never used before (such as a Mac instead of a PC), how would you go about learning to use the new computer?

   **c.** What other devices might your employer provide? Consider such items as smartphones or peripherals such as printers. How important is it for these devices to conform to the latest trends?

   **d.** Should you be able to use employer-provided equipment, such as a smartphone, for personal benefit? Does your answer differ if you have to pay for part or all of the device?

## team time//

# Which Mobile Device Is the Best?

## Problem

You've joined a small business that's beginning to evaluate its technology setup. Because of the addition of several new sales representatives and other administrative employees, the company needs to purchase many new computers. You're trying to decide which mobile devices would be better—laptop computers, tablet computers (iPads), smartphones with large screens (phablets), or a combination of these devices.

## Task

Split your class into teams of three and assign the following tasks:

- Member A explores the benefits and downfalls of laptop computers.
- Member B explores the benefits and downfalls of smartphones with large screens (phablets).
- Member C explores the benefits and downfalls of tablet computers.

## Process

1. Think about what the technology goals are for the company and what information and resources you will need to tackle this project.
2. Research and then discuss the components of each system you're recommending. Are any components better suited for the particular needs of certain types of employees (sales representatives versus administrative staff)? Consider all the input, output, processing, and storage devices. Are any special devices or peripherals required?
3. Consider the different types of employees in the company. Would a combination of devices be better than a single solution? If so, what kinds of employees would get which type of device?
4. As a team, write a summary position paper. Support your system recommendation for the company. Each team member should include why his or her type of computer will be part of the solution or not.

## Conclusion

Laptops, smartphones with large screens (phablets), and tablet computers have their own merits as computing systems. Being aware of the options in the marketplace, knowing how to analyze the trade-offs of different designs, and recognizing the different needs each type of computer fulfills allows you to become a better consumer as well as a better computer user.

## ethics project//

# Green Computing

Ethical conduct is a stream of decisions you make all day long. In this exercise, you'll research and then role-play a complicated ethical situation. The role you play may or may not match your own personal beliefs, but your research and use of logic will enable you to represent whichever view is assigned. An arbitrator will watch and comment on both sides of the arguments, and together, the team will agree on an ethical solution.

## Background

Green computing—conducting computing needs with the least possible amount of power and impact on the environment—is on everyone's minds. Although it's hard to argue with an environmentally conscious agenda, the pinch to our pocketbooks and the loss of some comforts sometimes make green computing difficult. Businesses, including colleges, need to consider a variety of issues and concerns before jumping into a complete green overhaul.

## Research Areas to Consider

- End-of-life management: e-waste and recycling
- Energy-efficient devices
- Renewable resources used in computer manufacturing
- Costs of green computing
- Government funding and incentives

## Process

1. Divide the class into teams.
2. Research the areas cited above and devise a scenario in which your college is considering modifying its current technology setup to a more green information technology (IT) strategy.
3. Team members should write a summary that provides background information for their character—for example, environmentalist, college IT administrator, or arbitrator—and that details their character's behaviors to set the stage for the role-playing event. Then, team members should create an outline to use during the role-playing event.
4. Team members should arrange a mutually convenient time to meet for the exchange, using a virtual meeting tool or by meeting in person.
5. Team members should present their case to the class or submit a PowerPoint presentation for review by the rest of the class, along with the summary and resolution they developed.

## Conclusion

As technology becomes ever more prevalent and integrated into our lives, more and more ethical dilemmas will present themselves. Being able to understand and evaluate both sides of the argument, while responding in a personally or socially ethical manner, will be an important skill.

# 3 Using the Internet: Making the Most of the Web's Resources

## Working and Playing on the Web

### The Internet and How It Works

**OBJECTIVES**

1. What is the origin of the Internet? **(pp. 76–77)**
2. How does data travel on the Internet? **(pp. 77–78)**

### Communicating and Collaborating on the Web

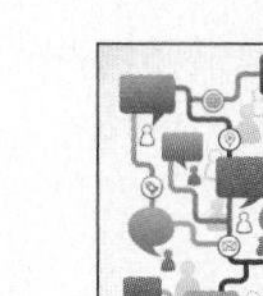

**OBJECTIVES**

3. How can I communicate and collaborate using Web 2.0 technologies? **(p. 79–84)**
4. How can I communicate using e-mail and instant messaging? **(pp. 79–81)**

**Sound Byte:** Blogging

### Web Entertainment

**OBJECTIVE**

5. What multimedia files are found on the web, and what software is needed to access those files? **(p. 85–86)**

### Conducting Business over the Internet: E-Commerce

**OBJECTIVE**

6. What is e-commerce, and what online safeguards are available? **(pp. 87–89)**

**Active Helpdesk:** Doing Business Online

## Using the Web Effectively

### Accessing and Moving Around the Web

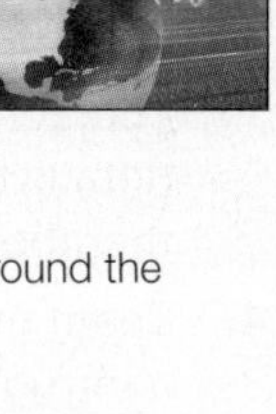

**OBJECTIVES**

7. What is a web browser, and what are a URL and its parts? **(pp. 93–96)**
8. How can I use hyperlinks and other tools to get around the web? **(pp. 96–97)**

**Sound Byte:** Welcome to the Web

### Searching the Web Effectively

**OBJECTIVE**

9. How do I search the Internet effectively, and how can I evaluate websites? **(pp. 100–103)**

**Active Helpdesk:** Using Subject Directories and Search Engines

**Active Helpdesk:** Getting Around the Web

**Sound Byte:** Finding Information on the Web

For all media in this chapter go to **pearsonhighered.com/techinaction** or **MyITLab**.

*(© dny3d/Fotolia; Marish/Shutterstock; Angela Waye/Shutterstock; Maxx-Studio/Shutterstock; © adimas/Fotolia; © HaywireMedia/Fotolia)*

# HOW COOL IS THIS?

Scan here for more info

Have you ever wanted to **share your computer screen** with someone but couldn't because you didn't know how or didn't have the right software? Now you can share your computer screen with anyone on **any device via the web** with one click, hassle-free, with **Screenleap (screenleap.com)**.

All you need to do is **click a link that generates a code**, then send the code to whomever you want to share your screen with; they will be able to view your screen immediately from their web browser on their smartphone, tablet, or PC. You can share your screen publicly, or privately to only a select few. There is also an extension to initiate sharing directly from your Gmail account. Using this technology may help you to **better communicate** with classmates or your professors when seeking or offering help. A **free account** will give you two hours of sharing time per day. So, share your screen with someone today with Screenleap! *(by-studio/fotolia; Courtesy of Google, Inc.)*

# Working and Playing on the Web

You most likely know at least a little bit about how to use the web's resources to communicate and collaborate with others, how to work with multimedia files, and how business is conducted over the web. In this section, we'll explore these and other topics. But first, let's start with a brief lesson on the history of the Internet.

## the internet and how IT WORKS

It's hard to imagine life without the **Internet**, the largest computer network in the world. The Internet is actually a network of networks that connects billions of computer users globally, but its beginnings were much more modest.

### The Origin of the Internet

**Why was the Internet created?** The concept of the Internet was developed in the late 1950s while the United States was in the midst of the Cold War with the Soviet Union (see Figure 3.1). At that time, the U.S. Department of Defense needed a computer network that wouldn't be disrupted easily in the event of an attack.

At the same time, researchers for the Department of Defense were trying to get different computers to work with each other using a common communications method that all computers could use. The Internet was created to respond to these two concerns: establishing a *secure* form of

**FIGURE 3.1** How the Internet Began.

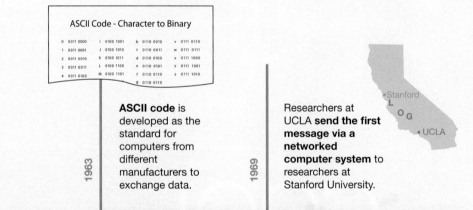

1958 The **Advanced Research Projects Agency (ARPA)** is established for the US Department of Defense. This agency creates the ARPANET—the beginnings of the Internet.

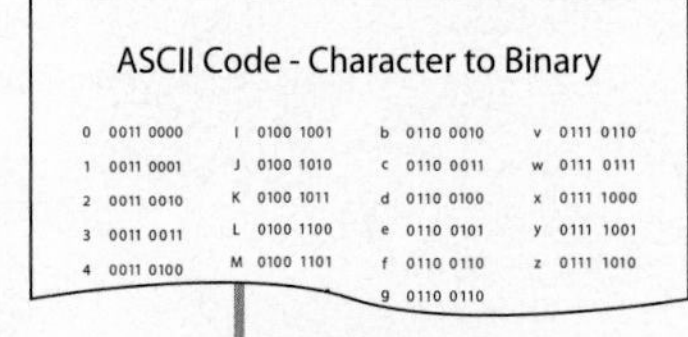

ASCII Code - Character to Binary

| 0 | 0011 0000 | I | 0100 1001 | b | 0110 0010 | v | 0111 0110 |
|---|---|---|---|---|---|---|---|
| 1 | 0011 0001 | J | 0100 1010 | c | 0110 0011 | w | 0111 0111 |
| 2 | 0011 0010 | K | 0100 1011 | d | 0110 0100 | x | 0111 1000 |
| 3 | 0011 0011 | L | 0100 1100 | e | 0110 0101 | y | 0111 1001 |
| 4 | 0011 0100 | M | 0100 1101 | f | 0110 0110 | z | 0111 1010 |
| | | | | g | 0110 0110 | | |

1963 **ASCII code** is developed as the standard for computers from different manufacturers to exchange data.

1964 A **new network scheme** is developed with multiple paths so if one communication path was destroyed (from a potential Soviet Union attack), the rest of the network would still be able to communicate.

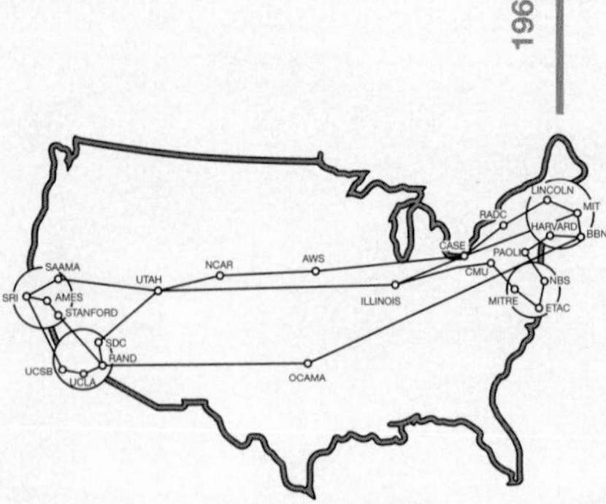


1969 Researchers at UCLA **send the first message via a networked computer system** to researchers at Stanford University.

Stanford
L
O G
UCLA

communications and creating a means by which *all* computers could communicate.

**Who invented the Internet?** The modern Internet evolved from an early U.S. government-funded "internetworking" project called the Advanced Research Projects Agency Network (ARPANET). ARPANET began as a four-node network involving UCLA, Stanford Research Institute, the University of California at Santa Barbara, and the University of Utah in Salt Lake City. The first real communication occurred in 1969 between the computer at Stanford and the computer at UCLA. Although the system crashed after the third letter of "Login" was transmitted, it was the beginning of a revolution. Many people participated in the creation of the ARPANET, but two men, Vinton Cerf and Robert Kahn, are generally acknowledged as the "fathers" of the Internet. These men earned this honor because in the 1970s they were primarily responsible for developing the communications protocols (standards) still in use on the Internet today.

**So are the web and the Internet the same thing?** Because the **World Wide Web** (**WWW** or the **web**) is what we use the most, we sometimes think of the Internet and the web as being interchangeable. However, the web is only a subset of the Internet, dedicated to broadcasting HTML pages; it is the means by which we access information over the Internet. The web is based on the Hypertext Transfer Protocol (HTTP), which is why you see an *http://* at the beginning of web addresses. What distinguishes the web from the rest of the Internet is its use of the following:

- Common communications protocols that enable computers to talk to each other and display information in compatible formats
- Special links that enable users to navigate from one place to another on the web

**Who created the web?** The web began in 1991. It was based on a protocol developed by Tim Berners-Lee, a physicist at the European Organization for Nuclear Research (CERN), who wanted a method for linking his research documents so that other researchers could access them. In conjunction with Robert Cailliau, Berners-Lee developed the basic architecture of the web and created the first **web browser**, software that lets you display and interact with text and other media on the web. The original browser could handle only text. Then, in 1993, the Mosaic browser, which could display graphics as well as text, was released. The once-popular Netscape Navigator browser evolved from Mosaic and heralded the beginning of the web's monumental growth.

## How the Internet Works

**How does the Internet work?** All computers and other devices such as tablets and smartphones that are connected to the Internet create a network of networks. These

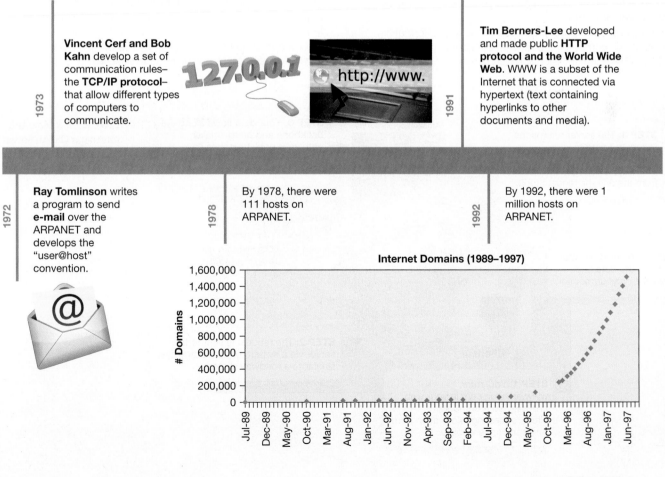

1973 **Vincent Cerf and Bob Kahn** develop a set of communication rules–the **TCP/IP protocol**–that allow different types of computers to communicate.

1991 **Tim Berners-Lee** developed and made public **HTTP protocol and the World Wide Web**. WWW is a subset of the Internet that is connected via hypertext (text containing hyperlinks to other documents and media).

1972 **Ray Tomlinson** writes a program to send **e-mail** over the ARPANET and develops the "user@host" convention.

1978 By 1978, there were 111 hosts on ARPANET.

1992 By 1992, there were 1 million hosts on ARPANET.

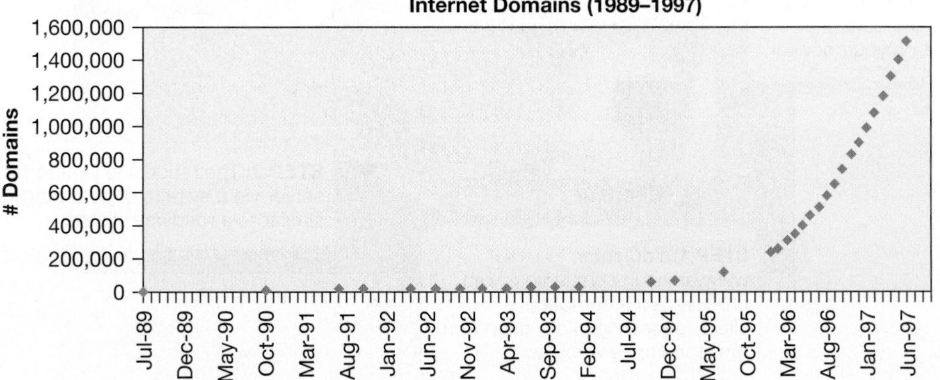


(Cristi180884/Shutterstock; Iznogood/Shutterstock; Matthias Pahl/Shutterstock; Alphaspirit/Shutterstock)

# BITS&BYTES

## Ever Heard of the Internet2?

Although the Internet2 may sound like a new and separate network meant to replace the Internet, this is not the case. The Internet2 is actually a consortium of U.S. leaders in education, research, industry, and government that seeks to expand the possibilities of the existing Internet by developing new technologies and applications and then deploying them to the public. These experimental technologies require a faster and more efficient Internet, so the researchers use separate data lines that support extremely high-speed communications—up to 8.8 terabits per second (Tbps). In fact, many of the Internet's current technologies are possible because of the research done by the Internet2 consortium.

Internet-connected devices communicate with each other in turns, just as we do when we ask a question or reply with an answer. Thus, a computer (or other device) connected to the Internet acts in one of two ways: Either it's a **client**, a computer that asks for data, or it's a **server**, a computer that receives the request and returns the data to the client. Because the Internet uses clients and servers, it's referred to as a **client/server network**.

When a client computer puts out a request for information from the server computer, the request travels along transmission lines. These transmission lines are similar to our highway system of roads, with some roads having different speed limits. The transmission lines with the fastest speeds are referred to as **Internet backbones**.

**How do computers talk to each other?** Suppose you want to order something from Amazon.com. Figure 3.2 illustrates what happens when you type **www.amazon.com** into your web browser and when Amazon's home page displays on your computer monitor. As you can see, the data request from your computer (the client computer) is sent via Internet communication pathways to a server computer. The server computer (in this case, Amazon's server) processes the request and returns the requested data to your client computer via Internet communication pathways. The data reply most likely takes a different route than did the data request. The web browser on your client computer interprets the data and displays it on its monitor.

**How does the data get sent to the correct computer?** Each time you connect to the Internet, your computer is assigned a unique identification number. This number, called an **Internet Protocol (IP) address**, is a set of four groups of numbers separated by periods, such as 123.45.245.91, and is commonly referred to as a *dotted quad* or *dotted decimal*. IP addresses are the means by which computers connected to the Internet identify each other. Similarly, each website is assigned a unique IP address. However, because the numbers that make up IP addresses are difficult for people to remember, websites are given text versions of their IP addresses. So, Amazon's website has an IP address of 72.21.211.176 and a name of **www.amazon.com**. When you type "www.amazon.com" into your browser, your computer (with its unique IP address) looks for Amazon's IP address (72.21.211.176). Data is exchanged between Amazon's server computer and your computer using these unique IP addresses. ■

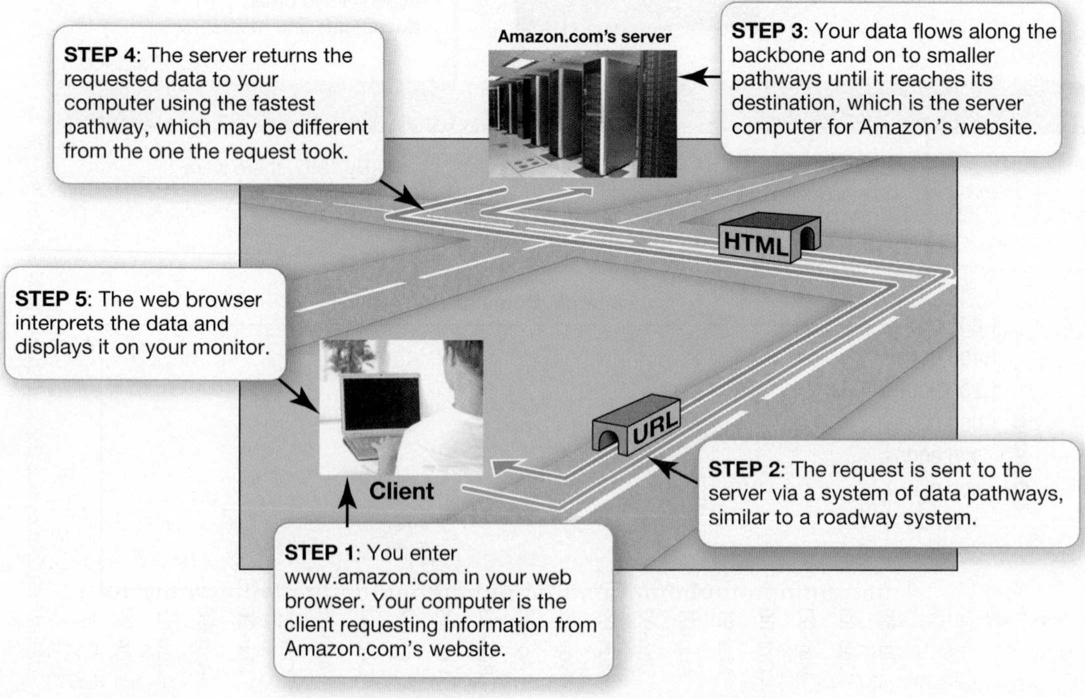

Amazon.com's server
STEP 3: Your data flows along the backbone and on to smaller pathways until it reaches its destination, which is the server computer for Amazon's website.
STEP 4: The server returns the requested data to your computer using the fastest pathway, which may be different from the one the request took.
HTML
STEP 5: The web browser interprets the data and displays it on your monitor.
URL
Client
STEP 2: The request is sent to the server via a system of data pathways, similar to a roadway system.
STEP 1: You enter www.amazon.com in your web browser. Your computer is the client requesting information from Amazon.com's website.


**FIGURE 3.2** How the Internet's Client/Server Model Works. *(Leo Lintang/Fotolia; Edhar/Shutterstock)*

# communicating and collaborating ON THE WEB

Over time, our use of the web has evolved from passively browsing web pages that were created for us to actively creating our own web content and sharing and collaborating on it with others. This new collaborative, user-created web content has been dubbed **Web 2.0**. Web 2.0 can be classified as the *social web,* in which the user is also a participant. Before Web 2.0 technologies were in place, we were unable to collaborate with others through web applications such as Google Docs, to rate and recommend products or services with Yelp, to tag a friend on social networks such as Facebook, or to share a video on YouTube or a favorite image on Pinterest. These new means of Web 2.0 communication are collectively called *social media* and include social networking, blogs, wikis, podcasts, and webcasts. Although **e-mail** (short for **electronic mail**) still remains the most widely used form of communication on the Internet, social media has truly changed how we communicate.

## Social Networking

**Who hasn't heard of Facebook or social networking?** As you probably know, **social networking** refers to using the web to communicate and share information among your friends and others. Social networking services such as Facebook and Twitter have become widely popular because they provide fun ways for users to communicate with their friends through wall posts, chats, tagged images, and tweets. Other social networking sites, such as YouTube, Flickr, and Pinterest, provide ways for users to show friends their favorite videos or images that they have taken themselves or have found on the web.

**How is social networking used in business?** In the business community, professionals often engage in in-person networking to locate and fill open job positions as well as to find clients. Today, networking also happens online. Professional, business-oriented online networks such as LinkedIn are helpful for members seeking potential clients, business opportunities, jobs, or job candidates. Like a true business network, these sites can help you meet other professionals through the people you already know. In addition, businesses use social networking for marketing and communicating directly with their customers. For example, companies may post special deals and offers on their Facebook page or solicit responses from followers that may help with product development or future marketing campaigns.

Figure 3.3 shows the various sites that are considered Web 2.0 social networking sites. As you can see, there is more to social networking than just Facebook and Twitter.

**What are some dos and don'ts of social networking?** When social networking sites first became popular, there was concern over privacy issues, especially for school-aged children who put personal information on their pages without considering the possibility of that information being misused by a stalker or identity thief. Although those concerns still exist, many of the most popular social networking sites have improved their privacy policies, thereby reducing, but not eliminating, such concerns. Still, users must be cautious about the type of content they post on these sites. Consider these precautions as you use social networking sites:

- Keep your personal information personal. The year you were born, your physical address, and the routines of your life (sports games, practices, work schedules) should not be broadcast to the general public.
- Know who your friends are, and know who can see the information you post. Review your privacy settings periodically, as sites change and update their privacy practices frequently.
- Do not post information such as your favorite teacher or your first pet's name because these are often used as security questions to verify your identity.
- Use caution when posting images, and know what images others are posting of you. Although privacy settings may offer some comfort, some images may be available for view through search engines and may not require site registration to be seen. Online images may become public property and subject to reproduction, and you might not want some—or any—of those images to be distributed.

Many employers and colleges use social networks as a means of gaining information about potential applicants before granting an interview or extending admission or a job offer. In fact, there have been instances of people being fired from their jobs and being expelled from school for using social media, such as Facebook, Twitter, and blogs, in a questionable way. Generally, questionable content on social media includes negative discussion about the poster's job, employer, or colleagues or inappropriate content about the poster. The responsibility for your content rests with you. Even though you may have strong privacy settings, you can't control what those who you allow to see your content do with it. Therefore, treat all information posted on the web as public, and avoid posting damaging words and pictures. Bottom line: Make sure your profile, images, and site content project an image that accurately represents you.

## E-Mail

**Why do I need e-mail?** Despite the increasing popularity of social networking, e-mail is still the primary means of communication over the Internet. E-mail is a written message sent or received over the Internet. E-mail is the primary method of electronic communication worldwide because it's fast and convenient. And because it's *asynchronous*, users do not need to be communicating at the same time. They can send and

FIGURE 3.3

## Types of Social Networking Sites

| | DESCRIPTION | SUGGESTED URLS |
|---|---|---|
| **Social Exchange Networks** | Allow users to connect with others, provide status updates | facebook.com<br>twitter.com |
| **Create Your Own Social Networks** | Allow users to create their own social network around a common topic; groups can be public or private | ning.com<br>mixxt.net |
| **Business-Related Social Networks** | Allow users to seek potential clients, business opportunities, jobs, or job candidates | linkedin.com |
| **Media Sharing Networks** | Allow users to share pictures and videos | youtube.com<br>flickr.com<br>picassa.google.com |
| **Information Sharing Networks** | Allow users to share information | delicious.com<br>wikipedia.org<br>slideshare.net |
| **Information Recommendations and Filtering (Bookmarking) Networks** | Allow users to post their opinion of a product, service, news, or web item for others to see and use | reddit.com<br>digg.com |

(Kevin Britland/Alamy; M4OS Photos/Alamy; © Anil Kumar / Alamy; Mixxt; Kristoffer Tripplaar/Alamy; PhotoEdit/Alamy; © PSL Images / Alamy M4OS Photos/Alamy; Web Pix/Alamy; PhotoEdit/Alamy;SlideShare, Inc.; M4OS Photos/Alamy; NetPics/Alamy)

respond to messages at their own convenience. E-mail is also convenient for exchanging and collaborating on documents via attachments.

**How private is e-mail?** Although e-mail is a more private exchange of information than public social networking sites, e-mails really are not private. Consider the following:

- Because e-mails can be printed or forwarded to others, you never know who may read your e-mail.
- Most e-mail content is not protected, so you should never use e-mail to send personal or sensitive information such as bank account or Social Security numbers. Doing so could lead to identity theft.
- Employers have access to e-mail sent from the workplace, so use caution when putting negative or controversial content in e-mail.
- Even after you've deleted a message, it doesn't really vanish. Many Internet service providers and companies archive e-mail, which can be accessed or subpoenaed in the event of a lawsuit or investigation.

**What are some tips on e-mail etiquette?** When you write a casual e-mail to friends, you obviously don't need to follow any specific e-mail guidelines (except to remember that your e-mail may be forwarded). But when you send e-mail for professional reasons, you should use proper e-mail etiquette. The following are a few guidelines (also see Figure 3.4):

- Be concise and to the point.
- Use the spell-checker and proofread your e-mail before sending it.
- Avoid using abbreviations such as *u*, *r*, *LOL*, and *BTW*.
- Include a meaningful subject line to help recipients prioritize and organize e-mails.
- Add a signature line that includes your contact information.
- Include only those people on the e-mail who truly need to receive it.

Following such guidelines maintains professionalism, increases efficiency, and might even help protect a company from lawsuits.

**Are there different types of e-mail systems?** There are two different types of e-mail systems:

1. **Web-based e-mail**, such as Yahoo! mail or Gmail, is managed with your web browser and allows you to access your e-mail from the web.
2. An **e-mail client** requires a program, such as Microsoft Outlook, to be installed on your computer. When you open the program, your e-mail is downloaded to your computer.

The primary difference between the two is access. Web-based e-mail allows you to access e-mail from any Internet-connected device, but you can't see your e-mail when you're offline. With an e-mail client, you view your e-mail on the computer on which the e-mail client software has been installed, but you can then view and manage your e-mail while you're offline. Both systems can be used together for the "best of both worlds." You can have a Gmail account, for example, so that you can read your e-mail from any computer connected to the

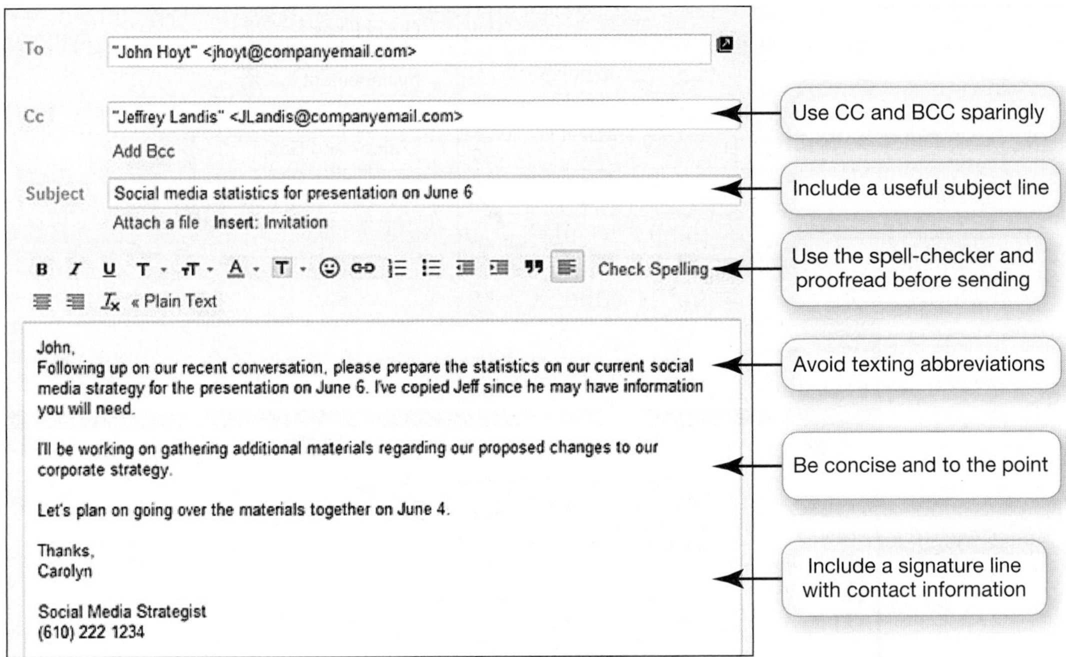

To
"John Hoyt" <jhoyt@companyemail.com>
Cc
"Jeffrey Landis" <JLandis@companyemail.com>
Add Bcc
Subject
Social media statistics for presentation on June 6
Attach a file Insert: Invitation
Check Spelling
« Plain Text
John,
Following up on our recent conversation, please prepare the statistics on our current social media strategy for the presentation on June 6. I've copied Jeff since he may have information you will need.
I'll be working on gathering additional materials regarding our proposed changes to our corporate strategy.
Let's plan on going over the materials together on June 4.
Thanks,
Carolyn
Social Media Strategist
(610) 222 1234
Use CC and BCC sparingly
Include a useful subject line
Use the spell-checker and proofread before sending
Avoid texting abbreviations
Be concise and to the point
Include a signature line with contact information


**FIGURE 3.4** Using simple guidelines of e-mail etiquette can promote a professional image and make your message more effective.

Internet, and you can also have Outlook installed on your primary computer and set up the program to display your Gmail account (see Figure 3.5).

## Instant Messaging

**Is instant messaging just for friends?** You've most likely used **instant messaging (IM)** services—programs that let you communicate in real time over the Internet. Although IM is most often used for conversations between friends, many businesses use IM as a means of instant communication between co-workers. Some IM systems provide mechanisms to hold conversations with more than one person, either through simultaneous individual conversations or with group chats. And some programs even let you conduct video chats using a webcam.

AIM, Google Chat, Windows Messenger, and Yahoo! Messenger are proprietary IM services, meaning you can IM or chat only with those who share the same IM service and are on your contact or buddy list. Another option is to chat with those you've "friended" on Facebook through Facebook's chat option. There are also universal chat services such as Trillian and Digsby that you install on your computer and that allow you to chat with users of all popular IMs, regardless of the service they use.

## Wikis

**What are wikis?** You've no doubt heard of Wikipedia (**wikipedia.org**), the popular collaborative online encyclopedia. Wikipedia is one example of a **wiki**, a web application that allows users to add, remove, or edit its content. Wiki content such as that found on Wikipedia is created collaboratively by multiple users, resulting in an emergent "common" opinion rather than the opinion of an individual writer. Because of wiki technology, Wikipedia's content can be updated continually.

## BITS&BYTES

### Outlook.com

With the release of Office 2013, Microsoft introduced Outlook.com, a free web-based e-mail service that is linked to your desktop Outlook data and can pull additional contact information from Facebook, Twitter, and LinkedIn as well as your calendar. Outlook.com is a combination of Hotmail and Windows Live (which no longer exist). All you need in order to access the web-based e-mail is a Windows account—which you already may have if you have access to OneDrive, Xbox Live, or have a current Hotmail or Windows Live account. Outlook.com offers a clean, ad-free inbox, with additional features borrowed from the installed version of Outlook that can simplify using e-mail. If you already have another web-based e-mail account (such as Gmail) and you don't want to switch your e-mail address, you can still enjoy the features of Outlook.com; just plug in your Gmail e-mail address, and it syncs automatically.

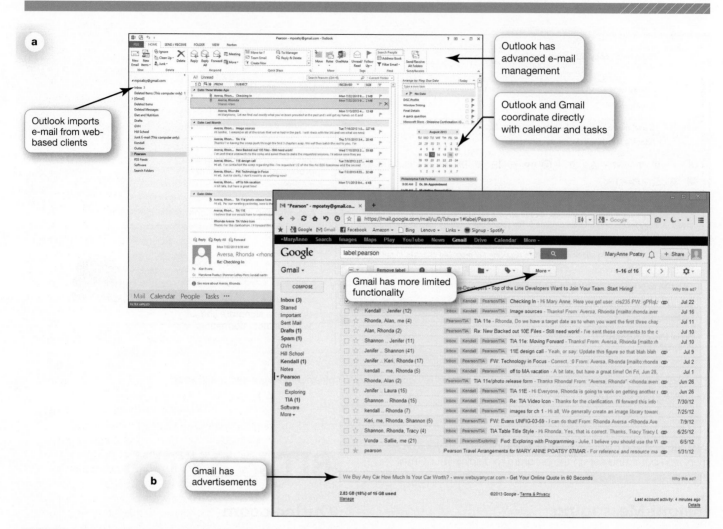

**FIGURE 3.5** (a) Client-Based and (b) Web-Based E-mail Systems *((b)Courtesy of Google, Inc.)*

**What else are wikis used for?** Wikis are not just used to create Wikipedia; they're also useful tools for business collaboration. Rather than needing to pass documents back and forth via e-mail and possibly losing track of which version is the most recent, wikis allow all who have access to the wiki page to post their ideas and modify the content of the current version of a single document (see Figure 3.6). Wikis provide the extra benefit of users being able to access, review, and even revert back to past versions at any time.

Some web-based document products, such as Google Docs (**docs.google.com**), have wiki-like features to promote similar online collaboration, and specific wiki software, such as Wikispaces (**wikispaces.com**) and MediaWiki (**mediawiki.org**), is available that you can download for free. The Wikimedia Foundation, which hosts Wikipedia, also hosts other collaborative projects, such as Wikibooks (textbooks), Wikiversity (learning tools),

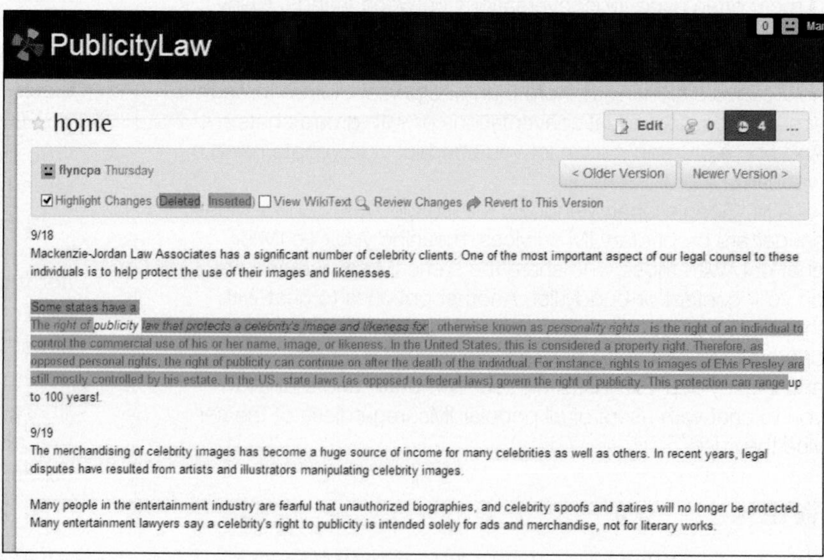


**FIGURE 3.6** Different users can collaborate on a wiki page. A member of this wiki's group has modified the original text. Text that the person deleted appears in red, while inserted text appears in green. *(Courtesy of Wikipedia)*

and Wikisource (a document library). These wiki-type collaborative efforts apply to a variety of other useful applications. For example, wikiHow (**wikihow.org**) is an online project that uses both wikis and the collaborative process to build a large, online how-to manual.

**Why isn't Wikipedia good to use as a source for a research paper?** The idea behind content that is managed and edited by many users, such as that found in Wikipedia and other large public wikis, is that the group will keep the content current and valid. However, because wikis are publicly editable, they can't be trusted completely. If a user adds erroneous content, the community of users can quickly catch and correct it, but if you used Wikipedia as a source, you may have referenced erroneous content before it was corrected. To help address these concerns, Wikipedia has implemented tighter access controls, requiring users who want editing privileges to register with the site, but the risks still remain. Citizendium (**citizendium.org**), another open wiki encyclopedia, requires contributors to provide real names and sign an ethics pledge, and all postings are monitored.

## Blogs

**Why do people write blogs?** A **blog** (short for **weblog**) is a personal log or journal posted on the web. Anyone can create a blog, and there are millions of blogs available to read, follow, and comment on. Blogs are generally written by a single author and are arranged as a listing of entries on a single page, with the most recent blog entry appearing at the top of the list. In addition, blogs are public. Blogs have searchable and organized content, making them user friendly. They're accessible from anywhere using a web browser.

Many people use blogs as a sort of personal scrapbook. Whenever the urge strikes, they report on their daily activities. Many other blogs focus on a particular topic. For example, the Movie Blog (**themovieblog.com**) contains reviews and opinions about movies, and engadget (**engadget.com**) is a blog devoted to discussing technogadgets. Many corporations, such as Walmart and Best Buy, have blogs written by employees. Technorati (**technorati.com**) and Blogcatalog (**blogcatalog.com**) are two of many blog directories that can help you find blogs that fit your interests.

**Are all blogs text-based?** The traditional form of a blog is primarily text-based but may also include images and audio. A **video log** (**vlog** or **video blog**) is a blog that uses video as the primary content (although it can also contain text, images, and audio). Vlogs are quickly becoming a popular means of personal expression, and many can be found by searching YouTube (**youtube.com**) and Tout (**tout.com**).

**How do I create a blog?** Many websites provide the tools you need to create your own blog. Two sites that offer free blog hosting are Blogger (**blogger.com**) and WordPress (**wordpress.com**). Such tools also let you add features like pictures or subpages to your blog. You can also choose to host your blog yourself so that the URL reflects your name or the name of your business. If you choose this option, you'll need your own website and a URL so people can access it.

SOUND BYTE
**Blogging**

In this Sound Byte, you'll see why blogs are one of today's most popular publishing mediums. You'll also learn how to create and publish your own blog.

**Are there any problems with blogs?** The popularity of blogs has brought about a new problem: *spam blogs* (*splogs*), which are artificially created blog sites filled with fake articles or stolen text (a tactic known as *blog scraping*). Splogs, which contain links to other sites associated with the splog's creator, have the intention of either increasing traffic to, or increasing search engine rankings for, these usually disreputable or useless websites. Although not really harmful, splogs are another unwanted form of content that continues to grow like weeds on the web.

## Podcasts and Webcasts

**What is a podcast?** A **podcast** is a form of digital media comprised of a series of audio or video files that are distributed over the Internet. There are podcasts for radio shows, audiobooks, magazines, and even educational programs, which you can download to any device that can play audio files. What makes podcasts different from other audio files found on the web is that podcasts deliver their content using **Really Simple Syndication (RSS)**. RSS is a format that sends the latest content of the podcast series automatically to an **aggregator** such as iTunes or Feedspot. An aggregator locates all the RSS series to which you've subscribed and automatically downloads only the new content to your computer or media player. If you have several favorite websites or podcasts, rather than needing to check each site for updated content, aggregators collect all the site updates in one place. These updates or changes to the content are then delivered automatically if you subscribe to the podcast, instead of you having to search for the latest content and download it yourself.

**Where can I find podcasts?** Most online news and radio sites offer podcasts of their programs. Although many podcasts are news related, others offer entertaining and educational content. For example, you can access lessons on yoga, foreign language classes, or DIY tips. Many schools supply students with course content updates through podcasts, and instructors sometimes create podcasts of their lectures. Figure 3.7 lists some websites where you can find podcasts.

**Can I create my own podcast?** It's simple to create a podcast. To record the audio content all you need is a computer with a microphone, and if you want to make a video podcast, you also need a webcam or video camera. Although high-end equipment will produce more sophisticated output, you certainly can use whatever equipment you might own. You may also need additional software to edit the audio and video

FIGURE 3.7

## Podcast Directories and Aggregators

**iTunes (itunes.com)**
- Software makes it easy to play, manage, and share your favorite podcasts

**Podfeed (podfeed.net)**
- Broad collection of podcasts

**Stitcher (stitcher.com)**
- Customize podcast playlists

**YouTube (youtube.com)**
- Good source for video blogs (vlogs)

content, depending on how professional you wish the podcast to be. After you've recorded and edited the podcast content, you need to export it to MP3 format. The free program Audacity (**audacity.sourceforge.net**) lets you both edit audio files and export them to MP3 format. All that's left is for you to create an RSS feed (tricky, but doable) and then upload the content to a site that hosts podcasts, such as iTunes, Podfeed, or Stitcher.

**What's a webcast?** A **webcast** is the (usually live) broadcast of audio or video content over the Internet. Unlike podcasts, which are prerecorded and made available for download, most webcasts are distributed in "real time," meaning that they're live or one-time events. Some webcasts are archived so they can be viewed at a later date. Webcasts are not updated automatically like podcasts, but some, such as Microsoft's On-Demand Webcasts, are RSS feeds.

Webcasts use continuous audio and video feeds, which let you view and download large audio and video files. Webcasts can include noninteractive content such as a simultaneous broadcast of a radio or television program, but more recent webcasts invite interactive responses from the viewing or listening audience. For example, ORLive (**orlive.com**) provides surgical webcasts that demonstrate the latest surgical innovations and techniques. Webcasts also are used in the corporate world to broadcast annual meetings and in the educational arena to transmit seminars.

Figure 3.8 lists the popular methods of online communication that we've discussed. ■

FIGURE 3.8

## Methods of Online Communication

**SOCIAL NETWORKING**
- Web 2.0 technology
- Lets you build an online network of friends
- Lets you share media content

**E-MAIL**

- Most common form of online communication
- Asynchronous (not having to be done at the same time)

**INSTANT MESSAGING**

- Real-time exchange
- Can be used with multiple persons simultaneously
- Video/audio chats available

**WIKIS**
- Great collaborative tool
- Content updated by many users
- Historical content kept, so you can revert to past versions

**BLOGS**

- Written by a single author
- Chronologic entries
- Searchable content
- May include images, audio, and video

**PODCASTS**

- Audio/video files delivered via RSS
- New RSS content collected with aggregator
- Can download and view content on portable media player

**WEBCASTS**

- Most often live, streamed broadcasts

(Ben Legend/Fotolia; Beboy/Fotolia; LiveStock/Shutterstock; Kheng Guan Toh/Shutterstock; ayzek/Shutterstock; 3drenderedlogos com/Shutterstock; Brisbane/Shutterstock)

# web ENTERTAINMENT

When you think of how you use the Internet for entertainment purposes, what comes to mind? Streaming audio and video, Internet radio, MP3s, interactive gaming, and smart TV are all favorite responses. What makes all these forms of web entertainment so popular is their multimedia content. **Multimedia** is anything that involves one or more forms of media in addition to text. It includes the following:

- *Graphics* such as drawings, charts, and photos (the most basic form of multimedia)
- *Audio files* such as the clips you hear when you visit websites, MP3 files you download, podcasts and webcasts, and live broadcasts you can listen to through Internet radio
- *Video files* ranging from simple, short video clips on sites such as YouTube (**youtube.com**) to movies and television shows on sites such as Hulu (**hulu.com**)

**What is streaming media?**
**Streaming media** is multimedia (audio and video) that is continuously fed to your browser so you avoid having to wait for the entire file to download completely before listening to or watching it. Without streaming media, you wouldn't be able to watch movies on Netflix or on demand from your cable provider, listen to live audio broadcasting, or even play some online games. Internet radio also uses streaming media to present a continuous stream of audio to its listeners. Pandora (**pandora.com**) enables you to personalize your audio stream by specifying a favorite artist, song, or composer that you want to hear. Then the service picks music with the same characteristics. In addition to Internet radio service, Spotify (**spotify.com**) lets you pick your own songs, build playlists, and share your playlists with others.

**Do I need anything besides a browser to view or hear multimedia on the web?** Most graphics on the web will appear in your browser without any additional software. However, to view and hear some multimedia files—for example, podcasts, YouTube videos, and audio files—you might need a **plug-in** (or **player**)—a special software component that adds a specific feature to an existing software program. Figure 3.9 lists the most popular plug-ins.

FIGURE 3.9

**Popular Plug-Ins and Players and Their Uses**

| PLUG-IN NAME | WHERE YOU GET IT | WHAT IT DOES |
|---|---|---|
| Adobe Reader | adobe.com | Views and prints portable document format (PDF) files |
| Flash Player | adobe.com | Plays animation and movies through web browsers |
| QuickTime Player | apple.com | Plays MP3, animation, music, musical instrument digital interface (MIDI), audio, and video files |
| Shockwave Player<br>ADOBE SHOCKWAVE PLAYER | adobe.com | Plays interactive games, multimedia, graphics, and streaming audio and video on the web |
| Silverlight | microsoft.com | Similar to Flash; plays web-based animations and videos |
| Windows Media Player | microsoft.com | Plays MP3 and WAV music files, movies, and live audio and video on broadcasts on the web |

(NetPhotos3/Alamy; NetPhotos3/Alamy; NetPhotos3/Alamy; N/A, Alamy; franck reporter/Shutterstock; Nicemonkey/Shutterstock)

# BITS&BYTES

## HTML5 Versus Flash

Adobe's Flash is a plug-in you're no doubt familiar with that is designed to run multimedia through web browsers. Flash has been the multimedia standard for decades and was at one time used with all browsers. However, in 2007, a controversy between Flash and HTML5 began when the Apple iPhone was introduced—and this controversy continued with the later introduction of the iPad. What was the problem? Both the iPhone and the iPad ran with an operating system that supported HTML5 rather than Flash. Flash-based YouTube videos, for example, would not play on an iPhone or an iPad.

Why would Apple choose HTML5 over Flash? HTML5—the fifth revision of the HTML standard—is open-source code, meaning the program code is available to the general public to use or modify, unlike Flash, which is owned by one company. The goal of HTML5 is to ease the handling of multimedia and graphical content on the web, to reduce or eliminate the need for plug-ins, and to become device independent. Although the major browsers support many of the new HTML5 elements, the standard itself is still a work in progress.

Because Flash had been so dominant for so long, it's taken a while for the HTML5 standard to catch on. But even Flash stalwarts such as YouTube, which was solely Flash dependent, added capability to run HTML5 video in 2011. Similarly, most Flash-dependent websites have incorporated HTML5 players or extensions. It's becoming clear that HTML5 is not going away soon. What do you think is the future for Flash?

**How do I get players and plug-ins?** If you purchased your computer within the past several years, most popular plug-ins probably came preinstalled on your computer. If a website requires a plug-in not installed on your computer, you are usually automatically directed to a site where you can download the plug-in free of charge. For example, to use streaming video, your browser might send you to the Adobe website, where you can download Flash Player.

**Is there any way to get multimedia web content to load faster?** When you're on the Internet, your browser keeps track of the sites you've visited so that it can load them faster the next time you visit them. This *cache* (temporary storage place) of the text pages, images, and video files from recently visited websites can make your web surfing more efficient, but it can also slow down your hard drive. Additionally, if you don't have your cache settings configured to check for updates to the web page, your browser may not load the most recent content. To keep your system running efficiently, consider doing the following:

- Delete your temporary Internet cache every month or so, depending on your usage.
- To ensure the most recent website content is displayed, click Refresh or press the F5 key if you revisit a site in the same browsing session.
- Clear your Internet cache manually or adjust the setting in your web browser so that it clears the cache automatically every time you exit the browser. ■

# conducting business over the internet: E-COMMERCE

It's hard to believe that only a few years ago, many people were scared to buy things online. Today, there is little hesitation, and you can buy nearly anything on the web, including big-ticket items such as homes and cars. **E-commerce**—short for **electronic commerce**—is the process of conducting business online. Figure 3.10 shows the most common items purchased through e-commerce transactions.

**Are there different types of e-commerce?** There are three types of e-commerce business models:

1. **Business-to-consumer (B2C)** transactions take place between businesses and consumers. Such transactions include those between customers and completely online businesses (such as **Amazon.com**) and those between customers and stores that have both an online and a physical presence, such as Target (**target.com**). Such businesses are referred to as *click-and-brick* businesses. Some click-and-bricks allow online purchases and in-store pickups and returns.
2. **Business-to-business (B2B)** transactions occur when businesses buy and sell goods and services to other businesses. An example is Omaha Paper Company (**omahapaper.com**), which distributes paper products to other companies.
3. **Consumer-to-consumer (C2C)** transactions occur when consumers sell to each other through sites such as eBay (**ebay.com**), Craigslist (**craigslist.org**), and Etsy (**etsy.com**).

**FIGURE 3.10** Top Five Online Consumer Purchases. *(© allegro/ Fotolia)*

**Social commerce** is a subset of e-commerce that uses social networks to assist in marketing and purchasing products. If you're on Facebook, you've no doubt noticed the many businesses that have Facebook pages asking you to "Like" them. Consumers are voicing their opinions on Facebook and other sites about products and services by providing ratings and reviews, and studies show that such peer recommendations have a major influence on buying behavior. When you see your friend on Facebook recommend a product or service, you're more likely to click through to that retailer and check out the product.

For example, after implementing the Facebook "Like" button, American Eagle noticed that Facebook-referred visitors spent 57 percent more than other online shoppers. Other peer-influenced e-commerce trends include group buying and individual customization. Groupon and LivingSocial are two popular deal-of-the-day group purchase websites that require a certain number of people to buy the discounted deal before the deal can go through. CafePress and Zazzle sell T-shirts and other items that are customized with your own graphic designs.

But e-commerce encompasses more than just shopping opportunities. Today, anything you can do inside your bank you can do online, and approximately 80 percent of U.S. households do some form of online banking. Many people use online services to check their account balances, pay bills online, and check stock and mutual fund performance. Credit card companies allow you to view, schedule, and pay your credit card bill; brokerage houses allow you to conduct investment activities online.

## E-Commerce Safeguards

**Just how safe are online transactions?** When you buy something online, you most likely use a credit or debit card; therefore, money is exchanged directly between your credit card company and the online merchant's bank. Because online shopping eliminates a salesclerk or other human intermediary from the transaction, it can actually be safer than traditional retail shopping.

**What precautions should I take when shopping online?** In addition to using some basic common computing sense such as having a firewall and up-to-date antivirus

ACTIVE HELPDESK

**Doing Business Online**

In this Active Helpdesk call, you'll learn about e-commerce and what e-commerce safeguards protect you when you're doing business online.

software on your computer and using strong passwords for all your online accounts, there are several important guidelines to follow to ensure your online shopping experience is a safe one (see Figure 3.11):

- **Look for visual indicators that the website is secure.** Check that the beginning of the URL changes from "http://" to "https://"—with the *s* standing for secure, indicating that the **secure sockets layer** protocol has been applied to manage the security of the website. Also, look for a small icon of a closed padlock in the toolbar (in both Internet Explorer and Firefox) and a green-colored address bar, indications that the site may be secure. (However, note that even if a site has these indicators, it still might not be safe. Consider the validity of the site before making a purchase.)
- **Shop at well-known, reputable sites.** If you aren't familiar with a site, investigate it with the Better Business Bureau (**bbb.org**) or at bizrate (**bizrate.com**). Make sure the company has a phone number and street address in addition to a website. You can also look for third-party verification such as that from TRUSTe or the Better Business Bureau. But let common sense prevail. Online deals that seem too good to be true are generally just that—and may be pirated software or illegal distributions.
- **Pay by credit card, not debit card.** Federal laws protect credit card users, but debit card users don't have the same level of protection. If possible, reserve one credit card for Internet purchases only; even better, use a prepaid credit card that has a small credit limit. For an extra layer of security, find out if your credit card company has a service that confirms your identity with an extra password or code that only you know to use when making an online transaction or that offers a one-time-use credit card number. Also, consider using a third-party payment processor such as PayPal or Google Wallet. PayPal also offers a security key that provides additional security to your PayPal account.
- **When you place an order, check the return policy, save a copy of the order, and make sure you receive a confirmation number.** Make sure you read and understand the fine print on warranties, return policies, and the retailer's privacy statements. If the site disappears overnight, this information may help you in filing a dispute or reporting a problem to a site such as the Better Business Bureau.
- **Avoid making online transactions when using public computers.** Public computers may have *spyware*

**FIGURE 3.11**

## Online Shopping Precautions

When shopping at home, use a firewall and antivirus software for general computer protection.

Don't shop on public WiFi networks, as they may contain spyware.

Check for visual indicators such as https:// in the URL, a closed padlock icon, and a green address bar.

Look for third-party verification from TRUSTe or the Better Business Bureau symbol.

Use a credit card, not a debit card, to protect transactions, or use a third-party payer such as PayPal or Google Wallet.

Create a strong password for all online accounts (one that includes numbers and other symbols such as @).

Deals that are too good to be true are usually just that.

Read and understand the fine print on warranties, return policies, and the retailer's privacy statements.

(beboy/Shutterstock; © Roy Wylam / Alamy; photoinnovation/Shutterstock; HANDOUT/KRT/Newscom; Maxx-Studio/Shutterstock; isak55/Shutterstock; Alhovik/Shutterstock; iQoncept/Shutterstock)

installed, programs that track and log your keystrokes and can retrieve your private information. Similarly, unless you have specific protection on your own notebook computer, avoid making wireless transactions on public hotspots.

Whether you're doing business, playing games, or communicating with friends or colleagues, the Internet makes these activities more accessible. The Internet can potentially make these experiences and activities more enriched as well, although you must take precautions for the safest of experiences. ■

**Before moving on to Part 2:**
- **Watch Replay Video 3.1** .
- Then check your understanding of what you've learned so far.

# BITS&BYTES

## Making Safe Online Payments Using PayPal and Google Wallet

When people first began making online purchases, many were not comfortable buying from sites like eBay because the sites required them to give personal financial information such as credit card numbers to strangers. PayPal (**paypal.com**) resolved that issue by serving as a payment intermediary that allows anyone to pay with credit cards and bank accounts without sharing their financial information. PayPal is now a standard means of payment for many online merchants and offers buyer protection and dispute resolution services. Figure 3.12 shows how PayPal works.

Google Wallet (**google.com/wallet**) offers similar services to PayPal. For example, you can pay directly from your bank account with Google Wallet. However, and you can only make purchases within the United States, and Google Wallet only provides customer support through forums and e-mail. PayPal has increased its customer service considerably, so that you can chat live with PayPal representatives when additional assistance is needed.

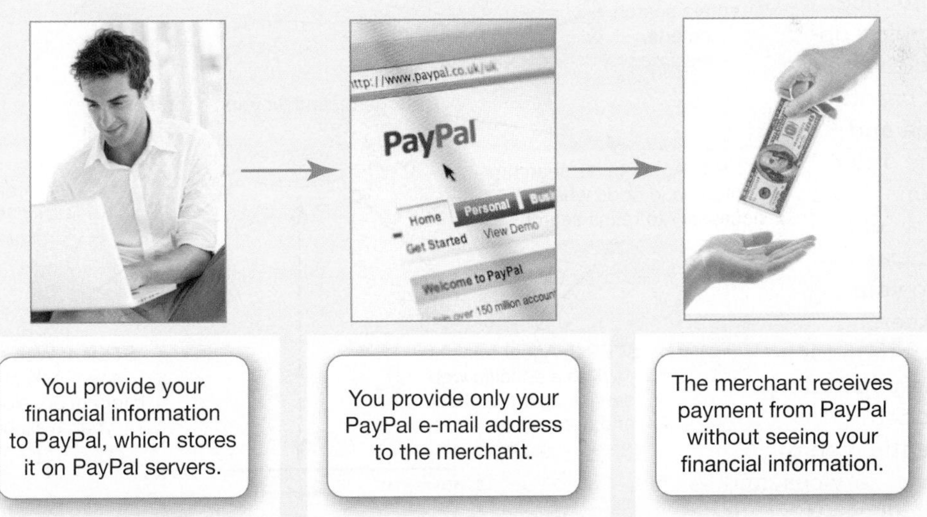

PayPal
Home
Personal
Get Started
View Demo
Welcome to PayPal
You provide your financial information to PayPal, which stores it on PayPal servers.
You provide only your PayPal e-mail address to the merchant.
The merchant receives payment from PayPal without seeing your financial information.


**FIGURE 3.12** How PayPal Works. *(Yuri Arcurs/Shutterstock; AKP Photos/Alamy; happydancing/Shutterstock)*

# DIG DEEPER Discovering the Semantic Web

Think about all the types of data on the web that you access manually, such as appointment times, transportation and entertainment schedules, and store locations and hours. It would seem that computers would be helpful in plugging through all this web data, but oddly, that is not the case. Web pages are designed for people to read, not for computers to manipulate. As yet, no reliable way exists for computers to process the meaning of data on a web page so that it can be used to see relationships or make decisions.

The **semantic web** (or **Web 3.0**) is an evolving extension of the web in which data is defined in such a way to make it more easily processed by computers. Right now, search engines function by recognizing keywords such as *office hours* and *dentist*, but they can't determine, for example, in which office and on what days Dr. Smith works and what his available appointment times are. By using a so-called "agent," the semantic web would enable computers to find that type of information, coordinate it with your other schedules and preferences, and then make the appointment for you.

The semantic web would also assist you in comparing products, prices, and shipping options by finding the best product option based on specified criteria and then placing the order for you. Additionally, the agent would record the financial transaction into your personal bookkeeping software and arrange for a technician to help install the software, if needed.

For the semantic web to work, businesses, services, and software would all use the same categorization structures so that similar information would share the same attributes, ensuring consistency of metadata throughout the web. The semantic web would build on this type of capability so that each website would have text and pictures (for people to read) and metadata (for computers to read) describing the information on the web (see Figure 3.13).

Although some of the semantic web's functionalities are beginning to emerge in technologies such as Siri in the current iPhone operating system, the majority of its functionality and implementation are still in development. The greatest challenge is recoding all the information currently available on the web into the type of metadata that computers can recognize. The very grandeur of that task means that we will not see a fully functional semantic web until sometime in the distant future. In the meantime, we can continue to benefit from each small step toward that goal.

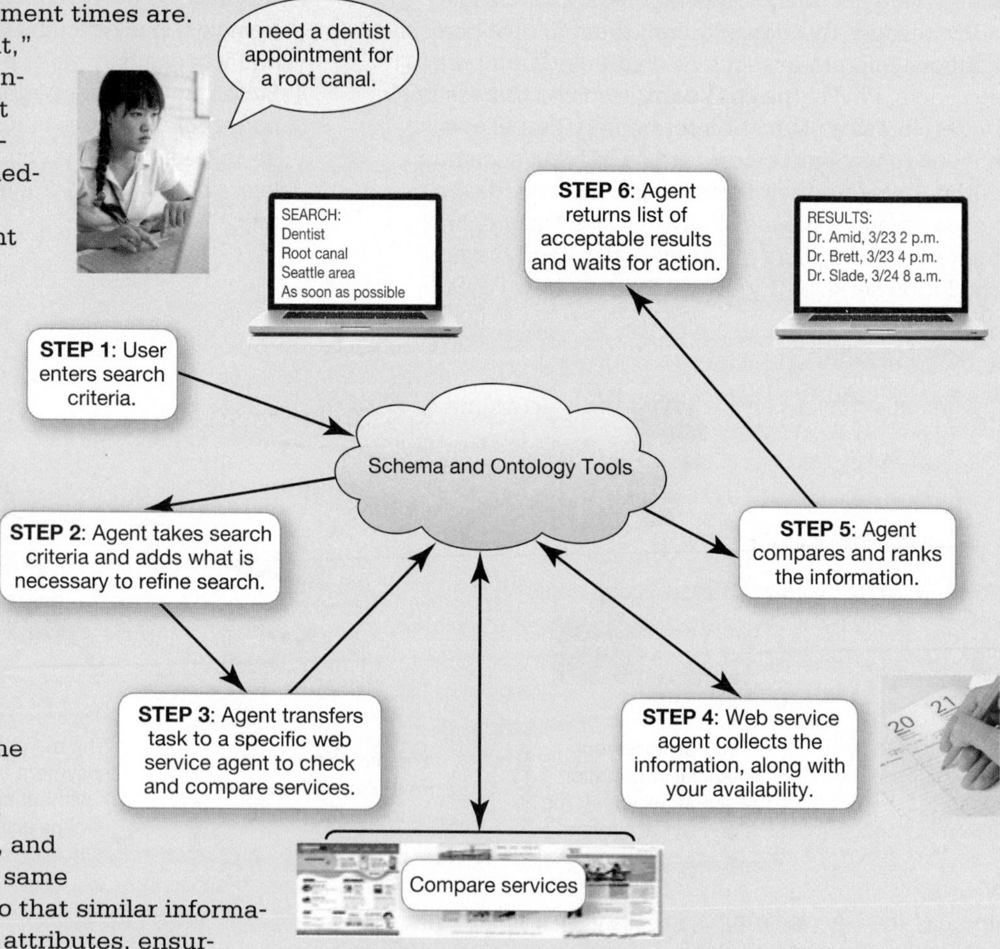


**FIGURE 3.13** The Semantic Web. *(William Casey/Shutterstock; Tomasz Sz/Shutterstock; nattstudio/Fotolia)*

# check your understanding//

For a quick review to see what you've learned so far, answer the following questions. Visit **pearsonhighered.com/techinaction** to check your answers.

## multiple choice

1. Which is NOT true about the Internet?
   - **a.** It is the largest computer network in the world.
   - **b.** It was created to establish a secure form of military communications.
   - **c.** It was developed as an additional means of commerce.
   - **d.** It was designed as a means for all computers to communicate with each other.
2. What do you need if you want to read, send, and organize e-mail from *any* computer connected to the Internet?
   - **a.** an e-mail client program
   - **b.** an e-mail server
   - **c.** an e-mail aggregator
   - **d.** a web-based e-mail account
3. Which is NOT an example of Web 2.0 technology?
   - **a.** e-mail
   - **b.** social networking
   - **c.** blogging
   - **d.** wiki
4. Which of the following is NOT a characteristic of a blog?
   - **a.** Blogs are used to express opinions.
   - **b.** Blogs are generally written by a single author.
   - **c.** Blogs are private and require password access.
   - **d.** Blogs are arranged as a listing of entries.
5. Which of the following would be the correct classification for Target.com?
   - **a.** B2B
   - **b.** C2C
   - **c.** B2C
   - **d.** Click-and-brick business

## true–false

_______ **1.** Deleted e-mails can be recovered—they don't really vanish.

_______ **2.** The first web browser was created by ARPANET.

## critical thinking

1. **Social Networking and Society**

   Social networking seems to have taken over our lives! Almost everyone is on Facebook and Twitter. But is this a good thing?
   - **a.** What advantages and disadvantages does social networking bring to your life and to society?
   - **b.** How are businesses using social networking?
2. **Mobile E-Commerce Safety**

   The text lists several ways to ensure your online transactions are secure and to reduce the risk of things going awry as you shop and sell online. However, surveys indicate that many feel that shopping from a mobile device, such as a smartphone, presents additional risks. Do you agree there are additional risks when conducting e-commerce from a mobile device? Why or why not?

**Continue** »

TRY THIS 

# Create a OneDrive Account to Store and Share Your Files in the Cloud

You probably have your favorite ways of moving your files around. Perhaps you have a USB drive or you e-mail files to yourself, or maybe you have a portable external hard drive. With any of these solutions, there can be confusion as to which is the most current version of the file if you have worked on it on multiple devices at different times. You also run the risk of losing your USB drive or deleting the e-mail attachment by mistake. These methods also make exchanging files difficult if you want to share your files or collaborate with a group.

A simpler solution is to use a web-based or cloud storage and sharing service such as OneDrive or Dropbox. OneDrive is part of Microsoft's Office 365 suite of web apps. With 7 GB of free storage space for new users, you can store thousands of files and get to them anytime you're online. Note: At the time this book went to press, Microsoft had announced changing the name of SkyDrive to OneDrive, but had not updated the website, so images still reflect SkyDrive.

**Step 1 Sign in to OneDrive:** Go to **onedrive.com**. Sign in to your Microsoft account. If you don't have a Microsoft account, creating one is easy. A Microsoft account will give you access to services such as OneDrive, Xbox LIVE, and **Outlook.com**.

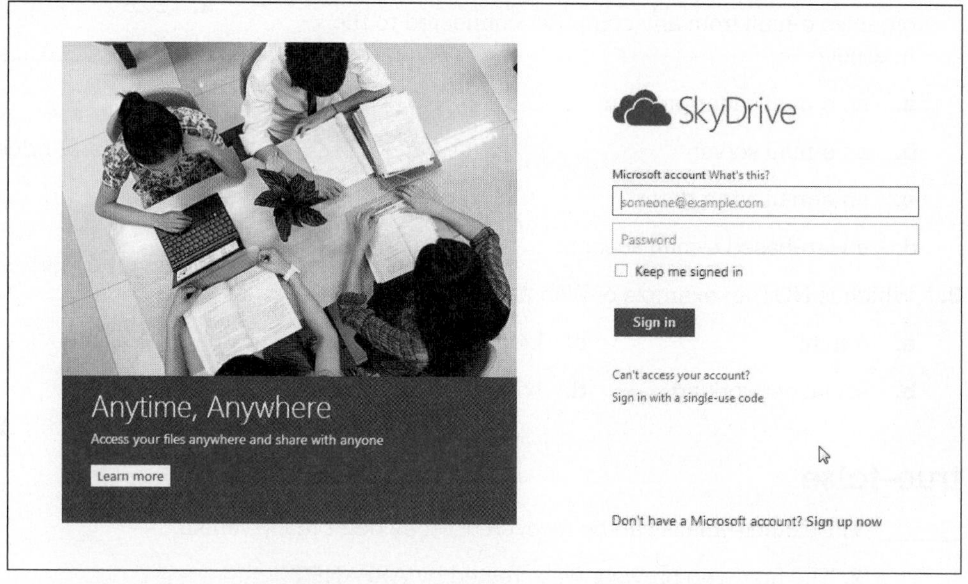


**Step 2 Create a Folder and Add Files:** Once you're in OneDrive, you can create a folder and then begin to add files.

- To create a folder: Click **Create** at the top of the page, click **Folder**, and then give your new folder a name. Click the new folder to open it.
- To add a file: Click **Upload** at the top of the page, then locate the file and click **Open**. To upload more than one file, hold the **Ctrl key** while you select each file.

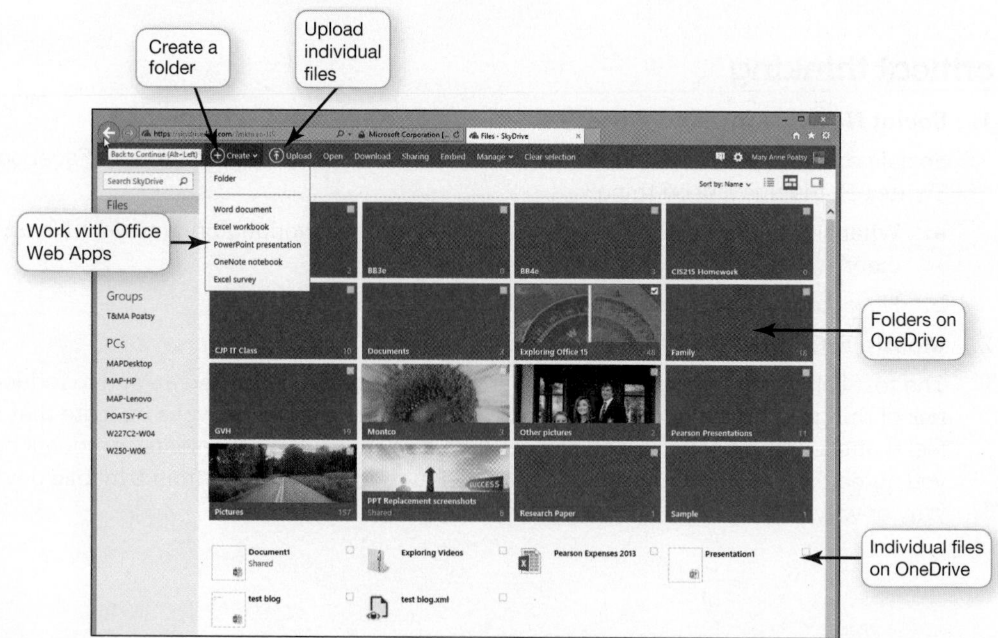

**Step 3 Share a File or Folder:** To share a file or folder, do the following:

- Right-click the file or folder that you want to share, and click **Sharing**.
- Fill in the e-mail form.
- Establish editing privileges by checking the **Recipients can edit** box, if desired, then click **Share**.

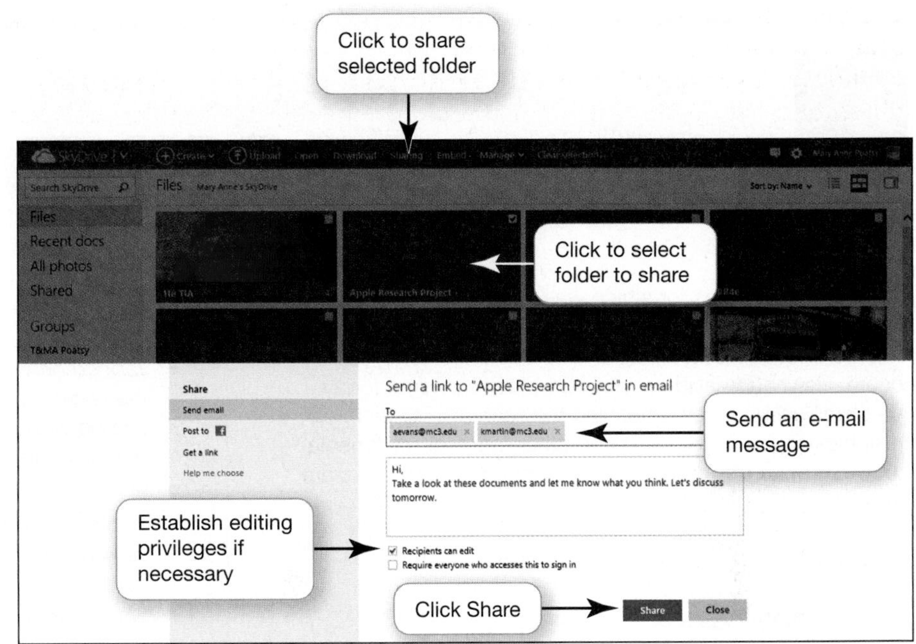


- To see what files that have been shared with you, click **Shared** in the left menu.

**Step 4 Sync with Your Smartphone:** If you have an iPhone, Android, or Windows Phone, you can access your documents wherever you go. You can download the One-Drive app, or you can always access OneDrive through your phone's browser at **onedrive .com**.

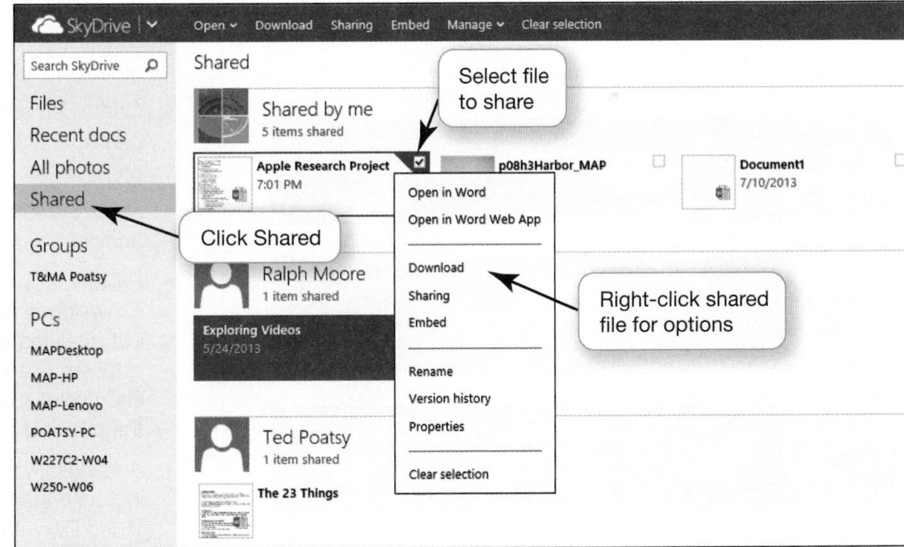

# Using the Web Effectively

You no doubt know how to use the web—to buy products, send e-mail, visit Facebook, and use Google—but do you know how to use it effectively? In this section, we'll look at ways to make your online experience more enjoyable, more productive, and even more efficient.

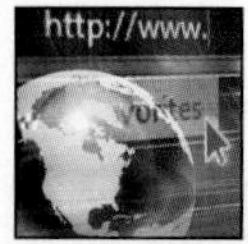


http://www.

## accessing and moving AROUND THE WEB

None of the activities for which we use the web could happen without an important software application: a web browser. Recall that a browser is software that lets you locate, view, and navigate the web. Most browsers today are *graphical* browsers, meaning they can display pictures (graphics) in addition to text and other forms of multimedia such as sound and video. The most common browsers are displayed in Figure 3.14.

### Web Browsers

**What features do browsers offer?** Most popular browsers share similar features that make the user experience more efficient (as shown in Figure 3.15). For example, most browsers include a built-in search box in which you can designate your preferred default search engine and tools for printing, page formatting, and security settings. Other features include the following:

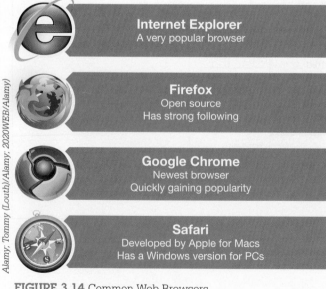

- *Tabbed browsing:* Web pages are loaded in "tabs" within the same browser window. Rather than having to switch among web pages in several open windows, you can flip between the tabs in one window. You may also save a group of tabs as a Favorites group if there are several tabs you often open at the same time.
- *Pinned tabs:* You can "dock" tabs to the taskbar (in Internet Explorer) or minimize and save them permanently (Google Chrome and Firefox) for easier navigation of your favorite sites.
- *Tear-off tabs:* An opened tab can be dragged away from its current window so it's then opened in a new window.
- *Thumbnail previews:* Another convenient navigation tool that most browsers share is providing thumbnail previews of all open web pages in open tabs.
- *Tab isolation:* With this feature, tabs are independent of each other, so if one crashes, it does not affect the other tabs.
- *Combined search and address bar:* With this feature, you can both type a website URL or search the web from the address bar.
- *SmartScreen filter:* Most browsers offer built-in protection against phishing, malware, and other web-based threats.
- *Privacy browsing:* Privacy features (such as InPrivate Browsing in Internet Explorer) let you browse the web without retaining a history trail, temporary Internet files, cookies, or usernames and passwords. These features are especially helpful when you use public computers at college or the public library, for example.
- *Add-ons:* Add-ons are small programs that customize and increase the functionality of the browser. Examples include Video DownloadHelper that converts web videos, like those found on YouTube, to files you can save, as well as a Facebook toolbar that integrates Facebook functionality into your browser.
- *Session Restore:* Brings back all your active web pages if the browser or system shuts down unexpectedly.

Open source
Has strong following

Newest browser
Quickly gaining popularity

Safari
Developed by Apple for Macs
Has a Windows version for PCs

(Pablo Fonseca Q./La Nacion de Costa Rica/Newscom; Lucia Lanpur/Alamy; Tommy (Louth)/Alamy; 2020WEB/Alamy)

A very popular browser

**FIGURE 3.14** Common Web Browsers

**FIGURE 3.15** Like most of the popular web browsers, Internet Explorer and Google Chrome include tabbed and privacy browsing and an address bar that doubles as a search bar. Pinned tabs make accessing your favorite sites even easier. *(Courtesy of NASA; Courtesy of the IRS)*

# BITS&BYTES

## Maxthon: A Great Alternative Brower

Not well known in the United States but quite popular elsewhere globally, Maxthon is a web browser that rivals our U.S. favorites. Maxthon has the convenient features of tabbed browsing, bookmarking capabilities, thumbnails of previously viewed sites, and privacy viewing, so you'll feel quite at home rather quickly. Since Maxthon is a cloud-based browser, when you access the browser on any device, all your settings are synced. Maxthon does have some unique features, such as Maxthon's dock—a sidebar that resides in the desktop, with customizable shortcut icons to your favorite websites. In addition, Maxthon enables you to use mouse gestures so that you can match a specific mouse movement with a specific command. In addition, super drag and drop enables you to drag and drop a link, image, or highlighted text into the search box rather than typing the content; night mode adjusts the brightness of the screen; "snap" enables you to take screen grabs; and SkyNote lets you save and access notes. If you haven't already, you may enjoy taking Maxthon for a test drive.

## URLs, Protocols, and Domain Names

**What do all the parts of a URL mean?** You gain initial access to a particular **website** by typing its unique address, or **Uniform Resource Locator** (**URL**, pronounced "you-are-ell"), in your browser. A website is comprised of many different web pages, each of which is a separate document with its own unique URL. Like a regular street address, a URL is comprised of several parts that help identify the web document it stands for (see Figure 3.16):

- the *protocol* (set of rules) used to retrieve the document;
- the **domain name**; and
- the *path* or subdirectory

Although every part of a URL is important information that ensures the web page you requested actually displays in your

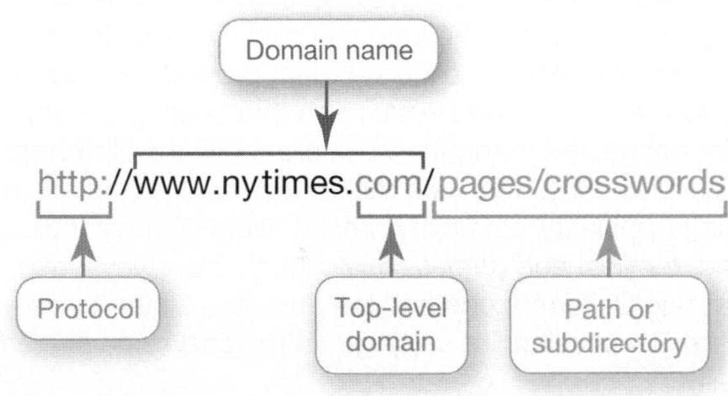


**FIGURE 3.16** The Parts of a URL

FIGURE 3.17

## Common Top-Level Domains and Their Authorized Users

| DOMAIN NAME | WHO CAN USE IT |
|---|---|
| .biz | Businesses |
| .com | Originally for commercial sites, but now can be used by anyone |
| .edu | Degree-granting institutions |
| .gov | Local, state, and federal U.S. governments |
| .info | Information service providers |
| .mil | U.S. military |
| .net | Originally for networking organizations, but no longer restricted |
| .org | Organizations (often not-for-profits) |

browser, you don't have to type in every part in the location or address bar of the browser. Most current browsers no longer require you to enter the http://protocol or the "www," and most don't even require the domain if it's a .com—the browser will enter those automatically.

**What's the protocol?** You're probably most familiar with URLs that begin with *http*, which is short for **Hypertext Transfer Protocol (HTTP)**. HTTP is the protocol that allows files to be transferred from a **web server**—a computer that hosts the website you're requesting—so that you can see it on your computer. The HTTP protocol is what the web is based on.

**Is HTTP the only protocol I need to use?** HTTP is the most common protocol, but it's not the only one. HTTP is part of the Internet protocol suite, a group of protocols that govern how information is exchanged on a network. Another protocol in that group is the **File Transfer Protocol (FTP)**. As its name implies, FTP was originally designed, before the HTTP protocol was developed, to transfer files from your computer to a web server. Today, FTP is often used when you have large files to upload or download. To connect to most FTP servers, you need a user ID and password. To upload and download files from FTP sites, you can use a browser or file transfer software such as WS_FTP, Fetch, or FileZilla.

BitTorrent, like FTP, is a protocol used to transfer files, though it's not part of the Internet protocol suite. To use BitTorrent, you install a software client program. It uses a *peer-to-peer networking system,* so that sharing occurs between connected computers that also have the BitTorrent client installed. BitTorrent was developed in 2001 and has been gaining popularity, especially among users who want to share music, movies, and games. Use caution, however, when accessing BitTorrent content. Because it is a peer-to-peer system, it's possible for copyrighted material to be shared illegally.

**What's in a domain name?** The domain name identifies the site's **host**, the location that maintains the computers that store the website files. For example, **www.berkeley.edu** is the domain name for the University of California at Berkeley website. The suffix in the domain name after the dot (such as "com" or "edu") is called the **top-level domain**. This suffix indicates the kind of organization to which the host belongs. Figure 3.17 lists the most frequently used top-level domains.

Each country has its own top-level domain. These are two-letter designations such as .za for South Africa and .us for the United States. A sampling of country codes is shown in Figure 3.18. Within a country-specific domain, further subdivisions can be made for regions or states. For instance, the .us domain contains subdomains for each state, using the two-letter abbreviation of the state. For example, the URL for Pennsylvania's website is **www.state.pa.us**.

**What's the information after the domain name that I sometimes see?** When the URL is the domain name, such as **www.nytimes.com**, you're requesting a site's home page. However, sometimes a forward slash and additional text follow the domain name, such as in **www.nytimes.com/pages/crosswords**. The information after each slash indicates a particular file or **path** (or **subdirectory**)

FIGURE 3.18

## Examples of Country Codes

| COUNTRY CODE | COUNTRY |
|---|---|
| .au | Australia |
| .ca | Canada |
| .jp | Japan |
| .uk | United Kingdom |

*Note:* For a full listing of country codes, refer to **iana.org/domains/root/db/**.

**FIGURE 3.19** Navigating a Web Page *(Courtesy of the U.S. Small Business Administration)*

within the website. In Figure 3.16, you would connect to the crossword page on the *New York Times* site.

## Hyperlinks and Beyond

**What's the best way to get around in a website?** As its name implies, the web is a series of interconnected paths, or links. You've no doubt moved around the web by clicking on **hyperlinks**, specially coded elements that let you jump from one web page to another within the same website or to another site altogether (see Figure 3.19). Generally, text that operates as a hyperlink appears in a different color (often blue) and is usually underlined, but sometimes images also act as hyperlinks. When you hover your cursor over a hyperlink, the cursor changes to a hand with a finger pointing upward.

**What other tools can I use to navigate a website?** To move back or forward one page at a time, you can use the browser's Back and Forward buttons (see Figure 3.19).

To help navigate more quickly through a website, some sites provide a **breadcrumb trail**—a navigation aid that shows users the path they have taken to get to a web page, or where the page is located within the website. It usually appears at the top of a page. Figure 3.19 shows an example of a breadcrumb trail. "Breadcrumbs" get their name from the fairy tale "Hansel and Gretel," in which the characters drop breadcrumbs on the trail to find their way out of a forest. By clicking on earlier links in a breadcrumb trail, you can go directly to a previously visited web page without having to use the Back button to navigate back through the website.

The History list on your browser's toolbar is also a handy feature. The History list shows all the websites and pages you've visited over a certain period of time. These sites are organized according to date and can go back as far as three weeks, depending on your browsing activity. To access the History list in Internet Explorer, click the star in the upper right-hand corner of the browser window and then click the History tab.

SOUND BYTE

**Welcome to the Web**

In this Sound Byte, you'll visit the web in a series of guided tours of useful websites. This tour serves as an introductory guide for web newcomers but is also a great resource for more experienced users.

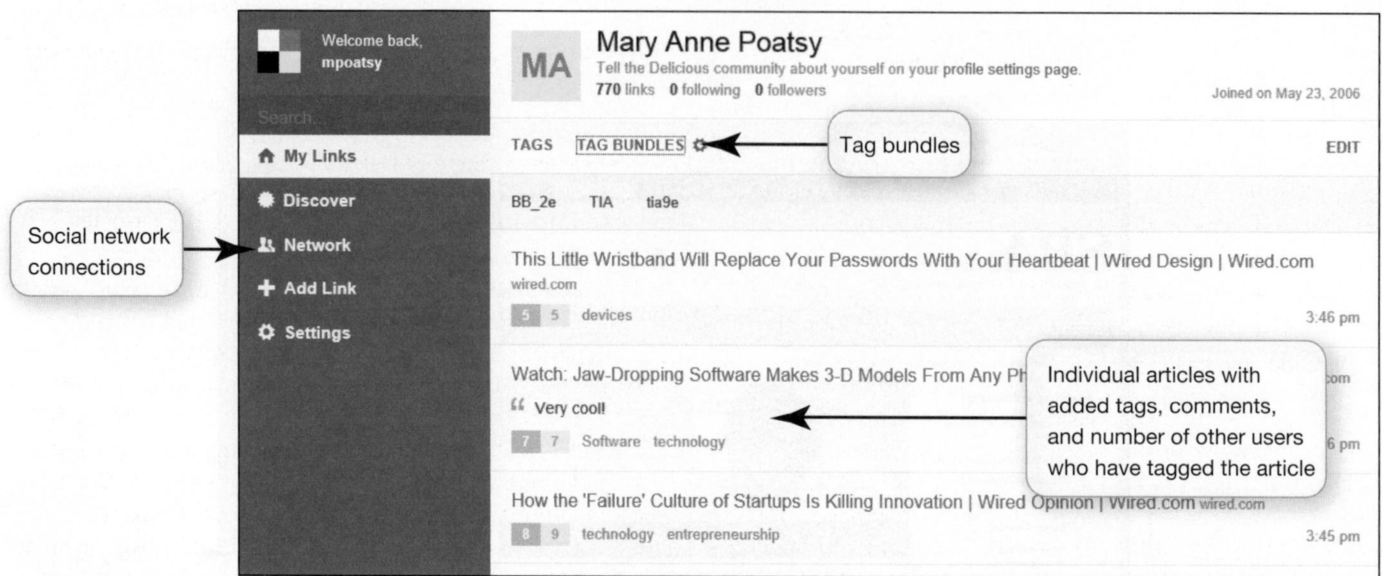


**FIGURE 3.20** Delicious is a social bookmarking website that allows you to organize and share your favorite websites. *(AVOS Systems, Inc., www.delicious.com)*

## Favorites, Live Bookmarks, and Tagging

**What's the best way to mark a site so I can return to it later?** If you want an easy way to return to a specific web page, you can use your browser's **Bookmarks** feature (Internet Explorer calls this feature **Favorites**). This feature places a marker of the site's URL in an easily retrievable list in your browser's toolbar. To organize the sites into categories, most browsers offer tools to create folders.

Favorites and Bookmarks are great for quickly locating those sites you use most, but they're accessible to you only when you're on your own computer. Although most browsers provide features that let you export the list of bookmarks to a file you can import to another computer or another browser, another way to access your Bookmarks and Favorites from any computer is to use MyBookmarks (**mybookmarks.com**), a free Internet service that stores your Bookmarks and Favorites online.

**What are live bookmarks? Live bookmark** is a feature in Firefox that adds the technology of RSS feeds to bookmarking. Safari and Internet Explorer also have built-in RSS readers, while Chrome requires that you add on an extension. Because the web is constantly changing, the site you bookmarked last week may subsequently change and add new content. Traditionally, you would notice the change only the next time you visited the site. Live bookmarks deliver content updates to you as soon as they become available using RSS, the same technology that updates blogs and podcasts that we described earlier in the chapter. Live bookmarks and RSS feeds are useful if you're interested in the most up-to-date news stories, sports scores, or stock prices.

**What is tagging? Tagging**, also known as **social bookmarking**, is like bookmarking your favorite website, but instead of saving it to your browser for only you to see, you're saving it to a social bookmarking site so that you can share it with others. A social bookmark or tag is a **keyword** or term that you assign to a web page, digital image, or video. A tag can be something you create to describe the digital content, or it can be a suggested term provided by the website. For example, as you were surfing the web you came across a web page with a great article on inexpensive places to go for spring break. You might tag the article with the term *vacations*. Others on the same social bookmarking site who are looking for websites about vacations may use *vacations* as the search term and find the article you tagged.

Delicious (**delicious.com**) is one of the original social bookmarking sites (see Figure 3.20). Delicious lets you group related links and organize them into "bundles." So if you've collected several links to websites about different places to go to over spring break, you can collect all those links into one bundle about vacations. Or if you want to see what links others may have found about interesting vacations, you could search Delicious with the term *vacations* to see other vacation-related bundles.

Another social bookmarking site is Diigo (**diigo.com**). Diigo differs from Delicious by allowing you to annotate the pages with highlights and sticky notes. Through Diigo, you can archive web pages so they are always available. ■

# trends in IT

## Doing Business on a Shoestring—Thanks to the Internet

Let's say you think that flip-flops in school colors would be a popular product. Your school's bookstore carries everything else with the school's colors and logo, but not flip-flops. You've asked your friends and several classmates, and most of them say they would buy flip-flops in the school's colors. So what do you do next? How do you move from product concept to selling a physical product?

Before the Internet, it would have been much more difficult and expensive to get your product produced and distributed. First, you would have had to find someone to design your flip-flops. Then, to make the flip-flops, you would have had to find a manufacturer, who may have required a high minimum order (maybe tens of thousands of pairs of flip-flops). You also would have needed a package design, marketing brochures, a company logo, a storage facility, and more. Finally, the largest hurdle would have been to convince a brick-and-mortar retailer, such as your campus bookstore, to carry your product.

Today, however, the Internet brings the power of the global economy right to your door (see Figure 3.21). For product design and manufacturing, you can visit a site like Alibaba (**alibaba.com**), which helps entrepreneurs locate manufacturers of all sorts of products. Many manufacturers are happy to work with small business owners to custom-design products. So if you find a flip-flop style you like, you probably can get it customized with your school colors.

But what happens if the bookstore doesn't want to sell your flip-flops? If this happens, you can set up a website to sell them yourself. Of course, you may need help doing this, in which case you can locate skilled professionals by using sites such as Guru (**guru.com**) or Elance (**elance.com**). You simply create a description of the job you need done (such as logo design for a flip-flop company), post it on the site, and invite freelancers to bid on your job. You then contact the freelancers who look promising, review samples of their work, and decide on someone who can help you—and at a competitive price. After your website is designed and up and running, you can place your business on social networking sites, such as Facebook, to help potential customers discover your product and spread the word about your great flip-flops. You probably already have lots of friends on Facebook who attend your school and would be good potential customers.

Another hurdle is determining where you'll store your product and who will package and ship it to customers. If your parents' basement isn't large enough, you can outsource warehousing and order fulfillment to **Amazon.com**. Amazon will (for a fee) warehouse your inventory and then package and ship it when customer orders are received. Orders don't have to come through Amazon's site (although that is an option); you can provide ordering information collected on your site to Amazon, and Amazon will take care of the rest.

Although there is always a cost to starting up a business, up-front costs are much lower when you take advantage of the global marketplace and the Internet. So, take that brilliant idea you have and turn it into a business today!

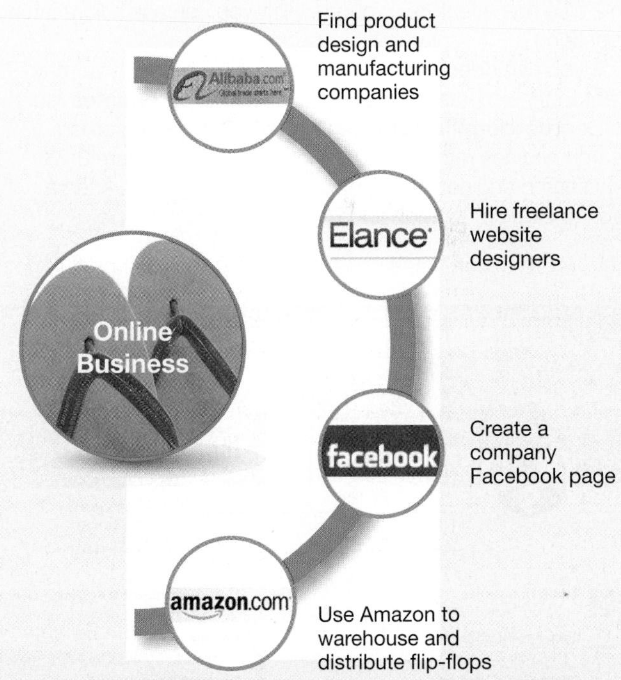


**FIGURE 3.21** By using the services of only a few websites, you can create and distribute products, such as your own line of custom flip-flops. *(M4OS Photos/Alamy; Elance, Inc.; Kevin Britland/Alamy; Anatolii Babii/Alamy; nito/Shutterstock)*

# searching the web EFFECTIVELY

You've most likely "Googled" something today, and if you did, your search is one of over five billion searches today. Google is the world's most popular **search engine**—a set of programs that searches the web for keywords (specific words you wish to look for or *query*) and then returns a list of the sites on which those keywords are found. In fact, Google has become so popular that its name is synonymous with looking for information on the web. Other popular search engines include Yahoo!, Bing, and Ask.com. But there are even more options for searching the web.

For some web searches, it might be better to use a **subject directory**, which is a structured outline of websites organized by topics and subtopics. By drilling down through the topics and subtopics, you can narrow down to a list of meaningful websites to look through. For example, if you wanted to know about exhibits of 3-D photography, you might click Arts>Visual Arts>Photography>3-D>Exhibits in a subject directory. In Yahoo's subject directory (**dir.yahoo.com**), the result would be a list of relevant websites about 3-D photography exhibits. The website ipl2 (**ipl2.org**) has a subject directory that combines resources from the Internet Public Library and the Librarians' Internet Index websites (see Figure 3.22). (ipl2 also has a feature through which you can ask a librarian a question.)

If you can't decide which search engine is best, you may want to try a metasearch engine. **Metasearch engines**, such as Dogpile (**dogpile.com**; see Figure 3.22), search other search engines rather than individual websites. Figure 3.23 lists search engines and subject directories that are alternatives to Google, Yahoo!, and Bing.

## Using Search Engines Effectively

**How do search engines work?** Search engines have three components:

1. The first component is a program called a *spider,* which constantly collects data on the web, following links in websites and reading web pages. Spiders get their name because they crawl over the web using multiple "legs" to visit many sites simultaneously.
2. As the spider collects data, the second component of the search engine, an *indexer program*, organizes the data into a large database.
3. When you use a search engine, you interact with the third component: the *search engine software*. This software searches the indexed data, pulling out relevant information according to your search.

The resulting list appears in your web browser as a list of hits—sites that match your search.

**Why don't I get the same results from all search engines?** Each search engine uses a unique formula, or *algorithm*, to formulate the search and create the resulting index of related sites. In addition, search engines differ in how they rank the search results. Most search engines rank their results based on the frequency of the appearance of your queried keywords in websites as well as the location of those words in the sites. This means that sites that include the keywords in their URL or site name most likely appear at the top of the results list. An important part of a company's marketing strategy

**FIGURE 3.22** ipl2 and Dogpile are alternatives to Google. ipl2 (**ipl2.org**) is a subject directory that lists resources by subject, and Dogpile (**dogpile.com**) is a metasearch engine that searches Google, Yahoo!, and Bing. *(Courtesy of iPL2; Courtesy of InfoSpace, Inc./Blucora)*

**FIGURE 3.23**

## Beyond Google: Alternative Search Engines and Subject Directories

| | |
|---|---|
| Bing **bing.com** | Web search engine from Microsoft |
| ChaCha **chacha.com** | Uses live people who help you search; free of charge. Also available by texting your questions to 242242. |
| CompletePlanet **aip.completeplanet.com** | "Deep web" directory that searches databases not normally searched by typical search engines. |
| Dogpile **dogpile.com** | Metasearch engine that searches Google, Yahoo!, and Bing. |
| Excite **excite.com** | Website that in addition to having keyword search capabilities includes links to information on a wide variety of topics including travel, weather, concert tickets, and top news items. |
| Info.com **info.com** | Metasearch engine that searches Google, Yahoo!, Bing, and Yandex (a Russian search engine). |
| InfoMine **infomine.ucr.edu** | Subject directory of academic resources with keyword search engine capabilities. |
| ipl2 **ipl2.org** | Subject directory that combines resources from the Internet Public Library and the Librarians' Internet Index websites. |
| Oolone **oolone.com** | Visual search engine that displays images rather than text as a result of a keyword search. |
| Open Directory Project **dmoz.org** | Human-edited subject directory with keyword search capabilities. Maintained by a global community of volunteer editors. |
| Yippy **yippy.com** | Metasearch engine that groups similar results into topics called clusters (for example, NBA, College Basketball, Photo Gallery, and Articles would be some resulting clusters if you use the search term *basketball*). Clicking on any of these clusters results in listing those sites specific to that subset of basketball. |

*Note: For a complete list of search engines, go to* **searchengineguide.com**.

is search engine optimization, which is designing the corporate website to ensure it ranks near the top of a search.

Search engines also differ as to which sites they search. For instance, Google and Bing search nearly the entire web, whereas specialty search engines search only sites that are relevant to a particular topic or industry. Specialty search engines exist for almost every industry or interest. DailyStocks (**dailystocks.com**) is a search engine used primarily by investors that searches for corporate information. Search Engine Watch (**searchenginewatch.com**) has a list of many specialty search engines, organized by industry.

**Can I use a search engine to search just for images and videos?** With the increasing popularity of multimedia, search engines such as Google, Bing, and Yahoo! let you search the web for digital images and audio and video files. After putting in your search term, select Video from Google's top menu to display only the search results that are videos. You can further narrow down the video selection by using the filtering tools. Blinkx (**blinkx.com**) is a video search engine that helps you sift through all the video posted on the web (see Figure 3.24).

**How can I refine my searches for better results?** You've probably searched for something on Google and gotten back a list of hits that includes thousands—even millions—of web pages that have no relevance to the topic you're interested in. Initially, Boolean operators were needed to help refine a search. **Boolean operators** are words such as *AND, NOT,* and *OR* that describe the relationships between keywords in a search. With the simple addition of a few words or constraints,

ACTIVE HELPDESK

**Using Subject Directories and Search Engines**

In this Active Helpdesk call, you'll play the role of a helpdesk staffer, fielding calls about how to search the Internet using search engines and subject directories, as well as how to use advanced search options to search the web more effectively.

ACTIVE HELPDESK

**Getting Around the Web**

In this Active Helpdesk call, you'll play the role of a helpdesk staffer, fielding calls about web browsers, URLs, and how to use hyperlinks and other tools to get around the web.

you can narrow your search results to a more manageable and more meaningful list.

**Are there other helpful search strategies?** Other strategies can help refine your searches when entering your search phrases:

- **Search for a phrase.** To search for an exact phrase, place quotation marks around your keywords. The search engine will look for only those websites that contain the words in *that exact order*. For example, if you want information on the movie *The Green Hornet* and you type these words without quotation marks, your search results will contain pages that include either of the words *Green* and *Hornet*, although not necessarily in that order. Typing *"The Green Hornet"* in quotation marks guarantees that search results will include this exact phrase.
- **Search within a specific website.** To search just a specific website, you can use the search keyword, then *site:* followed by the website's URL. For example, searching with *processor site:* www.wired.com returns results about processors from the Wired.com website. The same method works for entire classes of sites in a given top-level domain or country code.
- **Use a wild card.** The asterisk ("*") is a wild card, or placeholder, feature that is helpful when you need to search with unknown terms. Another way to think about the wild card search feature is as a "fill in the blank." For example, searching with *Congress voted * on the * bill* might bring up an article about the members of Congress who voted *no* on the *healthcare* bill or a different article about the members of Congress who voted *yes* on the *energy* bill.

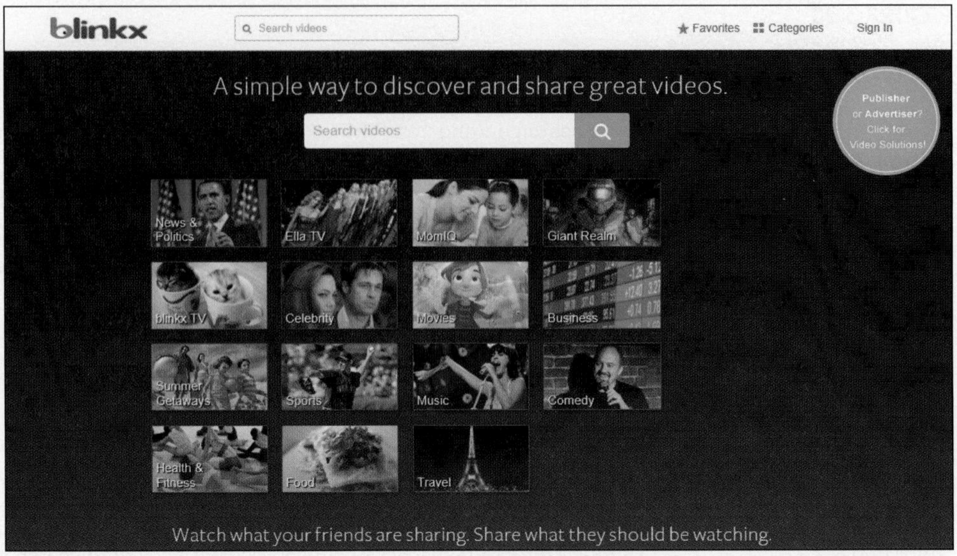

**FIGURE 3.24** Blinkx is a video search engine that helps you sift through the increasing number of videos on the web. *(Courtesy of Blinkx)*

# BITS&BYTES

## Searching to Do Good

Wouldn't it be great to benefit others just by searching the web? Now there's an easy way to "do good" with every search. Goodsearch (**goodsearch.com**) is a Yahoo!-powered search engine that donates half of its revenues (approximately a penny per search) to approved U.S. charities and schools that users designate. The money Goodsearch donates comes from the site's advertisers. More than 100,000 charitable organizations are being helped by Goodsearch, but if the organization you're interested in isn't on the list, as long as it's a registered U.S. not-for-profit organization, you can apply to have it added. Goodsearch has expanded its program to online shopping and dining out.

You can also contribute to your favorite charity by shopping online through Goodshop (**goodshop.com**). Instead of going directly to your favorite online store, go to Goodshop first, find and click through to the store of your choice, and start shopping. Participating stores donate up to 30% of the purchased amount. Similarly, through the GoodDining program, dine at a participating restaurant and a percentage of your bill will go to your cause. So, search, shop, and eat—and do some good!

**How else can I customize my searches?** Many other specialty search strategies and services are available. By clicking on Search tools in Google's menu at the top of a Google search, you can restrict search results by time, location, and even reading level (see Figure 3.25). You can also click on the Apps button in Google's main page, then click the "More" and "Even more from Google" options for all the specialized search products Google offers (see Figure 3.26):

- *Scholar* searches scholarly literature such as peer-reviewed papers, theses, and publications from academic organizations. Each search result contains bibliographic information as well.
- *Custom Search* lets you create a customized search engine to search only a selected set of sites tailored to your needs. You can add this specialized search engine to a website or blog or design it for a specific organization.
- *Google Shopping* lets you search by product rather than by company. So if you're interested in buying a digital camera, Google Shopping lists cameras by popularity and provides information on the stores that carry the cameras, along with the average price.

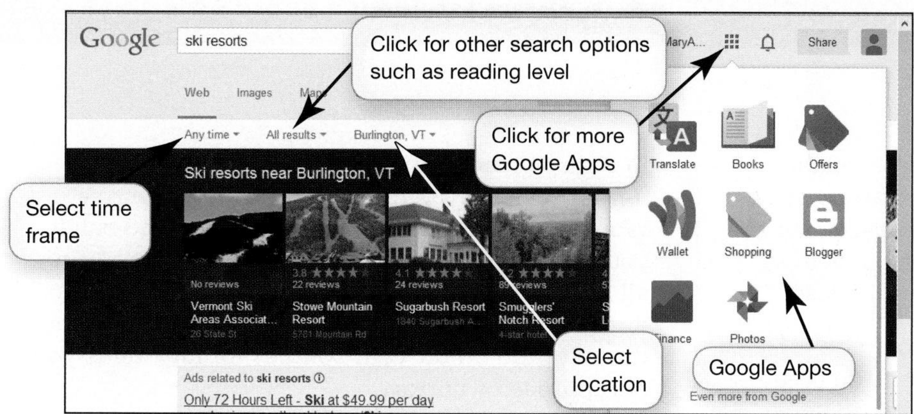


FIGURE 3.25 Use Google's search tools to restrict the time frame, the location, and even the reading level of your search results. *(Courtesy of Google, Inc.)*

- *Alerts* let you know by e-mail when content that you specify has been updated, so you can monitor a developing news story or be aware of breaking news about your favorite sports team, for example.

## Evaluating Websites

**How can I make sure a website is appropriate to use for research?** When you're using the Internet for research, you shouldn't assume that everything you find is accurate and appropriate to use. The following is a list of questions to consider before you use an Internet resource; the answers to these questions will help you decide whether you should consider a website to be a good source of information:

- **Authority:** Who is the author of the article or the sponsor of the site? If the author is well known or the site is published by a reputable news source (such as the *New York Times*), then you can feel more confident using it as a source than if you are unable to locate such information. *Note:* Some sites include a page with information about the author or the site's sponsor.
- **Bias:** Is the site biased? The purpose of many websites is to sell products or services or to persuade rather than inform. These sites, though useful in some situations, present a biased point of view. Look for sites that offer several sets of facts or consider opinions from several sources.
- **Relevance:** Is the information on the site current? Material can last a long time on the web. Some research projects (such as historical accounts) depend on older records. However, if you're writing about cutting-edge technologies, you need to look for the most recent sources. Therefore, look for a date on information to make sure it is current.
- **Audience:** For what audience is the site intended? Ensure that the content, tone, and style of the site match your needs. You probably wouldn't want to use information from a site geared toward teens if you're writing for adults, nor would you use a site that has a casual style and tone for serious research.
- **Links:** Are the links available and appropriate? Check out the links provided on the site to determine whether they're still working and appropriate for your needs. Don't assume that the links provided are the only additional sources of information. Investigate other sites on your topic, as well. You should also be able to find the same information on at least three different websites to help verify the information is accurate. ■

SOUND BYTE
**Finding Information on the Web**

In this Sound Byte, you'll learn how and when to use search engines and subject directories. Through guided tours, you'll learn effective search techniques, including how to use Boolean operators and metasearch engines.

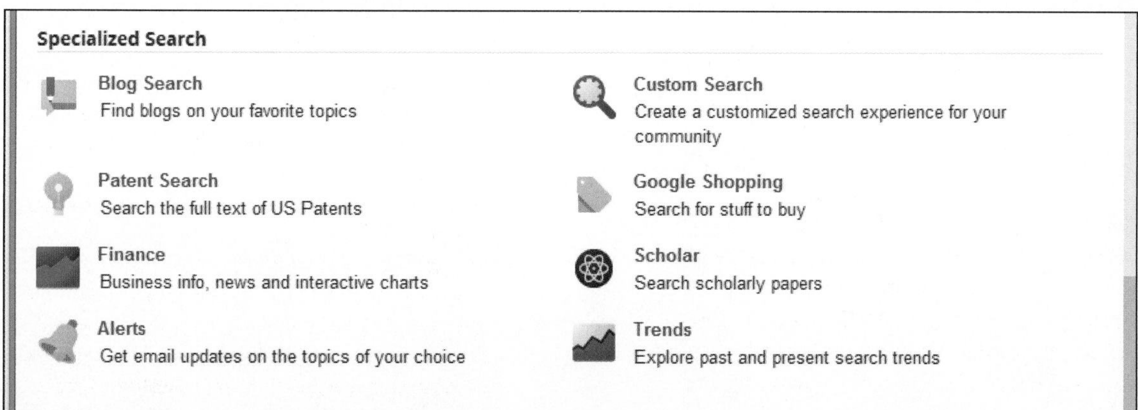


FIGURE 3.26 Google's Specialized Search Tools. *(Courtesy of Google, Inc.)*

# ethics in IT Plagiarism and Copyright Violation: What Can You Borrow from the Internet?

Despite having so much information easily available on the web, using it without receiving proper permissions is not only wrong but can also be illegal. So what can you borrow from the web and what must you seek permission to use? Consider these scenarios:

1. You find a political cartoon that would be terrific in a PowerPoint presentation you're creating for your civics class. You copy it into your presentation.
2. Your hobby is writing children's books, which you later sell online. Most of what you create is your content, but sometimes you borrow story ideas from other children's books and just change a few characters or situations. You do not obtain permission from the originators of the story ideas you borrow.
3. You're pressed for time and need to do research for a paper due tomorrow. You find information on an obscure website and copy it into your paper without documenting the source.
4. You download a song from the Internet and incorporate it into a PowerPoint presentation for a school project. Because you assume everyone knows the song, you don't credit it in your sources.

Which of the preceding scenarios represent copyright violations? Which represent plagiarism? The distinctions between these scenarios are narrow in some cases, but it's important to understand the differences.

*Plagiarism* occurs when you use someone else's ideas or words and represent them as your own. In today's computer society, it's easy to copy information from the Internet and paste it into a Word document, change a few words, and call it your own. To avoid plagiarism, properly crediting all information you obtain from the Internet by using quotation marks around all words you borrow directly, and credit your sources for any ideas you paraphrase or borrow.

WriteCheck (**writecheck.com**) is a website specifically for students to help check for plagiarism violations (see Figure 3.27). The site compares your document to a database of publications, books, and web content and identifies possible plagiarism violations. Although some common phrasing may be truly coincidental, real and purposeful plagiarism is reasonably easy to identify. Students can use WriteCheck before submitting an assignment to ensure their papers are free from plagiarism and avoid the serious consequences of this offense.

*Copyright violation* is more serious because it, unlike plagiarism, is punishable by law. Copyright law assumes that all original work is copyrighted even if the work does not display the copyright symbol (©). Copyright violation occurs when you use another person's material for your own personal economic benefit or when you take away from the economic benefit of the originator. In most cases, citing the source is not sufficient; you need to seek and receive written permission from the copyright holder.

There are exceptions to this rule. There is no copyright on government documents, so you can download and reproduce material from any government website. The British Broadcasting Corporation (BBC) is also beginning to digitize and

**FIGURE 3.27** Students can compare their work to a database of publications in sites such as WriteCheck to check for unintended plagiarism. *(Keith Morris/Alamy)*

make available its archives of material to the public without copyright restrictions. Teachers and students receive special consideration that falls under a provision called *academic fair use*. As long as the material is being used for educational purposes only, limited copying and distribution is allowed.

One standard applied to academic fair use is the effect the use has on the potential market. For example, a student can include a cartoon in a PowerPoint presentation without seeking permission from the artist. However, to avoid plagiarism, you still must credit your sources of information.

So, do you now know which of the four scenarios above are plagiarism or copyright violations? Let's review them.

1. You are not in violation because the use of the cartoon is for educational purposes and falls under the academic fair use provision. You must still credit the source, however.
2. You are in violation of copyright laws because you are presenting others' ideas for children's stories as your own and receiving personal economic benefit from them.
3. You are guilty of plagiarism because you copied content from another source and implied it was your own work.
4. Again, because your copying is for a school project, you are not in violation of copyright laws because of the academic fair use provision. However, it's always important to document your sources.

**Before moving on to the Chapter Review:**

- **Watch Replay Video 3.2** .
- Then check your understanding of what you've learned so far.

# check your understanding//

For a quick review to see what you've learned so far, answer the following questions. Visit **pearsonhighered.com/techinaction** to check your answers.

## multiple choice

1. What is the name for a list of links you've visited within a website?
   - **a.** favorites
   - **b.** breadcrumb trail
   - **c.** bookmarks
   - **d.** social bookmarks
2. Which is NOT a component of a search engine?
   - **a.** spider
   - **b.** indexer program
   - **c.** subject directory
   - **d.** search engine software
3. When using the Internet for research, you
   - **a.** can assume that everything you find is accurate and appropriate.
   - **b.** should evaluate sites for bias and relevance.
   - **c.** can assume the author is an authority on the subject matter.
   - **d.** can assume that the links provided on the site are the only additional sources of information.
4. Which of the following is not an Internet protocol?
   - **a.** ARPANET
   - **b.** HTTP
   - **c.** FTP
   - **d.** BitTorrent
5. Country codes are what part of a URL?
   - **a.** sub-top-level domain
   - **b.** top-level domain
   - **c.** path
   - **d.** protocol

## true–false

_______ **1.** A search engine that searches other search engines is called a SuperSearch engine.

_______ **2.** You can share your favorite sites with others through social bookmarking.

## critical thinking

**1. File-Swapping Ethics**

Downloading free music, movies, and other electronic media from the Internet, although illegal, still occurs on sites such as BitTorrent.

- **a.** Do you think you should have the ability to download free music files of your choice? Do you think the musicians who oppose online music sharing have made valid points?
- **b.** Discuss the differences you see between sharing music files online and sharing CDs with your friends.
- **c.** The current price to buy a song online is about $1. Is this a fair price? If not, what price would you consider fair?

**2. The Power of Google**

Google is the largest and most popular search engine on the Internet today. Because of its size and popularity, some people claim that Google has enormous power to influence a web user's search experience solely by its website-ranking processes. What do you think about this potential power? How could it be used in negative or harmful ways?

- **a.** Some websites pay search engines to list them near the top of the results pages. These sponsors therefore get priority placement. What do you think of this policy?
- **b.** What effect (if any) do you think that Google has on website development? For example, do you think website developers intentionally include frequently searched words in their pages so that they will appear in more hits lists?

**Continue**

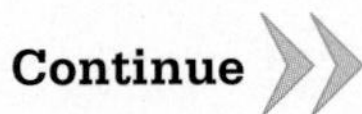

# 3 Chapter Review

## summary//

### The Internet and How It Works

**1. What is the origin of the Internet?**

- The Internet is the largest computer network in the world, connecting millions of computers.
- Government and military officials developed the early Internet as a reliable way to communicate in the event of war. Eventually, scientists and educators used the Internet to exchange research.
- Today, we use the Internet and the web (which is a part of the Internet) to shop, research, communicate, and entertain ourselves.

**2. How does data travel on the Internet?**

- A computer (or other device) connected to the Internet acts as either a client (a computer that asks for information) or a server (a computer that receives the request and returns the information to the client).
- Data travels between clients and servers along a system of communication lines or pathways. The largest and fastest of these pathways form the Internet backbone.
- To ensure that data is sent to the correct computer along the pathways, IP addresses (unique ID numbers) are assigned to all computers connected to the Internet.

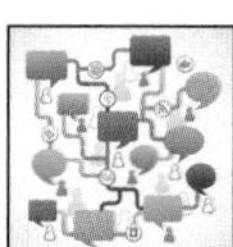

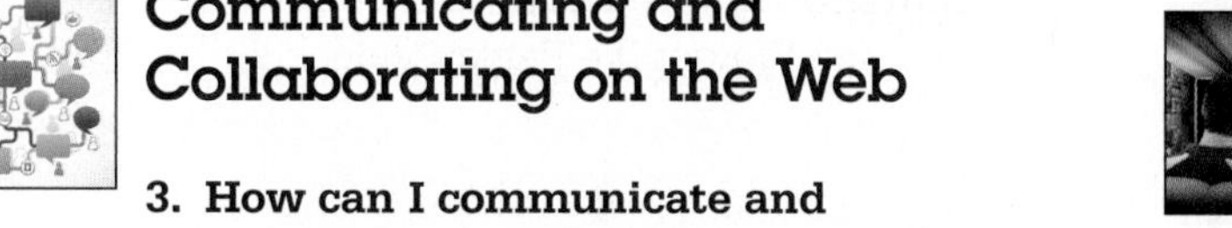

### Communicating and Collaborating on the Web

**3. How can I communicate and collaborate using Web 2.0 technologies?**

- Web 2.0 can be described as the social web, in which the user is also a participant. Before Web 2.0 technologies were in place, we were only able to be passive users of the web.
- Examples of Web 2.0 technologies include social networking, blogs, wikis, podcasts, and webcasts. Social networking enables you to communicate and share information with friends as well as meet and connect with others.
- Blogs are journal entries posted to the web that are generally organized by a topic or area of interest and are publicly available. Generally, one person writes the blog, and others can comment on the journal entries.
- Video logs are personal journals that use video as the primary content in addition to text, images, and audio.
- Wikis are a type of website that allows users to collaborate on content—adding, removing, or editing it.
- Podcasts are audio or video content that is available over the Internet. Users subscribe to receive updates to podcasts.
- Webcasts are broadcasts of audio or video content over the Internet. Most webcasts are distributed in real time, unlike podcasts that are usually prerecorded and made available for download.

**4. How can I communicate using e-mail and instant messaging?**

- Communication was one of the reasons the Internet was developed and is one of the primary uses of the Internet today.
- E-mail allows users to communicate electronically without the parties involved being available at the same time, whereas instant-messaging services are programs that enable you to communicate in real time with others who are online.

### Web Entertainment

**5. What multimedia files are found on the web, and what software is needed to access those files?**

- Multimedia is anything that involves one or more forms of media in addition to text, such as graphics, audio, and video clips.
- Sometimes you need a special software program called a *plug-in* (or *player*) to view and hear multimedia files. Plug-ins are often installed in new computers or are offered free of charge at developer's websites.

## Conducting Business over the Internet: E-Commerce

**6. What is e-commerce, and what online safeguards are available?**

- E-commerce is the business of conducting business online.
- E-commerce includes transactions between businesses (B2B), between consumers (C2C), and between businesses and consumers (B2C).
- Because more business than ever before is conducted online, numerous safeguards have been put in place to ensure that transactions are protected. Some important safeguards to keep in mind include looking for indicators that the website is secure; shopping at well-known, reputable sites; and avoiding making online transactions on public computers.

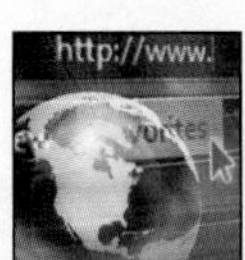


## Accessing and Moving Around the Web

**7. What is a web browser, and what are a URL and its parts?**

- Once you're connected to the Internet, in order to locate, navigate to, and view web pages, you need to install special software called a web browser on your system.
- The most common web browsers are Internet Explorer, Firefox, Google Chrome, and Safari.
- You gain access to a website by typing in its address, called a Uniform Resource Locator (URL).
- A URL is comprised of several parts, including the protocol, the domain, the top-level domain, and paths (or subdirectories).

**8. How can I use hyperlinks and other tools to get around the web?**

- One unique aspect of the web is that you can jump from place to place by clicking on specially formatted pieces of text or images called *hyperlinks*.
- You can also use the Back and Forward buttons, History lists, breadcrumb trails, and Favorites or Bookmarks to navigate the web.
- Favorites, live bookmarks, and social bookmarking help you return to specific web pages without having to type in the URL and help you organize the web content that is most important to you.

## Searching the Web Effectively

**8. How do I search the Internet effectively, and how can I evaluate websites?**

- A search engine is a set of programs that searches the web using specific keywords you wish to query and then returns a list of the websites on which those keywords are found.
- Search engines can be used to search for images, podcasts, and videos in addition to traditional text-based web content.
- A subject directory is a structured outline of websites organized by topic and subtopic. Metasearch engines search other search engines.
- Not all websites are equal, and some are better sources for research than others. To evaluate whether it is appropriate to use a website as a resource, determine whether the author of the site is reputable and whether the site is intended for your particular needs. In addition, make sure that the site content is not biased, the information on the site is current, and all the links on the site are available and appropriate. If multiple sites offer the same content, this is another indication that the information is accurate.

Be sure to check out the companion website for additional materials to help you review and learn, including a Tech Bytes Weekly newsletter—**pearsonhighered.com/techinaction**. And don't forget the Replay Videos.

# key terms//

aggregator **83**
blog (weblog) **83**
Bookmarks **98**
Boolean operators **101**
breadcrumb trail **97**
business-to-business (B2B) **87**
business-to-consumer (B2C) **87**
client **78**
client/server network **78**
consumer-to-consumer (C2C) **87**
domain name **95**
e-commerce (electronic commerce) **87**
e-mail (electronic mail) **79**
e-mail client **80**
Favorites **98**
File Transfer Protocol (FTP) **96**
host **96**
hyperlink **97**
Hypertext Transfer Protocol (HTTP) **96**
instant messaging (IM) **81**
Internet **76**
Internet backbone **78**
Internet Protocol (IP) address **78**
keyword **98**
live bookmark **98**

metasearch engine **100**
multimedia **85**
path (subdirectory) **96**
plug-in (player) **85**
podcast **83**
Really Simple Syndication (RSS) **83**
search engine **100**
secure socket layer **88**
semantic web (Web 3.0) **90**
server **78**
social commerce **87**
social networking **79**
streaming media **85**
subject directory **100**
tagging (social bookmarking) **98**
top-level domain **96**
Uniform Resource Locator (URL) **95**
video log (vlog or video blog) **83**
Web 2.0 **79**
web-based e-mail **80**
web browser (browser) **77**
webcast **84**
web server **96**
website **95**
wiki **81**
World Wide Web (WWW or the web) **77**

## making the transition to . . . next semester//

1. **Plagiarism**

   Policies Does your school have a plagiarism policy?

   a. Search your school's website to find the school's plagiarism policy. What does it say?

   b. How well do you paraphrase? Find some websites that help test or evaluate your paraphrasing skills.

   c. Create an account at WriteCheck. This website checks your written work against content on the web and produces an originality report. Submit at least three different drafts of your work to WriteCheck to check for any intended or unintended cases of plagiarism before submitting your final work for a grade. What were the results?

2. **Searching Beyond Google**

   While Google is probably your first choice among search engines, there are many other very good search engines that are worth knowing about. Conduct searches for inexpensive travel deals for spring break by using the search engines in the following list. Record your results and a summary of the differences among search engines. Would you choose to use any of these search engines again? Why or why not?

   a. Yippy.com

   b. Dogpile.com

   c. Chacha.com

## making the transition to . . . the workplace//

1. **Online Résumé Resources**

   Using a search engine, locate several web resources that offer assistance in writing a résumé. For example, the University of Minnesota (**umn.edu/ohr/careerdev/resources/resume**) has a résumé tutor that guides you as you write your résumé.

   a. What other websites can you find that help you write a résumé?

   b. Do these sites all offer the same services and have the same features?

2. **Evaluating Web 2.0 Content**

   You are aware of the guidelines you should use to evaluate the quality of content on a website, but you find yourself using other kinds of web content such as blogs, wikis, social networking sites, and social bookmarks. Visit **library.albany.edu/usered/eval/evalweb** and review the new guidelines for evaluating web content in the Web 2.0 environment. After reviewing the guidelines, describe the guidelines for evaluating web content at the following sites:

   a. Free research sites such as Google Scholar (**scholar.google.com**)

   b. Document repositories such as California Digital Library (**cdlib.org**)

   c. Blogs and wikis such as TechCrunch (**techcrunch.com**)

d. Social networking sites such as Twitter (**twitter.com**)
e. Social bookmarking sites such as Delicious (**delicious.com**)
f. Multimedia sites such as YouTube (**youtube.com**)

3. **Facebook Privacy and Security**

   You most likely share lots of information on Facebook with your friends and family. You're aware of the privacy and security settings, and may think you have your settings established just right. But the problem is that those settings are complex and change on a regular basis, so reviewing your settings is important to ensure you're not sharing too much. Conduct an Internet search to locate a guide to Facebook privacy that has been published by a reputable source within the past month. (If you're using Google, click on Search tools, click the Any time arrow, and then select Past month.) Go through the guide, and make any necessary changes to your Facebook privacy and security settings. Write a brief report that summarizes the steps in the guide, and note where you had to make changes. End the report by summarizing your thoughts about Facebook's privacy and security settings.

## team time//

# Collaborating with Technology

## Problem

Collaborating on projects with team members is a regular part of business and academia. Many great tools are available that facilitate online collaboration, and it's important to be familiar with them. In this Team Time, each team will create a group report on a specific topic, using online collaboration tools, and compare and rate the tools and the collaboration process.

## Process

Split your group into teams. To appreciate fully the benefits of online collaboration, each team should have at least five or six members. Each group will create a team report on a topic that is approved by your instructor. As part of the report, one group member should record the process the group took to create the report, including a review of the tools used and reflections on the difficulties encountered by the group.

1. Conduct a virtual meeting. Agree on an online meeting and video collaboration tool such as Skype, Google+ Hangouts, ooVoo, or Tinychat and conduct a group chat. In this phase, outline your group project strategy and delegate work responsibilities.
2. Share documents and collaborate online. Your group must create one document that is accessible to every member at all times. Gone are the days of e-mailing parts of documents to a group member who will assemble the parts. Explore document-sharing sites such as Google Docs, Evernote, OneDrive, or Dropbox and collaboratively create your group document. All members are responsible for reviewing the entire document.
3. After the group reports are created, the class should decide which online sharing site (such as Dropbox or OneDrive) will be used so teams can make their reports available to the other teams for comments.

## Conclusion

After all the team group reports have been completed and shared, discuss the following with your class: What is the benefit of using online collaboration technology to create group projects? How did collaboration technologies help or hinder the team process?

# Plagiarism

In this exercise, you'll research and then role-play a complicated ethical situation. The role you play may or may not match your own personal beliefs, but your research and use of logic will enable you to represent whichever view is assigned. An arbitrator will watch and comment on both sides of the arguments, and together the team will agree on an ethical solution.

## Problem

Plagiarism, or portraying another's work as your own, has been around for a long time and extends well beyond the classroom. For example, Nick Simmons, the son of Gene Simmons (from KISS) and a member of A&E's *Family Jewels* reality series, created a comic book series, *Incarnate*. Radical Publishing picked up the series but quickly stopped publication when Internet messages accused the author of copying from other similar series. Similarly, the Australian band Men at Work was cited for copying a melody from "Kookaburra Sits in the Old Gum Tree" for its 1980s hit "Down Under" and owes the owner years of royalties.

## Research Areas to Consider

- Plagiarism violations
- Comic book series *Incarnate*
- Australian band Men at Work
- Plagiarism consequences

## Process

1. Divide the class into teams.
2. Research the areas cited above and devise a scenario in which someone has violated plagiarism rules.
3. Team members should write a summary that provides background information for their character—for example, author, publisher, or arbitrator—and that details their character's behaviors to set the stage for the role-playing event. Then team members should create an outline to use during the role-playing event.
4. Team members should arrange a mutually convenient time to meet for the exchange, using a virtual meeting tool or by meeting in person.
5. Team members should present their case to the class or submit a PowerPoint presentation for review by the rest of the class, along with the summary and resolution they developed.

## Conclusion

As technology becomes ever more prevalent and integrated into our lives, more and more ethical dilemmas will present themselves. Being able to understand and evaluate both sides of an argument, while responding in a personally or socially ethical manner, will be an important skill.

# Technology in Focus

# The History of the Personal Computer

Ever wonder how big the first personal computer was or how much the first laptop weighed? Computers are such an integral part of our lives that we don't often stop to think about how far they've come or where they got their start. In just 40 years, computers have evolved from expensive, huge machines that only corporations could own to small, powerful devices that almost anyone can have. In this Technology in Focus feature, we look at the history of the personal computer.

**FIGURE 1** Timeline of Early Personal Computer Development

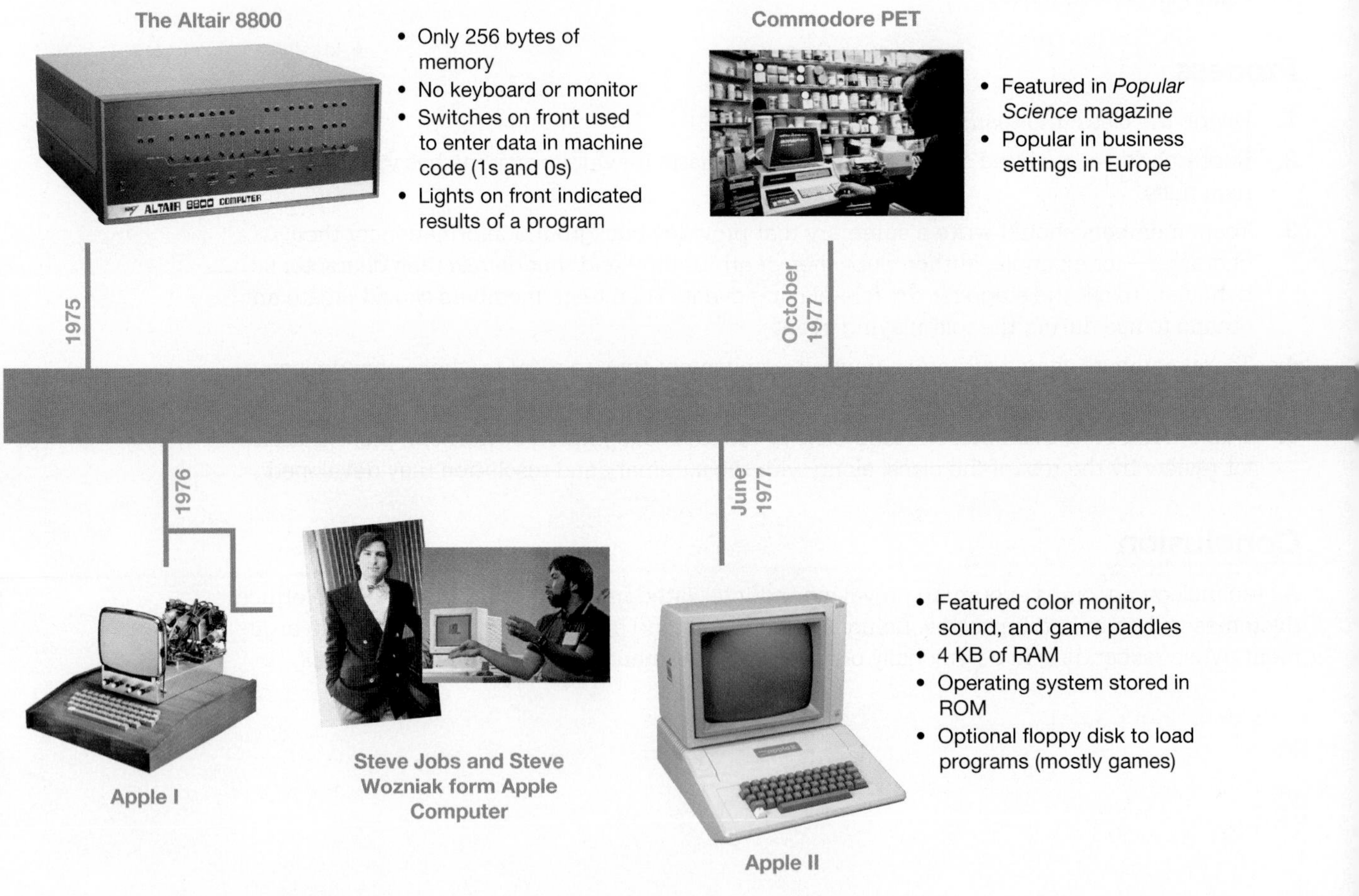

**1975 — The Altair 8800**

- Only 256 bytes of memory
- No keyboard or monitor
- Switches on front used to enter data in machine code (1s and 0s)
- Lights on front indicated results of a program

**1976 — Apple I**

**Steve Jobs and Steve Wozniak form Apple Computer**

**June 1977 — Apple II**

- Featured color monitor, sound, and game paddles
- 4 KB of RAM
- Operating system stored in ROM
- Optional floppy disk to load programs (mostly games)

**October 1977 — Commodore PET**

- Featured in *Popular Science* magazine
- Popular in business settings in Europe

(AP Photo/Heinz Nixdorf Museumsforum; SSPL/The Image Works; Marilyn K. Yee/New York Times Co./Getty Images; AP Photo/Steve Castillo; SSPL/Getty Images; Jerry Mason/Photo Researchers, Inc.)

## The First Personal Computer: The Altair

Our journey through the history of the personal computer starts in 1975. At that time, most people weren't familiar with the mainframes and supercomputers that large corporations and the government owned. With price tags exceeding the cost of buildings, and with few if any practical home uses, these monster machines weren't appealing to or attainable by average Americans.

However, in 1975, the first personal computer, the **Altair 8800** (see Figure 1), was born. At $395 for a do-it-yourself kit or $498 for a fully assembled unit (about $2,162 in today's dollars), the price was reasonable enough that computer fanatics could finally own their own computers.

The Altair was primitive by today's standards—no keyboard, no monitor, and completely not user friendly. Despite its limitations, computer enthusiasts flocked to the machine. Many who bought it had been taught to program, but until that point, they had access only to big, clumsy computers at their jobs. With the Altair, they could create their own programs. Within three months, 4,000 orders were placed for the machine.

The release of the Altair marked the start of the personal computer boom. In fact, two men whose names you might have heard were among the first Altair owners: Bill Gates and Paul Allen were so enamored by the "minicomputer" that they wrote a compiling program (a program that translates user commands into commands the computer can understand) for it. The two later convinced the Altair's developer to buy their program, marking the start of a company called Microsoft. We'll get to that story later. First, let's see what their rivals were up to.

## The Apple I and II

Around the time the Altair was released, **Steve Wozniak**, an employee at Hewlett-Packard, was dabbling with his own computer design. **Steve Jobs**, who was working for computer game manufacturer Atari at the time, liked Wozniak's prototypes and made a few suggestions. Together, the two built a personal computer, the **Apple I**, in Wozniak's garage (see Figure 1) and formed the Apple Computer Company in 1976.

A year later, in 1977, the **Apple II** was born (see Figure 1). The Apple II included a color monitor, sound, and game

**TRS-80**

November 1977

- Introduced by Radio Shack
- Monochrome display
- 4 KB of RAM
- Circuitry hidden under keyboard
- Wildly popular with consumers—sold 10,000 units in the first month

April 1981

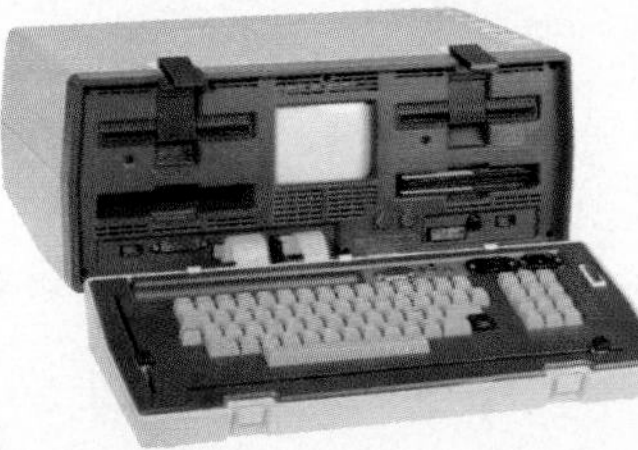

**Osbourne**

- First "portable" computer
- Weighed 24.5 pounds
- 5-inch screen
- 64 kilobytes of RAM
- Two floppy disk drives
- Preinstalled with spreadsheet and word processing software

**IBM PC (5150)**

August 1981

- Marketed to businesses and consumers
- 64 KB to 256 KB of RAM
- Floppy disk drives optional
- Hard disks not supported in early models

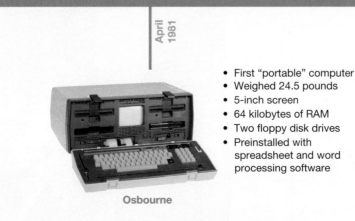

*(Interfoto/Alamy; Interfoto/Alamy; Science & Society Picture Library/Contributor/Getty Images)*

**Why Is It Called "Apple"?**

(Prisma Bildagentur AG/Alamy)

Steve Jobs wanted Apple Computer to be the "perfect" computer company. Having recently worked at an apple orchard, Jobs thought of the apple as the perfect fruit because it was high in nutrients, came in a nice package, and was not easily damaged. Thus, he and Wozniak decided to name their computer company Apple.

paddles. Priced around $1,300 (about $5,011 in today's dollars), one of its biggest innovations was that the operating system was stored in read-only memory (ROM). Previously, the operating system had to be rewritten every time the computer was turned on. The friendly features of the Apple II operating system encouraged less technically oriented computer enthusiasts to write their own programs.

An instant success, the Apple II would eventually include a spreadsheet program, a word processor, and desktop publishing software. These programs gave personal computers like the Apple functions beyond gaming and special programming and led to their popularity.

## Enter the Competition

Around the time Apple was experiencing success with its computers, a number of competitors entered the market. The largest among them were Commodore, Radio Shack, Osborne, and IBM. The **Commodore PET** (see Figure 1) was aimed at the business market and did well in Europe, while Radio Shack's **TRS-80** (see Figure 1) was clearly aimed at the U.S. consumer market. Just one month after its release in 1977, it had sold about 10,000 units.

### The Osborne: The Birth of Portable Computing

The Osborne Company introduced the first portable computer, the **Osborne**, in 1981 (see Figure 1). Although portable, the computer weighed 24.5 pounds. It featured a minuscule 5-inch screen and carried a price tag of $1,795 (about $4,612 today). The Osborne was an overnight success, and its sales quickly reached 10,000 units per month. However, despite the computer's popularity, the Osborne Company eventually closed. Compaq bought the Osborne design and in 1983 produced its own portable computer.

### IBM PCs

By 1980, IBM primarily made mainframe computers, which it sold to large corporations, and hadn't taken the personal computer seriously. In 1981, however, IBM released its first personal computer, the **IBM PC** (see Figure 1). Because many companies were familiar with IBM mainframes, they adopted the IBM PC. The term *PC* soon became the term used to describe all personal computers.

IBM marketed its PC through retail outlets such as Sears to reach home users, and it quickly dominated that market. In January 1983, *Time* magazine, playing on its annual person of the year issue, named the computer "1982 Machine of the Year."

## Other Important Advancements

It wasn't just personal computer hardware that was changing. At the same time, advances in programming languages and operating systems and the influx of application software were leading to more useful and powerful machines.

### The Importance of BASIC

The software industry began in the 1950s with programming languages such as FORTRAN, ALGOL, and COBOL. These languages were used mainly by businesses to create financial, statistical, and engineering programs. However, the 1964 introduction of **Beginners All-Purpose Symbolic Instruction Code (BASIC)** revolutionized the software industry. BASIC was a language that beginning programming students could easily learn. It thus became enormously popular—and the key language of the PC. In fact, **Bill Gates** and **Paul Allen** (see Figure 2) used BASIC to write their program for the Altair. As we noted earlier, this program led to the creation of **Microsoft**, a company that produced computer software.

**FIGURE 2** Bill Gates and Paul Allen are the founders of Microsoft. *(Doug Wilson/CORBIS)*

## The Advent of Operating Systems

Because data on the earliest personal computers was stored on audiocassettes, many programs weren't saved or reused. This meant that programs had to be rewritten whenever they were needed. In 1978, Steve Wozniak designed a 5.25-inch floppy disk drive so that programs could be saved easily and operating systems developed.

Operating systems are written to coordinate with the specific processor chip that controls the computer. At that time, Apples ran on a Motorola chip, whereas PCs (IBMs and so on) ran on an Intel chip. **Disk Operating System (DOS)**, developed by Wozniak and introduced in 1977, was the OS that controlled the first Apple computers. The **Control Program for Microcomputers (CP/M)**, developed by Gary Kildall, was the OS designed for the Intel 8080 chip (the processor for PCs).

In 1980, when IBM was entering the personal computer market, it approached Bill Gates at Microsoft to write an OS program for the IBM PC. Gates recommended that IBM investigate the CP/M OS, but IBM couldn't arrange a meeting with the founder, Gary Kildall. Microsoft reconsidered the opportunity to write an OS program and developed **MS-DOS** for IBM computers. Eventually, virtually all PCs running on the Intel chip used MS-DOS as their OS. Microsoft's reign as one of the dominant players in the personal computer landscape had begun.

## The Software Application Explosion: VisiCalc and Beyond

Because the floppy disk was a convenient way to distribute software, its inclusion in personal computers set off an application software explosion. In 1978, Harvard Business School student Dan Bricklin recognized the potential for a personal computer spreadsheet program. He and his friend Bob Frankston created the program **VisiCalc**, which became an instant success. Finally, ordinary home users could see the benefit of owning a personal computer. More than 100,000 copies of VisiCalc were sold in its first year.

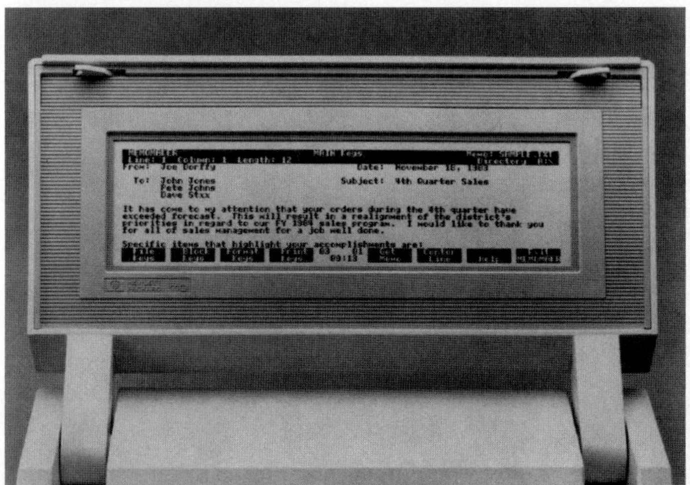

**FIGURE 3** This 1983 Hewlett-Packard computer used an early version of the MS-DOS operating system as well as the Lotus 1-2-3 spreadsheet program. *(Everett Collection / SuperStock)*

**FIGURE 4**

### Application Software Development

| YEAR | APPLICATION |
|---|---|
| 1978 | **VisiCalc:** First electronic spreadsheet application<br>**WordStar:** First word processing application |
| 1980 | **WordPerfect:** Best DOS–based word processor, was eventually sold to Novell and later acquired by Corel |
| 1983 | **Lotus 1-2-3:** Added integrated charting, plotting, and database capabilities to spreadsheet software<br>**Word for MS-DOS:** Introduced in the pages of *PC World* magazine on the first magazine-inserted demo disk |
| 1985 | **Excel:** One of the first spreadsheets to use a graphical user interface<br>**PageMaker:** The first desktop publishing software |

After VisiCalc, other electronic spreadsheet programs entered the market. **Lotus 1-2-3** came on the market in 1983, and **Microsoft Excel** entered the scene in 1985 (see Figure 3). These products became so popular that they eventually put VisiCalc out of business.

Meanwhile, word processing software was gaining a foothold in the industry. Until then, there were separate, dedicated word processing machines; personal computers, it was believed, were for computation and data management only. However, once **WordStar**, the first word processing application, became available for personal computers in 1979, word processing became another important use for the personal computer. Competitors such as **Word for MS-DOS** (the precursor to Microsoft Word) and **WordPerfect** soon entered the market. Figure 4 lists some of the important dates in application software development.

## The Graphical User Interface

Another important advancement in personal computers was the introduction of the **graphical user interface (GUI)**, which allowed users to interact with the computer more easily. Until that time, users had to use complicated command- or menu-driven interfaces. Apple was the first company to take full commercial advantage of the GUI, but the GUI was not invented by a computer company.

### Xerox: Birth of the GUI

In 1972, a few years before Apple launched its first personal computer, photocopier manufacturer **Xerox** was designing

**FIGURE 5** The Alto was the first computer to use a GUI, and it provided the basis for the GUI that Apple used. However, because of marketing problems, the Alto never was sold. *(Josie Lepe/MCT/Newscom)*

**FIGURE 6** The Lisa was the first computer to introduce a GUI to the market. Priced too high, it never gained the popularity it deserved. *(SSPL/The Image Works)*

a personal computer of its own. Named the **Alto** (see Figure 5), the computer included a word processor, based on the What You See Is What You Get (WYSIWYG) principle, that incorporated a file management system with directories and folders. It also had a mouse and could connect to a network. None of the other personal computers of the time had these features. For a variety of reasons, Xerox never sold the Alto commercially. Several years later, it developed the Star Office System, which was based on the Alto. Despite its convenient features, the Star never became popular because no one was willing to pay the $17,000 asking price.

## The Lisa and the Macintosh

Xerox's ideas were ahead of their time, but many of the ideas present in the Alto and Star would soon catch on. In 1983, Apple introduced the **Lisa**, the first successful personal computer brought to market that used a GUI (see Figure 6). Legend has it that Jobs had seen the Alto during a visit to Xerox in 1979 and was influenced by its GUI. He therefore incorporated a similar user interface into the Lisa, providing features such as windows, drop-down menus, icons, a file system with folders and files, and a point-and-click device called a mouse. The only problem with the Lisa was its price. At $9,995 (about $23,441 in today's dollars), few buyers were willing to take the plunge.

A year later, in 1984, Apple introduced the **Macintosh**, shown in Figure 7. The Macintosh was everything the Lisa was and then some, at about a third of the cost. The Macintosh was also the first personal computer to utilize 3.5-inch floppy disks with a hard cover, which were smaller and sturdier than the previous 5.25-inch floppies.

## The Internet Boom

The GUI made it easier for users to work on the computer. The Internet provided another reason for people to buy computers. Now people could conduct research and communicate in a new way. In 1993, the web browser **Mosaic** was introduced. This browser allowed users to view multimedia on the web, causing Internet traffic to increase by nearly 350%.

**FIGURE 7** The Macintosh became one of Apple's best-selling computers, incorporating a GUI along with other innovations such as the 3.5-inch floppy disk drive. *(Ed Kashi/CORBIS)*

Meanwhile, companies discovered the Internet as a means to do business, and computer sales took off. IBM–compatible PCs became the computer system of choice when, in 1995, Microsoft introduced **Internet Explorer**, a browser that integrated web functionality into Microsoft Office applications, and **Windows 95**, the first Microsoft OS designed to be principally a GUI OS.

About a year earlier, in 1994, a team of developers launched the **Netscape** web browser, which soon became a predominant player in browser software. However, pressures from Microsoft became too strong, and in 1998, Netscape announced it would no longer charge for the product and would make the code available to the public.

## Making the Personal Computer Possible: Early Computers

Billions of personal computers have been sold over the past three decades. But the computer is a compilation of parts, each of which is the result of individual inventions. Let's look at some early machines that helped to create the personal computer we know today.

### The Pascalene Calculator and the Jacquard Loom

From the earliest days of humankind, we have been looking for a more systematic way to count and calculate. Thus, the evolution of counting machines led to the development of the computer we know today. The **Pascalene** was the first accurate mechanical calculator. This machine, created by the French mathematician **Blaise Pascal** in 1642, used revolutions of gears, like odometers in cars, to count by tens. The Pascalene could be used to add, subtract, multiply, and divide. The basic design of the Pascalene was so sound that it lived on in mechanical calculators for more than 300 years.

Nearly 200 years later, **Joseph Jacquard** revolutionized the fabric industry by creating a machine that automated the weaving of complex patterns. Although not a counting or calculating machine, the **Jacquard loom** (shown in Figure 8) was significant because it relied on stiff cards with punched holes to automate the weaving process. Much later, this punch-card process would be adopted as a means for computers to record and read data.

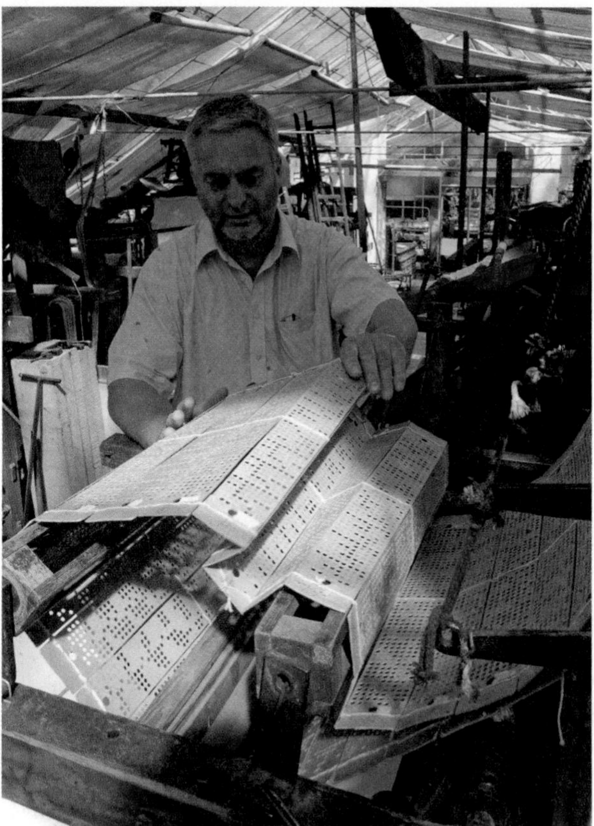

**FIGURE 8** The Jacquard loom used holes punched in stiff cards to make complex designs. This technique would later be used in punch cards that controlled the input and output of data in computers. *(JANEK SKARZYNSKI/AFP/Getty Images/Newscom)*

### Babbage's Engines

In 1834, **Charles Babbage** designed the first automatic calculator, called the **Analytical Engine** (see Figure 9). The machine was actually based on another machine called the **Difference Engine**, which was a huge steam-powered mechanical calculator that Babbage designed to print astronomical tables. Although the Analytical Engine was never developed, Babbage's detailed drawings and descriptions of the machine include components similar to those found in today's computers, including the store (akin to RAM) and the mill (a central processing unit) as well as input and output devices. This invention gave Charles Babbage the title of the "father of computing."

Meanwhile, Ada Lovelace, who was the daughter of poet Lord Byron and a student of mathematics (which was unusual for women of the time), was fascinated with Babbage's Engines. She translated an Italian paper on Babbage's machine and, at the request of Babbage, added her own extensive notes. Her efforts are thought to be the best description of Babbage's Engines.

### The Hollerith Tabulating Machine

In 1890, **Herman Hollerith**, while working for the U.S. Census Bureau, was the first to take Jacquard's punch-card concept and apply it to computing with his **Hollerith Tabulating Machine**. Until that time, census data had been tabulated manually in a long, laborious process. Hollerith's tabulating machine automatically read data that had been punched onto small punch cards, speeding up the tabulation process. Hollerith's machine became so successful that he left the Census Bureau in 1896 to start the Tabulating

FIGURE 9 The Analytical Engine, designed by Charles Babbage, was never fully developed but included components similar to those found in today's computers. *(Chris Howes/Wild Places Photography/Alamy)*

Machine Company. His company later changed its name to International Business Machines, or IBM.

## The Z1 and the Atanasoff–Berry Computer

German inventor **Konrad Zuse** is credited with a number of computing inventions. His first, in 1936, was a mechanical calculator called the **Z1**. The Z1 is thought to be the first computer to include certain features integral to today's systems, such as a control unit and separate memory functions.

In 1939, John Atanasoff, a professor at Iowa State University, and his student Clifford Berry built the first electrically powered digital computer, called the **Atanasoff–Berry Computer (ABC)**, shown in Figure 10. The computer was the first to use vacuum tubes, instead of the mechanical switches used in older computers, to store data. Although revolutionary at the time, the machine weighed 700 pounds, contained a mile of wire, and took about 15 seconds for each calculation. (In comparison, today's personal computers can perform billions of calculations in 15 seconds.) Most importantly, the ABC was the first computer to use the binary system and to have memory that repowered itself upon booting. The design of the ABC would be central to that of future computers.

## The Harvard Mark I

From the late 1930s to the early 1950s, **Howard Aiken** and **Grace Hopper** designed the Mark series of computers used by the U.S. Navy for ballistic and gunnery calculations. Aiken, an electrical engineer and physicist, designed the computer, while Hopper did the programming. The **Harvard Mark I**, finished in 1944, could add, subtract, multiply, and divide.

However, many believe Hopper's greatest contribution to computing was the invention of the **compiler**, a program that translates English-language instructions into computer language. The team was also responsible for a common computer-related expression. Hopper was the first to "debug" a computer when she removed a moth that had flown into the Harvard Mark I and had caused the computer to break down (see Figure 11). After that, problems that caused a computer not to run were called *bugs*.

## The Turing Machine

Meanwhile, in 1936, British mathematician **Alan Turing** created an abstract computer model that could perform logical operations. The **Turing Machine** was not a real machine but rather a hypothetical model that mathematically defined a mechanical procedure (or algorithm). Additionally, Turing's concept described a process by which the machine

FIGURE 10 The Atanasoff–Berry Computer laid the design groundwork for many computers to come. *(AP Photo/Frederick News-Post)*

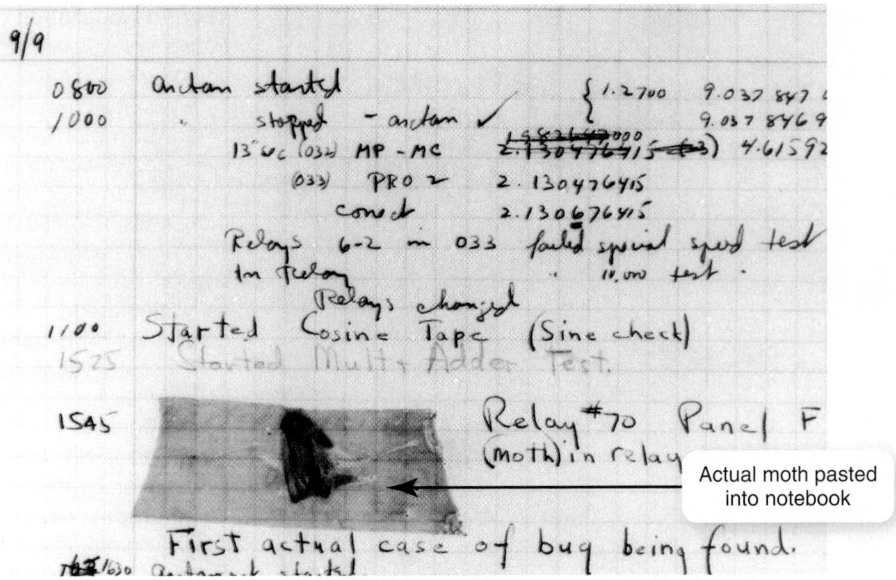


**FIGURE 11** Grace Hopper coined the term *computer bug* when a moth flew into the Harvard Mark I, causing it to break down. *(Naval History and Heritage Command, photo # NH 96566)*

could read, write, or erase symbols written on squares of an infinite paper tape. This concept of an infinite tape that could be read, written to, and erased was the precursor to today's RAM.

## The ENIAC

The **Electronic Numerical Integrator and Computer (ENIAC)**, shown in Figure 12, was another U.S. government–sponsored machine developed to calculate the settings used for weapons. Created by **John W. Mauchly** and **J. Presper Eckert** at the University of Pennsylvania, it was put into operation in 1944. Although the ENIAC is generally thought of as the first successful high-speed electronic digital computer, it was big and clumsy. The ENIAC used nearly 18,000 vacuum tubes and filled approximately 1,800 square feet of floor space. Although inconvenient, the ENIAC served its purpose and remained in use until 1955.

## The UNIVAC

The **Universal Automatic Computer**, or **UNIVAC**, was the first commercially successful electronic digital computer. Completed in 1951, the UNIVAC operated on magnetic tape (see Figure 13), setting it apart from its competitors, which ran on punch cards. The UNIVAC gained notoriety when, in a 1951 publicity stunt, it was used to predict the outcome of the Stevenson–Eisenhower presidential race. After analyzing only 5% of the popular vote, the UNIVAC correctly identified Dwight D. Eisenhower as the victor. After that, UNIVAC soon became a household word. The UNIVAC and computers like it were considered **first-generation computers** and were the last to use vacuum tubes to store data.

## Transistors and Beyond

Only a year after the ENIAC was completed, scientists at the Bell Telephone Laboratories in New Jersey invented

**FIGURE 12** The ENIAC took up an entire room and required several people to manipulate it. *(University of Pennsylvania/AP Images)*

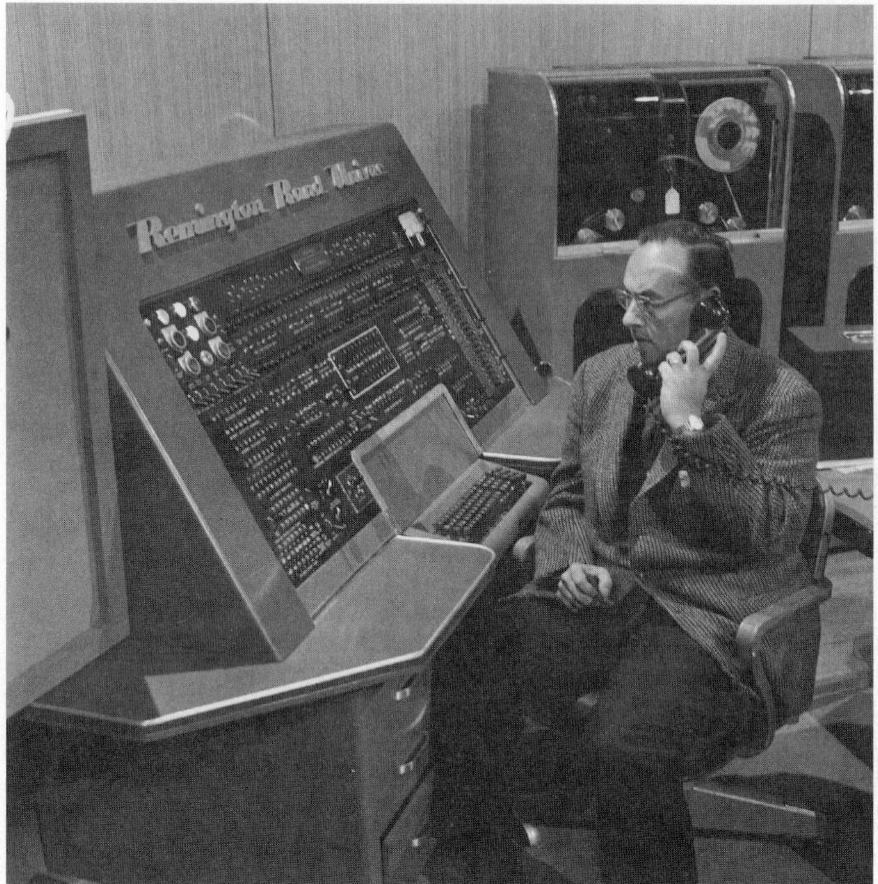


**FIGURE 13** UNIVACs were the first computers to use magnetic tape for data storage. *(CBS/Landov)*

the **transistor**, another means to store data (see Figure 14). The transistor replaced the bulky vacuum tubes of earlier computers and was smaller and more powerful than tubes. It was used in almost everything, from radios to phones. Computers that used transistors were referred to as **second-generation computers**. Still, transistors were limited as to how small they could be made.

A few years later, in 1958, **Jack Kilby**, while working at Texas Instruments, invented the world's first **integrated circuit**, a small chip capable of containing thousands of transistors. This consolidation in design enabled computers to become smaller and lighter. The computers in this early integrated-circuit generation were considered **third-generation computers**.

Other innovations in the computer industry further refined the computer's speed, accuracy, and efficiency. However, none was as significant as the 1971 introduction by the Intel Corporation of the **microprocessor chip**, a small chip containing millions of transistors (see Figure 15). The microprocessor functions as the central processing unit (CPU), or brains, of the computer. Computers that use a microprocessor chip are called **fourth-generation computers**. Over time, Intel and Motorola became the leading manufacturers of microprocessors. Today, the Intel Core i7 is one of Intel's most powerful processors.

As you can see, personal computers have come a long way since the Altair and have a number of inventions and people to thank for their amazing popularity. What will the future bring? ■

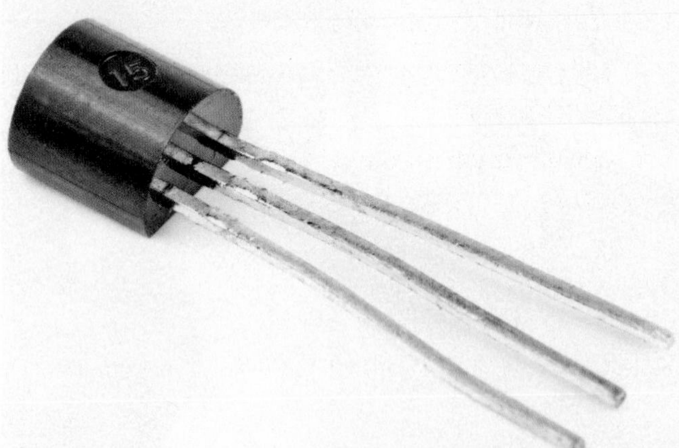

**FIGURE 14** Transistors were 1/10 the size of vacuum tubes, faster, and produced much less heat. *(borissos/Fotolia)*

**FIGURE 15** Today's microprocessors can contain billions of transistors. *(Tudor Voinea/Shutterstock)*

# check your understanding//

For a quick review of what you've learned, answer the following questions. Visit **pearsonhighered.com/techinaction** to check your answers.

## multiple choice

1. What was the name of the first web browser?
   - **a.** Mosaic
   - **b.** Internet Explorer
   - **c.** Netscape
   - **d.** Firefox
2. Which programming language revolutionized the software industry?
   - **a.** ALGOL
   - **b.** BASIC
   - **c.** COBOL
   - **d.** FORTRAN
3. Which invention replaced vacuum tubes in computers?
   - **a.** the integrated circuit
   - **b.** the transistor
   - **c.** the microprocessor chip
   - **d.** magnetic tape
4. Which computer was touted as the first personal computer?
   - **a.** Altair
   - **b.** Commodore PET
   - **c.** Lisa
   - **d.** Osborne
5. What was the importance of the Turing machine to today's computers?
   - **a.** It described a system that was a precursor to today's notebook computer.
   - **b.** It was the first electronic calculator and a precursor to the computer.
   - **c.** It was the first computer to have a monitor.
   - **d.** It described a process to read, write, and erase symbols on a tape and was the precursor to today's RAM.
6. Which computer first stored its operating system in ROM?
   - **a.** Apple I
   - **b.** Apple II
   - **c.** Lisa
   - **d.** Macintosh
7. What was the first spreadsheet application?
   - **a.** Lotus 1-2-3
   - **b.** Excel
   - **c.** WordStar
   - **d.** VisiCalc
8. Which components are a characteristic of second-generation computers?
   - **a.** transistors
   - **b.** vacuum tubes
   - **c.** integrated circuits
   - **d.** microprocessor chips
9. For what is the Atanasoff–Berry computer best known?
   - **a.** It was the first computer used to tabulate U.S. census data.
   - **b.** It was the first computer to use the binary system.
   - **c.** It was the first computer to incorporate a magnetic tape system.
   - **d.** It was the first computer used as a mechanical calculator.
10. Who are the founders of Microsoft?
    - **a.** Paul Allen and Bill Gates
    - **b.** Steve Jobs and Steve Wozniak
    - **c.** Steve Jobs and Bill Gates
    - **d.** Bill Gates and Steve Wozniak

# 4 Application Software: Programs That Let You Work and Play

## Programs That Let You Work

### The Nuts and Bolts of Software

**OBJECTIVES**

1. What's the difference between application software and system software? **(p. 124)**
2. What are the different ways I can access and use software? **(pp. 124–125)**

### Productivity and Business Software

**OBJECTIVES**

3. What kinds of applications are included in productivity software? **(pp. 126–134)**
4. What kinds of software do small and large businesses use? **(pp. 134–135)**

## Programs That Let You Play

### Multimedia and Entertainment Software

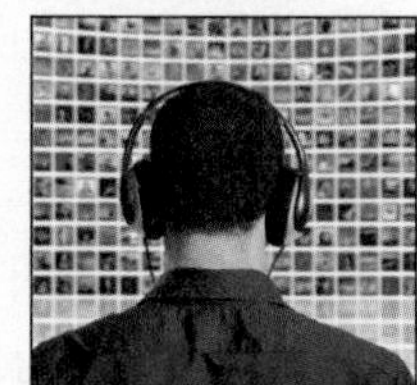

**OBJECTIVE**

5. What different types of multimedia and entertainment software are available? **(pp. 140–145)**

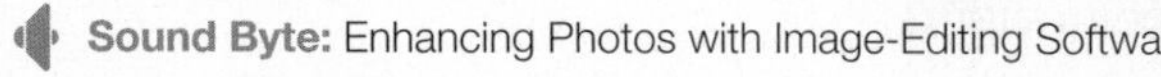

**Sound Byte:** Enhancing Photos with Image-Editing Software

**Active Helpdesk:** Choosing Software

### Managing Your Software

**OBJECTIVES**

6. What's important to know when buying software? **(pp. 146–149)**
7. How do I install and uninstall software? **(pp. 149–150)**

**Active Helpdesk:** Buying and Installing Software

For all media in this chapter go to **pearsonhighered.com/techinaction** or **MyITLab**.

*(Norebbo/Shutterstock; mmaxer/Shutterstock; IKO/Shutterstock; Timo Darco/Fotolia LLC)*

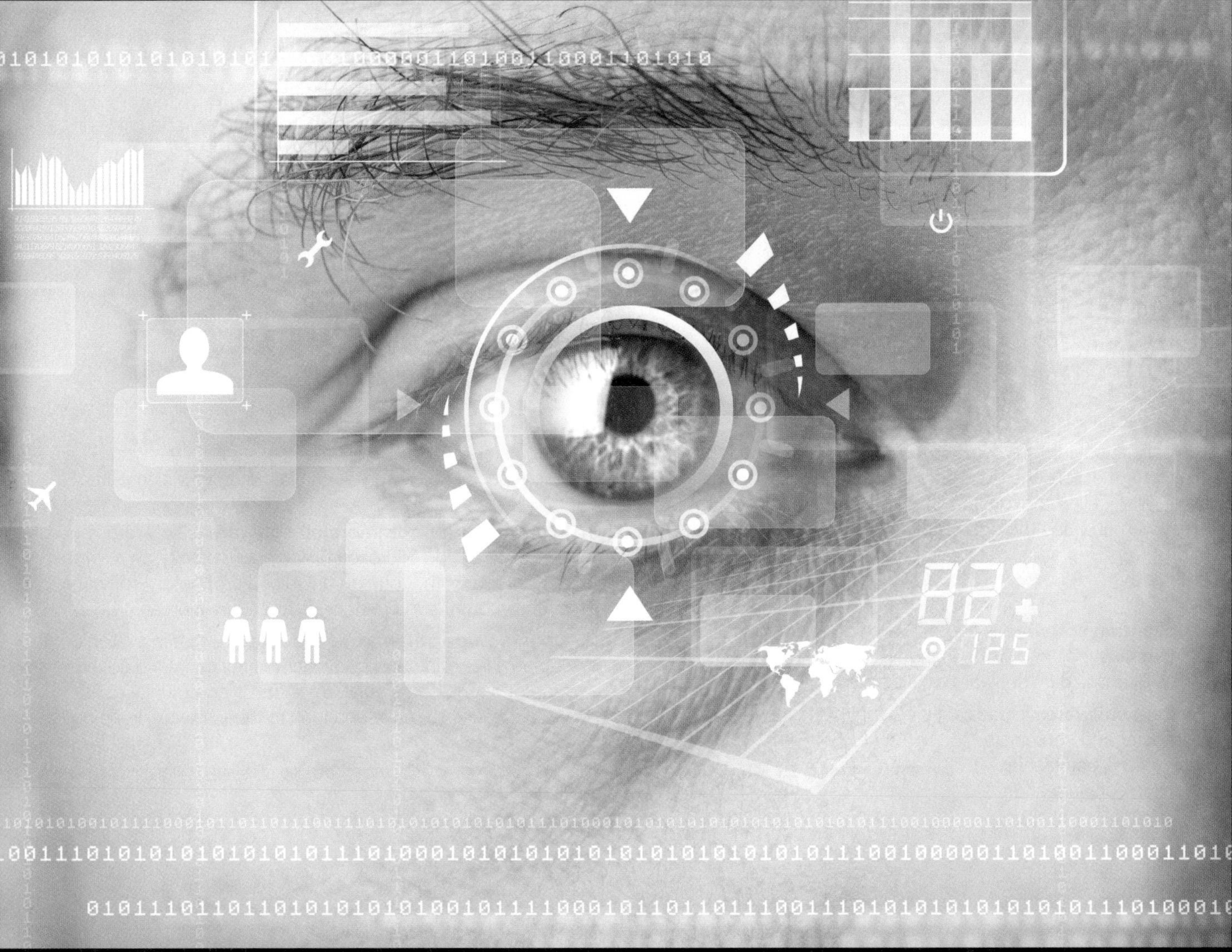

# HOW COOL IS THIS?

Scan here for more info

Ever watch a video on your smartphone only to **fall asleep** or to be interrupted and miss part of it? **Eye-tracking software** has been around for a while. It's been used with desktop computers to help the disabled and in some high-end cars to warn drivers of dozing off. But it has only recently been deployed on some mobile devices. Samsung's Galaxy S4 detects the presence of a user's face through the phone's front camera and then uses that information to **start or stop a video**. If you look away or close your eyes while the video is playing, for example, the **video will pause** until you look back to continue watching. And FocusAssist for iPad from Mindflash is meant to help you **focus and pay attention** during training videos. But these uses are only the tip of the iceberg, and experts agree that eye tracking has the potential to **transform** the way users interact with their mobile devices. With a **blink of an eye**, you could open or close apps, scroll through a webpage, take a picture, and so on. What possibilities do you see this technology presenting? *(© ra2 studio/Fotolia)*

# Programs That Let You Work

A computer without software is like a sandwich without filling. Although a computer's hardware is critical, a computer system does nothing without software. In this section, we'll look at programs created to help you work more effectively and efficiently. First, let's check out some software basics.

## the nuts and bolts of SOFTWARE

Technically speaking, the term **software** refers to a set of instructions that tells the computer what to do. An instruction set, also called a **program**, provides a means for us to interact with and use the computer, even if we lack specialized programming skills. Your computer has two main types of software:

1. **Application software** is the software you use to do tasks at home, school, and work. Figure 4.1 shows the various types of application software we'll discuss in this chapter.
2. **System software** includes software that helps run the computer and coordinate instructions between application software and the computer's hardware devices. System software includes the operating system (such as Windows and OS X) and utility programs (programs in the operating system that help manage system resources). We discuss system software in detail in Chapter 5.

Other types of software, such as web browsers, virus protection, and backup and recovery software, are used every day. We'll discuss these types of software elsewhere in this book.

**What software do I need to install on my computer?** Virtually every new computer comes with software preinstalled, including an operating system and some application software, depending on which computer you buy. If you need to add other software to your system, you'll need either to install the software yourself or to access it from the web. There are two types of software you can install on your computer:

1. **Proprietary (or commercial) software** is software you buy, such as the Microsoft Office applications you're probably familiar with. You can download proprietary software directly from the Internet, or you can buy it on a DVD.
2. **Open source software** is free software that is available with few licensing and copyright restrictions. One advantage of open source software is that a community of users continues to make changes to the software, keeping

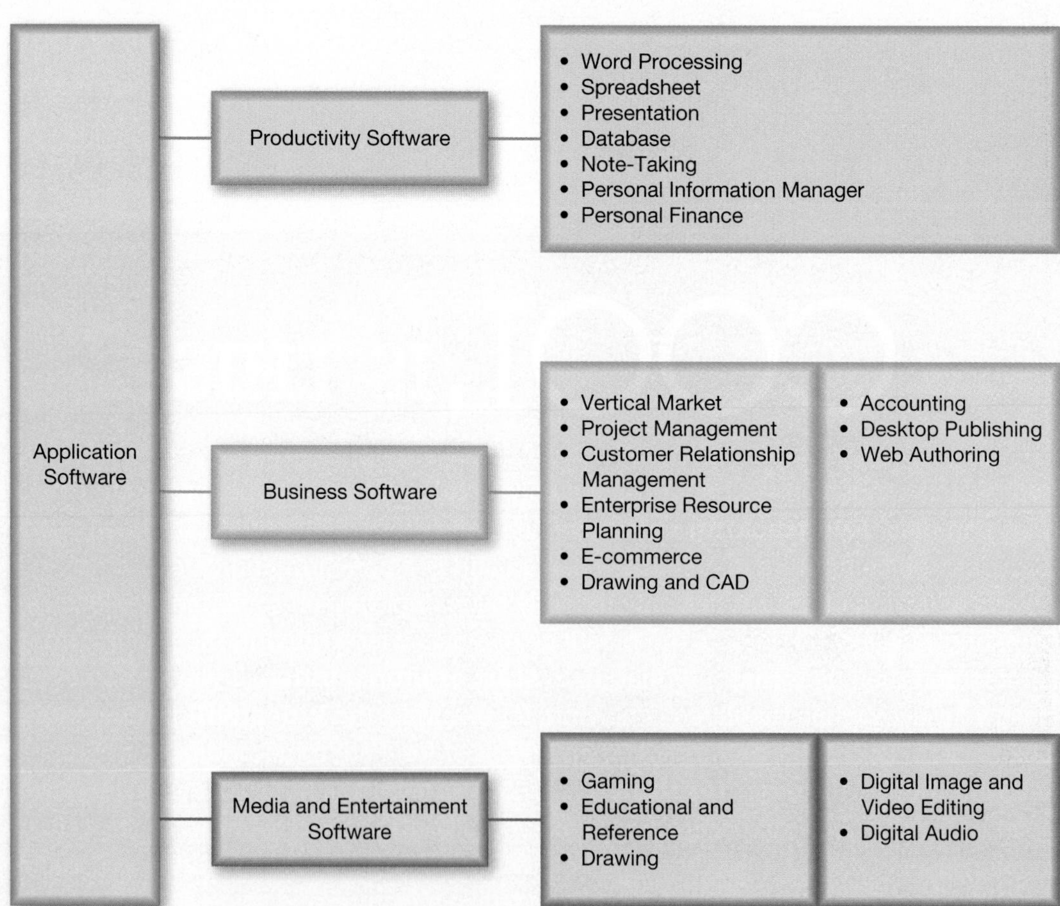

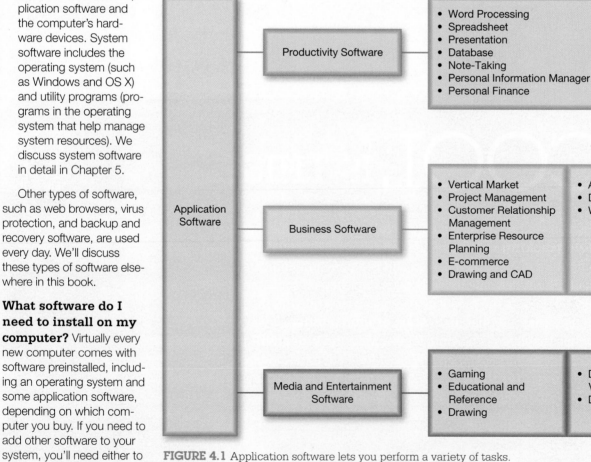

**FIGURE 4.1** Application software lets you perform a variety of tasks.

# trends in IT

## Mobile Commerce: What Have You Bought with Your Phone Lately?

Most people own a mobile device, so it's no surprise that companies regard *mobile commerce* (or m-commerce)—using applications on smartphones and tablets to buy and sell products—as a trend that shouldn't be ignored.

Although mobile commerce hasn't taken over traditional methods of e-commerce just yet, making purchases from mobile devices continues to rise. Some studies indicate that in a few years, the number of mobile online retail transactions in the United States will double and account for nearly a quarter of all e-commerce retail activity. The emergence of tablets and better functioning m-commerce apps has improved the mobile shopping experience. Consider two trends that have facilitated the growing acceptance of m-commerce:

1. *Mobile payments:* Instead of using your credit card or debit card to buy something, some retailers such as Starbucks and Target have mobile apps that enable you to pay for your super macchiato or Jason Wu dress just by showing your smartphone. Mobile wallets, such as Google Wallet and Square Wallet, have been slower to catch on, but industry experts anticipate that mobile wallets will become the primary payment method of the future.
2. *Mobile coupons and barcodes:* Many consumers use mobile device apps to look up information by scanning special quick response (QR) codes (such as the one shown on page 123) on products. Many stores also have virtual store loyalty cards on their apps that let you access coupons, product information, and store discount programs.

Although many mobile device owners feel it's not as safe to use their mobile devices to make purchases, it's just as safe as making purchases with your computer on the web. Time and education will help to relieve those fears.

**FIGURE 4.2** Have you made a payment using your smartphone instead of a credit card yet? *(Dai Sugano/MCT/Newscom)*

it current without needing to wait for periodic updates. However, unlike Microsoft Office and other proprietary applications, open source applications offer little or no formal support. Instead, they're supported from their community of users across websites and newsgroups.

**Can I use software directly from the web?** Another way to obtain software is through **Software as a Service (SaaS)**, in which the vendor hosts the software online and you access and use the software over the Internet without having to install it on your computer. With these **web-based applications**, you can collaborate online with others, avoiding the coordination mess that often occurs when transferring documents via e-mail. Although many web-based applications are not as fully featured as their installable counterparts, most work with files from other applications. ■

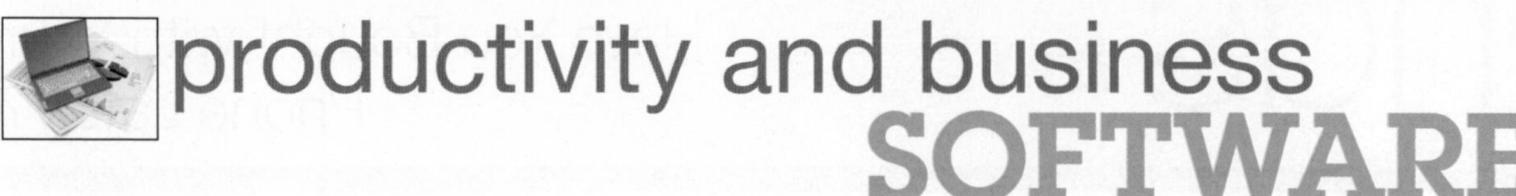

# productivity and business SOFTWARE

One reason computers are invaluable is that they make it easier to complete our daily tasks. **Productivity software** includes programs that let you perform various tasks required at home, school, and business and includes word processing, spreadsheet, presentation, database, and personal information manager programs.

## Bundled Productivity Software

**Is it better to buy software individually or in a bundled package?** For proprietary software, it's cheaper to buy a **software suite** than to buy each program individually. Software suites are available for all types of software. Productivity software suites include:

- *Microsoft Office:* the standard proprietary software suite for Windows. A version is also available for Apple computers.
- *Apache OpenOffice:* an open source productivity suite that provides functionality similar to that of Microsoft Office. You can download the installation file you'll need to run OpenOffice at **openoffice.org**.
- *Apple iWork:* a productivity suite made especially for Apple computers.

Microsoft Office Web Apps and Google Docs are examples of web-based productivity suites. Microsoft Office Web Apps are part of Microsoft Office 365 and are online versions of Word, Excel, PowerPoint, and OneNote but with less functionality than the installed versions. Google Docs (**docs.google.com**) includes word processing, spreadsheet, and presentation functionality, as well as forms and drawing applications. If you're looking for basic productivity software that you can access from any computer, Google Docs is sufficient. Figure 4.3 lists examples of productivity suites, along with the individual applications each suite offers.

The individual programs within a suite work well together because they share common features, toolbars, and menus. For example, when using applications in the Microsoft Office suite, you can seamlessly create a spreadsheet in Excel, import it into Access, and then link an Access query to a Word document. It would be much harder to do the same thing using different applications from a variety of software developers.

## Word Processing Software

**What are the most common word processing applications?** You've probably used **word processing software** to create and edit documents such as research papers, class notes, and résumés. Microsoft Word is the most popular word processing program that you can buy and install on your computer. If you're looking for a more affordable alternative, you might want to try an open source alternative such as Writer, a word processing program from the Apache OpenOffice suite (**openoffice.org**). Writer is similar to Microsoft Word. When saving a document in Writer, the default file format has an OpenDocument file (.odt) extension. However, by using

**FIGURE 4.3**

**Productivity Software Suites**

| PRODUCTIVITY SUITE | WORD PROCESSING | SPREADSHEET | PRESENTATION | DATABASE | NOTE-TAKING | PIM/E-MAIL |
|---|---|---|---|---|---|---|
| **Installed: Proprietary** | | | | | | |
| Microsoft Office | Word | Excel | PowerPoint | Access | OneNote | Outlook |
| Apple iWork | Pages | Numbers | Keynote | | | |
| **Installed: Open Source** | | | | | | |
| Apache OpenOffice | Writer | Calc | Impress | Base | | |
| **Web-Based** | | | | | | |
| Microsoft Office 365 | Word | Excel | PowerPoint | | OneNote | Outlook |
| Google Docs | Documents | Spreadsheets | Presentation | | | Gmail |
| Zoho | Writer | Sheet, Books | Show | Creator | Notebook | |
| ThinkFree | Document | Spreadsheet | Presentation | | Note | |

the Save As command, you can save files in other formats, such as .doc for Word.

**What special tools do word processing programs have that I might not know about?** You're probably familiar with the basic tools of word processing software, such as the spelling and grammar checking tools, the thesaurus, and the find-and-replace tool. But did you know you can translate words or phrases into another language or automatically correct your spelling as you type? You also can automatically summarize key points in a text document, add bibliographical references, and include illustrations with different picture styles.

**How can I make my documents look more professional?** With word processing software, you can easily change fonts, font styles, and sizes; add colors to text; adjust margins; add borders to portions of text or to entire pages; insert bulleted and numbered lists; and organize your text into columns. You also can insert pictures from your own files or from a gallery of images and graphics, such as clip art and SmartArt, which are included with the software.

You also can enhance the look of your document by creating an interesting background or by adding a "theme" of coordinated colors and styles. Figure 4.4 shows what a document can look like when you apply formatting options found in many word processing applications. (Note that although many of the open source and web-based applications have great formatting capabilities, most are not as fully featured as the installed version of Microsoft Word.)

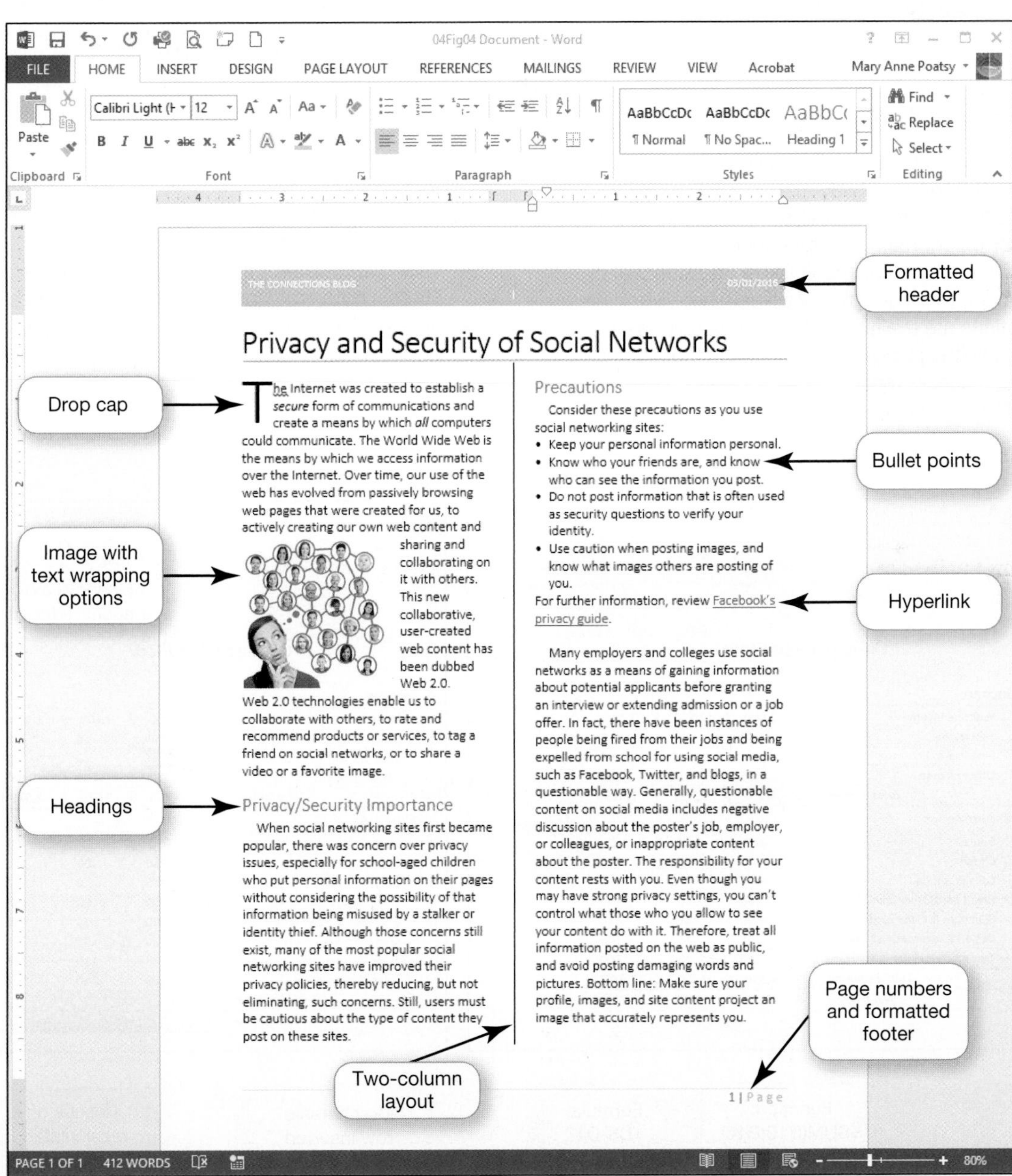


**FIGURE 4.4** Nearly every word processing application has formatting features that let you give your documents a professional look. *(Robert Kneschke/Fotolia)*

# BITS&BYTES

## Finding the Right Software

There are millions of applications, and new ones are developed and released every day. How can you find the right ones to meet your needs? What are the cool new applications or the ones that just don't work? The editors and analysts at *PC Magazine* have put together AppScout (**appscout.pcmag.com**), a site that provides reviews of the best software, websites, and web applications. Next time you're looking for a new application, check out AppScout.

## Spreadsheet Software

**Why would I use spreadsheet software?**
**Spreadsheet software** is software that lets you make calculations and perform numerical analyses. You can use it to track your expenses or create a simple budget, as shown in Figure 4.5a, for example. Microsoft Excel and Apache OpenOffice Calc are two examples of spreadsheet software. (Web-based options are available within the Google Docs and Office Web Apps suites.) One benefit of spreadsheet software is that it can automatically recalculate all formulas and functions in a spreadsheet when values for some of the inputs change. For example, as shown in Figure 4.5b, you can insert an additional row in your budget ("Membership") and change a value (for September Financial aid), and the results for "Total Expenses" and "Net Income" recalculate automatically.

Because automatic recalculation lets you immediately see the effects different options have on your spreadsheet, you can quickly test different assumptions. This is called *what-if analysis*. Look again at Figure 4.5b and ask, "If I don't get as much financial aid next semester, what impact will that have on my total budget?" The recalculated cells in rows 18 and 19 help answer your question. In addition to financial analysis, many spreadsheet applications have limited database capabilities to sort, filter, and group data.

**How do I use spreadsheet software?** The basic element in a spreadsheet program is the *worksheet,* which is a grid consisting of columns and rows. As shown in Figure 4.5a, the columns and rows form individual boxes called *cells*. Each cell can be identified according to its column and row position. For example, a cell in column A, row 1 is referred to as cell A1. You can enter several types of data into a cell:

- *Text:* Any combination of letters, numbers, symbols, and spaces. Text is often used as labels to identify the contents of a worksheet or chart.
- *Values and Dates:* Numerical data that represents a quantity or a date/time and is often the basis for calculations.
- *Formulas:* Equations that use addition, subtraction, multiplication, and division operators, as well as values and cell references. For example, in Figure 4.5a, you would use the formula =D8-D17 to calculate net income for November.

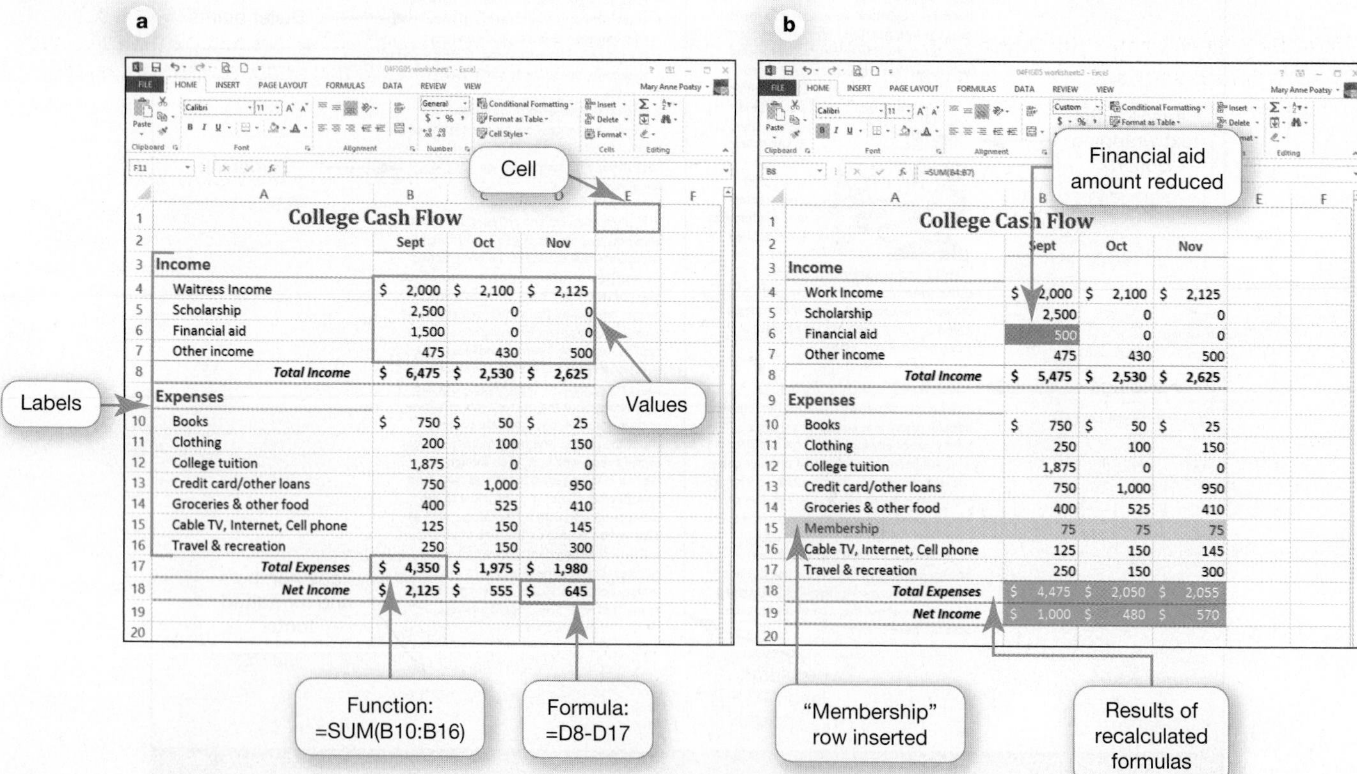


**FIGURE 4.5** Spreadsheet software lets you easily calculate and manipulate numerical data with the use of built-in formulas.

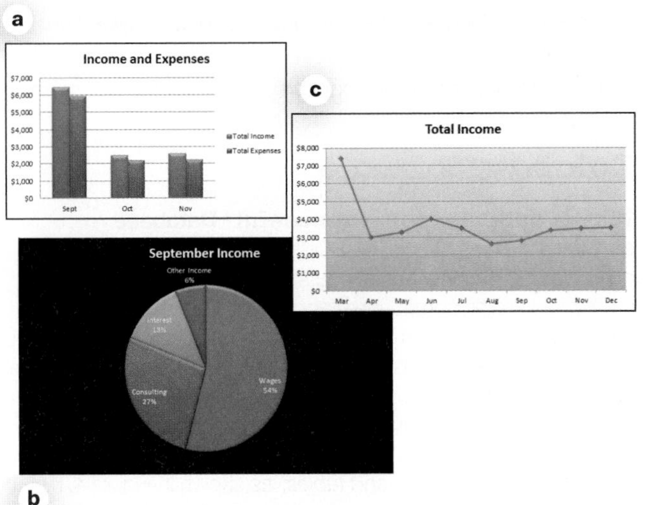


**FIGURE 4.6** (a) Column charts show comparisons. (b) Pie charts show how parts contribute to the whole. (c) Line charts show trends over time.

- *Functions:* Formulas that are preprogrammed into the spreadsheet software. Functions help you with calculations ranging from the simple (such as adding groups of numbers) to the complex (such as determining monthly loan payments), without requiring you to know the exact formula. In Figure 4.5a, to calculate the total of all expenses for September, you could use the built-in addition function, which would look like this: =SUM(B10:B16).

**What kinds of graphs and charts can I create with spreadsheet software?** As shown in Figure 4.6, most spreadsheet applications let you create a variety of charts,

| | | | 1 Year History | | |
|---|---|---|---|---|---|
| | | Current | Trend | High | Low |
| Microsoft | $ | 25.79 | | 30.54 | 20.26 |
| Apple | $ | 255.96 | | 261.09 | 125.83 |
| Intel | $ | 20.95 | | 22.84 | 15.72 |
| Hewlett Packard | $ | 46.05 | | 53.15 | 34.35 |
| Dell | $ | 13.24 | | 16.2 | 11.57 |

Sparklines

**FIGURE 4.7** Sparklines are tiny graphs that fit into a single cell.

including basic column charts, pie charts, and line charts, with or without 3-D effects. In addition to these basic charts, you can make stock charts (for investment analysis) and scatter charts (for statistical analysis) or create custom charts. A newer feature in Excel is *sparklines*—small charts that fit into a single cell and make it easy to show data trends (see Figure 4.7).

## Presentation Software

**How can software help with my presentations?** You've no doubt sat through presentations where the speaker used **presentation software** such as Microsoft PowerPoint (see Figure 4.8) to create a slide show. Because these applications are simple to use, you can produce high-quality presentations without a lot of training. With some of the capabilities in PowerPoint, you can embed online videos, add effects, and even trim video clips without the need for a separate video-editing program.

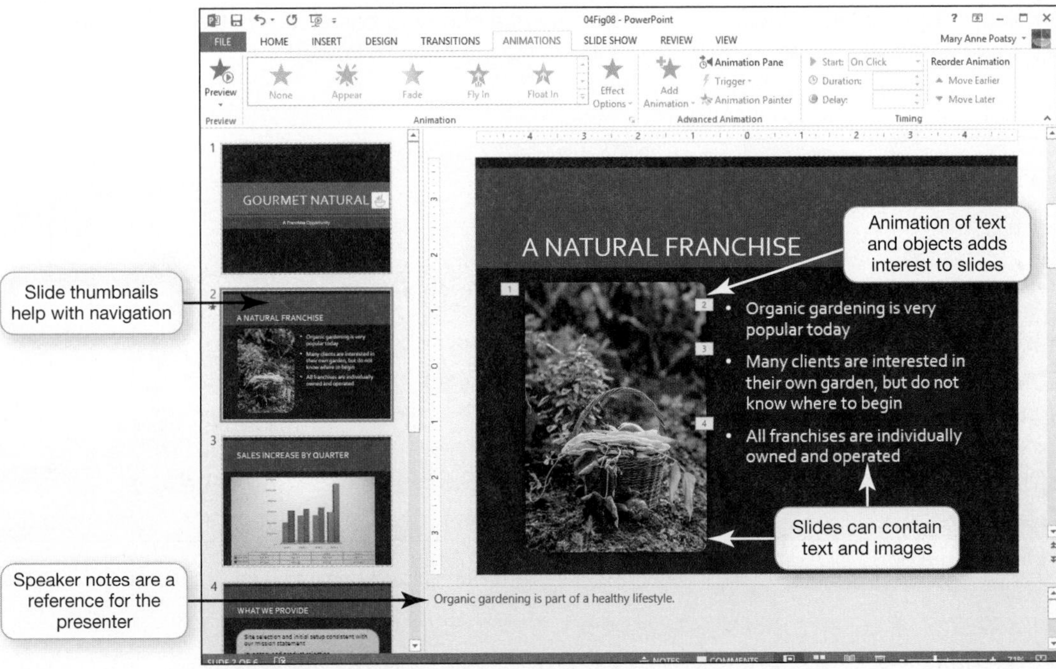


**FIGURE 4.8** You can use Microsoft PowerPoint to create dynamic presentations. *(© DIA/Fotolia)*

**What are some tips to make a great presentation?** Undoubtedly, you've seen at least one bad presentation. Don't make your audience suffer through another one! Here are some tips for designing good presentations:

- *Be careful with color:* Choose dark text on a light background or light text on a dark background. Avoid using clashing text and background colors.
- *Use bullets for key points:* Limit the number to four to six bulleted points per slide. Avoid full sentences and paragraphs.
- *Use images:* Images can convey a thought or illustrate a point. Make sure any text over an image can be read easily.
- *Consider font size and style:* Keep the font size large enough to read from the back of the room. Avoid script or fancy font styles. Use only one or two font styles per presentation.
- *Keep animations and/or background audio to a minimum:* They can be distracting.

## Database Software

**Why is database software useful? Database software** such as Oracle, MySQL, and Microsoft Access are powerful applications that let you store and organize data. As mentioned earlier, spreadsheet applications are easy to use for simple tasks such as sorting, filtering, and organizing data. However, you need to use a more robust, fully featured database application to manage larger and more complicated data that is organized in more than one table; to group, sort, and retrieve data; and to generate reports. Traditional databases are organized into *fields, records,* and *tables,* as shown in Figure 4.10.

# BITS&BYTES

## Alternatives to PowerPoint

PowerPoint is generally the go-to application for creating presentation visual aids. But there are several applications that offer a compelling alternative to PowerPoint that are worth a closer look. One cool alternative is Prezi (**prezi.com**), a web-based program that uses an innovative way to produce presentations. Rather than using a set of slides, Prezi uses a large canvas in which you connect ideas. By using the zoom and navigation features, you can move over the canvas, focusing on individual aspects, then zoom in on the finer details and zoom out to see the bigger concept. You can add videos as well as rotate the canvas for added visual interest.

Since images often make the presentation, consider using HaikuDeck (**www.haikudeck.com**). This app has search tools that match your slide content to a wealth of free art to illustrate your presentations. PowToon (**www.powtoon.com**) provides a library of cartoon-like characters that are easily animated to give your presentations more of a "storytelling" aspect rather than fact delivery. PowToon can be converted to video clips and then displayed on the web. Apache OpenOffice Impress and Zoho Show (**www.zoho.com**) are good open source and web-based alternatives, respectively, and are fairly similar to PowerPoint.

a

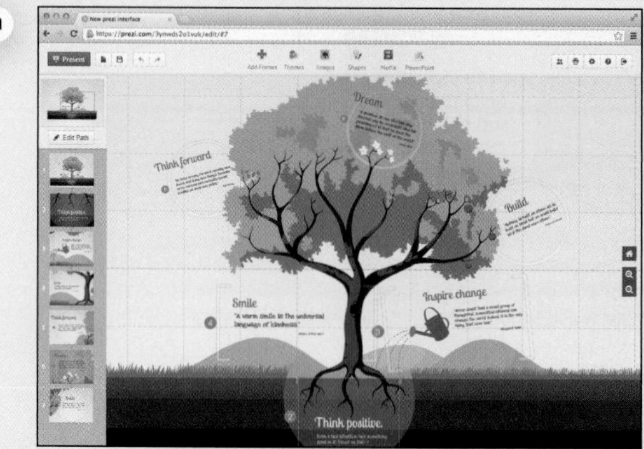


b

**FIGURE 4.9** (a) Prezi and (b) PowToon are alternatives to Microsoft PowerPoint for making interesting and distinct presentations. *(Courtesy of Prezi, Inc.; Courtesy of Powtoon)*

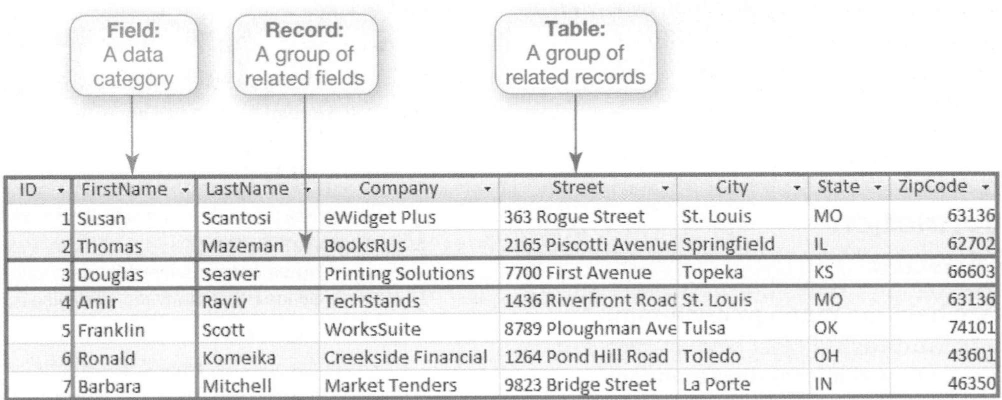


| ID | FirstName | LastName | Company | Street | City | State | ZipCode |
|---|---|---|---|---|---|---|---|
| 1 | Susan | Scantosi | eWidget Plus | 363 Rogue Street | St. Louis | MO | 63136 |
| 2 | Thomas | Mazeman | BooksRUs | 2165 Piscotti Avenue | Springfield | IL | 62702 |
| 3 | Douglas | Seaver | Printing Solutions | 7700 First Avenue | Topeka | KS | 66603 |
| 4 | Amir | Raviv | TechStands | 1436 Riverfront Road | St. Louis | MO | 63136 |
| 5 | Franklin | Scott | WorksSuite | 8789 Ploughman Ave | Tulsa | OK | 74101 |
| 6 | Ronald | Komeika | Creekside Financial | 1264 Pond Hill Road | Toledo | OH | 43601 |
| 7 | Barbara | Mitchell | Market Tenders | 9823 Bridge Street | La Porte | IN | 46350 |

**FIGURE 4.10** In databases, information is organized into fields, records, and tables.

**How do businesses use database software?** Businesses like Amazon, iTunes, Craigslist, and Pandora all rely on databases to keep track of products, clients, invoices, and personnel information. Often, some of that information is available to a home computer user. For example, at Amazon, you can access the history of all the purchases you've ever made on the site. FedEx, UPS, and other shipping companies also let you search their online databases for tracking numbers, allowing you to get instant information on the status of your packages.

## Note-Taking Software

**Is there software to help me take notes?** Microsoft OneNote is a popular note-taking and organizational tool you can use for research, brainstorming, and collaboration, as well as just organizing random bits of information. Using OneNote, you can organize your notes into tabbed sections (see Figure 4.11). In addition, you can access your OneNote notes from other Microsoft Office applications. For example, if you're writing a research paper in Word, click the OneNote icon in the Word ribbon to open OneNote, where you can add your notes—perhaps a reference to a website where you found some interesting research. Later, if you open OneNote and click on that reference, it will bring you to the exact spot in the Word document where you made the reference.

You can also add audio or video recordings of lectures to OneNote, and you can search for a term across all the digital notebooks you created during the semester to find common ideas such as key points that might appear on a test. There is also a OneNote app for the iPhone and iPad.

Several very good and functional free and online note-taking options are also available to help you take notes or to just jot down a quick reminder. Evernote (**evernote.com**), for example, lets you take notes via

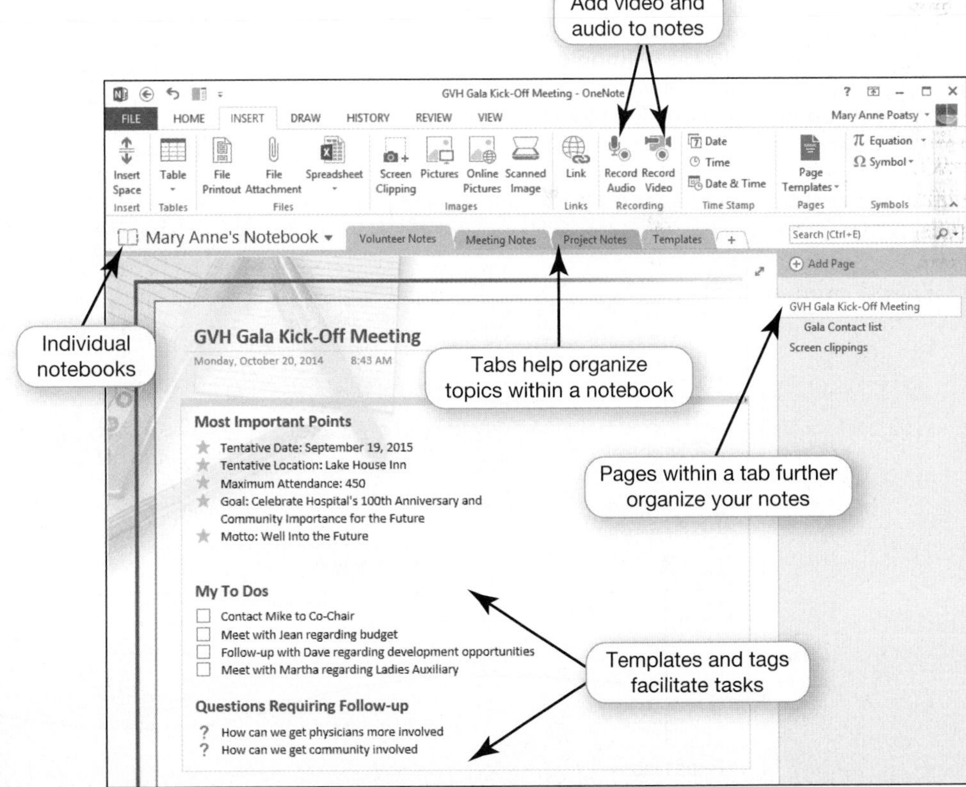


**FIGURE 4.11** Microsoft OneNote is a great way to collect and organize notes and other information. The files are readily searchable and easy to share.

the web, your phone, or your computer and then sync your notes between your devices. You can then share your notes with other Evernote users for easy collaboration. Figure 4.12 lists some popular alternative note-taking applications.

## Personal Information Manager Software

**How can software help me manage my e-mail, time, contact lists, and tasks?** Most productivity suites contain some form of **personal information manager (PIM) software** to help you manage e-mail, contacts, calendars, and tasks in one place. Microsoft Outlook (see Figure 4.13) is the most widely used PIM program. If you share a network at home or at work and are using the same PIM software as others on a common network, a PIM program simplifies sharing calendars and scheduling meetings.

Many web-based e-mail clients, such as Yahoo! and Google, also include coordinating calendar and contacts similar to Microsoft Outlook. Yahoo! includes Notepad for jotting down notes and tasks. Google's calendar and contacts sync with Outlook so you can access your Outlook calendar information by logging into Google. This gives you access to your schedule anywhere you have access to a computer and an Internet connection.

There are a wide variety of other to-do lists and simple organizers that work with all your mobile and computing devices. For example, Toodledo (**toodledo.com**) is a free program that coordinates well with Microsoft Outlook, and OmniFocus (**omnifocus.com**) is a more full-featured option for Mac devices.

FIGURE 4.12

### Beyond Microsoft OneNote: Alternative Note-Taking Applications

**Evernote (www.evernote.com)**

- Web-based
- Notes can be shared for easy collaboration
- Syncs notes between all devices

**Springpad (www.springpadit.com)**

- Automatically categorizes notes based on your categories
- Links with Facebook

**Simplenote (www.simplenoteapp.com)**

- Web-based, open source
- Notes organized by tags
- Mobile apps available

**Noteability (www.gingerlabs.com)**

- PDF annotations
- Advanced word processing
- Linked audio recordings to notes
- Auto-sync notes between devices

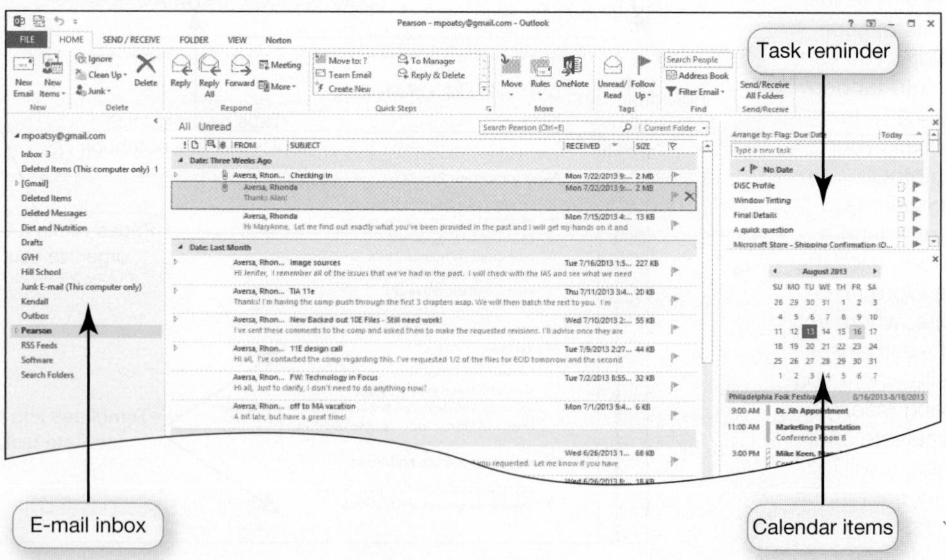


FIGURE 4.13 Microsoft Outlook includes common PIM features, such as a summary of appointments, a list of tasks, and e-mail messages.

# BITS&BYTES

## Productivity Software Tips and Tricks

Looking for tips on how to make better use of your productivity software? Some websites send subscribers periodic e-mails full of tips, tricks, and shortcuts for their favorite software programs:

- Microsoft's website includes many tips and tricks for its Office applications (**office.microsoft.com**).
- MakeTechEasier (**maketecheasier.com**) has tidbits for a variety of applications, including Windows and Mac products, Apache OpenOffice, and cellphone applications.
- GCFLearnFree.org (**gcflearnfree.org**) offers free instructional tutorials on a variety of technology topics, including Microsoft Office applications.
- You can also find tips as videos online. To take any videos from YouTube, TED, and other websites on the road with you for future off-line reference, check out TubeSock (**stinkbot.com**) to download, convert, and copy videos to your personal media player.

## Microsoft Office Productivity Software Features

**What tools can help me work more efficiently with productivity software?** Whether you're working on a word processing document, spreadsheet, database, or slide presentation, you can make use of several tools to increase your efficiency:

- A **wizard** walks you through the steps necessary to complete a complicated task. At each step, the wizard asks you questions. Based on your responses, the wizard helps you complete that portion of the task. When you install software, you're often guided by a wizard.
- A **template** is a predesigned form. Templates are included in many productivity applications. They provide the basic structure for a particular kind of document, spreadsheet, or presentation. Templates can include specific page layout designs, formatting and styles relevant to that particular document, and automated tasks (macros).
- A **macro** is a small program that groups a series of commands so that they will run as a single command. Macros are best used to automate a routine task or a complex series of commands that must be run frequently. For example, a teacher may write a macro to sort the grades in her grade book in descending order and to highlight grades that add up to less than a C average. Every time she adds the results of an assignment or a test, she can set up the macro to run through this series of steps.

## Personal Financial Software

**How can I use software to keep track of my finances? Financial planning software** helps you manage your daily finances. Financial planning programs include electronic checkbook registers and automatic bill payment tools. With these features, you can make recurring monthly payments, such as rent or student loans, with automatically scheduled online payments. The software records all transactions, including online payments, in the checkbook register. In addition, you can assign categories to each transaction and then use these categories to create budgets and analyze your spending patterns.

Intuit's installed and web-based products, Quicken and Mint (**mint.com**; see Figure 4.14), respectively, are the market leaders in financial planning software. Both are great at tracking and analyzing your spending habits and at offering advice on how to better manage your finances. With either, you also can track your investment portfolio. With Mint, you can monitor and update your finances from any computer with a private and secure setting. You can also access Mint on a smartphone and tablet, so your information is conveniently accessible. Mint also provides access to a network of other users with whom to exchange tips and advice.

**What software can I use to prepare my taxes? Tax preparation software**, such as Intuit TurboTax and H&R Block At Home, lets you prepare your state and federal taxes on your own instead of hiring a professional. Both programs offer a complete set of tax forms and instructions, as well as videos that contain expert advice on how to complete each form. Each company also offers free web-based versions of federal forms and instructions. In addition, error-checking features are built into the programs to catch mistakes. TurboTax

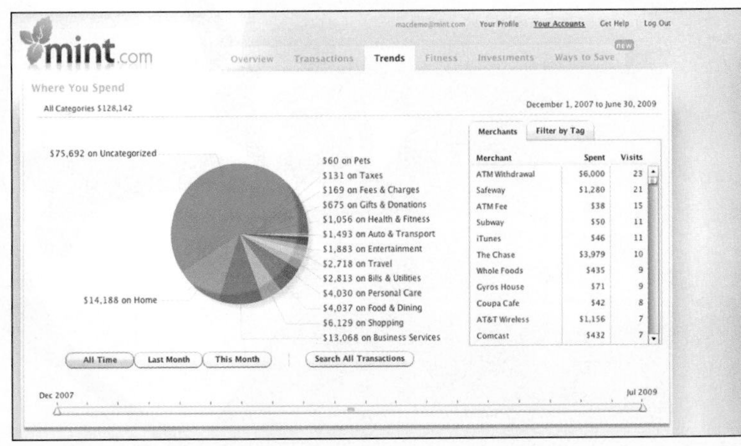


**FIGURE 4.14** Mint (**mint.com**) is an online financial management tool. An extensive online community provides helpful tips and discussions with other people in similar situations. *(Reprinted with permission © Intuit Inc. All rights reserved.)*

# ethics in IT

## Can I Borrow Software That I Don't Own?

As noted in the chapter, when you purchase software, you're purchasing a license to use it rather than purchasing the actual software. That license tells you how many times you can install the software, so it is important to read it. If you make more copies of the software than the license permits, you're participating in **software piracy** (see Figure 4.15). Historically, the most common way software has been pirated has been by borrowing installation CDs from others and installing the software on other computers. Larger-scale illegal duplication and distribution by counterfeiters are quite common as well. In addition, the Internet provides various ways to copy and distribute pirated software illegally.

Is it really a big deal to copy a program or two? As reported by the Business Software Alliance, nearly half of all software used is pirated. Not only is pirating software unethical and illegal, the practice has financial impacts on all software consumers. The financial loss to the software industry was estimated to be over $63 billion for 2012. This loss decreases the amount of money available for further software research and development, while increasing the up-front costs to legitimate consumers.

**FIGURE 4.15** Making more copies than the software license permits is pirating and is illegal. *(Igor Prole/Lepro/iStockphoto)*

To determine whether you have a pirated copy of software installed on your computer, conduct a software audit. The Business Software Alliance website (**bsa.org**) has several free third-party software audit tools that help you identify and track software installed on your computer and networks. These programs check the serial numbers of the software installed on your computer against software manufacturer databases of officially licensed copies and known fraudulent copies. Any suspicious software installations are flagged for your attention.

As of yet, there's no such thing as an official software police force, but if you're caught with pirated software, severe penalties do exist. A company or individual can pay up to $150,000 for each software title copied. In addition, you can be criminally prosecuted for copyright infringement, which carries a fine of up to $250,000, a five-year jail sentence, or both.

Efforts to stop groups involved with counterfeit software are in full force. Software manufacturers also are becoming more aggressive in programming mechanisms into software to prevent illegal installations. For instance, with many Microsoft products, installation requires you to activate the serial number of your software with a database maintained at Microsoft. This is different from the traditional "registration" that enrolled you voluntarily and allowed you to be notified of product updates. Failure to activate your serial number or attempting to activate a serial number used previously results in the software going into a "reduced functionality mode" after the 50th time you use it. Therefore, without activation or after activating a used serial number, you would not be able to save documents in Office.

can also run a check for audit alerts, file your return electronically, and offer financial planning guidance to help you plan and manage your financial resources effectively in the following year (see Figure 4.16).

Some financial planning applications also coordinate with tax preparation software. Both Quicken and Mint, for example, integrate seamlessly with TurboTax, so you never have to go through your debit card statements and bills to find tax deductions, tax-related income, or expenses. Many banks and credit card companies also offer online services that download a detailed monthly statement into Quicken and Mint. Remember, however, that the tax code changes annually, so you must obtain an updated version of the software each year.

## Small Business Software

**What kinds of software are helpful for small business owners?** If you have a small business or a hobby that produces income, you know the importance of keeping good records and tracking your expenses and income. **Accounting software** helps small business owners manage their finances more efficiently by providing tools for tracking accounts receivable and accounts payable. In addition, these applications offer inventory management, payroll, and billing tools. Examples of accounting applications are Intuit QuickBooks and Sage Peachtree. Both programs include templates for invoices, statements, and financial reports so that small business owners can create common forms and reports.

If your business requires the need for newsletters, catalogs, annual reports, or other large, complicated publications, consider using **desktop publishing (DTP) software**. Although many word processing applications include some of the features that are hallmarks of desktop publishing, specialized DTP software, such as Microsoft Publisher, QuarkXPress, and Adobe InDesign, allows professionals to design books and other publications that require complex layouts.

**What software do I use to create a web page? Web page–authoring software** allows even the novice to design interesting and interactive web pages without knowing any HTML code. Web page–authoring applications often include wizards, templates, and reference materials to help novices complete most web page–authoring tasks. More experienced users can take advantage of these applications' advanced features to make the web content current, interactive, and interesting. Microsoft Expression Web and Adobe Dreamweaver are two programs that both professionals and casual web page designers use.

Note that if you need to produce only the occasional web page, you'll find that many applications include features that let you convert your document into a web page. For example, in some Microsoft Office applications, you can choose to save a file as a web page.

## Software for Large and Specialized Businesses

**What types of software do large businesses use?** There is an application for almost every aspect of business. There are specialized programs for project management software, customer relationship management (CRM), enterprise resource planning (ERP), e-commerce, marketing and sales, finance, point of sale, security, networking, data management, and human resources, to name just a few. Figure 4.17 lists many of the common types of business-related software. Some applications are tailored to the specific needs of a particular company or industry. Software designed for a specific industry, such as property management software for real estate professionals, is called **vertical market software**.

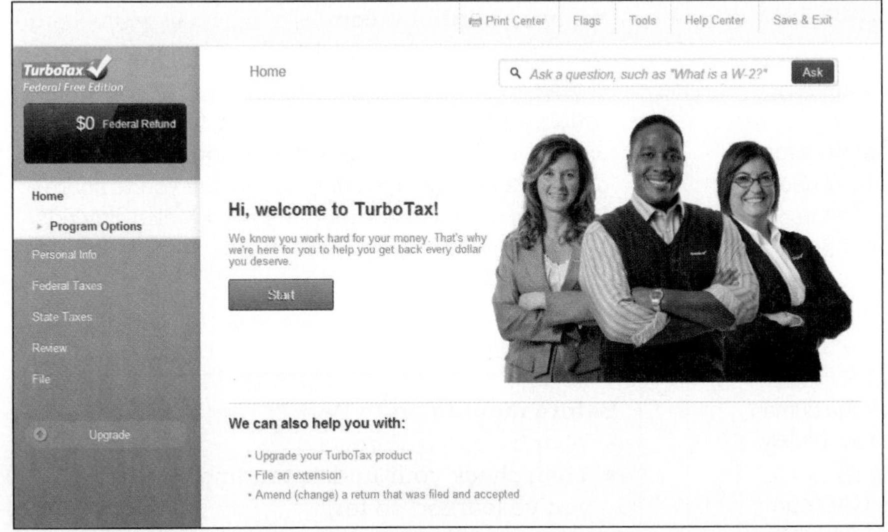


**FIGURE 4.16** Tax preparation software such as Intuit TurboTax lets you prepare and file your taxes using a guided, systematic process. *(Vika Sabo/Alamy)*

**What software is used to make 3-D models?** Engineers use **computer-aided design (CAD)** programs such as Autodesk's AutoCAD to create automated designs, technical drawings, and 3-D model visualizations. Here are some cool applications of CAD software:

- Architects use CAD software to build virtual models of their plans and readily visualize all aspects of design before actual construction.
- Engineers use CAD software to design everything from factory components to bridges. The 3-D nature of these programs lets engineers rotate their models and adjust their designs if necessary, eliminating costly building errors.
- CAD software also is used in conjunction with GPS devices for accurate placement of fiber optic networks around the country.

FIGURE 4.17

## Common Types of Large Business-Related Software

| PROJECT MANAGEMENT | CUSTOMER RELATIONSHIP MANAGEMENT (CRM) | ENTERPRISE RESOURCE PLANNING (ERP) |
|---|---|---|
| Creates scheduling charts to plan and track specific tasks and to coordinate resources |   Stores sales and client contact information in one central database |   Controls many "back office" operations and processing functions such as billing, production, inventory management, and human resources management |
| **E-COMMERCE** | **COMPUTER-AIDED DESIGN (CAD)** | **VERTICAL MARKET** |
|  Facilitates website creation and hosting services, shopping cart setup, and credit card–processing services |  Creates automated designs, technical drawings, and 3-D model visualizations for architecture, automotive, aerospace, and medical engineering industries |  Addresses the needs of businesses in a specific industry or market such as the real estate, banking, and automotive industries |

(John T Takai/Shutterstock; Toro Attila/Shutterstock; designdepot/Shutterstock; Helder Almeida/Shutterstock; cybrain/Shutterstock; nmedia/Shutterstock)

# BITS&BYTES

## Need to Work on Files Together? Try These Real-Time Collaboration Tools

You're part of a group working together on a project. You could share files via e-mail, but you've found that can lead to confusion, with multiple versions of the document being revised at the same time. Consider some of these other methods to share and collaborate on files:

- Skype (**skype.com**) lets users work together through video calling and share desktops remotely with other Skype users. This lets two users view the same file at the same time, and the remote user can follow the cursor on the screen of the host user to see exactly what the host user is doing, just as if they were working together in the same room.
- Google Docs (**docs.google.com**) and wikis allow multiple users to work together in real time on the same document and to communicate with project members via live text chat.
- Scribblar (**scribblar.com**) is a multiuser whiteboard with live audio chat, which is great for holding virtual brainstorm sessions.
- Dropbox (**dropbox.com**), OneDrive (**onedrive.com**), and Google Drive (**drive.google.com**) are online file storage systems that enable you to share files with others in addition to keeping files synced with any Internet-connected device.

- The medical engineering community uses CAD software to create anatomically accurate solid models of the human body, developing medical implants quickly and accurately.

The list of CAD applications keeps growing as more and more industries realize the benefits CAD can bring to their product development and manufacturing processes. ■

**Before moving on to Part 2:**

- **Watch Replay Video 4.1** .
- Then check your understanding of what you've learned so far.

# check your understanding//

For a quick review to see what you've learned so far, answer the following questions. Visit **pearsonhighered.com /techinaction** to check your answers.

## multiple choice

1. Software that is available on demand via the Internet is called
   - **a.** proprietary software.
   - **b.** Software as a Service (SaaS).
   - **c.** productivity software.
   - **d.** open source software.
2. What type of software enables you to create dynamic slide shows?
   - **a.** word processing
   - **b.** spreadsheet
   - **c.** presentation
   - **d.** database
3. Which type of program takes advantage of automatic recalculation and what-if analysis?
   - **a.** spreadsheet
   - **b.** database
   - **c.** CAD/CAM
   - **d.** project management
4. Which of the following is true about open source software?
   - **a.** The program code is confidential.
   - **b.** The program can be changed and freely distributed.
   - **c.** The program can be freely distributed as long as the program code is not changed.
   - **d.** The program code is subject to copyright protection.
5. Which program can you use to take notes in class?
   - **a.** Noteability
   - **b.** Evernote
   - **c.** OneNote
   - **d.** all of the above

## true–false

_____ **1.** System software is another term for application software.

_____ **2.** A wizard is a software tool that offers a step-by-step guide through complicated tasks.

## critical thinking

1. **Living on the Cloud**

   Cloud computing is becoming more popular, and many users are working from the cloud and not even realizing it. What kinds of software applications are you using that are completely web-based? Why do you use them instead of installed software applications? Envision a time when all software is web-based and describe how being totally on the cloud might be an advantage. What disadvantages might a cloud-based environment present?
2. **What's Your App?**

   Small applications are being developed every day for smartphones. If you have a smartphone, what apps are the most useful to you? If you don't own a smartphone, what kind of app do you think would be the most useful? Describe an app not currently available that would be your "killer app."

**Continue** »

TRY THIS

# Citing Website Sources

You've been assigned a research paper, and your instructor requires citations and a bibliography. In the past, you might have resorted to using websites such as Son of Citation Machine (**citationmachine.net**) or EasyBib (**easybib.com**) to create your citations and generate a bibliography. But did you know there are tools built right into Microsoft Word that do the same thing?

## To Add a New Citation and Source to a Document:

**Step 1** Click at the end of the sentence or phrase that you want to cite.

**Step 2** On the References tab, in the Citations & Bibliography group, click **Insert Citation**.

**Step 3** To add the source information, click **Add New Source**.

Note: To create a citation and fill in the source information later, click **Add New Placeholder**.

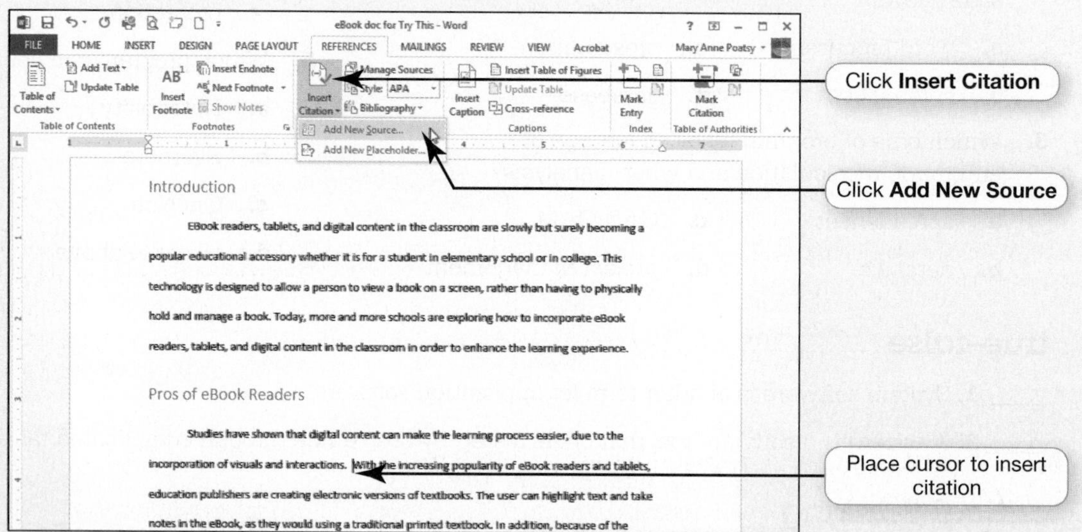
eBook doc for Try This - Word
FILE
HOME
INSERT
DESIGN
PAGE LAYOUT
REFERENCES
MAILINGS
REVIEW
VIEW
Acrobat
Mary Anne Poatsy
Insert Citation
Manage Sources
Style: APA
Bibliography
Add New Source...
Add New Placeholder...
Introduction
EBook readers, tablets, and digital content in the classroom are slowly but surely becoming a popular educational accessory whether it is for a student in elementary school or in college. This technology is designed to allow a person to view a book on a screen, rather than having to physically hold and manage a book. Today, more and more schools are exploring how to incorporate eBook readers, tablets, and digital content in the classroom in order to enhance the learning experience.
Pros of eBook Readers
Studies have shown that digital content can make the learning process easier, due to the incorporation of visuals and interactions. With the increasing popularity of eBook readers and tablets, education publishers are creating electronic versions of textbooks. The user can highlight text and take notes in the eBook, as they would using a traditional printed textbook. In addition, because of the
Click Insert Citation
Click Add New Source
Place cursor to insert citation

**Step 4** Begin to fill in the source information by clicking the arrow next to Type of Source.

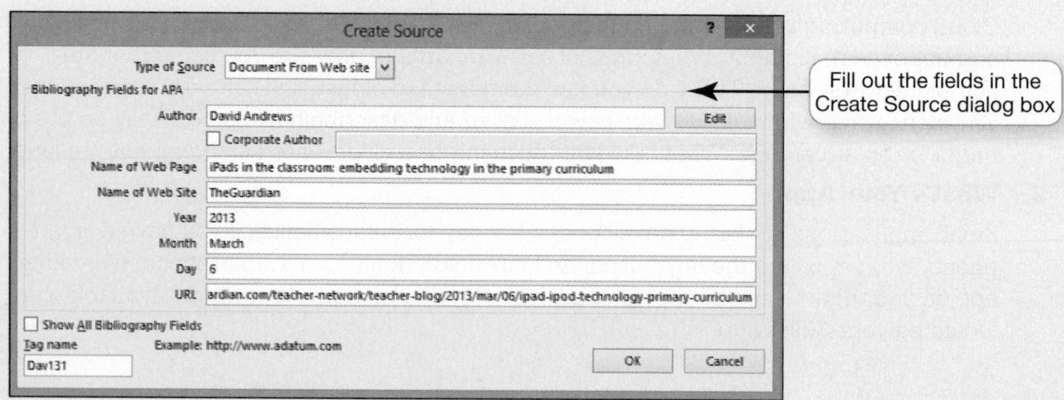
Create Source
Type of Source Document From Web site
Bibliography Fields for APA
Author David Andrews
Corporate Author
Name of Web Page iPads in the classroom: embedding technology in the primary curriculum
Name of Web Site TheGuardian
Year 2013
Month March
Day 6
URL ardian.com/teacher-network/teacher-blog/2013/mar/06/ipad-ipod-technology-primary-curriculum
Show All Bibliography Fields
Tag name
Example: http://www.adatum.com
Dav131
OK
Cancel
Fill out the fields in the Create Source dialog box

**Step 5** The citation will appear in your document.

Studies have shown that digital content can make the learning process easier, due to the incorporation of visuals and interactions. (Andrews, 2013) With the increasing popularity of eBook readers and tablets, education publishers are creating electronic versions of textbooks. The user can highlight text and take notes in the eBook, as they would using a traditional printed textbook. In addition, because of the software used with eBook readers and tablets, users can more easily search

The citation displays in text

## To Create a Bibliography:

You can create a bibliography at any point after you insert one or more sources in a document. Click where you want to insert a bibliography, usually at the end of the document. Then do the following:

**Step 1** On the References tab, in the Citations & Bibliography group, click **Bibliography**.

**Step 2** Click a predesigned bibliography format to insert the bibliography into the document.

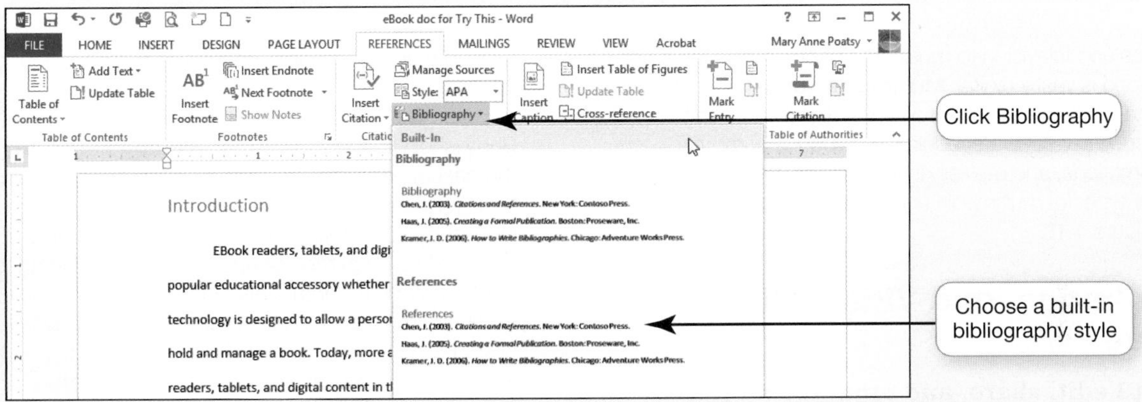


**Step 3** The bibliography is automatically generated.

**Step 4** You can update information in your sources and bibliography if information is added or changed by clicking on the **Bibliography** insert in the document and then clicking **Update Citations and Bibliography**.

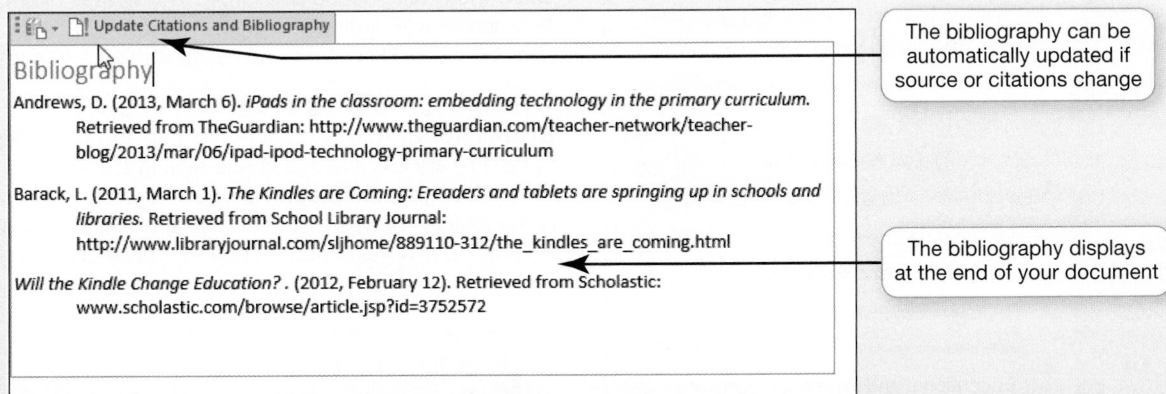

Update Citations and Bibliography
Bibliography
Andrews, D. (2013, March 6). iPads in the classroom: embedding technology in the primary curriculum. Retrieved from TheGuardian: http://www.theguardian.com/teacher-network/teacher-blog/2013/mar/06/ipad-ipod-technology-primary-curriculum
Barack, L. (2011, March 1). The Kindles are Coming: Ereaders and tablets are springing up in schools and libraries. Retrieved from School Library Journal: http://www.libraryjournal.com/sljhome/889110-312/the_kindles_are_coming.html
Will the Kindle Change Education? . (2012, February 12). Retrieved from Scholastic: www.scholastic.com/browse/article.jsp?id=3752572
The bibliography can be automatically updated if source or citations change
The bibliography displays at the end of your document

# Programs That Let You Play

While many programs help you be more productive, there are also programs that entertain you with audio, video, and digital images and through games, animations, and movies. Regardless of whether the software helps you work or play, it's important to know how to work with and manage the software so that you install it correctly and use it legally. This section discusses both aspects of entertainment software.

## multimedia and entertainment SOFTWARE

From movies and television to music and photography, the entertainment world is vastly digital. **Multimedia software** includes digital image- and video-editing software, digital audio software, and other specialty software required to produce computer games, animations, and movies. In this section, we look at several popular types of multimedia and entertainment software, as shown in Figure 4.18.

### Digital Image- and Video-Editing Software

**How can I edit, share, and organize digital images?** One great advantage of taking digital images is that you can easily manipulate them and then share them on the web. While Facebook is a great option for sharing images, Flickr (**flickr.com**) is a website specifically designed for sharing photos. It lets you organize your images and then share them publicly with millions of users or just with your closest friends and family. Discussion boards are also available so that people can leave comments about the images.

If you want to edit your photos before sharing, Adobe Photoshop Elements is **image-editing software** geared to the casual photographer. Image-editing software includes tools for basic modifications to digital photos such as removing red-eye; modifying contrast, sharpness, and color casts; or removing scratches or rips from scanned images of old photos. Many programs also include painting tools such as brushes, pens, and artistic media (such as paints, pastels, and oils) that let you create realistic-looking images. Some include templates so you can insert your favorite pictures into preformatted pages for digital scrapbooks or greeting cards. Google Picasa (**picasa.google.com**) is a popular application that not only lets you edit images but also helps to organize and share your digital images (see Figure 4.19). Picasa also stores your photos on the web.

Several other online photo-sharing and photo-storing sites, such as Snapfish (**snapfish.com**), Kodak (**kodak.com**), and Shutterfly (**shutterfly.com**), let you upload your digital images from your computer, create photo albums, and share them with friends and family. These sites offer printing services as well, letting you create customized cards, stationery, books, and even iPhone cases with your images.

**What image-editing programs might a professional use?** Adobe Photoshop and Corel PaintShop Photo Pro are fully featured image-editing applications. Gimpshop (**gimpshop.com**) is a free download that has most of the features offered by the for-pay applications, such as Photoshop and PaintShop Photo Pro. These offer sophisticated

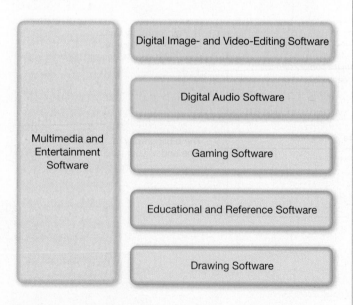

Multimedia and Entertainment Software
- Digital Image- and Video-Editing Software
- Digital Audio Software
- Gaming Software
- Educational and Reference Software
- Drawing Software

**FIGURE 4.18** There are many varieties of multimedia and entertainment software.

SOUND BYTE

**Enhancing Photos with Image-Editing Software**

In this Sound Byte, you'll learn tips and tricks on how to best use image-editing software. You'll learn how to remove the red-eye from photos and to incorporate borders, frames, and other enhancements to produce professional effects.

**FIGURE 4.19** You can create collages of your favorite images using Google Picasa. *(Mary Anne Poatsy)*

tools for tasks like layering images and masking images (hiding parts of layers to create effects such as collages). Designers use these more sophisticated tools to create the enhanced digital images used commercially in logos, in advertisements, and on book and CD covers.

### What software do I need to edit digital videos?

While it's easy to upload videos directly to YouTube or Facebook unedited, you can use **digital video–editing software** to help refine your videos. Although the most expensive products (such as Adobe Premiere Pro and Apple's Final Cut Pro) offer the widest range of special effects and tools, some moderately priced video-editing programs have enough features to keep the casual user happy. Windows Movie Maker and iMovie have intuitive drag-and-drop features that make it simple to create professional-quality movies with little or no training (see Figure 4.20).

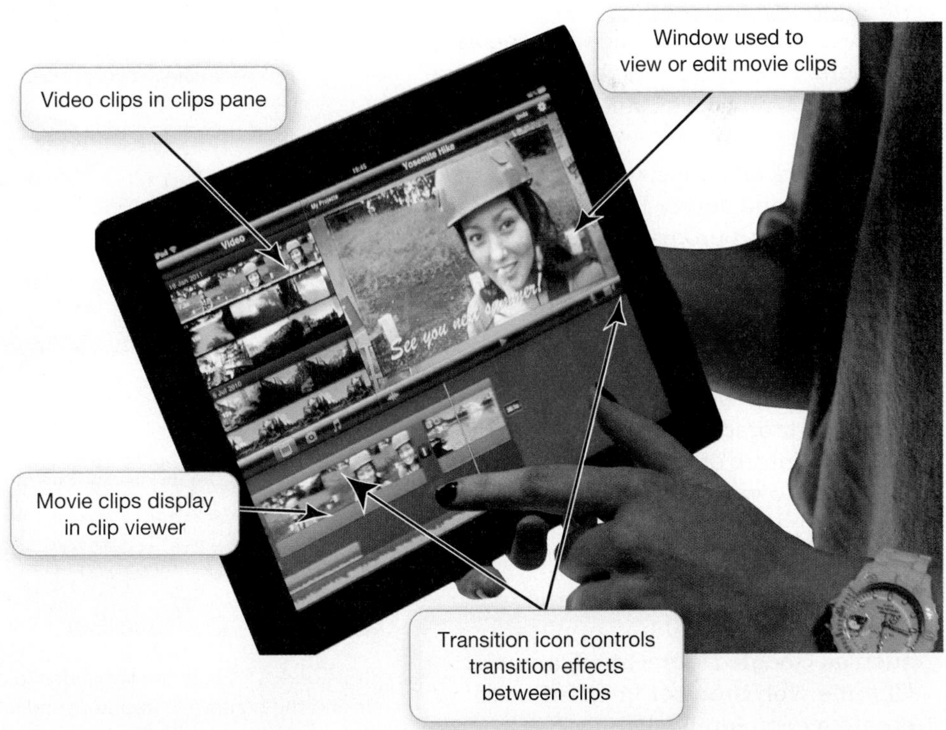


**FIGURE 4.20** Video-editing programs such as Apple iMovie make it easy to create and edit movies. *(Press Association/AP Images)*

# DIG DEEPER How Cloud Computing Works

Have you ever done any of the following?

- Posted pictures on Facebook that your friends accessed from their iPhone
- Used Dropbox or OneDrive to store your files instead of carrying around a flash drive
- Used Google Docs or Microsoft Office Web Apps to collaborate on a team project
- Used Carbonite to back up your data online

By doing any of these activities, you have participated in cloud computing. So what exactly is **cloud computing**?

Cloud computing refers to storing data, files, and applications on the web and being able to access and manipulate these files and applications from any Internet-connected device. Being able to work from the cloud eliminates the need to have everything stored on your own computer's drives and lets you access your pictures, music, files, and programs from any device as long as you have access to the Internet. In addition, cloud computing makes it easier to collaborate and communicate with others, and it can cut down on administrative tasks for organizations maintaining large amounts of computer hardware and software.

There are two sides to cloud computing:

1. The *front end* is the side we see as users. It involves a web browser like Internet Explorer, Firefox, or Google Chrome.
2. The *back end* consists of various data centers and server farms that house the files and programs you access "on the cloud" (see Figure 4.21). These data centers and server farms are warehouses full of computers and servers, and they are being created all over the world, providing us with "cloud storage." The computers in the data centers or server farms are designed to work together, adjusting to the varying degrees of demand placed on them at any time.

Google is one of the first true explorers in the cloud, building applications such as Google Docs, Gmail, and the Chrome web browser in an effort to create a completely virtual operating environment. A fully functioning operating environment would enable users to sign in on any computer and have "their" computer setup (desktop configurations and images, programs, files, and other personalized settings) display. Additionally, cloud computing would reduce the need for all of us to have the fastest computers with the most memory and storage capabilities. Instead, we could all have simple front-end terminals with basic input and output devices because the computers on the back end will be providing all the computing muscle.

The Chromebook is Google's first attempt at a notebook (called a netbook) where all the applications and files are stored on the web. Nothing is installed or saved to a hard drive, not even the operating system! All programs are accessed and all work is done through the web-based browser, so sending e-mail, editing photos, and working on documents are all done via web-based applications. Since the Chromebook requires an Internet connection to get most tasks done, users must be near a WiFi connection or pay for a data plan.

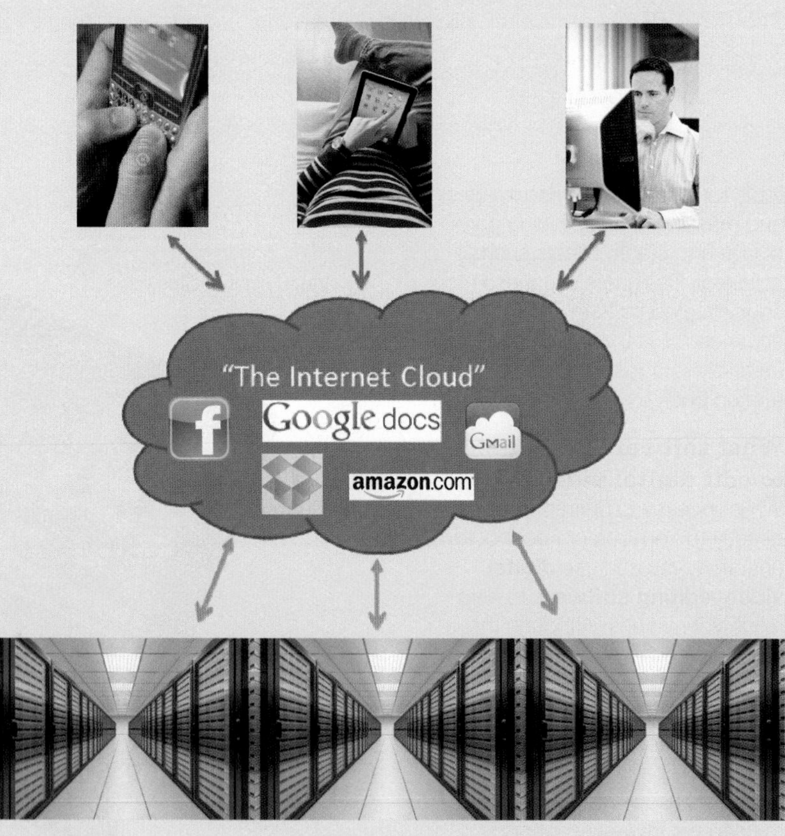


**FIGURE 4.21** There are two sides to cloud computing: the side we see as users and the banks of computers and servers that house the files and programs we access. *(Jupiterimages/Photos.com/Thinkstock; Neil Fraser/Alamy; Monashee Frantz/Alamy; zentilia/Shutterstock; PhotoEdit/Alamy; digitallife/Alamy; Google, Inc.; Anatolii Babii/Alamy; PhotoEdit/Alamy)*

There are some considerations with cloud computing of which you need to be aware:

- *Security and privacy:* Right now, the security of information stored on the web is built on trusting that the passwords we set and the security systems that the data centers put in place are able to keep our information away from unauthorized users. Caution is always warranted, as nothing is completely safe and private.
- *Backup:* Because even the devices in these large data centers and server farms inevitably will break down, the cloud computing systems have redundant systems to provide backup. However, for critical files that you must have, it might be a good idea not to completely rely on the cloud but to have your own offline backup system, as well.
- *Access issues:* With cloud computing, you access your files and programs only through the Internet. If you couldn't access the Internet due to a power failure or system failure with your Internet service provider, you wouldn't be able to access your files. Storing your most critical files and programs offline will help reduce the inconvenience and loss of productivity while access to the Internet is being restored.

Before relying on cloud computing, consider the above concerns against the advantages of the convenience of having your information when and where you want it and the ability to promote better collaboration.

## Digital Audio Software

**What's the difference between all the digital audio file types on my computer?** You probably have a variety of digital audio files stored on your computer, such as downloaded music files, audiobooks, or podcasts. These types of audio files have been *compressed* so they're more manageable to transfer to and from your computer and over the Internet. MP3, short for MPEG-1 Audio Layer 3, is a type of audio compression format and is the most common compressed digital format, but there are other compressed formats, such as AAC and WMA.

You may also see *uncompressed* audio files on your computer, such as WAV or AIFF files. Uncompressed files—the files found on audio CDs, for example—have not had any data removed, so the quality is a perfect representation of the audio as it was recorded. Unfortunately, the file size is much larger than that of compressed files. Compressed formats remove data such as high frequencies that the human ear does not hear in order to make the files smaller and easier to download and store. MP3 format, for example, makes it possible to transfer and play back music on iPods and other music players. A typical CD stores between 10 and 15 songs in uncompressed format, but with files in MP3 format, the same CD can store between 100 and 180 songs. The smaller file size not only lets you store and play music in less space, it also allows quick and easy distribution over the Internet. Ogg Vorbis (or just Ogg) is a free, open source audio compression format alternative to MP3. Some say that Ogg produces a better sound quality than MP3.

**What do I use to create my own audio files?** There are many digital audio applications that let you create and record your own audio files. With programs such as MAGIX Music Maker or Apple GarageBand, you can compose your own songs or soundtracks with virtual instruments, voice recorders, synthesizers, and special audio effects, and these will end up as uncompressed MIDI files. Other programs, such as Audacity and Cakewalk SONAR, let you record audio files.

**Can I edit audio files? Audio-editing software** includes tools that make editing audio files as easy as editing text files. Software such as the open source Audacity

## BITS&BYTES

### Mirror, mirror...

Sometimes when you download software, especially open source software, you must choose a download location. Each location in the list is a mirror site. A mirror site is a copy of a website or set of files hosted at a remote location. Software developers sometimes use geographically distributed mirror sites so that users can choose the mirror site closest to their location to expedite the download time. Mirror sites are also used as backups, so if a server goes down for some reason, users can access the software from a different site, ensuring the software is always accessible. Developers also use mirror sites to help offset issues associated with a sudden influx of traffic that would otherwise overload a single server.

ACTIVE HELPDESK

**Choosing Software**

In this Active Helpdesk call, you'll play the role of a helpdesk staffer, fielding calls about the different kinds of multimedia software, educational and reference software, and entertainment software.

(**audacity.sourceforge.net**) and Sony Sound Forge Pro (**sonycreativesoftware.com**) lets you perform such basic editing tasks as cutting dead air space from the beginning or end of a song or clipping a portion from the middle. You can also add special sound effects, such as echo or bass boost, and remove static or hiss from MP3 files. AudioAcrobat (**audioacrobat.com**), a web-based program, makes it easy to record and stream audio and video and hosts your audio files. These applications support recording sound files from a microphone or any source you can connect through the input line of a sound card.

## Gaming Software

**Can I make video games?** Now that video games represent an industry with revenue of more than $25 billion each year, designing and creating video games is emerging as a desirable career opportunity. Professionally created video games involve artistic storytelling and design, as well as sophisticated programming. Major production houses such as Electronic Arts use applications not easily available to the casual home enthusiast. However, you can use the editors and game engines available for games such as EverQuest, Oblivion, and Unreal Tournament to create custom levels and characters to extend the game.

If you want to try your hand at creating your own video games, multimedia applications such as Unity, Adobe Flash, and RPG Maker VX provide the tools you need to explore game design and creation. The program GameMaker (**yoyogames.com**) is a free product that lets you build a game without any programming; you drag and drop key elements of the new game creation into place. Alice (**alice.org**) is another free environment to check out; it lets you easily create 3-D animations and simple games (see Figure 4.22). See the Sound Byte on 3-D Programming the Easy Way in Chapter 10.

## Educational and Reference Software

**What fun educational and reference software should I check out?** If you want to learn more about a subject, you can turn to the web for many instructional videos and documents. But sometimes, it's best to use software for more complete or detailed instructions. Educational and reference software is available to help you master, study, design, create, or plan. As shown in Figure 4.23, there are software products that teach new skills such as typing, languages, cooking, and playing the guitar.

Students who will be taking standardized tests like the SAT often use test preparation software. In addition, many computer and online brain-training games and programs are designed to improve the health and function of your brain. Lumosity (**lumosity.com**) is one such site that has a specific "workout" program that you can play on your PC or smartphone. Brain Age$^2$ (**brainage.com**) has software for the Nintendo DS and is designed for players of all ages.

**What types of programs are available to train people to use software or special machines?** Many programs provide tutorials for popular computer applications (you may even use one in your course provided with MyITLab). These programs use illustrated systematic instructions to guide users through unfamiliar skills in an environment that acts like the actual software, without the software actually being installed.

Some training programs, known as **simulation programs**, allow you to experience or control the software as if it were an actual event. Such simulation programs include commercial and military flight training, surgical instrument training, and machine operation training. One benefit of simulated training programs is that they safely allow you to experience potentially dangerous situations such as flying a helicopter during high winds. Consequently, users of these training programs are more likely to take risks and learn from their mistakes—something they could not afford to do in real life. Simulated training programs also help prevent costly errors. Should something go awry, the only cost of the error is restarting the simulation program.

**Do I need special software to take courses online?** Although some courses are run from an individually developed website, many online courses are run using **course management software** such as Blackboard, Moodle, and Canvas. In addition to traditional classroom tools such as calendars and grade books, these programs provide special areas for students and instructors to exchange ideas and information through chat rooms, discussion forums, and e-mail. In addition, collaboration tools such as whiteboards and desktop sharing facilitate virtual office hour sessions. Depending on the content and course materials, you may need a password or special plug-ins to view certain videos or demos.

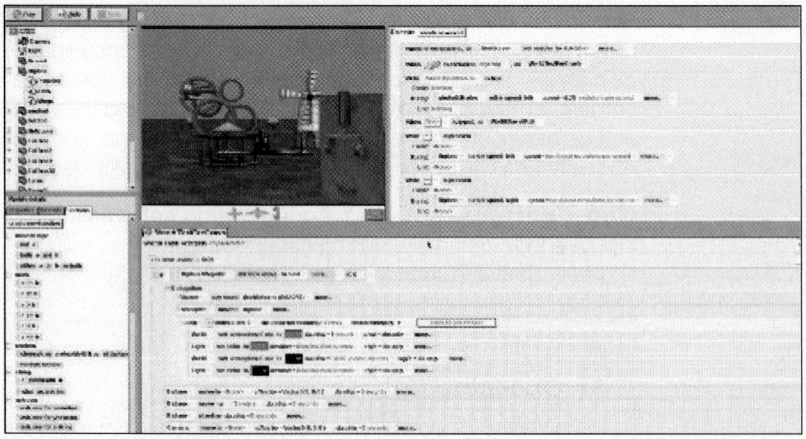

**FIGURE 4.22** Software programs such as that from Alice.org help students learn how to program as well as create 3-D animations and simple games. *(Courtesy of the Carnegie Mellon University Press)*

## Drawing Software

**What kind of software should I use to create illustrations? Drawing software** (or **illustration software**) lets you create or edit 2-D, line-based drawings. You can use it to create technical diagrams or original nonphotographic drawings, animations, and illustrations using standard tools such as pens, pencils, and paintbrushes. You also can drag geometric objects from a toolbar onto the canvas area to create images and can use paint bucket, eyedropper, and spray can tools to add color and special effects to the drawings.

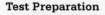

FIGURE 4.23

## Educational and Reference Software: A Sample of What's Available

**Test Preparation**

Designed to improve your performance on standardized tests

**Simulation**

Allows you to experience a real situation through a virtual environment

**Instructional**

Designed to teach you almost anything from playing a musical instrument to learning a language or cooking

**Trip Planning**

Generates maps and provides driving instructions; some incorporate hotel, restaurant, and other trip information

**Home Design/ Improvement**

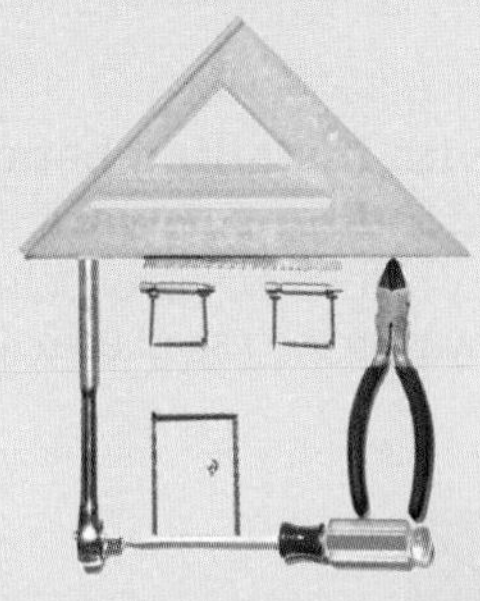

Provides 2-D or 3-D templates and images to let you better visualize indoor and outdoor remodeling projects and landscaping ideas

**Course Management**

Web-based software system that creates a virtual learning experience, including course materials, tests, and discussion boards

**Brain Training**

Features games and activities to exercise your brain to improve your memory, processing speed, attention, and multitasking capabilities

**Genealogy**

Helps chart the relationships between family members through multiple generations

(Amy Strycula/Alamy; Greg Pease/Getty Images; iQoncept/Shutterstock; almagami/Shutterstock; Zack Clothier/Shutterstock; Scott Maxwell/LuMaxArt/Shutterstock; julien tromeur/Fotolia; sassyphotos/Fotolia)

Adobe Illustrator includes tools that let you create professional-quality creative and technical illustrations such as muscle structures in the human body. Its warping tool allows you to bend, stretch, and twist portions of your image or text. Because of its many tools and features, Illustrator is the preferred drawing software program of most graphic artists.

**What kind of software can be used for home or landscape planning?** There are many software packages to help plan the layout of homes and landscapes, such as those offered by Broderbund. A simple, web-based and fairly full-featured free 3-D modeling application is Trimble's SketchUp (formerly owned by Google). SketchUp (**sketchup.com**) lets you create a 3-D image of your dream home (see Figure 4.24). ■

**FIGURE 4.24** SketchUp is a free, web-based 3-D modeling application. *(Archipoch/Shutterstock)*

# managing your SOFTWARE

It's important to know how to pick out the best software for your computer, how to get it onto your computer correctly, and how to take it off. We discuss all of these topics next.

## Getting Software

**Is discounted software for students available?** If you're a student, you can sometimes buy substantially discounted software that is no different from regularly priced software. Campus computer stores and college bookstores offer discounted prices to students who possess a valid student ID. Online software suppliers such as Journey Education Marketing (**journeyed.com**) and Academic Superstore (**academicsuperstore.com**) also offer popular software to students at reduced prices. Software developers, such as Microsoft and Apple, often offer their products to students at a discount so it's always good to check their websites before purchasing software or hardware.

**Can I get software for free legally?** In addition to open source software, discussed previously in the chapter, **freeware** is copyrighted software that you can use for free. Explore sites like FileHippo (**filehippo.com**) and MajorGeeks (**majorgeeks.com**) to see how many good freeware programs are available. However, while much legitimate freeware exists, some unscrupulous people use freeware to distribute viruses and malware. Be cautious when installing freeware, especially if you're unsure of the provider's legitimacy.

**Can I try new software before it's released?** Some software developers offer beta versions of their software free of charge. A **beta version** is an application that is still under development (see Figure 4.25). By distributing free beta versions, developers hope users will report errors, or bugs, they find in their programs. Many beta versions are available for a limited trial period and are used to help developers respond to issues before they launch the software on the market.

**Are there risks associated with installing beta versions, freeware, or downloading software from the Internet?** By their very nature, beta products are unlikely to be bug free, so you always run the risk of something

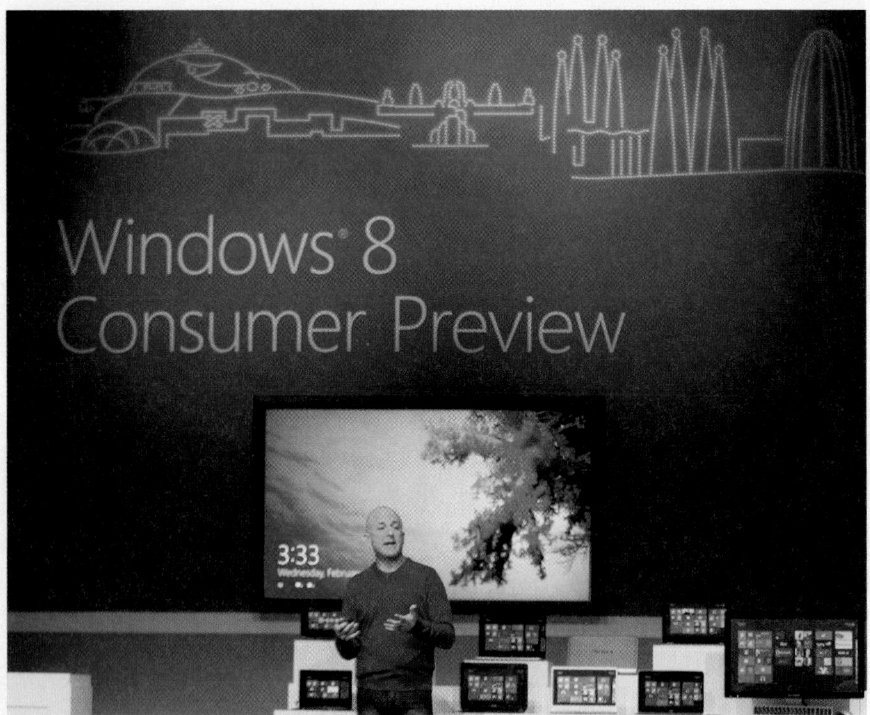


**FIGURE 4.25** Prior to releasing Windows 8, Microsoft released the beta version, named Consumer Preview, for users to try.

# BITS&BYTES

## How to Open Unknown File Types

Normally, when you double-click a file to open it, the program associated with the file runs automatically. For example, when you double-click a file with a .doc or.docx extension, the file opens in Microsoft Word. However, if the file has no extension or Windows has no application associated with that file type, an "Open with" dialog box appears and asks what program you want to use to open the file. In other cases, a document may open with a program other than the one you wanted to use. This is because many applications can open several file types, and the program you expected the file to open in is not currently the program associated with that file type. To assign a program to a file type or to change the program to open a particular file type, follow these instructions:

1. Use the search and navigation tools in File Explorer (previously called Windows Explorer) to locate the file you want to change. (For example, you can search for all Word files by searching for *.doc or *.docx.) Right-click on the file, and then point to **Open With**.
2. A list of programs installed on your computer appears. Click the program you want to use to open this file type. If you're sure the selected program is the one that should always be used for this file type, then instead select **Choose default program**, and make sure to check "**Use this app for all [extension] files**," and click the default program from the list.

When you double-click that file in the future, the file will open in the program you selected.

going awry with your system by installing and using beta versions. Unless you're willing to deal with potential problems, it may be best to wait until the last beta version is released—often referred to as the *gold version*. By that time, most of the serious bugs have been worked out.

As a precaution, you should be comfortable with the reliability of the source before downloading a freeware or beta version of software. If it's a reliable developer whose software you're familiar with, you can be more certain that a serious bug or virus isn't hiding in the software. Similarly, you should be sure that the software you're downloading is meant for your system and that your system has met all the necessary hardware and operating system requirements.

Before installing any software, it's always good to make sure your virus protection software is up to date. It's equally important that you back up your system as well as create a *restore point*. That way, if something does go awry, you can return your system to the way it was before you started. You can create a restore point by using Windows 8 System protection tools. To access the System protection tools, click System and Security from the Control Panel, and then click System. In the left pane, click System protection to display the System Properties dialog box. On the System Protection tab, click the Create button, and type a description for the restore point (such as "Before installing [name of software]") and click Create. You will be notified when the restore point is created.

## Software Licenses

**Don't I own the software I buy?** Most people don't understand that, unlike other items they purchase, the software they buy doesn't belong to them. The only thing they're actually purchasing is a license that gives them the right to use the software for their own purposes as the *only* user of that copy. The application is not theirs to lend.

A **software license**, also known as an **End User License Agreement (EULA)**, is an agreement between you, the user, and the software company (see Figure 4.26). You accept this agreement before installing the software on your machine. It's a legal contract that outlines the acceptable uses of the program and any actions that violate the agreement. Generally, the agreement states who the ultimate owner of the software is, under what circumstances copies of the software can be made, and whether the software can be installed on any other machine. Finally, the license agreement states what, if any, warranty comes with the software.

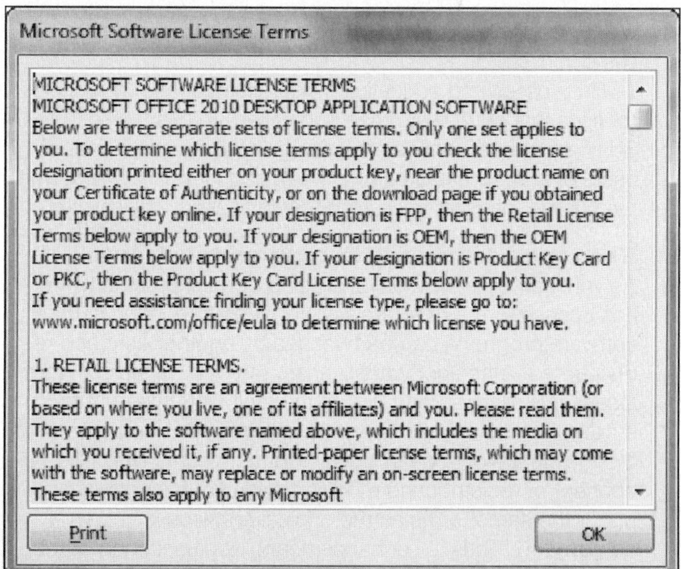


**FIGURE 4.26** You must accept the terms of the software license before using the product.

## BITS&BYTES

### Run versus Save When Downloading Software

When you download software from the web, often you're given the choice to run or save it (see Figure 4.27). What's the difference? When you select Run, the program is downloaded to your machine and generally stored in Temporary Internet Files. Then the file is "run," meaning that it is loaded into memory and the operating system runs it. Use the Run option when you need to use the downloaded file on a limited basis, such as a song or video that you only plan to watch once or twice. Some installation programs instead install the software on your machine in a permanent location when Run is selected.

When you select Save (or sometimes Save As) on a download, the file will be copied to your hard disk. There may be an AutoRun program associated with the file that starts the installation automatically. Otherwise, you may need to navigate to the stored location and execute (or run) the file independently. The big difference is that the saved file is not downloaded into a temporary location. Use Save when you want to keep the file for a longer period of time or when you want to control where the file or program is saved.

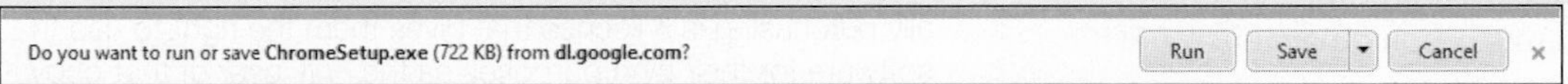

Do you want to run or save ChromeSetup.exe (722 KB) from dl.google.com?
Run
Save
Cancel

**FIGURE 4.27** When downloading software, you have the choice to Run or Save.

**Does a license only cover one installation?** Some software is purchased with a single license to cover one person's specific use. You can't share these licenses, and you can't "extend" the license to install the software on more than one of your computers. Many manufacturers are now offering licensing bundles to allow several computers in one household to be installed with a legal copy. For example, Apple offers a Family Pack Software License Agreement that permits a user to install the purchased software legally on as many as five computers in the same household, and some versions of Microsoft Office come with the ability to install the software on multiple computers in the same household.

Businesses and educational institutions often buy multiuser licenses that allow more than one person to use the software. Some multiuser licenses are per-seat and limit the number of users overall, whereas others, called *concurrent licenses,* limit the number of users accessing the software at any given time.

**Does open source software require a license?** As you learned earlier, anyone using open source software has access to the program's code. Therefore, open source software programs can be tweaked by another user and redistributed. A free software license, the *GNU General Public License,* is required and grants the recipients the right to modify and redistribute the software. Without such a license, the recipient would be in violation of copyright laws. This concept of redistributing modified open source software under the same terms as the original software is known as **copyleft**. Thus, all enhancements, additions, and other changes to copyleft software must also be distributed as free software.

## Getting the Right Software for Your System

**How do I ensure the software I buy will work on my computer?** Every software program has a set of **system requirements** that specify the minimum recommended standards for the operating system, processor, primary memory (random access memory, or RAM), and hard drive capacity. Sometimes there are other specifications for the video card, monitor, optical drive, and other peripherals. These requirements are printed on the software packaging or are available at the manufacturer's website. Before installing software on your computer, ensure that your system setup meets the minimum requirements as specified by the developer.

**When is it worth buying a newer version?** Periodically, software developers improve the functionality of their software by releasing a software upgrade. Although software developers suggest otherwise, there's no need to rush out and buy the latest version of a software program every time one is available. Depending on the software, some upgrades may not be sufficiently different from the previous version to make it cost-effective for you to buy the newest version. Unless the upgrade adds features that are important to you, you may be better off waiting to upgrade every other release. You also should consider whether you use the software frequently enough to justify an upgrade and whether your current system can handle the new system requirements of the upgraded version. In between upgrades, developers will make available software updates (sometimes referred to as software patches). Updates are usually downloaded and provide smaller enhancements to the software or fix program bugs.

**If I have an older version of software and someone sends me files from a newer version, can I still open them?** Software vendors recognize that people work on different versions of the same software. Vendors, therefore, make new versions backward compatible, meaning that the new versions can recognize (open) files created with older versions. However, some software programs are not forward compatible, so these older versions are not able to recognize files created on newer versions of the same software.

## Installing and Uninstalling Software

**What's the difference between a custom installation and a full installation?** Before you use most software, you must permanently place it, or install it, on your system. The installation process may differ slightly depending on whether you're installing the software from a DVD or downloading it from the web. One of the first steps in the installation wizard asks you to decide between a full installation and a custom installation. A **full installation** (often referred to as a *typical installation*) copies all the most commonly used files and programs from the distribution disc to your computer's hard drive. By selecting **custom installation**, you can decide which features you want installed on your hard drive. Installing only the features you want saves space on your hard drive.

**How do I start my programs in Windows 8?** Every program you install on your system gets a tile on the Start screen. The simplest way to start an application is by clicking the program tile on the Start screen. Alternatively, you can work from the desktop view in Windows 8. To easily access commonly used programs or newly installed programs, you can pin a shortcut to a program on the taskbar or to the Start screen. To place a program on the taskbar or pin it to the Start screen, right-click the program icon on your desktop or right-click the program tile on the Start screen. From the options that are displayed, select Pin to Taskbar or Pin to Start. Windows then places an icon for this program on the taskbar or a tile on the Start screen (see Figure 4.28). To uninstall a pinned icon from Start, right-click the icon and select Unpin from Start.

**How do I uninstall a program?** An application contains many different files—library files, help files, and other text files—in addition to the main file you use to run the program. By deleting only the main file, you're not ridding your system of all the pieces of the program. Windows 8 makes it easy to uninstall a program: Simply right-click on the program icon on the Start screen, then from the panel that displays at the bottom, click Uninstall. To uninstall a program from the desktop view in Windows 8, open the Control Panel, select Programs from the Control Panel, then click Uninstall a program.

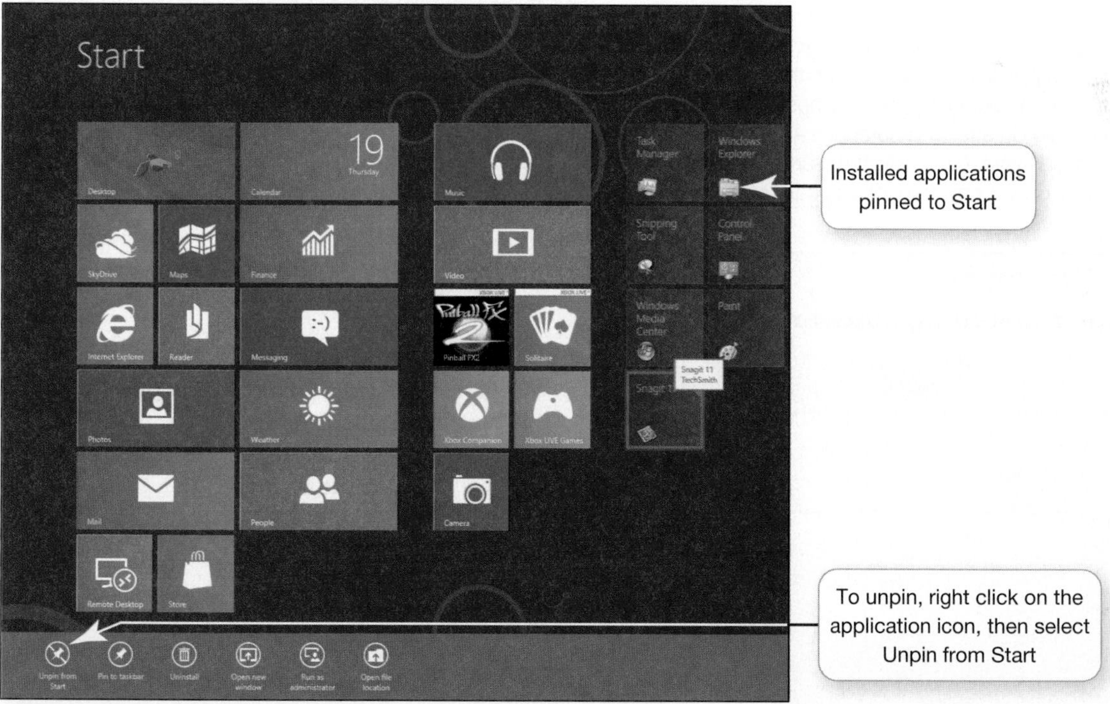
Start
Installed applications pinned to Start
To unpin, right click on the application icon, then select Unpin from Start

**FIGURE 4.28** By pinning an application to the Start screen in Windows 8, you have easy access to your most frequently used programs.

# BITS&BYTES

## Ridding Your Computer of "Bloat"

Manufacturers often include software on new computers that you don't want or need. Called ***bloatware***, this software can slow down your computer and degrade its performance. How do you get rid of it? Install an application such as PC Decrapifier (**pcdecrapifier.com**), or, if you'd rather do it yourself, consider some of these tips:

- *Uninstall preinstalled antivirus software:* If you have antivirus software on your old computer, you may be able to transfer the unexpired portion of your software license to your new computer. If this is the case, you can uninstall the preinstalled trial version on your new computer.
- *Uninstall unwanted toolbars:* Many computers come with Google, Bing, and other toolbars preinstalled. Go through Programs and Features in the Control Panel to uninstall any toolbars you don't want.
- *Remove manufacturer-specific software:* Some computer manufacturers install their own software. Some of these programs can be useful, but others are help features and update reminders that are also found in your operating system. You can remove any or all of these support applications and instead just check the manufacturer's website periodically for updates or new information.

Select the program you want to uninstall from the list, then click Uninstall.

**If my computer crashes, can I get the preinstalled software back?** Although some preinstalled software is not necessary to replace if your computer crashes, other software such as the operating system is critical to reinstall. Most manufacturers use a separate partition on the hard drive to hold an image, or copy, of the preinstalled software. However, it's not always possible to reboot from the partitioned hard drive, especially when your computer crashes, so one of the first things you should do after you purchase a new computer is create a recovery drive. Generally, the manufacturer will have placed a utility on your system, or you can use the Recovery utility included in Windows to create a recovery drive. You can access the Advanced Recovery tools in Windows 8.1 from the Control Panel by typing Recovery in the search box, and then clicking Create a recovery drive under System. Then, to create the recovery drive, insert a blank flash drive in a USB port and follow the steps in the wizard. Once the recovery drive has been made, label the flash drive and put it away in a safe place.

There is an application for almost anything you want or need to do on your computer, whether it is school or work related or just for entertainment purposes. And there are a variety of types of applications, such as proprietary, open source, web-based, and freeware. Have fun exploring all the various possibilities! ■

ACTIVE HELPDESK

**Buying and Installing Software**

In this Active Helpdesk call, you'll play the role of a helpdesk staffer, fielding calls about how to best purchase software or to get it for free, how to install and uninstall software, and where you can go for help when you have a problem with your software.

**Before moving on to the Chapter Review:**

- **Watch Replay Video 4.2**.
- **Then check your understanding of what you've learned so far.**

# check your understanding//

For a quick review to see what you've learned so far, answer the following questions. Visit **pearsonhighered.com/techinaction** to check your answers.

## multiple

1. The minimum set of recommended standards for a program is known as the
   - **a.** operating system.
   - **b.** system requirements.
   - **c.** setup guide.
   - **d.** installation specs.
2. Which of the following is an uncompressed audio file format?
   - **a.** AAC
   - **b.** WAV
   - **c.** MP3
   - **d.** WMA
3. Which of the following is considered a benefit of using simulation programs?
   - **a.** They allow users to experience potentially dangerous situations without risk.
   - **b.** They help to prevent costly errors.
   - **c.** They allow users to train on software that is not installed on their systems.
   - **d.** All of the above
4. Which of the following is NOT necessary to do before installing beta software?
   - **a.** creating a restore point
   - **b.** backing up your system
   - **c.** defragging the hard drive
   - **d.** ensuring your virus protection software is updated
5. Which software is best to use if you want to change the looks of your digital pictures?
   - **a.** image-editing program
   - **b.** video-editing program
   - **c.** media management software
   - **d.** All of the above

## true–false

_____ **1.** To delete an unwanted program from Windows 8, right-click the program tile from the Start screen and select Uninstall.

_____ **2.** When you buy software, you then own it and can do anything you'd like with it, including giving it to friends to install on their machines.

## critical thinking

1. **Educational and Reference Software**

   As a student, you use a wide variety of software—more than you probably realize. Create a list of all the software you're using or have used this semester, and note the category the software falls into. For example, you might use Blackboard as course management software or Microsoft Word as productivity or word processing software. Can you list at least 20 different software applications?
2. **Software Myths and Misconceptions**

   There are several myths and misconceptions about software, such as the 24-hour rule, the 80/20 rule, and the abandonment rule. The 24-hour rule claims a person can download software for 24 hours and then have the choice of deleting it or buying it. The 80/20 rule implies that for single-use licenses, a person can install software on both a work and home computer as long as work use is not more than 80% and home use is not more than 20%. The abandonment rule claims that one can use software if it is no longer supported or was created by a company that is no longer in business. Explain how you think each of these is a violation of copyright law.
3. **Can You Reuse Software?**

   Several years ago, you purchased Adobe Acrobat so you could create, edit, and mark up PDF documents. You have since changed computers, and your version of Acrobat is not compatible with the operating system on your new computer. You're required to purchase an upgrade of Adobe Acrobat to run on the new machine. Your sister wants to install the old version of Adobe Acrobat on her computer since you're not using it anymore. Do you think this will be legal to do? Why or why not?

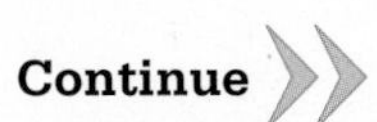

# 4 Chapter Review

## summary//

### The Nuts and Bolts of Software

**1. What's the difference between application software and system software?**

- The term *software* refers to a set of instructions that tells the computer what to do.
- Application software is the software you use to do everyday tasks at home, school, and work. Application software includes the following:
  - o Productivity software, such as word processing, finance, and personal information management programs
  - o Business software for small and large businesses
  - o Multimedia software, such as applications used for image and video editing, recording and editing digital audio, and gaming software
  - o Educational and reference software
- System software is the software that helps run the computer and coordinates instructions between application software and the computer's hardware devices. System software includes the operating system and utility programs.

**2. What are the different ways I can access and use software?**

- Some software comes preinstalled on your computer. You will need to add other software by installing the software or accessing the software from the web. There are two types of software that you can install on your computer:
  1. Proprietary (or commercial) software is software you buy.
  2. Open source software is program code that is free and publicly available with few licensing and copyright restrictions. The code can be copied, distributed, or changed without the stringent copyright protections of software products you purchase.
- Web-based applications are those that are hosted online by the vendor and made available to the customer over the Internet. This web-based distribution model is also referred to as Software as a Service (SaaS). Web-based applications are accessed via an Internet connection to the site that hosts the software.

### Productivity and Business Software

**3. What kinds of applications are included in productivity software?**

- Productivity software programs include the following:
  - o Word processing: to create and edit written documents
  - o Spreadsheet: to do calculations and numerical and what-if analyses easily
  - o Presentation: to create slide presentations
  - o Database: to store and organize data
  - o Note-taking: to take notes and easily organize and search them
  - o Personal information manager (PIM): to keep you organized by putting a calendar, address book, notepad, and to-do lists within your computer
- Individuals can also use productivity software to help with business-like tasks such as managing personal finances and preparing taxes.

**4. What kinds of software do small and large businesses use?**

- Businesses use software to help them with the following tasks:
  - o Finances and accounting
  - o Desktop publishing
  - o Web page authoring
  - o Project management
  - o Customer Relationship Management (CRM)
  - o Enterprise Resource Planning (ERP)
  - o E-commerce
- Businesses may use specialized business software (or vertical market software) that is designed for their specific industry.
- Some businesses also use specialized drawing software to create technical drawings and computer-aided design (CAD) software to create 3-D models.

## Multimedia and Entertainment Software

**5. What types of multimedia and entertainment software are available?**

- Multimedia software is software for playing, copying, recording, editing, and organizing multimedia files. Multimedia software includes the following:
  - o Digital image- and video-editing software
  - o Digital audio software
  - o Specialty software to produce computer games
- Educational and reference software is available to help you master, study, design, create, or plan.
  - o Simulation (training) programs let users experience or control the software as if it were the actual software or an actual event. Simulated programs safely allow users to experience potentially dangerous situations without the risks of experiencing the same situations in real life.
  - o Course management software provides traditional classroom tools such as discussion areas, assignment features, and grade books over the Internet.
  - o Drawing software includes a wide range of software programs that help you create and edit simple line-based drawings or create more-complex designs for both imaginative and technical illustrations.

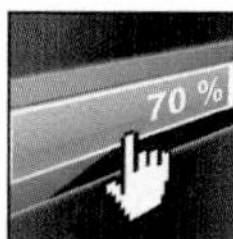


## Managing Your Software

**6. What's important to know when buying software?**

- You must purchase software unless it is freeware or open source.
- When you purchase software, you're actually purchasing the license to use it and therefore must abide by the terms of the licensing agreement you accept when installing the program.
- Before installing software on your computer, ensure that your system setup meets the system requirements that specify the minimum recommended standards for the operating system, processor, primary memory (RAM), and hard drive capacity. Sometimes, there are other specifications for the video card, monitor, optical drive, and other peripherals.

**7. How do I install and uninstall software?**

- When installing software, you are often given the choice between a full (typical) or custom installation.
  - o A full installation copies all the files and programs from the distribution disc to your computer's hard drive.
  - o A custom installation lets you decide which features you want installed on your hard drive.
- When uninstalling software, it's best to use the uninstall feature that comes with the operating system.
  - o In Windows 8, right-click on the program tile on the Start screen, then select Uninstall from the bottom tab that displays.
  - o Using the uninstall feature of the operating system when uninstalling a program will help you ensure that all additional program files are removed from your computer.
- Your system comes with preinstalled software, such as the operating system and possibly some files from the manufacturer.
- One of the first things you should do after you purchase a new computer is create a recovery drive that you can use to reboot the computer after a system failure and return the computer to the condition it was in when you first purchased it.

Be sure to check out the companion website for additional materials to help you review and learn, including a Tech Bytes Weekly newsletter—**pearsonhighered.com/techinaction.** And don't forget the Replay Videos .

# key terms//

accounting software **135**
application software **124**
audio-editing software **143**
beta version **146**
cloud computing **142**
computer-aided design (CAD) **135**
copyleft **148**
course management software **144**
custom installation **149**
database software **130**
desktop publishing (DTP) software **135**
digital video-editing software **141**
drawing software (illustration software) **144**
End User License Agreement (EULA) **147**
financial planning software **133**
freeware **146**
full installation **149**
image-editing software **140**
macro **133**
management software **144**
multimedia software **140**
open source software **124**
personal information manager (PIM) software **132**
presentation software **129**
productivity software **126**
program **124**
proprietary (commercial) software **124**
simulation programs **144**
software **124**
Software as a Service (SaaS) **125**
software license **147**
software piracy **134**
software suite **126**
spreadsheet software **128**
system requirements **148**
system software **124**
tax preparation software **133**
template **133**
vertical market software **135**
web-based applications **125**
web page–authoring software **135**
wizard **133**
word processing software **126**

## making the transition to . . . next semester//

1. **Going to the Cloud**

   You really like the concept of web-based computing and want to use as many web-based programs as possible. Write a brief paragraph discussing the programs you would use for productivity, file storage, collaboration, and communication. What are the benefits and drawbacks of each choice?

2. **Collaborating with Software**

   You've been assigned the dreaded group project. For once, you have a great group of students to work with, but none of your schedules line up so that you can meet in person. You decide to use web-based applications because they are great for collaborating online. Research different types of software you anticipate your group needing to use, including web-based productivity software, sites that enable sharing and storing files online, and sites to use for group video chats and group texting. Create a chart or list that identifies the best software for these needs.

3. **Using OneNote**

   You've been assigned a research paper, which will be very extensive. You're required to collect information for the paper throughout the semester, so you need a good system to keep your notes, readings, and data organized. You've heard OneNote is a great tool for just this type of project, but since you've never used the software, you don't know where to start. Go to **microsoft.com** and search for "Templates for OneNote." Find several good templates that will help you get started. What are the features of the templates that you chose? Discuss which template you would most likely use, and why.

## making the transition to . . . the workplace//

1. **Required Software for the Job**

   Almost every profession requires some use of technology and software. Identify the field you would like to enter upon graduation, and then after doing some research, compile a list of software applications you expect to use in your job. If possible, list a proprietary application, as well as open source and web-based alternatives. Note those applications for which you will need training. If your chosen field currently does not require software, discuss why that may be the case. Do you foresee a time when software may be helpful? If so, what kind of software might that be?

2. **Tracking Your Personal Finances**

   You are finally out on your own—graduated from college and working your first job. It's time to track how much you spend versus what you're earning. You really don't want to live paycheck to paycheck, and you want to begin a savings plan to build a rainy-day fund. Investigate online financial planning sites such as Mint (**mint.com**) and Yodlee (**yodlee.com**) and then choose the one that seems best. If you can, download a version of the software for your smartphone. Track your expenses for a few weeks, and identify areas in which you can cut back on your spending. What are the features of the software that you like? Discuss how this may or may not help you in your goal of achieving financial independence.

# Software for Startups

## Problem

You and your friends have decided to start Recycle Technology, a not-for-profit organization that would recycle and donate used computer equipment. In the first planning session, your group recognizes the need for certain software to help you with various parts of the business such as tracking inventory, designing notices, mapping addresses for pickup and delivery, and soliciting residents by phone or e-mail about recycling events, to name a few.

## Task

Split your class into as many groups of four or five as possible. Make some groups responsible for locating free or web-based software solutions and other groups responsible for finding proprietary solutions. Another group could be responsible for finding mobile app solutions. The groups will present and compare results with each other at the end of the project.

## Process

1. Identify a team leader who will coordinate the project and record and present results.
2. Each team is to identify the various kinds of software that Recycle Technology needs. Consider software that will be needed for all the various tasks required to run the organization such as communication, marketing, tracking, inventory management, and finance.
3. Create a detailed and organized list of required software applications. Depending on your team, you will specify either proprietary software or open source software.

## Conclusion

Most organizations require a variety of software to accomplish different tasks. Compare your results with those of other team members. Were there applications that you didn't think about, but that other members did? How expensive is it to ensure that even the smallest company has all the software required to carry out daily activities, or can the needs be met with free, open source products?

# Open Source Software

Ethical conduct is a stream of decisions you make all day long. In this exercise, you'll research and then role-play a complicated ethical situation. The role you play might or might not match your own personal beliefs, but your research and use of logic will enable you to represent the view assigned. An arbitrator will watch and comment on both sides of the arguments, and together, the team will agree on an ethical solution.

## Topic: Proprietary Software Versus Open Source Software

Proprietary software has set restrictions on use and can be very expensive, whereas open source software is freely available for users to use as is or to change, improve, and redistribute. Open source software has become acceptable as a cost-effective alternative to proprietary software—so much so that it is reported that the increased adoption of open source software has caused a drop in revenue to the proprietary software industry. But determining which software to use involves more than just reducing the IT budget.

## Research Areas to Consider

- Open source software (Linux, Apache OpenOffice suite, and Mozilla.org)
- Proprietary software (Microsoft Windows and Office, Apple Mac OS X and iWork)
- Copyright licensing
- Open source development

## Process

1. Divide the class into teams.
2. Research the areas cited above and devise a scenario in which someone is a proponent for open source software but is being rebuffed by someone who feels that "you get what you pay for" and is a big proponent of using proprietary software.
3. Team members should write a summary that provides background information for their character—for example: open source proponent, proprietary developer, or arbitrator—and that details their character's behaviors to set the stage for the role-playing event. Then, team members should create an outline to use during the role-playing event.
4. Team members should arrange a mutually convenient time to meet for the exchange, using a virtual meeting tool or by meeting in person
5. Team members should present their case to the class or submit a PowerPoint presentation for review by the rest of the class, along with the summary and resolution they developed.

## Conclusion

As technology becomes ever more prevalent and integrated into our lives, more and more ethical dilemmas will present themselves. Being able to understand and evaluate both sides of the argument, while responding in a personally or socially ethical manner, will be an important skill.

# 5 System Software: The Operating System, Utility Programs, and File Management

## Understanding System Software

### Operating System Fundamentals

**OBJECTIVES**

1. What software is included in system software? **(p. 160)**
2. What are the different kinds of operating systems? **(pp. 160–163)**
3. What are the most common operating systems? **(pp. 162–165)**

**Sound Byte:** Customizing Windows

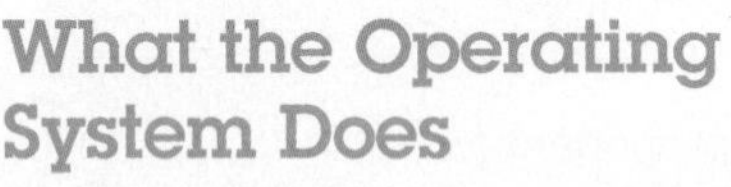

### What the Operating System Does

**OBJECTIVES**

4. How does the operating system provide a means for users to interact with the computer? **(p. 166)**
5. How does the operating system help manage resources such as the processor, memory, storage, hardware, and peripheral devices? **(pp. 167–171)**
6. How does the operating system interact with application software? **(p. 171)**

### The Boot Process: Starting Your Computer

**OBJECTIVE**

7. How does the operating system help the computer start up? **(pp. 172–174)**

**Active Helpdesk:** Starting the Computer: The Boot Process

## Using System Software

### The Windows Interface

**OBJECTIVE**

8. What are the main features of the Windows interface? **(pp. 178–183)**

### Organizing Your Computer: File Management

**OBJECTIVE**

9. How does the operating system help me keep my computer organized? **(pp. 184–188)**

**Sound Byte:** File Management

**Active Helpdesk:** Organizing Your Computer: File Management

### Utility Programs

**OBJECTIVE**

10. What utility programs are included in system software and what do they do? **(pp. 189–195)**

**Active Helpdesk:** Using Utility Programs

**Sound Byte:** File Compression

**Sound Byte:** Hard Disk Anatomy

**Sound Byte:** Letting Your Computer Clean Up After Itself

The information in this text is written for Windows 8.1. If you are still running Windows 8, your screens and task instructions may vary slightly.

For all media in this chapter go to **pearsonhighered.com /techinaction** or **MyITLab**.

*(Mary Anne Poatsy; Ferenc Szelepcsenyi/Shutterstock; Ivancovlad/Shutterstock; Bloomberg/Getty Images; Stanislav Popov/ Shutterstock; reji/Fotolia) (Redshinestudio/Fotolia)*

# HOW COOL IS THIS?

Are you **constantly switching** between devices during the day, such as a **laptop** at work, a **tablet** at home, and a **smartphone** wherever else you happen to be? Ever wish you could **pick up right where you left off** on your laptop browser when you open your smartphone browser? Just install **Google Chrome** on all your devices. Then make sure you **always log in** to the Chrome browser with your Google account. You can then set the Chrome browser to **sync between your devices**. You'll be able to access open tabs on your laptop computer when you go out to lunch and fire up your smartphone browser. Chrome also **syncs your bookmarks, history, and other browser preferences**, and these settings are all also saved in your Google account along with open tab information. So switch to Chrome on all your devices and you can **enjoy the same browsing experience** no matter which device you're using.

# Understanding System Software

As discussed in the previous chapter, your computer uses two basic types of software: application software and system software. **Application software** is the software you use to do everyday tasks at home and at work. **System software** is the set of programs that helps run the computer and coordinates instructions between application software and the computer's hardware devices. From the moment you turn on your computer to the time you shut it down, you're interacting with system software.

## operating system FUNDAMENTALS

System software consists of two primary types of programs: the *operating system* and *utility programs*. The **operating system (OS)** is a group of programs that controls how your computer functions. The OS:

- Manages the computer's hardware, including the processor, memory, and storage devices, as well as peripheral devices such as the printer;
- Provides a consistent means for application software to work with the central processing unit (CPU); and
- Is responsible for the management, scheduling, and coordination of tasks

You interact with your OS through the **user interface**—the *desktop, icons,* and *menus* that let you communicate with your computer.

A **utility program** is a small program that performs many of the general housekeeping tasks for your computer, such as system maintenance and file compression. A set of utility programs is bundled with each OS, but you can also buy standalone utility programs that often provide more features.

**Do all computers have operating systems?** Every computer, from the smallest laptop to the largest supercomputer, has an OS. Even cell phones, game consoles, cars, and some appliances have operating systems. The role of the OS is critical; the computer can't operate without it.

**Are all operating systems alike?** You're probably familiar with Microsoft Windows, Apple OS X, and perhaps the Android operating system if it's on your phone, but many other operating systems exist. Laptops, tablet computers, and smartphones all need specific operating systems designed to take advantage of their unique characteristics. However, as devices begin to converge in terms of functionality, and operating systems continue to become more powerful, developers such as Microsoft and Apple are making operating systems that have similar functionality (such as OS X and iOS) or single operating systems (such as Windows 8) that can run on multiple devices. Figure 5.1 lists a number of common operating systems.

When operating systems were originally developed, they were designed for a single user performing one task at a time

FIGURE 5.1

**Common Operating Systems**

| OS NAME | DEVELOPED BY | AVAILABLE ON |
|---|---|---|
| **Windows 8** | Microsoft | Laptops, tablets, desktops, all-in-ones, cell phones |
| **OS X 10.9 (Mavericks)** | Apple | Laptops, desktops, all-in-ones |
| **iOS 7** | Apple | Tablets, iPhones, iPod Touches |
| **Android 4.4** | Google | Cell phones, tablets |
| **Linux** | Open source | Laptops, desktops |

(© MONICA M. DAVEY/epa/Corbis; Kevork Djansezian/Getty Images; Bloomberg/Getty Images; tibbbb/Fotolia)

(that is, they were *single-user, single-task operating systems*). However, modern operating systems allow a single user to **multitask**—to perform more than one process at a time. And operating systems such as Windows and OS X provide networking capabilities as well, essentially making them *multiuser, multitasking operating systems*.

Operating systems can be categorized by the type of device in which they're installed, such as robots and specialized equipment with built-in computers, mainframes and network computers, mobile devices, and personal computers. Next, we'll look at these different types of operating systems.

## Real-Time Operating Systems

**Why do machines with built-in computers need an OS?** Machinery that performs a repetitive series of specific tasks in an exact amount of time requires a **real-time operating system (RTOS)**. Also referred to as *embedded systems,* RTOSs require minimal user interaction. This type of OS is a program with a specific purpose, and it must guarantee certain response times for particular computing tasks; otherwise, the machine is useless. The programs are written specifically for the needs of the devices and their functions. Therefore, there are no commercially available standard RTOS software programs. Devices that must perform regimented tasks or record precise results—such as measurement instruments found in the scientific, defense, and aerospace industries—require RTOSs. Examples include digital storage oscilloscopes and the Mars Reconnaissance Orbiter.

**Where else are RTOSs used today?** You also encounter RTOSs every day in devices such as fuel-injection systems in car engines, automobile "infotainment" systems, and some common appliances. RTOSs are also found in many types of robotic equipment. Television stations use robotic cameras with RTOSs that glide across a suspended cable system to record sports events from many angles (see Figure 5.2).

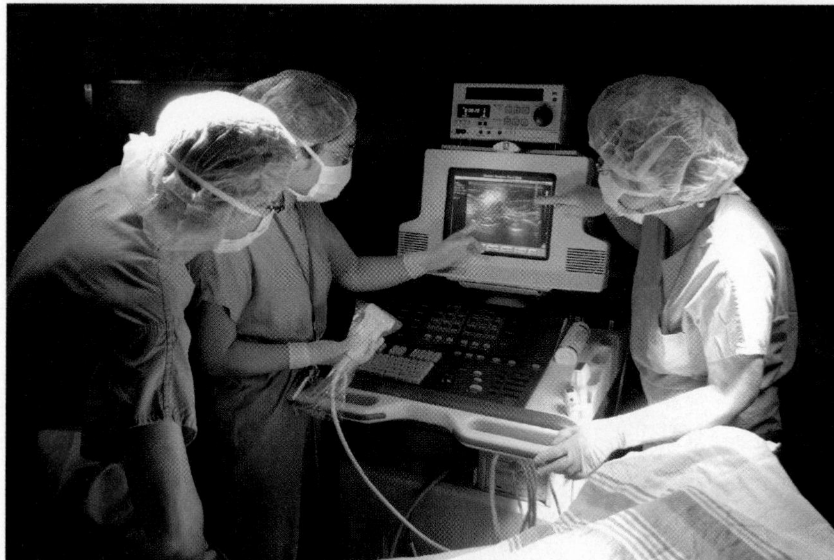

**FIGURE 5.2** Devices such as TV sky cameras, cars, and medical equipment use RTOSs. *(John Pyle/Cal Sport Media/Newscom; The Washington Post/Getty Images; Elfstrom/David Elfstrom/iStockphoto)*

## Operating Systems for Networks, Servers, and Mainframes

**What kind of operating systems do networks use?** A **multiuser operating system (or network operating system)** lets more than one user access the computer system at a time by handling and prioritizing requests from multiple users. Networks (groups of computers connected to each other so that they can communicate and share resources) need a multiuser OS because many users simultaneously access the server (the computer that manages network resources such as printing and communications). The latest versions of Windows and OS X can be considered network operating systems: They enable users to set up basic networks in their homes and small businesses.

In larger networks, a more robust network OS is installed on servers and manages all user requests. For example, on a network where users share a printer, the network OS ensures that the printer prints only one document at a time in the order the requests were made. Examples of network operating systems include Windows Server, Linux, and UNIX.

**What is UNIX? UNIX** is a multiuser, multitasking OS that is used as a network OS, although it's also often found on PCs. Developed in 1969 by Ken Thompson and Dennis Ritchie of AT&T's Bell Labs, the UNIX code was initially not proprietary—in other words, no company owned it. Rather, any programmer was allowed to use the code and modify it to meet his or her needs. UNIX is now a brand that belongs to the company The Open Group, but any vendor that meets testing requirements and pays a fee can use the UNIX name. Individual vendors then modify the UNIX code to run specifically on their hardware.

**What other kinds of computers require a multiuser OS?** Mainframes and supercomputers also require multiuser operating systems. Mainframes routinely support hundreds or thousands of users at time, and supercomputers are often accessed by multiple people working on complex calculations. Examples of mainframe operating systems include UNIX, Linux on System z, and IBM's z/OS, whereas the vast majority of supercomputers use Linux.

## Operating Systems for Mobile Devices

**What kind of OS does a smartphone use?** Figure 5.3 shows the most common operating systems found on smartphones such as the iPhone. Most smartphones have at least modest multitasking capabilities, such as letting you check e-mail while you're on a phone call. More advanced smartphones provide greater multitasking, such as letting you talk and use apps at the same time.

**What OS do tablets use?** Popular tablet operating systems include iOS, Android, and Windows (see Figure 5.4). iPads use iOS, whereas a number of different tablets (such as the Samsung Galaxy Tab and the Motorola Xoom) use versions of Android. The Kindle Fire also runs a customized version of Android. Until the release of Windows 8 in 2012, Microsoft didn't have a popular tablet OS, but the company has managed to grab a 4.5% market share releasing Windows 8, which is optimized for tablet devices.

**Do gaming consoles and iPods use an OS?** Gaming systems such as Microsoft's Xbox 360, the Nintendo Wii, and the Sony PlayStation, as well as personal media players such as the iPod, all require system software developed specifically for the particular device. The system software controls the physical aspects of the device (such as game controllers) as well as other application programs that come with the device. For example, the operating systems on gaming consoles control web browsing and file storage of media and photos as well as playing of DVDs and games.

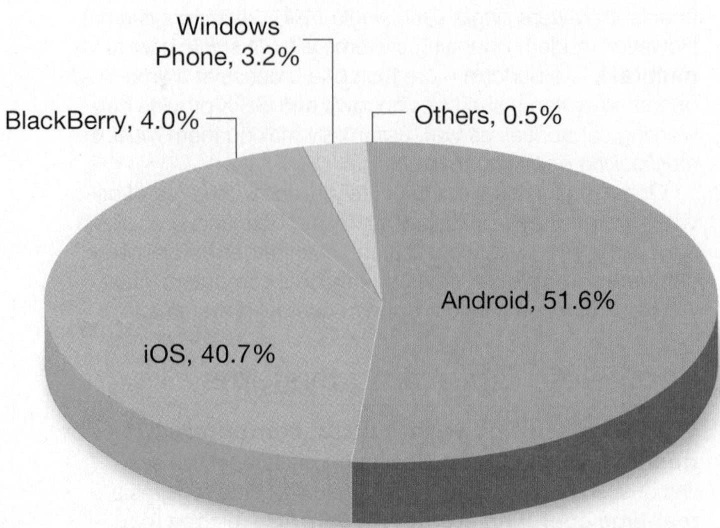


**FIGURE 5.3** Popular Smartphone Operating Systems *(Based on U.S. Market Share, August 2013, per comScore; Stats from http://www.latinospost.com/articles/29175/20131007/ios-vs-android-windows-phone-market-share-2013-news-google.htm)*

## Operating Systems for Personal Computers

**What are the most popular operating systems for personal computers?** Microsoft Windows, OS X, and Linux (an open source OS) are the top three operating systems for personal computers. Although they share similar features, each is unique.

**What's special about Windows?** Microsoft **Windows** is an operating environment that incorporates a user-friendly, visual interface like the one that was first introduced with Apple's OS. Over time, improvements in Windows have concentrated on increasing user functionality and friendliness, improving Internet capabilities, supporting home networks, and enhancing file privacy and security. The newest release of Microsoft's OS, **Windows 8**, provides a new interface optimized for touch-screen devices.

**What's the difference between the various editions of Windows 8 operating systems?** Windows 8 simplifies consumer choices because it's offered in only two versions: Windows 8 and Windows 8 Pro. For most users, Windows 8 is sufficient, as it now includes many features (such as remote access) that weren't included in Windows 7 Home Premium. However, Windows 8 doesn't include Media Center, which you may be used to seeing in previous versions of Windows. Media Center is now available only as an add-on package for Windows 8 Pro. Windows 8.1 is the latest release currently available of the Windows 8 OS.

**What's special about the Mac OS?** In 1984, **Mac OS** became the first commercially available OS to incorporate a **graphical user interface**, or **GUI**, with user-friendly point-and-click technology. Many Mac users have switched from Windows because of the "coolness" of the Mac OS, OS X. With the release of the Mountain Lion version, Apple added many of the popular and innovative features loved by iOS

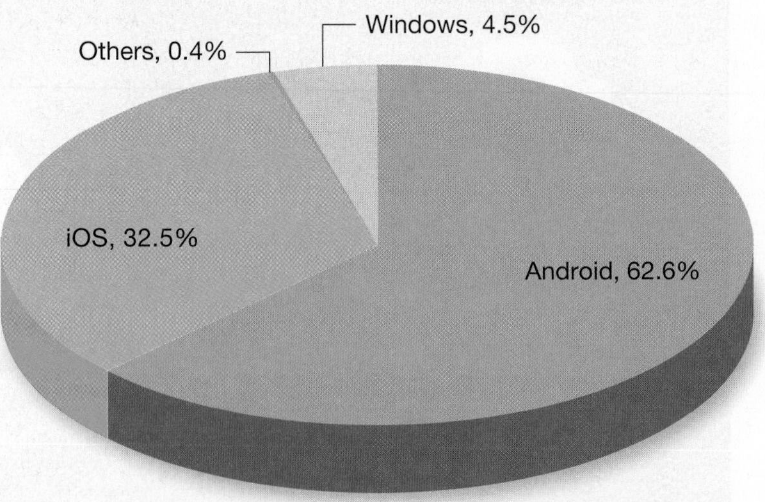


**FIGURE 5.4** Popular Tablet Operating Systems *(Based on Market Share, Second Quarter 2013, per IDC; Stats taken from http://news.yahoo.com/apple-once-dominant-tablet-market-share-collapsed-151513016.html)*

users, such as messages, reminders, notes, and a notification center. The latest version, Mavericks, was released in late 2013 and features interface and usability enhancements designed to dovetail with the iOS 7 upgrade released earlier that year. If you've been using Windows for a while, you shouldn't have any problems making the transition to OS X. You'll notice immediately that OS X uses the same desktop metaphors as Windows, including icons for folders and a Trash Can (similar to a Recycle Bin) for deleted documents. OS X also includes a window-based interface like the one in Windows.

OS X is based on the UNIX operating system, which is exceptionally stable and reliable. However, just as with any other OS, you still need to install updates as they become available and protect yourself from viruses, spyware, and other malicious software.

**What is Linux? Linux** is an open source OS designed for use on personal computers and as a network OS. Open source software is freely available for anyone to use or modify as he or she wishes. Linux began in 1991 as a part-time project of Finnish university student Linus Torvalds. It has since been tweaked by scores of programmers as part of the Free Software Foundation GNU Project (**gnu.org**).

Linux has a reputation as a stable OS that is not subject to crashes or failures. Because the code is open and available to anyone, Linux can be modified or updated quickly by hundreds of programmers around the world.

**What computers use Linux?** Linux is gaining popularity among computer manufacturers, which have begun to ship it with some of their latest PCs. Android, the tablet and phone OS, is Linux based. Because the overall size of Android is much smaller than that of Windows, many netbook users choose to use it in place of the factory-installed Windows OS (see Figure 5.5). Some Linux-based operating systems have been modified to run on iPods and gaming systems.

**Where can I get Linux?** Linux is available for download in various packages known as **distributions**, or **distros**. Distros include the underlying Linux kernel (the code that provides Linux's basic functionality) and special modifications to the OS, and may also include additional open source software (such as OpenOffice). A good place to start researching distros is **distrowatch.com**. This site tracks Linux distros and provides helpful tips for beginners on choosing one.

# BITS&BYTES

## Upgrading Your Operating System

If you've had your computer for a year or two, you may be wondering whether you should upgrade to the newest release of your OS (such as going from Windows 7 to Windows 8.1). Here are a few key things to consider before taking the plunge:

- **Is your current OS still supported?** When the company deploys new versions of operating systems, it may stop supporting older versions. If your current version will no longer be supported, it's best to upgrade to a newer version.
- **Are there significant features in the new version that you want?** Operating systems are often upgraded to provide extra security, better performance, and additional features intended to make your computer experience more efficient, and perhaps even more fun. But if the only features the new version offers are ones you don't need, you should reconsider upgrading.
- **Will your hardware work with the new version of the OS?** Check the minimum operating requirements (required RAM, processor speed, hard drive space, etc.) of the new version to ensure that your computer can handle the workload of the new OS. You'll also need to make sure drivers for the new OS are available for all your hardware devices and peripherals to ensure they'll work with it. Microsoft has made this easy with Windows 8.1 Upgrade Assistant, which you can download from Microsoft's website. The Upgrade Assistant scans your hardware, devices, and installed programs for compatibility, advises you on how to resolve any issues, and recommends what you should do before upgrading.
- **Is your application software compatible with the new version of the OS?** Usually, application software works fine with a new version of an OS. Sometimes it doesn't. Check with software vendors regarding compatibility. Most programs that run under Windows 7 will run from the desktop in Windows 8.1. And Windows 8.1 has an upgrade option in its install program that lets you install Windows 8.1 over an existing installation of Windows 7. This relieves you from having to install all your application software after upgrading.

Before starting the upgrade, back up all your data files so you won't lose anything accidentally during the upgrading process. File Recovery and other backup features in Windows make this job less of a hassle.

**Does it matter what OS is on my computer?** An OS is designed to run on specific CPUs. CPUs have different designs, which can require modifying the OS software to allow it to communicate properly with each CPU. The combination of an OS and a specific processor is referred to as a computer's **platform**.

For user convenience, computers and other devices usually come with an OS already installed. However, with some PCs, you can specify which OS you'd like installed when you order your device. For example, Windows and Linux can run on most of the hardware being sold today. Your choice of an OS in this case is mostly a matter of price and personal preference. However, Apple equipment—computers, iPhones, iPads, and iPod Touches—comes with Apple operating systems preinstalled.

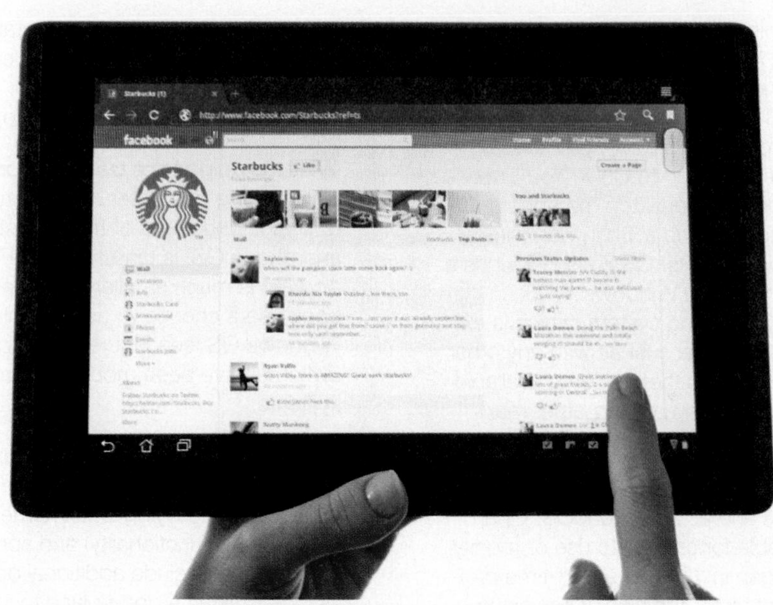

FIGURE 5.5 Developed by Google, the Android OS is based on Linux and runs easily on netbooks and tablets. *(Andrew Rubtsov / Alamy)*

Note that most *application software* is OS dependent. You need to make sure you get the correct version of the application software for your OS, such as Microsoft Office 2013 for Windows and Microsoft Office 2011 for OS X.

**Can I have more than one OS on my computer?** Many people run more than one OS on their computers because different operating systems offer different features. For example, Windows and Linux both run well on Apple computers. A standard utility included in OS X called Boot Camp lets you boot into either Windows or OS X. And if you want to run both OS X and Windows OS at the same time, you can create "virtual drives" using virtualization software such as Parallels or VMware Fusion.

In Windows, you can create a separate section of your hard drive (called a *partition*) and install another OS on it while leaving your original Windows installation untouched. After installing the second OS, when your computer starts, you're offered a choice of which OS to use.

SOUND BYTE
**Customizing Windows**

In this Sound Byte, you'll find out how to customize your desktop. You'll learn how to configure the desktop, set up a screen saver, change pointer options, customize the Start screen, and manage user accounts.

**How do operating systems use the "cloud"?** Now that broadband Internet access and providing computer resources via the Internet (so-called *cloud computing*) are becoming more commonplace, operating systems have features that are tied to cloud computing. Here are a few examples:

- Windows 8 features tighter integration with the cloud. Using your *Microsoft account,* Windows 8 stores your settings and keeps track of applications you've purchased from the Windows store online. You can easily access and store files online in your *OneDrive account*. You can also log into your Windows account from any Windows 8 machine and be able to see your familiar desktop and applications.
- Similarly, OS X Mavericks allows you to sign in with your *Apple ID,* which provides access to Apple's *iCloud* system. iCloud stores your content online and automatically pushes it out to all your Apple devices.
- Google has launched the *Google Chrome OS* (see Figure 5.6), which is a web-based OS. With the Chrome OS, virtually no files are installed on your computing device. Rather, the main functionality of the OS is provided by accessing the web through a web browser. Chrome OS is only available on certain hardware from Google's manufacturing partners, and these devices are called *Chromebooks*. The Chrome OS should not be confused with the *Google Chrome browser*. The browser is application software that can run in many different operating systems.

Another pioneer in accessing cloud-based storage and applications with a browser is the open source product eyeOS (**eyeos.com**). eyeOS allows companies to set up private clouds containing data and applications that can be accessed by their employees, partners, or customers. Using almost any computing device with a browser, users can access their data and applications through an Internet connection. ■

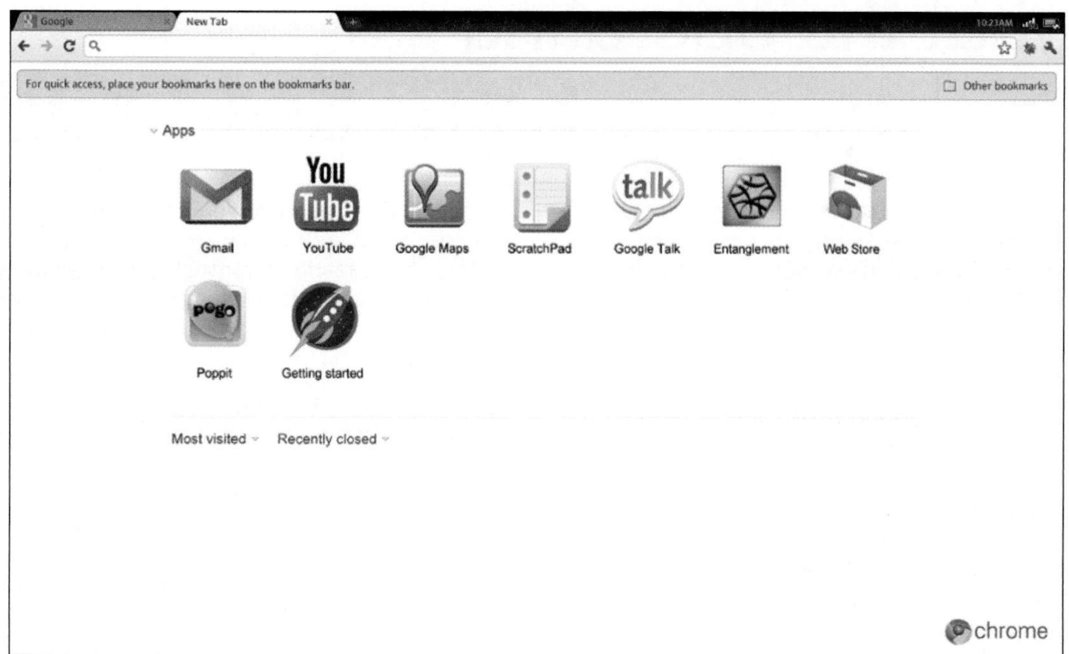


**FIGURE 5.6** The Google Chrome OS has a very minimalist look. *(Courtesy of Google, Inc.)*

# BITS&BYTES

## OS Market Share Battle: It's Still a Windows World

So who is winning the OS market share war? It depends on the type of device. For conventional desktop and laptop computers, hands down the winner is still various versions of Windows, with 89% of the market (see Figure 5.7). But as of October 2013, Windows only had a 4% market share on smartphones vs. Android's 81%. Clearly Microsoft is losing the phone OS wars.

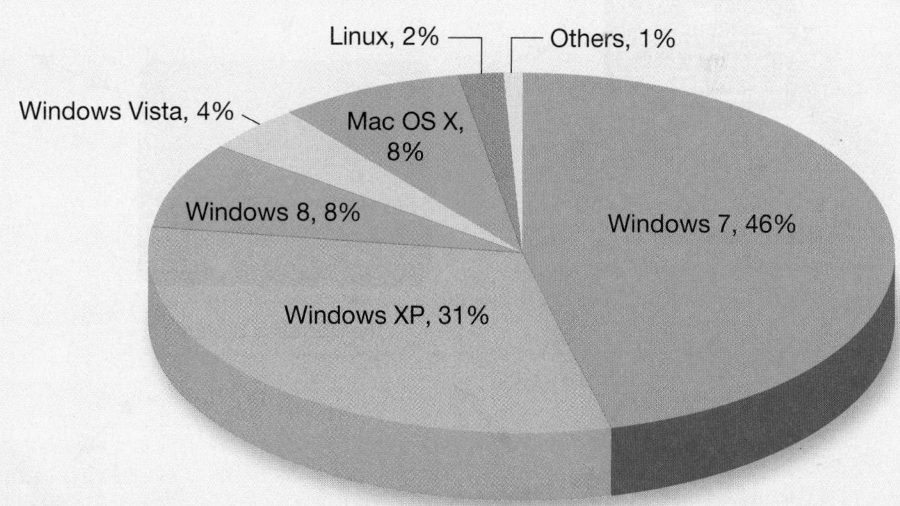


**FIGURE 5.7** Desktop/Laptop Operating Systems *(Based on Market Share, September 2013, per netmarketshare.com)*

# what the operating SYSTEM DOES

As shown in Figure 5.8, the OS is like an orchestra's conductor. It coordinates and directs the flow of data and information through the computer system. In this section, we explore the operations of the OS in detail.

## The User Interface

**How does the OS control how I interact with my computer?** The OS provides a user interface that lets you interact with the computer. The first personal computers used *Microsoft Disk Operating System* (*MS-DOS,* or just *DOS*), which had a command-driven interface, as shown in Figure 5.9a. A **command-driven interface** is one in which you enter commands to communicate with the computer system. The DOS commands were not always easy to understand; as a result, the interface proved to be too complicated for the average user. Therefore, PCs were used primarily in business and by professional computer operators.

The command-driven interface was later improved by incorporating a menu-driven interface, as shown in Figure 5.9b. A **menu-driven interface** is one in which you choose commands from menus displayed on the screen. Menu-driven interfaces eliminated the need for users to know every command because they could select most of the commonly used commands from a menu. However, they were still not easy enough for most people to use.

**What kind of interface do operating systems use today?** Current personal computer operating systems such as Microsoft Windows and OS X use a graphical user interface, or GUI (pronounced "gooey"). Unlike command- and menu-driven interfaces, GUIs display graphics and use the point-and-click technology of the mouse and cursor (or human finger), making them much more user-friendly.

Linux-based operating systems do not have a single default GUI interface. Instead, users are free to choose among many commercially available and free interfaces, such as GNOME and KDE, each of which provides a different look and feel.

## Processor Management

**Why does the OS need to manage the processor?** When you use your computer, you're usually asking the processor (also called the CPU) to perform

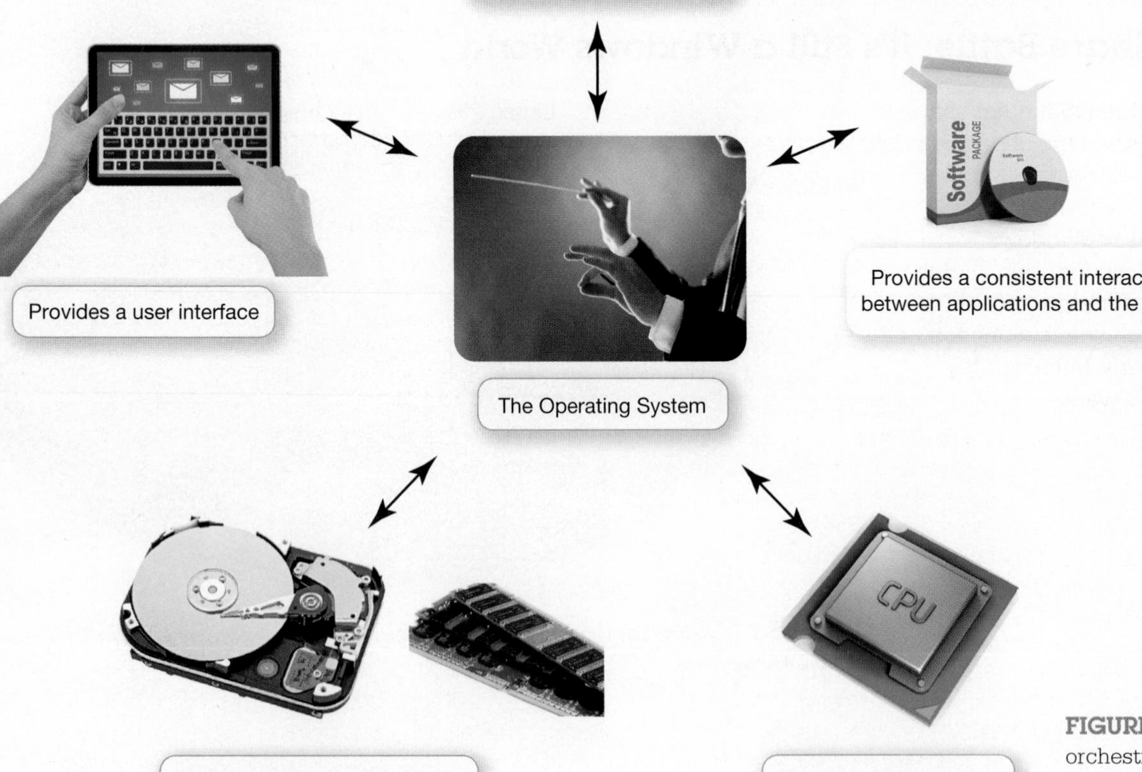


**FIGURE 5.8** The OS is the orchestra conductor of your computer, coordinating its many activities and devices.

(StockPhotosArt/Shutterstock; ra2studio/Shutterstock; Yuri Arcurs Media / SuperFusion / SuperStock; © Dukes - Fotolia; Roosmin/Shutterstock; Roosmin/Shutterstock)

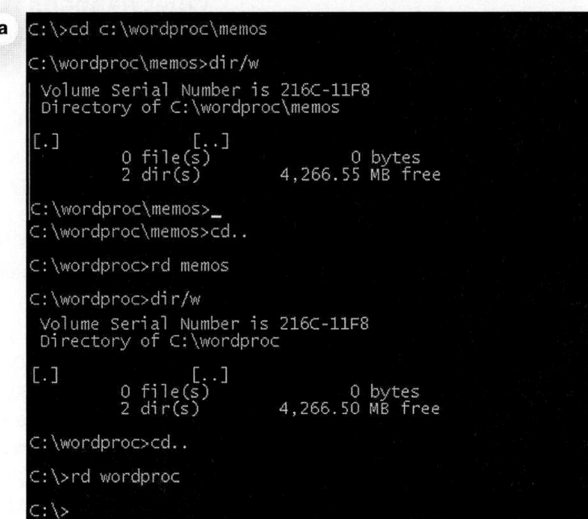

C:\>cd c:\wordproc\memos
C:\wordproc\memos>dir/w
Volume Serial Number is 216C-11F8
Directory of C:\wordproc\memos
[.] [..]
0 file(s) 0 bytes
2 dir(s) 4,266.55 MB free
C:\wordproc\memos>_
C:\wordproc\memos>cd..
C:\wordproc>rd memos
C:\wordproc>dir/w
Volume Serial Number is 216C-11F8
Directory of C:\wordproc
[.] [..]
0 file(s) 0 bytes
2 dir(s) 4,266.50 MB free
C:\wordproc>cd..
C:\>rd wordproc
C:\>


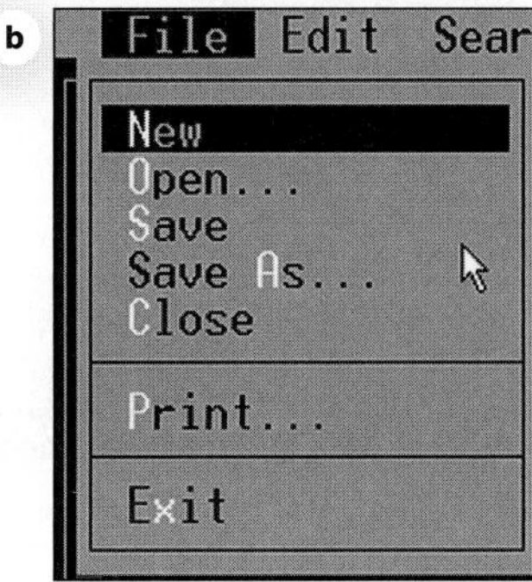


**FIGURE 5.9** (a) A command-driven interface. (b) A menu-driven interface.

several tasks at once. For example, you might be printing a Word document, chatting with your friends on Facebook, and watching a movie using the Blu-ray drive—all at the same time, or at least what appears to be at the same time. Although the CPU is powerful, it still needs the OS to arrange the execution of all these activities in a systematic way.

To do so, the OS assigns a slice of its time to each activity that requires the processor's attention. The OS must then switch among different processes millions of times a second to make it appear that everything is happening seamlessly. Otherwise, you wouldn't be able to watch a movie and print at the same time without experiencing delays in the process.

**How exactly does the OS coordinate all the activities?** When you create and print a document in Word while also watching a Blu-ray movie, for example, many different devices in the computer are involved, including your keyboard, mouse, Blu-ray drive, and printer. Every keystroke, every mouse click (or touch on the screen), and each signal to the printer and from the Blu-ray drive creates an action, or **event**, in the respective device (keyboard, mouse, Blu-ray drive, or printer) to which the OS responds.

Sometimes these events occur sequentially (such as when you type characters one at a time), but other events involve two or more devices working concurrently (such as the printer printing while you type and watch a movie). Although it looks as though all the devices are working at the same time, the OS in fact switches back and forth among processes, controlling the timing of events on which the processor works.

For example, assume you're typing and want to print a document. When you tell your computer to print your document, the printer generates a unique signal called an **interrupt** that tells the OS that it's in need of immediate attention. Every device has its own type of interrupt, which is associated with an **interrupt handler**, a special numerical code that prioritizes the requests. These requests are placed in the interrupt table in the computer's primary memory (RAM). The OS processes the task assigned a higher priority before processing a task assigned a lower priority. This is called **preemptive multitasking**.

In our example, when the OS receives the interrupt from the printer, it suspends the CPU's typing activity and Blu-ray activity and puts a "memo" in a special location in RAM called a *stack*. The memo is a reminder of what the CPU was doing before it started to work on the printer request. The CPU then retrieves the printer request from the interrupt table and begins to process it. On completion of the printer request, the CPU goes back to the stack, retrieves the memo it placed about the keystroke or Blu-ray activity, and returns to that task until it is interrupted again, in a very quick and seamless fashion, as shown in Figure 5.10.

**What happens if more than one document is waiting to be printed?** The OS also coordinates multiple activities for peripheral devices such as printers. When the processor receives a request to send information to the printer, it first checks with the OS to ensure that the printer is not already in use. If it is, the OS puts the request in another temporary storage area in RAM, called the *buffer*. The request then waits in the buffer until the **spooler**, a program that helps coordinate all print jobs currently being sent to the printer, indicates the printer is available. If more than one print job is waiting, a line (or *queue*) is formed so that the printer can process the requests in order.

## Memory and Storage Management

**Why does the OS have to manage the computer's memory?** As the OS coordinates the activities of the processor, it uses RAM as a temporary storage area for instructions and data the processor needs. The processor then accesses these instructions and data from RAM when it's ready to process them. The OS is therefore responsible for coordinating the space allocations in RAM to ensure there's

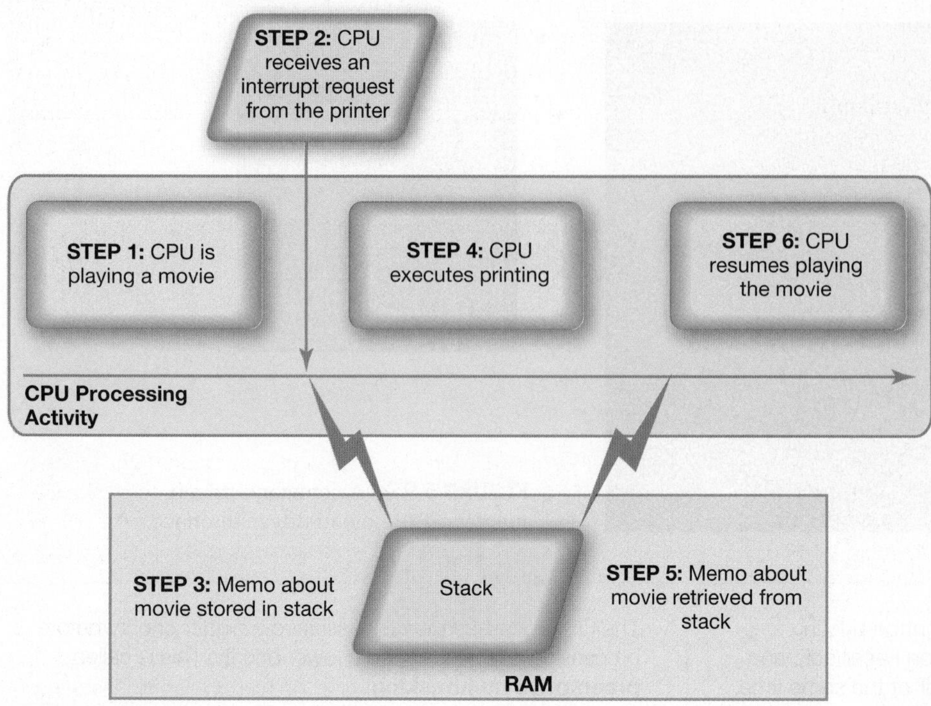
STEP 2: CPU receives an interrupt request from the printer
STEP 1: CPU is playing a movie
STEP 4: CPU executes printing
STEP 6: CPU resumes playing the movie
CPU Processing Activity
STEP 3: Memo about movie stored in stack
Stack
STEP 5: Memo about movie retrieved from stack
RAM

**FIGURE 5.10** How Preemptive Multitasking Works

enough space for all the pending instructions and data. The OS then clears the items from RAM when the processor no longer needs them.

**Can my OS ever run out of RAM?** RAM has limited capacity. Like most users, you'll add new software and peripherals to your computer over time. Most computers sold for home use have between 4 and 16 GB of RAM. If you have an older computer system with less RAM, it might be time to consider buying a new computer or adding more RAM. As you add and upgrade software and increase your usage of the computer system, you might find that the amount of RAM you have is no longer sufficient for your needs.

**What happens if my computer runs out of RAM?** When there isn't enough RAM for the OS to store the required data and instructions, the OS borrows from the more spacious hard drive. This process of optimizing RAM storage by borrowing hard drive space is called **virtual memory**. As shown in Figure 5.11, when more RAM is needed, the OS swaps out from RAM the data or instructions that haven't recently been used and moves them to a temporary storage area on the hard drive called the **swap file** (or **page file**). If the data or instructions in the swap file are needed later, the OS swaps them back into active RAM and replaces them in the hard drive's swap file with less active data or instructions. This process of swapping is known as **paging**.

**Can I ever run out of virtual memory?** Only a portion of the hard drive is allocated to virtual memory. You can manually change this setting to increase the amount of hard drive space allocated, but eventually your computer will become sluggish as it is forced to page more often. This condition of excessive paging is called **thrashing**. The solution to this problem is to increase the amount of RAM in your computer so that it won't be necessary for it to send data and instructions to virtual memory.

**How does the OS manage storage?** If it weren't for the OS, the files and applications you save to the hard drive and other storage locations would be an unorganized mess. Fortunately, the OS has a file-management system that keeps track of the name and location of each file you save and the programs you install. We'll talk more about file management later in this chapter.

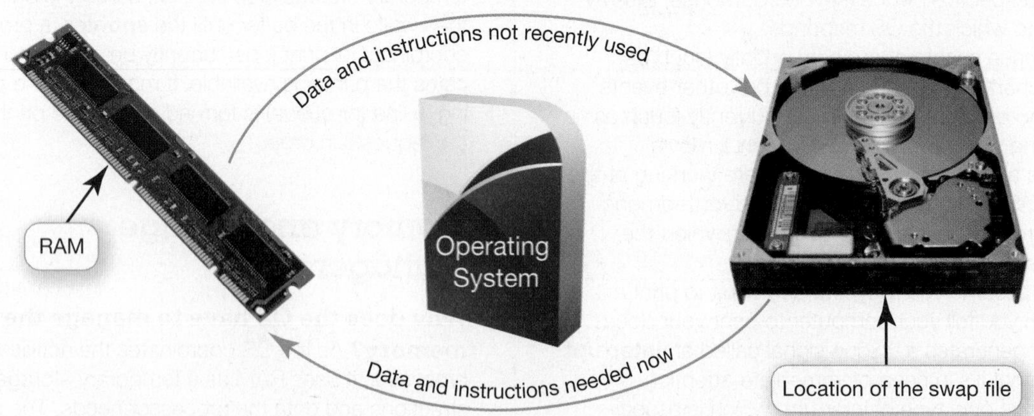
Data and instructions not recently used
RAM
Operating System
Data and instructions needed now
Location of the swap file

**FIGURE 5.11** Virtual memory borrows excess storage capacity from the hard drive when there isn't enough capacity in RAM. *(brontazavra/ Shutterstock; aPERFECT/Fotolia; Tim Dobbs/Shutterstock)*

## Hardware and Peripheral Device Management

**How does the OS manage the hardware and peripheral devices?** Each device attached to your computer comes with a special program called a **device driver** that facilitates communication between the device and the OS. Because the OS must be able to communicate with every device in the computer system, the device driver translates the device's specialized commands into commands the OS can understand, and vice versa. Devices wouldn't function without the proper device drivers because the OS wouldn't know how to communicate with them.

**Do I always need to install drivers?** Today, most devices, such as flash drives, mice, keyboards, and digital cameras, come with the driver already installed in Windows. The devices whose drivers are included in Windows are called Plug and Play devices. **Plug and Play (PnP)** is a software and hardware standard designed to facilitate the installation of new hardware in PCs by including in the OS the drivers these devices need in order to run. Because the OS includes this software, incorporating a new device into your computer system seems automatic. PnP lets you plug a new device into your computer, turn it on, and immediately play (use) the device (see Figure 5.12).

**What happens if the device is not PnP?** Sometimes you may have a device that is so new the drivers aren't yet available automatically in Windows. You'll then be prompted to insert the driver that was provided with the device or downloaded

FIGURE 5.12 A Windows message showing a successful driver install the first time an external hard drive was connected to the computer.

from the Internet. If you obtain a device secondhand and don't receive the device driver, or if you're required to update the device driver, you can often download the necessary driver from the manufacturer's website. You can also go to websites such as DriverZone (**driverzone.com**) to locate drivers.

**Can I damage my system by installing a device driver?** Occasionally, when you install a driver your system may become unstable (that is, programs may stop responding, certain actions may cause a crash, or the device or the entire system may stop working). Although this is uncommon, it can happen. Fortunately, to remedy the problem, Windows has a Roll Back Driver feature that removes a newly installed driver and replaces it with the last one that worked (see Figure 5.13).

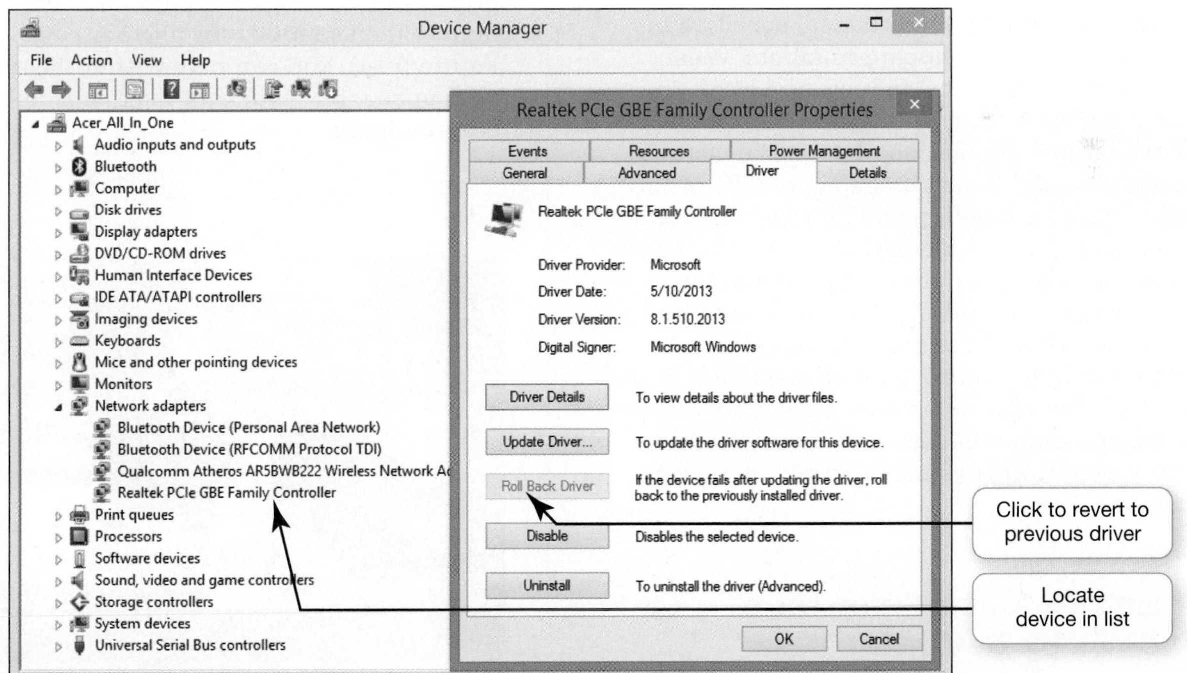


FIGURE 5.13 The Roll Back Driver feature in Windows removes a newly installed driver and replaces it with the last one that worked.

*>To access the Device Manager window, navigate to the desktop, right-click the Start button to display the shortcut menu, and select* **Device Manager**. *To display the Properties dialog box, double-click on a device. Click the* **Driver** *tab.*

# The Great Debate: Is Mac OS X Safer than Windows?

Many Mac users feel they are impervious to viruses and malware (software that can disable or interfere with the use of a computing device) because those are "just Windows problems." This means that Mac users often run their computers with only the basic protection provided by Apple in its operating system software. Are Mac users wild risk takers, or are they actually safe from hackers? As with many issues, it's a little bit of both.

## Threats Are Out There

Windows users have been bombarded by malware and virus attacks for decades. When you bought your last Windows machine, it invariably came with a trial version of third-party antivirus/anti-malware software. Running a Windows computer without antivirus/anti-malware software is just asking for trouble.

However, over the last several years, the attacks against Macs have also increased. Why weren't Macs attacked frequently in the past? Most malware is designed to steal sensitive information such as credit card numbers. When thieves expend the time, money, and effort to develop malware, they want to ensure that it targets the largest population of potential victims. Up until recently, Windows had over 90% of the market share for desktop and laptop computers. However, as OS X gains market share, Mac users are becoming a larger group of potential targets. In fact, in many affluent nations, Mac ownership has reached 20% of the market. And since Macs tend to cost more than Windows machines, it can be argued that Mac users may have more disposable income than other computer buyers. And wealthy people always make attractive targets for thieves.

## But Isn't OS X Just Safer Than Windows by Design?

To a certain extent, this is true. OS X does have certain design features that tend to prevent the installation and spread of malware. Apple has also designed current versions of iOS and OS X to prevent the installation of unapproved software (i.e., software not available on Apple's approved online outlets like the App Store). In addition, apps sold on the App Store are required to be designed using the access control technology known as *App Sandbox*.

When most software programs or apps are running, they have broad latitude to interact with the OS (such as Windows or OS X). Usually they have all the rights that the user has over the OS. So if hackers can design an exploit that takes advantage of a security flaw in an app, they can potentially gain extensive control over the computer using the access that the user has to the OS. As noted, Apple requires all approved apps to be "sandboxed" (developed to run in the App Sandbox environment). When an app is sandboxed, the developer defines what the app needs to do in order to interact with the OS. The OS then grants only those specific rights and privileges to the app and nothing else. By doing this, it severely limits what hackers can do in an OS if they breach the security of an app. It's like being in a high-walled sandbox (or playpen) as a child (see Figure 5.14). You can play within the confines of your space, but you can't make mischief outside certain limits.

**FIGURE 5.14** Just as sandboxes are designed to constrain children, toys, and sand to a specific area, Mac apps are also designed to limit access to the OS. *(© EduardSV – Fotolia.com)*

## So I'll Buy a Mac and Be Safe Forever, Right?

Alas, it's not that simple. Although it's more difficult to design exploits for OS X and iOS, it's not impossible. And a great deal of cybercrime relies on social engineering techniques like those used in scareware scams. *Scareware* is software designed to make it seem as if there is something wrong with your computer. The author of the scareware program then "persuades" you to buy a solution to the problem, acquiring your credit card number in the process. Scareware victims can be both Mac and PC users, so even if you own a Mac, you need to be aware of such scams and avoid falling prey to them (see Chapter 9).

## The Solution: Extra Security Precautions!

The current versions of OS X, iOS, and Windows all include some level of security tools and precautions. But there are a few things you should do to protect yourself:

1. **Make sure your software is set to download and install updates automatically**—As OS developers discover holes in their software's security, they provide updates to repair these problems.
2. **Use third-party antivirus/anti-malware software (even on a Mac).** Although no product will detect 100% of malware, detecting some is better than detecting none.
3. **Be aware of social engineering techniques.** Use vigilance when surfing the Internet so you don't fall prey to scams.

So, no OS is 100% safe. But if you're informed and proceed with caution, you can avoid a lot of schemes perpetrated by hackers and thieves.

## Software Application Coordination

**How does the OS help application software run on the computer?** Every computer program, no matter what its type or manufacturer, needs to interact with the CPU using computer code. For programs to work with the CPU, they must contain code the CPU recognizes. Rather than having the same blocks of code for similar procedures in each program, the OS includes the blocks of code—each called an **application programming interface (API)**—that application software needs in order to interact with the CPU. Microsoft DirectX, for example, is a group of multimedia APIs built into the Windows OS that improves graphics and sounds when you're playing games or watching videos on your PC.

ACTIVE HELPDESK

**Managing Hardware and Peripheral Devices: The OS**

In this Active Helpdesk call, you'll play the role of a helpdesk staffer, fielding calls about how the OS manages memory, storage, hardware, and peripheral devices.

**What are the advantages of using APIs?** To create applications that can communicate with the OS, software programmers need only refer to the API code blocks when they write an application. They don't need to include the entire code sequence. APIs not only prevent redundancies in software code, they make it easier for software developers to respond to changes in the OS. Software companies also take advantage of APIs to make applications in software suites (such as Microsoft Office) that have a similar interface and functionality. And since these applications share common APIs, data exchange is facilitated between two programs, such as inserting a chart from Excel into a Word document. ■

# the boot process: starting YOUR COMPUTER

Many things happen quickly between the time you turn on your computer and the time it's ready for you to start using it. As we discussed earlier, all data and instructions (including the OS) are stored in RAM while your computer is on. When you turn off your computer, RAM is wiped clean of all its data (including the OS). How does the computer know what to do when you turn it on if there is nothing in RAM? It runs through a special boot process (or start-up process) to load the OS into RAM. The term *boot,* from *bootstrap loader* (a small program used to start a larger program), alludes to the straps of leather, called *bootstraps,* that people used to use to help them pull on their boots. This is the source of the expression "pull yourself up by your bootstraps."

**What are the steps involved in the boot process?** As illustrated in Figure 5.15, the **boot process** consists of four basic steps. Let's look at each step in detail.

## Step 1: Activating BIOS

**What's the first thing that happens after I turn on my computer?** In the first step of the boot process, the CPU activates the **basic input/output system (BIOS)**. BIOS is a program that manages the exchange of data between the OS and all the input and output devices attached to the system. BIOS is also responsible for loading the OS into RAM from its permanent location on the hard drive. BIOS itself is stored on a read-only memory (ROM) chip on the motherboard. Unlike data stored in RAM, data stored in ROM is permanent and is not erased when the power is turned off.

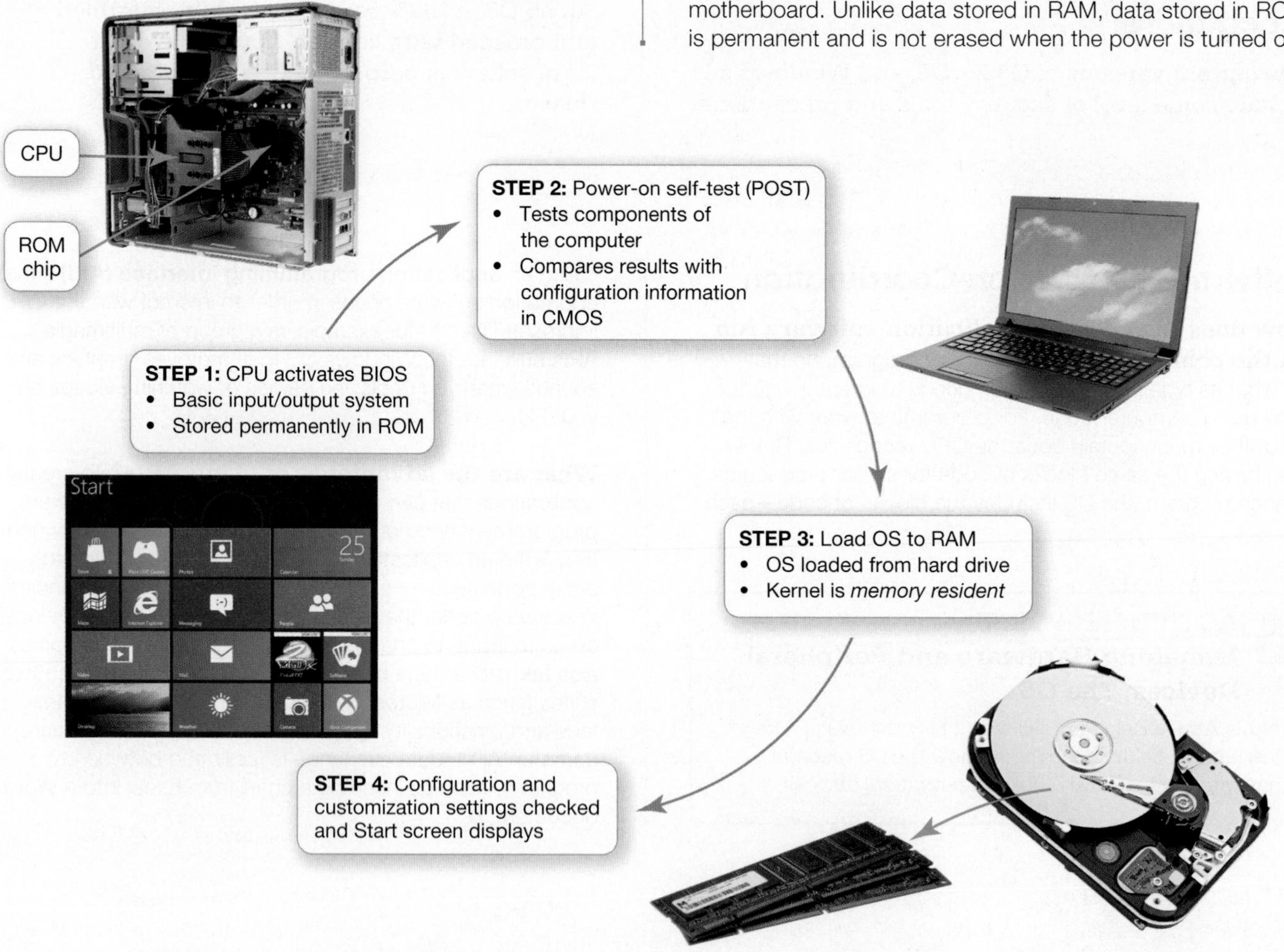

CPU

ROM chip

**STEP 1:** CPU activates BIOS
- Basic input/output system
- Stored permanently in ROM

**STEP 2:** Power-on self-test (POST)
- Tests components of the computer
- Compares results with configuration information in CMOS

**STEP 3:** Load OS to RAM
- OS loaded from hard drive
- Kernel is *memory resident*

**STEP 4:** Configuration and customization settings checked and Start screen displays

Start

**FIGURE 5.15** The Boot Process *(Kitch Bain/Shutterstock; Vtls/Shutterstock)*

## Step 2: Performing the Power-On Self-Test

**How does the computer determine whether the hardware is working properly?** The first job BIOS performs is to ensure that essential peripheral devices are attached and operational—a process called the **power-on self-test**, or **POST**. The BIOS compares the results of the POST with the various hardware configurations permanently stored in CMOS (pronounced "see-moss"). CMOS, which stands for *complementary metal-oxide semiconductor,* is a special kind of memory that uses almost no power. A little battery provides enough power so that the CMOS contents won't be lost after the computer is turned off. CMOS contains information about the system's memory, types of disk drives, and other essential input and output hardware components. If the results of the POST compare favorably with the hardware configurations stored in CMOS, the boot process continues.

## Step 3: Loading the OS

**How does the OS get loaded into RAM?** Next, BIOS goes through a preconfigured list of devices in its search for the drive that contains the **system files**, the main files of the OS. When it is located, the OS loads into RAM from its permanent storage location on the hard drive.

Once the system files are loaded into RAM, the **kernel** (or **supervisor program)** is loaded. The kernel is the essential component of the OS. It's responsible for managing the processor and all other components of the computer system. Because it stays in RAM the entire time your computer is powered on, the kernel is said to be *memory resident*. Other, less critical, parts of the OS stay on the hard drive and are copied over to RAM on an as-needed basis so that RAM is managed more efficiently. These programs are referred to as *nonresident*. Once the kernel is loaded, the OS takes over control of the computer's functions.

## Step 4: Checking Further Configurations and Customizations

**Is that it?** Finally, the OS checks the registry for the configuration of other system components. The **registry** contains all the different configurations (settings) used by the OS and by other applications. It contains the customized settings you put into place, such as mouse speed, as well as instructions as to which programs should be loaded first.

ACTIVE HELPDESK

**Starting the Computer: The Boot Process**

In this Active Helpdesk call, you'll play the role of a helpdesk staffer, fielding calls about how the operating system helps the computer start up.

**Why do I sometimes need to enter a login name and password at the end of the boot process?** The verification of your login name and password is called **authentication**. The authentication process blocks unauthorized users from entering the system. You may have your home computer set up for authentication, especially if you have multiple users accessing it. All large networked environments, like your college, require user authentication for access.

On a Windows 8 computer, the default setting is to input a password to log in to your **Microsoft account** after your computer has completely booted up. Because configuration settings are stored online and associated with a particular Microsoft account, this makes it easy for multiple people to share any Windows 8 computer while maintaining access to their individual settings and preferences.

**How do I know if the boot process is successful?** The entire boot process takes only a few minutes to complete. If the entire system is checked out and loaded properly, the process completes by displaying the login screen or the Start screen. The computer system is now ready to accept your first command.

## Handling Errors in the Boot Process

**What should I do if my computer doesn't boot properly?** Sometimes problems occur during the boot process. Here are some suggestions for solving a boot problem:

- If you've recently installed new software or hardware, try uninstalling it. (Make sure you use the Uninstall a program feature in the Control Panel to remove the software.) If the problem no longer occurs when rebooting, you can reinstall the device or software.
- Try accessing the Windows Advanced Options Menu (accessible by pressing the F8 key during the boot process). If Windows detects a problem in the boot process, it will add Last Known Good Configuration to the Windows Advanced Options Menu. Every time your computer boots successfully, a configuration of the boot process is saved. When you choose to boot with the Last Known Good Configuration, the OS starts your computer by using the registry information that was saved during the last shut down.
- Try refreshing your computer (new in Windows 8).

**What happens when a PC is "refreshed"?** Sometimes Windows does not boot properly or the system does not respond properly. You may even see messages related to "fatal exceptions." **Refresh your PC** is a new utility

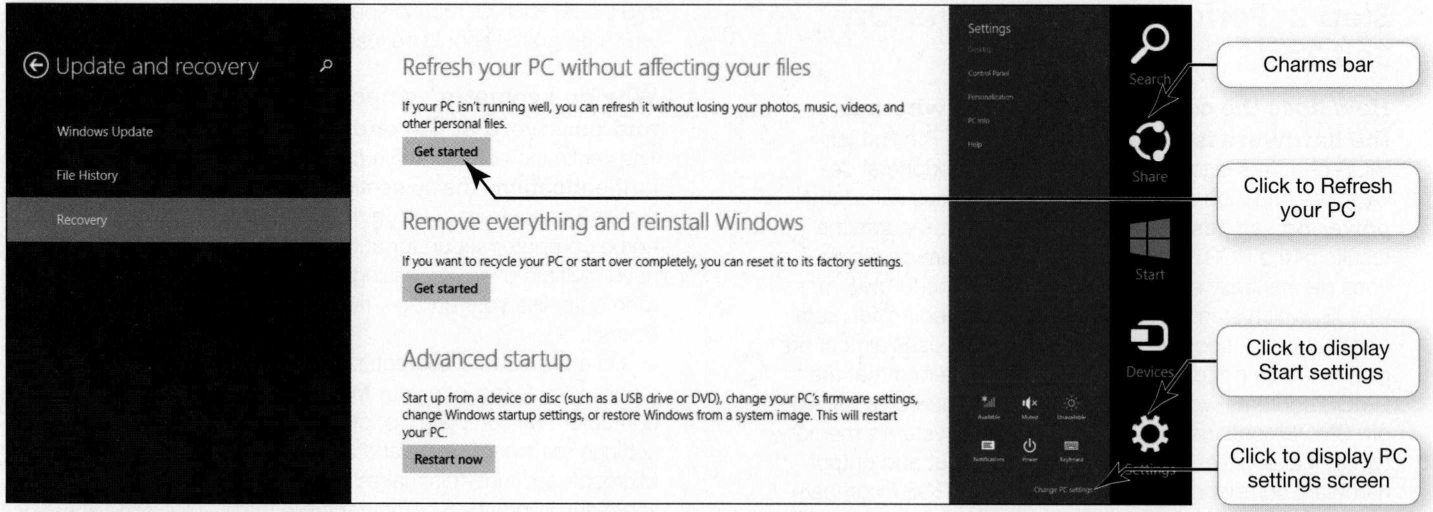


**FIGURE 5.16** The Update and recovery screen (an option on the PC settings screen) in Windows 8.1 provides access to the Refresh your PC option. *To access the Update and recovery screen, display the Charms bar on the Start screen (swipe from right, or point cursor to upper-right corner of screen), click* **Settings**, *then click* **Change PC Settings**. *On the PC Settings screen, click* **Update and recovery**, *then select* **Recover**.

program in Windows 8 that attempts to diagnose and fix errors in your Windows system files that are causing your computer to behave improperly (see Figure 5.16). When a PC is refreshed, the following occurs:

- Your data files (documents, music, videos, etc.) and personalization settings are not removed or changed.
- Apps that you have downloaded from the Windows Store are kept intact.
- Apps that you have downloaded from the Internet or installed from DVDs will be removed from your PC. Therefore, you'll need to reinstall them after the refresh.

It's recommended that you back up your PC prior to refreshing it as a precautionary measure. Finally, if all other attempts to fix your computer fail, try a System Restore to roll back to a past configuration. System Restore is covered in more detail later in this chapter.

**What should I do if my keyboard or another device doesn't work after I boot my computer?** Sometimes during the boot process, BIOS skips a device (such as a keyboard) or improperly identifies it. Your only indication that this problem has occurred is that the device won't respond after the system has been booted. When that happens, try rebooting. If the problem persists, check the OS's website for any patches (or software fixes) that may resolve the issue. If there are no patches or the problem persists, you may want to get technical assistance. ■

**Before moving on to Part 2:**

- **Watch Replay Video 5.1** .
- **Then check your understanding of what you've learned so far.**

# check your understanding//

For a quick review to see what you've learned so far, answer the following questions. Visit **pearsonhighered.com /techinaction** to check your answers.

## multiple choice

1. Which is NOT an example of a tablet OS?
   - **a.** iOS
   - **b.** UNIX
   - **c.** Android
   - **d.** Windows
2. You are most likely to find a Linux OS
   - **a.** in your automobile.
   - **b.** on a supercomputer.
   - **c.** on a smartphone.
   - **d.** on an iPad.
3. All of the following are key attributes of an operating system EXCEPT
   - **a.** it manages memory and storage.
   - **b.** it provides a user interface.
   - **c.** it manages the CPU.
   - **d.** it tracks connections to external networks.
4. Modern operating systems such as Windows and OS X use a ____________ interface.
   - **a.** command-driven
   - **b.** graphical user
   - **c.** menu-driven
   - **d.** text-based
5. The OS with the largest market share on tablet devices is
   - **a.** Linux
   - **b.** Windows
   - **c.** iOS
   - **d.** Android

## true–false

_______ **1.** Each device attached to your computer needs an interrupt file to communicate with the OS. (false)

_______ **2.** The second step of the boot process is the power-on self-test (POST). (true)

## critical thinking

1. **Market Dominance Shifts**

   Apple and Google are large corporations and have control of most of the OS market for tablet computing devices. Microsoft (also a large corporation) is currently fighting for market share in the tablet market with Windows 8. Does the size and market dominance of these three companies prevent more innovation by creating a barrier to entry to smaller OS companies? Why or why not? Apple's iOS had the biggest market share in tablets until 2013, when Android claimed the top spot. Why do you think the Android operating system is more popular than iOS?

2. **A Web-Based OS**

   OS interfaces have evolved from a text-based console format to the current GUI. Modern operating systems such as Windows and OS X are starting to include features that store and retrieve data from the cloud (the Internet). Many believe the OS of the future will be totally web-based and not require the installation of an OS on a specific device. Discuss the implications of this type of OS. What are the potential security issues of a totally web-based OS?

**Continue** »

TRY THIS 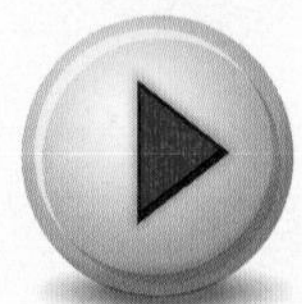

# Organizing Tiles on the Start Screen in Windows 8

The Start screen in Windows 8 is similar to the desktop in Windows 7 in that you can arrange the tiles on the Start screen to suit your needs, much like you can move around the icons on the Windows 7 desktop. You can even create groups of tiles and give each group a name. On a busy Start screen, this helps you keep your tiles organized so you can find the right app quickly. Let's create a small group for app tiles that take us out to the Internet. Note: At the time this book went to press, Microsoft had announced changing the name of SkyDrive to OneDrive, but had not updated the website, so images still reflect SkyDrive.

**Step 1** Locate the OneDrive tile on your Start screen. Left-click the tile (or press and hold) and drag it to the space between two groups of tiles. A faint vertical bar will appear, indicating that you wish to place that tile in its own group. Release the mouse button (or stop touching the screen). The OneDrive tile should now be alone in its own group.

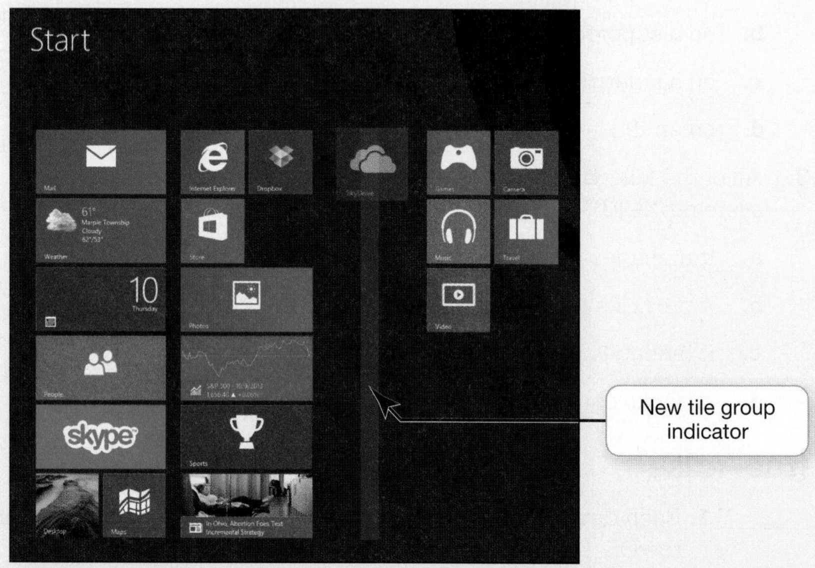


**Step 2** Locate the Internet Explorer and Store tiles. Left-click and drag (or press and drag) these tiles so they are in close proximity to the OneDrive tile. Release the mouse button (or stop pressing the screen) and these tiles should join the OneDrive tile in their own group. To name the group, right-click (or press and hold) one of the icons in the group. In the **Name group box** that appears above the group, enter *Internet Apps*. Left-click (or press) on any blank area of the Start screen.

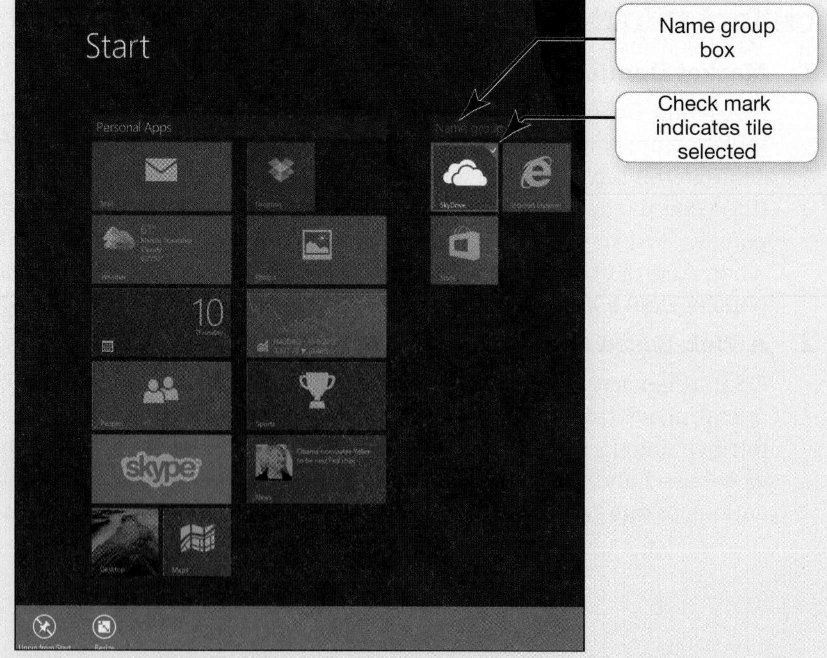

**Step 3** Perhaps you use OneDrive quite frequently. You may wish to make that tile larger. Right-click (or press and hold) the OneDrive tile to select it. At the bottom of the Start screen, select **Resize**, then select **Wide**.

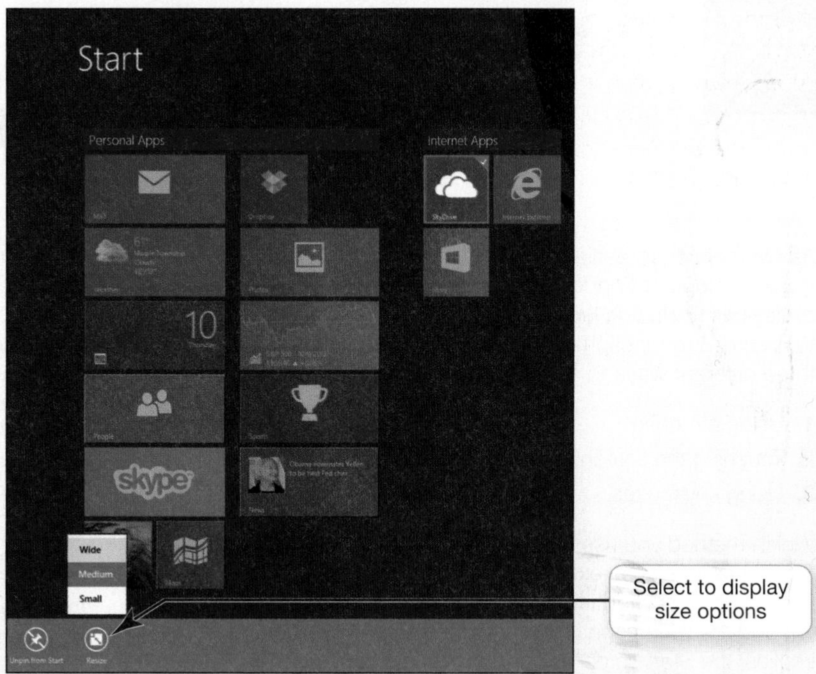


**Step 4** Notice that the OneDrive icon is now twice the size of the other two icons.

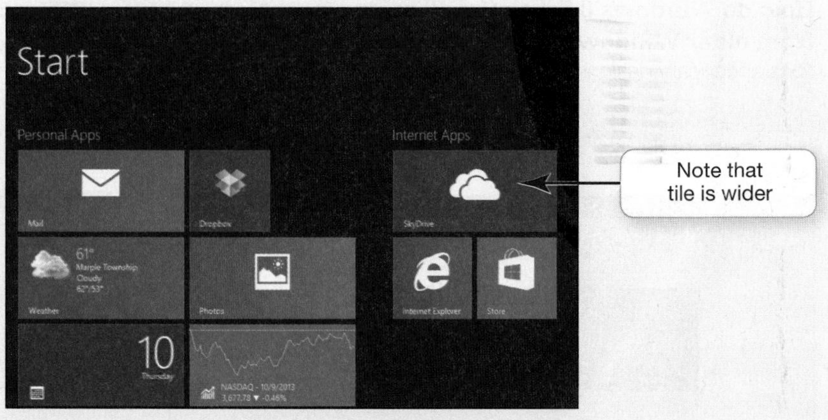

# Using System Software

Now that you know how system software works, let's explore how specific operating systems and their tools function.

## the windows INTERFACE

As we mentioned earlier, Windows 8 is a departure from previous versions of Windows because it's designed for a variety of devices, including laptops, phones, and tablets. To enable Windows 8 to function on all types of devices, there are often three different ways to accomplish tasks in Windows 8:

1. Using a mouse
2. Touching the screen (on touch-enabled devices)
3. Using keystrokes

Which method you use depends on the type of device you're using and, to a large extent, on your personal preferences.

The **Start screen** is the first interaction you have with the OS and the first image you see on your display. As its name implies, the Start screen is the place where you begin all of your computing activities. The Windows 8 Start screen provides you with access to your most used applications in one convenient screen.

**How do Windows 8 "optimized" programs differ from older Windows apps? Windows 8 apps** are applications specifically designed to run in the interface of Windows 8. The **Windows 8 interface** features large type with clean, readable block images inspired by metropolitan service signs such as those found on bus stations and subways.

Windows 8 apps either are preinstalled with Windows 8 (such as Photos, Messaging, and Calendar) or are available for download from the Windows Store (Microsoft's apps marketplace). You can launch Windows 8 apps by clicking or tapping on their icons on the Start screen.

Windows 8 apps are displayed full screen, without the distractions of borders or controls (such as scrollbars or menus). For example, Figure 5.17 shows Internet Explorer 11, which is a Windows 8 app. Notice that unlike older versions of Internet Explorer, there are no window borders or menus visible (see Figure 5.17a), as the application fills the entire screen. Controls and settings are contained on **app bars**, such as the Tabs bar (see Figure 5.17b), that float on screen above the app when you summon them or you need them. Right-clicking on a Windows 8 app screen (or swiping up from the bottom) usually displays the app bars.

**What are the main features of the Windows 8 Start screen?** The Start screen is based on the interface for Windows smartphones. The most useful feature of the Start

a

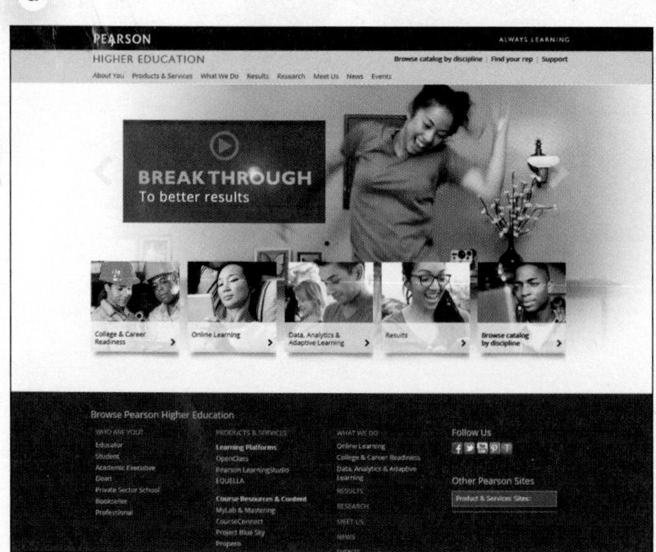


b

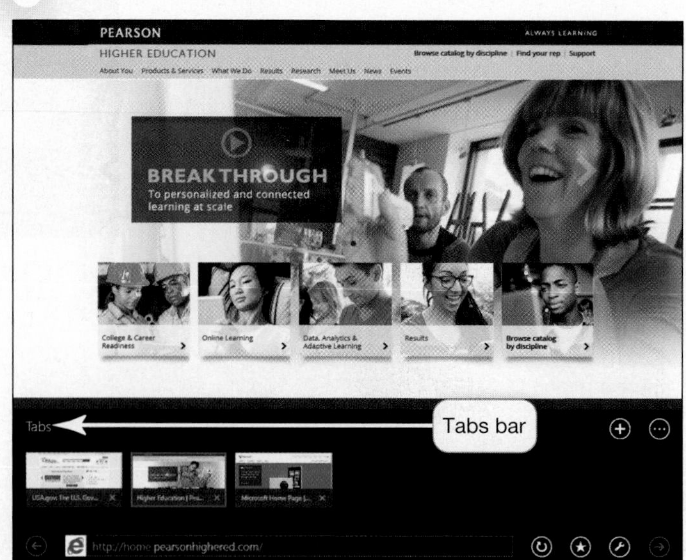


**FIGURE 5.17** (a) Internet Explorer 11, a Windows 8 app, displays full screen. (b) Right-clicking on the Internet Explorer 11 screen displays the open Tabs bar. *(© Pearson Education, Upper Saddle River, New Jersey; © Pearson Education, Upper Saddle River, New Jersey)*

screen is that it lets you customize it to meet your needs. (For more on customizing the Start screen, see the Try This feature on pages 176–177.) As such, the Start screen on your computer may be different from the Start screen on your friend's computer. And because your Windows 8 settings and preferences are saved in your Microsoft account, when you log on to any Windows 8 computer, you'll see your own personal settings, preferences, and applications reflected on the Start screen (see Figure 5.18).

For performing common tasks, such as searching or sharing information, Windows 8 has created special shortcuts called **charms**. Charms are located on the *Charms bar* (see Figure 5.18b), which you access by moving your cursor to the upper-right corner of the screen, swiping in from the right edge of the screen, or pressing the Windows key+C.

**Why can't I see tiles for certain applications on my Start screen?** Not all the Windows 8 apps and programs installed on your computer are visible on the Start screen. You can choose which applications are visible on the Start screen through a process called **pinning**. Usually, when you install a Windows 8 app or any other program on your computer, it pins the program (displays it) on the Start screen by default. If there is a tile on the Start screen you don't need, just right-click on it (or touch and hold) and select the Unpin from Start option that appears on the app bar at the bottom of the screen.

If you want to see all the applications installed on your computer, not just the ones pinned to your Start screen, click the All programs (apps) button that appears at the bottom of the Start screen (see Figure 5.18a). This displays the Apps screen (see Figure 5.19), which shows all Windows 8 apps and other programs installed on your computer.

**What happened to the Start button from Windows 7?** When using Windows 8.1 for the first time, you might be looking for the Start button, which is not initially displayed on the Start screen. If you leave the Start screen and go to the desktop, you will see the Start button (represented by the Windows 8 logo) in its familiar spot on the taskbar. However, this does not have the functionality of the old Windows 7 Start button. Instead of displaying a list of installed applications, the new Start button merely returns you to the Start screen. Once you have returned to the Start screen from the desktop, moving your cursor to the lower left-hand corner of the Start screen will display the Start button.

**How can I quickly access useful programs and tools that were available from the Windows 7 Start button?** Right-clicking on the Windows 8.1 Start button displays a menu of quick links to common administrative tasks and programs, such as Control Panel, File Explorer, and shutdown options

**Where is the Windows desktop?** If you've been using versions of Windows prior to Windows 8, you're used to the desktop being the first screen you see on your computer. The desktop from Windows 7 still exists, just in a slightly modified version. You can access the Windows 8 desktop via the

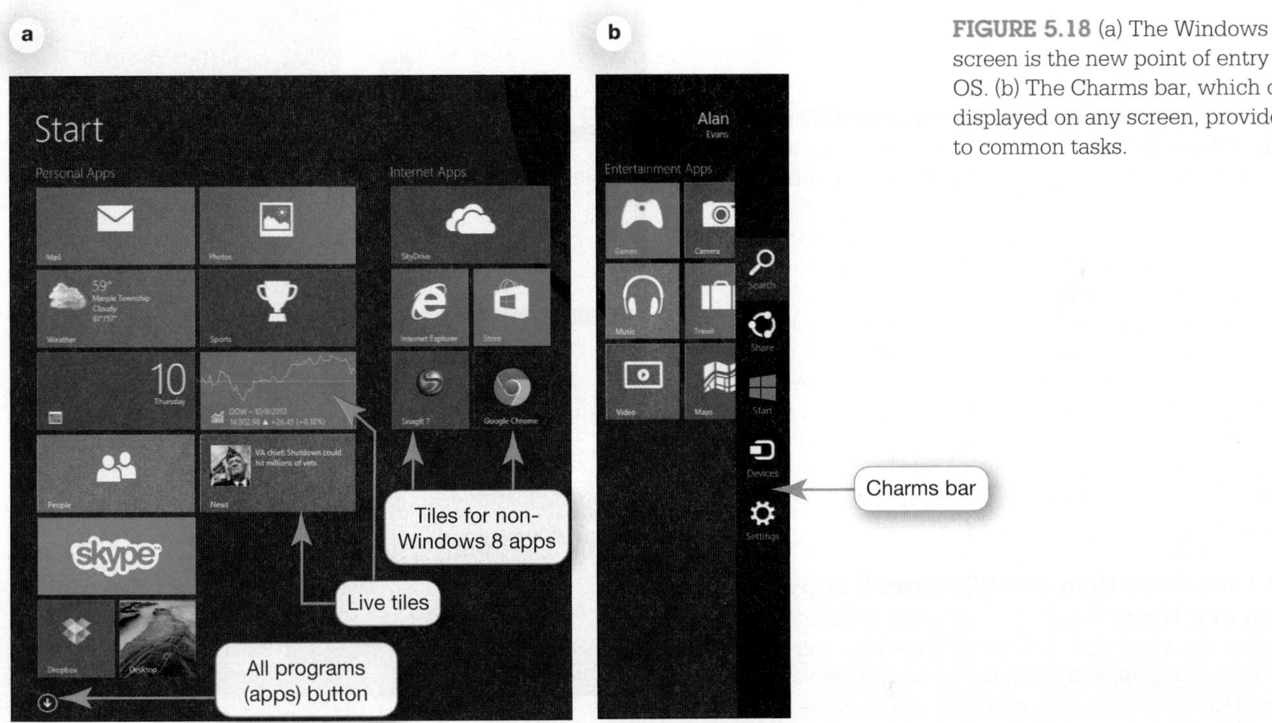


**FIGURE 5.18** (a) The Windows 8 Start screen is the new point of entry to the OS. (b) The Charms bar, which can be displayed on any screen, provides access to common tasks.

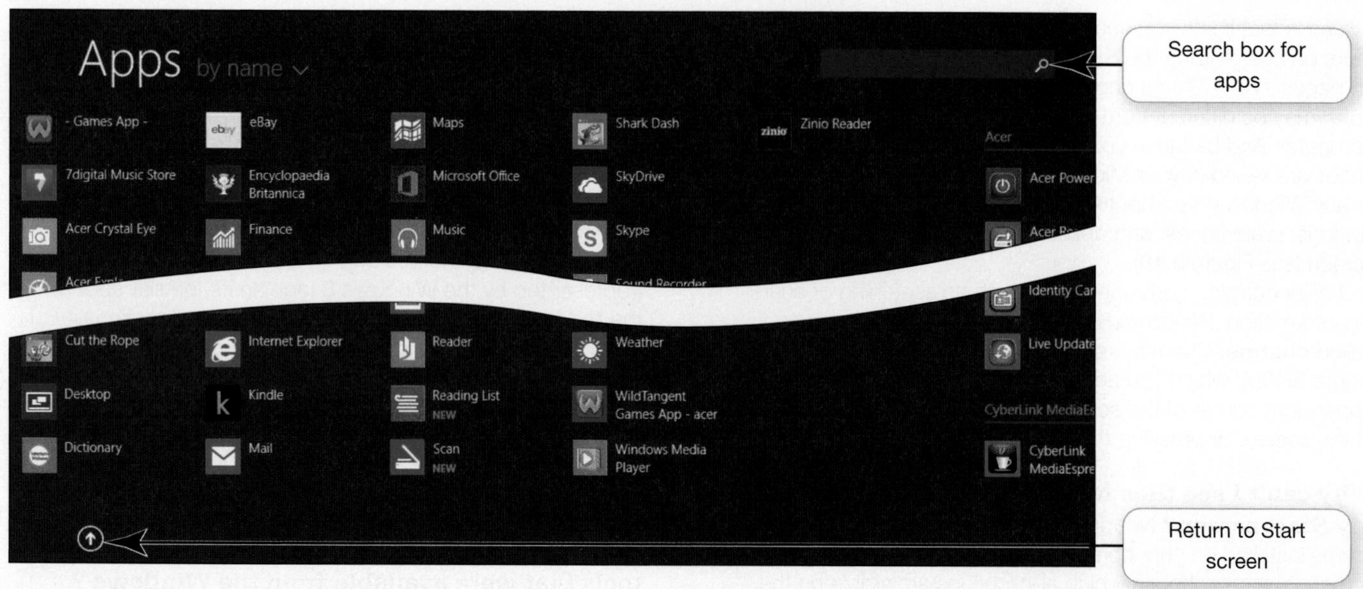


**FIGURE 5.19** The Windows 8 Apps screen shows all Windows 8 apps and other programs installed on your computer.

Desktop icon on the Start screen or by pressing the Windows key+D. Programs that have not been designed to run in the Windows 8 interface (like Microsoft Office 2010) will run on the Windows 8 desktop.

The desktop still has features like the taskbar. The **taskbar** displays open and favorite applications for easy access. You can point to an icon to preview windows of open files or programs, or move your mouse over a thumbnail to preview a full-screen image. Or, you can right-click an icon to view a Jump List—the most recently or commonly used files or commands for that application.

**How can I switch between apps in Windows 8?** If you want to go back to the last program you were using, just point your cursor to the upper-left corner of the screen and drag (or swipe) from the left. Drag the thumbnail image of your previous program to the middle of your screen and it will be available. Repeatedly swiping from the left will scroll backward through all your open programs.

For a list of open programs—so you can jump right to the correct one—position your cursor in the upper-left corner until the thumbnail appears, then move the cursor down (or swipe in from the left, and before you let go, swipe out again) to display a list of thumbnails of previous programs called a *switch list* (see Figure 5.20). Alternatively, pressing and holding the Alt key and then pressing the Tab key repeatedly also allows you to scroll through open apps.

**How can I see more than one Windows 8 app on my screen at a time?** Windows 8 apps can snap into place on either the left or right side of the screen, so you can easily display two apps at the same time. Just display the thumbnail list of running apps and click and drag the thumbnail of the second app you want to display to the left or right side of the screen. The app will snap into place while

**FIGURE 5.20** The thumbnails of open programs allow you to switch quickly between them. *(Alan Evans)*

## BITS&BYTES

### Touch Language for Windows 8

Because the main thrust of Windows 8 is to optimize Windows for touch-screen devices, the Windows developers needed to agree on a set of touch interactions they would use when programming Windows 8. If you're using Windows 8 on a touch-screen device, you may want to learn the gestures shown in Figure 5.21.

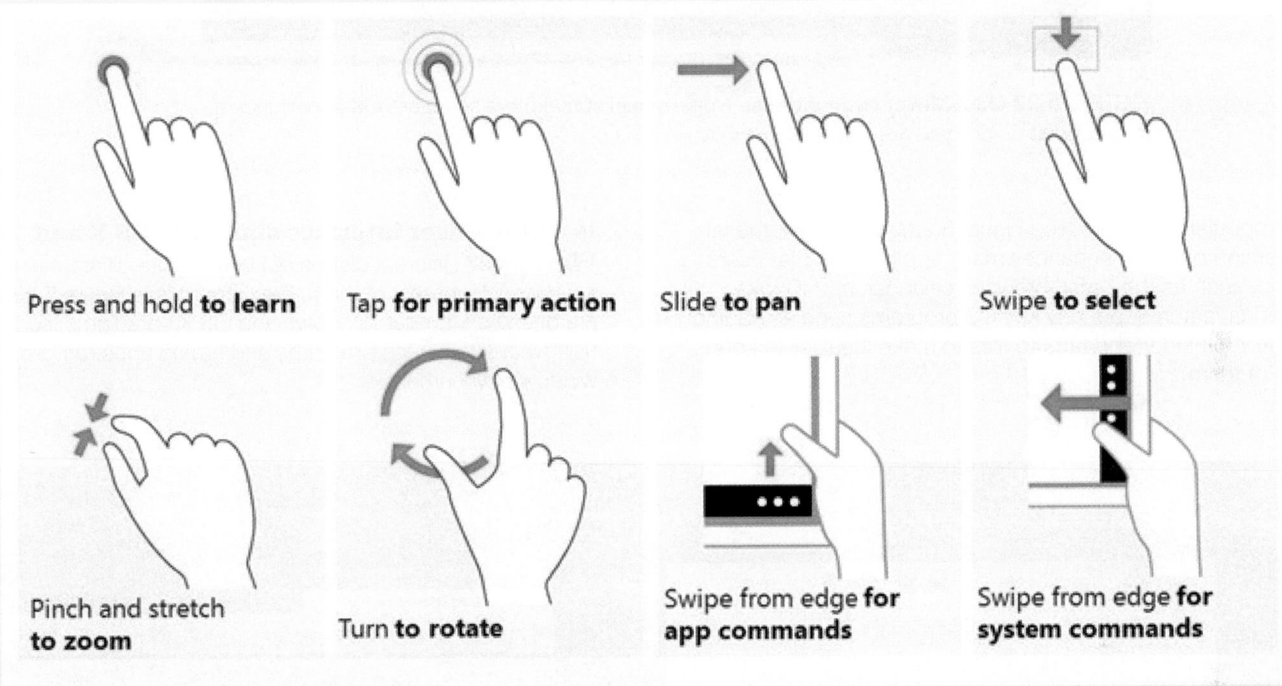


**FIGURE 5.21** Windows 8 Touch Gestures

still leaving the other app you had running visible, with each one taking up half the screen. You can resize the apps as necessary to allow one to take up more screen space than the other.

**How do I close a Windows 8 app?** When Windows 8 apps aren't displayed on the screen, Windows will suspend them temporarily so they don't use much memory or power. Therefore, theoretically, you don't ever need to shut down Windows 8 apps. However, most people prefer not to have endless apps running, and it may be inconvenient to scroll through a huge list of running apps to find the one you want. To close a Windows 8 app from within the app, press Alt+F4. Alternatively, you can move your cursor to the top of the screen until it turns into a hand, then left-click and drag down. The app will shrink to a small window. Drag it down to the bottom of the screen and release the mouse button to close the app. Right-clicking on a thumbnail of the app on the switch list also allows you to close an app, as does swiping from the top of the screen to the bottom with your finger.

**How does the Mac user interface compare with Windows 8?** Although the OS X and the Windows operating systems aren't compatible, they're extremely similar in terms of functionality. For example, as is the case with Windows, OS X programs appear in resizable windows and use menus and icons. However, instead of the Start screen, OS X features a Dock with icons on the bottom for your

**FIGURE 5.22** OS X Mavericks continues Apple's goal of making a seamless OS experience no matter what device you are using. *(Courtesy of Apple, Inc.)*

most popular programs (see Figure 5.22). Mavericks, the latest version of OS X, enhances many applications that users rely on, such as the Safari browser, calendar, and iBooks, and adds features to many key OS programs such as adding tabs to the Finder and tags to files to make it easier to keep track of them.

**Is a Linux user interface similar to OS X and Windows?** Different distros of Linux feature different user interfaces. But most of them, like Ubuntu (see Figure 5.23), are based on familiar Windows and OS X paradigms, such as using icons to launch programs and having apps run in a window environment. ■

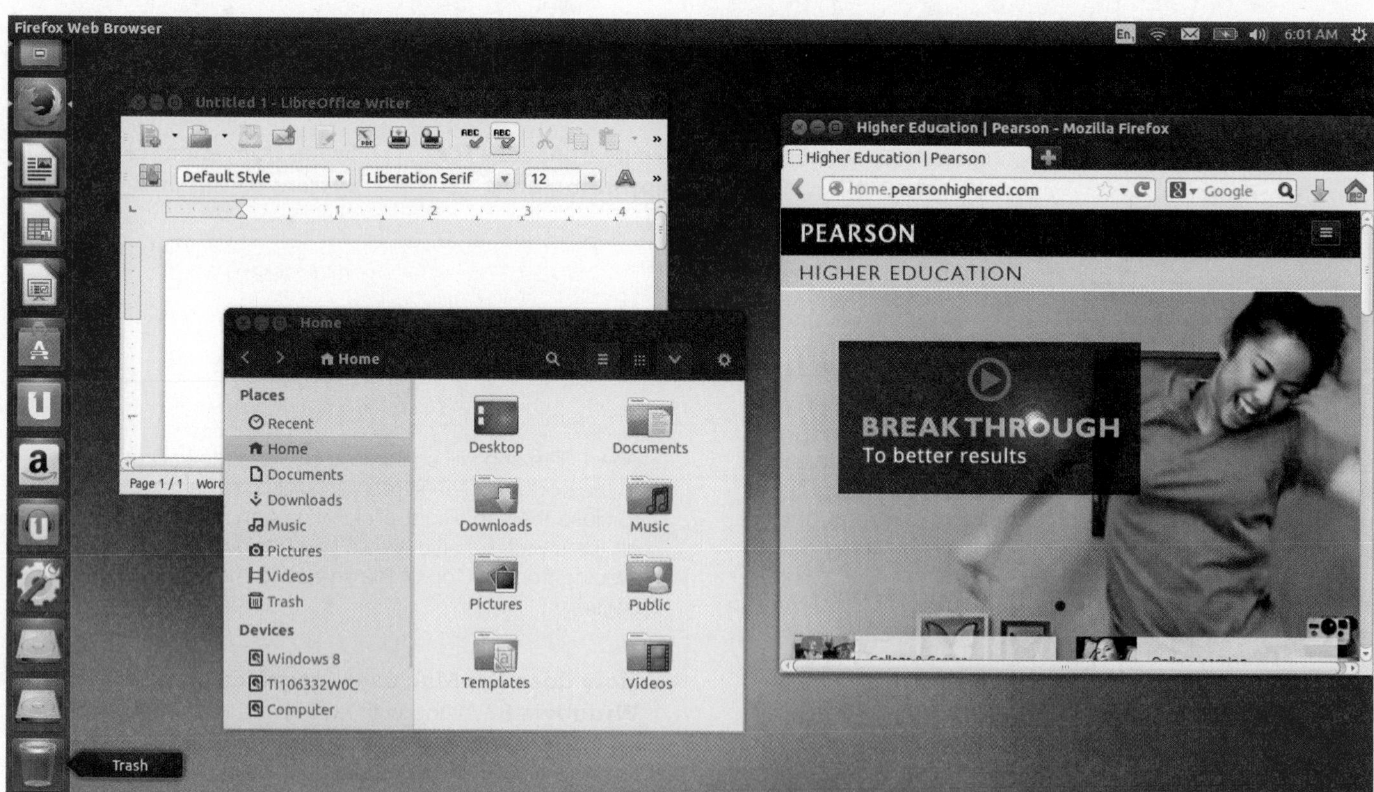


**FIGURE 5.23** The Ubuntu Linux user interface resembles the Windows desktop. *(Ubuntu Linux)*

# trends in IT

## Open Source Software: Why Isn't Everyone Using Linux?

Proprietary software such as Microsoft Windows and Apple's OS X is developed by corporations and sold for profit. This means that the **source code**, the actual lines of instructional code that make the program work, is not accessible to the general public. Without being able to access the source code, it's difficult for a user to modify the software or see exactly how the program author constructed various parts of the OS.

Restricting access to the source code protects companies from having their programming ideas stolen, and it prevents customers from using modified versions of the software. However, in the late 1980s, computer specialists became concerned that large software companies (such as Microsoft) were controlling a large portion of market share and driving out competitors. They also felt that proprietary software was too expensive and contained too many bugs (errors).

These people felt that software should be developed without a profit motive and distributed with its source code free for all to see. The theory was that if many computer specialists examined, improved, and changed the source code, a more full-featured, bug-free product would result. Hence, the open source movement was born.

So, if an OS such as Linux is free and relatively bug-free, why does Windows, which users must pay for, have such a huge market share? One reason is that corporations and individuals have grown accustomed to one thing that proprietary software makers can provide: technical support. It's almost impossible to provide technical support for open source software because anyone can freely modify it; thus, there is no specific developer to take responsibility for technical support. Similarly, corporations have been reluctant to install open source software extensively because of the cost of the internal staff of programmers that must support it.

Companies such as Red Hat, Ubuntu, and Xandros have been combating this problem. Red Hat offers a free, open source OS called Fedora (see Figure 5.24). In addition, Red Hat has modified the original Linux source code and markets a version, Red Hat Enterprise Linux, as a proprietary program. Fedora is the testing ground for what eventually goes into this proprietary program. Red Hat Enterprise Linux comes in versions for servers and desktops. Purchasers of Red Hat Enterprise Linux receive a warranty and technical support. Packaging open source software in this manner has made its use much more attractive to businesses. As a result, many web servers are hosted on computers running Linux.

**FIGURE 5.24** Companies like Red Hat provide free or low-cost Linux software, such as Fedora, but technical support is often not available (or not free). *(Paul Sakuma/AP Images)*

# organizing your computer: FILE MANAGEMENT

So far we've discussed how the OS manages the processor, memory, storage, and devices, and that it provides a way for applications and users to interact with the computer. An additional function of the OS is to enable **file management**, which provides an organizational structure to your computer's contents. In this section, we discuss how you can use this organizational structure to make your computer more organized and efficient.

## Organizing Your Files

**How does the OS organize files?** Windows organizes the contents of your computer in a hierarchical **directory** structure composed of *drives, libraries, folders, subfolders,* and *files*. The hard drive, represented as the C: drive, is where you permanently store most of your files. Each additional storage drive (optical drive, flash drive, or external hard drive) is given a unique letter (*D, E, F,* and so on). The C: drive is like a large filing cabinet in which all files are stored. As such, the C: drive is the top of the filing structure of your computer and is referred to as the **root directory**. All other folders and files are organized within the root directory. There are areas in the root directory that the OS has filled with files and folders holding special OS files. The programs within these files help run the computer and generally shouldn't be accessed.

**What exactly are files and folders?** In an OS, a **file** is a collection of program instructions or data that is stored and treated as a single unit. Files can be generated from an application such as a Word document or an Excel workbook. In addition, files can represent an entire application, a web page, a set of sounds, or an image. Files can be stored on the hard drive, a flash drive, online, or on any other permanent storage medium. As the number of files you save increases, it becomes more important to keep them organized in folders and libraries. A **folder** is a collection of files.

**How does the library work?** In Windows, a **library** gathers categories of files from different locations and displays them as if they were all saved in a single folder, regardless of where they are physically stored. For example, you might have pictures stored all over your computer, including your external hard drive. Rather than looking through each separate location to view your pictures, you can access all of them more easily by looking in the Pictures library. There are four default libraries: Documents, Music, Pictures, and Videos.

**How can I easily locate and see the contents of my computer?** In Windows, **File Explorer** (previously called Windows Explorer) is the main tool for finding, viewing, and managing the contents of your computer. It shows the location and contents of every drive, folder, and file. As illustrated in Figure 5.25, File Explorer is divided into two panes, or sections:

1. The *navigation pane* on the left shows the contents of your computer. It displays commonly accessed areas, organized by Favorites and Libraries (Documents, Music, Pictures, and Videos).
2. When you select a Favorite, Library, drive, or Homegroup, the files and folders of that particular area are displayed in the *details pane* on the right.

## BITS&BYTES

### How to Get the Most from Windows Libraries

To get the most out of using Windows libraries, consider the following tips:

- **Display libraries:** In Windows 8.1, Libraries are not displayed by default in File Explorer. To display Libraries, right-click on a blank space in the Navigation Pane and select *Show libraries* from the shortcut menu.
- **Add a new library:** To add a new library (such as one for your games), open File Explorer. In the Navigation Pane on the left side of the window, right-click on Libraries, click New, and then click Library. Type in a name for the new library. To add new locations to the library, open the new library, and click on Include a Folder.
- **Share or collaborate with libraries:** Say you have pictures saved on your laptop, your dad's desktop, and your mom's laptop. As long as all three computers are on the same Homegroup network, you can share each other's libraries by right-clicking the library name, pointing to Share With, and then clicking one of the two Homegroup options, depending on whether you want to allow editing privileges to those with whom you're sharing the library.
- **Create a backup library:** Do you store important data in a variety of folders on your computer? Even though it's best to back up your entire system, you might only need to back up specific folders. In that case, create a new library and call it "Backup." Add the folders you want to ensure are backed up to the library, and then point your backup software to that library.

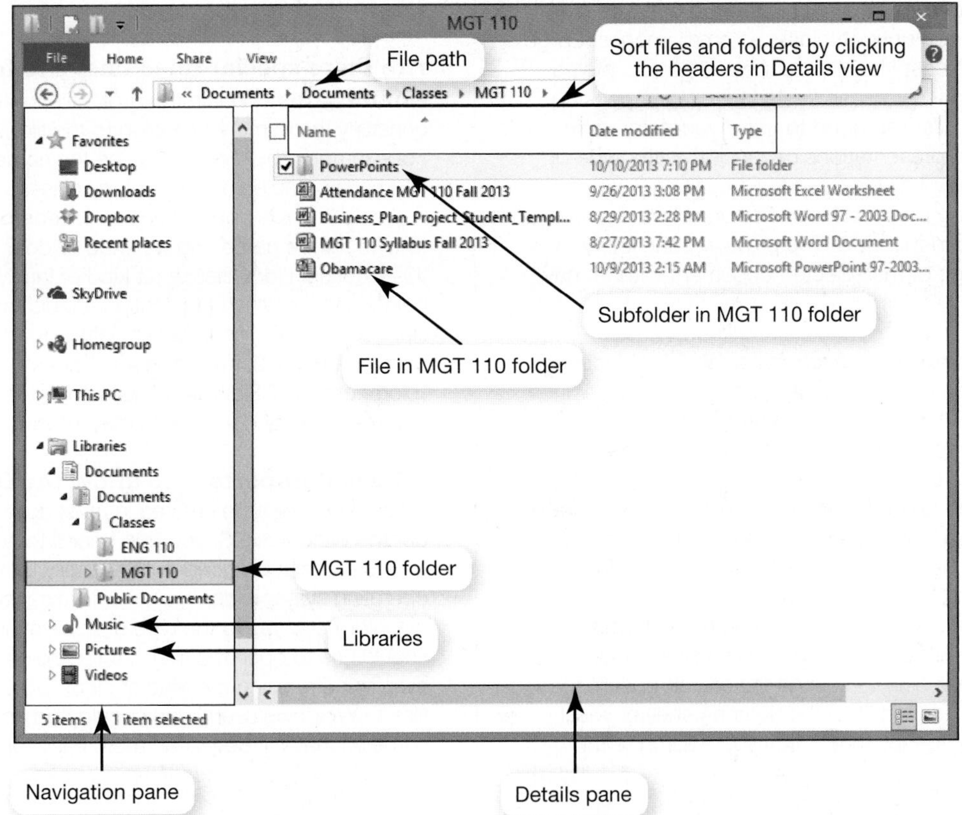


**FIGURE 5.25** File Explorer lets you see the contents of your computer.
> *Right-click on the Start button to display the menu, and then select* **File Explorer**.

**What are some tips on how best to organize my files?** Creating folders is the key to organizing files because folders keep related documents together. For example, you might create one folder called "Classes" to hold your class work. Inside the "Classes" folder, you could create subfolders for each of your classes (such as ENG 110 and MGT 110). Inside each of those subfolders, you could create further subfolders for each class's assignments, homework, and so on.

Grouping related files into folders makes it easier for you to identify and find files. Which would be easier—going to the MGT 110 folder to find a file or searching through the hundreds of individual files in the Documents library hoping to find the right one? Grouping files in a folder also allows you to move files more efficiently, so you can quickly transfer critical files needing frequent backup, for instance.

SOUND BYTE
**File Management**

In this Sound Byte, you'll examine the features of file management and maintenance. You'll learn the various methods of creating folders, how to turn a group of unorganized files into an organized system of folders with related files, and how to maintain your file system.

## Viewing and Sorting Files and Folders

**Are there different ways I can view and sort my files and folders?** When you open any folder in File Explorer, the ribbon at the top displays a View tab. Clicking on the View tab offers you different ways to view the folders and files. In some views, the folders are displayed as *Live Icons*. Live Icons allows you to preview the actual contents of a specific file or folder without actually opening the file. Live Icons can be displayed in a variety of views. Here are the two most useful views for students:

1. **Details view:** This is the most interactive view. As shown in Figure 5.25, files and folders are displayed in list form, and the additional file information is displayed in columns alongside the name of the file. You can sort and display the contents of the folder by any of the column headings, so you can sort the contents alphabetically by name or type, or hierarchically by date last modified or file size. Right-click the column heading area to modify the display of columns.

2. **Large Icons view:** As shown in Figure 5.26, Large Icons view shows the contents of folders as small images. Large Icons view is the best view to use if your folder contains picture files because you can see a few images peeking out of the folder. It's also good to use if your folder contains PowerPoint presentations because the title slide of the presentation will display, making it easier for you to distinguish among presentations. Additionally, a preview pane is available in this view. The preview pane lets you view the first page of the selected document without having to open it.

**What's the best way to search for a file?** In Windows 8, the Search app is the best way to search for files and the contents of folders. The Search app searches through your hard drive or other storage devices (DVD or flash drive) to locate files and folders that match the criteria you provide. Your search can be based on part of the name of the file or folder or just a word or phrase in it. You can also search for a file type by representing the file name as an asterisk (called a wildcard character) and typing the file extension (such as "*.xlsx" to search for Excel files). You access the Search app from the Charms bar or from File Explorer. OS X has a similar feature called Spotlight. Make sure to change the search option from Everywhere to Files (at the top of the Search panel) or you'll also see a list of web pages that match your search term.

## Naming Files

**Are there special rules I have to follow when I name files?** The first part of a file, or the **file name**, is generally the name you assign to the file when you save it. For example, "bioreport" may be the name you assign a report you have completed for a biology class.

In a Windows application, an **extension**, or **file type**, follows the file name and a period or dot (.). Like a last name, this extension identifies what kind of family of files the file belongs to, or which application should be used to read the file. For example, if "bioreport" is a spreadsheet created in Microsoft Excel 2013, it has an .xlsx extension, and its name is "bioreport.xlsx." Figure 5.27 lists some common file extensions and the types of documents they indicate.

**Why is it important to know the file extension?** When you save a file created in most applications running under the Windows OS, you don't need to add the extension to the file name; it is added automatically for you. Mac and Linux operating systems don't require file extensions. This is because the information as to the type of application the computer should use to open the file is stored inside the file itself. However, if you're using the Mac or Linux OS and will be sending files to Windows users, you should add an extension to your file name so that Windows can more easily open your files.

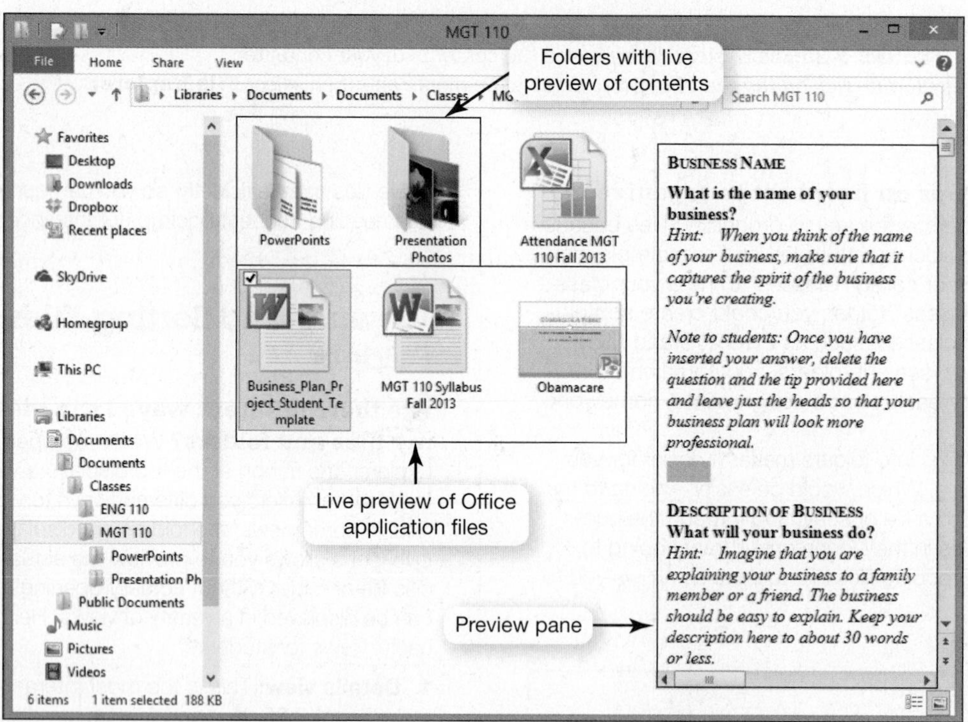


**FIGURE 5.26** The Large Icons view is a good way to display the contents of files and folders. The preview pane on the right lets you see the first page of your document without first opening it.
> *To access Large Icons view, click the* **View** *tab from the ribbon in File Explorer, and then select* **Large Icons** *view. To access the Preview pane, click that icon on the View tab of the ribbon.*

FIGURE 5.27

## Common File Name Extensions

| EXTENSION | TYPE OF DOCUMENT | APPLICATION |
|---|---|---|
| .docx | Word processing document | Microsoft Word 2007 and later |
| .xlsx | Workbook | Microsoft Excel 2007 and later |
| .accdb | Database | Microsoft Access 2007 and later |
| .pptx | Presentation | Microsoft PowerPoint 2007 and later |
| .pdf | Portable Document Format | Adobe Acrobat or Adobe Reader |
| .rtf | Text (Rich Text Format) | Any program that can read text documents |
| .txt | Text | Any program that can read text documents |
| .htm or .html | HyperText Markup Language (HTML) for a web page | Any program that can read HTML |
| .jpg | Joint Photographic Experts Group (JPEG) image | Most programs capable of displaying images |
| .zip | Compressed file | Various file compression programs |

Have you ever been sent a file by e-mail and couldn't open it? Most likely, that was because your computer didn't have the program needed to open the file. Sometimes, similar programs that you already have installed can be used to open the file, so it's helpful to know what the file extension is. Sites such as FILExt (**filext.com**) can help you identify the source program.

**Are there things I shouldn't do when naming my files?** Each OS has its own naming conventions, or rules, which are listed in Figure 5.28. Beyond those conventions, it's important that you name your files so that you can easily identify them. Files names can have as many as 255 characters, so don't be afraid to use as many characters as you need. A file name such as "BIO 101 Research Paper First Draft.docx" makes it very clear what that file contains.

Keep in mind, however, that all files must be uniquely identified, unless you save them in different folders or in different locations. Therefore, although files may share the same file name (such as "bioreport.docx" or "bioreport.xlsx") or share the same extension ("bioreport.xlsx" or "budget.xlsx"), no two files stored on the same device and folder can share *both* the same file name and the same extension.

FIGURE 5.28

## File-Naming Conventions

<table>
<tr><th></th><th>OS X</th><th>WINDOWS</th></tr>
<tr><td>File and folder name length</td><td>As many as 255 characters*</td><td>As many as 255 characters</td></tr>
<tr><td>Case sensitive?</td><td>Yes</td><td>No</td></tr>
<tr><td>Forbidden characters</td><td>Colon (:)</td><td>" / \ * ? <> | :</td></tr>
<tr><td>File extensions needed?</td><td>No</td><td>Yes</td></tr>
</table>

**Note: Although OS X supports file names with as many as 255 characters, many applications running on OS X still support only file names with a maximum of 31 characters.*

**How can I tell where my files are saved?** When you save a file for the first time, you give the file a name and designate where you want to save it. For easy reference, the OS includes libraries where files are saved unless you specify otherwise. In Windows, the default libraries are Documents for files, Music for audio files, Pictures for graphics files, and Videos for video files.

You can determine the location of a file by its **file path**. The file path starts with the drive in which the file is located and includes all folders, subfolders (if any), the file name, and the extension. For example, if you were saving a picture of Andrew Carnegie for a term paper for a U.S. History course, the file path might be C:\Documents\HIS182\Term Paper\Illustrations\ACarnegie.jpg.

As shown in Figure 5.29, "C:" is the drive on which the file is stored (in this case, the hard drive), and "Documents" is the file's primary folder. "HIS182," "Term Paper," and "Illustrations" are successive subfolders within the "Documents" main folder. Last comes the file name, "ACarnegie," separated from the file extension (in this case, "jpg") by a period. The backslash characters (\), used by Windows, are referred to as **path separators**. OS X files use a colon (:), whereas UNIX and Linux files use the forward slash (/) as the path separator.

ACTIVE HELPDESK

**Organizing Your Computer: File Management**

In this Active Helpdesk call, you'll play the role of a helpdesk staffer, fielding calls about the desktop, window features, and how the OS helps keep the computer organized.

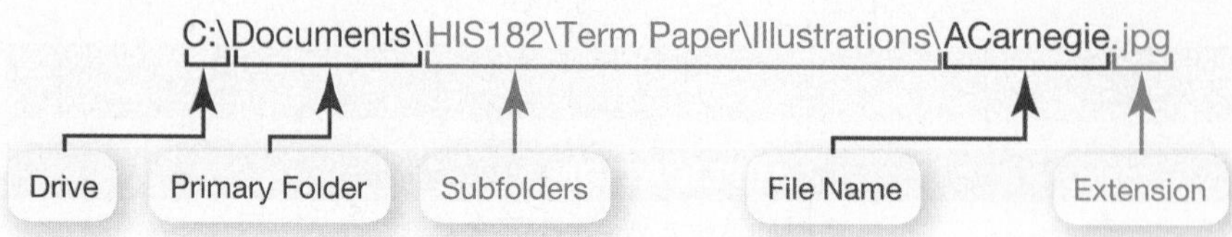


**FIGURE 5.29** Understanding File Paths

## Working with Files

**How can I move and copy files?** Once you've located your file with File Explorer, you can perform many other file-management actions such as opening, copying, moving, renaming, and deleting files. You open a file by double-clicking the file from its storage location. You can copy a file to another location using the Copy command. To move a file from one location to another, use the Cut command. You can access both of these commands easily by right-clicking on a file's name, which displays a shortcut menu.

**Where do deleted files go?** The **Recycle Bin** is a folder on the desktop, represented by an icon that looks like a recycling bin, where files deleted from the hard drive reside until you permanently purge them from your system. Unfortunately, files deleted from other drives don't go to the Recycle Bin but are deleted from the system immediately. In addition, files stored in the cloud are not cycled through the Recycle Bin. When you delete a file from a Dropbox or OneDrive folder, consider it gone forever!

Mac systems have something similar to the Recycle Bin, called Trash, which is represented by a wastebasket icon. To delete files on a Mac, drag the files to the Trash icon.

**How do I permanently delete files from my system?** Files placed in the Recycle Bin or the Trash remain in the system until they're permanently deleted. To delete files from the Recycle Bin permanently, select Empty Recycle Bin after right-clicking the desktop icon. On Macs, select Empty Trash from the Finder menu in OS X.

**What happens if I need to recover a deleted file?** Getting a file back after the Trash has been emptied still may be possible using one of two methods:

- File History is a Windows 8 utility that automatically backs up files (see page 196 for a further explanation of File History) and saves previous versions of files to a designated drive (such as an external hard drive). If you're using File History, you can restore previously deleted files or even previous versions of files you've changed.
- When the Trash is emptied, only the reference to the file is deleted permanently, so the OS has no easy way to find the file. The file data actually remains on the hard drive until it's written over by another file. You may be able to use a program such as FarStone's RestoreIT or Norton Ghost to try to retrieve files you think you've permanently deleted. These programs reveal files that are still intact on the hard drive and help you recover them. This is how they do it on *CSI*! ■

# BITS&BYTES

## Save Files in the Cloud Right from Your Apps

When you sign up for a Windows account, you automatically get free storage on OneDrive, Microsoft's cloud storage site. Taking advantage of this free storage space helps ensure that you have files available to you whenever you need them and have access to the Internet.

Fortunately, it's easy to save files to OneDrive in Windows 8. When you use the Save As command in an application, OneDrive now shows up as an option (see Figure 5.30) on the locations to which you can save files (assuming you're connected to the Internet). So instead of saving your research paper to the Documents folder on your C: drive, save it to a folder called Documents on OneDrive. Initially there won't be any folders in your OneDrive account, but just create any that you need. Using OneDrive will ensure availability of your files when you need them.

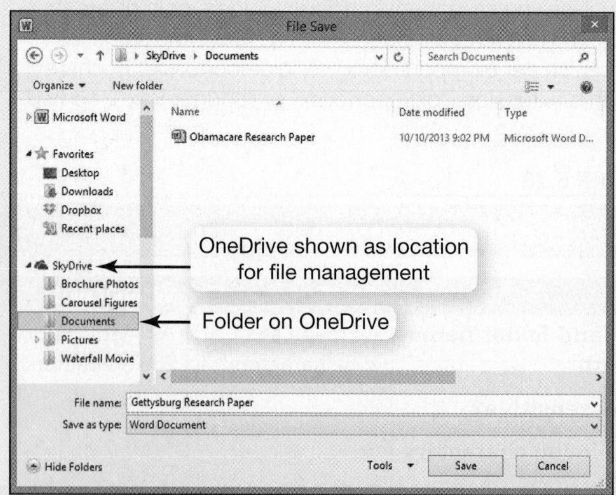


**FIGURE 5.30** As shown in this File Save dialog box, OneDrive now appears as a location in which you can create folders and save files.

# utility PROGRAMS

The main component of system software is the OS. However, *utility programs*—small applications that perform special functions on the computer—are also an essential part of system software. Utility programs come in three flavors:

1. Those that are included with the OS (such as System Restore)
2. Those sold as stand-alone programs (such as Norton antivirus)
3. Those offered as freeware (such as anti-malware software like Ad-Aware from Lavasoft)

Figure 5.31 lists some of the various types of utility programs available within the Windows OS as well as some alternatives available as stand-alone programs. In general, the basic utilities designed to manage and tune your computer hardware are incorporated into the OS. The stand-alone utility programs typically offer more features or an easier user interface for backup, security, diagnostic, or recovery functions. For some Windows programs, like Task Manager and Resource Monitor, no good stand-alone alternatives exist.

## Display Utilities

**How can I change the appearance of my Start screen and desktop?** You can personalize the Start screen and the lock screen (the screen that forces you to enter a password to resume using your computer) to suit your tastes. To do so, display the Charms bar, select Settings, choose Change PC settings, and then the PC and devices option. This provides you with access to personalization options such as changing pictures, colors, and backgrounds. This also provides you with access to the features you need to change the appearance of your desktop.

## The Programs and Features Utility

**What's the correct way to add new programs to my system?** When you download Windows 8 apps from the Windows Store, they automatically install on your computer. If you install non-Windows 8 programs, the program usually automatically runs a *wizard* that walks you through the installation process. If a wizard doesn't start automatically, open the Control Panel, click Programs, then click Programs and Features. This prompts the OS to look for the setup program of the new software, and it starts the installation wizard.

ACTIVE HELPDESK
**Using Utility Programs**

In this Active Helpdesk call, you'll play the role of a helpdesk staffer, fielding calls about the utility programs included in system software and what these programs do.

FIGURE 5.31

**Utility Programs Available Within Windows and as Stand-Alone Programs**

| WINDOWS UTILITY PROGRAM | STAND-ALONE ALTERNATIVES | WHAT IT DOES |
|---|---|---|
| File Explorer File Compression | WinZip, StuffIt | Reduces file size |
| Disk Cleanup | McAfee Total Protection | Removes unnecessary files from your hard drive |
| Error-Checking | SeaTools (free download from **seagate.com**) | Checks your hard drive for unnecessary or damaged files |
| Task Manager and Resource Monitor | None | Displays performance measures for processes; provides information on programs and processes running on your computer |
| Disk Defragmenter | Norton Utilities, iDefrag | Rearranges files on your hard drive to allow for faster access of files |
| System Restore | FarStone Snapshop, Acronis Backup and Security, Norton Ghost | Restores your system to a previous, stable state |
| File History, File Recovery | Acronis True Image, Norton Ghost | Backs up important files, makes a complete mirror image of your current computer setup |

In this section, we explore many of the utility programs you'll find installed on a Windows 8 OS. Unless otherwise noted, you can find Windows utilities in the Control Panel. We'll discuss antivirus and personal firewall utility programs in Chapter 9.

## File Compression Utilities

**Why would I want to use a file compression utility?** File compression makes a large file more compact, making it easier and faster for you to send large attachments by e-mail, upload them to the web, or save them onto a disc. As shown in Figure 5.32, Windows has a built-in **file compression utility** that takes out redundancies in a file (zips it) to reduce the file size. You can also obtain several stand-alone freeware and shareware programs, such as WinZip (for Windows) and StuffIt (for Windows or Mac), to compress your files.

**How does file compression work?** Most compression programs look for repeated patterns of letters and replace these patterns with a shorter placeholder. The repeated patterns and the associated placeholder are cataloged and stored temporarily in a separate file called the *dictionary*. For example, in the following sentence, you can easily see the repeated patterns of letters.

**The rain in Spain falls mainly on the plain.**

Although this example contains obvious repeated patterns (ain and the), in a large document, the repeated patterns may be more complex. The compression program's algorithm (a set of instructions designed to complete a solution in a step-by-step manner) therefore runs through the file several times to determine the optimal repeated patterns needed to obtain the greatest compression.

SOUND BYTE
**File Compression**

In this Sound Byte, you'll learn about the advantages of file compression and how to use Windows to compress and decompress files. This Sound Byte also teaches you how to find and install file compression shareware programs.

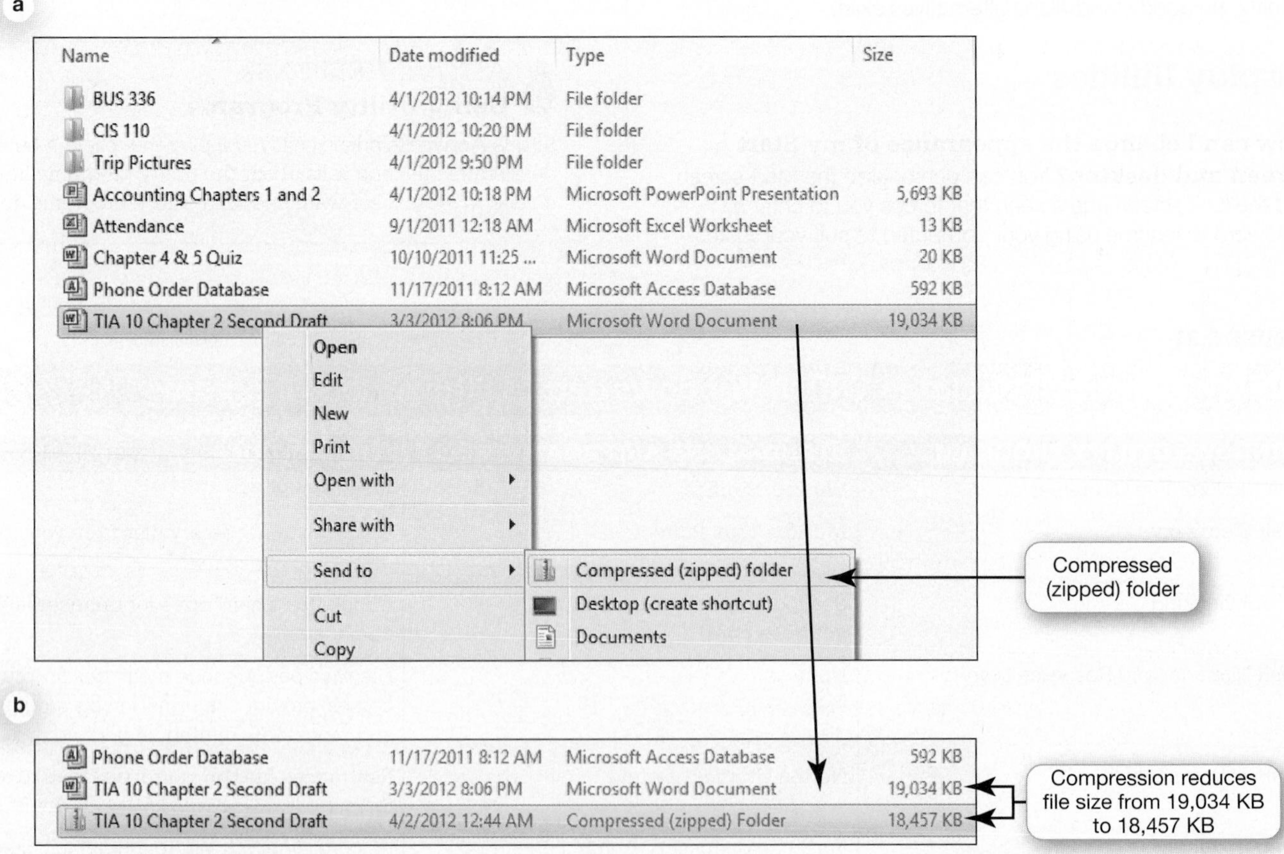


**FIGURE 5.32** (a) File compression is a built-in utility of the Windows OS. (b) Compressing the Word document reduces the file size from 19,034 KB to 18,457 KB.
> *To access the Windows file compression utility, right-click the file or folder that you want to compress, select* **Send to** *from the shortcut menu, and then select* **Compressed (zipped) folder**.

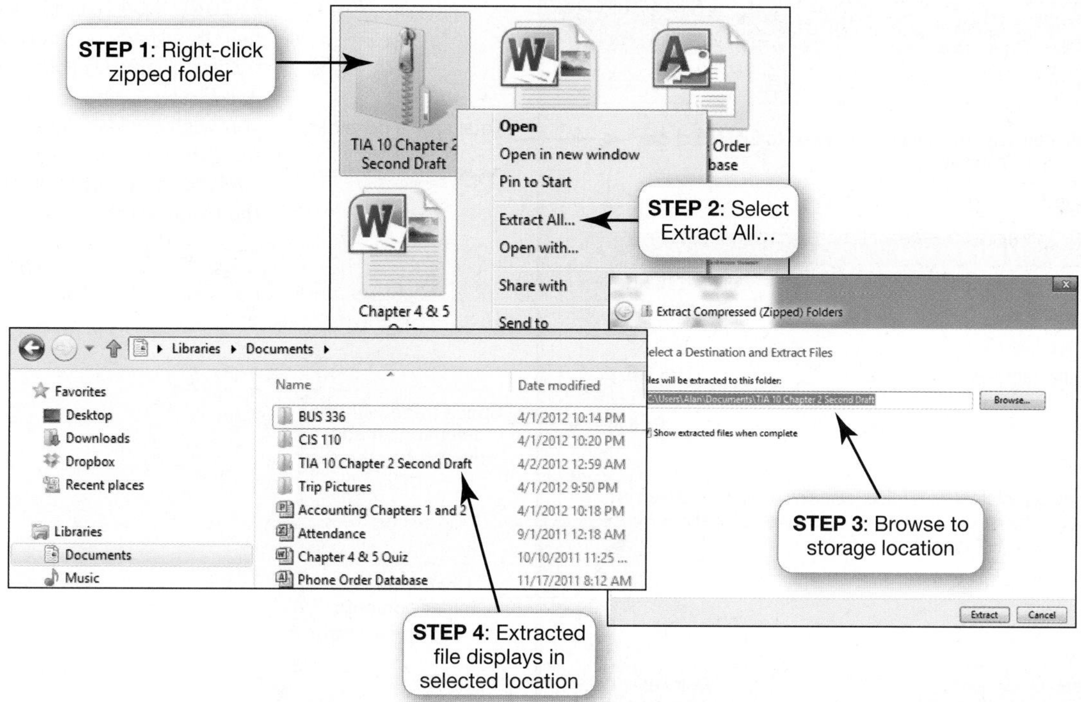


**FIGURE 5.33** The Extraction Wizard in Windows makes unzipping compressed folders and files easy.

**How effective are file compression programs?** Current compression programs can reduce text files by 50% or more, depending on the file. However, some files, such as PDF files, already contain a form of compression, so they don't need to be compressed further. Image files such as JPEG, GIF, and PNG files discard small variations in color that the human eye might not pick up. Likewise, MP3 files permanently discard sounds that the human ear can't hear. These graphic and audio files don't need further compression.

**How do I decompress a file I've compressed?** When you want to restore the file to its original state, you need to *decompress* the file. Generally, the program you used to compress the file can decompress the file as well (see Figure 5.33).

## System Maintenance Utilities

**What utilities can make my system work faster?** **Disk Cleanup** is a Windows utility that removes unnecessary files from your hard drive. These include files that have accumulated in the Recycle Bin as well as temporary files—files created by Windows to store data temporarily while a program is running. Windows usually deletes these temporary files when you exit the program, but sometimes it forgets to do this or doesn't have time because your system freezes or incurs a problem that prevents you from properly exiting a program.

Disk Cleanup also removes temporary Internet files (web pages stored on your hard drive for quick viewing) as well as offline web pages (pages stored on your computer so you can view them without being connected to the Internet). If not deleted periodically, these unnecessary files can slow down your computer.

**How can I control which files Disk Cleanup deletes?** When you run Disk Cleanup, the program scans your hard drive to determine which folders have files that can be deleted and calculates the amount of hard drive space that will be freed up by doing so. You check off which type of files you would like to delete, as shown in Figure 5.34.

**How can I diagnose potential errors or damage on my hard drive? Error-checking** is a Windows utility that checks for lost files and fragments as well as physical errors on your hard drive. Lost files and fragments of files occur as you save, resave, move, delete, and copy files on your hard drive. Sometimes the system becomes confused, leaving references on the **file allocation table**, or **FAT** (an index of all sector numbers in a table), to files that no longer exist or have been moved. Physical errors on the hard drive occur when the mechanism that reads the hard drive's data (which is stored as *1*s or *0*s) can no longer determine whether the area holds a *1* or a *0*. These areas are called *bad sectors*. Sometimes Error-checking can recover the lost data, but more often, it deletes the files that are taking up space.

Error-checking also makes a note of any bad sectors so that the system won't use them again to store data. To locate Error-checking in Windows 8.1, display File Explorer, right-click the disk you want to diagnose, select Properties, and select the Tools tab. On Macs, you can use the Disk Utility to test and repair disks. Disk Utility is located in the Utilities subfolder in the Applications folder on your hard drive.

**How can I check on a program that's stopped running?** If a program has stopped working, you can use the Windows **Task Manager** utility (see Figure 5.35) to check on the program or to exit the nonresponsive program.

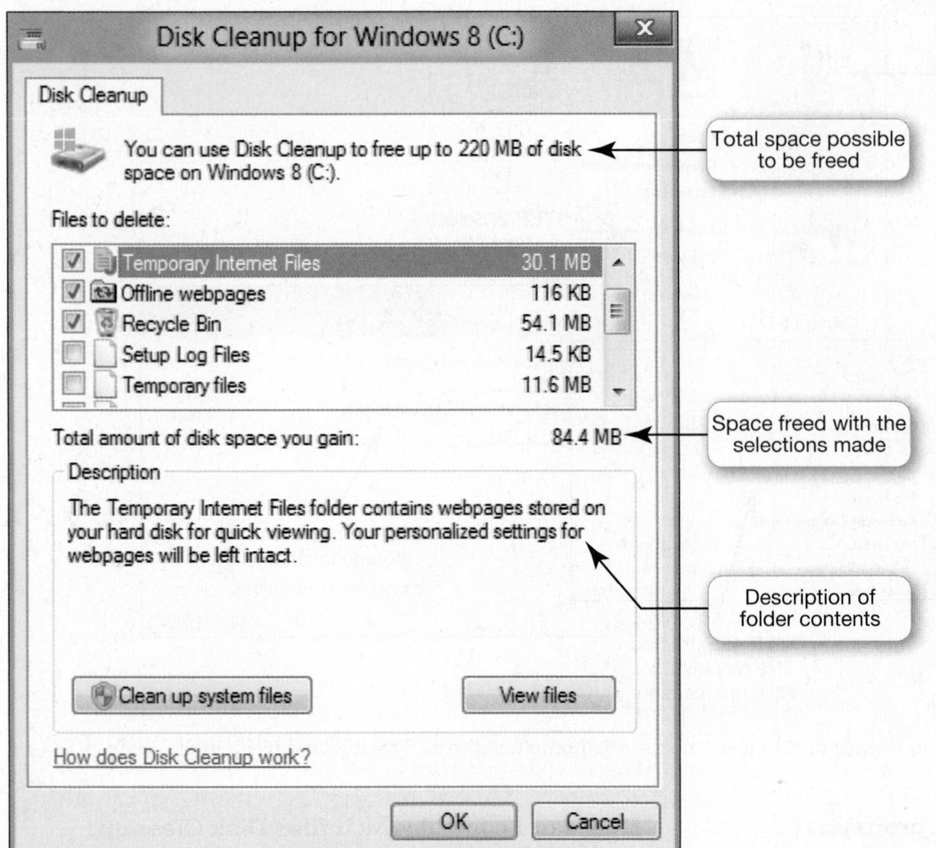


**FIGURE 5.34** Using Disk Cleanup will help free space on your hard drive.
> *Disk Cleanup is accessed by displaying File Explorer, right-clicking on the disk you wish to clean, selecting* **Properties** *from the shortcut menu, and then clicking the* **Disk Cleanup** *button on the General tab.*

In Windows 8.1, the Processes tab of Task Manager lists all the programs you're using and indicates their status. "Not responding" will be shown next to a program that stopped improperly. If the status section is blank (Figure 5.35), then the program is working normally. You can terminate programs that aren't responding by right-clicking the app name and selecting End Task from the shortcut menu.

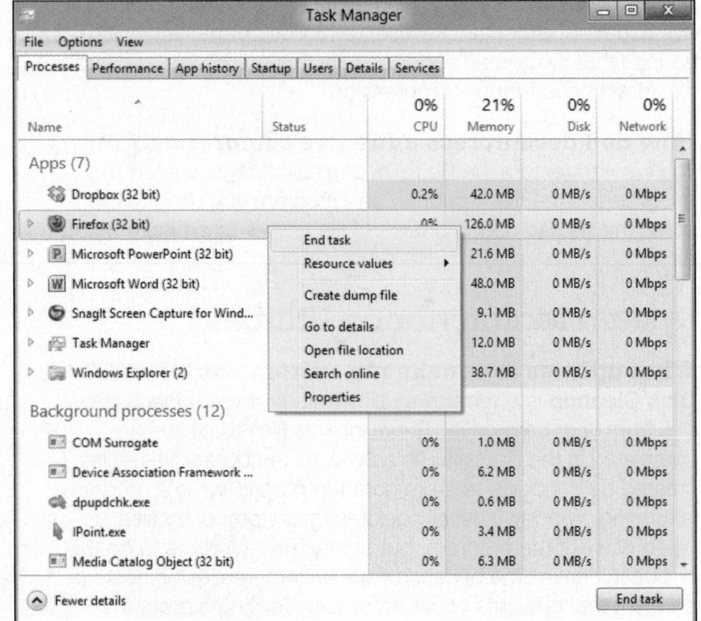


**FIGURE 5.35** You can use Windows 8.1 Task Manager to close nonresponsive programs.
> *Task Manager is accessed by holding down* **Ctrl**, **Alt**, *and* **Del** *or by right-clicking on the taskbar at the bottom of the desktop.*

## System Restore and Backup Utilities

**Is there an undo command for the system?** Suppose you've just installed a new software program and your computer freezes. After rebooting the computer, when you try to start the application, the system freezes once again. You uninstall the new program, but your computer continues to freeze after rebooting. What can you do now?

SOUND BYTE
**Hard Disk Anatomy**

In this Sound Byte, you'll watch a series of animations that show various aspects of a hard drive, including the anatomy of a hard drive, how a computer reads and writes data to a hard drive, and the fragmenting and defragmenting of a hard drive.

# DIG DEEPER How Disk Defragmenter Utilities Work

**Disk defragmenting** programs group together related pieces of files on the hard drive, allowing the OS to work more efficiently. To understand how disk defragmenter utilities work, you first need to understand the basics of how a hard disk drive stores files. A hard disk drive is composed of several platters, or round, thin plates of metal, covered with a special magnetic coating that records the data. The platters are about 3.5 inches in diameter and are stacked onto a spindle. There are usually two or three platters in any hard disk drive, with data stored on one or both sides. Data is recorded on hard disks in concentric circles called **tracks**. Each track is further broken down into pie-shaped wedges, each called a **sector** (see Figure 5.36). The data is further identified by **clusters**, which are the smallest segments within the sectors.

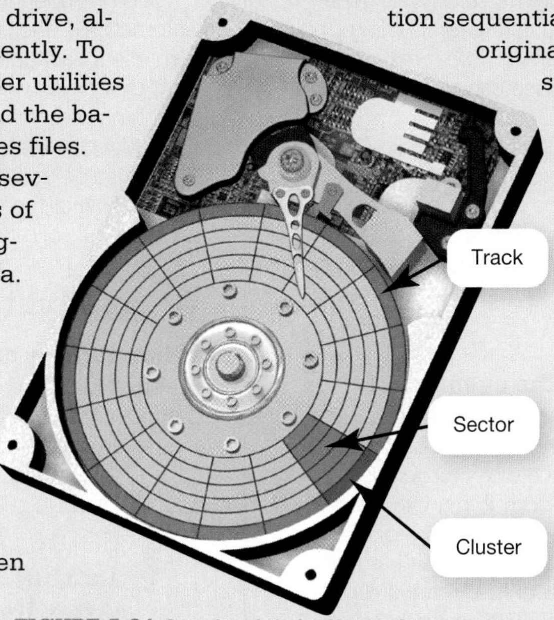

Track
Sector
Cluster

**FIGURE 5.36** On a hard disk platter, data is recorded onto tracks, which are further divided into sectors and clusters.

When you want to save (or write) a file, the bits that make up your file are recorded onto one or more clusters of the drive. To keep track of which clusters hold which files, the drive also stores an index of all sector numbers in a table. To save a file, the computer looks in the table for clusters that aren't already being used. It then records the file information on those clusters. When you open (or read) a file, the computer searches through the table for the clusters that hold the desired file and reads that file. Similarly, when you delete a file, you're actually not deleting the file itself but rather the reference in the table to the file.

So, how does a disk become fragmented? When only part of an older file is deleted, the deleted section of the file creates a gap in the sector of the disk where the data was originally stored. In the same way, when new information is added to an older file, there may not be space to save the new information sequentially near where the file was originally saved. In that case, the system writes the added part of the file to the next available location on the disk, and a reference is made in the table as to the location of this file fragment. Over time, as files are saved, deleted, and modified, the bits of information for various files fall out of order and the disk becomes fragmented.

Disk fragmentation is a problem because the OS isn't as efficient when a disk is fragmented. It takes longer to locate a whole file because more of the disk must be searched for the various pieces, slowing down your computer.

Defragmenting tools take the hard drive through a defragmentation process in which pieces of files scattered over the disk are placed together and arranged sequentially on it. Also, any unused portions of clusters that were too small to save data in before are grouped, increasing the available storage space on the disk. Figure 5.37 shows before and after shots of a fragmented disk that has gone through the defragmentation process.

The disk defragmentation utility in Windows 8 is set by default to automatically defragment the hard drive on a regular basis. Macs don't have a defragmentation utility built into the system. Those users who feel the need to defragment their Mac can use iDefrag, an external program from Coriolis Systems.

For more about hard disks and defragmenting, check out the Sound Byte "Hard Disk Anatomy."

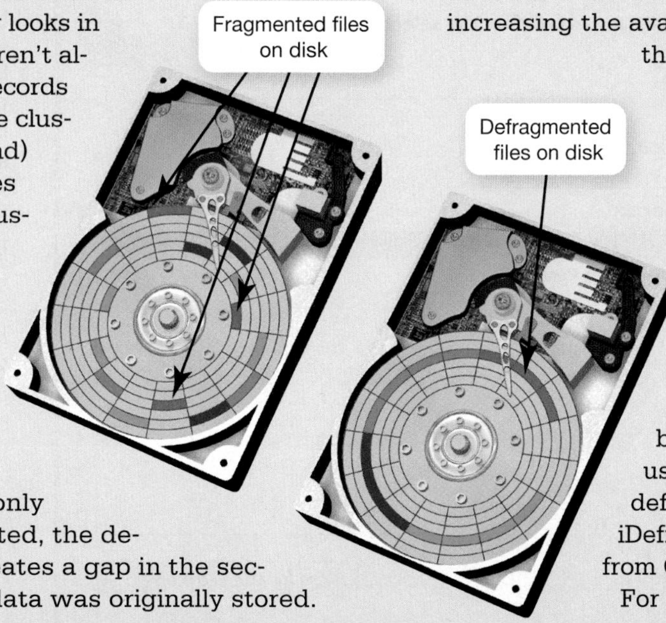

Fragmented files on disk
Defragmented files on disk

**FIGURE 5.37** Defragmenting the hard drive arranges file fragments so that they are located next to each other. This makes the hard drive run more efficiently.

Windows has a utility called **System Restore** that lets you roll your system settings back to a specific date when everything was working properly. A **system restore point**, which is a snapshot of your entire system's settings, is generated prior to certain events, such as installing or updating software, or automatically once a week if no other restore points were created in that time. You also can create a restore point manually at any time.

Should problems occur, if the computer was running just fine before you installed new software or a hardware device, you could restore your computer to the settings that were in effect before the software or hardware installation (see Figure 5.38). System Restore doesn't affect your personal data files (such as Word documents or e-mail), so you won't lose changes made to these files.

**How can I protect my data in the event something malfunctions in my system?** When you use the Windows 8.1 **File History** utility, you can have Windows automatically create a duplicate of your libraries, desktop, contacts, and favorites and copy it to another storage device, such as an external hard drive (see Figure 5.39). A backup copy protects your data in the event your hard drive fails or files are accidentally erased. Also, File History keeps copies of different version of your files. This means that if you need to go back to the second draft of your history term paper, even though you are now on your fifth draft, File History should allow you to recover it. File History needs to be turned on by the user and requires an external hard drive (or network drive) that is always connected to the computer to function.

Windows 8 also includes recovery tools that allow you to complete backups of your entire system (system image) that you can later restore in the event of a major hard drive crash.

OS X includes a backup utility called Time Machine that automatically backs up your files to a specified location. Apple also offers backup hardware called Time Capsules, which are hard disk drives with wireless connectivity, designed to work with Time Machine and record your backup data. Because Time Machine makes a complete image copy of your system, it can also be used to recover your system in the case of a fatal error. (For more information on backing up your files, see Chapter 9.)

## Accessibility Utilities

**What utilities are designed for users with special needs?** Microsoft Windows includes an Ease of Access Center, which is a centralized location for assistive technology and tools to adjust accessibility settings. In the Ease of

SOUND BYTE

**Letting Your Computer Clean Up After Itself**

In this Sound Byte, you'll learn how to use the various maintenance utilities within the OS. You'll also learn why maintenance tasks should be done on a routine basis to make your system more efficient.

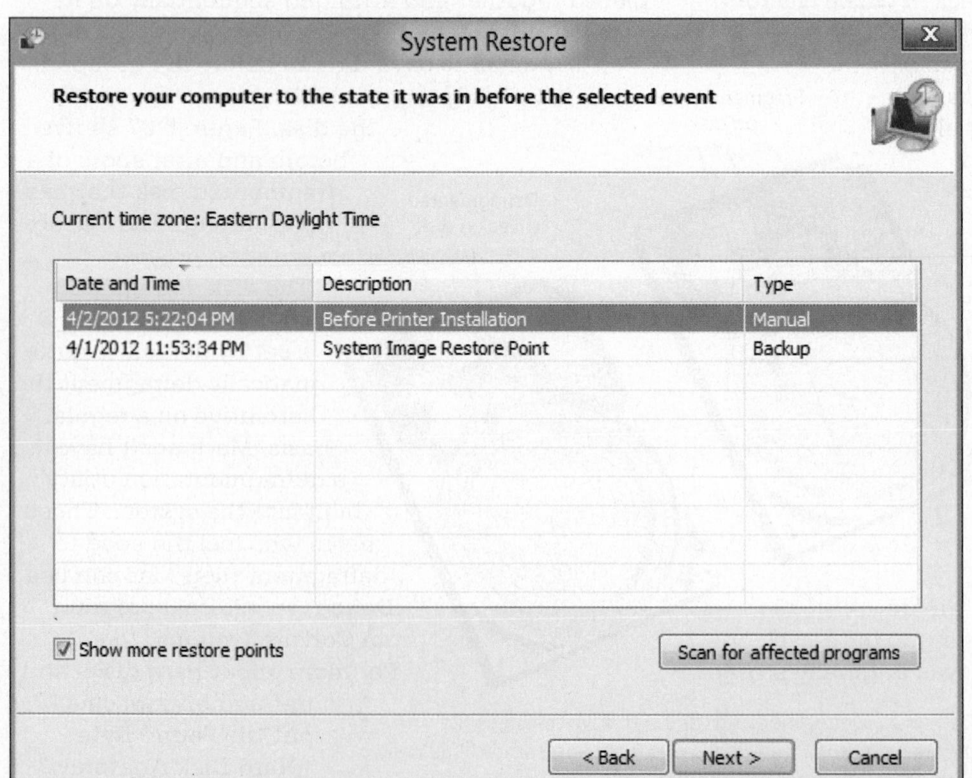


**FIGURE 5.38** This System Restore Wizard shows a restore point set manually by a user and automatically by Windows before a backup was run. Setting a restore point is good practice before installing any hardware or software.

> *The System Restore Wizard is found by right-clicking the* **Start** *button, choosing* **System**, *selecting the* **System Protection** *link, and then clicking the* **System Restore** *button. The* **System Restore Wizard** *appears, with the restore points shown on the second page of the Wizard.*

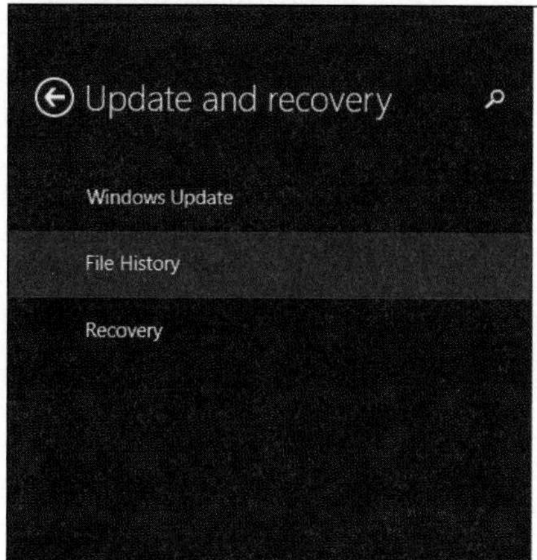


**FIGURE 5.39** Windows 8.1 File History set up to back up files to an external hard drive.
>*To access File History, display the charms bar, choose* **Settings**, *select* **Change PC Settings**, *choose* **Update and Recovery**, *and then select* **File History**.

Access Center, which is accessible from the Control Panel, you can find the tools to help users with disabilities, shown in Figure 5.40. The tools shown in the figure are just a sampling of the available tools. If you're not sure where to start or what settings might help, a questionnaire asks you about routine tasks and provides a personalized recommendation for settings that will help you better use your computer.

Whether you use Windows, OS X, Linux, or another operating system, a fully featured OS is available to meet your needs. As long as you keep the operating system updated and regularly use the available utilities to fine-tune your system, you should experience little trouble from your OS. ■

**Before moving on to the Chapter Review:**
- **Watch Replay Video 5.2.**
- **Then check your understanding of what you've learned so far.**

**FIGURE 5.40**

## Windows Ease of Access Tools

**MAGNIFIER**
- Creates a separate window that displays a magnified portion of the screen

**NARRATOR**
- Reads what is on screen
- Can read the contents of a window, menu options, or text you have typed

**SPEECH RECOGNITION**
- Allows you to dictate text and control your computer by voice

**ON-SCREEN KEYBOARD**
- Allows you to type with a pointing device

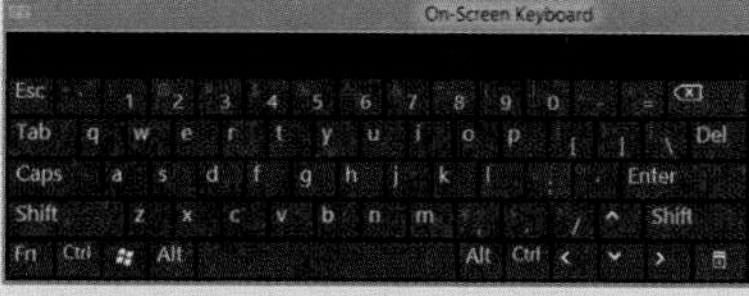


**HIGH CONTRAST**
- Color schemes invert screen colors for vision-impaired individuals

>*The Ease of Access Center is found by accessing the Control Panel and clicking* **Ease of Access**.

(Imagery Majestic/Fotolia; Anatoly Maslennikov/Fotolia; gilles lougassi/Fotolia)

## check your understanding//

For a quick review to see what you've learned so far, answer the following questions. Visit **pearsonhighered.com/techinaction** to check your answers.

### multiple choice

1. Which of the following is considered an accessibility utility?
   - **a.** System Restore
   - **b.** Disk Cleanup
   - **c.** File History
   - **d.** Speech Recognition
2. Apps not specifically designed for Windows 8 (such as Word 2010)
   - **a.** run on the desktop.
   - **b.** will not run in Windows 8.
   - **c.** can't be launched from the Start screen.
   - **d.** use a large amount of RAM.
3. The Windows app used for closing unresponsive apps is
   - **a.** Disk Manager.
   - **b.** Task Manager.
   - **c.** File Explorer.
   - **d.** Library Explorer.
4. The location of a file on a drive such as C:\Documents\CIS110\Homework\Termpaper.docx is known as the
   - **a.** document location.
   - **b.** file path.
   - **c.** file position.
   - **d.** file address.
5. The ________ utility automatically backs up files from your libraries.
   - **a.** Disk Cleanup
   - **b.** File History
   - **c.** System Restore
   - **d.** System Refresh

### true–false

_____ **1.** The main purpose of File Explorer is to help you organize and find files on your computer.

_____ **2.** System restore points can be created manually by a user at any time.

### critical thinking

1. **To Hackintosh or Not: That Is the Question**

   Using Mac's Boot Camp, or virtualization software such as VMware, it's easy (and legal) to install Windows on a Mac. It isn't quite as easy to install OS X on a PC, but it can be done. A PC that has been modified so that OS X can be run on it is called a *Hackintosh*. What are the benefits of tweaking a PC to run OS X? Is it okay to violate Apple's End User Licensing Agreement (EULA), which prohibits installation of OS X on non-Apple-branded equipment? If Apple changed its EULA to allow the installation of its software onto PCs, would that ultimately hurt Apple-branded computers?

2. **What App Is Best for You?**

   Consider your needs as a student. Perhaps you need a good note-taking app for class—one that can also record lectures if needed. Explore the Windows Store, Apple's App Store, and Google Play (for Android apps). What note-taking apps did you find? Which one looks like it would do the best job for you in the classroom? Would the selection of the perfect app influence your choice of hardware? Why or why not?

**Continue**

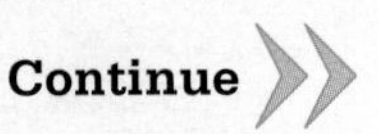

# 5 Chapter Review

## summary//

### Operating System Fundamentals

**1. What software is included in system software?**

- System software is the set of software programs that helps run the computer and coordinates instructions between application software and hardware devices. It consists of the operating system (OS) and utility programs.
- The OS controls how your computer system functions.
- Utility programs are programs that perform general housekeeping tasks for the computer, such as system maintenance and file compression.

**2. What are the different kinds of operating systems?**

- There are many different kinds of operating systems.
- Real-time operating systems (RTOSs) require no user intervention. They are designed for systems with a specific purpose and response time (such as robotic machinery).
- A multiuser operating system (network operating system) provides access to a computer system by more than one user at a time.
- Smartphones have their own specific operating systems, which allow the user to multitask.
- Tablets use operating systems (such as iOS, Android, and Windows 8) that allow interaction with touch-screen interfaces.
- Gaming consoles use operating systems developed specifically for those particular devices.
- Current operating systems for desktops, laptops, and netbooks have multitasking and networking capabilities.

**3. What are the most common operating systems?**

- Microsoft Windows is the most popular OS. It has evolved into a powerful multiuser OS. The most recent release is Windows 8.1.
- Another popular OS is the Mac OS, which is designed to work on Apple computers. Apple's most recent release, Mac OS X, is based on the UNIX OS.
- There are various versions of UNIX on the market, although UNIX is most often used on servers and networks.
- Linux is an open source OS based on UNIX and designed primarily for use on personal computers, although it is often used on servers and supercomputers.

### What the Operating System Does

**4. How does the operating system provide a means for users to interact with the computer?**

- The OS provides a user interface that enables users to interact with the computer.
- Most OSs today use a graphical user interface (GUI). Unlike the command- and menu-driven interfaces used many years ago, GUIs display graphics and use the point-and-click technology of the mouse and cursor (or touch-sensitive screens), making the OS more user-friendly. Common features of GUIs include windows, menus, and icons.

**5. How does the operating system help manage resources such as the processor, memory, storage, hardware, and peripheral devices?**

- When the OS allows you to perform more than one task at a time, it is multitasking. To provide for seamless multitasking, the OS controls the timing of the events on which the processor works.
- As the OS coordinates the activities of the processor, it uses RAM as a temporary storage area for instructions and data the processor needs. The OS is therefore responsible for coordinating the space allocations in RAM to ensure that there is enough space for the waiting instructions and data. If there isn't sufficient space in RAM for all the data and instructions, then the OS allocates the least necessary files to temporary storage on the hard drive, called *virtual memory.*
- The OS manages storage by providing a file-management system that keeps track of the names and locations of files and programs.
- Programs called *device drivers* facilitate communication between devices attached to the computer and the OS. Device drivers translate the specialized commands of devices to commands that the OS can understand, and vice versa, enabling the OS to communicate with every device in the computer system. Device drivers for common devices are included in the OS software.

**6. How does the operating system interact with application software?**

- All software applications need to interact with the CPU. For programs to work with the CPU, they must contain code that the CPU recognizes.

- Rather than having the same blocks of code appear in each application, the OS includes the blocks of code to which software applications refer. These blocks of code are called *application programming interfaces* (APIs).

## The Boot Process: Starting Your Computer

**7. How does the operating system help the computer start up?**

- When you start your computer, it runs through a special process called the *boot process*.
- The boot process consists of four basic steps: (1) The basic input/output system (BIOS) is activated when the user powers on the CPU. (2) In the POST check, the BIOS verifies that all attached devices are in place. (3) The OS is loaded into RAM. (4) Configuration and customization settings are checked.

## The Windows Interface

**8. What are the main features of the Windows interface?**

- In Windows 8, the Start screen provides your first interaction with the OS and is the first image you see on your monitor once the system has booted up. It provides you with access to your computer's apps, tools, and commonly used programs.
- The Windows 8 interface is designed for touch-screen devices.
- Windows 8 apps run full screen and feature commands hidden in app bars.
- Non-Windows 8 programs run on the desktop.

## Organizing Your Computer: File Management

**9. How does the operating system help me keep my computer organized?**

- The OS allows you to organize the contents of your computer in a hierarchical structure of directories that includes files, folders, libraries, and drives.
- File Explorer helps you manage your files and folders by showing the location and contents of every drive, folder, and file on your computer.
- Creating folders is the key to organizing files because folders keep related documents together.
- Following naming conventions and using proper file extensions are also important aspects of file management.

## Utility Programs

**10. What utility programs are included in system software and what do they do?**

- Some utility programs are incorporated into the OS; others are sold as stand-alone off-the-shelf programs.
- Common Windows utilities include those that enable you to adjust your display, add or remove programs, compress files, clean unnecessary files off your system, check for lost files and errors, restore your system to an earlier setting, back up your files, and check on programs that have stopped running.

Be sure to check out the companion website for additional materials to help you review and learn, including a Tech Bytes Weekly newsletter—**pearsonhighered.com/techinaction**. And don't forget the Replay Videos.

# key terms//

app bars **178**
application programming interface (API) **171**
application software **160**
authentication **173**
basic input/output system (BIOS) **172**
boot process **172**
charms **179**
cluster **193**
command-driven interface **166**
device driver **169**
directory **184**
Disk Cleanup **191**
Disk defragmenting **193**
distributions (distros) **163**
Error-checking **191**
event **167**
extension (file type) **186**
file **184**
file allocation table (FAT) **191**
file compression utility **190**
File Explorer **184**
File History **194**
file management **184**
file name **186**
file path **187**
folder **184**
graphical user interface (GUI) **162**
interrupt **167**
interrupt handler **167**
kernel (supervisor program) **173**
library **184**
Linux **163**
Mac OS **162**
menu-driven interface **166**
Microsoft account **173**

multitask **161**

multiuser operating system (network operating system) **161**

operating system (OS) **160**

paging **168**

path separator **187**

pinning **179**

platform **164**

Plug and Play (PnP) **169**

power-on self-test (POST) **173**

preemptive multitasking **167**

real-time operating system (RTOS) **161**

Recycle Bin **188**

Refresh your PC **173**

registry **173**

root directory **184**

sector **193**

source code **183**

spooler **167**

Start screen **178**

swap file (page file) **168**

system files **173**

System Restore **194**

system restore point **194**

system software **160**

taskbar **180**

Task Manager **191**

thrashing **168**

track **193**

UNIX **161**

user interface **160**

utility program **160**

virtual memory **168**

Windows **162**

Windows 8 **162**

Windows 8 apps **178**

Windows 8 interface **178**

## making the transition to . . . next semester//

1. **Upgrading to Windows 8.1**

   You have a laptop that is running Windows 7 and appears to be meeting your needs for your schoolwork. However, many of your friends are getting new touch-screen laptops and tablets with Windows 8.1. Research the differences between Windows 7 and Windows 8.1 and answer the following questions:

   **(a)** What features of Windows 8.1 (that are not available in Windows 7) would be important to enhancing your learning experience?

   **(b)** Would your current computer be able to run Windows 8.1 (assuming that you didn't need the touch-screen features of Windows 8.1)? Go to the Microsoft website and run the upgrade tool to make sure. Use the snipping tool to capture a screenshot of the results.

2. **Deciding on a New Computer**

   You decide it is time to buy a new computer. Decide whether you want a desktop, laptop, tablet, or netbook and then describe how the choice may affect the OS you get.

   **(a)** Discuss the advantages and disadvantages of Windows, Mac, and Linux operating systems.

   **(b)** Research whether you can use multiple operating systems on a single machine. Why might this be an important feature for you to consider?

   **(c)** Research how your smartphone might sync with your computer's OS.

   **(d)** Explain which OS would be most useful to you and why.

3. **Creating a Backup Plan**

   Your computer just shut down unexpectedly. Fortunately, you were able to get it back up and running without any loss of data. You realize that this was too close of a call, so you decide to back up your precious files once and for all. Research the specific steps you'll need to take to create a backup initially and then maintain a current backup as your files change. Include in your research what stand-alone programs or OS tools you'll need to use, as well as any hardware devices or accessories you'll require. Then research the process of creating a disk image. What's the difference between creating a system backup and a disk image?

## making the transition to . . . the workplace//

1. **Collaborating with Team Members**

   Your new job requires you to collaborate and work with sales and management teams within the United States as well as globally. Research the collaboration features of Windows 8.1 and OneDrive and prepare a synopsis of the ones you think would be most useful. Do the features on the list meet all your needs or do you need to purchase additional apps?

2. **Top-Five Utility Programs**

   Create a list of the top-five utilities you feel every computer should have. For each utility, discuss whether it is included in the OS and/or if there are alternatives that can be downloaded for free or that can be purchased as stand-alone programs. Then, for each recommendation, include a review of the utility that has been written in the past year—make sure you document your sources.

3. **Accessibility Features**

   Windows offers a lot of great accessibility tools for those needing extra assistance. The vice president of human resources at the company you work for has asked you to research some stand-alone accessibility programs to determine what else, if anything, is available. List software that is available to help those who have special computing needs.

## team time//

# Choosing the Best OS

## Problem

You're the owner of a technology consulting firm. Your current assignments include advising several start-up clients on their technology requirements. The companies include a fashion design company, a small financial planning company, and an IT networking firm. The companies are holding off on buying anything until they hear from you as to the hardware and software they should purchase. Obviously, one of the critical decisions for each company is the choice of OS.

## Task

Recommend the appropriate OS for each company.

## Process

1. Break up into teams that represent the three primary operating systems: Windows, Mac, or Linux. (Additional teams could be assigned to consider smartphone or tablet operating systems.)
2. As a team, research the pros and cons of your OS. What features does it have that would benefit each company? What features does it not have that each company would need? Why would your OS be the appropriate (or inappropriate) choice for each company? Why is your OS better (or worse) than either of the other options?
3. Develop a presentation that states your position with regard to your OS. Your presentation should have a recommendation and include facts to back it up.
4. As a class, decide which OS would be the best choice for each company.

## Conclusion

Because the OS is the most critical piece of software in the computer system, the selection should not be taken lightly. The OS that is best for a fashion design agency may not be best for a financial planning firm. An IT networking firm may have different needs altogether. It is important to make sure you consider all aspects of the work environment and the type of work being done to ensure a good fit.

# ethics project//

## OS Upgrades

In this exercise, you'll research and then role-play a complicated ethical situation. The role you play may or may not match your own personal beliefs, but your research and use of logic will enable you to represent whichever view is assigned. An arbitrator will watch and comment on both sides of the arguments, and together, the team will agree on an ethical solution.

### Problem

Software developers spend millions of dollars developing new versions of their OS products. Developers argue that new OS versions are needed to meet consumer demands for popular features (such as touch-screen computing). Consumers, however, often resent the constant cycle of upgrades, which require them to upgrade their skills to learn the new features. Developers also usually charge for major upgrades to software (such as from Windows 7 to Windows 8), and consumers are sometimes mystified about why they are paying for a new OS when the older version seems to be meeting their needs. Most schools feel they need to be teaching the most current version of an OS but are sometimes hard pressed to afford the upgrades.

### Research Areas to Consider

- Windows 8 features vs. Windows 7 features
- Software licensing agreements
- Costs for Windows 8 upgrades from older versions of Windows
- Costs for adding touch-screens to existing desktop computers

### Process

1. Divide the class into teams.
2. Research the areas cited above and devise a scenario in which a college is considering upgrading to Windows 8 from Windows 7 and needs to justify an increase in student fees to accomplish the upgrade.
3. Team members should write a summary that provides background information for their character—for example, representative of Microsoft, student, parent, teacher, or arbitrator—and that details their character's behaviors to set the stage for the role-playing event. Then, team members should create an outline to use during the role-playing event.
4. Team members should arrange a mutually convenient time to meet for the exchange, using a virtual meeting tool or by meeting in person.
5. Team members should present their case to the class or submit a PowerPoint presentation for review by the rest of the class, along with the summary and resolution they developed.

### Conclusion

As technology becomes ever more prevalent and integrated into our lives, more and more ethical dilemmas will present themselves. Being able to understand and evaluate both sides of the argument, while responding in a personally or socially ethical manner, will be an important skill.

# Technology in Focus

# Information Technology Ethics

The ethical choices we make have a far-reaching impact on our lives. In this Technology in Focus feature, we examine how technology and ethics affect each other. We'll discuss several key issues related to technology and ethics, including the following:

- Intellectual property rights
- Privacy
- E-commerce
- Free speech
- Computer abuse

But first, let's get started by asking an important question: What is ethics?

## What Is Ethics?

**Ethics** is the study of the general nature of morals and of the specific moral choices individuals make. Morals involve conforming to established or accepted ideas of right and wrong (as generally dictated by society) and are usually viewed as being black and white. Ethical issues often involve subtle distinctions, such as the difference between fairness and equity. Ethical principles are the guidelines you use to make decisions each day.

For example, say you stop to use a photocopier on campus. You discover a copy of the upcoming final exam for your psychology course that your teacher left behind in class. Do you give it back to your professor without looking at the questions? Do you share it with your friends so you can all get good grades on the final? Do you give a copy to your friend who really needs to pass the course in order to prevent losing his or her financial aid?

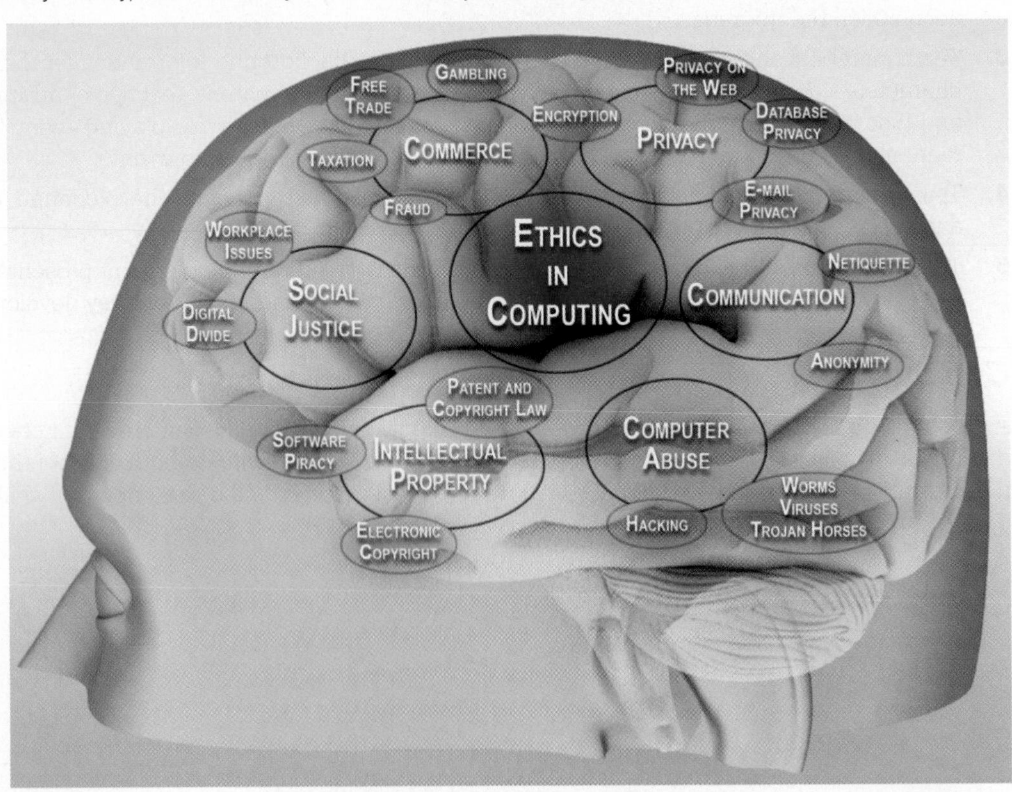


**Doesn't everyone have the same basic ethics?** There are many systems of ethical conduct. Figure 1 lists the five major ethical systems.

FIGURE 1

## Systems of Ethics

| ETHICAL SYSTEM | BASIC TENETS | EXAMPLES |
|---|---|---|
| **Relativism**  | • No universal moral truth<br>• Moral principles dictated by cultural tastes and customs | Topless bathing is prevalent in Europe but generally banned on public beaches in the United States |
| **Divine Command Theory**  | • God is all-knowing and sets moral standards<br>• Conforming to God's law is right; breaking it is wrong | Christians believe in rules such as the Ten Commandments |
| **Utilitarianism**  | • Actions are judged solely by consequences<br>• Actions that generate greater happiness are judged to be better than actions that lead to unhappiness<br>• Individual happiness is not important—consider the greater good | Using weapons of mass destruction ends a war sooner and therefore saves lives otherwise destroyed by conventional fighting |
| **Virtue Ethics**  | • Morals are internal<br>• Strive to be a person who behaves well spontaneously | A supervisor views the person who volunteered to clean up a park as a better person than the workers who are there because of court-ordered community service |
| **Deontology (Duty-Based)**  | • Focus on adherence to moral duties and rights<br>• Morals should apply to everyone equally | Human rights (like freedom of religion) should be respected for all people because human rights should be applied universally |

(Solomin Andrey/Fotolia; Sergey Galushko/Fotolia; kentoh/Fotolia; Alexmillos/Fotolia; Scanrail/Fotolia)

**Aren't laws meant to guide people's ethical actions?** Laws are formal, written standards designed to apply to everyone. Laws are enforced by government agencies and interpreted by the courts. However, it's impossible to pass laws that cover every possible behavior in which humans can engage. Therefore, ethics provide a general set of unwritten guidelines for people to follow.

**Is unethical behavior the same as illegal behavior?** Unethical behavior isn't necessarily illegal. Take the death penalty. In many U.S. states, putting convicted criminals to death for certain crimes is legal. However, many people consider it unethical to execute a human for any reason.

Not all illegal behavior is unethical, though. Civil disobedience, which is manifested by intentionally refusing to obey certain laws, is used as a form of protest to effect change. Gandhi's nonviolent resistance to the British rule of India, which led to India's establishment as an independent country, is an example of civil disobedience. Is it ever ethical for one country to control another country's people?

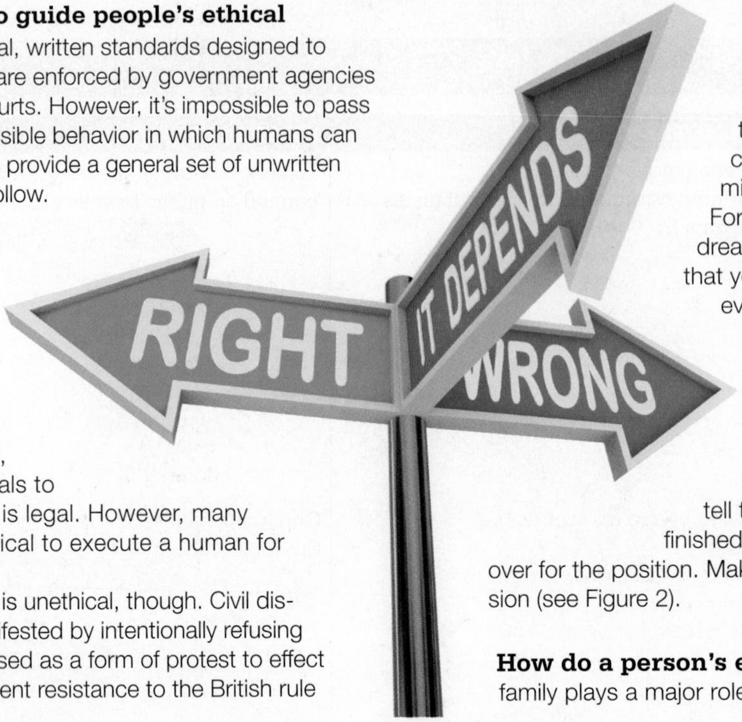

**FIGURE 2** It would be nice if there were signposts to ethical conduct, but the issues are complex. *(iQoncept/Shutterstock)*

Note that there is also a difference between *unethical* behavior and *amoral* behavior:

- *Unethical behavior* can be defined as not conforming to a set of approved standards of behavior. For instance, using your phone to text message a test answer to your friend during an exam is unethical.
- *Amoral behavior* occurs when a person has no sense of right and wrong and no interest in the moral consequences of his or her actions, such as when a murderer shows no remorse for his or her crime.

**Which system of ethics works best?** there is no universal agreement on which is the best system of ethics. Most societies use a blend of different systems. Regardless of the ethical system of the society in which you live, all ethical decisions are greatly influenced by personal ethics.

## Personal Ethics

**What are personal ethics?** Every day you say and do certain things, and each time, you're making decisions. As you choose your words and actions, you're following a set of **personal ethics**—a set of formal or informal ethical principles you use to make decisions in your life. Some people have a clear, well-defined set of principles they follow. Others' ethics are inconsistent or are applied differently in different situations.

It can be challenging to adhere to your own ethical principles if the consequences of your decisions might lead to an unhappy result. For example, to get the job of your dreams, should you say on your résumé that you've already finished your degree, even though you're still one credit short? Is this lying? Is such behavior justified in this setting? After all, you do intend to finish that last credit, and you would work really hard for this company if you were hired. If you tell the truth and state that you haven't finished college yet, you might be passed over for the position. Making this choice is an ethical decision (see Figure 2).

**How do a person's ethics develop?** Naturally, your family plays a major role in establishing the values you cherish in your own life, and these might include a cultural bias toward certain ethical positions (see Figure 3). Your religious affiliation is another major influence on your ethics because most religions have established codes of ethical conduct. How these sets of ethics interact with the values of the larger culture is often challenging. Issues such as abortion, the death penalty, and war often create conflict between personal ethical systems and the larger society's established legal–ethical system.

As you mature, your life experiences also affect your personal ethics. Does the behavior you see around you make sense within the ethical principles that your family, your church, or your first-grade teacher taught you? Has your experience led you to abandon some ethical rules and adopt others? Have you modified how and when you apply these laws of conduct depending on what's at stake?

**What if I'm not sure what my personal ethics are?** When you have a clear idea of what values are important to you, it may be easier to handle situations in your life that demand ethical action. Follow these steps to help define a list of personal values:

1. **Describe yourself.** Write down words that describe who you are, based on how others view you. Would a friend describe you as honest, or helpful, or kind? These keywords will give you a hint as to the values and behaviors that are important to you.
2. **List the key principles you believe in.** Make a list of the key principles that influence your decisions. For example, would you be comfortable working in a lab that used animals for medical research? If not, is it because

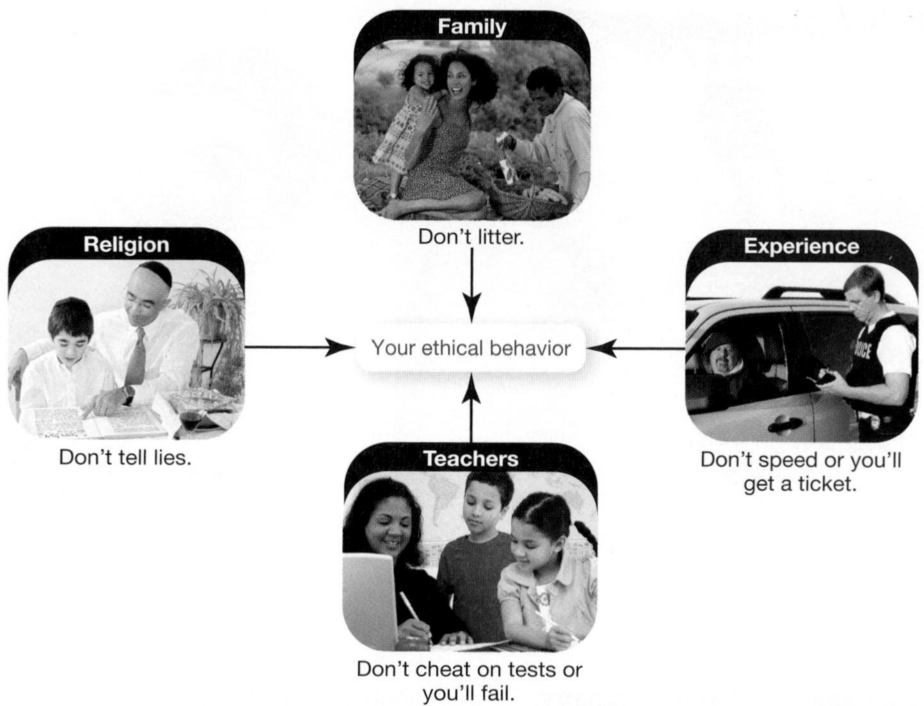


**FIGURE 3** Many different forces shape your personal ethics. *(Noam Armonn/Shutterstock; Shutterstock; Rachel Donahue/Getty Images; Rob Marmion/Shutterstock)*

you value protecting any living being? How important is it to you that you never tell a lie? Or do you feel it is kind to lie in some situations? List the key ideas you believe to be important in conducting your life. Do you always behave this way, or are you "flexible"? Are there situations in which your answers might change (say, if the medical research was to cure cancer or the lie was to protect someone's feelings)?

3. **Identify external influences.** Where did your key principles come from—your parents? Your friends? Spiritual advisors? Television and movies? You may want to question some of your beliefs once you actually identify where they came from.
4. **Consider "why."** After writing down your beliefs, think about *why* you believe them. Have you accepted them without investigation? Do they stand up in the context of your real-world experiences?
5. **Prepare a statement of values.** Distill what you have written into a short statement. By having a well-defined statement of the values you hold most important in your own life, which you can refer to in times of challenge, it will be easier for you to make ethical decisions.

**What are the benefits to ethical living?** Society has established its own set of rules of conduct in the form of laws. Ignoring or being inconsistent in following these rules can have an immediate impact. And more and more research is showing the health benefits of ethical living. When your day-to-day decisions are in conflict with your ethical principles, you often develop stress and anger.

Perhaps even happiness itself is a result of living ethically (see Figure 4). **Positive psychology** is a new focus in the field of psychology. Pioneered by Dr. Martin Seligman of the University of Pennsylvania, this field works to discover the *causes* of happiness instead of addressing the treatment of mental dysfunctions. Dr. Seligman's research has shown that by identifying your personal strengths and values and then aligning your life so that you can apply them every day, you can be happier (and suffer less depression)—an effect equivalent to that of antidepressant medication and therapy. Thus, finding a way to identify and then apply your ethics and values to your daily life can impact your health and happiness.

## Personal Ethics and Your Work Life

**How do employers affect personal ethics?** You may have a set of personal ethics that guide your behavior, but do your ethics change when you go to work? Of course, your employer expects you to follow the rules of conduct established for the business. However, this doesn't mean you need to blindly follow corporate practices that you feel are unethical or detrimental to society (see Figure 5).

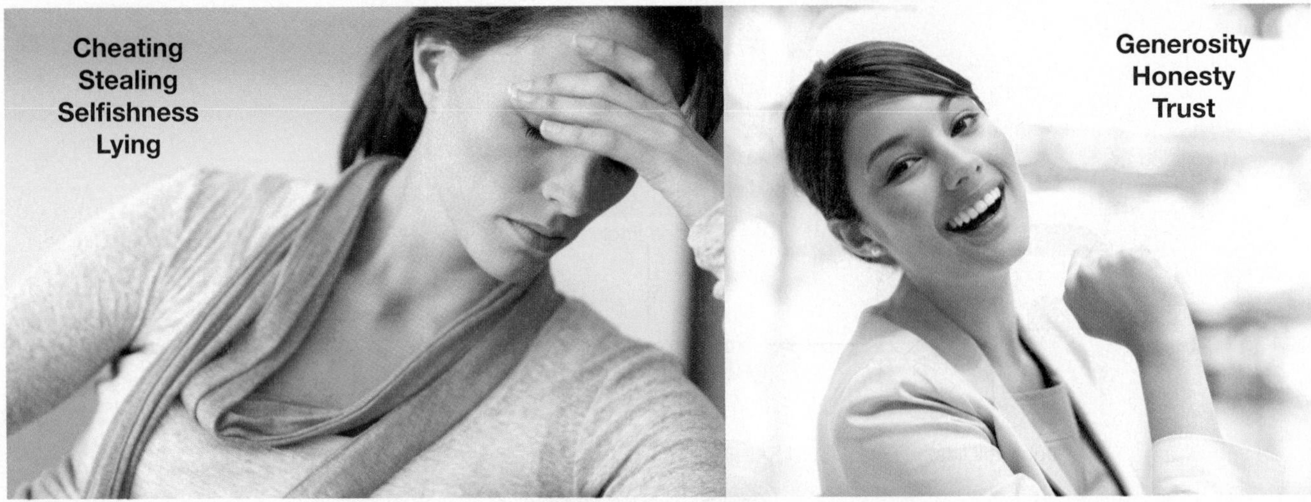


**FIGURE 4** The field of positive psychology shows that living and working ethically affects your happiness. *(Shutterstock; Shutterstock)*

**If you spot unethical behavior at your company, what do you do? Whistle-blowers** are people who report businesses to regulatory agencies for committing illegal acts or who expose unethical (but still legal) acts committed by their employers by publicizing unethical behavior through various media outlets. The Sarbanes–Oxley Act of 2002 requires companies to provide mechanisms for employees and third parties to report complaints, including ethics violations, anonymously. In addition, many businesses are using their websites to allow whistle-blowers to report wrongdoing anonymously, replacing previously used e-mail and telephone hotline systems, which did not shield employees from being identified. With an online system, it's easier for a company to sort and classify complaints and designate them for appropriate action.

**FIGURE 5** How should you respond if you see people in authority at work behaving unethically? *(Inspirestock/Corbis)*

**Should your employer have control over your conduct outside of the office?** Do behavior, integrity, and honesty off the job relate to job performance? They might. But even if they don't, from your employer's perspective, your actions could reflect poorly on your employer. Consider the Transportation Security Administration (TSA) officer who was fired from his job at Chicago's O'Hare airport for making racist remarks about certain types of passengers on his Facebook page. He claimed his remarks were just an exercise of his First Amendment right to free speech. Obviously, his TSA supervisors thought his comments reflected poorly on the agency. Therefore, although your ethics might dictate one mode of behavior, you need to consider how your employer might view your actions.

**How does making ethical choices in a business setting differ from making personal ethical choices?** Most personal ethical decisions involve few people. However, before making an ethical choice for a business, you need to consider the effect your choice will have on all of the business's stakeholders. **Stakeholders** are those people or entities who are affected by the operations of a business. Typical business stakeholders include customers, suppliers, employees, investors (shareholders), financial lenders, and society at large.

For instance, suppose you decide to cut costs in your restaurant by hiring workers "off the books" by paying them in cash. Although doing so might boost profits in the short term, the long-term impact on stakeholders can be severe. If you're caught avoiding paying payroll taxes by paying workers in cash, fines will be levied against your business, which may cause investors to lose money and may affect the company's ability to repay lenders. The negative publicity from being caught doing something illegal may cause a downturn in business, which, in turn, might force layoffs of employees or even closure of the business. Your simple decision on cutting costs isn't as simple as it may seem.

In summary, in a business environment, your behavior is guided by the ethical principles defined by the business owner or management, but you're ultimately guided by your own personal ethics.

## Technology and Ethics: How One Affects the Other

Because technology moves faster than rules can be formulated to govern it, how technology is used is often left up to the individual and the guidance of his or her personal ethics. In the rest of this Technology in Focus feature, we explore situations in which ethics and technology affect each other: social justice (brain technology), intellectual property (international piracy), privacy (personal privacy and technology), e-commerce (geolocation), electronic communication (free speech), and computer abuse (cyberbullying).

Ethical considerations are never clear-cut. They're complex, and reasonable people can have different, yet equally valid, views. We present alternative viewpoints in each setting for you to consider and discuss. Figure 6 summarizes the issues we'll be discussing.

FIGURE 6

### Ethics in Computing

| TOPIC | ETHICAL DISCUSSION | DEBATE ISSUE |
|---|---|---|
| **Social justice** | Does the deployment of technology to alter the human brain blur the lines between human and machine? | Will brain technology make some humans superior to others? |
| **Intellectual property** | Do entire countries support software piracy? | Can we impose our values and intellectual property laws on the world? |
| **Privacy** | Can employers peer into your personal profiles on social media sites? | Should personal privacy be protected? |
| **E-commerce** | Do geolocation devices and applications threaten privacy? | Do the benefits of geolocation devices and applications outweigh the risks? |
| **Electronic communication** | When does big business limit free speech? | Should companies allow the Chinese government to dictate when to curtail free speech? |
| **Computer abuse** | Whose responsibility is it to monitor cyberbullying? | Should parents bear all the responsibility of monitoring cyberbullying, or should it be in the hands of public officials? |

# SOCIAL JUSTICE

## Brain Technology: Creating Cyborgs?

### Summary of the Issue

A **cyborg**, short for "cybernetic organism," is an entity that contains both biological and artificial (e.g., electronic, mechanical, or robotic) components. How close are we to creating cyborgs in your lifetime? Perhaps closer than you think. Consider the sophisticated artificial limbs already available, the installation of which could technically classify an individual as a cyborg.

But most people aren't getting upset about prosthetic limbs. Altering the human brain raises eyebrows, though. Technological advances are being applied to the field of brain research at an increasing rate. Human brain and neurological tissue have a limited ability to regenerate and repair themselves, leading to severe handicaps after injuries or diseases that affect the brain and central nervous system, such as Parkinson's disease. Research is proceeding in three main areas:

1. **Brain–computer interfaces (BCIs):** BCIs work to establish a direct communication pathway between the brain and external devices, such as robotic limbs, computers, and wheelchairs, allowing thought to direct or control the device. In 2013, researchers at the University of Washington demonstrated the first human brain-to-brain interface. Computers were connected to two individuals by BCIs. Through the interfaces, one person was able to control the movement of the other person's arm just by thinking about moving it!
2. **Neurostimulation:** Techniques such as deep brain stimulation involve the transplantation of devices that transmit electrical impulses to the brain for treating movement disorders like Parkinson's disease as well as chronic pain. Repetitive transcranial magnetic stimulation (rTMS) is a noninvasive technique for changing brain activity by exposing it to magnetic fields and is used in treating migraines, strokes, depression, and Parkinson's disease.
3. **Neural stem cells:** Research is underway to determine how neural stem cells respond during strokes, multiple sclerosis, Parkinson's disease, and other neurological disorders. The goal is to develop effective therapies by producing or enhancing neural stem cells to make them more effective in resisting adverse events.

Outcomes of these fields of research have been focused on the treatment of severe medical conditions. However, military organizations are interested in applying BCIs to control fighter aircraft, drones, and other weapons systems. The gaming industry is also interested in BCI technology, since it could provide the capability for thought-controlled video games. And neurostimulation and neural stem cell research hold the potential for not just treating illnesses but possibly enhancing human brain function to allow humans to progress beyond their normal brain potential.

So how should technology be allowed to affect human brain function (Figure 7)? If we can create a smarter or more athletic human, should we do so? Where do we draw the line between humans and machines? If a smart bomb (a bomb guided by computer technology) zeroes in on a military target and destroys it, a machine is responsible for the carnage. But if the bomb is guided by a human being connected to it through a BCI, who bears the responsibility? Where do we separate the person from the machine if we reach this point?

## Questions to Think About and Research

1. Who is responsible for controlling the direction and outcomes of brain technology research?
2. If a missile controlled by a person connected to a weapons system through a BCI accidently destroys a civilian target, who is responsible—human or machine?
3. When do the benefits of medical research outweigh the risks of the technology being used in illegal, evil, or immoral ways?
4. Does enhancing our brain capabilities with technology make us less human?

## POINT

### Brain Technology Research Will Provide Medical "Miracles"

Advocates of brain technology research argue that it will allow for the treatment of currently untreatable catastrophic illnesses and injuries, thus alleviating human suffering.

1. Society will dictate what the acceptable uses of brain technology are, just as they have done for other types of advancements (such as atomic energy).
2. Technology is not responsible for the actions or the consequences of the actions of people. Governments can put controls in place to limit the uses of brain technology just as the United States and Russia have done with strategic arms limitation agreements for nuclear weapons.
3. Technology has provided new tools that allow us to exercise unprecedented control over neurological systems. Ignoring these areas of research provides no relief for afflicted individuals.

## COUNTERPOINT

### Brain Technology Will Radically Change Society if It Is Misused

Critics maintain that the directions brain research will take cannot be adequately controlled and that creating humans with enhanced capabilities poses too much of a danger to society.

1. No one can ultimately prevent or control the results of brain technology research from being used for military purposes.
2. If technology is used irresponsibly, it might create strife between the groups that have access to enhanced brain technology and those who do not.
3. Integrating technology into human beings and altering their body chemistry essentially destroys what it means to be human.

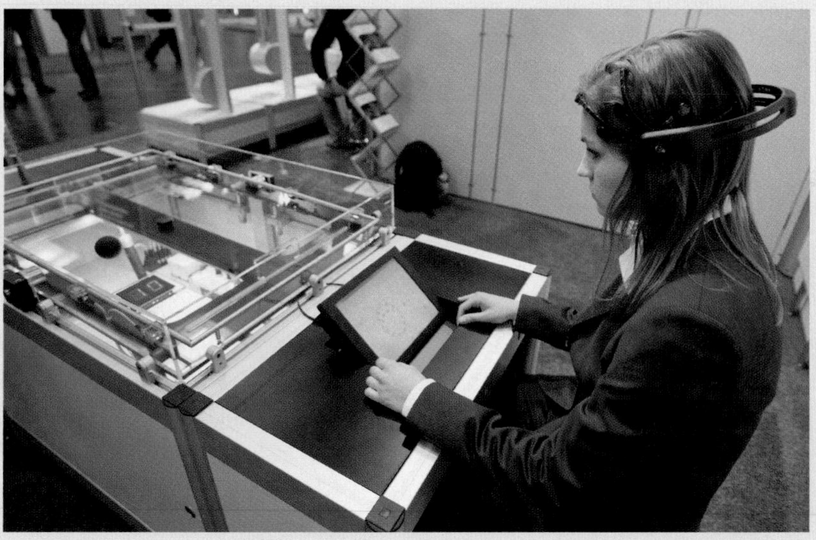

**FIGURE 7** A woman demonstrates control of an industrial machine using a BCI. When human brains directly control machines, which is responsible if something goes awry—human or machine? *(MATZEN/Reuters/Corbis)*

# International Pirates

## Summary of the Issue

Intellectual property (such as music, writing, and software) is protected by copyright law. But there have been challenges in enforcing these standards in other countries. What happens to fair trade if some countries refuse to enforce copyright laws? How should the trade partners of these countries respond?

The Business Software Alliance estimated that in 2011, 70% of computers in the Philippines and 77% of the computers in China ran on pirated software. For comparison, the estimated piracy levels in the United States and Sweden are 19% and 24%, respectively. This discrepancy means that many businesses in the Philippines and China don't have to spend money for operating system or productivity software, which gives them an advantage in the international marketplace. Although some companies, like Microsoft, continue to do business in China and the Philippines despite the high levels of piracy, smaller companies often can't survive there. For example, Tom Adams, chief executive of Rosetta Stone, pulled his company and its language training software products out of China. He describes China as a "kleptocratic society" and worries about the amount of theft of his software in that environment.

In fact, the chief executives of 12 major software companies—Microsoft, Adobe, Autodesk, Symantec, and others—have lobbied the U.S. administration and lawmakers to continue to put pressure on China to crack down on illegal copying. With a potential market of more than one billion people, and an increasing number of technology-hungry purchasers, companies dread the idea of missing out on the Chinese market. In 2010, talks between the United States and China resulted in promises by the Chinese government of stricter enforcement of antipiracy laws and implementation of aggressive antipiracy media campaigns. But to date, software companies have failed to see any significant increases in software sales in China, indicating the Chinese government's actions have been ineffective. On the other hand, the Philippines government is stepping up enforcement of copyright laws (see Figure 8) in an effort to get off the U.S. government's intellectual property watch list.

Many countries, such as Armenia, Bangladesh, Yemen, Libya, and Vietnam, have higher rates of piracy than China and the Philippines. The Business Software Alliance estimates the monetary losses from software piracy at more than $63 billion worldwide for 2011, although there is debate around the exact value.

Most people have had the opportunity to participate in the piracy of copyrighted materials through illegal peer-to-peer sharing and the use of torrents. This behavior is now multiplied to the level of nations, and the consequences are still being explored.

## Questions to Think About and Research

1. Should a government be penalized for failing to actively enforce the laws it has enacted within its own country? If so, what should the penalties be, and how should they be enforced?
2. Does each government have the right to make its own decision on a stand against piracy?
3. How can other countries respond to international piracy?
4. Does individual piracy have any connection to the enforcement of copyright laws on an international level?

## POINT

### International Copyright Protections Need to Be Vigorously Enforced

Artists and software developers depend on the integrity of the protection of intellectual property, both within the United States and internationally, to make a fair profit on their work.

1. If other countries do not fight piracy, artists and developers have a disadvantage in the marketplace.
2. By allowing massive piracy, some countries are stealing from others.
3. Every country needs to have a common understanding and enforcement of intellectual property laws for trade to be fair and beneficial to everyone.

## COUNTERPOINT

### Global Business Demands Understanding Other Cultures

Most countries have laws on their books regarding intellectual property. It is not the job of the United States to tell a foreign government how to conduct its internal affairs.

1. The existing laws on intellectual property have worked to serve the interests of these countries. If U.S. companies do not want to sell to the billion-person market of China, then that is their choice.
2. Piracy exists within the United States, so it is hypocritical to be chastising foreign governments for software piracy.
3. Companies can pursue restitution for piracy through the foreign court systems.

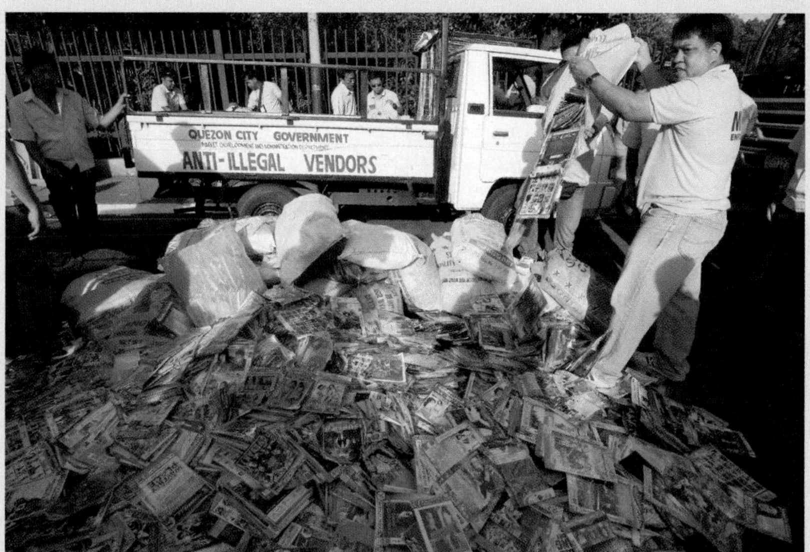


**FIGURE 8** A crackdown on pirated media in the Philippines underscores that issues of intellectual property play an important role in international trade.
*(© ROLEX DELA PENA/epa/Corbis)*

# Can Employers Peer into Your Personal Life?

## Summary of the Issue

Like respect and dignity, privacy is a basic human right. What, exactly, is privacy? Simply stated, privacy is the right to be left alone to do as one pleases. The idea of privacy is often associated with hiding something (a behavior, a relationship, or a secret). However, privacy really means not being required to explain your behavior to others. But social media sites such as Facebook are inherently about sharing information with others. Does this mean there is no such thing as personal privacy (see Figure 9) on social media sites?

Facebook and other social media allow you to set privacy filters on your personal information. You can choose to share information publically, share it with just with your friends, or keep it totally private. Employers now routinely check social media sites to gather publically shared information on prospective employees. But recently, many government agencies, such as police departments and some private employers, have been asking job seekers for access to their *private* Facebook information, as well.

Sometimes this is blatant, such as what happened to a Maryland corrections officer who was seeking reinstatement. During an interview, he was asked for his Facebook password. The interviewer then proceeded to log on to his account, purportedly to see if he had any gang affiliations.

Although this might seem like a legitimate reason for a prison system to screen candidates, the U.S. Senate disagrees. In 2012 and 2013, legislators proposed the Password Protection Act to prevent employers from demanding passwords to private sites from employees. The 2012 bill died in committee, and the 2013 bill was still in committee as of late 2013. In May 2012, Maryland became the first state to enact a law that prohibits employers from asking current and prospective employees for their access codes to social networking sites. Employers are currently prohibited from asking prospective employees information related to their gender, race, religion, age, and sexual orientation, but this information is often found in social media site profiles. Facebook has also warned employers against this practice, as it violates the terms-of-use agreement for the site.

Often, however, employer research is more subtle. For example, employers often encourage prospective employees to "friend" them on Facebook. Although these company profiles are set up specifically so that prospective employees can learn information about the company, once prospective employees "friend" the company, company representatives can often see more information about these would-be employees than what is visible in their public profile.

The American Civil Liberties Union (ACLU) and other privacy advocates have begun voicing opposition to these practices, citing erosion of personal privacy rights. You wouldn't give a prospective employer the keys to your house so they could poke around in your personal life. But doesn't it have almost the same effect if you let them see your private information in a social media profile?

Employers—especially small businesses—argue that hiring decisions are so critical that they need to gather as much information as possible and that people voluntarily surrendering passwords is not a violation of prospective employees' rights. But critics of these practices say that job seekers may feel powerless to refuse these invasions of their privacy for fear they'll be turned down for a job.

The control and privacy of information will continue to be a fine balancing act for the foreseeable future, with employers trying to gather intelligence while appeasing the concerns of privacy advocates. Leaving a trail of electronic breadcrumbs is to a certain extent inevitable. But cleaning up or hiding your "trail" is still important to many users, not because they're trying to hide something but because they value their basic right to privacy.

## Questions to Think About and Research

1. Should you be able to decide exactly what information on a social networking site you share with others? Would you be willing to pay for this privilege?
2. Do you know what your privacy settings are on the social media sites you use? Is there any information being shared publicly that you weren't aware was being shared?
3. Should employers be allowed to ask prospective employees for their passwords to social media sites? Is this practice still legal in the United States?
4. Is there any information on sites you use that you want to restrict potential employers from seeing? Do these sites allow you to restrict the information you wish to protect?

## POINT

### Employers Have No Right to Job Seekers' Private Social Media Information

The advocates of protecting privacy in the United States argue that the right to privacy is a basic human right that should be afforded to everyone. Personal privacy concerns should outweigh the business needs of a corporation.

1. Social media sites have an inherent duty to protect the data of their users.
2. If employers are screening private information, they might misuse or lose control of the data or violate current employment law.
3. Default privacy settings on social media sites should all be opt-in, allowing users the ultimate control over who views their data.

## COUNTERPOINT

### Employers Are Entitled to Gather Personal Information Directly Related to Employment

Advocates for unrestricted sharing of information feel that business concerns outweigh privacy concerns. Businesses should have the right to screen all data in social media sites to determine the character and fitness of employment candidates.

1. Volunteering password information does not violate an individual's right to privacy.
2. Users can make their own privacy decisions and choose not to post or share sensitive information (opt out).
3. In the digital age, loss of a certain amount of privacy is inevitable.

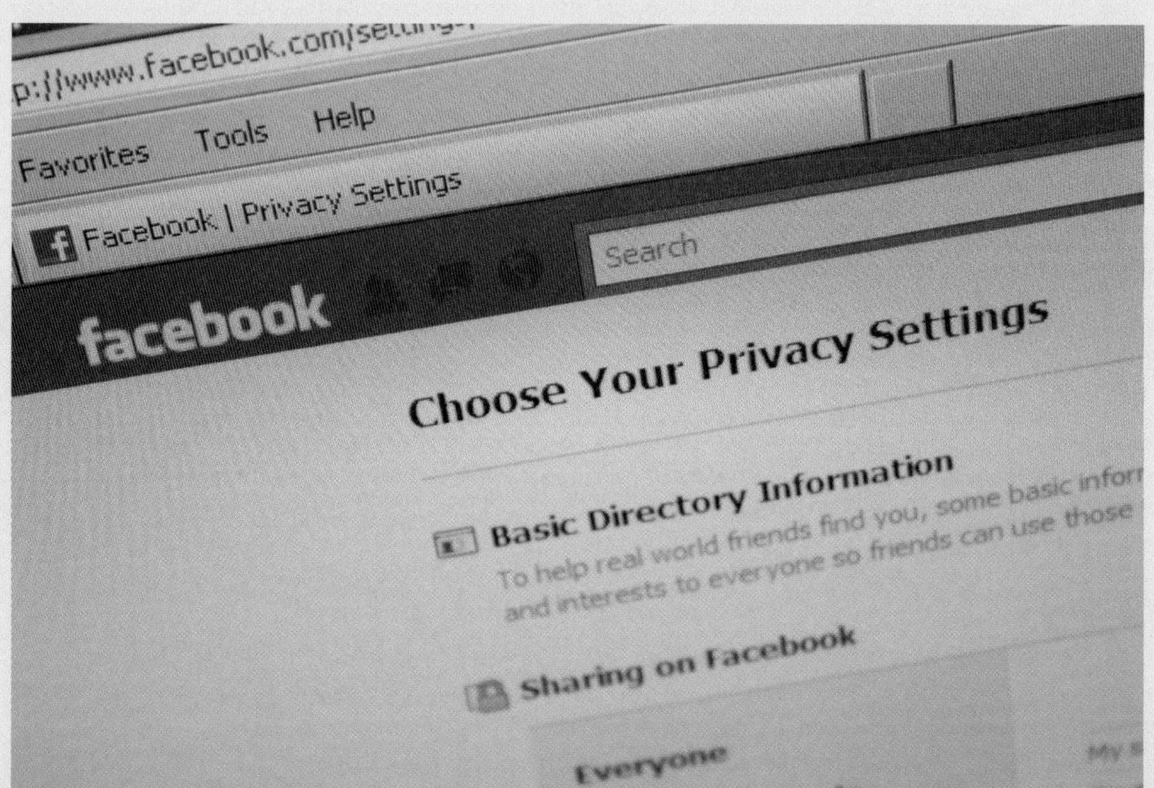


**FIGURE 9** What information are you sharing on Facebook and with whom? *(© digitallife / Alamy)*

# Geolocation: Who Knows Where You Are?

## Summary of the Issue

"Where are you?" is the burning social networking question these days, and your smartphone probably has the answer. The technology is called geolocation (see Figure 10), and smartphones have a GPS chip that can calculate your exact position. Services such as Foursquare, Gowalla, Brightkite, and Loopt are all hoping you'll use their geolocation services to find your friends or let your friends find you. Through the apps, you can receive recommendations of places to visit or things to do nearby. Businesses are using geolocation apps to promote their products and offer rewards for "checkins" to help drive customers to their location.

When you sign up on Foursquare and other social media sites, you can choose what information is publically available, such as your location or your Facebook profile. Foursquare is designed to make it convenient to see where your friends are and who's in the venue where you're currently "checked in." You might be cautious and choose to make personal and location information only accessible to your friends—or it might all be public. But what if another app you know nothing about is using your information in a way never intended by the social media sites you joined?

Consider the controversy that erupted around the iPhone app Girls Around Me. When the app was first launched, it used data from Foursquare to create a local map that showed how many individuals logged into Foursquare were in geographic locations near you. It also allowed you to view Facebook profiles of people around you if they had their Facebook profiles linked to their Foursquare account. The app developer, i-Free, promoted the app as a tool to see what was happening in a wider range of locations instead of just one at a time. It viewed its tool as a way to let users identify "hot spots" of activity that had a lot of people checked in. i-Free said the app was just like looking in the window of a location to see how crowded it was, but it was also aggregating publically available information provided by other social media services.

Critics of the app decried it as a tool for stalkers that provided more information than people could gain by glancing in a window. They argued that the app violated the privacy of Foursquare users because they had no knowledge of how the Girls Around Me app was using their information. Many detractors argued that just because you agreed to make certain information public on Foursquare doesn't mean you automatically agree to the use of that same information on other apps that might function in a different (and perhaps objectionable) way. Foursquare claimed that i-Free was violating the terms of its information-sharing agreement and changed its application programming interfaces (APIs) to effectively disable the Girls Around Me app. i-Free removed the app from the App Store for retooling. The app has been reintroduced, and Foursquare is permitting the app to access some of their users' information once again.

But the question remains, when you leave your home and announce your constant whereabouts through tweets and checkins, do you lose your privacy in exchange for fun and convenience? Although you can set certain levels of privacy in the apps, there is still the potential for someone with bad intentions (stalkers, robbers) to follow your updates. And do you really know how the information you make public will be used by other app creators? In addition to opening yourself up to potential stalking or robbery, geolocation devices also can track the activities you might not want publicized and that once documented can later be used against you.

It wasn't long ago that we were concerned about using our real names online, but now we're comfortable with sharing our exact location in a very public way. As Facebook CEO Mark Zuckerberg said, "People have really gotten comfortable not only sharing more information and different kinds, but more openly and with more people." But does such acceptance justify neglecting to maintain certain levels of privacy? Again, it seems that technology has moved more quickly than society can address the potential risks and dangers.

## Questions to Think About and Research

1. Do the benefits of geolocation outweigh the risks?
2. What other devices besides cell phones track and record our movements and locations as digital records?
3. How have social networks increased the risks of geolocation?
4. What risks do geolocation pose for college students? How can users mitigate those risks?

## POINT

### Geolocation Devices Do Not Threaten Privacy

The advocates of using geolocation devices with minimal concern for threatened privacy are those who believe the social norm has shifted and people have become comfortable with sharing more information.

1. Businesses are adopting geolocation apps as a part of their social media strategy in order to drive customers to their business. They would lose revenue if such activities ceased.
2. As the devices and apps become better and more precise, they may become useful as public safety and news-gathering devices.
3. Society may need to reevaluate its views about how much privacy is needed in people's digital lives, as well as the degree of an individual's responsibility for making sensible decisions about sharing information through the Internet.

## COUNTERPOINT

### Geolocation Devices Are a Threat to Privacy

The advocates for tighter privacy controls and awareness campaigns about the potential risks of using geolocation devices suggest that the threats are too big to ignore. Society has become too complacent with privacy issues.

1. Privacy settings on apps and GPS devices should be more restrictive in order to avoid broadcasting one's location and risking personal assault.
2. Laws and regulations will need to be created as to the use and distribution of digital location information.
3. Consumers need to be educated about geolocation and the ways it can affect them so that they are able to make informed choices.

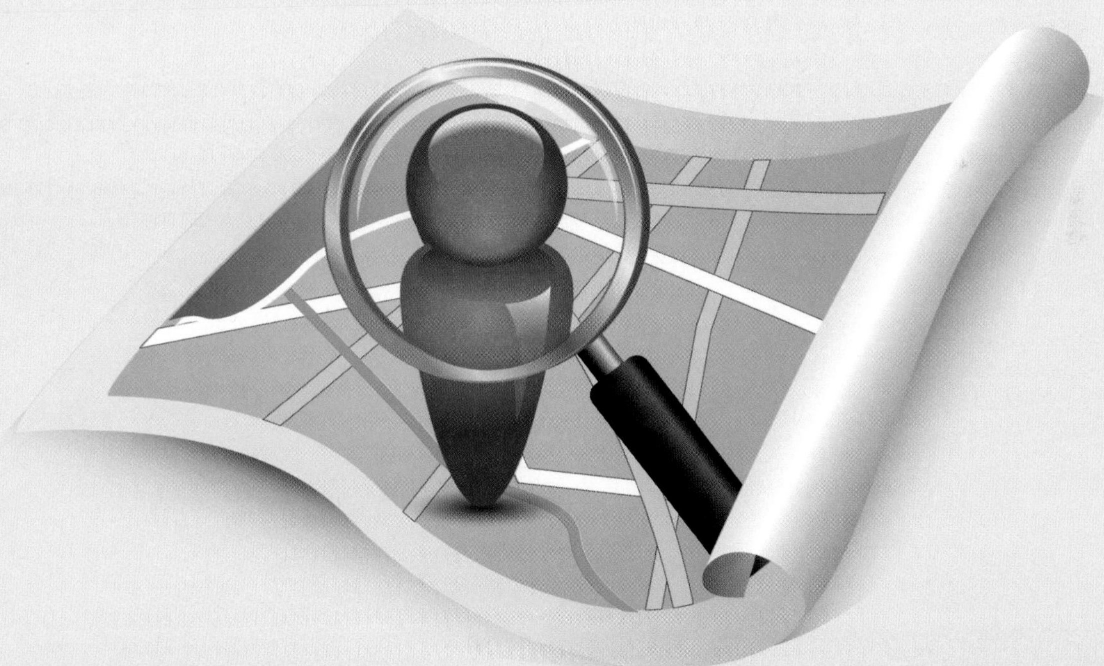

**FIGURE 10** Geolocation applications help you find cool places and businesses. But who do you want to find you with geolocation? *(© Cseke Timea/Fotolia)*

# Does Free Speech Have a Price?

## Summary of the Issue

In early 2006, when Google launched its search engine services in China, it conceded to the Chinese government's demands that it self-censor its search engine, restricting search results for sensitive information such as the details of the Tiananmen Square protests and of human rights groups. This decision prompted much discussion, with some condemning Google's decision for putting business profits over what they saw as basic human rights (see Figure 11). Google justified its actions by stating that a company must operate within the rules of the market in which it operates and that the benefits of increased access to information for people in China "outweighed our discomfort in agreeing to censor some results." And, compared with search results from **Baidu.com**, the leading Chinese search engine, Google was not censoring all information.

However, in 2010, Google announced that it was no longer willing to censor search results and moved the site to Hong Kong, where it hoped there would be less censorship. The departure was a reaction to a sophisticated, targeted cyberattack that Google believes was done to gather information on Chinese human rights activists. At that time, Google had about a 35% market share.

Microsoft had only a 1% share of the market, so it decided to partner with **Baidu.com** to provide English-language search results for China's largest search engine. Microsoft stated it would agree to abide by Chinese censorship laws (so search terms like *freedom* and *democracy* deliver filtered results), thereby respecting the laws of the countries where it operates. However, before honoring any censor requests, Microsoft insisted that Chinese authorities made legally binding requests in writing.

So how did it all work out? As of 2013, Google's market share has dropped to 3% in China, whereas **Baidu.com** has increased its market share to 63%. Microsoft's decision to keep censoring its searches appears to have paid off—at least from a monetary perspective. But is the financial result more important than the social implications of its behavior?

## Questions to Think About and Research

1. Is there anything else that Google could have done that would have a major impact on China's censorship laws?
2. Has Microsoft's compliance with censorship laws furthered the Chinese government's cooperation in combating software piracy in China? Are Microsoft's financial incentives even deeper than just Internet market share?
3. Can the U.S. government compel technology companies to take a firmer stance on free speech in China and elsewhere by instituting criminal charges if U.S. companies do not take reasonable steps to protect human rights?

## POINT

### U.S. Companies Should Comply with Local Laws in Foreign Countries

Those in favor of Microsoft's actions to remain in China feel that if a company chooses to operate in a foreign country, it knows the local laws and should be prepared to work within those laws as it does business. It is not the place of a company to try to change laws of foreign countries.

1. Microsoft conducts businesses in other countries that have censorship laws, so why not participate in China?
2. Working in China does not mean a company supports all of China's policies.
3. Microsoft's presence continues to advance the progress the Chinese government is making toward democracy. U.S. companies can ethically stay in China if they make an effort to improve human rights there. U.S. companies operating in China should agree on guidelines that respect human rights.
4. A U.S. company's presence has no impact on reform—reform must come from within.

## COUNTERPOINT

### U.S. Companies Should Put What Is Right Ahead of What Is Financially Expedient

Those in favor of Google's actions believe that international corporations should begin to take a firm stance against governments that do not promote basic human rights.

1. China will never change unless there are financial and political incentives to do so. Google's departure helps pressure the Chinese government.
2. Google's withdrawal from China threatens the viability of many advertising resellers in China. Will this added pressure help or hinder human rights efforts?
3. Google's decision to leave helps put pressure on China's government to play by global standards. China cannot expect to compete in the global marketplace while refusing to have a global exchange of ideas.

**FIGURE 11** Is free speech possible in countries (such as China) where information availability is restricted by law? *(kentoh/Shutterstock)*

# Cyberbullying: Who Should Protect Children from Each Other?

## Summary of the Issue

Cyberbullying is just like normal bullying, but it involves the use of digital technologies such as the Internet, cell phones, or video (see Figure 12). There are many types of cyberbullying, some of which might result in criminal charges depending on the type of incident:

- Bombarding a victim with harassing instant messages or text messages
- Stealing a password and then using the victim's account to embarrass the victim by sending harassing, threatening, or lewd messages while pretending to be the victim
- Spreading rumors or lies on social networking sites
- Posting embarrassing photos or videos on the web
- Infecting the victim's computer with malware, usually to spy on the victim

The effects of cyberbullying can be devastating. Infamous cases include Hannah Smith, the English girl who at 14 committed suicide after being repeatedly taunted on social networking sites, and Tyler Clementi, a Rutgers freshman who committed suicide after his roommate showed fellow students videos of him having sex.

Signs that a child is a victim of cyberbullying are often the same as the signs of depression. A child may:

- Suddenly lose interest in normal activities
- Be reluctant to go to school
- Lose his or her appetite
- Have trouble sleeping
- Appear upset after using the Internet
- Experience unusual mood swings (such as bursting into tears for no apparent reason)

Signs that a child might be perpetrating cyberbullying include the following:

- Using the Internet excessively
- Sending large volumes of text messages
- Clearing the computer screen when others enter a room
- Conducting clandestine Internet activities (refusal to say what he or she is doing)

Vigilance over children's online activities is obviously key to spotting both victims and perpetrators of cyberbullying.

But who is responsible for monitoring children? Parents obviously need to protect their children, but bullying usually doesn't happen until children are exposed to other children, such as in school. So should teachers shoulder the responsibility for detecting, reporting, and mitigating cyberbullying? Children often spend more time in school during the day than under the supervision of their parents. But cyberbullying activities don't just take place in school. Most children have access to the Internet at home and can carry on campaigns of terror from their bedrooms.

There is currently no federal law prohibiting cyberbullying, but the recently passed law against cyberstalking may cover this area. According to the Cyberbullying Research Center (**cyberbullying.us**), as of 2013, 49 states had antibullying laws on the books. However, only 47 state laws cover electronic harassment, and a mere 18 state laws cover cyberbullying. Many legislatures are reluctant to pass laws that instruct parents on how to raise their children because this tends to raise issues about personal freedom. Therefore, anti-cyberbullying laws tend to place the burden of detection on the schools. For instance, the Massachusetts law requires schools to provide age-appropriate education on bullying to students, to train school employees in detection and prevention of bullying, and to have plans developed for detecting and reporting bullying.

## Questions to Think About and Research

1. What level of responsibility should school employees have for protecting children from cyberbullying?
2. Should there be federal laws that make cyberbullying a crime? If so, how would these laws be enforced?
3. What types of education for children would be beneficial in preventing cyberbullying? When should these programs begin, and how often should children be required to participate?

## POINT

### Parents Must Protect Their Children from Cyberbullying

Proponents of parental responsibility for detecting and preventing cyberbullying feel that it's a personal behavior issue. Individuals are responsible for their own behavior as long as it doesn't harm others. Parents should be allowed to educate their children according to their own standards of behavior and preferences in terms of moral behavior (such as religion).

1. Parents are ultimately responsible for protecting their children.
2. Bullying is a personal behavior issue, and all decisions regarding personal freedom and behavior should be made by parents.
3. Because educating children about bullying is key to preventing it, the content of such training needs to be controlled by parents.

## COUNTERPOINT

### Schools Must Bear the Responsibility for Protecting Students from Cyberbullying

Cyberbullying affects society because it can severely damage an individual's self-esteem. Cyberbullying is similar to other hate crimes and should enlist public officials (such as educators) in enforcement of the laws.

1. Parents do not supervise their children 24/7 and therefore require help from other responsible adults to protect their children.
2. Parents need to be assured that publicly funded institutions such as schools and libraries are "safe havens" where their children will not be exposed to malicious activities.
3. Educators have better resources than most parents for teaching children about the serious effects of cyberbullying.

**FIGURE 12** Cyberbullying involves the use of digital technologies both to bully and to disseminate acts of bullying. *(Rawdon Wyatt/Alamy)*

## Using Computers to Support Ethical Conduct

Although there are many opportunities to use computers and the Internet unethically, we can also use technology to support ethical conduct. For example, many charitable organizations use the Internet and other technology tools for fundraising. When severe flooding wiped out 1,600 homes in Colorado in September 2013, the Salvation Army and other charities received many pledges via their websites.

Google Crisis Response is a project sponsored by Google that helps disseminate information before and after a crisis to coordinate relief efforts and provide updates to the public (see Figure 13). Google Person Finder, part of Google Crisis Response, helps individuals and organizations to provide information and updates on persons missing (or located) after a disaster.

Computing devices and the Internet provide many opportunities for you to start or get involved in ethical initiatives. Consider the Empty Bowls movement that was started by students at Wichita State University students. Local potters, students, and educators worked to create bowls and then guests were invited to consume a simple meal of bread and soup from them. For a donation to help local organizations feed the hungry, donors were encouraged to keep the bowls as a reminder of all the empty bowls in the world. This movement is now spreading across the United States through the website **emptybowls.net**. What can you and your fellow students do in your community?

Throughout your life, you'll encounter many ethical challenges relating to information technology. Your personal ethics—combined with the ethical guidelines your company provides and the general ethical environment of society—will guide your decisions.

For further information on ethics, check out the following websites:

- Ethics in Computing (**ethics.csc.ncsu.edu**)
- The Center for Ethics in Science and Technology (**ethicscenter.net**)
- Business Ethics: The Magazine of Corporate Responsibility (**business-ethics.com**)
- Council for Ethical Leadership at Capital University (**businessethics.org**)

**FIGURE 13** Tools provided by Google Crisis Response help disseminate information and locate lost individuals after a disaster such as the tornado in Moore, Oklahoma, in 2013. *(Courtesy of Google, Inc.)*

# check your understanding//

For a quick review of what you've learned, answer the following questions. Visit **pearsonhighered.com/techinaction** to check your answers.

## multiple choice

**1.** Which ethical theory focuses on adherence to moral duties and rights?

- **a.** deontology
- **b.** divine command theory
- **c.** utilitarianism
- **d.** virtue ethics

**2.** The ethical theory that states that deities are all-knowing and set moral truth is

- **a.** utilitarianism.
- **b.** virtue ethics.
- **c.** deontology.
- **d.** divine command theory.

**3.** Which ethical philosophy states that morals are internal?

- **a.** deontology
- **b.** virtue ethics
- **c.** relativism
- **d.** divine command theory

**4.** Which of the following statements is *false*?

- **a.** Individuals who have no sense of right or wrong exhibit amoral behavior.
- **b.** Ethical decisions are usually influenced by personal ethics.
- **c.** Unethical behavior is always illegal.
- **d.** Life experience affects an individual's personal ethics.

**5.** Unethical behavior

- **a.** is the same as illegal behavior.
- **b.** is based on civil disobedience.
- **c.** is different from illegal behavior.
- **d.** is governed by specific laws passed by legislative bodies.

**6.** The field of psychology that theorizes that happiness results from ethical living is known as

- **a.** principled psychology.
- **b.** positive psychology.
- **c.** moral psychology.
- **d.** affirmative psychology.

**7.** Which system of ethics is most widely agreed on to be the best system?

- **a.** utilitarianism
- **b.** relativism
- **c.** virtue ethics
- **d.** There is no universally agreed-on best system.

**8.** What should you do if you spot unethical behavior at your workplace?

- **a.** Nothing, as long as the behavior is legal.
- **b.** Report it to the police immediately.
- **c.** Follow company procedures for reporting unethical behavior.
- **d.** Start looking for a new job.

**9.** Which of the following actions would NOT help to identify your personal ethics?

- **a.** Describe yourself.
- **b.** Identify the influences of your work environment.
- **c.** Conduct a genealogic study of your extended family.
- **d.** Prepare a list of values that are most important to you.

**10.** Ethical decisions in business affect which of the following?

- **a.** the employees
- **b.** the business's clients and customers
- **c.** the suppliers and financial lenders
- **d.** all stakeholders

# 6 Understanding and Assessing Hardware: Evaluating Your System

## Evaluating Key Subsystems

### Your Ideal Computing Device

**OBJECTIVE**

1. What kind of computing device is best for me? **(pp. 224–225)**

### Evaluating the CPU Subsystem

**OBJECTIVE**

2. What does the CPU do, and how can I evaluate its performance? **(pp. 226–229)**

**Sound Byte:** Using Windows to Evaluate CPU Performance

### Evaluating the Memory Subsystem

**OBJECTIVES**

3. How does memory work in my computer? **(pp. 230–231)**
4. How do I evaluate how much memory I need? **(p. 232)**

**Sound Byte:** Memory Hierarchy Interactive

**Active Helpdesk:** Evaluating Your CPU and RAM

**Sound Byte:** Installing RAM

### Evaluating the Storage Subsystem

**OBJECTIVES**

5. What are the computer's storage devices? **(pp. 233–236)**
6. How do I evaluate my storage devices? **(pp. 236–238)**

**Sound Byte:** Optical Media Reading and Writing Interactive

**Sound Byte:** Installing a Blu-ray Drive

## Evaluating Other Subsystems and Making a Decision

### Evaluating the Video and Audio Subsystems

**OBJECTIVES**

7. What components affect the quality of video on my computer? **(pp. 242–244)**
8. How do I know if I need better video performance? **(p. 244)**
9. What components affect my computer's sound quality? **(pp. 246–247)**

**Active Helpdesk:** Evaluating Computer System Components

### Evaluating System Reliability and Making a Final Decision

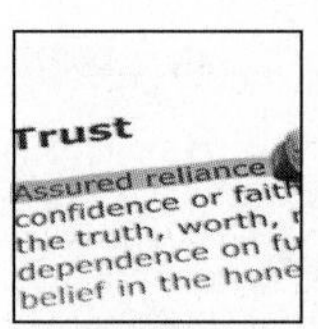


**OBJECTIVE**

10. How can I improve the reliability of my system? **(pp. 248–249)**

For all media in this chapter go to **pearsonhighered.com/techinaction** or MyITLab.

*(Radius Images/Alamy; nigel james/Alamy; joppo/Fotolia; Cobalt./Fotolia; Scanrail/Fotolia; SSilver/Fotolia; Ivelin Radkov/Alamy)*

# ow COOL IS THIS?

to create something really cool? The **Arduino microcontroller project** has
l an abundance of DIY (do-it-yourself) electronics projects and created an energized
nunity of do-it-yourselfers. This **small printed circuit board** is based on a
controller and includes everything you need: You **just plug it in and begin**
**DIY project**. The open-source hardware is licensed under the Creative Commons
e, so schematics are freely available to be changed or re-created as you wish.

**ilyPad variation of the Arduino**, designed by MIT engineer Leah Buechley, is
used to create wearable projects. Conductive thread runs from the Arduino output
o LEDs, and the **finished garments are washable**. One project is this turn-
l biking jacket. The Arduino LilyPad fires up an LED turn signal on your back to

# Evaluating Key Subsystems

It can be tough to know if your computer is the best match for your needs. New technologies emerge so quickly, and it's hard to determine whether they're expensive extras or tools you need. Do you need USB 3.0 instead of USB 2.0? Doesn't it always seem like your friend's computer is faster than yours anyway? Maybe you could get more out of newer technologies, but should you upgrade the system you have or buy a new machine? In this chapter, you'll learn how to measure your system's performance and gauge your needs so that you end up with a system you love.

## your ideal COMPUTING DEVICE

**When is the best time to buy a new computer?** There never seems to be a perfect time to buy. It seems that if you can just wait a year, computers will be faster and cost less. But is this actually true?

As it turns out, it is true. In fact, a rule of thumb often cited in the computer industry called **Moore's Law** describes the pace at which central processing units (CPUs) improve. Named for Gordon Moore, the cofounder of the CPU chip manufacturer Intel, this rule predicts that the number of transistors inside a CPU will increase so fast that CPU capacity will double about every two years. (The number of transistors on a CPU chip helps determine how fast it can process data.)

This rule of thumb has held true for over 45 years. Figure 6.1 shows a way to visualize this kind of exponential growth. If CPU capacity were put into terms of population growth, a group of 2,300 people at the start of CPU development would now be a country of over one billion! Moore himself has predicted that around the year 2020, CPU chips will be manufactured in a different way, thus changing or eliminating the effects of Moore's Law altogether.

In addition to the CPU becoming faster, other system components also continue to improve dramatically. For example, the capacity of memory chips such as dynamic random access memory (DRAM)—the most common form of memory found in personal computers—increases about 60% every year. Meanwhile, hard drives have been growing in storage capacity by some 50% each year.

**OK, things change fast. How do I know what's best for me?** Consider what kind of user you are and

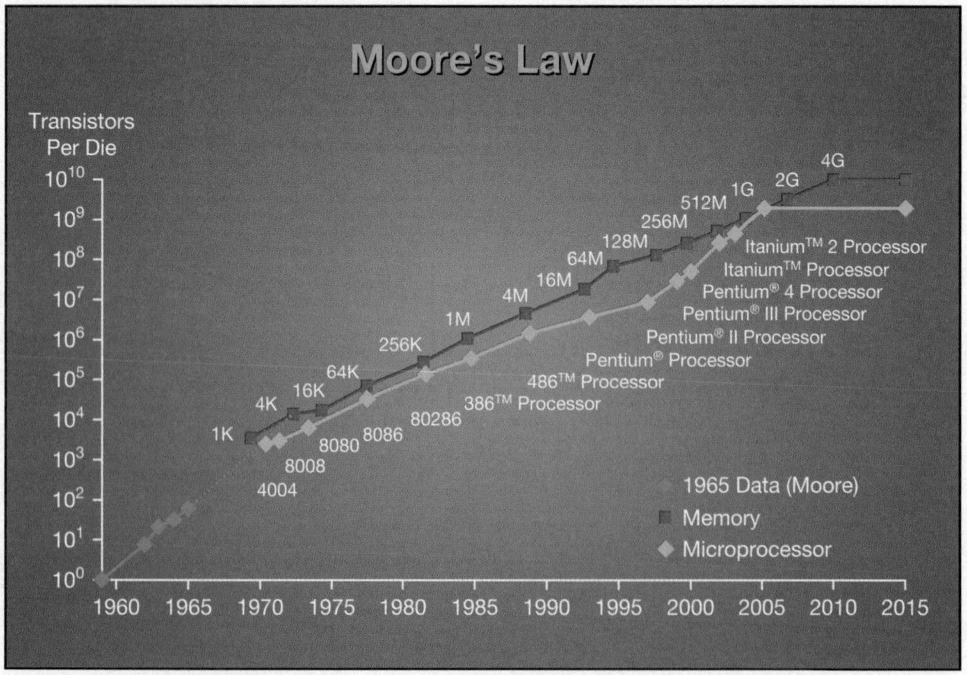


**FIGURE 6.1** Moore's Law illustrates the amazing pace of growth in CPU capabilities. *(Courtesy of the Intel Corporation)*

FIGURE 6.2

## What Kind of Technology User Are You?

**Casual User**

- Uses the computer primarily for Internet access
- Uses some software applications locally, like Microsoft Office
- Uses videos and software but does not create them

**Power User**

- Needs fast, powerful processing
- Needs fast storage and lots of it
- Creates videos and software programs

**Mobile User**

- Needs a lightweight device
- Needs a long battery life
- Is happy to sacrifice some capabilities for less weight

(Ilaszlo/Shutterstock; ColorBlind Images/Iconica/Getty Images; olly/Shutterstock)

what needs you have. For example, are you a power user who wants a machine for doing video editing and high-end gaming? Are you a more casual user, mainly using a device for word processing and Internet access? Are you on the move and need to bring your computer with you everywhere? Figure 6.2 shows a few different types of users—which type (or types) are you?

Now ask yourself, does your current computer match your needs? As we evaluate the pieces of your system, it'll become clear whether you need a few upgrades or perhaps a new machine better suited to you.

**How do I pick from all the types of devices available?** A huge number of choices are on the market (see Figure 6.3):

- Tablets (like the iPad or Galaxy)
- Ultrabooks (like the MacBook Air)
- Netbooks (which have a screen smaller than 10 inches and a small keyboard)
- Tablet PCs (which have a touch-enabled screen and a full keyboard)
- Laptops (or notebooks)
- Desktops

The main distinction among the available options is based on your need for mobility versus your need for processing power. If you're on the move all the time and have to have the lightest solution possible, an ultrabook may be best for you. At less than 3 pounds, they're great on weight but don't include an optical drive for DVDs/Blu-rays or much storage space. Even lighter are tablets like the iPad, but they also

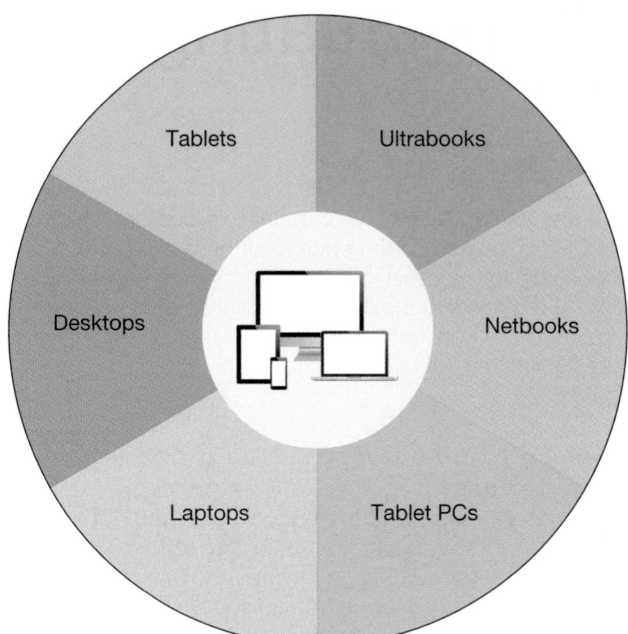


FIGURE 6.3 Range of Computing Devices *(© tpx/Fotolia)*

lack optical drives and may not be able to run all the software you need.

**Why would I consider buying a desktop?** Desktop systems are invariably a better value than lighter, more mobile computers. You'll find you get more computing power for your dollar, and you'll have more opportunity to upgrade parts of your system later. In addition, desktops often ship with a 24-inch or larger monitor, whereas lighter computers offer screens between 10 and 17 inches.

Desktop systems are also more reliable. Because of the vibration that a laptop experiences and the added exposure to dust, water, and temperature fluctuations that portability brings, laptops often have a shorter lifespan than desktop computers. You'll have less worry over theft or loss with a desktop, too. Manufacturers do offer extended warranty plans that cover laptop computers for accidental damage and theft; however, such plans can be costly.

**How long should I plan on keeping my computing device?** You should be able to count on two years, and maybe even four or five years. The answer depends in part on how easy it is to upgrade your system. Take note of the maximum amount of memory you can install in your device. Also, check whether you can upgrade your device's graphics capabilities down the road.

**How can I tell if my current system is good enough?** We'll begin by conducting a **system evaluation**. To do this, we'll look at your computer's subsystems, see what they do, and check how they perform during your typical workday. Then we'll compare that with what is available on the market, and the path forward for you will become clearer. Even if you're not in the market for a new computer, conducting a system evaluation will help you understand what you might want down the road. ■

# evaluating the CPU SUBSYSTEM

Let's start by considering your system's processor, or CPU. The CPU is located on the system motherboard and is responsible for processing instructions, performing calculations, and managing the flow of information through your computer. The dominant processors on the market are the Core family from Intel, featuring the i7, i5, and i3 (see Figure 6.4).

FIGURE 6.4 The Intel i5 and i7 CPU chips run many of the laptop and desktop offerings on the market today. *(David Caudery/PC Format Magazine/Future/Getty Images)*

**How can I find out what CPU my computer has?** If you have a PC, System Properties will show you the type of CPU you have installed. For example, the CPU in the computer in Figure 6.5 is an Intel i5 running at 2.6 GHz. AMD is another popular manufacturer of CPUs; you may have one of its processors, such as the FX-8150 or the Phenom X4. But more detailed information about your CPU, such as its number of cores and amount of cache memory, is not shown on this screen. Let's dive into that.

## How the CPU Works

**How does the CPU actually work?** The CPU is composed of two units: the *control unit* and the *arithmetic logic unit (ALU)*. The control unit coordinates the activities of all the other computer components. The ALU is responsible for performing all the arithmetic calculations (addition, subtraction, multiplication, and division). It also makes logic and comparison decisions, such as comparing items, to determine if one is greater than, less than, or equal to another.

FIGURE 6.5 The System Properties window identifies your computer's CPU as well as its speed. This computer has an Intel i5 running at 2.6 GHz.

>*To access your system settings, right-click the* ***Start*** *button. From the menu that displays, choose* ***System***.

Every time the CPU performs a program instruction, it goes through the same series of steps:

1. It *fetches* the required piece of data or instruction from random access memory (RAM), the temporary storage location for all the data and instructions the computer needs while it's running.
2. It *decodes* the instruction into something the computer can understand.
3. It *executes* the instruction.
4. It *stores* the result to RAM before fetching the next instruction.

This process is called a **machine cycle**. (We discuss the machine cycle in more detail in the Technology in Focus feature "Under the Hood" on page 303.)

## CPU Factors

**What makes one CPU different from another?** You pay more for a computer with an Intel i7 than one with an i5 because of its increased processing power. A CPU's processing power is determined by the following:

- Its *clock speed*
- Whether it has multiple *cores*
- Its amount of *cache memory*

**How does a CPU with a higher clock speed help me?** The **clock speed** of a CPU dictates how many instructions the CPU can process each second. It is measured in gigahertz (GHz), or billions of steps per second. The faster the clock speed, the more quickly the next instruction is processed. CPUs currently have clock speeds between 2.1 and 4 GHz. There is a huge difference between a computer with a 2.1 GHz CPU and one with a 4 GHz CPU.

Some users push their hardware to perform faster, **overclocking** their processor. Overclocking means that you run the CPU at a faster speed than the manufacturer recommends. It produces more heat, meaning a shorter lifetime for the CPU, and usually voids any warranty, but in gaming systems, you'll see this done quite often.

**How does a multi-core CPU help me?** A **core** on a CPU contains the parts of the CPU required for processing. As shown in Figure 6.6a, with multiple-core technology, two or more complete processors live on the same chip, enabling the independent execution of two sets of instructions at the same time. If you had a clone of yourself sitting next to you working, you could get twice as much done: That is the idea of multi-core processing. With multi-core processing, applications that are always running behind the scenes, such as virus protection software and your operating system (OS), can have their own dedicated processor, freeing the other processors to run other applications more efficiently. This results in faster processing and smoother multitasking.

CPUs began to execute more than one instruction at a time when **hyperthreading** was introduced in 2002. Hyperthreading provides quicker processing of information by enabling a new set of instructions to start executing *before the previous set has finished*. As shown in Figure 6.6b, hyperthreading allows two different programs to be processed at one time, but they're sharing the computing resources of the chip.

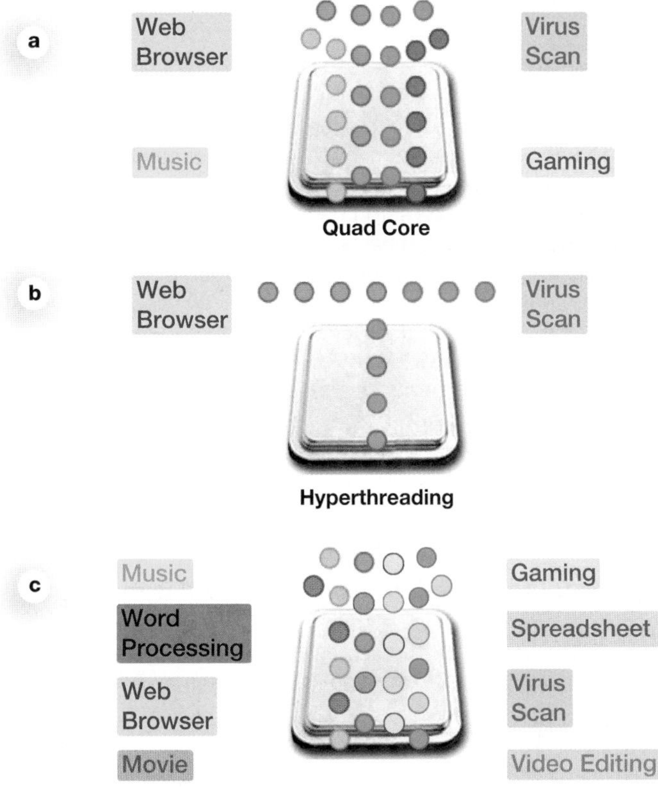


**FIGURE 6.6** (a) Intel Quad Core processors have four cores that are able to run four programs simultaneously. (b) Hyperthreading allows work on two processes to happen in one core at the same time. (c) So, a four-core hyperthreaded processor can be working on eight programs at one time.

All of the Intel Core processors have multiple cores *and* hyperthreading (see Figure 6.6c). The Intel i7-990X has six cores, each one using hyperthreading, so it simulates having 12 processors!

**How does more cache memory help me?** The CPU's **cache memory** is a form of RAM that gets data to the CPU for processing much faster than bringing the data in from the computer's RAM. There are three levels of cache memory, defined by their proximity to the CPU:

- *Level 1 cache* is a block of memory built on the CPU chip itself for storage of data or commands that have just been used. That gets the data to the CPU blindingly fast!
- *Level 2 cache* is located on the CPU chip but is slightly farther away and so takes somewhat longer to access than Level 1 cache. It contains more storage area than Level 1 cache.
- *Level 3 cache* is slower for the CPU to reach but is larger in size than Level 2 cache.

The more expensive the CPU, the more cache memory it will have.

**So how do I shop for a CPU?** You'll often see models of the same computer with just a different CPU varying in cost by $200 or more. Is the price difference worth it? It's hard to know because so many factors influence CPU performance. Picking the best CPU for the kind of work you do is easier if you research some performance benchmarks. **CPU benchmarks** are measurements used to compare performance between processors. Benchmarks are generated by running software programs specifically designed to push the limits of CPU performance. Articles are often published comparing CPUs, or complete systems, based on their benchmark performance. Investigate a few, using sites like **cpubenchmark.net**, before you select the chip that's best for you.

## Measuring the CPU

**How can I tell whether my current CPU is meeting my needs?** One way to determine whether your CPU is right for you is to watch how busy it is as you work. You can do this by checking out your **CPU usage**—the percentage of time your CPU is working.

Your computer's OS has utilities that measure CPU usage. These are incredibly useful, both for considering whether you should upgrade and for investigating if your computer's performance suddenly seems to drop off for no apparent reason.

On Windows systems, Task Manager lets you access this data (see Figure 6.7). The **CPU usage graph** records your CPU usage for the past minute. (Note that if you have multiple cores and hyperthreading, you'll see only one physical processor listed, but it will show that you have several virtual processors.) Of course, there will be periodic peaks of high CPU usage, but if your CPU usage levels are greater than 90% during most of your work session, a faster CPU will contribute a great deal to your system's performance.

To walk through using the Task Manager, check out the Try This on pages 240–241 and watch the "Using Windows to Evaluate CPU Performance" Sound Byte. Mac OS X has a similar utility named Activity Monitor, which is located in the Utilities folder in the Applications subfolder.

**How often do I have to be watching the CPU load?** Keep in mind that the workload your CPU experiences depends on how many programs are running at one time. Even though the CPU may meet the specs for each program separately, how you use your machine during a

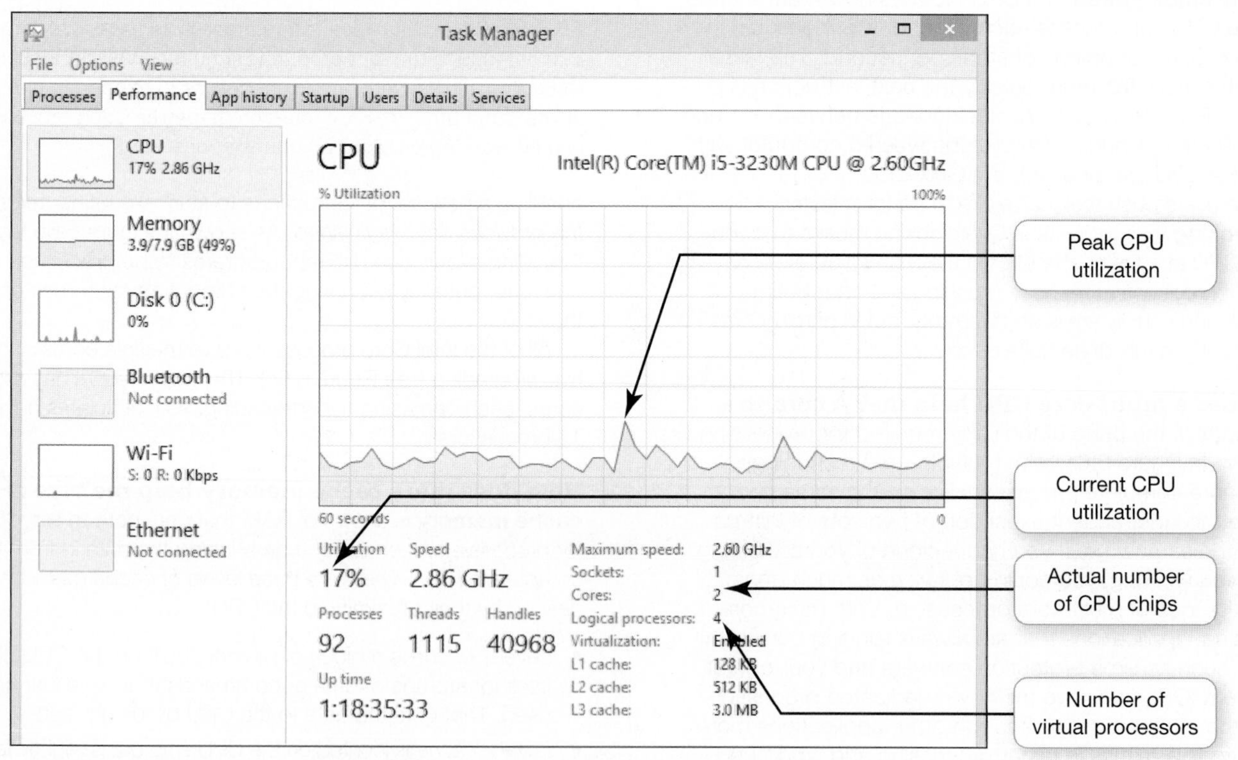


**FIGURE 6.7** The Performance tab of the Windows Task Manager utility shows you how busy your CPU is.

*>To access the Performance tab, right-click the **Start** button. From the menu, select **Task Manager**, and then click the **Performance** tab.*

# BITS&BYTES

## The Haswell Boost

The amount of power a CPU requires is very important to designers looking to extend the battery life of an ultrabook or tablet. Intel's newest generation of the Core CPU line, its fourth-generation processors, nicknamed "Haswell," gives systems up to a 50% boost in battery life. Since Haswell-based computers also see about a 40% increase in graphics performance, look for the fourth-generation Intel CPU for a system that is fast and can make it through the day on a single charge.

typical day may tax the CPU. If you're having slow response times or decide to measure CPU performance as a check, open the Task Manager and leave it open for a full day. Check in at points when you have a lot of open windows and when you have a lot of networking or disk-usage demand.

**So a better CPU means a better performing system?** Your CPU affects only the *processing* portion of the system performance, not how quickly data can move to or from the CPU. Your system's *overall* performance depends on many factors, including the amount of RAM installed as well as hard drive speed. Your selection of CPU may not offer significant improvements to your system's performance if there is a bottleneck in processing because of insufficient RAM or hard drive performance, so you need to make sure the system is designed in a balanced way. Figure 6.8 lists factors to consider as you decide which specific CPU is right for you. ■

SOUND BYTE

**Using Windows to Evaluate CPU Performance**

In this Sound Byte, you'll learn how to use the utilities provided by Windows to evaluate your CPU's performance. You'll also learn about shareware utilities (software that you can install and try before you purchase it) that expand on the capabilities the Task Manager utility provides.

FIGURE 6.8

### Evaluating the CPU

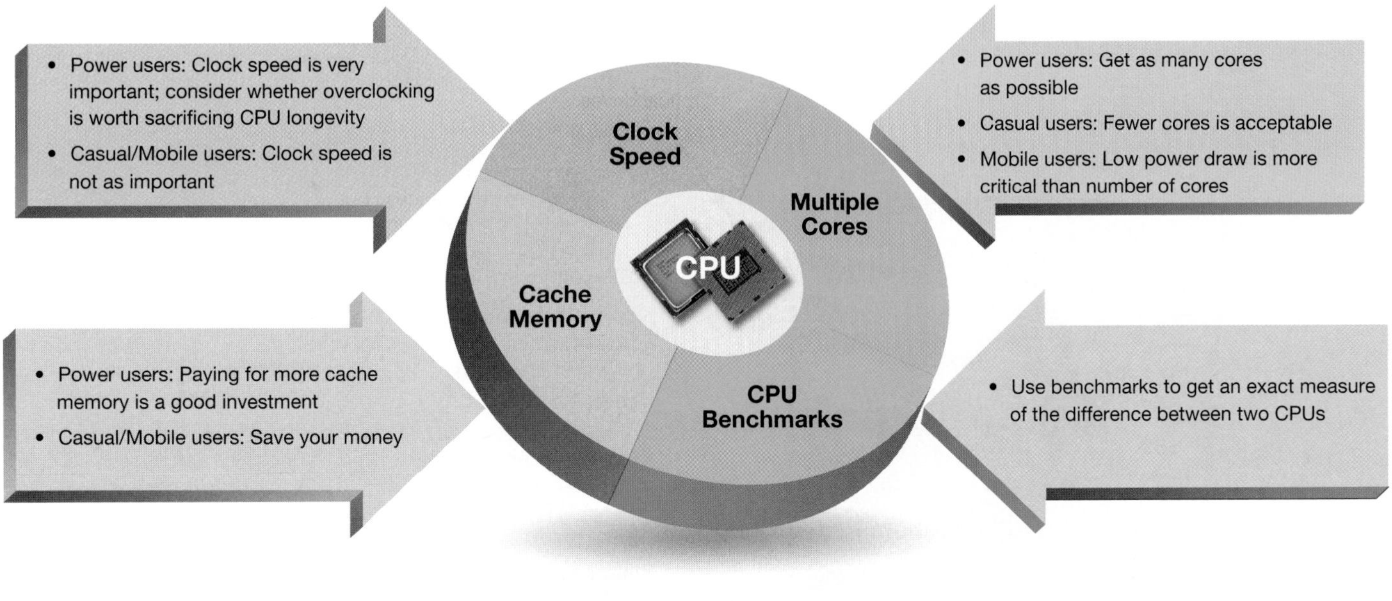

CPU

Clock Speed
- Power users: Clock speed is very important; consider whether overclocking is worth sacrificing CPU longevity
- Casual/Mobile users: Clock speed is not as important

Multiple Cores
- Power users: Get as many cores as possible
- Casual users: Fewer cores is acceptable
- Mobile users: Low power draw is more critical than number of cores

Cache Memory
- Power users: Paying for more cache memory is a good investment
- Casual/Mobile users: Save your money

CPU Benchmarks
- Use benchmarks to get an exact measure of the difference between two CPUs

# evaluating the MEMORY SUBSYSTEM

**Random access memory (RAM)** is your computer's temporary storage space. Although we refer to RAM as a form of storage, it really is the computer's short-term memory. It remembers everything that the computer needs in order to process data into information, such as data that has been entered and software instructions, but only when the computer is on. RAM is an example of **volatile storage**. When the power is off, the data stored in RAM is cleared out. This is why, in addition to RAM, systems always include **nonvolatile storage** devices for permanent storage of instructions and data. Read-only memory (ROM), for example, holds the critical start-up instructions. Hard drives provide the largest nonvolatile storage capacity in the computer system.

**Why not use a hard drive to store the data and instructions?** It's about one million times faster for the CPU to retrieve a piece of data from RAM than from a mechanical hard drive. The time it takes the CPU to grab data from RAM is measured in nanoseconds (billionths of seconds), whereas pulling data from a fast mechanical hard drive takes an average of 10 milliseconds (ms), or thousandths of seconds.

Figure 6.9 shows the various types of memory and storage distributed throughout your system: memory that is actually part of the CPU (such as CPU registers and cache), RAM, virtual memory, optical drives, and SSD and mechanical hard drives. Each of these has its own tradeoff of speed versus price. Because the fastest memory is so much more expensive, systems are designed with much less of it. This principle is influential in the design of a balanced computer system and can have a tremendous impact on system performance.

## The RAM in Your System

**Are there different types of RAM?** Yes, but in most current systems, the type of RAM used is double data rate 3 (DDR3) memory modules, available in several different speeds (1066 MHz, 1333 MHz, 1600 MHz). The higher the speed, the better the performance. DDR5 (double data rate 5) memory, which has an even faster data transfer rate, is seen in high-performance video graphics cards.

RAM appears in the system on **memory modules** (or **memory cards**), small circuit boards that hold a series of RAM chips and fit into special slots on the motherboard. Most memory modules in today's systems are packaged as a *dual inline memory module (DIMM)*, a small circuit board that holds several memory chips (see Figure 6.10).

**How can I tell how much RAM is installed in my computer?** The amount of RAM actually sitting on memory

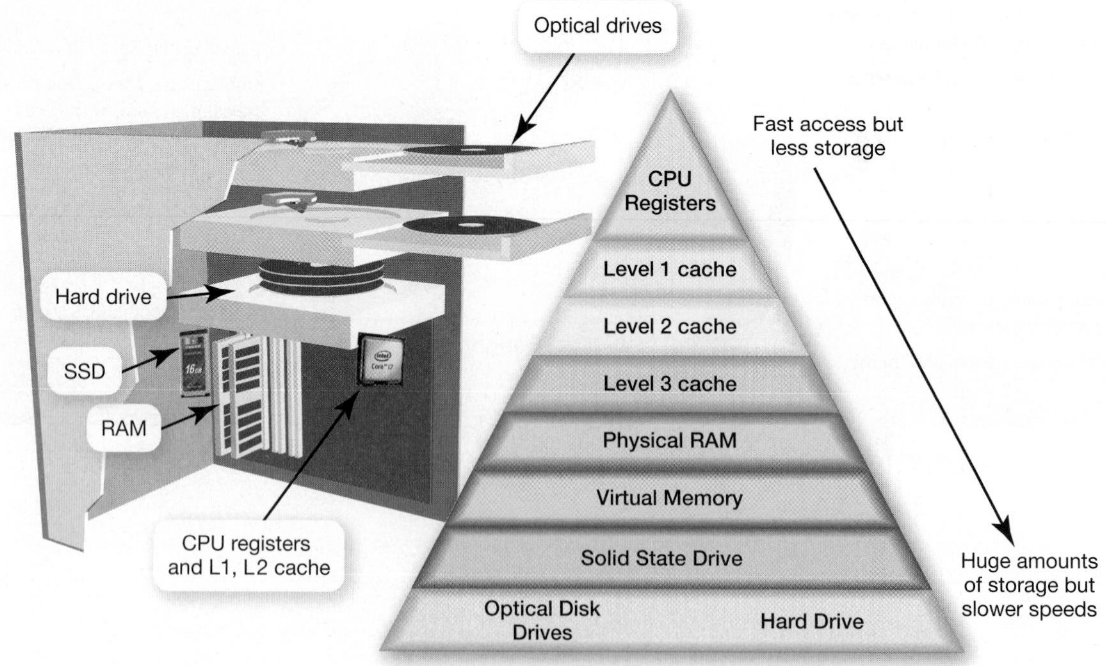


**FIGURE 6.9** A computer system's memory has many different levels, ranging from the small amounts in the CPU to the much slower but more plentiful storage of a mechanical hard drive.

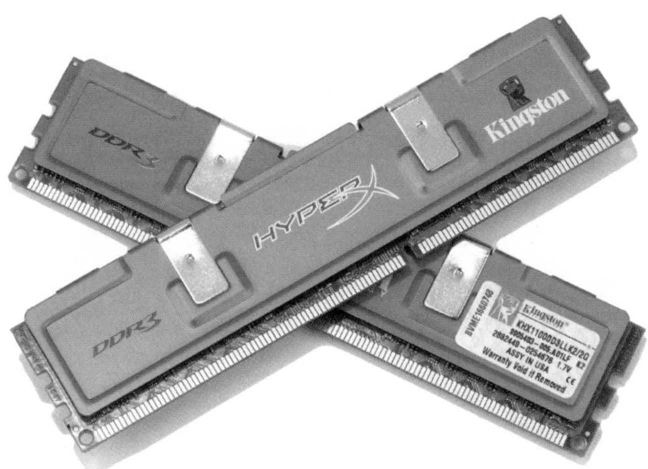


FIGURE 6.10 A DIMM memory module holds a series of RAM chips. *(Hugh Threlfall/Alamy)*

modules in your computer is your computer's **physical memory**. The easiest way to see how much RAM you have is to look in the System Properties window. (On a Mac, choose the Apple menu and then About This Mac.) This is the same tab you looked in to determine your system's CPU type and speed, and is shown in Figure 6.5. RAM capacity is measured in gigabytes (GB), and most machines sold today have at least 4 GB of RAM.

SOUND BYTE
**Memory Hierarchy Interactive**

In this Sound Byte, you'll learn about the different types of memory used in a computer system.

**How can I tell how my RAM is being used?** To see exactly how your RAM is being used, open the Resource Monitor and click on the Memory tab (see Figure 6.11). The Resource Monitor gives additional details on CPU, disk, network, and memory usage inside your system, and you can use it to see how you're using all the RAM you paid for!

Windows uses a memory-management technique known as **SuperFetch**. SuperFetch monitors the applications you use the most and preloads them into your system memory so that they'll be ready to be used when you want them. For example, if you have Microsoft Word running, Windows stores as much of the information related to Word in RAM as it can, which speeds up how fast your application responds. This is because pulling information from RAM is much faster than pulling it from the hard drive. You can watch this process at work using the Resource Monitor. Figure 6.11 shows how the 8 GB of installed RAM is being used:

- 1.5 GB is running programs.
- 2.15 GB is holding cached data and files ready for quick access.
- 4.4 GB is currently unused.

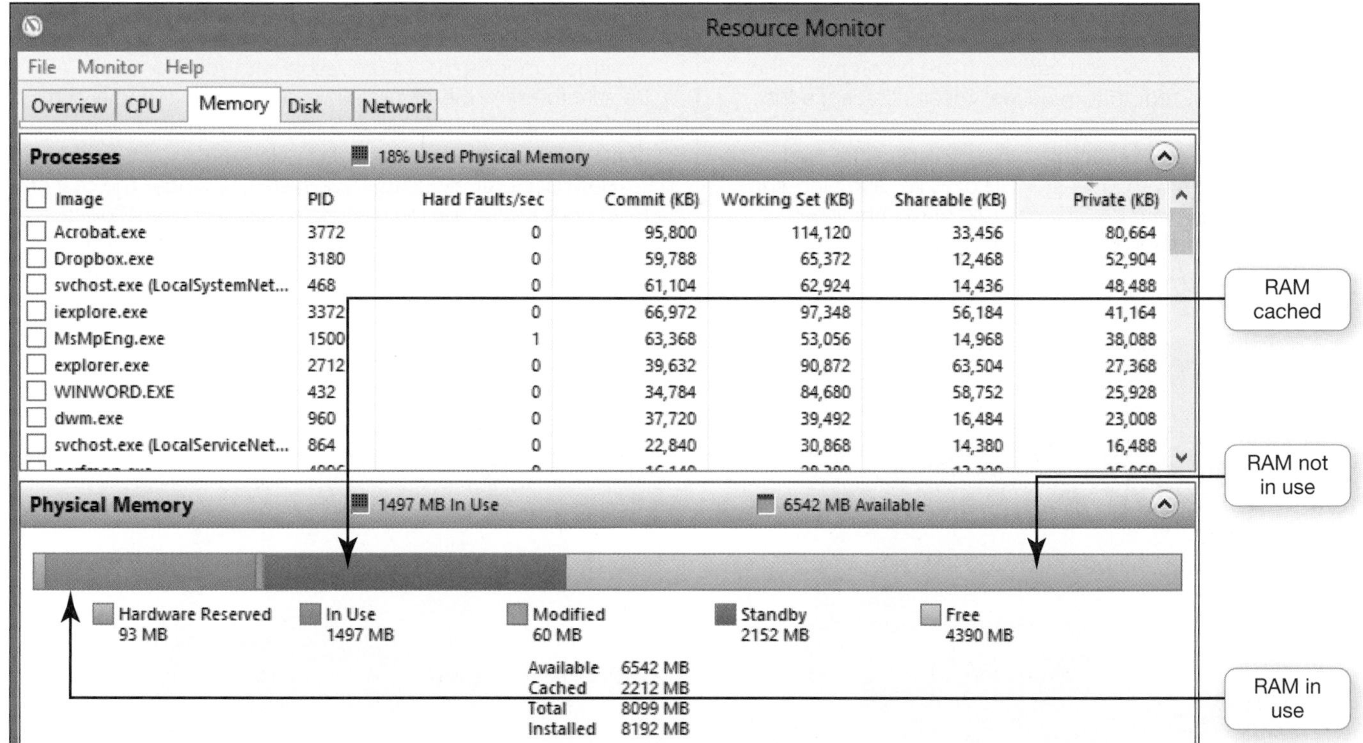


| Image | PID | Hard Faults/sec | Commit (KB) | Working Set (KB) | Shareable (KB) | Private (KB) |
|---|---|---|---|---|---|---|
| Acrobat.exe | 3772 | 0 | 95,800 | 114,120 | 33,456 | 80,664 |
| Dropbox.exe | 3180 | 0 | 59,788 | 65,372 | 12,468 | 52,904 |
| svchost.exe (LocalSystemNet... | 468 | 0 | 61,104 | 62,924 | 14,436 | 48,488 |
| iexplore.exe | 3372 | 0 | 66,972 | 97,348 | 56,184 | 41,164 |
| MsMpEng.exe | 1500 | 1 | 63,368 | 53,056 | 14,968 | 38,088 |
| explorer.exe | 2712 | 0 | 39,632 | 90,872 | 63,504 | 27,368 |
| WINWORD.EXE | 432 | 0 | 34,784 | 84,680 | 58,752 | 25,928 |
| dwm.exe | 960 | 0 | 37,720 | 39,492 | 16,484 | 23,008 |
| svchost.exe (LocalServiceNet... | 864 | 0 | 22,840 | 30,868 | 14,380 | 16,488 |



FIGURE 6.11 The Resource Monitor's Memory tab shows a detailed breakdown of how the computer is using memory.

*>To access the Resource Monitor, in the Task Manager, click the **Performance** tab, click **Open Resource Monitor**, and then click the **Memory** tab.*

ACTIVE HELPDESK

**Evaluating Your CPU and RAM**

In this Active Helpdesk call, you'll play the role of a helpdesk staffer, fielding calls about what the CPU does and how to evaluate its performance. You'll also field calls about how memory works and how to evaluate how much memory a computer needs.

SOUND BYTE

**Installing RAM**

In this Sound Byte, you'll learn how to select the appropriate type of memory to purchase, how to order memory online, and how to install it yourself. As you'll discover, the procedure is a simple one and can add great performance benefits to your system.

**How much RAM do I need?** At a minimum, your system needs enough RAM to run the OS. Running the 64-bit version of Windows 8.1 requires a minimum of 2 GB of RAM. However, because you run more applications at one time than just the OS, you'll want to have more RAM than just what's needed for the OS. For example, Figure 6.12 shows how much RAM is recommended for the OS, a web browser, and some software.

It's a good idea to have more than the minimum amount of RAM you need now so you can use more programs in the future. Remember, too, that "required" means these are the *minimum values* recommended by manufacturers; having more RAM often helps programs run more efficiently. New systems today ship with at least 4 GB of RAM, and high-end systems can come with 24 GB. The rule of thumb: When buying a new computer, buy as much RAM as you can afford.

FIGURE 6.12

**Sample RAM Allocation**

| APPLICATION | RAM RECOMMENDED |
|---|---|
| Windows 8.1 (64 bit) | 2 GB |
| Microsoft Office Professional 2013 | 2 GB |
| Internet Explorer 11 | 2 GB |
| iTunes 11 | 1 GB |
| Adobe Photoshop Elements 11 | 2 GB |
| **Total RAM recommended to run all programs simultaneously** | **9 GB** |

## Adding RAM

**Is there a limit to how much RAM I can add to my computer?** The motherboard is designed with a specific number of slots into which the memory cards fit, and each slot has a limit on the amount of RAM it can hold. To determine your specific system limits, check the system manufacturer's website.

In addition, the OS running on your machine imposes its own RAM limit. For example, the maximum amount of RAM for the 32-bit version of Windows 8.1 is 4 GB, whereas the maximum memory you can install using the 64-bit version of Windows 8.1 Pro is 192 GB.

**Is it difficult or expensive to add RAM?** Adding RAM is fairly easy (see Figure 6.13). Be sure that you purchase a memory module that's compatible with your computer. Also be sure to follow the installation instructions that come with the RAM module. Typically, you simply line up the notches and gently push the memory module in place.

RAM is a relatively inexpensive system upgrade. The cost of RAM does fluctuate in the marketplace as much as 400% over time, though, so if you're considering adding RAM, you should watch the prices of memory in online and print advertisements. ■

**FIGURE 6.13** Adding RAM to a computer is quite simple and relatively inexpensive. On a laptop, you often gain access through a panel on the bottom. *(Editorial Image, LLC/Alamy; Editorial Image, LLC/Alamy)*

# evaluating the STORAGE SUBSYSTEM

Remember, there are two ways data is stored on your computer: temporary storage and permanent storage. RAM is a form of temporary (or volatile) storage. The information residing in RAM is not stored permanently. It's critical to have the means to store data and software applications permanently.

Fortunately, several storage options exist. Storage devices include internal hard drives, SSDs, optical drives, and external hard drives. When you turn off your computer, the data that has been written to these devices will be available the next time the machine is powered on. These devices therefore provide *nonvolatile* storage.

## Mechanical Hard Drives

**What makes the hard drive such a popular storage device?** With storage capacities exceeding 4 terabytes (TB), a mechanical **hard drive** has the largest capacity of any storage device. And because it offers the most storage per dollar, the hard drive is also a more economical device than other options.

Today, most desktop system units are designed to support more than one internal hard drive. The Apple Mac Pro has room for four hard drives, and the Thermaltake Level 10 can support six hard drives. Each one simply slides into place when you want to add more storage.

**How is data stored on a hard drive?** A hard drive is composed of several coated, round, thin plates of metal stacked on a spindle. Each plate is called a **platter**. When data is saved to a hard drive platter, a pattern of magnetized spots is created on the iron oxide coating of each platter. When the spots are aligned in one direction, they represent a *1*; when they're aligned in the other direction, they represent a *0*. These *0*s and *1*s are *bits* (or *binary digits*) and are the smallest pieces of data that computers can understand. When data stored on the hard drive platter is retrieved (or read), your computer translates these patterns of magnetized spots into the data you have saved.

**How quickly does a hard drive find information?** The hard drive's **access time**, the time it takes a storage device to locate its stored data and make it available for processing, is faster than optical drives. Mechanical hard drive access times are measured in milliseconds (ms), meaning thousandths of seconds. For large-capacity drives, access times of approximately 12 to 13 milliseconds are typical. That's less than one-hundredth of a second. For comparison, a DVD drive can take over 150 milliseconds to access data.

## Solid-State Drives

**Do mechanical hard drives have the fastest access times?** A **solid-state drive (SSD)** uses electronic memory and has no mechanical motors or moving parts. Having no mechanical motors allows SSDs to offer incredibly fast access times, reaching data in only a tenth of a millisecond (0.1 ms). That's about 100 times faster than mechanical hard drives (see Figure 6.14)! SSDs also have a great advantage when booting up since a mechanical hard drive has to wait for motors to bring the plates up to the final rotation speed. The start-up time of SSDs is so fast, in fact, that most desktop and laptop systems offer an option to use at least one SSD. This "system drive" may only be 20 GB large, but it holds the operating system and means the wake-up time for the system will be very fast. In addition, SSDs run with no noise, generate very little heat, and require very little power, making them a popular option in ultrabooks.

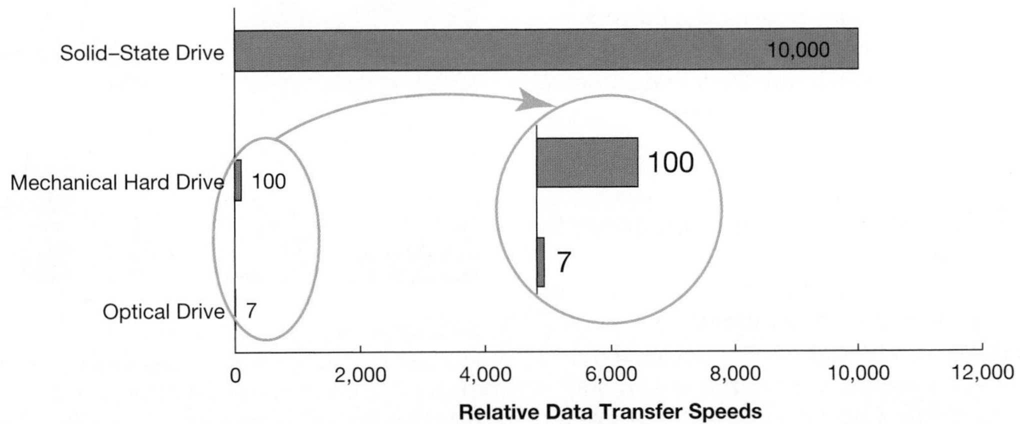


**FIGURE 6.14** Relative Data Transfer Speeds for Nonvolatile Storage Options

# DIG DEEPER How a Hard Drive Works

The thin metal platters that make up a hard drive are covered with a special magnetic coating that enables the data to be recorded onto one or both sides of the platter. Hard drive manufacturers prepare the disks to hold data through a process called *low-level formatting*. In this process, concentric circles, each called a **track**, and pie-shaped wedges, each called a **sector**, are created in the magnetized surface of each platter, setting up a gridlike pattern that identifies file locations on the hard drive. A separate process called *high-level formatting* establishes the catalog that the computer uses to keep track of where each file is located on the hard drive. More detail on this process is presented in the Dig Deeper feature "How Disk Defragmenter Utilities Work" in Chapter 5.

Hard drive platters spin at a high rate of speed, some as fast as 15,000 revolutions per minute (rpm). Sitting between the platters are special "arms" that contain read/write heads (see Figure 6.15). A **read/write head** moves from the outer edge of the spinning platter to the center, as frequently as 50 times per second, to retrieve (read) and record (write) the magnetic data to and from the hard drive platter. As noted earlier, the average total time it takes for the read/write head to locate the data on the platter and return it to the CPU for processing is called its *access time*. A new hard drive should have an average access time of approximately 12 ms.

Access time is mostly the sum of two factors—seek time and latency:

1. The time it takes for the read/write heads to move over the surface of the disk, moving to the correct track, is called the **seek time**. (Sometimes people incorrectly refer to this as access time.)
2. Once the read/write head locates the correct track, it may need to wait for the correct sector to spin to the read/write head. This waiting time is called **latency** (or **rotational delay**).

The faster the platters spin (or the faster the rpm), the less time you'll have to wait for your data to be accessed. Currently, most hard drives for home systems spin at 7,200 rpm.

The read/write heads don't touch the platters of the hard drive; rather, they float above them on a thin cushion of air at a height of 0.5 microinches. As a matter of comparison, a human hair is 2,000 microinches thick and a particle of dust is larger than a human hair. Therefore, it's critical to keep your hard drive free from all dust and dirt because even the smallest particle could find its way between the read/write head and the disk platter, causing a **head crash**—a stoppage of the hard drive that often results in data loss.

SSDs free you from worry about head crashes at all. The memory inside an SSD is constructed with electronic transistors, meaning there are no platters, no motors, and no read/write arms. Instead, a series of cells are constructed in the silicon wafers. If high voltage is applied, electrons move in and you have one state. Reverse the voltage and the electrons flow in another direction, marking the cell as storing a different value. The limiting factor for an SSD's lifespan is how many times data can be written to a cell. But the current generation of SSDs is proving to have very strong performance over time. Intel, one manufacturer of SSDs, says its drives will last five years when being written to heavily (20 GB per day).

Capacities for hard drives in personal computers can exceed 4,000 GB (4 TB). Increasing the amount of data stored in a hard drive is achieved either by adding more platters or by increasing the amount of data stored on each platter. How tightly the tracks are placed next to each other, how tightly spaced the sectors are, and how closely the bits of data are placed affect the measurement of the amount of data that can be stored in a specific area of a hard drive platter. Modern technology continues to increase the standards on all three levels, enabling massive quantities of data to be stored in small places.

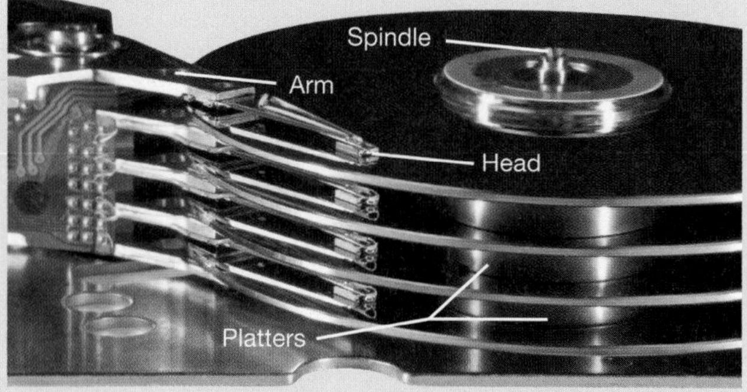


**FIGURE 6.15** The hard drive is a stack of platters enclosed in a sealed case. Special arms fit between each platter. The read/write heads at the end of each arm read data from and save data to the platters. *(skaljac/Shutterstock)*

SOUND BYTE
**Optical Media Reading and Writing Interactive**

In this Sound Byte, you'll learn about the process of storing and retrieving data from CD-RW, DVD, and Blu-ray discs.

Storage capacities for SSDs now range up to 2 TB, but such a large SSD is very expensive. Systems now often offer an SSD of 128 GB or 256 GB and then a mechanical hard drive, or two, to provide TBs of inexpensive slower storage space.

## Optical Drives

**How do optical drives work? Optical drives** are disc drives that use a laser to store and read data. Data is saved to a compact disc (CD), digital video disc (DVD), or Blu-ray disc (BD) (called **optical media**) within established tracks and sectors, just like on a hard drive. But optical discs store data as tiny pits that are burned into the disc by a high-speed laser. These pits are extremely small, less than 1 micron (a millionth of a meter).

Figure 6.16 shows how data is read from a disc by a laser beam, with the pits and nonpits (called *lands*) translating into the *1*s and *0*s of the binary code that computers understand. CDs and DVDs use a red laser to read and write data. Blu-ray discs get their name because they are read with a blue laser light, which has a shorter wavelength and can focus more tightly and pack more information on a disc. Blu-ray drives are the fastest optical devices on the market and deliver the high-definition quality video that larger displays and monitors demand.

**Why can I store data on some optical discs but not others?** All forms of optical media come in three formats:

1. *Prerecorded* discs are read-only (ROM), meaning you can't save any data onto them.
2. *Recordable* (R) formats allow you to write data to them, but only once.
3. *Rewriteable* (RW) discs let you write and rewrite data to them many times.

**Should I bother having an optical disc drive?** Traditionally, optical media delivered music and movies, but these are now available through streaming services. Likewise, in the past, software was often installed from a DVD, but now you buy almost all software online. Therefore, many lightweight systems have stopped including optical drives. For example, netbooks and ultrabooks are so thin and lightweight they often leave out an optical drive but may include a slot for an SD memory card to allow you to transfer files. You can buy

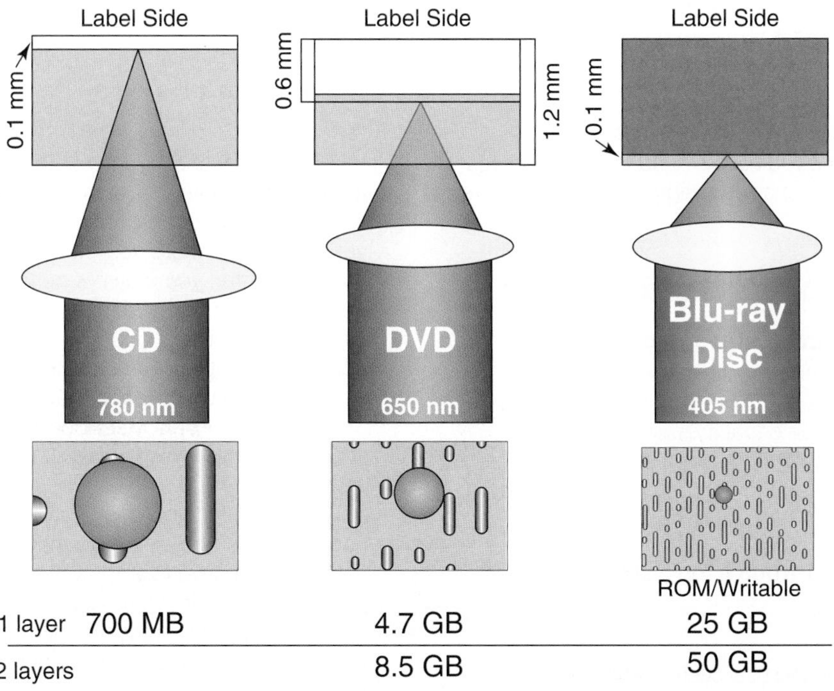


**FIGURE 6.16** Blu-ray lasers have a shorter wavelength and so can store a much higher density of information than CDs and DVDs.

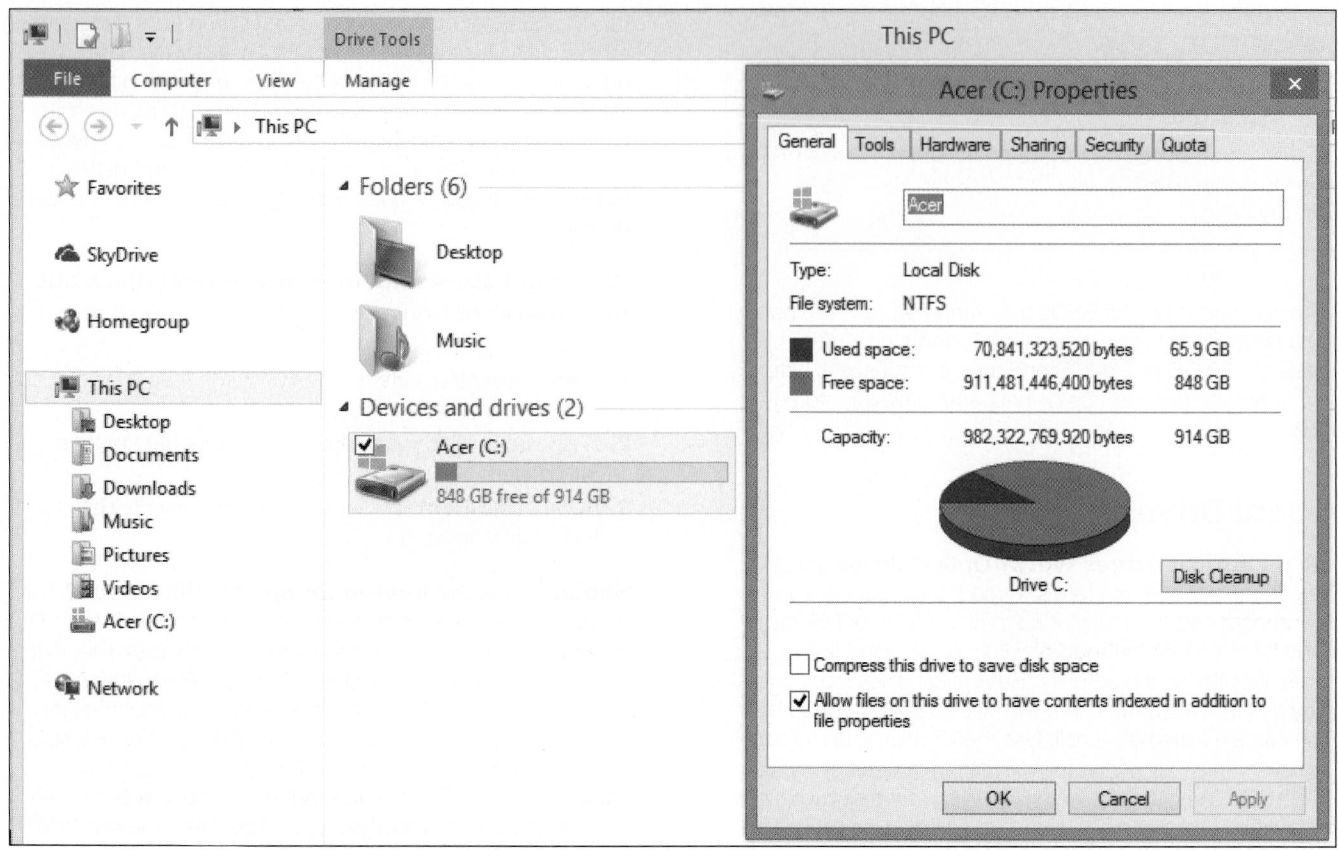


**FIGURE 6.17** In Windows, the free and used capacity of each device in the computer system is shown in the Computer window. The General tab of the Properties dialog box gives you more-detailed information.

>*To view the Computer window, launch File Explorer (previously called Windows Explorer), and then click* ***This PC****. To view the pie chart, right-click the* ***C drive****, and select* ***Properties****.*

external optical drives, but if you have a need for optical drives, you're probably better off purchasing a laptop computer; these have optical drives.

## Your Storage Capacity and Needs

**How do I know how much storage capacity I have?** Typically, hard drive capacity is measured in gigabytes (GB) or terabytes (1 TB = 1,000 GB). Windows displays the hard drives, their capacity, and usage information, as shown in Figure 6.17. To get a slightly more detailed view, select a drive and then right-click and choose Properties.

**How much storage do I need?** You need enough space to store the following:

- The OS
- The software applications you use, such as Microsoft Office, music players, and games
- Your data files
- Your digital music library, photos, videos of television shows and movies, and so on

Figure 6.18 shows an example of storage calculation. If you plan to have a system backup on the same drive, be sure to budget for that room as well. However, note that if you're going to store your data files online instead of on your computer, you may not need much hard drive space. For example, if you stream all the movies you watch from Netflix, keep all your data files in Microsoft OneDrive, and use online software like Google Docs to edit, you may need very little hard drive space. Most ultrabooks like the Dell XPS 13 or the Apple MacBook Air are configured with 128-GB drives. In fact, many Chromebooks have only a 16-GB drive.

Also note that you don't need an internal hard drive that has all the storage space you need. You can also add an external hard drive to your system, many of which use a USB port to connect. If you're looking to buy an external hard drive, the USB 3.0 standard is about 10 times faster than USB 2.0, so if your system supports USB 3.0, that's the better choice.

**Is it better to have one huge drive or several smaller drives?** It depends on what's important to you: speed or security. If you purchase two smaller drives, you can

FIGURE 6.18

## Sample Hard Drive Space Requirements

| APPLICATION/DATA | HARD DRIVE SPACE REQUIRED | HEAVY CLOUD STORAGE USER |
|---|---|---|
| Windows 8 (64 bit) | 20 GB | 20 GB |
| Microsoft Office 2013 Professional | 3.5 GB | 3.5 GB |
| Adobe Photoshop Elements 11 | 4 GB | 4 GB |
| Adobe Premiere Pro CC | 10 GB | 10 GB |
| Video library of movies | 80 GB (about 40 HD movies) | Streamed through online services |
| Music library | 50 GB (about 7,000 songs) | Stored in cloud (iCloud or Amazon Cloud Drive) |
| Photographs | 5 GB | Stored in iCloud or Dropbox |
| **Total storage in use** | **172.5 GB** | **37.5 GB** |
| Full backup | 172.5 GB | Done to cloud using Carbonite |
| **Total required** | **345 GB** | **37.5 GB** |

combine them using RAID technology. **RAID (redundant array of independent disks)** is a set of strategies for using more than one drive in a system (see Figure 6.19). RAID 0 and RAID 1 are the most popular options for consumer machines.

- When you run two hard drives in **RAID 0**, the time it takes to write a file is cut in half. If disk performance is very important—for example, when you're doing video editing or sound recording—using two files in RAID 0 could be important. RAID 0 is faster because every time data is written to a hard drive, it's spread across the two physical drives (see Figure 6.19a). The write begins on the first drive, and while the system is waiting for that write to be completed, the system jumps ahead and begins to write the next block of data to the second drive. This makes writing information to disk almost twice as fast as using

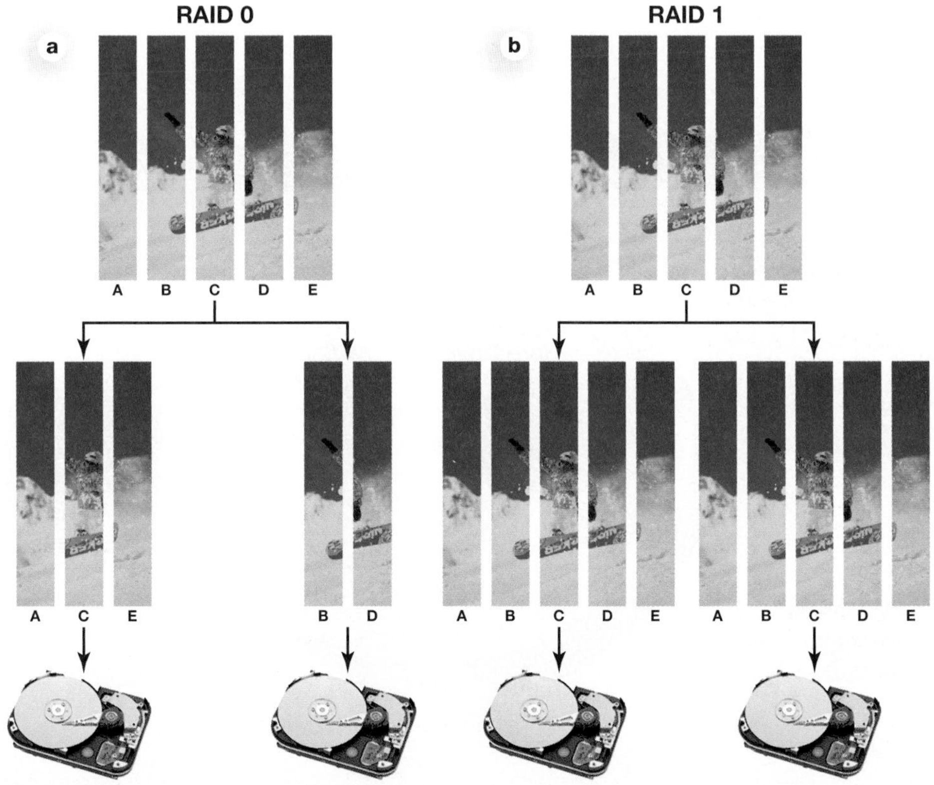


FIGURE 6.19 (a) A RAID 0 configuration speeds up file read/write time. (b) A RAID 1 configuration gives you an instant backup. *(World Pictures/Alamy; Ragnarock/Shutterstock)*

# BITS&BYTES

## How Much Storage to Buy?

No matter what kind of device you purchase, you'll have to decide how much storage you're willing to pay for. Does your Nexus 7 need 16 GB? 32 GB? Should the SSD drive in your ultrabook be 128 GB? 256 GB? 512 GB? When you make your decision, keep in mind two factors:

1. Whether you can add storage later using an SD card. If you can have a few SD cards to store music or photos, that will be a cheaper option.
2. How much usable storage is available in the device. For example, a 128-GB drive often provides much less available storage space after the operating system, the manufacturer software, and backup storage space are accounted for.

just one hard drive. The downside is that if either of these disks fail, you lose all your data because part of each file is on each drive. So RAID 0 is for those most concerned with performance.

SOUND BYTE

**Installing a Blu-ray Drive**

In this Sound Byte, you'll learn how to install a Blu-ray drive in your computer.

- If you're really paranoid about losing data, you should consider having two drives in RAID 1. In a **RAID 1** configuration, all the data written to one drive is instantly perfectly mirrored and written to a second drive (see Figure 6.19b). This provides you with a perfect, instant-by-instant backup of all your work. It also means that if you buy two 1-TB drives, you only have room to store 1 TB of data because the second 1-TB drive is being used as the "mirror."

RAID 0 and RAID 1 configurations are available on many desktop systems and are even beginning to appear on laptop computers.

**So how do my storage devices measure up?** Figure 6.20 summarizes the factors you should consider in evaluating your storage subsystem. ■

**Before moving on to Part 2:**
- **Watch Replay Video 6.1** .
- Then check your understanding of what you've learned so far.

FIGURE 6.20

## Evaluating Storage

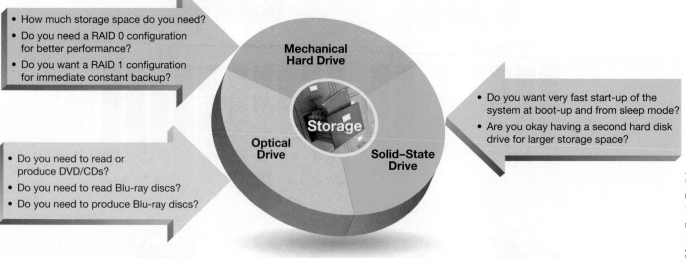

- How much storage space do you need?
- Do you need a RAID 0 configuration for better performance?
- Do you want a RAID 1 configuration for immediate constant backup?

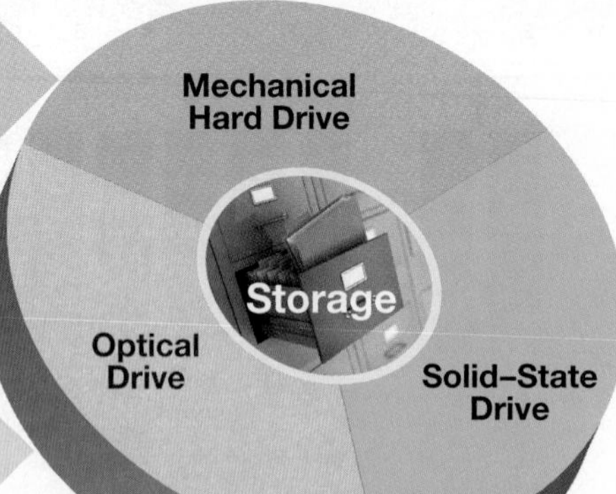


- Do you want very fast start-up of the system at boot-up and from sleep mode?
- Are you okay having a second hard disk drive for larger storage space?

- Do you need to read or produce DVD/CDs?
- Do you need to read Blu-ray discs?
- Do you need to produce Blu-ray discs?

(Maxim_Kazmin/Fotolia)

# check your understanding//

For a quick review to see what you've learned so far, answer the following questions. Visit **pearsonhighered.com/techinaction** to check your answers.

## multiple choice

**1.** Which statement about ultrabook computers is FALSE?

- **a.** Ultrabooks have the fastest optical drives.
- **b.** Ultrabooks are equipped with SSD drives for fast start-up.
- **c.** Ultrabooks typically weigh less than 3 pounds.
- **d.** Ultrabooks do not offer HDMI video output ports.

**2.** SSDs are classified as what type of storage?

- **a.** volatile
- **b.** nonvolatile
- **c.** video
- **d.** cache

**3.** When would you want to consider RAID 1 technology?

- **a.** When you need the fastest solution for writing data
- **b.** When you need an instant backup of your work
- **c.** If you think that SSDs are too expensive
- **d.** When you only want to have one hard disk drive

**4.** CPU benchmarks are used to

- **a.** compare system performance.
- **b.** compare processor performance.
- **c.** compare memory performance.
- **d.** compare storage system performance.

**5.** SuperFetch is a memory-management technique that

- **a.** determines the type of RAM your system requires.
- **b.** makes the boot-up time for the system very quick.
- **c.** preloads the applications you use most into system memory.
- **d.** defragments the hard drive to increase performance.

## true–false

_____ **1.** A quad core CPU with hyperthreading has eight virtual CPUs.

_____ **2.** SSD hard drives are primarily used for backup of data.

## critical thinking

**1. Types of Storage**

You can select between optical drives, portable drives, and SSD drives. There are a wide range of options. How will you decide the proper balance for your own computing needs?

**2. Emerging Technologies**

Touch screens are now available in a range of sizes, from smartphones to iPads to larger products like the Microsoft PixelSense. Windows 8 has a redesigned interface for support of touch screens. What other new technologies will become part of our collective experience? How will these technologies and devices change entertainment and how people interact with information? What future technologies would be on your wish list?

# Measure Your System Performance

Using the Windows Task Manager and the Resource Monitor can provide you with a lot of useful information about your computer system. Let's make sure you can use these Windows tools to keep an eye on your system performance.

**Step 1** Hold the Windows key and hit X. From the pop-up, select **Task Manager**. Click the **Performance** tab.

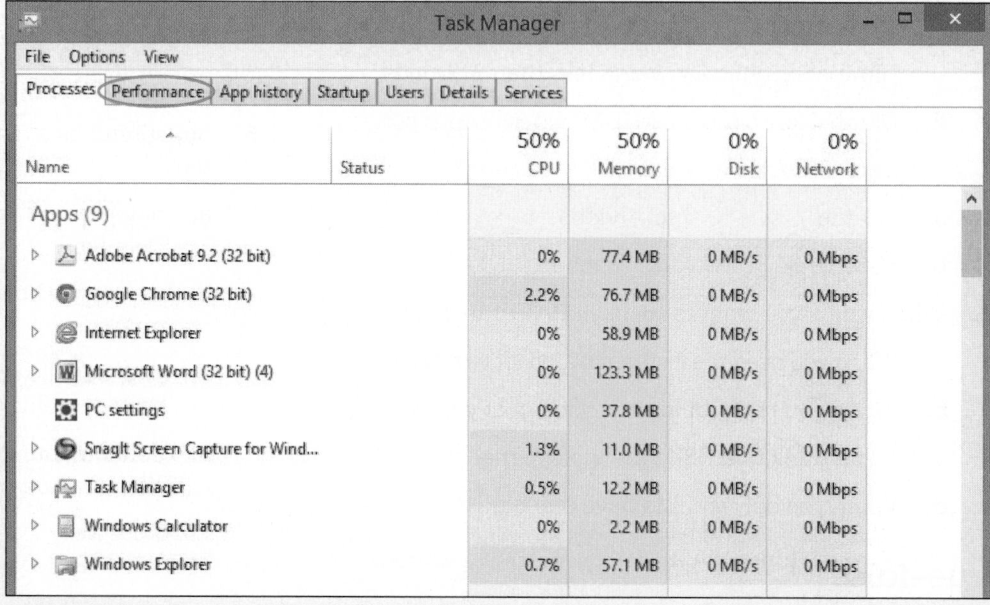


**Step 2** If you leave this window open while you work, you can pop in and check the history of how your CPU, disk, memory, and network are performing. Let's start by looking at **CPU** utilization.

This computer is only occasionally going over 50%, so the system isn't limited by CPU speed.

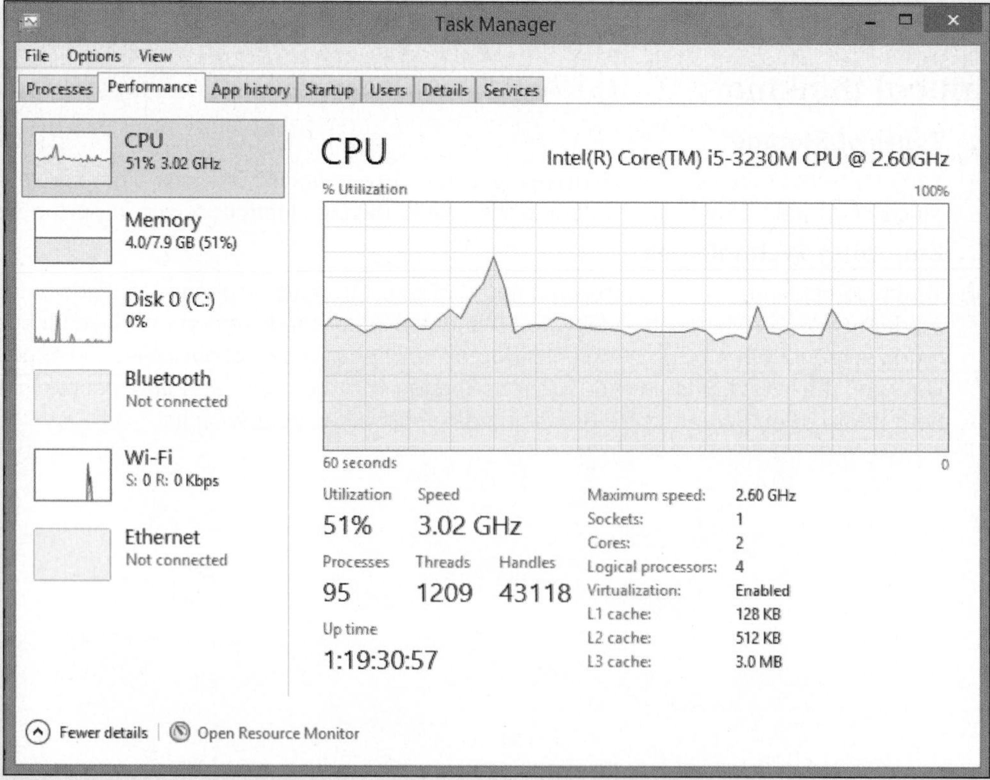

**Step 3** What about memory usage? Clicking on **Memory** in the left panel shows that we have 8 GB of memory installed in this computer. This computer is running Windows 8 and has the following applications open: Word, Excel, IE 11, Chrome Browser, Adobe Acrobat, and several Windows systems utilities.

Notice that memory usage is consistent at about 4 GB. Windows 8.1 is good at allocating memory to programs on an as-needed basis and keeping programs from taking up large amounts of memory when they are idle. We have plenty of available memory so this system isn't limited by memory capacity.

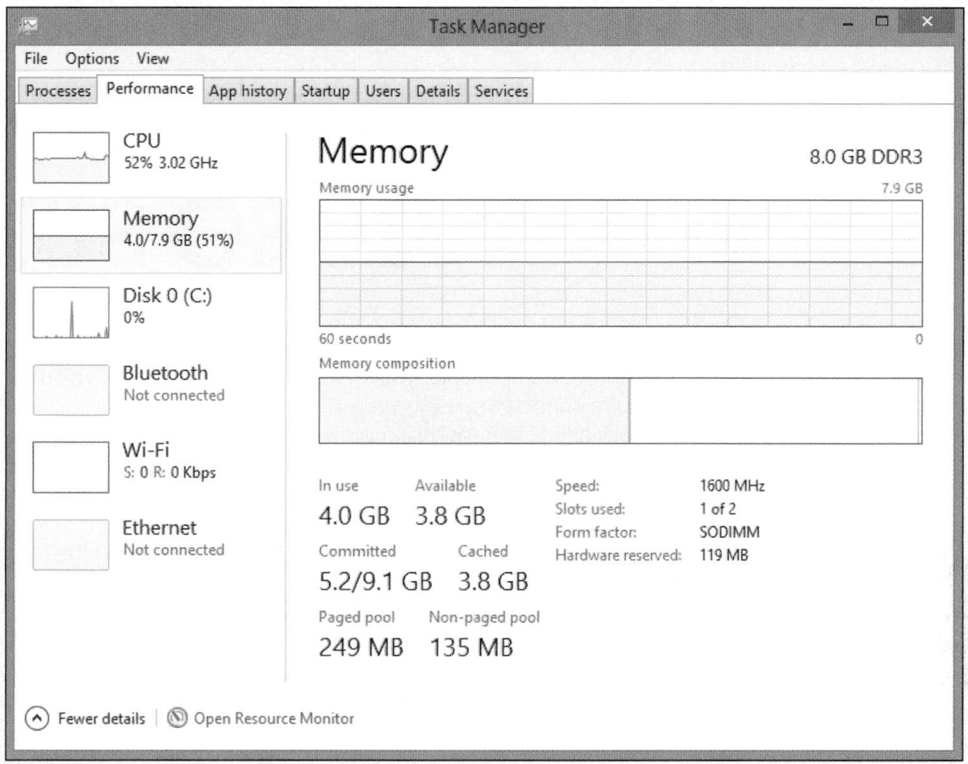


**Step 4** What about disk usage? Clicking on **Disk** in the left panel shows that we have one disk drive, a 1 TB internal hard drive. The lower graph shows the history of data moving back and forth to the disk, the disk transfer rate. The larger upper graph shows how active the disk is—what percentage of time it is reading and writing. If that is consistently high, upgrading to a faster, larger disk will have a big performance impact.

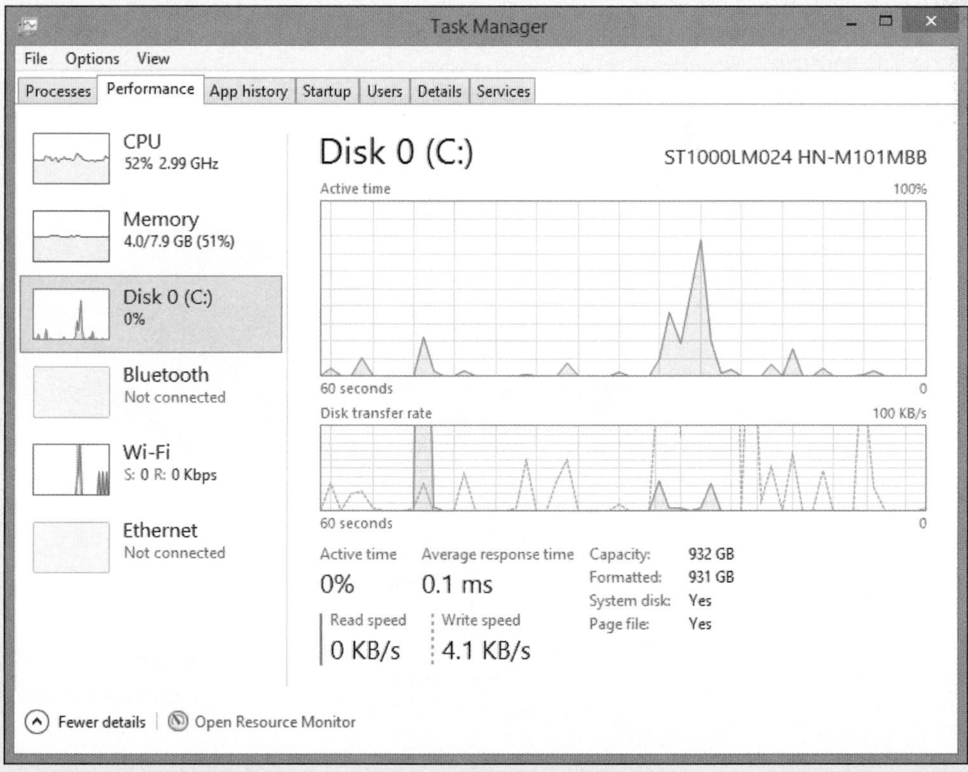

# Evaluating Other Subsystems and Making a Decision

The audio and video subsystems of your computer affect much of your enjoyment of the machine. Let's evaluate those subsystems and consider what state-of-the-art audio/video would add to your computing experience. Then let's consider how to make sure your system is reliable—nothing interferes with enjoying technology like a misbehaving computer!

## evaluating the VIDEO SUBSYSTEM

How video is displayed depends on two components: your video card and your monitor. If you're considering using your computer to display complex graphics, edit high-definition videos, or play graphics-rich games with a lot of fast action, you may want to consider upgrading your video subsystem.

### Video Cards

**What exactly is a video card?** A **video card** (or **video adapter**) is an expansion card that's installed inside the system unit to translate binary data into the images you view on your monitor. Modern video cards like the ones shown in Figures 6.21 and 6.22 let you connect video equipment using a number of different ports:

- *DVI ports* for digital LCD monitors
- *HDMI ports* for high-definition TVs, Blu-ray players, or gaming consoles
- *DisplayPort adapters,* a newer style port that can connect to digital monitors or projectors

**How much memory does my video card need?** All video systems include their own RAM, called **video memory**. Several standards of video memory are available, including graphics double data rate 3 (GDDR3) memory and the newer **graphics double data rate 5 (GDDR5)** memory.

The amount of video memory on your video card makes a big impact on the resolution the system can support and on how smoothly and quickly it can render video. Most new laptop computers come with video cards equipped with a minimum of 1 GB of video memory. For the serious gamer, 2 GB or more is essential, and cards with 3 GB are available. These high-end video cards allow games to generate smoother animations and more-sophisticated shading and texture.

**How can I tell how much memory my video card has?** You'll find information about your system's video card in the Advanced Settings of the Screen Resolution dialog box.

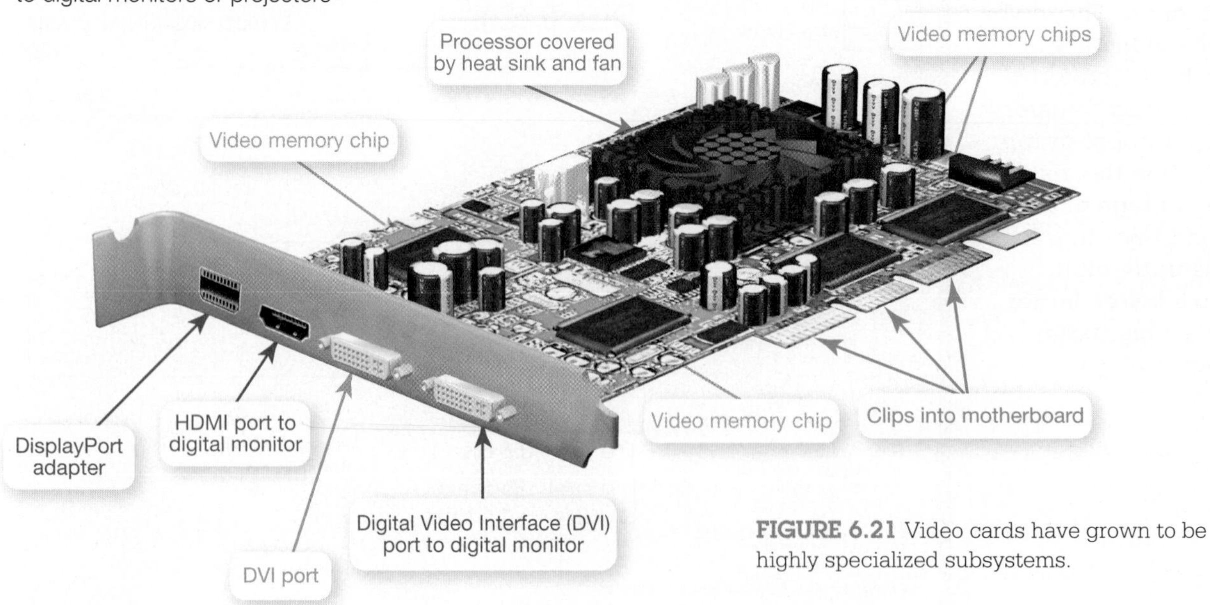


**FIGURE 6.21** Video cards have grown to be highly specialized subsystems.

**FIGURE 6.22** Video card processors produce so much heat that video cards have their own fan—or two. *(nikkytok/Fotolia)*

To get to the Screen Resolution dialog box, right-click on your desktop and select Screen Resolution. In the Screen Resolution dialog box, click the Advanced settings link. A window will appear that shows you the type of video card installed in your system, as well as its memory information.

**How does the CPU handle intensive video calculations?** Because displaying graphics demands a lot of computational work from the CPU, video cards come with their own **graphics processing unit (GPU)**. The GPU is a separate processing chip specialized to handle 3-D graphics and image and video processing with incredible efficiency and speed. When the CPU is asked to process graphics, it redirects those tasks to the GPU, significantly speeding up graphics processing. Figure 6.23 shows how the CPU can run much more efficiently when a GPU does all the graphics computations.

In addition, special lighting effects can be achieved with a modern GPU. Designers can change the type of light, the texture, and the color of objects based on complex interactions. Some GPU designs incorporate dedicated hardware to allow high-definition movies to be decoded or special physics engines to model water, gravity, and rigid body movements.

**Why do some people use more than one video card in the same system?** For users who are primarily doing text-based work, one video card is certainly enough. Computer gamers and users of high-end visualization software, however, often take advantage of the ability to install more than one video card at a time. Two or even three video cards can be used in one system.

The two major video chip set manufacturers, Nvidia and ATI, have each developed their own standards supporting the combining of multiple video cards. For Nvidia, this standard is named SLI; for ATI, it is called CrossFire. When the system is running at very high video resolutions, such as 1920 x 1200 or higher, multiple video cards working together provide the ultimate in performance. If you're buying a new system and might be interested in employing multiple video cards, be sure to check whether the motherboard supports SLI or CrossFire.

**Can I run a few monitors from one video card?** Working with multiple monitors is useful if you often have more than one application running at a time (see Figure 6.24) or even if you just want to expand your gaming experience. Some video cards can support up to six monitors from a

ACTIVE HELPDESK

**Evaluating Computer System Components**

In this Active Helpdesk call, you'll play the role of a helpdesk staffer, fielding calls about the computer's storage, video, and audio devices and how to evaluate whether they match your needs as well as how to improve the reliability of your system.

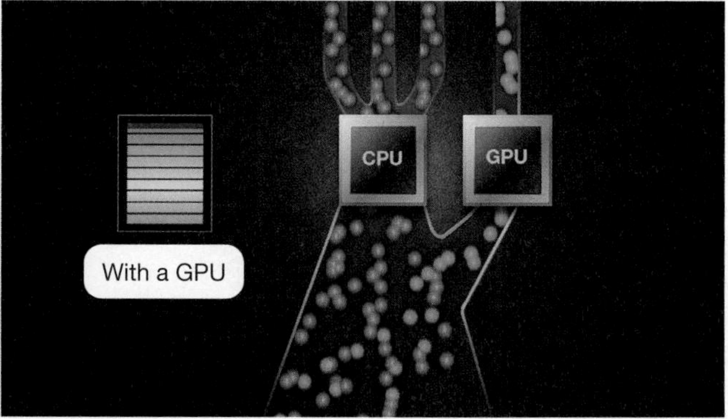


**Without a GPU** **With a GPU**

**FIGURE 6.23** The GPU is specialized to handle processing of photos, videos, and video game images. It frees up the CPU to work on other system demands.

**FIGURE 6.24** AMD Radeon technology supports six monitors, which can be combined in any way. *(© satopon / Fotolia)*

single card. The AMD Radeon graphics card, for example, lets you merge all six monitors to work as one screen or to combine them into any subset—for example, displaying a movie on two combined screens, Excel on one monitor, Word on another, and a browser spread across the final two.

**Can I have a 3-D experience from a computer monitor?** 3-D panels are available for desktop monitors and for some laptops. Using the 3-D wireless vision glasses included with the panels, the glasses make existing games or 3-D movies display in stereoscopic 3-D.

**How do I know if I'm putting too much demand on my video card?** If your monitor takes a while to refresh when you're editing photos or playing a graphics-rich game, then the video card could be short on memory or the GPU is being taxed beyond its capacity. You can evaluate this precisely using the software that came with your card. For example, AMD Overdrive software monitors the GPU usage level, the current temperature, and the fan speed.

Review the considerations listed in Figure 6.25 to see if it might be time to upgrade your video card. On a desktop computer, replacing a video card is fairly simple: Just insert the new video card in the correct expansion slot on the motherboard. The video card in a laptop is more difficult to upgrade since the display and keyboard usually have to be removed to replace the video card. Note that some very basic laptop systems have video adapters integrated into the motherboard, so these video cards can't be upgraded. ■

# BITS&BYTES

## Where's the Free TV?

Most major networks are streaming content for free so that you can catch episodes of most TV series on the go. Subscription channels like HBO and Showtime all have free streaming of content. If you have HBO at home, you can watch any show from the HBO GO website. If you're interested in more international viewing, head to Squid TV and select broadcasts from around the world. If you're looking for homemade shows, sites like Justin.tv and Ustream are filled with live and archived video webcasts. And if you want to make TV instead of just watching, you can webcast your own show from the Ustream webapp using your webcam or smartphone video camera.

**FIGURE 6.25**

**Evaluating the Video Card**

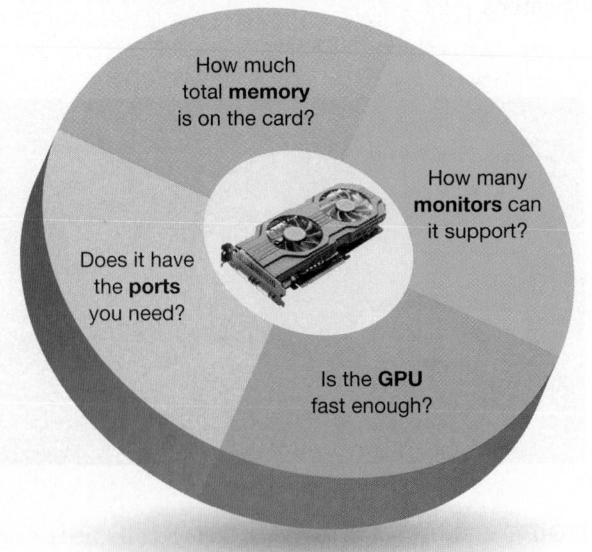
How much total **memory** is on the card?
How many **monitors** can it support?
Does it have the **ports** you need?
Is the **GPU** fast enough?

# trends in IT

## Thunderbolt: The New Standard for Data Transfer

Faster is always better, and the newest input/output standard, Thunderbolt, is faster than anything seen before. And speed isn't its only advantage.

Intel used fiber optics—the transmission of digital data through pure glass cable as thin as human hair—to develop the new input/output technology named Thunderbolt. Thunderbolt supports blazingly fast transfer rates of 10 Gb/s, zooming past even the theoretical limit of the new USB 3.0, which is 4.8 Gb/s. How fast is that? Intel says that Thunderbolt could transfer a full-length HD movie in under 30 seconds or in just 10 minutes copy a library of music that would take a solid year to play through. And Thunderbolt can supply much more power to devices than the USB standard allows. It also has a very slim connector design, allowing laptop designers to make their systems even thinner (see Figure 6.26).

Thunderbolt port

USB port

**FIGURE 6.26** Thunderbolt ports are very thin, allowing for new design options. *(Kendall Martin)*

But one of the greatest hopes that comes with Thunderbolt is that the technology will be able to replace a number of different ports, cleaning up the cluttered design we see now on the sides of laptops and the backs of desktop units. Apple has introduced Thunderbolt ports on its full line of systems. A Thunderbolt port looks like a single thin port that supports both the video standard DisplayPort and the bus standard PCI Express (see Figure 6.27). So Thunderbolt can connect monitors to computers using VGA, DisplayPort, DVI, or HDMI and can connect systems to external hard drives that use USB, FireWire, or eSATA. One Thunderbolt port can support several devices because the cables can be daisy-chained (connected one after another in a serial fashion), so having just one Thunderbolt port on a laptop allows you to connect up to six different peripherals to your system.

Thunderbolt technology also gives you a two-for-one deal, because each connector can support two separate channels to send and receive data, each one still operating at the full 10 Gb/s bandwidth.

What will this mean to laptop designers? Some speculate we'll see the heavy, heat-producing video cards currently integrated into gaming laptops become external graphics boxes. An incredibly thin, light laptop design would let you be wonderfully mobile all day, and then when you come home, you'd attach one cable. It would run from your Thunderbolt port to your 60-inch HDTV and then continue on to a separate graphics processor box. That same laptop would then be running a huge high-definition monitor with a high-resolution graphics and physics engine.

Apple is not the only company that uses the Intel technology. Hard-drive companies like LaCie and Western Digital, as well as audio/video processing companies like Avid and Apogee, now offer Thunderbolt products. And the USB community may need to put up a bit of a fight to keep their standard around. But the allure of incredible speed, great versatility, and small, thin packaging is going to make the Thunderbolt technology a trend to watch.

Could Thunderbolt make USB a thing of the past?

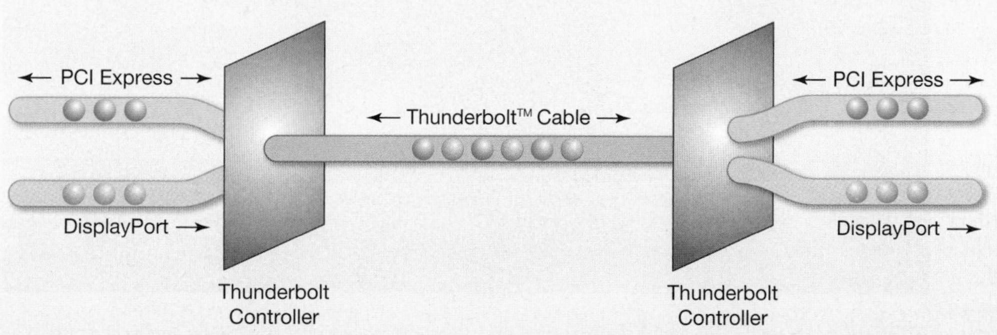


**FIGURE 6.27** Thunderbolt can carry two channels of information on the same connector.

# evaluating the AUDIO SUBSYSTEM

For many users, a computer's preinstalled speakers and sound card are adequate. However, if you often use your computer to play games, music, and video, you may want to upgrade your speakers or your sound card.

**What does the sound card do?** Like a video card, a **sound card** is an expansion card that attaches to the motherboard inside your system unit. A sound card enables the computer to drive the speaker system. Most desktop systems have a separate sound card, although low-end computers often have integrated the job of managing sound onto the motherboard itself. You can upgrade laptop sound cards using an ExpressCard solution, like the Creative Sound Blaster X-Fi.

**What does a basic sound card do for me?** Many computers ship with a **3-D sound card**. 3-D sound technology is better at convincing the human ear that sound is omnidirectional, meaning that you can't tell from which direction the sound is coming. This tends to produce a fuller, richer sound than stereo sound. However, 3-D sound is not surround sound.

**What is surround sound, then?** **Surround sound** is a type of audio processing that makes the listener experience sound as if it were coming from all directions by using multiple speakers. The current surround-sound standard is from Dolby. There are many formats available, including Dolby Digital EX and Dolby Digital Plus for high-definition audio. Dolby TrueHD is the newest standard. It features high-definition and lossless technology, which means that no information is lost in the compression process.

To create surround sound, another standard, Dolby Digital 7.1, takes digital sound from a medium (such as a Blu-ray disc) and reproduces it in eight channels. Seven channels cover the listening field with placement to the left front, right front, left rear, right rear, and center of the audio stage, as well as two extra speakers to the side, as shown in Figure 6.28. The eighth channel holds extremely low-frequency (LFE) sound data and is sent to a subwoofer, which can be placed anywhere in the room.

The name 7.1 surround indicates that there are seven speakers reproducing the full audio spectrum and one speaker handling just lower frequency bass sounds. There is also a 5.1 surround-sound standard, which has a total of six speakers—one subwoofer, a center speaker, and four speakers for right/left in the front and the back. If you have a larger space or want precise location of sounds, use the newer 7.1 system.

To set up surround-sound on your computer, you need two things:

1. A set of surround-sound speakers and, for the greatest surround-sound experience,
2. A sound card that is Dolby Digital compatible

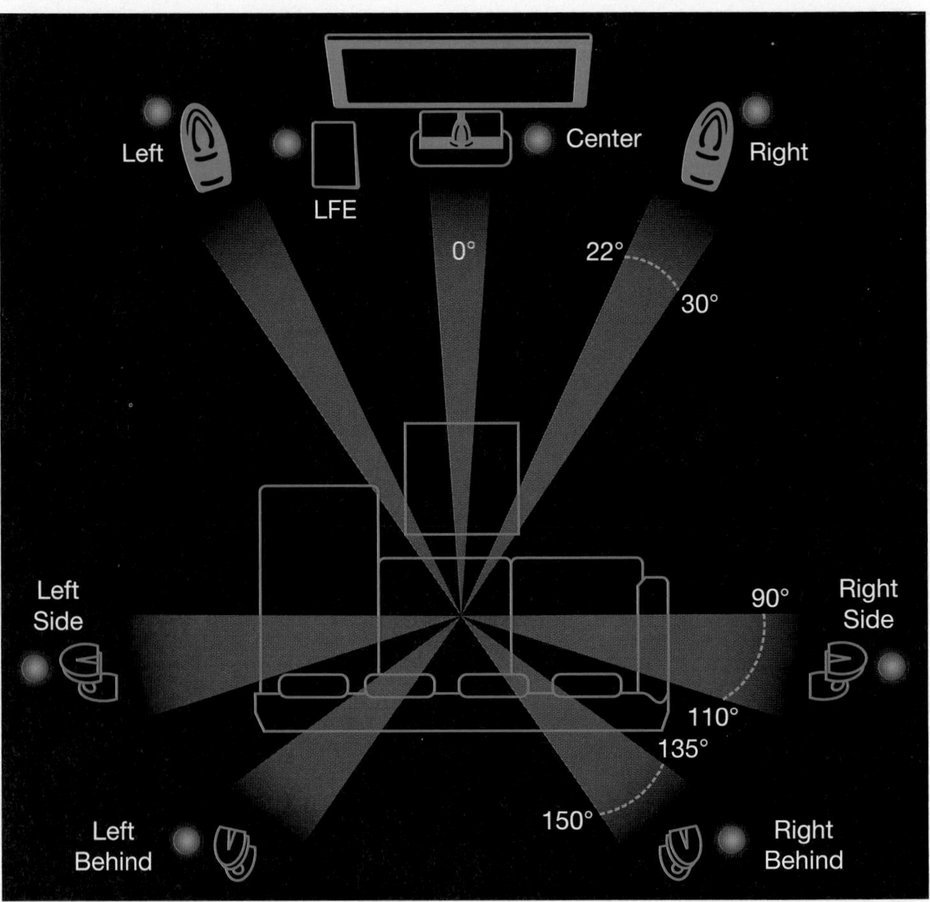


**FIGURE 6.28** Dolby Digital 7.1 surround sound gives you a better quality audio output.

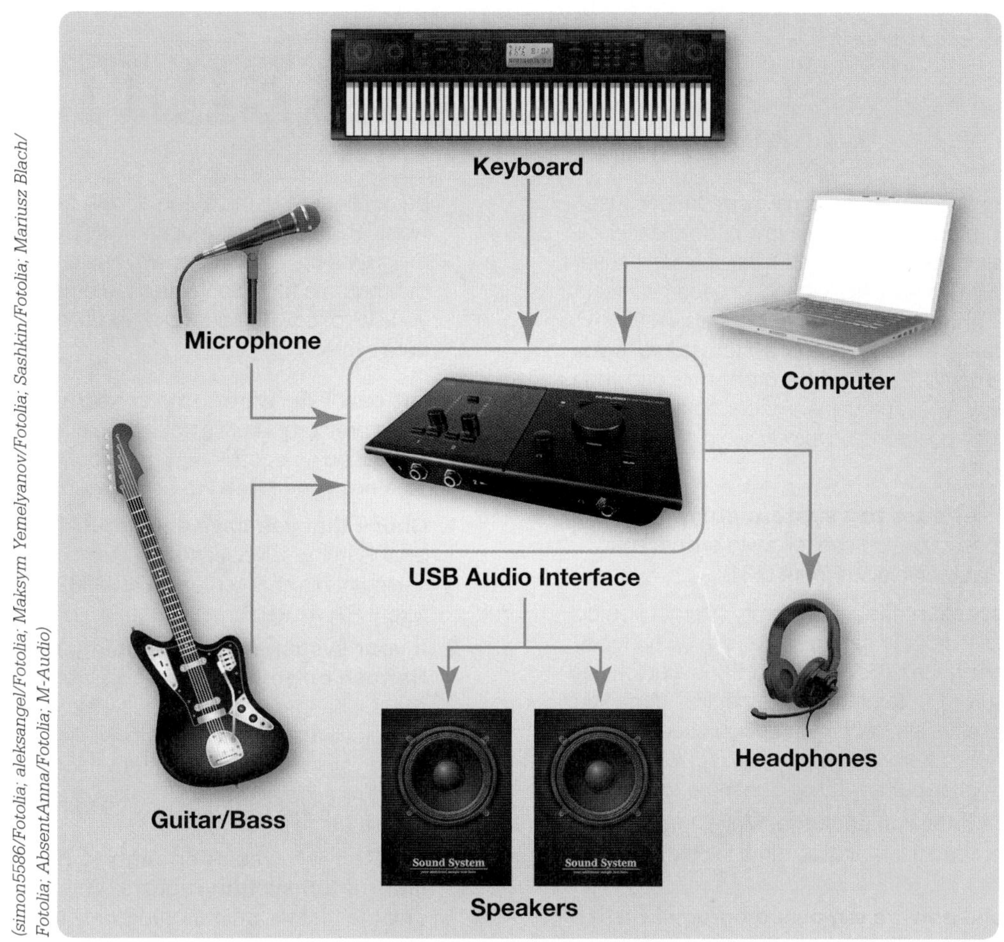


(simon5586/Fotolia; aleksangel/Fotolia; Maksym Yemelyanov/Fotolia; Sashkin/Fotolia; Mariusz Blach/Fotolia; AbsentAnna/Fotolia; M-Audio)

**FIGURE 6.29** Sample Home Recording Studio Setup

**Does it matter what kind of speakers my laptop has?** The limited size for speakers in a laptop and the added weight of circuitry to drive them means most people use headphones or ear buds for great audio instead of speakers. However, some laptops have built-in higher-quality speakers, like the Alienware line featuring Klipsch speakers and the HP series offering Beats speakers.

**What setup do I need if I want to use my computer for recording my band?** You can connect MIDI instruments, high-quality microphones, and recording equipment to your computer through an **audio MIDI interface** box. MIDI is an electronics standard that allows different kinds of electronic instruments to communicate with each other and with computers. The audio interface box attaches to your computer through a USB port and adds jacks for connecting guitars and microphones. You can edit and mix tracks through many different software packages, like Cakewalk or GarageBand. Figure 6.29 shows a simple home recording studio setup.

Figure 6.30 lists the factors to consider when deciding whether your audio subsystem meets your needs. ■

**FIGURE 6.30**

**Evaluating the Audio Subsystem**

Do you want to upgrade your **speaker** quality?

Do you want 7.1 or 5.1 **surround** sound?

**Audio**

Do you need an **audio MIDI interface** box?

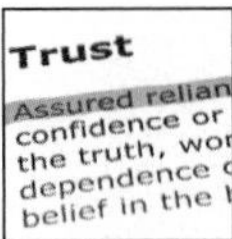


# evaluating system RELIABILITY

Many computer users decide to buy a new system because they're experiencing problems such as slow performance, freezes, and crashes. Over time, even normal use can cause your computer to build up excess files and to become internally disorganized. This excess, clutter, and disorganization can lead to deteriorating performance or system failure. If you think your system is unreliable, see if the problem is one you can fix before you buy a new machine. Proper upkeep and maintenance also may postpone an expensive system upgrade or replacement.

**What can I do to ensure my system stays reliable?** Here are several procedures you can follow to ensure your system performs reliably (see also Figure 6.31):

- **Clear out unnecessary files.** Temporary Internet files can accumulate quickly on your hard drive, taking up unnecessary space. Running the Disk Cleanup utility is a quick and easy way to ensure your temporary Internet files don't take up precious hard drive space. Likewise, you should delete any unnecessary files from your hard drive regularly because they can make your hard drive run more slowly.
- **Install a reliable antivirus package.** Make sure it's set to update itself automatically and to run a full system scan frequently.
- **Run spyware and adware removal programs.** These often detect and remove different pests and should be used in addition to your regular antivirus package.
- **Run the Disk Defragmenter utility on your hard drive.** When your hard drive becomes fragmented, its storage capacity is negatively affected. When you defragment (defrag) your hard drive, files are reorganized, making the hard drive work more efficiently. But remember that this only makes sense for mechanical drives. With no motors, there is no need to defrag an SSD drive.
- **Automate the key utilities.** The utilities that need to be run more than once, like Disk Cleanup, Disk Defragmenter, and the antivirus, adware, and spyware programs, can be configured to run automatically at any time interval you want. You can use Windows Task Scheduler or third-party programs like Norton Security Suite to set up a sequence of programs to run one after the other every evening while you sleep, so you can wake up each day to a reliable, secure system.

**What can I do when my system crashes?** Computer systems are complex. It's not unusual to have your system stop responding occasionally. If rebooting the computer doesn't help, you'll need to begin troubleshooting:

1. **Check that you have enough RAM.** You learned how to do this in the "Evaluating the Memory Subsystem" section earlier in this chapter (page 230–232). Systems with insufficient RAM often crash.
2. **If your system isn't responding, try doing a Windows Refresh on your system.** This Windows 8 utility removes all the changes you've made to the system and brings it back to the state it came to you from the factory. It removes all the applications from third-party vendors, but it won't remove personal files like your music, documents, or videos.
3. **If a Refresh wasn't enough to fix the problem, consider a full system restore.** Windows 8 automatically creates restore points before any major change to the system takes place, such as when you install a new program or change a device driver. You can also click on System and Security and manually create a restore point at any time. You can then select any restore point and bring your system back to the state it was in at that point. Open the Control Panel, click on System, and then select System Protection to learn more about System Restore.

   For Mac systems, the Mac OS X Time Machine, shown in Figure 6.32, provides automatic backup and enables you to look through and restore (if necessary) files, folders, libraries, or the entire system.

FIGURE 6.31

**Utilities to Keep Your System Reliable**

| TO AVOID THIS PROBLEM | USE THIS TOOL | FOR MORE INFO |
|---|---|---|
| Your hard drive is running low on space, making it run slowly | Disk Cleanup utility | Chapter 5 |
| Your system is slowing down; browsers or other programs are behaving strangely | Antivirus software<br>Spyware and adware removal software | Chapter 9 |
| Files are spread across many spots on the hard drive, making the hard drive run slowly | Disk Defragmenter utility | Chapter 5 |
| System not responding | Windows Refresh | Chapter 5 |

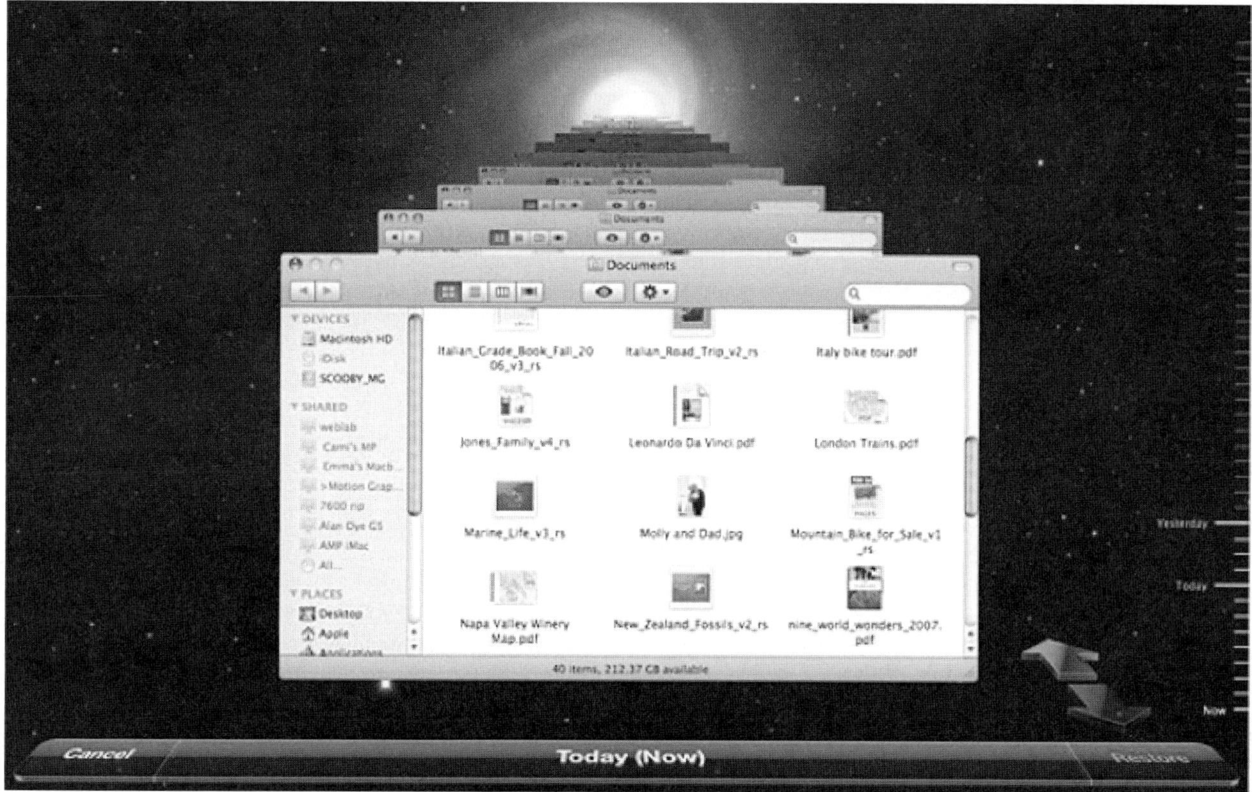


**FIGURE 6.32** Mac's Time Machine keeps copies of files, folders, and libraries and can restore your system back to any previous point in time. *(Courtesy of Apple, Inc.)*

4. **If you see an error code in Windows, visit the Microsoft Knowledge Base (support.microsoft.com).** This online resource helps users resolve problems with Microsoft products. For example, it can help you determine what an error code indicates and how you may be able to solve the problem.
5. **Search Google.** If you don't find a satisfactory answer in the Knowledge Base, try copying the entire error message into Google and searching the larger community for solutions.

**Can my software affect system reliability?** Having the latest version of software makes your system much more reliable. You should upgrade or update your OS, browser software, and application software as often as new patches (or updates) are reported for resolving errors. Sometimes these errors are performance related; sometimes they're potential system security breaches.

If you're having a software problem that can be replicated, use the Steps Recorder to capture the exact steps that lead to it. In Windows 8.1, display the Charms bar, select Search, then type "ste" in the search box. Now run the Steps Recorder and go through the exact actions that create the problem you're having. At any particular step, you can click the Add Comment button and add a comment about any part of the screen. The Steps Recorder then produces a documented report, complete with images of your screen and descriptions of each mouse movement you made. You can then e-mail this report to customer support to help technicians resolve the problem.

**How do I know whether updates are available for my software?** You can configure Windows so that it automatically checks for, downloads, and installs any available updates for itself, Internet Explorer, and other Microsoft applications such as Microsoft Office. From the Windows Control Panel, open System and Security and then Windows Update. Click Change Settings.

Many other applications now also include the ability to check for updates. Check under the Help menu of the product, and you'll often find a Check for Updates command.

**What if none of this helps? Is buying a new system my only option?** If your system is still unreliable after these changes, consider upgrading your OS to the latest version. There are often substantial increases in reliability with a major release of a new OS. However, upgrading the OS may require hardware upgrades such as additional RAM, an updated graphics processor, and even a larger hard drive. When you launch the Windows 8 upgrade from the web, it determines whether your hardware, applications, and devices will work with the new OS. ■

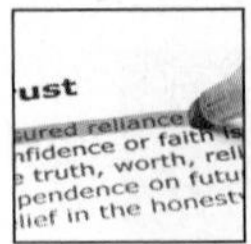

# making a final DECISION

Now that you've evaluated your computer system, you need to shift to questions of *value*. How closely does your system come to meeting your needs? How much would it cost to upgrade your current system to match what you'd ideally like your computer to do, not only today but also a few years from now? How much would it cost to purchase a new system that meets these specifications?

To know whether upgrading or buying a new system would have better value for you, you need to price both scenarios. Conduct a thorough system evaluation (Figure 6.33) to gather the data to help you decide. Purchasing a new system is an important investment of your resources, and you want to make a well-reasoned, well-supported decision.

## Getting Rid of Your Old Computer

**What should I do with my old computer?** Before you get rid of your computer, be sure to consider what benefit you might obtain by having two systems. Would you have a use for the older system? Would you be able to donate it?

FIGURE 6.33

### Key Items in System Evaluation

**CPU**

- What is your CPU usage level?

**RAM**

- Do you have at least 4 GB?

**Storage**

- Do you need an SSD start-up drive?
- Do you have a fast-access mechanical drive for large storage space?
- Do you need RAID 0 or RAID 1 storage drives for extra-fast performance or mirroring?

**Video**

- Do you have enough graphics memory?
- Is your GPU powerful enough?
- Do you have HDMI ports?
- How many monitors do you need to run simultaneously?

**Audio**

- Do you have 7.1 or 5.1 surround sound?

Also, before you decide to throw it away, consider the environmental impact (Figure 6.34). Mercury in LCD screens, cadmium in batteries and circuit boards, and flame retardants in plastic housings all are toxic. An alarming, emerging trend is that discarded machines are beginning to create an e-waste crisis.

**So how can I recycle my old computer?** Instead of throwing your computer away, you may be able to donate it to a nonprofit organization. Here are a few ways to do this:

- Many manufacturers, such as Dell, offer recycling programs and have formed alliances with nonprofit organizations to help distribute your old technology to those who need it.
- Sites like Computers with Causes (**computerswithcauses.org**) organize donations of both working and nonworking computers, printers, and mice.
- You can also take your computer to an authorized computer-recycling center in your area. The Telecommunications Industry Association provides an e-cycling information site you can use to find a local e-cycling center (**ecyclingcentral.com**).

For companies that need to retire large quantities of computers, the risk of creating an environmental hazard is serious. Firms like GigaBiter (**gigabiter.com**) offer a solution. GigaBiter eliminates security and environmental risks associated with electronic destruction by first delaminating the hard drive and then breaking down the computer e-waste into recyclable products. The result of the final step is a sand-like substance that is 100% recyclable.

**Can I donate a computer safely, without worrying about my personal data?** Before donating or recycling a computer, make sure you carefully remove all data from your hard drive. Built into Windows 8 is an option to help with this, Remove everything and reinstall Windows. It removes all user-installed applications and all of your personal data, and resets your PC settings back to the default values.

Becoming a victim of identity theft is a serious risk. Credit card numbers, bank information, Social Security numbers, tax records, passwords, and personal identification numbers (PINs) are just some of the types of sensitive information that we casually record to our computers' hard drives. Just deleting files that contain proprietary personal information is not protection enough. Likewise, reformatting or erasing your hard drive does not totally remove data, as was proved by two MIT graduate students. They bought more than 150 used hard drives from various sources. Although some of the hard drives had been reformatted or damaged so that the data was supposedly nonrecoverable, the two students were able to retrieve medical records, financial information, pornography, personal e-mails, and more than 5,000 credit card numbers!

# ethics in IT — Free Hardware for All

The open source software movement has flourished over the past decade. In response to increasing prices and the limitations placed on commercially available software, programmers began to donate time to design, develop, and support software systems. These products, like Gimp (a photo-editing tool), were then made freely available.

In the world of hardware, a similar but different approach called the open source hardware movement has flourished. Because hardware projects require materials and tools to assemble, products distributed as open source are not free in terms of cost, but they are free from any restrictions on how you modify them. Inexpensive hardware devices now span the range from the Digispark, a $9 microcontroller the size of a quarter, to the $35 Raspberry Pi, a full Linux-based computer the size of a credit card. Sample open source hardware projects include video game systems, audio equipment, and 3-D printers.

Is open hardware good for the world? Does it undermine the intellectual property of others who want to create hardware resources and sell them for a profit? What is the impact on developing countries if they have immediate access to hardware designs instead of being required to purchase these items from a for-profit company? Follow the future of open source hardware by keeping an eye on conferences like the Open Hardware Summit (**openhardwaresummit.org**), developer and supplier sites like littleBits (**littlebits.cc**), and homebrew blogs like Procrastineering (**procrastineering.blogspot.com**).

**FIGURE 6.34** An electronics garbage dump can cause environmental concerns, like the leaching of lead and mercury into the ground. *(Minnesota Public Radio, Tim Post/AP Photo)*

The U.S. Department of Defense suggests a seven-layer overwrite for a "secure erase." This means that you fill your hard drive seven times over with a random series of *1*s and *0*s. Fortunately, several programs exist for doing this. For PCs running Windows, look for utility programs like File Shredder or Eraser. Wipe is available for Linux, and ShredIt X can be used for Mac OS X. These programs provide secure hard drive erasures, either of specific files on your hard drive or of the entire hard drive. ■

**Before moving on to the Chapter Review:**

- **Watch Replay Video 6.2** .
- Then check your understanding of what you've learned so far.

# check your understanding//

For a quick review to see what you've learned so far, answer the following questions. Visit **pearsonhighered.com/techinaction** to check your answers.

## multiple choice

1. To document a problem you are having, you can use
   - **a.** Disk Cleanup.
   - **b.** Steps Recorder.
   - **c.** PC Decrapifier.
   - **d.** Resource Monitor.
2. Which is NOT a type of video port?
   - **a.** HDMI
   - **b.** DVI
   - **c.** USB 3.0
   - **d.** DisplayPort
3. When a computer is no longer useful, it can be
   - **a.** securely donated.
   - **b.** recycled.
   - **c.** turned into a sand-like substance.
   - **d.** all of the above.
4. To improve video performance, modern computers have a ________ in addition to the CPU.
   - **a.** GPU
   - **b.** VPU
   - **c.** DPU
   - **d.** APU
5. The faster data transfer port for computers today is the ________ port
   - **a.** USB 3.0
   - **b.** HDMI
   - **c.** Thunderbolt
   - **d.** DisplayPort

## true–false

_____ **1.** Windows Refresh is a utility to transfer files to a new system.

_____ **2.** GDDR5 memory is often used in external hard drives.

## critical thinking

**1. The Early Adopter**

We're all aware of the technology price curve: When first introduced, products have the highest prices and the most instability. As these products settle into the market, they become more reliable and the prices fall, sometimes very quickly. People who make those first-release purchases are called *early adopters*. What are the advantages to being an early adopter? What are the disadvantages? How do you decide at what point you should step into the technology price curve for any given product?

**2. A Green Machine**

Review the impacts on the environment of your computer during its entire lifecycle. How do the production, transportation, and use of the computer affect the increase of greenhouse gas emissions? How does the selection of materials and packaging impact the environment? What restricted substances (like lead, mercury, cadmium, and PVC) are found in your machine? Could substitute materials be used? How would the ultimate "green machine" be designed?

**Continue** 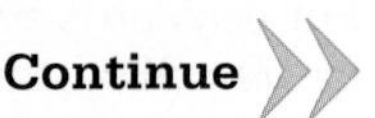

# 6 Chapter Review

## summary//

### Your Ideal Computing Device

**1. What kind of computer is best for me?**

- Review the types of computer devices available and consider what your needs are for weight, screen size, and processing power.
- Evaluate your computer system so you have clear data on what you currently have. Then you can compare it with what is on the market and make a decision to upgrade or purchase a new device.

### Evaluating the CPU Subsystem

**2. What does the CPU do, and how can I evaluate its performance?**

- You can find out what processor you have using the System Properties window.
- The CPU works by running a series of four steps: fetch, decode, execute, and store.
- CPUs are compared based on their clock speed, the number of cores they have, and their amount of cache memory.
- CPU benchmarks help you compare the overall performance of different CPUs.
- The CPU performance can be measured and recorded using the CPU usage graph of the Resource Monitor.

### Evaluating the Memory Subsystem

**3. How does memory work in my computer?**

- RAM is used to hold instructions and data because the CPU can access RAM much faster than it can access the hard drive.
- Memory modules are small circuit boards that hold a series of RAM chips in your system.

**4. How do I evaluate how much memory I need?**

- The System Properties window shows how much physical memory you have installed.
- The Resource Monitor shows how the installed RAM is being used by your system.
- You can easily install RAM in your system, though each system has a limit on how much RAM it can hold.

### Evaluating the Storage Subsystem

**5. What are the computer's storage devices?**

- Data is stored on mechanical hard drives, solid-state drives, and optical drives.
- There is a wide range of difference in access times and cost between different storage solutions, so most systems have a combination of types.

**6. How do I evaluate my storage devices?**

- The Properties dialog box in File Explorer (previously called Windows Explorer) displays information on the amount of storage available in your system.
- Compute the amount of storage you need for the software and data files you want to keep locally.
- Decide how many drives you want, what type each should be, and how you will configure them. RAID 0 is an option for combining drives for optimal performance. RAID 1 is an option for combining drives for immediate backup.

### Evaluating the Video and Audio Subsystems

**7. What components affect the quality of video on my computer?**

- The video card is key to video quality. Be aware of how much video memory is installed and what kind of GPU is used on the card.
- Some users install multiple video cards for high-end graphics performance.
- With only one card, you can run multiple monitors.

**8. How do I know if I need better video performance?**

- If you see long refresh times, you may want an upgraded video card. The software that comes with the card can run performance testing to give you specific data on how the card is doing.

**9. What components affect my computer's sound quality?**

- The sound card and speakers control the sound quality in your system.
- If you want surround sound, you may want to invest in a new sound card and additional speakers.

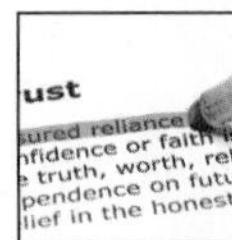

## Evaluating System Reliability and Making a Final Decision

**10. How can I improve the reliability of my system?**

- To make sure your system stays reliable, clear out unnecessary files, run antivirus software, run spyware and adware removal programs, run the Disk Defragmenter on mechanical hard drives, and use the Task Scheduler to automate these tasks.
- If your system is crashing often, check that you have enough RAM. Then consider doing a system refresh or even a full system restore.
- Keep your software updated. Use the Steps Recorder to capture problems as they happen and report them to the manufacturer.

Be sure to check out the companion website for additional materials to help you review and learn, including a Tech Bytes Weekly newsletter—**pearsonhighered.com/techinaction**
And don't forget the Replay Videos.

## key terms//

3-D sound card **246**
access time **233**
audio MIDI interface **247**
cache memory **227**
clock speed **227**
core **227**
CPU benchmarks **228**
CPU usage **228**
CPU usage graph **228**
graphics double data rate 5 (GDDR5) **242**
graphics processing unit (GPU) **243**
hard drive **233**
head crash **234**
hyperthreading **227**
latency (rotational delay) **234**
machine cycle **227**
memory module (memory card) **230**
Moore's Law **224**
nonvolatile storage **230**
optical drive **235**
optical media **235**
overclocking **227**
physical memory **231**
platter **233**
random access memory (RAM) **230**
read/write head **234**
redundant array of independent disks (RAID) **237**
RAID 0 **237**
RAID 1 **238**
sector **234**
seek time **234**
solid-state drive (SSD) **233**
sound card **246**
SuperFetch **231**
surround sound **246**
system evaluation **225**
track **234**
video card (video adapter) **242**
video memory **242**
volatile storage **230**

## making the transition to . . . next semester//

1. **Go Small or Stay Home**

   Manufacturers are releasing a number of systems that are trying to capitalize on size—or the lack of size! Explore some of the small form factor (SFF) computers appearing on the market.

   a. Research the Falcon Northwest FragBox and Tiki (**falcon-nw.com**).

   b. Compare that system with the Apple Mac mini and the Apple Mac Pro (**apple.com**).

   Why are these SFF computers appearing? What role do you see these systems fulfilling? What kind of performance and hardware would you recommend for such a system?

2. **How Does Your System Measure Up?**

   A number of tools are available to measure your system's performance. Explore the following tools and use one to gather data on your current system's performance.

   a. Windows 8 Resource Monitor: Use the Resource Monitor to collect data on CPU utilization and memory usage over a typical school day.

   b. Benchmarking suites: Examine a sample of consumer benchmarking programs like PassMark's PerformanceTest, Primate Lab's Geekbench, and Maxon's Cinebench. Which subsystems do each of these products evaluate?

3. **Storage on the Go**

   You will want to keep an archive of all your academic work so you can develop the best possible e-portfolio at graduation. Which type of portable hard drive is best suited to your needs? What size? Do you need built-in WiFi? Can the drive stream media content? Do you think you could store everything you produce in your academic career in a single cloud storage account?

## making the transition to . . . the workplace//

1. **Video Connections**

   You have a position in a pharmaceutical research firm. Your group does simulations of protein folding to predict if a new drug will be effective. You collaborate daily with a team in India using videoconferencing. Now you've found out you also have the responsibility of creating a series of training videos to teach the Indian team how to use the newest release of software. What video and processing hardware would your workstation need to tackle this? Specify the video card performance and the CPU and memory requirements this project would have.

2. **Let Me Tell You My Problem**

   You may be responsible for helping others solve various computer problems. Test out the Steps Recorder in Windows to see how the program can help you help them. From the Charms bar, search for "psr." Run the program and click Start Record. Then just click between different applications, visit the Control Panel, and add a comment. Save the file to your desktop and close the Steps Recorder. View the annotated report. How could you use the Steps Recorder to describe a problem or to gather information?

# Many Different Devices for Many Different Needs

## Problem

Even within one discipline, there are needs for a variety of types of computing solutions. Consider the Communications Department in a large university. Because it's an interdisciplinary area, there are some groups involved in video production, some groups producing digital music, and some groups creating scripts and screenplays. The department as a whole needs to decide on a complete computing strategy.

## Process

1. Split the class into teams.
2. Select one segment of the Communications Department that your team will represent: video production, digital music, or scripting. The video production team requires its labs to be able to support the recording, editing, and final production and distribution of digital video. The digital music group wants to establish a collegiate recording studio (after the model of the Drexel University recording label, Mad Dragon Records, at **maddragonmusic.com**). The scripting group needs to support a collaborative community of writers and voice-over actors.
3. Analyze the computing needs of that segment, with particular focus on how it needs to outfit its computer labs.
4. Price the systems you would recommend and explain how they will be used. What decisions have you made in order to guarantee they will still be useful in three years?
5. Write a report that summarizes your findings. Document the resources you used and generate as much enthusiasm as you can for your recommendations.

## Conclusion

The range of available computing solutions has never been so broad. It can be a cause of confusion for those not educated in technology. But with a firm understanding of the basic subsystems of computers, it is precisely this pace of change that is exciting. Being able to evaluate a computer system and match it to the current needs of its users is an important skill.

## ethics project//

# Benchmarking

In this exercise, you'll research and then role-play a complicated ethical situation. The role you play might not match your own personal beliefs; regardless, your research and use of logic will enable you to represent the view assigned. An arbitrator will watch and comment on both sides of the arguments, and together, the team will agree on an ethical solution.

## Problem

We've seen that for complex systems like computers, performance often is determined not by comparing the specifications of individual parts but by using benchmarks, software suites that test a full area of performance. There are benchmarks for battery life, for CPU performance, and for video performance. The results of these tests become a major force in marketing and selling the product.

There have been a number of claims of unethical conduct in the area of benchmarking. Companies have been accused of using out-of-date testing software to skew their results. Some companies have manipulated the settings on the machine to artificially raise their score (for example, turning off the display and wireless network before testing for battery life). Some companies have a pattern of making sure the systems sent out to magazines and other evaluators have better-performing components than you might get off the shelf in your own new system.

Where is the line between gaining a competitive edge and lying when it comes to hardware assessment?

## Research Areas to Consider

- SysMark2002
- BAPCo
- MobileMark
- 2009 Nobel Prize for Physics

## Process

1. Divide the class into teams.
2. Research the areas cited above from the perspective of either an Intel engineer working on a new CPU, an AMD engineer working on a competing CPU, or a benchmark designer.
3. Team members should write a summary that provides factual documentation for the positions and views their character takes around the issue of equitable testing of hardware. Then, team members should create an outline to use during the role-playing event.
4. Team members should arrange a mutually convenient time to meet for the exchange, using a virtual meeting tool or by meeting in person.
5. Team members should present their case to the class or submit a PowerPoint presentation for review by the rest of the class, along with the summary and resolution they developed.

## Conclusion

As technology becomes ever more prevalent and integrated into our lives, more and more ethical dilemmas will present themselves. Being able to understand and evaluate both sides of the argument, while responding in a personally or socially ethical manner, will be an important skill.

# 7 Networking: Connecting Computing Devices

## How Networks Function

### Networking Fundamentals

**OBJECTIVE**

1. What is a network, and what are a network's advantages and disadvantages? **(pp. 260–261)**

**Active Helpdesk:** Understanding Networking

### Network Architectures and Components

**OBJECTIVES**

2. What are the different ways to classify networks? **(pp. 262–264)**
3. Which type of network is most commonly found in the home? **(p. 264)**
4. What are the main components of every network? **(pp. 265–268)**

### Connecting to the Internet

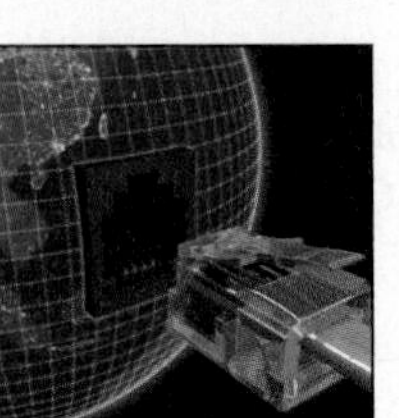

**OBJECTIVE**

5. What are my options for connecting to the Internet? **(pp. 269–272)**

**Sound Byte:** Connecting to the Internet

**Active Helpdesk:** Connecting to the Internet

## Your Home Network

### Installing and Configuring Home Networks

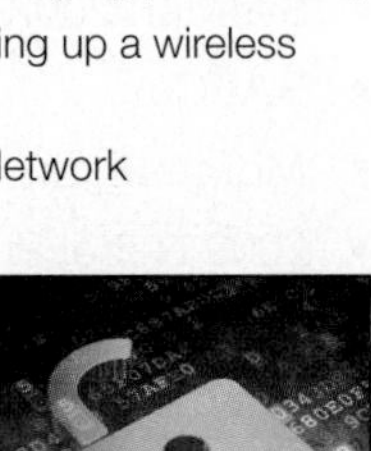

**OBJECTIVES**

6. How do I tell if my home network is up to date, and how do I identify the devices on the network? **(pp. 276–277)**
7. Besides computers, what other devices can I connect to a home network? **(pp. 277–284)**
8. How do I configure the software on my computer and set up other devices to get my network up and running? **(pp. 284–286)**
9. What problems might I encounter when setting up a wireless network? **(p. 286)**

**Sound Byte:** Installing a Home Computer Network

### Securing Wireless Networks

**OBJECTIVE**

10. Why are wireless networks more vulnerable to security risks than wired networks, and what special precautions are required to ensure my wireless network is secure? **(pp. 288–289)**

**Sound Byte:** Securing Wireless Networks

For all media in this chapter go to **pearsonhighered.com/techinaction** or **MyITLab**.

*(Sergej Khackimullin/Fotolia; AKS/Fotolia; ktdesign/Shutterstock; Norebbo/Shutterstock; Maksim Kabakou/Shutterstock) (Beboy/Fotolia LLC)*

# HOW COOL IS THIS?

Scan here for more info

Many of us have multiple wireless devices but often **no access to WiFi**, or we're too near the limit on our mobile device data plan to do what we want without costing a small fortune. Now, using **Karma WiFi**, you can travel with your own **personal hot spot**, and you can share the connection while **earning more data** as you do. All you need to do is buy a Karma device and set up an account. You get 1 GB of data, which is enough to watch a two-hour movie or listen to eight hours of music. When you've used that up, you can purchase more—no subscription needed. And you can stretch how often you need to buy more data by **sharing your connection**. As others connect to your Karma hot spot, you each earn a free 100 MB. You only share the connection—not your data—so the more you share, the more free bandwidth you accumulate. The

# How Networks Function

You access wired and wireless networks all the time—when you use an ATM, print out a document, or use the Internet (the world's largest network). It's important to understand the fundamentals of networking, such as how networks are set up, what devices are necessary to establish a network, and how you can access a network so that you can share, collaborate, and exchange information among your friends, family, and colleagues.

## networking FUNDAMENTALS

Many of today's homes have more than one computing device capable of connecting to the Internet. A typical family engages in many activities that involve sharing and accessing files over and from the Internet and using a variety of Internet-connected devices (see Figure 7.1). What makes all this technology transfer and sharing possible? A computer network!

A computer **network** is simply two or more computers that are connected via software and hardware so they can communicate with each other. Each device connected to a network is referred to as a **node**. A node can be a computer, a peripheral such as a printer or a game console, or a network device such as a router.

**What are the benefits of networks?** There are several benefits to having computers networked:

- *Sharing an Internet connection:* A network lets you share the high-speed Internet connection coming into your home.
- *Sharing printers and other peripherals:* Networks let you share printers and other peripheral devices. For example, say you have a laptop that isn't connected to a printer. To print a document from your laptop without a network, you would need to transfer the file using a flash drive or other device to another computer that's connected

Jackie watches a video she took while on vacation
Andy plays PlayStation online and uploads a video he made for school
Mom watches a lecture from her online course while she prepares a snack
Dad watches a streaming movie and checks fantasy football scores on his iPad
Andrea takes pictures of her dog and uploads them directly to Facebook

**FIGURE 7.1** With a home network, all family members can connect their computing devices whenever and wherever they want.

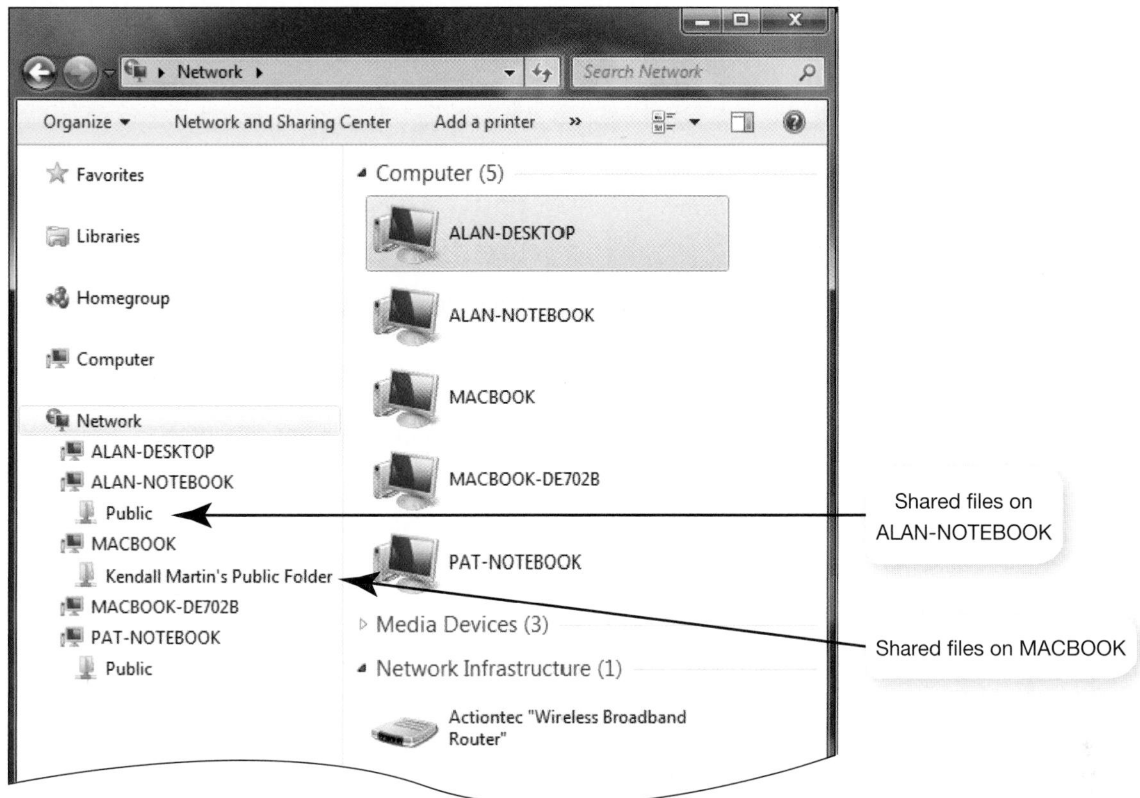


**FIGURE 7.2** File Explorer (previously called Windows Explorer) shows five networked computers set up for sharing.

to a printer or carry your laptop to the printer and connect your laptop to it. With a network, you can print directly from your device even if it's not physically connected to the printer.

- *Sharing files:* You can share files between networked computers without having to use portable storage devices such as flash drives to transfer the files. In addition, you can set sharing options in Windows or OS X that let the user of each computer on the network access files stored on any other computer on the network. For example, the Windows network in Figure 7.2 has five computers attached to it. ALAN-DESKTOP, ALAN-NOTEBOOK, and PAT-NOTEBOOK are running Windows. The two MACBOOKs are running OS X. The Public folders enable file sharing because the user of any computer on the network can access the Public folder's contents.
- *Common communications:* As illustrated in Figure 7.2, computers running different operating systems can communicate on the same network.

**Are there disadvantages to setting up networks?** Fortunately, after most home networks have been set up, there isn't much else that needs to be done to maintain or administer the network; therefore, the benefits of using a network outweigh the disadvantages. However, large networks involve an initial purchase of equipment to set them up. They also need to be administered, which can be costly and time consuming. **Network administration** involves tasks such as:

- Installing new computers and devices
- Monitoring the network to ensure it's performing efficiently
- Updating and installing new software on the network, and
- Configuring, or setting up, proper security for a network.

**How fast does data move through networks?** **Data transfer rate** (also called **bandwidth**) is the maximum speed at which data can be transmitted between two nodes on a network. **Throughput** is the actual speed of data transfer that is achieved. Throughput is always less than or equal to the data transfer rate. Data transfer rate and throughput are usually measured in *megabits per second (Mbps).* A megabit is one million bits. One of the main factors that determines how fast data moves is the type of network, which we'll discuss later in this chapter. ■

ACTIVE HELPDESK

**Understanding Networking**

In this Active Helpdesk call, you'll play the role of a helpdesk staffer, fielding calls about home networks—their advantages, their main components, and the most common types—as well as about wireless networks and how they are created.

# network ARCHITECTURES

The network you have in your home differs greatly in terms of its size, structure, and cost from the one on your college campus. This difference is based in part on their network architectures. **Network architectures**, or network designs, are classified according to:

- The distance between nodes
- The way in which the network is managed (or administered)
- The set of rules (or *protocol*) used to exchange data between network nodes, and
- The communications medium used to transport the data

Next we'll look at all of these factors plus the hardware that is often used on networks.

## Network Architectures Defined by Distance

**How does the distance between nodes define a network?** The distance between nodes on a network is one way to describe a network. The following are common types of networks (see Figure 7.3):

- A **personal area network (PAN)** is a network used for communication among devices close to one person, such as smartphones, notebooks, and tablets using wireless technologies such as Bluetooth and WiFi.
- A **local area network (LAN)** is a network in which the nodes are located within a small geographic area.

**FIGURE 7.3** Networks can be classified by the distance between their nodes. *(SiuWin/ Shutterstock)*

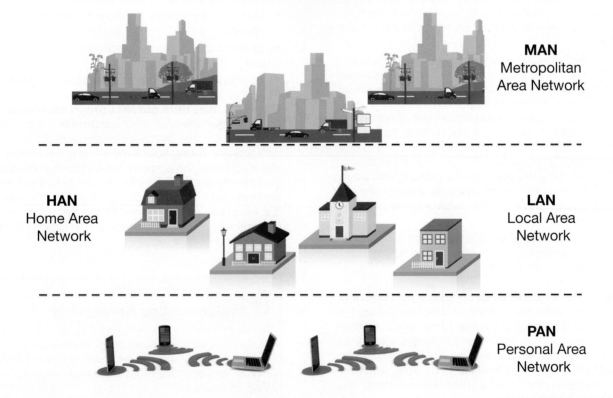

Examples include a network in a computer lab at school or at a fast-food restaurant.

- A **home area network (HAN)** is a specific type of LAN located in a home. HANs are used to connect all of a home's digital devices, such as computers, peripherals, phones, gaming devices, digital video recorders (DVRs), and televisions.
- A **metropolitan area network (MAN)** is a large network designed to provide access to a specific geographic area, such as an entire city. Many U.S. cities are now deploying MANs to provide Internet access to residents and tourists. Some MANs employ WiMAX wireless technology that extends local WiFi networks across greater distances.
- A **wide area network (WAN)** spans a large physical distance. The Internet is the largest WAN, covering the globe. A WAN is also a networked collection of LANs. If a school has multiple campuses located in different towns, each with its own LAN, connecting the LANs of each campus by telecommunications lines allows the users of the LANs to communicate. All the connected LANs would be described as a single WAN.

## Network Architectures Defined by Levels of Administration

**How does the level of administration define a network?** A network can be administered, or managed, in two main ways—centrally or locally (see Figure 7.4):

- *Central administration:* In a centrally administered network, tasks performed from one computer can affect the other computers on the network. A **client/server network** is an example. In a client/server network, a *client* is a computer on which users accomplish tasks and make requests, whereas the *server* is the computer that provides information or resources to the client computers as well as central administration for network functions such as printing. Most networks that have 10 or more nodes are client/server networks.
- *Local administration:* In a locally administered network, the configuration and maintenance of the network must be performed on each individual computer attached to the network. A **peer-to-peer (P2P) network** is an example. In a P2P network, each node connected on the network

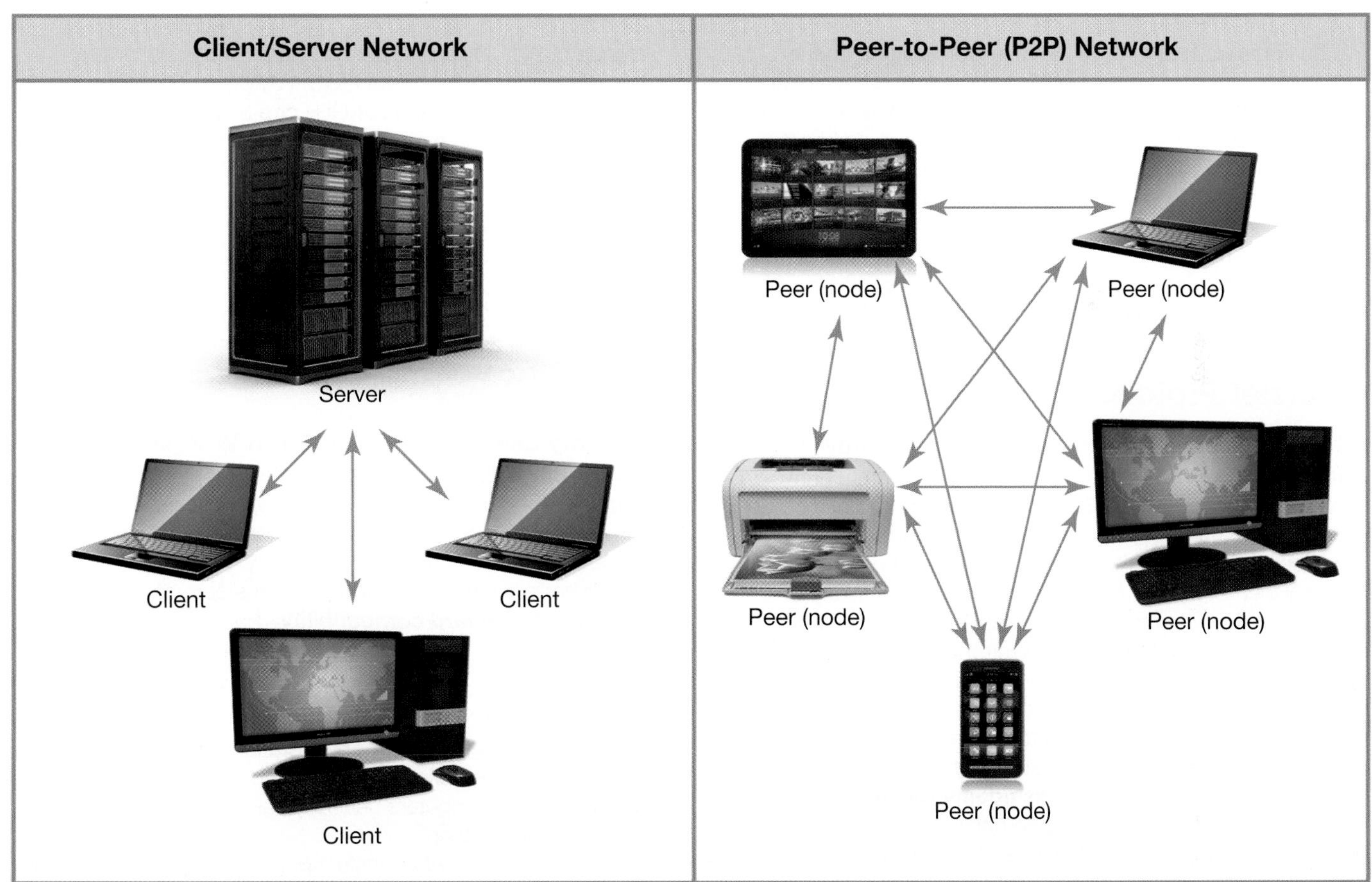


**FIGURE 7.4** Client/Server and P2P Networks. *(Scanrail/Fotolia; Scanrail/Fotolia; tuulijumala/Fotolia; Scanrail/Fotolia; Sashkin/Fotolia; Maksym Dykha/Fotolia)*

# BITS&BYTES

## PAN Clothing: Organization and Power for Portable Gear

Now that people carry so many portable computing devices, clothing designers are starting to offer clothing that facilitates the storage, transportation, charging, and networking of their digital gadgets. The Scottevest is one of a line of vests and jackets designed to hold iPods, smartphones, and even iPads. It also features a built-in PAN to help maintain connectivity of your devices. And because all the devices in your PAN need power, accessories such as the Voltaic Backpack (shown in Figure 7.5) help recharge your digital devices using renewable energy sources. So don't forget to consider the perfect fashion accessory for your latest digital acquisition!

**FIGURE 7.5** The Voltaic Backpack recharges your mobile devices using solar cells. *(Ashley Cooper/Alamy)*

can communicate directly with every other node on the network. Thus, all nodes on this type of network are peers (equals). When printing, for example, a computer on a P2P network doesn't have to go through the computer that's connected to the printer. Instead, it can communicate directly with the printer. Because they're simple to set up, cost less than client/server networks, and are easier to configure and maintain, P2P networks are the most common type of home network. Very small schools and offices may also use P2P networks.

## Ethernet Protocols

**What network standard is used in my home network?** The vast majority of home and corporate networks are Ethernet networks. An **Ethernet network** is so named because it uses the Ethernet protocol as the means (or standard) by which the nodes on the network communicate.

The Ethernet protocol was developed by the Institute of Electrical and Electronics Engineers (IEEE), which develops many standard specifications for electronic data transmission that are adopted throughout the world. Establishing standards for networking is important so that devices from different manufacturers will work well together. The standard for wired Ethernet networks is 802.3. The standard for wireless Ethernet networks, also known as **wireless fidelity (WiFi)**, is 802.11. The current version of wireless Ethernet is 802.11ac. Previous versions included 802.11n, 802.11g, 802.11b, and 802.11a.

**How is the 802.11ac version different from the previous versions?** The current wireless Ethernet standard, 802.11ac, is faster and has a better signal range than the earlier 802.11n standard. While the 802.11n standard operated at either a 2.4 GHz or a 5 GHz frequency, the 802.11ac standard operates at a 5 GHz frequency, and most prior standards operated only at the 2.4 GHz frequency. This means the 802.11ac standard is more resistant to signal interference. 802.11ad, also known as WiGig, was adopted by the Institute of Electrical and Electronics Engineers (IEEE) in late 2012 and is expected to deliver even faster speeds at 60 GHz frequencies. WiGig is not intended for home wireless networks but rather will act as a wireless link between devices, similar to but faster than Bluetooth.

**Will my device that has 802.11n WiFi still work on an 802.11ac network?** Devices using older standards, such as 802.11n, will still work with 802.11ac networks, but they'll operate with slower data transfer rates and may run into some frequency interference. The ability of current devices to use earlier standards in addition to the current standard is known as **backward compatibility**.

**Are there different standards for wired Ethernet?** The most commonly used wired Ethernet standard for home networks is the **gigabit Ethernet** standard. A data transfer rate of up to 1 gigabit per second (Gbps) is possible using this standard. Computers generally ship with gigabit Ethernet cards installed in them.

For even faster data transfer speeds, *10 gigabit Ethernet* is available. It provides a maximum data transfer rate of 10 Gbps. But 10 gigabit Ethernet networks are primarily used in businesses with large data throughput needs. ■

# network COMPONENTS

To function, all networks must include:

- A means of connecting the nodes on the network (cables or wireless technology)
- Special hardware devices that allow the nodes to communicate with each other and to send data
- Software that allows the network to run (see Figure 7.6)

## Transmission Media

**How do nodes connect to each other?** All network nodes are connected to each other and to the network by transmission media. **Transmission media** can be either wired or wireless; they establish a communications channel between the nodes on a network. The media used depend on the requirements of a network and its users.

**What transmission media is used on a wired network?** Wired networks use various types of cable (wire) to connect nodes (see Figure 7.7). The type of network and the distance between nodes determines the type of cable used:

- **Twisted-pair cable** is made up of copper wires that are twisted around each other and surrounded by a plastic jacket. Normal telephone cable is a type of twisted-pair cable, although phone cable won't work for connecting a LAN or HAN. A slightly different type of twisted-pair cable, called **unshielded twisted-pair (UTP) cable**, is used for networks. UTP is composed of four pairs of wires twisted around each other to reduce electrical interference.
- **Coaxial cable** consists of a single copper wire surrounded by layers of plastic. If you have cable TV, the cable running into your TV or cable box is most likely coaxial cable.
- **Fiber-optic cable** is made up of plastic or glass fibers that transmit data at extremely fast speeds.

**What type of cable is used in most wired home networks?** The most popular transmission media option for wired Ethernet networks is UTP cable. You can buy UTP cable in varying lengths with Ethernet connectors (called RJ-45 connectors) already attached. Ethernet connectors resemble standard phone connectors (called RJ-11 connectors) but are slightly larger and have contacts for eight wires (four pairs) instead of four wires.

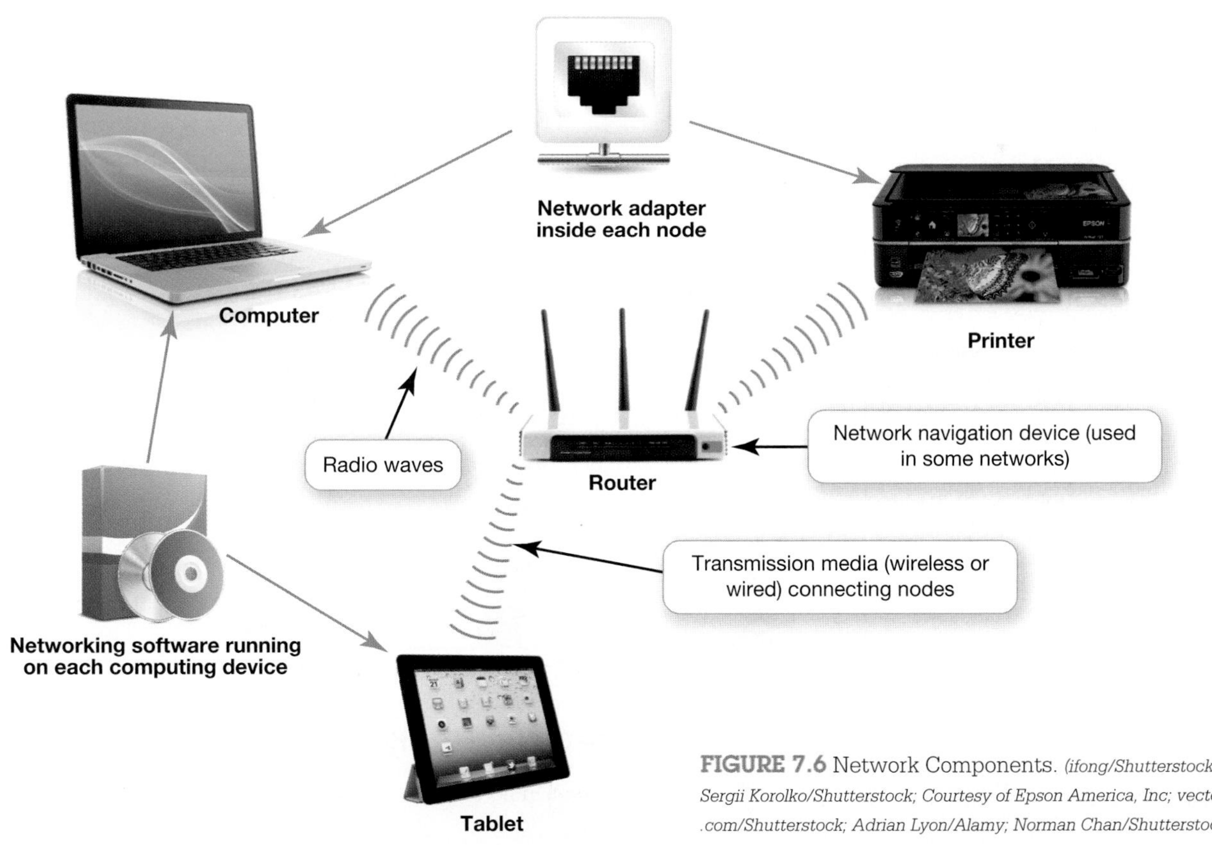


**FIGURE 7.6** Network Components. *(ifong/Shutterstock; Sergii Korolko/Shutterstock; Courtesy of Epson America, Inc; vectorlib.com/Shutterstock; Adrian Lyon/Alamy; Norman Chan/Shutterstock)*

FIGURE 7.7

## Wired Transmission Media

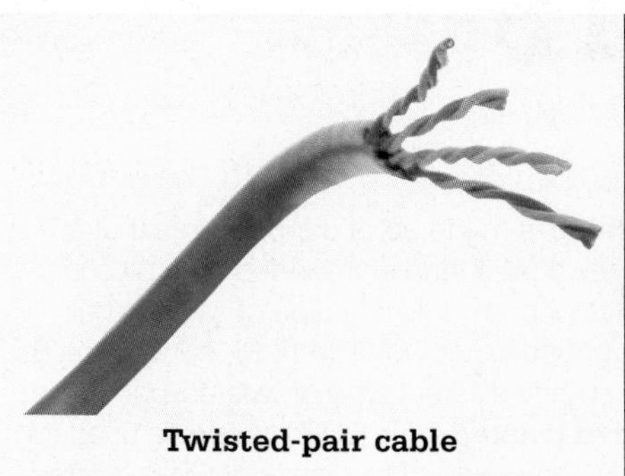
Twisted-pair cable

Coaxial cable

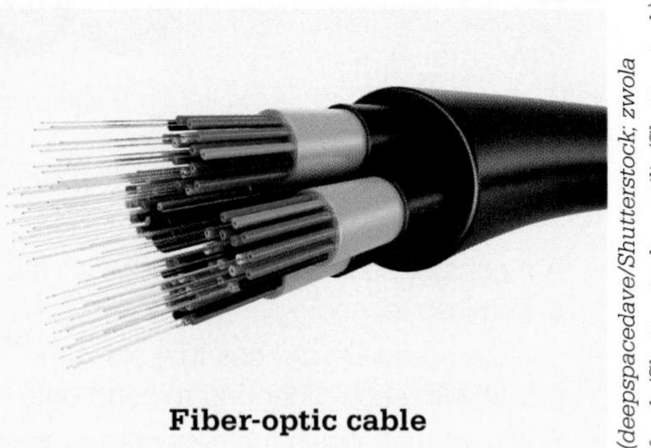
Fiber-optic cable

(deepspacedave/Shutterstock; zwola fasola/Shutterstock; zentilia/Shutterstock)

**Do all wired Ethernet networks use the same kind of UTP cable?** The three main types of UTP cable you would consider using in wired Ethernet home networks and their data transfer rates are as follows (also see Figure 7.8):

1. *Cat 5E:* Although Cat 5E cable is the cheapest of the three types and is sufficient for many home networking tasks, it was designed for 100 Mbps–wired Ethernet networks that were popular before gigabit Ethernet networks became the standard. Therefore, you should probably not install Cat 5E cable even though it's still available in stores.
2. *Cat 6:* Because **Cat 6 cable** is designed to achieve data transfer rates that support a gigabit Ethernet network, it's probably the best choice for home networking cable, though it's more expensive and more difficult to work with than Cat 5E cable.
3. *Cat 6a:* Cat 6a cable is designed for ultrafast Ethernet networks that run at speeds as fast as 10 Gbps. Installing a 10 gigabit Ethernet network in the home is probably unnecessary because today's home applications (even gaming and streaming media) don't require this rate of data transfer.

**What transmission media is used to connect nodes on a wireless network?** As noted earlier, *WiFi* is a standard for wireless transmissions using radio waves to connect computing devices to wireless networks and the Internet. With so many portable devices being connected to networks, a network with wireless connectivity is used in businesses as well as in most homes. However, note that wireless networks generally have decreased throughput compared with that of wired networks.

**Why are wireless networks slower than wired networks?** Some common reasons why wireless signals may have decreased throughput are:

- Wireless signals are more susceptible to interference from magnetic and electrical sources.
- Other wireless networks (such as your neighbor's network) can interfere with the signals on your network.

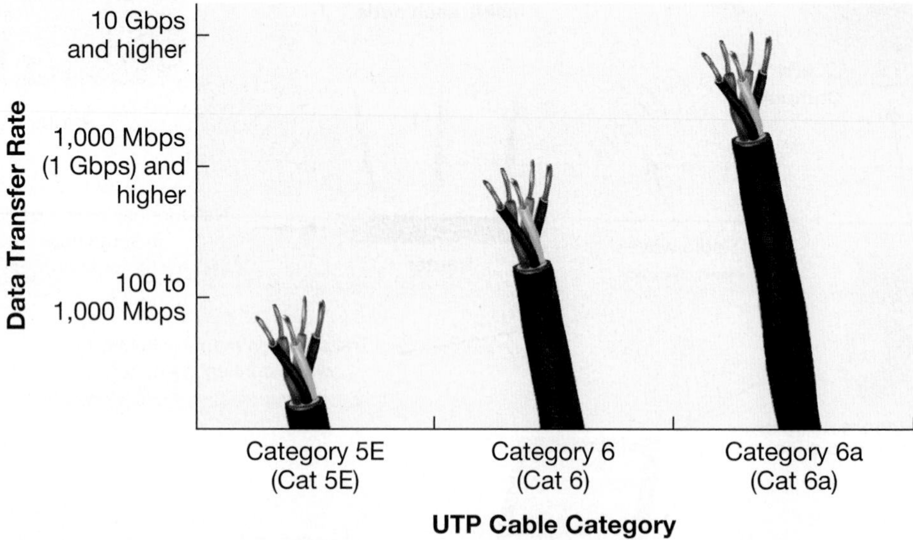


FIGURE 7.8 The three main UTP cable types used in home networks have different data transfer rates.

- Certain building materials (such as concrete and cinderblock) and metal (such as a refrigerator) can decrease throughput.
- Throughput varies depending on the distance between your networking equipment.
- Wireless networks usually use specially coded signals to protect their data, whereas wired connections don't protect their signals. This process of coding signals can slightly decrease throughput, although once coded, data travels at usual speeds.

**Can I have both wired and wireless nodes on the same network?** One network can support nodes with both wireless and wired connections. Most people use wireless connections for portable devices such as laptops. However, many of the devices connected to a network, such as printers and TVs, usually stay in one location. Although these devices probably feature wireless connectivity, hooking them up to wired connections lets you take advantage of the faster throughput achieved by wired connectivity. In situations where you want to achieve the highest possible throughput on your portable device, you may want to use a wired connection temporarily.

## Basic Network Hardware

**What hardware is needed for different nodes on the network to communicate?** For the different nodes on a network to communicate with each other and access the network, each node needs a **network adapter**. All desktop and laptop computers as well as smartphones, tablets, and many peripherals sold today contain network adapters installed *inside* the device. This type of integrated network adapter is referred to as a **network interface card (NIC)**. Different NICs are designed to use different types of transmission media. Most NICs included in computing devices today are built to use wireless media, but many can use wired media as well.

**What equipment do I need in order to hook up to broadband?** A broadband Internet connection requires a modem. Depending on the type of broadband service you have, you'll have either a cable modem or a DSL modem. Often, your Internet service provider will rent the appropriate modem to you or specify what type of modem you have to buy to work properly with the Internet service provider's technology. The modem translates the broadband signal into digital data and back again.

**What hardware is necessary to transmit data through a network?** Data is sent through a network in bundles called **packets**. For computers to communicate, these packets of data must be able to flow between network nodes. **Network navigation devices**, such as a router or a switch, facilitate and control the flow of data through a network:

- A **router** transfers packets of data between two or more networks. On a home network, you need a router to transfer data between your home network and the Internet, which is considered a separate network. To add WiFi to your home network, you need a router that features wireless capabilities.
- A **switch** acts like a traffic signal on a network (see Figure 7.9). All routers sold for home use have integrated

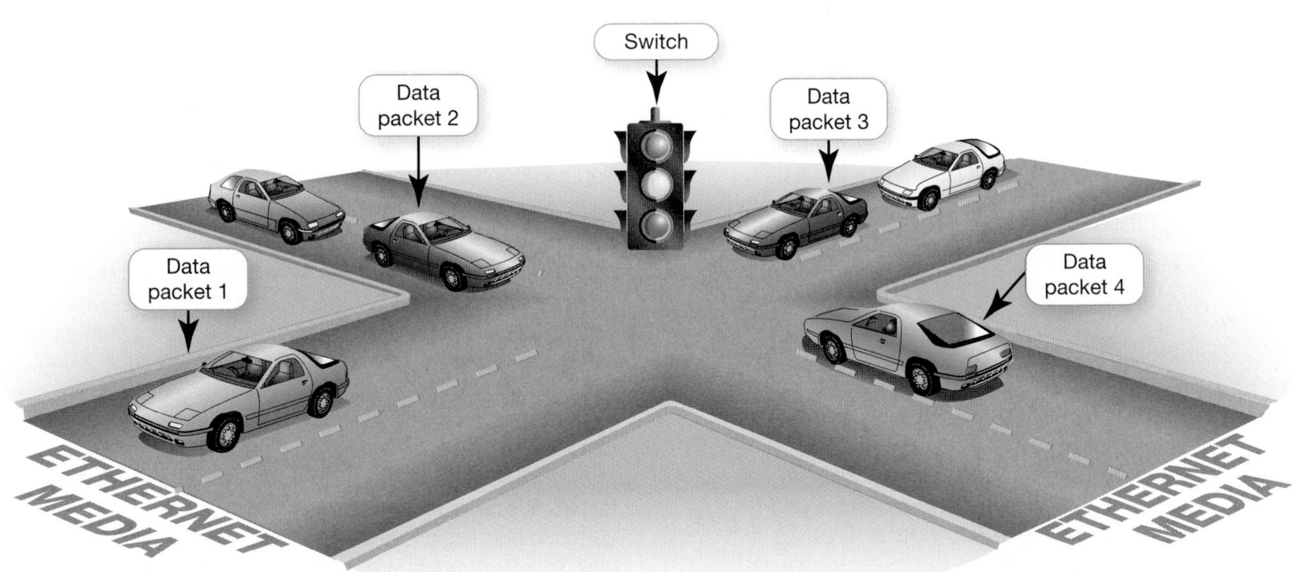


FIGURE 7.9 A simplified explanation of the function of switches is that, together with NICs, they act like traffic signals or traffic cops. They enforce the rules of the data road on an Ethernet network and help prevent data packets from crashing into each other. *(Luca di Filippo, iStockphoto)*

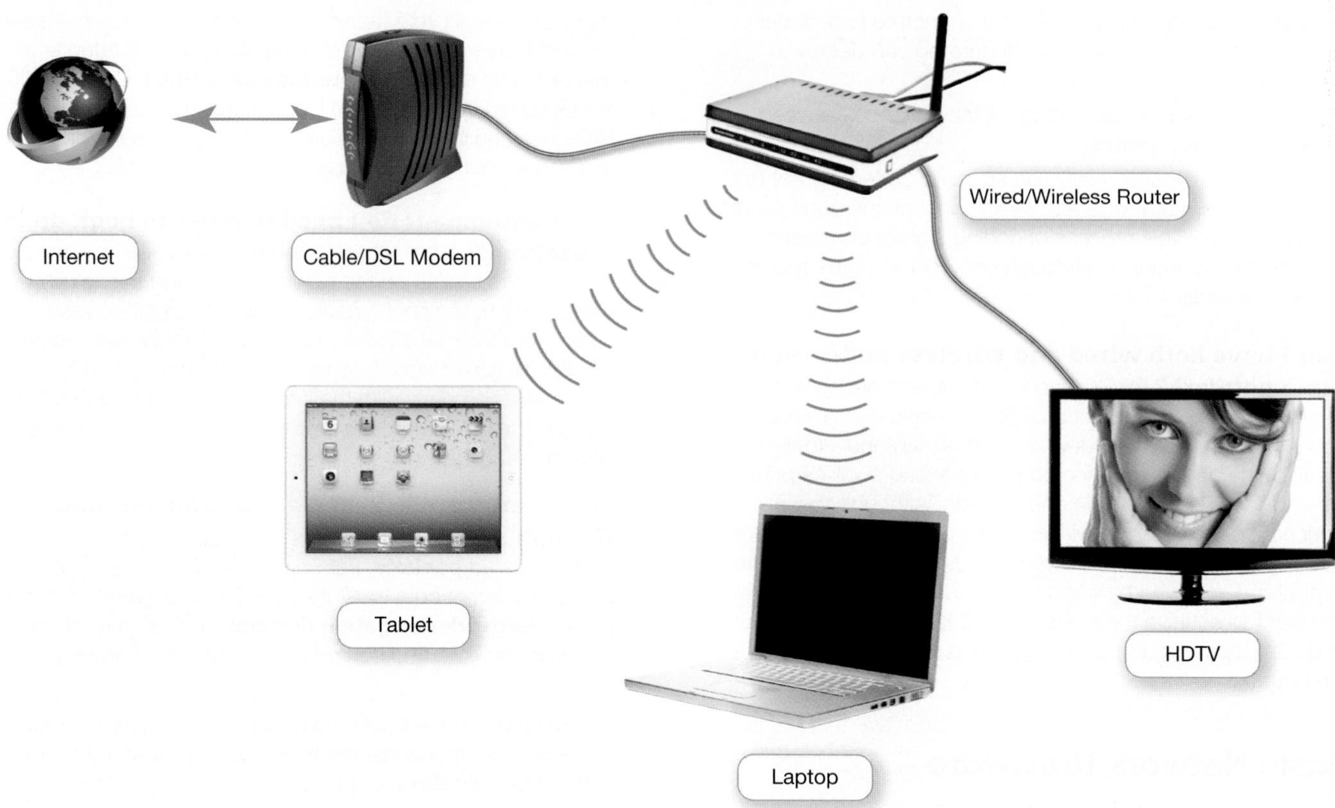


**FIGURE 7.10** A small network with a wired/wireless router attached. *(Beboy/Fotolia; Norman Chan/Shutterstock; S.Dashkevych/Shutterstock; IKO/Shutterstock; Luca di Filippo/iStockPhoto.com; duckycards/Jill Fromer/iStockphoto; Oleksiy Maksymenko/Alamy)*

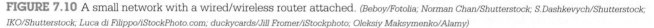

switches. Switches receive data packets and send them to their intended nodes on the same network (not between different networks). During the transmission process, data packets can suffer collisions; subsequently, the data in them is damaged or lost and the network doesn't function efficiently. The switch keeps track of the data packets and, in conjunction with NICs, helps the data packets find their destinations without running into each other. The switch also keeps track of all the nodes on the network and sends the data packets directly to the node for which they're headed. This keeps the network running efficiently.

**Where should you place the router on your network?** Your router should be connected directly to your broadband (cable/DSL) modem (see Figure 7.10). The connection should be an Ethernet cable running from an Ethernet port on your modem to the modem port on your router. Then, all computing devices—such as an HDTV, a tablet, and a laptop—are connected to the router via a wired or wireless connection. Some routers have integrated modems so that you only need one device.

## Network Software

**What network software do home networks require?** Because home networks are P2P networks, they need operating system software that supports P2P networking. Windows, OS X, and Linux all support P2P networking. You can connect computers running any of these operating systems to the same home network.

**Is the same network software used in client/server networks?** As opposed to P2P networks, the nodes on a client/server network don't communicate directly with each other; rather, they communicate through a centralized server. Communicating through a server is more efficient in a network with a large number of nodes, but it requires more complex software than is necessary for P2P networks. Therefore, the servers on client/server networks have specialized **network operating system (NOS)** software installed. This software handles requests for information, Internet access, and the use of peripherals for the rest of the network nodes. Examples of NOS software include Windows Server and SUSE Linux Enterprise Server. ■

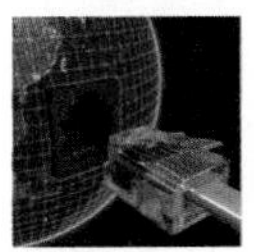

# connecting TO THE INTERNET

One of the main reasons for setting up a network is to share an Internet connection. Some businesses and large organizations have a dedicated connection to the Internet, but other businesses and homeowners purchase Internet access from **Internet service providers (ISPs)**. ISPs may be specialized providers, like Juno, or companies like Comcast that provide additional services, such as phone and cable TV. Broadband is the preferred way to access the Internet, but in some situations, cellular or dial-up access may be necessary.

## Wired Broadband Internet Connections

**What exactly is broadband Internet access? Broadband**, often referred to as high-speed Internet, refers to a type of connection that offers a means to connect to the Internet with faster throughput. Broadband usually has a data transmission rate that ranges from 1 to 50 Mbps. This high rate of access is in contrast to dial-up Internet access, which has a maximum transmission speed of 56 Kbps (kilobits per second).

**What types of broadband are available?** As shown in Figure 7.11, the standard wired broadband technologies in most areas are *cable*, *DSL (digital subscriber line)*, and *fiber-optic service*. *Satellite broadband* is used mostly in rural or mountain areas that can't get DSL, cable, or fiber-optic service.

There are also wireless broadband options. *Mobile broadband* is offered through many cell-phone service providers through 3G and 4G networks. *Wireless Internet* is also available via WiFi radio waves. We'll discuss these options later in the chapter.

SOUND BYTE

**Connecting to the Internet**

In this Sound Byte, you'll learn the basics of connecting to the Internet from home, including useful information on the various types of Internet connections and selecting the right ISP.

**How does cable Internet work? Cable Internet** is a broadband service that transmits data over the coaxial cables that also transmit cable television signals; however, cable TV and cable Internet are separate services. Cable TV is a one-way service in which the cable company feeds programming signals to your television. To bring two-way Internet connections to homes, cable companies had to upgrade their networks with two-way data-transmission capabilities.

**How does DSL work? DSL (digital subscriber line)** uses twisted-pair cable, the same as that used for regular telephones, to connect your computer to the Internet. The bandwidth of the wires is split into three sections, like a three-lane highway. One lane is used to carry voice data. DSL uses the remaining two lanes to send and receive data separately at much higher frequencies than voice data. Although DSL uses a standard phone line, having a traditional phone line in your house doesn't mean you have access to DSL service. Your local phone company must have special DSL technology to offer you the service.

**How does fiber-optic service work? Fiber-optic service** uses fiber-optic lines, which are strands of optically

FIGURE 7.11

**Comparing Common Wired Broadband Internet Connection Options**

| BROADBAND TYPE | TRANSMISSION MEDIUM | SPEED CONSIDERATIONS | AVERAGE AND MAXIMUM DOWNLOAD SPEEDS |
|---|---|---|---|
| **Cable** | Coaxial cable, similar to cable TV wire | Cable connections are shared, so speed can drop during high-usage periods | Average speed of 10 Mbps, with maximum of 30 Mbps |
| **DSL (Digital Subscriber Line)** | Copper wire phone line | Speed drops as distance from the main signal source increases | Average speed of 3.7 Mbps, with maximum of 15 Mbps |
| **Fiber-Optic** | Strands of optically pure glass or plastic | Transmits data via light signals, which do not degrade over long distances | Average speed of 50 Mbps, with maximum of 500 Mbps |

pure glass or plastic that are as thin as a human hair. They're arranged in bundles called *optical cables* and transmit data via light signals over long distances. Because light travels so quickly, this technology can transmit an enormous amount of data at superfast speeds. When the data reaches your house, it's converted to electrical pulses that transmit digital signals your computer can "read." Fiber-optic cable is not usually run inside the home. On a fiber-optic network, twisted-pair or coaxial cable is still used inside the home to transport the network signals.

**How does satellite Internet work?** To take advantage of **satellite Internet**, you need a satellite dish (see Figure 7.12), which is placed outside your home and connected to your computer with coaxial cable, the same type of cable used for cable TV. Data from your computer is transmitted between your personal satellite dish and the satellite company's receiving satellite dish by a satellite that sits in a geosynchronous orbit thousands of miles above the Earth.

**How do I choose which broadband connection option is best for me?** Depending on where you live, you might not have a choice of the broadband connection available. Check with your local cable TV provider, phone company, and satellite TV provider(s) to determine what broadband options are available and what the transfer rates are in your area.

Often, the most difficult decision is choosing between high-speed plans offered by the same company. For instance, at the time of printing, Verizon offered three different fiber-optic plans that featured download speeds from 15 to 500 Mbps. Although 15 Mbps is fine for every day browsing, e-mail, and shopping, it may not be fast enough for streaming HD movies or satisfying the needs of multiple devices on the Internet

**FIGURE 7.12** ISPs that offer satellite Internet can provide Internet access even in remote areas. *(Ilene MacDonald/Alamy)*

# BITS&BYTES

## Connecting to Wireless Networks on the Road? Beware of "Evil Twins"!

When you want to connect to a wireless network, you switch on your laptop, and the wireless network adapter finds a network called "free WiFi" or something similar. After connecting, you decide to buy some Kindle books from Amazon.com. You enter your credit card information, download the content, and enjoy a good read. Three days later, your credit card company calls asking about the $2,400 big-screen TV you just bought. The thing is, you didn't make this purchase; instead you probably fell prey to an "evil twin" wireless hotspot.

Hackers know the areas where people are likely to seek access to wireless networks. They'll often set up their own wireless "evil twin" networks in these areas with sound-alike names to lure unsuspecting web surfers to free Internet access. The hackers monitor traffic on these sites looking for sensitive information, such as credit card numbers and passwords that they can exploit.

How can you protect yourself? Check with authorized personnel hosting the hotspot to determine the name of the legitimate connection. Don't connect to a free hotspot that isn't legitimate. Lastly, it's better to not make online purchases, enter online passwords, or work with sensitive materials in free WiFi areas. Save those activities to a time when you can log on to a secure network that you can trust.

at the same time. Finally, you may also need to consider what other services you want bundled into your payment, such as phone or TV. Consulting with friends and neighbors about the plan they have and whether it's meeting their needs can help you decide on the right plan for you.

## Wireless Internet Access

**How can I access the Internet wirelessly at home?** To access the Internet wirelessly at home, you need to establish WiFi on your home network by using a router that features wireless capabilities. You also need the right equipment on your mobile device. Virtually all laptops, smartphones, game systems, and personal media players sold today are WiFi enabled and come with wireless capability built in.

**How can I access WiFi when I'm away from home?** When you're away from home, you need to find a WiFi hotspot. Many public places, such as libraries, hotels, airports, and fast-food and coffee shops, offer WiFi access. Most locations are free, though a few still charge or require a special password to access the connection. Websites like Wi-Fi-FreeSpot (**wififreespot.com**) and Wi-Fi Planet (**wi-fiplanet.com**) help you locate a free hotspot wherever you're planning to go. When you have to buy WiFi access, you can pay for a single session or a monthly membership through services such as Boingo (**boingo.com**). Boingo has over 400,000 hotspots worldwide, including airports, hotels, and restaurants.

Even wireless in-flight Internet service is available! Gogo (**gogoair.com**) is a wireless broadband network that provides coverage on participating airlines across the continental United States. So, when you are cleared to use your portable electronic devices, you can comfortably access wireless Internet from 35,000 feet.

**How can I access the Internet when WiFi isn't available?** There are often occasions when you're not in a WiFi hotspot but still need to access the Internet. In these instances, you may want to consider signing up for mobile broadband. **Mobile broadband** connects you to the Internet through the same cellular network that cell phones use to get 3G or 4G Internet access.

3G and 4G can be thought of as "WiFi everywhere" in that they provide Internet access to your mobile devices in the same way they provide voice service to your mobile phone. *3G* and *4G* refer to the third and fourth generations, respectively, of cell-phone networks. **4G** is the latest service standard and offers the fastest data-access speeds over cell-phone networks. To utilize the 3G or 4G capabilities of a mobile device, you need to sign up for an access plan with a mobile data provider such as Verizon or AT&T.

ACTIVE HELPDESK

**Connecting to the Internet**

In this Active Helpdesk call, you'll play the role of a helpdesk staffer. You'll field calls about various options for connecting to the Internet and how to choose an Internet service provider.

**How does mobile broadband Internet compare with wired Internet access?** 3G performs similarly to a standard DSL connection (roughly 3 Mbps). According to the standards set for 4G, the data transfer rate you would get while in a moving vehicle is approximately 100 Mbps; from a fixed location, you can expect up to a 1 Gbps data transfer rate. Some of the early 4G systems released in the market support less than the required 1 Gbps rate and are not fully compliant with the 4G standards, and so are being tagged as 4G LTE. They are still faster than 3G, however.

**How can I get 3G/4G service if my device doesn't have the right equipment?** Many devices such as the iPad, Kindle Fire, Chromebook, and some laptops are available with built-in 3G or 4G capabilities. If your device doesn't have built-in 3G or 4G equipment, you can buy a *USB modem*. USB modems fit into a USB port on your computer and let you access 3G or 4G networks. Like a smartphone, they also require a service plan.

Alternatively, instead of buying a USB modem that works on one device, you can buy a *mobile hotspot* (see Figure 7.13). These mobile hotspots let you connect more than one device

**FIGURE 7.13** A MiFi device turns your phone signal into a 4G LTE mobile hotspot for you and four of your friends. *(PRNewsFoto/Verizon Wireless/AP Photos)*

## BITS&BYTES

### How Do You Find Your WiFi?

**FIGURE 7.14** The WiFi Detector T-shirt and cap make a statement—a geeky statement. *(Courtesy of ThinkGeek.com)*

Detecting a nearby WiFi signal is important if your device doesn't have 3G/4G connectivity. Although most portable devices will display a list of available wireless networks, there are other ways to find WiFi:

- Some laptops have a built-in WiFi scanner that displays a row of lights on the case whenever a WiFi signal is available.
- There are WiFi keychain fobs that light up when they detect WiFi signals.
- ThinkGeek's WiFi Detector T-shirt and WiFi Detector baseball cap have a logo that lights up to indicate the signal strength of a nearby WiFi network (see Figure 7.14). Find your WiFi and look—well, look geeky while doing it!

to the Internet with either WiFi or mobile broadband. Mobile hotspots require you to purchase a data plan, but the monthly fee may be less than paying for individual monthly plans on multiple devices. So, if you have several mobile devices that need wireless Internet access, this may be the most economical and functional way to access the Internet while on the road.

## Dial-Up Connections

**Why would I ever want to consider a dial-up connection to the Internet?** Although about 70% of Internet users in the United States use high-speed Internet connections such as DSL, cable, or fiber-optic, there are still some areas (usually rural) where broadband service isn't available. A dial-up connection needs only a standard phone line and a modem to access the Internet. Therefore, some people choose to use a dial-up connection when there's no high-speed service in their area. Additionally, a dial-up connection is the least costly way to connect to the Internet, so for those who don't use the Internet frequently, the extra cost of broadband may be unnecessary.

**What are the disadvantages of dial-up?** The major downside to dial-up is speed. Dial-up modems transfer data about 600 times slower than a fiber-optic broadband connection. Also, dial-up uses a traditional phone line to connect to the Internet; therefore, unless you have a separate phone line just for your dial-up connection, when you're using dial-up, you tie up your phone line. ■

**Before moving on to Part 2:**

- **Watch Replay Video 7.1** .
- Then check your understanding of what you've learned so far.

# check your understanding//

For a quick review to see what you've learned so far, answer the following questions. Visit **pearsonhighered.com /techinaction** to check your answers.

## multiple choice

1. The current standard for home wireless Ethernet networks is
   - **a.** WiGig.
   - **b.** 802.3.
   - **c.** 802.11ac.
   - **d.** all of the above.
2. The type of network used for communication among a laptop and smartphone using Bluetooth is a
   - **a.** WAN.
   - **b.** PAN.
   - **c.** LAN.
   - **d.** MAN.
3. The fastest broadband Internet service is usually
   - **a.** fiber-optic.
   - **b.** DSL.
   - **c.** cable.
   - **d.** satellite.
4. The part of the network that establishes a communications channel between the nodes of the network is known as
   - **a.** network operating software.
   - **b.** transmission media.
   - **c.** a network navigation device.
   - **d.** a switch.
5. The device used to move data between two networks is called a
   - **a.** gateway.
   - **b.** switch.
   - **c.** wireless range extender.
   - **d.** router.

## true–false

_____ **1.** Actual data throughput is usually higher on wired networks than on wireless networks.

_____ **2.** A network interface card (NIC) is necessary for a mobile device to connect to a wireless network.

## critical thinking

1. **Using Online Storage**

   Sneakernet is jargon for physically transporting files from one location to another, as in using a flash drive. Think about the advantages and disadvantages of sneakernet devices versus online storage systems, such as Dropbox and OneDrive. Defend your preferred method of carrying and sharing files.

2. **Body Area Networks**

   There are small devices used in the medical industry that track vital signs and monitor heart rhythms, breathing rates, and other critical information. These devices form a body area network (BAN), connecting wirelessly to an Internet-connected device that relays the information to a medical technician or to emergency services. Do you think BANs are useful? Are there concerns or risks that BANs might present?

**Continue**

# TRY THIS  Testing Your Wired and Wireless Internet Connection Speeds

## Testing Your Wired Internet Connection Speed

Your ISP may have promised you certain downloading and uploading data speeds. How can you tell if you're getting what was promised? Numerous sites on the Internet, such as **speedtest.net** and **broadband.gov**, test the speed of your Internet connection. You can then see how your results compare with others, as well as determine whether you're getting the results promised by your ISP.

**Step 1** Go to **speedtest.net**, then click **Begin Test**.
*(Courtesy of Ookla.)*

**Step 2** The program will display a "signal" being sent as a small data file is downloaded from a remote server to your location. Then the speed is measured as a data file is uploaded back from your location to the remote server. When the test is done, your results display, along with the location of the server that was used in the test.
*(Courtesy of Ookla.)*

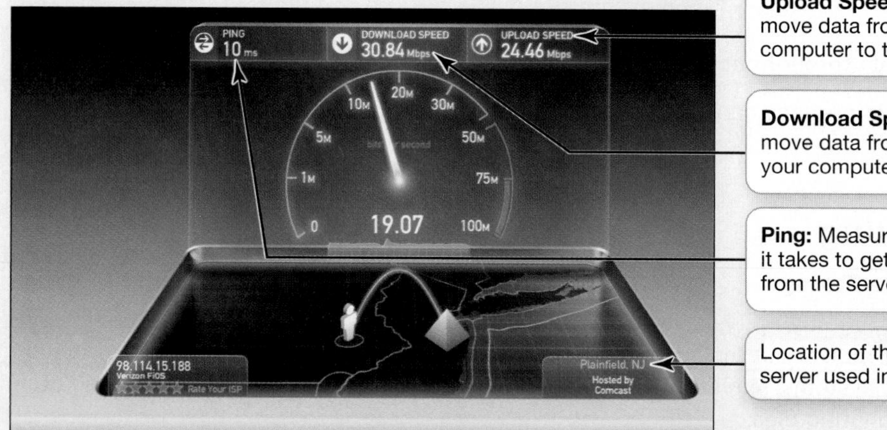

**Step 3** You can access more information about your results and how they compare with global averages by clicking the My Results box at the top-right corner of the test screen. Note that many factors can influence your Internet speeds, so be sure to run the test at several different times of the day over the course of a week before complaining to your ISP about not getting your promised speed. *(Courtesy of Ookla.)*

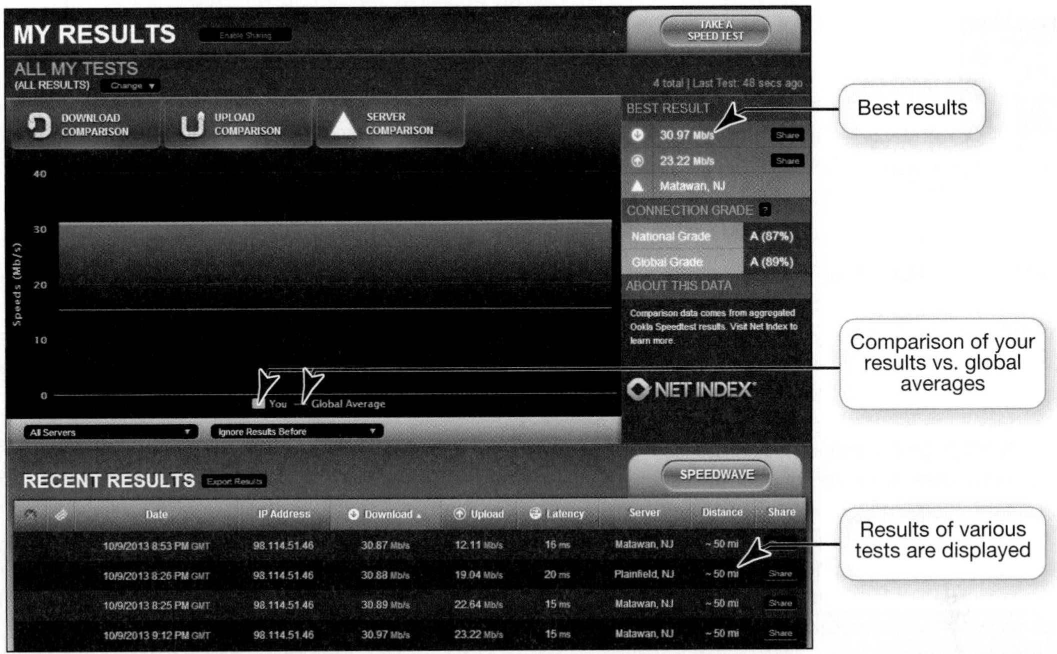


## Testing Your Wireless Internet Connection Speed

You know wireless Internet speeds are usually slower than wired connections, but what's the actual speed of your wireless connection? You can install various utilities, such as Net Meter (available at **download.cnet.com**), on your computer that show the throughput you're achieving on your computer's wireless connection to your network over a period of time. The performance of your WiFi connection depends on several factors, including the quality of the signal strength and which WiFi standard (802.11 b/g/n) your router and NIC are using.

**Step 1** Go to **download.cnet.com**. In the Find Software box on the left, type **Net Meter** and press Enter. Net Meter will display at the top of the list of search results (scroll down if necessary).

**Step 2** Select **Net Meter** in the displayed list, then click **Download Now**. Follow the steps in the Net Meter Setup Wizard to install the program on your computer.

**Step 3** Once the program is installed, select **Continue Evaluation**. (You can evaluate the program free for 30 days.) Then run Net Meter. Net Meter shows the maximum connection that is currently being achieved on your wireless network. *(Courtesy of Hoo Technologies)*

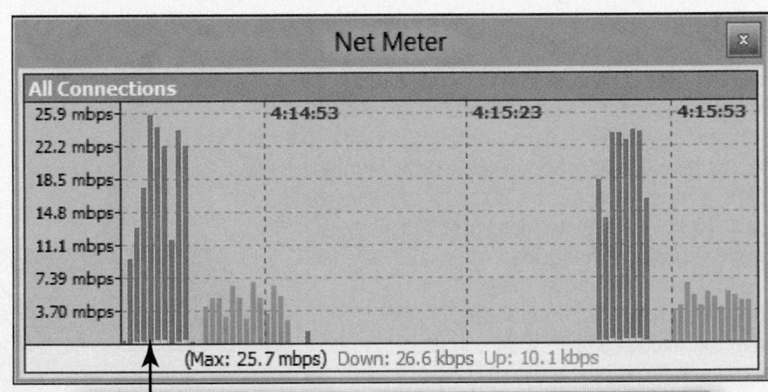

# Your Home Network

You know what a network is and the advantages of having one. In this section, we look at installing or updating a home network and keeping it safe.

## installing and configuring HOME NETWORKS

Now that you understand the basic components of a network and your Internet connection options, you're ready to install a network in your home. If you already have a network in your home, it's useful to examine your network settings and configuration to make sure they're still meeting your needs, especially if you've added new devices.

Only a few years ago, most home networks included just a few computers and a printer. However, a network that can manage those devices is often very different from one that can support the smartphones, gaming consoles, tablets, and smart TVs many homes have added to their networks since. If you're using any of these additional devices and you haven't updated your network equipment or setup in a while, it may be time to do so.

### Planning Your Home Network

**Where do I start?** One of the first things you should do to evaluate your network is list all the devices you're using, as well as any devices you think you may add in the near future. Then determine whether your network is sufficiently up to date to support all your devices.

**What wireless Ethernet standard should my network be using?** For a home network to run most efficiently and to provide the fastest experience, it's best that all network nodes—computers, network adapters (NICs), routers, and so on—use the latest Ethernet standard. Devices that support the 802.11n standard have been around for a while, so if you've bought a laptop or other portable device in the past few years, it most likely has an 802.11n NIC. However, the newest wireless standard 802.11ac is now supported on many devices.

However, your router may still be supporting the 802.11n standard. If you have the fastest 802.11ac NIC in your laptop but the router is the slower 802.11n standard, then data will be sent at the speeds supported by the lower standard. If you haven't updated your router in a while, you may want to consider getting an 802.11ac router (Figure 7.15) to get the fastest connection speeds.

Additionally, the higher standard gives your wireless signal more range, so if you feel that some of your devices aren't connecting properly to the Internet from certain parts of your home, you may want to upgrade to the higher standard.

**How can I tell what wireless standard my router supports?** You may be able to tell whether your router is supporting the faster 802.11ac standard just by looking at it. Many routers have the wireless standard indicated on the device. If you're still not sure, you can search for more information on your router by entering the model number into a search engine. If your router is provided by your ISP and it's an older standard, you should consider having your ISP provide you with a new router.

**How can I tell what network adapters are installed in my computer?** To see which network adapters are installed in your Windows computer, use the Device Manager utility (see Figure 7.16), which lists all the adapters. If you can't tell which wireless standard the adapter supports from the list, search the Internet for information on your specific adapter to determine its capability. The Device Manager can also alert you if there's a problem with the adapter.

**FIGURE 7.15** 802.11ac wireless routers offer the fastest connection speeds and a greater wireless signal range. *(Scanrail/Fotolia LLC)*

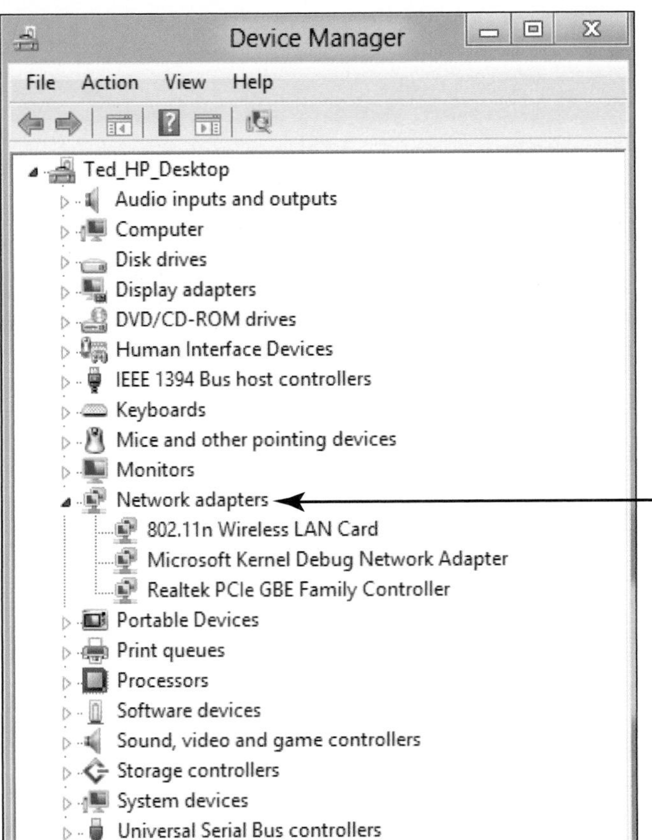


**FIGURE 7.16** The Windows Device Manager shows the wireless and wired network adapters installed on a computer.

> *To access the Device Manager, right-click the Start button to display the shortcut menu, and select* ***Control Panel****. Then click* ***Hardware and Sound****, and select* ***Device Manager*** *from the* ***Devices and Printers*** *group.*

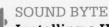

SOUND BYTE

**Installing a Home Computer Network**

Installing a network is relatively easy if you watch someone else do it. In this Sound Byte, you'll learn how to install the hardware and to configure Windows for a wired or wireless home network.

## Connecting Devices to a Router

**How can I directly connect multiple devices to my router?** Most home routers have three or four Ethernet ports on the back to support wired connections. If you have a lot of devices (such as a game console, an HDTV, and a laptop) in your home that you use at the same time, you might want to connect some of them via a wired connection to increase the bandwidth to each device.

If you need additional ports for plugging in wired connections to your network, you can buy a stand-alone switch and plug that into one of the ports on your router (see Figure 7.17). This will give you additional ports for making wired connections. However, don't mistakenly buy another router with an embedded switch and try adding that to your network. The two routers will cause conflicts as they fight for control over network navigation.

**How many wireless devices can connect to a router in a home network?** Most home wireless routers can support up to 253 wireless connections at the same time, although most home networks have far fewer. Regardless of how many devices your home network has, they all share bandwidth when they're connected to a router. Therefore, the more devices actively transmitting data that you connect to a single router, the smaller the portion of the router's bandwidth each device receives.

To look at this another way, say you have a pizza that represents your router's bandwidth. You can cut the pizza into six or eight pieces (that is, you can connect either six or eight devices to the network). If you cut the pizza into eight pieces, each person who gets a slice receives a smaller portion than if you had cut the pizza into six pieces. Similarly, when you connect eight devices to the network, each device has less bandwidth than it would if only six devices were connected to the network.

**Are wireless routers for Windows and OS X networks different?** All routers that support the 802.11n standard should work with computers running Windows or OS X. However, Apple has designed routers

**FIGURE 7.17** You can add additional ports to your network by connecting a switch to your router. *(Sergey Dashkevich/Fotolia LLC; © vladimirs - Fotolia.com; alarich/Shutterstock)*

**FIGURE 7.18** The AirPort Express router can be used for home networks to support devices running iOS, OS X and Windows. *(Apple/MCT/Newscom)*

that are optimized for working with Apple computers. So if you're connecting Apple computers to your network, you may want to use the Apple AirPort Extreme router for larger home networks, or the AirPort Express for smaller networks (see Figure 7.18). Windows machines can also connect to an AirPort router, so it's a great choice for households with both Apples and PCs. The AirPort Extreme uses the newest 802.11ac technology for the fastest data transfers. In addition, it offers the option of creating a guest network, which can use a different password or no password at all, keeping all your networked devices and files secure.

### How do I know what's connected to my router?

To determine what's connected to your router, you need to log in to an account associated with your router's IP address. You can find your router's IP address on the router manufacturer's website. Once you know it, type it into a web browser. You may need to enter a user name and password, but eventually you'll get to a configuration page that lists what wired and wireless devices are in your network. You may be surprised at all the various devices associated with your network.

Figure 7.19 shows a router network listing with wired (desktop computer) and wireless (TiVo DVR, laptop, iPhone, and iPads) devices connected in a home network. You'll notice that each device also has an IP address. You can think of your network as an apartment building. The router's IP address is the building's street address, while the IP addresses of the individual devices connected to the router are the apartment numbers. Each device needs an IP address so the router knows to which device to send information.

**FIGURE 7.19** Wired and wireless connections can use the same router.

## BITS&BYTES

### Mesh Networks: An Emerging Alternative

Have you ever heard of a *mesh network*? This emerging technology uses small radio transmitters instead of wireless routers as its network nodes. What is so great about mesh networks is that only one node needs to physically connect to a network connection, and then all other nodes can share wirelessly with each other. This connection sharing between nodes can extend almost endlessly, since one wired node can share its Internet connection wirelessly with other nearby nodes, and then those nodes can share their connection wirelessly with nodes closest to them—thus creating a "mesh" of connectivity. The truly wireless aspect of mesh networks poses several advantages to the wireless networks that are in place today: they are easier to install since few wires need to be run; they can accommodate more nodes; and they enable wireless networks to be created in outdoor and unstructured venues.

In developing nations as well as in some areas in the United States, mesh networks have helped to provide access to the Internet in a much more timely and inexpensive manner than waiting for the physical connections to be established. Mesh networks also can help promote cellular communications during times of disasters when traditional communications are halted. And if you have an Android mobile phone, you can participate in the "Serval Mesh," which allows users to send and receive information without depending on established cellular networks.

## Network-Attached Storage Devices

**What can I attach to my network to facilitate file sharing and backup of data?** **Network-attached storage (NAS) devices** are specialized devices designed to store and manage all network data. Although data can always be stored on individual hard drives in computers on a network, NAS devices provide for centralized data storage and access.

Popular for years on business networks, NAS devices are now being widely marketed for home networks (see Figure 7.20). You can think of them as specialized external hard drives, and many of them actually resemble external hard drives. NAS devices connect directly to the network through a router or switch. Specialized software is installed on computers attached to the network to ensure that all data saved to an individual computer is also stored on the NAS device as a backup.

For Apple computers, the Time Capsule is a wireless router combined with a hard drive that facilitates the backup of all computers connected to the network. The Time Capsule looks very similar to the AirPort router, and it works in conjunction with the Time Machine backup feature of OS X. If you buy a Time Capsule, you won't need to buy an AirPort router (or other router) because the Time Capsule also fulfills this function on your network. When the Time Capsule is installed on your network, Macs connected to the network will ask the user if they want to use the Time Capsule as their source for Time Machine backups. The Time Capsule is another type of NAS device.

**FIGURE 7.20** A network-attached storage device provides centralized data storage and access. *(Leslie Wilk / Alamy)*

# trends in IT

# Where Should You Store Your Files? The Cloud Is Calling!

You need to store your files where they're backed up regularly and secure. You also need to access your files whenever you need them. So should you store your files on your home network? That might work if your network-attached storage is accessible via the Internet. The latest trend, however, is to store your files in the cloud. Deciding which cloud option to use depends on a number of factors.

## For Files Currently Being Used

Having the latest version of a file accessible on any device you use is important. However, constantly saving a file on multiple devices or carrying around a flash drive can be cumbersome and time consuming. When you store your files on the cloud, you avoid the hassle of saving the same file on multiple devices.

A popular web-based application for storing files on the cloud is Dropbox. Dropbox supports computers running Windows, OS X, and Linux, as well as many smartphones and tablets. After installing the Dropbox software on your devices, any files you save in the Dropbox folder are accessible to all your other devices via the Internet. You can also share folders in Dropbox with other Dropbox users, making it ideal for group projects.

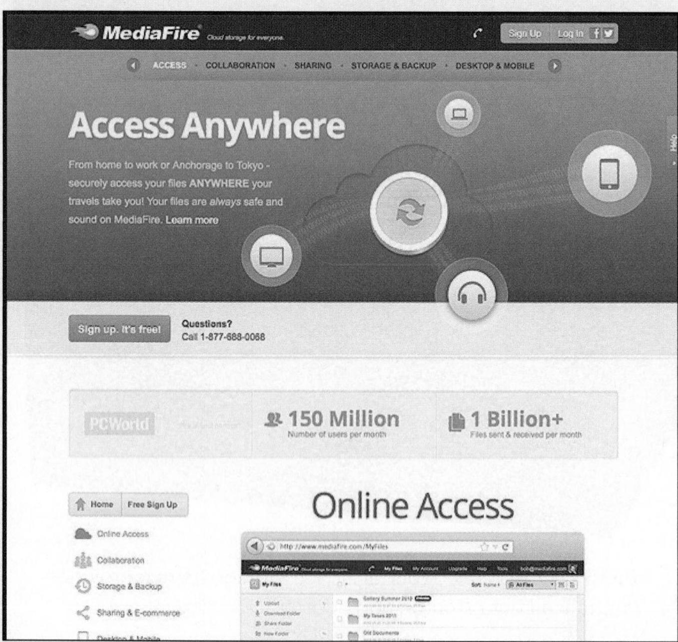


**FIGURE 7.21** MediaFire offers free storage and file sharing.
*(Courtesy of MediaFire)*

Dropbox storage capacity is limited to between 2 GB and 18 GB for free accounts. Other alternatives include Microsoft OneDrive, which provides 7 GB of free space, Google Drive, which provides 15 GB of free space, and Apple iCloud and Amazon Cloud Drive, which each offer 5 GB of free storage.

## For Media on the Go

You might like to view or listen to your media on the go, and storing it out in the cloud and streaming it over the Internet to your device may make a lot of sense. Companies like Apple and Amazon with their iCloud and Cloud Drive offerings let you store your media files on their servers. Since both iCloud and Cloud Drive offer limited amounts of space for free, these might not be the best options for large media collections.

## For Large Media Collections That Need to Be Shared

For large media collections that you want to share with others, sites like ADrive and MediaFire (Figure 7.21) are popular choices. Both MediaFire and ADrive offer up to 50 GB of storage for free. You can easily share files with other people on either site. You can also post links to the files directly to Facebook or Twitter from MediaFire. However, with the MediaFire free account, you can't upload files larger than 200 MB. This limit won't impact music or photos, but if you're planning on uploading HD movies, you'll need a pay account. MediaFire does not allow sharing of any copyrighted content.

The advantage of these sites is the amount of free storage and the sharing capabilities. The drawback is that they can't play streaming media (like iCloud and Cloud Drive can), so you need to download files before playing them.

When you choose which option is best for you, make sure to carefully investigate the site's file backup policies. Some free accounts don't feature guaranteed backups of your media, or the site might delete files that you haven't accessed for a certain period of time. The pay accounts generally guarantee that the files are backed up regularly. So don't ignore backup policies—you want your files to be there when you need them!

## Home Network Servers

**Besides external hard drives, are there other NAS devices I could use on my network?** A more sophisticated type of NAS device is a **home network server**. Home network servers are specialized devices designed to store files, share files across the network, and back up files on computers connected to the network. All computers connected to the network can access the server.

Home network servers (see Figure 7.22) often look like oversized external hard drives. They are configured with operating systems like Windows Server 2012 Essentials and connect directly as a node on your network. Home servers have more sophisticated functionality than NAS devices and often handle the following tasks:

- Automatically back up all computers connected to the network
- Act as a repository for files to be shared across the network
- Function as an access gateway to allow any computer on the network to be accessed from a remote location via the Internet (see Figure 7.23)

FIGURE 7.22 Home network servers can perform a variety of tasks that simplify file management on a home network. *(Sashkin/Fotolia)*

Note that even though these devices are servers, they don't convert a home P2P network into a client/server network because these servers don't perform all the functions performed on client/server networks. Also note that you can access the media stored on your Windows Server 2012 Essentials server through your Xbox One as long as the Xbox is also connected to your home network.

## Digital Entertainment Devices on a Network

**What kinds of digital entertainment devices can connect directly to the network?** A **network-ready device** (or Internet-ready device) can be connected directly to a network, either through a wired or wireless connection. Most game consoles, Blu-ray players, and DVRs, as well as many televisions (smart TVs) and home theater systems, are network ready. A device that is not network ready requires that the device be connected directly to another computer via a cable on the network.

**Why should I connect digital entertainment devices to my network?** One reason for connecting entertainment devices to your network is to access and share digital content between devices on your network. Connecting these devices to your network also gives them access to the Internet so you can access a lot of entertainment content, including movies, videos, and music available online.

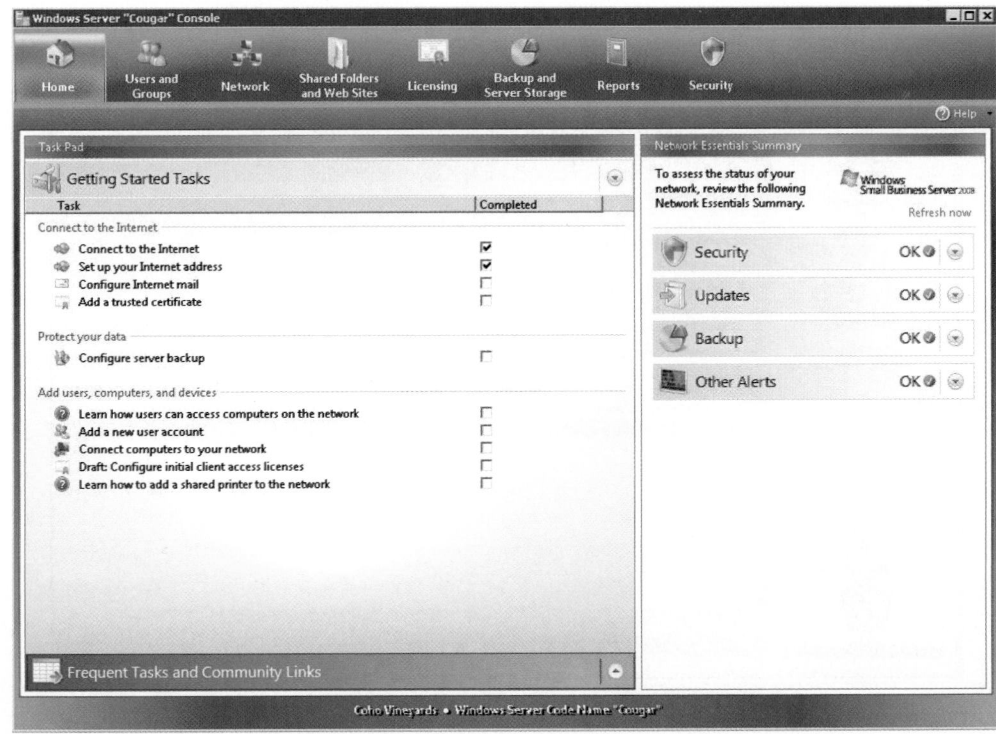


FIGURE 7.23 Windows Server 2012 Essentials home page. *(ItGroove Professional Services, Ltd.)*

You can also use gaming devices to play multiplayer games with players in the next room or all over the world. The content you access is either downloaded or streamed to your devices. Newer smart TVs and other smart devices (such as Blu-ray players, game consoles, and home theater systems) are continually adding apps and video services so that you can play games, view on-demand and online videos, listen to Internet radio, and access social networking sites (see Figure 7.24). Some smart devices also feature an integrated web browser that lets you access the web directly, without the use of apps.

**FIGURE 7.24** Smart TVs have their own apps and let you directly access the web so you can play games, connect with your social networking accounts, and view on-demand and online videos. *(STANCA SANDA / Alamy)*

**What if I don't have a smart TV?** You can get the same services on your existing television by using a Blu-ray player like the Sony 3-D Blu-ray Disc player. These Blu-ray players feature integrated wireless connectivity to receive streaming media from various ISPs in addition to having high-definition resolution and the capability to display 3-D video. Some set-top boxes, such as the LG Smart TV Upgrader, also provide the same types of connectivity as a Blu-ray player. Alternatively, you can use devices such as Apple TV or Google Chromecast that enable you to send Internet-based media to your traditional TV.

**Why should I connect my DVR to my network?** You may have a DVR, like the TiVo Premiere, which you use to record HDTV programs. Connecting your TiVo to your network makes it possible to receive downloads of movies directly to your TiVo from services such as Netflix and Amazon Instant Video. And some home network servers, like the Hewlett Packard MediaSmart servers, now work in conjunction with TiVo devices to provide them with additional storage. The TiVo Desktop software (see Figure 7.25), which you download from **tivo.com**, lets you transfer

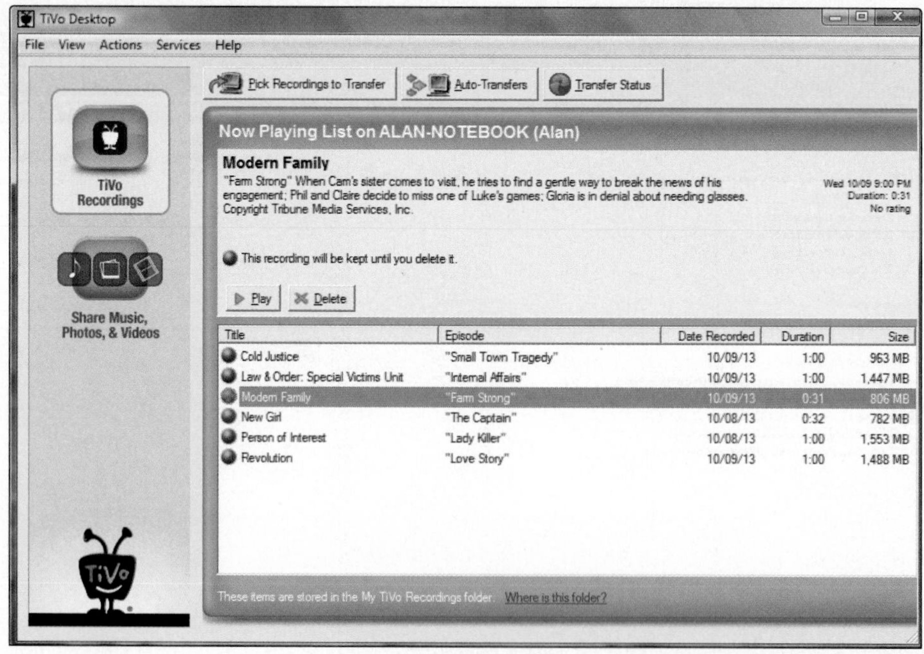


**FIGURE 7.25** The TiVo Desktop software facilitates transfer of recorded shows to portable devices so you can enjoy your content on the go. *(TiVo® and the TiVo logo are trademarks of TiVo Inc. and its subsidiaries worldwide)*

FIGURE 7.26 The Remote Play feature of the PS Vita 4 lets you access PS4 features, like the PlayStation Store, directly from your Vita. *(Kyodo/AP Images)*

shows recorded on your TiVo to your computer or portable devices.

**Why should I connect my gaming consoles to my home network?** Current gaming systems, like the PlayStation 4 (PS4), can function as a total entertainment platform when connected to the Internet through your network. The PS4 has a built-in Blu-ray drive and can play Blu-ray discs, DVDs, and music files. You can download movies, games, and videos from the Internet directly to the PS4. You can also use it to share media across your network and to import photos or video from cameras and phones.

If you have a PS Vita, you can use an application called Remote Play (see Figure 7.26) to access features of your PS4 from your Vita. You can use the Vita to turn your PS4 on and off; access photos, music, and video files; play games; and browse the Internet. Media is transmitted from your PS4 and displayed on the Vita screen.

## Specialized Home-Networking Devices

**How can I use my home network to share photos?** Digital picture frames that display photos are popular, and some, such as the Kodak Pulse Digital Frame, come with built-in wireless adapters for easy connection to home networks. Featuring a touch-screen interface, this frame can access photos stored on your network or on an online photo-sharing site and display them. You can even set up an e-mail address for the picture frame so that friends and family can e-mail pictures directly to the frame.

**How can I use my home network to enhance my home security?** Monitoring cameras, both for indoor and outdoor use, are now available for the home that feature wireless connectivity so you can keep track of your home while you're away. You can connect these cameras to your network and monitor them in real time through software like the Logitech Alert System using portable devices such as an iPhone or Android phone (see Figure 7.27).

FIGURE 7.27 Logitech security systems can help you monitor your home's security from your mobile devices. *(Logitech)*

The software can be configured to alert you via e-mail or text message when the cameras detect movement, such as a vehicle entering your driveway. Some systems also allow you to receive alerts when there is a lack of movement. This can be useful for monitoring an aging relative or for monitoring the arrival of children coming home from school.

As time goes on, many more types of entertainment devices and home gadgets will be connected to your home network.

## Configuring Software for Your Home Network

**How do I set up a Windows home network for the first time?** In Windows, the process of setting up a network is fairly automated, especially if you're using the same version of Windows on all your computers. The Windows examples in this section assume all computers are running Windows 8.1. You can launch the Windows network setup wizards from the Network and Sharing Center, which you access via the Network and Internet group in the Control Panel. Before configuring the computers to the network, do the following:

1. Make sure there are network adapters on each node.
2. For any wired connections, plug all the cables into the router, nodes, and so on.
3. Make sure your broadband modem is connected to your router and that the modem is connected to the Internet.
4. Turn on your equipment in the following order (allowing the modem and the router about one minute each to power up) and configure:
   a. Your broadband modem
   b. Your router
   c. All computers and peripherals (printers, scanners, and so on)

You can add other devices, such as TVs, Blu-ray players, and gaming consoles, to the network after you configure the computers.

After you've completed the previous steps, open the Network and Sharing Center from the Control Panel (see Figure 7.28):

- If your computer has a wired connection to the network, you should automatically be connected. You should give the network the same secured name you give to your router (see *Troubleshooting Wireless Network Problems on page 286*).
- If you're connecting wirelessly, click Connect to a Network in the Network and Sharing Center. The Networks panel opens on the right side of your screen, displaying the wired and wireless connection options. You will need to enter your security passphrase to connect to your wireless network initially.

**How do I share files with other computers on my network?** For ease of file and peripheral sharing, Windows 7 created a feature known as *homegroup* that has carried over to Windows 8. The homegroup is a software device that makes it easier to allow computers on a Windows 8 network to share peripherals and information. To create a homegroup after connecting your first Windows 8 computer to your network, complete the steps outlined in Figure 7.29.

**What if I don't have the same version of Windows on all my computers?** Computers with various versions of Windows can coexist on the same network. Always set up the computers running the newest version of Windows first. Then consult the Microsoft website for guidance on how to configure computers with previous versions of Windows.

**How do I connect a mobile device to a wireless network?** Connecting a mobile device, regardless of its operating system, to a wireless network is an easy process these days. When you boot up your device, your device will display a list of available networks that the NIC in your device detects. On Macs, the list pops up in the network login screen. On Windows 8 machines, you can click on the Internet access icon in the system tray to display available networks, or click the Settings charm button in Windows 8, to display network

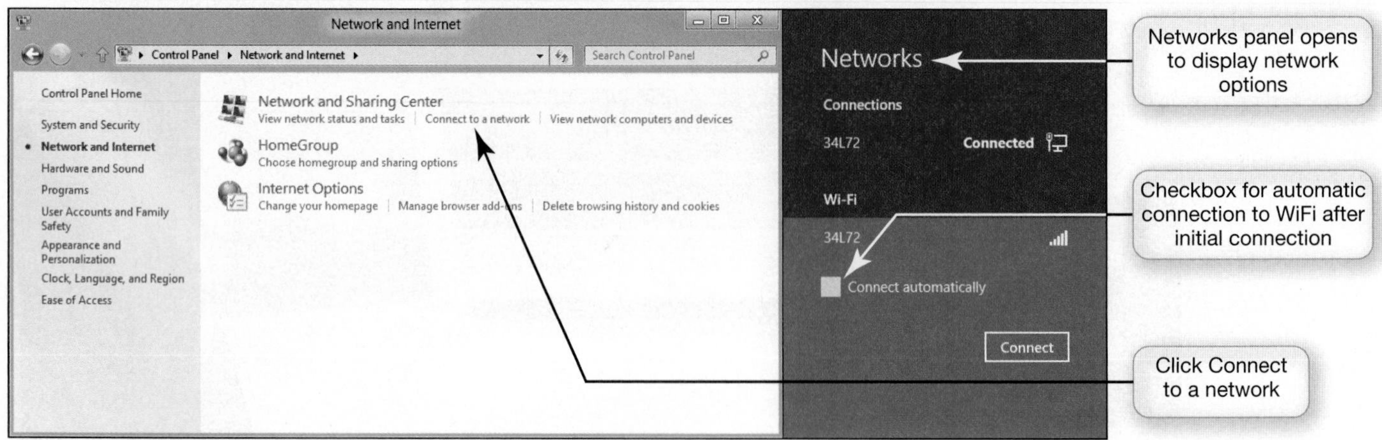


**FIGURE 7.28** Connecting a Windows 8.1 computer to a network for the first time is fairly automated.

FIGURE 7.29

## Creating a Homegroup in Windows 8

### CREATING A HOMEGROUP IN WINDOWS 8

**Step 1:** Click **Create a homegroup** in the HomeGroup window (accessed from the Network and Internet group in the Control Panel).

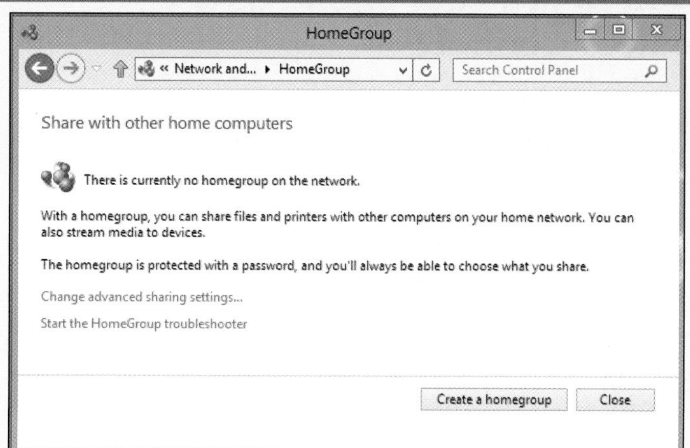


**Step 2:** Choose the sharing options for computers that belong to the homegroup. You can choose to share pictures, music, videos, documents, and printers with other Windows computers that belong to the homegroup. Although these are global settings for every computer in the homegroup, you can change these settings on individual computers if you wish.

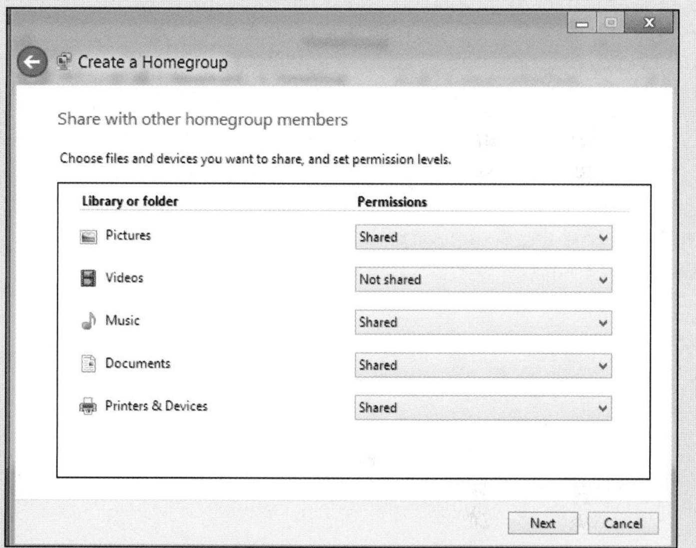


**Step 3:** Windows generates a password. All other computers added to the network will need this password to join the homegroup. Once you've created the homegroup on the first computer, it will belong to that homegroup. You can then begin connecting other Windows computers to the network and join them to the homegroup you created.

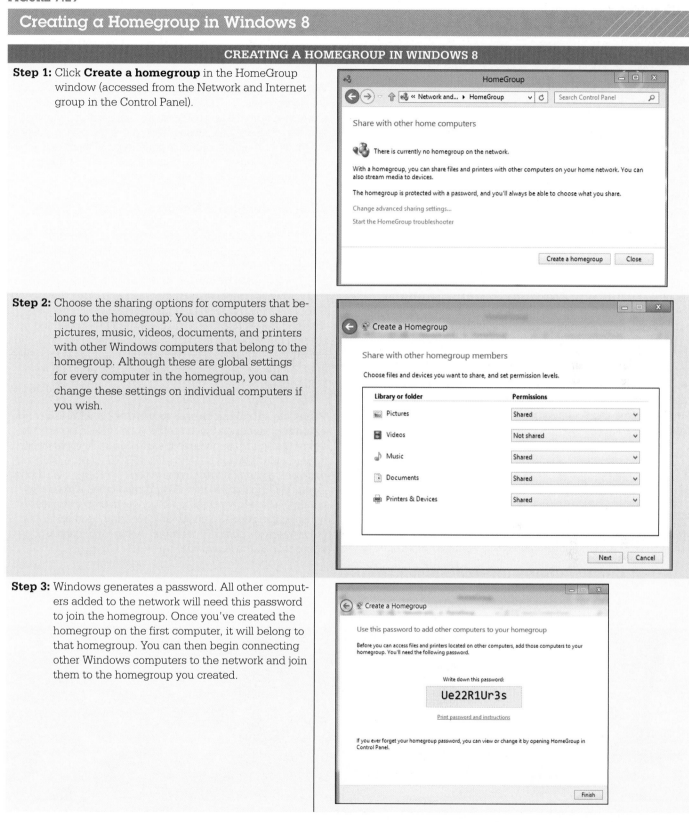

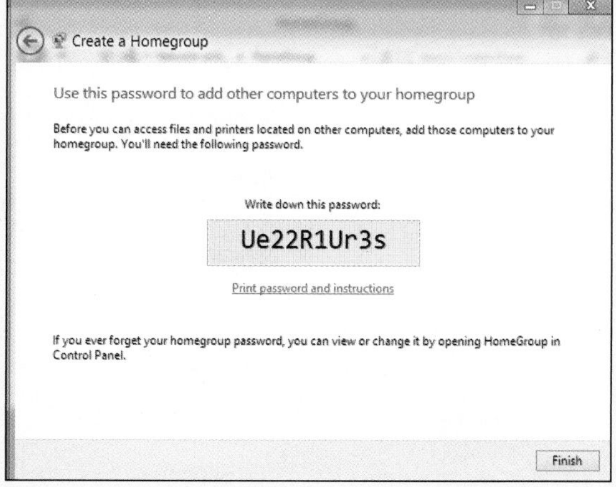

## BITS&BYTES

### Want to Use Your Phone as a Remote Control?

Companies are developing apps that let your portable devices act as remote controls. In fact, apps exist to allow both iOS and Android devices to control televisions, DVRs, and cable boxes over your WiFi network. Using a tablet or phone as a remote control offers a color, touch-sensitive interface for controlling your electronics. Check the manufacture's website for more details on downloading these apps.

connections. If there is a padlock icon next to the network name, this means that the network is secure and will require a password. Enter the password for the network in the password box, and click the Join button. For unsecure networks, you don't need a password. Checking the "Remember this network" check box will make any network a preferred network, enabling the computer to connect to the network automatically when that network is available. You can have multiple preferred networks, such as your home, school, work, and local coffee shop networks.

## Troubleshooting Wireless Network Problems

**What types of problems can I run into when installing wireless networks?** The maximum range of 802.11n or 802.11ac wireless devices is about 350 feet. But as you go farther away from your router, the throughput you achieve decreases. Obstacles between wireless nodes also decrease throughput. Walls, floors, and large metal objects (such as refrigerators) are the most common sources of interference with wireless signals.

**What if a node on the network seems slow?** Repositioning the node within the same room (sometimes even just a few inches from the original position) can affect communication between nodes. If this doesn't work, move the device closer to the router or to another room in your house. If these solutions don't work, consider using a dual-band N router or adding a wireless range extender to your network.

**What's a dual-band N router?** A dual-band N router allows for simultaneous support for both 2.4 GHz and 5 GHz frequency bands for 802.11n and all prior 802.11 standards (a, b, and g). Traditional routers only support one signal band at a time, so they're more likely to experience interference by outside devices (such as cell phones or microwave ovens) using the same bandwidth. Dual-band N routers allow for simultaneous access to both frequencies and therefore provide maximum flexibility in setting up a home network. For example, data transfers can be set to run on the 2.4 GHz side without impacting the performance of 802.11n clients that might be streaming video on the 5 GHz band.

**What's a wireless range extender?** A **wireless range extender** is a device that amplifies your wireless signal to extend to parts of your home that are experiencing poor connectivity. For example, as shown in Figure 7.30, Laptop C on the back porch can't connect to the wireless network even though Computer B in the den can. By placing a range extender in the den, where there is still good connectivity to the wireless network, the wireless signal is amplified and beamed farther out to the back porch. This allows Laptop C to make a good connection to the network. ■

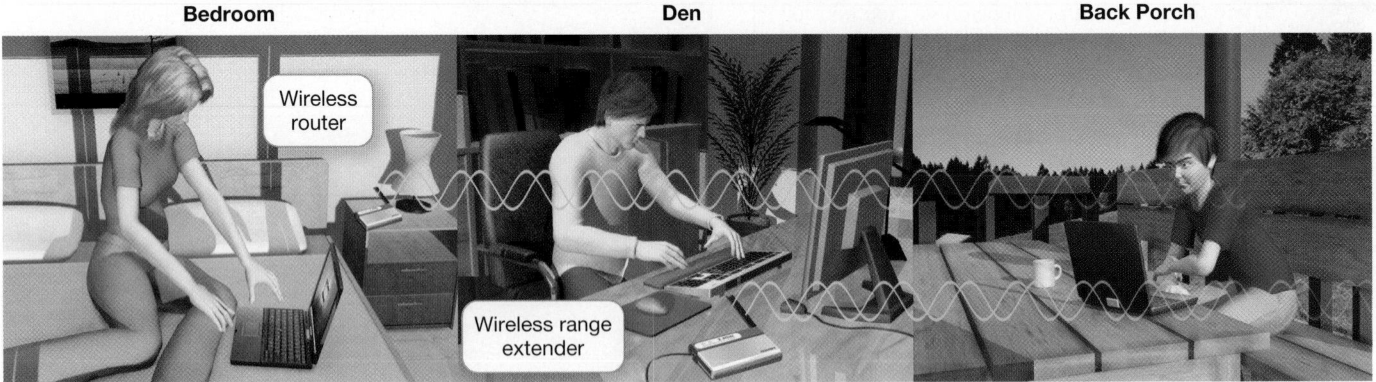


**FIGURE 7.30** Because a wireless range extender is installed in the den, Laptop C on the back porch can now connect to the wireless network.

# ethics in IT

# Sharing Your Internet Connection with Your Neighbors: Legal? Ethical? Safe?

With the advances in wireless equipment, signals can travel well beyond the walls of your home. This makes it possible for a group of neighbors to share a wireless signal and potentially save money by splitting the cost of one Internet connection among them. However, before jumping into this venture, you need to weigh a few issues carefully:

- **State and local laws:** You probably aren't legally prohibited from sharing an Internet connection, but check on state and local laws. Most laws are designed to prohibit piggy using a network without the network owner's consent. However, if you're giving neighbors permission to share your connection, you probably aren't violating any piggybacking laws.
- **ISP restrictions:** The terms of your agreement with your ISP might prohibit you from sharing your connection with people outside your household. If you aren't allowed to share the type of account you have now, your ISP probably offers an account (such as a small business account) that lets you share a connection, but it will most likely be more expensive. You might be able to share a personal account without being detected by your ISP, but that would be unethical because you should be paying for a higher level of access.
- **Range of access:** You also need to consider whether the shared access should be open to all neighbors or just to the neighbors contributing to the cost of the Internet connection (see Figure 7.31). You could leave the connection open, like the connections at your local coffee shop, and let anyone who finds it log on and surf. You could register your free hotspot with a service like JiWire (**jiwire.com**), and then people would be able to find it. However, neighbors who are helping pay for the connection might not want to fund free surfing for everyone. Make sure you work this out before proceeding.
- **Security:** If you're going to host a free and open hotspot, you need to make sure you set it up safely. You want to maintain a secure network for you and your neighbors while still allowing the occasional visiting surfer to use the connection. There are WiFi sharing services such as Fon (**corp.fon.com**) and Chillifire (**chillifire.net**) that provide hardware and software that let you configure your hotspot so your network remains secure.

Although offering free access to anyone will earn you lots of good karma, additional risks exist because you don't know what mischief or criminal activities someone might engage in while connected to the Internet through your account. Think carefully before you proceed down the sharing path, and make sure you set up your hotspot to protect your internal network.

**FIGURE 7.31** The first network listed is the home network; the other networks are from neighbors (and have much weaker signals).

# securing wireless NETWORKS

All computers that connect to the Internet, whether or not they're on a network, need to be secured from intruders. This is usually accomplished by using a firewall, which is a hardware or software solution that helps shield your network from prying eyes. (We discuss firewalls at length in Chapter 9.) Wireless networks present special vulnerabilities; therefore, you should take additional steps to keep your wireless network safe. If you're setting up a new network, it's wise to take these precautions *as you set up your network*. If you have a network already installed, check to be sure you've followed the guidelines discussed here.

**Why is a wireless network more vulnerable than a wired network?** With a wired network, it's fairly easy to tell if a **hacker**, someone who breaks into computer systems to create mischief or steal information, is using your network. However, the newer wireless 802.11 networks have wide ranges that may extend outside your house. This makes it possible for a hacker to access your network without your knowledge.

Also, in some areas where residences are close together, wireless signals can reach a neighbor's residence. Most wireless network adapters are set up to access the strongest wireless network signal detected. **Piggybacking** is connecting to a wireless network without the permission of the owner. This practice is illegal in many jurisdictions but often happens inadvertently between neighbors.

**Why should I be worried about someone logging onto my wireless network without my permission?** If your neighbor is using your network connection, his or her usage could be slowing down your connection speed. Some neighbors might even be computer savvy enough to penetrate your unprotected wireless network and steal personal information, just as any other hackers would. And any cyberattacks or illegal behavior a hacker initiates from your wireless network could get you in trouble with the authorities.

**How is my wireless network vulnerable?** Packets of information on a wireless network are broadcast through the airwaves. Savvy hackers can intercept and decode information from your transmissions that may allow them to bypass standard protections, such as a firewall, that you have set up on your network. Therefore, to secure a wireless network, take the additional precautions described in the Sound Byte "Securing Wireless Networks" and summarized as follows:

1. **Change your network name (SSID).** Each wireless network has its own name to identify it, known as the **service set identifier (SSID)**. Unless you change this name when you set up your router, the router uses a default network name that all routers from that manufacturer use (such as "Wireless" or "Netgear"). Hackers know the default names and access codes for routers. If you haven't changed the SSID, it's advertising the fact that you probably haven't changed any of the other default settings for your router either.
2. **Disable SSID broadcast.** Most routers are set up to broadcast their SSIDs so that other wireless devices can find them. If your router supports disabling SSID broadcasting, turn it off. This makes it more difficult for a hacker to detect your network and nearly impossible for a neighbor to inadvertently connect to your network.
3. **Change the default password on your router.** Routers have default user names and passwords. Hackers can use these to access your router and break into your network. Change the password on your router to something hard to guess. Use at least eight characters that are a combination of letters, symbols, and numbers.
4. **Turn on security protocols.** Most routers ship with security protocols such as Wired Equivalent Privacy (WEP) or Wi-Fi Protected Access (WPA). Both use encryption (a method of translating your data into code) to protect data in your wireless transmissions. WPA is a much stronger protocol than WEP, so enable WPA if you have it; enable WEP if you don't.
5. **Create a passphrase.** When you enable these protocols, you're forced to create a security encryption key (passphrase). When you attempt to connect a node to a security-enabled network for the first time, you're required to enter the security key. The security key or passphrase (see Figure 7.32) is the code that computers on your network need to decrypt (decode) data transmissions. Without this key, it's extremely difficult, if not impossible, to decrypt the data transmissions from your network. The Windows 8 Connect to a Network dialog box shows all wireless networks within range. Moving your cursor over the network name will reveal details about the network such as whether it's a secured network. Clicking on a network name allows you to connect to it or prompts you for more information such as the SSID name and security key.

SOUND BYTE
**Securing Wireless Networks**

In this Sound Byte, you'll learn some simple steps to secure your wireless network against intruders.

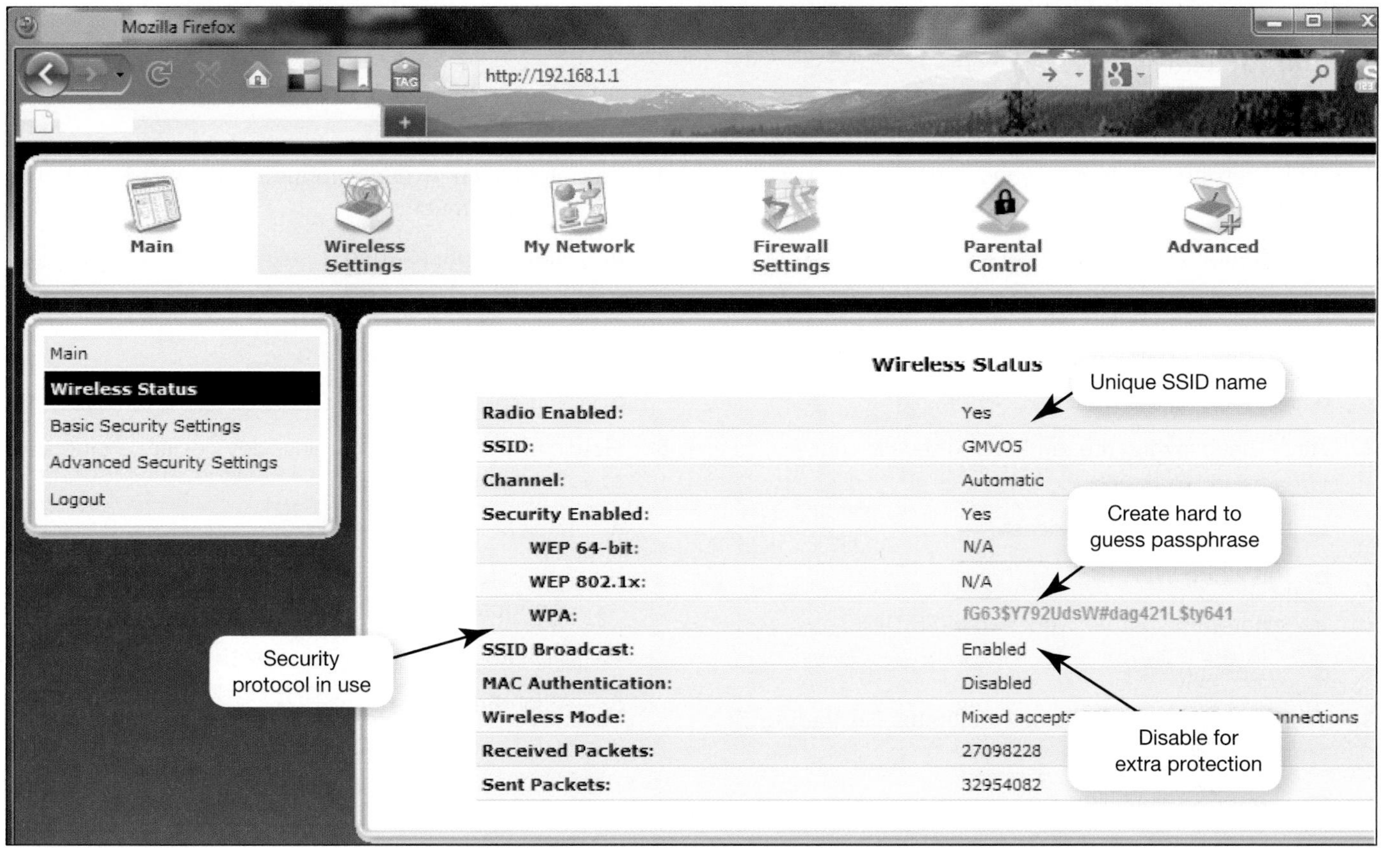


**FIGURE 7.32** By accessing your router, you can configure the security protocols available on your router and change the SSID. *(Courtesy of the Mozilla Foundation)*

6. **Implement media access control.** Each network adapter on your network has a unique number (like a serial number) assigned to it by the manufacturer. This is called a media access control (MAC) address, and it's a number printed right on the network adapter. Many routers allow you to restrict access to the network to only certain MAC addresses. This helps ensure that only authorized devices can connect to your network.
7. **Limit your signal range.** Many routers allow you to adjust the transmitting power to low, medium, or high. Cutting down the power to low or medium could prevent your signal from reaching too far away from your home, making it tougher for interlopers to poach your signal.
8. **Apply firmware upgrades.** Your router has read-only memory that has software written to it. This software is known as **firmware**. As bugs are found in the firmware (which hackers might exploit), manufacturers issue patches, just as the makers of operating system software do. Periodically check the manufacturer's website and apply any necessary upgrades to your firmware.

If you follow these steps, you'll greatly improve the security of your wireless network. In Chapter 9, we'll explore many other ways to keep your computer safe from malicious individuals on the Internet and ensure that your digital information is secure. ■

**Before moving on to the Chapter Review:**
- **Watch Replay Video 7.2** .
- Then check your understanding of what you've learned so far.

# check your understanding//

For a quick review to see what you've learned so far, answer the following questions. Visit **pearsonhighered.com/techinaction** to check your answers.

## multiple choice

**1.** When setting up a home network, the router is attached

- **a.** directly to the broadband modem.
- **b.** directly to the NIC in each device.
- **c.** directly to the Internet.
- **d.** directly to the Ethernet switch.

**2.** All of the following are methods to secure your wireless network except

- **a.** disabling SSID broadcast.
- **b.** enabling WPA.
- **c.** changing your network name (SSID).
- **d.** disabling WEP.

**3.** Which network-ready device facilitates file sharing and data backup?

- **a.** home network server
- **b.** Time Capsule
- **c.** network-attached storage
- **d.** all of the above

**4.** To share files between computers on a Windows home network, you must

- **a.** enable groupsharing.
- **b.** create a homegroup.
- **c.** enable Windows sharing.
- **d.** None of the above

**5.** How can you tell what wireless devices are connected to your router?

- **a.** Look at the router itself.
- **b.** Log in to the router's IP address and check the configuration page.
- **c.** Look at the device wireless settings.
- **d.** All of the above.

## true–false

_____ **1.** A dual-band N router is an option when trying to improve wireless network performance.

_____ **2.** Home network servers are a specialized type of NAS device.

## critical thinking

**1. Protecting Yourself on Public Wireless Networks**

Many people use free public wireless networks to access the Internet. But many public networks don't have adequate security or may be under surveillance by hackers. To protect your sensitive data, there are certain activities you should not engage in while on public networks. What types of activities should you avoid on a public network? What types of information should you only process on your secure home network?

**2. Evaluating Your Network Configuration**

Write down all the devices you believe currently connect to your home network, either wired or wirelessly. Make sure you consider smartphones, tablets, laptops, desktops, gaming consoles, DVRs, smart TVs, and printers. Are there devices (such as printers or TVs) that are not currently able to connect directly to your network that you might want to replace? If so, note those devices, and describe the advantages a network-ready replacement would bring. Are there other devices you might also want to consider adding to your network that you don't currently have, such as a home-monitoring system? If so, why would they be helpful?

# 7 Chapter Review

## summary//

### Networking Fundamentals

**1. What is a network, and what are a network's advantages and disadvantages?**

- A computer network is simply two or more computers that are connected using software and hardware so they can communicate.
- Advantages of networks include allowing users to
  - share an Internet connection,
  - share printers and other peripheral devices,
  - share files, and
  - communicate with computers regardless of their operating system.
- Disadvantages for larger networks are that they require administration and that they may require costly equipment.

### Network Architecture and Components

**2. What are the different ways to classify networks?**

- Networks can be defined by the distance between nodes:
  - A personal area network (PAN) is used for communication among personal mobile devices using Bluetooth or WiFi wireless technologies.
  - A local area network (LAN) connects nodes that are located in a small geographic area.
  - A home area network (HAN) is a specific type of LAN located in a home.
  - A metropolitan area network (MAN) is a large network in a specific geographic area.
  - A wide area network (WAN) spans a large physical distance.
- Networks are classified by administration:
  - Central: A client/server network contains two types of computers: a client computer on which users perform specific tasks and a server computer that provides resources to the clients and central control for the network. Most networks that have 10 or more nodes are client/server networks.
  - Local: Peer-to-peer (P2P) networks enable each node connected to the network to communicate directly with every other node. Most home networks are P2P networks.

**3. Which type of network is most commonly found in the home?**

- Ethernet networks are the most common networks used in home networking.
- Most Ethernet networks use a combination of wired and wireless connections, depending on the data throughput required. Wired connections usually achieve higher throughput than wireless connections.
- Wired Ethernet home networks use the gigabit Ethernet standard.
- Wireless Ethernet networks are identified by a protocol standard: 802.11 a/b/g/n/ac.
  - 802.11ac is the newest standard.
  - WiGig (802.11ad) is a new wireless link between devices. WiGig is similar to but faster than Bluetooth.

**4. What are the main components of every network?**

- To function, any network must contain a number of components:
  - A means of connecting the nodes on the network (cables or wireless technology)
  - Special hardware devices that allow the nodes to communicate with each other and to send data
  - Software that allows the network to run

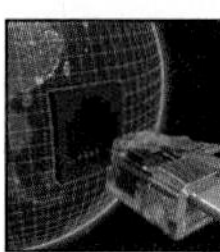

### Connecting to the Internet

**5. What are my options for connecting to the Internet?**

- Wired networks use various types of cable to connect nodes. The type of network and the distance between the nodes determines the type of cable used. Broadband connections include the following types:
  - Cable transmits data over coaxial cable that is also used for cable television.
  - DSL uses twisted-pair wire, similar to that used for telephones.
  - Fiber-optic cable uses glass or plastic strands to transmit data via light signals.
  - Satellite is a connection option for those who do not have access to faster broadband technologies. Data is transmitted between a satellite dish and a satellite that is in a geosynchronous orbit.

- WiFi allows users to connect to the Internet wirelessly but is not as fast as a wired connection.
  - Mobile broadband is a 3G or 4G service delivered by cell-phone networks.
- Dial-up is the cheapest means of accessing the Internet, but it is also the slowest.

## Installing and Configuring Home Networks

**6. How do I tell if my home network is up to date, and how do I identify the devices on the network?**

- Most home network routers should support both wireless and wired access to the Internet.
- For a home network to run efficiently, all nodes such as NICs and routers should use the same Ethernet standard.
- The Device Manager utility in Windows lists all adapters installed on your computer.

**7. Besides computers, what other devices can I connect to a home network?**

- All devices are connected to your router, either wirelessly or with a wired connection. Wired connections deliver better throughput than wireless.
- To add additional ports to your network, you can connect a switch to your router.
- Network-attached storage (NAS) devices let you store and share data files such as movies and music, as well as provide a central place for file backups. Home network servers can be used instead of an NAS device if your needs require more sophisticated functionality than NAS devices.
- Connecting digital entertainment devices (such as gaming consoles) lets you stream movies and other entertainment directly from the Internet.

**8. How do I configure the software on my computer and set up the devices required to get my network up and running?**

- The latest versions of Windows make it easy to set up wired and wireless networks.
  - Plug in the modem, the router, and all cables, and then switch on the modem, router, and computers (in that order).
  - Launch the Network and Sharing Center, and select the appropriate links for setup.
  - Make sure each computer has a distinct name, and ensure that all computers are in the same homegroup.
  - Devices such as gaming consoles each have their own setup procedures for connecting to wireless networks but usually require the same information as that needed for connecting a computer to a secured wireless network.

**9. What problems might I encounter when setting up a wireless network?**

- You may not get the throughput you need through a wireless connection. Therefore, you may need to consider a wired connection for certain devices.
- Distance from the router, as well as walls, floors, and large metal objects between a device and the router, can interfere with wireless connectivity.
- To solve connectivity problems, dual-band N routers allow for simultaneous support for devices running on both the 2.4 GHz and 5 GHz frequency bands for 802.11n standards. Wireless range extenders can amplify signals to improve connectivity in areas of poor signal strength.

## Securing Wireless Networks

**10. Why are wireless networks more vulnerable to security risks than wired networks, and what special precautions are required to ensure my wireless network is secure?**

- Wireless networks are even more susceptible to hacking than wired networks because the signals of most wireless networks extend beyond the walls of your home.
- Neighbors may unintentionally (or intentionally) connect to the Internet through your wireless connection, and hackers may try to access it.
- To prevent unwanted intrusions into your network, you should change the default password on your router to make it tougher for hackers to gain access, use a hard-to-guess SSID (network name), disable SSID broadcasting to make it harder for outsiders to detect your network, enable security protocols such as WPA or WEP, create a network passphrase, implement media access control, limit your signal range, and apply firmware upgrades.

Be sure to check out the companion website for additional materials to help you review and learn, including a Tech Bytes Weekly newsletter—**pearsonhighered.com/techinaction**. And don't forget the Replay Videos.

# key terms//

4G **271**
backward compatibility **264**
bandwidth **261**
broadband **269**
cable Internet **269**
Cat 6 cable **266**
client/server network **263**
coaxial cable **265**
data transfer rate **261**
digital subscriber line (DSL) **269**
Ethernet network **264**
fiber-optic cable **265**
fiber-optic service **269**
firmware **289**
gigabit Ethernet **264**
hacker **288**
home area network (HAN) **263**
home network server **281**
Internet service provider (ISP) **269**
local area network (LAN) **262**
metropolitan area network (MAN) **263**
mobile broadband **271**
network **260**
network adapter **267**
network administration **261**
network architecture **262**
network-attached storage (NAS) device **279**
network interface card (NIC) **267**
network navigation device **267**
network operating system (NOS) **268**
network-ready device **281**
node **260**
packet **267**
peer-to-peer (P2P) network **263**
personal area network (PAN) **262**
piggybacking **288**
router **267**
satellite Internet **270**
service set identifier (SSID) **288**
switch **267**
throughput **261**
transmission media **265**
twisted-pair cable **265**
unshielded twisted-pair (UTP) cable **265**
wide area network (WAN) **263**
wireless fidelity (WiFi) **264**
wireless range extender **286**

# making the transition to . . . next semester//

1. **Dormitory Networking**

   Often, you and your college suitemates are all on the Internet at the same time downloading movies or other large files, which causes your network's performance to slow down considerably. You realize you need to update your router to the faster 802.11ac standard. In addition, you've agreed to buy a printer that you all can share, and someone has suggested also getting shared backup storage.

   **a.** Research network-ready laser printers on sites such as **hp.com**, **epson.com**, and **brother.com**. What network-ready printer would you recommend? Why?

   **b.** Research 802.11ac wireless routers at sites such as **netgear.com**, **home.cisco.com/en-us/home**, and **dlink.com**. What router do you think will meet your needs? Why?

   **c.** What would you recommend to address backup needs? Would you recommend individual external devices, an NAS device, a home network server, or cloud storage? What is the rationale for your choice?

2. **Connecting Your Computer to Public Networks**

   You're working for a local coffee shop that offers free wireless access to customers. Your supervisor has asked you to create a flyer for patrons that warns them of the potential dangers of surfing the Internet in public places. Conduct research about using public hotspots to access the Internet. Prepare a flyer that lists specific steps that customers can take to protect their data when surfing on publicly accessible networks.

# making the transition to . . . the workplace//

1. **Mesh Networks**

   In the Bits & Bytes feature on page 279, you read about mesh networks and how they can offer a viable solution to providing Internet access to economically depressed and undeveloped areas around the world. In addition, mesh networks are providing Internet access that is less susceptible to government intervention. Investigate how mesh networks have been used by political activists. Do you think these types of networks serve a positive purpose? Why or why not?

2. **Putting Computers to Work on Research Projects**

   Most computer central processing units (CPUs) use only a fraction of their computing power most of the time. Many medical research companies (such as those seeking cures for cancer and AIDS) could benefit from "borrowing" computer CPU time when computers are not being used or are being underutilized. Virtual supercomputers (which are really networks of computers) can be created using software installed on tens of thousands of computers. This type of computing is also known as *grid* or *distributed computing*. These virtual computing nets can be harnessed to solve complex problems when the individual computer owners are not using their computers. Assume that you are working for a business that has 100 computers and you would like to participate in a grid-computing project. Investigate IBM's World Community Grid (WCG; **worldcommunitygrid.org**). Prepare a report for your boss that does the following:

   **a.** Describes the WCG and its objectives

   **b.** Lists current projects on which the WCG is working

   **c.** Describes the process for installing the WCG software on the company's computers

   **d.** Suggests a strategy for publicizing the company's participation in the WCG project that will encourage your employer's customers to participate

# Providing Wireless Internet Access to the Needy

## Problem

Wireless Internet access in the home is very desirable. However, not everyone is able to afford it, and this can put families, especially ones with school-aged children, at a disadvantage. Providing Internet access to the underprivileged is a way of closing the "digital divide" that exists between those who can afford Internet access and those who cannot.

## Task

You're volunteering for a charity that wants to begin installing wireless networks in homes for needy families. The project is funded by charitable grants with the objective of providing basic broadband Internet access and simple networking capabilities at no cost to the recipients. The assumption is that each family already has two laptop computers (provided through another charity) that have 802.11ac wireless capabilities. You've volunteered to research potential network and Internet solutions.

## Process

Break the class into three teams. Each team will be responsible for investigating one of the following issues:

1. **Internet service providers:** Research ISPs that serve the town where your school is located (don't forget to include satellite providers). Compare and contrast their lowest-cost broadband access. Compare maximum upload and download speeds as well as costs. Be sure to consider the cost of the modems—whether they're purchased up front or rented on a monthly basis. Make sure to select what your group considers the best deal.
2. **Networking equipment and network-ready peripherals:** Each home needs to be provided with an 802.11ac-capable wireless router (to share the Internet access), a network-ready all-in-one printer, and a Blu-ray player capable of streaming digital video (for educational programs and movies). Research at least three different options for each of these devices. Since this is a grant and money is limited, be sure to consider price as well as functionality.
3. **Security:** The wireless networks need to be secured to keep hackers and piggybackers out. Work in conjunction with the group that is researching routers to determine the best type of router to purchase since it needs to support a strong wireless security protocol such as WPA. Make sure to consider what other types of protection are needed on the network, such as antivirus software, anti-malware software, and firewalls.

Present your findings to your class and come to a consensus about the solution you would propose for the charity. Provide your instructor with a report on your area suitable for presentation to the CEO of the charity.

## Conclusion

Providing technology to underserved populations on a cost-effective basis will go a long way toward closing the digital divide and ensuring that disadvantaged youth have the Internet access they need to pursue their education and compete effectively in today's society.

# Firing Employees for Expressing Views on Social Media Sites

In this exercise, you'll research and then role-play a complicated ethical situation. The role you play may or may not match your own personal beliefs; regardless, your research and use of logic will enable you to represent the view assigned. An arbitrator will watch and comment on both sides of the arguments, and together the team will agree on an ethical solution.

## Problem

The largest network, the Internet, provides the capability for vast social interaction. Social media sites such as Facebook, YouTube, and Twitter, as well as blogs and wikis, give everyone convenient ways to express their opinions. However, employers often are intolerant of employees who freely express negative opinions or expose inside information about their employers on social media sites. Given that most jurisdictions in the United States use the doctrine of employment at will (that is, employees can be fired at any time for any reason, or even no reason), many employers are quick to discipline or terminate employees who express opinions with which the company disagrees. When such cases come to court, the courts often find in favor of the employers. It's clear that individuals must exercise extreme care when posting work-related content.

## Research Areas to Consider

- Ellen Simonetti and Delta Airlines
- Fired for blogging about work
- Free speech
- Joyce Park or Michael Tunison

## Process

1. Divide the class into teams.
2. Research the areas cited above and devise a scenario in which someone has complained about an employee blogging about a sensitive workplace issue such as cleanliness at a food manufacturing facility or employee romances.
3. Team members should write a summary that provides background information for their character—for example, employee, human resources manager, or arbitrator—and that details their character's behaviors to set the stage for the role-playing event. Then, team members should create an outline to use during the role-playing event.
4. Team members should arrange a mutually convenient time to meet for the exchange, using a virtual meeting tool or by meeting in person.
5. Team members should present their case to the class or submit a PowerPoint presentation for review by the rest of the class, along with the summary and resolution they developed.

## Conclusion

As technology becomes ever more prevalent and integrated into our lives, more and more ethical dilemmas will present themselves. Being able to understand and evaluate both sides of the argument, while responding in a personally or socially ethical manner, will be an important skill.

# Technology in Focus Under the Hood

Some people are drawn to understanding things in detail; others are happy just to have things work. If you use a computer, you may not have been tempted to "look under the hood." However, if you can understand the hardware inside a computer, you'll have some real advantages:

- You won't have to pay a technician to fix or upgrade your computer. You'll be able to fine-tune it yourself, and you'll be able to make your investment in your computer last longer.
- You'll be able to evaluate new advances in technology. For example, what's the impact of a new type of memory or a new processor?
- If you're a programmer, you'll be able to write more efficient and faster programs.

And if you're preparing for a career in information technology, understanding computer hardware is critical for you. In this Technology in Focus feature, we'll build on what you've learned about computer hardware in other chapters and go "under the hood" to look at the components of your system unit in more detail. Let's begin by looking at the building blocks of computers: switches.

(Lepp/Corbis)

## Switches

How does a computer process the data you input? A computer system can be viewed as an enormous collection of on/off switches. These simple on/off switches are combined in different ways to perform addition and subtraction and to move data around the system.

### Electrical Switches

To process data into information, computers need to work in a language they understand. Computers understand only two states of existence: on and off. Inside a computer, these two possibilities, or states, are defined using the two numbers *1* and *0*; the language represented by these numbers is called **binary language** because just two numbers are used. Everything a computer does, such as processing data or printing a report, is broken down into a series of *0*s and *1*s. **Electrical switches** are the devices inside the computer that are flipped between the two states of *1* and *0*, signifying "on" and "off."

You use various forms of switches every day. The light switch in your kitchen either is ON, allowing current to flow to the light bulb, or OFF. Another switch you use each day is

**FIGURE 1** Water faucets can be used to illustrate binary switches.

a water faucet. As shown in Figure 1, shutting off the faucet so that no water flows could represent the value 0, whereas turning it on could represent the value 1.

Computers are built from a huge collection of electrical switches. The history of computers is really a story about creating smaller and faster sets of electrical switches so that more data can be stored and manipulated quickly.

**Vacuum Tubes.** The earliest generation of electronic computers used **vacuum tubes** as switches. Vacuum tubes act as switches by allowing or blocking the flow of electrical current. The problem with vacuum tubes is that they take up a lot of space, as shown in Figure 2. The first high-speed digital computer, the Electronic Numerical Integrator and Computer (ENIAC), was deployed in 1945. It used nearly 18,000 vacuum tubes as switches and was about half the size of a basketball court! In addition to being large, the vacuum tubes produced a lot of heat and burned out frequently.

Since the introduction of ENIAC's vacuum tubes, two major revolutions have occurred in the design of switches, and consequently computers, to make them smaller and faster:

1. The invention of the *transistor*
2. The fabrication of *integrated circuits*

**Transistors. Transistors** are electrical switches built out of layers of a special type of material called a **semiconductor**. A semiconductor is any material that can be controlled either to conduct electricity or to act as an insulator (to prohibit electricity from passing through). Silicon, which is found in common sand, is the semiconductor material used to make transistors (see Figure 3).

By itself, silicon doesn't conduct electricity particularly well, but if specific chemicals are added in a controlled way to the silicon, it begins to behave like a switch. The silicon allows electrical current to flow easily when a certain voltage is applied; otherwise, it prevents electrical current from flowing, thus behaving as an on/off switch. This kind of behavior is exactly what's needed to store digital information—the *0*s (off) and *1*s (on) of binary language.

The first transistors were much smaller than vacuum tubes, produced little heat, and could quickly be switched from on to off, thereby allowing or blocking electrical current. They also were less expensive than vacuum tubes.

It wasn't long, however, before transistors reached their limits. Continuing advances in technology began to require more transistors than circuit boards could reasonably handle. Something was needed to pack more transistor capacity into a smaller space. Thus, integrated circuits, the next technical revolution in switches, were developed.

**FIGURE 2** Early computers were constructed using vacuum tubes (see inset). The difference in size achieved by moving from tubes to transistors allowed computers to become desktop devices instead of room-sized machines. *(© CORBIS)*

**Integrated Circuits. Integrated circuits** (or **chips**) are tiny regions of semiconductor material that support a huge number of transistors (see Figure 4). Most integrated circuits are no more than a quarter inch in size yet can hold billions of transistors.

This advancement has enabled computer designers to create small yet powerful **microprocessors**, which are the chips that contain a central processing unit (CPU). The Intel 4004, the first complete microprocessor to be located on a single integrated circuit, was released in 1971, marking the beginning of the true miniaturization of computers. The Intel 4004 contained slightly more than 2,300 transistors. Today, more than 2 billion transistors can be manufactured in a space as tiny as the nail of your little finger!

## Number Systems

How can simple switches be organized so that they let you use a computer to pay your bills online or write an essay? How can a set of switches describe a number or a word or

**FIGURE 3** This silicon wafer has the transistor circuitry for hundreds of devices etched on it. *(Justin Sullivan/Staff/Getty Images)*

give a computer the command to perform addition? Recall that to manipulate the on/off switches, the computer works in binary language, which uses only two digits, *0* and *1*. Let's look at how numbering systems work so that we can begin to understand this more deeply.

## The Base-10 Number System

A **number system** is an organized plan for representing a number. Although you may not realize it, you're already familiar with one number system. The **base-10 number system**, also known as **decimal notation**, is the system you use to represent all of the numeric values you use each day. It's called base 10 because it uses 10 digits—0 through 9—to represent any value.

To represent a number in base 10, you break the number down into groups of ones, tens, hundreds, thousands, and so on. Each digit has a place value depending on where it appears in the number. For example, using base 10, in the whole number 6,954 there are 6 sets of thousands, 9 sets of hundreds, 5 sets of tens, and 4 sets of ones. Working from right to left, each place in a number represents an increasing power of 10, as follows:

$$6{,}954 = (6 * 1{,}000) + (9 * 100) + (5*10) + (4*1)$$
$$= (6 * 10^3) + (9 * 10^2) + (5 * 10^1) + (4 * 10^0)$$

Note that in this equation, the final digit *4* is represented as $4 * 10^0$ because any number raised to the zero power is equal to 1.

**FIGURE 4** An integrated circuit is packaged in a small case but holds billions of transistors. *(Gudellaphoto/Fotolia)*

## The Base-2 (or Binary) Number System

Anthropologists theorize that humans developed a base-10 number system because we have 10 fingers. However, computer systems are not well suited to thinking about numbers in groups of 10. Instead, computers describe a number in powers of 2 because each switch can be in one of two positions: on or off (see Figure 5). This numbering system is referred to as the **binary number system**.

The binary number system is also referred to as the **base-2 number system**. Even with just two digits, the binary number system can still represent all the values that a base-10 number system can. Instead of breaking the number down into sets of ones, tens, hundreds, and thousands, as is done in base-10 notation, the binary number system describes a number as the sum of powers of 2—ones, twos, fours, eights, and sixteens. Binary numbers are used to represent every piece of data stored in a computer: all of the numbers, all of the letters, and all of the instructions that the computer uses to execute work.

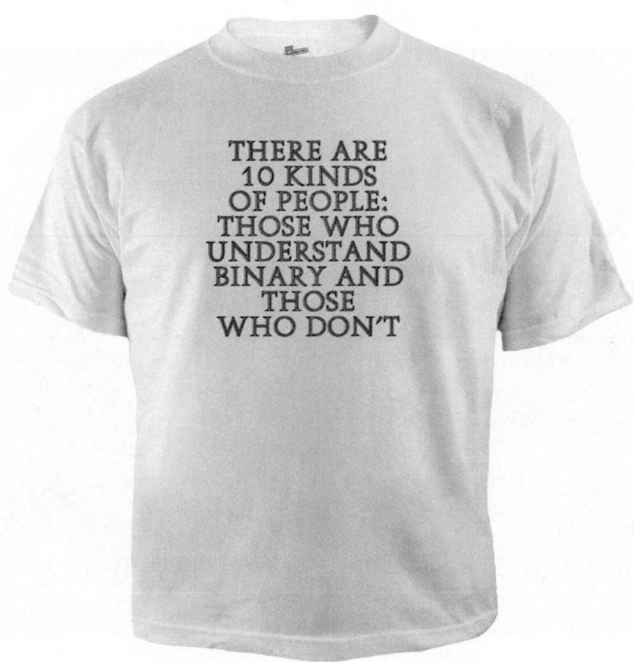


**FIGURE 5** Computer humor—the value *2* is written as *10* in binary! *(GroovyGearShop.com/CafePress.com)*

**Representing Integers.** In the base-10 number system, a whole number is represented as the sum of *1*s, *10*s, *100*s, and *1,000*s—that is, sums of powers of 10. The binary system works in the same way, but describes a value as the sum of groups of *1*s, *2*s, *4*s, *8*s, *16*s, *32*s, *64*s, etc.—that is, powers of 2: 1, 2, 4, 8, 16, 32, 64, and so on.

Let's look at the number 67. In base 10, the number 67 would be six sets of *10*s and seven sets of *1*s, as follows:

**Base 10:** $67 = (6 * 10^1) + (7 * 10^0)$

One way to figure out how 67 is represented in base 2 is to find the largest possible power of 2 that could be in the number 67. Two to the eighth power is 256, and there are no groups of 256 in the number 67. Two to the seventh power is 128, but that is bigger than 67. Two to the sixth power is 64, and there is a group of 64 inside a group of 67.

| | | | | |
|---|---|---|---|---|
| **67 has** | 1 | **group of** | 64 | **That leaves 3 and** |
| **3 has** | 0 | **groups of** | 32 | |
| | 0 | **groups of** | 16 | |
| | 0 | **groups of** | 8 | |
| | 0 | **groups of** | 4 | |
| | 1 | **group of** | 2 | **That leaves 1 and** |
| **1 has** | 1 | **group of** | 1 | **Now nothing is left** |

So, the binary number for 67 is written as 1000011 in base 2:

**Base 2:**
$$\begin{aligned}67 &= 64 + 0 + 0 + 0 + 0 + 2 + 1\\ &= (1 * 2^6) + (0 * 2^5) + (0 * 2^4) + (0 * 2^3) +\\ &\quad (0 * 2^2) + (1 * 2^1) + (1 * 2^0)\\ &= (1000011)_{\text{base 2}}\end{aligned}$$

It's easier to have a calculator do this for you! Some calculators have a button labeled DEC (for decimal) and another labeled BIN (for binary). Using Windows 8, you can access the Scientific Calculator that supports conversion between decimal (base 10) and binary (base 2) by accessing Search from the Charms bar and typing "calc" on the Start screen. From the App search results, choose the Calculator. From the Calculator menu, select View and then Programmer. You can enter your calculation in decimal and instantly see the binary representation in 64 bits, as shown in Figure 6.

SOUND BYTE
**Where Does Binary Show Up?**

In this Sound Byte, you'll learn how to use tools to work with binary, decimal, and hexadecimal numbers. (These tools come with the Windows operating system.) You'll also learn where you might see binary and hexadecimal values when you use a computer.

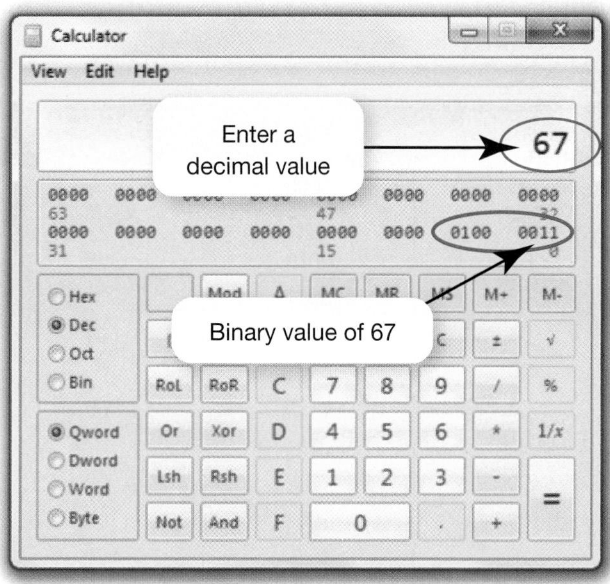


**FIGURE 6** The Windows Calculator in Programmer mode instantly converts values from decimal to binary.

**Hexadecimal Notation.** A large integer value becomes a very long string of *1*s and *0*s in binary! For convenience, programmers often use **hexadecimal notation** to make these expressions easier to use. Hexadecimal is a base-16 number system, meaning it uses 16 digits to represent numbers instead of the 10 digits used in base 10 or the 2 digits used in base 2. The 16 digits it uses are the 10 numeric digits, 0 to 9, plus six extra symbols: A, B, C, D, E, and F. Each of the letters A through F corresponds to a numeric value, so that A equals 10, B equals 11, and so on (see Figure 7). Therefore, the value 67 in decimal notation is 1000011 in binary or 43 in hexadecimal notation. It is much easier for computer scientists to use the 2-digit 43 than the 7-digit string 1000011. The Windows Calculator in Programmer view also can perform conversions to hexadecimal notation. (You can watch a video that shows you how to perform conversions between bases using the Windows Calculator in the Sound Byte titled, "Where Does Binary Show Up?")

**Representing Characters: ASCII.** We've just been converting integers from base 10, which *we* understand, to base 2 (binary state), which the computer understands. Similarly, we need a system that converts letters and other symbols that *we* understand to a binary state the computer understands. To provide a consistent means for representing letters and other characters, certain codes dictate how to represent characters in binary format. Most of today's personal computers use the American National Standards Institute (ANSI, pronounced "AN-see") standard code, called the **American Standard Code for Information Interchange** (ASCII, pronounced "AS-key"), to represent each letter or character as an 8-bit (or 1-byte) binary code.

Each binary digit is called a **bit** for short. Eight binary digits (or bits) combine to create one **byte**. We've been converting base-10 numbers to a binary format. In such cases, the binary format has no standard length. For example, the binary format for the number *2* is two digits (10), whereas the binary

FIGURE 7

## Sample Hexadecimal Values

| DECIMAL NUMBER | BINARY VALUE | HEXADECIMAL VALUE |
|---|---|---|
| 00 | 0000 | 00 |
| 01 | 0001 | 01 |
| 02 | 0010 | 02 |
| 03 | 0011 | 03 |
| 04 | 0100 | 04 |
| 05 | 0101 | 05 |
| 06 | 0110 | 06 |
| 07 | 0111 | 07 |
| 08 | 1000 | 08 |
| 09 | 1001 | 09 |
| 10 | 1010 | A |
| 11 | 1011 | B |
| 12 | 1100 | C |
| 13 | 1101 | D |
| 14 | 1110 | E |
| 15 | 1111 | F |

format for the number *10* is four digits (1010). Although binary numbers can have more or fewer than 8 bits, each single alphabetic or special character is 1 byte (or 8 bits) of data and consists of a unique combination of a total of eight *0*s and *1*s.

The ASCII code represents the 26 uppercase letters and 26 lowercase letters used in the English language, along with many punctuation symbols and other special characters, using 8 bits. Figure 8 shows several examples of the ASCII code representation of printable letters and characters.

**Representing Characters: Unicode.** Because it represents letters and characters using only 8 bits, the ASCII code can assign only 256 (or $2^8$) different codes for unique characters and letters. Although this is enough to represent English and many other characters found in the world's languages, ASCII code can't represent all languages and symbols,

FIGURE 8

## ASCII Standard Code for a Sample of Letters and Characters

| ASCII CODE | REPRESENTS THIS SYMBOL | ASCII CODE | REPRESENTS THIS SYMBOL |
|---|---|---|---|
| 01000001 | A | 01100001 | a |
| 01000010 | B | 01100010 | b |
| 01000011 | C | 01100011 | c |
| 01011010 | Z | 00100011 | # |
| 00100001 | ! | 00100100 | $ |
| 00100010 | " | 00100101 | % |

*Note: For the full ASCII table, see* ***ascii-code.com****.*

*(Courtesy of the American National Standards Institute)*

because some languages require more than 256 characters and letters. Thus, a new encoding scheme, called **Unicode**, was created. By using 16 bits instead of the 8 bits used in ASCII, Unicode can represent nearly 1,115,000 code points and currently assigns more than 96,000 unique character symbols (see Figure 9).

The first 128 characters of Unicode are identical to ASCII, but because of its depth, Unicode is also able to represent the alphabets of all modern and historic languages and notational systems, including such languages and writing systems as Tibetan, Tagalog, and Canadian Aboriginal syllabics. As we continue to become a more global society, it's anticipated that Unicode will replace ASCII as the standard character formatting code.

**Representing Decimal Numbers.** The binary number system can also represent a decimal number. How can a string of *1*s and *0*s capture the information in a value such as 99.368? Because every computer must store such numbers in the same way, the Institute of Electrical and Electronics Engineers (IEEE) has established a standard called the *floating-point standard* that describes how numbers with fractional parts should be represented in the binary number system. Using a 32-bit system, we can represent an incredibly wide range of numbers.

The method dictated by the IEEE standard works the same for any number with a decimal point, such as the number −0.75. The first digit, or bit (the sign bit), is used to indicate whether the number is positive or negative. The next 8 bits store the magnitude of the number, indicating whether the number is in the hundreds or millions, for example. The standard says to use the next 23 bits to store the value of the number.

**Interpretation.** *All* data inside the computer is stored as bits:

- **Positive and negative integers** can be stored using signed integer notation, with the first bit (the sign bit) indicating the sign and the rest of the bits indicating the value of the number.

FIGURE 9 The written languages of the world require thousands of different characters, shown here. The Unicode Code Chart (**unicode.org/charts**) shows how Unicode provides a system allowing digital representation of over 1,100,000 unique characters.

## SOUND BYTE
### Binary Numbers Interactive

This Sound Byte helps remove the mystery surrounding binary numbers. You'll learn about base conversion among decimal, binary, and hexadecimal systems interactively, using colors, sounds, and images.

- **Decimal** numbers are stored according to the IEEE floating-point standard.
- **Letters and symbols** are stored according to the ASCII code or Unicode.

These number systems and codes exist so that computers can store different types of information in their on/off switches. No matter what kind of data you input in a computer—a color, a musical note, or a street address—that data will be stored as a pattern of *1*s and *0*s. The important lesson is that the interpretation of *0*s and *1*s is what matters. The same binary pattern could represent a positive number, a negative number, a fraction, or a letter.

How does the computer know which interpretation to use for the *1*s and *0*s? When your mind processes language, it takes the sounds you hear and uses the rules of English, along with other clues, to build an interpretation of the sound as a word. If you're in New York City and hear someone shout, "Hey, Lori!" you expect that someone is saying hello to a friend. If you're in London and hear the same sound—"Hey! Lorry!"—you jump out of the way because a truck is coming at you! You knew which interpretation to apply to the sound because you had some other information—the fact that you were in England.

Likewise, the CPU is designed to understand a specific language or set of instructions. Certain instructions tell the CPU to expect a negative number next or to interpret the following bit pattern as a character. Because of this extra information, the CPU always knows which interpretation to use for a series of bits.

# How the CPU Works

Any program you run on your computer is actually a long series of binary code describing a specific set of commands the CPU must perform. These commands may be coming from a user's actions or may be instructions fed from a program while it executes. Each CPU is somewhat different in the exact steps it follows to perform its tasks, but all CPUs must perform a series of similar general steps. These steps, also illustrated in Figure 10, are referred to as a CPU **machine cycle (or processing cycle)**:

1. **Fetch:** When any program begins to run, the *1*s and *0*s that make up the program's binary code must be "fetched" from their temporary storage location in random access memory (RAM) and moved to the CPU before they can be executed.
2. **Decode:** Once the program's binary code is in the CPU, it is decoded into commands the CPU understands.
3. **Execute:** Next, the CPU actually performs the work described in the commands. Specialized hardware on the CPU performs addition, subtraction, multiplication, division, and other mathematical and logical operations.
4. **Store:** The result is stored in one of the **registers**, special memory storage areas built into the CPU, which are the most expensive, fastest memory in your computer. The CPU is then ready to fetch the next set of bits encoding the next instruction.

No matter what program you're running and no matter how many programs you're using at one time, the CPU performs these four steps over and over at incredibly high speeds. Shortly, we'll look at each stage in more detail. But first, let's examine components that help the CPU perform its tasks.

## The Control Unit

The CPU, like any part of the computer system, is designed from a collection of switches. How can the simple on/off switches of the CPU "remember" the fetch-decode-execute-store sequence of the machine cycle?

The **control unit** of the CPU manages the switches inside the CPU. It is programmed by CPU designers to remember the sequence of processing stages for that CPU and how each switch in the CPU should be set (i.e., on or off) for each stage. With each beat of the system clock, the control unit moves each switch to the correct on or off setting and then performs the work of that stage.

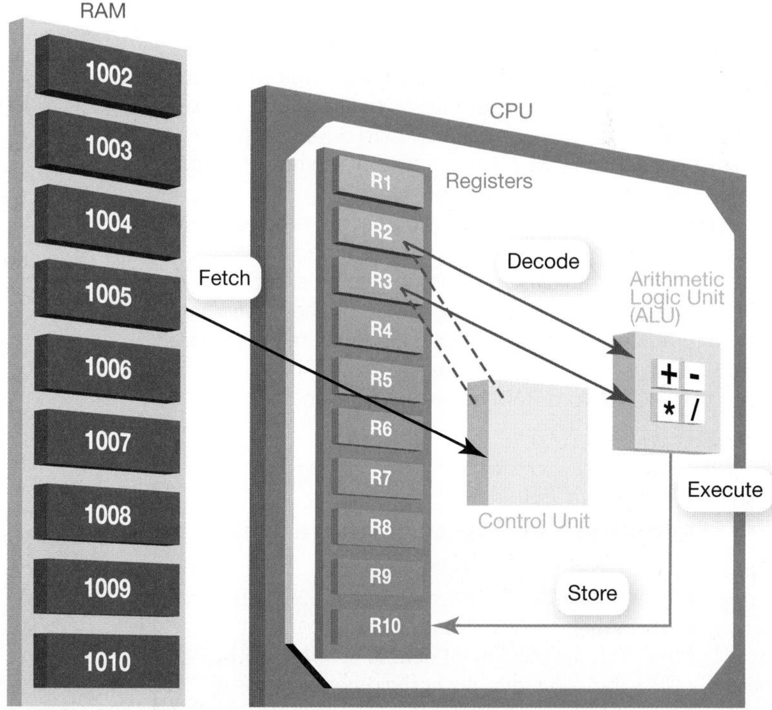


**FIGURE 10** The CPU Machine Cycle.

## The System Clock

To move from one stage of the machine cycle to the next, the motherboard uses a built-in **system clock**. This internal clock is actually a special crystal that acts like a metronome, keeping a steady beat and controlling when the CPU moves to the next stage of processing.

These steady beats or "ticks" of the system clock, known as the **clock cycle**, set the pace by which the computer moves from process to process. The pace, known as **clock speed**, is measured in hertz (Hz), which describes how many times something happens per second. Today's system clocks are measured in gigahertz (GHz), or a billion clock ticks per second. Therefore, in a 3 GHz system, there are 3 billion clock ticks each second.

Let's now look at each of the stages in the machine cycle in a bit more depth.

(Steve Young/Fotolia LLC)

### Stage 1: The Fetch Stage

The data and program instructions the CPU needs are stored in different areas in the computer system. Data and program instructions move between these areas as they're needed by the CPU for processing. Programs are permanently stored on the hard drive because it offers nonvolatile storage. However, when you launch a program, it—or sometimes only its essential parts—is transferred from the hard drive into RAM.

The program moves to RAM because the CPU can access the data and program instructions stored in RAM more than 1 million times faster than if they're left on the hard drive. In part, this is because RAM is much closer to the CPU than the hard drive is. Another reason for the delay in transmission of data and program instructions from the hard drive to the CPU is the relatively slow speed of mechanical hard drives. The read/write heads have to sweep over the spinning platters, which takes time. Even nonmechanical SSD hard drives have slower access speeds than RAM. RAM is a type of memory that gives very fast direct access to data.

As specific instructions from the program are needed, they're moved from RAM into registers (the special storage areas located on the CPU itself), where they wait to be executed.

The CPU's storage area isn't big enough to hold everything it needs to process at the same time. If enough memory were located on the CPU chip itself, an entire program could be copied to the CPU from RAM before it was executed. This would add to the computer's speed and efficiency because there would be no delay while the CPU stopped processing operations to fetch instructions from RAM to the CPU. However, including so much memory on a CPU chip would make these chips extremely expensive. In addition, CPU design is so complex that only a limited amount of storage space is available on the CPU itself.

**Cache Memory.** The CPU doesn't actually need to fetch every instruction from RAM each time it goes through a cycle. Another layer of storage, called **cache memory**, has even faster access to the CPU than RAM. Cache memory consists of small blocks of memory located directly on and next to the CPU chip. These memory blocks are holding places for recently or frequently used instructions or data that the CPU needs the most. When these instructions or data are stored in cache memory, the CPU can retrieve them more quickly than if it had to access them in RAM.

Modern CPU designs include several types of cache memory:

- **Level 1 cache:** If the next instruction to be fetched isn't already located in a CPU register, instead of looking directly to RAM to find it, the CPU first searches Level 1 cache. **Level 1 cache** is a block of memory built onto the CPU chip to store data or commands that have just been used.
- **Level 2 cache:** If the command is not located in Level 1 cache, the CPU searches Level 2 cache. Depending on the design of the CPU, **Level 2 cache** is either located on the CPU chip but slightly farther away from the CPU than Level 1 or is located on a separate chip next to the CPU and therefore takes somewhat longer to access. Level 2 cache contains more storage area than Level 1 cache. For the Intel Core i7, for example, Level 1 cache is 64 kilobytes (KB) and Level 2 cache is 1 megabyte (MB).

  Only if the CPU doesn't find the next instruction to be fetched in either Level 1 or Level 2 cache will it make the long journey to RAM to access it.
- **Level 3 cache:** The current direction of processor design is toward increasingly large multilevel CPU cache structures. Today, CPUs such as Intel's Core i7 processors have an additional third level of cache memory storage called **Level 3 cache**. On computers with Level 3 cache, the CPU checks this area for instructions and data after it looks in Level 1 and Level 2 cache but before it makes the longer trip to RAM (see Figure 11). Level 3 cache holds between 2 and 12 MB of data. With 12 MB of Level 3 cache, there is storage for some entire programs to be transferred to the CPU for execution.

As an end user of computer programs, you do nothing special to use cache memory. The advantage of having more cache memory is that you'll experience better performance because the CPU won't have to make the longer trip to RAM to get data and instructions as often. Unfortunately, because it's built into the CPU chip or motherboard, you can't upgrade cache; it's part of the original design of the CPU. Therefore, as with RAM, when buying a computer, it's important to consider the one with the most cache memory, everything else being equal.

SOUND BYTE

**Computer Architecture Interactive**

In this Sound Byte, you'll take animated tours that illustrate many of the hardware concepts introduced in this chapter. Along the way, you'll learn about the machine cycle of the CPU, the movement of data between RAM and the CPU, and the hierarchy of the different types of memory in computer systems.

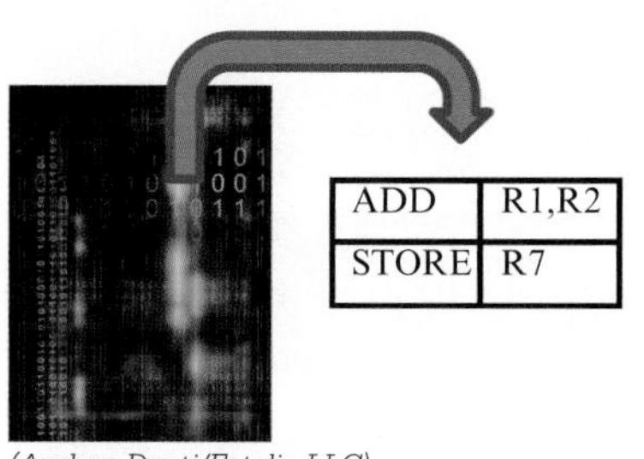

(Andrea Danti/Fotolia LLC)

## Stage 2: The Decode Stage

The main goal of the decode stage is for the CPU's control unit to translate (or **decode**) the program's instructions into commands the CPU can understand. The collection of commands that a specific CPU can execute is called the **instruction set** for that system. Each CPU has its own unique instruction set. For example, the AMD FX 8350 eight-core processor in a Gamer Mage system has a different instruction set than the fourth-generation Intel Core i5 used in a Dell Inspiron notebook. The control unit interprets the code's bits according to the instruction set the CPU designers laid out for that particular CPU. The control unit then knows how to set up all the switches on the CPU so that the proper operation will occur.

Because humans are the ones who write the initial instructions, all the commands in an instruction set are written in a language called **assembly language**, which is easier for humans to work with than binary language. Many CPUs have similar assembly commands in their instruction sets, including the following commands:

| CPU INSTRUCTION | FUNCTION |
| --- | --- |
| ADD | Add |
| SUB | Subtract |
| MUL | Multiply |
| DIV | Divide |
| MOVE | Move data to RAM |
| STORE | Move data to a CPU register |
| EQU | Check if equal |

CPUs differ in the choice of additional assembly language commands selected for the instruction set. Each CPU design team works to develop an instruction set that is both powerful and speedy.

However, because the CPU knows and recognizes only patterns of *0*s and *1*s, it can't understand assembly language directly, so these human-readable instructions are translated into binary code. The control unit uses these long strings of binary code called **machine language** to set up the hardware in the CPU for the rest of the operations it needs to perform. Machine language is a binary code for computer instructions, much like the ASCII code is a binary code for letters and characters. Similar to each letter or character having its own unique combination of *0*s and *1*s assigned to it, a CPU has a table of codes consisting of combinations of *0*s and *1*s for each of its commands. If the CPU sees a particular pattern of bits arrive, it knows the work it must do. Figure 12 shows a few commands in both assembly language and machine language.

# BITS&BYTES

## Using a Little Hideaway

Taking data you think you'll be using soon and storing it nearby is a simple but powerful idea. This strategy shows up in places in your computer system other than cache memory. For example, when you're browsing web pages, it takes longer to download images than text. Your browser software automatically stores images on your hard drive so that you don't have to download them again if you want to go back and view a page you've already visited. Although this cache of files is not related to the cache storage space designed into the CPU chip, the idea is the same. The word cache is derived from the French word cacher, which means "to hide." A little bit of memory space used as a hideaway can give performance a big boost.

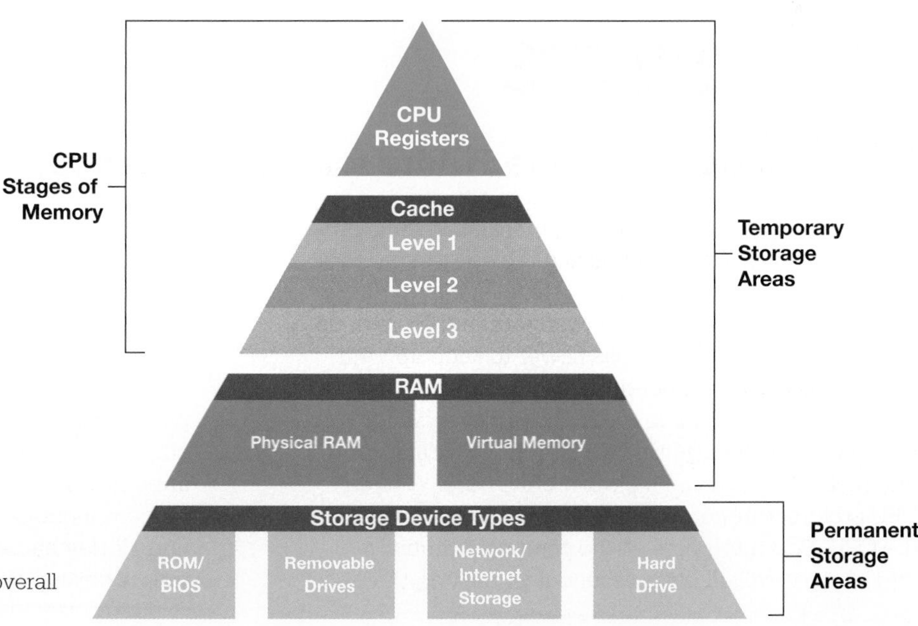


**FIGURE 11** The CPU has multiple stages of internal memory, which is just a part of the overall hierarchy of a computer's memory storage.

FIGURE 12

**Representations of Sample CPU Commands**

| HUMAN LANGUAGE FOR COMMAND | CPU COMMAND IN ASSEMBLY LANGUAGE (LANGUAGE USED BY PROGRAMMERS) | CPU COMMAND IN MACHINE LANGUAGE (LANGUAGE USED IN THE CPU'S INSTRUCTION SET) |
|---|---|---|
| Add | ADD | 1110 1010 |
| Subtract | SUB | 0001 0101 |
| Multiply | MUL | 1111 0000 |
| Divide | DIV | 0000 1111 |

(Taras Livyy/Fotolia LLC)

### Stage 3: The Execute Stage

The **arithmetic logic unit (ALU)** is the part of the CPU designed to perform mathematical operations such as addition, subtraction, multiplication, and division and to test the comparison of values such as *greater than, less than,* and *equal to*. For example, in calculating an average, the ALU is where the addition and division operations would take place.

The ALU also performs logical OR, AND, and NOT operations. For example, in determining whether a student can graduate, the ALU would need to ascertain whether the student had taken all required courses AND obtained a passing grade in each of them. The ALU is specially designed to execute such calculations flawlessly and with incredible speed.

The ALU is fed data from the CPU's registers. The amount of data a CPU can process at a time is based in part on the amount of data each register can hold. The number of bits a computer can work with at a time is referred to as its **word size**. Therefore, a 64-bit processor can process more information faster than a 32-bit processor.

(John Takai/Fotolia LLC)

### Stage 4: The Store Stage

In the final stage, the result produced by the ALU is stored back in the registers. The instruction itself will explain which register should be used to store the answer.

Once the entire instruction has been completed, the next instruction will be fetched, and the fetch-decode-execute-store sequence will begin again.

## Making CPUs Even Faster

Knowing how to build a CPU that can run faster than the competition can make a company rich. However, building a faster CPU isn't easy. A new product launch must take into

## BITS&BYTES

### Forget CPUs: SoC Is the Future for Mobile Devices!

Since consumers are demanding more powerful mobile devices such as smartphones and tablets, the pressure is on for chip designers to create smaller chips. But the chips also need to be more powerful than the previous generation and consume less power to keep up with software and communication demands.

Intel and other chip manufacturers have risen to the challenge by migrating away from CPUs and introducing SoC (system on a chip) architecture. Whereas CPU architecture requires additional chips to support the CPU, SoC integrates all the computer circuitry into a single chip. This is essential for making the "brains" of small computing devices such as tablets and smartphones.

In the fall of 2013, Intel announced the X1000 in its line of Quark SoC, which is one-fifth the size of Intel's Atom processor. The X1000 consumes only 10 percent of the power that an Atom requires, while offering a 30 percent boost in performance. Tablets featuring this chip are expected in early 2014. At the same time, Intel announced a new 20nm phone chip that offers a 50 percent increase in performance, LTE (4G) capability, and 12-day battery life. Thanks to SoC design, the future is getting smaller every year!

consideration the time it will take to design, manufacture, and test that processor. When the processor finally hits the market, it must be faster than the competition if the manufacturer hopes to make a profit. To create a CPU that will be released 36 months from now, it must be built to perform at least twice as fast as anything currently available.

Processor manufacturers can increase CPU performance in many different ways:

- Using *pipelining*
- Designing the CPU's instruction set so that it contains *specialized instructions for handling multimedia and graphics*
- Including *multiple independent processing paths* inside the CPU

Let's explore each of these methods in more detail.

## Pipelining

As an instruction is processed, the CPU runs sequentially through the four stages of processing: fetch, decode, execute, and store. **Pipelining** is a technique that allows the CPU to work on more than one instruction (or stage of processing) at the same time, thereby boosting CPU performance.

For example, without pipelining, it may take four clock cycles to complete one instruction (one clock cycle for each of the four processing stages). However, with a four-stage pipeline, the computer can process four instructions at the same time. The ticks of the system clock (the clock cycle) indicate when all instructions move to the next process. Using pipelining, a four-stage processor can potentially run up to four times faster because some instruction is finishing every clock cycle rather than waiting four cycles for each instruction to finish. In Figure 13a, a non-pipelined instruction takes four clock cycles to be completed, whereas in Figure 13b, the four instructions have been completed in the same time using pipelining.

There is a cost to pipelining a CPU, however. The CPU must be designed so that each stage (fetch, decode, execute, and store) is independent. This means that each stage must be able to run at the same time that the other three stages are running. This requires more transistors and a more complicated hardware design.

## Specialized Multimedia Instructions

Each design team that develops a new CPU tries to imagine what users' greatest needs will be in four or five years. Currently, several processors on the market reflect this consideration by incorporating specialized multimedia instructions into the basic instruction set.

Hardware engineers have redesigned the chip so that the instruction set contains new commands customized to speed up the work needed for video and audio processing. For example, Intel has integrated into its second-generation Core processor the Advanced Encryption Standard (AES) instruction set. These seven new instructions work to allow the CPU to deliver faster data protection.

## Multiple Processing Efforts

Many high-end server systems use a set of completely separate CPU chips on one motherboard. These server

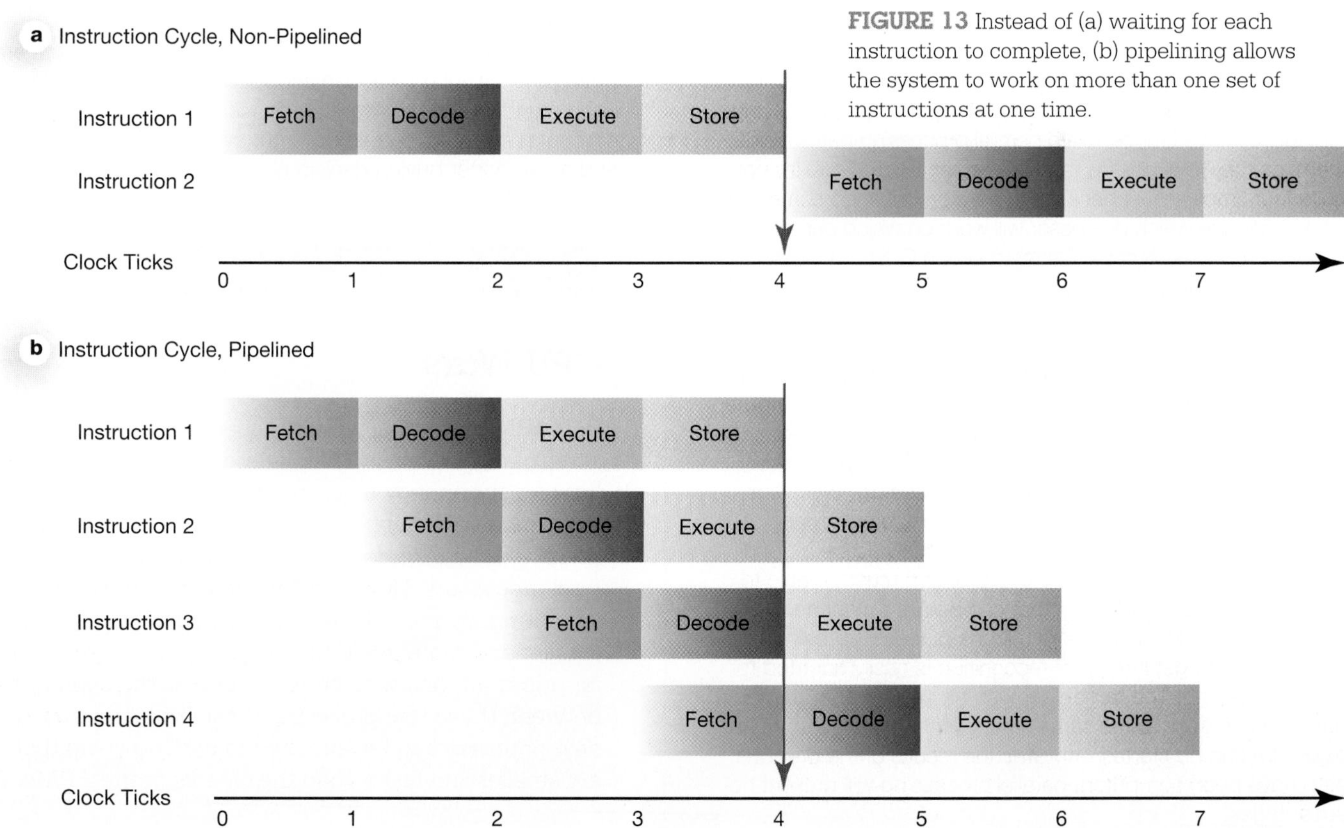


**FIGURE 13** Instead of (a) waiting for each instruction to complete, (b) pipelining allows the system to work on more than one set of instructions at one time.

# BITS&BYTES

## Today's Supercomputers: Faster than Ever

Supercomputers are the biggest and most powerful type of computer. Scientists and engineers use these computers to solve complex problems or to perform massive computations. Some supercomputers are single computers with multiple processors, whereas others consist of multiple computers that work together.

The Tianhe-2 was recently ranked as the world's fastest supercomputer. It features a whopping 3,120,000 cores and runs the Linux operating system. Tianhe-2 is deployed at the National Supercomputer Center in Guangzho, China. Since it was developed by the National University of Defense Technology, the assumption is that it will be used primarily for weapons system research.

The rankings of supercomputers change frequently as new models are deployed or older models are upgraded. You can keep up with the rankings at **top500.org**.

**FIGURE 14** The Tianhe-2 in China is the world's faster supercomputer . . . for now! Check **top500.org** for the latest rankings. *(Hongtao/Xinhua Press/Corbis)*

systems can later be scaled so that they can accommodate large numbers of processors with multiple cores, like the Tianhe-2 supercomputer, which uses Intel Xeon IvyBridge and Phi processors to provide 3,120,000 computing cores of power!

In personal computers, Intel uses *multi-core processing* in its Core processor line of chips. Chips with quad-core processing capabilities have four separate parallel processing paths inside them, so they're almost as fast as four separate CPUs. It's not quite four times as fast because the system must do some extra work to decide which processor will work on which part of the problem and to recombine the results each CPU produces.

Six-core processors, like the Intel i7 Extreme Edition, and even eight-core CPUs (like the AMD FX) are available as well, executing six (or eight) separate processing paths. Multiprocessor systems are often used when intensive computational problems need to be solved in such areas as computer simulations, video production, and graphics processing.

Certain types of problems are well suited to a parallel-processing environment. In **parallel processing**, there is a large network of computers, with each computer working on a portion of the same problem simultaneously. To be a good candidate for parallel processing, a problem must be able to be divided into a set of tasks that can be run simultaneously. For example, a problem where millions of faces are being compared with a target image for recognition is easily adapted to a parallel setting. The target face can be compared with many hundreds of faces at the same time. But if the next step of an algorithm can be started only after the results of the previous step have been computed, parallel processing will present no advantages.

In the future, you can expect CPUs to continue to get smaller and faster and to consume less power. This fits with the current demands of consumers for more powerful portable computing devices.

At the most basic level of binary *1*s and *0*s, computers are systems of switches that can accomplish impressive tasks. By understanding the hardware components that make up your computer system, you can use your system more effectively and make better buying decisions.

# BITS&BYTES

## CPU Wars

The ARM processor, which is used in tablets and smartphones, was a CPU contender that challenged Intel for supremacy in the market. Microsoft even released a version of Windows 8 for the ARM processor, since it consumes less power and is cheaper than Intel processors. However, Intel responded recently by launching its line of Quark processors, which are even smaller and more powerful than ARM processors. Look for prices on tablets to begin to drop as the competition between these two processors heats up! And expect new processors to be launched in coming years that are smaller and faster than the Quarks or the ARMs.

# check your understanding//

For a quick review of what you've learned, answer the following questions. Visit **pearsonhighered.com/techinaction** to check your answers.

## multiple choice

1. Which part of the CPU is specifically designed to perform mathematical operations?
   - **a.** fetch module
   - **b.** ALU
   - **c.** registers
   - **d.** cache memory
2. What is another name for the base-2 number system?
   - **a.** decimal notation
   - **b.** binary number system
   - **c.** hexadecimal notation
   - **d.** integer system
3. Which encoding scheme can represent the alphabets of all modern and historic languages?
   - **a.** base-2 number system
   - **b.** Unicode
   - **c.** ASCII
   - **d.** scientific
4. A multi-core processor like the Intel i7 (containing four cores)
   - **a.** processes data almost as fast as four separate CPUs.
   - **b.** processes data faster than four separate CPUs because of pipelining.
   - **c.** processes data faster than 16 separate CPUs because of parallel processing.
   - **d.** is a software setting you can use to speed up CPU processing.
5. To regulate the internal timing of a computer system, the motherboard uses
   - **a.** a system clock.
   - **b.** software simulation.
   - **c.** RAM.
   - **d.** a register.
6. Special areas of memory storage located very close to the CPU are known as
   - **a.** switches.
   - **b.** semiconductors.
   - **c.** registers.
   - **d.** caches.
7. Which is the correct set of steps in the machine cycle?
   - **a.** execute, store, fetch, decode
   - **b.** store, fetch, execute, decode
   - **c.** execute first instruction, execute second instruction, execute third instruction
   - **d.** fetch, decode, execute, store
8. All data inside the computer is stored as
   - **a.** words.
   - **b.** numbers.
   - **c.** binary patterns.
   - **d.** cache memory.
9. Which statement about pipelining is TRUE?
   - **a.** Pipelining does not boost CPU performance.
   - **b.** Pipeline design is only used in computers in conjunction with parallel processing.
   - **c.** Pipelining allows a less complicated hardware design.
   - **d.** Pipelining allows the computer to process multiple instructions simultaneously.
10. From fastest to slowest, which is the fastest sequence of accessing memory?
    - **a.** registers, RAM, Level 1 cache, Level 2 cache
    - **b.** registers, Level 1 cache, Level 2 cache, RAM
    - **c.** Level 1 cache, Level 2 cache, RAM, registers
    - **d.** Level 2 cache, Level 1 cache, registers, RAM

# 8 Digital Devices and Media: Managing a Digital Lifestyle

## Mobile Devices

### Digital Convergence

**OBJECTIVE**

1. How is the trend of digital convergence seen in the market? **(p. 312)**

### Telephony: Smartphones and Beyond

**OBJECTIVES**

2. What hardware and software comprise a typical smartphone? **(pp. 313–316)**
3. How do I synchronize information between my phone and my computer, and how do mobile Internet data plans work? **(pp. 316–319)**
4. What do I need to keep my smartphone secure? **(p. 319)**
5. How does digital telephony support VoIP services? **(pp. 319–320)**

**Sound Byte:** Smartphones Are Really Smart

**Sound Byte:** Connecting with Bluetooth

**Active Helpdesk:** Keeping Your Data on Hand

### Tablets, Netbooks, and Ultrabooks

**OBJECTIVE**

6. What distinguishes the performance of tablets, netbooks, and ultrabooks? **(pp. 322–323)**

## The Digital Information Age

### Digital Defined

**OBJECTIVE**

7. What advantage do digital formats have over analog signals? **(pp. 327–328)**

### Digital Media

**OBJECTIVES**

8. How is the digital format changing the way media is created and distributed? **(pp. 329–334)**
9. How do I work with digital images and videos? **(pp. 335–340)**

**Active Helpdesk:** Using Portable Media Players

For all media in this chapter go to **pearsonhighered.com /techinaction** or MyITLab.

*(kuroji/Fotolia; Scanrail/Fotolia; Frankie Angel/Alamy; Tetra Images/Getty Images; Oleksiy Maksymenko/Getty Images)*

# HOW COOL IS THIS?

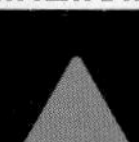

Scan here for more info

Ever heard of **3D printing**? If not, you soon will, as it is maturing into a technology that is set to launch a **hardware revolution**. First-generation 3D printing consisted of "extruded plastic printing"—melting plastic down and then pushing it into a mold to shape it. Form 1 is a 3D printer that goes beyond the extruded plastic of first generation 3D printing using a new, more accurate technique. The printer's laser draws on the surface of a pool of **liquid plastic resin**. The small spots where the laser hits harden. Layer by layer, a specific shape can be formed. The accuracy and resolution of this approach far exceeds earlier 3D printers, and **different colors, transparencies, and flexibility** can be incorporated to create much more sophisticated printable parts. As cool as Form 1 is, how it was funded is even cooler. Founders used the crowd-funding site **Kickstarter** to ask for $100,000 in pledges. Supporters gave almost **$3 million** in one month! *(© ZUMA Press, Inc./Alamy)*

# Mobile Devices

For many of us, our phone is our lifeline to the world, and if not our phone, then our laptop or iPad. We live in a digital world, and our devices have evolved to let us communicate anywhere we go, 24/7. In this section, we'll check out a number of mobile devices and their features. But first, we look at digital convergence.

## digital CONVERGENCE

**Digital convergence**, the use of a single unifying device to handle media, Internet, entertainment, and telephony needs, is exemplified in the range of devices now on the market. You see digital convergence in the evolution of smartphones, which now let you do just about anything a computer can do. The push to digital convergence is seen in the migration of digital devices into environments like the cabin of your car. The Tesla S features a 17-inch touch-screen display, shown in Figure 8.1a, that controls all of the electronics systems of the car, including a high-definition camera watching as you back up, and provides Internet access, mobile communications, and navigation. Even some refrigerators, like the one shown in Figure 8.1b, now include LCD touch-screen displays and network adapters so that they can play music and display family photos and recipes from websites such as **epicurious.com**.

In fact, devices are beginning to converge so much that an organization has been created to standardize them. The Digital Living Network Alliance (**dlna.org**) is an organization working to standardize different kinds of appliances and network devices used in our homes. As our appliances, cars, and homes become designed to communicate over a common network, how we manage our media, control our living spaces, and communicate with our families will continue to change.

**How have mobile devices converged?** As more and more computing power is available in mobile processors, mobile devices have evolved to be able to do multiple tasks. Smartphones can now videoconference like laptops. Tablets such as the iPad are touch sensitive like smartphones. Netbooks and ultrabooks both run traditional desktop operating systems and are lightweight. All these devices have significant overlap in the tasks they can perform, so learning the differences will be important in finding the device that's just right for you. Let's start by taking a look at smartphones. ■

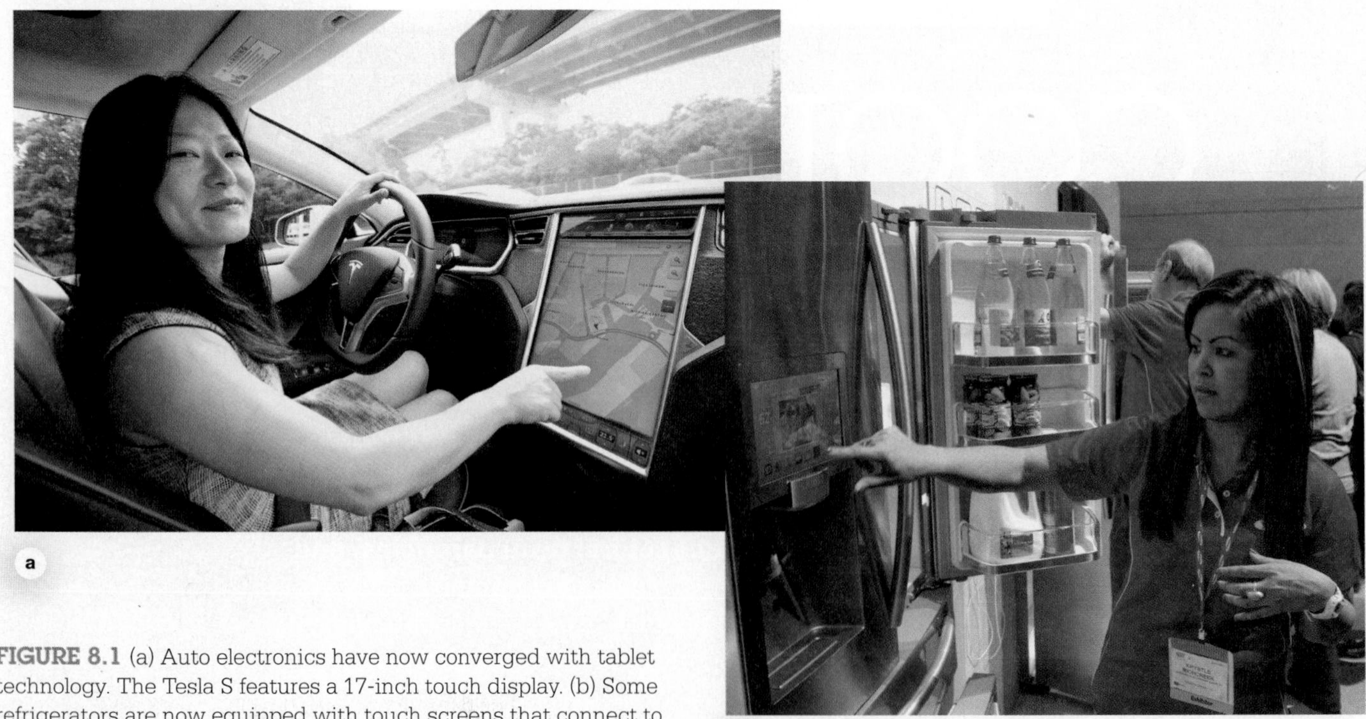

**FIGURE 8.1** (a) Auto electronics have now converged with tablet technology. The Tesla S features a 17-inch touch display. (b) Some refrigerators are now equipped with touch screens that connect to the Internet. *(Kyodo / AP Images; Steve Marcus/Reuters/Landov)*

# telephony: smartphones AND BEYOND

Communication has changed radically in the digital age. Chapter 3 discussed the use of wikis, blogs, and other web-based tools for connecting people and their ideas. All of these software applications are dependent on digital information.

Hardware devices that support communication also have evolved because of digital technologies. **Telephony**, the use of equipment to provide voice communications over a distance, has shifted from an analog science to a digital one. In this section, we examine smartphones and Voice over Internet Protocol (VoIP) devices to see how they're changing to meet modern communication needs.

## Smartphone Basics

**What makes a smartphone a smartphone?** A smartphone does more than let you make and answer phone calls. In fact, smartphones illustrate the power of digital convergence (see Figure 8.2). They incorporate functions and features, such as the following, that used to be available only in separate, dedicated devices:

- Internet access
- Personal information management (PIM) features
- Voice recording features
- The ability to play and organize music files
- GPS services
- Digital image and video capture
- Computing power to run programs like word processors or even video-editing software

Examples of smartphones include the iPhone and the HTC Thunderbolt.

**Isn't every phone a smartphone now?** All phones that use mobile, cellular technology can be called **cellular (cell) phones**. Although many cell phones on the market are considered smartphones, less powerful cell phones are available. Called **feature phones**, these inexpensive phones have modest processors, simpler interfaces, and often no touch screen. As more features are integrated into every cell phone product, though, it becomes difficult to distinguish a smartphone from a feature phone. Most providers, like AT&T or Verizon, label a smartphone as one that has sufficient power so that you can use Internet features easily. In addition, you often have to purchase a data plan with a smartphone. In this chapter, we'll use the term *cell phone* to refer to all cellular phones and *smartphones* to refer to the more powerful type of cell phone that can run more complex applications.

## Smartphone Components

**Are smartphones computers?** All cell phones—smartphones and feature phones—have the same components as any computer: a processor (central processing unit, or CPU), memory, and input and output devices, as shown in Figure 8.3. Cell phones require their own operating system (OS) software and have their own application software. So, in effect, all cell phones are computers.

Smartphones use a CPU and an interface so powerful that they can take on many of the same tasks as much more expensive computers: videoconferencing, recording and editing high-definition (HD) video, and broadcasting live-streaming video.

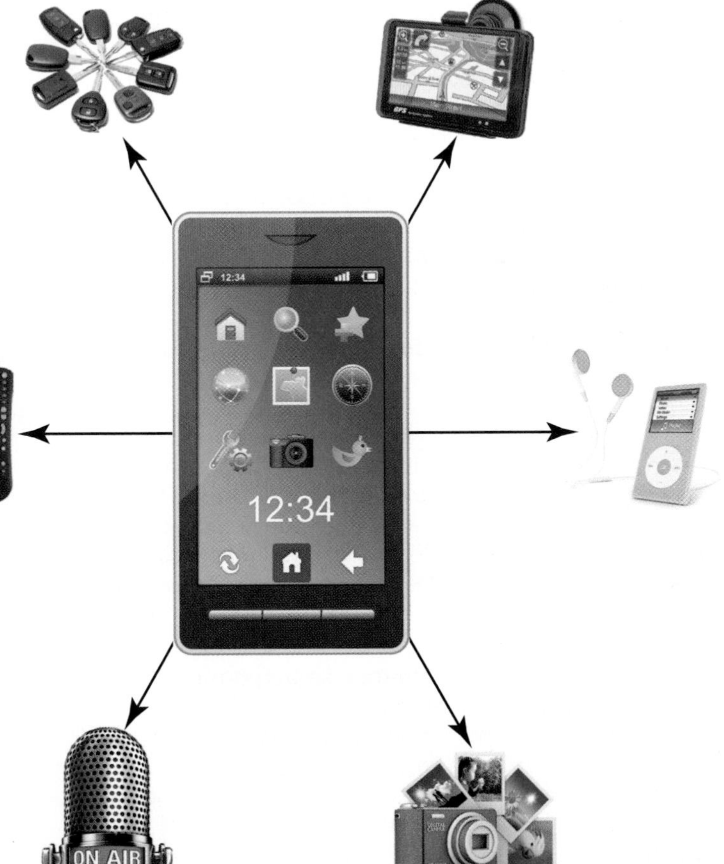


(fsketch/Fotolia; Maxx-Studio/Shutterstock; You can more/Shutterstock; MrGarry/Shutterstock; frank_peters/Shutterstock; gielmichal/Shutterstock; Bartosz Zakrzewski/Shutterstock)

**FIGURE 8.2** Digital convergence has brought us single devices like smartphones that play the role of many separate devices.

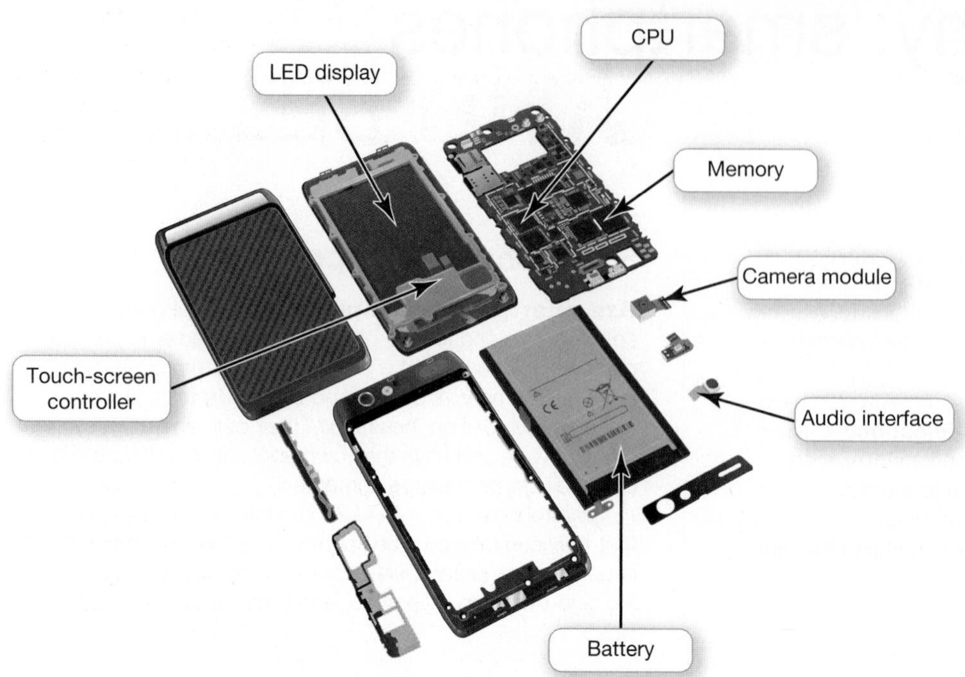


**FIGURE 8.3** Inside your smartphone, you'll find a CPU; a memory chip; input devices such as a microphone, a camera, and a touch screen; and output devices such as a display screen.

**What kind of processor is inside a smartphone?** Although the processor in a cell phone is not as fast or as high-powered as the processor in a desktop computer, it's still responsible for a great number of tasks. The processor coordinates sending all of the data among the other electronic components inside the phone. It also runs the cell phone's OS, which provides a user interface so that you can change phone settings, store information, play games, and so on. Popular processors for smartphones include the Qualcomm Snapdragon and the Apple A5. These use dual-core processing technology, which used to be reserved for high-end computer systems.

**Is there a standard OS for smartphones?** There are a number of operating systems in the smartphone market now. Many smartphones use the Android OS. Apple's iPhone uses iOS, a version of the OS X operating system used in Apple's computers. Microsoft is also now in the running with the Windows Phone 8 mobile OS. These operating systems are required to translate the user's commands into instructions for the processor. Figure 8.4 illustrates some of the user interfaces featured among smartphone operating systems.

**What does the memory inside a smartphone do?** Your phone's memory stores all of the phone's information and programs. The OS is stored in read-only memory (ROM), the phone's permanent memory, because the phone would be useless without that key piece of software. Other phone data, such as ring tones and contact lists, is stored in separate internal memory chips.

Many smartphones let you add additional memory through micro SD flash cards (see Figure 8.5). Micro SD cards are easy to install inside a phone, and some models have external slots for an SD card. Not all smartphones

**FIGURE 8.4**

## Mobile Operating Systems

| OPERATING SYSTEM | MANUFACTURER | USER INTERFACE |
|---|---|---|
| iOS | Apple | |
| Windows Phone 8 | Microsoft | |
| Android | Used by HTC, Samsung | |
| BlackBerry OS | BlackBerry | |

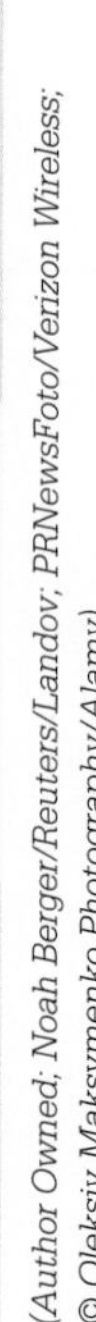

(Author Owned; Noah Berger/Reuters/Landov; PRNewsFoto/Verizon Wireless; © Oleksiy Maksymenko Photography/Alamy)

**SOUND BYTE**

**Smartphones Are Really Smart**

In this Sound Byte, you'll learn how to use a smartphone as a powerful tool to communicate, calculate, and organize your workload.

allow memory upgrades in this way, however. For example, iPhones don't let you add memory.

**FIGURE 8.5** Micro SD flash cards add memory to some phones. *(Clifford Farrugia/Alamy)*

**What input and output devices do smartphones use?** The primary input devices for a smartphone are its microphone and touch pad. Some phones, such as the BlackBerry Porsche (see Figure 8.6a), offer both a touch screen and a built-in keyboard. The Apple iPhone provides a software-based keyboard (see Figure 8.6b) that supports more than 40 languages. And a smartphone's digital camera is also an input device, capturing photos and video.

Cell-phone output devices include a speaker and a liquid crystal display (LCD). Higher-end models include full-color, high-resolution LCD screens. Newer on the market are OLED (organic light-emitting diode) displays, which allow very bright, sharp imaging and draw less power than LCD screens.

**What smartphone software is available?** A smartphone OS comes with a standard collection of software, such as a to-do list, contact manager, and calendar. Modified versions of application software such as Microsoft Word, Excel, Outlook, and PowerPoint are available for some high-end smartphones. Manufacturers also have web-based software stores, like the App Store for the Apple iPhone and the App World for RIM's BlackBerry devices (see Figure 8.7). Software applications are available for Android through Google Play. The Android developer community holds competitions to spur the creation of new software applications for Android-based phones.

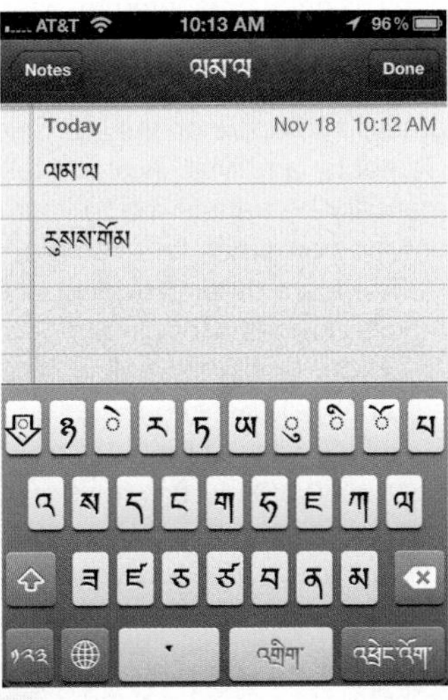


**FIGURE 8.6** (a) The BlackBerry Porsche includes a touch screen and a built-in keyboard. (b) The Apple iPhone has a touch keyboard that supports more than 40 languages. *(BlackBerry/MarketFotoPress EPN/Newscom; Jae C. Hong/AP Images)*

## How Cell Phone Technology Works

**What's "cellular" about a cell phone?** As noted earlier, the term *cell phone* is short for *cellular phone*. A set of connected "cells" makes up a cellular network. Each cell is a geographic area centered on a **base transceiver station**, which is a large communications tower with antennas, amplifiers, receivers, and transmitters. When you place a call on a cell phone, a base station picks up the request for service. The station then passes the request to a central location called a **mobile switching center**. The reverse process occurs when you receive an incoming call. A telecommunications company builds its network by constructing a series of cells that overlap in an attempt to guarantee that its cell-phone customers have coverage no matter where they are.

As you move during your phone call, the mobile switching center monitors the strength of the signal between your cell phone and the closest base station. When the signal is no longer strong enough between your cell phone and the base station, the mobile switching center orders the next base station to take charge of your call. When your cell phone "drops out," it may be because the distance between base stations is too great to provide an adequate signal.

**FIGURE 8.7** Google Play, the Windows Store, and Apple's App Store are some of the many online stores delivering software for mobile devices. *(Associated Press; © Kevin Britland/Alamy; © Anatolii Babii/Alamy)*

## BITS&BYTES

### Talking to Yourself

It may look like you are talking to yourself, but more and more we are talking to our phone OS! Voice recognition capabilities on smartphones are improving quickly. Want to book a restaurant reservation? Using iPhone's Siri, all you need to do to book a restaurant reservation through Open Table is say "Make a reservation at Olive Garden for 6 next Saturday." And if you say "Read my new messages," your iPhone will read your most recent incoming texts. Android can connect successive questions, so it can handle "Who is Hillary Clinton?" followed by "Who is her husband?" So if you have a spare moment, ask your phone "What's the answer to life, the universe, and everything?"

**How do cell phones use digital signals?** When you speak into a cell phone, a series of digital processing steps occur:

1. Sound enters the microphone as a sound wave. Because these sound waves need to be *digitized* (that is, converted into a sequence of *1*s and *0*s that the cell phone's processor can understand), an **analog-to-digital converter chip** converts your voice's sound waves into digital signals.
2. Next, the digital data must be *compressed*, or squeezed, into the smallest possible space so that it will transmit more quickly to another phone. The processor can't perform the mathematical operations required at this stage quickly enough, so there's a specialized chip called the **digital signal processor** included in the cell phone that handles the compression work.
3. Finally, the digital data is *transmitted* as a radio wave through the cellular network to the destination phone.

When you receive an incoming call, the digital signal processor decompresses the incoming message. An amplifier boosts the signal to make it loud enough, and it is then passed on to the speaker.

## Synchronizing

**What's the best way to synchronize data between my phone and computer?** The process of updating your data so your to-do lists, schedules, and other files on your cell phone and computer are the same is called **synchronizing,** or **syncing**. There are two main ways to transfer information between your phone and computer:

1. *Wired:* Use a micro SD card or a USB cable to directly transfer data.
2. *Wireless:* Use a wireless connection to transfer data.

SOUND BYTE

**Connecting with Bluetooth**

In this Sound Byte, you'll learn what freedoms Bluetooth affords you and how to use Bluetooth devices.

**How does a wired transfer of data work?** Almost all phones are designed with a USB port. Some have a mini-USB connector, while other models require a special cable to connect the phone to a standard USB port. Once connected using a USB data cable, your phone will appear on your computer like an additional flash drive, and you can drag and drop files to it. You can also charge your phone through the USB cable.

If your phone supports a high-density micro SD card, you can easily remove the card and slip it directly into a flash card reader in your computer.

**How do I transfer information to and from my phone wirelessly?** Most smartphones on the market today are Bluetooth-enabled, meaning they include a small Bluetooth chip that allows them to transfer data wirelessly to any other Bluetooth-enabled device. **Bluetooth** technology uses radio waves to transmit data signals over distances up to approximately 300 feet (for Bluetooth 4). Bluetooth 4 devices are the newest on the market and are almost twice as fast as Bluetooth 3 devices.

Another way to wirelessly transfer data to your phone is to use a wireless connection to a cloud service. A number of web services are now available to synchronize your e-mail, files, contacts, and calendars instantly and wirelessly. SugarSync, for example, wirelessly syncs folders of data and photos on your Android phone to your home computers automatically (see Figure 8.8). These web services follow the model of cloud computing, where Internet-based services and resources are distributed to users instead of being installed as an application on the user's computer. Apple's iOS has cloud support integrated into applications like Calendar, iTunes, PhotoStream, Contacts, and Mail. A photo taken on your iPhone will automatically be transferred to your iPad and your home Windows or Mac computer, for example.

There are other providers of wireless synchronization for mobile devices. Google Sync works with a range of devices. All of your Google e-mail, calendar events, and contacts are automatically backed up online instantly on the Google servers. Even the Amazon Kindle uses wireless synchronization so that if you read a bit further in your e-book on your phone, when you get to your office the Kindle software on your PC will have automatically updated to bookmark the new page you're on.

## Text Messaging

**What does SMS stand for? Short message service (SMS)**—often just called *text messaging*—is a technology that lets you send short text messages (up to 160 characters) over cellular networks. You can send SMS messages to other mobile devices or to any e-mail address.

Companies now support texting in many ways—for example, your bank may allow you to text commands to request account balances or details about your last transaction and the bank will text the requested information back to you.

**How does SMS work?** SMS uses the cell-phone network to transmit messages. When you send an SMS message, an SMS calling center receives the message and delivers it to the appropriate mobile device using something called *store-and-forward* technology. This technology allows users to send SMS messages to any other SMS device in the world.

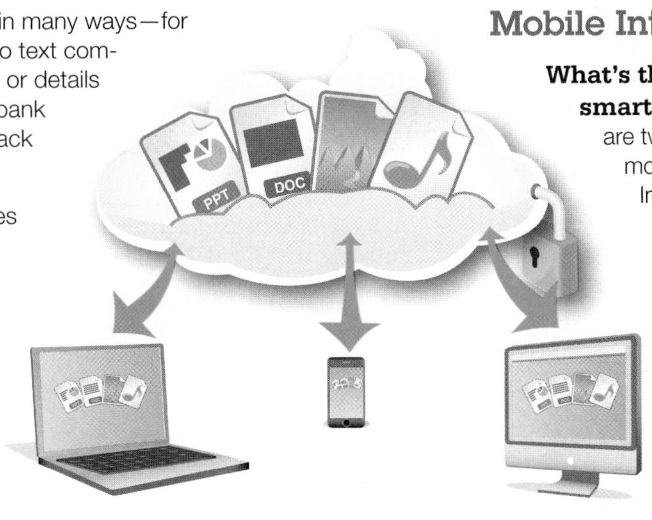

**Is the same technology used to send and receive photos and videos?** SMS technology lets you send only text messages. However, an extension of SMS called **multimedia message service (MMS)** lets you send messages that include text, sound, images, and video clips to other phones or e-mail addresses. MMS messages actually arrive as a series of messages; you view the text, then the image, then the sound, and so on. You can then choose to save just one part of the message (such as the image), all of it, or none of it. MMS users can subscribe to financial, sports, and weather services that will "push" information to them, sending it automatically to their phones in MMS format.

FIGURE 8.8 A cloud service lets you keep the information on your phone instantly in sync with your other computing devices.

# BITS&BYTES

## Texting for Change

Can texting impact social change? Texting is now being used to address serious social issues because it is the choice communication mode of people age 14 to 30. Studies show that texts reach the teenage population at 11 times the effectiveness of e-mail. The average number of monthly texts a teenager sends and receives is over 3,500 a month. This holds true across a wide range of socioeconomic categories.

Crisis texting hotlines are opening to reach and respond to violence, rape, and bullying that young people experience. The site DoSomething.org (**dosomething.org**) opened a Crisis Text Line to organize their response to crisis text messages they were receiving. In addition, police around the country are establishing anonymous texting tip lines to take advantage of the prevalence of texting.

## Mobile Internet

**What's the best way to connect my smartphone to the Internet?** There are two ways smartphones (and most mobile devices) can connect to the Internet:

1. Using a WiFi network
2. Using the cellular phone system (a 3G or 4G connection)

A major advantage of WiFi is that it offers a faster data-transfer speed. However, there may not always be a WiFi signal available where you are. Cellular networks are much more widely available, whether you're in your car or just walking down the street.

For devices like tablets, manufacturers will offer one model that can only connect to the Internet using WiFi and another model that costs more but can connect with either WiFi or cellular 3G/4G.

**Who sells cellular Internet service for my smartphone?** Just as you have an Internet service provider (ISP) for Internet access for your desktop or laptop computer, you must have a **wireless Internet service provider** (or **wireless ISP**) to connect your smartphone to the Internet. Phone companies (such as T-Mobile, Verizon, and AT&T) double as wireless ISPs. Most wireless ISPs also offer free login to their network of WiFi hotspots if you're a cellular customer.

**How do I purchase Internet time?** Providers measure your Internet usage not according to how much time you're on the Internet but according to how much data you download and upload. An Internet connectivity plan is known as a **data plan**. You pay one monthly price and are allowed data transfers up to some fixed limit per month, such as 2 GB or 500 MB. If you exceed your data limit in a month, the fee for the extra data usage is usually very expensive.

Understanding your data usage is complicated. A cellular data plan is for Internet data transfer, not texting. Providers require a separate texting plan. Note that all the data transfer you do using WiFi (instead of the 3G/4G network) do not count as part of your data plan usage.

**How big a data plan do I need to buy?** Before subscribing to a data plan, you should assess your needs:

- How often will you be able to use WiFi access, and how often will you need to use the cellular network?
- How often do you download apps, stream music, or play online games?
- Do you use your phone to watch streaming video?
- Do you use your smartphone's Internet access to download files attached to e-mails or from your company website?

Begin by estimating how much data you transfer up and down from the Internet each month. To do so, you can use an online estimator supplied by your provider like the one from AT&T shown in Figure 8.9. Apps such as My Data Usage Pro or 3G Watchdog are also available for any smartphone to keep track of data usage for you.

Be sure you select a plan that provides adequate service at a good price. Remember, most providers require each device using cellular Internet to be covered by a data plan.

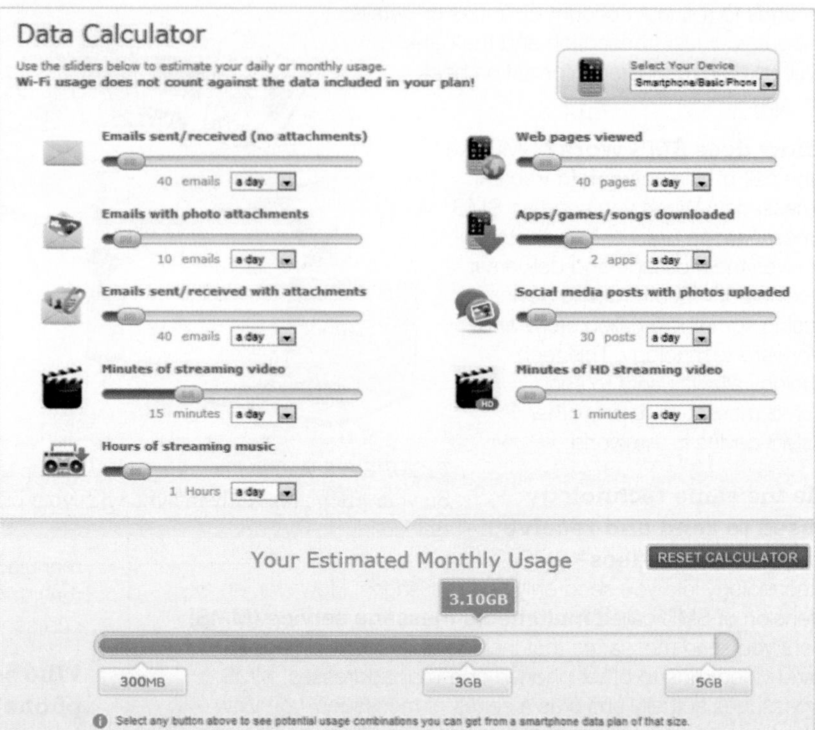


**FIGURE 8.9** Online tools can help you estimate your monthly data usage. *(Courtesy of AT&T)*

**At what speed is digital information transferred to my smartphone?** Although broadband speeds of 50 megabits per second (Mbps) are achievable at home using a cable or fiber-optic connection, your smartphone will connect at a much lower speed. The exact speed will depend on which technology you're using: WiFi, 3G cellular, or 4G cellular (see Figure 8.10).

We discussed WiFi networks in depth in Chapter 7. These networks typically run at speeds of 4 to 5 Mbps. Currently, there are two cellular data-transfer standards:

1. *3G:* 3G brought mobile device data-transfer rates as high as 3.8 Mbps (or more, under ideal conditions). 3G is more reliable than WiFi and is less susceptible to interference. 3G blankets most major urban areas with connectivity.
2. *4G:* 4G networks are now rolling out across the United States. The promise of 4G is incredible: mobile connection speeds of up to 100 Mbps! Currently, most providers can't deliver true 4G speeds; their 4G networks deliver speeds of 6 Mbps to 13 Mbps. These options, often named "4G LTE," are faster than 3G but don't meet the rate required to be true 4G, so they're referred to as "near 4G" networks. The expansion of 4G will usher in a new generation of mobile devices.

**How do I set my phone to use a WiFi connection?** It will be slightly different for each mobile OS, but in general, you turn on the setting that allows your phone to look for a network. If a network is found, the phone will try to log in. If the network has security protection, you'll be prompted for a password before joining. Most smartphones then display a special icon to show that you're using a WiFi connection instead of a 3G/4G signal.

## BITS&BYTES

### Want to Read That Voicemail?

Consider using Google Voice. Google Voice automatically transcribes your voice messages to text so if you're at a noisy concert, you can still check in on that last call. The transcription makes it easy to search for information left in a voice message. If you want, the transcribed calls can be e-mailed to you and you can text back a response right from the e-mail. You can sign up for a free Google Voice phone number at **google.com/voice**.

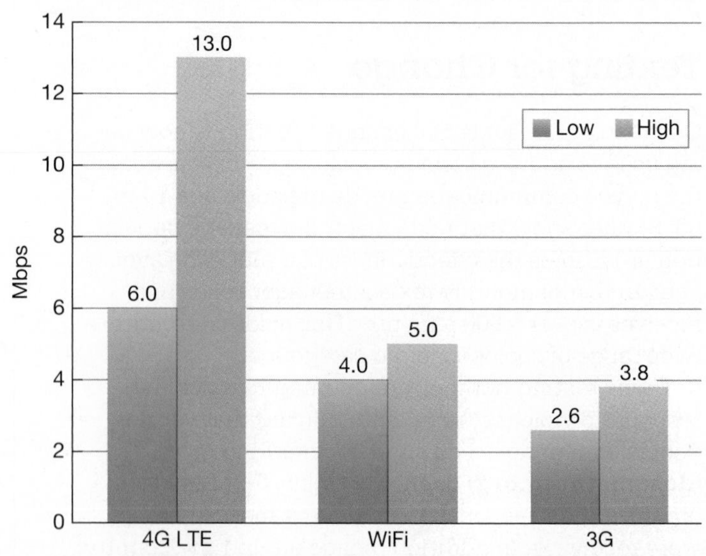


**FIGURE 8.10** The range of speeds you achieve when connecting to the Internet with your smartphone or mobile device depends on the type of connection.

ACTIVE HELPDESK

**Keeping Your Data on Hand**

In this Active Helpdesk call, you'll play the role of a help-desk staffer fielding calls about smartphones—what you can use them for, what internal components and features they have, and how you can synchronize these mobile devices with your computer.

Some people choose to leave their phone in the mode where it's looking for a WiFi network so it will always use a WiFi signal if it is available, saving them on data plan usage. This does use more battery life, though, so turn off WiFi detection if you're trying to extend your battery.

**Can I use my 3G/4G signal to create a WiFi hotspot for my other devices?** As mentioned in Chapter 7, if a WiFi spot isn't available, there are devices that will instantly create a mobile hotspot for you. MiFi (pronounced "my fy") devices are often available free with a new account from major Internet providers like Verizon and AT&T. These devices connect to the Internet through the wireless phone network and then distribute the WiFi signal over an area of 30 feet. These personal hot spots can then support up to 10 WiFi-enabled devices.

Another approach is **tethering**, which makes sure that as long as you have a 3G/4G signal, your computer can access the Internet even when it tells you there are no available wireless networks. Several phones offer this capability. For example, an iPhone can connect to your notebook computer through wireless Bluetooth and then provide Internet access through its 4G network signal. Check with your provider, though, because they may charge an extra fee for tethering.

## Smartphone Security

**Can I get a virus on my smartphone?** Viruses can indeed infect smartphones. Over half of users say they send confidential e-mails using their phones, and one-third of users access bank account or credit card information on their phones, so smartphones are the next most likely realm of attack by cybercriminals. Although viruses plaguing smartphones have not yet reached the volume of viruses attacking PC operating systems, with the proliferation of mobile devices, virus attacks are expected to increase.

Kaspersky, McAfee, and F-Secure are among leading companies currently providing antivirus software for mobile devices. Products are designed for specific operating systems; for example, Kaspersky Mobile Security has versions for Android phones and tablets, Windows phones, and BlackBerry devices. Often, businesses will have their information technology department install and configure an antivirus solution like this for all the phones used in the organization.

If no antivirus program is available for your phone's OS, the best precautions are commonsense ones. Check the phone manufacturer's website frequently to see whether your smartphone needs any software upgrades that could patch security holes. In addition, remember that you shouldn't download ring tones, games, or other software from unfamiliar websites.

**How do I keep my phone number private?** If you're concerned about widely distributing your phone number and potentially inviting lots of unwanted calls, consider using a virtual phone number. A virtual phone number is a phone number you create that can be assigned to ring on existing phone numbers. Companies such as Telusion (**tossabledigits.com**) will sell you a virtual number. Then, when you're filling out a registration form for some web service, you can input your virtual phone number in the web form instead of giving out your number. When you set up the virtual account, you can restrict the hours that you will receive calls from that number, and if you're receiving many unwanted calls, you can disable the virtual number without affecting your cell- or smartphone service.

## VoIP

**Is the cellular network the only way to place phone calls?** Cell phone service is still not 100% reliable, and dropped calls and poor reception are a problem in some areas. As an alternative, a fully digital phone service called **Voice over Internet Protocol (VoIP)** is available.

**How is VoIP different from regular telephone service?** VoIP is a form of voice-based Internet communication that turns a standard Internet connection into a means to place phone calls, including long-distance calls (see Figure 8.11). Traditional telephone communications use analog voice data and telephone connections. In contrast, VoIP uses technology similar to that used in e-mail to transmit your voice data digitally over the Internet.

**Who are some VoIP providers?** Skype is one very well-known provider. Creating a VoIP account with Skype (**skype.com**) is simple (see the Try This in Chapter 1, pages 12–13). Skype requires that both callers and receivers have the

**FIGURE 8.11** VoIP technology lets your computing device behave like a phone or video phone, using the Internet instead of the telephone system to transmit data. *(jd-photodesign/Fotolia)*

company's free software installed on their device (computer, tablet, or phone). With Skype you can place a phone call, make an HD-video call, and even share screens between users. Calls to other Skype users are free, and you can place low-cost calls to non-Skype users. Other VoIP service providers, such as Vonage (**vonage.com**), are a bit more complicated to set up and are not free. Major ISPs, like Comcast and Verizon, also provide VoIP phone services as an option you can package with your Internet or cable television plan.

**What do I need to use VoIP?** VoIP calls can be placed from anywhere you have Internet access. Any Android or iOS phone or tablet can also be used as a VoIP device. There are also standalone VoIP phones sold, sometimes called *IP phones*.

**What are the advantages and disadvantages of VoIP?** For people who make many long-distance phone calls, the advantage of VoIP is that it's free or low cost. Portability is another advantage: As long as you're connected to the Internet, you can sign on to your VoIP service and make your call.

Although VoIP is affordable and convenient, it does have drawbacks:

- Some people regard sound quality and reliability issues as VoIP's primary disadvantages.
- Another drawback when using VoIP at home is the loss of service if power is interrupted.
- Another issue with VoIP is security risks. Having a hacker break in to a VoIP system to make unauthorized calls is a serious but avoidable problem. Encryption services that convert data into a form not easily understood by unauthorized people are being deployed to help protect calls made over the Internet.

VoIP continues to enjoy explosive growth, and the technology will continue to improve.

**What new features come with using VoIP?** If you set up a VoIP service as your home telephone system, you can have your telephone messages automatically bundled up as e-mails and sent to your account. If you're watching television and a call comes in, it can be displayed on the screen with caller ID information. Some learning management systems also use VoIP. For example, if you're using MyITLab with this course, you can call your professor through VoIP without having his or her personal phone number.

## Smartphone GPS

**Does my smartphone contain a GPS chip?** Today every cell- and smartphone has to include a GPS chip. The Federal Communications Commission (FCC) mandated this to enable the complete rollout of the Enhanced 911 (E911) program. E911 automatically gives dispatchers precise location information for any 911 call. It also means your phone records may include this precise tracking information, which indicates where you are when you make a call.

**How does GPS work?** Built and operated by the U.S. Department of Defense, the **global positioning system (GPS)** is a network of 21 satellites (plus 3 working spares) that constantly orbits the Earth. GPS devices use an antenna to pick up the signals from these satellites and use special software to transform those signals into latitude and longitude. Using the information obtained from the satellites, GPS devices determine geographical location anywhere on the planet to within 3 feet (see Figure 8.12). The exact accuracy depends on such things as atmospheric conditions and interference from obstacles like mountains or buildings.

**Can I track a family member using the GPS chip in his or her phone?** Cell-phone providers offer plans (for a monthly fee) that allow you to track where a phone is at any given time. For example, AT&T's Family Map service lets parents track all the phones on their family plan in real time. Locations of all phones are displayed over the web on a map or to an app for your phone, or the service will send an automatic text message alert with the phones' locations at a specific time each day. So a parent could have a text or e-mail sent with his or her daughter's phone location each day at 3 p.m. to be sure she made it home from school. The person being tracked can't turn off the service. ■

**FIGURE 8.12** GPS computes your location anywhere on Earth from a system of orbiting satellites.

# tablets, netbooks, and ULTRABOOKS

The best way to navigate all the mobile devices on the market is to be aware of the boundaries between types of devices. In this section, we'll look at what changes when you move from one type of device to another.

## Tablets

**How do tablets compare with smartphones?** *Tablets* are very light, very portable devices. The top-selling tablets include the Apple iPad and the Samsung Galaxy, but there are over 75 tablets on the market (see Figure 8.13). The main difference between any tablet and a smartphone is screen size. Whereas smartphones usually have displays that are less than 5 inches, tablets come with screen sizes between 7 and 10 inches. But manufacturers are beginning to make even larger phones, offering a "phablet" model of phone, with screen sizes almost 6 inches. The larger screen allows for a larger virtual keyboard and higher resolution.

In most other regards, smartphones and tablets are similar. They have the following features:

- Similar operating systems: Whether iOS or Android, common operating systems operate on smartphones and tablets.
- Similar processors: The processing power of smartphones and tablets is often the same.
- Touch-screen interfaces: Smartphones and tablets are both equipped with touch-screen interfaces.
- Long battery life: Most tablets and smartphones run at least 10 hours on a single charge.
- Similar software applications: Most apps available for one device are available for the other.
- Similar Internet connectivity: Both offer 3G/4G as well as WiFi connectivity.
- Bluetooth: Both can be connected over Bluetooth to printers, keyboards, and other peripherals.

**FIGURE 8.13** iPad...Xoom...Galaxy? There are over 75 tablets on the market now. Finding the right digital device can be a challenge. *(oliver leedham/Alamy)*

**Can tablets function as a communication device?** Although tablets are currently not able to make cell-phone calls, they can easily place audio or video phone calls if connected to a WiFi network. A VoIP application like Skype is required for that. There are also apps available that allow tablets to handle texting. HeyWire, for example, supports free national and international texting from a range of devices, including tablets as well as phones.

## Netbooks

**Why would I want a netbook instead of a tablet?** A tablet runs a mobile OS. A *netbook*, on the other hand, uses a full traditional OS, like Windows 8. This means you can't run programs like Microsoft Office on a tablet, but you can on a netbook. In addition, a netbook has a physical keyboard. Netbooks weigh 2 pounds or less and are inexpensive compared with both tablets and ultrabooks, so they are a good option if you're looking for value. Many models are available for under $300.

**Why wouldn't I want a netbook?** The processing power and memory on a netbook makes it difficult to run software that does a lot of computation. Netbooks also have very small screens (usually 10 inches or less). The screen resolution and small keyboard may not work for your needs, so be sure to try one out before making a purchase.

## Ultrabooks

**How are ultrabooks different from laptops?** *Ultrabooks* are a newer category of full-featured computers that focus on offering a very thin, lightweight computing solution. Ultrabooks don't offer optical drives, for example, allowing a very thin profile. Most ultrabooks offer SSD drives and so have very fast response times on boot up and restoring from hibernation. They weigh in at under 3 pounds even though they feature the same operating systems and CPUs as heavier, larger laptops. They also include full-size keyboards and

13- to 15-inch screens. Examples include the Apple Macbook Air and the Asus Zenbook.

**How are ultrabooks different from tablets?** Whereas tablets share a lot in common with smartphones, ultrabooks are lightweight laptops. They are good choices when you want to run a traditional OS, have a lot of computing power, and aren't concerned with touch-screen features. Figure 8.14 summarizes how tablets and ultrabooks compare.

FIGURE 8.14

**Tablets Versus Ultrabooks**

| FEATURE | TABLET | ULTRABOOK |
|---|---|---|
| **Operating System** | Mobile OS (iOS, Android, Windows) | Traditional OS (Windows or OS X) |
| **Interface** | Touch screen | Non-touch screen and full-size keyboard |
| **Screen Size** | 7 to 10 inches | 13 to 15 inches |
| **Processing Power** | Mobile processor | Full quad-core Intel i5, i7 |
| **Storage** | ≤ 128 GB | 128 to 500 GB |
| **Software** | Specialized applications custom designed for touch interface | Standard versions of software for desktop environments (Microsoft Office, etc.) |

## Making a Choice

**With all these choices, how do I know which device is best for me?** Use these guidelines to determine what best fits your personal needs for this particular device. Consider the following:

- **Screen size and style of keyboard:** You can adapt these with accessories (add a Bluetooth keyboard or connect to a larger external monitor), but most of the time these will determine how you interact with your device. Do you want a touch-based interface? Is a physical keyboard important, or is a software keyboard sufficient?
- **Weight:** Does an additional 2 pounds matter? The price of an ultrabook is several hundred dollars more than an equivalent laptop.
- **Number of devices:** Is this your only computing device? As technology prices fall, you may be able to have more than one device. You might find an affordable solution that includes both a very mobile device and a second more powerful one.

Figure 8.15 summarizes several different mobile device categories. ■

# BITS&BYTES

## The Fabulous Phablet

You may have noticed that the screens of smartphones are growing. In fact, the latest generation has grown into a cross between a phone and a tablet, creating a new category (and a new word): the *phablet*. These touch-screen phones sport screens larger than 5.5 inches. Especially in emerging global markets in China and India, the phablet is increasingly the tool of choice because one device is taking the place of having both a phone and a separate home computer.

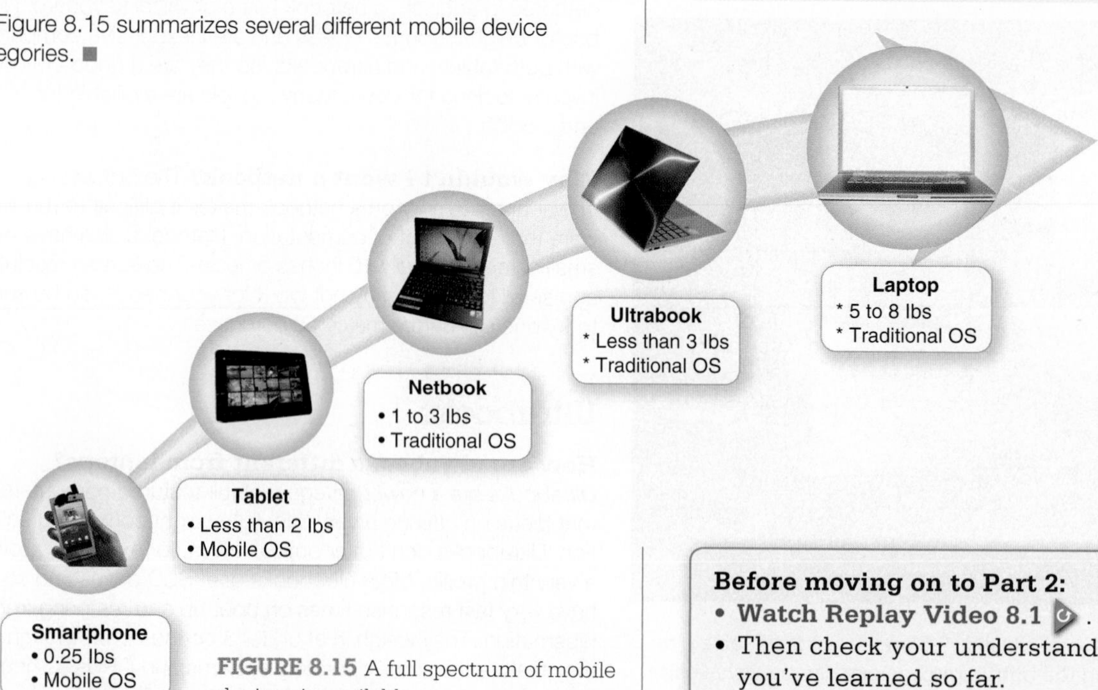


FIGURE 8.15 A full spectrum of mobile devices is available.

(Peter Dazeley/Getty Images; Bloomberg/Getty Images; Ethan Miller/Getty Images, Inc.; Josep lago/Getty Images, Inc.; Sean Gallup/Getty Images, Inc.)

**Before moving on to Part 2:**
- **Watch Replay Video 8.1** .
- Then check your understanding of what you've learned so far.

# check your understanding//

For a quick review to see what you've learned so far, answer the following questions. Visit **pearsonhighered.com /techinaction** to check your answers.

## multiple choice

1. The operating system of your cell phone or smartphone is stored in
   - **a.** read-only memory.
   - **b.** the display.
   - **c.** the digital signal processor.
   - **d.** random access memory.
2. VoIP is phone service that
   - **a.** requires a fiber-optic connection.
   - **b.** works over an Internet connection.
   - **c.** is only available for calls within the United States.
   - **d.** has extremely high quality but is very expensive.
3. Which service allows you to use your cell phone or smartphone to send messages that contain images?
   - **a.** MMS
   - **b.** ISP
   - **c.** SMS
   - **d.** MiFi
4. When there are no available wireless networks, your phone
   - **a.** cannot reach the Internet.
   - **b.** can create a wireless network if you have a data plan.
   - **c.** can use VoIP to still send e-mail.
   - **d.** can use tethering to connect your computer to the Internet .
5. There are several categories of mobile devices because
   - **a.** we do not yet have digital convergence.
   - **b.** there is a range of trade-offs between weight and performance.
   - **c.** everyone wants the fastest processor.
   - **d.** no one has designed a digital device that works well for travel.

## true–false

_____ **1.** Digital convergence means that all cellular networks will become 4G.

_____ **2.** Watching streaming video on your phone does not impact your data usage but downloading apps does.

## critical thinking

1. **The Ultimate Style**

   As mobile devices continue to evolve, they have become lighter and smaller, and we are beginning to see a convergence of computing and clothing.
   - **a.** What would the ultimate convergent mobile clothing be for you? Is there a limit in weight, size, or complexity?
   - **b.** Can you imagine uses for technology in fashion that would support better health? Better social relationships? A richer intellectual life?
2. **Tracking**

   With the evolution of mobile devices has come the ability to locate family members in real time. By tracking his or her cell-phone location, a child or spouse can be located to within a few feet. People can also choose to broadcast their location through social media sites. What are the benefits and costs of this level of tracking? Does it impact your feelings about privacy? Is there value in going "dark"—disabling location-aware devices?

**Continue**

# TRY THIS — Creating and Publishing a Movie

You've just taken some fantastic video and photos on a trip to the zoo, and you'd like to organize the media and put it on your Facebook page. What should you do? Try Movie Maker!

## Before You Start

a. Before starting, make sure you have several video clips and photos available. If you don't have any of your own, you can use the sample photos and video clips provided with Windows.
b. Movie Maker is part of the Windows Essentials package that is an add-on to Windows (this means it does not come preinstalled in Windows). To install Movie Maker, go to Microsoft's Windows Essentials website (**windows.microsoft.com/en-US/windows-live/essentials-home**) and click the **Download now** link. Once installed, there should be a tile on the Windows 8 Start Screen for Movie Maker. Click (or touch) this tile to launch Movie Maker.

**Step 1** The first step is to import your video clips and photos to Movie Maker. On the **Home tab** of the Ribbon, click the **Add Videos and Photos** icon.

**Step 2** In the dialog box that appears, browse to where your media files are saved, select the files you wish to import, and then click the **Open** button. The files you've added will appear in the Media window.

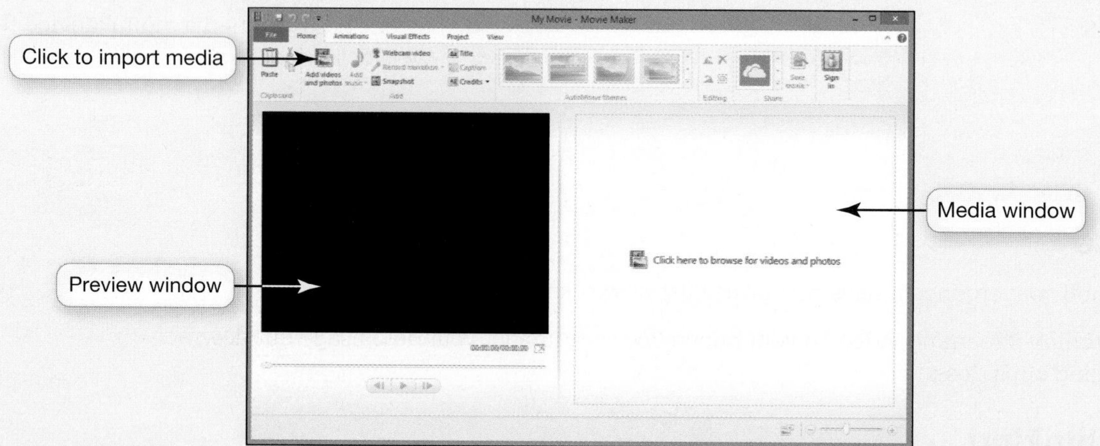


**Step 3** In your movie, the video clips and pictures will display in the order shown in the media window (timeline). Click and drag your media to the spot in the timeline where you want it to appear.

**Step 4** On the **Home tab** of the Ribbon, click the **Add music** icon and browse to a location on your storage device where you have music files. Select the music file you wish to add as a soundtrack for your movie, and then click the **Open** button.

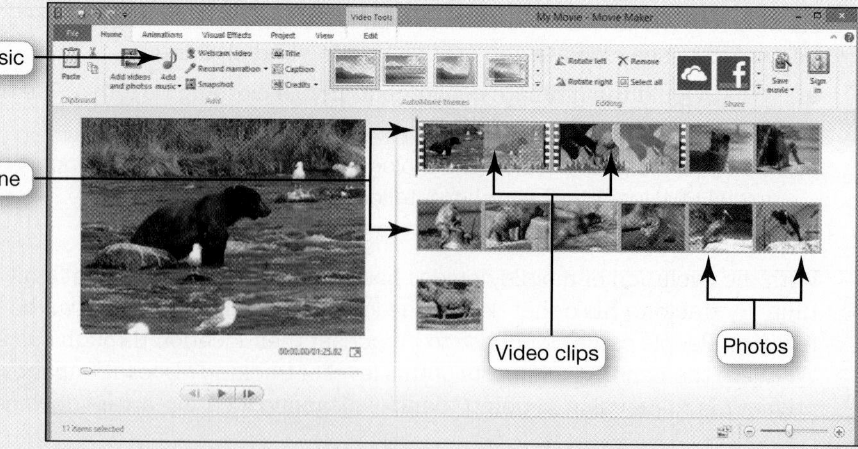

**Step 5** AutoMovie themes will add transitions between clips and title or credit slides based on predesigned templates. Just click on one of the available themes in the **AutoMovie themes** group on the **Home tab** to apply that theme to your movie.

**Step 6** Alternatively, you can manually add a title slide or credit slides by clicking on the appropriate icons on the **Home tab**. Just click on the slide in the preview window to enter a title for your slide.

**Step 7** To preview your movie, click the **Play** button under the Preview window.

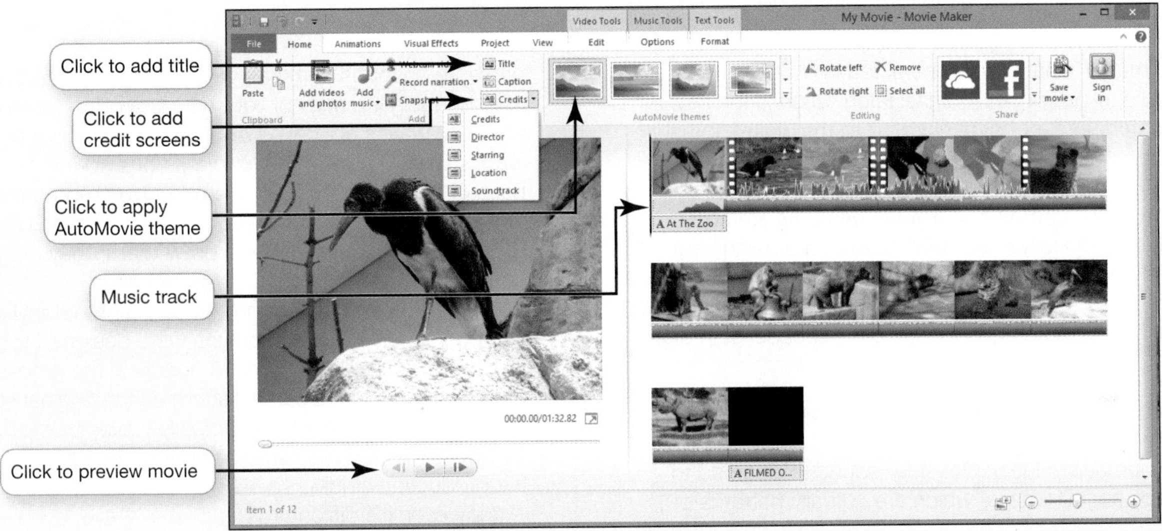


**Step 8** When you're satisfied with your movie, go to the **Home tab** and click the **Save movie** icon to save it.

**Step 9** To publish your movie on Facebook, go to the **Home tab**, and click the **Facebook** icon in the Share group. Select an appropriate resolution for your movie, and log on to your Facebook account (if necessary). Movie Maker will add your movie to your Facebook page.

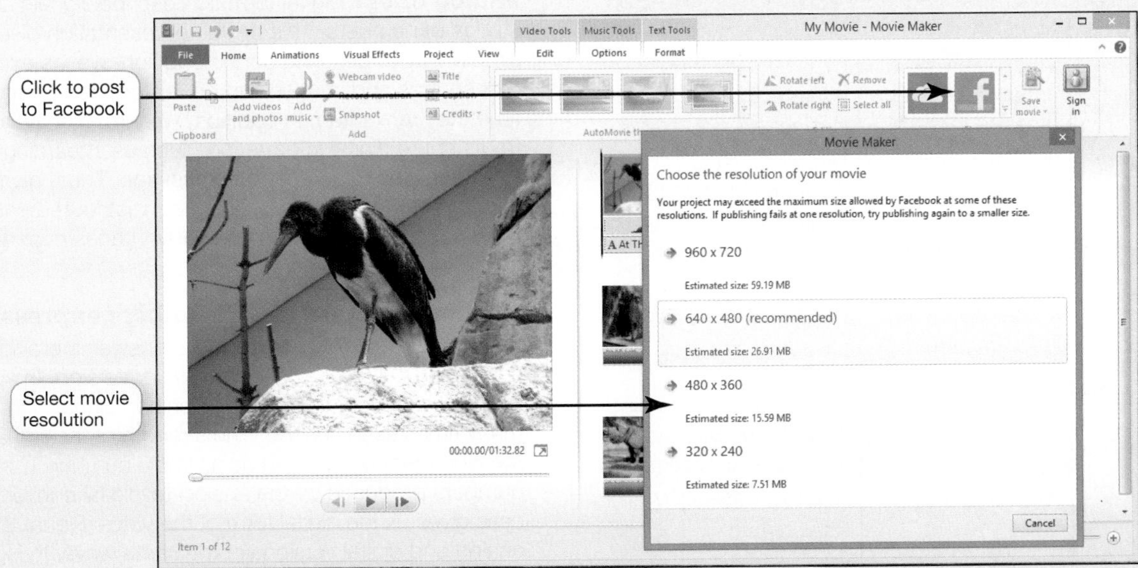

# The Digital Information Age

Do you really understand how all the digital technology you use every day actually works? Do you realize how many revolutionary changes are happening in all kinds of media as we continue to use digital formats? Let's take a closer look at what it means to be "digital" and the advantages it brings us.

## digital DEFINED

Today, no matter what you're interested in—music, movies, TV, radio, stock prices—digital information is the key. All forms of entertainment have migrated to the digital domain (see Figure 8.16). Phone systems and TV signals are now digital streams of data. MP3 files encode digital forms of music, and digital cameras and video cameras are now commonplace. In Hollywood, feature films are being shot entirely with digital equipment, and many movie theaters use digital projection equipment. Satellite radio systems such as SiriusXM satellite radio and HD Radio are broadcast in digital formats.

**How is digital different from analog?** Any kind of information can be digitized (measured and converted to a stream of numeric values). Consider sound. It's carried to your ears by sound waves, which are actually patterns of pressure changes in the air. Images are our interpretation of the changing intensity of light waves around us. These sound and light waves are called **analog** waves or continuous waves. They illustrate the loudness of a sound or the brightness of the colors in an image at a given moment in time. They're continuous signals because you would never have to lift your pencil off the page to draw them; they are just long, continuous lines.

First-generation recording devices such as vinyl records and analog television broadcasts were designed to reproduce these sound and light waves. A needle in the groove of a vinyl record vibrates in the same pattern as the original sound wave. Analog television signals are actually waves that tell an analog TV how to display the same color and brightness as is seen in the production studio.

However, it's difficult to describe a wave, even mathematically. The simplest sounds, such as that of middle C on a piano, have the simplest shapes, like the one shown in Figure 8.17a. However, something like the word *hello* generates a highly complex pattern, like the one shown in Figure 8.17b.

**What advantages do digital formats have over analog ones?** Digital formats describe signals as long strings of numbers. This digital representation gives us a simple way to describe sound and light waves exactly so that sounds and images can be reproduced perfectly any time they're wanted. In addition, we already have easy ways to distribute digital information, such as streaming movies or attaching files to a Facebook message. Thus, digital information can be reproduced exactly and distributed easily; both these reasons give digital huge advantages over an analog format.

**How can a sequence of numbers express complicated analog shapes?** The answer is provided by something called *analog-to-digital conversion*. In analog-to-digital conversion, the incoming analog signal is measured many times each second. The strength of the signal at each measurement is recorded as a simple number. The series of numbers produced by the analog-to-digital conversion process gives us the digital form of the wave. Figure 8.18 shows analog and digital versions of the same wave. In Figure 8.18a, you see the original, continuous analog wave. You could draw that wave without lifting your pencil from the page. In

FIGURE 8.16

**Analog Versus Digital Entertainment**

| | ANALOG | DIGITAL |
|---|---|---|
| **Publishing** | Magazines, books | E-books, e-zines |
| **Music** | Vinyl record albums and cassette tapes | CDs, MP3 files, and streaming music stations |
| **Photography** | 35-mm single-lens reflex (SLR) cameras<br>Photos stored on film | Digital cameras, including digital SLRs<br>Photos stored as digital files |
| **Video** | 8-mm, VHS, and Hi8 camcorders<br>Film stored on tapes | HD digital video (DV) cameras<br>Film stored as digital files; distributed on DVD and Blu-ray discs and streamed |
| **Radio** | AM/FM radio | HD Radio, SiriusXM satellite radio |
| **Television** | Analog TV broadcast | High-definition digital television (HDTV) |

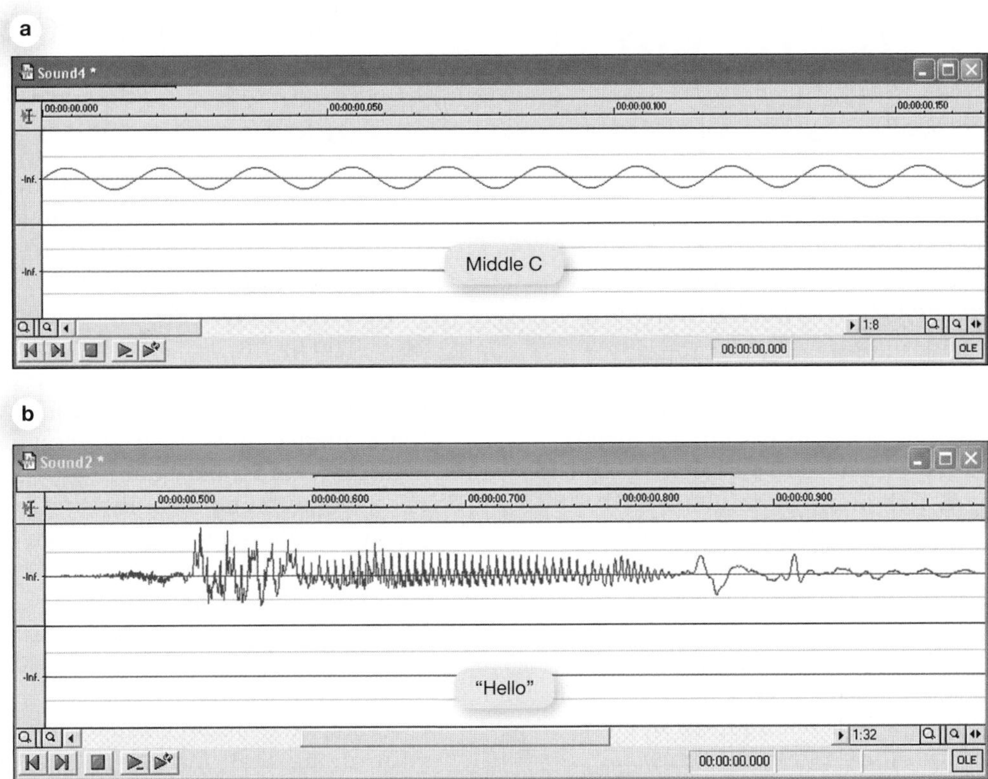


**FIGURE 8.17** (a) This is an analog wave showing the simple, pure sound of a piano playing middle C. (b) This is the complex wave produced when a person says "Hello."

Figure 8.18b, the wave has been digitized and is no longer a single line; instead, it is represented as a series of points or numbers.

**How has the change from analog to digital technologies affected our lifestyles?** When the market for communication devices for entertainment media—like photos, music, and video—switched to a digital standard, we began to have products with new and useful capabilities. Small devices can now hold huge collections of a variety of types of information. We can interact with our information any time we like in ways that, prior to the conversion to digital media, had been too expensive or too difficult to learn. The implications of the shift to digital media are continually evolving. ■

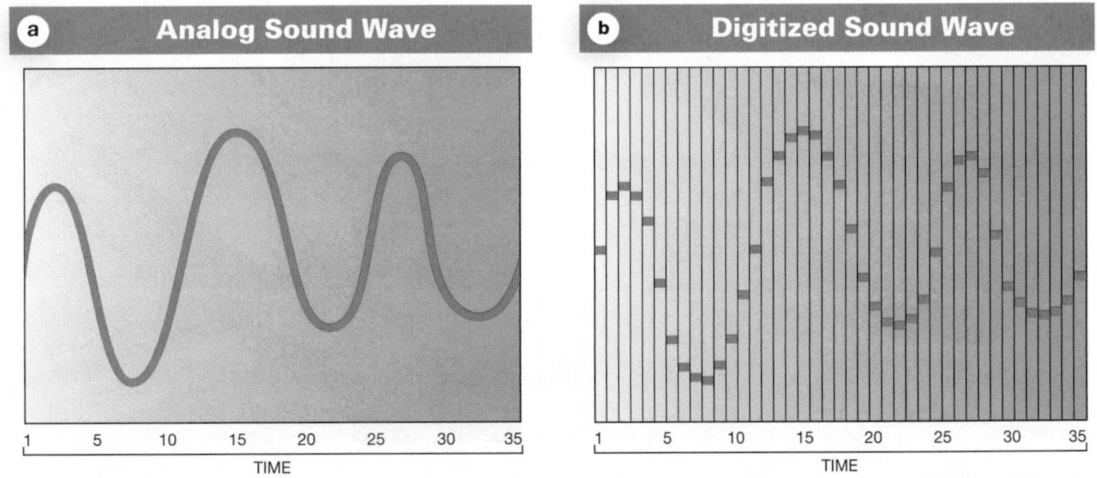


**FIGURE 8.18** (a) A simple analog wave. (b) A digitized version of the same wave. *(Courtesy of SONY Creative Software.; Courtesy of SONY Creative Software.)*

# trends in IT

## NFC Chips: Do You Have a Digital Wallet?

Your mobile device performs many tasks, and now, thanks to near field communication (NFC) technology, it will feature yet another form of convergence: the integration of your wallet into your phone. How so? NFC technology allows a device with an NFC chip (such as a smartphone) to communicate with another NFC device (such as a checkout machine) with a single touch. In fact, with NFC, you can forget your wallet: Financial transactions can be processed just by bringing the devices within an inch of each other.

Because NFC has such a short range (up to 1.5 inches), it is being used for secure credit card transactions. Both MasterCard and Visa are piloting programs that would allow cell phones to "tap and go," meaning phone owners would no longer need to carry physical credit cards. Instead, they could simply tap their phone near an NFC checkout device and have it automatically transmit the proper loyalty card information, select and process any coupon offers, and pay all at once (see Figure 8.19).

In countries like Japan, Spain, and Germany, NFC ticketing programs are already in place. The Deutsche Bahn rail system allows users to tap their phones to an NFC tag when they get on the train and to another on departing. The fare is automatically calculated and billed to their credit card monthly. Marketing agencies are also using NFC. An NFC chip can be stored inside a poster, for example. When a passerby touches his or her phone to a specific spot, a coupon or a website address can be transmitted.

NFC can handle identification verification as well. The swipe cards that verify your identity for entry into secure areas can be replaced using NFC to exchange stored virtual credentials. The same technology can be used to open door locks or any system where a user name and password are used. So, opening a cabinet or logging into a computer can all be managed with a tap of your NFC-enabled phone.

Several mobile applications, such as Google Wallet and Isis, are available for NFC sales transactions. These programs conduct NFC transactions as well as collect your loyalty cards, gift cards, receipts, boarding passes, tickets, and keys within your phone. Currently not all service providers will enable the NFC chip on your smartphone, however, so check before you buy a new phone.

Imagine a time soon when you're out to dinner with friends and need to split the bill. Your NFC phone is already linked to your credit card, and you simply tap your friend's phone to transfer him his share of the bill. Some are predicting the worldwide NFC market will grow to be worth $50 billion over the next few years, making this a trend to watch.

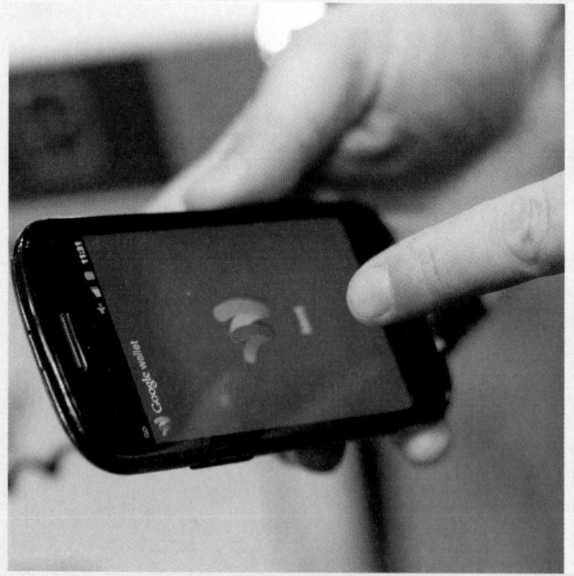

**FIGURE 8.19** NFC-equipped phones will shift how we handle financial transactions and identify ourselves.
*(AP Photo/File)*

# digital MEDIA

The entertainment industry has become an all-digital field. The publishing industry, the music recording industry, photography, and film production have all seen radical changes in how content is created and how it is distributed to an audience. Let's look at these forms of entertainment and how they affect you.

## Digital Publishing

**Are printed books dead?** The publishing industry is migrating to digital materials. **Electronic text (e-text)** is textual information captured digitally so that it can be stored, manipulated, and transmitted by electronic devices. With the increasing usage of e-text, the market for printed materials is changing dramatically. In fact, Amazon now sells more Kindle e-books than printed books each year. Several authors, such as Stieg Larsson and James Patterson, have each sold over one million e-books.

**What electronic devices are trying to replace books? E-readers** (see Figure 8.20) are devices that can display e-text and have supporting tools, like note taking, bookmarks, and integrated dictionaries. They are selling at a brisk pace with a dizzying range of offerings in the market, including the Amazon Kindle and Fire, Barnes and Noble NOOK, and Sony Reader.

**FIGURE 8.20** E-readers are popularizing the digital e-book. *(Kristoffer Tripplaar/Alamy)*

Tablets are also helping to popularize the digitized e-book and electronic versions of major magazines and newspapers. In the U.S. book market, e-books seem to be settling in at between 20 to 30% of total book sales.

**What features make e-readers popular?** One big allure of digital publishing is distribution. Ease of access to digital books is very attractive. Even a 1,000-page book can be delivered to your e-reader in under a minute. An incredible array of titles is available—over one million books are available in the Amazon Kindle store alone. In addition, there are millions of texts without copyright that are available for free.

The basic features of e-readers offer many advantages over paper books:

- Integrated dictionaries pull up a definition just by your highlighting a word. The Kindle, for example, can work with both English and German dictionaries—a help in reading foreign works.
- Note taking and highlighting are supported, and you can search the text for your own notes or for specific terms. You can also easily share the notes you make on the book with others.
- URL links or links to a glossary are often live in the book.
- Bookmarks are immediately pushed through cloud technology so you can read on one device and pick up with the most current bookmark on another device.

**Do I need a dedicated device just for reading e-texts?** There are free software download versions of the Kindle and the NOOK that run on either PC or Apple computers. You can also download certain texts that have no copyrights and read them directly on a computer either as a PDF file or by using browser add-ons like MagicScroll.

**How is digital text displayed?** There are two popular technologies used for representing digital text:

1. *Electronic ink:* **Electronic ink (E Ink)** is a very crisp, sharp grayscale representation of text. The "page" is composed of millions of microcapsules with white and black particles in a clear fluid. Electronic signals can make each spot appear either white or black. E Ink devices reflect the light that shines on the page, like ordinary paper. E Ink gives great contrast and is much easier to read in direct sunlight. Examples of devices using E Ink include high-contrast screens like the Amazon Kindle Paperwhite (see Figure 8.21a) and the Barnes and Noble NOOK.
2. *Backlit monitors:* Another option for presenting e-text is the high-resolution backlit monitors seen in readers like the iPad or the Amazon Fire (see Figure 8.21b). These screens illuminate themselves instead of depending on

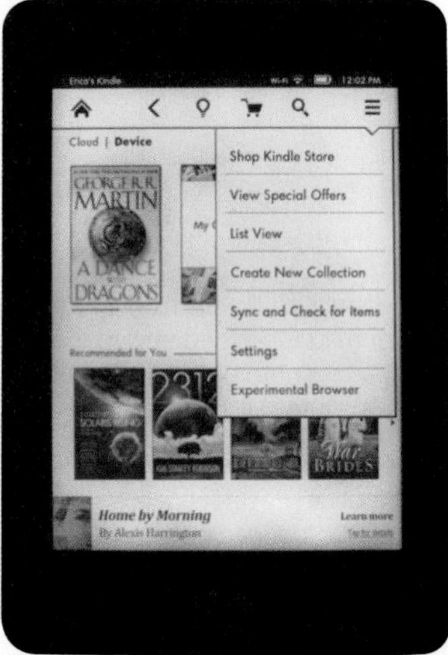

**FIGURE 8.21** The two main technologies for e-text display are (a) E Ink grayscale displays, like on the Amazon Kindle, and (b) high-resolution backlit color screens, like on the Amazon Fire. *(David McNew/Alamy; EMMANUEL DUNAND/Getty Images)*

room lighting conditions. They display color materials, like magazines, with great clarity and full color. The glass does reflect glare, though, which makes them hard to use in bright, direct sunlight. Some people experience more fatigue when reading from a backlit device than when using E Ink. Also note that E Ink readers have a battery life of a month or two on a charge, whereas high-resolution color readers hold a charge for 8 to 10 hours.

Be sure to try both under a variety of conditions before you make a purchasing decision.

**What kinds of file formats are used in electronic publishing?** Digital formats for publishing vary. Amazon uses a proprietary format (.azw extension), so books purchased for a Kindle are not transportable to a non-Kindle device. An open format also exists, ePub. Some e-readers support the ePub file format. There is an ePub reader plugin available for the browser Firefox and several stand-alone software ePub readers like Stanza.

**Where do I buy e-books?** There are a number of vendors associated with e-reader devices:

- Amazon sells the Kindle device, and it connects directly to the Amazon Kindle store.
- The Barnes and Noble NOOK device works with the Barnes and Noble e-bookstore.
- There are many publishers selling e-books online that can be read on any kind of device.
- Textbooks can be purchased in e-book format directly from the publisher; for example, the technology publisher O'Reilly has an online e-bookstore. Another option is a company like CourseSmart, which offers a year-long subscription to a digital text that times out and disappears from your device after your subscription is up.

**What if I just want to borrow a book from a library?** Libraries are now including e-book and audio book lending as part of their mission (see Figure 8.22). There is never a late fee; the book just times out and disappears from your device when the borrowing period expires. Products like the Overdrive Media Console (**search.overdrive.com**) let you search to find which area library has the book you want. When you log in to the library website, you can download a text any time of day or night. Libraries have a specific number of copies of each e-book title available, so you may be added to a waiting list if all the copies are checked out, just like with paper books. However, there is a lot of friction between publishers and libraries on how to handle the impact of lending electronically. It's so convenient that some publishers are refusing to allow their e-books to be distributed through libraries.

**Can I borrow an e-book from a friend?** Lending of e-books is now becoming a popular feature of e-reader systems. The Barnes & Noble NOOK, for example, has a Lend Me feature on certain books. An eligible book can be loaned once for a period of 14 days.

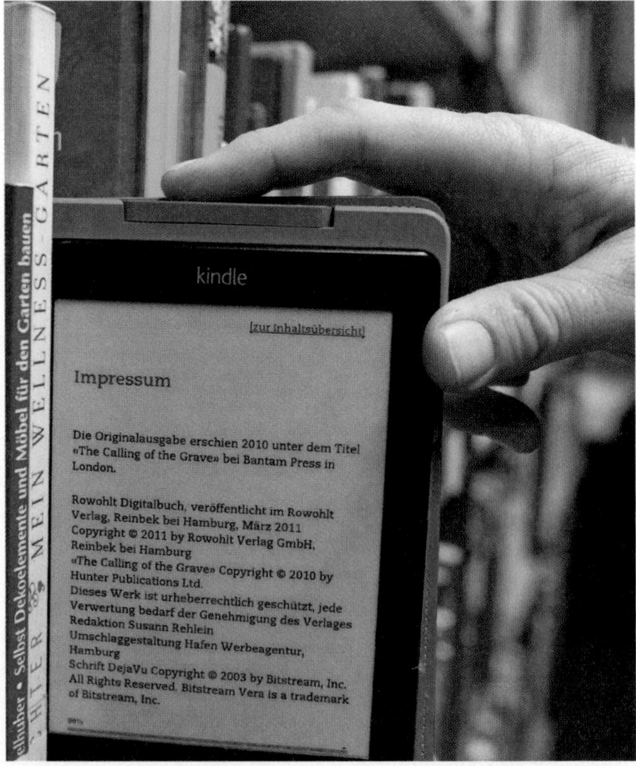


**FIGURE 8.22** E-books and audio books can be borrowed for free at most public libraries. *(Alex Ehlers/dpa/picture-alliance/Newscom)*

**Where can I find free e-books?** A great source of free reading is Project Gutenberg (**gutenberg.org**). This repository site is a collection of over 42,000 free books in ePub, Kindle, and PDF formats. It contains books that are free in the United States because their copyrights have expired. The catalog includes many classic titles like *War and Peace* by Leo Tolstoy or mystery novels by Agatha Christie.

**How can I publish my own works?** Self-publishing is much easier in the age of digital texts. There are many options available:

- Self-publish into the *Amazon Kindle Store* in a matter of minutes and earn up to a 70% royalty on sales.
- Use a company like *Smashwords* (**smashwords.com**). It accepts a Microsoft Word document from you and then makes your book available through a number of vendors like the Apple iBooks store, Barnes & Noble, and the Sony Reader store. Your book can also be distributed as an app to mobile marketplaces like Google Play or the Apple App Store.
- Use a site like *Lulu* (**lulu.com**) to do social marketing for your book so that you can promote it. In addition, it offers services from editors, designers, and marketers.

## Digital Music

**How is digital music created?** The sound waves created by instruments need to be turned into a string of digital information to record digital music. Figure 8.23 shows the process of digitally recording a song:

1. Playing music creates analog waves.
2. A microphone feeds the sound waves into a chip called an *analog-to-digital converter (ADC)* inside the recording device.
3. The ADC digitizes the waves into a series of numbers.
4. This series of numbers can be recorded onto CDs or DVDs, saved in a file, or sent electronically.
5. On the receiving end, a playback device such as a mobile device or a DVD player is fed that same series of numbers. Inside the playback device is a *digital-to-analog converter (DAC)*, a chip that converts the digital numbers to a continuous analog wave.
6. That analog wave tells the receiver how to move the speaker cones to reproduce the original waves, resulting in the same sound as the original.

More precisely, the digital wave will be *close* to exact. How accurate it is, or how close the digitized wave is in shape to the original analog wave, depends on the sampling rate of the ADC. The **sampling rate** specifies the number of times the analog wave is measured each second. The higher the sampling rate, the more accurately the original wave can be recreated. The improved sound quality higher sampling can afford also depends on the quality of the output device and

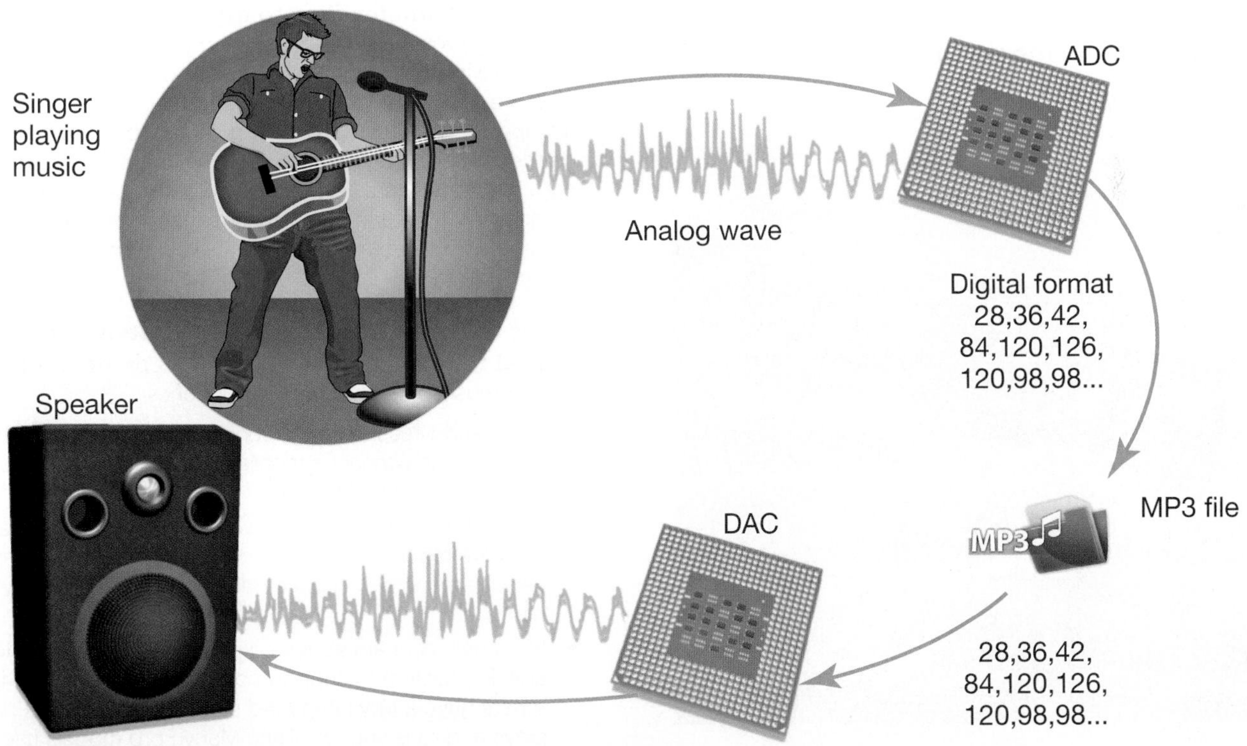


**FIGURE 8.23** During the complete recording process, information changes from analog form to digital data and then back again to analog sound waves. *(Ben Chams/Fotolia)*

speakers, of course. However, higher sampling rates also produce much more data and therefore result in bigger files. For example, sound waves on CDs are sampled at a rate of approximately 44,000 times a second. This produces a huge list of numbers for even a single minute of a song.

**What file types store digital music?** You're no doubt familiar with the MP3 file format used to store digital music, but many others exist, such as AAC and WMA. If you buy a song from the iTunes Store, for example, you receive an AAC-format file. There are also many formats, such as DivX, MPEG-4 (which usually has an .mp4 extension), WMV, and XviD, which hold both video and audio information. All file formats compete on sound and video quality and *compression*, which relates to how small the file can be and still provide high-quality playback. Be sure to check what kind of files your audio device understands before you store music on it.

**How do I know how much digital media my device can hold?** The number of songs or hours of video a device like an iPod (see Figure 8.24) can hold depends on how much storage space it has. Less expensive mobile devices use built-in flash memory ranging from 2 to 64 GB, whereas more expensive models use built-in hard drives, which provide as much as 160 GB of storage.

Another factor that determines how much music a player can hold is the quality of the MP3 music files. The size of an MP3 file depends on the digital sampling of the song. The same song could be sampled at a rate anywhere between 64 kbps and 320 kbps. The size of the song file will be five times larger if it is sampled at 320 kbps rather than the lower sampling rate of 64 kbps. The higher the sampling rate, the better quality the sound—but the larger the file size.

**How do you control the size of an MP3 file?** If you are *ripping*, or converting, a song from a CD to a digital MP3 file, you can select the sampling rate yourself. You decide by considering what quality sound you want, as well as how many songs you want to fit onto your MP3 player. For example, if your player has 1 GB of storage and you have ripped songs at 192 kbps, you could fit about 694 minutes of music onto the player. The same 1 GB could store 2,083 minutes of music if it were sampled at 64 kbps. Whenever you are near your computer, you can connect your player and download a different set of songs, but you always are limited by the amount of storage your player has.

**FIGURE 8.24** Apple reports over 350 million iPods have been sold since they were first introduced. *(Bloomberg/Getty Images)*

ACTIVE HELPDESK

**Using Portable Media Players**

In this Active Helpdesk call, you'll play the role of a helpdesk staffer, fielding calls about portable media players, what they can carry, and how they store data.

**What if I want to access more music than my device has room for?** Some of the devices that use flash memory allow you to add storage capacity by purchasing removable flash memory cards. You can also use a service that streams the music to you over WiFi or 3G/4G networks. Services like Spotify and GooglePlay have subscription plans that let you listen to any of the millions of tracks in their catalog. The music is not yours to own, however—if you cancel your subscription, you no longer have access to the music. But because it's streamed to you, it doesn't take up space on your device drive. Some streaming services offer options that also let you download music so that you can still play the songs on your playlist even if you're not in range of Internet access.

**How do I transfer files to my music device?** To move large volumes of data between your computer and your music device, you want a high-speed port. Most devices use a USB port, which lets you transfer files quickly. Cloud services are appearing that automatically push music to your mobile device. Apple's iOS operating system supports iCloud technology. This means that as soon as you purchase a new song from iTunes, it's automatically pushed to all your registered iTunes devices—your Mac, your PC, your iPad and iTouch, and your iPhone.

**What if I want a lot of people to listen to my digital music?** You have a number of options for listening to your music other than with headphones:

- Many audio receivers now come with a port or a dock so that you can connect a mobile device directly to them as another audio input source.
- Networked audio/video receivers have the hardware and software required to connect to your home network and use streaming services like Pandora or Spotify to play music.
- Most new cars are equipped with an auxiliary input to the speaker system to support connecting a mobile device; others have a fully integrated software system that displays and runs your playlists. Many Ford models use the Microsoft Sync system that allows you to navigate through your playlists with just voice commands.

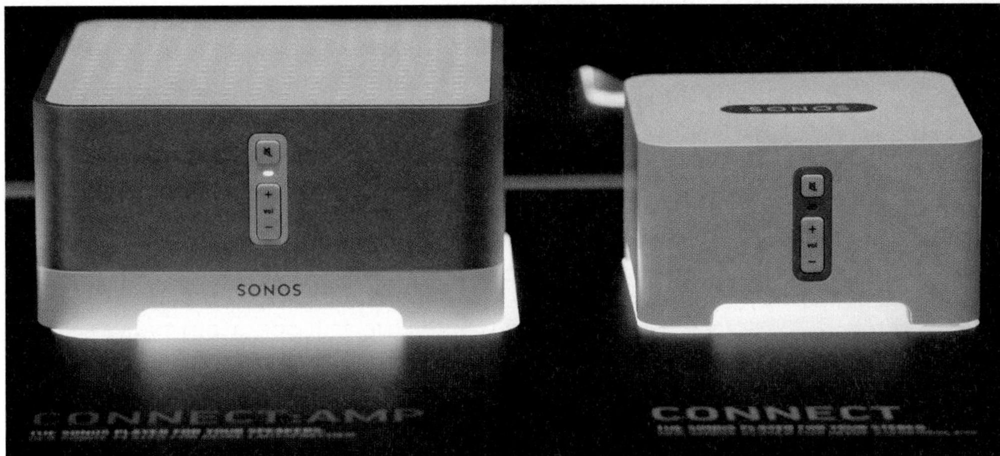


**FIGURE 8.25** Sonos is a multiroom system that streams music wirelessly throughout your home.
*(Robert Schlesinger/dpa/picture-alliance/Newscom)*

- There are alarm clocks and home speaker docks that can mate, even wirelessly, with a mobile device and that broadcast brilliant sound (see Figure 8.25).

**If I don't pay for a music download, is it illegal?** Although you need to pay for most music you download, some artists post songs for free. Business models are still evolving as artists and recording companies try to meet audience needs while also protecting their own intellectual property rights. Several different approaches exist. One is to deliver something called *tethered downloads*, in which you pay for the music and own it but are subject to restrictions on its use.

Another approach is to offer *DRM-free* music, which is music without any **digital rights management (DRM)**. DRM is a system of access control that allows only limited use of material that's been legally purchased. It may be that the song can only run on certain devices or a movie can only be viewed a certain number of times. A DRM-free song can be placed on as many computers or players as you wish. These song files can be moved freely from system to system.

**Will streaming music services eliminate radio stations?** The Internet allows artists to release new songs to their fans immediately (on sites such as Facebook) and without relying on radio airtime. This opens up new channels for artists to reach an audience and changes the amount of power radio stations have in the promotion of music. Many radio stations have increased listenership by making their stations available through Internet sites and by broadcasting in high-definition quality.

**What if I want to publicize my band's music?** Digital music has made distributing your own recordings very simple. You can make your own creations available using sites like ReverbNation (**reverbnation.com**). You can quickly create a web page for your band, post your songs, and start building a fan base through Facebook. ReverbNation will send you reports detailing who's listening to your music and what they're saying about it. ReverbNation is also a way to connect with independent recording labels and to find places that want to book your band.

# BITS&BYTES

## Need Money for Your Band? Try Indiegogo

What if your band has already built up a fan base but just needs to have the up-front money to go into the studio to record? Indiegogo (**indiegogo.com**) is a crowd-funding website specializing in creative projects and causes. Musicians have a platform to go to their fan base and raise money before a recording session or a tour, or even when tragedy strikes. When cellist Mike Block had a serious accident, he used Indiegogo to raise money to pay off his medical bills. Mike offered copies of an upcoming album or personal lessons as rewards to funders. He raised over $48,000 using Indiegogo and was able to repay years of accumulated medical expenses.

## Digital Photography

**What is "analog" photography?** Before digital cameras hit the market, most people used some form of 35-mm single-lens reflex (SLR) camera. When you take a picture using a traditional SLR camera, a shutter opens, creating an aperture (a small window in the camera) that allows light to hit the 35-mm film inside. Chemicals coating the film react when exposed to light. Later, additional chemicals develop the image on the film, and the image is printed on special light-sensitive paper. A variety of lenses and processing techniques, special equipment, and filters are needed to create printed photos taken with traditional SLR cameras.

**What's different about digital photography?** Digital cameras do not use film. Instead, they capture images on electronic sensors called *charge-coupled device (CCD) arrays* and then convert those images to digital data, long series of numbers that represent the color and brightness of millions of points in the image. Unlike traditional cameras, digital cameras allow you to see your images the instant you shoot them. Most camera models can now record digital video as well as digital photos.

# DIG DEEPER The Shift to Digital Music: A Bumpy Ride

The shift to digital music wasn't an easy transition for the recording industry. The initial MP3 craze was fueled by sites such as MP3.com, which originally stored its song files on a public server with the permission of the original artists or recording companies. Therefore, you weren't infringing on a copyright by downloading songs from sites such as MP3.com.

Napster was a file-exchange site created to correct some of the annoyances found by users of MP3.com (see Figure 8.26). One such annoyance was the limited availability of popular music in MP3 format. Napster differed from MP3.com because songs or locations of songs were not stored in a central public server but instead were "borrowed" directly from other users' computers. This process of users transferring files between computers is referred to as **peer-to-peer (P2P) sharing**. Napster also provided a search engine dedicated to finding specific MP3 files. This direct search and sharing eliminated the inconvenience of searching links only to find them unavailable.

The problem with Napster was that it was so good at what it did. The rapid acceptance and use of Napster—at one point, it had nearly 60 million users—led the music industry to sue the site for copyright infringement, and Napster was closed in June 2002. Napster has since merged with Rhapsody as a streaming music service.

The music industry has needed to reinvent itself since the demise of Napster. The initial reaction of the recording industry was to continue to enforce its absolute ownership over digital forms of its music. The industry even filed legal actions against individuals who had downloaded large amounts of music from Internet sites. This heavy-handed reaction to the new era of digital music ultimately backfired and left the music industry scrambling. Overall music sales have dropped significantly each year for the last decade. The recording industry is still trying to counter losing CD sales. The approach they took early on did not allow them to adapt quickly enough to the new business models required by the shift to digital technologies.

P2P sharing sites are still operating today. Napster was "easy" to shut down because it used a central index server that queried other Napster computers for requested songs. Current P2P protocols (such as BearShare) differ from Napster in that they don't limit themselves to sharing only MP3 files. Video files are easily obtainable on P2P sites. More importantly, these sites don't have a central computer acting to index all this information. Instead, they operate in a true P2P sharing environment in which computers connect directly to other computers. This makes them a prime source of unwanted viruses and spyware.

The argument these P2P networks make to defend their legality is that they do not run a central server like the original Napster but only facilitate connections between users. Therefore, they have no control over what the users choose to trade. These legal nuances weren't enough to keep the LimeWire service active, and it was shut down by court order in 2010. Note that not all P2P file sharing is illegal. For example, it is legal to trade photos or movies you've created with other users over a P2P site.

People who oppose such file-sharing sites contend that the sites know their users are distributing files illegally and breaking copyright laws. Be aware that having illegal content on your computer, deliberately or by accident, is a criminal offense in many jurisdictions.

**FIGURE 8.26** Napster was one of the original P2P music-sharing sites.
*(Mike Fanous/Getty Images)*

**How do I select a digital camera?** The first question to answer is whether you want a compact "point-and-shoot" camera or a more expensive digital SLR. If you decide you want a digital SLR, you have a number of options. Some digital SLRs let you switch among different lenses and offer features important to serious amateur and professional photographers. Although having such flexibility in selection of lenses is a great advantage, most of these cameras are also larger, heavier, and use more battery power than the fixed-lens models. Think about how you'll be using your camera and decide which model will serve you best in the long run. One great resource to use is Digital Photography Review (**dpreview.com**), a site that compares cameras and provides feedback from owners.

**What determines the image quality of a digital camera?** The overall image quality is determined by many factors:

- The quality of the lenses used
- The image sensor size
- The file format and compression used
- The color management software included
- The camera's **resolution**, or the number of data points it records for each image captured

A digital camera's resolution is measured in megapixels (MP). The word *pixel* is short for *picture element*, which is a single dot in a digital image. Point-and-shoot models typically offer resolutions from 10 to 15 MP. Professional digital SLR cameras, such as the Nikon D800, can take photos at resolutions as high as 36 MP.

If you're interested in making only 5" × 7" or 8" × 10" prints, a lower-resolution camera is fine. However, low-resolution images become grainy and pixelated when pushed to larger size. For example, if you tried to print an 11" × 14" enlargement from an 8 MP image taken using your smartphone's camera, the image would look grainy; you would see individual dots of color instead of a clear, sharp image. The 16 to 24 MP cameras on the market now have plenty of resolution to guarantee sharp, detailed images even with enlargements as big as 11" × 14".

But the size of the image sensor that actually captures the light is also very critical. Larger sensors demand larger cameras and larger lenses. Professional digital cameras use a full-frame sensor, the size of a 35 mm negative. Smartphones need to use a very compact sensor (typically about 4.5 mm) and pair that with a wider angle lens to be able to capture the full scene.

**What file formats are used for digital images?** To fit more photos on the same size flash memory card, digital cameras let you choose from several different file types in order to compress the image data into less memory space. When you choose to compress your images, you'll lose some of the detail, but in return you'll be able to fit more images on your flash card. The most common file types supported by digital cameras are raw uncompressed data (RAW) and Joint Photographic Experts Group (JPEG):

- *RAW files* have different formats and extensions depending on the manufacturer of a particular camera. The RAW file records all of the original image information, so it's larger than a compressed JPEG file.
- *JPEG files* can be compressed just a bit, keeping most of the details, or compressed a great deal, losing some detail. Most cameras let you select from a few different JPEG compression levels.

Often, cameras also support a very low-resolution storage option that provides images that aren't useful for printing but are so small that they're easy to e-mail. Even people who have slow Internet connections are able to quickly download and view such images on screen.

**Why not just use the camera on my smartphone?** The cameras on smartphones are improving in resolution—Nokia now offers a 41 MP camera phone, shown in Figure 8.27—but they often employ smaller image sensors and inferior lenses compared to stand-alone cameras. In addition, many features that photographers rely on often aren't available in smartphone cameras, such as different types of autofocus, image stabilization algorithms, and smile shutter, which waits to take a shot until your subject is smiling.

**What's the best way to transfer my photos to my computer?** Digital cameras have a built-in USB port you can use to copy the image files to your computer. Another option is to transfer the flash card from your camera directly to a built-in memory card reader on your computer. Some camera models support wireless network connections so

**FIGURE 8.27** Nokia CEO introduces its 41 MP camera phone, the Nokia 1020. *(JUSTIN LANE/EPA/Newscom)*

that you can transfer the images without the fuss of connecting any cables.

**Can I make my old photos digital?** You can use a scanner to turn your hand-drawn sketches or old photos into digital files. Most scanner software lets you store the converted images as TIFF files or in compressed form as JPEG files. Some scanners include hardware that lets you scan film negatives or slides as well or even insert a stack of photos to be scanned in sequence.

Scanner quality is measured by its resolution, which is given in dots per inch (dpi). Most modern scanners can digitize a document at resolutions as high as 9600 × 9600 dpi in either color or grayscale mode. Scanners also typically support optical character recognition (OCR). OCR software converts pages of handwritten or typed text into electronic files. You can then open and edit these converted documents with word processing programs such as Microsoft Word.

**How can I share my digital photos?** You've probably shared a number of photos on Facebook already. Other options include creating online albums at sites such as Picasa, which let you share your photos without having to print them. You can also design electronic scrapbooks on a number of digital scrapbooking sites such as **cottagearts.net**.

Of course, you can carry and display your photos on your tablet and smartphone. You can also connect your iPad wirelessly to your TV and deliver slide shows of your photos, complete with musical soundtracks you've selected. If you have networked your home, a TV connected to your network can display all the photos and videos stored on your computer.

**What are the best options for printing digital photos?** If you want to print photos, you have two main options:

1. **Use a photo printer:** The most popular and inexpensive ones are inkjet printers. Some inkjet printers can print high-quality color photos, although they vary in speed, quality, and features. Dye-sublimation printers are another option. If you're interested in a printer to use for printing only photos, a dye-sublimation printer is a good choice. However, some models print only specific sizes, such as 4" × 6" prints, so be sure the printer you buy will fit your long-term needs.
2. **Use a photo-printing service:** Most photo-printing labs, including the film-processing departments at stores such as Target, offer digital printing services. The paper and ink used at these labs are higher quality than what is available for home use and produce heavier, glossier prints that won't fade. You can send your digital photos directly to local merchants such as CVS and Walgreens for printing using Windows Photo Gallery. Online services, such as Flickr (**flickr.com**) and Shutterfly (**shutterfly.com**), store your images and allow you to create hard-copy prints, albums, mugs, T-shirts, or calendars.

## Digital Video

**What devices, sites, and other sources provide digital video content?** Digital video surrounds us:

- Television is broadcast in digitally formatted signals.
- The Internet delivers a huge amount of digital video through YouTube, communities like Vimeo (**vimeo.com**), and webcasting sites like Ustream (**ustream.tv**).
- Sites like Hulu (**hulu.com**) rebroadcast many current television shows as well as films and movie trailers.
- Many pay services are available to deliver digital video to you. These include on-demand streaming from cable providers, iTunes, Netflix's Instant Watch films, and Amazon's Instant Video download service.
- And, of course, you can create your own digital video. Although you can buy dedicated digital camcorders to record digital video, many smartphones now record HD video. Webcams also work as inexpensive devices for creating digital video.

**How do I record my own digital video?** Video equipment for home use stores information in a digital video format. Such cameras don't require any tapes; they store hours of video on built-in hard drives or flash cards. Some models even record directly to DVD. You can easily transfer video files to your computer and, using video-editing software, edit the video at home. You can save (or write) your final product on a CD or DVD and play it in your home DVD system or on your computer. For true videophiles, cameras and burners are available for HD video format.

**What if I decide to add special effects and a sound track?** Video-editing software presents a storyboard or timeline with which you can manipulate your video file, as shown in Figure 8.28. You can review your clips frame by frame or

**FIGURE 8.28** Adobe Premiere Elements allows you to build a movie from video clips and to add sound tracks and special effects. *(Adobe Premiere Elements screenshot(s) reprinted with permission from Adobe Systems Incorporated)*

FIGURE 8.29

## Typical File Formats for Digital Video

| FORMAT | FILE EXTENSION | NOTES |
|---|---|---|
| QuickTime | .qt<br>.mov | You can download the QuickTime player without charge from **apple.com/quicktime**. The Pro version allows you to build your own QuickTime files. |
| Moving Picture Experts Group (MPEG) | .mpg<br>.mpeg<br>.mp4 | The MPEG-4 video standard was adopted internationally in 2000; it's recognized by most video player software. |
| Windows Media Video | .wmv | This is a Microsoft file format recognized by Windows Media Player (included with the Windows OS). |
| Microsoft Video for Windows | .avi | This is a Microsoft file format recognized by Windows Media Player (included with the Windows OS). |
| RealMedia | .rm | This format is from RealNetworks and is popular for streaming video. You can download the player for free at **real.com**. |
| Adobe Flash Video | .flv | This is the Adobe Flash video format, sometimes embedded in Shockwave files (*.swf). |

trim them at any point. You can add titles, audio tracks, and animations; order each segment on the timeline in whichever sequence you like; and correct segments for color balance, brightness, or contrast. Examine online tutorial resources such as Izzy Video podcasts (**izzyvideo.com**) to learn how to make the most impact with the editing and effects you apply to your raw video footage.

**What kinds of files will I end up with?** Once you're done editing your video file, you can save or export it in a variety of formats. Figure 8.29 shows some of the popular video file formats in use today, along with the file extensions they use.

Your choice of file format for your finished video will depend on what you want to do with the video. For example, the QuickTime streaming file format is a great choice if your file is really large and you plan to post it on the web. The Microsoft AVI format is a good choice if you're sending your file to a wide range of users because it's the standard video format for Windows Media Player.

Different compression algorithms will have different results on your particular video. Try several to see which one does a better job of compressing your particular file. A **codec** (*co*mpression/*dec*ompression) is a rule, implemented in either software or hardware, that squeezes the same audio and video information into less space. Some information will be lost using compression, and there are several different codecs to choose from, each claiming better performance than its competitors. Commonly used codecs include MPEG-4, H.264, and DivX. There's no one codec that's always superior—a codec that works well for a simple interview may not do a good job compressing a live-action scene.

**What if I want to produce a DVD with a full menuing system?** You can use special authoring software such as Pinnacle Studio HD or Adobe Encore. These DVD/Blu-ray software packages often include preset selections for producing video for specific mobile devices. These programs can also create final discs that have animated menu systems and easy navigation controls, allowing the viewer to move quickly from one movie or scene to another. Home DVD and Blu-ray players, as well as gaming systems such as PlayStation and Xbox, can read these discs.

**What's the quickest way to get my video out to viewers?** The quickest way to get your video content out is to broadcast. Webcasting, or broadcasting your video live to an audience, is an option that has become simple to do. All you need is a webcam (see Figure 8.30), and sites like **justin.tv** or **ustream.tv** will let you quickly set up to webcast

FIGURE 8.30 Webcams are small enough to make them part of any activity. *(© ZUMA Press, Inc. / Alamy)*

# ethics in IT

## Managing Your Copyrights: Copyleft Might Simplify Your Life

You just returned from your trip to the Grand Canyon, and your friends are raving about the photos you took. You decide to put them on Flickr so others can see them. You also think that someone might see your photos and want to use them in a commercial publication such as a magazine. Because you own the copyright to your photos, you control how they can be used—and you want to protect your rights. You add a disclaimer to Flickr indicating that all rights are reserved on your photos. Anyone who wants to use them will need to contact you and request permission.

All of a sudden, you're bombarded by requests for permission to use your photos. A high school student in Illinois wants to feature one on her travel blog. A church in Georgia wants to use a photo for its newsletter. An ad agency in Seattle wants to modify your sunrise photo and use it in an ad. How are you going to manage all these permission requests?

**Copyleft**, a play on the word *copyright*, is designed for this situation. *Copyleft* is a term for various licensing plans that enable copyright holders to grant certain rights to the work while retaining other rights. Creative Commons (**creativecommons.org**), a nonprofit organization, has developed various licenses you can use based on the rights you wish to grant. Simply decide which type of license best fits your goals for the work, and Creative Commons provides you with HTML you can use to add the specific licensing information to your site.

The advantage to using Creative Commons licenses is that people won't constantly send you permission requests to use your work. The licenses explain how your work can be used. Also, many advocates of copyleft policies feel that creativity is encouraged when people are free to modify other people's work instead of worrying about infringing on copyright.

Opponents of Creative Commons licenses complain that the licenses have affected their livelihoods. If millions of images are out on Flickr with Creative Commons licenses that permit free commercial use, professional photographers might have a tougher time selling their work. Furthermore, Creative Commons licenses are irrevocable. If you make a mistake and select the wrong license for your work, or you later find out a work is valuable and you've already selected a license that allows commercial use, you're out of luck.

Each of us needs to carefully consider the value of our intellectual property and decide how best to conduct our digital livelihood. Understanding the meaning of copyright, and copyleft, is both important so that you respect the rights of others and so that you can simplify your life in granting permission rights to the works you create.

your video as it is captured to a live Internet audience. You can also display an interactive chat next to the video feed. Both the chat and the video are captured and archived for viewers who missed the live broadcast. Most smartphones record video at a quality good enough to directly webcast from your phone, and most laptops have an integrated webcam.

You may want to take time and produce a more polished video. When you have it just right, you can upload it to video-sharing sites like YouTube or Metacafe.

Of course, it's illegal for you to upload videos you don't own. You also can't take a piece of a copyrighted video and post it publicly. The Ethics in IT section in this chapter presents several legal and ethical situations that are important for you to be aware of as a content creator in the digital age.

**How is HD different from "plain" digital?** *HD* stands for **high definition**. It is a standard of digital television signal that guarantees a specific level of resolution and a specific *aspect ratio*, which is the rectangular shape of the image. A 1080 HDTV displays 1,920 vertical lines and 1,080 horizontal lines of video on the screen, which is over six times as many pixels as a standard definition TV. The aspect ratio used is 16:9, which makes the screen wider, giving it the same proportions as the rectangular shape of a movie theater screen (see Figure 8.31). This allows televisions to play movies in the widescreen format for which they were created, instead of "letterboxing" the film with black bars on the top and the bottom of the screen.

**What types of connectivity are provided on modern TV sets?** A typical HDTV set has multiple HDMI connectors, allowing game consoles, Blu-ray players, and cable boxes to be connected and to produce the highest-quality output. HDMI is a single cable that carries all of the video and all of the audio information.

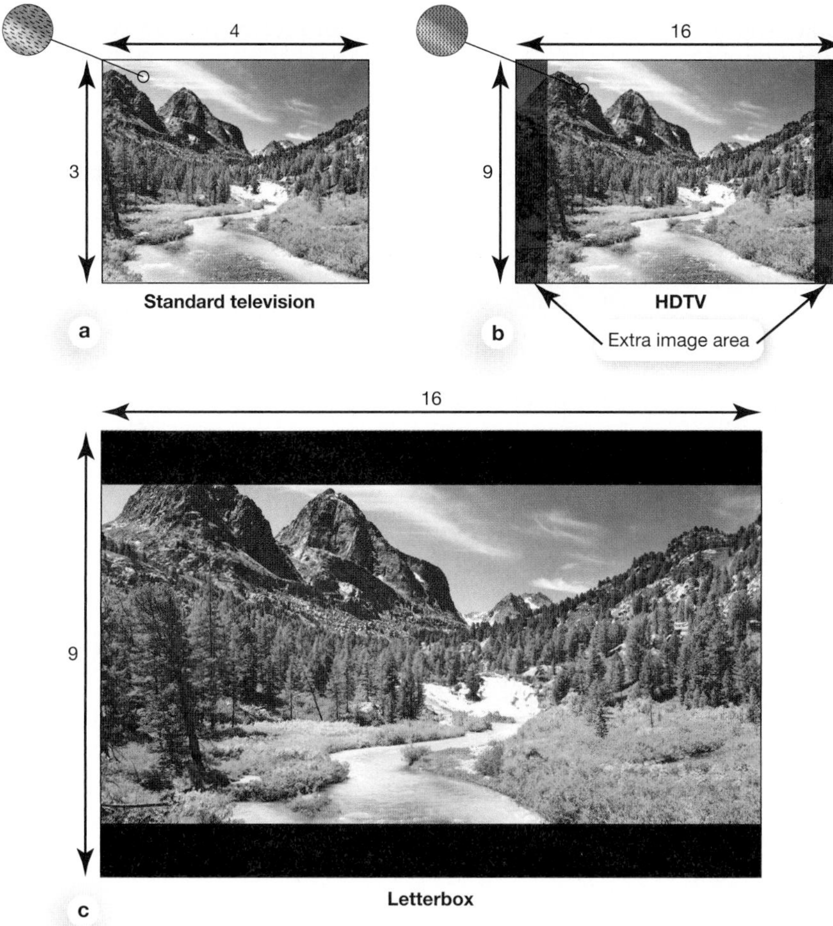

**FIGURE 8.31** (a) Standard-definition TV has a more "square" aspect ratio, whereas (b) HDTV matches the 16:9 ratio used in the motion picture industry without resorting to (c) letterboxing. *(Pichugin Dmitry/Shutterstock)*

Many TV sets have a built-in SD card reader. This allows users to display slide shows of photographs captured by their digital cameras. A PC VGA port is also included on most sets to allow you to feed your computer's output video signal directly to the television.

**What are the advantages to watching digital video on my TV?** Other information services can be integrated with the broadcast; so, for example, if a telephone call came through during the show, a pop-up could appear identifying the caller. Additional content can be delivered in real time with the broadcast, explaining the background of characters or pulling up behind-the-scenes info. In the future, there will be more interactivity integrated so you can participate in live polls or chats on screen as the show is broadcast.

**Can I record the digital video that comes over my TV?** There are a variety of digital video recorders (DVRs) available that record in HD. Models like TiVo even recommend new shows you might like based on what you've been watching. You can also install personal video recording (PVR) software on your computer. Programs like XBMC (**xbmc.org**) let you use your computer to view the schedule program guide, select shows to record (without commercials), and then watch them from anywhere you have Internet access.

**Can I get digital video to watch on my portable device?** Many DVR units, like TiVo, support software that lets you transfer recorded shows to files on your PC and format them for viewing on a mobile device. There are also devices like Slingbox that take the video from your TV and broadcast it to you over the Internet. With Slingbox, you can be in another room, or another country, and control and watch your home TV on your notebook or your smartphone (see Figure 8.32). ■

**Before moving on to Chapter Review:**
- **Watch Replay Video 8.2** .
- Then check your understanding of what you've learned so far.

**FIGURE 8.32** Slingbox can send your digital television content to your tablet, notebook, or phone, wherever you may be. *(HANDOUT/MCT/Newscom)*

# check your understanding//

For a quick review to see what you've learned so far, answer the following questions. Visit **pearsonhighered.com/techinaction** to check your answers.

## multiple choice

1. Which is *not* a factor that determines the quality of images taken with a digital camera?
   - **a.** lens quality
   - **b.** resolution
   - **c.** file format
   - **d.** type of battery
2. The quickest way to distribute your band's new song to a lot of listeners is to
   - **a.** use an application to post it on Facebook.
   - **b.** e-mail the song to local radio stations.
   - **c.** hand out CDs that you burned.
   - **d.** You cannot legally distribute music freely.
3. P2P is an acronym for
   - **a.** packet-to-packet networking.
   - **b.** peer-to-peer sharing.
   - **c.** person-to-person texting.
   - **d.** power-to-people delivery.
4. An analog signal is different from a digital signal because
   - **a.** it is continuous.
   - **b.** it has only specific discrete values.
   - **c.** it is easier to duplicate.
   - **d.** it is easier to transmit.
5. The open format for publishing of e-books that is optimized for mobile devices is
   - **d.** ePub.
   - **b.** raw.
   - **c.** azw.
   - **d.** pdf.

## true–false

_____ **1.** Digital music files must be converted to the MP3 format if they are transferred to a mobile device.

_____ **2.** High-definition video requires that the video has the specific aspect ratio of 16:9.

## critical thinking

1. **Reinvent Yourself**

   The arrival of digital information has forced major shifts in several industries, such as publishing, music recording, and film. How has each industry reacted? Have they each found ways to reinvent the products and services they deliver to match the challenge of the digital age? What other industries have had to realign their business models because of digital information?

2. **Too Much Media?**

   As a manager, what concerns might you have about your employees' use of corporate bandwidth to download and view media files? Do you think it would benefit your business to block certain file transfers or certain sites? As a manager, are there concerns you might have if employees have digital cameras on their smartphones? Would your answers be different in an academic setting?

**Continue**

# 8 Chapter Review

## summary//

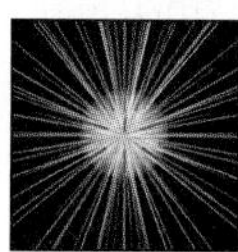

### Digital Convergence

**1. How is the trend of digital convergence seen in the market?**

- Digital convergence has brought us single devices with the capabilities that used to require four or five separate tools.

### Telephony: Smartphones and Beyond

**2. What hardware and software comprise a typical smartphone?**

- Like a traditional computer, a smartphone has a central processor, memory, and an OS. These components work in the same way as in a computer to process information and support communications, software applications, and other services.

**3. How do I synchronize information between my phone and my computer, and how do mobile Internet data plans work?**

- Information can be synched between devices using either wired or wireless solutions.
- A wired synch requires either a micro SD card or a USB cable to connect the device directly to the computer.
- A wireless synch can be done using Bluetooth or WiFi or by connecting to a cloud service.
- Mobile data plans allow your device to have access at almost any location.
- Data transfers occur at either 3G or 4G speeds, depending on your device and provider. Fees are tied to the amount of data you transfer each month.

**4. What do I need to keep my smartphone secure?**

- Viruses can infect smartphones, so using an antivirus software package is important. Check the manufacturer's website frequently for updates and practice safe habits by not downloading or opening files from unknown sources.

**5. How does digital telephony support VoIP services?**

- VoIP allows inexpensive communication using a computer or a WiFi-enabled phone. Because it's based on a digital format for information, it can support services like automatic delivery of phone messages to an e-mail account or texts to a mobile device.

### Tablets, Netbooks, and Ultrabooks

**6. What distinguishes the performance of tablets, netbooks, and ultrabooks?**

- Mobile devices differ in terms of size and weight, input (physical keyboard, software keyboard on a touch screen), and OS (mobile OS or traditional OS).
- Netbooks and ultrabooks can run traditional software packages like Microsoft Office, whereas tablets run new versions of productivity software made to take advantage of the features of the tablet.

## Digital Defined

**7. What advantage do digital formats have over analog signals?**

- Digital media is based on a series of numeric data, number values that were measured from the original analog waveform. As a string of numbers, a digital photo or video file can be easily processed by modern computers.

## Digital Media

**8. How is the digital format changing the way media is created and distributed?**

- The increased use of digital information has led to a period of greater creativity and control of our data. In a digital format, information is easy to carry, manipulate, and exchange. This has led to revolutionary changes in communication, entertainment media, and mobile computing.
- Digital publishing is allowing a variety of new distribution methods into the industry. E-readers and online bookstores are bringing changes to the models of how to sell printed materials.
- Digital music is created by combining pure digital sounds with samples of analog sounds. It has meant changes for the recording industry, for performers, and for music listeners. It's now inexpensive to carry a music library, to create new songs, and to distribute them worldwide.

**9. How do I work with digital images and video?**

- Digital cameras allow you to instantly capture and transfer images to your devices, computers, and cloud storage sites.
- Using software for video production, you can create polished videos with titles, transitions, a sound track, and special effects and distribute them on DVDs.
- You can also use a webcam to stream live video to sites that will "broadcast" it over the Internet.

Be sure to check out the companion website for additional materials to help you review and learn, including a Tech Bytes Weekly newsletter— **pearsonhighered.com/techinaction**. And don't forget the Replay Videos .

# key terms//

analog **326**
analog-to-digital converter chip **316**
base transceiver station **315**
Bluetooth **316**
cellular (cell) phone **313**
codec **337**
copyleft **338**
data plan **317**
digital convergence **312**
digital rights management (DRM) **333**
digital signal processor **316**
electronic ink (E Ink) **329**
electronic text (e-text) **329**
e-reader **329**
feature phone **313**
global positioning system (GPS) **320**
high definition **338**
mobile switching center **315**
multimedia message service (MMS) **317**
peer-to-peer (P2P) sharing **334**
resolution **335**
sampling rate **331**
short message service (SMS) **316**
synchronizing (or syncing) **316**
telephony **313**
tethering **319**
Voice over Internet Protocol (VoIP) **319**
wireless Internet service provider (wireless ISP) **317**

## making the transition to . . . next semester//

1. **Choosing Mobile Devices to Fit Your Needs**

   As a student, which devices discussed in this chapter would have the most immediate impact on the work you do each day? Which would provide the best value (that is, the greatest increase in productivity and organization per dollar spent)? Consider the full range of devices, from cell phones or smartphones to laptop systems.

2. **Ready . . . Set . . . Act!**

   As a student, you often give presentations or take on student teaching assignments. What steps would you follow to create a digital video recording of one of your presentations? What tools would you need to record? What kind of file would you end up producing? How would you distribute the video to a live Internet audience? How would you make a DVD of the performance?

3. **Author, Author**

   As a new author of fantasy stories, you have written a collection of short fiction. You decide to publish the collection yourself. What options are there for you to use? How do they compare and contrast? What legal issues do you need to be aware of? Compare self-publishing with services like Book Country (**bookcountry.com**) and Author Solutions (**authorsolutions.com**), which provide additional services but keep a percentage of earned royalties.

## making the transition to . . . the workplace//

1. **Subscription Versus Ownership**

   With the arrival of reliable, fast, networked digital information, businesses can track the location and status of all kinds of objects, such as cars and bicycles. This is introducing a new business model different from individual ownership—now, using a car can become a "subscription" service.

   What options are there for "subscribing" to a car instead of owning one? How about for a bicycle? Are there other businesses you can identify that would be able to take advantage of digital information and become subscription services instead of vendors of a physical product? What are the advantages to the consumer of subscription over ownership? What are the drawbacks?

2. **Everyone Is a Writer**

   Now that digital publishing is so accessible to everyone, how should a publishing business respond? Are there ways that existing publishing houses can take advantage of the easy access readers have to publish extensions of stories? What about in the fields of video or music—how might a business encourage the involvement of the fan base of a movie or a band by using the media-creation tools available?

3. **Mobile Devices on the Highway**

   Mobile devices used in vehicles are becoming the norm in today's society. Consider the following:

   **a.** Several car manufacturers provide Bluetooth option packages for their vehicles. What are the advantages to having Bluetooth connectivity in your car? Are there any disadvantages?

   **b.** Examine the Microsoft Sync software package. List the features and services it provides. If you were a salesperson with a territory that you covered by car, how would Sync help you?

team time//

# "And One Will Rule Them All"

## Problem

Digital convergence posits the dream of one device that can do it all, for everyone. But there are so many different mobile devices saturating the market that many people are left in a state of confusion. Either they are buying too many devices and not using them, or they are paralyzed from buying anything because of the dilemma of too many choices.

## Task

For each client scenario described as follows, the group will select the minimum set of devices that would support and enhance the client's life.

## Process

1. Consider the following three clients:
   - A retired couple who now travels for pleasure a great deal. They want to be involved in their grandchildren's lives and will need support for their health, finances, and personal care as they age.
   - A young family with two children, two working parents, and a tight budget.
   - A couple in which each individual is a physician and each adores technology.
2. Make two recommendations for your clients in terms of digital technologies that will enhance their business or their lifestyle. Discuss the advantages and disadvantages of each technology. Consider value, reliability, computing needs, training needed, and communication needs as well as expandability for the future.
3. As a group, prepare a final report that considers the costs, availability, and unique features of the recommendations you have made for your clients.
4. Bring the research materials from the individual team meetings to class. Looking at the clients' needs, make final decisions as to which digital technologies are best suited for each client.

## Conclusion

Digital information has allowed the development of a new style of living, both at home and at work. With so many digital solutions on the market today, recommending digital communication, media management, and mobility options needs to focus on converging to the minimum set of tools that will enhance life without adding complication to it.

# When Everyone Has a Voice

In this exercise, you'll research and then role-play a complicated ethical situation. The role you play might or might not match your own personal beliefs; in either case, your research and use of logic will enable you to represent the view assigned. An arbitrator will watch and comment on both sides of the arguments, and together the team will agree on an ethical solution.

## Background

Much of the world's population is now equipped with Internet-ready camera phones. Sensors on these phones could measure for viruses or compute pollution indexes, while the cameras could be used to document a range of human behavior. This could create changes in political movements, art, and culture as everyone's experience is documented and shared.

## Research Areas to Consider

- Evgeny Morozov RSA Animate
- Mobilebehavior.com
- The Witness Project
- Center for Embedded Networked Sensing

## Process

1. Divide the class into teams.
2. Research the areas cited above and devise a scenario in which mobile access could make an impact politically or environmentally, positively or negatively.
3. Team members should write a summary that provides background information for their character—for example: business owner, politician, reporter, or arbitrator—and that details their character's behaviors to set the stage for the role-playing event. Then team members should create an outline to use during the role-playing event.
4. Team members should arrange a mutually convenient time to meet for the exchange, using a virtual meeting tool or by meeting in person.
5. Team members should present their case to the class or submit a PowerPoint presentation for review by the rest of the class, along with the summary and resolution they developed.

## Conclusion

As technology becomes ever more prevalent and integrated into our lives, more and more ethical dilemmas will present themselves. Being able to understand and evaluate both sides of the argument, while responding in a personally or socially ethical manner, will be an important skill.

# 9 Securing Your System: Protecting Your Digital Data and Devices

## Major Threats to Your Digital Assets

### Cybercrime and Identity Theft

**OBJECTIVE**

1. What is cybercrime, and who perpetrates it? **(pp. 348–349)**

### Protecting Yourself from Computer Viruses

**OBJECTIVES**

2. What are the types of viruses from which I need to protect my computer? **(pp. 350–352)**
3. What can I do to protect my computer from viruses? **(pp. 353–355)**

**Active Helpdesk:** Avoiding Computer Viruses

**Sound Byte:** Protecting Your Computer

### Protecting Digital Assets from Hackers

**OBJECTIVES**

4. How can hackers attack my computing devices, and what harm can they cause? **(pp. 356–359)**
5. What is a firewall, and how does it keep my computer safe from hackers? **(pp. 360–362)**
6. How do I create secure passwords and manage all of my passwords? **(pp. 362–364)**
7. How can I surf the Internet anonymously and use biometric authentication devices to protect my data? **(pp. 364–366)**

**Active Helpdesk:** Understanding Firewalls

**Sound Byte:** Installing a Personal Firewall

## Protecting Your Digital Property from Yourself

### Managing Online Annoyances

**OBJECTIVE**

8. How do I manage online annoyances such as spyware and spam? **(pp. 370–375)**

### Keeping Your Data Safe

**OBJECTIVES**

9. What data do I need to back up, and what are the best methods for doing so? **(pp. 376–380)**
10. What is social engineering, and how do I avoid falling prey to phishing? **(pp. 381–383)**

**Sound Byte:** Managing Computer Security with Windows Tools

### Protecting Your Physical Computing Assets

**OBJECTIVE**

11. How do I protect my physical computing assets from environmental hazards, power surges, and theft? **(pp. 384–386)**

**Sound Byte:** Surge Protectors

For all media in this chapter go to **pearsonhighered.com/techinaction** or **MyITLab**.

*(iKandy/Shutterstock; Dimitri Vervits/ImageState/Alamy; Lauren Nicole/Getty Images; D. Hurst/Alamy; SVLuma/Shutterstock; Shutterstock)*

# HOW COOL IS THIS?

Scan here for more info

You have a lot of **information** in your **cell phone**. What happens if you **lose your phone**, damage it beyond repair, or want to **switch phones**? Transferring data can be very time-consuming, or even impossible, if you lose your phone. Apple's iOS devices do a good job of backing up your settings either in iTunes or iCloud. But what about backing up Android devices? Not all settings and apps are backed up on Google's sites. So, apps like **Helium (Premium)** provide a solution by allowing you to **back up settings**, contacts, notes, tasks, bookmarks, calendars, music, videos, and photos from your Android phone to popular **cloud sites** such as Dropbox, Box, or Google Drive. Then, if your phone is ever lost, stolen, or damaged, or if you are just upgrading to the latest model, you can easily **transfer** your information to a new or replacement phone. So install a backup app on your Android phone today and enjoy some peace of mind!

*(bannosuke/Fotolia; Courtesy of Google, Inc.)*

# Major Threats to Your Digital Assets

The media is full of stories about malicious computer programs damaging computers, criminals stealing people's identities online, and attacks on corporate websites bringing major corporations to a standstill. These are examples of cybercrime. In this part of the chapter, we'll discuss the three most serious types of cybercrime you need to worry about: identity theft, computer viruses, and hackers.

## cybercrime and IDENTITY THEFT

**Cybercrime** is any criminal action perpetrated primarily through the use of a computer. The existence of cybercrime means that computer users must take precautions to protect themselves. The FBI maintains a website (**fbi.gov/about-us/investigate/cyber/cyber**) specifically to inform the public about types of cybercrimes and methods of protecting yourself.

**Who perpetrates computer crimes? Cybercriminals** are individuals who use computers, networks, and the Internet to perpetrate crime. Anyone with a computer and the wherewithal to arm him- or herself with the appropriate knowledge can be a cybercriminal.

**What kinds of cybercrimes are conducted over the Internet?** The Internet Crime Complaint Center (IC3) is a partnership between the FBI and the National White Collar Crime Center (NW3C). In 2012 (the latest year for which data was available at this book's publication), the IC3 received almost 289,000 complaints related to Internet crime. Four common categories of complaints received are shown in Figure 9.1. FBI–related scams involve people pretending to represent official organizations, such as the FBI or Homeland Security, to defraud. Nonauction scams involve running auctions of merchandise that does not really exist, wherein the perpetrators just collect funds and disappear without delivering the promised goods. Advance fee fraud involves

FIGURE 9.1

**Common Types of Cybercrimes Reported to the IC3 in 2012**

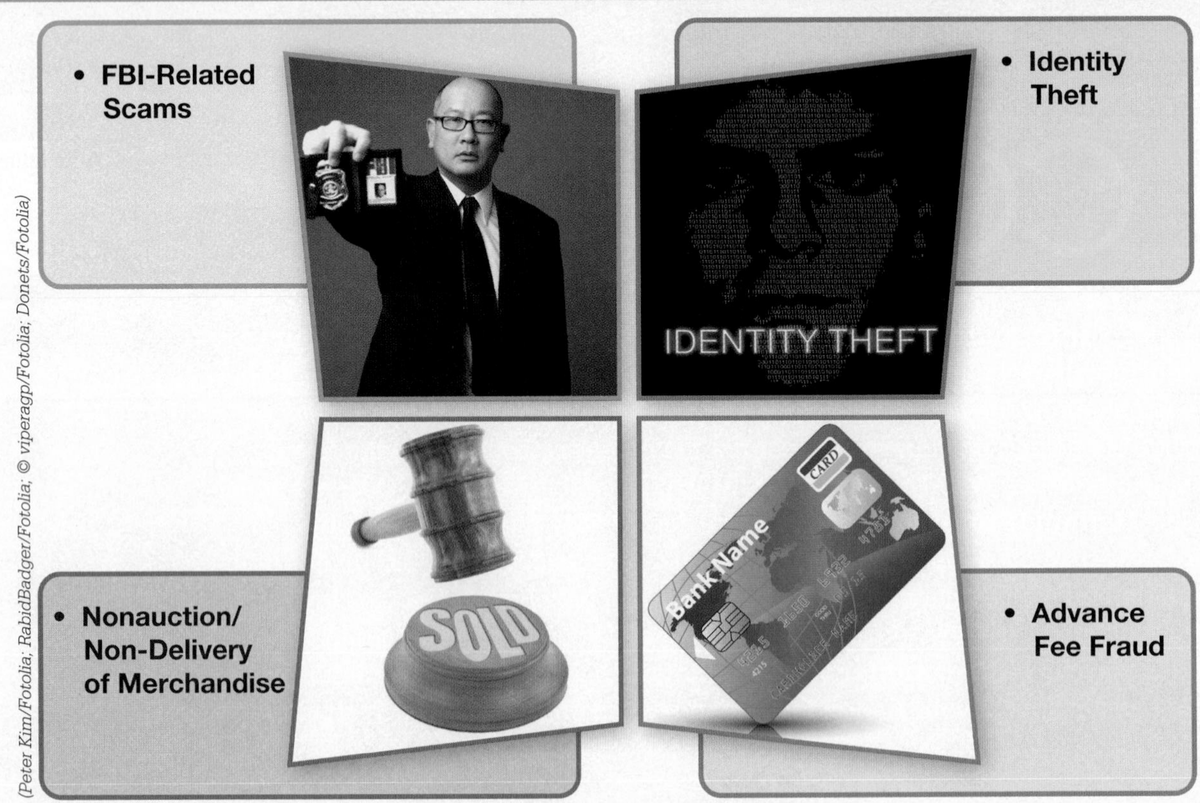


(Peter Kim/Fotolia; RabidBadger/Fotolia; © viperagp/Fotolia; Donets/Fotolia)

convincing individuals to send money as a "good faith" gesture to enable them to receive larger payments in return. The scammers then disappear with the advance fees. Although these complaints relate to some type of fraud, other complaints received involve equally serious matters such as computer intrusions (hacking), child pornography, and blackmail.

**What is the most financially damaging cybercrime plaguing individuals?** Theft of personal data such as bank account numbers and credit/debit card numbers is of most concern to individuals because this information is usually used for fraudulent purposes. **Identity theft** occurs when a thief steals personal information such as your name, address, Social Security number, birth date, bank account number, and credit card information and runs up debts in your name. Many victims of identity theft spend months, or even years, trying to repair their credit and eliminate fraudulent debts.

**What types of scams do identity thieves perpetrate?** The nefarious acts cover a wide range:

- Counterfeiting your existing credit and debit cards
- Requesting changes of address on your bank and credit card statements, which makes detecting fraudulent charges take longer
- Opening new credit cards and bank accounts in your name and then writing bad checks and not paying off the credit card balances (ruining your credit rating in the process)
- Obtaining medical services under your name (you might lose coverage later if the thief's treatment exceeds the limits of your policy's covered services)
- Buying a home with a mortgage in your name, then reselling the house and absconding with the money (leaving you with the debt)

Many people believe that the only way your identity can be stolen is by a computer. However, the Federal Trade Commission (**ftc.gov**) has identified other methods thieves use to obtain others' personal information:

- Stealing purses and wallets, in which people often keep personal information such as their ATM PIN codes
- Stealing mail or looking through trash for bank statements and credit card bills
- Posing as bank or credit card company representatives and tricking people into revealing sensitive information over the phone
- Installing skimming devices on ATM machines that record information, such as account numbers and passcodes

Although foolproof protection methods don't exist, there are precautions that will help you minimize your risk, which we'll discuss later in this chapter.

**With all the news coverage about identity theft and other cybercrimes, aren't people being more cautious?** Although most people are aware of spam, a survey by the Messaging Anti-Abuse Working Group (MAAWG) found that half of e-mail users in North America and Europe have opened spam, some of which are designed to trick you into divulging sensitive information. The MAAWG also discovered that 46% of people who opened spam did so intentionally—out of idle curiosity, to follow links to unsubscribe to unwanted e-mails (which only brings more spam), or because they are interested in the product being touted.

**Does cybercrime include the theft of computing devices?** Although theft of computer equipment is not classified as a cybercrime (it is considered larceny), the theft of tablets, smartphones, notebook computers, and other portable computing devices is on the rise. The resale value for used electronic equipment is high, and the equipment can be easily sold online. ■

# computer VIRUSES

A computer **virus** is a computer program that attaches itself to another computer program (known as the *host* program) and attempts to spread to other computers when files are exchanged. Creating and disseminating computer viruses is one of the most widespread types of cybercrimes. Some viruses cause only minor annoyances, whereas others cause destruction or theft of data. Many viruses are designed to gather sensitive information such as credit card numbers.

**Why are viruses such a threat to my security?** Computer viruses are threatening because they are engineered to evade detection. Viruses normally attempt to hide within the code of a host program to avoid detection. And viruses are not just limited to computers. Smartphones, tablet computers, and other devices can be infected with viruses. Viruses such as SpyEye Mobile Banking are used to trick users into downloading an infected file to their phones, which then steals their online banking information.

**I have an Apple computer, so I don't need to worry about viruses, do I?** This is a popular misconception! Everyone, even Apple users, needs to worry about viruses. As the OS X and iOS operating systems have gained market share, the amount of virus attacks against Apple operating systems is on the rise.

**What do computer viruses do?** A computer virus's main purpose is to replicate itself and copy its code into as many other host files as possible. This gives the virus a greater chance of being copied to another computer system so that it can spread its infection. However, computer viruses require human interaction to spread. Although there might be a virus in a file on your computer, a virus normally can't infect your computer until the infected file is opened or executed.

Although virus replication can slow down networks, it's not usually the main threat. The majority of viruses have secondary objectives or side effects, ranging from displaying annoying messages on the computer screen to destroying files or the contents of entire hard drives.

## Catching a Virus

**How does my computer catch a virus?** If your computer is exposed to a file infected with a virus, the virus will try to copy itself and infect a file on your computer.

Downloading infected audio and video files from peer-to-peer file-sharing sites is a major source of virus infections. Shared flash drives are also a common source of virus infection, as is e-mail. Just opening an e-mail message usually won't infect your computer with a virus, although some new viruses are launched when viewed in the preview pane of your e-mail software. Downloading and running (executing) a file that's attached to the e-mail are common ways that your computer becomes infected. Thus, be extremely wary of e-mail attachments, especially if you don't know the sender. Figure 9.2 illustrates the steps by which computer viruses are often passed from one computer to the next:

1. An individual writes a virus program, attaches it to a music file, and posts the file to a file-sharing site.
2. Unsuspecting Bill downloads the "music file" and infects his computer when he listens to the song.
3. Bill sends his cousin Fred an e-mail with the infected "music file" and contaminates Fred's tablet.
4. Fred syncs his phone with his tablet and infects his phone when he plays the music file.
5. Fred e-mails the file from his phone to Susan, one of his colleagues at work. Everyone who copies files from Susan's infected work computer, or whose computer is networked to Susan's computer, risks spreading the virus.

**What types of viruses exist?** Although thousands of computer viruses and variants exist, they can be grouped into six broad categories based on their behavior and method of transmission.

## Boot-Sector Viruses

**What are boot-sector viruses?** A **boot-sector virus** replicates itself onto a hard drive's master boot record. The **master boot record** is a program that executes whenever a computer boots up, ensuring that the virus will be loaded into memory immediately, even before some virus protection programs can load. Boot-sector viruses are often transmitted by a flash drive left in a USB port. When the computer boots up with the flash drive connected, the computer tries to launch a master boot record from the flash drive, which is usually the trigger for the virus to infect the hard drive.

## Logic Bombs and Time Bombs

**What are logic bombs and time bombs?** A **logic bomb** is a virus that is triggered when certain logical conditions are met, such as opening a file or starting a program a certain number of times. A **time bomb** is a virus that is triggered by the passage of time or on a certain date. For example, the Michelangelo virus was a famous time bomb that was set to trigger every year on March 6, Michelangelo's birthday. The effects of logic bombs and time bombs range from the display of annoying messages on the screen to the reformatting of the hard drive, which causes complete data loss.

## Worms

**What is a worm?** Although often called a virus, a **worm** is subtly different. Viruses require human interaction to spread, whereas worms take advantage of file transport methods, such

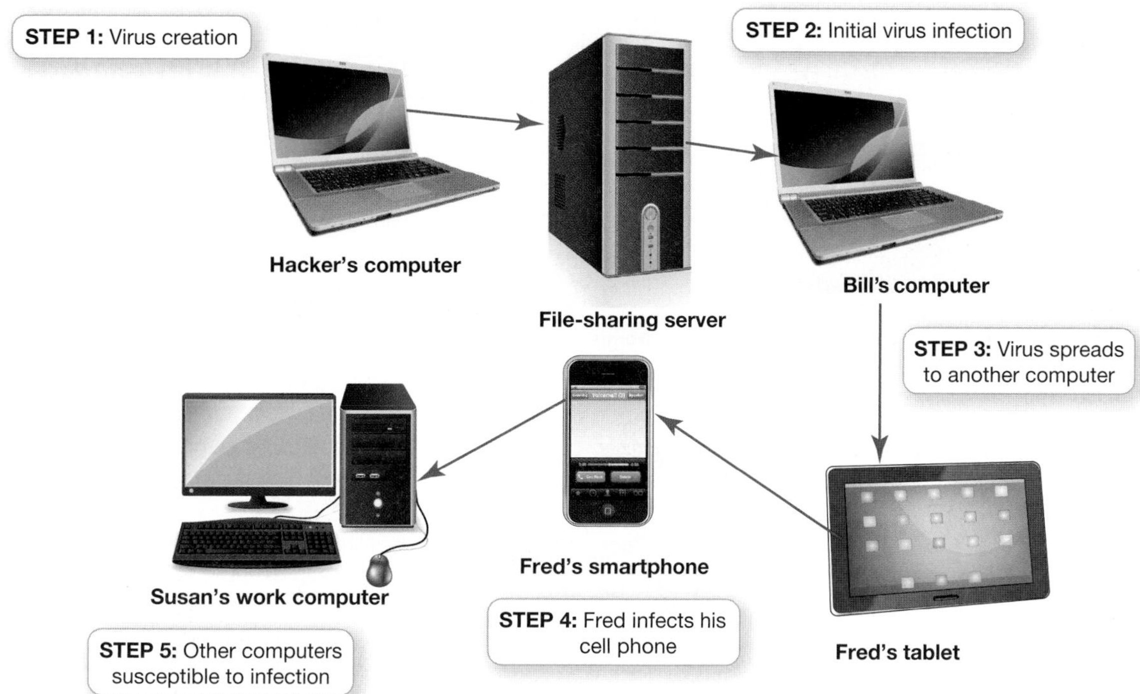


**FIGURE 9.2** Computer viruses are passed from one unsuspecting user to the next.

as e-mail or network connections, to spread on their own. A virus infects a host file and waits until that file is executed to replicate and infect a computer system. A worm, however, works independently of host file execution and is much more active in spreading itself. When the Palevo worm broke out in 2013, it was reported to be infecting 500 computers per hour. It spread through Yahoo! Messenger and used contacts in Yahoo! Messenger accounts to spread itself to other victims.

## Script and Macro Viruses

**What are script and macro viruses?** Some viruses are hidden on websites in the form of scripts. A **script** is a series of commands—actually, a miniprogram—that is executed without your knowledge. Scripts are often used to perform useful, legitimate functions on websites, such as collecting name and address information from customers. However, some scripts are malicious. For example, you might click a link to display a video on a website, which causes a script to run that infects your computer with a virus.

A **macro virus** is a virus that attaches itself to a document that uses macros. A *macro* is a short series of commands that usually automates repetitive tasks. However, macro languages are now so sophisticated that viruses can be written with them. In 1999, the Melissa virus became the first major macro virus to cause problems worldwide.

## E-Mail Viruses

**What is an e-mail virus?** In addition to being a macro virus, the Melissa virus was the first practical example of an e-mail virus. **E-mail viruses** use the address book in the victim's e-mail system to distribute the virus. In the case of the Melissa virus, anyone opening an infected document triggered the virus, which infected other documents on the victim's computer. Once triggered, the Melissa virus sent itself to the first 50 people in the e-mail address book on the infected computer.

## Encryption Viruses

**What are encryption viruses?** When **encryption viruses** infect your computer, they run a program that searches for common types of data files, such as Microsoft Word and Excel files, and compresses them using a complex encryption key that renders your files unusable. You then receive a message that asks you to send money to an account if you want to receive the program to decrypt your files. The flaw with this type of virus, which keeps it from being widespread, is that law enforcement officials can trace the payments to an account and may possibly be able to catch the perpetrators. Figure 9.3 summarizes the major categories of viruses.

## Additional Virus Classifications

**How else are viruses classified?** Viruses can also be classified by the methods they take to avoid detection by antivirus software:

- A **polymorphic virus** changes its own code or periodically rewrites itself to avoid detection. Most polymorphic viruses infect a particular type of file such as .EXE files, for example.
- A **multipartite virus** is designed to infect multiple file types in an effort to fool the antivirus software that is looking for it.

FIGURE 9.3

## Major Categories of Viruses

| | | |
|---|---|---|
| 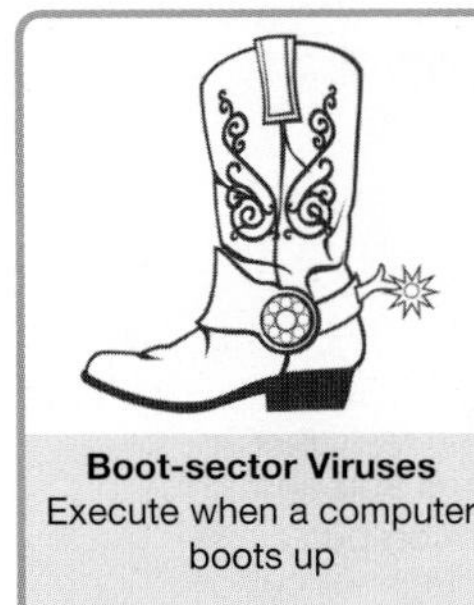 **Boot-sector Viruses** Execute when a computer boots up |  **Logic Bombs/Time Bombs** Execute when certain conditions or dates are reached |  **Worms** Spread on their own with no human interaction needed |
|  **Script and Macro Viruses** Series of commands with malicious intent |  **E-mail Viruses** Spread as attachments to e-mail, often using address books |  **Encryption Viruses** Hold files "hostage" by encrypting them; ask for ransom to unlock them |

*(tribalium81/Fotolia; LoopAll/Fotolia; dedMazay/Fotolia; Theo Malings/Fotolia; Beboy/Fotolia; Andrea Danti/Fotolia)*

- **Stealth viruses** temporarily erase their code from the files where they reside and then hide in the active memory of the computer. This helps them avoid detection if only the hard drive is being searched for viruses. Fortunately, current antivirus software scans memory as well as the hard drive.

## Virus Symptoms

**How can I tell if my computer is infected with a virus?** Sometimes it can be difficult to definitively tell whether your computer is infected with a virus. However, if your computer displays any of the following symptoms, it may be infected with a virus:

1. Existing program icons or files suddenly disappear. Viruses often delete specific file types or programs.
2. You start your browser and it takes you to an unusual home page (i.e., one you didn't set) or it has new toolbars.
3. Odd messages, pop-ups, or images are displayed on the screen, or strange music or sounds play.
4. Data files become corrupt. (However, note that files can become corrupt for reasons other than a virus infection.)
5. Programs stop working properly, which could be caused by either a corrupted file or a virus.
6. Your system slows down or takes a long time to boot up. ■

ACTIVE HELPDESK

**Avoiding Computer Viruses**

In this Active Helpdesk call, you'll play the role of a helpdesk staffer, fielding calls about different types of viruses and what users should do to protect their computer from them.

# BITS&BYTES

## CAPTCHA: Keeping Websites Safe from Bots

Automated programs called *bots* (or web robots) are used to make tasks easier on the Internet. For example, search engines use bots to search and index web pages. Unfortunately, bots can also be used for malicious or illegal purposes because they can perform some computing tasks faster than humans. For example, bots can be used on ticket-ordering sites to buy large blocks of high-demand concert tickets. They are also often used to post spam in the comment sections of blogs. Fortunately, website owners can deploy CAPTCHA software (see Figure 9.4) to prevent such bot activities.

CAPTCHA (Completely Automated Public Turing Test to Tell Computers and Humans Apart) programs generate distorted text and require that it be typed into a box. Because bots can't yet be programmed to read distorted text, which most people can, the CAPTCHA program can verify that a human is performing the task being tested. If you want to try integrating a CAPTCHA program into your website (to protect your e-mail address), go to **google.com/recaptcha**, which offers free CAPTCHA tools to help you protect your data.

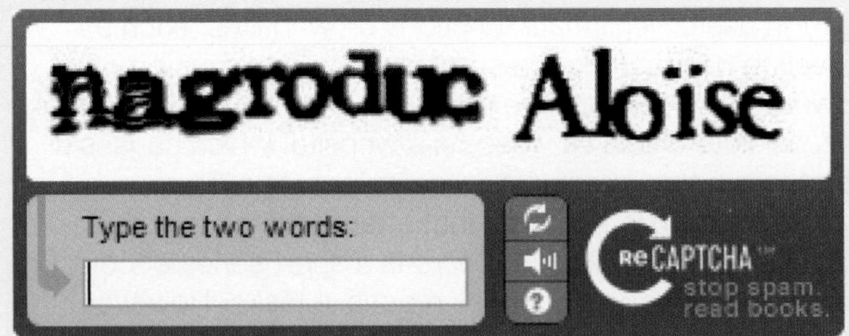


FIGURE 9.4 CAPTCHA programs like this one verify that a human, not a bot, is performing the requested task. *(Courtesy of the Carnegie Mellon University Press)*

# preventing virus INFECTIONS

**Antivirus software** is specifically designed to detect viruses and protect your computer and files from harm. Symantec, Kaspersky, AVG, and McAfee are among the companies that offer highly rated antivirus software packages. Antivirus protection is also included in comprehensive Internet security packages such as Norton Internet Security, Kaspersky Internet Security, and McAfee Total Protection. These software packages also help protect you from threats other than computer viruses. For example, Windows 8 includes Windows Defender, which defends against malware as well as viruses.

## Antivirus Software

**How often do I need to run antivirus software?** Although antivirus software is designed to detect suspicious activity on your computer at all times, you should run an active virus scan on your entire system at least once a week. By doing so, all files on your computer will be checked for undetected viruses.

Current antivirus programs run scans in the background when your CPU is not being heavily utilized. But you can also configure the software to run scans at times when you aren't using your system—for example, when you're asleep (see Figure 9.5). (However, it's important to note that your computer has to be on and not in sleep mode for these virus scans to take place.) Alternatively, if you suspect a problem, you can launch a scan and have it run immediately.

**How does antivirus software work?** The main functions of antivirus software are as follows:

- *Detection:* Antivirus software looks for virus signatures in files. A **virus signature** is a portion of the virus code that's unique to a particular computer virus. Antivirus software scans files for these signatures when they're opened or executed and identifies infected files and the type of virus infecting them.
- *Stopping virus execution:* If the antivirus software detects a virus signature or suspicious activity, such as the

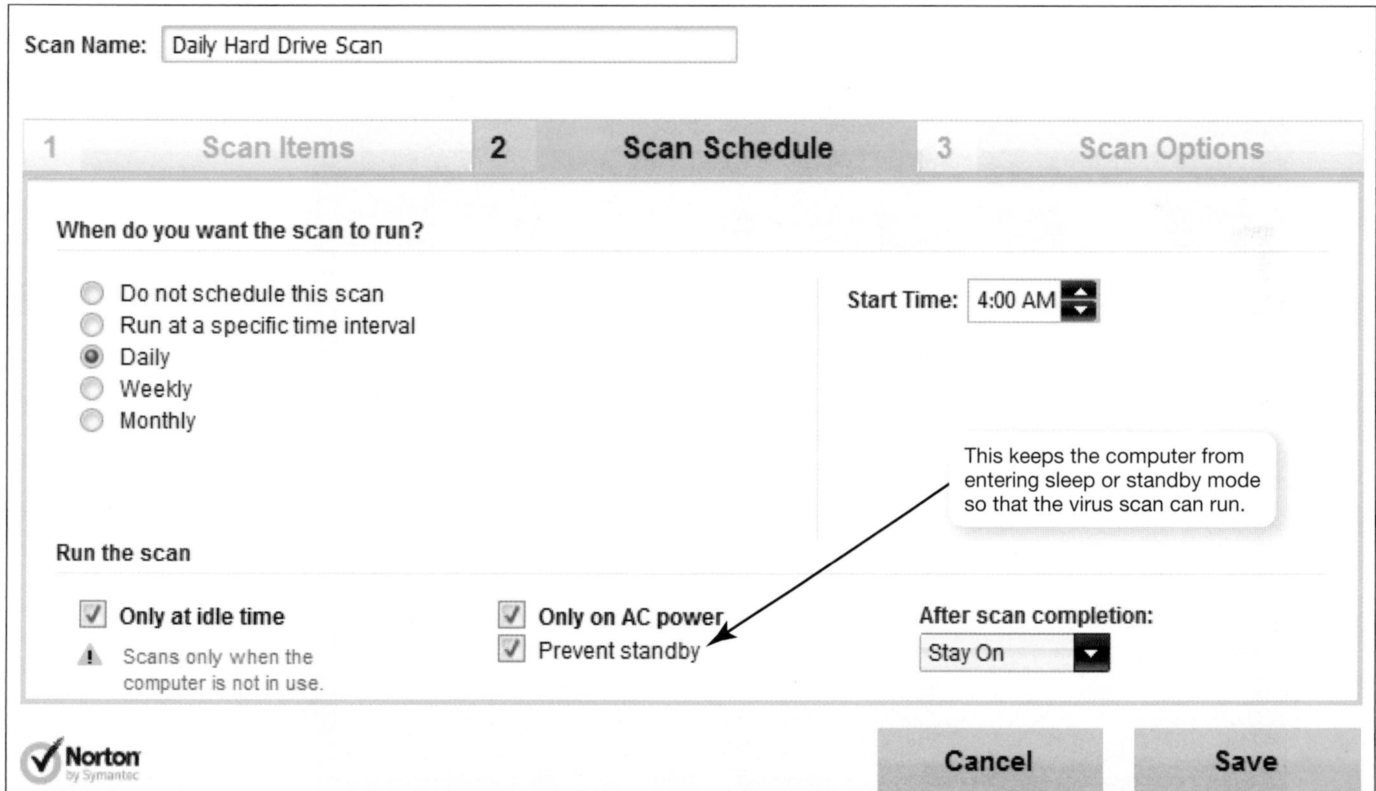


**FIGURE 9.5** In Norton Internet Security, you can set up virus scans to run automatically. This computer will be scanned every day at 4 a.m. *(Reprinted with permission of Symantec Corporation)*

launch of an unknown macro, it stops the execution of the file and virus and notifies you that it has detected a virus. It also places the virus in a secure area on your hard drive so that it won't spread to other files; this procedure is known as **quarantining**. Usually, the antivirus software then gives you the choice of deleting or repairing the infected file. Unfortunately, antivirus programs can't always fix infected files to make them usable again. You should keep backup copies of critical files so that you can restore them in case a virus damages them irreparably.

- *Prevention of future infection:* Most antivirus software will also attempt to prevent infection by inoculating key files on your computer. In **inoculation**, the antivirus software records key attributes about your computer files, such as file size and date created, and keeps these statistics in a safe place on your hard drive. When scanning for viruses, the antivirus software compares the attributes of the files with the attributes it previously recorded to help detect attempts by virus programs to modify your files.

**Does antivirus software always stop viruses?** Antivirus software catches *known* viruses effectively. However, new viruses are written all the time. To combat unknown viruses, modern antivirus programs search for suspicious virus-like activities as well as virus signatures. To minimize your risk, you should keep your antivirus software up to date.

**My new computer came with antivirus software installed, so shouldn't I already be protected?** Most new computers do come with antivirus software preinstalled. However, these are usually trial versions of the software that only provide updates to the software for a limited period of time, usually 90 or 180 days. After that, you have to buy a full version of the software to ensure you remain protected from new viruses.

**How do I make sure my antivirus software is up to date?** Most antivirus programs have an automatic update feature that downloads updates for virus signature files every time you go online (see Figure 9.6). Also, the antivirus software usually shows the status of your update subscription so that you can see how much time you have remaining until you need to buy another version of your software.

**What should I do if I think my computer is infected with a virus?** Boot up your computer using the antivirus installation disc. This should prevent most virus programs from loading and will allow you to run the antivirus software directly from your disk drive. (*Note:* If you download your antivirus software from the Internet, copy it to a DVD in case you have problems in the future.) If the software does detect viruses, you may want to research them further to determine whether your antivirus software will eradicate them completely or whether you'll need to take additional manual steps to eliminate the viruses. Most antivirus company websites, such as the Symantec site (**symantec.com**), contain archives of information on viruses and provide step-by-step solutions for removing them.

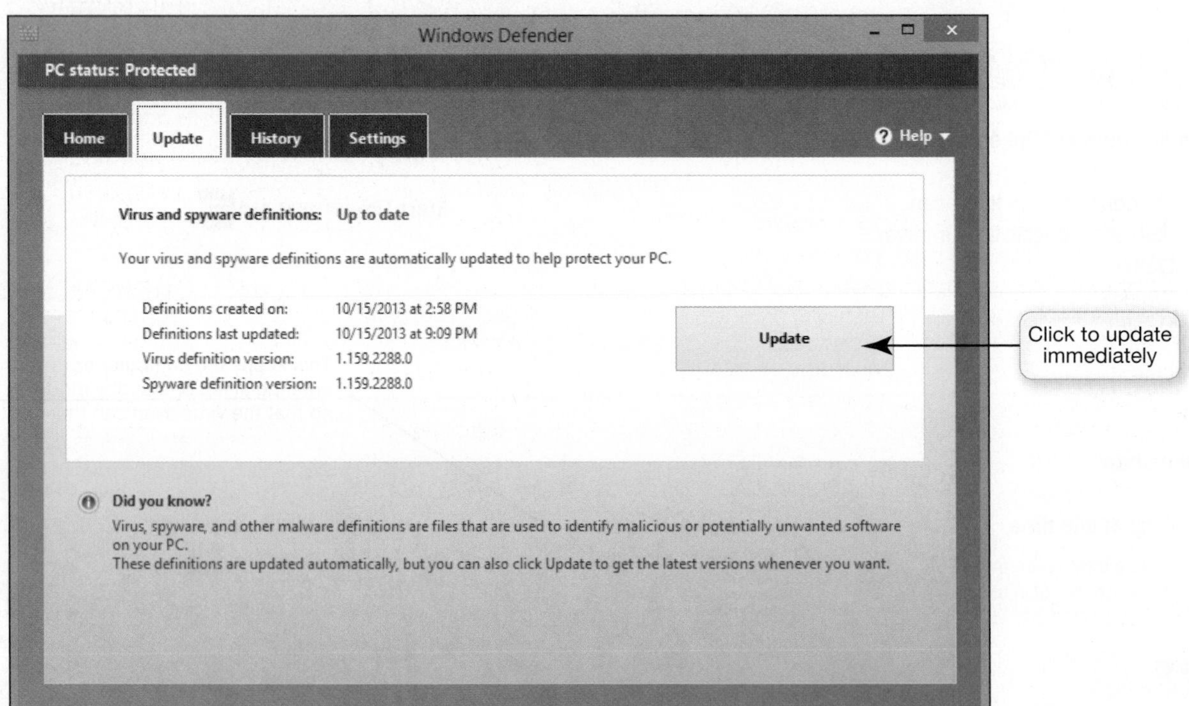


**FIGURE 9.6** Antivirus software, such as Windows Defender, provides for automatic updates but also allows manual updates.

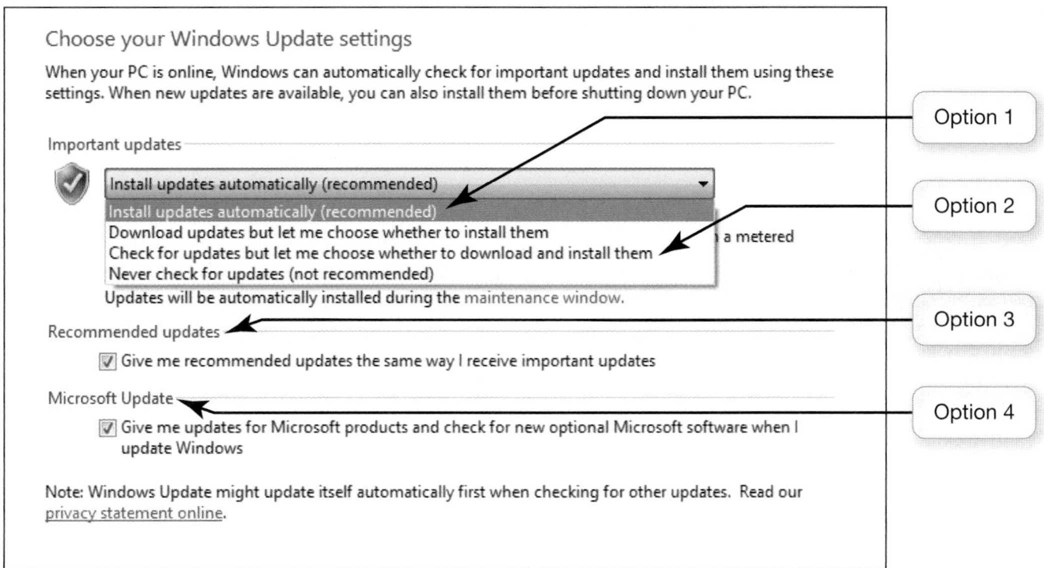


**FIGURE 9.7** The Windows Update screen makes it easy for users to configure Windows to update itself.

*>To enable automatic updates, access the Control Panel, select* **System and Security**, *click the* **Windows Update** *link, and then click the* **Change Settings** *link.*

**How do I protect my phone from viruses?** Because smartphones and other mobile devices run operating systems and contain files, they are susceptible to infection by viruses. Cybercriminals are now hiding viruses in legitimate-looking apps for download to mobile devices. Most antivirus software companies now offer antivirus software specifically designed for mobile devices, such as Lookout Mobile Security, which Samsung is now installing on its Android phones.

## Software Updates

**Why does updating my operating system (OS) software help protect me from viruses?** Many viruses exploit weaknesses in operating systems. Malicious websites can be set up to attack your computer by downloading harmful software onto your computer. According to research conducted by Google, this type of attack, known as a **drive-by download**, affects almost 1 in 1,000 web pages. To combat these threats, make sure your OS is up to date and contains the latest security patches. You can update your Windows OS with an automatic update utility called Windows Update. When you enable automatic updates, your computer searches for updates on the Microsoft website every time it connects to the Internet. Mac OS X has a similar utility for gathering updates.

SOUND BYTE

**Protecting Your Computer**

In this Sound Byte, you'll learn how to use a variety of tools to protect your computer, including antivirus software and Windows utilities.

**Do OS updates only happen automatically?** The default option in Windows is to receive updates automatically. There are several other options you can choose from in Windows, as shown in Figure 9.7. The following options are noteworthy:

- *Option 1: Install updates automatically.* Selecting this option will automatically download and install updates at a time you have specified. *We strongly recommend that you select this option.*
- *Option 2: Check for updates but let me choose whether to download and install them.* This is an appropriate choice only if you have low bandwidth Internet access. Because downloads over dial-up can take a long time, you need to control when they will occur. But you need to be extra vigilant with this option because you may forget to install important updates.
- *Option 3: Give me recommended updates.* This option ensures you receive recommended (optional) updates as well as critical (necessary) updates.
- *Option 4: Microsoft Update.* This option ensures you receive updates for other Microsoft products besides Windows, such as Microsoft Office.

If you keep both your antivirus and OS software up to date, you'll help prevent viruses from infecting your computer. ■

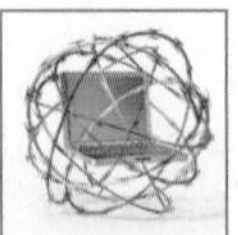

# understanding HACKERS

Although there's a great deal of disagreement as to what a hacker actually is, especially among hackers themselves, a **hacker** is most commonly defined as anyone who unlawfully breaks into a computer system—either an individual computer or a network (see Figure 9.8).

**Are there different kinds of hackers?** Some hackers are offended by being labeled as criminals and therefore attempt to classify different types of hackers as follows:

- **White-hat hackers** (or **ethical hackers**) break in to systems for nonmalicious reasons, such as to test system security vulnerabilities or to expose undisclosed weaknesses. They believe in making security vulnerabilities known either to the company that owns the system or software or to the general public, often to embarrass a company into fixing a problem.
- **Black-hat hackers** break into systems to destroy information or for illegal gain. The terms *white hat* and *black hat* are references to old Western movies in which the heroes wore white hats and the outlaws wore black hats.
- **Grey-hat hackers** are a bit of a cross between black and white—they often illegally break into systems merely to flaunt their expertise to the administrator of the system they penetrated or to attempt to sell their services in repairing security breaches.

FORTUNES TOLD
WILDT
"Oh, we used to use a crystal ball, but hacking into your credit files is much more informative!"

**FIGURE 9.8** Hackers can find lots of personal information about you on the Internet. *(Wildt, Chris/Cartoonstock)*

Regardless of the hackers' opinions, the laws in the United States and in many other countries consider *any* unauthorized access to computer systems a crime.

## Problems Hackers Can Cause

**Could a hacker steal my debit card or bank account number?** Hackers often try to break in to computers or websites that contain credit card information. If you perform financial transactions online, such as banking or buying goods and services, you probably do so using a credit or debit card. Credit card and bank account information can thus reside on your hard drive or an online business's hard drive and may be detectable by a hacker.

Aside from your home computer, you have personal data stored on various websites. For example, many sites require that you provide a login ID and password to gain access. Even if this data isn't stored on your computer, a hacker may be able to capture it when you're online by using a *packet analyzer (sniffer)* or a *keylogger* (a program that captures all keystrokes made on a computer).

**What's a packet analyzer?** Data travels through the Internet in small pieces called *packets*. The packets are identified with an IP address, in part to help identify the computer to which they are being sent. Once the packets reach their destination, they're reassembled into cohesive messages.
A **packet analyzer (sniffer)** is a program deployed by hackers that looks at (or sniffs) each packet as it travels on the Internet—not just those addressed to a particular computer, but all packets coming across a particular network. For example, a hacker might sit in a coffee shop and run a packet sniffer to capture sensitive data (such as debit/credit card numbers) from patrons using the coffee shop's free wireless network. Wireless networks such as these can be particularly vulnerable to this type of exploitation if encryption of data isn't enabled when the networks are set up. (This topic was covered in more detail in Chapter 7.)

**What do hackers do with the information they "sniff"?** Once a hacker has your debit/credit card information, he or she can use it to purchase items illegally or can sell the number to someone who will. If a hacker steals the login ID and password to an account where you have your bank card information stored (such as eBay or Amazon), he or she can also use your account to buy items and have them shipped to him- or herself instead of to you. If hackers can gather enough information in conjunction with your credit card information, they may be able to commit identity theft.

Although this sounds scary, you can easily protect yourself from packet sniffing by installing a firewall (which we discuss later in this chapter) and using data encryption on a wireless network (which was covered in Chapter 7).

## Trojan Horses and Rootkits

**Besides stealing information, what other problems can hackers cause if they break into my computer?** Hackers often use individuals' computers as a staging area for mischief. To commit widespread computer attacks, for example, hackers need to control many computers at the same time. To this end, hackers often use Trojan horses to install other programs on computers. A **Trojan horse** is a program that appears to be something useful or desirable, like a game or a screen saver, but while it runs, it does something malicious in the background, without your knowledge (see Figure 9.9).

**What damage can Trojan horses do?** Often, the malicious activity perpetrated by a Trojan horse program is the installation of a backdoor program or a rootkit. **Backdoor programs** and **rootkits** are programs (or sets of programs) that allow hackers to gain access to your computer and take almost complete control of it without your knowledge. Using a backdoor program, hackers can access and delete all the files on your computer, send e-mail, run programs, and do just about anything else you can do with your computer. A computer that a hacker controls in this manner is referred to as a **zombie**. Zombies are often used to launch *denial-of-service attacks* on other computers.

## Denial-of-Service Attacks

**What are denial-of-service attacks?** In a **denial-of-service (DoS) attack**, legitimate users are denied access to a computer system because a hacker is repeatedly making requests of that computer system through a computer he or she has taken over as a zombie. A computer system can handle only a certain number of requests for information at one time. When it is flooded with requests in a DoS attack, it shuts down and refuses to answer any requests for information, even if the requests are from a legitimate user. Thus, the computer is so busy responding to the bogus requests for information that authorized users can't gain access.

**Couldn't a DoS attack be traced back to the computer that launched it?** Launching a DoS attack on a computer system from a single computer is easy to trace. Therefore, most savvy hackers use a **distributed denial-of-service (DDoS) attack**, which launches DoS attacks from more than one zombie (sometimes thousands of zombies) at the same time.

Figure 9.10 illustrates how a DDoS attack works. A hacker creates many zombies and coordinates them so that they begin sending bogus requests to the same computer at the same time. Administrators of the victim computer often have a great deal of difficulty stopping the attack because it comes from so many computers. Often, the attacks are coordinated automatically by botnets. A **botnet** is a large group of software programs (called *robots* or *bots*) that runs autonomously on zombie computers. Some botnets have been known to span 1.5 million computers.

Because many commercial websites receive revenue from users, either directly (such as via subscriptions to online games) or indirectly (such as when web surfers click on advertisements), DDoS attacks can be financially distressing for the owners of the affected websites.

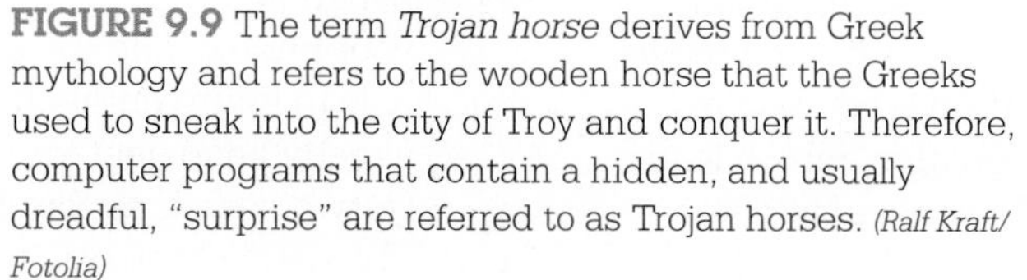

**FIGURE 9.9** The term *Trojan horse* derives from Greek mythology and refers to the wooden horse that the Greeks used to sneak into the city of Troy and conquer it. Therefore, computer programs that contain a hidden, and usually dreadful, "surprise" are referred to as Trojan horses. *(Ralf Kraft/ Fotolia)*

## How Hackers Gain Computer Access

**How exactly does a hacker gain access to a computer?** Hackers can gain access to computers directly or indirectly:

- Direct access involves sitting down at a computer and installing hacking software. It's unlikely that such an attack would occur in your home, but it's always a wise precaution to set up your computer so that it requires a password for a user to gain access.
- The most likely method a hacker will use to access a computer is to enter indirectly through its Internet connection.

Many people forget that their Internet connection is a two-way street. Not only can you access the Internet, but people on the Internet can access your computer. Think of your computer as a house. Common sense tells you to lock your home's doors and windows to deter theft when you aren't there. Hooking your computer up to the Internet without protection is like leaving the front door to your house wide open. Your computer obviously doesn't have doors and windows like a house, but it does have logical ports.

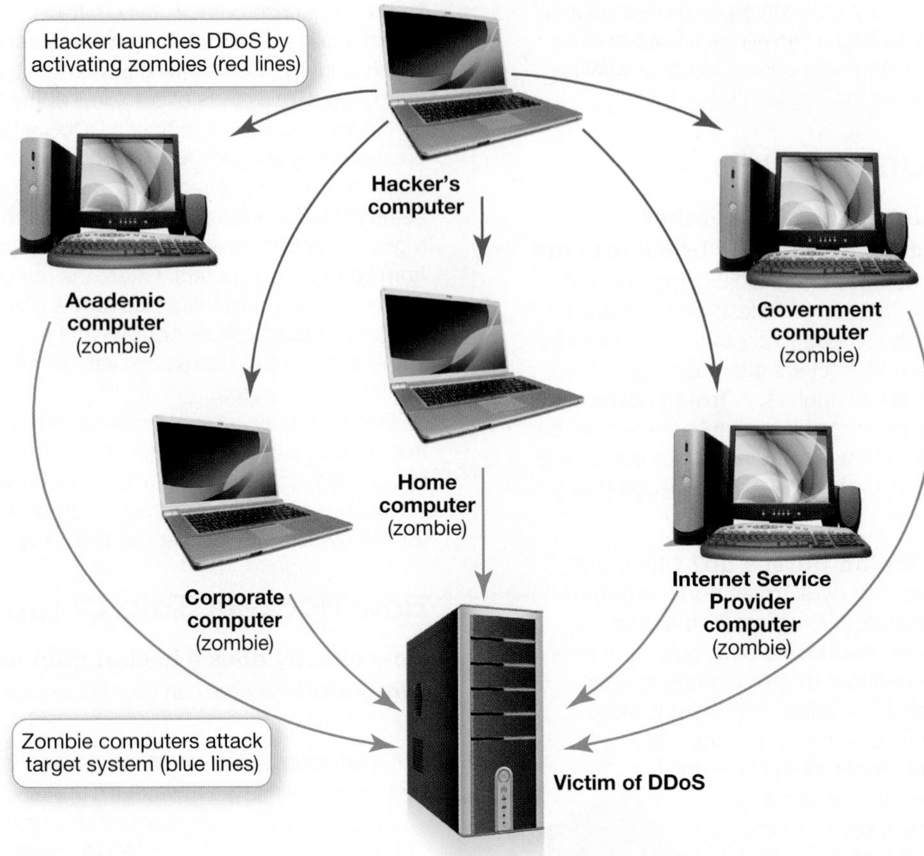


**FIGURE 9.10** Zombie computers are used to facilitate a DDoS attack.

# BITS&BYTES

## Are Your Photos Helping Criminals Target You?

All cell phones today contain GPS chips. The cameras in phones often use information gathered from the GPS chips to encode information onto photos in the form of geotags. A **geotag** is a piece of data attached to a photo that indicates your latitude and longitude when you took the photo. Geotagging is useful for applications that can take advantage of this information, but problems arise when you share geotagged photos on the web.

If you post a lot of photos, cybercriminals and cyberstalkers can use the information from the geotags on your photos to figure out the patterns of your movements. They may be able to ascertain when you're at work or that you're currently on vacation, which leads them to determine prime times for burglarizing your home. Some sites such as Facebook and Twitter have measures in place to limit the amount of geotagged information that can be seen in photos in order to prevent their users from unwittingly revealing personal information. However, many photo-sharing sites don't have such protections in place.

The safest thing to do is not tag your photos with geotags in the first place. It's usually easy to disable location tracking on your smartphone. For instance, on the iPhone, on the Settings screen, select General, then Location Services, and choose Off. So stop geotagging your photos, and make it tougher for the cybercriminals to figure out your movements. For photos that already have geotags, you can remove them using software such as BatchPurifier or Geotag Remover.

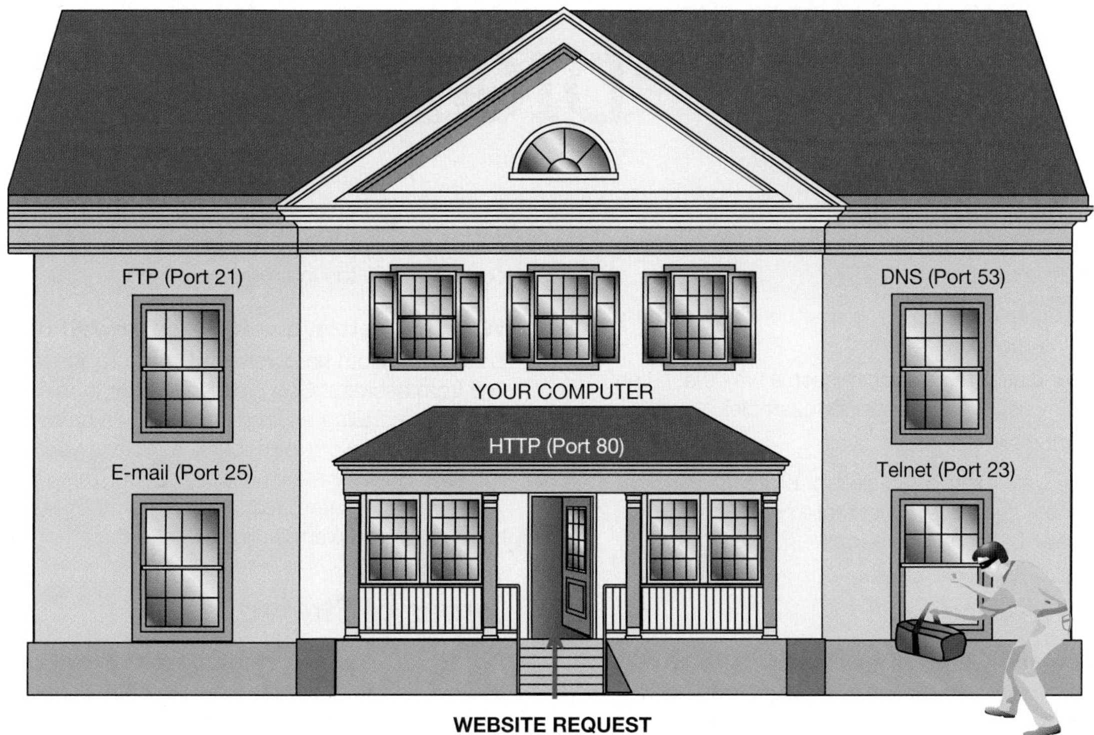


**FIGURE 9.11** Open logical ports are an invitation to hackers.

**What are logical ports? Logical ports** are virtual—that is, not physical—communications gateways or paths that allow a computer to organize requests for information, such as web page downloads or e-mail routing, from other networks or computers. Unlike physical ports, such as USB ports, you can't see or touch a logical port; it's part of a computer's internal organization.

Logical ports are numbered and assigned to specific services. For instance, logical port 80 is designated for hypertext transfer protocol (HTTP), the main communications protocol for the web. Thus, all requests for information from your browser to the web flow through logical port 80. Open logical ports, like open windows in a home, invite intruders, as illustrated in Figure 9.11. Unless you take precautions to restrict access to your logical ports, other people on the Internet may be able to access your computer through them.

Fortunately, you can thwart most hacking problems by installing a firewall, which we discuss next. ■

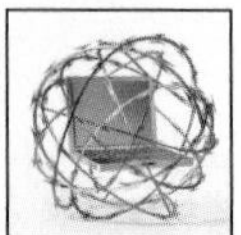

# restricting access to your DIGITAL ASSETS

Keeping hackers at bay is often just a matter of keeping them out. You can achieve this by:

- Preventing hackers from accessing your computer (usually through your Internet connection)
- Protecting your digital information in such a way that it can't be accessed (by using passwords, for example)
- Hiding your activities from prying eyes

In this section, we explore strategies for protecting access to your digital assets and keeping your Internet-surfing activities from being seen by the wrong people.

## Firewalls

**What is a firewall?** A **firewall** is a software program or hardware device designed to protect computers from hackers. It's named after a housing construction feature that slows the spread of fires from house to house. A firewall specifically designed for home networks is called a **personal firewall**. By using a personal firewall, you can close open logical ports to invaders and potentially make your computer invisible to other computers on the Internet.

**Which is better, a software firewall or a hardware firewall?** Both hardware and software firewalls will protect you from hackers. One type isn't better than the other. Although installing either a software or a hardware firewall on your home network is probably sufficient, you should consider installing both for maximum protection. This will provide you with additional safety, just as wearing multiple layers of clothing helps keep you warmer in the winter than a single layer.

## Types of Firewalls

**What software firewalls are there?** Both Windows and OS X include reliable firewalls. The Windows Action Center is a good source of information about the security settings on your computer (see Figure 9.12), including the status of your firewall. Security suites such as Norton Internet Security, McAfee Internet Security, and ZoneAlarm Internet Security

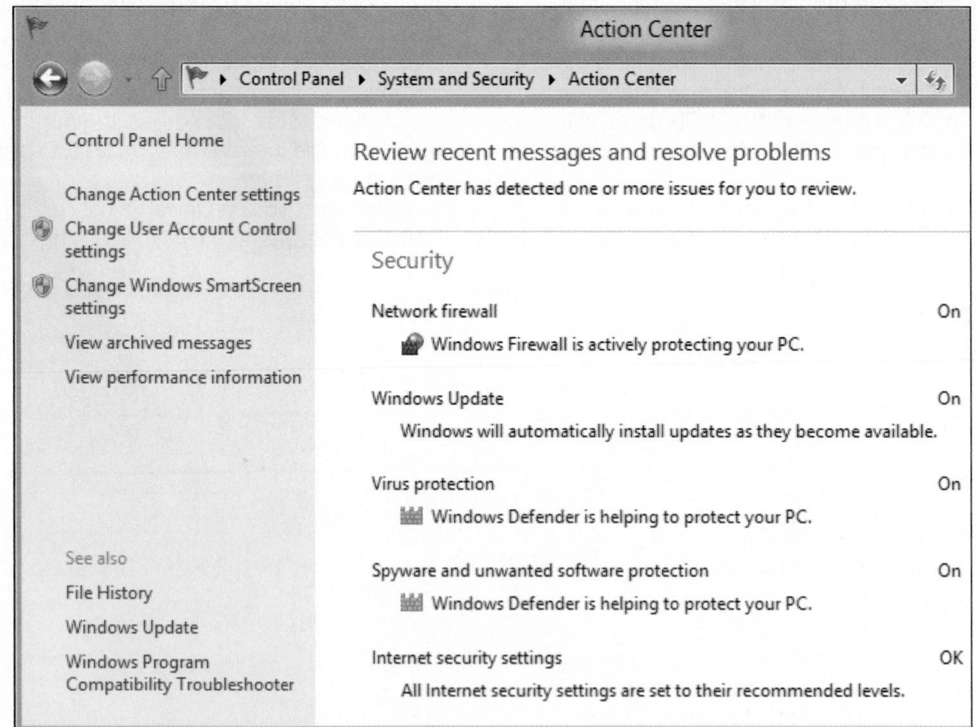


**FIGURE 9.12** The security section of the Windows Action Center provides the status of programs protecting your computer.

*>To view the Action Center, access the Control Panel, select* **System and Security**, *and then click the* **Action Center** *link.*

Suite also include firewall software. Although the firewalls that come with Windows and OS X will protect your computer, firewalls included in security suites often come with additional features such as monitoring systems that alert you if your computer is under attack.

If you're using a security suite that includes a firewall, the suite should disable the firewall that came with your OS. Two firewalls running at the same time can conflict with each other and cause your computer to slow down or freeze up.

**What are hardware firewalls?** You can also buy and configure hardware firewall devices. Many routers sold for home networks include firewall protection. Just like software firewalls, the setup for hardware firewalls is designed for novices, and the default configuration on most routers keeps unused logical ports closed. Documentation accompanying routers can assist more-experienced users in adjusting the settings to allow access to specific ports if needed.

## How Firewalls Work

**How do firewalls protect you from hackers?** Firewalls are designed to restrict access to a network and its computers. Firewalls protect you in two major ways:

1. By blocking access to logical ports and
2. By keeping your computer's network address secure

**How do firewalls block access to your logical ports?** Certain logical ports are very popular in hacker attacks. To block access to logical ports, firewalls examine data packets that your computer sends and receives. Data packets contain information such as the address of the sending and receiving computers and the logical port that the packet will use. Firewalls can be configured so that they filter out packets sent to specific logical ports in a process known as **packet filtering**. Firewalls are also often configured to ignore requests that originate from the Internet asking for access to certain ports. This process is referred to as **logical port blocking**. By using filtering and blocking, firewalls keep hackers from accessing your computer (Figure 9.13).

**How do firewalls keep your network address secure?** Every computer connected to the Internet has a unique address called an *Internet Protocol address (IP address)*. Data is routed to the correct computer on the Internet based on the IP address. This is similar to how a letter finds its way to your mailbox. You have a unique postal address for your home. If a hacker finds out the IP address of your computer, he or she can locate it on the Internet and try to break into it. This is similar to how a conventional thief might target your home after finding out you collect antique cars by using your street address to locate your house.

Your IP address for your home network is assigned to your router by your Internet service provider (ISP), but each device on your home network also has an IP address. Firewalls use a process called **network address translation (NAT)** to assign internal IP addresses on a network. The internal IP addresses are used only on the internal network and therefore can't be detected by hackers. For hackers to access your computer, they must know your computer's internal IP address. With a NAT–capable router/firewall installed on your network, hackers are unable to access the internal IP address assigned to your computer, so your computer is safe. You can use NAT in your home by purchasing a hardware firewall with NAT capabilities. Many routers sold for home use are also configured as firewalls, and many feature NAT.

ACTIVE HELPDESK

**Understanding Firewalls**

In this Active Helpdesk call, you'll play the role of a helpdesk staffer, fielding calls about how hackers can attack networks and what harm they can cause as well as what a firewall does to keep a computer safe from hackers.

## Knowing Your Computer Is Secure

**How can I tell if my computer is at risk?** For peace of mind, you can visit websites that offer free services that test your computer's vulnerability. One popular site is Gibson Research Corporation (**grc.com**). The company's ShieldsUP and LeakTest programs are free and easy to run and can pinpoint security vulnerabilities in a system connected to the Internet. If you get a clean report from these programs, your

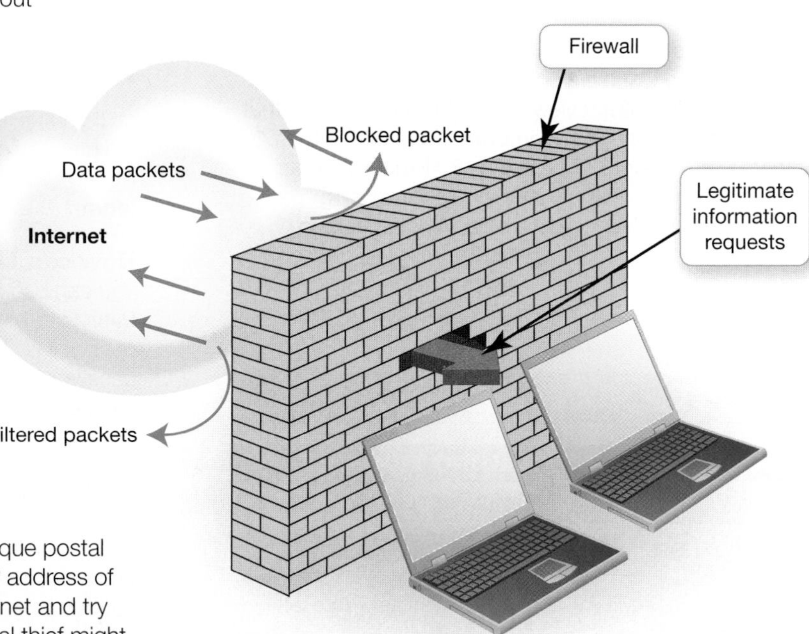


**FIGURE 9.13** Firewalls use filtering and blocking to keep out unwanted data and keep your network safe. *(Intelligent Computer Solutions)*

SOUND BYTE

**Installing a Personal Firewall**

Firewalls provide excellent protection against hackers on a home network. In this Sound Byte, you'll learn how to install and configure software firewalls to protect your computer.

system is probably not vulnerable to attack. See the Try This section in this chapter (page 368) for instructions on how to test your system.

**What if I don't get a clean report from the testing program?** If the testing program detects potential vulnerabilities and you don't have a firewall, you should install one as soon as possible. If the firewall is already configured and common ports (such as those shown in Figure 9.14) are identified as being vulnerable, consult your firewall documentation for instructions on how to close or restrict access to those ports.

## Password Protection and Password Management

**How can I best use passwords to protect my computer?** You no doubt have many passwords you need to remember to access your digital life. However, creating strong passwords—ones that are difficult for hackers to guess—is an essential piece of security that people sometimes overlook. Password-cracking programs have become more sophisticated. In fact, some commonly available programs can test more than one million password combinations per second! Creating a secure password is therefore more important than ever.

Many people use extremely weak passwords. The Imperva Application Defense Center, a computer-security research organization, conducted a review of 32 million passwords that were used at the website **rockyou.com**. More than 345,000 people were using "12345," "123456," or "123456789" as their password. And almost 62,000 people were using "password"! Passwords such as these are easy for hackers to crack.

**FIGURE 9.14**

**Common Logical Ports**

| PORT NUMBER | PROTOCOL USING THE PORT |
|---|---|
| 21 | FTP (File Transfer Protocol) control |
| 23 | Telnet (unencrypted text communications) |
| 25 | SMTP (Simple Mail Transfer Protocol) |
| 53 | DNS (domain name system) |
| 80 | HTTP (Hypertext Transfer Protocol) |
| 443 | HTTPS (HTTP with Transport Layer Security [TLS] encryption) |

Websites that need to be very secure, such as those for financial institutions, usually have strong defenses to prevent hackers from cracking passwords. But sites that need less security, such as casual gaming or social networking sites, might have less protection. Hackers attack poorly defended sites for passwords because many people use the same password for every site they use. So if a hacker can get your password from a poorly secured gaming site, they might be able to access your bank account with the same password.

## Creating Passwords

**What constitutes a strong password?** Strong passwords are difficult for someone to guess. Follow these guidelines to create strong passwords (see Figure 9.15):

- Don't use easily deduced components related to your life, such as parts of your name, your pet's name, your street address, or the name of the website or institution for which you are creating the password (i.e., don't use "Citibank" for your online banking password).
- Use a password that is at least 14 characters long. Longer passwords are more difficult to deduce. Consider using a passphrase that is even longer (see the Bits & Bytes on page 364).
- Don't use words found in the dictionary.
- Use a mix of upper- and lowercase letters and symbols (such as # or %).
- Never tell anyone your password or write it down in a place where others might see it, like in your wallet or purse.
- Change your passwords on a regular basis, such as monthly or quarterly. Your school or your employer probably requires you to change your password regularly. This is also a good idea for your personal passwords.
- Don't use the same password for every account you have.

If you have trouble thinking of secure passwords, there are many password generators available for free, such as the Strong Password Generator (**strongpasswordgenerator .com**).

**How can I check the strength of my passwords?** You can use online password strength testers, such as the Password Meter (**passwordmeter.com**), to evaluate your passwords. The Password Meter provides guidelines for good passwords and shows you how integrating various elements, such as symbols, affects the strength score of your password.

**How do I restrict access to my computer?** Windows, OS X, and most other operating systems have built-in password (or passcode) protection for files as well as the entire desktop. After a certain period of idle time, your computer is automatically password locked, and your password must be entered to gain access to the computer. This provides excellent protection from casual snooping if you need to walk away from your computer for a period of time. If someone attempts to log on to your computer without your password, that person won't be able to gain access. It's an especially good idea to use passwords on laptop computers, smartphones, and

FIGURE 9.15

## Strong and Weak Password Candidates

| PASSWORD | RATING | GOOD POINTS | BAD POINTS |
|---|---|---|---|
| Joysmithl022 | Poor | • Contains upper- and lowercase letters<br>• Contains letters and numbers | • Less than 14 characters<br>• Contains name and birth date |
| test44drive6car | Mediocre | • 15 characters in length | • Contains three words found in the dictionary<br>• Numbers repeated consecutively |
| 8$RanT%5ydTTtt& | Better | • Good length<br>• Contains upper- and lowercase letters<br>• Contains symbols | • Upper- and lowercase letters repeated consecutively<br>• Still contains one dictionary word (rant) |
| 7R3m3mB3R$5%y38 | Best | • All good points from above<br>• Dictionary word (remember) has 3s instead of Es | • None |

tablets because this provides additional protection of your data if your device is lost or stolen.

Windows 8 allows you to use picture passwords. You select a picture and then draw three gestures on it—either straight lines, circles, or taps. This picture then works as an additional method for accessing your computer. You just unlock your computer by repeating the gestures (see Figure 9.16). But if you forget your gestures, you can always access your computer via the conventional password.

## Managing Your Passwords

**How can I remember all of my complex passwords?** Good security practices suggest that you have different passwords for all the different websites that you access and that you change your passwords frequently. The problem with well-constructed passwords is that they can be hard to remember. Fortunately, password-management tools are now available. They take the worry out of forgetting passwords because the password-management software does the remembering for you.

**Where can I obtain password-management software?** Most current Internet security suites and web browsers make it easy to keep track of passwords by providing password-management tools. For example, Internet Explorer (IE) will remember passwords for you. When you go to a website that requires a login, IE will display a dialog box prompting you to have IE remember the password for the site (see Figure 9.17). Then, when you return to the site and type in your user name, IE will fill in the password information for you using a process known as auto complete. However, there are some passwords that you shouldn't have your browser remember, such as your online banking password. So be selective when using this feature.

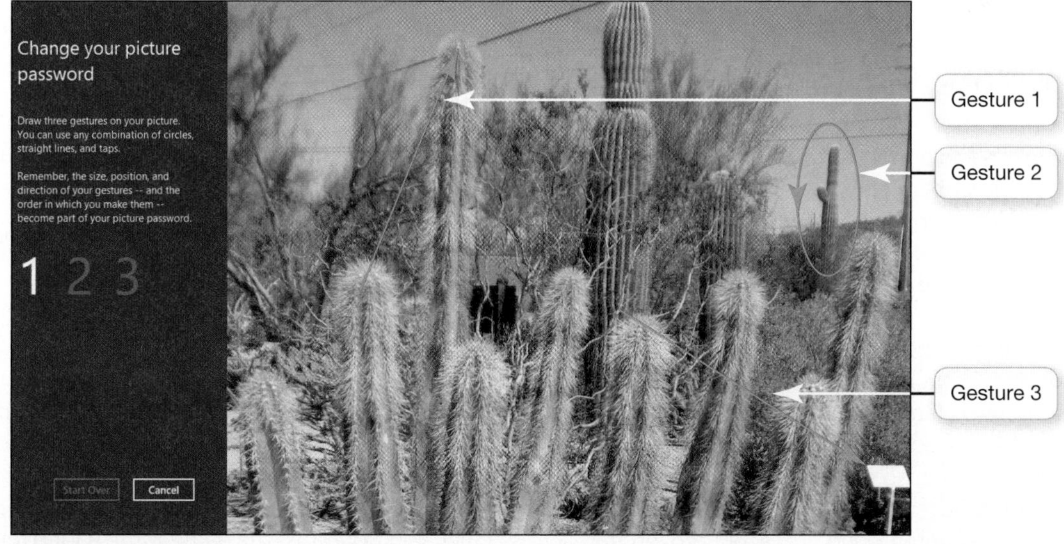


FIGURE 9.16 Drawing three gestures on your picture (and repeating them once) sets your picture password options in Windows 8.

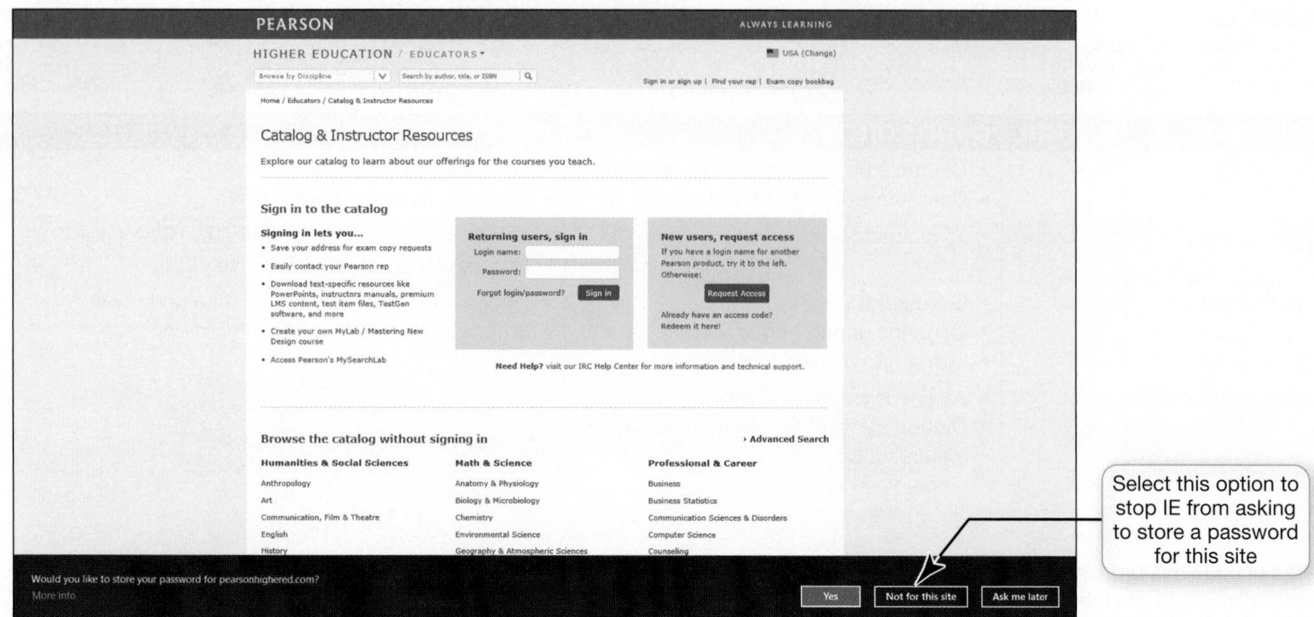


**FIGURE 9.17** The password bar in IE 11 displays whenever you type in a password for a website for which IE hasn't yet stored the password.

## Anonymous Web Surfing: Hiding from Prying Eyes

**Should I be concerned about surfing the Internet on shared, public, or work computers?** If you use shared computers in public places such as libraries, coffee shops, or student unions, you never know what nefarious tools have been installed by hackers on a public computer. When you browse the Internet, traces of your activity are left behind on that computer, often as temporary files. A wily hacker can glean sensitive information long after you've finished your surfing session. In addition, many employers routinely review the Internet browsing history of employees to ensure workers are spending their time on the Internet productively.

**What tools can I use to keep my browsing activities private when surfing the Internet?** The current versions of Google Chrome, Firefox, and Internet Explorer include privacy tools (called Incognito,

# BITS&BYTES

## Can't Remember Passwords? Try a Passphrase Instead!

Sure, Tr4h&nj9$WsD2# is a hard-to-guess password. It's also difficult for most people to remember. It's often easier for people to remember a phrase than random strings of characters and numbers. Therefore, *passphrases* can be a useful alternative to passwords.

A passphrase is a string of words that makes some sense to the individual using it so it will be easier to remember. Passphrases usually span 25 or more characters, making them much longer than passwords, which are typically 10 to 14 characters long. Longer passphrases are harder to crack, so the longer the better.

Passphrases should have meaning only to you. You should not use famous quotes, song lyrics, old proverbs or really any phrase that is in common usage or has been published. A phrase related to a memorable event in your past usually works best, such as:

- myfirstcatwasnamedblackieandwanderedupto ourdoorwhenIwasfive
- IfirstwentwaterskiinginMainewithmyfriend Scottin1997

Unless you have published a memoir with this information in it, personal events should be unknown to other people. Most people find a phrase easier to remember than a complex password. But as with passwords, you should change your passphrase periodically, and don't use the same phrase for every website/system that you access.

Private Browsing, and InPrivate, respectively) that help you surf the web anonymously (see Figure 9.18). When you choose to surf anonymously, all three browsers open special versions of their browser windows that are enhanced for privacy. When surfing in these windows, records of websites you visit and files you download don't appear in the web browser's history files. Furthermore, any temporary files generated in that browsing session are deleted when you exit the special window.

**Are there any other tools I could use to protect my privacy?** Portable privacy devices, such as the Ironkey Personal Flash Drive (**ironkey.com**), provide an even higher level of surfing privacy. Simply plug the device into an available USB port on the machine on which you'll be working. All sensitive Internet files, such as cookies, passwords, Internet history, and browser caches, will be stored on the privacy device, not on the computer you're using. Privacy devices such as these often come preloaded with software designed to shield your IP address from prying eyes, making it difficult (if not impossible) for hackers to tell where you're surfing on the Internet. These privacy devices also have password-management tools that store all of your login information and encrypt it so it will be safe if your privacy device falls into someone else's hands.

**Is there anything else I can do to keep my data safe on shared computers?** Another free practical solution is to take the Linux OS with you on a flash drive and avoid using the public or work computer's OS. The interfaces of many Linux distros look almost exactly like Windows and are easy to use. There are several advantages to using a Linux-based OS on a public or work computer:

- Your risk of picking up viruses and other malicious programs is significantly reduced because booting a computer from a flash drive completely eliminates any interaction with the computer's OS. This, in turn, significantly reduces the chance that your flash drive will become infected by any malware running on the computer.
- Virus and hacking attacks against Linux are far less likely than attacks against Windows. Because Windows has about 90% of the OS market, people who write malware tend to target Windows systems.
- When you run software from your own storage medium, such as a flash drive, you avoid reading and writing to the hard disk of the computer. This significantly enhances your privacy because you don't leave traces of your activity behind.

Pendrivelinux (**pendrivelinux.com**) is an excellent resource that offers many different versions of Linux for download and includes step-by-step instructions on how to install them

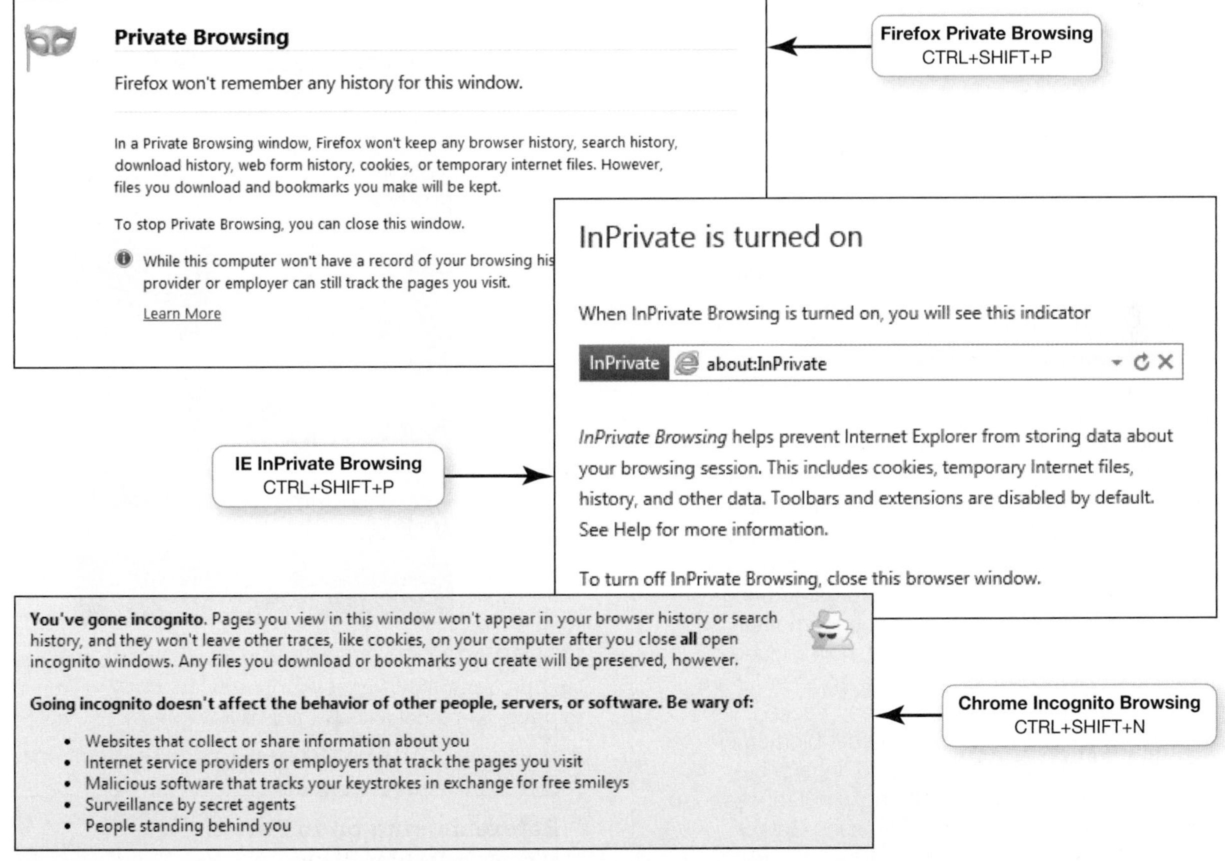


**FIGURE 9.18** The recent versions of the Firefox, Internet Explorer, and Google Chrome browsers all feature privacy tools for web surfing. *((a) Courtesy of the Mozilla Foundation; (c) Courtesy of the Mozilla Foundation)*

on your flash drive (see Figure 9.19). If you're a Mac user, the gOS version of Linux provides a close approximation of OS X, so you can feel right at home.

**Do I need to take special precautions with my tablet devices?** Tablets like the iPad run their own proprietary operating systems that differ from the operating systems deployed on laptop and desktop computers. Although tablet operating systems do contain security features, they may not be robust enough to satisfy business users who have a great deal of confidential information on their tablets, especially when the devices are connected to wireless networks. Third-party software developers are now offering many apps to enhance tablet security. Comprehensive suites like IPVanish (**ipvanish.com**) offer features such as government-grade encryption of data, enhanced e-mail security, and anonymous web surfing. So look for security apps that are specifically designed for your tablet device if you often deal with sensitive data on your tablet, such as online banking.

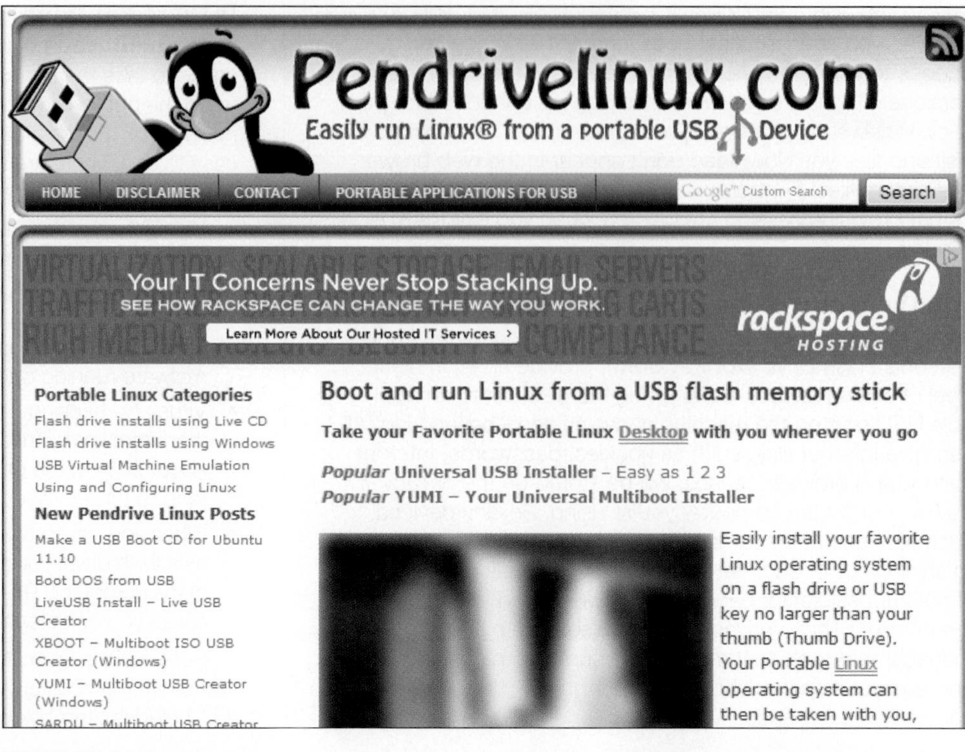


**FIGURE 9.19** **Pendrivelinux.com** can help you load a version of Linux onto a flash drive. *(Courtesy of USB Pen Drive Linux)*

## Biometric Authentication Devices

**Besides passwords, how else can I restrict the use of my computer?** A **biometric authentication device** is a device that reads a unique personal characteristic such as a fingerprint or the iris pattern in your eye and converts its pattern to a digital code (see Figure 9.20). When you use the device, your pattern is read and compared to the one stored on the computer. Only users having an exact fingerprint or iris pattern match are allowed to access the computer.

Because no two people have the same biometric characteristics (fingerprints and iris patterns are unique), these devices provide a high level of security. They also eliminate the human error that can occur in password protection. You might forget your password, but you won't forget to bring your fingerprints when you're working on your computer! Some smartphones, such as the iPhone 5s, now include fingerprint readers. But since Touch ID (the Apple software for fingerprint identification) has already been hacked, you might be safer using a regular password. Other biometric devices, including voice authentication and fingerprint–recognition systems, are now widely offered in notebooks, tablets, and smartphones (such as the Samsung Galaxy phones).

Make sure to use some (or all) of these methods to keep your activities from prying eyes and to restrict access to your digital information. ■

**FIGURE 9.20** Face recognition software is now available on laptops. You might forget your password, but you won't forget to bring your face! *(© Jochen Tack/Alamy).*

**Before moving on to Part 2:**

- **Watch Replay Video 9.1** .
- Then check your understanding of what you've learned so far.

## check your understanding//

For a quick review to see what you've learned so far, answer the following questions. Visit **pearsonhighered.com /techinaction** to check your answers.

### multiple choice

1. When a hacker steals personal information with the intent of impersonating another individual to commit fraud, it is known as
   a. impersonation theft.
   b. scareware theft.
   c. identity theft.
   d. malware theft.
2. Viruses that activate on certain dates or with the passage of time are known as
   a. boot-sector viruses.
   b. script viruses.
   c. time bombs.
   d. encryption viruses.
3. Firewalls work by closing __________ in your computer.
   a. logical ports
   b. software gaps
   c. logical doors
   d. backdoors
4. An attack that renders a computer unable to respond to legitimate users because it is being bombarded with data requests is known as a __________ attack.
   a. stealth
   b. backdoor
   c. scareware
   d. denial-of-service
5. A large group of software programs used to launch coordinated DoS attacks is known as a __________.
   a. rootkit
   b. botnet
   c. Trojan horse
   d. zombienet

### true–false

_____ **1.** Cybercrime is any crime that is carried out with the aid of a computer.

_____ **2.** Hackers that break into systems for nonmalicious reasons, such as to test security systems, are known as black-hat hackers.

### critical thinking

1. **Protecting Your Data from Viruses and Malware**

   Consider the following:

   a. What security software are you using on your personal computers? (Make sure to list all devices.) Is the security software up to date? If you don't have security software on a certain device (such as your phone), research available software to determine what might be appropriate to protect your device.

   b. Have you or a family member ever been the victim of a virus or malware attack? If so, how did you eradicate the problem? Were data or files lost because of the infection?

2. **Password Protection**

   You know from reading this chapter that secure passwords are essential to protecting your digital information. Consider the following:

   a. How many online accounts do you have that have passwords? List them. Are the passwords for these accounts secure, based on the suggestions proposed in this chapter? Do you change your passwords on a regular basis?

   b. How do you keep track of all of your passwords? Do you use password-management features in your browser? If so, which browser are you using? If you don't use password-management in your browser, what methodology do you use for remembering and tracking your passwords? Have you replaced your passwords with passphrases for added security?

**Continue**

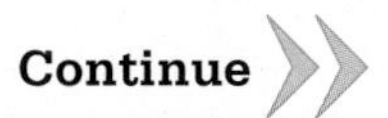

# TRY THIS 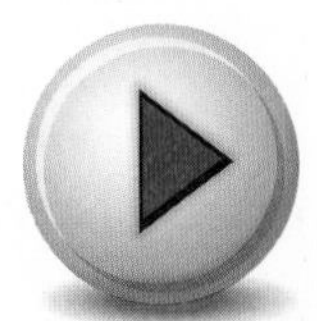 Testing Your Network Security

A properly installed firewall should keep you relatively safe from wily hackers. But how do you know if your computer system is safe? Many websites help test your security. In this exercise, we'll use tools provided by Gibson Research Corporation (**grc.com**) to test the strength of your protection.

**Step 1** Open a web browser and navigate to **grc.com**. From the pull-down Services menu at the top of the screen, select **ShieldsUP!** *(Courtesy of the Gibson Research Corporation)*

**Step 2** On the ShieldsUP! welcome screen, click the **Proceed** button. *(Courtesy of the Gibson Research Corporation)*

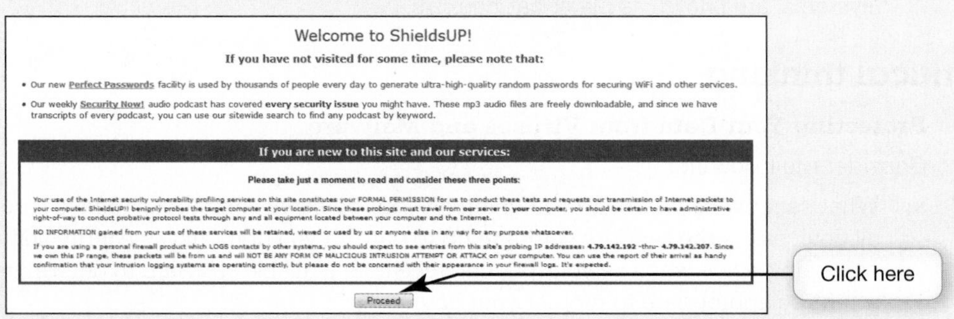


**Step 3** Click the **Common Ports** link to begin the security test. It will take a few moments for the results to appear, depending on the speed of your Internet connection. *(Courtesy of the Gibson Research Corporation)*

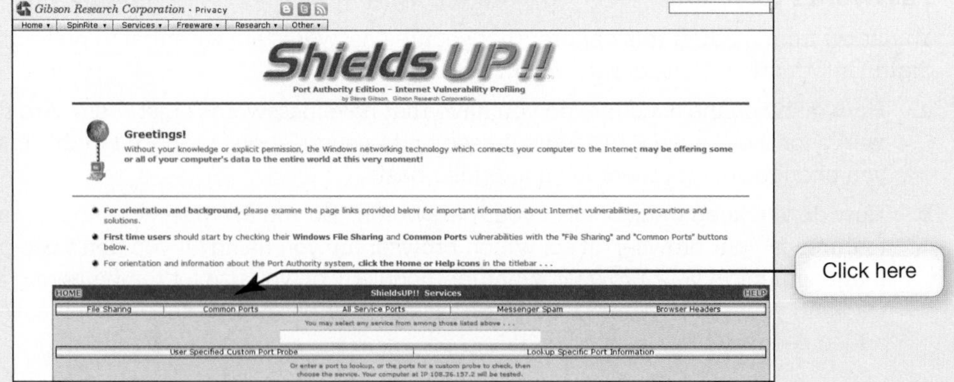

**Step 4** Hopefully, you'll see a report indicating that your computer has passed the TruStealth analysis test. This means that your computer is very safe from attack. However, don't panic if your results say **failed for true stealth analysis**. Consider these common issues:

- Ports that only report as being closed will result in a TruStealth analysis failure. As long as all common ports are reporting as stealth or closed, you are well protected. However, if any ports report as being open, this means your computer could be exposed to hackers. Consult your firewall documentation to resolve the problem.
- Another common failure on the TruStealth test is ping reply. This means GRC attempted to contact your computer using a method called ping and it replied to the GRC computer. This is not a serious problem. It just means it's a little easier for a hacker to tell your computer network is there, but that doesn't mean that a hacker can break in. Often your ISP has your home modem configured to reply to ping requests to facilitate remote diagnostics if there is ever a problem with your modem. As long as your ports are closed (or stealthed), your system should still be secure. *(Courtesy of the Gibson Research Corporation)*

**Port Authority Edition – Internet Vulnerability Profiling**
by Steve Gibson, Gibson Research Corporation.

**Checking the Most Common and Troublesome Internet Ports**

This Internet Common Ports Probe attempts to establish standard TCP Internet connections with a collection of standard, well-known, and often vulnerable or troublesome Internet ports on **YOUR** computer. Since this is being done from **our** server, successful connections demonstrate which of your ports are "open" or visible and soliciting connections from passing Internet port scanners.

**Your computer at IP:**

**108.36.157.2**

**Is being profiled. Please stand by. . .**

Total elapsed testing time: 4.995 seconds

**TruStealth Analysis**

Your system has achieved a **perfect** "TruStealth" rating. **Not a single packet** — solicited or otherwise — was received from your system as a result of our security probing tests. Your system ignored and refused to reply to repeated Pings (ICMP Echo Requests). From the standpoint of the passing probes of any hacker, this machine does not exist on the Internet. Some questionable personal security systems expose their users by attempting to "counter-probe the prober", thus revealing themselves. But your system wisely remained silent in every way. Very nice.

| Port | Service | Status | Security Implications |
|---|---|---|---|
| 0 | <nil> | Stealth | There is NO EVIDENCE WHATSOEVER that a port (or even any computer) exists at this IP address! |
| 21 | FTP | Stealth | There is NO EVIDENCE WHATSOEVER that a port (or even any computer) exists at this IP address! |
| 22 | SSH | Stealth | There is NO EVIDENCE WHATSOEVER that a port (or even any computer) exists at this IP address! |
| 23 | Telnet | Stealth | There is NO EVIDENCE WHATSOEVER that a port (or even any computer) exists at this IP address! |

# Protecting Your Digital Property from Yourself

Often, we can be our own worst enemies when using computing devices. If you're not careful, you might be taken in by thieves or scam artists who want to steal your digital and physical assets. Being aware of the tricks and traps that criminals use allows you to take steps to avoid being scammed.

## managing online ANNOYANCES

Surfing the web, using social networks, and sending and receiving e-mail have become common parts of most of our lives. Unfortunately, the web has become fertile ground for people who want to advertise their products, track our browsing behaviors, or even con people into revealing personal information. In this section, we'll look at ways in which you can manage, if not avoid, these and other online headaches.

### Malware: Adware and Spyware

**What is malware? Malware** is software that has a malicious intent (hence the prefix *mal*). There are three primary forms of malware: adware, spyware, and viruses. Adware and spyware are not physically destructive like viruses and worms, which can destroy data. Known collectively as *grayware*, most malware is intrusive, annoying, or objectionable online programs that are downloaded to your computer when you install or use other online content such as a free program, game, or utility.

**What is adware? Adware** is software that displays sponsored advertisements in a section of your browser window or as a pop-up box. It's considered a legitimate, though sometimes annoying, means of generating revenue for those developers who do not charge for their software or information. Fortunately, because web browsers such as Firefox, Safari, and Internet Explorer have built-in pop-up blockers, the occurrence of annoying pop-ups has been greatly reduced.

Some pop-ups, however, are legitimate and increase the functionality of the originating site. For example, your account balance may pop up on your bank's website. To control which sites to allow pop-ups on, you can access the pop-up blocker settings in your browser (see Figure 9.21) and add websites for which you allow pop-ups. Whenever a

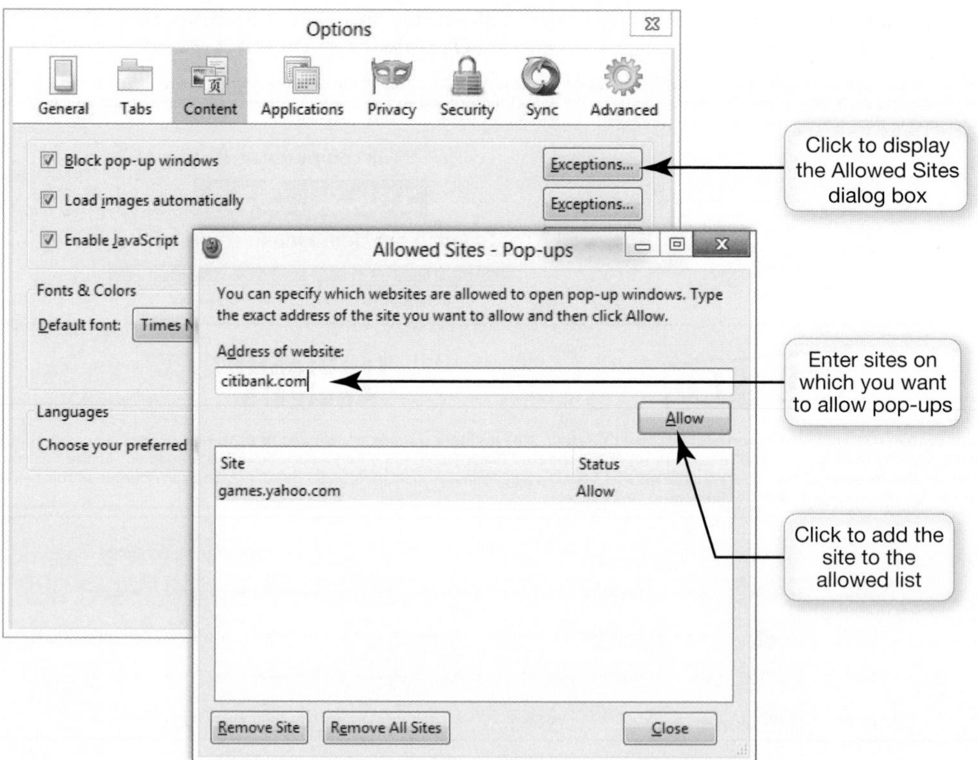


**FIGURE 9.21** Firefox's Allowed Sites - Pop-ups dialog box lets you control which sites you'll allow to display pop-ups. *(Courtesy of the Mozilla Foundation)*

*>To display the pop-up blocker in Firefox, from the Tools menu, select* **Options***, and then click the* **Content** *tab.*

pop-up is blocked, the browser displays an information bar or plays a sound to alert you. If you feel the pop-up is legitimate, you can choose to accept it.

**What is spyware? Spyware** is an unwanted piggyback program that usually downloads with other software you install from the Internet and that runs in the background of your system. Without your knowledge, spyware transmits information about you, such as your Internet-surfing habits, to the owner of the program so that the information can be used for marketing purposes. Many spyware programs use tracking cookies (small text files stored on your computer) to collect information. One type of spyware program known as a **keystroke logger (key logger)** monitors keystrokes with the intent of stealing passwords, login IDs, or credit card information.

**Can I prevent spyware from spying on me?** Anti-spyware software detects unwanted programs and allows you to delete the offending software easily. Most Internet security suites now include anti-spyware software. You can also obtain stand-alone anti-spyware software and run it on your computer to delete unwanted spyware. Because so many variants of spyware exist, your Internet security software may not detect all types that attempt to install themselves on your computer. Therefore, it's a good idea to install one or two additional stand-alone anti-spyware programs on your computer.

Because new spyware is created all the time, you should update and run your anti-spyware software regularly. Windows comes with a program called Windows Defender, which scans your system for spyware and other potentially unwanted software. Malwarebytes Anti-Malware, Ad-Aware, and Spybot–Search & Destroy (all available from **download.com**) are other anti-spyware programs that are easy to install and update. Figure 9.22 shows an example of Malwarebytes in action.

## Spam

**How can I best avoid spam?** Companies that send out **spam**—unwanted or junk e-mail—find your e-mail address either from a list they purchase or with software that looks for e-mail addresses on the Internet. Unsolicited instant messages are also a form of spam, called *spim*. If you've used your e-mail address to purchase anything online, open an online account, or participate in a social network such as Facebook, your e-mail address eventually will appear on one of the lists that spammers get.

One way to avoid spam in your primary account is to create a free e-mail address that you use only when you fill out forms or buy items on the web. For example, both Windows Mail and Yahoo! let you set up free e-mail accounts. If your free e-mail account is saturated with spam, you can abandon that account with little inconvenience. It's much less convenient to abandon your primary e-mail address.

Another way to avoid spam is to filter it. A **spam filter** is an option you can select in your e-mail account that places known or suspected spam messages into a special folder (called "Spam" or "Junk Mail"). Most web-based e-mail

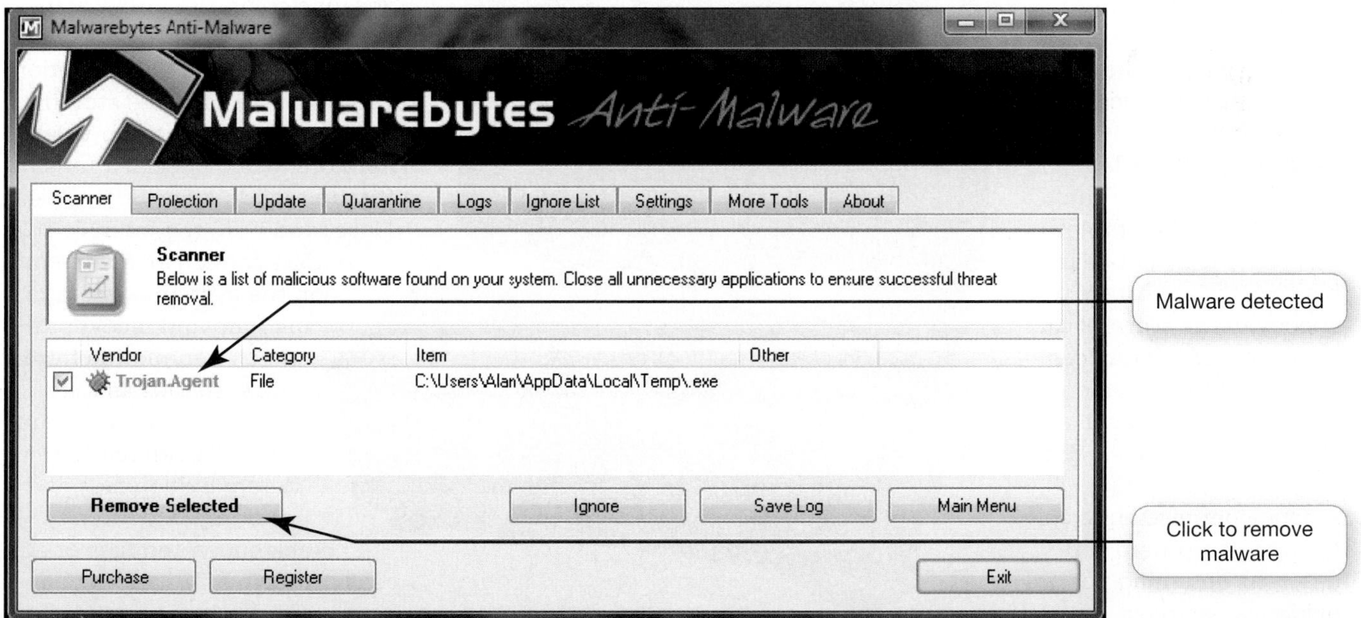


**FIGURE 9.22** After performing a routine scan of a computer, Malwarebytes returns a log of problems found on the system. *(Courtesy of Malwarebytes)*

# DIG DEEPER Computer Forensics: How It Works

On law enforcement TV shows, you often see computer technicians working on suspects' computers to assist detectives in solving crimes. It may look simple, but the science of computer forensics is a complex step-by-step process that ensures evidence is collected within the confines of the law.

*Forensic* means that something is suitable for use in a court of law. There are many branches of forensic science. For example, forensic pathologists provide evidence about the nature and manner of death in court cases involving deceased individuals. **Computer forensics** involves identifying, extracting, preserving, and documenting computer evidence. Computer forensics is performed by individuals known as *computer forensic scientists*, who rely primarily on specialized software to collect their evidence.

## Phase 1: Obtaining and Securing Computer Devices

The first step in a computer forensics investigation is to seize the computer equipment that law enforcement officials believe contains pertinent evidence. Police are required to obtain a warrant to search an individual's home or place of business. Warrants must be very specific by spelling out exactly where detectives can search for evidence and exactly what type of evidence they're seeking. If a warrant indicates that the police may search an individual's home for his laptop computer, they can't then confiscate a tablet computer they notice in his car. It is important to specify in the warrant all types of storage devices where potential evidence might be stored, such as external hard drives, flash drives, and servers.

Once permission to collect the computers and devices containing possible evidence has been obtained, law enforcement officials must exercise great care when collecting the equipment. They need to ensure that no unauthorized persons are able to access or alter the computers or storage devices. The police must make sure the data and equipment are safe; if the equipment is connected to the Internet, the connection must be severed without data loss or damage. It's also important for law enforcement officials to understand that they may not want to power off equipment because potential evidence contained in RAM may be lost. After the devices are collected and secured, the computer forensic scientists take over the next phase of the investigation.

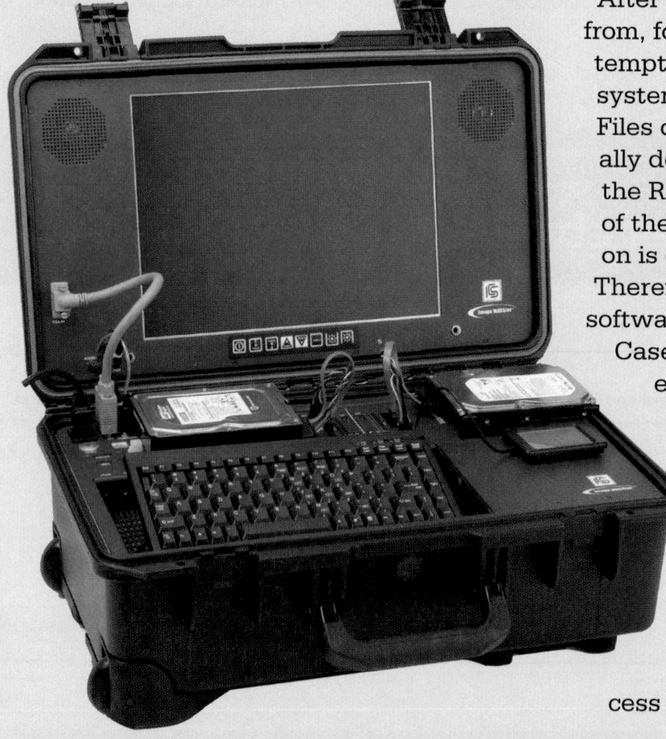

FIGURE 9.23 Portable devices like the RoadMASSter 3 Data Acquisition and Analysis tool make it easy to copy storage devices at crime scenes. *(Intelligent Computer Solutions)*

## Phase 2: Cataloging and Analyzing the Data

It's critical to preserve the data exactly as it was found, or attorneys may argue that the computer evidence was subject to tampering or altering. Because just opening a file can alter it, the first task is to make a copy of all computer systems and storage devices collected (see Figure 9.23). The investigators then work from the copies to ensure that the original data always remains preserved exactly as it was when it was collected.

After obtaining a copy to work from, forensics professionals attempt to find every file on the system, including deleted files. Files on a computer aren't actually deleted, even if you empty the Recycle Bin, until the section of the hard disk they're stored on is overwritten with new data. Therefore, using special forensic software tools such as SIFT, EnCase, and FTK, the forensic scientists catalog all files found on the system or storage medium and recover as much information from deleted files as they can. Forensic software like FTK can readily detect hidden files and perform procedures to crack encrypted files or access protected files and reveal their contents.

The most important part of the process is

documenting every step. Forensic scientists must clearly log every procedure performed because they may be required to provide proof in court that their investigations did not alter or damage information contained on the systems they examined. Detailed reports should list all files found, how the files were laid out on the system, which files were protected or encrypted, and the contents of each file. Finally, computer forensic professionals are often called on to present testimony in court during a trial.

Criminals are getting more sophisticated and are now employing anti-forensics techniques to foil computer forensic investigators. Although techniques for hiding or encrypting data are popular, the most insidious anti-forensics techniques are programs designed to erase data if unauthorized persons (i.e., not the criminal) access a computer system or if the system detects forensics software in use. When computer forensic investigators detect these countermeasures, they must often use creative methods and custom-designed software programs to retrieve and preserve the data.

Computer forensics is an invaluable tool to law enforcement in many criminal investigations, but only if the correct procedures are followed and the appropriate documentation is prepared.

services, such as Hotmail and Yahoo!, offer spam filters (see Figure 9.25). Microsoft Outlook also features a spam filter.

You can also buy third-party programs that provide some control over spam, including SPAMfighter, which you can download at **download.com**.

**How do spam filters work?** Spam filters and filtering software can catch as much as 95% of spam by checking incoming e-mail subject headers and senders' addresses against databases of known spam. Spam filters also check your e-mail for frequently used spam patterns and keywords, such as "for free" and "over 21." Spam filters aren't perfect, and you should check the spam folder before deleting its contents because legitimate e-mail might end up there by mistake. Most programs let you reclassify e-mails that have been misidentified as spam (see Figure 9.24).

**How else can I prevent spam?** Here are a few other ways you can prevent spam:

1. Before registering on a website, read its privacy policy to see how it uses your e-mail address. Don't give the site permission to pass on your e-mail address to third parties.
2. Don't reply to spam to remove yourself from the spam list. By replying, you're confirming that your e-mail address is active. Instead of stopping spam, you may receive more.
3. Subscribe to an e-mail forwarding service such as VersaForward (**versaforward.com**) or Sneakemail (**sneakemail.com**). These services screen your e-mail messages, forwarding only those messages you designate as being okay to accept.

## Cookies

**What are cookies? Cookies** are small text files that some websites automatically store on your hard drive when you visit them. When you log on to a website that uses cookies, a cookie file assigns an ID number to your computer. The unique ID is intended to make your return visit to a website more

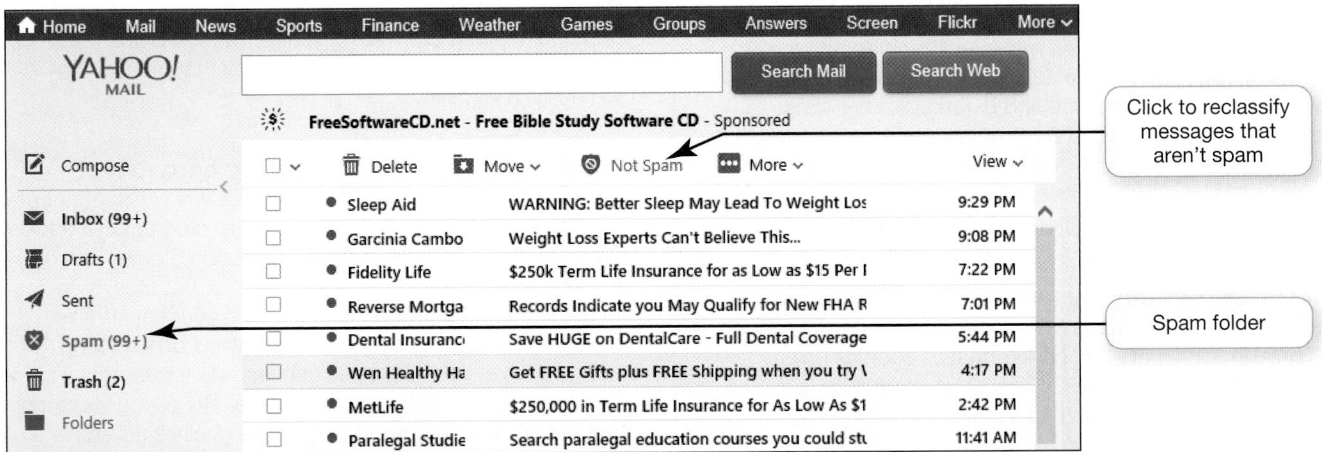


**FIGURE 9.24** In Yahoo! Mail, messages identified as spam are directed into a folder called "Spam" for review and deletion. *(Courtesy of Yahoo, Inc.)*

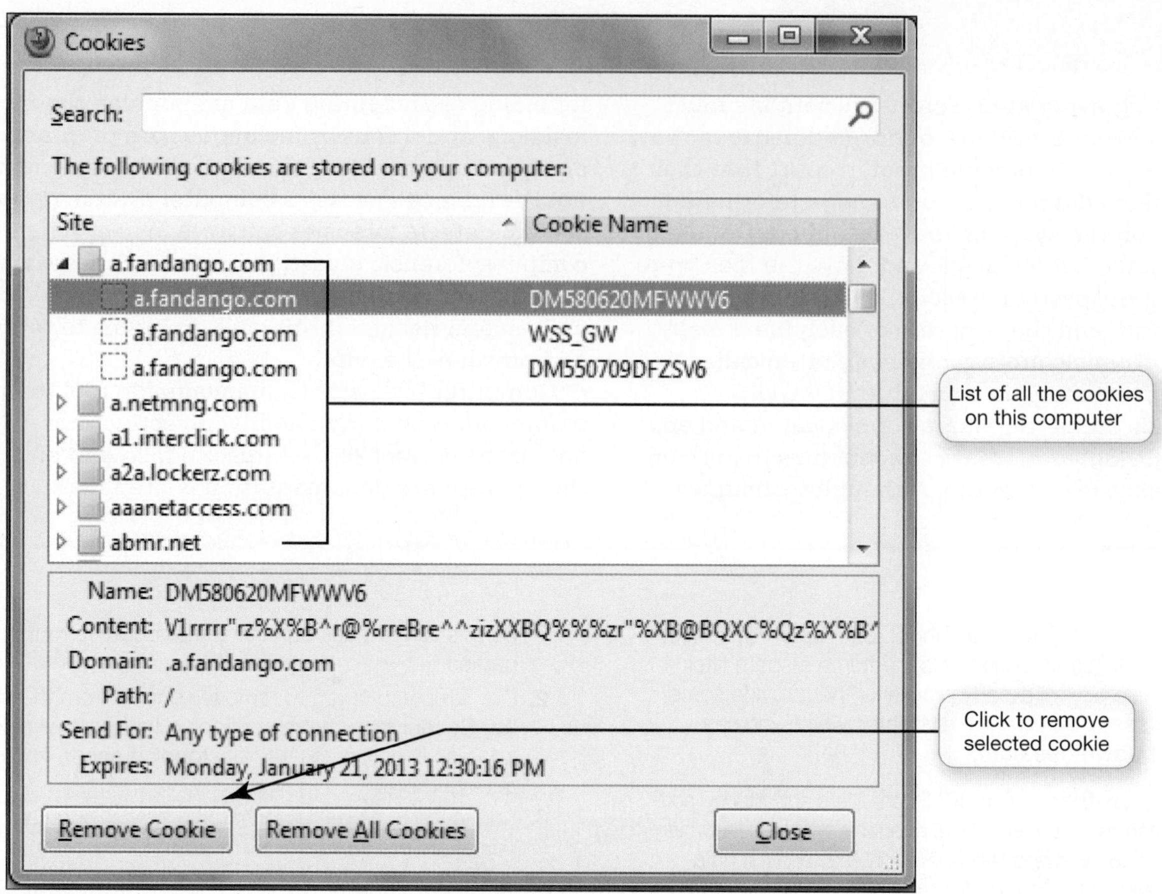


**FIGURE 9.25** Tools are available, either through your browser (Firefox is shown here) or as separate programs, to distinguish between cookies you want to keep and cookies you don't want on your system. *(Courtesy of the Mozilla Foundation)*

*>On the Firefox menu toolbar, click* **Tools**, *click Options, choose the* **Privacy tab**, *and then click the* **remove individual cookies** *link to display the Cookies dialog box.*

efficient and better geared to your interests. The next time you log on to that site, the site marks your visit and keeps track of it in its database.

**What do websites do with cookie information?** Cookies can provide websites with information about your browsing habits, such as the ads you've opened, the products you've looked at, and the time and duration of your visits. Companies use this information to determine the traffic flowing through their website and the effectiveness of their marketing strategy and placement on websites. By tracking such information, cookies enable companies to identify different users' preferences.

**Can companies get my personal information when I visit their sites?** Cookies do not go through your hard drive in search of personal information such as passwords or financial data. The only personal information a cookie obtains is the information you supply when you fill out forms online.

**Do privacy risks exist with cookies?** Some sites sell the personal information their cookies collect to web advertisers who are building huge databases of consumer preferences and habits, collecting personal and business information such as phone numbers, credit reports, and the like. The main concern is that advertisers will use this information indiscriminately, thus invading your privacy. And you may feel your privacy is being violated by cookies that monitor where you go on a website.

**Should I delete cookies from my hard drive?** Cookies pose no *security* threat because it is virtually impossible to hide a virus or malicious software program in a cookie. Because they take up little room on your hard drive, and offer you small conveniences on return visits to websites, there is no great reason to delete them. Deleting your cookie files could actually cause you the inconvenience of reentering data you have already entered into website forms. However, if you're uncomfortable with the accessibility of your personal information, you can periodically delete cookies (as shown in Figure 9.25) or configure your browser to block certain types of cookies. Software such as Cookie Pal (**kburra.com**) also can help you monitor cookies. ■

# ethics in IT You're Being Watched ... But Are You Aware You're Being Watched?

Think you aren't being closely watched by your employer? Think again! A recent survey of employers by the American Management Association and the ePolicy Institute revealed that, of the employers surveyed:

- 73% monitored e-mail messages
- 66% monitored web surfing
- 48% monitored activities using video surveillance
- 45% monitored keystrokes and keyboard time
- 43% monitored computer files in some other fashion

As you can see, there is a high probability that you're being monitored while you work and when you access the Internet via your employer's Internet connection.

The two most frequently cited reasons for employee monitoring are to prevent theft and to measure productivity. Monitoring for theft isn't new—monitoring cameras have been around for years, and productivity monitoring has been used for assembly line workers for decades. However, the Internet has led to a new type of productivity drain of concern to employers. **Cyberloafing**, or cyberslacking, means using your computer for nonwork activities while you're being paid to do your job. Examples of cyberloafing activities include playing games and using social networks. Some employees even do multiple nonwork tasks at the same time, which is known as *multishirking*.

**FIGURE 9.26** George Orwell was right—at least when you're at work! It's legal for employers to monitor your computer usage. *(SVLuma/Shutterstock)*

Estimates of business productivity losses due to cyberloafing top $50 billion annually.

Do you have a right to privacy in the workplace? Laws such as the 1986 Electronic Communications Privacy Act (ECPA), which prohibits unauthorized monitoring of electronic communications, have been interpreted by the courts in favor of employers. The bottom line is that employers who pay for equipment and software have the *legal* right to monitor their usage (see Figure 9.26).

So, is it *ethical* for employers to monitor their employees? Certainly, it seems fair that employers ensure they're not the victims of theft and that they're getting a fair day's work from their employees, just as employees have an obligation to provide a fair effort for a fair wage. The ethical issue is whether employees are adequately informed of monitoring policies. Employers have an ethical responsibility (and a legal one as well, depending on the jurisdiction) not to place monitoring devices in sensitive locations such as bathrooms and dressing areas. However, in many states, the employer does not legally need to inform employees in advance that they're being monitored. Conscientious employers include monitoring disclosures in published employee policies to avoid confusion and conflict.

The bottom line? Because employers may have a legal right to monitor you in the workplace, operate under the assumption that everything you do on your work computer is subject to scrutiny and behave accordingly. Do your online shopping at home!

# keeping your DATA SAFE

People are often too trusting or just plain careless when it comes to protecting private information about themselves or their digital data. In this section, we discuss ways to keep your data safe from damage, either accidental or intentional, and to keep unscrupulous individuals from tricking you into revealing sensitive information.

## Protecting Your Personal Information

If a complete stranger walked up to you on the street and asked you for your address and phone number, would you give it to him or her? Of course you wouldn't! But many people are much less careful when it comes to sharing sensitive information online. And often people inadvertently share information that they really only intended to share with their friends. With cybercrimes like identify theft rampant, you need to take steps to protect your personal information.

**What information should I never share on websites?** A good rule of thumb is to reveal as little information as possible, especially if the information would be available to everyone. Figure 9.27 gives you some good guidelines.

Your Social Security number, phone number, date of birth, and street address are four key pieces of information that identity thieves need to steal an identity. This information should never be shared in a public area on any website.

**How can I tell who can see my information on a social network?** Social networking sites like Facebook make privacy settings available in your profile settings. If you've never changed your default privacy settings in Facebook, you're probably sharing information more widely than you should.

**How can I protect my information on Facebook?** To begin, you need to change your privacy settings in your profile from some of the default options. In general, it's a bad idea to make personal information available to the public, although this is a default setting for some items in Facebook (see Figure 9.28). It's a good idea to set most of the options in your profile's Basic Information section to Friends or to Only Me because, presumably, these are personal details you should wish to share only with friends.

In the Contact Information section, restricting this information only to friends or to yourself is imperative. You don't want scammers contacting you via e-mail or snail mail and trying to trick you into revealing sensitive information.

## Backing Up Your Data

**How might I damage the data on my computer?** The data on your computer faces three major threats:

1. Unauthorized access
2. Tampering
3. Destruction

As noted earlier, a hacker can gain access to your computer and steal or alter your data. However, a more likely scenario is that you'll lose your data unintentionally. You may accidentally delete files. You may drop your laptop on the ground, causing the hard drive to break and resulting in complete data loss. A virus from an e-mail attachment you opened

FIGURE 9.27

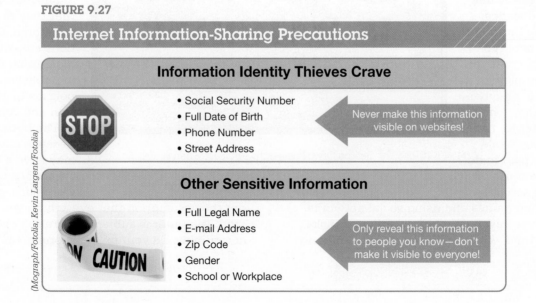

**Internet Information-Sharing Precautions**

**Information Identity Thieves Crave**

STOP

- Social Security Number
- Full Date of Birth
- Phone Number
- Street Address

Never make this information visible on websites!

**Other Sensitive Information**

CAUTION

- Full Legal Name
- E-mail Address
- Zip Code
- Gender
- School or Workplace

Only reveal this information to people you know—don't make it visible to everyone!

(Mograph/Fotolia; Kevin Largent/Fotolia)

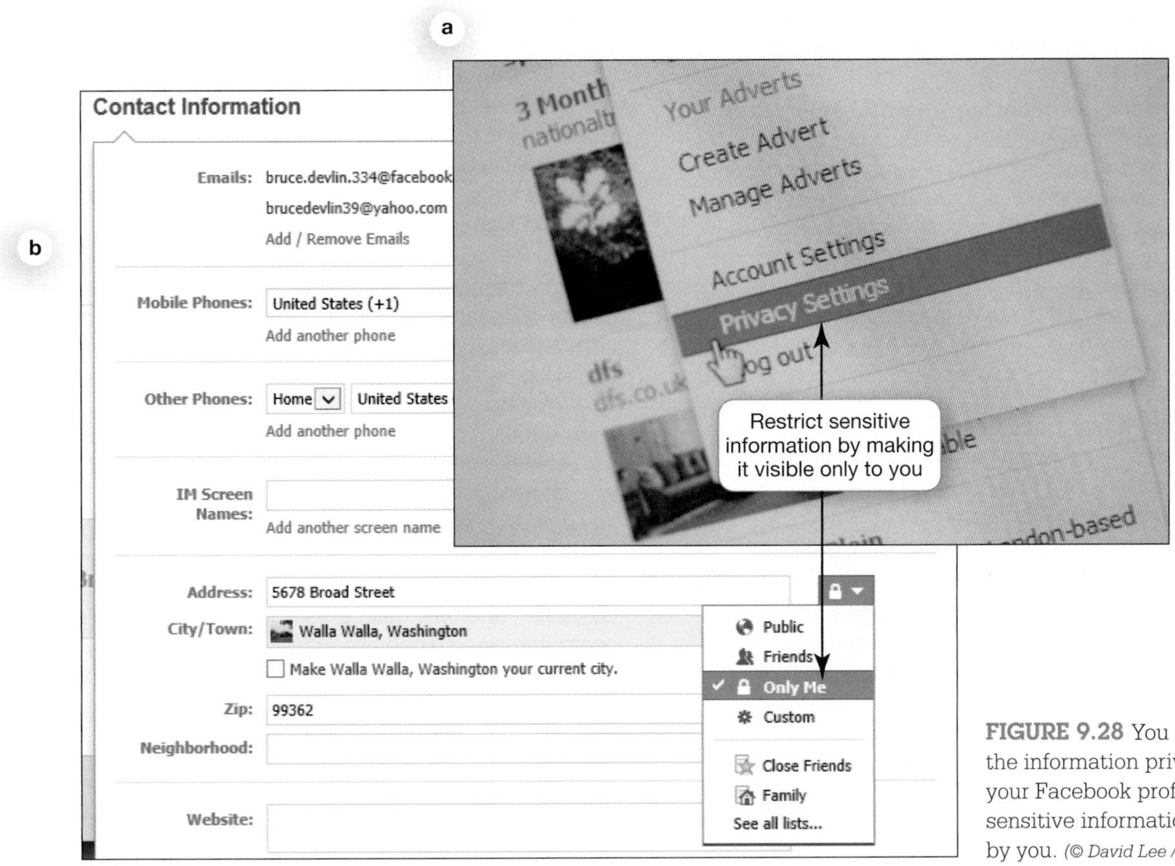

Restrict sensitive information by making it visible only to you

FIGURE 9.28 You should review the information privacy settings in your Facebook profile to ensure your sensitive information can only be seen by you. *(© David Lee / Alamy)*

may destroy your original file. Your house may catch fire and destroy your computer. Because many of these possibilities are beyond your control, you should have a strategy for backing up your files (see Figure 9.29). **Backups** are copies of files that you can use to replace the originals if they're lost or damaged.

**What types of files do I need to back up?** Two types of files need backups:

1. **Program files** include files used to install software, usually found on DVDs or downloaded from the Internet. As long as you have the DVDs in a safe place, you shouldn't need to back up these program files. If you've downloaded a program file from the Internet, however, you should make a copy of the program installation files on a removable storage device as a backup.
2. **Data files** include files you've created or purchased, such as research papers, spreadsheets, music and photo files, contact lists, address books, e-mail archives, and your Favorites list from your browser.

**What types of backups can I perform?** There are two main options for backing up files:

1. An **incremental backup** (or **partial backup**) involves backing up only files that have changed or have been created since the last backup was performed. Using backup

FIGURE 9.29

## An Effective Backup Strategy

### Files to Back Up

- **Program files:** Installation files for productivity software (i.e., Microsoft Office)
- **Data files:** Files you create (term papers, spreadsheets, etc.)

### Types of Backups

- **Incremental (partial):** Only backs up files that have changed
- **Image (system):** Snapshot of your entire computer, including system software

### Where to Store Backup Files

- Online (in the cloud)
- External hard drives
- Network-attached storage devices or home servers

software that has an option for incremental backups will save time because backing up files that haven't changed is redundant.

2. An **image backup** (or **system backup**) means that all system, application, and data files are backed up, not just the files that changed. Although incremental backups are more efficient, an image backup ensures you capture changes to application files, such as automatic software updates, that an incremental backup might not capture. The idea of imaging is to make an exact copy of the setup of your computer so that in the event of a total hard drive failure you could copy the image to a new hard drive and have your computer configured exactly the way it was before the crash.

**Where should I store my backups?** To be truly secure, backups must be stored away from where your computer is located and should be stored in at least two different places. You wouldn't want a fire or a flood destroying the backups along with the original data. You have three main choices for where to back up your files (see Figure 9.30):

1. *Online (in the cloud):* The beauty of online storage is that you don't need to be at your home computer or lug around your external hard drive to access your data. More important, because the information is stored online, it's in a secure, remote location, so data is much less vulnerable to the disasters that could harm data stored in your computer or external hard drive. Free storage options include Microsoft OneDrive (**onedrive.com**) and ADrive (**adrive.com**). However, image backups probably won't fit within the storage limits offered by free providers. For a fee, companies such as Carbonite (**carbonite.com**) and IBackup (**ibackup.com**) provide larger storage capacity.
2. *External hard drives:* External hard drives, or even large-capacity flash drives, are popular backup options that are usually connected to a single computer. Although convenient and inexpensive, using external hard drives for backups still presents the dilemma of keeping the hard drive in a safe location. Also, external hard drives can fail, possibly leading to loss of your backed-up data. Therefore, using an external hard drive for backups is best done in conjunction with an online backup strategy for added safety.
3. *Network-attached storage (NAS) devices and home servers:* NAS devices are essentially large hard drives connected to a network of computers instead of one computer, and they can be used to back up multiple computers simultaneously. Home servers also act as high-capacity NAS devices for automatically backing up data and sharing files.

FIGURE 9.30

## A Comparison of Typical Data Backup Locations

| BACKUP LOCATION | PROS | CONS |
|---|---|---|
| Online (in the Cloud) | • Files stored at a secure, remote location<br>• Files/backups accessible anywhere through a browser | • Most free storage sites don't provide enough space for image backups |
| External Hard Drive | • Inexpensive, one-time cost<br>• Fast backups with USB 3.0 devices connected directly to your computer | • Could be destroyed in one event (fire/flood) with your computer<br>• Can be stolen<br>• Slightly more difficult to back up multiple computers with one device |
| Network-Attached Storage (NAS) Device and Home Server | • Makes backups much easier for multiple computing devices | • More expensive than a stand-alone external hard drive<br>• Could be destroyed in one event (fire/flood) with your computer<br>• Can be stolen |

(mipan/Fotolia; © Prapass Wannapinij/Fotolia; © darkdesigns/Fotolia)

**How often should I back up my data files?** You should back up your data files every time you make changes to them, which can be difficult to remember to do. Fortunately, most backup software can be configured to do backups automatically so you don't forget to perform them. For example, with the Windows 8 File History utility, you can have Windows automatically save your data files from your libraries, desktop, contacts, and favorites to an external hard drive or NAS device. The default setting for File History saves files you changed every hour to the backup location you specify. File History even keeps previous versions of the file on the backup drive so you can revert to a previous version of the file if you need to do so.

To set up File History, you first need to connect an external hard drive to your computer or a NAS device to your network. You can then access File History through the Control Panel (in the System and Security group) and set it up (see Figure 9.31). Once configured, your data files will be backed up as often as you indicate. You can also restore files that you've backed up from the File History utility.

**How often should I create an image backup?** Because your program and OS files don't change as often as your data files, you can perform image backups on a less frequent basis. You might consider scheduling an image backup of your entire system on a weekly basis, but you should definitely perform one after installing new software.

**How do I perform an image backup?** Windows 8 includes the System Image Backup utility, which provides a quick and easy way to perform image backups. You can access this utility from the System Image Backup link on the File History screen (see Figure 9.31). Before starting this utility, make sure your external hard drive or NAS device is connected to your computer or network and is powered on. To set it up, follow these steps:

1. The first screen displayed (see Figure 9.32a) shows a list of available backup devices. Select a device (usually an external hard drive), and click Next to proceed.

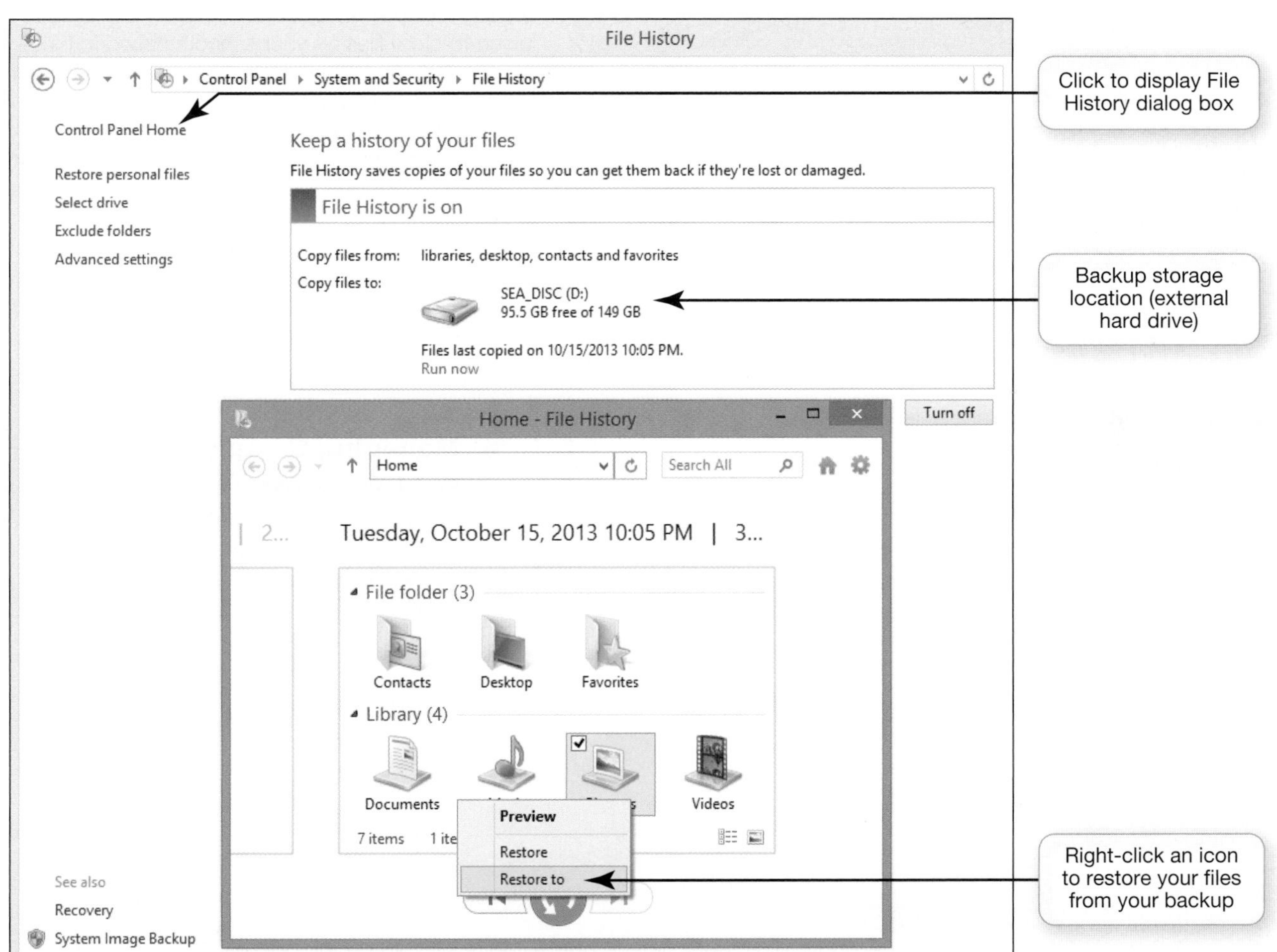


**FIGURE 9.31** You can use the Windows 8 File History utility to back up files and restore files from a previous backup.
>*Access the Control Panel, select the* **System and Security** *group, and then click the* **File History** *link.*

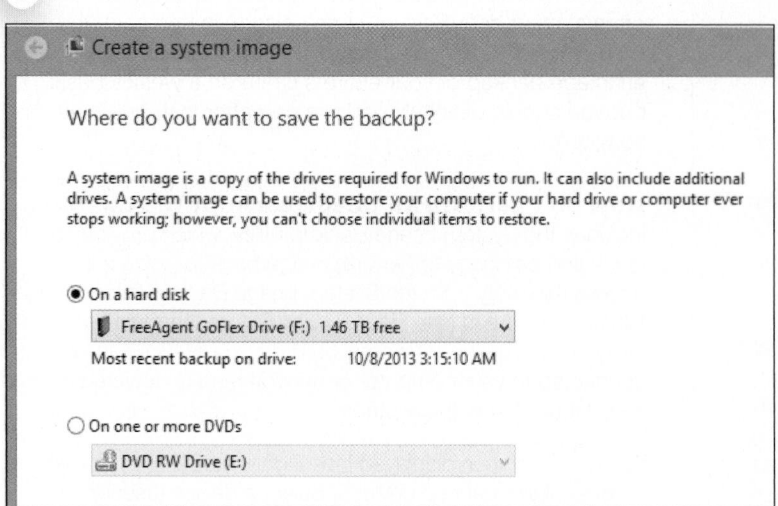
a
Create a system image
Where do you want to save the backup?
A system image is a copy of the drives required for Windows to run. It can also include additional drives. A system image can be used to restore your computer if your hard drive or computer ever stops working; however, you can't choose individual items to restore.
On a hard disk
FreeAgent GoFlex Drive (F:) 1.46 TB free
Most recent backup on drive: 10/8/2013 3:15:10 AM
On one or more DVDs
DVD RW Drive (E:)

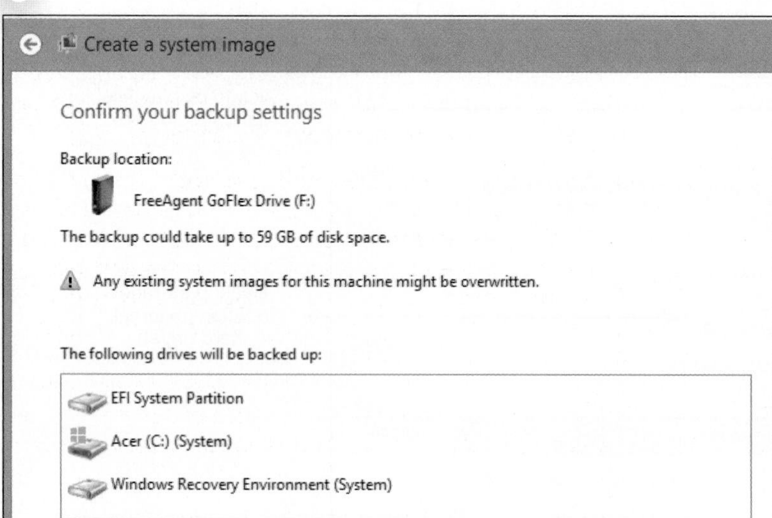
b
Create a system image
Confirm your backup settings
Backup location:
FreeAgent GoFlex Drive (F:)
The backup could take up to 59 GB of disk space.
Any existing system images for this machine might be overwritten.
The following drives will be backed up:
EFI System Partition
Acer (C:) (System)
Windows Recovery Environment (System)

**FIGURE 9.32** The System Image Backup utility allows you to perform an image backup. (a) Select your backup destination. (b) Review options and start the backup.

2. On the following screen (see Figure 9.32b), you can review your settings Windows decides what to include in your system image backup: all data files and system files on all partitions on your hard drive. When you click the Start Backup button, your system image backup is created on the drive you selected.

From the File History screen, you can access advanced recovery tools (such as creating a system repair backup and System Restore) by clicking the Recovery link. A system repair backup is a copy of files that you can use to boot your computer in case of a serious Windows error.

**What about backing up Apple computers?** For OS X users, backups are very easy to configure. The Time Machine feature in OS X detects when an external hard drive is connected to the computer or a NAS device is connected to your network. You're then asked if you want this to be your backup drive. If you answer yes, all of your files (including OS files) are automatically backed up to the external drive or NAS device.

**Should I back up my files that are stored on my school's network?** Most likely, if you're allowed to store files on your school's network, these files are backed up regularly. You should check with your school's network administrators to determine how often they're backed up and how you would request that files be restored from the backup if they're damaged or deleted. But don't rely on these network backups to bail you out if your data files are lost or damaged. It may take days for the network administrators to restore your files. It's better to keep backups of your data files yourself, especially homework and project files, so that you can immediately restore them. ■

SOUND BYTE

**Managing Computer Security with Windows Tools**

In this Sound Byte, you'll learn how to monitor and control your computer security using features built into the Windows OS.

# social ENGINEERING

**Social engineering** is any technique that uses social skills to generate human interaction that entices individuals to reveal sensitive information. Social engineering often doesn't involve the use of a computer or face-to-face interaction. For example, telephone scams are a common form of social engineering because it is often easier to manipulate someone when you don't have to look at them.

**How does social engineering work?** Most social engineering schemes use a pretext to lure their victims. **Pretexting** involves creating a scenario that sounds legitimate enough that someone will trust you. For example, you might receive a phone call during which the caller says he is from your bank and that someone tried to use your account without authorization. The caller then tells you he needs to confirm a few personal details such as your birth date, Social Security number, bank account number, and whatever other information he can get out of you. The information he obtains can then be used to empty your bank account or commit some other form of fraud. The most common form of pretexting in cyberspace is *phishing*.

## BITS&BYTES

### I Received a Data Breach Letter ... Now What?

Data breaches are becoming more common, and companies that are the subject of data breaches now routinely notify customers of data breaches...usually by physical letter, but sometimes via e-mail. Here's what you should do if you receive such a letter:

1. Take it seriously. 22.5% of recipients of these letters become the victim of identity theft per a study by Javelin Strategy and Research.
2. Contact one of the three big credit bureaus (Equifax, Experian, and TransUnion) and have a fraud alert put on your credit report. This alerts people accessing your credit report that your identity information has been stolen and that the person who is applying for credit in your name might be an imposter.
3. For even better security, contact all three credit bureaus and have a credit freeze put on your credit reports. This prevents anyone (even you) from getting credit in your name. You can always unfreeze your accounts later if you need to apply for credit yourself.
4. Review your credit reports regularly. You are entitled to one free credit report per year from each of the three big agencies. Go to **annualcreditreport.com** and request a report from one of the agencies. Repeat the process every 4 months from a different agency. Review the reports for any suspicious activity.

## Phishing and Pharming

**How are phishing schemes conducted? Phishing** (pronounced "fishing") lures Internet users to reveal personal information such as credit card numbers, Social Security numbers, or other sensitive information that could lead to identity theft. The scammers send e-mail messages that look like they're from a legitimate business such as an online bank. The e-mail usually states that the recipient needs to update or confirm his or her account information. When the recipient clicks on the provided link, he or she goes to a website. The site looks like a legitimate site but is really a fraudulent copy that the scammer has created. Once the e-mail recipient enters his or her personal information, the scammers capture it and can begin using it.

**Is pharming a type of phishing scam?** Pharming is much more insidious than phishing. Phishing requires a positive action by the person being scammed, such as going to a website mentioned in an e-mail and typing in personal information. **Pharming** occurs when malicious code is planted on your computer, either by viruses or by your visiting malicious websites, which then alters your browser's ability to find web addresses. Users are directed to bogus websites even when they enter the correct address of the real website. You end up at a fake website that looks legitimate but is expressly set up for the purpose of gathering information.

**How can I avoid being caught by phishing and pharming scams?** Follow these guidelines to avoid falling prey to such schemes:

- Never reply directly to any e-mail asking you for personal information.
- Don't click on a link in an e-mail to go to a website. Instead, type the website address in the browser.
- Check with the company asking for the information and only give the information if you're certain it's needed.
- Never give personal information over the Internet unless you know the site is secure. Look for the closed padlock, *https*, or a certification seal such as Norton Secured to help reassure you that the site is secure.
- Use phishing filters. The latest versions of Firefox, Chrome, and Internet Explorer have phishing filters built in, so each time you access a website, the phishing filter checks for the site's legitimacy and warns you of possible web forgeries.
- Use Internet security software on your computer that's constantly being updated.

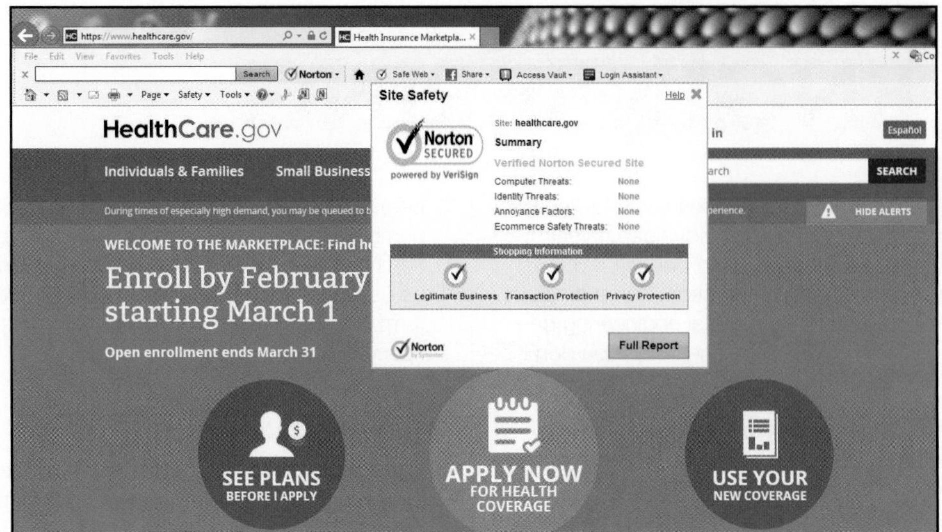


FIGURE 9.33 Not sure whether you're on the Healthcare.gov website or a cleverly disguised phishing site? Norton Site Safety reassures you that all is well. *(Courtesy of HealthCare.gov; Courtesy of the Symantec Corporation)*

Most Internet security packages can detect and prevent pharming attacks. The major Internet security packages—for example, McAfee and Norton (see Figure 9.33)—also offer phishing-protection tools. When you have the Norton Toolbar displayed in your browser, you're constantly informed about the legitimacy of the site you are visiting.

## Scareware

**What is scareware? Scareware** is a type of malware that downloads onto your computer and tries to convince you that your computer is infected with a virus (see Figure 9.34) or other type of malware. Pop-ups, banners, or other annoying types of messages will flash on your screen saying frightening things like, "Your computer is infected with a virus . . . immediate removal is required." You're then directed to a website where you can buy fake removal or antivirus tools that provide little or no value. Panda Security estimates that scareware scams generate in excess of $34 million a month for cybercriminals. Some scareware even goes so far as to encrypt your files and then demand that you pay to have them unencrypted, which is essentially extortion.

Scareware is a social engineering technique because it uses people's fear of computer viruses to convince them to part with their money. Scareware is often designed to be extremely difficult to remove from your computer and to interfere with the operation of legitimate security software. Scareware is usually downloaded onto your computer from infected websites or Trojan horse files.

**How do I protect myself against scareware?** Most Internet security suites, antivirus, and anti-malware software packages now detect and prevent the installation of scareware. But make sure you never click on website banners or pop-up boxes that say "Your computer might be infected, click here to scan your files" because these are often the starting points for installing malicious scareware files on your computer. ■

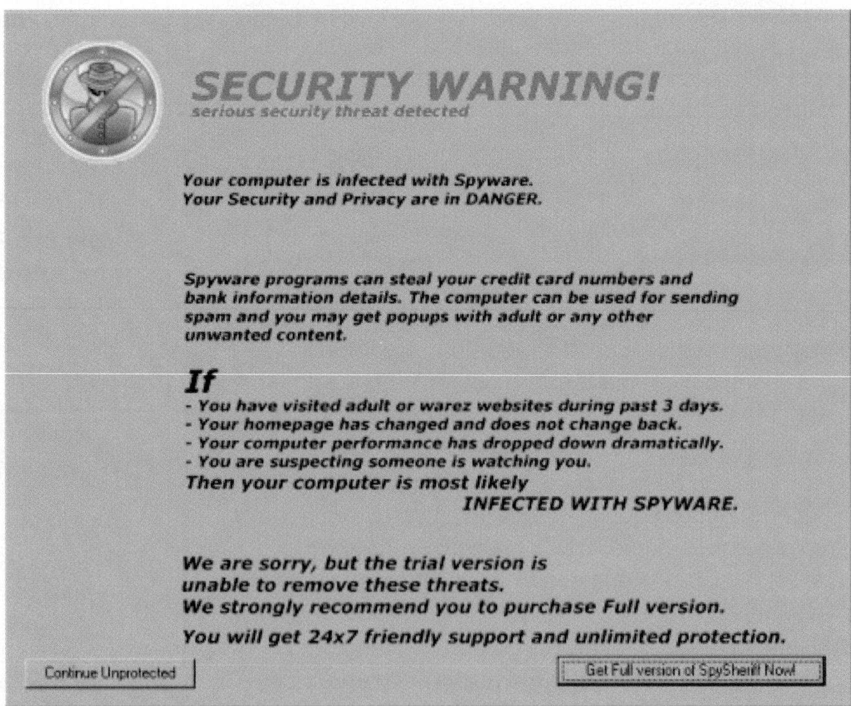


FIGURE 9.34 Preying on people's fears, scareware attempts to convince you that your computer is infected with a virus and you need to purchase a "solution." *(Courtesy of McAfee, Inc.)*

# trends in IT

## Computers in Society: Spear Phishing: The Bane of Data Breaches

Most people have vast amounts of personal data residing in the databases of the various companies with which they conduct business. Amazon.com has your credit card and address information. Your bank has your Social Security number, birth date, and financial records. Your local supermarket probably has your e-mail address from when you joined its loyalty club to receive grocery discounts. All this data in various places puts you at risk when companies responsible for keeping your data confidential suffer a data breach.

A **data breach** occurs when sensitive or confidential information is copied, transmitted, or viewed by an individual who isn't authorized to handle the data. Data breaches can be intentional or unintentional. Intentional data breaches occur when hackers break into digital systems to steal sensitive data. Unintentional data breaches occur when companies controlling data inadvertently allow it to be seen by unauthorized parties, usually due to some breakdown in security procedures or precautions.

Unfortunately, data breaches appear to be quite common, as there always seems to be another one in the news. In April 2013, Living Social, a daily deal website, notified 50 million customers that its systems had been breached and that names, e-mail addresses, and dates of birth had been exposed. Fortunately, the system that held customer credit card information had not been hacked. Data breaches such as this one pose serious risks to the individuals whose data has been compromised, even if financial data is not involved. The data thieves now have the basis with which to launch targeted social engineering attacks even if they just have contact information, such as e-mail addresses.

With regular phishing techniques, cybercriminals just send out e-mails to a wide list of e-mail addresses, whether they have a relationship with the company or not. For example, a criminal might send out a general phishing e-mail claiming that a person's Citibank checking account had been breached. People who receive this e-mail that don't have any accounts at Citibank should immediately realize this is a phishing attack and ignore the instructions to divulge sensitive data.

But when cybercriminals obtain data on individuals that includes information about which companies those individuals have a relationship with, they can engage in much more targeted attacks known as **spear phishing**. Spear phishing e-mails are sent to people known to be customers of a company and have a much greater chance of successfully getting individuals to reveal sensitive data. If cybercriminals obtain a list of e-mail addresses of customers from Barclays Bank, for example, they can ensure that the spear phishing e-mails purport to come from Barclays and will include the customer's full name. This type of attack is much more likely to succeed in fooling people than just random e-mails sent out to thousands of people who might not have a relationship with the company mentioned in the phishing letter.

So how can you protect yourself after a data breach? You need to be extra suspicious of any e-mail correspondence from companies involved in the data breach. Companies usually never contact you by e-mail or phone asking you to reveal sensitive information or reactivate your online account by entering confidential information. Usually, these requests come via regular snail mail.

So, if you receive any e-mails or phone calls from companies you deal with purporting to have problems with your accounts, your best course of action is to delete the e-mail or hang up the phone. Then contact the company that supposedly has the problem by a phone number that you look up yourself either in legitimate correspondence from the company (say, the toll-free number on your credit card statement) or in the phone book. The representatives from your company can quickly tell if a real problem exists or if you were about to be the victim of a scam.

# protecting your physical COMPUTING ASSETS

Your computer, tablet, and phone aren't useful to you if they're damaged. Therefore, it's essential to select and ensure a safe environment for these devices. This includes protecting them from environmental factors, power surges, power outages, and theft.

## Environmental Factors

**Why is the environment critical to the operation of my computer equipment?** Computers are delicate devices and can be damaged by the adverse effects of abuse or a poor environment. Sudden movements, such as a fall, can damage your computing device's internal components. You should make sure that your computer sits on a flat, level surface, and if it's a laptop or a tablet, you should carry it in a protective case.

Electronic components don't like excessive heat or excessive cold. Don't leave computing devices and phones in a car during especially hot or cold weather because components can be damaged by extreme temperatures. Unfortunately, computers generate a lot of heat, which is why they have fans to cool their internal components. Chill mats that contain cooling fans and sit underneath laptop computers are useful accessories for dissipating heat. Make sure that you place your desktop computer where the fan's intake vents, usually found on the rear of the system unit, are unblocked so air can flow inside.

Naturally, a fan drawing air into a computer also draws in dust and other particles, which can wreak havoc on your system. Therefore, keep the room in which your computer is located as clean as possible. Finally, because food crumbs and liquid can damage keyboards and other computer components, consume food and beverages away from your computer.

**FIGURE 9.35** Surge protectors such as this one are critical for protecting your electronic devices. *(aberenyi/Fotolia)*

## Power Surges

**What is a power surge?** Power surges occur when electrical current is supplied in excess of normal voltage. Old or faulty wiring, downed power lines, malfunctions at electric company substations, and lightning strikes can all cause power surges. A **surge protector** is a device that protects your computer against power surges (see Figure 9.35).

Note that you should replace your surge protectors every two to three years. Also, after a major surge, the surge protector will no longer function and must be replaced. And it's wise to buy a surge protector that includes indicator lights, which illuminate when the surge protector is no longer functioning properly. Don't be fooled by old surge protectors—although they can still function as multiple-outlet power strips, they deliver power to your equipment without protecting it.

**Besides my computer, what other devices need to be connected to a surge protector?** All electronic devices in the home that have solid-state components, such as TVs, stereos, printers, and smartphones (when charging), should be connected to a surge protector. However, it can be inconvenient to use individual surge protectors on everything. A more practical method is to install a **whole-house surge protector** (see Figure 9.36). Whole-house surge protectors function like other surge protectors, but they protect *all* electrical devices in the house. Typically, you'll need an electrician to install a whole-house surge protector, which will cost $300 to $400 (installed).

**Is my equipment 100% safe when plugged into a surge protector?** Lightning strikes can generate such high voltages that they can overwhelm a surge

SOUND BYTE

**Surge Protectors**

In this Sound Byte, you'll learn about the major features of surge protectors and how they work. You'll also learn about the key factors you need to consider before buying a surge protector, and you'll see how easy it is to install one.

FIGURE 9.36 A whole-house surge protector is usually installed at the breaker panel or near the electric meter.

protector. As tedious as it sounds, unplugging electronic devices during an electrical storm is the only way to achieve absolute protection.

## Deterring Theft

**What do I need to worry about if my computing device is stolen?** Because they're portable, laptops, tablets, and phones are easy targets for thieves. You have four main security concerns with mobile devices:

1. Keeping them from being stolen
2. Keeping data secure in case they are stolen
3. Finding a device if it is stolen
4. Remotely recovering and wiping data off a stolen device

## Keep Them Safe: Alarms

**What type of alarm can I install on my mobile device?** Motion alarm software is a good, inexpensive theft deterrent. Free software such as LAlarm (**lalarm.com**) is effective for laptops. Apps such as Motion Alarm and Alarmomatic help secure your iPad or iPhone. Alarm software either detects motion, like your device being picked up, or sounds near your device and then sets off an ear-piercing alarm until you enter the disable code. Thieves normally don't like it when attention is drawn to their activities, so alarms can be a very effective theft deterrent.

## Keeping Mobile Device Data Secure

**How can I secure the data on my mobile devices?** Encrypting the data on your mobile device can make it extremely difficult, if not impossible, for thieves to obtain sensitive data from your stolen equipment. *Encryption* involves transforming your data using an algorithm that can only be unlocked by a secure code (or key). Encrypted data is impossible to read unless it's decrypted, which requires a secure password, hopefully known only to you.

Safe is an app that provides 256-bit encryption, which is very hard to crack, for data and images on your iPhone and iPad. If your password is not entered, no one can access the data and images on your iPhone or iPad. Mobile StrongBox is a similar app for Android devices. SensiGuard and SafeHouse are available for laptop computers to provide encryption for files or even entire hard drives.

## Software Alerts and Data Wipes

**How can my computer help me recover it when it is stolen?** You've probably heard of LoJack, the theft-tracking device used in cars. Similar systems now exist for computers. Tracking software such as LoJack for Laptops (**absolute.com**), PC PhoneHome, and Mac PhoneHome (**brigadoonsoftware.com**) enables your computer to alert authorities to the computer's location if it is stolen. A similar tracking app for Android and iOS devices is iHound.

To enable your mobile device to help with its own recovery, you install the tracking software on your device. The software contacts a server at the software manufacturer's website each time the device connects to the Internet. If your device is stolen, you notify the software manufacturer. The software manufacturer instructs your device to transmit tracking information, such as an IP address, WiFi hotspot, or cell tower location, that will assist authorities in locating and retrieving the mobile device.

**What if the thieves find the tracking software and delete it?** The files and directories holding the software aren't visible to thieves looking for such software, so they probably won't know the software is there. Furthermore, the tracking software is written in such a way that even if the thieves tried to reformat the hard drive, it would detect the reformat and hide the software code in a safe place in memory or on the hard drive. This works because some sectors of a hard drive are not rewritten during most reformatting. That way, the tracking software can reinstall itself after the reformatting is complete.

**What if my device can't be recovered by the authorities?** In the event that your laptop can't be recovered, software packages are available that provide for remote recovery and deletion of files. LoJack for Laptops has these features and allows you to lock your device to keep the thieves from accessing it or to remotely wipe its contents by deleting all your data from your laptop.

**FIGURE 9.37** The Find My iPhone app can really help if your iOS device goes astray. You can play a sound to help you find it (if it's misplaced where you are), display a message on the device (Lost Mode), or erase all data on the device. *(Courtesy of Apple, Inc.)*

**FIGURE 9.38**

## Computer Security Checklist

### Virus and Spyware Protection

- Is antivirus and anti-spyware software installed on all your devices?
- Is the antivirus and anti-spyware software configured to update itself automatically and regularly?
- Is the software set to scan your device on a regular basis (at least weekly) for viruses and spyware?

### Firewall

- Do all your computers and tablets have firewall software installed and activated before connecting to the Internet?
- Is your router also able to function as a hardware firewall?
- Have you tested your firewall security by using the free software available at grc.com?

### Software Updates

- Have you configured your operating systems (Windows, OS X, iOS) to install new software patches and updates automatically?
- Is other software installed on your device, such as Microsoft Office or productivity apps, configured for automatic updates?
- Is the web browser you're using the latest version?

### Protecting Your Devices

- Are all computing devices protected from electrical surges?
- Do your mobile devices have alarms or tracking software installed on them?

For all iOS devices, Apple offers the Find My iPhone service, which is now part of iCloud. Enabling this service on your device provides you with numerous tools that can assist you in recovering and protecting your mobile devices. Did you forget where you left your iPad? Just sign in with your Apple ID at the iCloud website to see a map showing the location of your iPad (see Figure 9.37). You can also remotely send a message to be displayed on your lost device, such as your phone number and a reward offer, so that someone who finds it will know what to do. If you can't recover the device, you can remotely password lock it so no one can use it or, if necessary, wipe all the data off the device to completely protect your privacy. With iOS 7, additional security is in place to keep thieves from using your phone. Your Apple ID and password are required to turn off Find My iPhone or to use the phone again after it has been erased.

**How can I ensure that I've covered all aspects of protecting my digital devices?** Figure 9.38 provides a guide to ensure you haven't missed critical aspects of security. If you've addressed all of these issues, you can feel reasonably confident that your data and devices are secure. ■

**Before moving on to the Chapter Review:**
- **Watch Replay Video 9.2.**
- Then check your understanding of what you've learned so far.

# check your understanding//

For a quick review to see what you've learned so far, answer the following questions. Visit **pearsonhighered.com /techinaction** to check your answers.

## multiple choice

1. A technique that uses illegally obtained information about individuals to perform targeted attacks in the hopes of getting them to reveal sensitive information is known as
   **a.** spear phishing.
   **b.** pretexting.
   **c.** keystroke logging.
   **d.** logic bombing.

2. A backup of all files on your computer, which is essentially a snapshot of exactly how your computer looks at a particular point in time, is known as a(n)
   **a.** total backup.
   **b.** incremental backup.
   **c.** image backup.
   **d.** global backup.

3. Software that transmits information about you, such as your Internet surfing habits, back to a third party is known as
   **a.** scareware.
   **b.** spyware.
   **c.** adware.
   **d.** trackingware.

4. Small text files that some websites automatically store on your computer's hard drive are known as
   **a.** greyware.
   **b.** spam.
   **c.** adware.
   **d.** cookies.

5. A social engineering technique in which you send people an e-mail for the purpose of inducing them into revealing sensitive information is known as
   **a.** pretexting.
   **b.** phishing.
   **c.** pharming.
   **d.** key logging.

## true–false

_____ **1.** Sending e-mails to lure people into revealing personal information is a technique known as pharming.

_____ **2.** Using a surge protector will even protect your computer from massive surges such as lightning strikes.

## critical thinking

**1. Restricting Information to Keep You Safe**

Many countries, such as China, have laws that control the content of the Internet and restrict their citizens' access to information. The United States, with the exception of specific areas such as cyberbullying and child pornography, doesn't currently take steps to restrict its citizens' access to the Internet. Unfortunately, this freedom of information does carry some cost because some information on the web can potentially be dangerous to the general public.

**a.** Do you think the U.S. government should censor information on the web, such as instructions for making weapons, to protect the general public? Why or why not? If you think there should be some censorship, do you think such a law would violate the First Amendment right to free speech? Explain your answer.

**b.** Would you be willing to live with a lower level of information access to increase your sense of well-being? What topics do you feel would make you feel more secure if they were censored?

**Continue**

# 9 Chapter Review

## summary//

### Cybercrime and Identity Theft

**1. What is cybercrime, and who perpetrates it?**

- Cybercrime, is any type of crime perpetrated via a computer or a website.
- Major types of cybercrime are identity theft, credit card fraud, computer viruses, illegal access of computer systems, and auction fraud.
- Cybercriminals use computers, the Internet, and computer networks to commit their crimes.

### Protecting Yourself from Computer Viruses

**2. What are the types of viruses from which I need to protect my computer?**

- A computer virus is a program that attaches itself to another program and attempts to spread to other computers when files are exchanged.
- Computer viruses can be grouped into six categories: (1) boot-sector viruses, (2) logic bombs and time bombs, (3) worms, (4) scripts and macro viruses, (5) e-mail viruses, and (6) encryption viruses. Once run, viruses perform their malicious duties in the background and are often invisible to the user.

**3. What can I do to protect my computer from viruses?**

- The best defense against viruses is to install antivirus software. You should update the software on a regular basis and configure it to examine all e-mail attachments for viruses. You should periodically run a complete virus scan on your computer to ensure that no viruses have made it onto your hard drive.

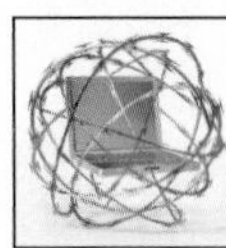

### Protecting Digital Assets from Hackers

**4. How can hackers attack my computing devices, and what harm can they cause?**

- A hacker is defined as anyone who breaks into a computer system unlawfully. Hackers can use software to break into almost any computer connected to the Internet, unless proper precautions are taken.
- Once hackers gain access to a computer, they can potentially (1) steal personal or other important information, (2) damage and destroy data, or (3) use the computer to attack other computers.

**5. What is a firewall, and how does it keep my computer safe from hackers?**

- Firewalls are software programs or hardware devices designed to keep computers safe from hackers. By using a personal firewall, you can close to invaders open logical ports and potentially make your computer invisible to other computers on the Internet.

**6. How do I create secure passwords and manage all of my passwords?**

- Secure passwords contain a mixture of upper- and lowercase letters, numbers, and symbols and are at least 14 characters long. Passwords should not contain words that are in the dictionary or easy-to-guess personal information, like your pet's name.
- Online password checkers can be used to evaluate the strength of your passwords.
- Utilities built into web browsers and Internet security software can be used to manage your passwords and alleviate the need to remember numerous complex passwords.

**7. How can I surf the Internet anonymously and use biometric authentication devices to protect my data?**

- The current versions of popular browsers include tools, such as Google Chrome's Incognito feature, that hide your surfing activities by not recording websites that you visit or files that you download in your browser's history files.
- Biometric authentication devices use a physical attribute that is not easily duplicated to control access to data files or computing devices. Some laptops and smartphones today feature fingerprint readers and facial-recognition software to control access.

## Managing Online Annoyances

**8. How do I manage online annoyances such as spyware and spam?**

- The web is filled with annoyances such as spam, pop-ups, cookies, spyware, and scams such as phishing that make surfing the web frustrating and sometimes dangerous.
- Installing anti-malware software tools helps to prevent, detect, and/or reduce spam, adware, and spyware.

## Keeping Your Data Safe

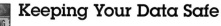

**9. What data do I need to back up, and what are the best methods for doing so?**

- Data files created by you, such as Word and Excel files, or purchased by you, such as music files, need to be backed up in case they're inadvertently deleted or damaged. Application software, such as Microsoft Office, may need to be reinstalled if files are damaged, so backups, such as the DVDs the application came on, must be maintained.
- An incremental backup means only files that have changed or been created since the last backup was performed will be backed up. Image backups copy all system, application, and data files regardless of whether they changed since the last backup.
- Websites such as ADrive and OneDrive are great for backing up individual files. External hard drives are popular choices for holding image backups of your entire system, as are online (cloud) storage sites. Windows and OS X contain solid backup tools that help automate backup tasks.

**10. What is social engineering, and how do I avoid falling prey to phishing?**

- Social engineering schemes use human interaction, deception, and trickery to fool people into revealing sensitive information such as credit card numbers and passwords.
- Phishing schemes usually involve e-mails that direct the unwary to a website that appears to be legitimate, such as a bank site, but that is specifically designed to capture personal information for committing fraud. To avoid phishing scams, you should never reply directly to any e-mail asking you for personal information and never click on a link in an e-mail to go to a website.
- Don't fall for scareware scams that attempt to frighten you by pretending there is something wrong with your computer.

## Protecting Your Physical Computing Assets

**11. How do I protect my physical computing assets from environmental hazards, power surges, and theft?**

- Computing devices should be kept in clean environments free from dust and other particulates and should not be exposed to extreme temperatures (either hot or cold).
- You should protect all electronic devices from power surges by hooking them up through surge protectors, which will protect them from most electrical surges that could damage the devices.
- Mobile devices can be protected from theft by installing software that will (1) set off an alarm if the computer is moved; (2) help recover the computer, if stolen, by reporting the computer's whereabouts when it is connected to the Internet; and/or (3) allow you to lock or wipe the contents of the digital device remotely.

Be sure to check out the companion website for additional materials to help you review and learn, including a Tech Bytes Weekly newsletter—**pearsonhighered.com/techinaction**. And don't forget the Replay Videos.

# key terms//

adware **370**
antivirus software **353**
backdoor program **357**
backup **377**
biometric authentication device **366**
black-hat hacker **356**
boot-sector virus **350**
botnet **357**
computer forensics **372**
cookie **373**
cybercrime **348**
cybercriminal **348**
cyberloafing **375**
data breach **383**
data file **377**
denial-of-service (DoS) attack **357**
distributed denial-of-service (DDoS) attack **357**
drive-by download **355**
e-mail virus **351**
encryption virus **351**
firewall **360**
geotag **358**
grey-hat hacker **356**
hacker **356**
identity theft **349**
image backup (system backup) **378**
incremental backup (partial backup) **377**
inoculation **354**
keystroke logger (keylogger) **371**
logical port **359**
logical port blocking **361**
logic bomb **350**
macro virus **351**
malware **370**
master boot record **350**
multipartite virus **351**
network address translation (NAT) **361**
packet analyzer (sniffer) **356**
packet filtering **361**
personal firewall **360**
pharming **381**
phishing **381**
polymorphic virus **351**
pretexting **381**
program file **377**
quarantining **354**
rootkit **357**
scareware **382**
script **351**
social engineering **381**
spam **371**
spam filter **371**
spear phishing **383**
spyware **371**
stealth virus **352**
surge protector **384**
time bomb **350**
Trojan horse **357**
virus **350**
virus signature **353**
white-hat hacker (ethical hacker) **356**
whole-house surge protector **384**
worm **350**
zombie **357**

## making the transition to . . . next semester//

1. **Backup Procedures**

   You know you should have a good backup strategy in place for your key data. Consider the following:

   **a.** How often do you back up critical data files, such as homework files? What type of device do you use for backing up files? Where do you store the backups to ensure they won't be destroyed if a major disaster (such as a fire) destroys your computer? Do you use online sites for file backups?

   **b.** List the applications (such as Microsoft Office) that are currently installed on your computer. Where is the media (DVDs) for your application software stored? For any software you purchased in an Internet download, have you burned a copy of the installation files to DVD/Blu-ray disc in case you need to reinstall the software?

   **c.** Have you ever made an image backup of your entire system? If so, what software do you use for image backups? If not, research image backup software on the Internet and find an appropriate package to use. Suppose you need to purchase an additional backup device to hold your image backup. Find one that is appropriate. What is the total cost of the software and hardware you will need to implement your image backup strategy?

2. **Shouldn't Protection Be Included?**

   The Uniform Commercial Code, which governs business in every state except Louisiana, covers the implied warranty of merchantability. The warranty's basic premise is that a company selling goods guarantees that its products will do what they are designed to do (i.e., a car will transport you from place to place) and that there are no significant defects in the product. But computers are routinely sold with only trial versions of anti-malware software.

   **a.** Computer hardware manufacturers don't make OS software, but they sell computers that would be unusable without an OS. What responsibility do they have in regard to providing anti-malware protection to their customers?

   **b.** Does the failure of OS manufacturers to include anti-malware tools constitute a breach of the implied warranty of merchantability? Why or why not?

3. **Botnet Awareness**

   Botnets are serious computer infestations that affect large numbers of computers at one time. Still, many students are unaware of this threat even as botnets strike college campuses. Research botnets and prepare a short flyer for your classmates that explains the threats posed by botnets and the software that can be used to detect them.

## making the transition to . . . the workplace//

1. **Tracking Employees**

   Many corporations provide mobile devices to their employees who work outside the office. With apps such as Footprints (from Sollico Software) and GPS tracking (from LOCiMOBILE), it's easy for employers to track the whereabouts of their employees by tracking the location of their mobile devices. Consider the following:

   **a.** How would you feel about your boss tracking your movements during the day? Should employers have to disclose to employees that they're being tracked? Should employers have the right to track employees to ensure they're not slacking off during work hours?

   **b.** Should the tracking software have an option to allow employees to disable the tracking feature temporarily? Under what circumstances should it be permissible for an employee to turn off employer tracking?

2. **Computer Security Careers**

   Computer security professionals are among the highest-paid employees. Using employment sites such as **Monster.com**, **computerjobs.com**, and **dice.com**, research computer security jobs available in the state where your school is located (try searching "computer security"). Select three entry-level computer security jobs from different employers and prepare a document comparing the following: What are the educational requirements? What job skills are required? How much prior work experience are firms looking for? Are programming skills required?

team time//

# Protecting a Network

## Problem

Computer networks with high-speed connections to the Internet are common in most businesses and government agencies today. However, along with easy access to computing devices and the web comes the danger of theft of digital assets.

## Task

An alumnus of your school has just been placed in charge of the computer department of his county government offices. The network contains a mixture of computers running Windows 7, Windows Vista, and OS X. Lacking recent experience in computing threats, he approached your instructor for help in ensuring that his computers and network are adequately protected from viruses, malware, and hackers. Because the county is currently experiencing a spending freeze, he is hoping that there may be free software available that can adequately shield his employees' computers from harm.

## Process

1. Break the class into three teams. Each team will be responsible for investigating one of the following issues:
   a. **Antivirus software:** Research alternatives that can be used to protect the computers in the office from virus infection. Find at least three alternatives and support your recommendations with reviews (from publications such as *PC Magazine* or *PC World*) that evaluate free packages and compare them to commercial solutions.
   b. **Anti-malware software:** Research free packages that will offer protection from malware. Locate at least three alternatives and determine whether the recommended software can be updated automatically. (Many free versions require manual updates.) Most companies that provide free malware protection also offer commercial packages (for a fee) that provide automatic updates. You may want to recommend that the county purchase software to ensure that a minimum of employee intervention is needed to keep the software up to date.
   c. **Firewalls:** Determine if the firewall software provided with Windows 7, Windows Vista, and OS X is reliable. If your research shows that it is reliable, prepare documentation (for all three operating systems) for the county employees to check and see if their firewalls are properly configured. If you determine that additional firewall software is needed, research free firewall software and locate at least three software options that can be deployed by the county.
2. Present your findings to the class and discuss the pros and cons of free and commercial software. Provide your instructor with a report suitable for eventual presentation to the manager of the county office network.

## Conclusion

With the proliferation of viruses and malware, it is essential to protect computers and networks in businesses and government offices from destruction and disruption. Free alternatives might work, but you should ensure that you have done adequate research to determine the best possible protection solution for your particular situation.

## ethics project//

# Content Control: Censorship to Protect Children

In this exercise, you'll research and then role-play a complicated ethical situation. The role you play might or might not match your own personal beliefs; in either case, your research and use of logic will enable you to represent the view assigned. An arbitrator will watch and comment on both sides of the arguments, and together, the team will agree on an ethical solution.

## Problem

Many parents use web-filtering software (also known as content-control software) to protect their children from objectionable content on the Internet. However, the software is also widely used in libraries, schools, and other public places where people other than parents are making decisions about what information to restrict. In 2000, the U.S. federal government began requiring libraries to use content-control software as a condition to receiving federal funds under the provisions of the Children's Internet Protection Act (CIPA). Libraries that don't receive federal funds don't have to install filtering software unless their state (like Virginia) passes laws requiring them to do so to receive state funding. Upon installation of the software, it's up to the library administrators to decide what content is restricted, as guided by the provisions of laws such as CIPA. Therefore, content restriction can vary widely from library to library.

## Research Areas to Consider

- U.S. Supreme Court case *United States v. American Library Association* (2003)
- Content-control software and First Amendment rights
- Violation of children's free speech rights
- Children's Internet Protection Act (CIPA)

## Process

1. Divide the class into teams.
2. Research the areas cited above and devise a scenario in which someone has complained about objectionable content not being blocked or about innocuous content that was inappropriately blocked.
3. Team members should write a summary that provides background information for their character—for example, library patron, library administrator, or arbitrator—and that details their character's behaviors to set the stage for the role-playing event. Then, team members should create an outline to use during the role-playing event.
4. Team members should arrange a mutually convenient time to meet for the exchange, using a virtual meeting tool or by meeting in person.
5. Team members should present their case to the class or submit a PowerPoint presentation for review by the rest of the class, along with the summary and resolution they developed.

## Conclusion

As technology becomes ever more prevalent and integrated into our lives, more and more ethical dilemmas will present themselves. Being able to understand and evaluate both sides of the argument, while responding in a personally or socially ethical manner, will be an important skill.

# Technology in Focus

# Careers in IT

It's hard to imagine an occupation in which computers aren't used in some fashion. Even such previously low-tech industries as waste disposal and fast food use computers to manage inventories and order commodities. In this Technology in Focus feature, we explore various information technology (IT) career paths open to you.

(Carol and Mike Werner/Alamy)

## Rewards of Working in Information Technology

There are many great reasons to work in the exciting, ever-changing field of IT. In this section, we'll explore some reasons why IT fields are so attractive to graduates looking for entry-level positions.

## IT Workers Are in Demand

If you're investigating a career with computers, the first question you may have is, "Will I be able to get a job?" Consider the following:

- According to projections by the U.S. Department of Labor's Bureau of Labor Statistics, computer-related jobs

FIGURE 1

## High-Growth IT Jobs*

| OCCUPATION | MEDIAN PAY ($) | TOP PAY ($) | 10-YEAR GROWTH RATE (%) | TOTAL NEW JOBS |
|---|---|---|---|---|
| Software developers | 90,530 | 143,330 | 30 | 270,900 |
| Computer systems analysts | 77,740 | 119,070 | 22 | 120,400 |
| Computer support specialists | 46,260 | 76,970 | 18 | 110,000 |
| Network and computer systems administrators | 69,160 | 108,090 | 28 | 96,600 |
| Information security analysts, web developers, and computer network architects | 75,660 | 119,940 | 22 | 65,700 |
| Computer programmers | 71,380 | 114,180 | 12 | 43,700 |
| Database administrators | 73,490 | 115,660 | 31 | 33,900 |
| Computer and information research scientists | 100,660 | 153,120 | 19 | 5,300 |

*Excerpted from* Occupational Outlook Handbook*, 2012 Edition, Bureau of Labor Statistics*

are expected to be among the fastest-growing occupations through 2020 (see Figure 1).

- In 2013, *US News and World Report* published a list of the best careers to consider based on employment opportunity, good salary, work-life balance, and job security. Computer systems analyst, software developer, and web developer were included among the top 10 careers. Three other IT careers—computer programmer, IT manager, and computer systems administrator—were in the top 25.
- According to the National Association of Colleges and Employers (NACE) 2013 Starting Salaries for New College Graduates Survey, the average starting salary for computer science majors is $64,100 and was the fourth highest average salary on the list, trailing those of petroleum, chemical, and computer engineering.

The number of students pursuing computer science degrees also has been increasing over the past several years. A recent report by the Computing Research Association revealed that the number of computer science majors increased by 29.2% in 2012. Yet, shortages of computing professionals in the United States are still projected over the next 5 to 10 years. What does all this mean? In terms of job outlook, now is a perfect time to consider an IT career.

## IT Jobs Pay Well

As you can see from Figure 1, median salaries in IT careers are robust. But what exactly affects your salary in an IT position? Your skill set and your experience level are obvious answers, but the size of an employer and its geographic location are also factors. Large companies tend to pay more, so if you're pursuing a high salary, set your sights on a large corporation. But remember that making a lot of money isn't everything—be sure to consider other quality-of-life issues such as job satisfaction. Of course, choosing a computer career isn't a guarantee you'll get a high-paying job. Just as in any other profession, you'll need appropriate training and on-the-job experience to earn a high salary.

So how much can you expect to start out earning? Although starting salaries for some IT positions (computer desktop support and helpdesk analysts) are in the modest range ($41,000 to $45,000), starting salaries for students with bachelor's degrees in IT are fairly robust. But IT salaries vary widely, depending on experience level, the geographic location of the job, and the size of the employer.

To obtain the most accurate information, you should research salaries yourself in the geographic area where you expect to work. **Salary.com** provides a free salary wizard to help you determine what IT professionals in your area are making compared with national averages. You can add information such as your degree and the size of the company to your search selection to fine-tune the figures further.

Figure 2 shows that for an entry-level programming position in Chicago, you could expect to earn a salary of between $47,098 and $75,966 at a company of 500 to 1,000 employees. Hundreds of IT job titles are listed in **Salary.com**, so you can tailor your search to the specific job, location, and industry in which you're interested.

## IT Jobs Are Not Going "Offshore"

In the global economy in which we now operate, job outlook includes the risk of jobs being outsourced, possibly to other countries. **Outsourcing** is a process whereby a business hires a third-party firm to provide business services (such as customer-support call centers) that were previously handled by in-house employees. **Offshoring** occurs when the outsourcing firm is located (or uses employees) outside the United States.

India, China, and Romania and other former Eastern Bloc countries are major players in providing outsourcing services for U.S. companies. The big lure of outsourcing and offshoring is cost savings: Considering that the standard of living and salaries are much lower in many countries than they are in the United States, offshoring is an attractive option for many U.S. employers.

However, outsourcing and offshoring don't always deliver the cost savings that CEOs envision. Demand for personnel overseas has led to increased costs (primarily due to wage

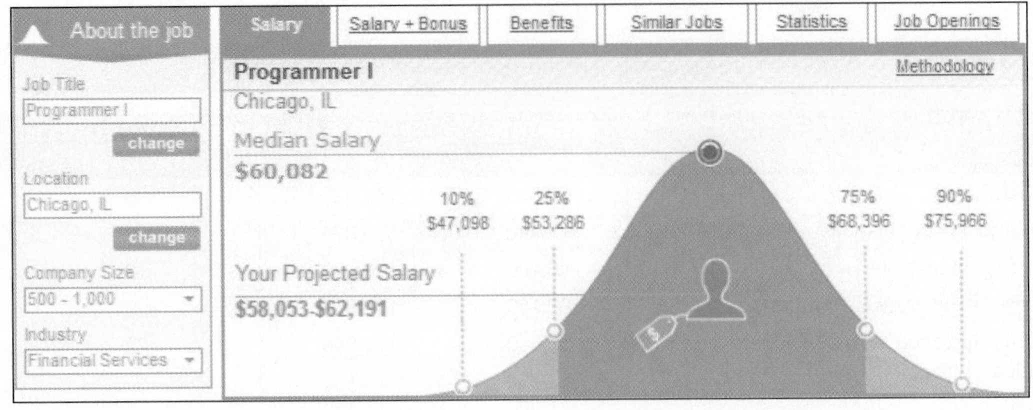


**FIGURE 2** The salary wizard at **Salary.com** is easy to tailor to your location. *(Courtesy of Kenexa)*

increases) for service providers in foreign markets. Furthermore, other, less-tangible factors can outweigh the cost savings from outsourcing. Communications problems can arise between internal and external employees, for example, and cultural differences between the home country and the country doing the offshoring can result in software code that needs extensive rework by in-house employees. Data also can be less secure in an external environment or during the transfer between the company and an external vendor. Although outsourcing and offshoring won't be going away, companies are approaching these staffing alternatives with more caution and are looking more to U.S. companies to provide resources.

So, many IT jobs are staying in the United States. According to *InformationWeek* magazine, most jobs in the following three categories (see Figure 3) will stay put:

1. *Customer interaction:* Jobs that require direct input from customers or that involve systems with which customers interface daily
2. *Enablers:* Jobs that involve getting key business projects accomplished, often requiring technical skills beyond the realm of IT, and good people skills
3. *Infrastructure jobs:* Jobs that are fundamental to moving and storing the information that U.S.-based employees need to do their jobs

In addition, jobs that require specific knowledge of the U.S. marketplace and culture, such as social media managers, are also very likely not to be offshored.

**FIGURE 3**

## Jobs That Will Likely Remain Onshore

| CUSTOMER INTERACTION | ENABLERS | INFRASTRUCTURE JOBS |
|---|---|---|
| Web application developers | Business process analysts | Network security |
| Web interface designers | Application developers (when customer interaction is critical) | Network installation technicians |
| Database and data warehouse designers/developers | Project managers (for systems with customers and business users who are located predominantly in the United States) | Network administrators (engineers) |
| Customer relationship management (CRM) analysts | | Wireless infrastructure managers and technicians |
| Enterprise resource planning (ERP) implementation specialists | | Disaster recovery planners and responders |

## Women Are in High Demand in IT Departments

Currently, women make up about 25% of the IT workforce (per the National Center for Women and Information Technology). This presents a huge opportunity for women who have IT skills, because many IT departments are actively seeking to diversify their workforces. In addition, although a salary gender gap (the difference between what men and women earn for performing the same job) exists in IT careers, it's smaller than in most other professions.

## You Have a Choice of Working Location

In this case, location refers to the setting in which you work. IT jobs can be office-based, field-based, project-based, or home-based. Because not every situation is perfect for every individual, you can look for a job that suits your tastes and requirements. Figure 4 summarizes the major job types and their locations.

## You Constantly Meet New Challenges

In IT, the playing field is always changing. New software and hardware are constantly being developed. You'll need to work hard to keep your skills up to date. You'll spend a lot of time in training and self-study trying to learn new systems and

FIGURE 4

## Where Do You Want to Work?

| TYPE OF JOB | LOCATION AND HOURS | SPECIAL CONSIDERATIONS |
|---|---|---|
| **Office-based**  | Report for work to the same location each day and interact with the same people on a regular basis; requires regular hours of attendance (such as 9 a.m. to 5 p.m.) | May require working beyond "normal" working hours; may also require workers to be on call 24/7 |
| **Field-based**  | Travel from place to place as needed and perform short-term jobs at each location | Involves a great deal of travel and the ability to work independently |
| **Project-based**  | Work at client sites on specific projects for extended periods of time (weeks or months) | Can be especially attractive to individuals who like workplace situations that vary on a regular basis |
| **Home-based (telecommuting)**  | Work from home | Involves very little day-to-day supervision and requires an individual who is self-disciplined |

(Mardis Coers/Fotolia; Harvepino/Fotolia; Nestor Costa/Fotolia; Paul Maguire/Fotolia)

techniques. Many individuals thrive in this type of environment because it keeps their jobs from becoming dull or routine.

## You Work in Teams

When students are asked to describe their ideal jobs, many describe jobs that involve working in teams. Despite what some people think, IT professionals are not locked in lightless cubicles, basking in the glow of their monitors and working alone on projects. Most IT jobs require constant interaction with other workers, usually in team settings. People skills are highly prized by IT departments. If you have good leadership and team-building skills, you'll have the opportunity to exercise them in an IT job.

## You Don't Need to Be a Mathematical Genius

Certain IT careers such as programming involve a fair bit of math. But even if you're not mathematically inclined, you can explore many other IT careers. IT employers also value such attributes as creativity, marketing, and artistic style, especially in jobs that involve working on the Internet or with social media.

## IT Skills Are Transferable

Most computing skills are transferable from industry to industry. A networking job in the clothing manufacturing industry uses the same primary skill set as a networking job for a supermarket chain. Therefore, if something disastrous happens to the industry you're in, you should be able to switch to another industry without having to learn an entirely new skill set. Combining business courses with IT courses will also make you more marketable when changing jobs. For example, as an accounting major, if you minor in IT, employers may be more willing to hire you because working in accounting today means constantly interfacing with management information systems and manipulating data.

## Challenges of IT Careers

Although there are many positive aspects of IT careers, there can be some challenges. The discussions that follow aren't meant to discourage you from pursuing an IT career but merely to make you aware of exactly what challenges you might face in an IT department.

### Stress

Most IT jobs are hectic (see Figure 5). Whereas the average American works 42 hours a week, a survey by *InformationWeek* revealed that the average IT staff person works 45 hours a week and is on call for another 24 hours. On-call time (hours an employee must be available to work in the event of a problem) has been increasing because most IT systems require 24/7 availability.

### Women Are in the Minority

A majority of IT jobs are filled by men, so some women view IT departments as *Dilbert*-like microcosms of antisocial geeks and don't feel like they would fit in. Unfortunately, some mostly male IT departments do suffer from varying degrees of gender bias. Although some women may thrive on the challenge of enlightening these male enclaves and bringing them into the twenty-first century, others might find it difficult to work in such environments.

### Lifelong Learning Is Required

Although the constantly changing nature of IT can alleviate boredom, keeping up with the changes can also cause some stress. You'll need to take training courses, do self-study, and perhaps take additional college courses, such as getting a graduate degree, to keep up with the vast shifts of technology.

## Choosing Your Realm of IT

Figure 6 shows an organizational chart for a modern IT department at a large corporation that should help you understand the variety of careers available and how they interrelate. The chief information officer (CIO) has overall responsibility for the development, implementation, and maintenance of information systems and its infrastructure. Usually, the CIO reports to the chief operating officer (COO).

The responsibilities below the CIO are generally grouped into two units:

1. Development and integration (responsible for the development of systems and websites)
2. Technical services (responsible for the day-to-day operations of the company's information infrastructure and network, including all hardware and software deployed)

In large organizations, responsibilities are distinct and jobs are defined more narrowly. In medium-sized organizations, there can be overlap between position responsibilities. At a small company, you might be the network administrator, database administrator, computer support technician, and social media manager all at the same time. Let's look at the typical jobs found in each department.

### Working in Development and Integration

Two distinct paths exist in this division:

1. Web development
2. Systems development

Because everything involves the web today, there's often a great deal of overlap between these paths.

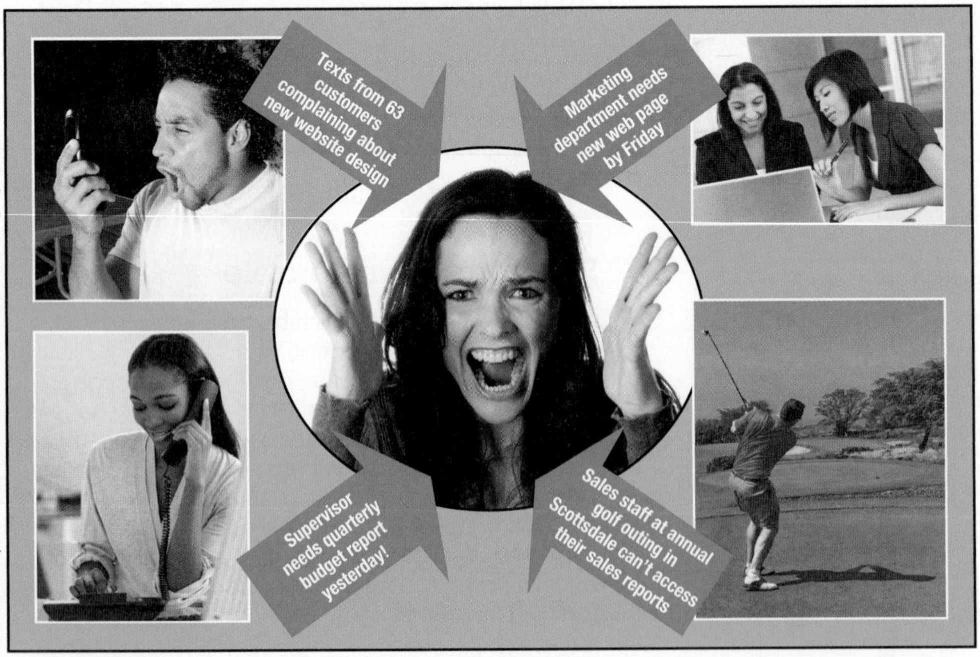

**FIGURE 5** Stress comes from multiple directions in IT jobs.

(Jenn Mackenzie/Shutterstock; Johan Larson/Shutterstock; Stephen Coburn/Shutterstock; wavebreakmedia/Shutterstock; LWPhotography/Shutterstock)

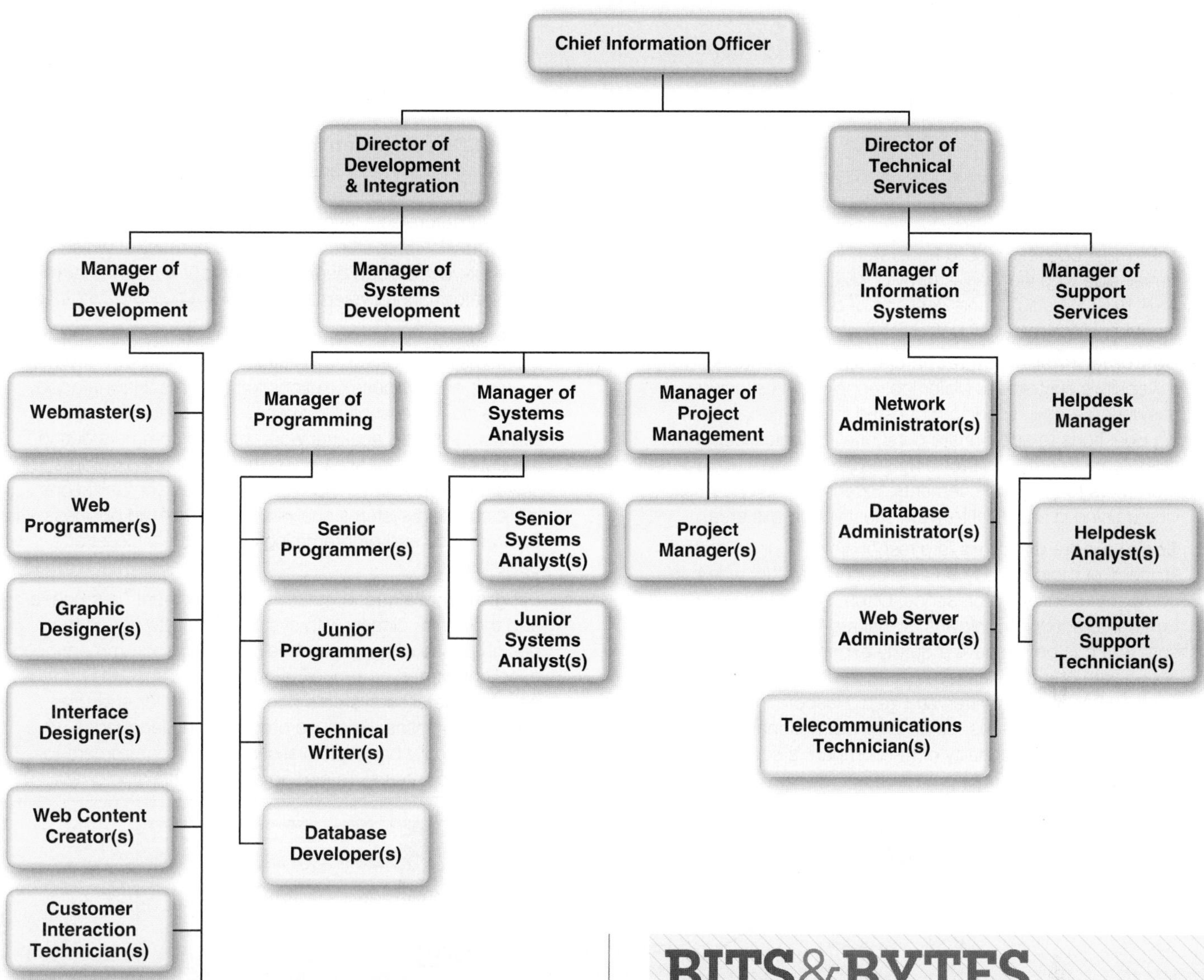


**FIGURE 6** This chart represents a typical structure for an IT department at a large corporation.

**Web Development.** When most people think of web development careers, they usually equate them with being a webmaster. Webmasters used to be individuals who were solely responsible for all aspects of a company's website. However, today's webmasters usually are supervisors with responsibility for certain aspects of web development. At smaller companies, they may also be responsible for tasks that other individuals in a web development group usually do, such as the following:

- **Web content creators** generate the words and images that appear on the web. Journalists, other writers, editors, and marketing personnel prepare an enormous amount of web content, whereas **video producers**, **graphic designers**, and **animators** create web-based multimedia. Web content creators have a thorough understanding of their own fields as well as HTML, PHP, and JavaScript.

## BITS&BYTES

### Matching a Career to Your Skills

Are you unsure about which career you'd like to pursue? Many online tools, such as the Skills Profiler from America's Career InfoNet (**careerinfonet.org**), can help you identify careers based on your skills. The Skills Profiler asks you to identify your skills in seven categories and then rate your skills in each area you selected. The program then compiles a skills profile for you and suggests job titles for you to explore.

Regardless of whether you choose to pursue a career in IT, you should visit the Bureau of Labor Statistics site (**bls.gov**). One of the site's most useful features is the *Occupational Outlook Handbook*. Aside from projecting job growth in various career fields, it describes typical tasks workers perform, the amount of training and education needed, and salary estimates.

- **Interface designers** work with graphic designers and animators to create a look and feel for the site and make it easy to navigate.
- **Web programmers** build web pages to deploy the materials that the content creators develop. They wield software tools such as Adobe Dreamweaver and Microsoft Expression to develop the web pages. They also create links to databases using products such as Oracle and SQL Server to keep information flowing between users and web pages. They must possess a solid understanding of client- and server-side web languages (HTML, XML, Java, JavaScript, ASP, PHP, Silverlight, and Perl) and of development environments such as the Microsoft .NET Framework.
- **Customer interaction technicians** provide feedback to a website's customers. Major job responsibilities include answering e-mail, sending requested information, funneling questions to appropriate personnel (technical support, sales, and so on), and providing suggestions to web programmers for site improvements. Extensive customer service training is essential to work effectively in this area.
- **Social media directors** are responsible for directing the strategy of the company on all social media sites where the company maintains a presence. Often, supervising customer interaction technicians, social media directors make sure that customers have a quality experience while interacting with company employees and customers on sites such as Facebook, Twitter, and Yelp. Responding to comments left on such sites, developing promotional strategies, and designing functionality of the company's social media sites are common job responsibilities.

As you can see in Figure 7, many different people can work on the same website. Web programming jobs often require a four-year college degree in computer science, whereas graphic designers often are hired with two-year art degrees.

**Systems Development.** Ask most people what systems developers do and they'll answer "programming." However, programming is only one aspect of systems development. Because large projects involve many people, there are many job opportunities in systems development, most of which require four-year college degrees in computer science or management information systems:

- **Systems analysts** gather information from end users about problems and existing information systems. They document systems and propose solutions to problems. Having good people skills is essential to success as a systems analyst. In addition, systems analysts work with programmers during the development phase to design appropriate programs to solve the problem at hand. Therefore, many organizations insist on hiring systems analysts who have solid business backgrounds and programming experience (at least at a basic level).
- **Programmers** attend meetings to document user needs, and they work closely with systems analysts during the design phase of program development. Programmers need excellent written communication skills because they often generate detailed systems documentation for end-user training purposes. Because programming languages are mathematically based, it is essential for programmers to have strong math skills and an ability to think logically.

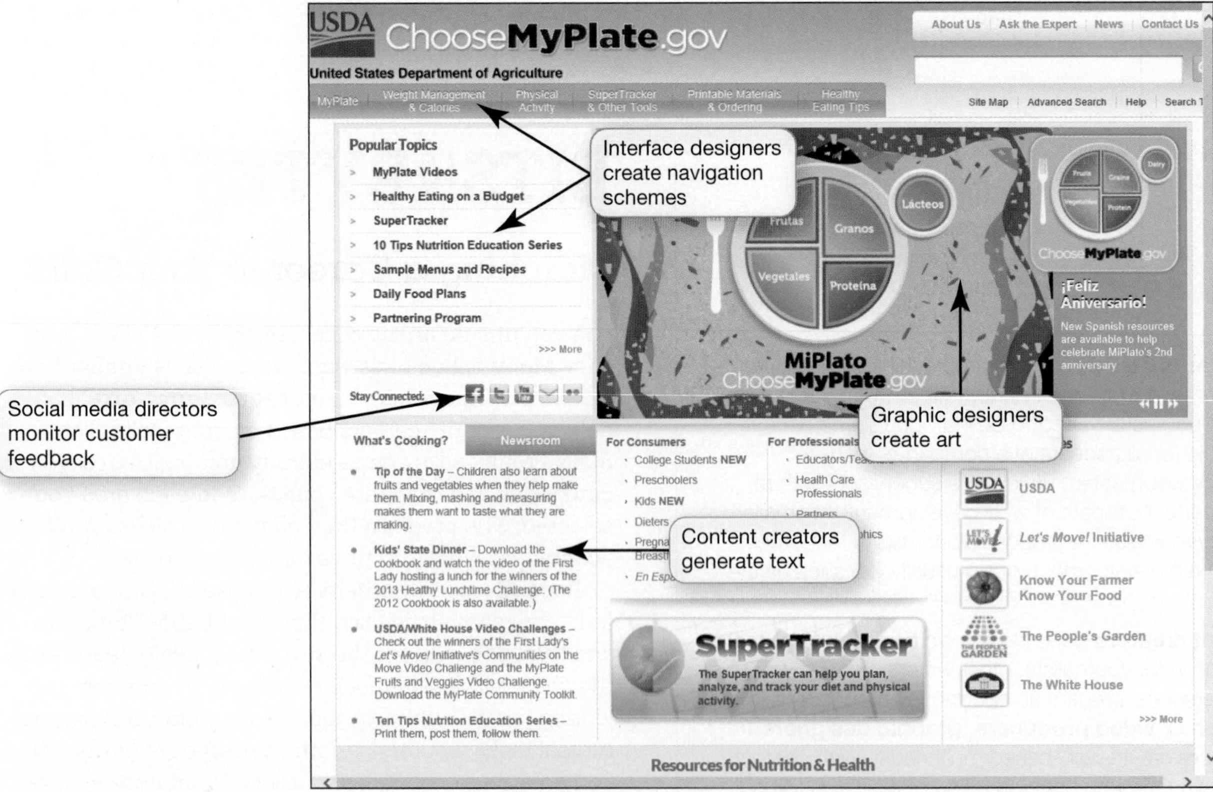


**FIGURE 7** It takes a team to create and maintain a website. *(Courtesy of the United States Department of Agriculture)*

• Programmers build the software that solves problems
• Systems analysts document systems and propose solutions
Project Team
• Project managers supervise, organize, and coach team members
• Database developers ensure data is accessible when it's needed

**FIGURE 8** There are many important team members in systems development. *(Bah69/Fotolia; Rob/Fotolia; FotoLuminate/Fotolia; HaywireMedia/Fotolia)*

- **Project managers** manage the overall systems development process: assigning staff, budgeting, reporting to management, coaching team members, and ensuring deadlines are met. Project managers need excellent time management skills because they're often pulled in several directions at once. They usually have prior experience as programmers or systems analysts. Many project managers obtain master's degrees to supplement their undergraduate degrees.

In addition to these key players, the following people are also involved in the systems development process:

- **Technical writers** generate systems documentation for end users and for programmers who may make modifications to the system in the future.
- **Network administrators** help the programmers and analysts design compatible systems, because many systems are required to run in certain environments (UNIX or Windows, for instance) and must work in conjunction with other programs.
- **Database developers** design and build databases to support the software systems being developed.

Large development projects may have all of these team members on the project. Smaller projects may require an overlap of positions, such as a programmer also acting as a systems analyst. As shown in Figure 8, team members work together to build a system.

## Working in Technical Services

Technical services jobs are vital to keeping IT systems running. The people in these jobs install and maintain the infrastructure behind the IT systems and work with end users to make sure they can interact with the systems effectively. There are two major categories of technical services careers:

1. Information systems
2. Support services

Note that these also are the *least likely* IT jobs to be outsourced because hands-on work with equipment and users is required on a regular basis.

**Information Systems.** The information systems department keeps the networks and telecommunications up and running at all times. Within the department, you'll find a variety of positions.

- **Network administrators** (sometimes called *network engineers*) are involved in every stage of network planning and deployment (see Figure 9). They decide what equipment to buy and what media to use, they determine the network's topology, and they help install the network (by supervising contractors or doing it themselves). Network administrators plan disaster-recovery strategies (such as what to do if a fire destroys the server room). When equipment and cables break, network administrators must fix the problem. They also obtain and install updates to network software and evaluate new equipment to determine whether the network should be upgraded. In addition, they monitor the network's performance and often develop policies regarding network usage, security measures, and hardware and software standards.

**FIGURE 9** At smaller companies, network administrators may be fixing a user's computer in the morning, installing and configuring a new network operating system in the afternoon, and troubleshooting a wiring problem (shown here) in the evening. *(ArtPix/Alamy)*

# trends in IT

## Get in the Game: Careers in Game Development

The video gaming industry in the United States has surpassed the earning power of the Hollywood movie industry. In 2012, U.S. consumers bought just under $15 billion worth of video games and accessories, whereas Hollywood took in just over $10.8 billion. Although some aspects of game development, such as scenery design and certain aspects of programming, are being sent offshore, the majority of game development requires a creative team whose members need to work in close proximity. Therefore, it's anticipated that most game development jobs will stay in the United States.

Consoles such as the Xbox One and the PlayStation 4 generate demand for large-scale games. The popularity of mobile devices such as smartphones and tablets is driving demand for lower-end, casual game applications. Casual games are games that can be played relatively quickly, such as puzzle games (see Figure 10). Demand for family-friendly games without violence, sex, and profanity is on the rise. With all this demand, there are many opportunities for careers in game development.

Game development jobs usually are split along two paths: designers and programmers.

- **Game designers** tend to be artistic and are responsible for creating 2-D and 3-D art, game interfaces, video sequences, special effects, game levels, and scenarios. Game designers must master software packages such as Autodesk 3ds Max, Autodesk Maya, NewTek LightWave 3D, Adobe Photoshop, and Adobe Flash.
- **Game programmers** are responsible for coding the scenarios developed by the designers. Using languages and toolsets such as Objective-C, Unity, Apple Xcode, C, C++, Assembly, and Java, programmers build the game and ensure that it plays accurately.

Aside from programmers and designers, play testers and quality-assurance professionals play the games with the intent of breaking them or discovering bugs within the game interfaces or worlds. **Play testing** is an essential part of the game development process because it assists designers in determining which aspects of the game are most intriguing to players and which parts of the game need to be repaired or enhanced.

No matter what job you may pursue in the realm of gaming, you'll need to have a two- or four-year college degree. If you're interested in gaming, look for a school with a solid animation or 3-D art program or a computer game–programming curriculum. Programming requires a strong background in math and physics to enable you to realistically program environments that mimic the real world. Proficiency with math (especially geometry) also helps with design careers.

For more information on gaming careers, check out the International Game Developers Association site (**igda.org**) and the Game Career Guide (**gamecareerguide.com**).

**FIGURE 10** Plants vs. Zombies, which has you grow plants to fend off encroaching zombie hordes, is an example of a popular casual game available for many different platforms. *(Vinod Kurien/Alamy)*

- **Database administrators (DBAs)** install and configure database servers and ensure that the servers provide an adequate level of access to all users.
- **Web server administrators** install, configure, and maintain web servers and ensure that the company maintains Internet connectivity at all times.
- **Telecommunications technicians** oversee the communications infrastructure, including training employees to use telecommunications equipment. They are often on call 24 hours a day.

**Support Services.** As a member of the support services team, you interface with users (external customers or employees) and troubleshoot their computer problems. Support service positions include the following:

- **Helpdesk analysts** staff the phones, respond to Internet live chats, or respond to e-mails and solve problems for customers or employees, either remotely or in person. Often, helpdesk personnel are called on to train users on the latest software and hardware.

- **Computer support technicians** go to a user's location and fix software and hardware problems. They also often have to chase down and repair faults in the network infrastructure.

As important as these people are, they may receive a great deal of abuse by angry users whose computers are not working. When working in support services, you need to be patient and not be overly sensitive to insults!

Technical services jobs often require a two-year college degree or training at a trade school or technical institute. At smaller companies, job duties tend to overlap between the helpdesk and technician jobs. These jobs are in demand and require staffing in local markets, so they are staying onshore. You can't repair a computer's power supply if you are located in another country!

## Preparing for a Job in IT

A job in IT requires a robust skill set and formal training and preparation. Most employers today have an entry-level requirement of a college degree, a technical institute diploma, appropriate professional certifications, experience in the field, or a combination of these. How can you prepare for a job in IT?

1. **Get educated.** Two- and four-year colleges and universities normally offer three degrees to prepare students for IT careers: computer science, management information systems, and information technology (although titles vary). Alternatives to colleges and universities are privately licensed technical (or trade) schools. Generally, these programs focus on building skill sets rapidly and qualifying for a job in a specific field. The main advantage of technical schools is that their programs usually take less time to complete than college degrees. However, to have a realistic chance of employment in IT fields other than networking or web development, you should attend a degree-granting college or university.
2. **Investigate professional certifications.** Certifications attempt to provide a consistent method of measuring skill levels in specific areas of IT. Hundreds of IT certifications are available, most of which you get by passing a written exam. Software and hardware vendors (such as Microsoft and Cisco) and professional organizations (such as the Computing Technology Industry Association) often establish certification standards. Visit **microsoft.com**, **cisco.com**, **comptia.org**, and **sun.com** for more information on certifications.
3. **Get experience.** In addition to education, employers want you to have experience, even for entry-level jobs. While you're still completing your education, consider getting an internship or part-time job in your field of study. Many schools will help you find internships and allow you to earn credit toward your degree through internships.
4. **Do research.** Find out as much as you can about the company and the industry it's in before going on an interview. Start with the company's website, and then expand your search to business and trade publications such as *BusinessWeek* and *Inc.* magazines.

## Getting Started in an IT Career

Training for a career is not useful unless you can find a job at the end of your training. Here are some tips on getting a job:

1. **Use the career resources at your school.** Many employers recruit at schools, and most schools maintain a placement office to help students find jobs. Employees in the placement office can help you with résumé preparation and interviewing skills and can provide you with leads for internships and jobs.
2. **Develop relationships with your instructors.** Many college instructors still work in or previously worked in the IT industry. They can often provide you with valuable advice and industry contacts.
3. **Start networking.** Many jobs are never advertised but instead are filled by word of mouth. Seek out contacts in your field and discuss job prospects with them. Find out what skills you need, and ask them to recommend others in the industry with whom you can speak. Professional organizations such as the Association for Computing Machinery (ACM) offer one way to network. These organizations often have chapters on college campuses and offer reduced membership rates for students. Figure 11

**FIGURE 11**

**Professional Organizations**

| ORGANIZATION NAME | PURPOSE | WEBSITE |
|---|---|---|
| Association for Computing Machinery (ACM) | Oldest scientific computing society; maintains a strong focus on programming and systems development | **acm.org** |
| Association for Information Systems (AIS) | Organization of professionals who work in academia and specialize in information systems | **aisnet.org** |
| Association of Information Technology Professionals (AITP) | Heavy focus on IT education and development of seminars and learning materials | **aitp.org** |
| Institute of Electrical and Electronics Engineers (IEEE) | Provides leadership and sets engineering standards for all types of network computing devices and protocols | **ieee.org** |
| Information Systems Security Association (ISSA) | Not-for-profit, international organization of information security professionals and practitioners | **issa.org** |

FIGURE 12

## Resources for Women in IT

| ORGANIZATION NAME | PURPOSE | WEBSITE |
|---|---|---|
| Anita Borg Institute for Women and Technology | Organization whose aim is to "increase the impact of women on all aspects of technology" | **anitaborg.org** |
| Association for Women in Computing (AWC) | A not-for-profit organization dedicated to promoting the advancement of women in computing professions | **awc-hq.org** |
| The Center for Women in Technology (CWIT) | An organization dedicated to providing global leadership in achieving women's full participation in all aspects of IT | **cwit.umbc.edu** |
| *Diversity/Careers in Engineering & Information Technology* | An online magazine whose articles cover career issues of technical professionals who are members of minority groups, women, or people with disabilities | **diversitycareers.com** |
| Women in Technology International (WITI) | A global trade association for tech-savvy, professional women | **witi.com** |

lists major professional organizations you should consider investigating.

If you're a woman and are thinking about pursuing an IT career, many resources and groups cater to female IT professionals and students (see Figure 12). The oldest and best-known organization is the Association for Women in Computing, founded in 1978.

4. **Check corporate websites for jobs.** Many corporate websites list current job opportunities. For example, Google provides searchable job listings by geographic location. Check the sites of companies in which you are interested and then do a search on the sites for job openings or, if provided, click their employment links.
5. **Visit online employment sites.** Most of these sites allow you to store your résumé online, and many sites allow employers to browse résumés to find qualified employees. Begin looking at job postings on these sites early in your education because these job postings detail the skill sets employers require. Focusing on coursework that will provide you with desirable skill sets will make you more marketable. Figure 13 lists employment sites as well as sites that offer other career resources.

The outlook for IT jobs should continue to be positive in the future. We wish you luck with your education and job search.

# BITS&BYTES

## Certifications: How Important Are They?

Employees with certifications generally earn more than employees who aren't certified. However, most employers don't view a certification as a substitute for a college degree or a trade school program. You should think of certifications as an extra edge beyond your formal education that will make you more attractive to employers. To ensure you're pursuing the right certifications, ask employers which certifications they respect, or explore online job sites to see which certifications are listed as desirable or required.

FIGURE 13

## Resources for IT Employment

| SITE NAME | URL |
|---|---|
| CareerBuilder | **careerbuilder.com** |
| ComputerJobs.com | **computerjobs.com** |
| ComputerWork.com | **computerwork.com** |
| Dice | **dice.com** |
| Gamasutra | **gamasutra.com** |
| JustTechJobs | **justtechjobs.com** |
| LinkedIn | **linkedin.com** |
| Monster | **monster.com** |
| TechCareers | **techcareers.com** |

# check your understanding//

For a quick review of what you've learned, answer the following questions. Visit **pearsonhighered.com /techinaction** to check your answers.

## multiple choice

**1.** The individuals responsible for generating images for websites are referred to as

- **a.** network administrators.
- **b.** graphic designers.
- **c.** web programmers.
- **d.** interface designers.

**2.** What type of job involves working at client locations and the ability to work with little direct supervision?

- **a.** field-based
- **b.** project-based
- **c.** office-based
- **d.** home-based

**3.** Which position is *not* typically a part of the information systems department?

- **a.** helpdesk analyst
- **b.** telecommunications technician
- **c.** network administrator
- **d.** web server administrator

**4.** Outsourcing is thought to be an attractive option for many companies because of

- **a.** the emphasis on employee training.
- **b.** the cost savings that can be realized.
- **c.** increased data security.
- **d.** decreased travel and entertainment costs.

**5.** Which of the following IT positions is responsible for directing a company's strategy on sites such as Facebook, Twitter, and Yelp?

- **a.** project manager
- **b.** customer interaction technician
- **c.** social media director
- **d.** social web analyst

**6.** Which of the following statements about IT careers is *false*?

- **a.** IT employers typically prefer experience to certification.
- **b.** Women who have IT skills have ample opportunities for securing IT employment.
- **c.** Many IT jobs are staying in the United States.
- **d.** Most IT jobs require little interaction with other people.

**7.** Which task is *not* typically performed by a network administrator?

- **a.** developing network usage policies
- **b.** installing networks
- **c.** planning for disaster recovery
- **d.** web programming

**8.** Interface designers are the people responsible for

- **a.** orchestrating the company strategy in online venues.
- **b.** providing feedback to website customers.
- **c.** creating the look and feel of a website.
- **d.** deploying the materials prepared by content creators.

**9.** If you are artistic and have mastered software packages such as Adobe Photoshop, Autodesk 3ds Max, and Autodesk Maya, you might consider a career as which of the following?

- **a.** game programmer
- **b.** game designer
- **c.** game tester
- **d.** web designer

**10.** Which position is *not* a part of the systems development department?

- **a.** systems analyst
- **b.** project manager
- **c.** programmer
- **d.** database administrator

# 10 Behind the Scenes: Software Programming

## Understanding Software Programming

### The Importance of Programming

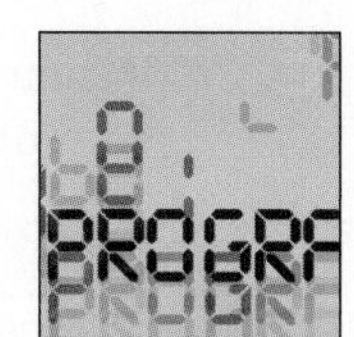

**OBJECTIVE**

1. Why do I need to understand how to create software? **(p. 408)**

### The Life Cycle of an Information System

**OBJECTIVE**

2. What is a system development life cycle, and what are the phases in the cycle? **(pp. 409–411)**

### The Life Cycle of a Program

**OBJECTIVES**

3. What is the life cycle of a program? **(p. 412)**
4. What role does a problem statement play in programming? **(pp. 412–414)**
5. How do programmers create algorithms and move from algorithm to code? **(pp. 414–426)**
6. What steps are involved in completing the program? **(pp. 426–427)**

**Active Helpdesk:** Understanding Software Programming

**Sound Byte:** Programming for End Users

**Sound Byte:** Looping Around the IDE

## Programming Languages

### Many Languages for Many Projects

**OBJECTIVE**

7. How do programmers select the right programming language for a specific task? **(pp. 431–432)**

### Exploring Programming Languages

**OBJECTIVE**

8. What are the most popular programming languages for different types of application development? **(pp. 433–440)**

**Sound Byte:** 3D Programming the Easy Way

For all media in this chapter go to **pearsonhighered.com/techinaction** or **MyITLab**.

*(Stockbyte/Getty Images; Dondesigns/iStockphoto/Getty; S.John/Fotolia; Erik Dreyer/Stone/Getty Images)*

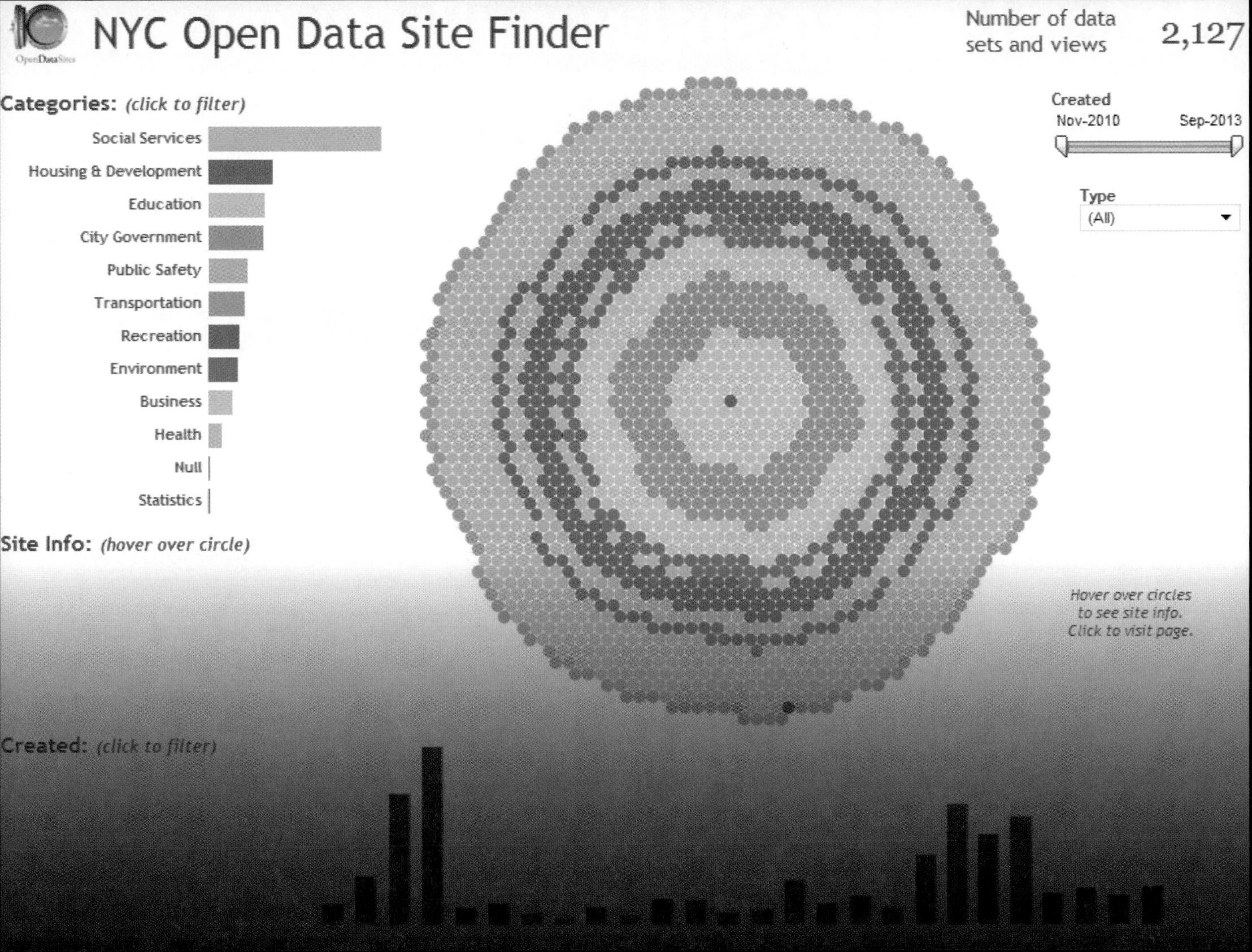

NYC Open Data Site Finder

Number of data sets and views 2,127

Categories: *(click to filter)*

Social Services
Housing & Development
Education
City Government
Public Safety
Transportation
Recreation
Environment
Business
Health
Null
Statistics

Created
Nov-2010 Sep-2013

Type
(All)

Site Info: *(hover over circle)*

*Hover over circles to see site info. Click to visit page.*

Created: *(click to filter)*

# HOW COOL IS THIS?

Scan here for more info

Most major cities now have made a commitment to make the data they use to govern open and transparent—to human eyes and to your programs. Websites format information so it is useful for communicating with humans, but **web services** format the information in a way that makes it easy to communicate the data **to your program**. Chicago, Philadelphia, and other major cities have opened up thousands of government records through **Open Data initiatives**. Using this data, users can do such things as create a program to visualize neighborhood crime statistics, track their city's snowplows, or compare the current school budget expenditures.

In New York City, the Open Data movement has made over 2,000 data sets available—enough that the **Open Data Site Finder** shown here is made available to users to make their job of locating data easier. For example, users can click on the purple area of the site finder and zoom down to see the 698 web services with data related to New York City social services. Each individual service provides the specific data to your program so you can **write a web app or mobile tool** that really has an **impact in your community**. Consider your own community. What kind of web app do you think it needs? Get started working on it—the data is waiting for you. *(Courtesy of Tableau Software; Courtesy of OpenDataSites)*

# Understanding Software Programming

Every day we face a wide array of tasks. Some tasks are complex and require creative thought and a human touch. But tasks that are repetitive, work with electronic information, and follow a series of clear steps are candidates for automation with computers—automation achieved through programming. In this part of the chapter, we'll look at some of the basics of programming.

## the importance of PROGRAMMING

A career in programming offers many advantages—jobs are plentiful, salaries are strong, and telecommuting is often easy to arrange. But even if you're not planning a career in programming, knowing the basics of programming is important to help you use computers productively.

**Why would I ever need to create a program?** Computer programs already exist for many tasks. For example, if you want to write a paper, Microsoft Word has already been designed to translate the tasks you want to accomplish into computer instructions. However, for users who can't find an existing software product to accomplish a task, programming is mandatory (see Figure 10.1). For example, imagine that a medical company comes up with a new smart bandage designed to transmit medical information about a wound directly to a diagnostic mobile monitor, like a doctor's phone. No software product exists that will accumulate and relay information in just this manner. Therefore, a team of programmers will have to create smart bandage software.

**If I'm not going to be a programmer, why should I learn about programming?** If you plan to use only existing, off-the-shelf software, having a basic knowledge of programming enables you to add features that support your personal needs. For example, most modern software applications let you automate features by using custom-built miniprograms called *macros*. By creating macros, you can execute a complicated sequence of steps with a single command. Understanding how to program macros enables you to add custom commands to, for example, Word or Excel and lets you automate frequently performed tasks, providing a huge boost to your productivity. And if you plan to create custom applications from scratch, having a detailed knowledge of programming will be critical to the successful completion of your projects. ■

**FIGURE 10.1** Congressman Bill Shuster takes a 33-mile ride to the Pittsburgh International Airport in a driverless car. Software both controls and drives the car with no human input at all. Legal in a number of states, driverless technology is here. *(AP Photo/Keith Srakocic)*

# the life cycle of an INFORMATION SYSTEM

Generally speaking, a *system* is a collection of pieces working together to achieve a common goal. Your body, for example, is a system of muscles, organs, and other groups of cells working together. An **information system** includes data, people, procedures, hardware, and software that help in planning and decision making. Information systems help run an office and coordinate online-purchasing systems and are behind database-driven applications used by Amazon and Netflix. But how are these complicated systems developed?

## The System Development Life Cycle

**Why do I need a process to develop a system?** Because teams of people are required to develop information systems, there needs to be an organized process to ensure that development proceeds in an orderly fashion. Software applications also need to be available for multiple operating systems, to work over networked environments, and to be free of errors and to be well supported. Therefore, a process often referred to as the **system development life cycle (SDLC)** is used.

**What steps constitute the SDLC?** There are six steps in a common SDLC model, as shown in Figure 10.2. This system is sometimes referred to as a "waterfall" system because each step is dependent on the previous step being completed before it can be started.

1. *Problem and Opportunity Identification:* Corporations are always attempting to break into new markets, develop new customers, or launch new products. At other times, systems development is driven by a company's desire to serve its existing customers more efficiently or to respond to problems with a current system. Whether solving an existing problem or exploiting an opportunity, large corporations typically form a development committee to evaluate systems development proposals. The committee decides which projects to take forward based on available resources such as personnel and funding.
2. *Analysis:* In this phase, analysts explore the problem or need in depth and develop a program specification. The **program specification** is a clear statement of the goals and objectives of the project. The first feasibility assessment is also performed at this stage. The feasibility assessment determines whether the project should go forward. If the project is determined to be feasible, the analysis team defines the user requirements and recommends a plan of action.
3. *Design:* The design phase generates a detailed plan for programmers to follow. The proposed system is documented using flowcharts and data-flow diagrams. Flowcharts are visual diagrams of a process, including the decisions that need to be made along the way. **Data-flow diagrams** trace all data in an information system from the point at which data enters the system to its final resting place (storage or output). The data-flow diagram in Figure 10.3 shows the flow of concert ticket information.

   The design phase details the software, inputs and outputs, backups and controls, and processing requirements of the problem. Once the system plan is designed, a company evaluates existing software packages to determine whether it needs to develop a new piece of software or if it can buy something already on the market and adapt it to fit its needs.
4. *Development:* It is during this phase that actual programming takes place. This phase is also the first part of the program development life cycle, described in detail later in the chapter. The documentation work is begun in this phase by technical writers.

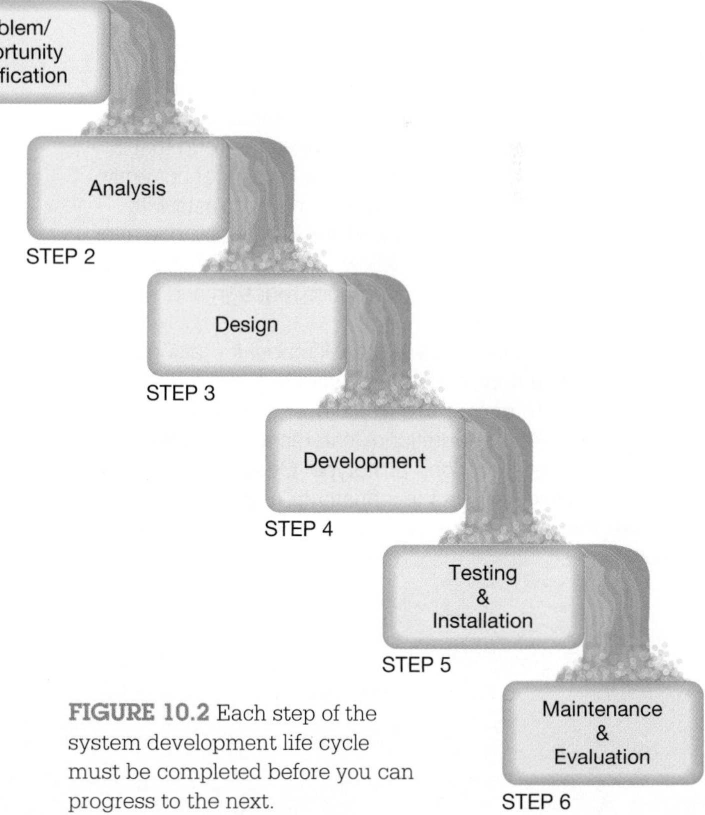


**FIGURE 10.2** Each step of the system development life cycle must be completed before you can progress to the next.

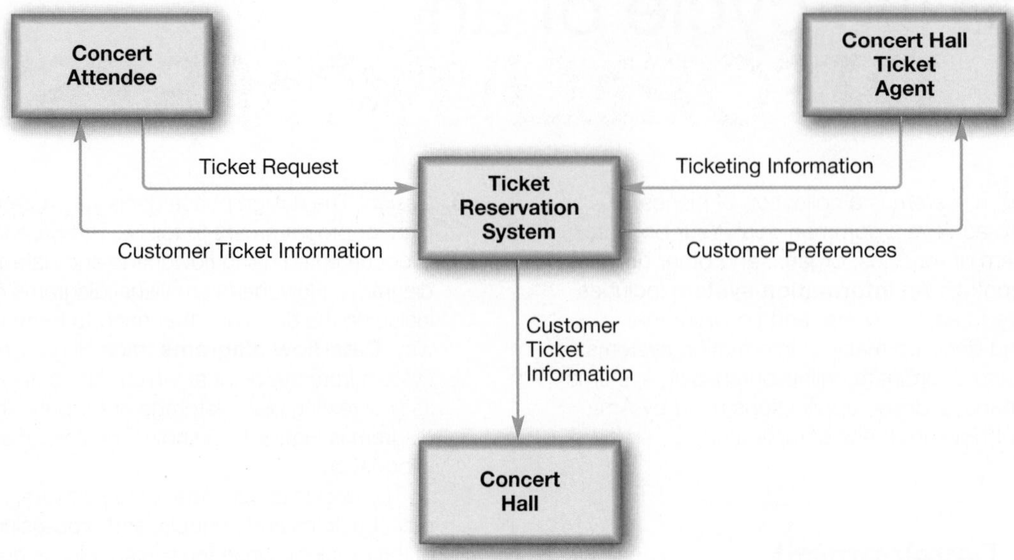


**FIGURE 10.3** Data-flow diagrams illustrate the way data travels in an information system.

5. *Testing and Installation:* Testing the program ensures it works properly. It is then installed for official use.
6. *Maintenance and Evaluation:* In this phase, program performance is monitored to determine whether the program is still meeting the needs of end users. Errors that weren't detected in the testing phase but that are discovered during use are corrected. Additional enhancements that users request are evaluated so that appropriate program modifications can be made.

The waterfall model is an idealized view of software development. Most developers follow some variation of it. For example, a design team may "spiral," where a group that's supporting the work of another group will work concurrently with the other group on development. This contrasts with workflows in which the groups work independently, one after the other. Often there is a "backflow" up the waterfall, because even well-designed projects can require redesign and specification changes midstream.

Some people criticize the waterfall model for taking too long to provide actual working software to the client. This may contribute to **scope creep**, an ever-changing set of requests from clients for additional features as they wait longer and longer to see a working prototype. Other developmental models are being used in the industry to address these issues (see the Bits & Bytes sidebar, "The More Minds, the Better"). ■

**BITS&BYTES**

## The More Minds, the Better

In each phase of the SDLC, a style of interaction called *joint application development (JAD)* can be useful in creating successful, flexible results. JAD is popular because it helps designers adapt quickly to changes in program specifications. In JAD, the customer is intimately involved in the project, right from the beginning. Slow communication and lengthy feedback time make the traditional development process extremely time-consuming. In JAD "workshops," there are no communication delays. Such workshops usually include end users, developers, subject experts, observers (such as senior managers), and a facilitator. The facilitator enforces the rules of the meeting to make sure all voices are heard and that agreement is reached as quickly as possible. Also called *accelerated design* or *facilitated team techniques*, JAD's goal is to improve design quality by fostering clear communication. For more details, search the Internet using keywords like *JAD, JAD methodology,* and *JAD tutorial*.

# the life cycle of a PROGRAM

**Programming** is the process of translating a task into a series of commands that a computer will use to perform that task. It involves identifying which parts of a task a computer can perform, describing those tasks in a highly specific and complete manner, and, finally, translating this description into the language spoken by the computer's central processing unit (CPU).

Programming often begins with nothing more than a problem or a request, such as, "Can you tell me how many transfer students have applied to our college?" A proposal will then be developed for a system to solve this problem, if one does not already exist. Once a project has been deemed feasible and a plan is in place, the work of programming begins.

**How do programmers tackle a programming project?** Each programming project follows several stages, from conception to final deployment. This process is sometimes referred to as the **program development life cycle (PDLC)**:

1. *Describing the Problem:* First, programmers must develop a complete description of the problem. The problem statement identifies the task to be automated and describes how the software program will behave.
2. *Making a Plan:* The problem statement is next translated into a set of specific, sequential steps that describe exactly what the computer program must do to complete the work. The steps are known as an **algorithm**. At this stage, the algorithm is written in natural, ordinary language (such as English).
3. *Coding:* The algorithm is then translated into programming code, a language that is friendlier to humans than the *1*s and *0*s that the CPU speaks but is still highly structured. By coding the algorithm, programmers must think in terms of the operations that a CPU can perform.
4. *Debugging:* The code then goes through a process of debugging in which the programmers repair any errors found in the code.
5. *Testing and Documentation:* The software is tested by both the programming team and the people who will use the program. The results of the entire project are documented for the users and the development team. Finally, users are trained so that they can use the program efficiently.

Figure 10.4 illustrates the steps of a program life cycle.

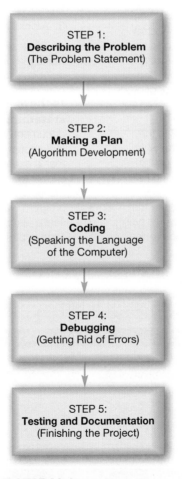

STEP 1:
**Describing the Problem**
(The Problem Statement)

STEP 2:
**Making a Plan**
(Algorithm Development)

STEP 3:
**Coding**
(Speaking the Language of the Computer)

STEP 4:
**Debugging**
(Getting Rid of Errors)

STEP 5:
**Testing and Documentation**
(Finishing the Project)

**FIGURE 10.4** The stages that each programming project follows, from conception to final deployment, are collectively referred to as the program development life cycle (PDLC).

Now that you have an overview of the process involved in developing a program, let's look at each step in more detail.

## Describing the Problem: The Problem Statement

**Why is a problem statement necessary?** The **problem statement** is the starting point of programming work. It's a clear description of what tasks the computer program must accomplish and how the program will execute those tasks and respond to unusual situations. Programmers develop problem statements so they can better understand the goals of their programming efforts.

**What kind of problems can computer programs solve?** As noted above, tasks that are repetitive, work with electronic information, and follow a series of clear steps are good candidates for computerization. This might sound as if computers only help us with the dullest and most simplistic tasks. However, many sophisticated problems can be broken down into a series of easily computerized tasks. For example, pharmaceutical companies design drugs using complex computer programs that model molecules. Using simulation software to perform "dry" chemistry, chemists can quickly "create" new drugs and determine whether they will have the desired pharmacological effects. Scientists then select the most promising choices and begin to test those compounds in the "wet" laboratory.

**What kinds of problems can computers *not* solve?** Computers can't yet act with intuition or be spontaneously creative. They can attack highly challenging problems, such as making weather predictions or playing chess, but only in a way that takes advantage of what computers do best—making fast, reliable computations. Computers don't "think" like humans do. They can only follow instructions and algorithms.

**How do programmers create problem statements?** The goal in creating a useful problem statement is to have programmers interact with users to describe three things relevant to creating a useful program:

1. **Data** is the raw input that users have at the start of the job.
2. **Information** is the result, or output, that the users require at the end of the job.

3. **Method**, described precisely, is the process of how the program converts the inputs into the correct outputs.

For example, say you want to compute how much money you'll earn working at a parking garage. Your salary is $7.50 per hour for an eight-hour shift, but if you work more than eight hours a day, you get time and a half, which is $11.25 per hour, for the overtime work. To determine how much money you make in any given day, you could multiply this in your mind, write it on a piece of paper, or use a calculator; alternatively, you could create a simple computer program to do the work for you. In this example, what are the three elements of the problem statement?

1. *Data (Input):* the data you have at the beginning of the problem, which is the number of hours you worked and the pay rate.
2. *Information (Output):* the information you need to have at the end of the problem, which is your total pay for the day.
3. *Method (Process):* the set of steps that take you from your input to your required output. In this case, the computer program would check if you worked more than eight hours. This is important because it would determine whether you would be paid overtime. If you didn't work overtime, the output would be $7.50 multiplied by the total number of hours you worked ($60.00 for eight hours). If you did work overtime, the program would calculate your pay as eight hours at $7.50 per hour for the regular part of your shift, plus an additional $11.25 multiplied by the number of overtime hours you worked.

**How do programmers handle bad inputs?** In the problem statement, programmers also must describe what the program should do if the input data is invalid or just gibberish. This part of the problem statement is referred to as **error handling**.

The problem statement also includes a **testing plan** that lists specific input numbers that the programmers would typically expect the user to enter. The plan then lists the precise output values that a perfect program would return for those input values. Later, in the testing process, programmers use the input and output data values from the testing plan to determine whether the program they created works the way it should. We discuss the testing process later in this chapter.

**Does the testing plan cover every possible use of the program?** The testing plan can't list every input the program could ever encounter. Instead, programmers work with users to identify the categories of inputs that will be encountered, find a typical example of each input category, and specify what kind of output must be generated. In the parking garage pay example, the error-handling process would describe what the program would do if you happened to enter "–8" (or any other nonsense character) for the number of hours you worked. The error handling would specify whether the program would return a negative value, prompt you to reenter the input, or shut down.

We could expect three categories of inputs in the parking garage example. The user might enter:

1. A negative number for hours worked that day
2. A positive number equal to or less than eight
3. A positive number greater than eight

The testing plan would describe how the error would be managed or how the output would be generated for each input category.

**Is there a standard format for a problem statement?** Most companies have their own format for documenting a problem statement. However, all problem statements include the same basic components: the data that is expected to be provided (inputs), the information that is expected to be produced (outputs), the rules for transforming the input into output (processing), an explanation of how the program will respond if users enter data that doesn't make sense (error handling), and a testing plan. Figure 10.5 shows a sample problem statement for our parking garage example.

FIGURE 10.5

**Complete Problem Statement for the Parking Garage Example**

| | PROBLEM STATEMENT | | |
|---|---|---|---|
| **Program Goal** | Compute the total pay for a fixed number of hours worked at a parking garage. | | |
| **Input** | Number of hours worked (a positive number) | | |
| **Output** | Total pay earned (a positive number) | | |
| **Process** | Total pay earned is computed as $7.50 per hour for the first eight hours worked each day. Any hours worked consecutively beyond the first eight are calculated at $11.25 per hour. | | |
| **Error Handling** | The input (number of hours worked) must be a positive real number. If it is a negative number or another unacceptable character, the program will force the user to reenter the information. | | |
| **Testing Plan** | **INPUT** | **OUTPUT** | **NOTES** |
| | 8 | 8*7.50 | Testing positive input |
| | 3 | 3*7.50 | Testing positive input |
| | 12 | 8*7.50 + 4*11.25 | Testing overtime input |
| | –6 | Error message/ask user to reenter value | Handling error |

ACTIVE HELPDESK

**Understanding Software Programming**

In this Active Helpdesk call, you'll play the role of a helpdesk staffer, fielding calls about the life cycle of a program, the role a problem statement plays in programming, how programmers create algorithms and move from algorithm to code to the *1*s and *0*s a CPU can understand, and the steps involved in completing the program.

SOUND BYTE

**Programming for End Users**

In this Sound Byte, you'll be guided through the creation of a macro in the Microsoft Office suite. You'll learn how Office enables you to program with macros in order to customize and extend the capabilities it offers.

## Making a Plan: Algorithm Development

**How does the process start?** Once programmers understand exactly what the program must do and have created the final problem statement, they can begin developing a detailed algorithm—a set of specific, sequential steps that describe in natural language exactly what the computer program must do to complete its task. Let's look at some ways in which programmers design and test algorithms.

**Do algorithms appear only in programming?** Although the term *algorithm* may sound like it would fall only under the domain of computing, you design and execute algorithms in your daily life. For example, say you're planning your morning. You know you need to

1. Get gas for your car,
2. Pick up a mocha latte at the café, and
3. Stop by the bookstore and buy a textbook before your 9 a.m. accounting lecture

You quickly think over the costs and decide it will take $150 to buy all three. In what order will you accomplish all these tasks? How do you decide? Should you try to minimize the distance you'll travel or the time you'll spend driving? What happens if you forget your credit card?

Figure 10.6 presents an algorithm you could develop to make decisions about how to accomplish these tasks. This algorithm lays out a specific plan that encapsulates all of the choices you need to make in the course of completing a particular task and shows the specific sequence in which these tasks will occur. At any point in the morning, you could gather your current data (your inputs)—"I have $20 and my Visa card, but the ATM machine is down"—and the algorithm would tell you unambiguously what your next step should be.

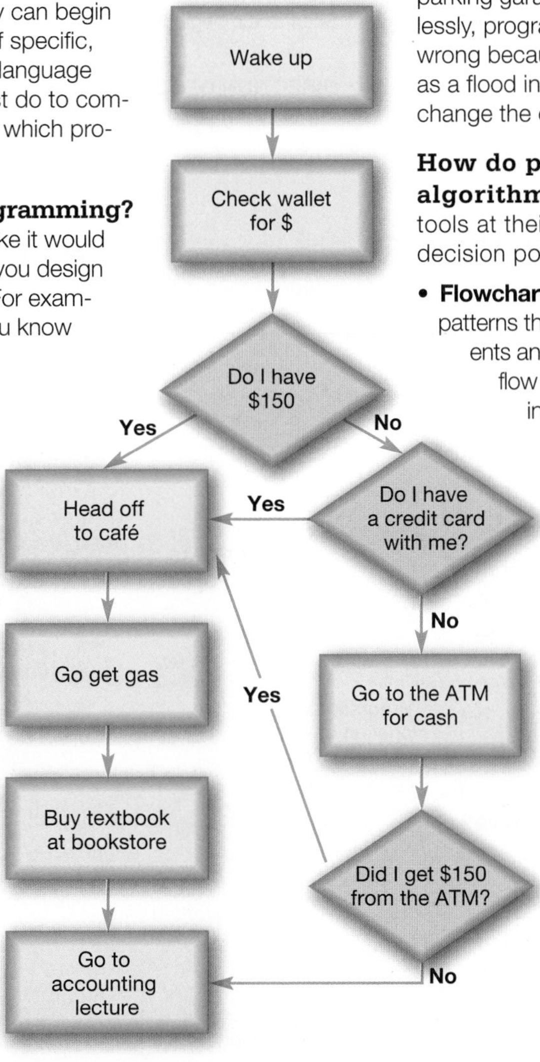

**FIGURE 10.6** An algorithm you might use to plan your morning would include all of the decisions you might need to make and would show the specific sequence in which these steps would occur.

**What are the limitations of algorithms?** An algorithm is a series of steps that's completely known: At each point, we know *exactly* what step to take next. However, not all problems can be described as a fixed sequence of predetermined steps; some involve random and unpredictable events. For example, although the program that computes your parking garage take-home pay each day works flawlessly, programs that predict stock prices are often wrong because many random events (inputs), such as a flood in India or a shipping delay in Texas, can change the outcomes (outputs).

**How do programmers represent an algorithm?** Programmers have several visual tools at their disposal to help them document the decision points and flow of their algorithms:

- **Flowcharts** provide a visual representation of the patterns the algorithm comprises. Figure 10.6 presents an example of a flowchart used to depict the flow of an algorithm. Specific shape symbols indicate program behaviors and decision types. Diamonds indicate that a yes/no decision will be performed, and rectangles indicate an instruction to follow. Figure 10.7 lists additional flowcharting symbols and explains what they indicate. Many software packages make it easy for programmers to create and modify flowcharts. Microsoft Visio is one popular flowcharting program.
- **Pseudocode** is a text-based approach to documenting an algorithm. In pseudocode, words describe the actions that the algorithm will take. Pseudocode is organized like an outline, with differing levels of indentation to indicate the flow of actions within the program. There is no standard vocabulary for pseudocode. Programmers use a combination of common words in their natural language and the special words that are commands in the programming language they're using.

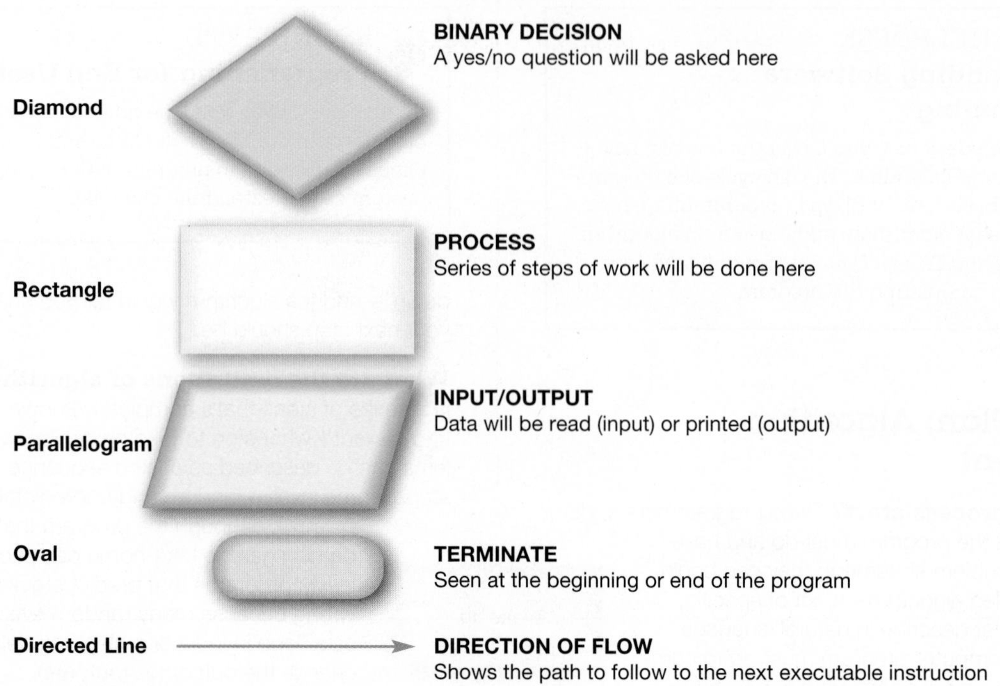


**FIGURE 10.7** Standard Symbols Used in Flowcharts

# Developing the Algorithm: Decision Making and Design

**How do programmers handle complex algorithms?** When programmers develop an algorithm, they convert the problem statement into a list of steps the program will take.

Problems that are complex involve choices, so they can't follow a sequential list of steps. Algorithms therefore include **decision points**, places where the program must choose from a list of actions based on the value of a certain input.

Figure 10.8 shows the steps of the algorithm in our parking garage example. If the number of hours you worked in a given day is eight or less, the program performs one simple calculation: It multiplies the number of hours worked by $7.50. If you worked more than eight hours in a day, the program takes a different path and performs a different calculation.

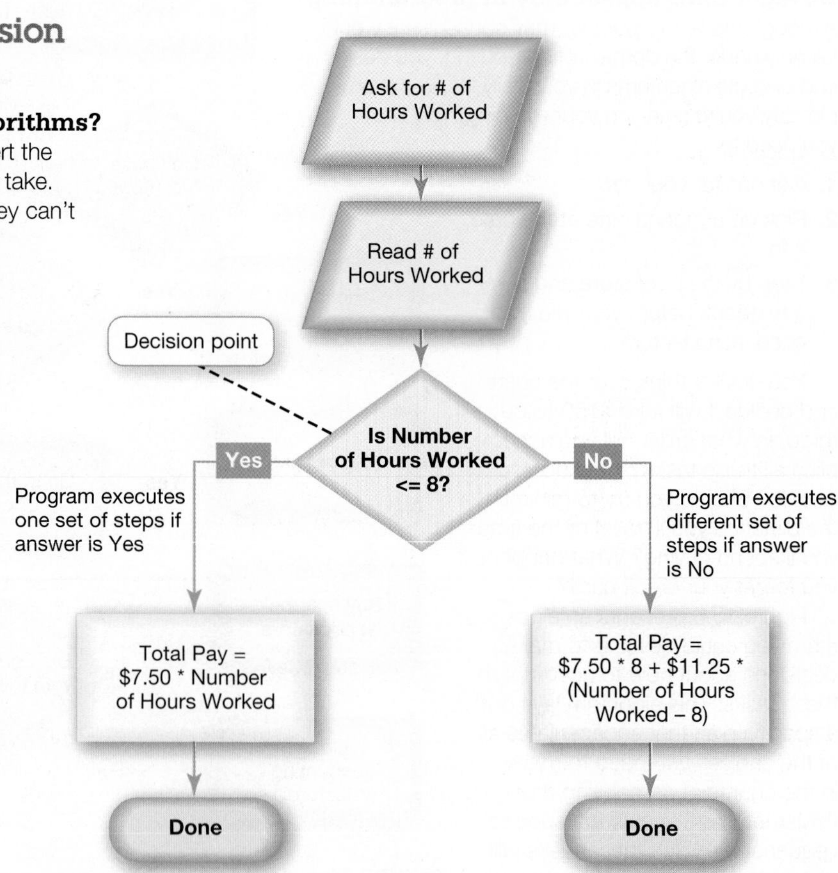


**FIGURE 10.8** Decision points force the program to travel down one branch of the algorithm or another.

**What kinds of decision points are there?** There are two main types of decisions that change the flow of an algorithm:

1. *Binary decisions:* One decision point that appears often in algorithms is like a "fork in the road." Such decision points are called **binary decisions** because they can be answered in one of only two ways: *yes* (true) or *no* (false). For example, the answer to the question, "Did you work at most eight hours today?"(Is number of hours worked <= 8 hours?), shown in Figure 10.8, is a binary

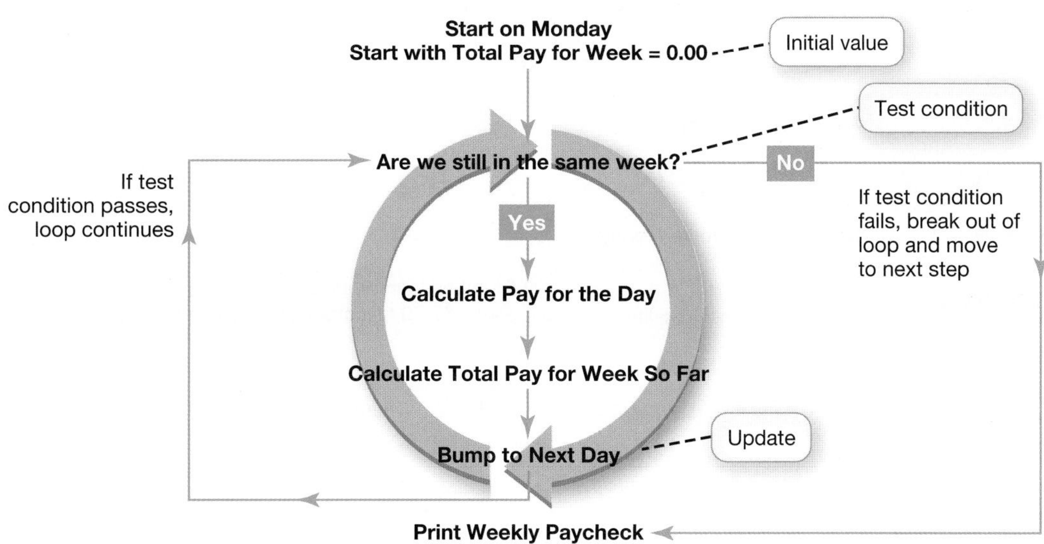


**FIGURE 10.9** We stay in the loop until the test condition is no longer true. We then break free from the loop and move on to the next step in the algorithm, which is outside of the loop.

decision because the answer can be only *yes* or *no*. If the answer is *yes*, the program follows one sequence of steps; if the answer is *no*, it follows a different path.

2. *Loops:* A second decision point that often appears in algorithms is a repeating loop. In a **loop**, a question is asked, and if the answer is *yes*, a set of actions is performed. Once the set of actions has finished, the question is asked again, creating a loop. As long as the answer to the question is *yes*, the algorithm continues to loop around and repeat the same set of actions. When the answer to the question is *no*, the algorithm breaks free of the looping and moves on to the first step that follows the loop.

In our parking garage example, the algorithm would require a loop if you wanted to compute the total pay you earned in a full week of work rather than in just a single day. For each day of the week, you would want to perform the same set of steps. Figure 10.9 shows how the idea of looping would be useful in this part of our parking garage program. On Monday, the program would set the Total Pay value to $0.00. It would then perform the following set of steps:

1. Read the number of hours worked that day.
2. Determine whether you qualified for overtime pay.
3. Compute the pay earned that day.
4. Add that day's pay to the total pay for the week.

On Tuesday, the algorithm would loop back, repeating the same sequence of steps it performed on Monday, adding the amount you earned on Tuesday to the Total Pay amount. The algorithm would continue to perform this loop for each day (seven times) until it hits Monday again. At that point, the decision "Are we still in the same week?" would become false. The program would stop, calculate the total pay for the entire week of work, and print the weekly paycheck.

As you can see, there are three important features to look for in a loop:

1. A beginning point, or **initial value**. In our example, the total pay for the week starts at an initial value of $0.00.
2. A set of actions that will be performed. In our example, the algorithm computes the daily pay each time it passes through the loop.
3. A **test condition**, or a check to see whether the loop is completed. In our example, the algorithm should run the loop seven times, no more and no fewer.

Every higher-level programming language supports both making binary yes/no decisions and handling repeating loops. **Control structures** is the general term used for keywords in a programming language that allow the programmer to direct the flow of the program based on a decision.

**How do programmers create algorithms for specific tasks?** It's difficult for human beings to force their problem-solving skills into the highly structured, detailed algorithms that computing machines require. Therefore, several different methodologies have been developed to support programmers, including *top-down design* and *object-oriented analysis*.

## Top-Down Design

**What is top-down design? Top-down design** is a systematic approach in which a problem is broken into a series of high-level tasks. In top-down design, programmers apply the same strategy repeatedly, breaking each task into successively more detailed subtasks. They continue until they have a sequence of steps that are close to the types of commands allowed by the programming language they'll use for coding. Previous coding experience helps programmers know the

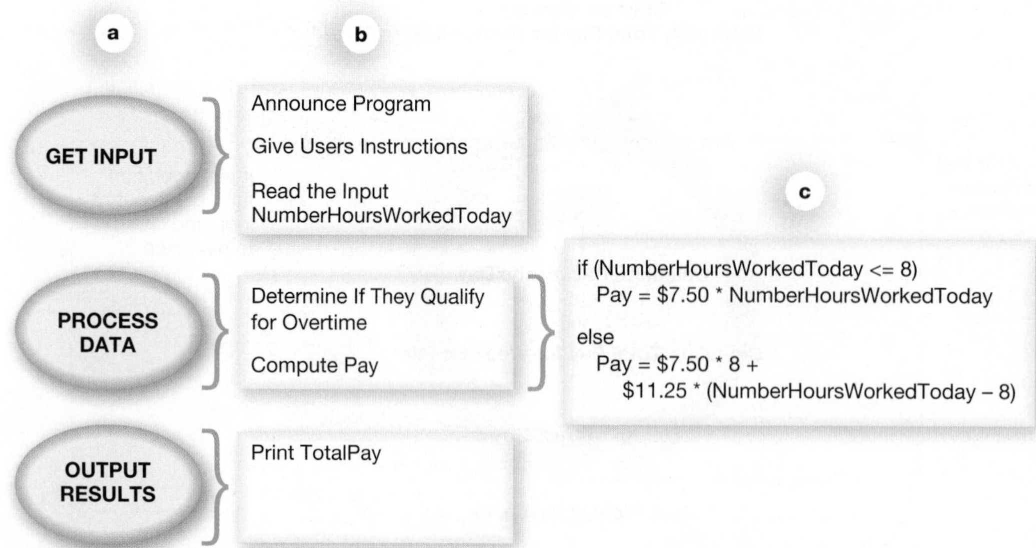


**FIGURE 10.10** (a) A top-down design is applied to the highest level of task in our parking garage example, (b) the tasks are further refined into subtasks, and (c) subtasks are refined into a sequence of instructions—an algorithm.

appropriate level of detail to specify in an algorithm generated by top-down design.

**How is top-down design used in programming?** Let's consider our parking garage example again. Initially, top-down design would identify three high-level tasks: Get Input, Process Data, and Output Results (see Figure 10.10a).

Applying top-down design to the first operation, Get Input, we'd produce the more detailed sequence of steps shown in the first step of Figure 10.10b: Announce Program, Give Users Instructions, and Read the Input NumberHours WorkedToday. When we try to refine each of these steps, we find that they are just print-and-read statements and that most every programming language will support them. Therefore, the operation Get Input has been converted to an algorithm.

Next, we move to the second high-level task, Process Data, and break it into subtasks. In this case, we need to determine whether overtime hours were worked and to compute the pay accordingly. We continue to apply top-down design on all tasks until we can no longer break tasks into subtasks, as shown in Figure 10.10c.

## Object-Oriented Analysis

**What is object-oriented analysis?** With **object-oriented analysis**, programmers first identify all the categories of inputs that are part of the problem the program is meant to solve. These categories are called **classes**. With the object-oriented approach, the majority of design time is spent identifying the classes required to solve the problem, modeling them, and thinking about what relationships they need to be able to have with each other. Constructing the algorithm becomes a process of enabling the objects to interact. For example, the classes in our parking garage example might include a TimeCard class and an Employee class.

## BITS&BYTES

### Competitive Coding

College hackathons—coding events that take place in a single day or a single weekend—are more popular than ever. The PennApps Hackathon at the University of Pennsylvania sees over 1,000 programmers attend from over 100 universities. The recent grand prize was $10,000, but in all, over $30,000 was given away along with sought-after meetings with engineers at Google, Dropbox, and more. Hackathons to create software with a purpose are appearing more and more too. The National Day of Civic Hacking (**hackforchange.org**) and Random Hacks of Kindness (**rhok.org**) are both hackathons to help develop solutions to local and global needs.

Hackathons can help you build your programming skills incredibly quickly. If you don't have a team, most hacakthons link you up with other programmers on the spot. Visit Challenge Post (**challengepost.com**) to find the coding events nearest you—and join in the competition!

Classes are defined by

- Information (data) with the class and
- Actions (methods) associated with the class

For example, as shown in Figure 10.11, *data* for an Employee would include a Name, Address, and Social Security Number, whereas the *methods* for the Employee would be GoToWork(), LeaveWork(), and CollectPay(). The data of the class describes the class, so classes are often characterized as nouns, whereas methods are often characterized as verbs—the ways that the class acts and communicates with other classes.

Programmers may need to create several different examples of a class. Each of these examples is an **object**. In Figure 10.11, John Doe, Jane Doe, and Bill McGillicutty are each Employee objects (specific examples of the Employee class). Each object from a given class is described by the same pieces of data and has the same methods; for example, John, Jane, and Bill are all Employees and can use the GoToWork(), LeaveWork(), and CollectPay() methods. However, because they all have different pay grades (PayGrade 5, PayGrade 10, and PayGrade 4, respectively) and different Social Security numbers, they are all unique objects.

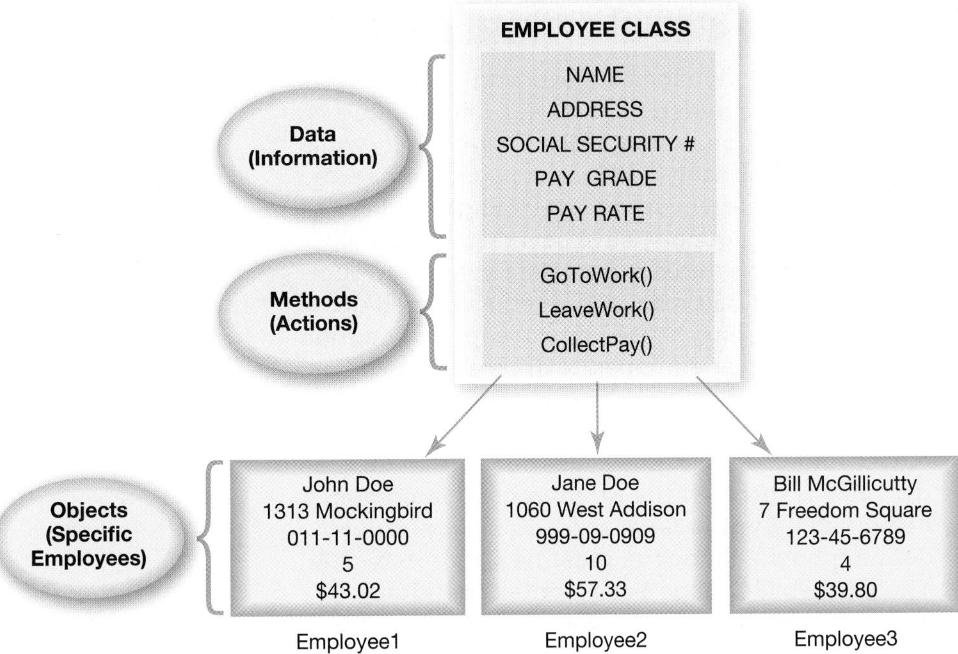


**FIGURE 10.11** The Employee class includes the complete set of information (data) and actions (methods or behaviors) that describe an Employee.

**Why would a developer select the object-oriented approach over top-down design?** An important aspect of object-oriented design is that it leads to **reusability**. Object-oriented analysis forces programmers to think in general terms about their problem, which tends to lead to more general and reusable solutions. Because object-oriented design generates a family of classes for each project, programmers can easily reuse existing classes from other projects, enabling them to produce new code quickly.

**How does a programmer take advantage of reusability?** Programmers must study the relationships between objects. Hierarchies of objects can be built quickly in object-oriented languages using the mechanism of inheritance. **Inheritance** means that a new class can automatically pick up all the data and methods of an existing class and then can extend and customize those to fit its own specific needs.

The original class is called the **base class**, and the new, modified class is called the **derived class**, as illustrated in Figure 10.12. You can compare this with making cookies.

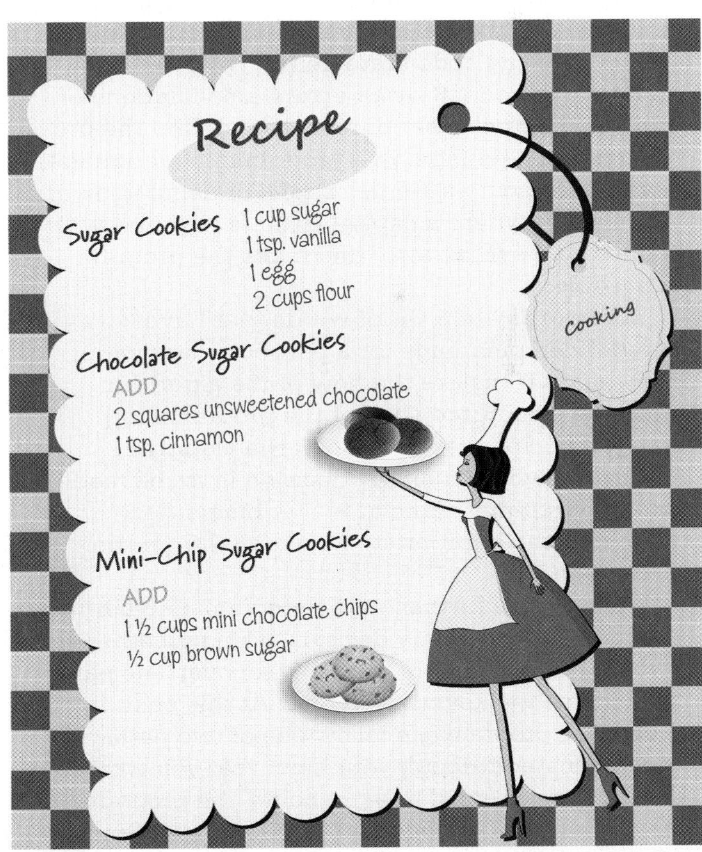


**FIGURE 10.12** In object-oriented programming, a single base class—for example, Sugar Cookies—helps you quickly create many additional derived classes, such as Chocolate and Mini-Chip Sugar Cookies. *(Nataliya Dolotko/Fotolia)*

# DIG DEEPER

## The Building Blocks of Programming Languages: Syntax, Keywords, Data Types, and Operators

Programming languages are evolving constantly. New languages emerge every year, and existing languages change dramatically. Therefore, it would be extremely difficult and time consuming for programmers to learn every programming language. However, all languages have several common elements: rules of syntax, a set of keywords, a group of supported data types, and a set of allowed operators. By learning these four concepts, a programmer will be better equipped to approach any new language.

The transition from a well-designed algorithm to working code requires a clear understanding of the rules (syntax) of the programming language being used. **Syntax** is an agreed-on set of rules defining how a language must be structured. The English language has a syntax that defines which symbols are words (for example, *gorilla* is a word but *allirog* is not) and what order words and symbols (such as semicolons and commas) must follow.

Likewise, all programming languages have a formal syntax that programmers must follow when creating code **statements**, which are sentences in a code. **Syntax errors** are violations of the strict, precise set of rules that define the programming language. In a programming language, even misplacing a single comma or using a lowercase letter where a capital letter is required will generate a syntax error and make the program unusable.

**Keywords** are a set of words that have predefined meanings for a particular language. Keywords translate the flow of the algorithm into the structured code of the programming language. For example, when the algorithm indicates where a binary decision must be made, the programmer translates that binary decision into the appropriate keyword(s) from the language.

To illustrate further, in the programming language C++, the binary decision asking whether you worked enough hours to qualify for overtime pay would use the keywords **if else**. At this point in the code, the program can follow one of two paths: If you indicated through your input that you worked fewer than or equal to eight hours, the program takes one path; if not (else), it follows another. Figure 10.13 shows this binary decision in the algorithm and the corresponding lines of C++ code that use the "if else" keywords.

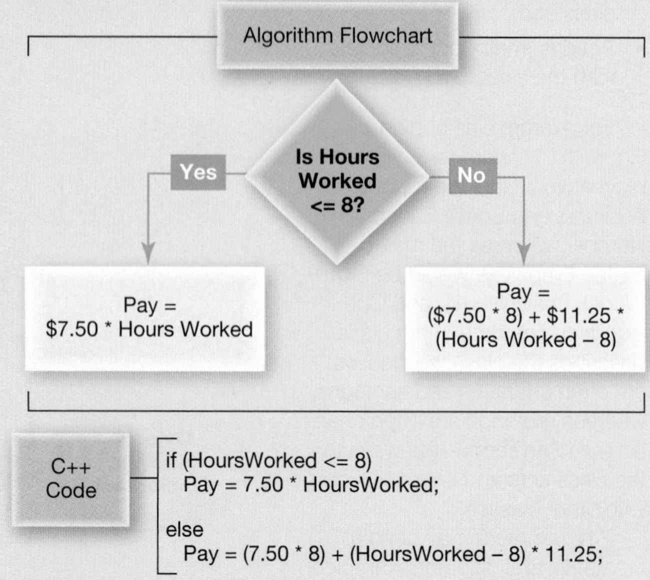


**FIGURE 10.13** The binary decision in the algorithm has been converted into C++ code.

Loops are likewise translated from algorithm to code by using the appropriate keyword from the language. For example, in the programming language Visual Basic, programmers use the keywords **For** and **Next** to implement a loop. After the keyword For, an input or output item is given a starting value. Then the statements, or "sentences," in the body of the loop are executed. When the command Next is run, the program returns to the For statement and increments the value of the input or output item by 1. It then tests that the value is still inside the range given. If it is, the body of the loop is executed again. This continues until the value of the input or output item is outside the range listed. The loop is then ended, and the statement that follows the loop is run.

In the parking garage example, the following lines of Visual Basic code loop to sum up the total pay for the entire week:

```
For Day = 1 to 7
    Total Pay = Total Pay + Pay;
Next Day
```

In this statement, the starting value of the input item Day is 1, and the program loops through until Day equals 7. Then, when Day equals 8, we move out of the loop, to the line of code that comes after the loop.

Often, a quick overview of a language's keywords can reveal the unique focus of that language. For example, the language C++ includes the keywords *public, private,* and *protected,* which indicate that the language includes a mechanism for controlling security.

Each time programmers want to store data in their program, they must ask the OS for storage space at a RAM location. **Data types** describe the kind of data being stored at the memory location. Each programming language has its own data types (although there is some degree of overlap). For example, C++ includes data types that represent integers, real numbers, characters, and Boolean (true–false) values. These C++ data types show up in code statements as *int* for integer, *float* for real numbers, *char* for characters, and *bool* for Boolean values.

Because it takes more room to store a real number such as 18,743.23 than it does to store the integer 1, programmers use data types in their code to indicate to the OS how much memory it needs to allocate. Programmers must be familiar with all the data types available in the language so that they can assign the most appropriate one for each input and output value, without wasting memory space.

**Operators** are the coding symbols that represent the fundamental actions of the language. Each programming language has its own set of operators. Many languages include common algebraic operators such as +, –, *, and / to represent the mathematical operations of addition, subtraction, multiplication, and division, respectively. Some languages, however, introduce new symbols as operators. The language APL (short for A Programmer's Language) was designed to solve multidimensional mathematical problems. APL includes less familiar operators such as rho, sigma, and iota, each representing a complex mathematical operation. Because it contains many specialized operators, APL requires programmers to use a special keyboard (see Figure 10.14).

Programming languages sometimes include other unique operators. The C++ operator >>, for example, is used to tell the computer to read data from the keyboard or from a file. The C++ operator && is used to tell the computer to check whether two statements are both true. "Is your age greater than 20 AND less than 30?" is a question that requires the use of the && operator.

In the following C++ code, several operators are being used. The > operator checks whether the number of hours worked is greater than 0. The && operator checks that the number of hours worked is simultaneously positive AND less than or equal to 8. If that happens, then the = operator sets the output Pay to equal the number of hours multiplied by $7.50:

```
if (Hours > 0 && Hours <= 8)
    Pay = Hours * 7.50;
```

Knowing operators such as these, as well as the other common elements described earlier, helps programmers learn new programming languages.

**FIGURE 10.14** APL requires programmers to use an APL keyboard that includes the many specialized operators in the language.

For example, you have a basic recipe for sugar cookies (base class: Sugar Cookies). However, in your family, some people like chocolate-flavored sugar cookies (derived class: Chocolate Sugar Cookies), and others like mini-chip sugar cookies (derived class: Mini-Chip Sugar Cookies). All the cookies share the attributes of the basic sugar cookie. However, instead of creating two entirely new recipes—one for chocolate cookies and one for mini-chip cookies—the two varieties inherit the basic sugar cookie (base class) recipe; the recipe is then customized to make the chocolate and mini-chip sugar cookies (derived classes).

## Coding: Speaking the Language of the Computer

**How is a person's idea translated into CPU instructions?** Once programmers create an algorithm, they select the best programming language for the problem and then translate the algorithm into that language. Translating an algorithm into a programming language is the act of **coding**. Programming languages are somewhat readable by humans but then are translated into patterns of *1*s and *0*s to be understood by the CPU.

Although programming languages free programmers from having to think in binary language—the *1*s and *0*s that computers understand—they still force programmers to translate the ideas of the algorithm into a highly precise format. Programming languages are quite limited, allowing programmers to use only a few specific keywords, while demanding a consistent structure.

**How exactly do programmers move from algorithm to code?** Once programmers have an algorithm, in the form of either a flowchart or a series of pseudocode statements, they identify the key pieces of information the algorithm uses to make decisions:

- What steps are required for the calculation of new information?
- What is the exact sequence of the steps?
- Are there points where decisions have to be made?
- What kinds of decisions are made?
- Are there places where the same steps are repeated several times?

SOUND BYTE
**Looping Around the IDE**

In this Sound Byte, you'll work in the Microsoft Visual Studio IDE with the C++ programming language and examine how the basic control structures of programming languages work.

Once programmers identify the required information and the flow of how it will be changed by each step of the algorithm, they can begin converting the algorithm into computer code in a specific programming language.

**What exactly is a programming language?** A **programming language** is a kind of "code" for the set of instructions the CPU knows how to perform. Computer programming languages use special words and strict rules so that programmers can control the CPU without having to know all its hardware details.

**What kinds of programming languages are there?** Programming languages are classified into several major groupings, sometimes referred to as *generations*. With each generation of language development, programmers have been relieved of more of the burden of keeping track of what the hardware requires. The earliest languages—assembly language and machine languages—required the programmer to know a great deal about how the computer was constructed internally and how it stored data. Programming is becoming easier as languages continue to become more closely matched to how humans think about problems.

**How have modern programming languages evolved?** There are five major categories of languages:

1. A **first-generation language (1GL)** is the actual **machine language** of a CPU, the sequence of bits (*1*s and *0*s) that the CPU understands.
2. A **second-generation language (2GL)** is also known as an **assembly language**. Assembly languages allow programmers to write their programs using a set of short, English-like commands that speak directly to the CPU and that give the programmer direct control of hardware resources.
3. A **third-generation language (3GL)** uses symbols and commands to help programmers tell the computer what to do. This makes 3GL languages easier for humans to read and remember. Most programming languages today, including BASIC, FORTRAN, COBOL, C/C++, and Java, are considered third generation.
4. **Fourth-generation languages (4GLs)** include database query languages and report generators. **Structured Query Language (SQL)** is a database programming language that is an example of a 4GL. The following SQL command would check a huge table of data on the employees and build a new table showing all those employees who worked overtime:

```
SELECT EmployeeName, TotalHours FROM
EMPLOYEES WHERE "TotalHours" Total
More Than 8
```

to collect and process the information for the next day. When the seventh day of data has been processed, the Day variable will be bumped up to the next value, 8. This causes the program to fail the test (Day <= 7?). At that point, the program exits the loop, prints the results, and quits.

**Are there ways in which programmers can make their code more useful for the future?** One aspect of converting an algorithm into good code is the programmer's ability to design general code that can easily be adapted to new settings. Sections of code that will be used repeatedly, with only slight modification, can be packaged into reusable "containers" or components. Depending on the language, these reusable components are referred to as *functions, methods, procedures, subroutines, modules,* or *packages*.

In our program, we could create a function that implements the overtime pay rule. As it stands in Figure 10.16, the code works only in situations in which the hourly pay is exactly \$7.50 and the bonus pay is exactly \$11.25. However, if we rewrote this part of the processing rules as a function, we could have code that would work for any base pay rate and any overtime rate. If the base pay rate or overtime rate changed, the function would use whichever values it was given as input to compute the output pay variable. Such a function, as shown in Figure 10.17, may be reused in many settings without changing any of the code.

## Compilation

**How does a programmer move from code in a programming language to the 1s and 0s the CPU can understand? Compilation** is the process by which code is converted into machine language—the language the CPU can understand. A **compiler** is a program that understands both the syntax of the programming language and the exact structure of the CPU and its machine language. It can "read" the **source code**, which comprises the instructions programmers have written in the higher-level language and can translate the source code directly into machine language—the binary patterns that will execute commands on the CPU. You can learn more about the details of the binary number system in the Technology in Focus section, "Under the Hood" (see page 298).

Each programming language has its own compiler. It's a program that you purchase and install just like any other software on your system. Separate versions of the compiler are required if you want to compile code that will run on separate processor types. One version of a compiler would create finished programs for a Sun SPARC T5 processor, for example, and another version of the compiler would create programs for an Intel i7 CPU.

At this stage, once the compiler has generated the executable program, the programmers have a program to distribute. An **executable program**, the binary sequence that instructs

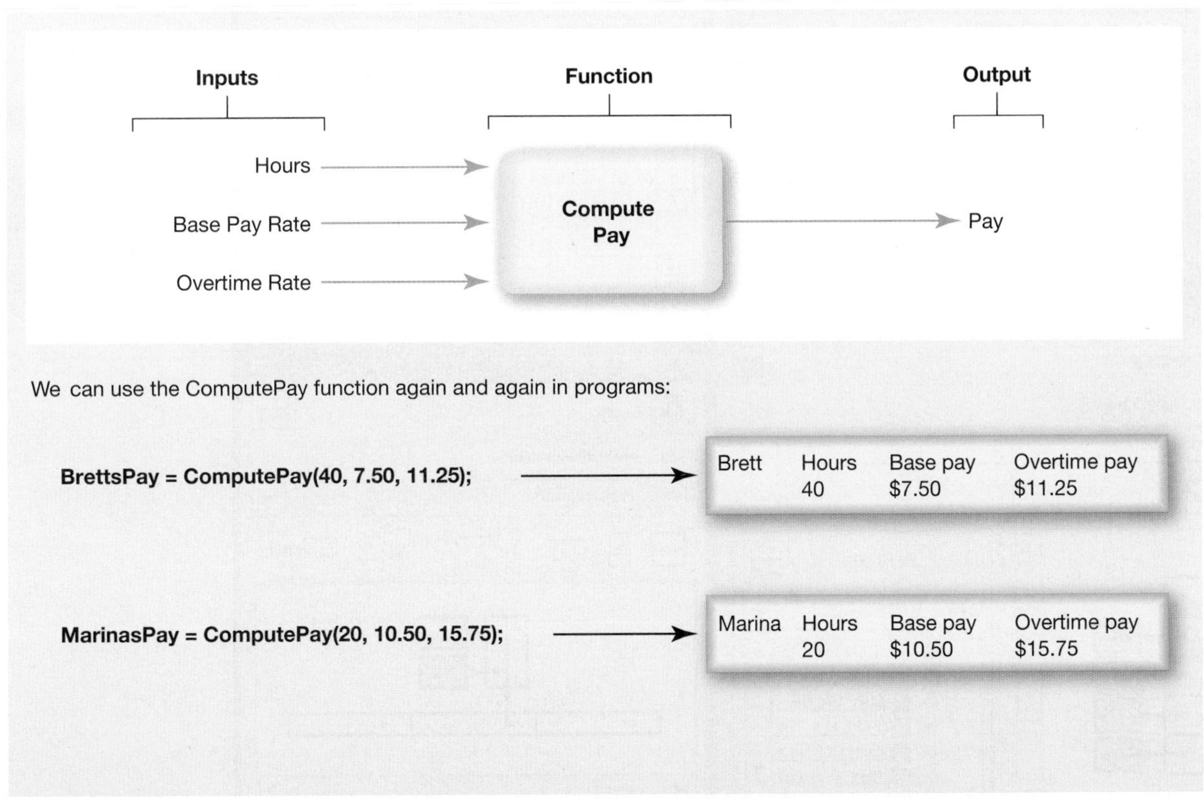


**FIGURE 10.17** A function is a reusable component that can be used in different settings.

the CPU to run their code, can't be read by human eyes because they're pure binary codes. They're stored as *.exe or *.com files on Windows systems.

**Does every programming language have a compiler?** Some programming languages don't have a compiler but use an interpreter instead. An **interpreter** translates the source code into an intermediate form, line by line. Each line is then executed as it's translated. The compilation process takes longer than the interpretation process because in compilation, all the lines of source code are translated into machine language before any lines are executed. However, the finished compiled program runs faster than an interpreted program because the interpreter is constantly translating and executing as it goes.

If producing the fastest executable program is important, programmers will choose a language that uses a compiler instead of an interpreter. For development environments in which many changes are still being made to the code, interpreters have an advantage because programmers don't have to wait for the entire program to be recompiled each time they make a change. With interpreters, programmers can immediately see the results of their program changes as they're making them.

## Coding Tools: Integrated Development Environments

**What tools make the coding process easier?** Modern programming is supported by a collection of tools that make the writing and testing of software easier. An **integrated development environment (IDE)** is a developmental tool that helps programmers write and test their programs. One IDE can often be configured to support many different languages. Figure 10.18 shows the IDE jGRASP working with Java code.

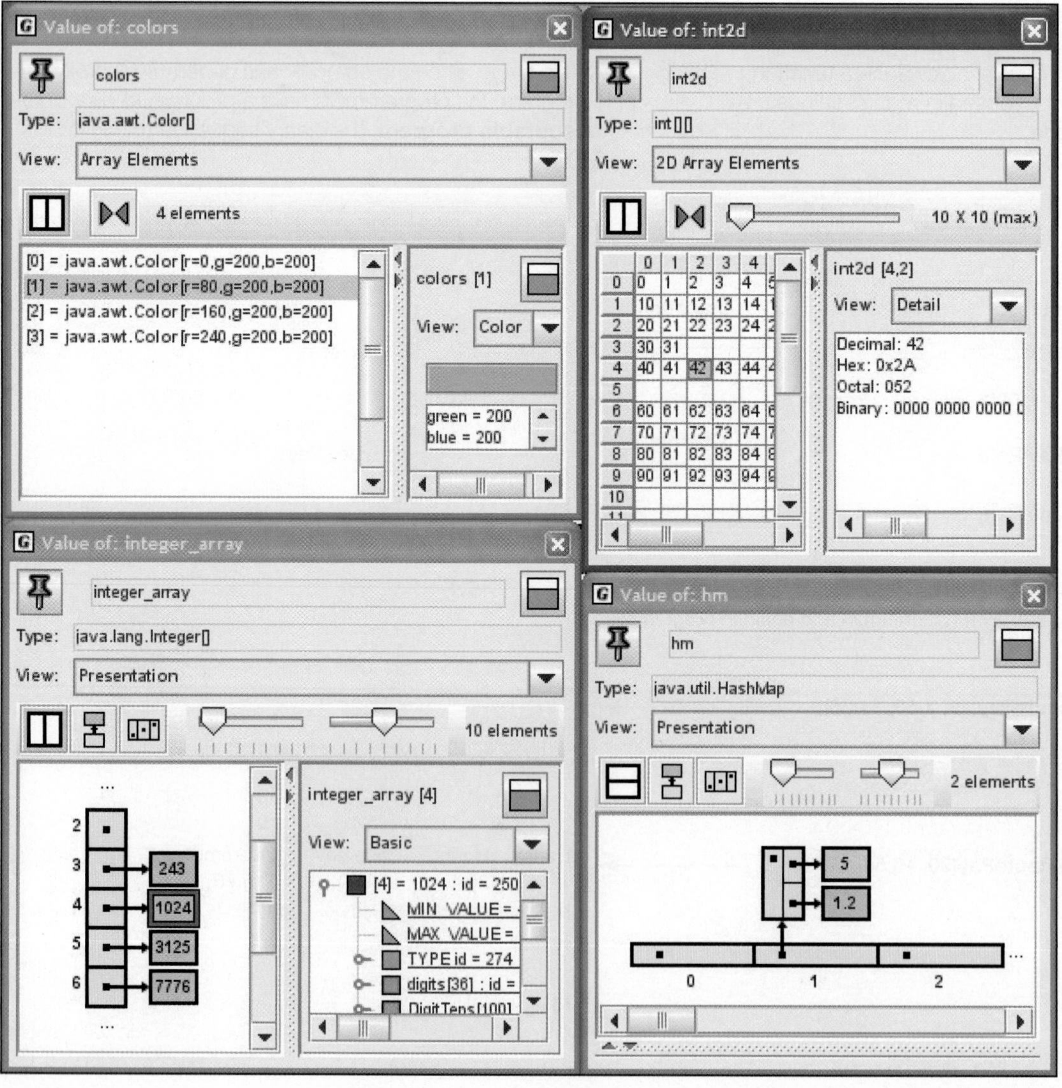


**FIGURE 10.18** The jGRASP IDE is a free tool that helps the programmer visualize the code as it runs to help eliminate logical errors. *(Courtesy of Auburn University)*

**How does an IDE help programmers when they're typing the code? Code editing** is the step in which a programmer physically types the code into the computer. An IDE includes an **editor**, a special tool that helps programmers as they enter the code, highlighting keywords and alerting the programmers to typos. Modern IDE editors also automatically indent the code correctly, align sections of code appropriately, and apply color to code comments to remind programmers that these lines won't be executed as code. In addition, IDEs provide auto-completion of code, suggest solutions to common errors, and more.

**How does the IDE help programmers after code editing is finished?** Editing is complete when the entire program has been keyed into the editor. At that time, the programmer clicks a button in the IDE, and the compilation process begins. The IDE shows how the compilation is progressing, which line is currently being compiled, how many syntax errors have been identified, and how many warnings have been generated. A warning is a suggestion from the compiler that the code might not work in the way the programmer intended even though there's no formal syntax error on the line.

A syntax error is a violation of the strict, precise set of rules that define the language. Programmers create syntax errors when they misspell keywords (such as typing BEEGIN instead of BEGIN) or use an operator incorrectly (such as typing x = , y + 2 instead of x = y + 2). Once compilation is finished, the IDE presents all of the syntax errors in one list. The programmer can then click any item in the list to see a detailed explanation of the type of error. When the programmer double-clicks an item in the list, the editor jumps to the line of code that contains the error, enabling the programmer to repair syntax errors quickly.

**FIGURE 10.19** Debugging—the process of correcting errors in a program—combines logic with an understanding of the problem to be solved. *(ARTSILENSEcom/Shutterstock)*

## Debugging: Getting Rid of Errors

**What is debugging?** Once the program has compiled without syntax errors, it has met all of the syntax rules of the language. However, this doesn't mean that the program behaves in a logical way or that it appropriately addresses the task the algorithm described. If programmers made errors in the strategy used in the algorithm or in how they translated the algorithm to code, problems will occur. The process of running the program over and over to find and repair errors and to make sure the program behaves in the way it should is termed **debugging** (see Figure 10.19).

**How do programmers know the program has solved the problem?** At this point in the process, the testing plan that was documented as part of the problem statement becomes critically important to programmers. The testing plan clearly lists input and output values, showing how the users expect the program to behave in each input situation. It's important that the testing plan contain enough specific examples to test every part of the program.

In the parking garage problem, we want to make sure the program calculates the correct pay for a day when you worked eight or fewer hours and for a day when you worked more than eight hours. Each of these input values forces the program to make different decisions in its processing path. To be certain the program works as intended, programmers try every possible path.

For example, once we can successfully compile the example code for the parking garage problem, we can begin to use our testing plan. The testing plan indicates that an input of 3 for NumberHoursWorkedToday must produce an output of Pay = 3 * $7.50 = $22.50. In testing, we run the program and make sure that an input value of 3 yields an output value of $22.50. To check that the processing path involving overtime is correct, we input a value of 12 hours. That input must produce Pay = 8 * $7.50 + (12 – 8) * $11.25 = $105.00.

A complete testing plan includes sample inputs that exercise all the error handling required as well as all the processing paths. Therefore, we would also want to check how the program behaves when NumberHoursWorkedToday is entered as –6.

**If the testing plan reveals errors, why does the program compile?** The compiler can't think through code or decide whether what the programmer wrote is logical. The compiler can only make sure that the specific rules of the language are followed.

For example, if in the parking garage problem we happened to type the if statement as

```
if (NumberHoursWorkedToday > 88)
   //Use the Overtime Pay rule
```

instead of

```
if (NumberHoursWorkedToday > 8)
   //Use the Overtime Pay rule
```

the compiler wouldn't see a problem. It doesn't seem strange to the compiler that you only get overtime after working 88 hours a day. These **logical errors** in the problem are caught only when the program executes.

Another kind of error caught when the program executes is a **runtime error**. For example, it's easy for a programmer to accidentally write code that occasionally divides by zero, a big "no-no" mathematically! That kind of forbidden operation generates a runtime error message.

## BITS&BYTES

### Many Languages on Display

At the 99 Bottles of Beer site **99-bottles-of-beer.net**, you can find a simple program that displays the lyrics to the song "99 Bottles of Beer on the Wall." If you've ever sat through round after round of this song on a long school bus trip, you know how repetitive it is. That means the code to write this song can take advantage of looping statements. This site presents the program in more than 1,400 different languages. Also check out the Rosetta Code wiki (**rosettacode.org/wiki/Rosetta_Code**) to see solutions to many other programming problems in a wide variety of languages.

**Are there tools that help programmers find logic errors?** Most IDEs include a tool called a **debugger** that helps programmers dissect a program as it runs. The debugger pauses the program while it's executing and allows the programmer to examine the values of all the variables. The programmer can then run the program in slow motion, moving it forward just one line at a time. This lets the programmer see the exact sequence of steps being executed and the outcome of each calculation. He or she can then isolate the precise place in which a logical error occurs, correct the error, and recompile the program.

## Testing and Documentation: Finishing the Project

**What is the first round of testing for a program?** Once debugging has detected all the runtime errors in the code, it's time for users to test the program. This process is called *internal testing*. In internal testing, a group within the software company uses the program in every way it can imagine—including how the program was intended to be used and in ways only new users might think up. The internal testing group makes sure the program behaves as described in the original testing plan. Any differences in how the program responds are reported back to the programming team, which makes the final revisions and updates to the code.

The next round of testing is *external testing*. In this testing round, people like the ones who eventually will purchase and use the software must work with it to determine whether it matches their original vision.

**What other testing does the code undergo?** Before its final commercial release, software is often provided free or at a reduced cost in a **beta version** to certain test sites or to interested users. By providing users with a beta version of software, programmers can collect information about remaining errors in the code and make a final round of revisions before officially releasing the program. Often, popular software packages like Microsoft Windows and Microsoft Office are available for free beta download for months before the official public release.

**What happens if problems are found after beta testing?** The manufacturer will make changes before releasing the product to other manufacturers, for installation on new machines, for example. That point in the release cycle is called **release to manufacturers** (or **RTM**). After the RTM is issued, the product is in **general availability** (or **GA**) and can be purchased by the public.

Users often uncover problems in a program even after its commercial release to the public. These problems are addressed with the publication of software updates or **service packs**. Users can download these software modules to repair errors identified in the program code. To make sure you have the latest service pack for your Windows OS, visit the Windows Service Pack Center **(windows.microsoft.com/en-US/windows/downloads/service-packs)**.

**After testing, is the project finished?** Once testing is complete, but before the product is officially released, the work of **documentation** is still ahead. At this point, technical writers create internal documentation for the program that describes the development and technical details of the software, how the code works, and how the user interacts with the program. In addition, the technical publishing department produces all the necessary user documentation that will be distributed to the program's users. User training begins once the software is distributed. Software trainers take the software to the user community and teach others how to use it efficiently. ■

**Before moving on to Part 2:**
- **Watch Replay Video 10.1** .
- **Then check your understanding of what you've learned so far.**

# check your understanding//

For a quick review to see what you've learned so far, answer the following questions. Visit **pearsonhighered.com/techinaction** to check your answers.

## multiple choice

1. Compiling a program turns
   - **a.** top-down design into object-oriented design.
   - **b.** a first-generation language into a fourth-generation language.
   - **c.** source code into an executable program.
   - **d.** none of the above.
2. The step of the SDLC in which we document the transfer of data from the point where it enters the system to its final storage or output is the
   - **a.** problem and opportunity identification phase.
   - **b.** analysis phase.
   - **c.** design phase.
   - **d.** development phase.
3. The life cycle of a program begins with describing a problem and making a plan. Then the PDLC requires
   - **a.** coding, debugging, and testing.
   - **b.** process, input, and output.
   - **c.** data, information, and method.
   - **d.** an algorithm.
4. A yes/no decision point in an algorithm is called a
   - **a.** loop.
   - **b.** binary decision.
   - **c.** test condition.
   - **d.** control structure.
5. In object-oriented analysis, classes are defined by their
   - **a.** objects and data.
   - **b.** data and methods.
   - **c.** operators and objects.
   - **d.** behaviors and keywords.

## true–false

_____ **1.** Object-oriented design promotes a high level of reuse of existing code.

_____ **2.** Inheritance means that a unique class must be constructed from scratch to represent each new set of attributes.

## critical thinking

**1. Feeling Out of Sorts**

An algorithm can be described as a fixed series of predecided steps. Often, one type of job can be accomplished with a variety of different algorithms. Consider sorting a set of 100 numbers. There are over 30 different algorithms for sorting such a set. How many ways can you think of to do the sorting? Which would be fastest? Does it depend on the particular set of numbers you are given to sort?

**2. Class Hierarchy**

A common test for deciding the structure of a class hierarchy is the "is a" versus "has a" test. For example, a motorcycle "has a" sidecar, so Sidecar would be a data field of a Motorcycle object. However, a motorcycle "is a" kind of vehicle, so Motorcycle would be a subclass of the base class Vehicle. Use the "is a" versus "has a" test to decide how a class structure could be created for computer peripherals. For example, consider that printers are a type of peripheral and that there are laser printers, inkjet printers, 3-D printers, color printers, black-and-white printers, and thermal printers. Work to separate the unique features into objects and to extract the most common features into higher-level classes.

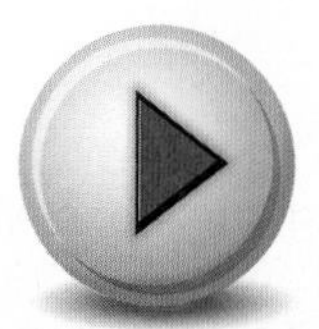

# Programming with Corona

Programming for mobile devices does not have to be complicated. In this Try This, we will use the product Corona to create an application that could be run on any iOS or Droid device.

**NOTE:** You need to be confident in installing and uninstalling demo software to your system to proceed. Refer to Chapter 4, page 149, if you need more support. Also, be aware that you will be asked to provide an e-mail address to qualify for the free trial version of Corona. *(Courtesy of Corona Labs, Inc.)*

**Step 1** From **notepad-plus-plus.org**, click **Download** and install the editor Notepad++. Launch Notepad++ and click **File->New**. *(Courtesy of Don Ho)*

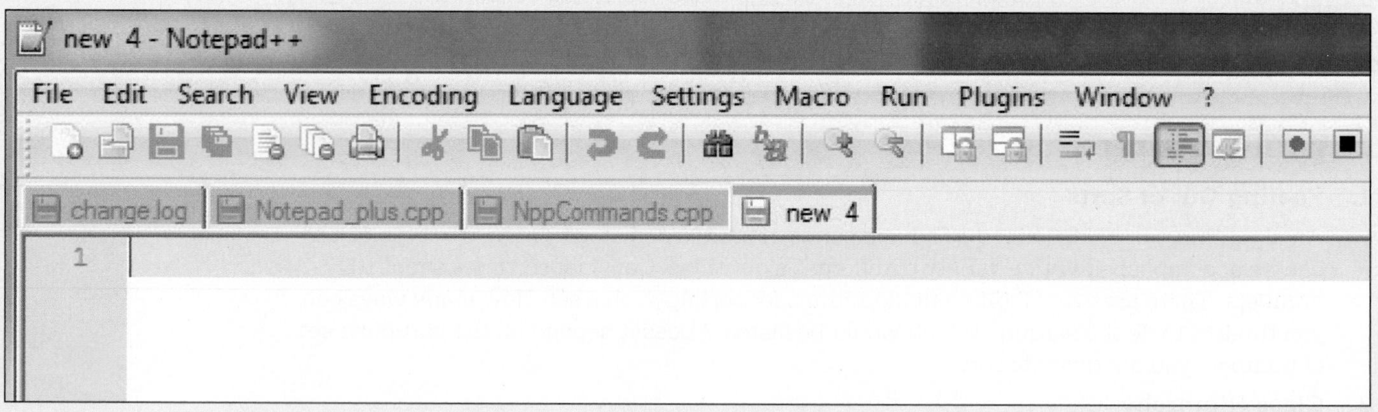


**Step 2** Head to **coronalabs.com/products/corona-sdk**. Download and install the free trial version of the Corona SDK.

**Step 3** Run the Corona simulator . Click the **Continue Trial** button. *(Courtesy of Corona Labs, Inc.)*

**Step 4** In Notepad++, type the following:

```
myText = display.newText( "TECH IN ACTION", 20, 40, native.systemFont, 36 )
myText:setTextColor( 255,97,3 )
```

**Step 5** In Notepad++, now click **File-> Save As**. In the **Save As Type** dropdown, select **LUA source file (*.lua)** and save this file with the name **main**. The file main.lua is now created.

**Step 6** Move to the Corona Simulator window and click **File->Open Project**. Then navigate to **main.lua** and open it.

You have just written a complete iPhone application! You can also run it on an iPad or any Android phone or tablet. Click **View->View As** and see how the program output looks on a few different devices.

**Step 7** Play with changing the color by altering the values in setTextColor. Try adding the line **myText.rotation = 45**.

*(LOVE graphic/Shutterstock)*

Visit **docs.coronalabs.com/api** to see the full set of built-in methods available. Have fun programming! *(Courtesy of Corona Labs, Inc.)*

# Programming Languages

Earlier in the chapter, you learned about the five main categories (generations) of programming languages. In this section, we discuss the specific programming languages that are members of these different generations.

## many languages for MANY PROJECTS

In any programming endeavor, programmers want to create a solution that meets several objectives. The software needs to:

- Run quickly
- Be reliable
- Be simple to expand later when the demands on the system change
- Be completed on time
- Be finished for the minimum possible cost

Because it's difficult to balance these conflicting goals, many programming languages have been developed. Although programming languages often share common characteristics, each language has specific traits that allow it to be the best fit for certain types of projects. The ability to understand enough about each language to match it to the appropriate style of problem is an exceptionally powerful skill for programmers.

**What languages are popular today?** One quick way to determine which languages are popular is to examine job postings for programmers. As of this writing, the languages most in demand include C/C++ and Java. In specific industries, certain languages tend to dominate the work. In the banking and insurance industries, for example, the programming language COBOL is still common, although most other industries rarely use it anymore. The Tiobe Index, shown in Figure 10.20, uses a number of different techniques to get a feel for which languages are popular in the software industry at certain times.

| Position Sep 2013 | Position Sep 2012 | Change in Position | Programming Language |
|---|---|---|---|
| 1 | 1 | = | C |
| 2 | 2 | = | Java |
| 3 | 4 | ↑ | C++ |
| 4 | 3 | ↓ | Objective-C |
| 5 | 6 | ↑ | PHP |
| 6 | 5 | ↓ | C# |
| 7 | 7 | = | (Visual) Basic |
| 8 | 8 | = | Python |
| 9 | 11 | ↑↑ | JavaScript |
| 10 | 14 | ↑↑↑↑ | Transact-SQL |
| 11 | 15 | ↑↑↑↑ | Visual Basic .NET |
| 12 | 9 | ↓↓↓ | Perl |
| 13 | 10 | ↓↓↓ | Ruby |
| 14 | 12 | ↓↓ | Delphi/Object Pascal |
| 15 | 16 | ↑ | Pascal |
| 16 | 13 | ↓↓↓ | Lisp |
| 17 | 19 | ↑↑ | PL/SQL |
| 18 | 24 | ↑↑↑↑↑↑ | R |
| 19 | 20 | ↑ | MATLAB |
| 20 | 25 | ↑↑↑↑↑ | COBOL |

**FIGURE 10.20** When attacking a problem, you can choose from many different programming languages. This chart of the Tiobe Index shows how popular certain languages are at specific times. *(Courtesy of Tiobe Software)*

**How do I know which language to study first?** A good introductory programming course will emphasize many skills and techniques that will carry over from one language to another. You should find a course that emphasizes design, algorithm development, debugging techniques, and project management. All of these aspects of programming will help you in any language environment.

**Pascal** is the only modern language that was specifically designed as a teaching language, but it's no longer taught frequently at the college level. Many colleges and universities have opted to have students begin with Java, C++, or Python.

**How does anyone learn so many languages?** Professional programmers can become proficient at new languages because they've become familiar with the basic components, discussed in this chapter's Dig Deeper feature, that are common to all languages: syntax, keywords, operators, and data types.

## Selecting the Right Language

**How do programmers know which language to select for a specific project?** A programming team considers several factors before selecting the language it will use for a specific project:

- *Space available:* Not all languages produce code that takes up the same amount of space. Therefore, the target language should be well matched to the amount of space available for the final program. For example, if the program will be embedded in a chip for use in a cell phone, it's important for the language to create space-efficient programs.
- *Speed required:* Although poorly written code executes inefficiently in any language, some languages can execute more quickly than others. Some projects require a focus on speed rather than size. These projects require a language that produces code that executes in the fastest possible time.
- *Organizational resources available:* Another consideration is the resources available in a manager's group or organization. Selecting a language that's easy to use and that will be easy to maintain if there's a turnover in programmers is an important consideration.
- *Type of target application:* Certain languages are customized to support a specific environment (UNIX or Windows, for instance). Knowing which languages are most commonly used for which environments can be helpful.

**What languages do programmers use if they want to build an application for Windows?** Software programs that run under the Windows OS are extremely popular. These programs often have a number of common features—scroll bars, title bars, text boxes, buttons, and expanding or collapsing menus, to name a few. Several languages include customized controls that make it easy for programmers to include these features in their programs. The same is true for the OS X operating system.

**Can I just point and click to create an application?** Many languages have a development environment that features a drag and drop-style interface for designing the visual layout of an application. Programmers use a mouse to lay out the screen and position scroll bars and buttons. The code needed to explain this to the computer is then written automatically. **Visual programming languages**, like Scratch and AppInventor, go even further. They use graphical blocks to represent control elements and variables. Programming consists of clicking together these blocks to define program behavior. ■

## BITS&BYTES

### Coding for Zombies

There are an incredible number of free courses available for the latest programming technologies. Rails for Zombies from Code Academy is one such course. The free interactive coding environment runs right in your browser and teaches you to create a Twitter-like program for Zombies using the Ruby on Rails web application framework. Also, explore course providers like Coursera, Udacity, and edX. They offer courses complete with quizzes, video lectures, and live discussion on topics like Python, Web Programming, and Java.

# ethics in IT — When Software Runs Awry

In the field of software programming, mistakes can be costly. Consider these examples:

- In 1996, Europe's newest unmanned rocket, the Ariane 5, had to be destroyed seconds after launch, along with its cargo of four scientific satellites. Cost: $500 million. The problem occurred when the guidance computer tried to convert rocket velocity from a 64-bit to a 16-bit value. Programmers had not properly coded for this, and an overflow error resulted. When the guidance system shut down, control passed to the backup unit, which also failed because it was running the same algorithm.
- When one switch in the AT&T network had a minor problem in 1990, system software fired off a message to the other 113 AT&T switching centers. This sparked a cascade of shutdowns, bringing down the entire network for nine hours. An estimated 75 million phone calls were missed, and over 200,000 airline reservations were lost. A single line of code in a large software upgrade was in error and led to the shutdown.
- In 2007, Los Angeles International Airport grounded 17,000 planes. For over eight hours, no one was authorized to enter or leave the United States through LAX. Software on a network card was sending faulty data and brought the entire Customs and Border Protection network to a halt.

Could better software engineering practices have prevented these failures? Many different factors contributed to this set of accidents, including the following:

- Simple programming errors
- Inadequate safety engineering
- Poor human–computer interaction design
- Inadequate or inappropriate testing
- Too little focus on safety by the manufacturing organization
- Inadequate reporting structure at the company level

Who should be held responsible for defective software? Is it the corporate management, who did not institute a defined software process? Is it the production managers, who forced tight schedules that demanded risky software engineering practices? What about the software engineers who wrote the defective code? What about the users of the software? Can they be held responsible for accidents? What if they made changes to the system?

Organizations of engineers and software designers have tried to define ethical standards that will minimize the risk of negative impact from their work. The very first article of the code of ethics of the Institute of Electrical and Electronics Engineers (IEEE) alerts engineers to their responsibility for making decisions that protect the health and safety of others. The Association for Computing Machinery (ACM) and the IEEE have established eight principles for ethical software engineering practices:[1]

1. *Public:* Software engineers shall act consistently with the public interest.
2. *Client and Employer:* Software engineers shall act in a manner that is in the best interests of their client and employer consistent with the public interest.
3. *Product:* Software engineers shall ensure that their products and related modifications meet the highest professional standards possible.
4. *Judgment:* Software engineers shall maintain integrity and independence in their professional judgment.
5. *Management:* Software engineering managers and leaders shall subscribe to and promote an ethical approach to the management of software development and maintenance.
6. *Profession:* Software engineers shall advance the integrity and reputation of the profession consistent with the public interest.
7. *Colleagues:* Software engineers shall be fair to and supportive of their colleagues.
8. *Self:* Software engineers shall participate in lifelong learning regarding the practice of their profession and shall promote an ethical approach to the practice of the profession.

Can you think of other steps the software industry could take to make sure its work contributes positively to our society?

[1] "Software Engineering Code of Ethics and Professional Practice," by IEEE-CS/ACM Joint Task Force on Software Engineering Ethics and Professional Practices. Copyright © 2011 by the Institute of Electrical and Electronics Engineers. Reprinted by permission.

# exploring programming LANGUAGES

All programming languages have many features in common. Let's take a tour of many of the popular languages and learn what makes each one special for particular situations.

## Visual Basic

**Why do programmers choose Visual Basic?** Programmers often like to build a **prototype**, or small model, of their program at the beginning of a large project. Prototyping is a form of **rapid application development (RAD)**, an alternative to the waterfall approach of systems development that was described at the beginning of this chapter. Instead of developing detailed system documents before they produce the system, developers create a prototype first, then generate system documents as they use and remodel the product.

Prototypes for Windows applications are often coded in Microsoft **Visual Basic (VB)**, a powerful programming language used to build a wide range of Windows applications. One strength of VB is its simple, quick interface, which is easy for a programmer to learn and use. It has grown from its roots in the language BASIC (short for Beginner's All-purpose Symbolic Instruction Code) to become a sophisticated and full-featured object-oriented language.

VB is designed for building object-oriented applications for Windows, the web, and mobile devices. Figure 10.21 shows how the interface of VB makes it easy to drag and drop entire programming components into an application. VB and the .NET Framework are both part of Visual Studio, which provides a complete set of developer tools.

**How does the Microsoft .NET Framework help programmers?** The Microsoft .NET (pronounced "dot net") Framework is a software development environment designed to let websites "talk" to each other easily. The .NET Framework includes **web services**, programs that a website uses to make information available to other websites. Web services provide a standard way for software to interact. For example, a web application could use the Google web service to search for information or to check the spelling of a word. The Google web service returns the requested information to your program in a standard format.

## C and C++

**What languages do programmers use if the problem requires a lot of "number crunching"?** A Windows application that demands raw processing power to execute difficult repetitive numerical calculations is most often a candidate for C/C++. For example, applications that simulate human cells and drug interactions have to solve elaborate mathematical equations many thousands of times each second, and are, therefore, excellent candidates for programming using C/C++. Several companies sell C/C++ design tools equipped with an environment that makes Windows programming as visual as with VB.

**Why was the C language developed?** The predecessor of C++, **C**, was originally developed for system programmers. It was defined by Brian Kernighan and Dennis Ritchie of AT&T Bell Laboratories in 1978 as a language that would make accessing the operating system easier. It provides higher-level programming language features (such as *if* statements and *for* loops) but still allows programmers to manipulate the system memory and CPU registers directly. This mix of high- and low-level access makes C highly attractive to "power" programmers. Most modern operating systems (Windows, OS X, and Linux) were written in C.

The **C++** language takes C to an object-oriented level. Bjarne Stroustrup, the developer of C++, used all the same symbols and keywords as C, but he extended the language with additional keywords, better security, and more support for the reuse of existing code through object-oriented design.

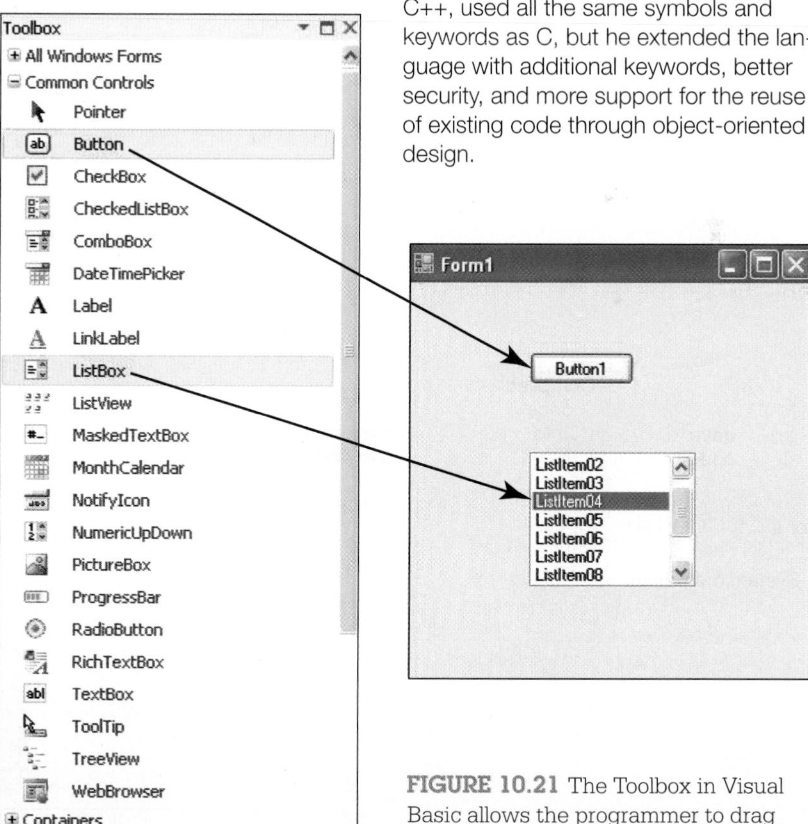


**FIGURE 10.21** The Toolbox in Visual Basic allows the programmer to drag and drop any of the items shown here into a program.

**Are C and C++ natural choices for when I'm looking to learn my first language?** Neither C nor C++ was intended as a teaching language. The notation and compactness of these languages make them relatively difficult to master. They're in demand in industry, however, because C/C++ can produce fast-running code that uses a small amount of memory. Programmers often choose to learn C/C++ because their basic components (operators, data types, and keywords) are common to many other languages.

## Java and C#

**What language do programmers use for applications that need to collect information from networked computers? Java** would be a good choice for these types of applications. James Gosling of Sun Microsystems introduced Java in the early 1990s. It quickly became popular because its object-oriented model enables Java programmers to benefit from its large set of existing classes. For example, a Java programmer could begin to use the existing "network connection" class with little attention to the details of how that code itself was implemented. Classes exist for many graphical objects, such as windows and scroll bars, and for network objects such as connections to remote machines. Observing Java's success, Microsoft released a language named **C#** (pronounced "see sharp") that competes with Java.

**Can a Java application work on any type of computer?** An attractive feature of Java is that it's **architecture neutral**. This means that Java code needs to be compiled only once, after which it can run on many CPUs (see Figure 10.22). The Java program doesn't care which CPU, OS, or user interface is running on the machine on which it lands. This is possible because the target computer runs a Java Virtual Machine (VM), software that can explain to the Java program how to function on any specific system. A Java VM installed with Microsoft Internet Explorer, for example, allows Internet Explorer to execute any **Java applet** (small Java-based program) it encounters on the Internet. Although Java code doesn't perform as fast as C++, the advantage of needing to compile only once before a program can be distributed to any system is extremely important.

## Objective C

**What's the most popular language for writing OS X applications? Objective C** is the language most often used to program applications to run under OS X. It's an object-oriented style of language, a superset of the C language, so it includes all the keywords of C and then adds more keywords and features. It's often used together with a library called Cocoa. The Cocoa library, or framework, lets users program for the OS X graphical user interface. The Cocoa Touch extension introduces a framework of methods that support gesture recognition for touch devices like the iPhone or iPad.

**Is there a favorite IDE for Objective C?** Many different IDE tools support Objective C, but OS X ships with a tool named Xcode (see Figure 10.23) that's often used to develop Objective C applications for OS X. Xcode is available free from the online Mac App Store.

## HTML

**What's the most basic language for developing web applications?** A document that will be presented on

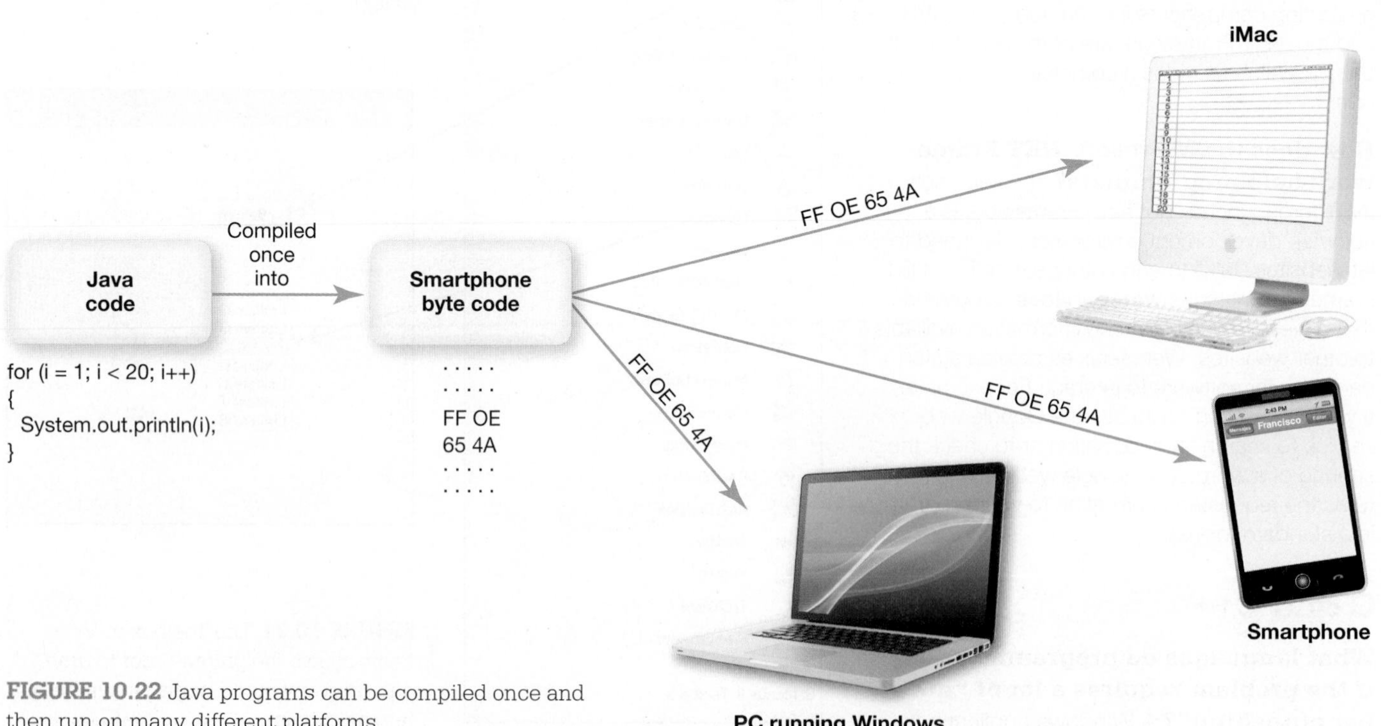


FIGURE 10.22 Java programs can be compiled once and then run on many different platforms.

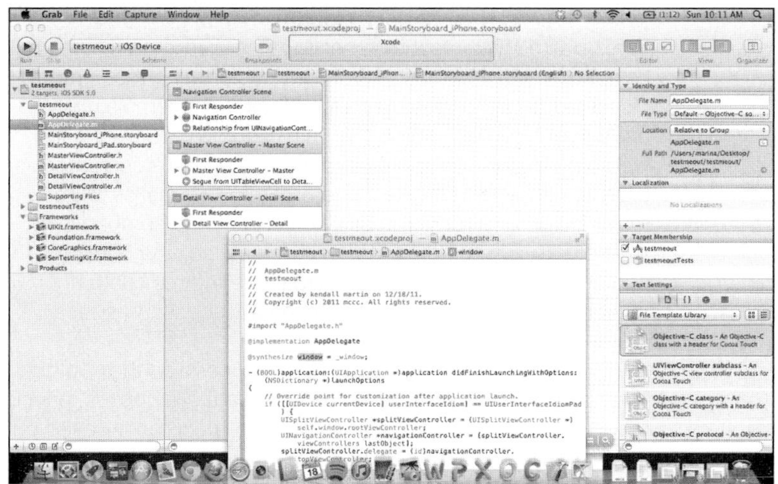

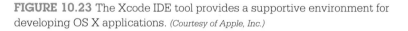

FIGURE 10.23 The Xcode IDE tool provides a supportive environment for developing OS X applications. *(Courtesy of Apple, Inc.)*

the web must be written using special symbols called *tags*. Tags control how a web browser will display the text, images, and other content tagged in **Hypertext Markup Language (HTML)**.

Although knowledge of HTML is required to program for the web, HTML itself isn't a programming language. HTML is just series of tags that modify the display of text. HTML was the original standard defining these tags. Many good HTML tutorials are available on the web at sites such as Learn the Net **(learnthenet.com),** Webmonkey **(webmonkey.com),** and the World Wide Web Consortium **(w3.org).** These sites include lists of the major tags that can be used to create HTML and XHTML documents.

**Are there tools that help programmers write in HTML?** Several different programs are available to assist in the generation of HTML. Adobe Dreamweaver and Microsoft Expression Web present web page designers with an interface that's similar to a word processing program. Web designers can quickly insert text, images, and hyperlinks, as shown in Figure 10.24. The program automatically inserts the corresponding HTML tags. For simple, static web pages, no programming is required.

**Will HTML continue evolving?** Yes, and the next release of HTML will be called HTML5. It's still being finalized in committee at the time of this writing, but it's a significant move toward standardizing HTML and adapting it to the times. For example <audio> and <video> tags allow pages to easily integrate media and let designers more easily support manipulating those elements. HTML5 will eliminate the need to install third-party browser plug-ins and will support features like drag-and-drop elements and document editing.

## JavaScript and VBScript

**Which programming languages do programmers use to make complex web pages?** To make their web pages more visually appealing and interactive, programmers use scripting languages to add more power and flexibility to their HTML code. A **scripting language** is a simple programming language that's limited to performing a set of specialized tasks. Scripts allow decisions to be made and calculations to be performed. Several popular scripting languages work well with HTML, including JavaScript, VBScript, and PHP (Hypertext Preprocessor).

**JavaScript** is a scripting language that's often used to add interactivity to web pages. JavaScript is not as fully featured as Java, but its syntax, keywords, data types, and operators are subsets of Java's. In addition, JavaScript has a set of classes that represent the objects often used on web pages: buttons, check boxes, and drop-down lists.

The JavaScript button class, for example, describes a button with a name and a type—for example, whether it's a regular button or a Submit or Reset button. The language includes behaviors, such as click(), and can respond to user actions. For example, when a user moves his or her mouse over a button and clicks to select it, the button "knows" the user is there and jumps in and performs a special action (such as playing a sound).

**Are there other scripting languages besides JavaScript?** Programmers who are more familiar with Visual Basic than Java or C++ often use **VBScript**, a subset of Visual Basic, to introduce dynamic decision making into web pages. **Dynamic decision making** means that the page can decide how to display itself based on the choices the reader makes. PHP, discussed in the following section, is another scripting language that has become extremely popular. It's a free, open-source product that runs very efficiently on multiple platforms, including Windows, UNIX, and Linux.

## ASP, JSP, and PHP

**How are interactive web pages built?** To build websites with interactive capabilities, programmers use **Active Server Pages (ASP)**, **JavaServer Pages (JSP)**, or the scripting language **PHP (Hypertext Preprocessor)**

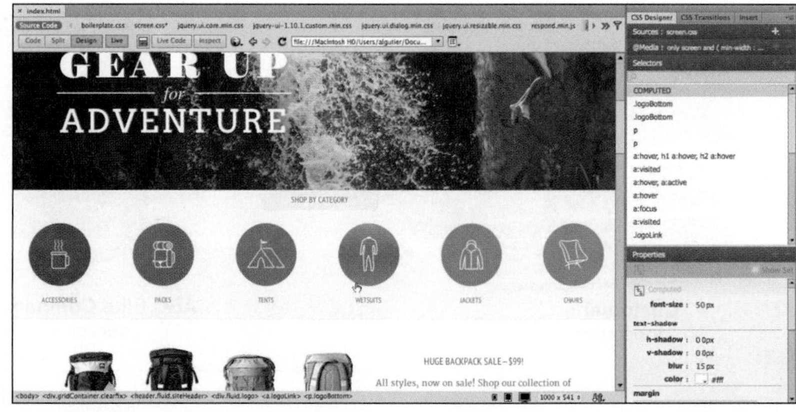


FIGURE 10.24 Adobe Dreamweaver is a popular tool for creating web pages. *(Adobe Dreamweaver screenshot reprinted with permission from Adobe Systems Incorporated)*

## BITS&BYTES

### The Best Résumé

Ever heard of GitHub? It's an online site for storing and managing software. One aspect of GitHub is that you can easily find projects or people who excite you and follow their work. For example, you can follow a specific person and get notifications of his or her work or even watch a specific project. When the project or work of a particular person is updated, you'll see that right away in your GitHub dashboard. You can also establish teams or "organizations" and work with multiple developers. Fork a copy of the code for a project you admire, and when you add a new feature, send out a request to have it pulled back into the original code.

And what's really cool is that your GitHub activity becomes a brilliant component of your résumé. A graph documents the contributions you have made over the previous year and allows an employer to actually see and use your body of work. A solid portfolio of your coding projects in GitHub is a smart investment in marketing yourself down the road.

to adapt the HTML page to the user's selections. The user supplies information that's translated into a request by the main computer at the company that owns the website, often using a database query language such as SQL. Scripting code in ASP, JSP, or PHP controls the automatic writing of the custom HTML page that's returned to the user's computer.

**What does additional programming bring to a web page?** The most advanced web pages interact with the user, collecting information and then customizing the content displayed based on the user's feedback. For example, the client/server type application shown in Figure 10.25 shows the web page of the ABC Bike Company collecting a customer bicycle inquiry for red bikes. The program then asks ABC's main server for a list of red bicycles sold by the company. An ASP program running on the server creates a new HTML page and delivers that to the user's browser, telling the customer what red bikes (including details such as model and size) are currently sold by ABC.

Thus, ASP programs can have HTML code as their output. They use what the user has told them (via the list boxes, check boxes, and buttons on the page) to make decisions. Based on those results, the ASP program decides what HTML to write. A small example of ASP writing its own HTML code is shown in Figure 10.26.

## AJAX and XML

**What if a programmer wants to create a web application that smoothly updates and communicates with other computers?** Many websites feature elaborate animations that interact with visitors. They may reach out to several other web resources to gather information or request services like translation. The collection of technologies referred to as **AJAX (Asynchronous JavaScript and XML)** and the continued evolution of HTML5, allow such web applications to update information on a page without requiring the user to do a page refresh or leave the page. By using existing technologies to do more processing in the browser, users have a more responsive experience.

**How do programs gather information from other computers?** The markup language called

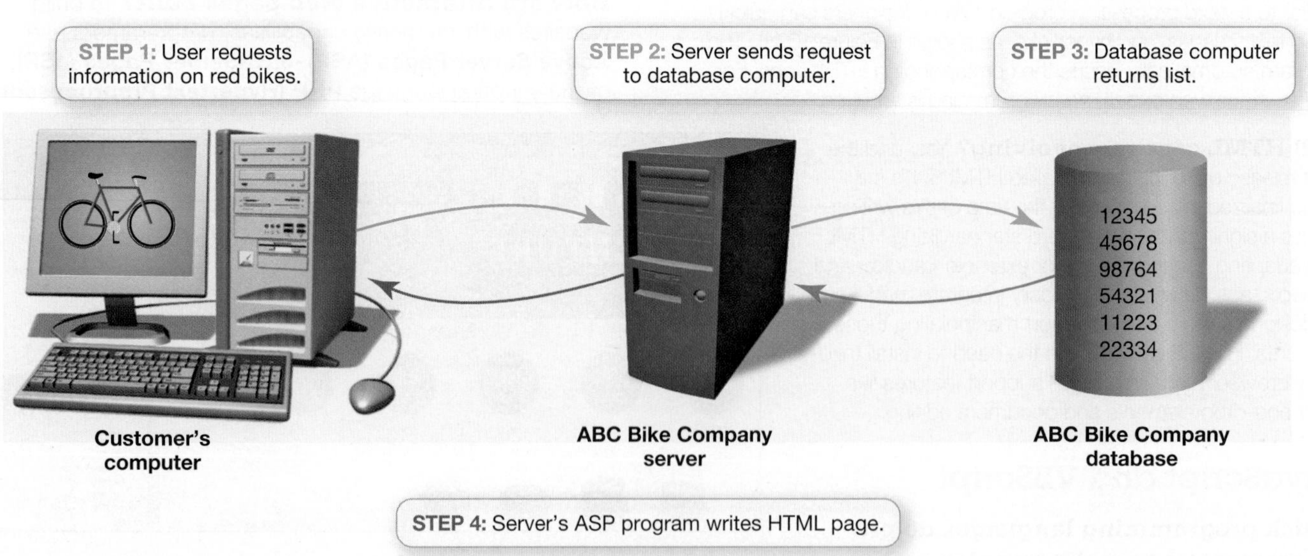
STEP 1: User requests information on red bikes.
STEP 2: Server sends request to database computer.
STEP 3: Database computer returns list.
12345
45678
98764
54321
11223
22334
Customer's computer
ABC Bike Company server
ABC Bike Company database
STEP 4: Server's ASP program writes HTML page.

**FIGURE 10.25** An online store is an example of the client/server type of Internet application.

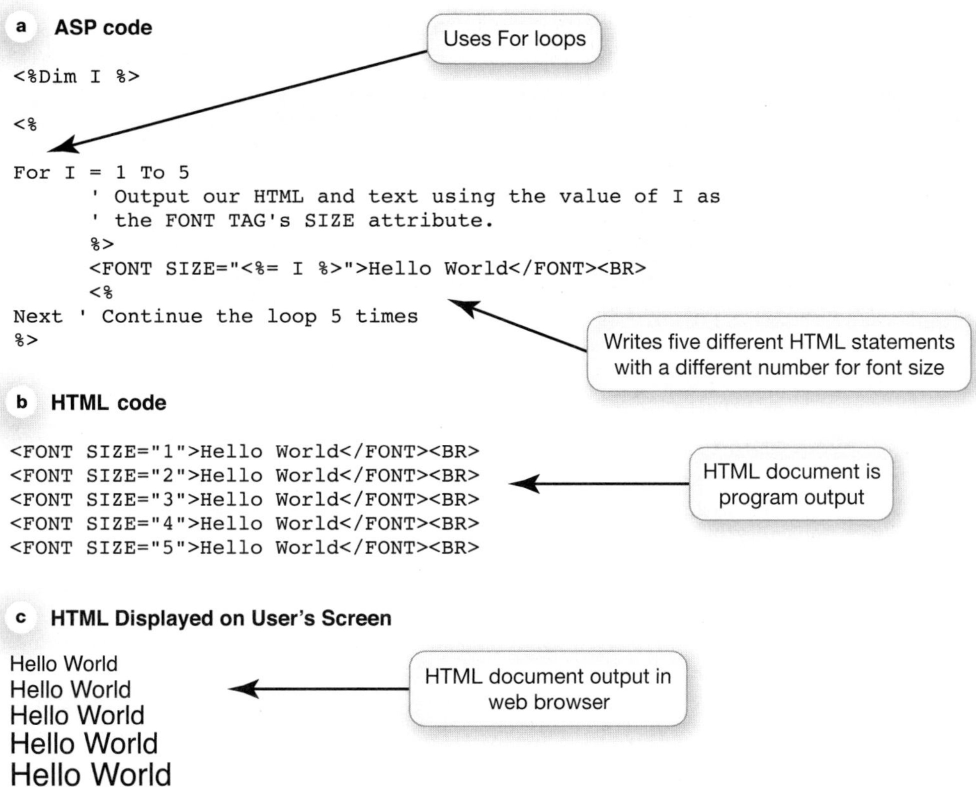

a ASP code
Uses For loops
<%Dim I %>
<%
For I = 1 To 5
' Output our HTML and text using the value of I as
' the FONT TAG's SIZE attribute.
%>
<FONT SIZE="<%= I %>">Hello World</FONT><BR>
<%
Next ' Continue the loop 5 times
%>
Writes five different HTML statements with a different number for font size
b HTML code
<FONT SIZE="1">Hello World</FONT><BR>
<FONT SIZE="2">Hello World</FONT><BR>
<FONT SIZE="3">Hello World</FONT><BR>
<FONT SIZE="4">Hello World</FONT><BR>
<FONT SIZE="5">Hello World</FONT><BR>
HTML document is program output
c HTML Displayed on User's Screen
Hello World
Hello World
Hello World
Hello World
Hello World
HTML document output in web browser


**FIGURE 10.26** An ASP program can (a) write HTML code as its (b) output. (c) This image illustrates how the HTML page would show up in a browser. *(Copyright © 2012, 2011, 2010, 2009, 2008 Pearson Education, Inc., publishing as Prentice Hall. All rights reserved. ISBN: 0132838737, p. 498)*

**eXtensible Markup Language (XML)** enables designers to define their own data-based tags, making it much easier for a program running on a server computer (a web service) to transfer the key information on its page to another site. When websites communicate with humans, HTML works well because the formatting it controls is important. People respond immediately to the visual styling of textual information; its layout, color, size, and font design all help to transfer the message of the page to the reader. When computer programs want to communicate with each other, however, all of these qualities just get in the way.

With XML, groups can agree on standard systems of tags that represent important data elements. For example, the XML tags <stock> and </stock> might delimit key stock quote information. Mathematicians have created a standardized set of XML tags named MathML for their work, and biometrics groups continue to refine XML standards to describe and exchange data such as DNA and face scans. Without XML, a website that wanted to look up current stock pricing information at another site would have to retrieve the HTML page, sort through the formatting information, and try to recognize which text on the page identified the data needed. **JSON** (short for JavaScript Object Notation) is another standard for exchanging information between a server computer process and a client. The information is delivered as a series of names and their values, making it easy for programs to parse and easy for humans to read.

Figure 10.27 shows a table of popular programming languages and technologies with their features and the typical settings in which they're used.

SOUND BYTE

**3-D Programming the Easy Way**

In this Sound Byte, you'll create a three-dimensional game using the visual drag-and-drop interface provided by Alice, a free software package. This program teaches all the concepts of programming with none of the pain of learning syntax.

## Mobile Applications

**How do programmers build applications for mobile devices?** Special languages and supporting tools are speeding the development of applications for mobile devices like smartphones and tablets. Programmers need to be able to take advantage of specific features like GPS capability, compasses, software keyboards, and touch-sensitive screens. In addition, the user interface has to take the smaller screen size of mobile devices into account.

**What development tools are used for creating mobile apps for Apple's iOS platform?** To start a complex project like an iPhone app requires a detailed prototype. Each of the many screens, all the user interface elements,

FIGURE 10.27

## Popular Programming Languages

| PROGRAMMING LANGUAGE | FEATURES | TYPICAL SETTING |
|---|---|---|
| **C/C++ and C#** | • Can create compact code that executes quickly<br>• Provides high- and low-level access | • Used in industrial applications such as banking and engineering |
| **Java** | • Is architecture neutral<br>• Is object oriented | • Used to create applets that can be delivered over the web |
| **Objective C** | • Has a framework for writing iOS applications | • Used to create applications for OS X and Apple mobile devices |
| **Visual Basic** | • Is easy to learn and use<br>• Is object oriented<br>• Has a drag-and-drop interface | • Used in prototype development<br>• Used to design graphical user interfaces |
| **WEB TECHNOLOGIES** | **FEATURES** | **TYPICAL SETTING** |
| **AJAX** | • Uses a combination of existing technologies like JavaScript, CSS, and XML | • Creates websites that can update without the user refreshing the page |
| **HTML5** | • Latest version of HTML; currently a "living standard" | • Introduces tags like <video> and supports drag and drop |
| **VBScript** | • Is similar in syntax to Visual Basic<br>• Has classes that represent buttons, drop-down lists, and other web page components | • Creates code that lives on the client machine and adds interaction to web pages |
| **XML** | • Enables users to define their own tags | • Facilitates exchange of information from web services |
| **JSON** | • Format defined with name/value pairs | • Very common format for exchange of information from web services |

and all the content need to be organized and linked smoothly. Often, programmers begin with a prototype, created quickly with drag-and-drop elements using products like MockApp or Interface Builder. MockApp (**mockapp.com**) is a template that uses PowerPoint or Keynote to construct a working simulation of your application. Interface Builder is part of the Apple Xcode development tool; it requires a bit more expertise to use than MockApp but can also rapidly create a prototype.

When it's time to begin writing the code for an iOS app, programmers turn to Objective C and use the Apple Xcode development toolset (see Figure 10.28). Xcode lets designers code and debug the behavior of the application and simulate the application in a software version of the target device. After the program is running, its performance can be profiled for speed, memory usage, and other possible problems.

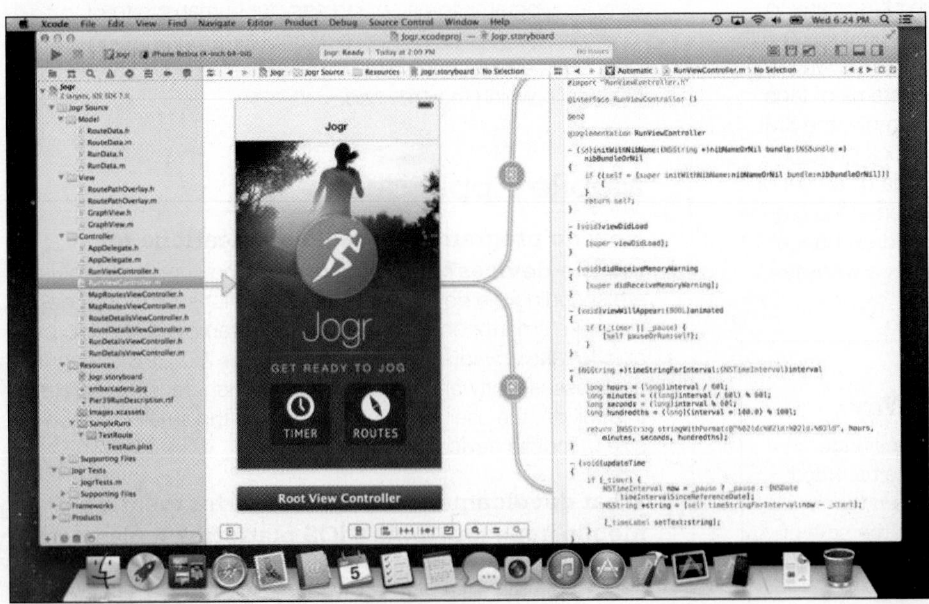


**Are there other tools for building apps for Android devices?** Yes, the Android software development kit (SDK) is required to build apps targeting Android smartphones and tablets. There are many ways programmers work with the Android SDK, including using well-known IDEs like Eclipse with special plug-ins for Android like the Android Development Tools. Information on the latest version of the Android SDK, as well as tutorials, guides, and other resources, is available at the Android Developers page (**developer.android.com**).

FIGURE 10.28 Xcode integrates all the tools required to program iOS applications from scratch. *(Courtesy of Apple, Inc.)*

# trends in IT

## Emerging Technologies: Unite All Your Video Game Design Tools

Unity is a game-development environment that supports home videogame production by combining many tools into one package, giving you what you need to edit, test, and play your game idea quickly. It can generate real-time shadowing effects, for example, and has preprogrammed scripts integrated. After you've polished your production, Unity allows you to publish for web, mobile, or console platforms. With over 500,000 developers using Unity, and over 60 million installs of the Unity browser plug-in, the potential of this tool is amazing (see Figure 10.29).

You'll start with the built-in Unity editor so you can quickly assemble a 3-D environment. Unity gives you access to its Asset Store right from the editor window. Art assets are supplied so that you instantly have materials to create your own landscape. Tutorials and sample projects are available, as well as character models and textures. Grab a sound effect or some code to simulate a great explosion effect. If you create assets you'd like to distribute, you can put them up for sale within the Asset Store.

Unity incorporates lighting control and shading and the application of textures in order to develop rich terrains. Its built-in physics engine lets objects respond to gravity, friction, and collisions. One example is the "wheel collider," a module that simulates the traction of real car tires. Audio processing is included, with effects like echo, reverb, and a chorus filter, as are tools to make real-time networking available from your game.

Programming is handled through several flexible scripting languages—JavaScript, C#, and an implementation of Python named Boo. It has a visual interface that lets you drag and drop objects to set variables, or you can choose to sync with an external IDE like Visual Studio. There's an integrated debugger so that you can pause your game, check variable values, and quickly repair errors. When it's time to optimize the performance before your final release, you can use the built-in profiler: It reports statistics on where the processing time is being spent so that you can fine tune game play.

Unity is available in a free downloadable version (**unity3d.com**) and in a pay version, Unity 3D Pro. The Pro version adds features but also can be licensed and used by companies. The free version of Unity can be used to create games that can be sold—there is no royalty or revenue sharing required. And there are modules that let you easily port your code to a number of target platforms: PC, iOS, Android, and web as well as Xbox 360, PS3, and Wii.

You'll also find an active community to support you as you learn. The Unify Community offers a Scriptswiki (**unifycommunity.com/wiki**) to organize the many tutorials, tips, and programming resources that users have contributed. There is a dedicated IRC (Internet Relay Chat) channel for live chatting with Unity users. If you need help distributing your finished game, you can join Union, a service that brings your game to new markets for you.

If you're interested in video game development, architectural visualizations, or just creating interactive animations, download Unity and realize the power of programming.

**FIGURE 10.29** Unity is a free game engine that can build web, mobile, or console games. *(Courtesy of Unity Technologies)*

**I'm not a programmer, but can I make a simple app?** Absolutely. If you have even a little programming experience, tools like Corona produce amazing games and apps quickly (see the Try This on pages 428–429 for more information). Tens of millions of apps constructed using Corona have been downloaded, including the overnight sensation Bubble Ball created by 14-year-old Robert Nay (**naygames.com**). Code can be deployed for an iOS device, an Android device, or even the Barnes & Noble Nook using Corona. The advantage of Corona is that it supports a wide range of features like networking support to Facebook, easy animation, multimedia, and a physics engine, but requires only simple programming syntax.

If your goal is to make a mobile app that's very simple or even specific to one occasion, like a wedding, there are web-based products that make that quick and easy. Magmito (**magmito.com**) supports developing a simple app with text and graphics and requires no programming knowledge.

**Does an application need to be rewritten for every kind of mobile device?** Programming environments like Corona and Magmito support publishing an application to several different types of devices. Although these tools can be great time savers for very simple applications, for programmers using specific features that make that device unique or for those concerned with extracting ultimate performance, custom programming for each environment still is required.

## The Next Great Language

**What will the next great language be?** It is never easy to predict which language will become the next "great" language. Software experts predict that as software projects continue to grow in size, the amount of time needed to compile a completed project will also grow. It's not uncommon for a large project to require 30 minutes or more to compile. Interpreted languages, however, take virtually no compile time because compilation occurs while the code is being edited. As projects get larger, the capability to be compiled instantaneously will become even more important. Thus, interpreted languages such as Python, Ruby, and Smalltalk could become more important in the coming years.

**Will all languages someday converge into one?** Certain characteristics of modern programming languages correspond well with how programmers actually think. These traits support good programming practices and are emerging as common features of most modern programming languages. The object-oriented paradigm is one example. Both Visual Basic and COBOL have moved toward supporting objects.

There will always be a variety of programming languages, however. Figure 10.30, in which the artist tries to give each language a "personality," illustrates that idea in a lighthearted fashion.

**FIGURE 10.30** There will always be a variety of languages, each with its own personality. *(Luis Guillermo Restrepo Rivas)*

Forcing a language to be so general that it can work for any task also forces it to include components that make it slower to compile, produce larger final executables, and require more memory to run. Having a variety of languages and mapping a problem to the best language create the most efficient software solutions.

**So what do I do if I want to learn languages that will be relevant in the future?** No particular set of languages is best to learn, and there is no one best sequence in which to learn them. The Association for Computing Machinery (**acm.org**) encourages educators to teach a core set of mathematical and programming skills and concepts, but school and university departments are free to offer a variety of languages.

When you're selecting which programming languages to study, some geographical and industry-related considerations come into play. For example, in an area in which a large number of pharmaceutical companies exist, there may be a demand for Massachusetts General Hospital Utility Multi-Programming System (MUMPS).This language is often used to build clinical databases, an important task in the pharmaceutical industry. Review the advertisements for programmers in area newspapers and investigate resources such as ComputerJobs (**computerjobs.com**) to identify languages in demand in your area.

Regardless of whether you pursue a career in programming, having an understanding of how software is created will help you in many IT careers. Software is the set of instructions that allows us to make use of our hardware. Programming skills give you the power to understand, create, and customize a computer system. ■

**Before moving on to the Chapter Review:**

- **Watch Replay Video 10.2** .
- Then check your understanding of what you've learned so far.

# check your understanding//

For a quick review to see what you've learned so far, answer the following questions. Visit **pearsonhighered.com /techinaction** to check your answers.

## multiple choice

1. Selecting the right programming language for a project depends on
   - **a.** who you have working for you and what they know.
   - **b.** the final requirements for performance and space used.
   - **c.** the environment of the finished project.
   - **d.** all of the above.
2. Which language is best for creating iOS-based mobile applications?
   - **a.** C/C++
   - **b.** Objective C
   - **c.** Java
   - **d.** ASP
3. Which is NOT an advantage of Java?
   - **a.** Java is architecture neutral.
   - **b.** Java needs to compile only once prior to distribution.
   - **c.** Java supports network communications.
   - **d.** Java performs faster than C++.
4. Which is TRUE about XML?
   - **a.** XML supports the development of rich multimedia.
   - **b.** XML makes it possible to update web pages without refreshing.
   - **c.** XML enables designers to define their own data-based tags.
   - **d.** XML has classes that represent drop-down lists and other web elements.
5. HTML5 features helpful new tags like
   - **a.** <audio> and <video>
   - **b.** <movie> and <actor>
   - **c.** <metaheader>
   - **d.** <div>

## true–false

_____ **1.** When producing the fastest executable program is essential, programmers use a language with an interpreter.

_____ **2.** Programmers often use JavaScript for client-side code in web applications.

## critical thinking

1. **Something for Nothing**

   The open source software movement depends on the participation of a number of people from all over the world. Some individuals donate time by writing code; others do testing or documentation. Projects are then made available free to users. Does the open source movement threaten or strengthen the software industry? Could it replace the existing business model for distributing software? Are there any benefits to working for free and giving your intellectual property away?

2. **Gathering Insights**

   There are many different ways to decide which programming languages are the most popular today. The Google Trends beta tool lets you compare search patterns and usage across specific regions, categories, or time periods. How would Google Trends help you determine the most popular programming languages? If you didn't have a tool such as Google Trends available, where would you go to conduct a survey on which programming languages are popular? What individuals would you survey? How would you expect their answers to differ from one another?

**Continue**

# 10 Chapter Review

## summary//

### The Importance of Programming

**1. Why do I need to understand how to create software?**

- Programming skills allow you to customize existing software products to accomplish required tasks.
- A beginning-level knowledge of programming will let you create macros, customized mini-programs that speed up redundant tasks.

### The Life Cycle of an Information System

**2. What is a system development life cycle, and what are the phases in the cycle?**

- An information system includes data, people, procedures, hardware, and software.
- The set of steps followed to ensure that development proceeds in an orderly fashion is the system development life cycle (SDLC). There are six steps in the SDLC waterfall model:
  1. A problem or opportunity is identified.
  2. The problem is analyzed, and a program specification document is created to outline the project objectives.
  3. A detailed plan for programmers to follow is designed using flowcharts and data-flow diagrams.
  4. Using the developed plan, programmers develop the program, and the program is then documented.
  5. The program is tested to ensure that it works and that it's installed properly.
  6. Ongoing maintenance and evaluation ensure a working product.

### The Life Cycle of a Program

**3. What is the life cycle of a program?**

- The problem statement identifies the task to be computerized and describes how the software program will behave.
- An algorithm is developed that specifies the sequence of steps that the program must take to complete the work.
- The algorithm is then translated into highly structured programming code.
- The code goes through the processes of debugging, in which the programmers find and repair any errors in the code.
- Testing is performed by the programming team and by the people who will use the program.
- The results of the entire project are documented for the users and the development team.

**4. What role does a problem statement play in programming?**

- The problem statement is an explicit description of what tasks the computer program must accomplish and how the program will execute these tasks and respond to unusual situations.
- The problem statement describes the input data that users will have at the start of the job, the output that the program will produce, and the exact processing that converts these inputs to outputs.
- The problem statement identifies potential errors and plans to address these errors.

**5. How do programmers create algorithms and move from algorithm to code?**

- Programmers create an algorithm by converting a problem statement into a list of steps and identifying where decision points occur.
- Yes/no binary decisions are common, and often a pattern of a repeating action loop is recognized.
- Algorithms are documented in the form of a flowchart or in pseudocode.
- Programmers use either top-down or object-oriented analysis to produce the algorithm.
- Computer code uses special words and strict rules to enable programmers to control the CPU without having to know all of its hardware details.
- Programming languages are classified in several major groupings, sometimes referred to as *generations,* with the first generation being machine language—the binary code of *1*s and *0*s that the computer understands. Assembly language is the next generation; it uses short, English-like commands that speak directly to the CPU and give the programmer direct control of hardware

resources. Each successive generation in language development has relieved programmers of some of the burden of keeping track of what the hardware requires and more closely matches how humans think about problems.
- Compilation is the process by which code is converted into machine language, the language the CPU can understand. A compiler is a program that understands both the syntax of the programming language and the exact structure of the CPU and its machine language. It can translate the instructions written by programmers in the higher-level language into machine language, the binary patterns that will execute commands on the CPU.
- Each programming language has its own compiler. Separate versions are required to compile code that will run on each different type of processor.

**6. What steps are involved in completing the program?**

- If programmers make errors in the algorithm or in translating the algorithm to code, problems will occur. Programmers debug the program by running it constantly to find errors and to make sure the program behaves the way it should.
- Once debugging has detected all the code errors, users—both within the company and outside the company—test the program in every way they can imagine, both as the program was intended to be used and in ways only new users might think up.
- Before its commercial release, software is often provided at a reduced cost or at no cost in a beta version to certain test sites or to interested users for a last round of testing.
- Once testing is complete, technical writers create internal documentation for the program and external documentation that will be provided to users of the program. User training, which begins once the software is distributed, teaches the user community how to use the software efficiently.

## Many Languages for Many Projects

**7. How do programmers select the right programming language for a specific task?**

- A programming team reviews several considerations before selecting the language to be used. Certain languages are best used for certain problems.
- The target language should be well matched to the amount of space available for the final program.
- Some projects require the selection of a language that can produce code that executes in the fastest possible time.
- Selecting a language with which the programmers are familiar is also helpful.

## Exploring Programming Languages

**8. What are the most popular programming languages for different types of application development?**

- Visual Basic, C/C++, and Java are languages that enable programmers to include control features such as scroll bars, title bars, text boxes, buttons, and expanding and collapsing menus.
- Objective C is a language used in programming applications for mobile devices using iOS and applications that will run under OS X.
- Programmers use HTML tags to structure web pages. HTML5, in development as of this writing, includes more advanced tags like <video>.
- For more complex web development, scripting programs such as JavaScript, PHP, and VBScript are popular.
- AJAX is a programming solution that uses a combination of technologies to create websites that can update without the user refreshing the page.
- XML and JSON allow programmers to create their own tags so that web pages can exchange information, not just formatting details.

Be sure to check out the companion website for additional materials to help you review and learn, including a Tech Bytes Weekly newsletter—**pearsonhighered.com/techinaction**. And don't forget the Replay Videos.

# key terms//

Active Server Pages (ASP) **435**
AJAX (Asynchronous JavaScript and XML) **436**
algorithm **411**
architecture neutral **434**
assembly language **420**
base class **417**
beta version **426**
binary decision **414**
C **433**
C++ **433**
C# **434**
class **416**
code editing **425**
coding **420**
comment **421**
compilation **423**
compiler **423**
control structure **415**
data **411**
data-flow diagram **409**
data type **419**
debugger **426**
debugging **425**
decision point **414**
derived class **417**
documentation **426**
dynamic decision making **435**
editor **425**
error handling **412**
executable program **423**
eXtensible Markup Language (XML) **437**
fifth-generation language (5GL) **421**
first-generation language (1GL) **420**
flowchart **413**
For **418**
fourth-generation language (4GL) **420**
general availability (GA) **426**
Hypertext Markup Language (HTML) **435**
if else **418**
information **411**
information system **409**
inheritance **417**
initial value **415**
integrated development environment (IDE) **424**
interpreter **424**
Java **434**
Java applet **434**
JavaScript **435**
JavaServer Pages (JSP) **435**
JSON **437**
keyword **418**
logical error **425**
loop **415**
machine language **420**
method **412**
Next **418**
object **417**
Objective C **434**
object-oriented analysis **416**
operator **419**
Pascal **430**
PHP (Hypertext Preprocessor) **435**
portability **421**
problem statement **411**
program development life cycle (PDLC) **411**
program specification **409**
programming **411**
programming language **420**
prototype **433**
pseudocode **413**
rapid application development (RAD) **433**
release to manufacturers (RTM) **426**
reusability **417**
runtime error **425**
scope creep **410**
scripting language **435**
second-generation language (2GL) **420**
service pack **426**
source code **423**
statement **418**
Structured Query Language (SQL) **420**
syntax **418**
syntax error **418**
system development life cycle (SDLC) **409**
test condition **415**
testing plan **412**
third-generation language (3GL) **420**
top-down design **415**
variable **421**
variable declaration **421**
VBScript **435**
Visual Basic (VB) **433**
visual programming languages **431**
web service **433**

## making the transition to . . . next semester//

1. **Interview Ready**

   There are many puzzles posted online that allegedly have been given as part of the interview processat tech companies like Google or Facebook. (For a collection, look at the book *Algorithms for Interviews* by Adnan Aziz and Amit Prakash.) Here are a few sample questions that could come up in assessing your ability to create algorithms. Prepare solutions to each.

   **a.** What method would you use to look up a word in a dictionary?

   **b.** Imagine you have a closet full of shirts. It's very hard to find a particular shirt, so what can you do to organize your shirts for easy retrieval?

   **c.** You have eight balls, all of the same size. Seven of them weigh the same, but one of them weighs slightly more. Can you find the ball that is heavier by using a balance and only two weighings?

2. **Reuse, Reuse, Reuse**

   One key to being an efficient programmer is to reuse code. Programmers often use collections of prewritten code modules named application programming interfaces (APIs) to add functionality to their program with relatively little work. Research the set of APIs available from Google by visiting Google Developers page (**developers.google.com**) and the Google Code Playground (**code.google.com/apis/ajax/playground**).

## making the transition to . . . the workplace//

1. **Learning All Those Languages**

   We discussed languages that are designed to support specific kinds of projects—3-D video game design, web applications, and mobile devices. In the workplace, you're expected to be fluent in many languages and to learn new languages easily. How do you become expert in so many different languages? Explore three programming environments: the Unity game engine, Ruby on Rails, and the Corona SDK. What similarities do all three have? What differences? Use YouTube tutorials and **codeacademy.org** resources to build a picture of their similarities and differences.

2. **Accessibility**

   Web designers and programmers can take specific steps to allow visually impaired users to access websites more easily. Examine the information on accessibility at Adobe's Accessibility resource center (**adobe.com/accessibility**). What does accessibility mean in a software context? Explore the details of existing assistive technologies, such as screen readers. What are the legal requirements with which websites must comply in order to meet the needs of persons with disabilities? Why is maximizing accessibility important to everyone?

team time//

# Working Together for Change

## Problem

You and your team have just been selected to write a software program that tells a vending machine how to make proper change from the bills or coins the customer inserts. The program needs to deliver the smallest possible amount of coins for each transaction.

## Task

Divide the class into three teams: Algorithm Design, Coding, and Testing. The responsibilities of each team are outlined as follows.

## Process

1. The Algorithm Design team must develop two documents. The first document should present the problem as a top-down design sequence of steps. The second document should use object-oriented analysis to identify the key objects in the problem. Each object needs to be represented as data and behaviors. Inheritance relationships between objects should be noted, as well. You can use flowcharts to document your results.

   Consider using a product such as Microsoft Visio or the open source program Dia to create a visual representation of your objects and their relationships to each other.
2. The Coding team needs to decide which programming language would be most appropriate for the project. This program needs to be fast and to take up only a small amount of memory. Use the web to collect information about the language you select, and be sure you have enough information to defend your selection.

   You may also consider using a product such as Visual Logic to try to develop the code for a prototype of the system (**visuallogic.org** offers a free demo version). This language, based on Visual Basic, lets you write code free from many constraints of syntax. Programs in Visual Logic look like flowcharts but actually execute!
3. The Testing team must create a testing plan for the program. What set of inputs would you test with to be sure the program is completely accurate? Develop a table listing combinations of inputs and correct outputs.
4. As a group, discuss how each team would communicate its results to the other teams. Once one team has completed its work, are the team members finished or do they need to interact with the other teams? How would the tools of a site such as SourceForge (**sourceforge.net**) help your development team across the life of the project?

## Conclusion

Any modern programming project requires programming teams to produce an accurate and efficient solution to a problem. The interaction of the team members within the team as well as with the other teams is vital to successful programming.

# Software That Kills

In this exercise, you'll research and then role-play a complicated ethical situation. The role you play might not match your personal beliefs, but your research and use of logic will enable you to represent the view assigned. An arbitrator will watch and comment on both sides of the argument, and together, the team will agree on an ethical solution.

## Problem

The Therac-25 was a computerized radiation-therapy machine. Between 1985 and 1987, six people were killed or badly harmed due to a flaw in its software. Although the therapeutic dose was expected to be about 200 rads, it was later estimated that one patient had received doses of radiation in the 15,000- to 20,000-rad range. (Doses of 1,000 rads can be fatal.) The error-prone software remained on the market for more than 18 months before the problem was recognized, acknowledged, and solved.

Does this situation indicate criminal conduct? Or is it not a criminal act but rather a situation that needs to be resolved in civil court (for monetary damages)? Should this incident be seen as an example of the price society pays for using complex technology and that no blame should be assigned?

## Research Areas to Consider

- Therac-25 case resolution
- 2010 Toyota recalls for unanticipated acceleration
- Software errors in avionic software systems
- ACM ethical guidelines

## Process

1. Divide the class into teams.
2. Research the areas cited above from the perspective of one of the following people: a software developer, the people impacted, and the arbitrator.
3. Team members should write a summary that provides factual support for their character's position regarding the fair and ethical design and use of technology. Then, team members should create an outline to use during the role-playing event.
4. Team members should arrange a mutually convenient time to meet for the exchange, using a virtual meeting tool or by meeting in person.
5. Team members should present their case to the class or submit a PowerPoint presentation for review by the rest of the class, along with the summary and resolution they developed.

## Conclusion

As technology becomes ever more prevalent and integrated into our lives, ethical dilemmas will present themselves to an increasing extent. Being able to understand and evaluate both sides of the argument, while responding in a personally or socially ethical manner, will be an important skill.

# 11 Behind the Scenes: Databases and Information Systems

## Database Basics

### Database Building Blocks

**OBJECTIVES**

1. What is a database, and why is using one beneficial? **(pp. 450–453)**
2. What do database management systems do? **(pp. 453–454)**
3. What components make up a database? **(pp. 454–457)**

**Active Helpdesk:** Using Databases

### Database Types

**OBJECTIVE**

4. What types of databases are there? **(pp. 458–459)**

### Database Functions

**OBJECTIVE**

5. How do relational databases organize and manipulate data? **(pp. 460–469)**

**Sound Byte:** Creating an Access Database

**Sound Byte:** Improving an Access Database

## How Businesses Use Databases

### Database Warehousing and Storage

**OBJECTIVE**

6. What are data warehouses and data marts, and how are they used? **(pp. 470–473)**

### Business Intelligence Systems

**OBJECTIVE**

7. What is a business intelligence system, and what types of business intelligence systems are used by decision makers? **(pp. 474–478)**

### Data Mining

**OBJECTIVE**

8. What is data mining, and how does it work? **(pp. 479–482)**

For all media in this chapter go to **pearsonhighered.com/techinaction** or **MyITLab.**

(*Marek Uliasz/Alamy; Kheng Ho Toh/Alamy; Juri Samsonov/Fotolia; Mira/Alamy; S.John/Fotolia; S.John/Fotolia*)

# HOW COOL IS THIS?

Scan here for more info

Have you used your finger to write or draw on a **touch screen** and wished there were a way to make your **strokes more accurate**? Researchers at Carnegie Mellon and Microsoft teamed up to create **DrawAFriend** to do just that. This iPhone drawing game lets friends take turns drawing faces of celebrities or mutual friends from Facebook. While one player traces over a photo, the other player sees only the keystrokes and guesses the subject's name, in Hangman-like style.

The game generates a **huge database of touches** that the researchers have used to create an algorithm to correct the "fat finger" problem associated with touch screens. The algorithm automatically refines touch strokes, allowing for more precise sketches.

This is an example of how **big data**—the collection of a large amount of specific data—is used to solve a problem by observing patterns in the data. Data patterns become more precise as more data is collected, allowing for **better solutions**. In the game's first five months, DrawAFriend generated nearly 20,000 images, each with specific stroke information, that have enabled continued refinements to the algorithm. So play DrawAFriend and help improve touch-screen accuracy as you do! *(Vincenzo Lombardo/Getty Images)*

# Database Basics

You interact with databases every day—when you retrieve a friend's phone number from your contacts, post to your Facebook page, or add a song to your iTunes playlist. In this part of the chapter, we'll look at the basics of databases and how databases can be used to provide relevant information quickly and easily.

## database building BLOCKS

A **database** is a collection of related data that can be stored, sorted, organized, and queried. Many actions we do every day, such as use an ATM, shop online, and make an airplane reservation, generate data that needs to be stored, managed, and used by others. Most likely, a database has been created that receives and stores our generated data and that enables that data to be processed and used by others. By creating an organized structure for data, databases make data more meaningful and therefore more useful. Databases effectively turn data into information.

**Why do I need to know about databases?** Since you interact with databases every day, understanding how databases work and what you can do with databases will help you use the ones you interact with more effectively. For example, *categorizing, sorting,* and *filtering* are key attributes of most databases. If a database isn't set up correctly or if you don't know how to use the database, you may not get the type of information you're looking for.

StubHub, the online ticket-exchange platform (see Figure 11.1), is an example of a database. Sellers list tickets on StubHub. They specify the categories the tickets fall into (sports, concerts, theater) and other details, such as day, time, and seat location of the event, and set a price. Buyers then access the website, using its filters to narrow down to the type of ticket they're looking to purchase. If the database doesn't have the right categories for sellers to choose from, buyers won't be able to locate the tickets they want.

### Databases Versus Lists

**Do I need databases for managing all types of data?** Not every situation in which related data needs to be

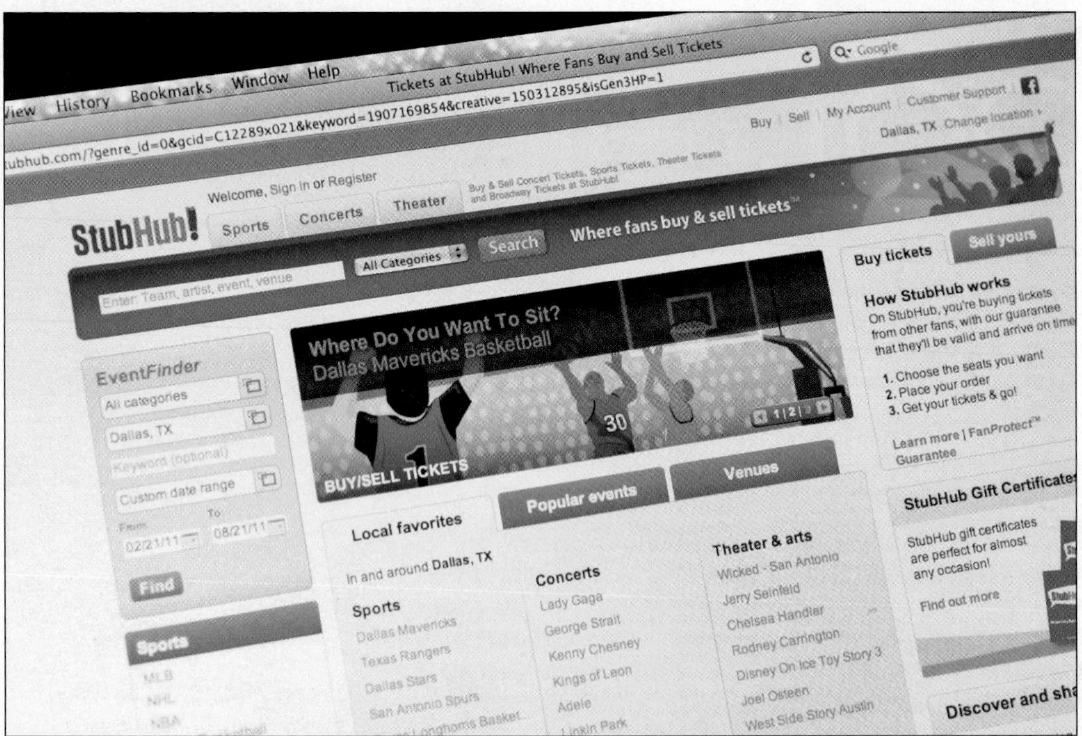


**FIGURE 11.1** StubHub is a database that provides for the exchange of tickets between sellers and buyers. *(NetPhotos/ Alamy)*

# BITS&BYTES

## Music Database Helps You Find New Music

Having good music at hand is easy thanks to music databases such as Pandora and Spotify. The *Music Genome Project* makes it possible for these applications to provide music based on specific preferences. Using almost 400 attributes such as "female lead vocalist" or "club rap roots," the Music Genome Project analyzes, categorizes, and organizes songs into a database that Pandora and Spotify access.

With Pandora (**pandora.com**), you create radio stations that play music with attributes similar to those you provide. For example, if you enjoy music from The Zac Brown Band or you like the song "Wake Me Up," you would enter these as "seeds." Pandora then plays randomly selected songs with attributes similar to the seeds you provided.

Spotify (**spotify.com**) offers music, but in a less random way. With Spotify, you can search to find the songs or artists you want to listen to (see Figure 11.2). Moreover, Spotify incorporates a social networking aspect by informing you what songs your friends are listening to and by sharing playlists from users who choose to make their lists public. Spotify also offers Artist Radio, which acts similarly to Pandora's random music generator.

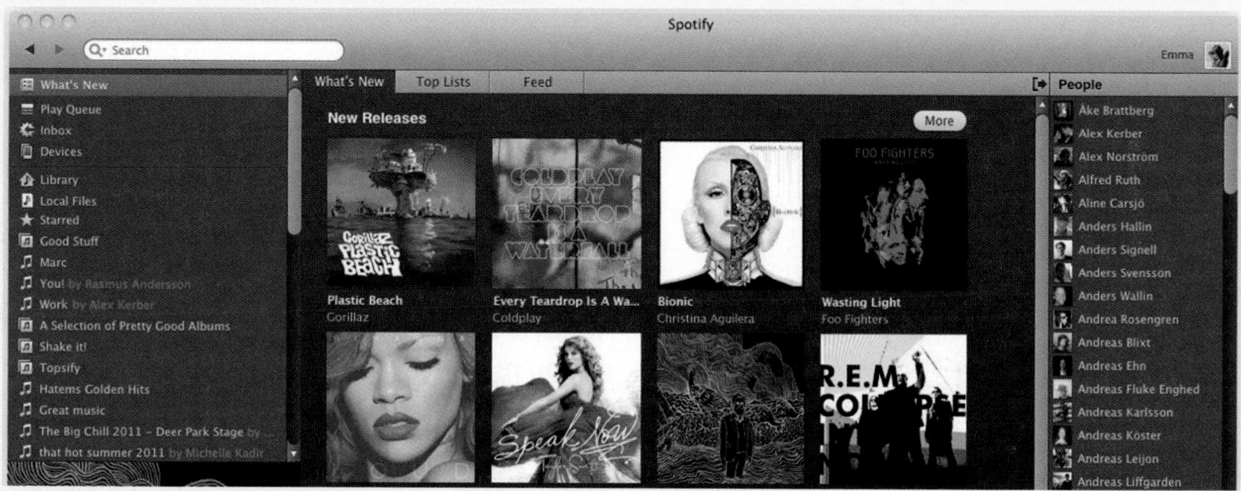


**FIGURE 11.2** Spotify lets you create and share your playlists or listen to those created by your friends or others. *(Handout/MCT/Newscom)*

turned into organized information demands the complexity of a database. For simple tasks, lists are adequate. Most word processing and spreadsheet applications have tools to help you create simple lists. A table you create in Microsoft Word can serve as a list, as can a spreadsheet you create in Microsoft Excel.

Figure 11.3 shows a simple "Books to Buy" list you might create in Excel before beginning college. This list works well because it's simple and suited to just one purpose: to provide you with a list of books you need to buy for a particular semester. If all the information that needs to be tracked were as simple as the information in Figure 11.3, there would be little need for databases.

**When is a list not sufficient for organizing data?** If complex information needs to be organized or more than one person needs to access it, a list isn't an efficient solution. For example, when you enrolled in college, you provided to a number of people basic information about yourself, including your name and address as well as the classes you wished to take. Your school also tracks other information about you, such as your residence hall assignment and meal plan preferences. Consider the lists shown in Figure 11.4. Figure 11.4a is a list the registrar's office might use to keep track of students and the classes they're taking. Figure 11.4b is a list the Housing and Dining manager might use to track a student's assigned housing and his or her selected meal plan.

**What's the problem with lists?** Lists can lead to inefficiencies due to repetition of data and errors from inconsistently entered or updated data. Consider Figure 11.4 again:

1. There is a great deal of duplicated data in the two lists. For example, each time Julio Garza registers for a class, his

| | A | B | C | D |
|---|---|---|---|---|
| 2 | **Books To Buy** | | | |
| 3 | | | | |
| 4 | **Class** | **Title** | **Author** | **Bought** |
| 5 | American Literature 1 | Anthology of American Literature, Volume 1 | McMichael et al. | |
| 6 | American Literature 1 | Moby Dick | Melville | Yes |
| 7 | American Literature 1 | The Last of the Mohicans | Cooper | Yes |
| 8 | English Composition 1 | The Academic Writer's Handbook | Rosen | |
| 9 | English Composition 1 | The Write Stuff: Thinking Through Essays | Sims | Yes |
| 10 | Intro to Business | Better Business | Solomon, Poatsy, Martin | Yes |

**FIGURE 11.3** A basic list created as a spreadsheet in Microsoft Excel or as a table in Microsoft Word is often sufficient to organize simple data.

name and address are entered. He also provides the same data to the Housing and Dining manager when he makes his residence hall and meal plan selections. Such unnecessary extra copies of data in a database, referred to as **data redundancy**, can be problematic, especially when a school has thousands of students. Imagine the time wasted by entering data multiple times, semester after semester, as well as the time required for the database to search through the duplicated information. Consider, too, the increased likelihood that someone will make a data-entry mistake. Additionally, if data is entered multiple times, as is Arthur Stinson's in the list in Figure 11.4a, any reports (such as student bills) generated based on this list will be inaccurate because of the duplicate data. In this case, Arthur could be sent multiple bills for his classes.

2. Each time the information in the list changes, multiple lists must be updated. If a student moves, his or her data will need to be updated in all the lists that contain his or her address. It would be easy to overlook one or more lists or even one or more rows in the same list. Moreover, it wouldn't be possible to easily tell which data is correct. This would lead to a state of **data inconsistency**, when

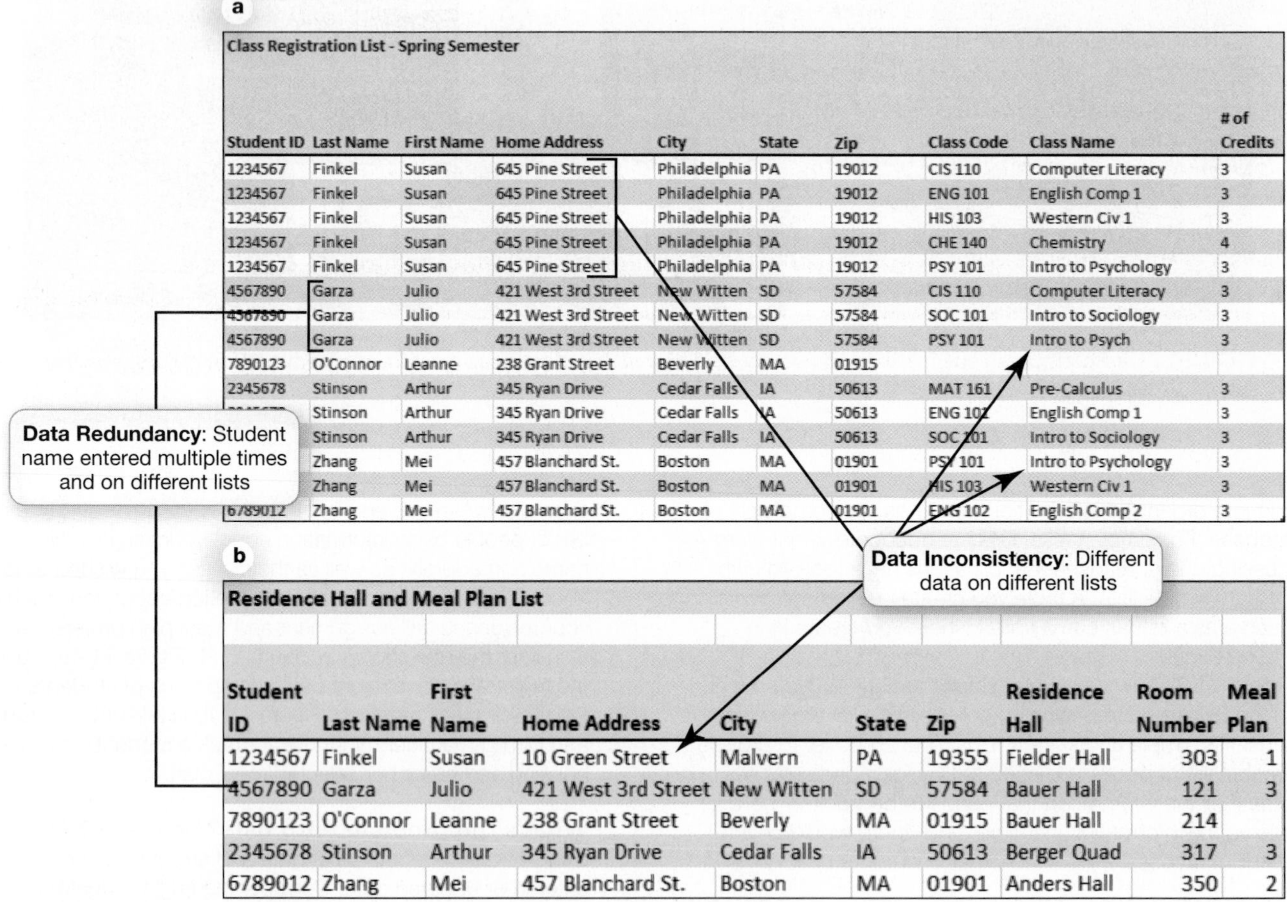


**Class Registration List - Spring Semester**

| Student ID | Last Name | First Name | Home Address | City | State | Zip | Class Code | Class Name | # of Credits |
|---|---|---|---|---|---|---|---|---|---|
| 1234567 | Finkel | Susan | 645 Pine Street | Philadelphia | PA | 19012 | CIS 110 | Computer Literacy | 3 |
| 1234567 | Finkel | Susan | 645 Pine Street | Philadelphia | PA | 19012 | ENG 101 | English Comp 1 | 3 |
| 1234567 | Finkel | Susan | 645 Pine Street | Philadelphia | PA | 19012 | HIS 103 | Western Civ 1 | 3 |
| 1234567 | Finkel | Susan | 645 Pine Street | Philadelphia | PA | 19012 | CHE 140 | Chemistry | 4 |
| 1234567 | Finkel | Susan | 645 Pine Street | Philadelphia | PA | 19012 | PSY 101 | Intro to Psychology | 3 |
| 4567890 | Garza | Julio | 421 West 3rd Street | New Witten | SD | 57584 | CIS 110 | Computer Literacy | 3 |
| 4567890 | Garza | Julio | 421 West 3rd Street | New Witten | SD | 57584 | SOC 101 | Intro to Sociology | 3 |
| 4567890 | Garza | Julio | 421 West 3rd Street | New Witten | SD | 57584 | PSY 101 | Intro to Psych | 3 |
| 7890123 | O'Connor | Leanne | 238 Grant Street | Beverly | MA | 01915 | | | |
| 2345678 | Stinson | Arthur | 345 Ryan Drive | Cedar Falls | IA | 50613 | MAT 161 | Pre-Calculus | 3 |
| [illegible] | Stinson | Arthur | 345 Ryan Drive | Cedar Falls | IA | 50613 | ENG 101 | English Comp 1 | 3 |
| [illegible] | Stinson | Arthur | 345 Ryan Drive | Cedar Falls | IA | 50613 | SOC 101 | Intro to Sociology | 3 |
| [illegible] | Zhang | Mei | 457 Blanchard St. | Boston | MA | 01901 | PSY 101 | Intro to Psychology | 3 |
| [illegible] | Zhang | Mei | 457 Blanchard St. | Boston | MA | 01901 | HIS 103 | Western Civ 1 | 3 |
| 6789012 | Zhang | Mei | 457 Blanchard St. | Boston | MA | 01901 | ENG 102 | English Comp 2 | 3 |

**Residence Hall and Meal Plan List**

| Student ID | Last Name | First Name | Home Address | City | State | Zip | Residence Hall | Room Number | Meal Plan |
|---|---|---|---|---|---|---|---|---|---|
| 1234567 | Finkel | Susan | 10 Green Street | Malvern | PA | 19355 | Fielder Hall | 303 | 1 |
| 4567890 | Garza | Julio | 421 West 3rd Street | New Witten | SD | 57584 | Bauer Hall | 121 | 3 |
| 7890123 | O'Connor | Leanne | 238 Grant Street | Beverly | MA | 01915 | Bauer Hall | 214 | |
| 2345678 | Stinson | Arthur | 345 Ryan Drive | Cedar Falls | IA | 50613 | Berger Quad | 317 | 3 |
| 6789012 | Zhang | Mei | 457 Blanchard St. | Boston | MA | 01901 | Anders Hall | 350 | 2 |

**FIGURE 11.4** (a) A class registration list and (b) a list of residence hall assignments are two lists a college might create to keep track of student information.

different versions of the same data appear in different places in a database. Notice in Figure 11.4 that Susan Finkel's address on the registrar's list differs from that on the Housing and Dining list. It's impossible to tell which address is correct, resulting in data inconsistency.

3. Correct data can be entered into a list but in an inconsistent format. Look at students Julio Garza and Mei Zhang in Figure 11.4a. Both are registered for PSY 101, but two different course names appear: *Intro to Psychology* and *Intro to Psych*. Are these the same course? Which name is correct? Confusion arises when data is inconsistently entered. Establishing data consistency is difficult to do with a list.

**Aside from data redundancy and inconsistency, are there any other problems with using lists instead of databases?** Other problems that occur when using simple lists to organize data are as follows:

- *Inappropriate data:* In Figure 11.4b, each student has selected one of the college's three meal plans. What if someone enters a nonexistent meal plan? This is not only wrong, it can also be confusing to anyone viewing the list. With a list, there are few checks to make sure that data entered is valid.
- *Incomplete data:* In Figure 11.4, Leanne O'Connor has enrolled in the college but hasn't yet registered for courses or chosen a meal plan. It's difficult to tell by looking at her record whether data relating to her course registration and meal plan is available and just wasn't entered or is truly missing.

**Can't I just exercise caution and set rules for creating and updating lists?** Carefully following the rules when you create and update a list like the ones in Figure 11.4 can address many of the problems mentioned, but there's still room for error. Being careful doesn't avoid the problems of data redundancy and inconsistency. And even if you could surmount these problems, it's difficult to share a list with other users and have the data remain consistent. Therefore, for any complex data that needs to be organized or shared, using a database is the most practical and efficient way to avoid the pitfalls associated with using lists.

## Advantages of Using Databases

**How do databases make our lives easier?** Databases provide several main advantages: They manage large amounts of data efficiently, they enable information sharing, and they promote data integrity.

**How can databases manage large amounts of data efficiently?** Often, large amounts of data are complex and need to be organized in specific ways in order to be used most efficiently. Figure 11.4 illustrates some issues that can occur when complex data is put in list format. The more data you have, the more likely you are to store that data in multiple lists or tables in a database.

ACTIVE HELPDESK

**Using Databases**

In this Active Helpdesk call, you'll play the role of a helpdesk staffer, fielding calls about databases, their benefits, their components, and how relational databases organize and manipulate data.

A database has mechanisms to manage large amounts of data and to keep it accurate as it's updated and manipulated.

**How do databases make information sharing possible?** With a database, only one file is maintained. Because of this, databases provide **data centralization**. There is no need for multiple lists, as there was when the individual college offices each maintained their own independent lists. A centralized database becomes a shared source that everyone can access (see Figure 11.5). Each department that needs to use student information accesses it from the same set of data. A centralized database also increases efficiency because there are no files to reconcile with each other. In addition, many databases also provide the ability to control who has access to the data, so security of data isn't diminished because it's centralized.

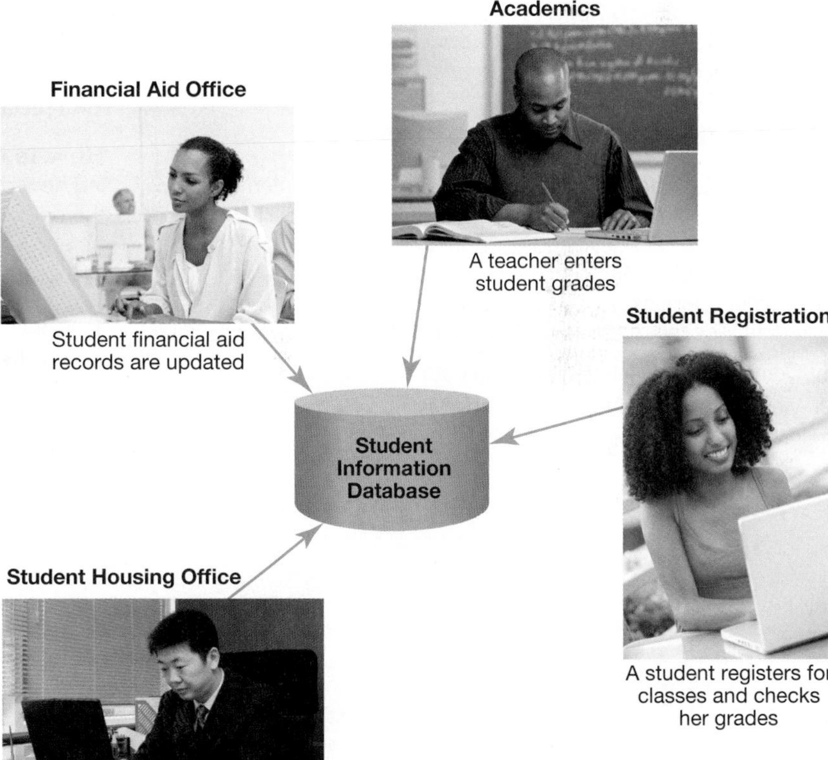


**FIGURE 11.5** A database centralizes data so that only one copy of relevant data must be maintained. All database users therefore access the same up-to-date information. *(wavebreakmedia/Shutterstock; AVAVA/Shutterstock; Monkey Business Images/Shutterstock; Tan Kian Khoon/Shutterstock)*

**How do databases promote data integrity? Data integrity** means that the data contained in the database is accurate and reliable. Data centralization goes a long way toward ensuring data integrity. Instead of data being stored in multiple lists that have to be maintained, in a database, data is stored in only one place. When multiple lists are kept, information may become inconsistent because each list is maintained separately. If an address changes, it needs to be changed in only one place in a database, whereas with multiple lists, it's quite possible that data will be updated in one list and not in another, as was illustrated with a change in address for Susan Finkel in Figure 11.4.

**Are there any disadvantages associated with databases?** Databases can be more time consuming and expensive to set up and administer than lists. Great care must be exercised in the design of databases to ensure they'll function as intended. Although average individuals can design small databases, it's helpful to have an experienced **database administrator** (or **database designer**)—an IT professional who is responsible for designing, constructing, and maintaining databases—for larger databases. Database administrators (DBAs) review and manage data on an ongoing basis to ensure the data is flowing smoothly into and out of the database. Figure 11.6 shows a view of the MySQL Enterprise Dashboard screen, a tool used primarily by DBAs when reviewing the performance of a database. DBAs can monitor table usage and CPU utilization to help determine whether database performance is acceptable.

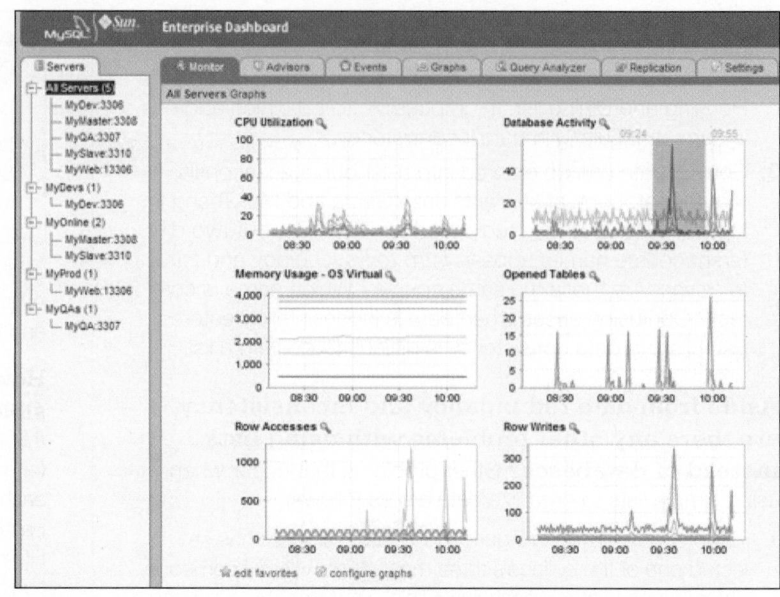


**FIGURE 11.6** The Enterprise Dashboard in MySQL helps DBAs review database performance. *(Courtesy of Oracle)*

## Database Management Systems

**How are databases created?** Databases are created and managed using a **database management system (DBMS)**. A DBMS is specially designed application software (such as Oracle Database or Microsoft Access) that interacts with the user, other applications, and the database to capture and analyze data. The four main operations of a DBMS are as follows:

1. Creating databases and entering data
2. Viewing (or browsing) and sorting data
3. Querying (extracting) data
4. Outputting data

In this section we look at the considerations required in creating and maintaining a database. But first, you need to understand some basic database terminology.

## Database Terminology

**How is data stored in a database?** Understanding how databases store information requires knowing the unique terminology developed to describe databases. As shown in Figure 11.7, databases have three main components:

1. *Fields:* A database stores each category of information in a **field**. Fields are displayed in columns. Each field is identified by a **field name**, which is a way of describing the information in the field. In Figure 11.7, there are seven different fields (Student ID, Last Name, First Name, Address, City, State, and Zip Code).

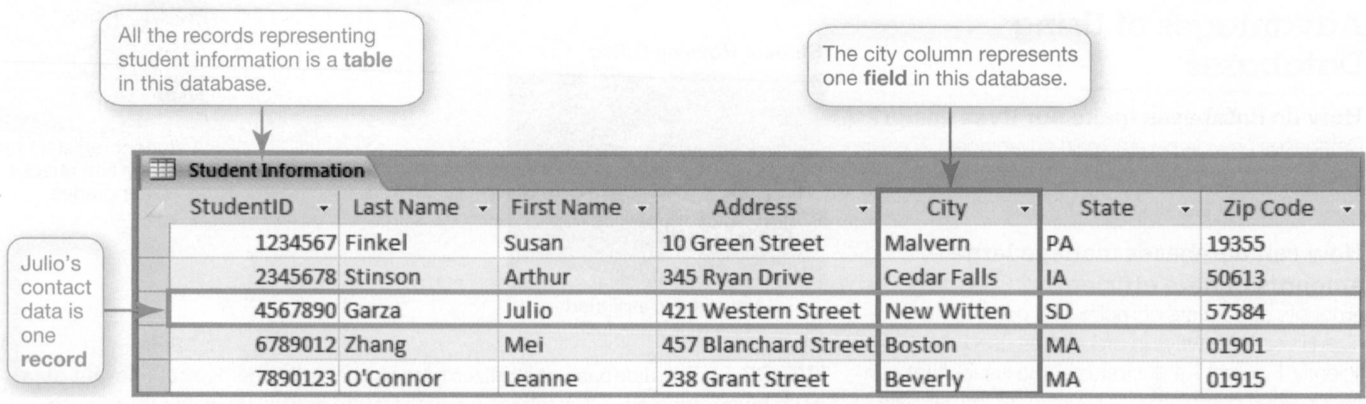


Student Information

| StudentID | Last Name | First Name | Address | City | State | Zip Code |
|---|---|---|---|---|---|---|
| 1234567 | Finkel | Susan | 10 Green Street | Malvern | PA | 19355 |
| 2345678 | Stinson | Arthur | 345 Ryan Drive | Cedar Falls | IA | 50613 |
| 4567890 | Garza | Julio | 421 Western Street | New Witten | SD | 57584 |
| 6789012 | Zhang | Mei | 457 Blanchard Street | Boston | MA | 01901 |
| 7890123 | O'Connor | Leanne | 238 Grant Street | Beverly | MA | 01915 |

**FIGURE 11.7** In a database, a category of information is stored in a field. A group of related fields is called a record, and a group of related records is called a table.

2. *Records:* A group of related fields is called a **record**. For example, in Figure 11.7, a student's ID, name, and complete address comprise a record.
3. *Tables (Files):* A group of related records is called a **table** (or **file**). Tables are usually organized by a common subject. Figure 11.7 shows a table (called "Student Information") that contains records representing contact information for students.

## Planning and Creating the Database

**How do I create a database with a DBMS?** To create a database with a DBMS, you must first describe the data to be captured. This description is contained in the database's files and is referred to as the **data dictionary** (or the **database schema**). The data dictionary is like a map of the database and defines the features of the fields in the database. You need to build a data dictionary entry for each field you'll use in a database before you enter data into the database. This forces you to consider up front the data you need to capture.

The attributes that define the data in the data dictionary include the following:

- The field name
- The *data type* (type of data in the field, such as text, numeric, or date/time)
- The description of the field (optional)
- Any properties (decimals, formatting, etc.) of that particular type of data
- The *field size* (the expected length of data for each field)

These attributes are **metadata**: data that describes other data. Metadata is an integral part of the data dictionary. Describing the data in this way helps to categorize it and sets parameters for entering valid data into the database (such as a 10-digit number in a phone number field). In addition to describing the specific features of the data to be entered in the database, the data dictionary describes relationships between the data, how the data will be indexed (which speeds up access to the data), and what kind of output may be required of the database.

**How do I include data dictionary details in a database?** The information from the data dictionary is used to create the tables in the database. In Microsoft Access, tables can be created in Datasheet View or Design View. As shown in Figure 11.8, Design View gives you a detailed view of the field name, data type, and other data elements—known as **field properties** in an Access database table—which were all defined in the data dictionary.

**How are database tables created?** Database tables are simple to create using four basic steps:

1. Input field names. Field names must be unique within a table. For example, in the table in Figure 11.8a, the field name "StateAbbreviation" is used to store the abbreviation for the state where the student lives. Sometimes the field name used to create the table may not be the best to display on forms and reports. The Caption property in Microsoft Access lets you display a field name of your choice that might be more meaningful, such as Last Name instead of LastName. In Figure 11.8a, the caption "State" is used as the caption for the StateAbbreviation field.
2. Define the data type for each field. For the "State" field in Figure 11.8a, you use a Short Text data type because state names are expressed using text characters.
3. Set a maximum field size for the field. For the State field in Figure 11.8a, the Field Size property is set to "2" (two characters). Therefore, the data would be restricted to the two-letter state abbreviations such as "DE" (the default, in this case), "MA," "TX," and the like.
4. Set a **default value** for a field, if necessary. A default value is the value the database automatically uses for the field unless the user enters another value. Default values are useful for field data that's frequently the same. For example,

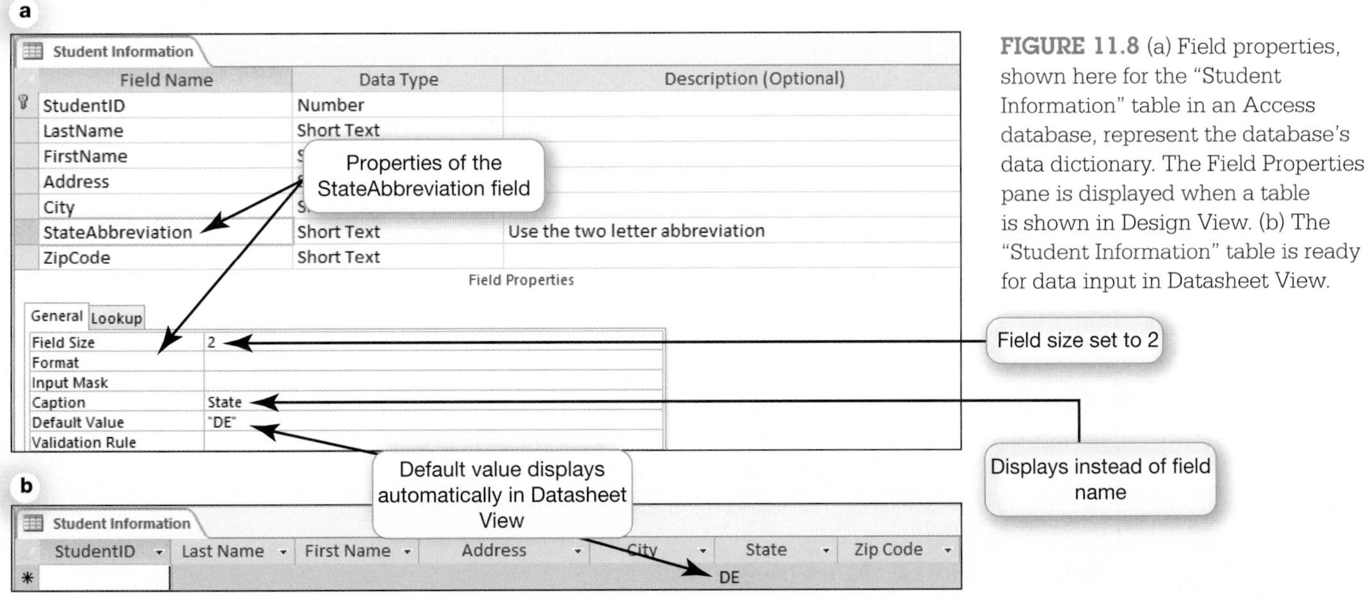


**FIGURE 11.8** (a) Field properties, shown here for the "Student Information" table in an Access database, represent the database's data dictionary. The Field Properties pane is displayed when a table is shown in Design View. (b) The "Student Information" table is ready for data input in Datasheet View.

setting a default value for a "State" field saves users from having to enter that value for each student if most students live in the same state.

You need to repeat these steps for each field in the table. When completed, the resulting table, shown in Datasheet View in Figure 11.8b, is ready for data entry.

**How do I know what fields are needed in my database?** Careful planning is required to identify each distinct category of data you need to capture. Each field should describe a unique piece of data and should not combine two separate pieces of data. For example, first and last names are separate pieces of data, and you'd want to create a separate field for each rather than having one field for "Name." For instance, suppose you want to send an e-mail message to students addressing all of them by their first name (such as "Dear Geri"). If Geri's first and last names are in the same field in the database, extracting just her first name for the salutation will be difficult. Similarly, if the name data is combined, it will be difficult to sort by last name (unless the data is inputted with last name first). Separating the data into individual fields allows for better filtering and sorting of all data.

**What happens if I need to add or delete fields from the database?** The purpose of planning the database ahead of time is to avoid having to change the structure of the database. Once relationships between the data are established and data is entered in the database, it's difficult to add and delete fields. It's often best to add sample or limited amounts of data to test your database before you fully populate (enter data into) it.

**Are there specific rules for establishing field names?** The following are some guidelines in establishing field names:

- Field names must be unique within a table. For example, you can't have two fields labeled "Name" in one table; they must be different, such as "FirstName" and "LastName."
- It's helpful to distinguish similarly named fields in different tables to avoid confusion if those fields appear together in other components of the database. For example, in a college database, there may be separate tables for Student and Faculty. In each table, there will be fields for "FirstName" and "LastName." Those fields may be used together in the same report that details a student's schedule. To avoid confusion, it would be better to use field names with some notation that distinguishes the table that the field is from, such as "S_LastName" and "S_FirstName" in the Student table and "F_LastName" and "F_FirstName" in the Faculty table.
- It is best practice to not use spaces in field names because they can cause errors when the objects are involved in programming tasks. Underscores or CamelCase notation can be used in lieu of spaces. Of course, if you want field names to *display* with spaces then the caption field property should be used.

Creating a data dictionary will help you plan for these types of naming arrangements.

**Can any type of data be entered in any field?** As noted earlier, when fields are created in the database, the user assigns each field a **data type** (or **field type**). The data type indicates what type of data can be stored in the field and prevents the wrong type of data from being entered into the field. Data types for Microsoft Access include text, numbers, and hyperlinks. Figure 11.9 lists the most common data types, with examples of each.

FIGURE 11.9

**Common Data Types in Microsoft Access**

| DATA TYPE | USED TO STORE | EXAMPLES |
|---|---|---|
| Short Text | Letters, symbols, or combinations of letters, symbols, and numbers (up to 255 characters). Short text also contains numbers that can't be used in calculations, such as phone numbers and zip codes. | Cecilia<br>PSY 101<br>(610) 555-1212 |
| Long Text | Long blocks of text (up to 65,535 characters). | Four score and seven years ago our fathers brought forth on this continent, a new nation, conceived in Liberty, and dedicated to the proposition that all men are created equal. |
| Number and Currency | Numeric data that can be used in calculations or that is represented as currency. | 512<br>1.789<br>$1,230 |
| Date/Time | Dates and times in standard notation. Data may be used in calculations, such as calculating the number of days between today and your next birthday. | 2/21/2016<br>10:48:01 |
| Calculated | Results of a calculation; often involves numeric or date/time data from other fields in the database. | Price * Quantity * .06 |
| OLE Object | Pictures, charts, or files from another Windows-based application. | JPG file<br>Word document |
| Hyperlink | Alphanumeric data stored as a hyperlink address to a web page, an e-mail address, or an existing file. | pearsonhighered.com<br>techinactionname@email.com |

SOUND BYTE

**Creating an Access Database**

In this Sound Byte, you'll learn how to create an Access database to catalog a collection of CDs and DVDs. The Sound Byte will take you through a systematic process that will result in a fully functional small database.

**How much data can be entered into a field?** As noted above, **field size** defines the maximum number of characters that a field can hold. As a rule, you should tailor the field size to match the maximum length of the data it contains. If a numeric field has a size of 5, it can hold a number that has up to 5 digits (from 1 to 99999). It is important to ensure that the selected field length is long enough to enable storage of the longest possible piece of data that might be entered into the field. Otherwise, data may be truncated (a portion of it chopped off and lost) during data entry.

## Using Primary Keys

**Can fields have the same values in the same table?** It's possible that two students live in the same town or have the same last name, so it's possible for different fields to have the same values. However, to keep records distinct, each record must have one field that has a value unique to that record. This unique field is called a **primary key field**. For example, as shown in Figure 11.10, in the "Student Information" table, the primary key field is "Student ID." Establishing a primary key and ensuring that it's unique makes it impossible to duplicate records.

**What makes a good primary key?** The most important constraint is that the primary key be unique, though there are other considerations. Social Security numbers, although unique to individuals, aren't a good choice because people often don't want them used for fear of identity theft if the data were misused. Other common numbers that might be used to identify data within a specific organization (such as a credit card number or driver's license number) also have their own flaws as universal unique identifiers.

In practice, primary keys don't have to be numbers that already represent something. In most instances, the number used to represent a record is some form of serial number that begins with the first record and increases serially as each new record is generated. For example, when you place an order with **Amazon.com**, your transaction gets a unique order number. This number is a primary key in Amazon's database. It's essential to have a unique number for each order because it would be difficult to keep track of the order without one. Many database programs have a means of automatically generating a unique identifier that has no meaning outside of the database system. In Microsoft Access, for example, this unique identifier is the AutoNumber data type.

**Is there a way to ensure data is organized efficiently?** You create database tables for two reasons: to hold unique data about a subject and to describe unique events or transactions. In databases, the goal is to reduce data redundancy by recording data only once. The process to ensure data is organized most efficiently is called data **normalization**. For example, normalization would remove issues such as the data redundancy shown in Figure 11.3 by separating data into two distinct student information and course information tables. ■

Student Information

| Student ID | Last Name | First Name | Address | City | State | Zip Code |
|---|---|---|---|---|---|---|
| 1234567 | Finkel | Susan | 645 Pine Street | Philadelphia | PA | 19012 |
| 3456789 | Finkel | Susan | 25 Maywood Road | Darien | CT | 06820 |
| 6789012 | Zhang | Mei | 457 Blanchard Street | Boston | MA | 01901 |
| 2345678 | Stinson | Arthur | 345 Ryan Drive | Cedar Falls | IA | 50613 |
| 4567890 | Garza | Julio | 421 Western Street | New Witten | SD | 57584 |

Same name, different Student ID

**FIGURE 11.10** The "StudentID" field makes an ideal primary key field because even students with the same name won't have the same ID number.

# database TYPES

Many different types of electronic databases have been used since the invention of the computer. The three major types of databases currently in use are *relational, object-oriented,* and *multidimensional*. Of these three, relational databases have the largest market share, but the market share of multidimensional databases is growing at a fast pace. Microsoft Access is the most popular relational database software.

## Relational Databases

**What is a relational database?** A **relational database** operates by organizing data into various tables based on logical groupings. For example, all student address and contact information would be grouped into one table, while the housing and dining information is grouped into a separate table. It would be redundant to have the same student contact information also included in the housing and dining table, so there needs to be some way in which the student contact information can be linked to the housing and dining information. In relational databases, a link between tables that defines how the data is related is referred to as a **relationship**. A common field between the two tables is used to create the link. In Figure 11.11, "StudentID" is the common field in the "Residence Assignments" and "Student Information" tables, and "ResidenceID" is the common field in the "Residence Halls" and "Residence Assignments" tables. The common field in one table is that table's *primary key,* and the common field in the related table is called a **foreign key**.

Because data is changed continually in a database, it's important to ensure that the data in related tables is synchronized and that a record isn't added or modified in one table and not the other. To prevent orphan records and to keep related data synchronized, you have the option of enforcing **referential integrity** for each relationship. Referential integrity means that for each value in the foreign key table there is a corresponding value in the primary key table.

For instance, if you attempt to enter a student's record in the "Residence Assignments" table with a StudentID number that doesn't exist in the "Student Information" table (the primary key table) and referential integrity is being enforced, an error message will display. You first would need to add the student to the "Student Information" table and then enter the student in the "Residence Assignments" table.

**Are there different types of relationships in relational databases?** A relationship in relational databases can take one of three forms:

1. A **one-to-many relationship** is characterized by a record appearing only once in one table while having the capability of appearing many times in a related table. For example, as shown in Figure 11.11, the "1" next to ResidenceID in the "Residence Halls" table indicates there is only one instance of each ResidenceID in the "Residence Halls" table, and the "∞" next to ResidenceID in the "Residence Assignments" table indicates that many records can have the same ResidenceID in the "Residence Assignments" table. There is only one of each residence hall, but each residence hall will be listed for each student who will be living there. One-to-many relationships are the most common type of relationship in relational databases.

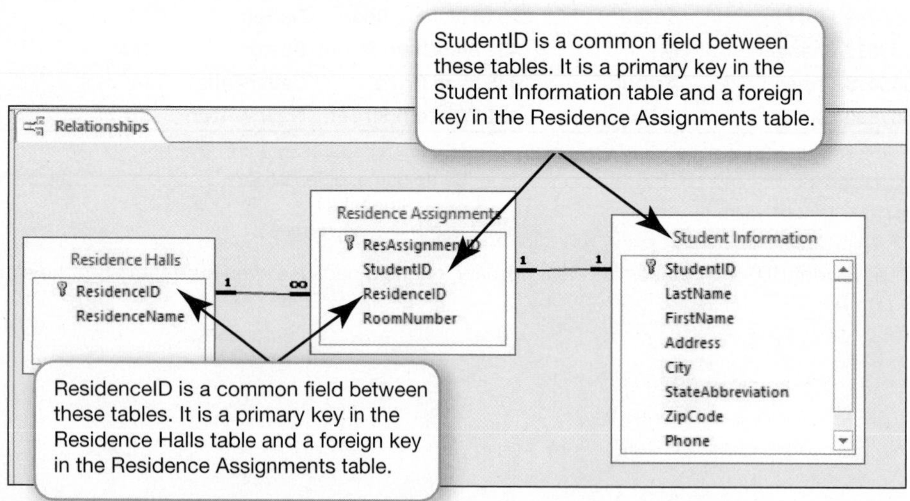


**FIGURE 11.11** The foreign key field is the same as the primary key field in a related table.

2. A **one-to-one relationship** indicates that for each record in a table there is only one corresponding record in a related table. For example, each student is assigned a room. Because a student can only live in one residence hall at a time, a one-to-one relationship is established, as shown in Figure 11.11 by the "1" next to the StudentID field in both the "Residence Assignments" table and the "Student Information" table.
3. A **many-to-many relationship** is characterized by records in one table being related to multiple records in a second table and vice versa. For instance, a table of students could be related to a table of student employers. The employers could employ many students, and students could work for more than one employer.

Relational databases are great for data that can fit into tables and be organized into fields and records. But some data, such as graphics, video, or audio files, are handled better in an object-oriented database.

## Object-Oriented Databases

**What is an object-oriented database?** An **object-oriented database** stores data in objects rather than in tables. Objects contain not only data but also methods for processing or manipulating that data. This allows object-oriented databases to store more types of data than relational databases and to access that data faster.

For example, a "student" object that contains data about the courses a student is taking might also store the instructions for generating a bill for the student based on his or her course load. Because object-oriented databases store the instructions for doing computations in the same place as they store the data, they can usually process requests for information faster than can relational databases (which would only store the student information).

**Why would I use an object-oriented database?** Object-oriented databases are more adept at handling **unstructured data** such as audio clips (including MP3 files), video clips, pictures, and extremely large documents. Data of this type is known as a **binary large object (BLOB)** because it's encoded in binary form. In comparison, relational databases are best for the storage of **structured (analytical) data** (such as "Bill" or "345").

Because businesses today need to store a greater variety of data, object-oriented databases are becoming more popular. Many relational database systems have been expanded to include object-oriented components. For a business to use its data in an object-oriented database, the data needs to undergo a costly conversion process. However, the faster access and reusability of the database objects can provide advantages for large businesses.

Object-oriented databases also need to use a query language to access and manage data. A **query language** is a specially designed computer language used to manipulate data in or extract data from a database. Many object-oriented databases use **Object Query Language (OQL)**, which is similar in many respects to **Structured Query Language (SQL)**, a standard language used to construct queries to extract data from relational databases.

## Multidimensional Databases

**What is a multidimensional database?** A **multidimensional database** stores data that can be analyzed from different perspectives, called dimensions. This distinguishes it from a relational database, which stores data in tables that have only two dimensions (fields and records). Multidimensional databases organize data in a cube format. Each data cube has a *measure attribute,* which is the main type of data that the cube is tracking. Other elements of the cube are known as *feature attributes,* which describe the measure attribute in some meaningful way.

For example, sales of automobiles (measure attribute) could be categorized by various dimensions such as region, automobile model, or sales month—all feature attributes (see Figure 11.12). In addition, the database could be constructed to define different levels within a particular feature attribute (such as state and town within a region).

**What are the advantages of multidimensional databases?** The two main advantages of multidimensional databases are as follows:

1. They can be customized to provide information to a variety of users based on their needs.
2. They can process data much faster than pure relational databases can.

The need for processing speed is critical when deploying a large database accessed via the Internet. Therefore, large databases such as eBay are usually designed as multidimensional databases. Oracle Corporation has morphed its relational database into a multidimensional database. This was primarily in response to customers who were using an Oracle database for applications deployed on the web and who needed better ways of storing and accessing image, audio, and video files. ■

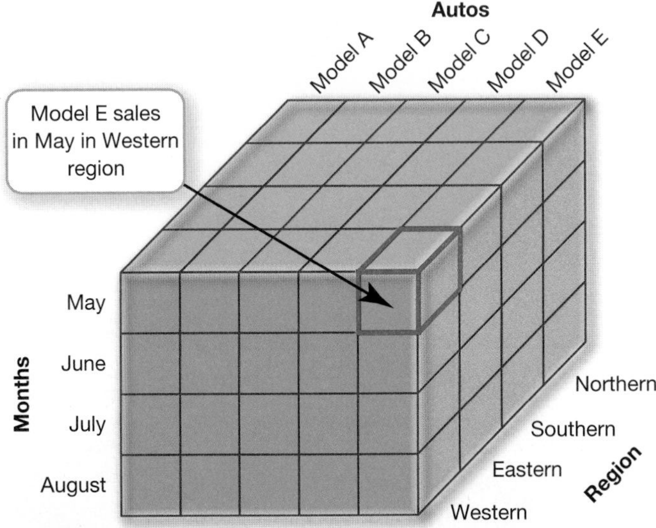


**FIGURE 11.12** Multidimensional databases store data in at least three dimensions.

# database FUNCTIONS

Once you've designed and tested your database to ensure that it works properly, you can begin creating individual records in (or populating) the database. After the database has been populated with data, users can employ certain methods to extract subsets of data from the database and then output the data in a meaningful and presentable format. In this section, we look at these database functions.

## Inputting Data

**How do I get data into the database?** You can key data directly into the database. However, because a great deal of data already exists in some type of electronic format, such as word processing documents, spreadsheets, and web-based sources, most databases can import data electronically from other files, which can save an enormous amount of keying and reduces the amount of data-entry errors.

When importing data, the data must exactly match the format of the database. Most databases usually apply filters to the data to determine whether it's in the correct format as defined by the data dictionary. Nonconforming data is flagged (either on-screen or in a report) so that you can modify the data to fit the database's format.

**How can I make manual entry into a database more efficient? Input forms** are used to control how new data is entered into a shared database. Figure 11.13 shows an example of an input form for the "Student Information" table. Each field has a label that indicates the data to be placed in the field. The data is inputted into the blank boxes. Notes have been added to the form to guide the users. In addition to being used to input new data, input forms are used to make changes to existing data in the database. Because a form can be configured to display individual records, making changes to data by using a form ensures that the change is made to the right record.

## Data Validation

**How can I ensure that only valid data is entered into a field? Validation** is the process of ensuring that data entered into a field meets specified guidelines. A **validation rule** is generally defined as part of the data dictionary and is specified in the field properties. Violations of validation rules usually result in an error message displayed on the screen with a suggested action so that the error can be addressed. Common validation rules include the following:

- *Range check:* A **range check** ensures that the data entered into the field falls within a certain range of values. For instance, you could set a **field constraint** (a property that must be satisfied for an entry to be accepted into



**FIGURE 11.13** Input forms are used to enter data into tables.

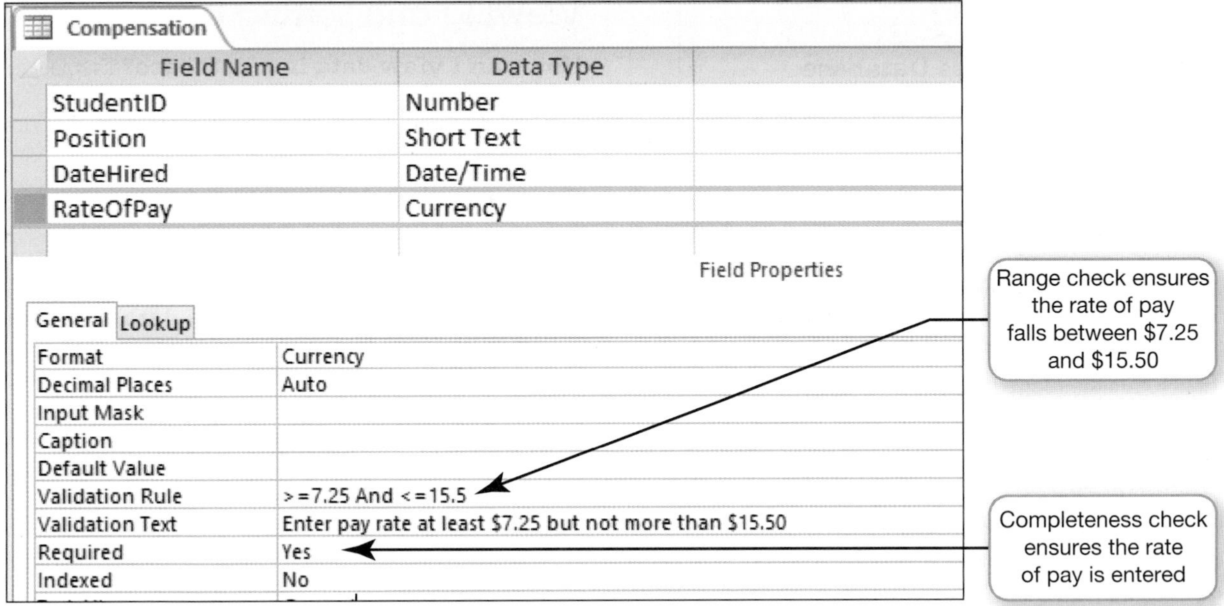


**FIGURE 11.14** Validation rules help ensure correct data is entered.

the field) to restrict the rate of pay to fall within a certain range. Figure 11.14 shows a range check in the Field Properties pane for an Access database. A validation rule restricts the entries for a student's rate of pay for his or her campus job to amounts between $7.25 and $15.50. If users tried to enter a rate of pay less than $7.25 or greater than $15.50, they would be notified of a range error and the input would not be accepted, as shown in Figure 11.15.

- *Completeness:* A **completeness check** ensures that all required fields have been completed. For example, Figure 11.14 shows the "Required" property set to "Yes," so when data is not entered in the field, as is the case in Figure 11.16, the database performs a completeness check, notices the blank "Rate of Pay" field, and displays an error message to alert the user of the omission.
- *Consistency check:* A **consistency check** compares the values of data in two or more fields to see if those values are reasonable. For example, your birth date and the date you enrolled in school are often in a college's database. It's not possible for you to have enrolled in college before you were born. Furthermore, most college students are at least 16 years old. Therefore, a consistency check on these fields might ensure that your birth date is at least 16 or more years before the date when you enrolled in college.

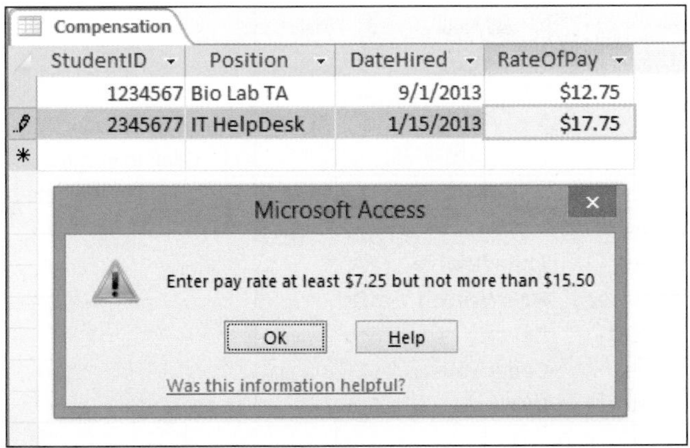


**FIGURE 11.15** Access users see this pop-up when they enter a value that falls outside the stated range of acceptable values. The displayed message is generated from the text typed in the Validation Text property.

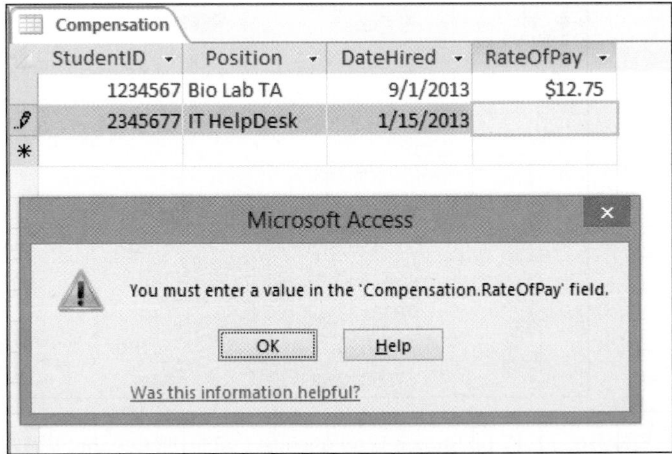


**FIGURE 11.16** Access users see this pop-up when they do not enter a value in a field that has been indicated as being required.

SOUND BYTE

**Improving an Access Database**

In this Sound Byte, you'll learn how to create input forms, queries, and reports to simplify maintenance of your CD and DVD database. You'll follow along step by step, using Microsoft Access wizards to create and modify queries to suit your needs.

- *Alphabetic and numeric checks:* An **alphabetic check** confirms that only textual characters (such as "Robin") are entered in a field. A **numeric check** confirms that only numbers are entered in the field. With these checks in place, "$J2.5n" would not be accepted as the price of a product or as a first name. Setting the data type as "Number" (or "Currency") or "Short Text" or "Long Text" will help ensure that numeric or text information is entered, respectively.

## Viewing and Sorting Data

**How can I view data in a database?** Displaying the tables on-screen and browsing through all the data is an option with most databases. In many instances, you'll only want to view the data one record at a time and not display all the data in an entire table. Forms are used to display individual records, either alone or in conjunction with other related data.

**How can I reorder records in a database?** You can easily sort data into ascending or descending order. Figure 11.17a shows an Access database table in which the records were inputted in no particular order. By highlighting a column (in this case "Last Name") and then clicking Ascending on the Ribbon, the database displays the records in alphabetical order by last name, as shown in Figure 11.17b.

a

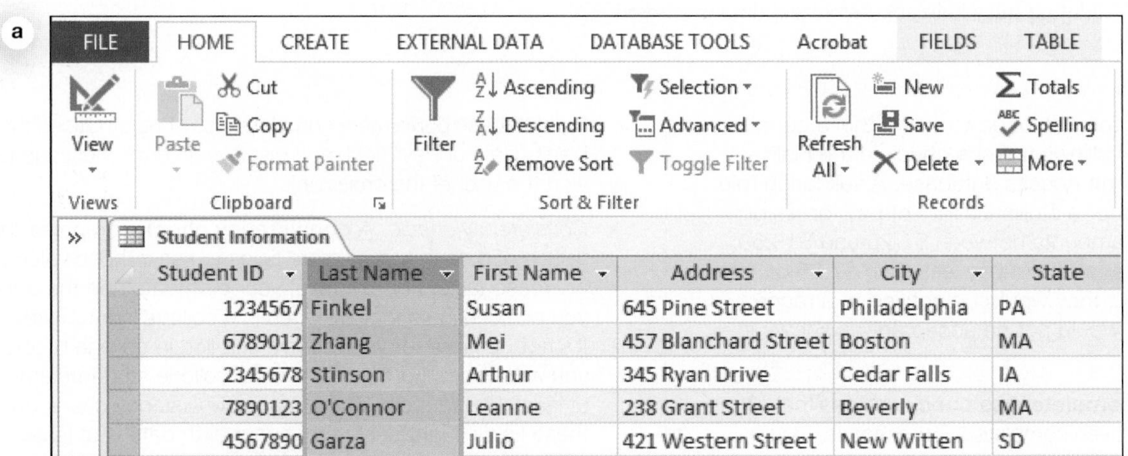


b

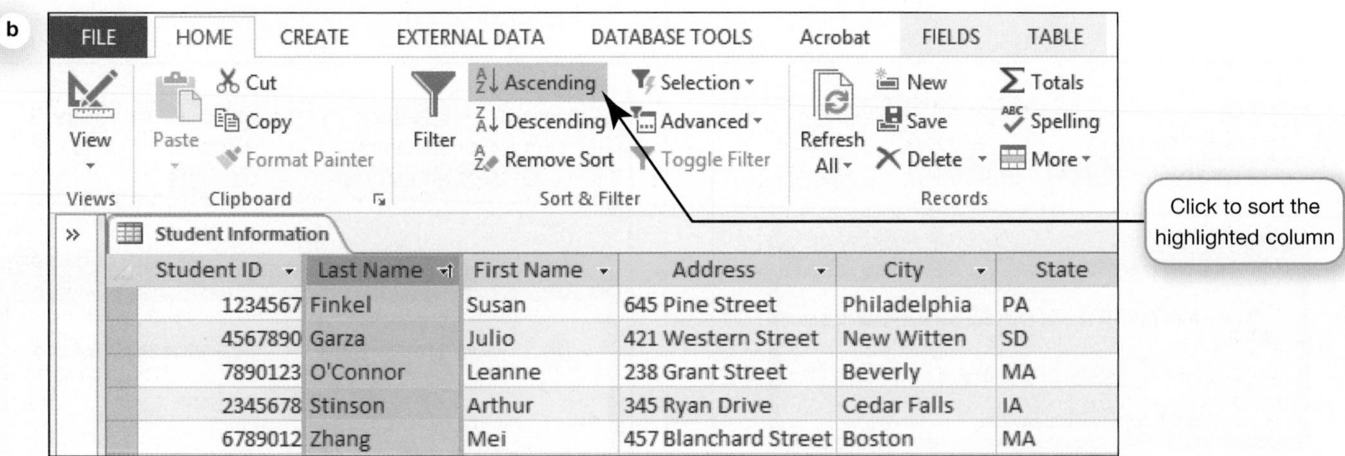


**FIGURE 11.17** (a) Shown is an unsorted table. Notice that the "Last Name" column is selected (highlighted) for sorting. (b) Selecting the sorting option "Ascending" produces the sorted output with the records sorted in ascending alphabetical order by last name.

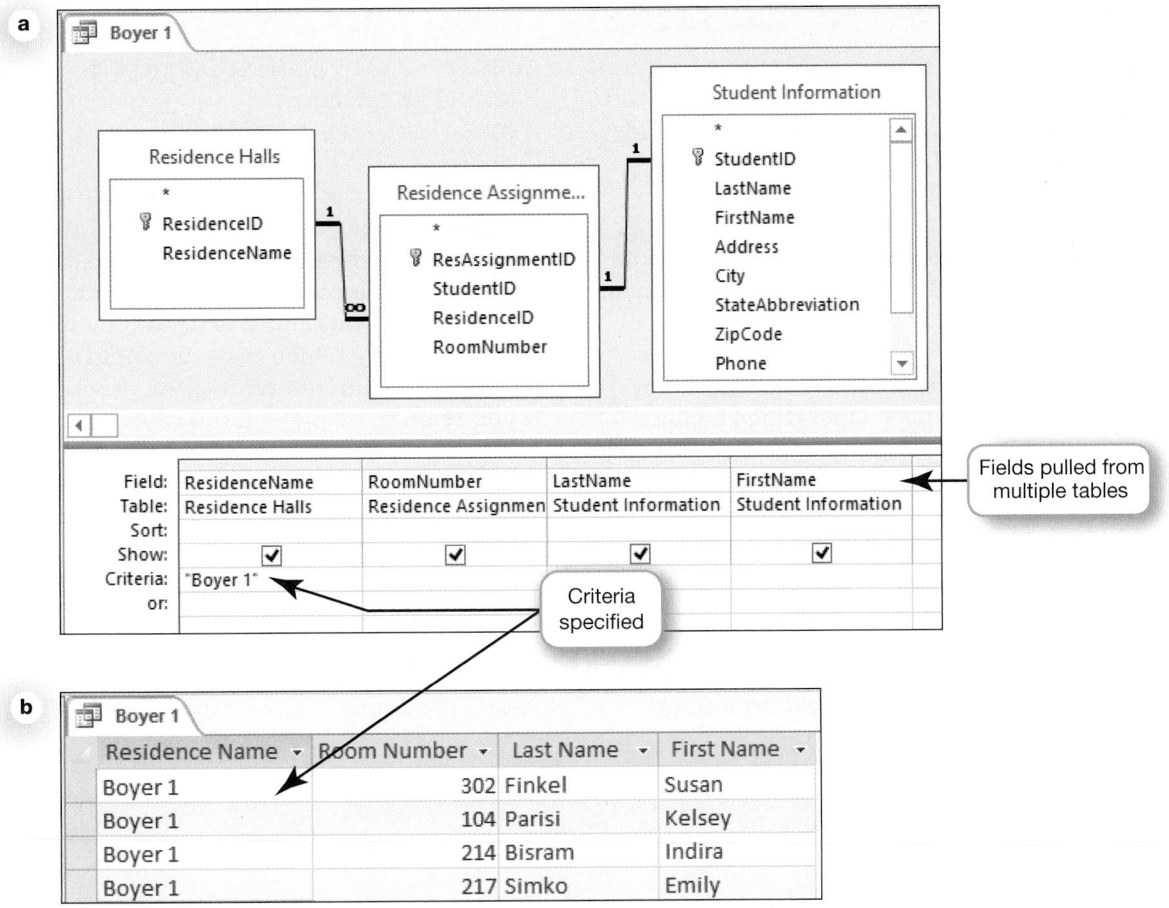


FIGURE 11.18 (a) When creating a query, you can specify fields from multiple tables as well as specific criteria within a field. (b) The outcome reflects those records meeting the specified criteria.

## Extracting or Querying Data

**What if I want to display only a certain subset of data in a database?** There are two ways to display only those records that match particular criteria:

1. *Use a filter:* A **filter** temporarily displays records that match certain criteria. When you apply a filter, you can't save the results, so filters are useful if you don't need to review the results at another time. Filters can only be applied to fields in one table, so if you need to combine fields from multiple tables to achieve your subset of data, queries would be a better option.
2. *Create a query:* A database **query** is a way of retrieving information that defines a particular subset of data. However, unlike a filter, a query can be used to extract data from one or multiple tables. When you create a query, you choose the fields that should be included in the results and specify the criteria for selecting records. For example, as shown in Figure 11.18a, if you wanted to create a list of students living in the Boyer 1 dorm and their room numbers, you would need to pull information from the "Student Information" table (FirstName and LastName), "Residence Halls" table (ResidenceName), and "Residence Assignments" table (RoomNumber). Then you'd need to specify to see only those records pertaining to a specific dorm, in this case Boyer 1. Figure 11.18b displays the results for this query.

**Do I have to learn a query language to develop queries for my database?** All modern DBMSs contain a query language that the software uses to retrieve and display records. A query language consists of its own vocabulary and sentence structure that you use to frame the requests. Query languages are similar to full-blown programming languages but are usually much easier to learn. The most popular query language used today is SQL. Modern database systems provide wizards or other mechanisms to guide you through the process of creating queries. Figure 11.18a shows an example of an Access query being created in Design View that allows you to easily select query elements. You can also create a query using a Simple Query Wizard in Microsoft Access. When you use the Simple Query Wizard or Design View, you're actually using SQL commands without realizing it.

However, you may want to create your own SQL queries in Access, modify existing queries at the SQL language level,

# DIG DEEPER Structured Query Language (SQL)

To extract records from a database, you use a query language. Almost all relational and object-oriented databases today use Structured Query Language, or SQL. Oracle, Microsoft SQL Server, Microsoft Access, IBM DB2, and MySQL are examples of popular databases that use SQL.

SQL uses relational algebra to extract data from databases. **Relational algebra** is the use of English-like expressions that have variables and operations, much like algebraic equations. Variables include table names, field names, or selection criteria for the data you wish to display. Operations include directions such as *select* (which enables you to pick variable names), *from* (which tells the database which table to use), and *where* (which enables you to specify selection criteria). The two most common queries used to extract data using relational algebra are select queries and join queries.

A **select query** displays a subset of data from a table (or tables) based on the criteria you specify. A typical select query has the following format:

```
SELECT (Field Name 1, Field Name 2, …)
FROM (Table Name)
WHERE (Selection Criteria)
```

The first line of the query contains variables for the field names you want to display. The FROM statement enables you to specify the table name from which the data will be retrieved. The last line (the WHERE statement) is used only when you wish to specify which records need to be displayed (such as all students with GPAs greater than 3.3). If you wish to display all the rows (records) in the table, then you don't use the WHERE statement (see Figure 11.19).

Suppose you want to create a phone list that includes all students from the Student Information table in Figure 11.19a. The SQL query you would send to the database would look like this:

```
SELECT (FirstName, LastName, CellPhone)
FROM (Student Information Table)
```

**a**

Student Information

| Student ID | LastName | FirstName | HomeAddress | City | State | Zip Code | CellPhone |
|---|---|---|---|---|---|---|---|
| 1234567 | Finkel | Susan | 645 Pine Street | Philadelphia | PA | 19012 | (610) 555-2367 |
| 4567890 | Garza | Julio | 421 Western Street | New Witten | SD | 57584 | (454) 555-6512 |
| 7890123 | O'Connor | Leanne | 238 Grant Street | Beverly | MA | 01915 | (303) 555-8723 |
| 2345678 | Stinson | Arthur | 345 Ryan Drive | Cedar Falls | IA | 50613 | (427) 555-2398 |
| 6789012 | Zhang | Mei | 457 Blanchard Street | Boston | MA | 01901 | (302) 555-4976 |

Query applied to this table

SELECT (FirstName, LastName, CellPhone)
FROM (Student Information Table)

Produces this output

**b**

| FirstName | LastName | CellPhone |
|---|---|---|
| Susan | Finkel | (610) 555-2367 |
| Julio | Garza | (454) 555-6512 |
| Leanne | O'Connor | (303) 555-8723 |
| Arthur | Stinson | (427) 555-2398 |
| Mei | Zhang | (302) 555-4976 |

Query applied to this table

SELECT (FirstName, LastName, CellPhone)
FROM (Student Information Table)
WHERE (State = MA)

Produces this output

**c**

| FirstName | LastName | CellPhone |
|---|---|---|
| Leanne | O'Connor | (303) 555-8723 |
| Mei | Zhang | (302) 555-4976 |

**FIGURE 11.19** When the query on the left is applied to the (a) "Student Information" table, it restricts the output to (b) only a phone list. The query on the right, which uses a WHERE statement, further restricts the phone list to (c) only students from Massachusetts.

Figure 11.19b shows the output from this query.

What if you want a phone list that shows only students from Massachusetts? In that case, you would add a WHERE statement to the query, as follows:

```
SELECT (FirstName, LastName, CellPhone)
FROM (Student Information Table)
WHERE (State = MA)
```

This query restricts the output to students who live in Massachusetts, as shown in Figure 11.19c. Notice that the "State" field in the "Student Information" table can be used by the query (in this case, as a limiting criterion) but that the contents of the "State" field aren't required to be displayed in the query results. This explains why the output shown in Figure 11.19c doesn't show the "State" field.

When you want to extract data that is in two or more tables, you use a **join query**. The query actually links (or joins) the two tables using the common field in both tables and extracts the relevant data from each. The format for a simple join query for two tables is as follows:

```
SELECT (Field Name 1, Field Name 2)
FROM (Table 1 Name, Table 2 Name)
WHERE (Table 1 Name.Common Field Name =
  Table 2 Name.Common Field Name)
AND (Selection Criteria)
```

Notice how similar this is to a select query, although the FROM statement must now contain two table names. In a join query, the WHERE statement is split into two parts. In the first part (right after WHERE), the relation between the two tables is defined by identifying the common fields between the tables. The second part of the statement (after AND) is where the selection criteria are defined.

The AND means that both parts of the statement must be true for the query to produce results (i.e., the two related fields must exist and the selection criteria must be valid). Figure 11.20 illustrates using a join query for the "Student Information" and "Roster Master" tables to produce a class roster for students.

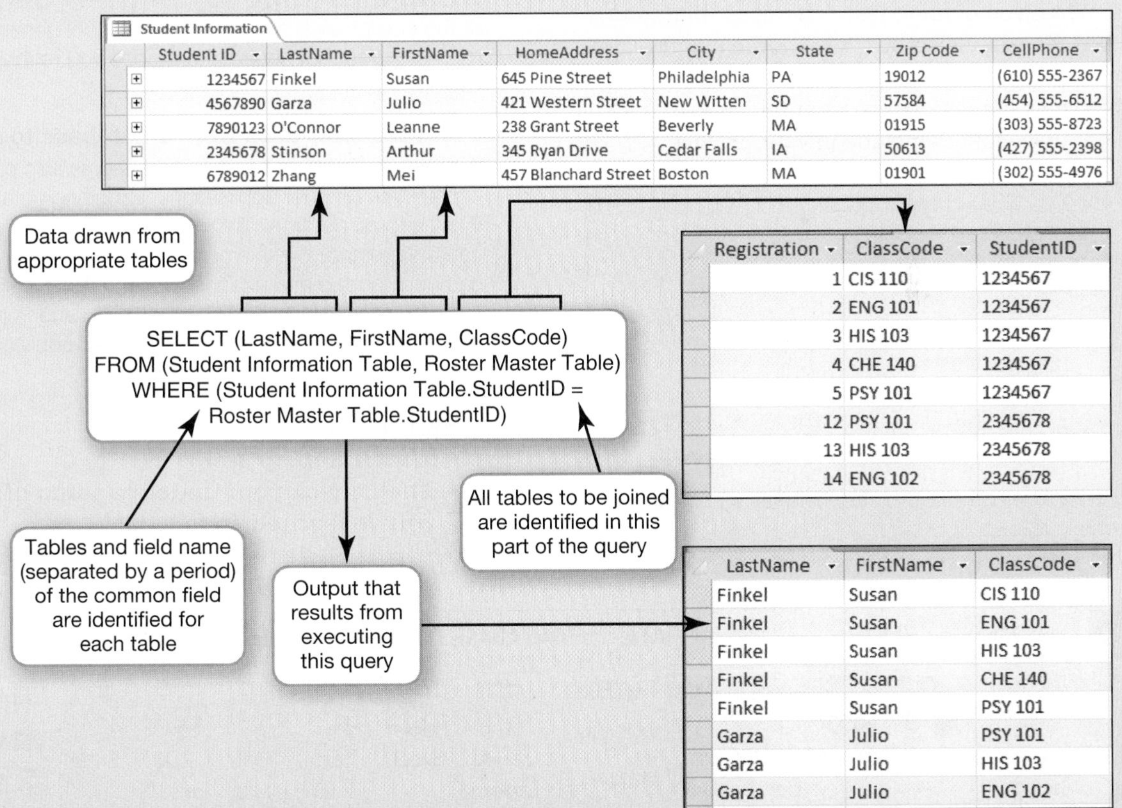


**FIGURE 11.20** This join query will display a student roster for each student in the "Student Information" table. Notice that the WHERE statement creates the join by defining the common field (in this case, StudentID) in each table.

```
SELECT [Residence Halls].ResidenceName, [Residence Assignments].RoomNumber,
[Student Information].LastName, [Student Information].FirstName
FROM [Student Information]
INNER JOIN ([Residence Halls]
INNER JOIN [Residence Assignments]
ON [Residence Halls].ResidenceID = [Residence Assignments].ResidenceID)
ON [Student Information].StudentID = [Residence Assignments].StudentID
WHERE ((([Residence Halls].ResidenceName)="Boyer 1"));
```

**FIGURE 11.21** The SQL View window in Access shows the SQL code for the query in Figure 11.18. Although it's a relatively simple select statement, it's much easier to create the query using the Access tools provided.

*>To display SQL code for a query, open a query and select* **SQL View** *from the View drop-down list on the Home tab of the Ribbon.*

or view the SQL code that the wizard created. Figure 11.21 shows the SQL code that the query in Figure 11.18 created.

## Outputting Data

**How do I get data out of a database?** The most common form of output for any database is a viewable (or printable) electronic report. You can use data in tables to create reports, or you can generate reports based on queries you create. Although you can print tables and the results of queries directly, when you create a report you can make other adjustments to how the information is displayed, such as grouping like information and including aggregate information such as totals. Businesses routinely summarize the data within their databases and compile summary data reports. For instance, at the end of each semester, your school generates a grade report for you that shows the grades you received for the classes you took.

**Can I transfer data from a database to another software application?** Database systems also can be used to export data to other applications. Exporting data involves putting it into an electronic file in a format that another application can understand. For example, as shown in Figure 11.23, data can be imported and exported among Access and Microsoft Word and Excel, as well as converted to and from other formats such as PDF and XML for use with other applications. ■

**Before moving on to Part 2:**
- **Watch Replay Video 11.1.**
- **Then check your understanding of what you've learned so far.**

# BITS&BYTES

## iTunes Smart Playlists—They're Just Queries!

Ever built a smart playlist in iTunes? If so, you've created a database query. iTunes is just a relational database that manages your media. A smart playlist (see Figure 11.22) allows you to define multiple criteria to create a playlist. Say you want all songs in the genre Rock, except for the artist Pink and the album *Monkey Business*. When you define these criteria as "match all" in the Smart Playlist dialog box, you'll get a smart playlist that contains the music you want. You have built a query that tells iTunes exactly what music to extract from the database and to include in your playlist.

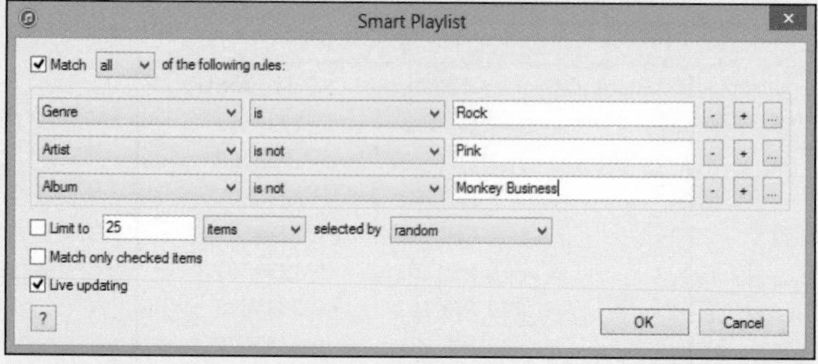


**FIGURE 11.22** The iTunes Smart Playlist dialog box creates a database query. *(Courtesy of Apple, Inc.)*

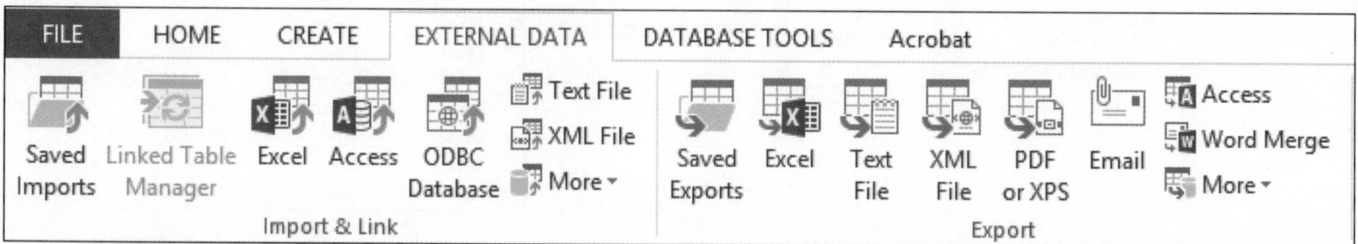


**FIGURE 11.23** Data can be imported and exported between Access and other Microsoft Office applications as well as converted to PDF, XML, and other formats for use with other applications.

# check your understanding//

For a quick review to see what you've learned so far, answer the following questions. Visit **pearsonhighered.com /techinaction** to check your answers.

## multiple choice

1. Two lists showing the same data about the same person is an example of
   - **a.** data redundancy.
   - **b.** data inconsistency.
   - **c.** data disparity.
   - **d.** data irregularity.
2. Which of the following is *not* an advantage of using databases instead of lists?
   - **a.** Data can be easily shared among users.
   - **b.** Data-entry errors can be minimized with databases.
   - **c.** Data integrity can be ensured with a database.
   - **d.** Databases are easier to build and maintain than lists.
3. A field that has a unique entry for each record in a database table is called the
   - **a.** logical key.
   - **b.** master field.
   - **c.** crucial field.
   - **d.** primary key.
4. A(n) __________ database organizes data in two-dimensional tables.
   - **a.** relational
   - **b.** object-oriented
   - **c.** rectangular
   - **d.** multidimensional
5. When just one residence hall can be listed for multiple students in a database, which type of relationship should be established between the database tables?
   - **a.** one-to-none relationship
   - **b.** many-to-many relationship
   - **c.** one-to-many relationship
   - **d.** one-to-one relationship

## true–false

_____ **1.** A query is used to extract information from a database.

_____ **2.** Relational databases are best used when storing unstructured data.

## critical thinking

1. **Databases Are Everywhere**

   Think about specific examples of databases you interact with regularly. Try to list at least 10 different ones. Discuss the specific advantages these databases have in your daily life, as well as some of the precautions you may need to take to ensure your privacy.

2. **Social Networks as Face-Recognition Databases**

   Facebook relies on underlying databases to establish relationships between users. The social network is able to suggest image tags by comparing an untagged image to information it has gathered from profile pictures and other photos in which tags have been added. Google+ has a similar feature. What privacy issues, if any, do you feel are generated with these types of database capabilities?

**Continue** »

# Using Excel's Database Functions

Databases are great for organizing lots of data, but they can be difficult to understand and to learn how to use. If your data is "flat"—that is, if it doesn't need to be divided into multiple tables—you can use Excel's database functions to organize your data. Excel is able to work with an enormous amount of data. Whether you're using Excel 2007, 2010, or 2013, you're allowed 1,048,576 rows and 16,384 columns on one worksheet, with a theoretical limit of 255 worksheets. If your computer had enough memory, you could process a lot of data!

Excel includes several useful database functions: sorting one or multiple columns, applying filters, and applying data validation. All the database commands in Excel are on the Data tab.

## Sorting in Alphabetical Order

Excel lets you sort one column of data in alphabetical or numerical order.

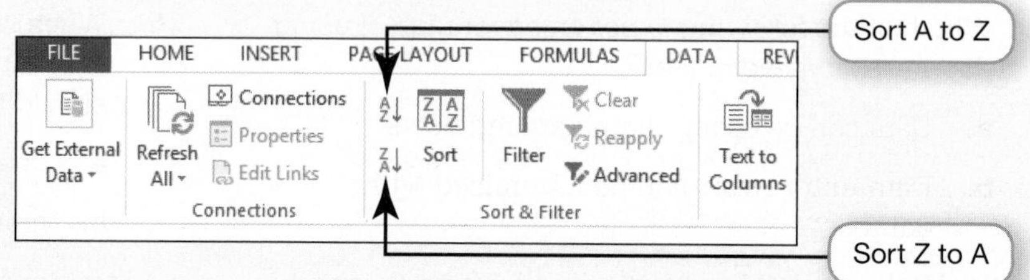


**Step 1** Place your cursor anywhere in the column you want to sort.

**Step 2** In the Sort & Filter group, click **Sort A to Z** or **Sort Z to A**, depending on whether you want to sort in ascending or descending order.

## Applying Filters

When you want to isolate a subset of data, you should apply a filter.

**Step 1** Click anywhere in the table, then click **Filter** in the Sort & Filter group. Filter arrows will display next to each column heading.

**Step 2** Click the filter arrow beside the column heading for the column you want to filter.

**Step 3** Remove the checkmark from Select All, and then click the filter value(s) you'd like to apply. Click **OK**.

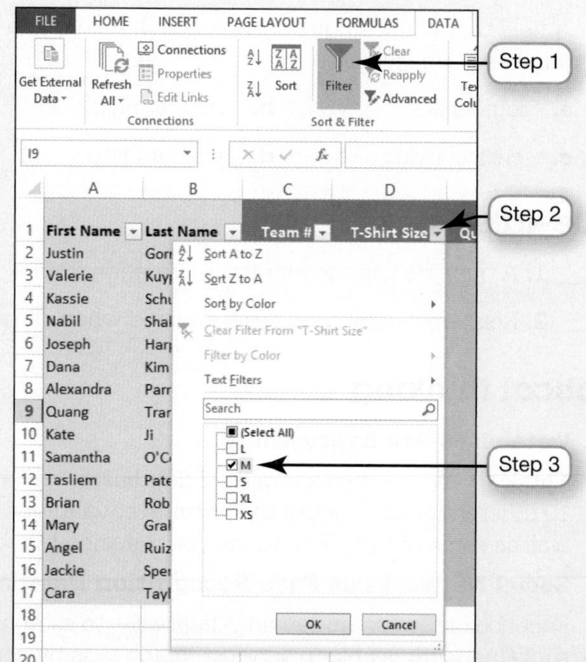


**Step 4** Review the data to ensure the filter has been applied correctly. (Note: To remove the filter, click **Filter** in the Sort & Filter group to unselect the option.)

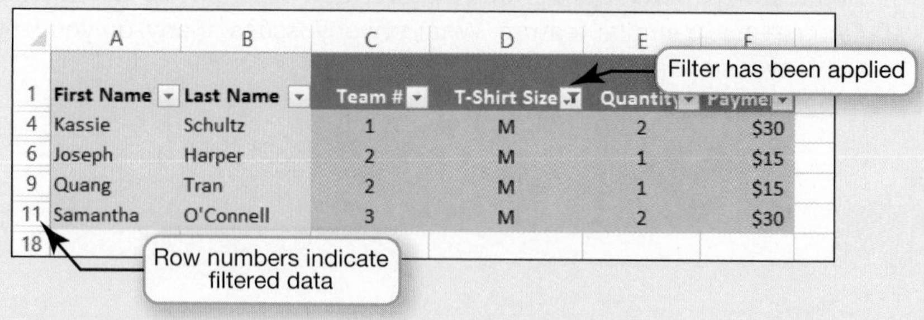

## Applying Data Validation

Using the Data Validation tool, you can apply rules to data so that you can ensure the proper data is being entered.

**Step 1** Click **Data Validation** in the Data Tools group to display the Data Validation dialog box.

**Step 2** On the **Settings** tab in the Data Validation dialog box, choose the type of data value to be allowed and the value limits in the **Data** and **Maximum** boxes. (Note: Depending on the criteria selected in the Allow field, the criteria in the Data box and other limits will vary.)

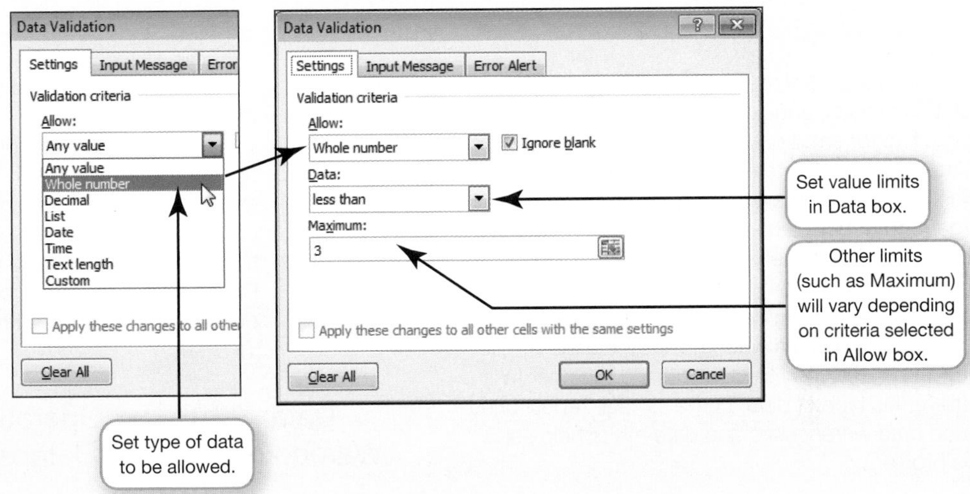


**Step 3** On the **Error Alert** tab, select the style of error message you want displayed (Stop, Warning, or Information), and then type the title of the error message and the error message text. Click **OK**.

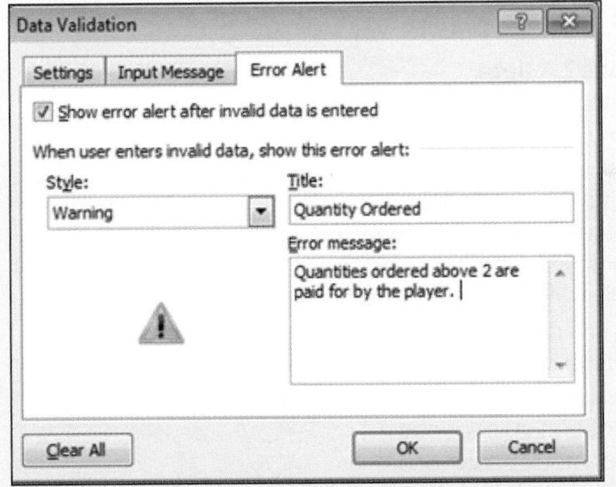


**Step 4** Test the data validation by entering an unacceptable value. When an unacceptable value is entered, an error message like the one shown here displays.

| B | C | D | E | F | G | H | I | J |
|---|---|---|---|---|---|---|---|---|
| Last Name | Team # | T-Shirt Size | Quantity | Payment | | | | |
| Schultz | 1 | M | 3 | $30 | | | | |
| Kuyper | 1 | L | 2 | $30 | | | | |
| Gormley | 1 | XL | | | | | | |
| Shakh | 1 | XL | | | | | | |
| Kim | 2 | S | | | | | | |
| Parrish | 2 | S | | | | | | |
| Harper | 2 | M | | | | | | |
| Tran | 2 | M | | | | | | |
| Patel | 3 | S | | | | | | |
| O'Connell | 3 | M | 2 | $30 | | | | |
| Robinson | 3 | L | 1 | $15 | | | | |

Quantity Ordered

Quantities ordered above 2 are paid for by the player.

Continue?

Yes No Cancel Help

Was this information helpful?

# How Businesses Use Databases

Large organizations accumulate massive amounts of data—both internal and external. By using *data warehousing*, *data marts*, and *data mining*, these organizations can use databases to tap into this wealth of information, improving their internal operations as well as their customer relationships. In this section, we'll look at how they do just that.

## data warehousing AND STORAGE

At the simplest level, data is stored in a single database on a database server, and you retrieve the data as needed. This works fine for small databases and simple enterprises where all the data you're interested in is in a single database. Problems can arise, however, when the organization gets much larger and department-specific data is stored in separate databases. Traditionally, the individual databases are used by different areas of the business and kept separate; however, the benefits of accessing data from all databases are being recognized. The problem with most databases is that they aren't designed to be accessed together to retrieve this type of data. Large storage repositories called *data warehouses* and *data marts* help solve this problem.

### Data Warehouses

**What is a data warehouse?** A **data warehouse** is a large-scale collection of data that contains and organizes in one place all the data from an organization's multiple databases. Individual databases contain a wealth of information, but each database's information usually pertains to one area in the organization. For instance, the order database at Amazon.com contains information about book orders, such as the buyer's name, address, and payment information and the book's name. However, the order database doesn't contain information on inventory levels of books, nor does it list suppliers from which out-of-stock books can be obtained. Data warehouses, therefore, consolidate information from various operational systems to present an enterprise-wide view of business operations.

**Is data in a data warehouse organized the same way as in a normal database?** Data in the data warehouse is organized by *subject*. Most databases focus on one specific operational aspect of business operations. For example, a large electronics retailer sells many types of electronics, such as TVs and cell phones. Different departments in the retailer are responsible for each type of product and track the products they sell in different databases (one database for TV sales and one for cell phone sales, for example), as shown in Figure 11.24.

These databases capture specific information about each type of electronics. The "TV Sales" database captures information such as TV features, extended warranty details (and costs), and the cost of the TV because this information is pertinent to determining the ultimate value of TV sales. The "Cell Phone Sales" database captures information such as data plan details, calling plan features (and costs), and phone costs.

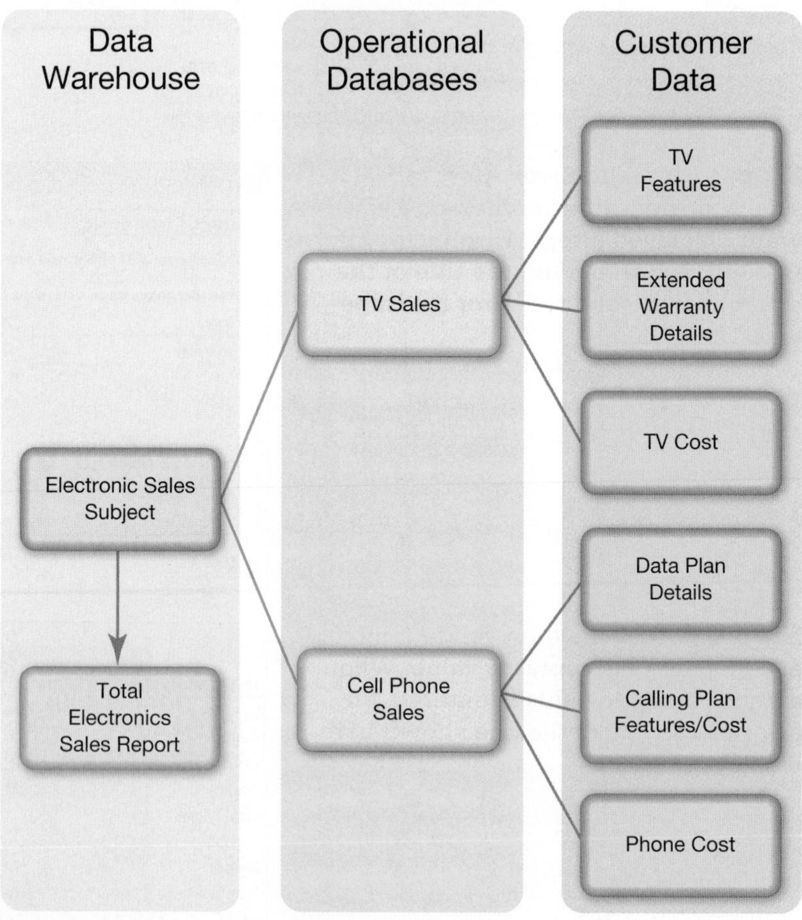


**FIGURE 11.24** Data from individual databases is drawn together in a data warehouse. Managers can then produce comprehensive reports that would be impossible to create from the individual databases.

# trends in IT

## Emerging Technologies: Can Your Business Partner Deliver the Goods? Enhanced Databases Can Help You Decide!

Suppose you manufacture T-shirts, and to keep costs low, you'd like to explore Vietnamese T-shirt manufacturers. You could use the terms "Vietnamese T-shirt manufacturers" in a search engine, and you'd probably find many leads. The information in the leads available online may be factually correct, but how do you determine how reliable these suppliers are? Alibaba.com and Panjiva are two online business-to-business databases that help to navigate these transactions.

Developed to respond to business needs, Alibaba.com (**alibaba.com**) is one of the world's largest online business-to-business databases (see Figure 11.25). Alibaba.com specializes in matching suppliers with buyers for all types of manufactured goods and raw materials. With the global nature of business, databases such as those maintained by Alibaba are essential tools that assist businesspeople in managing their global businesses.

Panjiva (**panjiva.com**) is a website that also has a searchable database, this one of over 1.5 million suppliers. The founders of Panjiva decided to make their database different. They gather data that indicates the reliability of suppliers from sources such as government agencies, independent certification companies, nonprofit organizations, and customers. Using the reliability information, Panjiva then creates ratings for companies (on a scale of 1 to 100) based on specific business performance criteria such as number of shipments to the U.S. market, the company's environmental record, and their capability to deliver shipments within promised time frames. Companies such as Home Depot that subscribe to Panjiva's database can feel more comfortable about doing business with suppliers that Panjiva has rated for reliability.

Databases with enhanced information are the wave of the future in the business world. So, before you make that next crucial business decision, ask yourself how much you really know about your prospective business partner. If you don't know enough, then find a database that can make you feel more at ease.

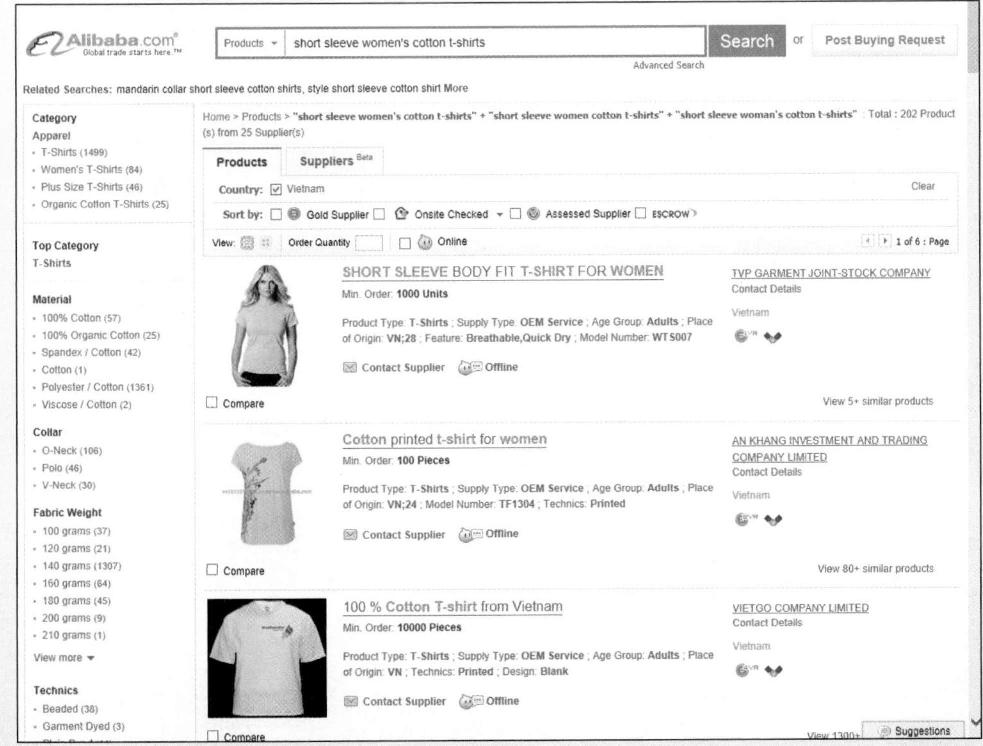


**FIGURE 11.25** Using the Alibaba database, a search for short-sleeved women's cotton T-shirts in Vietnam results in over 200 links to vendors selling some type of women's T-shirt. *(Courtesy of Alibaba)*

However, data on total electronic devices sold (and the resulting revenue generated) is critical to the management of the electronics retailer no matter what types of products are involved. Therefore, an electronics retailer's data warehouse would have a subject called "Electronics Sales Subject" (see Figure 11.24) that would contain information about *all* electronic devices sold throughout the company. "Electronics Sales Subject" is a database that contains information from the other databases the company maintains. However, all data in the "Electronics Sales Subject" database is specifically related to electronics sales (as opposed to, say, appliances, which the retailer also carries).

From the "Electronics Sales Subject" database, it's easy for managers to produce comprehensive reports, such as the "Total Electronics Sales Report," as shown in Figure 11.24, which can contain information pertaining to all types of electronics sales.

**Do data warehouses capture data from only one time period?** Data warehouse data is **time-variant data**, meaning it doesn't all pertain to one period in time. The warehouse contains current values, such as amounts due from customers, as well as historical data. If you want to examine the buying habits of a certain type of customer, you need data about both current and prior purchases. Having time-variant data in the warehouse enables you to analyze the past, examine the present in light of historical data, and make projections about the future.

## Populating Data Warehouses

**How are data warehouses populated with data?** Source data for data warehouses can come from three places:

1. *Internal sources:* Sales, billing, inventory, and customer databases all provide a wealth of information. Spreadsheets and other ad hoc analysis tools may contain data that can be loaded into the data warehouse.
2. *External sources:* Vendors and suppliers often provide data regarding product specifications, shipment methods and dates, billing information, and so on.
3. *Clickstream data:* Software used on company websites to capture information about each click that users make as they navigate through the site is referred to as **clickstream data**. Using clickstream data-capture tools, a company can determine which pages users visit most often, how long users stay on each page, which sites directed users to the company site, and user demographics.

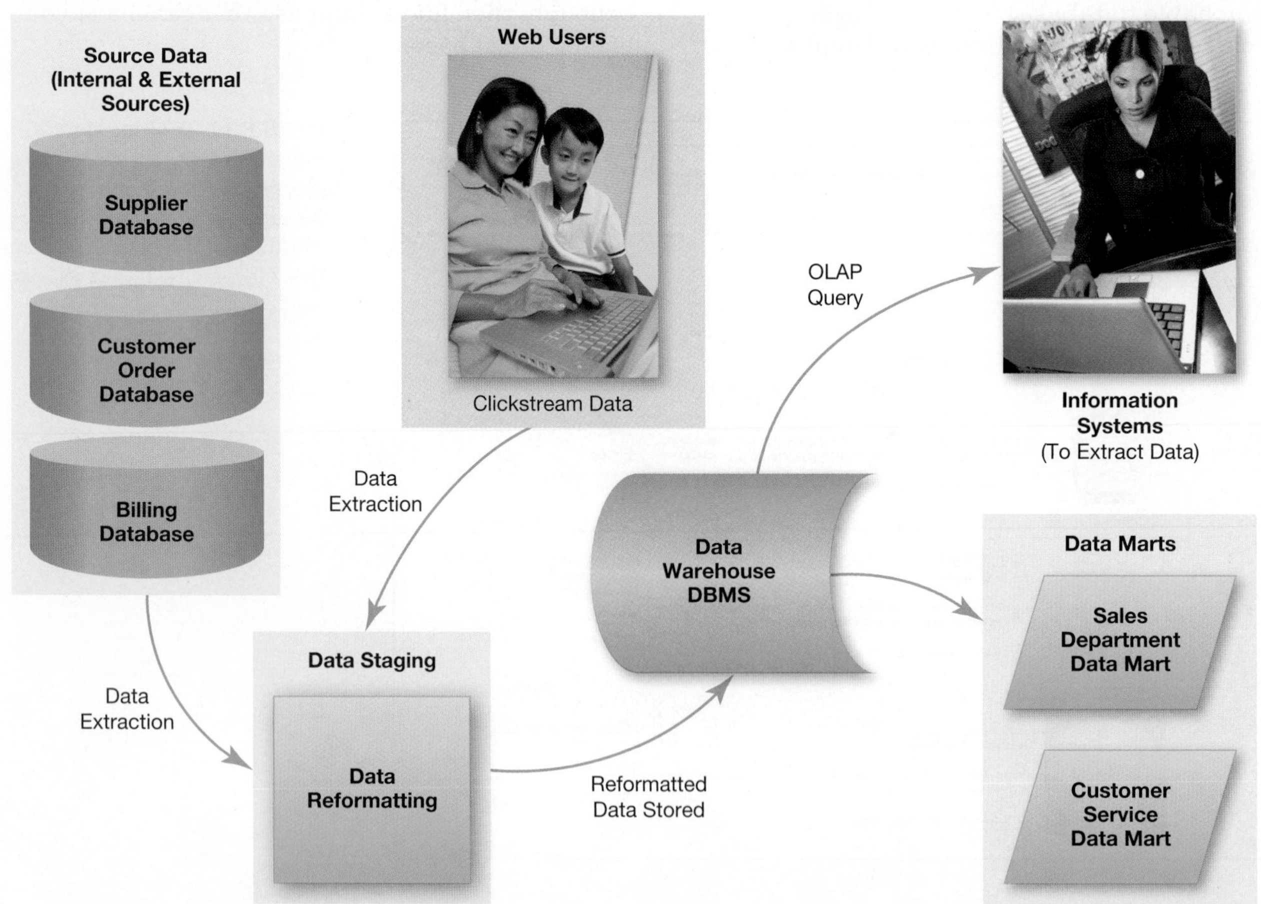


**FIGURE 11.26** This figure shows an overview of the data warehouse process. *(Bikeriderlondon/Shutterstock; REDAV/Shutterstock)*

Such data can provide valuable clues as to what a company needs to improve on its site to stimulate sales.

## Data Staging

**Does all source data fit into a data warehouse?** Although two source databases might contain similar information (such as customer names and addresses), the format of the data is most likely different in each database. Therefore, source data must be "staged" before entering the data warehouse. **Data staging** consists of three steps:

1. Extraction of the data from source databases
2. Transformation (reformatting) of the data
3. Storage of the data in the data warehouse

Many different software programs and procedures may have to be created to extract the data from varied sources and reformat it for storage in the data warehouse. The nature and complexity of the source data determine the complexity of the data-staging process.

**How can data stored in the data warehouse be extracted and used?** Managers can query the data warehouse in much the same way you would query an Access database. However, because there is more data in the data warehouse, special software is needed to perform such queries. **Online analytical processing (OLAP)** software provides standardized tools for viewing and manipulating data in a data warehouse. The key feature of OLAP tools is that they enable flexible views of the data, which the software user can easily change.

## Data Marts

**What if a smaller amount of data is needed?** Small slices of the data warehouse, each called a **data mart**, are often created so that companies can analyze a related set of data that is grouped together and separated out from the main body of data in the data warehouse. Whereas data warehouses have an enterprise-wide depth, the information in data marts pertains to a single component of the business.

For instance, if you need accurate sales-related information and you don't want to wade through customer service data, accounts payable data, and product shipping data to get it, a data mart that contains information relevant only to the sales department can be created to make the task of finding this data easier. An overview of the data-warehousing process is illustrated in Figure 11.26. Data staging is vital because different data must be extracted and then reformatted to fit the data structure defined in the data warehouse's DBMS. Data can be extracted using powerful OLAP query tools, or it can be stored in specialized data marts for use by specific employee groups.

Now that you understand how databases are created and how data is stored in large-scale repositories, in the next section we'll explore the types of information systems that utilize databases to provide business intelligence to managers. ■

# business intelligence SYSTEMS

Making intelligent decisions about developing new products, creating marketing strategies, and buying raw materials requires timely, accurate information. An **information system** is a software-based solution used to gather and analyze information. A system that delivers up-to-the-minute sales data on shoes to the computer of Zappos's president is one example of an information system. Databases, data warehouses, and data marts are integral parts of information systems because they store the information that makes information systems functional.

**Are all information systems the same?** All information systems perform similar functions, including acquiring data, processing that data into information, storing the data, and providing the user with a number of output options with which to make the information meaningful and useful (see Figure 11.27).

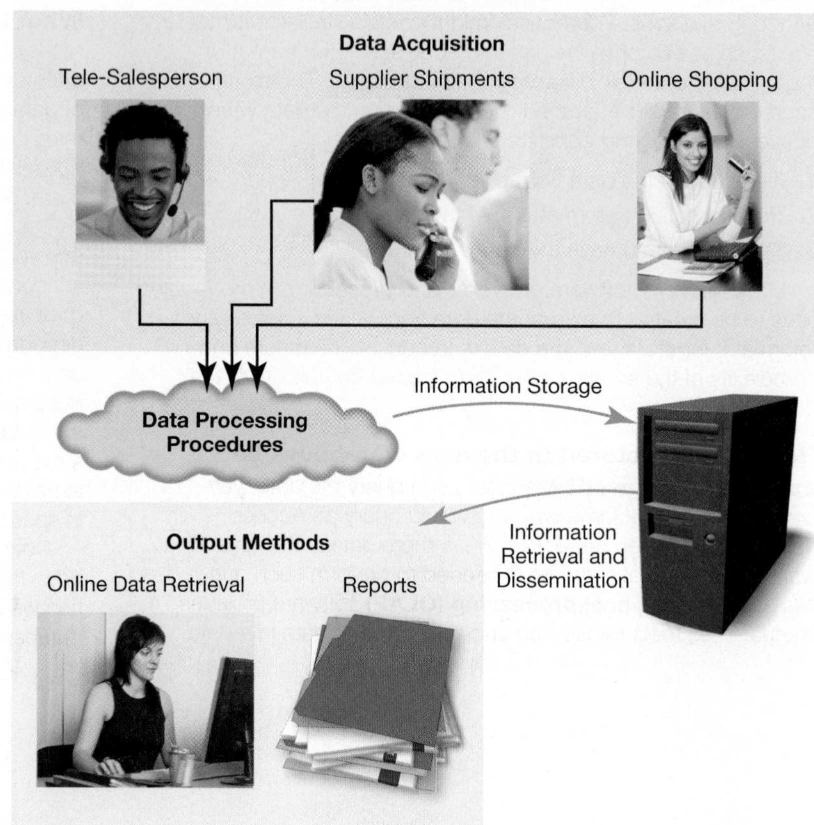


**FIGURE 11.27** Information systems acquire data, process that data into information, store the data, and provide the user with a number of output options to make the information useful. *(wavebreakmedia/Shutterstock; wavebreakmedia/Shutterstock; Michael Jung/Shutterstock; Raisa Kanareva/Shutterstock)*

**What information systems are used by business managers?** Most information systems fall into one of five categories:

1. Office support systems
2. Transaction-processing systems
3. Management information systems
4. Decision support systems
5. Enterprise resource planning (ERP) systems

Each type of system almost always involves the use of one or more databases. Management information systems, decision support systems, and enterprise resource planning systems are often classified as business intelligence systems. **Business intelligence systems** are used to analyze and interpret data in order to enable managers to make informed decisions about how best to run a business. Data warehouses and data marts are key components of business intelligence systems because they enable access to information gathered from multiple sources. Increased access to information usually enables business intelligence systems to provide better information to managers in a timely fashion, which can lead to enhanced decision making.

In the following sections, we'll examine each of the five types of systems in greater detail.

## Office Support Systems

**What does an office support system accomplish?** An **office support system (OSS)** is designed to improve communications and assist employees in accomplishing their daily tasks. Microsoft Office is an example of an OSS because it assists employees with routine tasks such as maintaining an employee phone list in Excel, designing a sales presentation in PowerPoint, and writing customer letters using Word.

Modern OSSs include e-mail, word processing, spreadsheet, database, and presentation programs. Office support systems have their roots in manual, paper-based systems developed before computers. A paper listing of employee phone extensions typed by an administrative assistant is an example of an early OSS. A modern OSS might publish this directory on the company's intranet (its internal network).

## Transaction-Processing Systems

**What is a transaction-processing system?** A **transaction-processing system (TPS)** keeps track of everyday business activities. For example, colleges have

TPSs in place to track transactions that occur frequently, such as registering students for classes, accepting tuition payments, and printing course catalogs. When computers were introduced to the business world, they often were first put to work hosting TPSs.

**How are transactions entered into a TPS?** Transactions can be entered manually or electronically. When you buy gas at a pay-at-the-pump terminal, the pump captures your credit card data and transmits it to a TPS, which records a sale (gallons of gas and dollar value). Transactions are processed either in batches or in real time. Various departments in an organization then access the TPSs to extract the information they need to process additional transactions, as shown in Figure 11.28.

**What is batch processing? Batch processing** means that transaction data is accumulated until a certain point is reached and then several transactions are processed at once. Batch processing is appropriate for activities that aren't time sensitive. For example, you may not receive a bill for each charge you make at the bookstore. Instead, the college may collect your charges and batch them together into one monthly billing. It's more efficient to batch and process all requests periodically.

**When are TPS transactions processed?** For most activities, processing and recording transactions in a TPS occur in real time. **Real-time processing** means that the database is updated while the transaction is taking place. For instance, when you register for classes online, if spots are still available for the classes you want, the database immediately records your registration in the class to ensure you have a spot. This **online transaction processing (OLTP)** ensures that the data in the TPS is current.

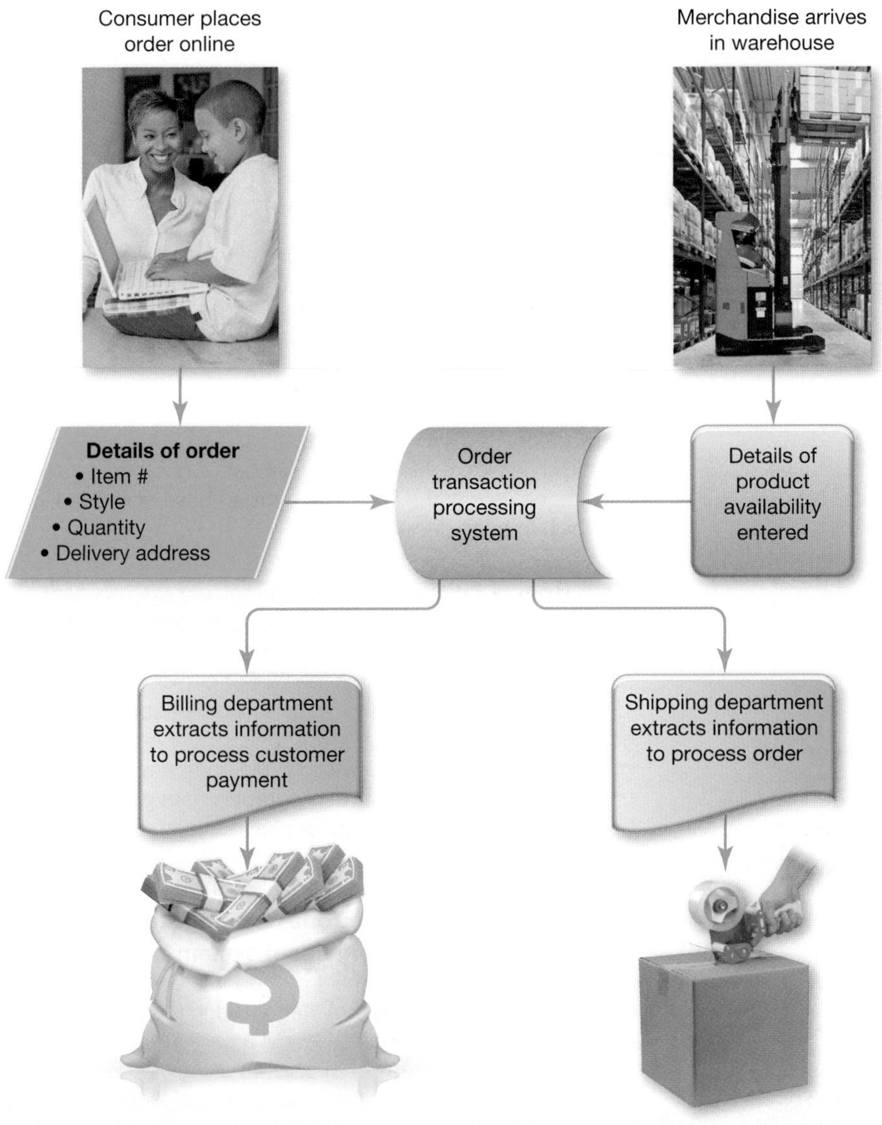

**FIGURE 11.28** Transaction-processing systems help capture and track critical business information needed for successful completion of business transactions such as selling merchandise over the Internet. *(Bikeriderlondon/Shutterstock; Penka Todorova Vitkova/Shutterstock; Chuck Rausin/Shutterstock; Natykach Nataliia/Shutterstock)*

## Management Information Systems

**What is a management information system?** A **management information system (MIS)** provides timely and accurate information that enables managers to make critical business decisions. MISs were a direct outgrowth of TPSs. Managers quickly realized that the data contained in TPSs could be an extremely powerful tool only if the information could be organized and outputted in a useful form. Today's MISs are often included as a feature of TPSs.

**What types of reports are generated by MISs?** MISs generate three types of reports:

1. A **detail report** provides a list of the transactions that occurred during a certain time period. For example, during registration at your school, the registrar might receive a detail report that lists the students who registered for classes each day. Figure 11.29a shows an example of a detail report on daily enrollment.
2. A **summary report** provides a consolidated picture of detailed data. These reports usually include some calculation (totals) or visual displays of information (such as charts and graphs). Figure 11.29b shows an example of a summary report displaying total daily credits enrolled by division.

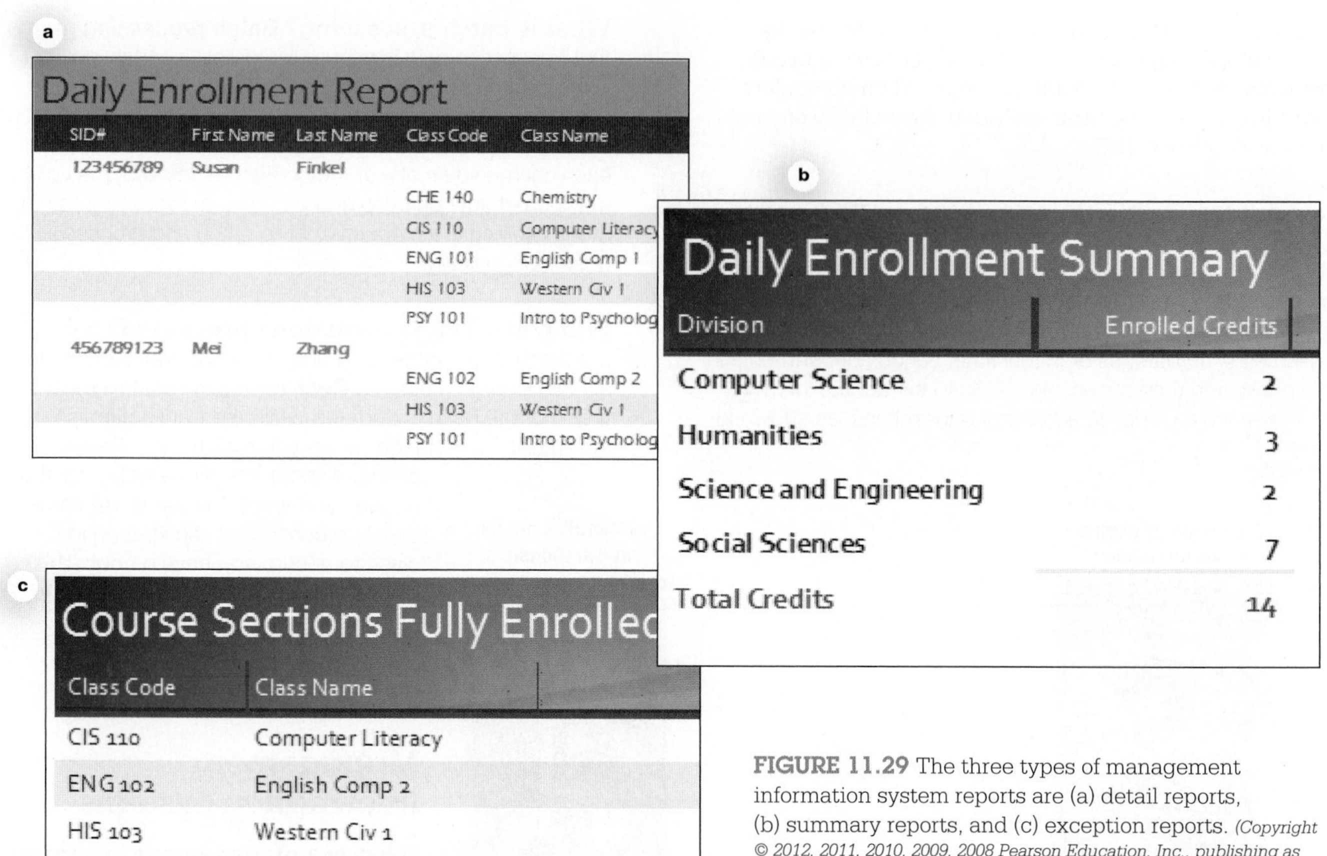

a

**Daily Enrollment Report**

| SID# | First Name | Last Name | Class Code | Class Name |
|---|---|---|---|---|
| 123456789 | Susan | Finkel | | |
| | | | CHE 140 | Chemistry |
| | | | CIS 110 | Computer Literac |
| | | | ENG 101 | English Comp 1 |
| | | | HIS 103 | Western Civ 1 |
| | | | PSY 101 | Intro to Psycholog |
| 456789123 | Mei | Zhang | | |
| | | | ENG 102 | English Comp 2 |
| | | | HIS 103 | Western Civ 1 |
| | | | PSY 101 | Intro to Psycholog |

b

**Daily Enrollment Summary**

| Division | Enrolled Credits |
|---|---|
| Computer Science | 2 |
| Humanities | 3 |
| Science and Engineering | 2 |
| Social Sciences | 7 |
| Total Credits | 14 |

c

**Course Sections Fully Enrollec**

| Class Code | Class Name |
|---|---|
| CIS 110 | Computer Literacy |
| ENG 102 | English Comp 2 |
| HIS 103 | Western Civ 1 |

**FIGURE 11.29** The three types of management information system reports are (a) detail reports, (b) summary reports, and (c) exception reports. *(Copyright © 2012, 2011, 2010, 2009, 2008 Pearson Education, Inc., publishing as Prentice Hall. ISBN: 0132838737, p 544)*

3. An **exception report** shows conditions that are unusual or that need attention by system users. The registrar at your college may get an exception report when all sections of a course are full, indicating that it may be time to schedule additional sections. Figure 11.29c shows an example of such an exception report.

## Decision Support Systems

**What is a decision support system?** A **decision support system (DSS)** is another type of business intelligence system designed to help managers develop solutions for specific problems. A DSS for a marketing department might provide statistical information on customer attributes, such as income levels or buying patterns, that would assist managers in making advertising strategy decisions. A DSS not only uses data from databases and data warehouses, it also enables users to add their own insights and experiences and apply them to the solution.

**What does a DSS look like?** DBMSs, while playing an integral part of a DSS, are supplemented by additional software systems in a DSS. In a DSS, the user interface provides the means of interaction between the user and the system. An effective user interface must be easy to learn. The other major components of a DSS are internal and external data sources, model management systems, and knowledge-based systems. As shown in Figure 11.30, these systems work together to provide the user of the DSS with a broad base of information on which to base decisions.

**How does a DSS get data?** Internal and external data sources provide a stream of data that is integrated into the DSS for analysis. Internal data sources are maintained by the same company that operates the DSS. For example, internal TPSs can provide a wealth of statistical data about customers, ordering patterns, inventory levels, and so on. An external data source is any source not owned by the company that owns the DSS, such as customer demographic data purchased from third parties, mailing lists, or statistics compiled by the government.

**What function does a model management system perform?** A **model management system** is software that assists in building management models in a DSS. A management model is an analysis tool that, through the use of internal and external data, provides a view of a particular business situation for the purposes of decision making. Models can be built to describe any business situation, such as the classroom space requirements for next semester or a listing of alternative sales outlet locations. Model management systems typically contain financial and statistical analysis tools that are used to analyze the data provided by models or to create additional models.

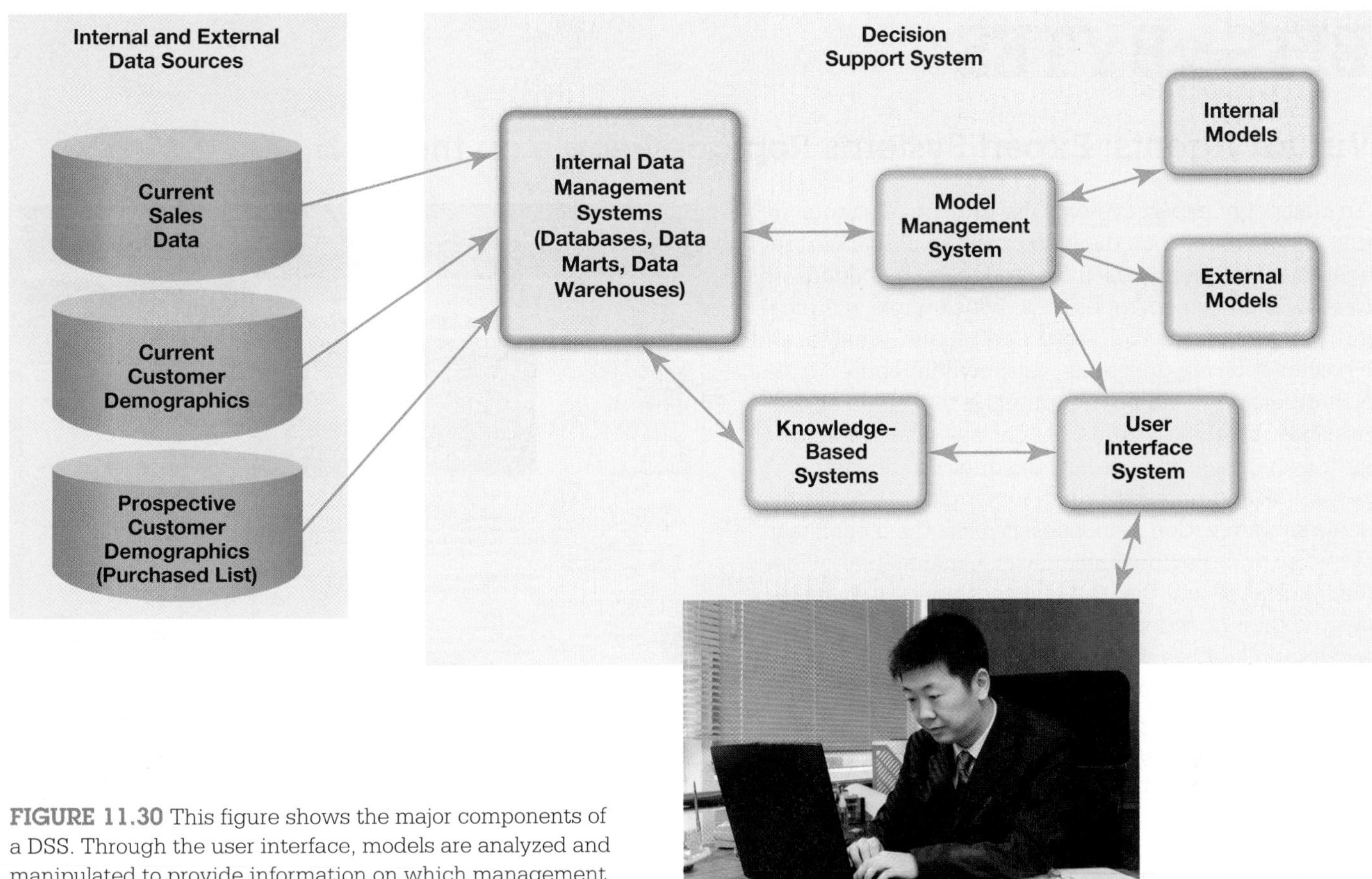


**FIGURE 11.30** This figure shows the major components of a DSS. Through the user interface, models are analyzed and manipulated to provide information on which management decisions are based. *(Tan Kian Khoon/Shutterstock)*

**What is a knowledge-based system, and how is it used in a DSS?** A **knowledge-based system** provides intelligence that supplements the user's own intellect and makes the DSS more effective. It could be an **expert system** that tries to replicate the decision-making processes of human experts in order to solve specific problems. For example, an expert system might be designed to take the place of a physician in a remote location. A physician expert system would ask the patient about symptoms just as a live physician would, and the system would make a diagnosis based on the algorithms programmed into it.

Another type of knowledge-based system is a **natural language processing (NLP) system**. NLP systems enable users to communicate with computer systems using a natural spoken or written language instead of using a computer programming language. Individuals just speak to the computer and it understands what they're saying, without users needing to use specific computer commands. Siri, the personal assistant application currently on Apple's iPhone 5, is an NLP system.

All knowledge-based systems fall under the science of artificial intelligence. **Artificial intelligence (AI)** is the branch of computer science that deals with the attempt to create computers that think like humans. To date, no computers have been constructed that can replicate the thinking patterns of a human brain, because scientists still do not fully understand how humans store and integrate knowledge and experiences to form human intelligence.

**How does a knowledge-based system help in the decision-making process?** Databases and the models provided by model management systems tend to be extremely analytical and mathematical in nature. If we relied solely on databases and models to make decisions, answers would be derived with a "yes or no" mentality, allowing no room for human thought. Fortunately, human users are involved in these systems, providing an opportunity to inject human judgment into the decision-making process.

The knowledge-based system also provides an opportunity to introduce experience into the mix. Knowledge-based systems support the concept of fuzzy logic. Normal logic is highly rigid: If "x" happens, then "y" will happen. **Fuzzy logic** enables the interjection of experiential learning into the equation by considering probabilities. Whereas an algorithm in a database has to be specific, an algorithm in a knowledge-based system could state that if "x" happens, 70% of the time "y" will happen.

For instance, managers at Best Buy would find it extremely helpful if their DSS informed them that 45% of customers who bought an iPad also bought a Smart Cover for it. This could

## BITS&BYTES

### Virtual Agents: Expert Systems Replace People on the Web

An offshoot of expert systems are the virtual agents that you encounter on the web or on the phone. Virtual agents are frequently used to interface with a database to answer customers' questions. For example, a typical virtual agent on the web features a picture, a name, and a box for entering questions, as shown in Figure 11.31. No virtual agent can be programmed to contain all the possible questions a human might ask. Therefore, the virtual agent software breaks the question down into key words and phrases, which it compares to a database containing question responses. It picks the most likely response and provides the answer. Customers provide feedback as to whether the response adequately answered their question. Usually, if results from the virtual agent aren't satisfactory or if customers need more information, they can connect to a live customer service agent. Virtual agents, although not perfect, save companies money by answering common questions without using expensive human labor.

**FIGURE 11.31** Spike, Gonzaga University's sports team mascot, has been transformed into a virtual agent to direct people to the appropriate page of the school's website. *(Courtesy of Gonzaga University.)*

suggest that designing a discount program for Smart Covers bought with iPads might spur sales. Fuzzy logic enables a system to be more flexible and to consider a wider range of possibilities than would conventional algorithmic thinking.

## Enterprise Resource Planning Systems

**What does an enterprise resource planning system do?** An *enterprise* is any business entity, large or small. All businesses have data and information to manage, and large, complex organizations can benefit from managing that information with a central piece of software. An **enterprise resource planning (ERP) system** is a software system that accumulates in a central location all information relevant to running a business and makes it readily available to whoever needs it to make decisions. ERP systems use a common database to store and integrate information. This enables the information to be used across multiple areas of an enterprise.

Human resource functions (such as the management of hiring, firing, promotions, and benefits) and accounting functions (such as payroll) are often the first processes integrated into an ERP system. Historically, human resource records and accounting records were kept in separate databases, but having the information reside in one database makes the management and compensation of employees more streamlined. If manufacturing operations were then integrated into the ERP system, the data that was already in place regarding the employees and payroll could be easily used for determining the cost of running an assembly line or for scheduling workers to run the assembly line. ■

# trends in IT

## Computers in Society: User-Populated Databases

Web 2.0 applications are about making it easy for users to create and disseminate their own content. So if you have a database that needs populating, why not seek help from the web community to populate it, especially if it's designed as a resource for the masses?

Yelp (**yelp.com**) is conceived as the "yellow pages" for the twenty-first century. Yelp is free to use, and anyone can write a review of a business and post it to the site. Users can easily search the site, find service providers in their area, and see what ratings consumers have given them. Thinking about going to a Mexican restaurant in the downtown San Jose area that you've never visited (see Figure 11.32)? A quick search on Yelp will lead to more than 57 restaurants that fit these criteria. Surely you'll be able to find one that fits your budget and that other people enjoyed visiting.

However, Yelp is not without its critics. Because it allows anonymous posting, some people argue that businesses may try to increase their ratings by posting their own positive reviews. And Yelp actively markets to businesses to pay for placement of ads on its site that some users may mistake for unsponsored reviews. (To avoid this kind of consumer misinterpretation, the Federal Communications Commission [FCC] now requires commercial websites to clearly identify reviews that are sponsored, but some consumers remain oblivious.)

An alternative to Yelp that addresses these concerns is Angie's List. Angie's List (**angieslist.com**) focuses primarily on service companies and health care professionals, not entertainment and food service businesses. Members pay a monthly fee to access the reviews on Angie's List. What do you get for your fee? Angie's List doesn't permit anonymous reviews. This is a big benefit for business owners because it makes it easier to contact dissatisfied customers and try to resolve issues. Angie's List also has a verification process with reviewers to ensure that businesses don't report on themselves. And businesses don't pay to advertise on Angie's List; they make it on the site only when they're reviewed by a consumer.

Both Yelp and Angie's List are searchable databases, but whereas most companies usually populate databases themselves, these websites rely on users to create their content. The databases still need to be well designed to capture this content, and processes need to be in place to review the data entered for appropriateness. By harnessing the power of large groups of users to populate a database, the database owners can reap the rewards of saving time, effort, and money.

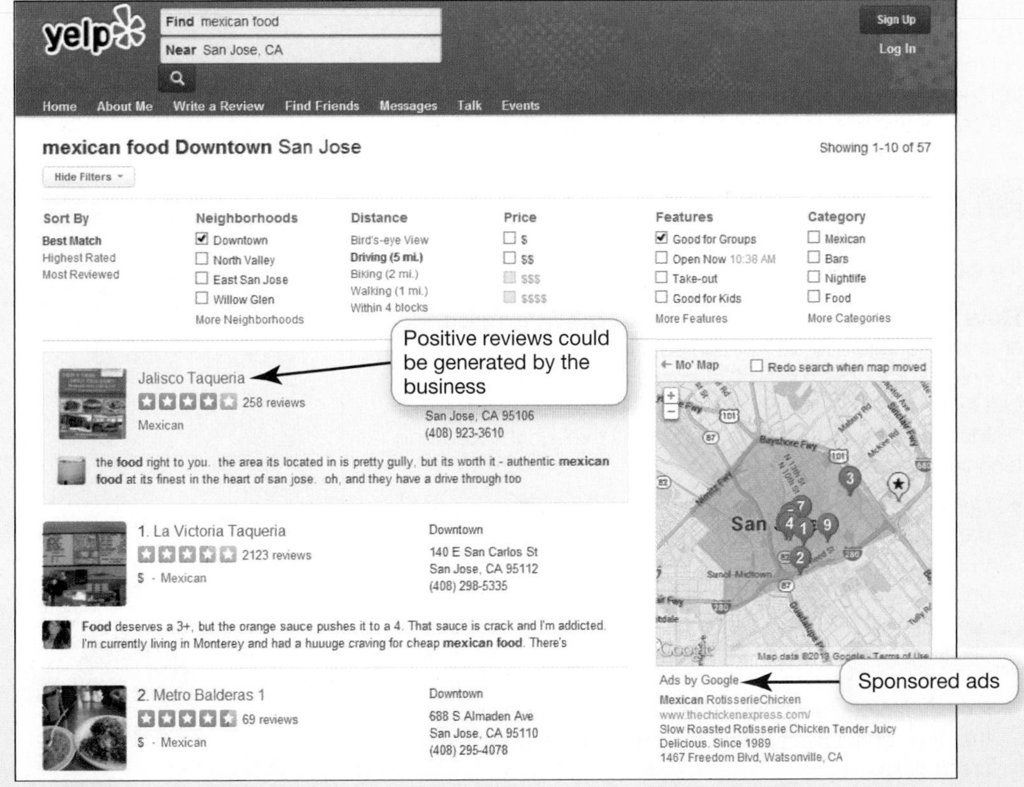


**FIGURE 11.32** Yelp's database is populated with reviews created by users. *(Courtesy of Yelp)*

# data MINING

Just because you have captured data in an organized fashion and have stored it in a format that seems to make sense doesn't mean that an analysis of the data will automatically reveal everything you need to know. Trends can sometimes be hard to spot if the data isn't organized or analyzed in a particular way. To make data work harder, companies employ data-mining techniques.

**Data mining** is the process by which great amounts of data are analyzed and investigated. The objective is to spot significant patterns or trends within the data that would otherwise not be obvious. For instance, by mining student enrollment data, a school may discover that there's been a consistent increase in new engineering-degree students who are women.

**Why do businesses mine their data?** The main reason businesses mine data is to understand their customers better. If a company can better understand the types of customers who buy its products and can learn what motivates its customers to do so, it can market effectively by concentrating its efforts on the populations most likely to buy. You may have noticed that products are frequently moved around in supermarkets. This is usually the result of data mining. With electronic scanning of bar codes, each customer's purchase is recorded in a database. By classifying the data and using *cluster analysis,* supermarket managers can determine which products people usually purchase with other products. The store then places these products close to each other so that shoppers can find them easily. For instance, if analysis shows that people often buy potato chips with soft drinks, it makes sense to place these items in the same aisle.

**How do businesses mine their data?** Data mining enables managers to sift through data in several ways. Each technique produces different information on which managers can then base their decisions.

Managers make their data meaningful through the following techniques (see Figure 11.33):

- *Classification:* Before mining, managers define data classes they think will be helpful in spotting trends. They then apply these class definitions to all unclassified data to prepare it for analysis. For example, "good credit risk" and "bad credit risk" are two data classes managers could establish to determine whether to grant car loans to applicants. Managers would then identify factors, such as credit history and yearly income, that they could use to classify applicants as good or bad credit risks.
- *Estimation:* When managers classify data, the record either fits the classification criteria or it doesn't. Estimation

**FIGURE 11.33**

**Data-Mining Techniques**

**Classification**
Define data classes to help spot trends, then apply the class definitions to all unclassified data.

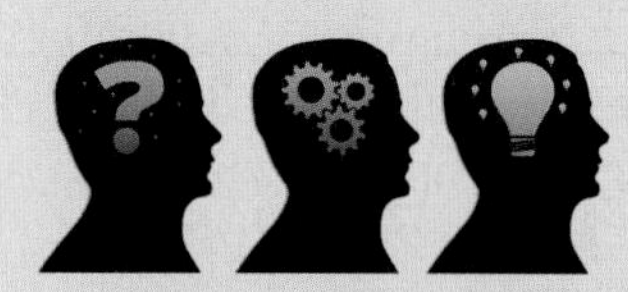

**Estimation**
Assign a value to data based on some criterion.

**Affinity Grouping (or Association Rules)**
Determine which data goes together.

**Clustering**
Organize data into similar subgroups, or clusters, without using predefined classes.

**Description and Visualization**
Describe data so that managers can interpret it in new and different ways.

(Dreaming Andy/Fotolia; kbuntu/Fotolia; Franck Boston/Fotolia; Gallo Images/Fotolia; Lvnel/Fotolia)

# ethics in IT

## Data, Data Everywhere—But Is It Protected?

As databases have become commonplace, an ever-increasing amount of information about you and your habits has been placed into various databases. How much of this data is protected (see Figure 11.34)? Consider the following:

- In April 2013, the U.S. National Security Agency, in an effort to protect against national security threats, ordered Verizon to turn over the metadata of telephone calls made in the United States within a three-month period. This court order generated wide discussion as to the privacy rights U.S. citizens have not only with respect to phone data (both wired and wireless) but also with digital communications.
- Every credit card purchase generates a record of that transaction, and both the merchant from whom you purchased the item and the credit card company have gathered information about your buying habits. In March 2012, private customer information was improperly exposed from all the major credit card brands, potentially affecting millions of credit card holders.
- Many companies such as Target collect e-mail addresses so they can correspond with customers, but the e-mails don't come directly from those companies. Large marketing companies such as Epsilon are hired to manage customer e-mail programs. Unfortunately, in March 2011 Epsilon's database servers suffered an attack that exposed millions of individuals' e-mail addresses to hackers.

Inadvertently exposing information to inappropriate or unauthorized individuals is known as a *data breach*. What responsibility do companies have in safeguarding your data? Should they inform you that your data might be shared with other corporations and obtain your permission before sharing it? How should consumers be compensated (and by whom) if their data is misused?

**FIGURE 11.34** Think about all the data about you that is stored in databases. Do you feel your privacy is protected? *(UK Stock Images Ltd/Alamy)*

### What Can You Do?

Providing information and having it recorded in databases are part of our way of life now. Because refusing to give information out at all is bound to be impractical, ask the following questions related to data you're providing:

- **For what purpose is the data being gathered?** When the clerk at the electronics superstore asks for your zip code, ask why he or she wants it.
- **Are the reasons for gathering the data legitimate or important to you?** You might not want to share your information for marketing purposes, but might want to in order to initiate a product warranty. Similarly, disclosing personal information to your pharmacist may be important for receiving good care and therefore is important to you. If you don't see the advantage, then ask more questions or don't reveal the information.
- **How will the collected information be protected?** Ask about data protection policies before you give information. Most websites provide access to their data protection policies when they ask you for information. If an organization doesn't have a data protection policy, be wary of giving them sensitive information. Data protection doesn't just refer to keeping data secure; it also means restricting access to the data to employees of the organization who need to use that data. A shipping clerk might need to see your address, for example, but doesn't need to see your credit card information.

- **Will the collected information be used for purposes other than the purpose for which it was originally collected?** This might be covered in a data protection policy. If it isn't, ask about it. Will your information be sold to or shared with other companies? Will it be used for marketing other products to you?
- **Could the information asked for be used for identity theft?** Identity thieves usually need your Social Security number and your birth date to open credit card accounts in your name. Be especially wary when asked for this information, and make sure there is a legitimate need for it. Most organizations and businesses are shying away from using Social Security numbers to track customers because of the risk of identity theft. And do you really need an e-mail from someone on your birthday advertising a product? It really isn't worth exposing your birth date to potential misuse.
- **Are organizations safeguarding your data?** Don't just consider new requests for information. Think about organizations, such as banks, that already have your information. Have they been in the news lately because of a major data breach? (Is your bank a customer of Epsilon, for instance?) You might want to consider switching institutions if yours has a poor record of data security.

Think carefully before providing information and be vigilant about monitoring your data when you can. It may make the difference between invasion of privacy and peace of mind.

enables managers to assign a value to data based on some criterion. For example, assume a bank wants to send out credit card offers to people who are likely to be granted a credit card. The bank may run the customers' data through a program that assigns a score based on where they live, their household income, and their average bank balance. This provides managers with an estimate of the most likely credit card prospects to target.

- *Affinity grouping (or association rules):* When mining data, managers can determine which data goes together. In other words, they can apply affinity grouping or association rules to the data. For example, suppose analysis of a sales database indicates that two items are bought together 60% of the time. Based on this data, managers might decide that these items should be pictured on the same page of their website.
- *Clustering:* Clustering involves organizing data into similar subgroups, or clusters. It's different from classification in that there are no predefined classes. The data-mining software makes the decision about what to group, and it's up to managers to determine whether the clusters are meaningful. For example, the data-mining software may identify clusters of customers with similar buying patterns. Further analysis of the clusters may reveal that certain socioeconomic groups have similar buying patterns.
- *Description and visualization:* Often, the purpose of data mining is to describe data so that managers can interpret it in new and different ways. For example, if large amounts of data revealed that right-handed women who live in rural environments never take philosophy courses, it would most likely spark a heated discussion about the reasons why. It would certainly provide plenty of opportunities for additional study on the part of psychologists, sociologists, and college administrators!

As we continue to accumulate data, the development of faster and bigger databases will be a necessity. You can expect to interact with more and more databases every year, even if you don't realize you're doing so. While you may never have to create a database, understanding how databases work will enable you to interact with them more effectively. ■

**Before moving on to the Chapter Review:**
- **Watch Replay Video 11.2** .
- Then check your understanding of what you've learned so far.

# check your understanding//

For a quick review to see what you've learned so far, answer the following questions. Visit **pearsonhighered.com /techinaction** to check your answers.

## multiple choice

1. Which best describes a data warehouse?
   - **a.** a building that stores computer servers
   - **b.** a software program that assists with file management
   - **c.** a collection of all the data from an organization's databases
   - **d.** a database that organizes data from multiple organizations
2. Which of the following is a component of data staging?
   - **a.** extraction of data from source databases
   - **b.** transformation of the data
   - **c.** storage of the data in the data warehouse
   - **d.** all of the above
3. A system that's designed to help perform routine daily tasks is known as (a)n
   - **a.** data mart.
   - **b.** office support system.
   - **c.** data warehouse.
   - **d.** decision support system.
4. Which would *not* be a feature or component of a transaction-processing system?
   - **a.** batch processing
   - **b.** real-time processing
   - **c.** virtual processing
   - **d.** online transaction processing
5. The process of analyzing and investigating large amounts of data to spot trends is called
   - **a.** data mining.
   - **b.** batch processing.
   - **c.** transaction processing.
   - **d.** data marting.

## true–false

_____ **1.** Fuzzy logic uses approximate data gathered by experiences rather than fixed and exact facts.

_____ **2.** Customer demographic data purchased from a third party is an example of an internal data source.

## critical thinking

1. **Database Privacy Policies**

   Most likely, you've provided personal information to various companies when you became their customer. Companies have an ethical responsibility to protect sensitive data obtained from customers. Think about a retailer that you've done business with recently. What personal information did you provide to that retailer? What personal information should a company not be allowed to disclose to others? What information does the company have of yours that you don't care if they share with (or sell to) other companies?

2. **Social Security Database**

   The U.S. Social Security Administration (SSA) maintains a large database containing a great deal of information on the personal income of individuals that would be of value to marketing professionals for targeted marketing. Currently, the SSA is prohibited from selling this information to third parties. However, the SSA and other government agencies face increasing pressure to find ways to generate revenue or decrease expenses.

   - **a.** Do you favor a change in the laws that would permit the SSA to sell names and addresses with household income information to third parties? Why or why not?
   - **b.** Would it be acceptable for the SSA to sell income information to marketing firms if it did not include personal information but only included income statistics for certain geographic areas? How is this better (or worse) than selling personal information?

**Continue** »

# 11 Chapter Review

## summary//

### Database Building Blocks

**1. What is a database, and why is using one beneficial?**

- Databases are electronic collections of related data that can be organized so that data is more easily accessed and manipulated. Properly designed databases cut down on data redundancy and duplicate data by ensuring relevant data is recorded in only one place. This also helps eliminate data inconsistency, which comes from having different data about the same transaction recorded in different places.
- When databases are used, multiple users can share and access information at the same time.
- Databases are used any time complex information needs to be organized or when more than one person needs to access the information. In these cases, lists (which are used to keep track of simple information) are no longer efficient.

**2. What do database management systems do?**

- Database management systems (DBMSs) are specially designed applications (such as Microsoft Access) that interact with the user, other applications, and the database itself to capture and analyze data.
- The main operations of a DBMS are creating databases, entering data, viewing (or browsing) data, sorting (or indexing) data, extracting (or querying) data, and outputting data.
- A query language is used to extract records from a database. Almost all relational databases today use Structured Query Language, or SQL. However, most DBMSs include wizards that enable you to query the database without learning a query language.
- The most common form of output for any database is a printed report.

**3. What components make up a database?**

- The three main components of a database are fields, records, and tables.
- A category of information in a database is stored in a field. Each field is identified by a field name, which is a way of describing the field. Fields are assigned a data type that indicates what type of data can be stored in the field. Common data types include text, numeric, computational, date, memo, object, and hyperlink.
- A group of related fields is a record.
- A group of related records is a table or file.
- To keep records distinct, each record must have one field that has a value unique to that record. This unique field is a primary key (or a key field).

### Database Types

**4. What types of databases are there?**

- The three major types of databases currently in use are relational, object-oriented, and multidimensional.
- Relational databases are characterized by two-dimensional tables of data in which a common field is maintained in each of two tables and the information in the tables is linked by this field.
- Object-oriented databases store data in objects, not in tables. The objects also contain instructions about how the data is to be manipulated or processed.
- Multidimensional databases represent data in three-dimensional cubes to enable faster retrieval of information from the database.

### Database Functions

**5. How do relational databases organize and manipulate data?**

- Relational databases operate by organizing data into various tables based on logical groupings. Because not all of the data in a relational database is stored in the same table, a methodology must be implemented to link data between tables. In relational databases, the links between tables that define how the data is related are referred to as relationships.
- To establish a relationship between two tables, both tables must have a common field (or column). Once linked, information can be drawn from multiple tables through the use of queries (for on-screen viewing of data) or report generators (used to produce printed reports).

## Database Warehousing and Storage

**6. What are data warehouses and data marts, and how are they used?**

- A data warehouse is a large-scale collection of data that contains and organizes in one place all the relevant data for an organization. Data warehouses often contain information from multiple databases.
- Because it can be difficult to find information in a large data warehouse, small slices of the data warehouse, called data marts, are often created. The information in data marts pertains to a single department within the organization, for example.
- Data warehouses and data marts consolidate information from a wide variety of sources to provide comprehensive pictures of operations or transactions within a business.

## Business Intelligence Systems

**7. What is a business intelligence system, and what types of business intelligence systems are used by decision makers?**

- Business intelligence systems are used to analyze and interpret data in order to enable managers to make informed decisions about how best to run a business.
- An office support system (OSS) is designed to assist employees in accomplishing their day-to-day tasks and improve communications.
- A transaction-processing system (TPS) is used to keep track of everyday business activities.
- A management information system (MIS) provides timely and accurate information that enables managers to make critical business decisions.
- A decision support system (DSS) is designed to help managers develop solutions for specific problems.
    - A model management system is software that assists in building analysis tools for DSSs.
    - A knowledge-based system provides intelligence to make the DSS more effective. There are several kinds of knowledge-based systems. An expert system tries to replicate the decision-making process of human experts to solve specific problems. A natural language processing (NLP) system uses natural spoken or written language rather than a computer programming language to communicate with a computer. Lastly, artificial intelligence (AI) attempts to create computers that think like humans.
- An enterprise resource planning (ERP) system is a large software system that gathers information from all parts of a business and integrates it to make it readily available for decision making.

## Data Mining

**8. What is data mining, and how does it work?**

- Data mining is the process by which large amounts of data are analyzed to spot otherwise hidden trends. Through processes such as classification, estimation, affinity grouping, clustering, and description (visualization), data is organized so that it provides meaningful information that can be used by managers to identify business trends.

Be sure to check out the companion website for additional materials to help you review and learn, including a Tech Bytes Weekly newsletter—**pearsonhighered.com/techinaction**. And don't forget the Replay Videos.

# key terms//

alphabetic check **462**
artificial intelligence (AI) **477**
batch processing **475**
binary large object (BLOB) **459**
business intelligence systems **474**
clickstream data **472**
completeness check **461**
consistency check **461**
database **450**
database administrator (database designer) **454**
database management system (DBMS) **454**
data centralization **453**
data dictionary (database schema) **455**
data inconsistency **452**
data integrity **454**
data mart **473**
data mining **480**
data redundancy **452**
data staging **473**
data type (field type) **456**
data warehouse **470**
decision support system (DSS) **476**
default value **455**
detail report **475**
enterprise resource planning (ERP) system **478**
exception report **476**
expert system **477**
field **454**
field constraint **460**
field name **454**
field properties **455**
field size **457**
filter **463**
foreign key **458**
fuzzy logic **477**
information system **474**
input forms **460**
join query **465**
knowledge-based system **477**
management information system (MIS) **475**
many-to-many relationship **459**
metadata **455**
model management system **476**
multidimensional database **459**
natural language processing (NLP) system **477**
normalization **457**
numeric check **462**
object-oriented database **459**
Object Query Language (OQL) **459**
office support system (OSS) **474**
one-to-many relationship **458**
one-to-one relationship **459**
online analytical processing (OLAP) **473**
online transaction processing (OLTP) **475**
primary key field **457**
query **463**
query language **459**
range check **460**
real-time processing **475**
record **455**
referential integrity **458**
relational algebra **464**
relational database **458**
relationship **458**
select query **464**
structured (analytical) data **459**
Structured Query Language (SQL) **459**
summary report **475**
table (file) **455**
time-variant data **472**
transaction-processing system (TPS) **474**
unstructured data **459**
validation **460**
validation rule **460**

## making the transition to . . . next semester//

1. **Designing Your Own Database**

   Students at your school want to collect and refurbish used computer equipment and donate it to underprivileged individuals. You offer to create a database to facilitate the tracking of the donated equipment. Determine the following:

   **a.** What fields do you need in your database to capture information about the clients donating the computing equipment? What would be the primary key of the "client" table? Explain your choice.

   **b.** What fields do you need to identify and categorize equipment? What would be a good primary key to use for the "computer inventory" table? Explain your choice.

   **c.** Design a table that tracks the donations. What fields from the other tables should be included in the "donation transaction" table? Justify your answer.

2. **Library Databases**

   Through your college library, you have access to many online research databases. Assume you were to conduct a research paper on data and privacy. Using your college's online databases, find five articles that would provide relevant information for your paper. List the article title, author and journal information, and a link to the article.

## making the transition to . . . the workplace//

1. **Data Marts**

   You work in the IT group of a chain of sporting goods stores, which has 40 locations in seven states. The 40 locations are organized into four regions (north, south, east, and west) with 10 stores in each. Regional managers are responsible for inventory, sales, and marketing for their region. The company has been processing all transactions electronically, and it has captured all the data in a large data warehouse. Unfortunately, there is so much information in the data warehouse that extracting meaningful data has become difficult. You've just been placed on the team that will design a new data strategy for the company.

   **a.** What type of data marts would you suggest setting up? Who will benefit from the data marts you suggest?

   **b.** For the data marts you identified, what data should be stored in each data mart? Explain how the regional managers could make use of that information to manage their group of stores.

2. **Recovering from a Data Breach**

   You work in the marketing department of XYZ Drugs that has an established buyer loyalty program. XYZ Drugs collects customer e-mail addresses and has engaged ABC Marketing to routinely send out marketing e-mails. ABC has just informed XYZ that its servers suffered a data breach and that all the names and e-mail addresses of XYZ's customers in ABC's database were compromised. You're working to inform XYZ's customers of the possible consequences of the data breach.

   **a.** What are the risks that XYZ's customers face from the data breach?

   **b.** What steps should the customers take to mitigate these risks? You need to be tactful and careful in your suggestions to customers because you want them to continue to trust XYZ with their personal information.

   **c.** Prepare a list of precautions customers can take with their personal data to avoid being victims of these types of data breaches. Try searching on the Internet for ideas using search terms such as "data breach protection" or "e-mail breach safeguards."

# Redesigning Facebook

## Problem

Facebook is the most popular social media site—it's also a database. But as with any product, there is always room for improvement. Facebook management has made decisions about what data they require from users who create Facebook accounts. They also have set up specific areas to display what management considers to be pertinent information on a user's main Facebook page. But perhaps you as a user would have designed Facebook differently.

## Task

Your class has volunteered to work as a focus group for Facebook as part of a nationwide project to assess the usefulness of the information it gathers. Users often provide unique perspectives, and they should be consulted whenever possible during the design, implementation, and updating of websites. As heavy users of Facebook, management feels that student input is invaluable to ensuring currency and usability of its features.

## Process

1. Divide the class into small groups.
2. Your group members should examine their individual Facebook accounts. Pay particular attention to the profile area of your account. What fields in the profile do you consider to be most useful? Which fields do you think are unnecessary and could be eliminated? What fields are missing from the profile that you think would be useful to you and your friends?
3. Investigate your account settings and application settings, paying particular attention to items that are displayed on the main page of your account. What changes would you make to these settings? Are options missing that you would find helpful in configuring your Facebook page?
4. Present your group's findings to the class. Compare your suggestions to those of other groups. Be sure to think about the needs of other groups of users (such as your parents, grandparents, or teenagers).
5. Prepare a list of recommendations for improvements to the current Facebook home page and settings pages. Clearly indicate how the proposed changes will benefit both users and the management of Facebook (retaining users, being able to better target advertising to users, and so on).

## Conclusion

Facebook will most likely experience competition in the future from other social networking sites that will want to poach its huge base of users. To remain competitive, Facebook needs to consider the input of users like you to ensure that it delivers a cutting-edge product with features its customers want and need.

## ethics project//

# Private Information on Public Databases

In this exercise, you'll research and then role-play a complicated ethical situation. The role you play might not match your own personal beliefs, but your research and use of logic will enable you to represent the view assigned. An arbitrator will watch and comment on both sides of the arguments, and together, the team will agree on an ethical solution.

## Problem

As more tasks in our lives are conducted online, there is a tremendous amount of data accumulated about us in online databases. Unfortunately, much of this material is accessible in databases that are searchable by anyone with Internet access or to anyone willing to pay a small fee. Websites such as **spokeo.com** and **411.com** comb through publicly accessible databases to compile information on individuals. These databases include social networking sites (Facebook or LinkedIn), online phone books, business sites where you have accounts, and government (federal, state, and local) websites. There is probably a lot of information about you available on sites such that could expose you to risks such as identify theft.

## Research Areas to Consider

- Electronic information privacy
- Electronic Privacy Information Center (**epic.org**)
- Protecting your online privacy
- Protecting yourself on Facebook
- Protecting yourself from data breaches

## Process

1. Divide the class into teams.
2. Research the areas cited above and devise a scenario in which someone has complained about a website (such as **spokeo.com**) providing information that led to his or her identity being stolen.
3. Team members should write a summary that provides background information for their character—for example, victim of identity theft, website owner, or arbitrator—and that details their character's behaviors to set the stage for the role-playing event. Then, team members should create an outline to use during the role-playing event.
4. Team members should arrange a mutually convenient time to meet for the exchange, using a virtual meeting tool or by meeting in person.
5. Team members should present their case to the class or submit a PowerPoint presentation for review by the rest of the class, along with the summary and resolution they developed.

## Conclusion

As technology becomes ever more prevalent and integrated into our lives, ethical dilemmas will present themselves to an increasing extent. Being able to understand and evaluate both sides of the argument, while responding in a personally or socially ethical manner, will be an important skill.

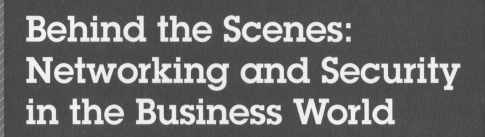

# 12 Behind the Scenes: Networking and Security in the Business World

## Client/Server Networks and Topologies

### Client/Server Network Basics

**OBJECTIVES**

1. What are the advantages of a business network? **(p. 492)**
2. How does a client/server network differ from a peer-to-peer network? **(p. 493)**
3. What are the different classifications of client/server networks? **(pp. 493–495)**
4. What components are needed to construct a client/server network? **(p. 496)**

### Servers and Network Topologies

**OBJECTIVES**

5. What do the various types of servers do? **(pp. 497–498)**
6. What are the various network topologies, and why is network topology important in planning a network? **(pp. 500–504)**

**Active Helpdesk:** Using Servers

**Sound Byte:** Network Topology and Navigation Devices

## Setting Up Business Networks

### Transmission Media

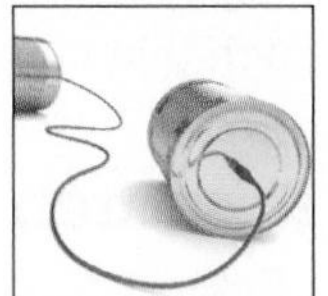

**OBJECTIVE**

7. What types of transmission media are used in client/server networks? **(pp. 508–510)**

### Network Adapters and Network Navigation Devices

**OBJECTIVES**

8. How do network adapters enable computers to participate in a client/server network? **(pp. 511–512)**
9. What devices assist in moving data around a client/server network? **(pp. 513–514)**

### Network Operating Systems

**OBJECTIVE**

10. What software needs to run on computers attached to a client/server network, and how does this software control network communications? **(p. 515)**

### Client/Server Network Security

**OBJECTIVE**

11. What measures are employed to keep large networks secure? **(pp. 518–522)**

**Sound Byte:** A Day in the Life of a Network Technician

For all media in this chapter go to **pearsonhighered.com/techinaction** or **MyITLab**.

(Alex Slobodkin/Getty Images; mostafa fawzy/Fotolia; iLexx/Getty Images; Creativeye99/Getty Images; Alex Slobodkin/Getty Images; Reuben Schulz/Getty Images)

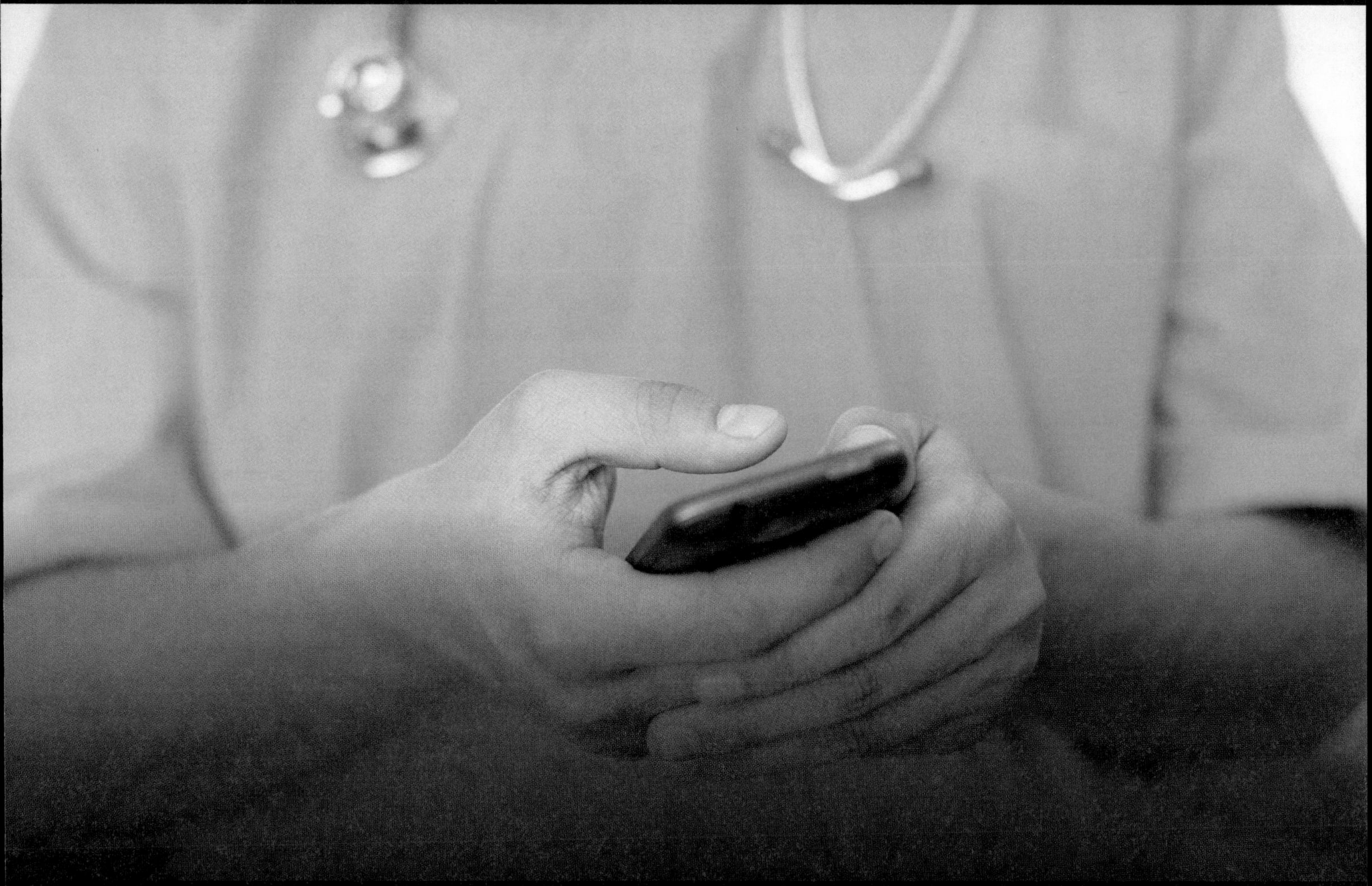

# HOW COOL IS THIS?

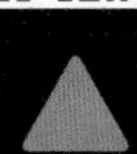

SMS **text messaging** is not encrypted or secure. But many **employees** want to use texting in the workplace, such as a nurse texting a doctor an update on a patient. So how does a business protect its **sensitive information**? Social collaboration tools designed for business and featuring **high-grade security protocols** are now appearing in the workplace. Software such as Jive, Cisco's WebEx Social, and Novell's Vibe collaboration platform are being deployed so workers who text colleagues can **effectively communicate without sacrificing security**. So expect to use secure, proprietary social networking tools at work someday soon! *(gpointstudio/Getty Images)*

# Client/Server Networks and Topologies

You learned about peer-to-peer networks and home networking in Chapter 7. In this chapter, you'll expand your knowledge about networks by delving into the client/server networks typically used in businesses.

## client/server network BASICS

Recall that a *network* is a group of two or more computing devices (or nodes) that are configured to share information and resources such as printers, files, and databases. Businesses such as your school or an insurance company gain advantages from deploying networks, similar to the advantages gained with a home network.

### Networking Advantages

**What advantages do businesses gain from networks?** Networked computers have many advantages over individual stand-alone computers (see Figure 12.1):

- **Networks enable expensive resources to be shared.** Networks enable people to share peripherals such as printers or share resources such as an Internet connection. Without a network, each computer would have to be individually connected to a printer and to the Internet. Attaching the computers to a network avoids the cost of providing each computer with duplicate resources.
- **Networks facilitate knowledge sharing.** The databases you learned about in Chapter 11 become especially powerful when deployed on a network. Networked databases can serve the needs of many people at one time and can increase the availability of data. Your college's databases are much more useful when all college employees can look up student records at the same time.
- **Networks enable software sharing.** Installing a new version of software on everyone's desktop in a business with 800 employees can be time consuming. However, if the computers are networked, all employees can access the same copy of a program from the server. Although the business must still purchase a software license for each user, with a network it can avoid having to install the program on every computer.
- **Networks enable enhanced communication.** Social networking tools, e-mail, and instant messaging are powerful applications when deployed on a network, especially one that's connected to the Internet. Business colleagues can easily exchange information with each other and can share valuable data by transferring files to other users.

**FIGURE 12.1**

**Benefits of Business Networks**

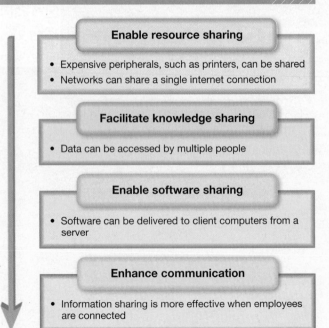

**Enable resource sharing**
- Expensive peripherals, such as printers, can be shared
- Networks can share a single internet connection

**Facilitate knowledge sharing**
- Data can be accessed by multiple people

**Enable software sharing**
- Software can be delivered to client computers from a server

**Enhance communication**
- Information sharing is more effective when employees are connected

**Are there disadvantages to using networks?** Because business networks are often complex, additional personnel are usually required to maintain them. These people, called **network administrators**, have training in computer and peripheral maintenance and repair, networking design, and the installation of networking software.

Another disadvantage is that operating a network requires special equipment and software. However, most companies feel that the cost savings of peripheral sharing and the ability to give employees simultaneous access to information outweigh the costs associated with network administrators and equipment.

### Comparing Client/Server and Peer-to-Peer Networks

**Where do I find client/server networks?** Aside from the smallest networks—such as peer-to-peer (P2P) networks, which are typically used in homes and small businesses—the majority of computer networks are based on the client/server model of computing. As you learned in Chapter 7, a **client /server network** (also called a **server-based network**) contains servers as well as client computers. A *server* is a computer that both stores and shares resources on a network, whereas a *client* is a computer that requests those resources.

Recall that in a P2P network, each node connected to the network communicates directly with every other node rather than using a server to exercise central control over the network. Many tasks that individual users must handle on a P2P network can be handled centrally at the server in a client/server network.

For instance, data files are normally stored on a server. Therefore, backups for all users on a business network can be performed by merely backing up all the files on that server. Security, too, can be exercised over the server instead of on each user's computer; this way, the server, not the individual user, coordinates data security. Therefore, client/server networks are said to be **centralized**. P2P networks, on the other hand, are **decentralized**.

**Why do businesses use client/server networks?** The main advantage of a client/server relationship is that it makes data flow more efficiently than in P2P networks. Servers can respond to requests from a large number of clients at the same time. In addition, servers can be configured to perform specific tasks, such as handling e-mail or database requests, efficiently.

**Why aren't P2P networks used more in business settings?** P2P networks become difficult to administer when they're expanded beyond 10 users. Each computer may require updating if there are changes to the network, which isn't efficient with large numbers of computers. And as noted previously, security can't be implemented centrally on a P2P network but instead must be handled by each user.

Figure 12.2 shows a small client/server arrangement. The server in this figure provides printing and Internet-connection services for all the client computers connected to the network. The server is performing tasks that would need to be done by each of the client computers in a P2P network. This frees resources on the client computers so that they can more efficiently perform processor-intensive tasks such as viewing a video or accessing a database.

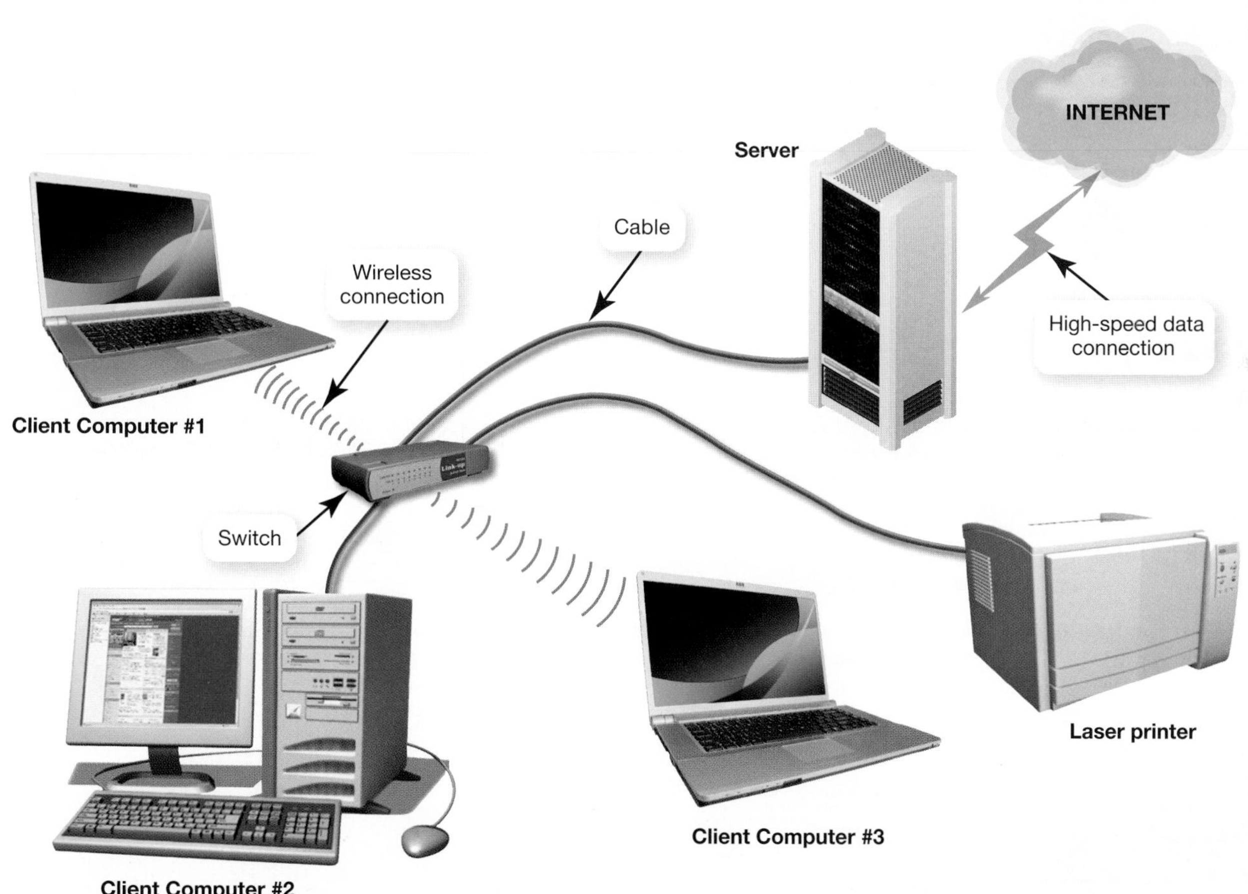


**FIGURE 12.2** This small client/server network enables users to share a printer and an Internet connection.

**Besides having a server, what makes a client/server network different from a P2P network?** Client/server networks also have increased scalability. **Scalability** means that more users can be added easily without affecting the performance of the other network nodes. Because servers handle the bulk of the printing, Internet access, and other tasks performed on the network, it's easy to accommodate more users by installing additional servers to help with the increased workload. Installing additional servers on a network is relatively simple and can usually be done without disrupting services for existing users.

## Types of Client/Server Networks

As you learned in Chapter 7, networks are generally classified according to their size and the distance between the physical parts of the network. Figure 12.3 lists the five most common types of client/server network classifications.

FIGURE 12.3

**Classifications of Client/Server Networks**

| NETWORK TYPE | DESCRIPTION | WHERE USED IN BUSINESS |
|---|---|---|
| PAN (Personal Area Network)  | Devices used by one person connected via wireless media | Usually by employees traveling on business |
| LAN (Local Area Network)  | A network consisting of nodes covering a small geographic area | In small businesses or self-contained units of a large business (such as one or more floors of the same office building) |
| HAN (Home Area Network)  | A type of small LAN installed in a home | Not usually deployed by businesses, except small home-based businesses |
| WAN (Wide Area Network)  | Two or more LANs connected together, often over long distances | Connecting business LANs over long distances such as between branches in two cities |
| MAN (Metropolitan Area Network)  | WANs constructed by municipalities to provide connectivity in a specific geographic area | Although not deployed by businesses, employees often use them while traveling |

(Drubig-photo/Fotolia; Whitehoune/Fotolia; Maridav/Fotolia; mostafa fawzy/Fotolia; Kamaga/Fotolia)

**What are the most common types of client/server networks encountered in businesses?** The two types of client/server networks most commonly encountered in businesses are *local area networks (LANs)* and *wide area networks (WANs)*:

- **Local area network (LAN)**: A LAN is generally a small group of computers and peripherals linked together over a relatively small geographic area. The computer lab at your school or the network serving the floor of the office building where you work is probably a LAN.
- **Wide area network (WAN)**: A WAN comprises large numbers of users over a wider physical area or separate LANs that are miles apart. Businesses often use WANs to connect two or more geographically distant locations. For example, a college might have a west and an east campus located in two different towns. The LAN at the west campus is connected to the LAN at the east campus, forming one WAN connected either by dedicated telecommunications lines or by satellite links. Students on both campuses can share data and collaborate through the WAN.

**What other sort of networks do businesses use?** An **intranet** is a private network set up by a business or an organization that's used exclusively by a select group of employees, customers, suppliers, volunteers, or supporters. It can facilitate information sharing, database access, group scheduling, videoconferencing, and other employee collaborations. An intranet isn't accessible by unauthorized individuals; a firewall protects it from unauthorized access through the Internet.

An area of an intranet that only certain corporations or individuals can access is called an **extranet**. The owner of an extranet decides who will be permitted to access it. For example, a company's customers and suppliers may be permitted to access information on the company's extranet.

Extranets are useful for enabling **electronic data interchange (EDI)**, which allows the exchange of large amounts of business data (such as orders for merchandise) in a standardized electronic format. Walmart has an extranet that allows its employees, vendors, and contractors to easily share information. Other uses of extranets include providing access to catalogs and inventory databases and sharing information among partners or industry trade groups.

**How is information kept secure on intranets and extranets?** Intranets and extranets often use virtual private networks to keep information secure. A **virtual private network (VPN)** uses the public Internet communications infrastructure to build a secure, private network among various locations. Although WANs can be set up using private leased communications lines, these lines are expensive and tend to increase in price as the distance between points increases. VPNs use special security technologies and protocols that enhance security, enabling data to traverse the Internet as securely as if it were on a private leased line. Installing and configuring a VPN requires special hardware such as VPN-optimized routers and firewalls. In addition, VPN software must be installed on users' computing devices.

**How do VPNs work?** The main technology for achieving a VPN is called **tunneling**. In tunneling, data packets are placed inside other data packets. The format of these external data packets is encrypted and can be understood only by the sending and receiving hardware, which is known as a *tunnel interface*. The hardware is optimized to seek efficient routes of transmission through the Internet.

## BITS&BYTES

### U.S. Military Brings Its Own Network—by Plane!

Battlefield communications need to be secure to keep enemy combatants from eavesdropping on carefully laid plans. Therefore, using public Internet communications is out of the question. And the most secure wireless communications are those that are transmitted via line-of-site technology, which presents a problem on the battlefield where terrain such as hills can prevent line-of-site communication between military units. But the U.S. military has a solution: put the network in planes!

Starting in 2014, Net-T (or network tactical) software upgrades will be applied to the advanced sensor and targeting pods that are carried by a wide variety of U.S. military aircraft. Net-T provides the capability for troops on the ground to communicate with each other by routing signals through the aircraft. The soldiers in the field use Remotely Operated Video Enhanced Receiver 5 (ROVER-5) tablet computing devices. Before Net-T, soldiers were only able to communicate with the aircraft. Now they will be able to communicate securely with other units of troops on the battlefield and share information such as video surveillance, maps, and troop deployment scenarios without using traditional radio or satellite communication. Using this secure network will help ensure that communications are not intercepted by the enemy.

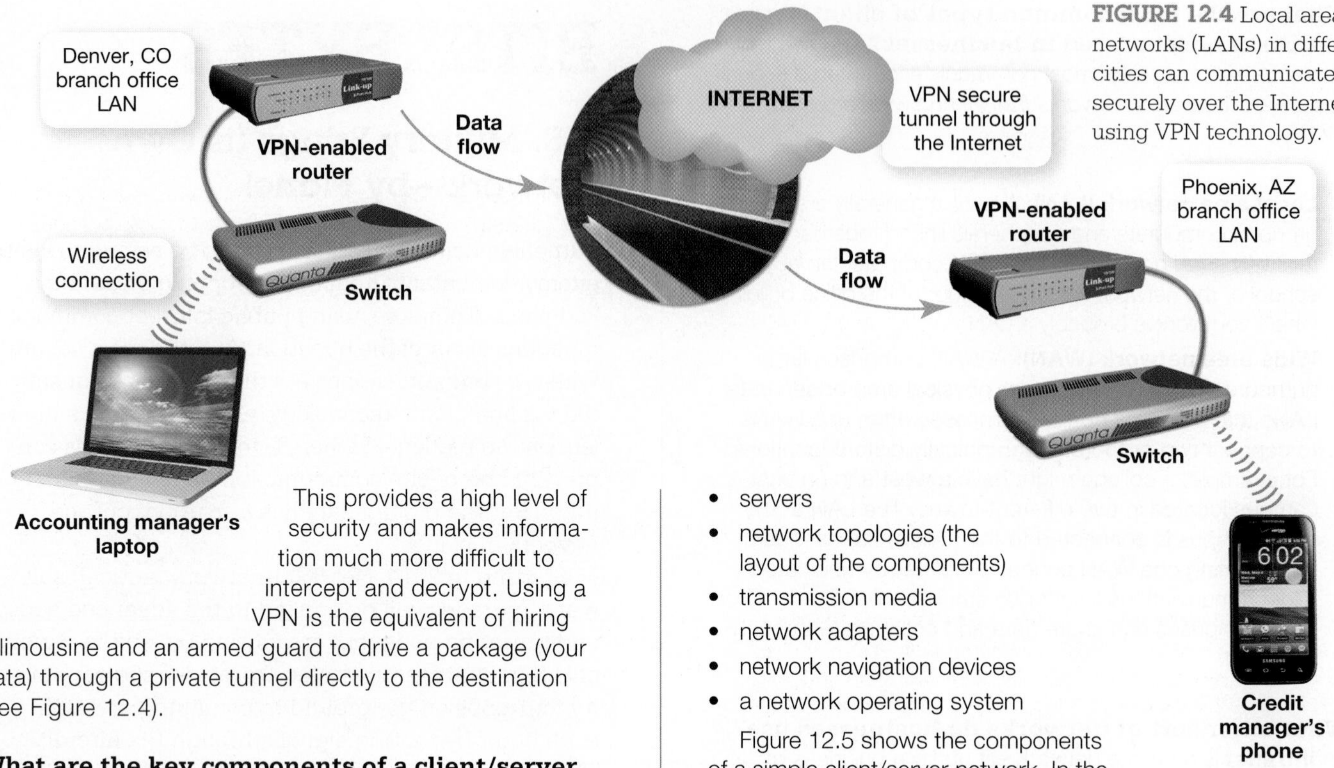

FIGURE 12.4 Local area networks (LANs) in different cities can communicate securely over the Internet using VPN technology.

This provides a high level of security and makes information much more difficult to intercept and decrypt. Using a VPN is the equivalent of hiring a limousine and an armed guard to drive a package (your data) through a private tunnel directly to the destination (see Figure 12.4).

**What are the key components of a client/server network?** The key components of a client/server network are as follows:

- servers
- network topologies (the layout of the components)
- transmission media
- network adapters
- network navigation devices
- a network operating system

Figure 12.5 shows the components of a simple client/server network. In the following sections, we'll explore each component in more detail. ■

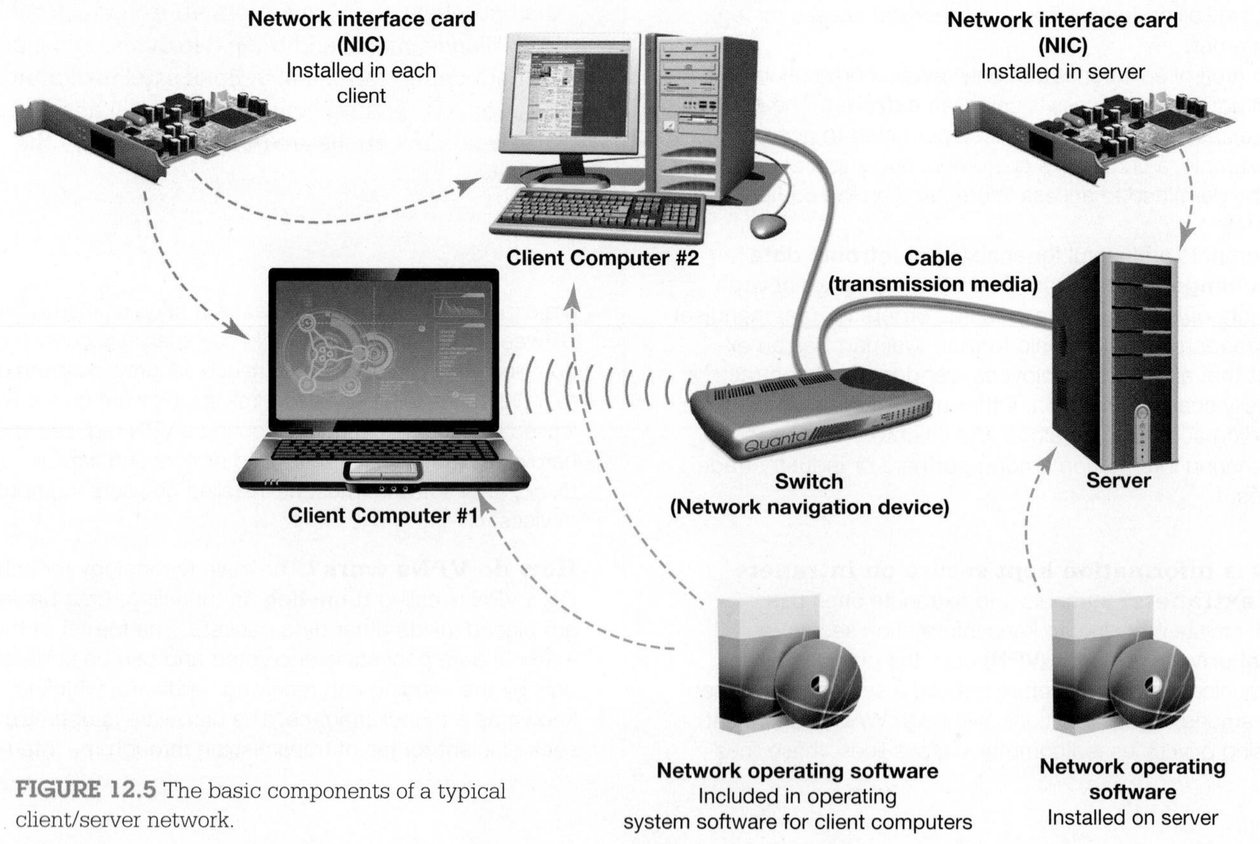


FIGURE 12.5 The basic components of a typical client/server network.

# SERVERS

Servers are the workhorses of the client/server network. They interface with many network users and assist them with a variety of tasks. The number and types of servers on a client/server network depend on the network's size and workload. Small networks (such as the one pictured in Figure 12.2 on page 493) would have just one server to handle all server functions.

**What types of servers are found on larger client/ server networks?** A **dedicated server** is a server used to fulfill one specific function, such as handling e-mail. When more users are added to a network, dedicated servers are also added in order to reduce the load on the main server. Once dedicated servers are deployed, the original main server can become a dedicated server.

**What functions do dedicated servers handle?** Any task that's repetitive or demands a lot of time from a computer's processor (CPU) is a good candidate to relegate to a dedicated server. Common types of dedicated servers are authentication servers, file servers, print servers, application servers, database servers, e-mail servers, communications servers, web servers, and cloud servers. Servers are connected to a client/server network so that all client computers that need to use their services can access them, as shown in Figure 12.6.

## Authentication and File Servers

**What are authentication and file servers?** An **authentication server** is a server that keeps track of who is logging on to the network and which services on the network are available to each user. Authentication servers also act as overseers for the network. They manage and coordinate the services provided by all other dedicated servers located on the network.

A **file server** is a server that stores and manages files for network users. On the network at your workplace or school, you may be provided with space on a file server to store files you create.

FIGURE 12.6

**Major Categories of Servers**

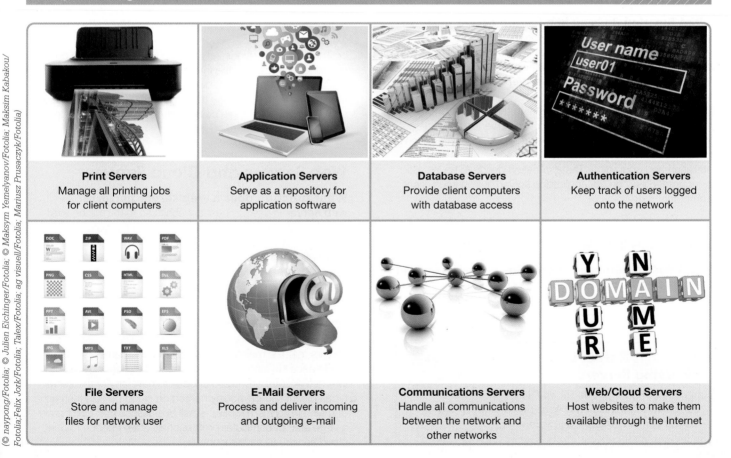

**Print Servers**
Manage all printing jobs for client computers

**Application Servers**
Serve as a repository for application software

**Database Servers**
Provide client computers with database access

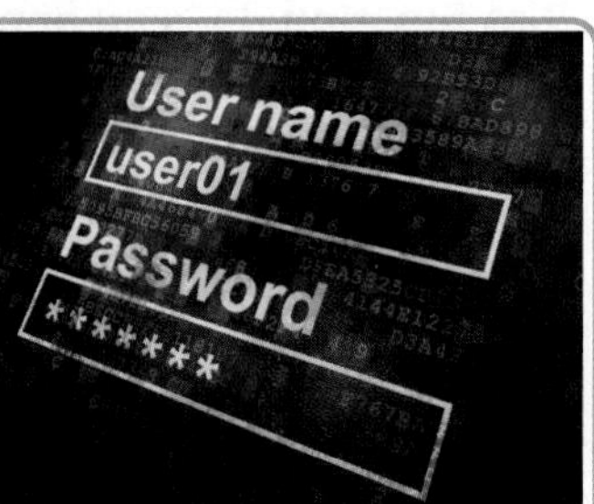


**Authentication Servers**
Keep track of users logged onto the network

**File Servers**
Store and manage files for network user

**E-Mail Servers**
Process and deliver incoming and outgoing e-mail

**Communications Servers**
Handle all communications between the network and other networks

**Web/Cloud Servers**
Host websites to make them available through the Internet

## Print Servers

**How does a print server function? Print servers** manage all client-requested printing jobs for all printers on a network, which helps client computers complete more productive work by relieving them of printing duties. When you tell your computer to print a document, it passes off the task to the print server. This frees the CPU on your computer to do other jobs.

**How does the printer know which documents to print?** A **print queue** (or *print spooler*) is a software holding area for print jobs. When the print server receives a printing request from a client computer, it puts the job into a print queue on the print server. Normally, each printer on a network has its own uniquely named print queue. Jobs receive a number when they enter the queue and go to the printer in the order in which they were received. Thus, print servers organize print jobs into an orderly sequence to make printing more efficient on a shared printer.

Another useful aspect of print servers is that network administrators can set them to prioritize print jobs. Different users and types of print jobs can be assigned different priorities so that higher-priority jobs will be printed first. For instance, in a company in which documents are printed on demand for clients, you would want those print jobs to take precedence over routine employee correspondence.

## Application Servers

**What function does an application server perform?** In many networks, all users run the same application software on their computers. In a network of thousands of personal computers, installing application software on each computer is time-consuming. An **application server** acts as a repository for application software.

When a client computer connects to the network and requests an application, the application server delivers the software to the client computer. Because the software doesn't reside on the client computer itself, this eases the task of installation and upgrading. The application needs to be installed or upgraded only on the application server, not on each client computer.

## Database Servers

**What does a database server do?** A **database server** provides client computers with access to information stored in databases. Often, many people need to access a database at the same time. For example, multiple college advisers can serve students at the same time because the advisers all have access to the student information database. This is made possible because the database resides on a database server that each adviser's computer can access through the network. If the database were on a stand-alone computer instead of a network, only one adviser could use it at a time.

ACTIVE HELPDESK
**Using Servers**

In this Active Helpdesk call, you'll play the role of a helpdesk staffer, fielding calls about various types of servers and client/server software.

## E-Mail Servers

**How is e-mail handled on a large client/server network?** The sole function of an **e-mail server** is to process and deliver incoming and outgoing e-mail. The volume of e-mail on a large network could quickly overwhelm a server that was attempting to handle other functions as well. On a network with an e-mail server, when you send or receive an e-mail, it goes through the e-mail server, which then handles the routing and delivery of your message.

## Communications Servers

**What types of communications does a communications server handle?** A **communications server** handles all communications between the network and other networks, including managing Internet connectivity. All requests for information from the Internet and all messages being sent through the Internet pass through the communications server. Because Internet traffic is substantial at most organizations, the communications server has a heavy workload.

The communications server often is the only device on the network connected to the Internet. E-mail servers, web servers, and other devices needing to communicate with the Internet usually route all their traffic through the communications server. Providing a single point of contact with the outside world makes it easier to secure the network from hackers.

## Web Servers and Cloud Servers

**What function does a web server perform?** A **web server** is used to host a website so that it will be available through the Internet. Web servers run specialized software such as Apache HTTP Server or Microsoft Internet Information Services (IIS) that enable them to host web pages. Not every large network has a web server; many businesses use a third-party web-hosting company to host their websites instead.

**What is a cloud server?** Servers no longer need to be physically located at a company's offices. **Cloud servers** are servers that are maintained by hosting companies, such as Rackspace Hosting, and are connected to networks via the Internet. A company could choose to have any of the server types discussed previously hosted on cloud servers instead of maintaining them locally. Small businesses that don't have a large staff of computer professionals often choose to use cloud servers to save money. ■

# trends in IT

## Virtualization: Making Servers Work Harder

Servers have historically been deployed on client/server networks as dedicated machines that perform one specific task. But today there are good reasons why some businesses may consider having servers perform multiple tasks.

Computers produce a lot of heat and take up physical space. As a company grows, continually adding servers may exceed the available floor space and cooling capacity of a company's data center. And budgets may limit a company's ability to purchase additional dedicated servers when needed.

Dedicated servers are mission critical when those servers handle processor-intensive operations. For instance, a major online retailer would have dedicated web servers handling e-commerce traffic so that customers could purchase items quickly and efficiently. But small businesses don't necessarily require the computing power of a dedicated server for all of their computing needs. In addition, today's powerful multi-core processors allow computers to process data more quickly and efficiently than single-core machines. Sometimes just dedicating a computer to one task, such as an authentication server, might not come close to fully utilizing that server's computing potential. For all of these reasons, *virtualization* was born.

**Virtualization** involves using specialized software to make individual physical servers behave as though they are more than one physical device (see Figure 12.7). Each virtual server can operate as a separate device and can even run its own operating system (OS). Therefore, you could have a virtual e-mail server running Windows and a virtual web server running Linux on the same physical server.

Creating virtual servers requires running specialized virtualization software on a physical server. The physical server then becomes known as the *host*. Virtual servers running on a host machine are known as *guest servers*. The computing power of the CPU is split between the guests running on the host. Therefore, it wouldn't be practical to run dozens of guest environments on one host because the computing power would become diluted. However, it's very possible to run two or three guest servers on one multi-processor physical server as long as the applications running on the virtual servers aren't overly processor intensive. VMware, Microsoft Hyper-V Server, and XenServer are popular virtualization software packages.

Virtualization is a great way to provide backup servers at a low cost. Mission-critical servers, such as web servers, need to be running and available to customers at all times. If a web server for an e-commerce business fails, the company is unable to sell products until the server is repaired. With virtual servers, you could have a copy of your web server running virtually on two separate physical machines (say server 1 and 2). If server 1 breaks, you could immediately have the virtual copy of your web server on physical server 2 take over, and the company could still be processing orders and conducting business.

Although virtualization isn't the perfect solution for every business situation, it does offer intriguing possibilities and effective solutions for specific needs. Many companies today are actively exploring virtualization as a way to extend their computing resources and save money.

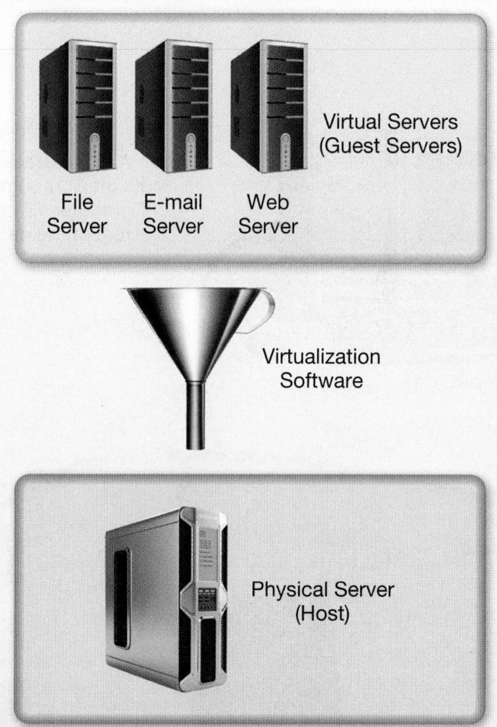


**FIGURE 12.7** Virtualization software allows one physical server to appear to be multiple separate servers capable of handling three different processes.

# network TOPOLOGIES

Just as buildings have different floor plans depending on their uses, networks have different layouts according to their purpose. **Network topology** refers to the physical or logical arrangement of computers, transmission media (cable), and other network components. *Physical topology* refers to the layout of the "real" components of the network, whereas *logical topology* refers to the virtual connections among network nodes. Logical topologies usually are determined by network protocols instead of the physical layout of the network or the paths that electrical signals follow on the network.

**What are network protocols?** A **protocol** is a set of rules for exchanging communications. Although many people think that Ethernet is a type of network topology, it's actually a communications protocol. Therefore, an Ethernet network could be set up using almost any type of physical topology.

In this section, we'll explore the most common network topologies (bus, ring, and star) and discuss when each topology is used. The type of network topology used is important because it can affect a network's performance and scalability. Knowing how the basic topologies work—and knowing the strengths and weaknesses of each one—will help you understand why particular network topologies were chosen on the networks you use.

## Bus Topology

**What does a bus topology look like?** In a **bus** (or **linear bus**) **topology**, all computers are connected in sequence on a single cable, as shown in Figure 12.8. This topology has largely become legacy technology because star topologies are more efficient on Ethernet networks, and a bus topology isn't designed to easily support wireless connections. However, bus topologies are still found in some manufacturing facilities where groups of computer-controlled machines are connected.

Each computer on the bus network can communicate directly with every other computer on the network. **Data collisions**, which happen when two computers send data at the same time and the sets of data collide somewhere in the connection media, are a problem on all networks. When data collides, it's often lost or damaged. A limitation of bus

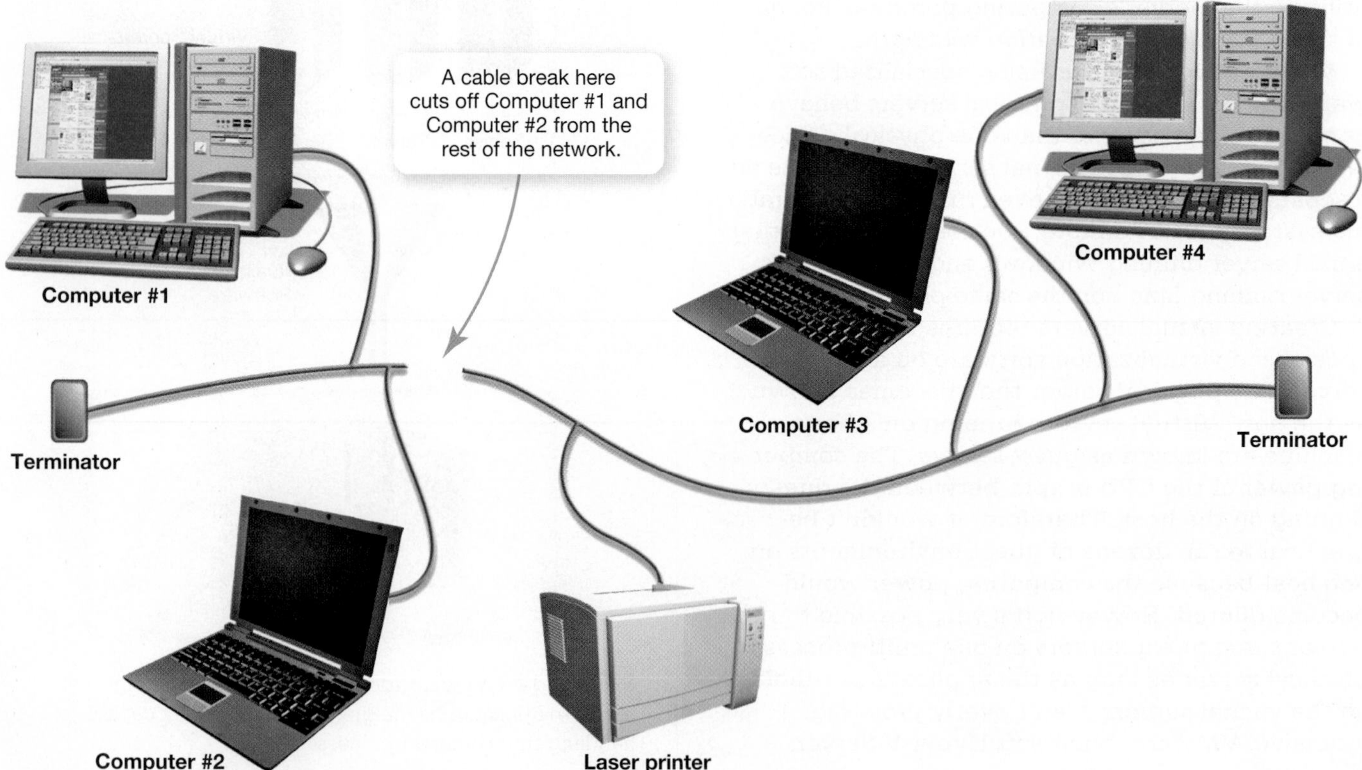


**FIGURE 12.8** In a linear bus topology, all computers are connected in a sequence.

networks is that data collisions can occur fairly easily because a bus network is essentially composed of one main communication medium (a single cable).

Because two signals transmitted at the same time on a bus network may cause a data collision, an **access method** has to be established to control which computer is allowed to use the transmission media at a certain time. Computers on a bus network behave like a group of people having a conversation. The computers "listen" to the network data traffic on the media. When no other computer is transmitting data (that is, when the "conversation" stops), the computer knows it's allowed to transmit data. This means of taking turns "talking" prevents data collisions.

**How does data get from point to point on a bus network?** The data is broadcast throughout the network via the media to all devices connected to the network. The data is broken into small segments, each called a *packet*. Each packet contains the address of the computer or peripheral device to which it's being sent. Each computer or device connected to the network listens for data that contains its address. When it "hears" data addressed to it, it takes the data off the media and processes it.

The devices (nodes) attached to a bus network do nothing to move data along the network. This makes a bus network a **passive topology**. The data travels the entire length of the medium and is received by all network devices. The ends of the cable in a bus network are capped off by terminators (as shown in Figure 12.8). A **terminator** is a device that absorbs a signal so that it's not reflected back onto parts of the network that have already received it.

**What are the advantages and disadvantages of bus networks?** The simplicity and low cost of bus network topology are its key advantages. As shown in Figure 12.8, the major disadvantage is that if there is a break in the cable, the bus network is effectively disrupted because some computers are cut off from others on the network. Also, because only one computer can communicate at a time, adding a large number of nodes to a bus network limits performance and causes delays in sending data.

## Ring Topology

**What does a ring topology look like?** Not surprisingly, given its name, the computers and peripherals in a **ring** (or **loop**) **topology** are laid out in a configuration resembling a circle, as shown in Figure 12.9. Data flows around the circle from device to device in one direction only. Because data is passed

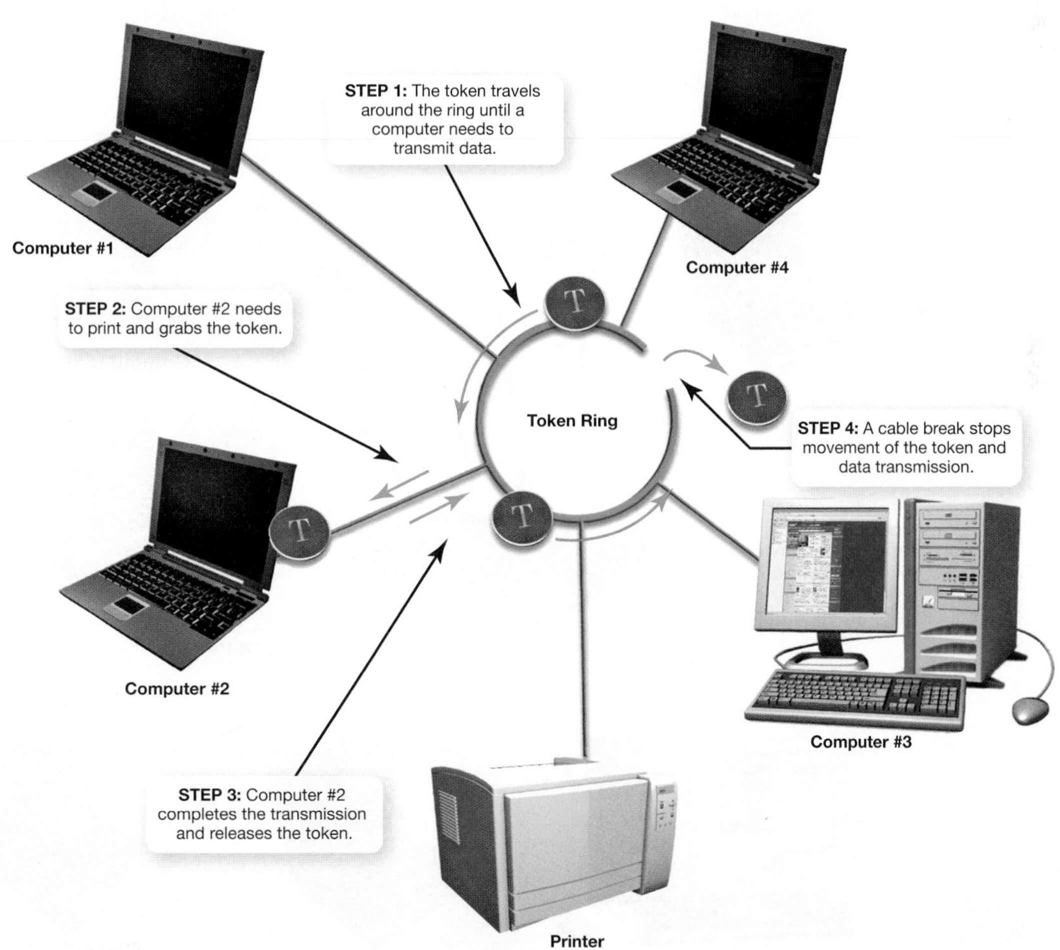
STEP 1: The token travels around the ring until a computer needs to transmit data.
Computer #1
Computer #4
STEP 2: Computer #2 needs to print and grabs the token.
T
Token Ring
STEP 4: A cable break stops movement of the token and data transmission.
Computer #2
Computer #3
STEP 3: Computer #2 completes the transmission and releases the token.
Printer

**FIGURE 12.9** A ring topology provides a fair allocation of resources.

using a special data packet called a **token**, this type of topology was once commonly called a *token-ring topology*.

**How does a token move data around a ring?** A token is passed from computer to computer around the ring until it's grabbed by a computer that needs to transmit data. The computer "holds" on to the token until it has finished transmitting data. Only one computer on the ring can "hold" the token at a time, and usually only one token exists on each ring.

If a node has data to send, such as a document that needs to go to the printer, it waits for the token to be passed to it. The node then takes the token out of circulation and sends the data to its destination. When the receiving node receives a complete transmission of the data (in this example, when the document is received by the printer), it transmits an acknowledgment to the sending node. The sending node then generates a new token and starts it going around the ring again. This is called the **token method** and is the access method that ring networks use to avoid data collisions.

A ring topology is an **active topology**, which means that nodes participate in moving data through the network. Each node on the network is responsible for retransmitting the token or the data to the next node on the ring. Large ring networks have the capability to use multiple tokens to help move data faster.

**What are the advantages and disadvantages of a ring topology?** A ring topology provides a fairer allocation of network resources than does a bus topology. By using a token, a ring network enables all nodes on the network to have an equal chance to send data. One "chatty" node can't monopolize the network bandwidth as easily as in a bus topology because it must pass the token on after sending a batch of data. In addition, a ring topology's performance remains acceptable even with large numbers of users.

As shown in Figure 12.9, one disadvantage of a ring network is that if one computer fails, the entire network can come to a halt because the failed computer is unavailable to retransmit tokens and data. Another disadvantage is that problems in the ring can be hard for network administrators to find. It's easier to expand a ring topology than a bus topology, but adding a node to a ring causes the ring to cease to function while the node is being installed.

## Star Topology

**What is the layout for a star topology?** A **star topology** is the most widely deployed client/server network topology because it offers the most flexibility for a low price. In a star topology, the nodes connect to a central communications device called a *switch* in a pattern resembling a star, as shown in Figure 12.10. The switch receives a signal from the sending node and retransmits it to the node on the network that needs to receive the signal. Each network node picks up only the

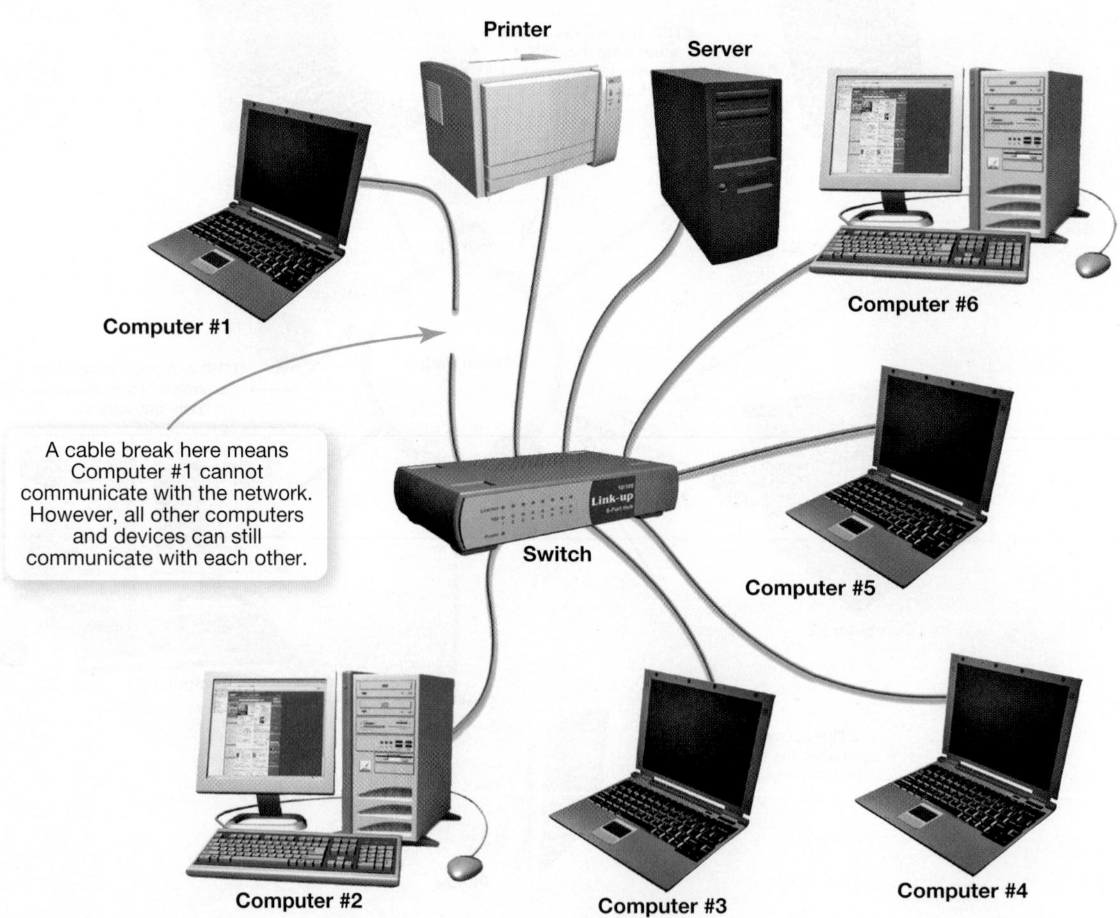


FIGURE 12.10 In a star topology, network nodes are connected through a central switch.

SOUND BYTE

**Network Topology and Navigation Devices**

In this Sound Byte, you'll learn about common network topologies, the types of networks they are used with, and various network navigation devices.

transmissions addressed to it. Because the switch retransmits data signals, a star topology is an active topology. The only drawback is that if the switch fails, the network no longer functions. However, it's relatively easy to replace a switch.

**How do computers on a star network avoid data collisions?** Because most star networks are Ethernet networks, they use the method used on all Ethernet networks to avoid data collisions: **CSMA/CD** (short for *carrier sense multiple access with collision detection*). With CSMA/CD, a node connected to the network uses carrier sense (that is, it "listens") to verify that no other nodes are currently transmitting data signals. If the node doesn't hear any other signals, it assumes that it's safe to transmit data. All devices on the network have the same right (that is, they have multiple access) to transmit data when they deem it safe. It's therefore possible for two devices to begin transmitting data signals at the same time. If this happens, the two signals collide.

**What happens when the signals collide?** As shown in Figure 12.11, when two nodes (#1 and #2) begin transmitting data signals at the same time (Step 1), signals collide, and a node on the network (#3) detects the collision. Node #3 then sends a special signal called a **jam signal** to all network nodes, alerting them that a collision has occurred (Step 2). The original nodes #1 and #2 then stop transmitting and wait a random amount of time before retransmitting their data signals (Step 3). The wait times need to be random; otherwise, both nodes would start retransmitting at the same time and another collision would occur.

**What are the advantages and disadvantages of a star topology?** The major advantages of a star network are as follows:

- The failure of one computer doesn't affect the rest of the network. This is extremely important in a large network, where having one disabled computer affect the operations of several hundred other computers would be unacceptable.
- It's easy to add nodes to star networks.
- Performance remains acceptable even with large numbers of nodes.
- Centralizing communications through a switch makes troubleshooting and repairs easier. Technicians can usually pinpoint a communications problem just by examining the switch, as opposed to searching for a particular length of cable that has broken in a ring network.

The disadvantage of star networks used to be cost. Because of the complexity of the layout of star networks, they require more cable and used to be more expensive than bus or ring networks. However, the price of cable has fallen and

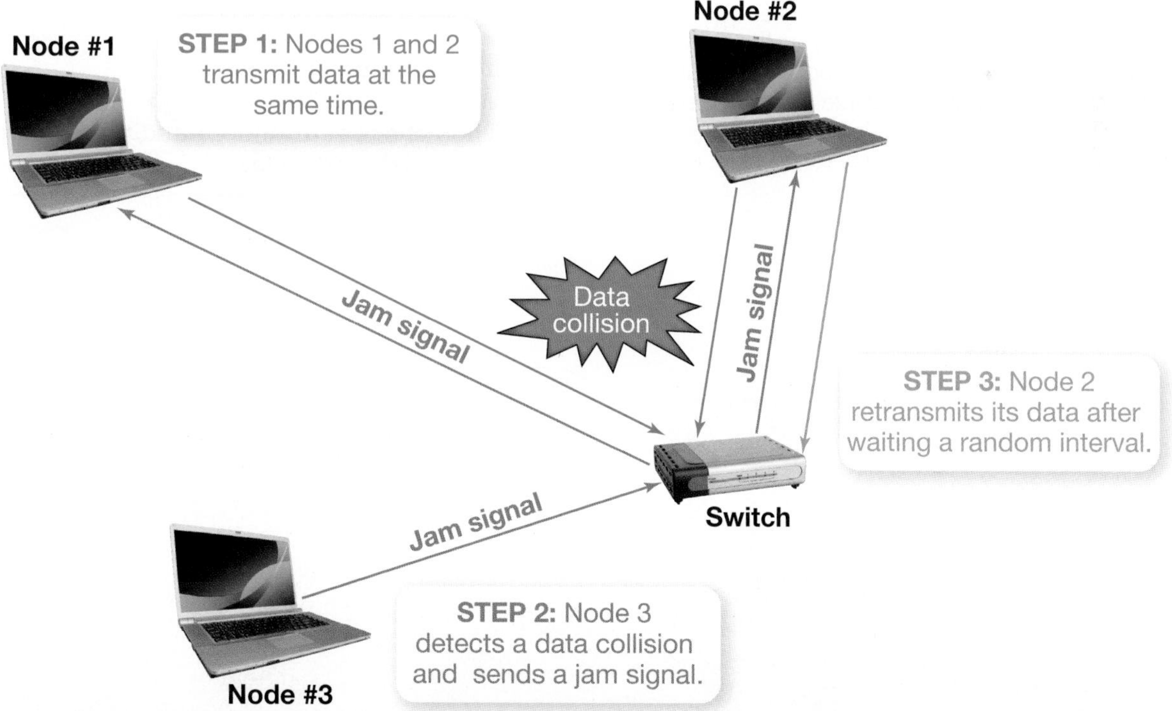


FIGURE 12.11 Jam signals are used to handle data collisions on an Ethernet network.

FIGURE 12.12

## Advantages and Disadvantages of Bus, Ring, and Star Topologies

| TOPOLOGY | ADVANTAGES | DISADVANTAGES |
|---|---|---|
| **Bus** | • Uses a minimal amount of cable.<br>• Installation is easy, reliable, and inexpensive. | • Breaks in the cable can disable the network.<br>• Large numbers of users decrease performance because of high volumes of data traffic. |
| **Ring** | • Allocates access to the network fairly.<br>• Performance remains acceptable even with many users. | • Adding/removing nodes disables the network.<br>• Failure of one node can bring down the network.<br>• Problems in data transmission can be difficult to find. |
| **Star** | • Failure of one node doesn't affect other nodes on the network.<br>• Centralized design simplifies troubleshooting and repairs.<br>• High scalability: Adding computers is easy.<br>• Performance remains acceptable even with many users. | • Requires more cable (and possibly higher installation costs) than a bus or ring topology.<br>• The switch is a single point of failure; if it fails, all computers connected to it are affected. |

wireless nodes are replacing many wired nodes on networks, removing cost as a barrier in most cases.

## Comparing Topologies

**Which topology is the best one?** Figure 12.12 lists the advantages and disadvantages of bus, ring, and star topologies. Star topologies are the most common, mainly because large networks are constantly adding new users. The ability to add new users easily—by installing an additional switch—without affecting users already on the network is the deciding factor. Bus topologies have become all but extinct now that most home networks utilize a star topology. Ring topologies are still popular in certain businesses where fair allocation of network access is a major requirement of the network.

**Can topologies be combined within a single network?** Because each topology has its own unique advantages, topologies are often combined to construct business networks. Combining multiple topologies into one network is known as constructing a **hybrid topology**. For instance, fair allocation of resources may be critical for reservation clerks at an airline (thereby requiring a ring network), but the airline's purchasing department may require a star topology. ■

**Before moving on to Part 2:**
- **Watch Replay Video 12.1** .
- Then check your understanding of what you've learned so far.

# check your understanding//

For a quick review to see what you've learned so far, answer the following questions. Visit **pearsonhighered.com /techinaction** to check your answers.

## multiple choice

1. Which of the following is *not* an advantage of installing a network in a business?
   - **a.** enables peripheral sharing
   - **b.** enables software sharing
   - **c.** decentralization of files and data
   - **d.** centralization of files and data
2. Why are client/server networks usually installed in businesses?
   - **a.** Security is weaker on client/server networks.
   - **b.** They do not require dedicated servers like P2P networks.
   - **c.** They are more scalable than P2P networks.
   - **d.** Client/server networks are cheaper to install.
3. To manage connections with outside networks, which server would a client/server network include?
   - **a.** Internet
   - **b.** authentication
   - **c.** communications
   - **d.** application
4. Which type of network topology is least popular?
   - **a.** bus
   - **b.** Ethernet
   - **c.** ring
   - **d.** star
5. A network consisting of nodes covering a small geographic area is known as a:
   - **a.** MAN
   - **b.** WAN
   - **c.** SAN
   - **d.** LAN

## true–false

_____ **1.** Client/server networks are more difficult to administer than P2P networks.

_____ **2.** An authentication server is used to host databases on a client/server network.

## critical thinking

1. **Acceptable-Use Internet Policies**

   Most schools have drafted acceptable-use policies for computers and Internet access to inform students and employees of the approved uses of college computing assets. Consider the following areas of a potential college policy:
   - **a.** Should college employees be allowed to use their computers and Internet access for personal tasks (such as checking personal e-mail or accessing Facebook)? If so, how much time per day is reasonable for employees to spend on personal tasks?
   - **b.** Should student computer and Internet usage be monitored to ensure compliance with the personal use policies? Should the college inform students that they're being monitored? What should the penalties be for violating these policies?
2. **Wireless Access**

   Many cities are considering providing MANs for their citizens and visitors. Consider the following:
   - **a.** If access is not free, how much should residents pay? Should visitors pay more or less than residents? Should there be discounts for low-income households?
   - **b.** If access is free, how should the city pay for the costs of providing Internet access?

**Continue** »

# Sharing Folders on a Home Network

Creating a HomeGroup in Windows lets you share folders and files with all computers on a network that belong to that HomeGroup. When you set up your Windows 8 computer, you're asked to create a HomeGroup and are provided with instructions for having other Windows 8 or Windows 7 computers join that HomeGroup. In this tutorial, you'll learn how to share a folder from a Windows 8 machine.

**Step 1** Ensure that all the computers on your network are members of the same HomeGroup. (**Note:** Only Windows 7 and 8 support HomeGroups.) To check if a computer is in a HomeGroup, launch Control Panel, click the **Network and Internet** link, then click the **HomeGroup** link. If you see a screen like the one below, your computer is in a HomeGroup.

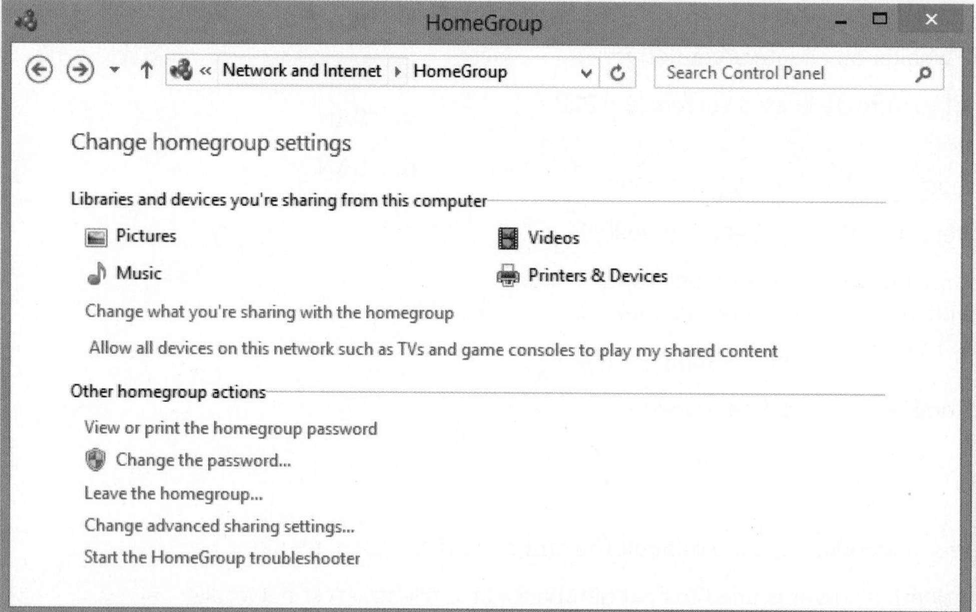


**Step 2** If there's a computer on your network that hasn't joined a HomeGroup, you need to obtain the HomeGroup password from the computer on which you set up your HomeGroup (most likely your Windows 8 computer). Navigate to the HomeGroup screen (as shown in Step 1) on your Windows 8 computer and click the **View or print the homegroup password** link to display the HomeGroup password. Write it down and use it to have your other computers join the HomeGroup.

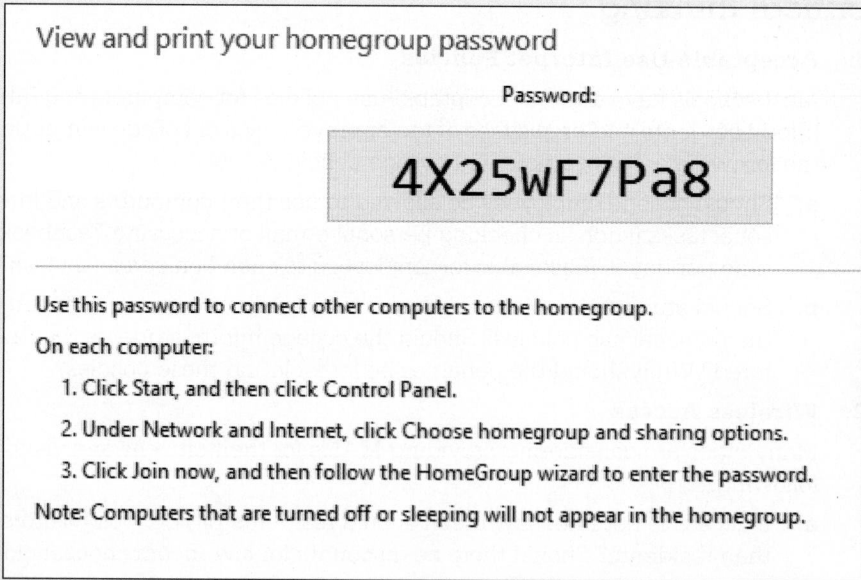

View and print your homegroup password
Password:
4X25wF7Pa8
Use this password to connect other computers to the homegroup.
On each computer:
1. Click Start, and then click Control Panel.
2. Under Network and Internet, click Choose homegroup and sharing options.
3. Click Join now, and then follow the HomeGroup wizard to enter the password.
Note: Computers that are turned off or sleeping will not appear in the homegroup.

**Step 3** Open File Explorer (previously Windows Explorer), navigate to the folder you wish to share with your HomeGroup, and left-click to select it. On the File Explorer ribbon, click the **Share** tab, and then select either **Homegroup (view)** or **Homegroup (view and edit)** to share the folder with your HomeGroup. The Homegroup (view) option only allows other members of the HomeGroup the ability to see and open the files in the folder. The Homegroup (view and edit) option gives other members of the HomeGroup the ability to add or delete files from the folder.

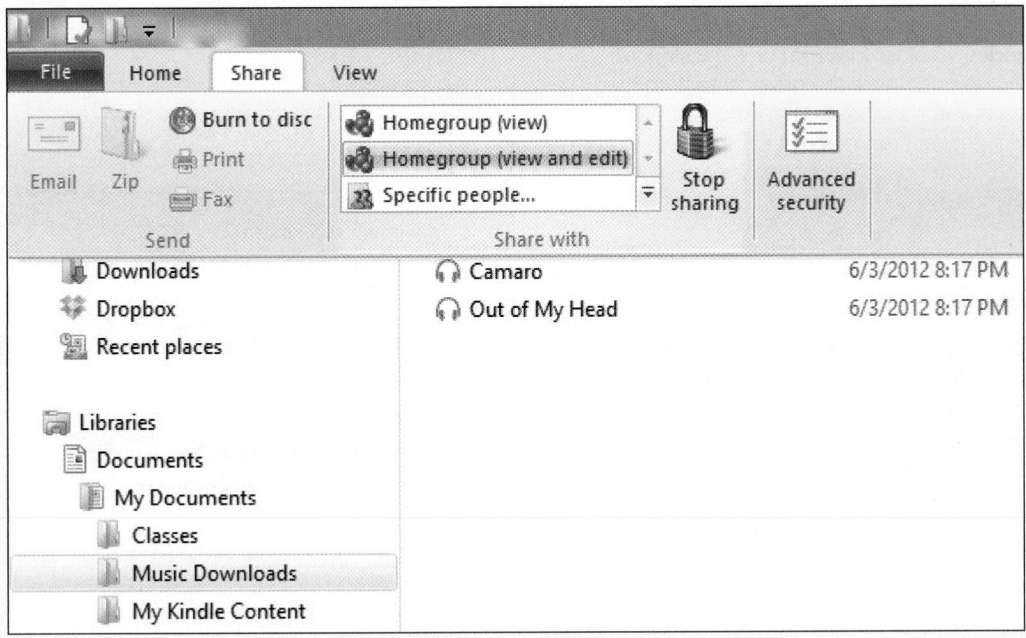


**Step 4** Launch File Explorer on another computer in the HomeGroup (a Windows 7 computer is shown below). Under Network in the **Navigation** pane, find the name of the computer on which you shared the folder. Navigate through the directory structure until you find the shared folder. You should now have access to the files.

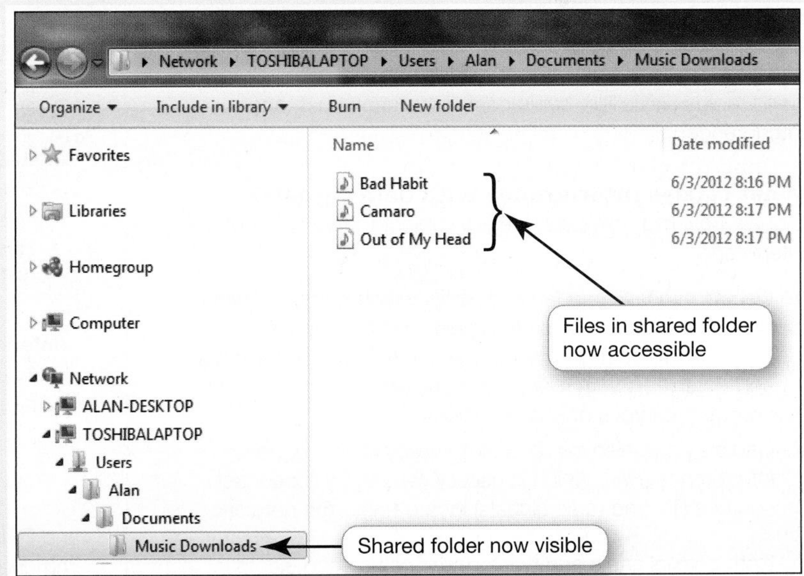

# Setting Up Business Networks

Setting up business networks is similar to configuring home networks. You need to consider the type of transmission media, ensure all nodes have network adapters, and install the appropriate network communication devices.

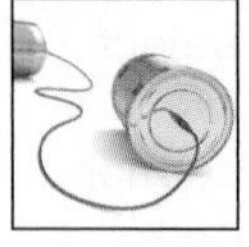

## transmission MEDIA

**Transmission media**, whether for wired or wireless communications technology, comprise the physical system that data takes to flow between devices on the network. Without transmission media, network devices would be unable to communicate. Most corporate networks contain a combination of wired and wireless media.

### Wired Transmission Media

**Why are wired connections used in business networks?** Wired connections are popular in business networks because they generally provide higher throughput and better security than wireless connections. Desktop computers still provide more computing power for less money than laptops, which makes desktop computers popular choices for business networks. Because desktops aren't often moved around, they're usually connected to a network with a wired connection.

**What are the important factors in choosing a cable type?** For business networks, the three main cable types that are used are *twisted-pair, coaxial,* and *fiber-optic*. Although each cable type is different, the same six factors always need to be considered when choosing a cable type (see Figure 12.13): maximum run length, bandwidth, bend radius (flexibility), cable cost, installation cost, and interference.

**What causes interference with data signals?** Signals traveling down a cable are subject to two types of interference:

1. *Electromagnetic interference (EMI)*, which is caused when the cable is exposed to strong electromagnetic fields, can distort or degrade signals on the cable. Fluorescent lights and machinery with motors or transformers are the most common sources of EMI emissions.
2. Cable signals also can be disrupted by *radio frequency interference (RFI),* which is usually caused by broadcast sources (TV and radio signals) located near the network.

Both coaxial cable and twisted-pair cable send electrical impulses down conductive material to transmit data signals, making them more subject to interference. Fiber-optic cable transmits data signals as pulses of light. Because EMI and RFI don't affect light waves, fiber-optic cable is virtually immune to interference.

In the sections that follow, we'll discuss the characteristics of each of the three major types of cable. We'll also discuss the use of wireless media as an alternative to cable.

FIGURE 12.13

**Factors to Consider When Choosing Network Cable**

**Maximum run length**
- How far a cable can run before data signal degrades
- Distance between nodes determines run length needed

**Bandwidth**
- Amount of data transmitted across medium
- Measured in bits per second (BPS)

**Flexibility (bend radius)**
- How much a cable can be bent before it is damaged
- Lots of corners? Need cable with a high bend radius.

**Cable cost**
- Cost is different for each cable type
- Budget may limit choice of cable type

**Installation cost**
- Twisted-pair and coaxial cable are inexpensive to install (low $)
- Fiber-optic cable requires special training and equipment (high $)

**Interference**
- Twisted-pair most susceptible to interference
- Fiber-optic immune to interference

(Maridav/Fotolia; Victoria/Fotolia; Nicholas Piccillo/Fotolia; Ion Popa/Fotolia; auremar/Fotolia; ermess/Fotolia)

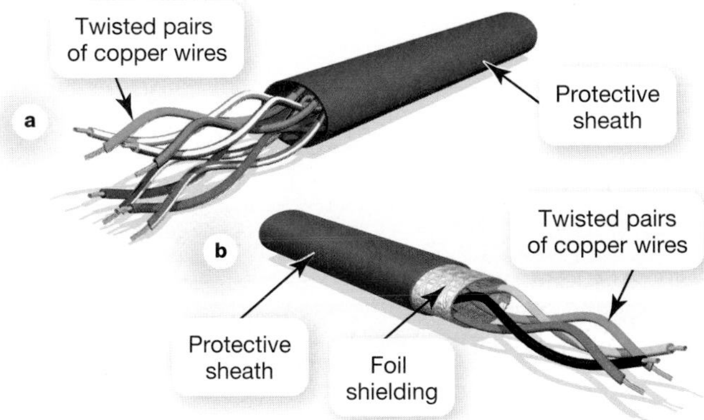


FIGURE 12.14 Anatomy of (a) unshielded twisted-pair (UTP) cable and (b) shielded twisted-pair (STP) cable.

## Twisted-Pair Cable

**Why are the wires in twisted-pair cable twisted?** **Twisted-pair cable** consists of pairs of copper wires twisted around each other and covered by a protective sheath (jacket). The twists are important because they cause the magnetic fields that form around the copper wires to intermingle, making them less susceptible to outside interference. The twists also reduce the amount of crosstalk interference (the tendency of signals on one wire to interfere with signals on a wire next to it).

If the twisted-pair cable contains a layer of foil shielding to reduce interference, it's called **shielded twisted-pair (STP) cable**. Most home networks use unshielded twisted-pair (UTP) cable that doesn't have the foil shielding. UTP cable is more susceptible to interference than STP cable. Figure 12.14 shows illustrations of both types of twisted-pair cable. Because of its lower price, UTP is used in business networks unless significant sources of interference must be overcome, such as in a production environment where machines create magnetic fields.

## Coaxial Cable

**Is coaxial cable still used in business networks?** Although not as popular as it once was, coaxial cable is still used in some manufacturing facilities where machinery creates heavy electrical interference. **Coaxial cable** (as shown in Figure 12.15) consists of four main components:

1. A core (usually copper) is in the very center and is used for transmitting the signal.
2. A solid layer of nonconductive insulating material (usually a hard, thick plastic) surrounds the core.
3. A layer of braided metal shielding covers the insulation to reduce interference with signals traveling in the core.
4. An external jacket of lightweight plastic covers the internal cable components to protect them from damage.

## Fiber-Optic Cable

**What does fiber-optic cable look like?** As shown in Figure 12.16, **fiber-optic cable** is composed of the following:

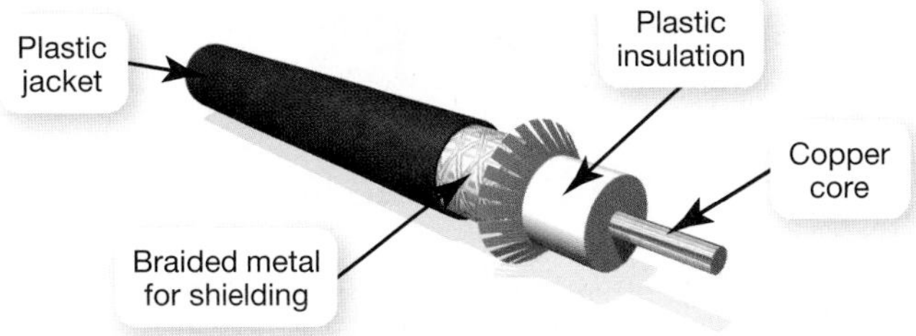


FIGURE 12.15 Coaxial cable consists of four main components: a core, an insulated covering, a braided metal shielding, and a plastic jacket.

- A glass (or plastic) fiber (or a bundle of fibers called a core) through which the data is transmitted
- A protective layer of glass or plastic cladding is wrapped around the core to protect it
- For additional protection, it has an outer jacket (sheath), which is often made of a durable material such as Kevlar (the substance used to make bulletproof vests)

Data transmissions can pass through fiber-optic cable in only one direction. Therefore, at least two fibers (or cores) are contained in most fiber-optic cables to enable transmission of data in both directions.

## Wireless Media Options

**What wireless media options are there?** Most business networks use the same Ethernet standards as home networks. Therefore, the wireless options for business networks are very similar to those available for home networks. *Wireless access points* are installed to provide coverage wherever employees will be working with portable devices, such as in conference rooms.

## Comparing Transmission Media

**Which medium is best for business networks?** Network engineers specialize in the design and deployment of networks and are responsible for selecting the appropriate

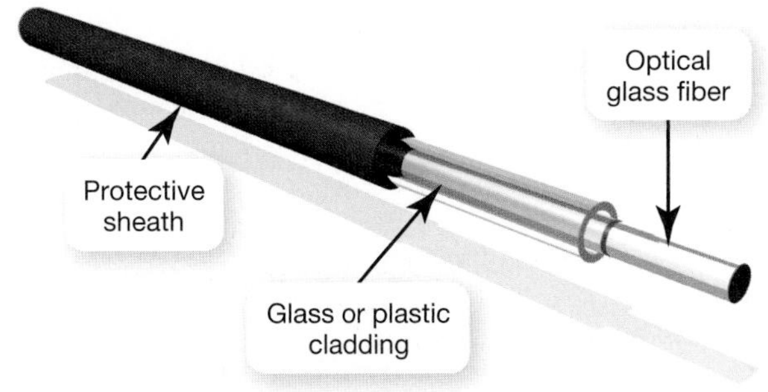


FIGURE 12.16 Fiber-optic cable is made up of a glass or plastic fiber (or a bundle of fibers), a glass or plastic cladding, and a protective sheath.

# BITS&BYTES

## Go Green with Mobile Apps

Many people want to support green initiatives and sustainability. The U.S. Environmental Protection Agency (EPA) hosts the My Green Apps website to make it easier to find useful apps that support green lifestyles (see Figure 12.17). The site currently lists almost 300 existing apps that can help individuals or groups switch to a greener lifestyle or track progress in daily green living activities.

If you can't locate an app that meets your needs, you can suggest one for development. Visitors to the website can vote on whether they think suggested apps are a useful idea. Software developers may well develop an app that gets a substantial number of votes. So visit **epa.gov/mygreenapps** today and find an app to help you live greener . . . or suggest a new one that will benefit everyone.

**FIGURE 12.17** The EPA's My Green Apps website provides information about apps that help you go green and even encourages you to suggest ideas for new apps. *(Courtesy of the United States Environmental Protection Agency)*

network topologies and media types. Their decision as to which transmission medium a network will use is based on the topology selected, the length of the cable runs needed, the amount of interference present, and the need for wireless connectivity.

As noted above, most large networks use a mix of media types. For example, fiber-optic cable may be appropriate for the portion of a network that traverses the factory floor, where interference from magnetic fields is significant. However, UTP cable may work fine in a general office area. Wireless media may be required in areas where employees are likely to connect their portable computing devices or where it's impractical or expensive to run cable. ■

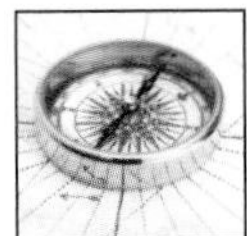

# network ADAPTERS

As noted in Chapter 7, client and server computers and peripherals need an interface to connect with and communicate on the network. **Network adapters** are devices that perform specific tasks to enable nodes to communicate on a network. Network adapters are installed inside computers and peripherals. These adapters are referred to as *network interface cards (NICs)*.

**What do network adapters do?** Network adapters perform three critical functions:

1. **They generate high-powered signals to enable network transmissions.** Digital signals generated inside the computer are fairly low powered and would not travel well on cable or wireless network media without network adapters. Network adapters convert the signals from inside the computer into higher-powered signals that have no trouble traversing the network media.
2. **They're responsible for breaking the data into packets and transmitting and receiving data.** They also are responsible for receiving incoming data packets and, in accordance with networking protocols, reconstructing them, as shown in Figure 12.18.
3. **They act as gatekeepers for information flowing to and from the client computer.** Much like a security guard in a gated community, a network adapter is responsible for permitting or denying access to the client computer (the community) and controlling the flow of data (visitors).

You should note that there won't always be the same number of response packets as there are request packets. The number of packets depends on the volume of the data being sent. A simple response may have less data than a complex one.

**Are there different types of network adapters?** Although there are different types of network adapters, almost without exception Ethernet is the standard communications protocol used on most client/server networks. Therefore, the adapter cards that ship with computers today are Ethernet compliant.

**Do wireless networks require network adapters?** A computing device that connects to a network using wireless access needs to have a special network adapter card, called

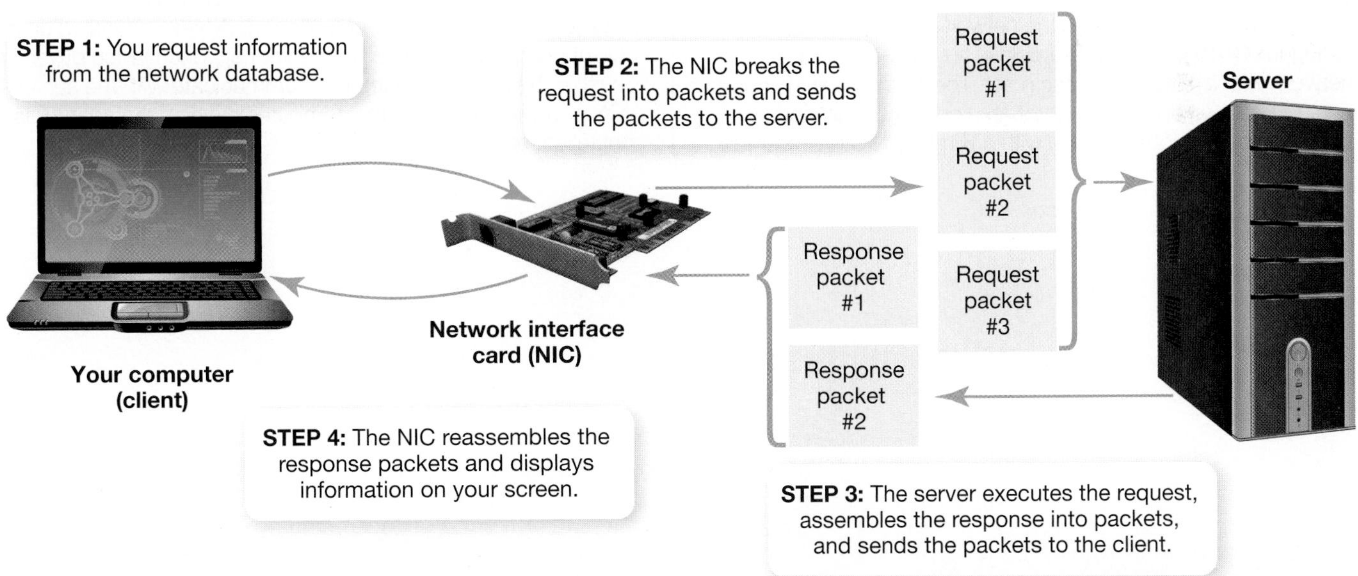
STEP 1: You request information from the network database.
STEP 2: The NIC breaks the request into packets and sends the packets to the server.
Request packet #1
Request packet #2
Request packet #3
Server
Response packet #1
Response packet #2
Network interface card (NIC)
Your computer (client)
STEP 4: The NIC reassembles the response packets and displays information on your screen.
STEP 3: The server executes the request, assembles the response into packets, and sends the packets to the client.

**FIGURE 12.18** A network interface card (NIC) is responsible for breaking down data into packets, preparing packets for transmission, receiving incoming data packets, and reconstructing them.

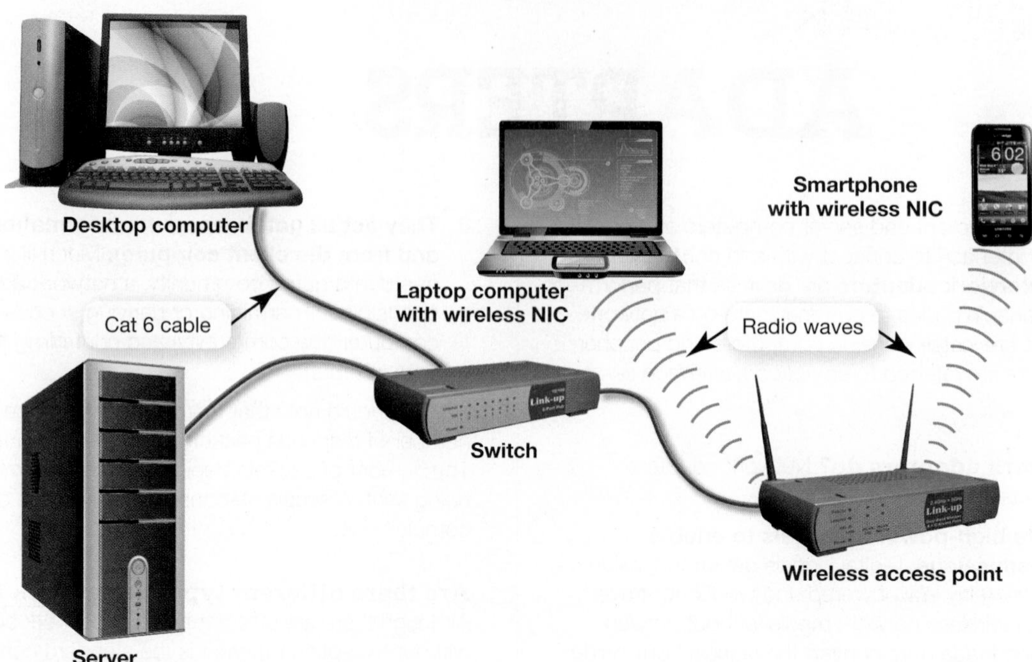


FIGURE 12.19 This small business network has an added wireless access point.

a **wireless network interface card (wireless NIC)**, installed in it. Laptop computers and other portable computing devices contain wireless NICs.

To allow wireless connections, a network also must be fitted with devices called wireless access points. A **wireless access point (WAP)** gives wireless devices a sending and receiving connection point to the network.

Figure 12.19 shows an example of a typical corporate network with a wireless access point. The access point is connected to the wired network through a conventional cable. When a laptop or other device with a wireless NIC is powered on near a wireless access point, it establishes a connection with the access point using radio waves. Many devices can communicate with the network through a single wireless access point.

**Do network adapters require software?** Special communications software called a **device driver** is installed on all client computers in the client/server network. Device drivers enable the network adapter to communicate with the server's OS and with the OS of the computer in which the adapter is installed. ■

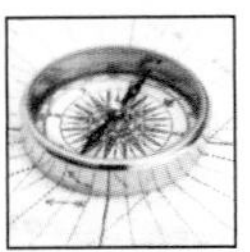

# network navigation DEVICES

As mentioned earlier, data flows through the network in packets. Data packets are like postal letters. They don't get to their destinations without some help. In this section, we explore the various conventions and devices that help speed data packets on their way through the network.

## MAC Addresses

**How do network adapters know where to send data packets?** Each network adapter has a physical address, similar to a serial number on an appliance. This address is called a **media access control (MAC) address**, and it's made up of 6 two-position characters, such as 01:40:87:44:79:A5. (Don't confuse this MAC with the Apple computers of the same name.) The first three sets of characters (in this case, 01:40:87) specify the manufacturer of the network adapter, and the second set of characters (in this case, 44:79:A5) makes up a unique address. Because all MAC addresses must be unique, there is an IEEE (Institute of Electrical and Electronics Engineers) committee responsible for allocating blocks of numbers to network adapter manufacturers.

**Are MAC addresses the same as IP addresses?** MAC addresses and IP (Internet Protocol) addresses are not the same thing. A MAC address is used for identification purposes *internally* on a network. An IP address is the address *external* entities use to communicate with your network. Think of it this way: The postal carrier delivers a package (data packet) to your dorm building based on its street address (IP address). The dorm's mail clerk delivers the package to your room because it has your name on it (MAC address) and not that of your neighbor. Both pieces of information are necessary to ensure that the package (or data) reaches its destination.

**How are data packets packaged for transmission?** Data packets aren't necessarily sent alone. Sometimes groups of data packets are sent together in a package called a **frame**. A frame is a container that can hold multiple data packets. This is similar to placing several letters going to the same postal address in a big envelope. While the data packets are being assembled into frames, the network operating system (NOS) software assigns the appropriate MAC address to the frame. The NOS keeps track of all devices and their addresses on the network. Much like an envelope that's entrusted to the postal service, the frame is delivered to the MAC address that the NOS assigned to the frame.

**What delivers the frames to the correct device on the network?** In a small bus network, frames just bounce along the transmission medium until the correct client computer notices that the frame is addressed to it and pulls the signal off the medium. However, this is inefficient in a larger network. Therefore, many types of devices have been developed to deliver data to its destination efficiently. These devices are designed to route signals and exchange data with other networks.

**Are MAC addresses useful for anything besides identifying a particular network device?** On networks with wireless capabilities, MAC addresses can be used to enhance network security. Because each MAC address is unique, you can input a list of authorized MAC addresses into the router. If someone who is using an unauthorized network

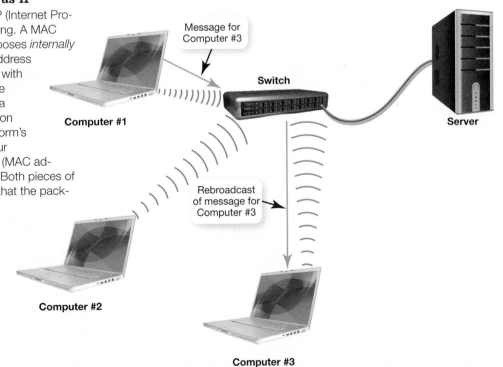

**FIGURE 12.20** Switches rebroadcast messages—but only to the devices to which the messages are addressed.

adapter attempts to connect to the network, he or she will be unable to make a connection.

## Switches and Bridges

**Which devices are used to route signals through a single network?** Switches are used to send data on a specific route through the network. A **switch** makes decisions, based on the MAC address of the data, as to where the data is to be sent and rebroadcasts it to the appropriate network node. This improves network efficiency by helping ensure that each node receives only the data intended for it. Figure 12.20 shows a switch being used to rebroadcast a message.

**Do all Ethernet networks need a switch?** Switches are needed on Ethernet networks whether they are installed in a home or a business. (Routers sold for home use have switches built in to them.)

**Are switches sufficient for moving data efficiently across all sizes of networks?** When a corporate network grows in size, performance can decline because many devices compete for transmission time on the network media. To solve this problem, a network can be broken into multiple segments known as *collision domains*. A **bridge** is a device that's used to send data between different collision domains, depending on where the recipient device is located, as indicated in Figure 12.21. Signals received by the bridge from Collision Domain A are forwarded to Collision Domain B only if the destination computer is located in that domain. (Note that most home networks contain only one segment and therefore do not require bridges.)

## Routers

**What device does a network use to move data to another network?** Whereas switches and bridges perform their functions within a single network, as you learned in Chapter 7, a **router** is designed to send information between two networks. To accomplish this, the router must look at higher-level network addresses (such as IP addresses), not MAC addresses. When the router notices data with an address that doesn't belong to a device on the network from which it originated, it sends the data to another network to which it is attached or out to the Internet. ■

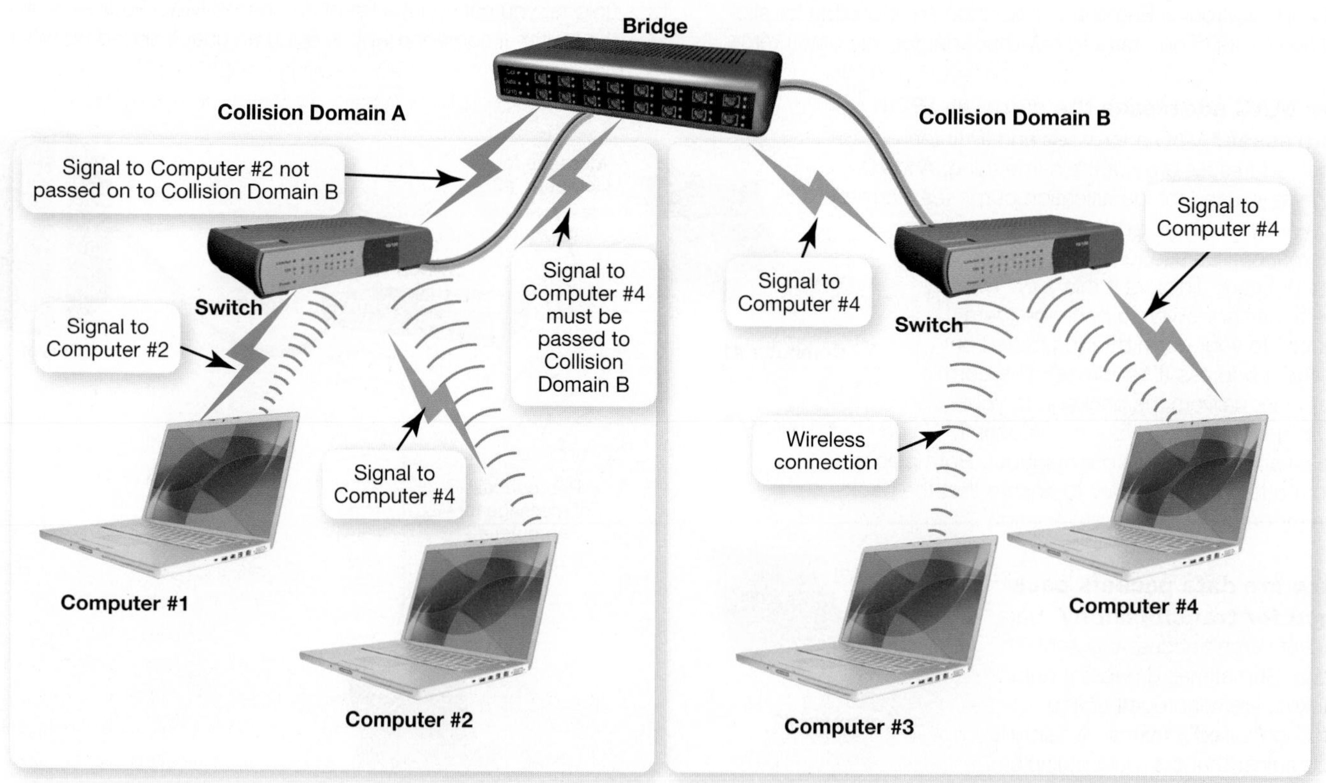


**FIGURE 12.21** Bridges are devices used to send data between different network collision domains.

# network operating SYSTEMS

Merely using media to connect computers and peripherals does not create a client/server network. Special software known as a **network operating system (NOS)** needs to be installed on each client computer and server that's connected to the network to provide the services necessary for them to communicate. The NOS provides a set of common rules (a *protocol*) that controls communication among devices on the network. Modern operating systems, such as Windows and OS X, include NOS client software as part of the basic installation. However, large networks, such as those found in businesses, require more sophisticated NOS server software.

**Why is a NOS needed on large networks?** OS software is designed to facilitate communication between the software and hardware components of your computer. NOS software is specifically designed to provide server services, network communications, management of network peripherals, and storage. NOSs that include server software include Windows Server, Linux, UNIX, and SUSE Linux Enterprise Server. NOS software is installed on servers.

To provide network communications, the client computers must run a small part of the NOS in addition to their OS. Windows and OS X contain network communication capabilities; therefore, no other NOS software is usually installed on these client computers.

**Do P2P networks need special NOS software?** The software that P2P networks require is built into the Windows, Linux, and Macintosh operating systems. So if you have a simple P2P network, there is no need to purchase specialized NOS software.

**How does the NOS control network communications?** Each NOS has its own proprietary communications language, file-management structure, and device-management structure. The NOS also sets and controls the protocols for all devices wishing to communicate on the network. Proprietary protocols from one vendor's NOS won't work with another vendor's NOS.

However, because the Internet uses an open protocol (called TCP/IP) for communications, many corporate networks use TCP/IP as their standard networking protocol regardless of the manufacturer of their NOS. All modern NOSs support TCP/IP.

**Can a network use two different NOSs?** Many large corporate networks use several different NOSs at the same time. This is because different NOSs provide different features, some of which are more useful in certain situations than others. For instance, although the employees of a corporation may be using a Windows environment for their desktops and e-mail, the file servers and web servers may be running a Linux NOS. ■

## BITS&BYTES

### The Doctor Isn't In: Virtual Doctors

There is a shortage of physicians in the United States, especially in rural areas. Even if there are plenty of general practitioners in your area, is there an orthopedic surgeon or a neurologist available for a timely consult after your car accident? In the future, computer networks are likely to provide solutions to these problems through an emerging field known as telemedicine.

Initiatives such as Cisco's HealthPresence are helping patients get care locally, regardless of where doctors are actually located. Exam stations containing equipment and software can be installed in office parks, malls, or even mobile tractor-trailer facilities. The exam stations are often staffed with nurses or physicians' assistants who are in much greater supply than physicians. Patients visit the exam stations locally, while the doctors work remotely.

This telemedicine technology uses two-way video conferencing to enable the doctors and patients to see each other and converse. Medical equipment such as blood pressure cuffs; pulse meters; and ear, nose, and throat scopes are integrated with the video conferencing equipment so that patient vital signs can be transmitted to the doctors. Software deployed with the equipment is designed to facilitate the review and generation of electronic patient records.

So, the next time you need a doctor, maybe you won't have to wait for hours in a waiting room. A computer solution may be just what the doctor ordered!

# DIG DEEPER The OSI Model: Defining Protocol Standards

The Institute of Electrical and Electronics Engineers (IEEE) has taken the lead in establishing worldwide networking protocols, including a standard of communications called the **Open Systems Interconnection (OSI)** reference model. The OSI model, which has been adopted throughout the computing world, provides the protocol guidelines for all modern networks. All modern network operating system (NOS) protocols are designed to interact in accordance with the standards set out in the OSI model.

The OSI model divides communications tasks into seven processes, called layers. Each layer of an OSI network has a specific function and knows how to communicate with the layers above and below it. Figure 12.22 shows the layers of the OSI model and their functions.

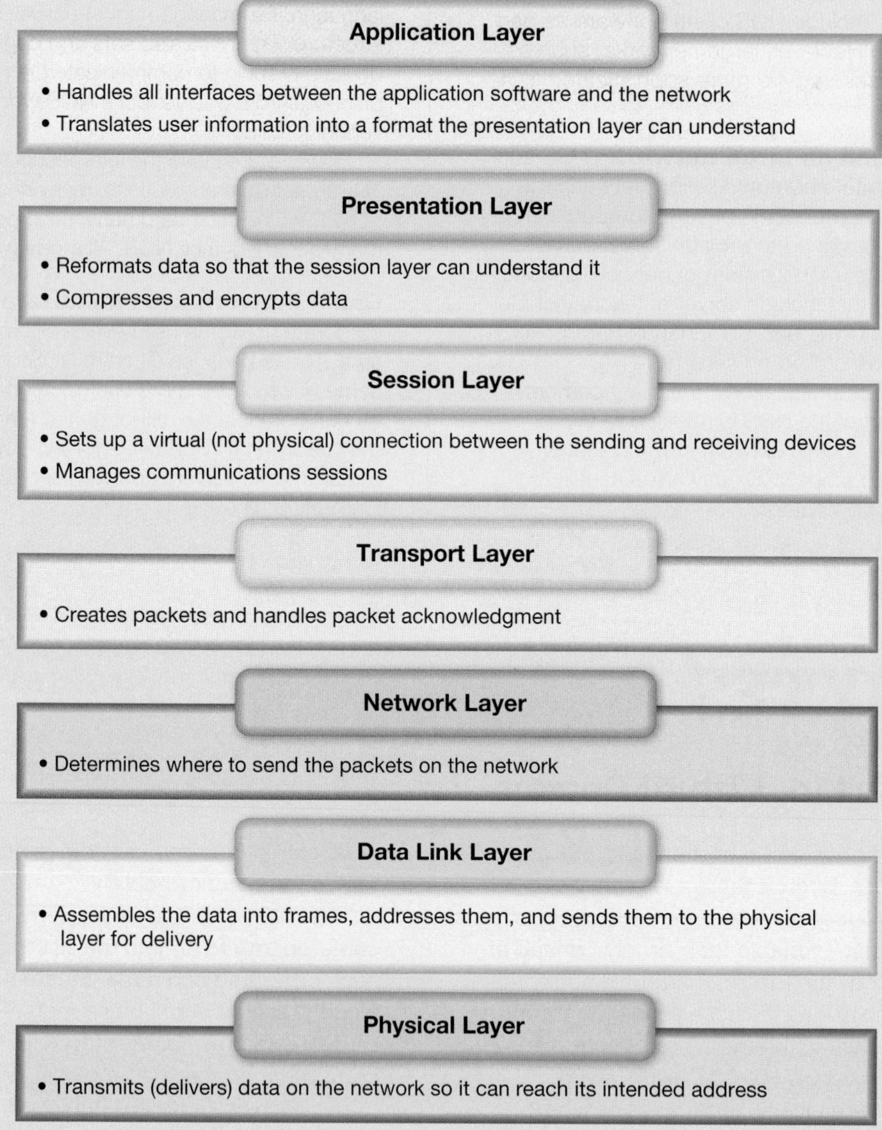

Application Layer
• Handles all interfaces between the application software and the network
• Translates user information into a format the presentation layer can understand
Presentation Layer
• Reformats data so that the session layer can understand it
• Compresses and encrypts data
Session Layer
• Sets up a virtual (not physical) connection between the sending and receiving devices
• Manages communications sessions
Transport Layer
• Creates packets and handles packet acknowledgment
Network Layer
• Determines where to send the packets on the network
Data Link Layer
• Assembles the data into frames, addresses them, and sends them to the physical layer for delivery
Physical Layer
• Transmits (delivers) data on the network so it can reach its intended address

**FIGURE 12.22** Layers of the OSI Model and Their Functions

This layering approach makes communications more efficient because specialized pieces of the NOS perform specific tasks. The layering approach is akin to assembly-line manufacturing. Producing thousands of cars per day would be difficult if one person had to build a car on his or her own. However, by splitting up the work of assembling a car into specialized tasks and assigning the tasks to people who perform them well, greater efficiency is achieved. By handling specialized tasks and communicating only with the layers above and below them, OSI layers make communications more efficient

Let's look at how each OSI layer functions by following an e-mail you create and send to your friend through the layers:

- *Application layer:* Handles all interaction between the application software and the network. It translates the data from the application into a format that the presentation layer can understand. For example, when you send an e-mail, the application layer takes the e-mail message you created in Microsoft Outlook, translates it into a format your network can understand, and passes it to the presentation layer.
- *Presentation layer:* Reformats the data so that the session layer can understand it. It also handles data encryption (changing the data into a format that makes it harder to intercept and read) and compression, if required. In our e-mail example, the presentation layer notices that you selected an encryption option for the e-mail message and encrypts the data before sending it to the session layer.
- *Session layer:* Sets up a virtual (not physical) connection between the sending and receiving devices. It then manages the communication between the two. In our e-mail example, the session layer would set up the parameters for the communications session between your computer and the Internet service provider (ISP) where your friend has her e-mail account. The session layer then tracks the transmission of the e-mail until it's satisfied that all the data in the e-mail was received at your friend's ISP.
- *Transport layer:* Breaks up the data into packets and sequences them appropriately. It also handles acknowledgment of packets (that is, it determines whether the packets were received at their destination) and decides whether packets need to be sent again. In our e-mail example, the transport layer breaks up your e-mail message into packets and sends them to the network layer, making sure that all the packets reach their destination.
- *Network layer:* Determines where to send the packets on the network and identifies the best way to route them there. In our e-mail example, the network layer examines the address on the packets (the address of your friend's ISP) and determines how to route the packets so they get to the ISP and can ultimately get to the receiving computer.
- *Data link layer:* Responsible for assembling the data packets into frames, addressing the frames, and delivering them to the physical layer so they can be sent on their way. It's the equivalent of a postal worker who reads the address on a piece of mail and makes sure it's sent to the proper recipient. In our e-mail example, the data link layer assembles the e-mail data packets into frames, which are addressed with appropriate routing information that it receives from the network layer.
- *Physical layer:* Takes care of delivering the data. It converts the data into a signal and transmits it over the network so that it can reach its intended address. In our e-mail example, the physical layer sends the data over the Internet to its ultimate destination (your friend's ISP).

By following standardized protocols set forth by the OSI model, NOS software can communicate happily with the computers and peripherals attached to the network as well as with other networks.

# client/server network SECURITY

A major advantage that client/server networks have over P2P networks is that they offer a higher level of security. With client/server networks, users can be required to enter a user ID and a password to gain access to the network. The security can be centrally administered by network administrators, freeing individual users of the responsibility of maintaining their own data security, as they must do on a P2P network.

In the following sections, we'll explore the challenges network administrators face in keeping a client/server network secure.

**What sources of security threats do all network administrators need to watch for?** Threats can be classified into three main groups:

1. *Human errors and mistakes:* Everyone makes mistakes. For example, a member of the computer support staff could mistakenly install an old database on top of the current one. Even physical accidents fall into this category; for example, someone could lose control of a car and drive it through the wall of the main data center.
2. *Malicious human activity:* Malicious actions can be perpetrated by current employees, former employees, or third parties. For example, a disgruntled employee could introduce a virus to the network, or a hacker could break into the student database server to steal credit card records.
3. *Natural events and disasters:* Some events—such as floods and fires—are beyond human control. All can lead to the inadvertent destruction of data.

Because networks are vulnerable to such security threats, one of the network administrator's key functions is to keep network data secure.

## Authentication

**How do network administrators ensure that only authorized users access the network?** **Authentication** is the process whereby users prove they have authorization to use a computer network. For example, correctly entering the user ID and password on your college network proves to the network that you have authorized access. The access is authorized because the ID was generated by a network administrator when you became an authorized user of the network.

However, authentication can also be achieved through the use of biometric devices (discussed later in this chapter) and through possessed objects. A **possessed object** is any object that users carry to identify themselves and that grants them access to a computer system or computer facility. Examples include identification badges, magnetic key cards, and smart keys (similar to flash drives).

**Can hackers use my account to log in to the network?** If a hacker knows your user ID and password, he or she can log in and impersonate you. Impersonation can also happen if you fail to log out of a terminal on a network and someone comes along and uses your account. Sometimes network user IDs are easy to figure out because they have a certain pattern, such as your last name and the first initial of your first name.

If a hacker can deduce your user ID, he or she might use a software program that tries millions of combinations of letters and numbers as your password in an attempt to access your account. Attempting to access an account by repeatedly trying different passwords is known as a **brute force attack**. To prevent these attacks from succeeding, network administrators often configure accounts so that they'll disable themselves after a set number of login attempts using invalid passwords have been made.

## Access Privileges

**How can I gain access to everything on a network?** The simple answer is that you can't! When your account is set up on a network, certain access privileges are granted to indicate which systems you're allowed to use. For example, on your college network, your access privileges probably include the ability to access the Internet. However, you definitely weren't granted access to the grade-entering system, because this would enable you to change your grades.

**How does restricting access privileges protect a network?** Because network access accounts are centrally administered on the authentication server, it's easy for the network administrator to set up accounts for new users and grant them access only to the systems and software they need. The centralized nature of the network-access creation and the ability to restrict access to certain areas of the network make a client/server network more secure than a P2P network.

**Aside from improper access, how else do data theft and destruction occur?** A major problem that portable devices such as flash drives pose is theft of data or intellectual property. Because these devices are so easy to conceal and have such large memory capacity, it's easy for a disgruntled employee to walk out the front door with stacks of valuable documents tucked in his or her pocket. Industrial espionage has never been easier—and no spy cameras are needed!

Flash drives can also introduce viruses or other malicious programs to a network, either intentionally or unintentionally. Secure Network Technologies, a security consulting firm, decided to test a client's security procedures by leaving 20 flash drives at random locations around the client's office. By the end of the day, employees had picked up 15 of the flash drives and plugged them into computers on the company network. The flash drives contained a simple program to display images as well as a Trojan horse program. While the employees were viewing the images, the Trojan horse program enabled the consultants to access the company network and steal or compromise data. It isn't hard to imagine hackers leaving flash drives around your school that could act as "skeleton keys" to your school's network.

**How should network administrators protect their networks from portable storage devices?** To head off problems with portable storage devices, the following actions should be taken:

- Educate employees about the dangers posed by portable media devices.
- Create policies regulating the use of portable media devices in the workplace.
- Install security measures such as personal firewalls or antivirus software to protect all computers in the company. The firewalls should be able to prevent malicious programs from running, even if they're introduced to a computer via a flash drive.
- Limit and monitor the use of portable media devices. Although Microsoft networking software allows network administrators to shut off access to the USB ports on computers, this prevents employees from using flash drives and other USB devices for legitimate purposes.
- Inform employees that their use of portable media devices is being monitored. This alone will often be enough to scare employees away from connecting untrusted devices to the network.

Other software products, such as DeviceLock and Safend Data Protection Suite, can be deployed on a network to provide options such as detailed security policies. Such products can also monitor USB device connections and track which users have connected devices to the network (including devices other than flash drives).

## Physical Protection Measures

**What physical measures are used to protect a network?** Restricting physical access to servers and other sensitive equipment is critical to protecting a network. Where are the servers that power your college network? They're most likely behind locked doors to which only authorized personnel have access. Likewise, the network's switches are securely tucked away in ceilings, walls, or closets, safe from anyone who might tamper with them in an attempt to sabotage the network or breach its security.

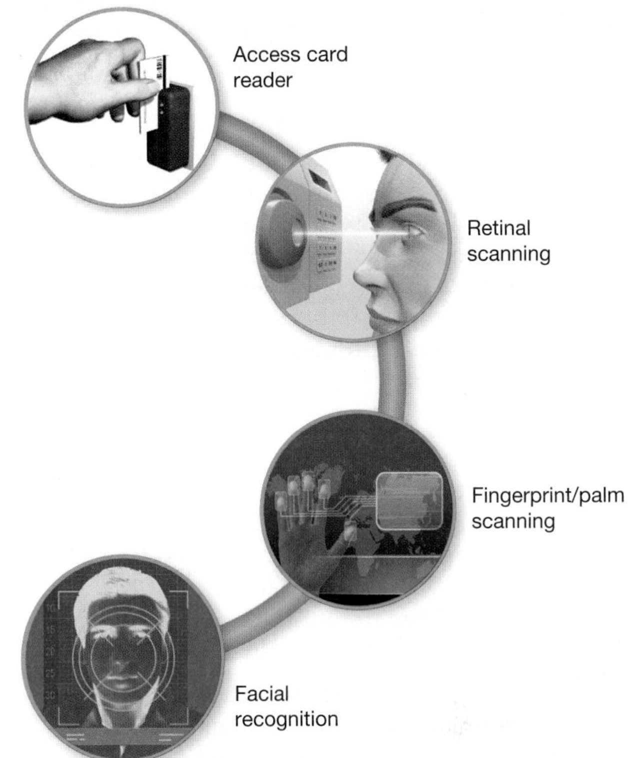


**FIGURE 12.23** Access card readers provide a relatively inexpensive solution to security for areas needing low-level security. Biometric authentication devices, such as fingerprint/palm, retinal, and facial-recognition scanners, are used to protect high-security areas, such as a server room. *(twobee/Fotolia)*

As shown in Figure 12.23, a number of different devices can be used to control access:

- An **access card reader** is a relatively cheap device that reads information from a magnetic strip on the back of a credit card–like access card, such as your student ID card. The card reader, which can control the lock on a door, is programmed to admit only authorized personnel to the area. Card readers are easily programmed by adding authorized ID card numbers.
- A **biometric authentication device** uses a unique characteristic of human biology to identify authorized users.

SOUND BYTE

**A Day in the Life of a Network Technician**

In this Sound Byte, you'll learn firsthand about the exciting, fast-paced job of a computer technician. Interviews with network technicians and tours of networking facilities will provide you with a deeper appreciation for the complexities of the job.

# ethics in IT

# How Should Companies Handle Data Breaches?

Data breaches occur all too frequently, and it seems we're always seeing reports in the media about yet another hacker obtaining supposedly private information. Many companies have sensitive data about you. But what is their ethical responsibility to protect your data? And what should a company do for its customers when a data breach occurs?

## Data Confidentiality

The objective for any company that possesses sensitive data should be **information assurance**, which means ensuring information systems are adequately secured against tampering. The five key attributes of secure information systems are as follows:

1. *Availability:* The extent to which a data-processing system is able to receive and process data. A high degree of availability is usually desirable.
2. *Integrity:* A quality that an information system has if the processing of information is logical and accurate and the data is protected against unauthorized modifications or destruction.
3. *Authentication:* Security measures designed to protect an information system against acceptance of a fraudulent transmission of data by establishing the validity of a data transmission or message or the identity of the sender.
4. *Confidentiality:* The assurance that information isn't disclosed to unauthorized persons, processes, or devices.
5. *Nonrepudiation:* A capability of security systems that guarantees that a message or data can be proven to have originated from a specific person and to have been processed by the recipient. The sender of the data receives a receipt for the data, and the receiver of the data gets proof of the sender's identity. The objective of nonrepudiation is to prevent either party from later denying having handled the data.

From your perspective, you are probably the most concerned about authentication and confidentiality. Companies that have your data shouldn't share it with unauthorized parties and should keep unauthorized people out of their databases. Unfortunately, you have very little control over authentication safeguards. That's the responsibility of the company that holds your data.

Some devices read fingerprints or palm prints when you place your hand on a scanning pad. Other devices shine a laser beam into your eye and read the unique patterns of your retina. Facial-recognition systems store unique characteristics of an individual's face for later comparison and identification. When an authorized individual uses a device for the first time, his or her fingerprints, retinal patterns, or face patterns are scanned and stored in a database.

Financial institutions and retail stores are considering using such devices to attempt to eliminate the growing fraud problems of identity theft and counterfeiting of credit and debit cards. If fingerprint authorization were required at the supermarket to make a purchase, a thief who stole your wallet and attempted to use your credit card would be unsuccessful.

**What are the problems with biometric devices?** The biometric devices currently on the market don't always function as intended. Facial-recognition and retinal-scanning systems can sometimes be fooled by pictures or videos of an authorized user. Researchers have fooled biometric fingerprint readers by using fingers made out of modeling clay, using the fingers of cadavers, or having unauthorized persons breathe on the sensor, which makes the previous user's fingerprint visible.

Next-generation fingerprint readers will use specially designed algorithms that will detect moisture patterns on a person's fingers. Another approach may involve readers that detect an electrical current when a finger touches the reader, which is possible because the human body conducts electrical current. Future retinal readers may check whether a person blinks or if his or her pupils contract when a bright light shines on them.

## Authentication Failures

The data breaches that occur usually represent authentication failures—unauthorized people gain access to data. Clearly, when this happens, a corporation has failed in its responsibility to protect its customers' data. No system is ever 100% safe against breaches, but most systems are adequately protected against all but the most determined hackers. But what ethical responsibilities does a company have to its customers after a data breach?

The first thing a company should do is admit the problem and inform its customers. The Federal Trade Commission (FTC) recommends the following course of action for companies who experience data breaches:

1. Notify the appropriate law enforcement agencies.
2. Notify other affected businesses, such as banks and credit card companies. These companies can then monitor the affected accounts for fraudulent activity.
3. Notify the individuals affected. The company should explain what happened, what information was compromised, who to contact in the organization, and what customers should do to protect themselves (which will vary based on the information compromised).

How can you be aware of a data breach if the company that suffered it never tells you that your data was exposed? You should monitor websites such as the Privacy Rights Clearinghouse (**privacyrights.org/data-breach**) and Open Security Foundation's DataLossDB (**datalossdb.org**), which track data breaches. This might be the fastest way to find out if your information has been compromised so you can take action. The FTC website on identity theft (**consumer.ftc.gov/features/feature-0014-identity-theft**) provides good guidelines to follow when your data has been exposed.

Granting customers free identity-theft protection is one of the more common forms of compensation offered to placate customers after a data breach, but not every company does it. Some companies merely stop at notifying customers and offer nothing in terms of compensation for the inconvenience.

Although companies may behave ethically after a data breach, your best protection is still your own vigilance!

## Firewalls

**Are Internet connections on client/server networks vulnerable to hackers?** Just like a home network, any company's network that's connected to the Internet can attract hackers. For this reason, a well-defended business network, just like a well-defended home network, includes a firewall. Firewalls can be composed of software or hardware, and many sophisticated firewalls include both. Routers are often equipped to act as hardware firewalls.

**Does a firewall on a client/server network work the same way as a personal firewall installed on a home network does?** Although a firewall on a business network may contain a few extra security options, making it even harder to breach than a personal firewall, the firewalls for business networks work on the same basic principles as a personal firewall. At a minimum, most firewalls work as packet screeners. **Packet screening** involves having an *external screening router* examining incoming data packets to ensure that they originated from or are authorized by valid users on the internal network. Unauthorized or suspect packets are discarded by the firewall before they reach the network.

Packet screening also can be configured for outgoing data to ensure that requests for information to the Internet are from legitimate users. This is done by an *internal screening router* and helps detect Trojan horse programs that may have been installed by hackers. Trojan horses often try to disguise where they're sending data from by using bogus IP addresses on the packets the programs send instead of using an authorized IP address belonging to the network.

With packet screening in place, packets going into and out of the network are checked to ensure they're either from or

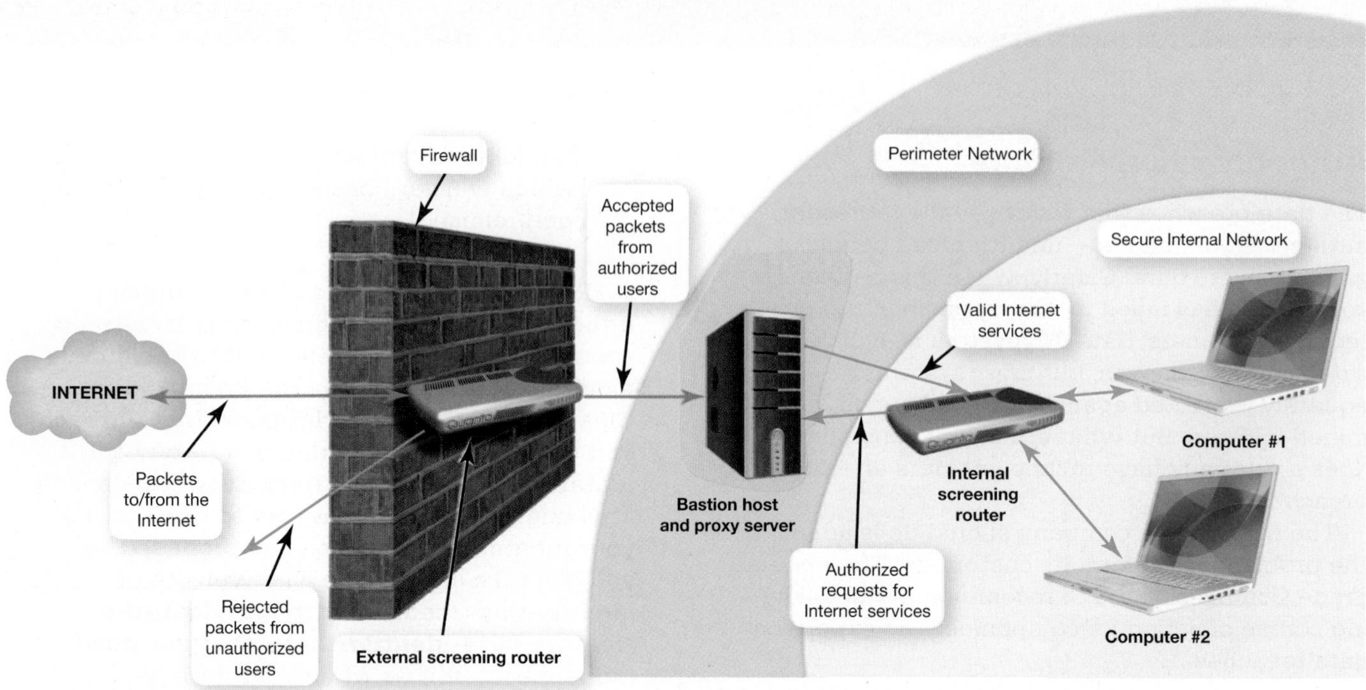


**FIGURE 12.24** Business firewalls provide sophisticated protection from hackers.

addressed to a legitimate IP address on the network. If the addresses aren't valid addresses on the network, the firewall (or the screening routers) discards them.

**What other security measures does the firewall on a client/server network use?** To increase security even further, most large networks add a **bastion host**, which is a heavily secured server located on a special perimeter network between the company's secure internal network and the firewall.

To external computers, the bastion host gives the appearance of being the internal network server. Hackers can waste a lot of time and energy attacking the bastion host. However, even if a hacker breaches the bastion host server, the internal network isn't vulnerable because the bastion host isn't on the internal network. Moreover, during the time the hackers spend trying to penetrate the bastion host, network administrators can detect and thwart their attacks.

**How do bastion hosts help protect systems from hackers?** Bastion hosts are a type of honey pot. A **honey pot** is a computer system that's set up to attract unauthorized users by appearing to be a key part of a network or a system that contains something of great value.

Bastion hosts are often configured as proxy servers. A **proxy server** acts as a go-between, connecting computers on the internal network with those on the external network (the Internet). All requests from the internal network for Internet services are directed through the proxy server. Similarly, all incoming requests from the Internet must pass through the proxy server. It's much easier for network administrators to maintain adequate security on one server than it is to ensure that security is maintained on hundreds or thousands of computers in a college network, for example.

Figure 12.24 shows a network secured by a firewall, a bastion host and proxy server, and a screening router. Now that you know a bit more about business networks, you should be able to comfortably navigate the network at your college or your place of employment and understand why certain security measures have been taken to protect network data. ■

**Before moving on to the Chapter Review:**

- **Watch Replay Video 12.2** .
- Then check your understanding of what you've learned so far.

# check your understanding//

For a quick review to see what you've learned so far, answer the following questions. Visit **pearsonhighered.com /techinaction** to check your answers.

## multiple choice

1. Which of the following is necessary in every client/ server network?
   - **a.** bastion host
   - **b.** firewall
   - **c.** transmission media
   - **d.** application server
2. Fiber-optic cable most likely would be used in a business network when
   - **a.** saving money is more important than speed.
   - **b.** electrical or magnetic interference is present.
   - **c.** very short cable runs are required.
   - **d.** the installation budget is very limited.
3. NOS software is needed
   - **a.** on all computers in a client/server network.
   - **b.** only on the servers in a client/server network.
   - **c.** only if a communications server is deployed on a client/server network.
   - **d.** only when configuring a network in a star topology.
4. On client/server networks, switches
   - **a.** transfer data between two networks.
   - **b.** route data between two collision domains on a single network.
   - **c.** move data efficiently from node to node on the internal network.
   - **d.** are necessary only in networks using the ring topology.
5. Correctly entering the user ID and password on your college network is an example of
   - **a.** authentication.
   - **b.** scalability.
   - **c.** packet screening.
   - **d.** virtualization.

## true–false

_____ **1.** Bridges are used to route data between two different networks.

_____ **2.** Two different types of network operating software can be deployed on the same network.

## critical thinking

1. **Biometric Access to Networks**

   Biometric security devices are still expensive. But there are usually parts of any organization that need to be more secure than others, and you can often justify the cost of these devices for certain areas. Consider the following organizations and prepare a paper discussing which areas of the following businesses could most benefit from installing biometric security devices:
   - **a.** Financial institution (bank)
   - **b.** Public university that conducts scientific research
   - **c.** Pharmaceutical company
2. **Monitoring Computer Usage in the Workplace**

   Software tools for monitoring computer usage are readily available on the Internet, often for free (such as Best Free Keylogger). In most jurisdictions, it's legal for employers to install monitoring software on computer equipment they provide to employees. It's usually illegal for employees to install monitoring software on computers owned by their employers for purposes of monitoring computer usage of co-workers or bosses. Do you think this double standard is fair? What circumstances do you think would justify an employee monitoring other employees' computer usage? Should whistleblowers have the right to conduct computer-usage monitoring? Fully explain your answers.

**Continue**
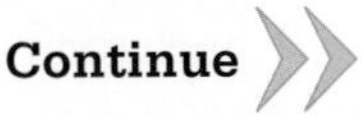

# Chapter Review

## summary//

### Client/Server Network Basics

**1. What are the advantages of a business network?**

- Networks enable resources, such as printers, to be shared, avoiding the cost of providing these resources to individual employees.
- Networks facilitate knowledge sharing between employees because multiple people can access data at the same time.
- Software can be shared from a network server, thereby reducing the costs of installation on each user's computer.
- Information sharing is more effective when employees are connected via networks.

**2. How does a client/server network differ from a peer-to-peer network?**

- In a peer-to-peer network, each node connected to the network can communicate directly with every other node on the network. In a client/server network, a separate device (the server) exercises control over the network.
- Data flows more efficiently in client/server networks than in peer-to-peer networks.
- In addition, client/server networks have increased scalability, meaning users can be added to the network easily.

**3. What are the different classifications of client/server networks?**

- Local area networks (LANs) are small groups of computers (as few as two) and peripherals linked together over a small geographic area. A group of computers in rooms on one floor of a campus building is most likely a LAN.
- Wide area networks (WANs) comprise large numbers of users (or of separate LANs) that are miles apart and linked together. Colleges often use WANs to connect two or more campuses in separate towns.

**4. What components are needed to construct a client/server network?**

- Client/server networks have many of the same components as peer-to-peer networks as well as some components specific to client/server networks, including servers, a network topology, transmission media, network adapters, network navigation devices, and network operating system (NOS) software.

### Servers and Network Topologies

**5. What do the various types of servers do?**

- Dedicated servers are used on large networks to increase efficiency.
- Authentication servers control access to the network and ensure that only authorized users can log in.
- File servers provide storage and management of user files.
- Print servers manage and control all printing jobs initiated on a network.
- Application servers provide access to application software.
- Database servers store database files and provide access to users who need the information in the databases.
- E-mail servers control all incoming and outgoing e-mail traffic.
- Communications servers are used to control the flow of information from the internal network to outside networks.
- Web servers are used to host websites.
- Cloud servers provide storage and access to data on the Internet.

**6. What are the various network topologies, and why is network topology important in planning a network?**

- In a bus topology, all nodes are connected to a single linear cable.
- Ring topologies are made up of nodes arranged roughly in a circle. The data flows from node to node in a specific order.
- In a star topology, nodes are connected to a central communication device (a switch) and branch out like points of a star.
- A hybrid topology blends two or more topologies in one network.
- Each topology has its own advantages and disadvantages. Topology selection depends on two

main factors: (1) the network budget and (2) the specific needs of network users, such as speed or fair allocation of resources.

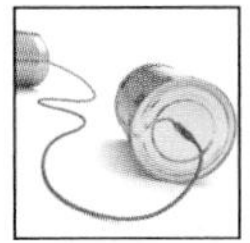

## Transmission Media

**7. What types of transmission media are used in client/server networks?**

- In addition to wireless media, three main cable types are used: twisted-pair cable, coaxial cable, and fiber-optic cable.
- Twisted-pair cable consists of pairs of wires twisted around each other in order to reduce interference.
- Coaxial cable is the same type of cable used by your cable TV company to run a signal into your house.
- Fiber-optic cable uses bundles of glass or plastic fiber to send signals using light waves. It provides the largest bandwidth but is expensive and difficult to install.
- Wireless media uses radio waves to send data between nodes on a network.

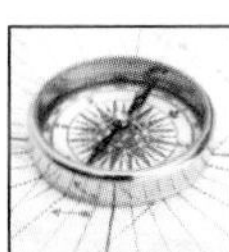

## Network Adapters and Network Navigation Devices

**8. How do network adapters enable computers to participate in a client/server network?**

- Without a network adapter, a computer could not communicate on a network. A network adapter provides three critical functions. First, it takes low-power data signals generated by the computer and converts them into higher-powered signals that can traverse network media easily. Second, it breaks the data generated by the computer into packets and packages them for transmission across the network media. Last, it acts as a gatekeeper to control the flow of data to and from the computer.

**9. What devices assist in moving data around a client/server network?**

- Switches are devices that read the addresses of data packets and retransmit a signal to its destination instead of to every device connected to the switch.
- Bridges are devices used to send data between two different segments (collision domains) of the same network.
- Routers are used to route data between two different networks, such as between a business network and the Internet.

## Network Operating Systems

**10. What software needs to run on computers attached to a client/server network, and how does this software control network communications?**

- Network operating system (NOS) software needs to be installed on each computer and server connected to a client/server network in order to provide the services necessary for the devices to communicate.
- The NOS provides a set of common rules (called a protocol) that controls communication between devices on the network.

## Client/Server Network Security

**11. What measures are employed to keep large networks secure?**

- Access to most networks requires authentication procedures, such as having users enter a user ID and password, to ensure that only authorized users access the network.
- The system administrator defines access privileges for users so that they can access only specific files.
- Network equipment is physically secured behind locked doors, which are often protected by biometric authentication devices. Biometric devices, such as fingerprint/palm, facial-recognition, and retinal scanners, use unique physical characteristics of individuals for identification purposes. Firewalls are employed to keep hackers from attacking networks through Internet connections. Packet screeners review traffic going to and from the network to ascertain whether the communication was generated by a legitimate user.

Be sure to check out the companion website for additional materials to help you review and learn, including a Tech Bytes Weekly newsletter—
**pearsonhighered.com/techinaction**
And don't forget the Replay Videos .

# key terms//

access card reader **519**
access method **501**
active topology **502**
application server **498**
authentication **518**
authentication server **497**
bastion host **522**
biometric authentication device **519**
bridge **514**
brute force attack **518**
bus (linear bus) topology **500**
centralized **493**
client/server network (server-based network) **493**
cloud server **498**
coaxial cable **509**
communications server **498**
CSMA/CD **503**
data collision **500**
database server **498**
decentralized **493**
dedicated server **497**
device driver **512**
electronic data interchange (EDI) **495**
e-mail server **498**
extranet **495**
fiber-optic cable **509**
file server **497**
frame **513**
honey pot **522**
hybrid topology **504**
information assurance **520**
intranet **495**
jam signal **503**
local area network (LAN) **495**
media access control (MAC) address **513**
network adapter **511**
network administrator **492**
network operating system (NOS) **515**
network topology **500**
Open Systems Interconnection (OSI) **516**
packet screening **521**
passive topology **501**
possessed object **518**
print queue **498**
print server **498**
protocol **500**
proxy server **522**
ring (loop) topology **501**
router **514**
scalability **494**
shielded twisted-pair (STP) cable **509**
star topology **502**
switch **514**
terminator **501**
token **502**
token method **502**
transmission media **508**
tunneling **495**
twisted-pair cable **509**
virtual private network (VPN) **495**
virtualization **499**
web server **498**
wide area network (WAN) **495**
wireless access point (WAP) **512**
wireless network interface card (wireless NIC) **512**

## making the transition to . . . next semester//

1. **A Truly Wireless Campus**

   Most schools have wireless networks mainly for students. School employees are still using desktop computers with wired connections because they are cheaper than laptops (for the same amount of computing power) and don't require as much maintenance and repair. Assuming your school decides to provide all employees with portable computing devices, draft a plan that answers these questions:

   **a.** Which two departments should be converted to wireless first?

   **b.** What benefits will the employees in these departments gain from wireless connectivity?

   **c.** How will wireless devices allow these employees to better serve or interact with the students?

   **d.** What guidelines should the school establish for use of the devices when they are off campus?

   **e.** What precautions should the school take to help recover the devices in the event they are lost or stolen?

2. **Establishing Virtual Servers**

   You and three friends want to market a new line of clothing to college students. One of your friends works in IT and tells you that you'll need a database server, an authentication server, an application server, and a web server to run your business effectively. You need to conserve cash, so you're wondering whether you can use one server plus virtualization software to run all four of these servers. Investigate the following:

   **a.** Determine what types of virtualization software are available and prepare a comparison of the features of three different software packages. Is there any software you can use for free (open source) or will you need to buy proprietary software?

   **b.** Investigate servers available from companies such as Dell, Apple, and Hewlett Packard. Prepare a comparison of the features and costs of at least three different servers. Which one do you think is right for your business?

## making the transition to . . . the workplace//

1. **Transitioning to Cloud Hosting**

   The network administrator at the company for which you work has just quit. The company network has authentication, web, and database servers. The owner has asked you to investigate whether it's feasible to use cloud servers to host the network.

   Investigate companies such as Rackspace Hosting (**rackspace.com**), GoGrid (**www.gogrid.com**), and NetDepot (**netdepot.com**). Consider the following:

   **a.** Do these companies offer turnkey services that will manage entire networks? If turnkey services aren't available, what servers can be hosted by these companies? What would be the cost of hosting services?

   **b.** Research cloud hosting. What risks are posed by having servers hosted in the cloud?

   **c.** Do you think it's feasible to use cloud-hosting services and not hire a local network administrator? What potential problems do you see arising with this scenario?

2. **Protecting Company Vehicle Data**

   Your company provides automobiles to its outside sales force. All of the vehicles are equipped with extensive computer systems (to control vehicle functions), GPS navigation, and telephone communications systems. These systems have been tied together by the manufacturer to allow the integration of vehicle-related and communications data (known as telematics). The telematics can be downloaded and forwarded to management for analysis. Data such as locations visited, driving style (average speed, etc.), seatbelt usage, and even the radio stations listened to is available for analysis. Consider the following:

   **a.** What is the best way to inform employees that their driving habits may be monitored?

   **b.** Who at the company should have access to the information (if anyone should)?

   **c.** An outside company is interested in purchasing access to the vehicle data for a marketing study it is doing on driving habits. Does the company have a duty to the employees to protect their privacy and not sell the data to third parties?

team time//

# Developing a Bring-Your-Own-Device Policy

## Problem

Employees, especially in developing economies, are often bringing their own computing device (BYOD) to work and using their personal devices to access company networks, databases, and the Internet. While this can have benefits to the company such as keeping equipment costs down and increasing employee morale (since they use a device with which they're already comfortable), BYOD can present unique challenges for data security.

## Task

X-Rocket, a local sports shoe company, has experienced a large rise in BYOD by its employees. It is concerned about the security of data that may be on the devices and potentially losing control of it. The X-Rocket CEO has asked your professor to assist him in constructing a BYOD policy for his company.

## Process

1. Divide the class into small teams.
2. Research BYOD security issues. Review BYOD policies that are in place for businesses and schools. Consider what types of devices (laptops, phones, tablets, etc.) might be used to access company data. Draft a BYOD policy for X-Rocket employees that clearly sets forth the company's expectations with regards to personal devices.
3. Meet as a class to discuss each group's findings. Do you feel most employees are aware of the security issues related to BYOD? Would most employees know that they need to take precautions to avoid storing company data on their personal devices in case they are lost or stolen? Try to obtain a consensus about which precautions are the most important ones for employees to take to protect the company's data.
4. Have each group prepare a multimedia presentation (PowerPoint, video, etc.) to educate the employees about the security risks of BYOD. Make sure that the presentations adequately explain any potentially unfamiliar concepts (such as what exactly is meant by BYOD) to ensure all viewers of the presentation will be on an equal footing.

## Conclusion

Having personal computing devices and bringing them to work is fast becoming the norm in the twenty-first century. But the best defense against loss of control of company data is to understand the consequences of accessing data with and storing data on personal computing devices.

# ethics project//

## Using Wireless Networks Without Permission

In this exercise, you'll research and then role-play a complicated ethical situation. The role you play might not match your own personal beliefs, but your research and use of logic will enable you to represent the view assigned. An arbitrator will watch and comment on both sides of the argument, and together, the team will agree on an ethical solution.

### Problem

Piggybacking occurs when people use a wireless network without the permission of the owner. Although piggybacking is illegal in many jurisdictions, it's often hard to detect. Piggybacking often happens inadvertently when people trying to connect to their own home network accidentally connect to their neighbor's wireless network. With the proliferation of wireless networks, many businesses have set up networks for their customers. However, because of the close proximity of many businesses to each other in areas such as shopping centers, the potential for inadvertent (or intentional) piggybacking of wireless networks exists. Sharing wireless connections between two entities (whether they be two households or two businesses) may violate the terms of service of the Internet service provider. And although wireless networks can be secured, it's often easier on the customers to leave them completely open, which can encourage piggybacking.

### Research Areas to Consider

- Detecting wireless piggybacking
- Piggybacking laws (legality of piggybacking)
- Securing wireless networks

### Process

1. Divide the class into teams.
2. Research the areas cited above and devise a scenario in which the owner of a coffee shop at a shopping center has accused the proprietor of the sandwich shop next door of encouraging the sandwich shop's patrons to piggyback on the coffee shop's wireless network.
3. Team members should write a summary that provides background information for their character—for example, coffee shop owner, sandwich shop owner, and shopping center manager (arbitrator)—and that details their character's behaviors to set the stage for the role-playing event. Then, team members should create an outline to use during the role-playing event.
4. Team members should arrange a mutually convenient time to meet for the exchange, using a virtual meeting tool or meeting in person.
5. Team members should present their case to the class or submit a PowerPoint presentation for review by the rest of the class, along with the summary and resolution they developed.

### Conclusion

As technology becomes ever more prevalent and integrated into our lives, ethical dilemmas will present themselves to an increasing extent. Being able to understand and evaluate both sides of the argument, while responding in a personally or socially ethical manner, will be important skills.

# 13 Behind the Scenes: How the Internet Works

## Inner Workings of the Internet

### The Management of the Internet

**OBJECTIVE**

1. Who owns, manages, and pays for the Internet? **(p. 532)**

### Internet Networking, Data Transmission, and Protocols

**OBJECTIVES**

2. How do the Internet's networking components interact? **(pp. 533–534)**
3. What data transmissions and protocols does the Internet use? **(pp. 535–536)**

### Internet Identity: IP Addresses and Domain Names

**OBJECTIVE**

4. Why are IP addresses and domain names important for Internet communications? **(pp. 537–542)**

**Active Helpdesk:** Understanding IP Addresses, Domain Names, and Protocols

## Coding and Communicating on the Internet

### HTML, XML, and Other Web Building Blocks

**OBJECTIVE**

5. What web technologies are used to develop web applications? **(pp. 546–550)**

**Sound Byte:** Creating Web Pages with HTML

### Communications Over the Internet

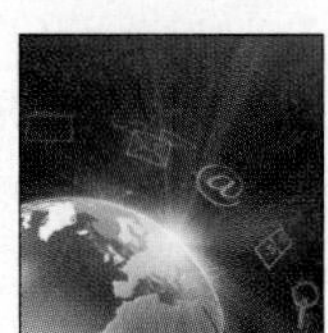

**OBJECTIVE**

6. How do e-mail and instant messaging work, and how is information using these technologies kept secure? **(pp. 551–555)**

**Active Helpdesk:** Keeping E-Mail Secure

For all media in this chapter go to **pearsonhighered.com/techinaction** or **MyITLab**.

(Adimas/Fotolia; Toria/Shutterstock; Matthias Pahl/Shutterstock; Phil Banko/Getty Images; Fry Design Ltd/Getty Images)

# HOW COOL IS THIS?

The creation of massively open online courses, or **MOOCs**, is shaking up the world of higher education. Kevin Struck, associate professor of Classical Studies at the University of Pennsylvania, has taught about 1,500 students in his 15 years at Penn. His first MOOC offering, Greek and Roman Mythology, was taken by **54,000 students** worldwide. The record attendance in a MOOC is an introduction to computer science class that ran with over 300,000 students. MOOC offerings are **free to take**, are available in multiple languages, and come from some of the best universities and best professors in the world.

Looking for the best MOOC for you? Head to **CourseTalk.org** to find classes by searching across all of the top MOOC providers, Coursera, edX, and Udacity, along with ratings and reviews. *(AP Photo / Matt Slocum)*

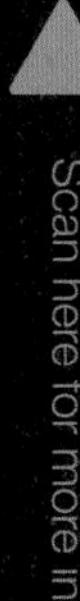

# Inner Workings of the Internet

We use the Internet so routinely that it may not have occurred to you to ask some fundamental questions about how it's administered. In this part of the chapter, we'll discuss this and other topics.

## the management of the INTERNET

To keep a massive network like the Internet functioning at peak efficiency, it must be governed and regulated. However, no single entity is in charge of the Internet. In addition, new uses for the Internet are created every day by a variety of individuals and companies.

**Who owns the Internet?** The local networks that constitute the Internet are owned by different entities, including individuals, universities, government agencies, and private companies. Government entities such as the National Science Foundation (NSF), as well as many privately held companies, own pieces of the communications infrastructure (the high-speed data lines that transport data between networks) that makes the Internet work.

**Does anyone manage the Internet?** Several nonprofit organizations and user groups, each with a specialized purpose, are responsible for the Internet's management. Figure 13.1 shows major organizations that play a role in the governance and development of the Internet.

Many of the functions handled by these nonprofit groups were previously handled by U.S. government contractors because the Internet developed out of a defense project. However, because the Internet serves the global community, assigning responsibilities to organizations with global membership is the best way to guarantee worldwide engagement in determining the direction of the Internet.

**Who pays for the Internet?** The National Science Foundation (NSF), which is a U.S. government–funded agency, still pays for a large portion of the Internet's infrastructure and funds research and development for new technologies. The primary source of NSF funding is federal taxes. Other countries also pay for Internet infrastructure and development. ■

FIGURE 13.1

Major Organizations in Internet Governance and Development

| ORGANIZATION | PURPOSE | WEB ADDRESS |
|---|---|---|
| Internet Society | Professional membership society that provides leadership for the orderly growth and development of the Internet | **internetsociety.org** |
| Internet Engineering Task Force (IETF) | A subgroup of the Internet Society that researches new Internet technologies to improve its capabilities and keep the infrastructure functioning smoothly | **ietf.org** |
| Internet Architecture Board (IAB) | Technical advisory group to the Internet Society and an IETF committee; provides direction for the maintenance and development of Internet protocols | **iab.org** |
| Internet Corporation for Assigned Names and Numbers (ICANN) | Organization responsible for managing the Internet's domain name system and the allocation of IP addresses | **icann.org** |
| World Wide Web Consortium (W3C) | Consortium of organizations that sets standards and develops protocols for the web | **w3.org** |

# internet NETWORKING

There is no magic involved in the Internet—just a series of communication transactions that enable the Internet to function as a global network. In this section, we explore the various networks that make up the Internet, explain how they connect to each other, and examine the workings of Internet data communications.

## Internet Data Routes

**How are computers connected to the Internet?** As a "network of networks," the Internet is similar to the U.S. highway system, where smaller roads feed into larger, faster highways. The main paths of the Internet, along which data travels the fastest, are known collectively as the **Internet backbone**. The Internet backbone is a collection of large national and international networks, most of which are owned by commercial, educational, or government organizations. These backbone providers, which are required to connect to other backbone providers, have the fastest high-speed connections. Figure 13.2 shows a typical Internet backbone provided by a single company. Large U.S. companies that provide backbone connectivity include Verizon, AT&T, and Sprint.

**How do the Internet service providers (ISPs) that form the Internet backbone communicate?** A backbone is typically a high-speed fiber-optic line, designated as an **optical carrier (OC) line**. OC lines come in a range of speeds, from 0.052 Gbps for OC-1 to the fastest OC-768, which runs at almost 40 Gbps.

Backbone ISPs initially connected with T lines. A **T line** carried digital data over twisted-pair wires. T-1 lines, which were the first to be used, transmit data at a throughput rate of 1.544 Mbps. T-3 lines, which were developed later, transmit data at 45 Mbps.

The bandwidth of the connections between ISPs and end users depends on the amount of data traffic required. Whereas your home might connect to the Internet with cable

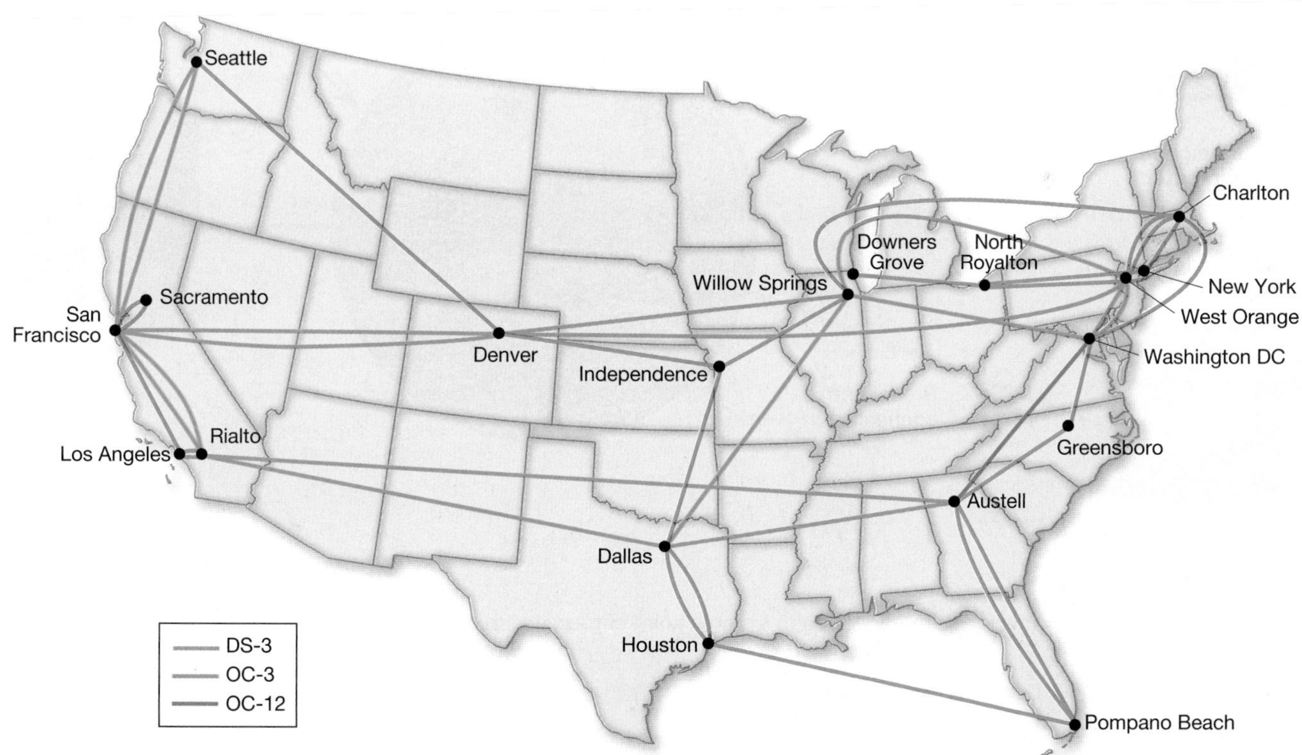


**FIGURE 13.2** A typical Internet backbone provided by a single company.

or fiber-optic lines, the volume of Internet traffic at your college probably requires it to use an OC line to move data to the school's ISP. Large companies usually must connect to their ISPs using high-throughput OC lines.

**How are ISPs connected to each other?** ISPs like Verizon and Comcast are connected together through an **Internet exchange point (IXP)**. A typical IXP is made up of one or more network switches to which ISPs connect. As you'll recall from Chapter 7, *switches* are devices that send data on a specific route through a network. By connecting directly to each other through IXPs, networks can reduce their costs and improve the speed and efficiency with which data is exchanged.

**How do individuals connect to an ISP?** Individual Internet users enter an ISP through a **point of presence (POP)**, which is a bank of modems, servers, routers, and switches (see Figure 13.3) through which many users can connect to an ISP simultaneously. ISPs maintain multiple POPs throughout the geographic area they serve.

## The Network Model of the Internet

**What type of network model does the Internet use?** The majority of Internet communications follows the **client/server model** of network communications. The clients are devices such as computers, tablets, and smartphones that use browsers to request services such as web pages. Various types of servers from which clients can request services are deployed on the networks that make up the Internet:

- **Web servers**: computers that run specialized operating systems, enabling them to host web pages and other information and to provide requested information to clients.
- **Commerce servers**: computers that host software that enables users to buy goods and services over the web. These servers generally use special security protocols to protect sensitive information, such as credit card numbers, from being intercepted.
- **File servers**: computers that are deployed to provide remote storage space or to act as storehouses for files that users can download. Cloud service providers offering online storage services have a huge collection of file servers. ■

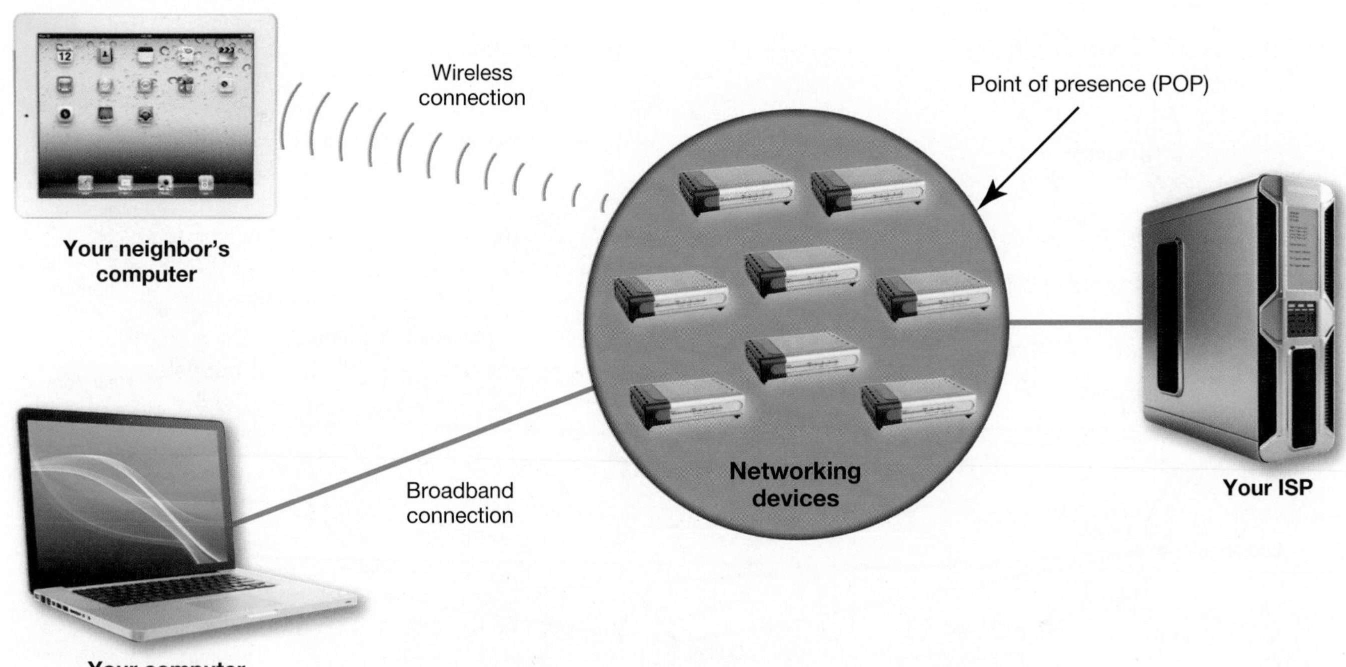


**FIGURE 13.3** Home users connect to their ISPs through a single point of presence that can handle many simultaneous connections.

# data transmission and PROTOCOLS

Just like any other network, the Internet follows standard protocols to send information between computers. A **computer protocol** is a set of rules for exchanging electronic information. If the Internet is the information superhighway, then protocols are the rules of the road.

**Why were Internet protocols developed?** The idea of a protocol is that anyone can use it on his or her computer system and be able to communicate with any other computer using the same protocol. The most common Internet tasks—communicating, collaborating, creating content, seeking information, and shopping—are all executed the same way on any system following accepted Internet protocols.

When common communication protocols are followed, networks can communicate even if they have different topologies, transmission media, or operating systems. To accomplish the early goals of the Internet, protocols needed to be written and agreed on by users. Each protocol had to be an **open system**, meaning its design would be made public for access by any interested party. This was in direct opposition to the **proprietary system** (private system) model that was the norm at the time.

**Were there problems developing an open system Internet protocol?** Agreeing on common standards was relatively easy. The tough part was developing a new method of communication because the technology available in the 1960s—circuit switching—was inefficient for computer communication.

## Circuit Switching

**Why don't we use circuit switching to connect two computers?** Circuit switching has been used since the early days of the telephone for establishing communication. In **circuit switching**, a dedicated connection is formed between two points (such as two people on phones), and the connection remains active for the duration of the transmission. This method of communication is important when communications must be received in the order in which they're sent, like phone conversations.

When applied to computers, however, circuit switching is inefficient. As a computer processor performs the operations necessary to complete a task, it transmits data in a group, or burst. The processor then begins working on its next task and ceases to communicate with output devices or other networks until it's ready to transmit data in the next burst. Circuit switching is inefficient for computers because either the circuit would have to remain open, and therefore unavailable to any other system, with long periods of inactivity, or it would have to be reestablished for each burst.

## BITS&BYTES

### Who Opened Your Ports?

If you get curious about what TCP/IP and UDP ports are currently being used on your system, consider trying out the freeware CurrPorts. It displays a listing of all the open TCP/IP ports, along with details like the name of the application that opened it, its current status (Listening, Waiting, etc.), and the time it was created. It also automatically highlights suspicious ports owned by unknown applications.

## Packet Switching

**If they don't use circuit switching, what do computers use to communicate? Packet switching** is the communications methodology that makes computer communication efficient. Packet switching doesn't require a dedicated communications circuit to be maintained. With packet switching, data is broken into smaller chunks called **packets** (or **data packets**). The packets are sent over various routes at the same time. When the packets reach their destination, they're reassembled by the receiving computer. This technology resulted from one of the original goals of creating the Internet: If an Internet node is disabled or destroyed, the data can travel an alternate route to its destination.

**What information does a packet contain?** Packet contents vary, depending on the protocol being followed. At a minimum, all packets must contain the following:

1. An address to which the packet is being sent
2. The address from where the packet originates
3. Reassembly instructions, if the original data is split between packets, and
4. The data that's being transmitted

Sending a packet is like sending a letter. Assume you're sending a large amount of information in written format from your home in Philadelphia to your aunt in San Diego. The information is too large to fit in one small envelope, so you mail three different envelopes to your aunt. Each envelope includes your aunt's address, your return address, and the information being sent inside it. The pages of the letters in each envelope are numbered so that your aunt will know in which order to read them.

Each envelope may not find its way to San Diego by the same route. However, even if the letters are routed through different post offices, they'll all eventually arrive in your aunt's mailbox. Your aunt will then reassemble the message in the right order and read it. The process of sending a message through the Internet works in much the same way. This process is illustrated in Figure 13.4, which traces an e-mail message sent from a computer in Philadelphia to a computer in San Diego.

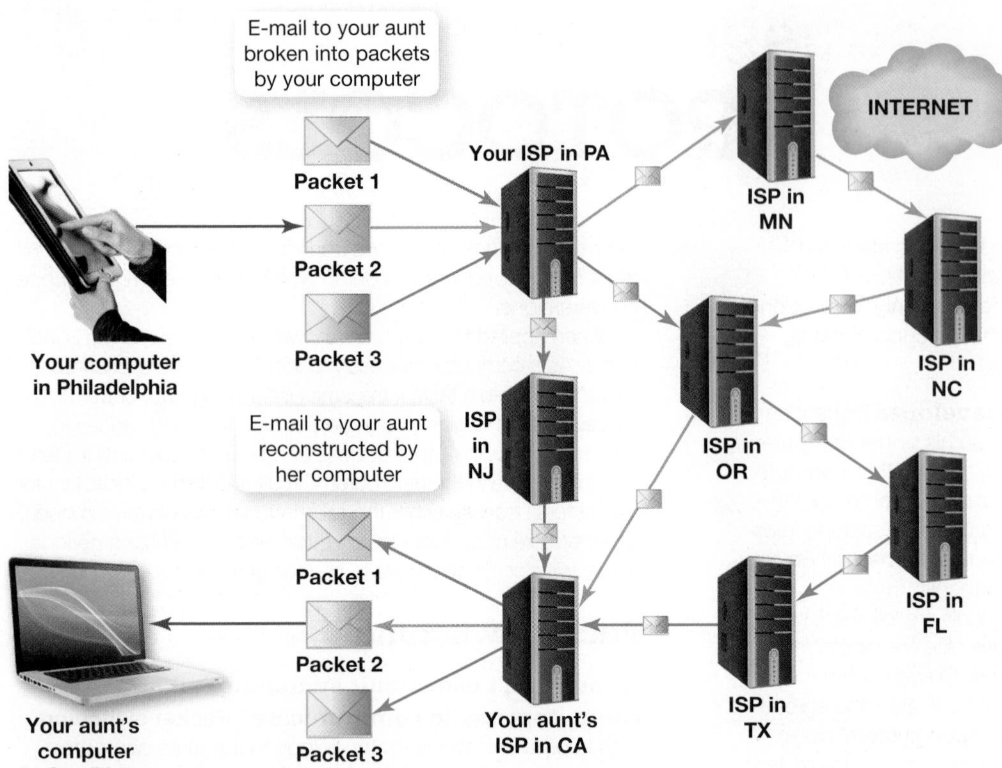

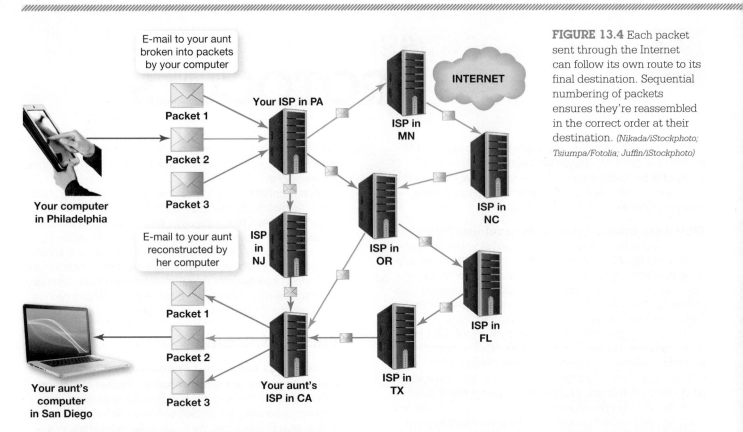

**FIGURE 13.4** Each packet sent through the Internet can follow its own route to its final destination. Sequential numbering of packets ensures they're reassembled in the correct order at their destination. *(Nikada/iStockphoto; Tsiumpa/Fotolia; Juffin/iStockphoto)*

**Why do packets take different routes, and how do they decide which route to use?** The routers that connect ISPs with each other monitor traffic and decide on the most efficient route for packets to take to their destination. The router works in the same way a police officer does while directing traffic. To ensure a smooth flow of traffic, police officers are deployed in areas of congestion, directing drivers along alternate routes to their destinations. The Try This exercise in this chapter uses the Windows utility tracert to show you the details on the exact route your request takes to the destination server.

## TCP/IP

**What protocol does the Internet use for transmitting data?** Although many protocols are available on the Internet, the main suite of protocols used is **TCP/IP**. The suite is named after the original two protocols that were developed for the Internet: the **Transmission Control Protocol (TCP)** and the **Internet Protocol (IP)**. Although most people think that the TCP/IP suite consists of only two protocols, it actually comprises many interrelated protocols, the most important of which are listed in Figure 13.5.

**Which particular protocol actually sends the information?** The Internet Protocol (IP) is responsible for sending the information from one computer to another. The IP is like a postal worker who takes a letter (a packet of information) that was mailed (created by the sending computer) and sends it on to another post office (router), which in turn routes it to the addressee (the receiving computer). The postal worker never knows whether the recipient actually receives the letter. The only thing the postal worker knows is that the letter was handed off to an appropriate post office that will assist in completing the delivery of the letter. ■

**FIGURE 13.5**

### TCP/IP Protocol Suite—Main Protocols

| | |
|---|---|
| Internet Protocol (IP) | Sends data between computers on the Internet |
| Transmission Control Protocol (TCP) | Prepares data for transmission and provides for error checking and resending of lost data |
| User Datagram Protocol (UDP) | Prepares data for transmission; lacks resending capabilities |
| File Transfer Protocol (FTP) | Enables files to be downloaded to a computer or uploaded to other computers |
| Telnet | Enables user to log in to a remote computer and work on it as if sitting in front of it |
| Hypertext Transfer Protocol (HTTP) and HTTP Secure (HTTPS) | Transfers Hypertext Markup Language (HTML) data from servers to browsers; HTTPS is an encrypted protocol for secure transmissions |
| Simple Mail Transfer Protocol (SMTP) | Used for transmission of e-mail messages across the Internet |
| Dynamic Host Configuration Protocol (DHCP) | Takes a pool of IP addresses and shares them with hosts on a network on an as-needed basis |

# internet identity: IP addresses and DOMAIN NAMES

Each computer, server, or device connected to the Internet is required to have a unique identification number, or IP address. However, because humans are better at remembering and working with words than with numbers, the numeric IP addresses were given more "human," word-based addresses. Thus, domain names were born. In this section, we'll look at both IP addresses and domain names.

## IP Addresses

**What is an IP address?** You'll recall from Chapter 3 that an **IP address** is a unique identification number that defines each computer, service, or other device connected to the Internet. IP addresses fulfill the same function as street addresses. For example, to send a letter to Rosa Juarez's house in Metamora, Illinois, you have to know her address. Rosa might live at 456 Walnut Street, which isn't a unique address because many towns have a Walnut Street, but 456 Walnut Street, Metamora, IL 61548 *is* a unique address.

The numeric zip code is the unique postal identification for a specific geographic area. IP addresses must be registered with the **Internet Corporation for Assigned Names and Numbers (ICANN)** to ensure they're unique and haven't been assigned to other users. ICANN is responsible for allocating IP addresses to network administrators.

**What does an IP address look like?** A typical IP address is expressed as follows:

```
197.169.73.63
```

An IP address in this form is called a **dotted decimal number** (or a **dotted quad**). The same IP address in binary form is as follows:

```
11000101.10101001.01001001.00111111
```

Each of the 4 numbers in a dotted decimal number is referred to as an **octet**. This is because each number would have 8 positions when shown in binary form. Because 32 positions are available for IP address values (4 octets with 8 positions each), IP addresses are considered 32-bit numbers. A position is filled by either a *1* or a *0*, resulting in 256 (which is $2^8$) possible values for each octet, from *0* to *255*. The entire 32-bit address can represent 4,294,967,296 values (or $2^{32}$), which is quite a few Internet addresses!

## BITS&BYTES

### What's Your IP Address?

Curious as to what your IP address is? Go to Google and type "what is my ip" (see Figure 13.6). Google will show your IP address at the top of the search results. If you want additional information, such as the geographic location of an IP address or even the telephone area code associated with it, visit **whatismyipaddress.com**.

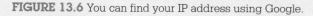

**FIGURE 13.6** You can find your IP address using Google.

# DIG DEEPER Connection-Oriented Versus Connectionless Protocols

The Internet Protocol is responsible only for sending packets on their way. The packets are created by either the TCP or the **User Datagram Protocol (UDP)**. You don't decide whether to use TCP or UDP. The choice of protocol is made for you by the developers of the computer programs you're using or by the other protocols that interact with your data packet (such as those listed in Figure 13.5).

As explained earlier, data transmission between computers is highly efficient if connections don't need to be established (as in circuit switching). However, there are benefits to maintaining a connection, such as reduced data loss. The difference between TCP and UDP is that TCP is a *connection-oriented* protocol, whereas UDP is a *connectionless* protocol.

A **connection-oriented protocol** requires two computers to exchange control packets, thereby setting up the parameters of the data-exchange session, before sending packets that contain data. This process is referred to as **handshaking**. TCP uses a process called a **three-way handshake** to establish a connection, as shown in Figure 13.7:

1. Your computer establishes a connection to the ISP and announces it has e-mail to send.
2. The ISP server responds that it's ready to receive the e-mail.
3. Your computer then acknowledges the ready state of the server and begins to transmit the e-mail.

A **connectionless protocol** doesn't require any type of connection to be established or maintained between two computers exchanging information. Just like a letter that's mailed, the data packets are sent without notifying the receiving computer or receiving any acknowledgment that the data was received. UDP is the Internet's connectionless protocol.

Besides establishing a connection, TCP provides for reliable data transfer, ensuring that all the data packets are delivered to the receiver free from errors and in the correct order. TCP achieves reliable data transfer by using acknowledgments and providing for the retransmission of data, as shown in Figure 13.8.

Assume that two systems, X and Y, have established a connection. When Y receives a data packet that it can read from X, it sends back a **positive acknowledgment (ACK)**. If X doesn't receive an ACK in an appropriate period of time, it resends the packet. If the packet is unreadable (damaged in transit), Y sends a **negative acknowledgment (NAK)** to X, indicating the packet wasn't received in understandable form. X then retransmits that packet. Acknowledgments ensure that the receiver has received a complete set of data packets. If a packet is unable to get through after being resent several times, the user is generally presented with an error message, indicating the communications were unsuccessful.

STEP 1:
I want to send e-mail.
STEP 2:
Okay, I'm ready to receive.
STEP 3:
Here's the e-mail message for Aunt Sally.
Your computer
Your ISP's server

**FIGURE 13.7** Two computers establish communication using a three-way handshake.

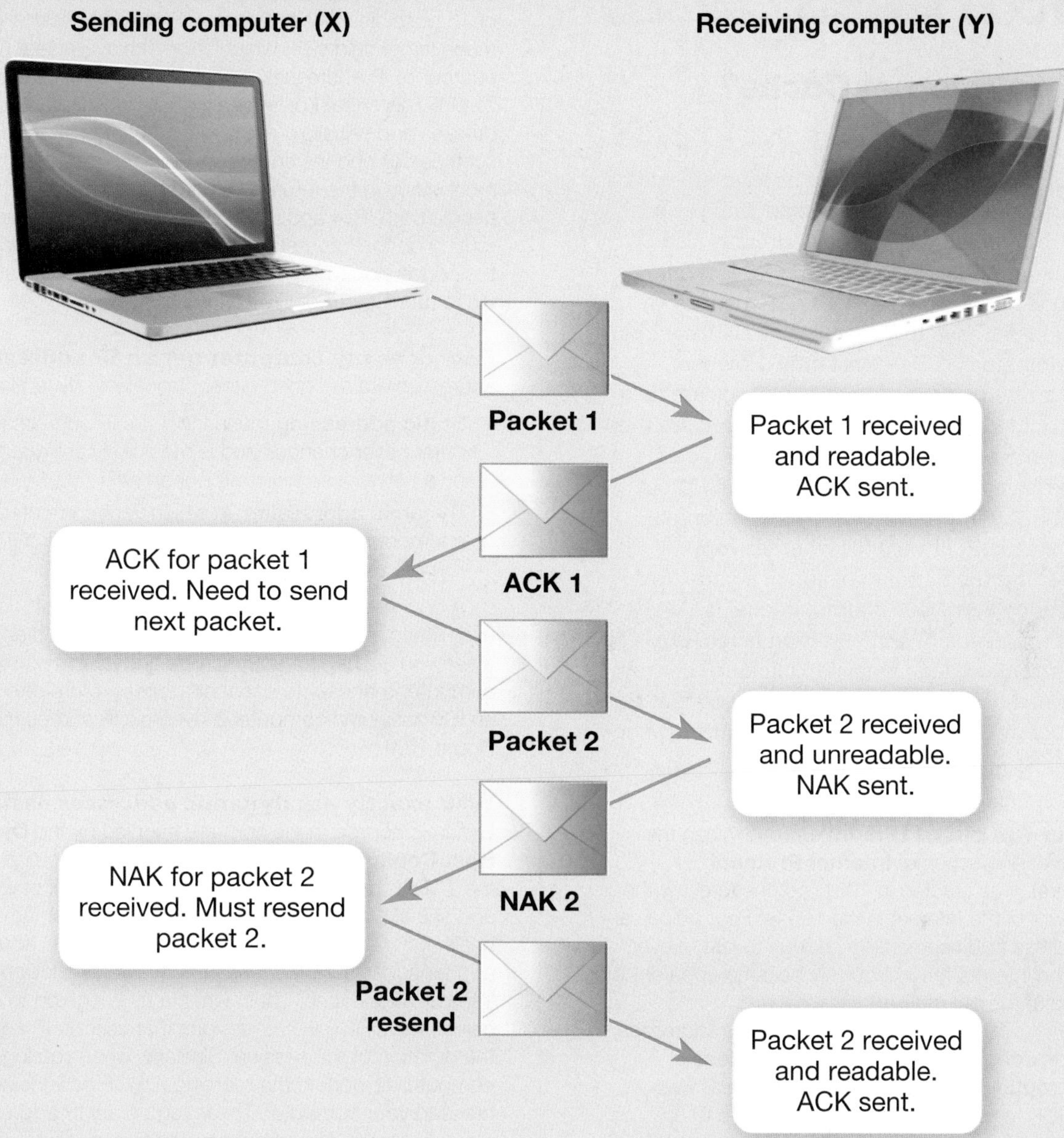
Sending computer (X)
Receiving computer (Y)
Packet 1
Packet 1 received and readable. ACK sent.
ACK 1
ACK for packet 1 received. Need to send next packet.
Packet 2
Packet 2 received and unreadable. NAK sent.
NAK 2
NAK for packet 2 received. Must resend packet 2.
Packet 2 resend
Packet 2 received and readable. ACK sent.

**FIGURE 13.8** Positive (ACK) and negative (NAK) packet acknowledgments provide reliable data transfer.

You may wonder why you wouldn't always want to use a protocol that provides for reliable data transfer. On the Internet, speed is often more important than accuracy. For certain applications (such as e-mail), it's important that your message be delivered completely and accurately. For streaming multimedia, it's not always important to have every frame delivered accurately because most streaming media formats provide for correction of errors caused by data loss. However, it's extremely important for streaming media to be delivered at a high rate of speed. Therefore, a protocol such as TCP, which uses handshakes and acknowledgments, would probably not be appropriate for transmitting a movie trailer over the Internet; in this instance, the Real-time Transport Protocol (RTP) would be better.

# BITS&BYTES

## What Is an Internet Cache?

Your **Internet cache** is a section of your hard drive that stores information that you may need again, such as IP addresses and frequently accessed web pages. However, caching of domain name addresses also takes place in domain name system (DNS) servers. This helps speed up Internet access time because a DNS server doesn't have to query master DNS servers for top-level domains (TLDs) constantly. However, caches have limited storage space, so entries are held in the cache only for a fixed period of time and are then deleted. The time component associated with cache retention is known as the *time to live (TTL)*. Without caches, surfing the Internet would take a lot longer.

Beware—you can't always tell whether your browser is loading the current version of a page from the web or a copy from your Internet cache. If a website contains time-sensitive information (such as a snow day alert on a college website), clicking the browser's Reload or Refresh button will ensure that the most current copy of the page loads into your browser.

**Will we ever run out of IP addresses?** When the original IP addressing scheme, **Internet Protocol version 4 (IPv4)**, was created in 1981, no one foresaw the explosive growth of the Internet in the 1990s. Four billion values for an address field seemed like enough to last forever. However, as the Internet grew, it quickly became apparent that we were going to run out of IP addresses.

Because IPv4 offers only a fixed number of IP addresses, a different addressing scheme, known as **classless interdomain routing (CIDR)**, pronounced "cider," was developed. CIDR, or *supernetting,* allows a single IP address to represent several unique IP addresses by adding a **network prefix**, represented by a slash and a number, to the end of the last octet. The network prefix identifies how many of the possible 32 bits in a traditional IP address are to be used as the unique identifier, leaving the remaining bits to identify the specific host. For example, in the IP address 206.13.01.48/25, "/25" is the network prefix. It indicates that the first 25 bits are used as the unique network identifier; the remaining 7 bits identify the specific host site.

**Are there other Internet addressing systems?** **Internet Protocol version 6 (IPv6)** is an IP addressing scheme developed by the IETF to make IP addresses longer, thereby providing more available IP addresses. IPv6 uses 128-bit addressing instead of 32-bit addressing. An IPv6 address would have the following format:

XXXX : XXXX : XXXX : XXXX : XXXX : XXXX : XXXX : XXXX

where each digit X is a **hexadecimal digit**. Hexadecimal is a base-16 number system, and each hexadecimal digit is one of 16 possible values: 0–9 or A–F. Hex addressing provides a much larger field size, which will make available a much larger number of IP addresses (approximately 340 followed by 36 zeros). This should provide a virtually unlimited supply of IP addresses and will allow many different kinds of non-PC devices such as cell phones and home appliances to join the Internet more easily in the future. All modern operating systems can handle both IPv4 and IPv6 addresses. Although the majority of routing on the Internet still takes place using IPv4 addresses, the conversion to IPv6 addressing should accelerate now that we're running out of IPv4 addresses.

**How does my computer get an IP address?** IP addresses are assigned either statically or dynamically:

- **Static addressing** means that the IP address for a computer never changes and is most likely assigned manually by a network administrator or an ISP.
- **Dynamic addressing**, in which your computer is assigned a temporary address from an available pool of IP addresses, is more common.

A connection to an ISP could use either method. If your ISP uses static addressing, then you were assigned an IP address when you applied for your service and had to configure your computer manually to use that address. More often, though, an ISP assigns a computer a dynamic IP address, as shown in Figure 13.9.

**How exactly are dynamic addresses assigned?** Dynamic addressing is normally handled by the **Dynamic Host Configuration Protocol (DHCP)**, which belongs to the TCP/IP protocol suite. DHCP takes a pool of IP addresses and shares them with hosts on the network on an as-needed basis. ISPs don't need to maintain a pool of IP addresses for all their subscribers because not everyone is logged on to the Internet at one time. Thus, when a user logs on to an ISP's server, the DHCP server assigns that user an IP address for the duration of the session. Similarly, when you log on to your computer at work in the morning, DHCP assigns an IP address to your computer. These temporary IP addresses may or may not be the same from session to session.

**What are the benefits of dynamic addressing?** Although having a static address would seem to be convenient, dynamic addressing provides a more secure environment by keeping hackers out of computer systems. Imagine

ACTIVE HELP DESK

**Understanding IP Addresses, Domain Names, and Protocols**

In this Active Helpdesk call, you'll play the role of a helpdesk staffer, fielding calls about which data transmissions and protocols the Internet uses and why IP addresses and domain names are important for Internet communications.

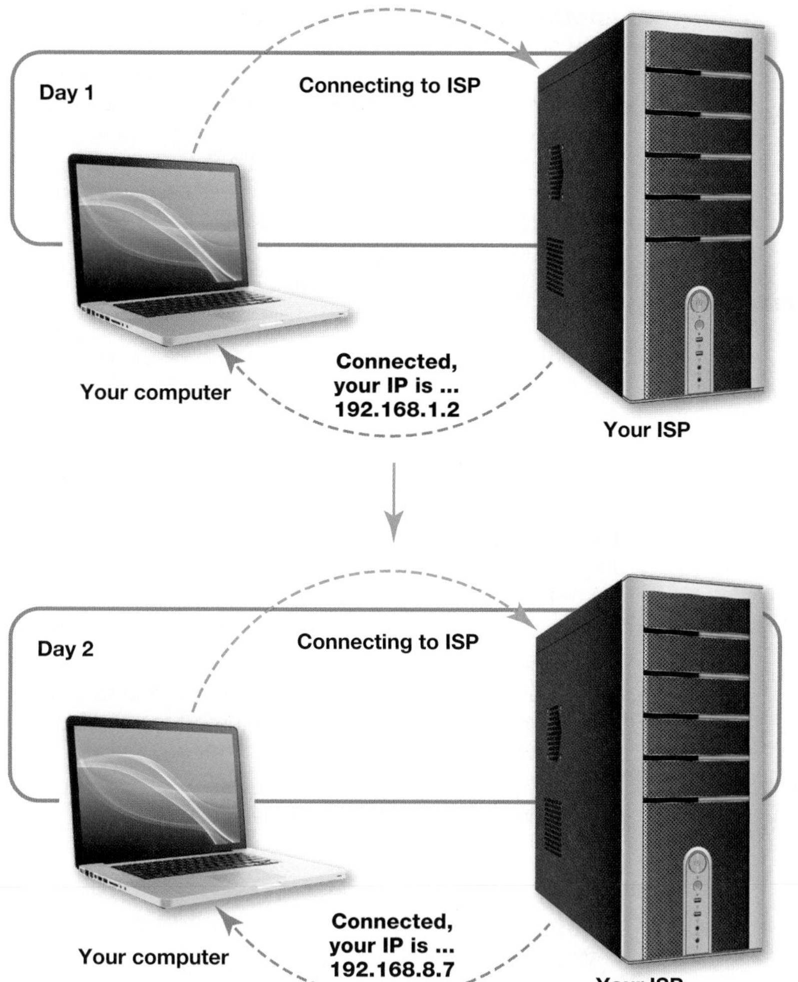


**FIGURE 13.9** With dynamic IP addressing, your IP address changes every time you connect to the Internet.

how hard it would be for burglars to find your home if you changed your address every day!

## Domain Names

**I've been on the Internet, so why have I never seen IP addresses?** As you learned in Chapter 3, a *domain name* is a name that takes the place of an IP address, making it easier for people to remember. For example, google.com is a domain name. The server where Google's main website is deployed has an IP address (such as 66.249.64.55), but it's much easier for you to remember to tell your browser to go to **google.com**.

**How are domains organized?** Domains are organized by level. As you'll recall from Chapter 3, the portion of the domain name after the dot is the *top-level domain (TLD)*. The TLDs are standardized pools such as .com and .org established by ICANN (see Figure 13.10).

Within each top-level domain are many second-level domains. A **second-level domain** is a domain that's directly below a top-level domain. For example, in **dropbox.com**, *dropbox* is the second-level domain to the .com TLD. A second-level domain needs to be unique within its own TLD but not necessarily unique to all top-level domains. For example, mynewIdeaWebsite.com and mynewIdeaWebsite.org could be registered as separate domain names.

**Who controls domain name registration?** ICANN assigns companies or organizations to manage domain name registration. Because names can't be duplicated within a TLD, one company is assigned to oversee each TLD and to maintain a listing of all registered domains. VeriSign

# BITS&BYTES

## Server in the Cloud

If you want to build a web application (a program that allows a user to send and receive information to a web browser), you may start by buying and maintaining a server computer in your home to host it. That means you have to get up in the middle of the night if the hard drive crashes, or risk angry user e-mails in the morning! What if your site becomes wildly popular and suddenly you need to expand to three or four servers to handle the load?

Using the free Google App Engine service avoids such problems. The server for your application is hosted by Google and is automatically scaled up or down as the demand for it changes. Using App Engine frees you from the worries of maintaining hardware too. And you can test out your ideas and then go live to users at no cost and only pay for services once your usage begins to take off. Your application can live at a domain name you make up, or you can serve your app from an available name off of the **appspot.com** domain. Explore more about Google App Engine at **developers.google.com/appengine**.

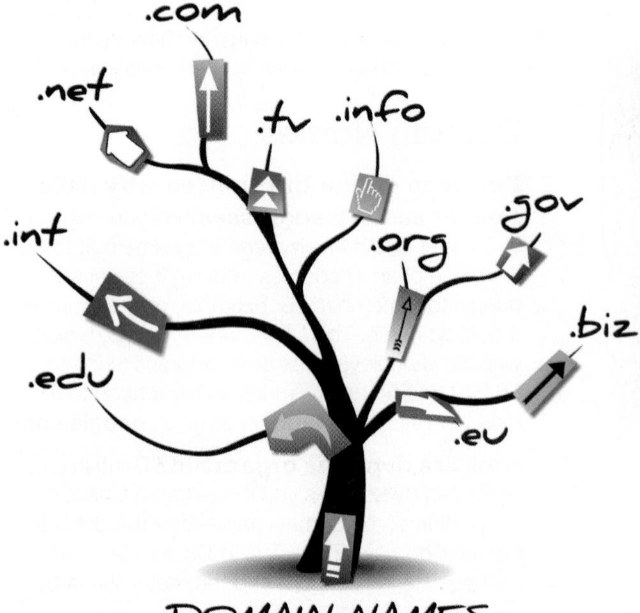
.com
.net
.tv
.info
.gov
.int
.org
.biz
.edu
.eu
DOMAIN NAMES

**FIGURE 13.10** The number of generic top-level domains has grown to include .museum and .job. ICANN is responsible for organizing TLD names.

is the current ICANN-accredited domain name registrar for the .com and .net domains. VeriSign provides a database that lists all the registered .com and .net domains and their contact information. You can look up any .com or .net domain at Network Solutions (**networksolutions.com**) to see whether it's registered and, if so, who owns it.

Country-specific domains (such as .au for Australia) are controlled by groups in those countries. You can find a complete list of country-code TLDs on the Internet Assigned Numbers Authority website (**iana.org**).

**How does my computer know the IP address of another computer?** When you enter a URL in your browser, your computer converts the URL to an IP address. To do this, your computer consults a database maintained on a **domain name system (DNS) server** that functions like a phone book for the Internet.

Your ISP's web server has a default DNS server (one that's convenient to contact) that it goes to when it needs to translate a URL to an IP address (illustrated in Figure 13.11). It uses the following steps:

1. Your browser requests information from a website (for example, ABC.com).
2. Your ISP doesn't know the address of ABC.com, so your ISP must request the address from its own default DNS server.
3. The default DNS server doesn't know the IP address of ABC.com either, so it queries one of the 13 root DNS servers maintained throughout the Internet. Each **root DNS server** knows the location of all the DNS servers that contain the master listings for an entire top-level domain.
4. The root server provides the default DNS server with the appropriate IP address of ABC.com.
5. The default DNS server stores the correct IP address for ABC.com for future reference and returns it to your ISP's web server.
6. Your computer then routes its request to ABC.com and stores the IP address in cache for later use. ■

**Before moving on to Part 2:**

- **Watch Replay Video 13.1.**
- **Then check your understanding of what you've learned so far.**

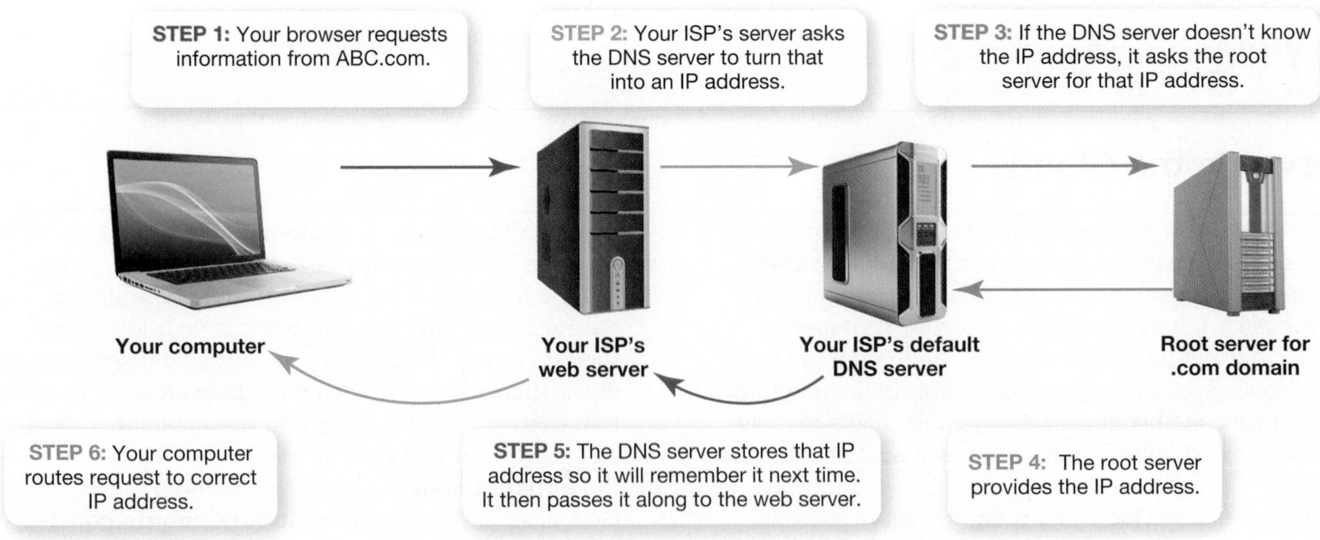
STEP 1: Your browser requests information from ABC.com.
STEP 2: Your ISP's server asks the DNS server to turn that into an IP address.
STEP 3: If the DNS server doesn't know the IP address, it asks the root server for that IP address.
Your computer
Your ISP's web server
Your ISP's default DNS server
Root server for .com domain
STEP 6: Your computer routes request to correct IP address.
STEP 5: The DNS server stores that IP address so it will remember it next time. It then passes it along to the web server.
STEP 4: The root server provides the IP address.

**FIGURE 13.11** DNS servers in action.

# check your understanding//

For a quick review to see what you've learned so far, answer the following questions. Visit **pearsonhighered.com /techinaction** to check your answers.

## multiple choice

1. Which is *not* a common protocol used on the Internet?
   - **a.** TCP
   - **b.** IP
   - **c.** HTTP
   - **d.** PGP
2. Packet switching sends information between two points
   - **a.** by breaking it into small chunks and sending the chunks across different routes.
   - **b.** by finding one route between the two points and sending the data.
   - **c.** by encrypting the data, then sending it.
   - **d.** differently for each company using it.
3. ISPs are connected to each other at
   - **a.** Internet exchange points.
   - **b.** points of presence.
   - **c.** Internet intersections.
   - **d.** DNS convergence points.
4. The main suite of Internet protocols used to transmit data is called
   - **a.** DNS.
   - **b.** XML.
   - **c.** HTTP.
   - **d.** TCP/IP.
5. A __________ takes the place of an IP address because it's easier for humans to recall than a long string of numbers.
   - **a.** DNS
   - **b.** CGI
   - **c.** domain name
   - **d.** HTML

## true–false

_____ **1.** The Internet is primarily managed by U.S. government agencies.

_____ **2.** Proprietary protocols are managed by the U.S. government.

## critical thinking

1. **Addresses for All**

   Why is IPv6 needed? How many devices do you have that are looking for an IP address when you walk onto campus? Some predictions state that by 2020, more than 30 billion devices will be connected to the Internet. What opportunities and what challenges will that bring?

2. **The Perfect Packet**

   In packet switching, data is broken up into smaller bundles. How small should a packet be for the best performance? Is it better to have many more very small packets or just a few packets? How would you decide, and would the answer be the same for all types of information?

**Continue** »

# TRY THIS — Ping Me

Several programs that help you understand networking are part of your Windows operating system but aren't on your desktop. In this Try This, we'll use the **ping** command and the **tracert** command to get some detailed info about the Internet.

**Step 1** In Windows 7, click the **Start** button, and in the search box, type **command**. Select the program **Command Prompt**. In Windows 8, display the Charms bar, and select **Search**. Type **command** in the search box. Click the **Command Prompt** icon from the search results.

```
Command Prompt
Microsoft Windows [Version 6.1.7601]
Copyright (c) 2009 Microsoft Corporation.  All rights reserved.

C:\Users\Kendall>
```

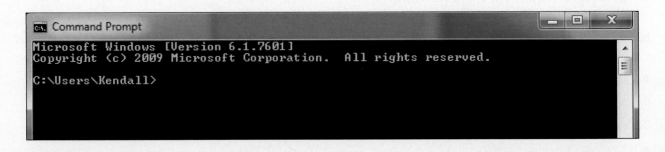

**Step 2** Type **ping google.com**, and press **Enter**. Ping is a utility that sends a packet of information to a specific computer and measures the time it takes to travel a round trip to the destination and back. You can use ping to test an IP address or a computer name. Ping will send a few packets and then report back to you the minimum, maximum, and average round trip times in milliseconds, as shown here.

```
C:\Users\Kendall>ping google.com

Pinging google.com [74.125.228.70] with 32 bytes of data:
Reply from 74.125.228.70: bytes=32 time=15ms TTL=252
Reply from 74.125.228.70: bytes=32 time=17ms TTL=252
Reply from 74.125.228.70: bytes=32 time=14ms TTL=252
Reply from 74.125.228.70: bytes=32 time=16ms TTL=252

Ping statistics for 74.125.228.70:
    Packets: Sent = 4, Received = 4, Lost = 0 (0% loss),
Approximate round trip times in milli-seconds:
    Minimum = 14ms, Maximum = 17ms, Average = 15ms
```

**Step 3** Now let's try another utility, tracert. Type: **tracert google.com**, and press **Enter**. Tracert traces the route that the packet takes from your computer to the destination computer and back. Here we see it starting off on a home system and jumping on to a computer that ISP Verizon operates in the Philadelphia area. The packet makes one more hop on the Verizon system, then jumps onto backbone network IAD8.ALTER.NET, and then begins to step down to local computers until it reaches google [74.125.228.6].

Tracert displays the total number of hops to reach the destination. Here we see it took 10 hops to reach **google.com**. It also shows the round-trip time for a packet to travel to each hop. Tracert sends three packets to each point and reports the round-trip time for each one.

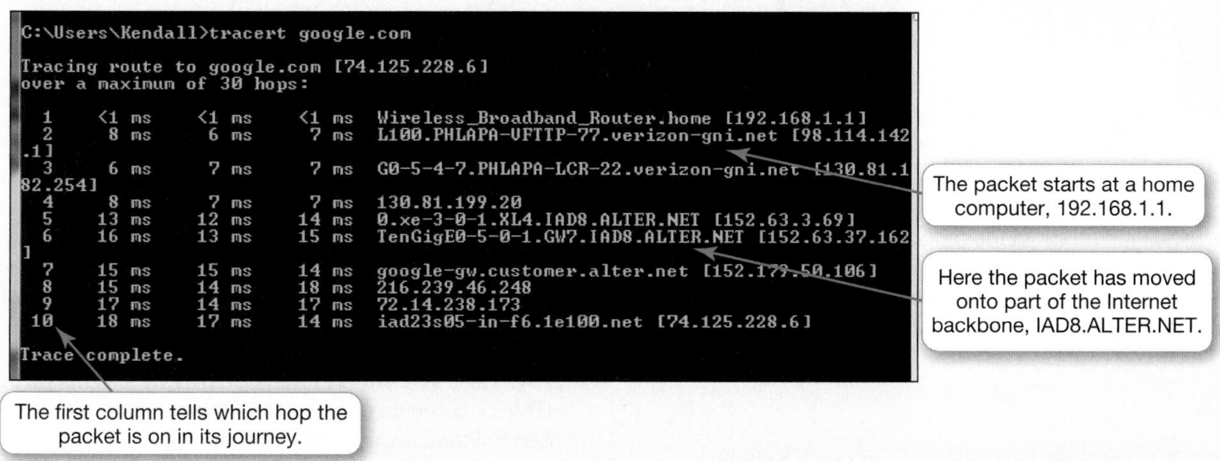
C:\Users\Kendall>tracert google.com
Tracing route to google.com [74.125.228.6]
over a maximum of 30 hops:
1 <1 ms <1 ms <1 ms Wireless_Broadband_Router.home [192.168.1.1]
2 8 ms 6 ms 7 ms L100.PHLAPA-VFTTP-77.verizon-gni.net [98.114.142.1]
3 6 ms 7 ms 7 ms G0-5-4-7.PHLAPA-LCR-22.verizon-gni.net [130.81.182.254]
4 8 ms 7 ms 7 ms 130.81.199.20
5 13 ms 12 ms 14 ms 0.xe-3-0-1.XL4.IAD8.ALTER.NET [152.63.3.69]
6 16 ms 13 ms 15 ms TenGigE0-5-0-1.GW7.IAD8.ALTER.NET [152.63.37.162]
7 15 ms 15 ms 14 ms google-gw.customer.alter.net [152.179.50.106]
8 15 ms 14 ms 18 ms 216.239.46.248
9 17 ms 14 ms 17 ms 72.14.238.173
10 18 ms 17 ms 14 ms iad23s05-in-f6.1e100.net [74.125.228.6]
Trace complete.
The packet starts at a home computer, 192.168.1.1.
Here the packet has moved onto part of the Internet backbone, IAD8.ALTER.NET.
The first column tells which hop the packet is on in its journey.

**Step 4** Now let's try to reach a location far away from home base.

At the prompt, type **tracert www.cityoflondon.gov.uk**, and press **Enter**.

In the following figure, a computer in Philadelphia is trying to reach a computer in London, **cityoflondon.gov.uk**. As shown here, the packet starts at home and then moves to a Verizon computer in Philadelphia. Then it jumps onto the Internet backbone and travels to Washington. Next there is a much longer trip time, 85 ms. This is probably as the packet moves across the Atlantic Ocean.

The packet finally reaches **cityoflondon.gov.uk** [86.54.118.84]. The series of timed-out requests after that are caused by the packet being denied by the firewall of that computer. You can press Ctrl+C at any point to stop the command.

Using ping and tracert is helpful when a website isn't reachable. You can see exactly where the connection is failing. If you see that your connection is timing out after line 1, it means there's a problem connecting to your ISP—call them! If the timeout is happening several hops later, there's probably nothing your ISP can do to help.

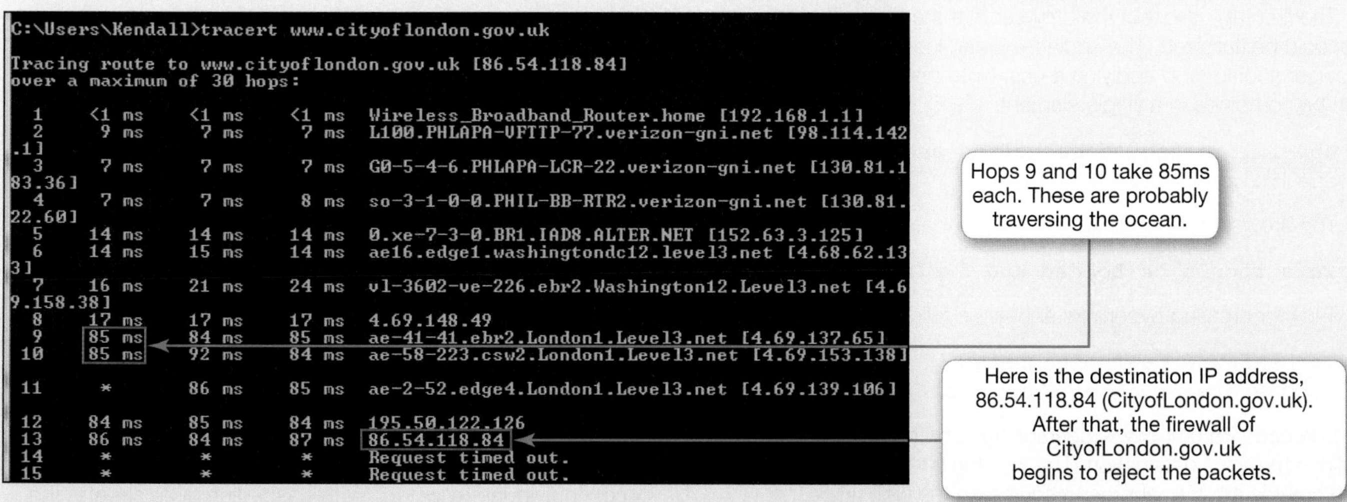
C:\Users\Kendall>tracert www.cityoflondon.gov.uk
Tracing route to www.cityoflondon.gov.uk [86.54.118.84]
over a maximum of 30 hops:
1 <1 ms <1 ms <1 ms Wireless_Broadband_Router.home [192.168.1.1]
2 9 ms 7 ms 7 ms L100.PHLAPA-VFTTP-77.verizon-gni.net [98.114.142.1]
3 7 ms 7 ms 7 ms G0-5-4-6.PHLAPA-LCR-22.verizon-gni.net [130.81.183.36]
4 7 ms 7 ms 8 ms so-3-1-0-0.PHIL-BB-RTR2.verizon-gni.net [130.81.22.60]
5 14 ms 14 ms 14 ms 0.xe-7-3-0.BR1.IAD8.ALTER.NET [152.63.3.125]
6 14 ms 15 ms 14 ms ae16.edge1.washingtondc12.level3.net [4.68.62.133]
7 16 ms 21 ms 24 ms vl-3602-ve-226.ebr2.Washington12.Level3.net [4.69.158.38]
8 17 ms 17 ms 17 ms 4.69.148.49
9 85 ms 84 ms 85 ms ae-41-41.ebr2.London1.Level3.net [4.69.137.65]
10 85 ms 92 ms 84 ms ae-58-223.csw2.London1.Level3.net [4.69.153.138]
11 * 86 ms 85 ms ae-2-52.edge4.London1.Level3.net [4.69.139.106]
12 84 ms 85 ms 84 ms 195.50.122.126
13 86 ms 84 ms 87 ms 86.54.118.84
14 * * * Request timed out.
15 * * * Request timed out.
Hops 9 and 10 take 85ms each. These are probably traversing the ocean.
Here is the destination IP address, 86.54.118.84 (CityofLondon.gov.uk). After that, the firewall of CityofLondon.gov.uk begins to reject the packets.

# Coding and Communicating on the Internet

The web uses special languages such as *HTML* and protocols such as *HTTP* to facilitate communication between computers that use different system and application software. Communication between any two points on the Internet is possible because of HTML and communication protocols. In this part of the chapter, we'll explore these topics.

# HTML, XML, and other web BUILDING BLOCKS

Let's examine in more detail the programming languages and communication protocols that support the Internet. We introduced some of these ideas in Chapter 10. Now we'll explore them in a bit more depth.

## HTML

**How are web pages formatted?** Web pages are text documents formatted using HTML (Hypertext Markup Language). HTML isn't a programming language; rather, it's a set of rules for marking up blocks of text so that a browser knows how to display them.

Blocks of text in HTML documents are surrounded by pairs of **HTML tags** (such as <b> and </b>, which indicate bolding). HTML tags surround and define HTML content. Each pair of tags and the text between them are collectively referred to as an **element**. The elements are interpreted by the browser, and appropriate effects are applied to the text. The following is an element from an HTML document:

```
<i>This should be italicized.</i>
```

The browser would display this element as:

*This should be italicized.*

The first tag, <i>, tells the browser that the text following it should be italicized. The ending </i> tag indicates that the browser should stop applying italics. Note that multiple tags can be combined in a single element:

```
<b><i>This should be bolded and
italicized.</i></b>
```

The browser would display this element as:

***This should be bolded and italicized.***

Tags for creating hyperlinks appear as follows:

```
<a href=www.pearsonhighered
.com>Pearson Higher Education</a>
```

The code <a href=www.pearsonhighered.com> defines the link's destination. The <a> tag is the anchor tag and creates a link to another resource on the web. Here the link is to the **www.pearsonhighered.com** web page. The text between the open and close of the anchor tag, Pearson Higher Education, is the link label. The link label is the text (or image) that's displayed on the web page as clickable text for the hyperlink.

**How do I see the HTML coding of a web page?** HTML documents are merely text documents with tags applied to them. If you want to look at the HTML coding behind any web page, just right-click and select View Source from the shortcut menu, and the HTML code for that page will display, as shown in Figure 13.12.

**What is the current HTML standard?** As we discussed in Chapter 10, HTML5 is the current version of the HTML standard. At the time of this writing, it's still under finalization. However, many devices and browsers are already HTML5 enabled. HTML5 modernizes a number of features in HTML such as:

- Reducing the need for external plug-ins (like Flash)
- Supporting better error handling
- Introducing new tags to support media, like <video> and <audio>
- Making it easier to draw graphics

**How can developers easily change the formatting of HTML elements?** A **cascading style sheet** is a list of rules that defines in one single location how to display HTML elements. Style rules enable a web developer to define a kind of formatting for each HTML element and apply it to all those elements on a set of web pages. Essentially, a template is created on which the formatting for many web pages within a site will be based. When a global change is necessary, the developer only needs to change the style on the style sheet, and all the elements in the web document will update automatically (see Figure 13.13).

For example, a web page has an <h1> heading tag, and all <h1> tags in the web page are formatted with a white background and an orange border. Before cascading style sheets, if you wanted to change the border color from orange to yellow, you had to change the background color of each individual <h1> tag. With cascading style sheets, the change from orange to yellow only needs to happen once on

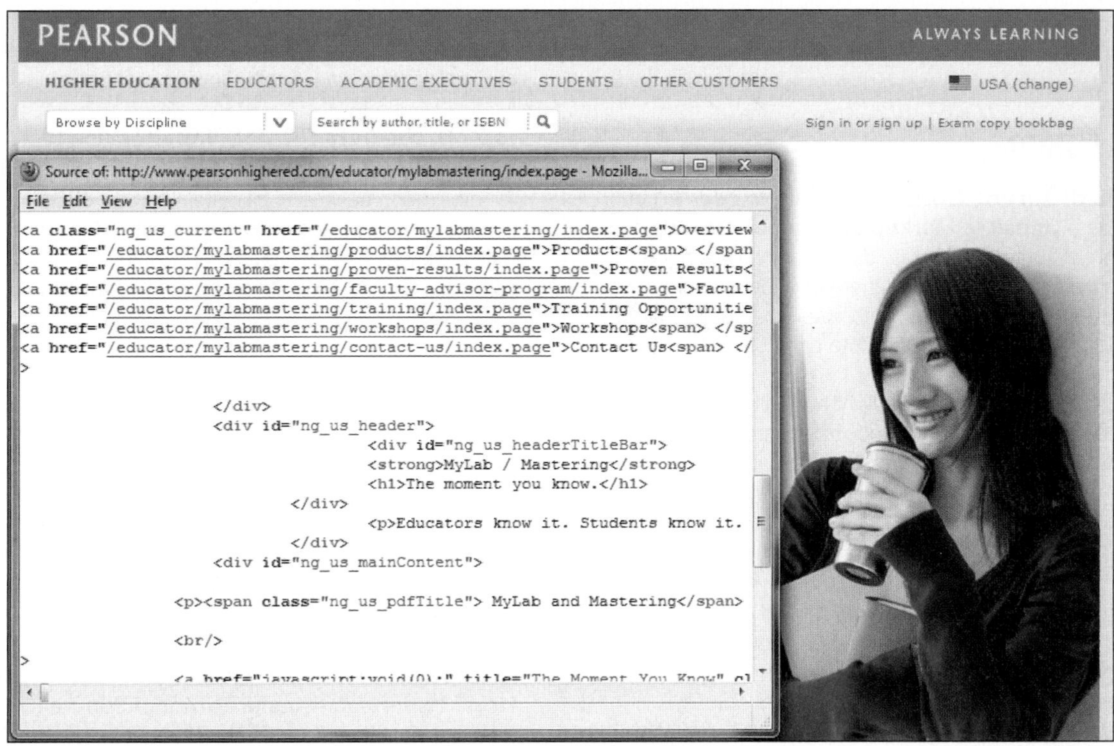


**FIGURE 13.12** You can view the source code of a website by right-clicking and selecting View Source from the shortcut menu.

the style sheet; all the <h1> tags on the web pages then update to yellow without individual changes needing to be made.

**Where does the cascading come in?** In web documents, there are different layers of styles:

- External: stored in a separate file
- Embedded: stored inside the current HTML document
- Inline: stored within a single line inside the HTML document

Therefore, it's possible that different rules can be created for the same type of element located in different places (external, embedded, or inline). In other words, in an external style sheet, there might be a rule that defines the background color for all paragraphs as blue. In an embedded style sheet, a rule for the background color for all paragraphs might be white. And in an inline style sheet, the background color might be light pink. Eventually, all these style sheets must be merged to form one style sheet for the document. This creates conflicts among rules. Therefore, each type of rule is understood to have a specific weight so that when the rules are collected and merged, the rule or style with a higher weight overrides the rule or

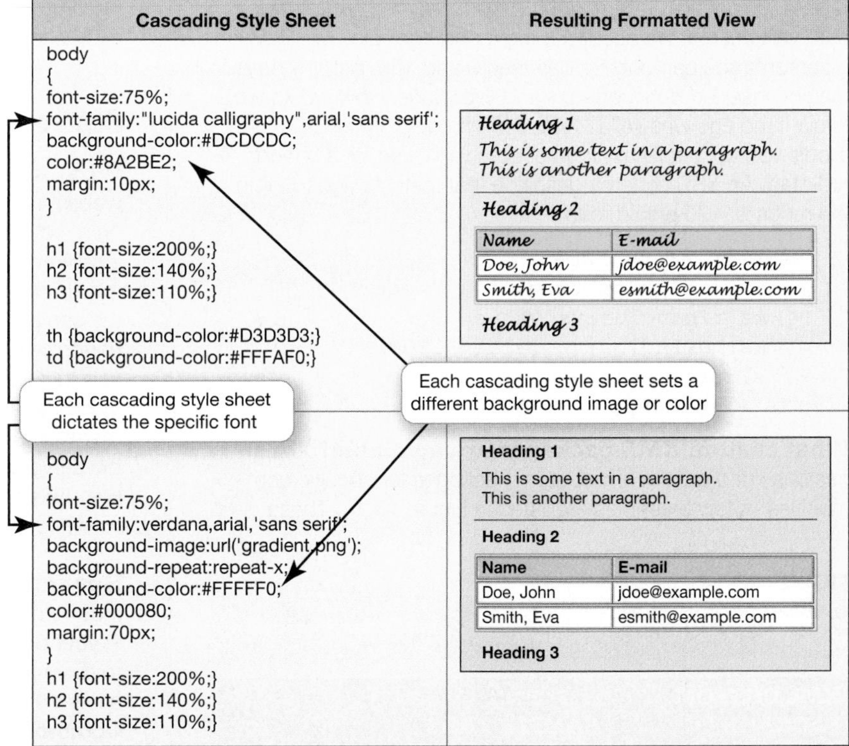


**FIGURE 13.13** Cascading style sheets allow developers to create formatting templates. Just as all the pages of this book have a similar look and feel, one style sheet can control the formatting of many web pages.

style with a lower weight. This hierarchy of competing styles creates a "cascade" of styles ranked according to their assigned weights.

## XML and JSON

**How is XML different from HTML?** As you learned in Chapter 10, the **eXtensible Markup Language (XML)** describes the content in terms of what data is being described rather than how it's to be displayed. Instead of being locked into standard tags and formats for data, users can build their own markup languages to accommodate particular data formats and needs.

For example, say you want to capture a credit card number. In HTML, the paragraph tags (<p> and </p>) are used to define text and numeric elements. Almost any text or graphic can fall between these tags and be treated as a paragraph. The HTML code could appear as:

```
<p>1234567890123456</p>
```

The browser will interpret the data contained within the <p> and </p> tags as a separate paragraph. However, the paragraph tags tell us nothing about the data contained within them. A better approach lies in creating tags that actually *describe* the data contained within them. Using XML we could create a "credit card number" tag that's used exclusively for credit card data:

```
<credit_card_number>1234567890123456
</credit_card_number>
```

In addition, HTML tags don't provide any methodology for data validation. If we needed a tag for an age field, we know a person's age can only be between 0 and 120, but any data may be inserted between <p> and </p> tags. How would we know if the age was valid? *XML schema diagrams (XSDs)* allows you to specify all kinds of data validation for a specific XML tag. An XSD schema definition that restricts age to be in the range 0, 120 would read:

```
<xs:simpleType name= "age">
 <xs:restriction base="xs:integer">
   <xs:minInclusive value="0"/>
   <xs:maxInclusive value="120"/>
 </xs:restriction>
</xs:simpleType>
```

**What custom XML packages are available?** XML has spawned quite a few custom packages for specific communities. A few examples are listed in Figure 13.14. These packages illustrate the goal of XML—information exchange standards that can be easily constructed and customized to serve a growing variety of online applications.

**FIGURE 13.14**

**XML Custom Packages**

| XML CUSTOM PACKAGE | SAMPLE TAGS |
|---|---|
| MathML | <times>, <power>, <divide> |
| X3D | <viewpoint>, <shape>, <scene> |
| MusicML | <score>, <beat>, <measure>, <clef> |

**Is XML the only format websites use to speak to each other?** There is another very popular format used to transfer information between computers named **JSON**. It stands for JavaScript Object Notation and is a data interchange standard that is easy for humans to read and write. JSON is faster and easier to use than XML. It consists of name and value pairs like:

```
"firstName" : "Kendall"
```

## Web Browser Protocols

**Which Internet protocol does a browser use to send requests?** The **Hypertext Transfer Protocol (HTTP)** was created especially for the transfer of hypertext documents across the Internet. (Recall that *hypertext* documents are documents in which text is linked to other documents or media.)

**How does a browser safeguard secure information? Hypertext Transfer Protocol Secure (HTTPS)** ensures that data is sent securely over the web. HTTPS is actually an acronym that's the combination of HTTP and **Secure Sockets Layer (SSL)**, a network security protocol. **Transport Layer Security (TLS)** is an updated extension of SSL. These protocols provide data integrity and security for transmissions over the Internet. Commerce servers use security protocols to protect sensitive information from interception by hackers.

## Server-Side Applications

**What are server-side applications?** As you'll recall, the web is a client/server network. The type of program that runs on a web server rather than on your computer is referred to as a **server-side program**. Server-side program execution can require many communication sessions between the client and the server to achieve the goal, but server-side programs can perform very complex operations.

**What are popular server-side interfaces?** Several methods of designing programs are available that execute on the server and give a web page more sophisticated capabilities. Two of the most popular are *CGI (Common Gateway Interface)* and *ASP.NET (Active Server Pages)*.

**How does CGI make a web page more interactive?** Most browser requests merely result in a file being displayed in your browser. To make a website interactive, you may need to run a program that performs a certain action (such as gathering a name and address and adding it to a database). The **Common Gateway Interface (CGI)** provides a methodology by which your browser can request that a program file be executed instead of just being delivered to the browser. This enables functionality beyond the simple display of information.

SOUND BYTE

**Creating Web Pages with HTML**

Creating simple web pages using Microsoft Word is relatively easy. In this Sound Byte, you'll learn the basics of web page creation by setting up a website featuring a student résumé.

**What programming language is used to create a CGI program?** CGI files can be created in almost any programming language, and the programs created are referred to as **CGI scripts**. Perl is a common language used to create CGI scripts, but other languages, like Python, offer libraries to support it. Almost any task can be accomplished by writing a CGI script. One common task is to collect a user's answers in a form and to create and send out an e-mail message with that information.

**How are CGI programs executed?** On most web servers, a directory called a **cgi-bin** is created by the network administrator who configures the web server. All CGI scripts are placed into this directory. The web server knows that all files in this directory aren't just to be read and sent but also need to be run.

Let's take an example, as shown in Figure 13.15:

**Step 1.** A button on bookworlds.com's website may say, "Click Here to Join Mailing List."

**Step 2.** Clicking the button may execute a script file, called "mailinglist.pl," from the cgi-bin directory on the web server hosting the site.

**Step 3.** This file generates a form that's sent to your browser. The form includes fields for a name and e-mail address and a Submit button.

**Step 4.** After you fill in the fields and click the Submit button, the mailinglist.pl program sends the information back to the server. The server then records the information in a database.

## Client-Side Applications

**What are client-side applications?** A **client-side program** is a program that runs on the client computer and requires no interaction with a web server. Once a web server processes a web page and sends the page to the client computer that requested it, the receiving computer can't get new data from the server unless a new request is made. If interactivity is required on a web page, this exchange of data between the client and server can make the interactivity inefficient and slow. Often it's more efficient to run programs on your computer (the client). Therefore, client-side programs are created.

**How is client-side programming done?** There are two main approaches to client-side programming:

1. An **HTML embedded scripting language**, which tucks programming code directly within the HTML of a web page. The most popular embedded language is *JavaScript*.
2. An **applet**, which is a small application actually located on the server. When requested, the applet is downloaded to the client. It's there ready to run when needed without additional data transfers between the client and server. The Java language is the most common language used to create applets for use in browsers.

**Isn't there a delay as an applet downloads?** You may experience some delay in functionality while waiting for a Java applet to download to your computer, but once the applet arrives, it can execute all its functions without further communication with the server. Games are often sent to your browser as applets. Let's look at an example, as shown in Figure 13.16:

**Step 1.** Your browser makes contact with a game on the game site ArcadePod (**arcadepod.com**) and makes your request to play a game.

**Step 2.** The web server returns the Java applet that contains all the code to run the game on your computer.

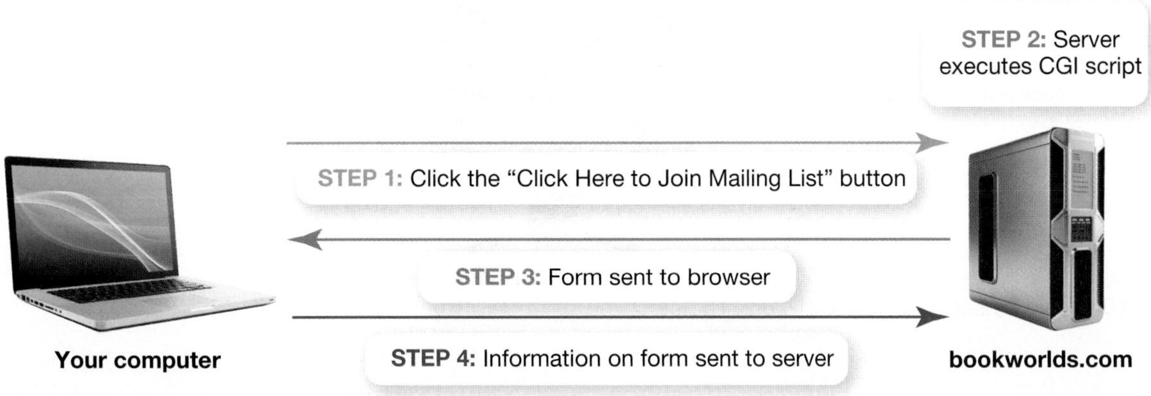


**FIGURE 13.15** Information flow when a CGI program is run.

**Step 3.** Your computer executes the applet code, and the game runs on your computer.

**What are some scripting technologies? Dynamic HTML (DHTML)** is a combination of technologies—HTML, cascading style sheets, and JavaScript—that's used to create lively and interactive websites. DHTML technologies allow a web page to change (that is, to be dynamic) after it's been loaded. Such change generally occurs in response to user actions, such as when you click your mouse or mouse over objects on a page. DHTML also brings special effects to otherwise static web pages without requiring users to download and install plug-ins or other special software.

**What is JavaScript? JavaScript** is a commonly used scripting language for creating DHTML effects. JavaScript is often confused with the Java programming language because of the similarity in their names. However, though they share some common elements, the two languages are different.

With JavaScript, HTML documents can be made responsive to mouse clicks and typing. For example, JavaScript is often used to validate the information you input in a web form, for example, to make sure you filled in all required fields.

When JavaScript code is embedded in an HTML document, it's downloaded to the browser with the HTML page. All actions dictated by the embedded JavaScript commands are executed on the client computer. Without JavaScript and other scripting languages, web pages would be lifeless.

**How does JavaScript control the components of a web page?** Just as cascading style sheets organize and combine the attributes of objects on a web page, JavaScript uses the **Document Object Model (DOM)** to organize the objects and page elements. The Document Object Model defines every item on a web page—including graphics, tables, and headers—as an object. Then with DOM, similar to cascading style sheets, web developers can easily change the look and feel of these objects.

**Where is web programming headed?** Web pages can interact with servers at times other than when a page is being fetched. Web pages can have an ongoing exchange of information, communicating with the server and updating information on the page without requiring the user to do a page refresh or leave the page. AJAX is the acronym for Asynchronous JavaScript and XML, a group of technologies that facilitates the creation of this style of web applications. There are a huge number of web application frameworks now available, like Ruby on Rails. These packages make it simpler to create an application that talks to a web server, queries a database, and then presents information in a nicely formatted template. ■

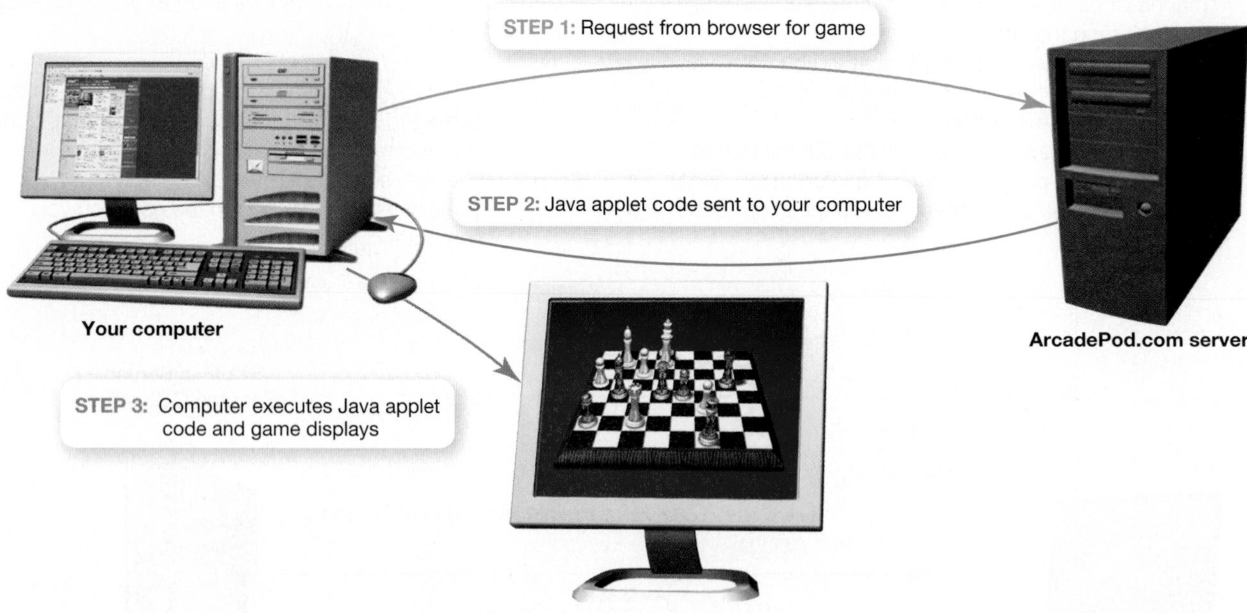
STEP 1: Request from browser for game
STEP 2: Java applet code sent to your computer
Your computer
ArcadePod.com server
STEP 3: Computer executes Java applet code and game displays

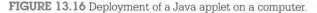

**FIGURE 13.16** Deployment of a Java applet on a computer.

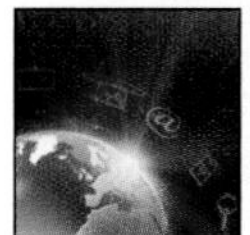

# communications over THE INTERNET

In this section, we explore electronic communications media and how to keep your information exchanges efficient and secure.

## E-Mail

**Who invented e-mail?** In 1971, Ray Tomlinson, a computer engineer who worked on the development of the ARPANET, the precursor to the Internet, created e-mail. E-mail grew from a simple program that Tomlinson wrote to enable computer users to leave text messages for each other on a single machine. The logical extension of this was sending text messages between machines on the Internet. E-mail became the most popular application on ARPANET; by 1973, it accounted for 75% of all data traffic.

**How does e-mail travel the Internet?** Just like other kinds of data that flow along the Internet, e-mail has its own protocol. The **Simple Mail Transfer Protocol (SMTP)** is responsible for sending e-mail along the Internet to its destination. SMTP is part of the Internet Protocol suite. As in most other Internet applications, e-mail is a client/server application. On the way to its destination, your mail will pass through **e-mail servers**—specialized computers whose sole function is to store, process, and send e-mail.

**Where are e-mail servers located?** If your ISP provides you with an e-mail account, it runs an e-mail server that uses SMTP. For example, as shown in Figure 13.17, say you're sending an e-mail message to your friend Cheyenne. Cheyenne uses Verizon as her ISP. Therefore, your e-mail to her is addressed to Cheyenne@verizon.net.

Let's follow that e-mail:

**Step 1.** When you send the e-mail message, your ISP's e-mail server receives it.

**Step 2.** The e-mail server reads the domain name (verizon.net) and communicates with a DNS server to determine the location of verizon.net.

**Step 3.** The DNS server turns the domain name into the associated IP address.

**Step 4.** The e-mail message is forwarded to verizon.net, and it arrives at an e-mail server maintained by Cheyenne's ISP.

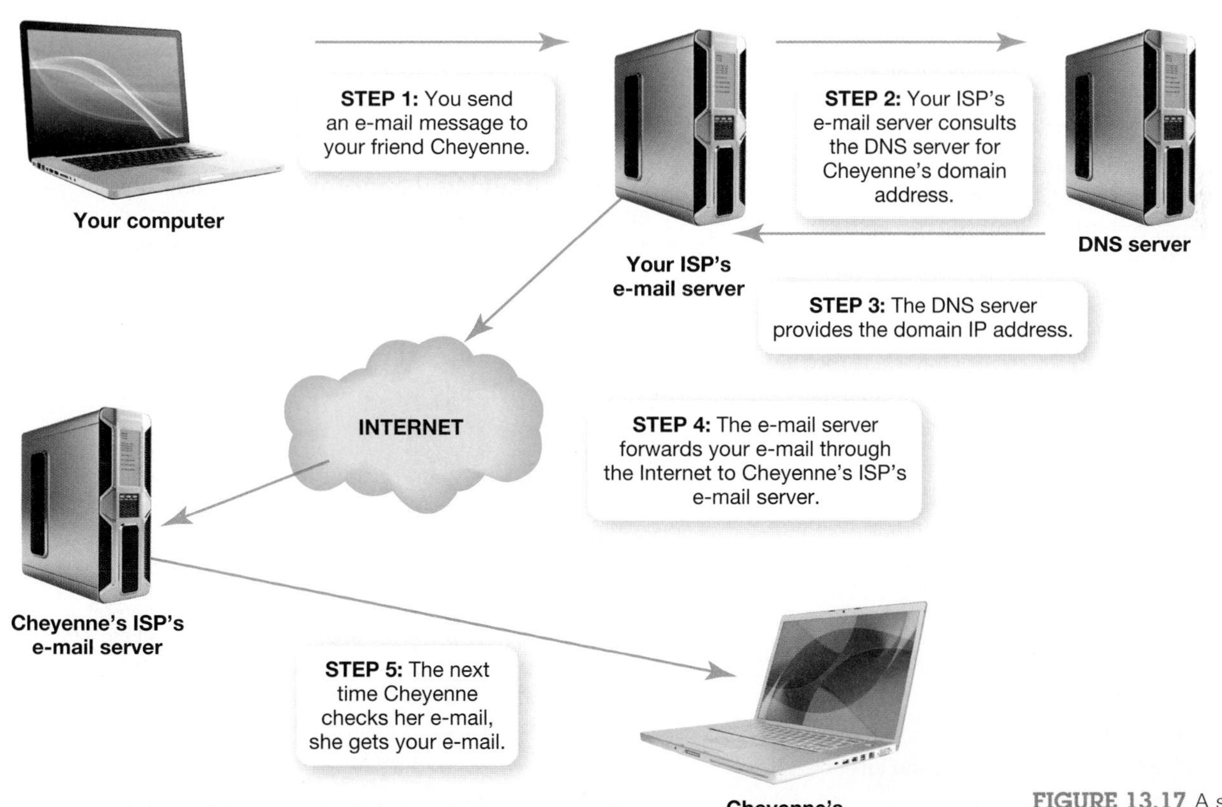


**FIGURE 13.17** A sample route an e-mail takes on the Internet.

**Step 5.** The e-mail is then stored on Cheyenne's ISP's e-mail server. The next time Cheyenne checks her e-mail, she'll receive your message.

**How are we able to send files as attachments?** SMTP was designed to handle text messages. When the need arose to send files by e-mail, the **Multipurpose Internet Mail Extensions (MIME)** specification was introduced. All e-mail client software now uses this protocol to attach files. E-mail is still sent as text, but the e-mail client using the MIME protocol now handles the encoding and decoding for the users. When attaching a file, your e-mail client transparently encodes and decodes the file for transmission and receipt.

# BITS&BYTES

## Gmail Features You Should Know About

Many individuals use Gmail because it's free. But free doesn't mean it isn't full featured. Gmail has some very useful tricks that can save you time, aggravation, and money. Here are a few to consider:

- **Priority inbox:** Enable this feature and Gmail will predict automatically which e-mails are important by watching which e-mails you read and respond to. You can also downgrade or upgrade the importance of an e-mail so your priority inbox becomes fine-tuned over time.
- **Inbox tabs:** Your inbox can be much more manageable using Inbox tabs. Categories like Promotions automatically catch and sort all the offers that are mailed to you.
- **Free phone calls and video calls:** Install the voice and video chat plug-in for Gmail, and you can call anyone in the United States or Canada directly from Gmail—for free! Just click the Call Phone or Start Video Call options in the Chat section of your Gmail screen to initiate the call.
- **Attach money:** Instead of just attaching a file, how about attaching some money? You can tie your Gmail account to a Google Wallet account and send money with just a click.
- **Big files:** You can send files up to 10 GB in size, as long as the files are stored in your Google Drive account.

For even more useful features, click the Labs option on your Gmail settings menu to see the latest and greatest features deployed by Google.

## E-Mail Security: Encryption

**Can other people read my e-mail?** E-mail is highly susceptible to being read by unintended parties because it's sent in plain text. Additionally, copies of your e-mail messages may exist, temporarily or permanently, on numerous servers as the messages make their way through the Internet. To protect your sensitive e-mail messages, encryption practices are available.

**How do I encrypt my e-mail?** Many e-mail services offer built-in encryption. Hushmail (**hushmail.com**) and Comodo SecureEmail (**comodo.com**) offer free versions of their secure e-mail services. You can sign up on their websites and experiment with sending encrypted e-mail. And you don't need to abandon your current e-mail accounts—just use your secure account when you require secure communications.

**How does encryption work? Encryption** refers to the process of coding your e-mail so that only the person with the key to the code (the intended recipient) can decode (or decipher) the message. There are two basic types of encryption:

1. *Private-key encryption*
2. *Public-key encryption*

**What is private-key encryption?** In **private-key encryption**, only the two parties involved in sending the message have the code. This could be a simple shift code where letters of the alphabet are shifted to a new position (see Figure 13.18). For example, in a two-position right-shift code, the letter ***a*** becomes *c*, *b* becomes *d*, and so on. Alternatively, it could be a more complex substitution code (*a* = *h*, *b* = *r*, *c* = *g*, etc.). The main problem with private-key encryption is key security. If someone steals a copy of the code or is savvy about decoding, the code is broken.

**What is public-key encryption?** In **public-key encryption**, two keys, known as a **key pair**, are created. You use one key for coding and the other for decoding.

A = C
B = D
C = E
D = F
E = G
F = H
G = I
H = J
I = K
J = L
K = M
L = N
M = O
N = P
O = Q
P = R
Q = S
R = T
S = U
T = V
U = W
V = X
W = Y
X = Z
Y = A
Z = B

The word **C O M P U T E R** using the two-position code at the left now becomes:

**E Q O R W V G T**

This is difficult to interpret without the code key at the left.

**FIGURE 13.18** Writing the word *COMPUTER* using a two-position right-shift encryption code results in *EQORWVGT*.

# ethics in IT

## Web Browsing: Not as Private as You May Think

Keeping track of where you've been on the Internet can be quite a challenge. Think about how many websites you visited this week. Can you remember them all? Tools built into browser software help us remember. For example, in Internet Explorer and Firefox, the History feature tracks all the sites you've visited over a period of time using the same browser on the same computer. If you have a Google account and use the Google Toolbar (an add-on for Internet Explorer and Firefox), the Google Web History feature tracks your entire browsing history regardless of what computer you may be using (as long as you're logged into your Google account and use the toolbar). But how private is your browsing history?

Most individuals in our society value privacy. But having your browsing habits recorded by the software you're using is tantamount to having someone looking over your shoulder and watching exactly what you're doing. Did you browse to a site today that you wouldn't want your parents, teacher, or boss to know about? If you haven't cleared the history file in your browser, anyone could easily call up the history in your browser and see it (see Figure 13.19).

Google Web History is even more of a conundrum. Your entire browsing history is contained in your Google file for all computers that you use (at home, school, and work). If you're browsing the web at the local coffee shop and haven't taken measures to secure your data transmissions on your notebook, any hacker could potentially intercept and gain access to your entire browsing history. This could reveal places where you have financial resources and help direct hackers to websites where they can attempt to access your accounts. Many people would feel that their privacy was severely violated if their entire web browsing history were seen by a stranger even if that person didn't use that information in a malicious way.

So, where does convenience stop and privacy start? This is one of the thorny ethical dilemmas we face in today's wired world. Having a browser history is convenient when you can't remember the name of a site you visited last week. But having a list of all the sites you visited could be downright embarrassing if your boss looked through it and found out you were surfing the "jobs available" section of a competitor's website. Do you really want the next person to use the computer in the lab at school to know what you were shopping for on the Internet?

Although users can erase browser histories and a Google Web History, this isn't automatic and requires user intervention. The current versions of browsers contain features called InPrivate Browsing (Internet Explorer), Incognito mode (Chrome), and Private Browsing (Firefox) that allow you to surf the web without the browser retaining your history.

Where does convenience end and privacy begin? What do you think?

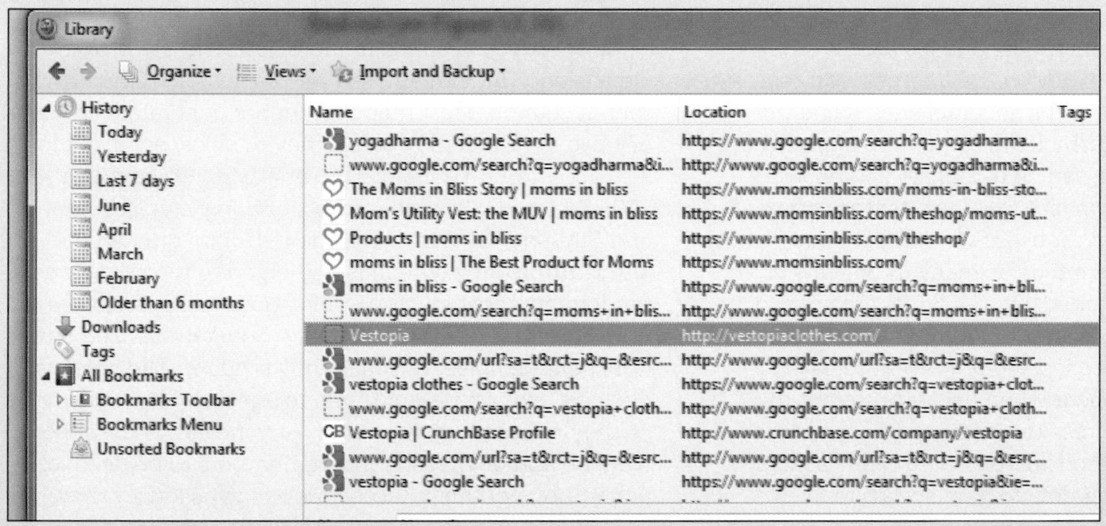


**FIGURE 13.19** Nothing embarrassing in this Firefox Web History. But what's lurking in your browser's history?

ACTIVE HELPDESK

**Keeping E-Mail Secure**

In this Active Helpdesk call, you'll play the role of a helpdesk staffer, fielding calls about how e-mail works and how messages are kept secure.

The key for coding is generally distributed as a **public key**. You can place this key on your website, for instance. Anyone wishing to send you a message can then download your public key and code the message using your public key.

When you receive the message, you use your **private key** to decode it. You're the only one who ever possesses the private key, and therefore it's highly secure. The keys are generated in such a way that they can work only with each other. The private key is generated first. The public key is then generated using a complex mathematical formula, often using values from the private key. The computations are so complex that they're considered unbreakable. Both keys are necessary to decode a message. If one key is lost, the other key can't be used by itself.

**Which type of encryption is used on the Internet?** Public-key encryption is the most commonly used encryption on the Internet. Public-key packages such as **Pretty Good Privacy (PGP)** are available for download at sites such as CNET Downloads (**download.cnet.com**), and you can usually use them free of charge (although there are now commercial versions of PGP). After obtaining the PGP software, you can generate key pairs to provide a private key for you and a public key for the rest of the world.

**What does a key look like?** A key is a binary number. Keys vary in length, depending on how secure they need to be. A 12-bit key has 12 positions and might look like this:

```
100110101101
```

Longer keys are more secure because they have more values that are possible. A 12-bit key provides 4,096 different possible values, whereas a 40-bit key allows for 1,099,511,627,776 possible values. The key and the message are run through a complex algorithm in the encryption program that converts the message into unrecognizable code. Each key turns the message into a different code.

**Is a private key really secure?** Because of the complexity of the algorithms used to generate key pairs, it's impossible to deduce the private key from the public key. However, that doesn't mean your coded message can't be cracked. As you learned in Chapter 12, a brute force attack occurs when hackers try every possible key combination to decode a message. This type of attack can enable hackers to deduce the key and decode the message.

**What kind of key is considered safe?** In the early 1990s, 40-bit keys were thought to be completely resistant to brute force attacks and were the norm for encryption. However, in 1995, a French programmer used a unique algorithm of his own and 120 workstations simultaneously to attempt to break a 40-bit key. He succeeded in just eight days. After this, 128-bit keys became the standard. However, using supercomputers, researchers have had some success cracking 128-bit encryption. Therefore, strong encryption now calls for 256-bit keys. It's believed that even with the most powerful computers

## BITS&BYTES

### Random Numbers: We Wouldn't Have Encryption Without Them!

E-mail encryption, SSL encryption, and just about anything we do to achieve privacy on the Internet requires random numbers. Encryption is accomplished using random number sequences, which are sequences of numbers in which no patterns can be recognized. Even for an e-commerce transaction (say, buying a textbook from **BarnesandNoble.com**) that uses SSL encryption to encode your credit card number, as many as 368 bits of random data might be needed. Only 128 bits are needed for the encryption key, but other random data is needed to create authentication codes and to prevent replay attacks. Replay attacks occur when hackers attempt to copy packets traveling across the Internet and to extract data (such as encryption codes) from them. The hackers then can replay (reuse) the data to gain access to networks or transactions.

So where do all these random numbers come from? Generating true random sequences is more difficult than it sounds. Most random number generators are really pseudo-random because they're all based on some sort of pattern to generate the numbers. However, in 1998, Mads Haahr of the School of Computer Science and Statistics at Trinity College in Dublin created the site **random.org**, which is dedicated to providing true random numbers for web applications such as encryption algorithms. The numbers are generated based on atmospheric noise, which is truly random. The noise is gleaned from radios not tuned to a particular station, so they're broadcasting static. Anyone can access the website and download random numbers to be used for encryption or other vital services such as lottery drawings. For more information, check out **random.org**.

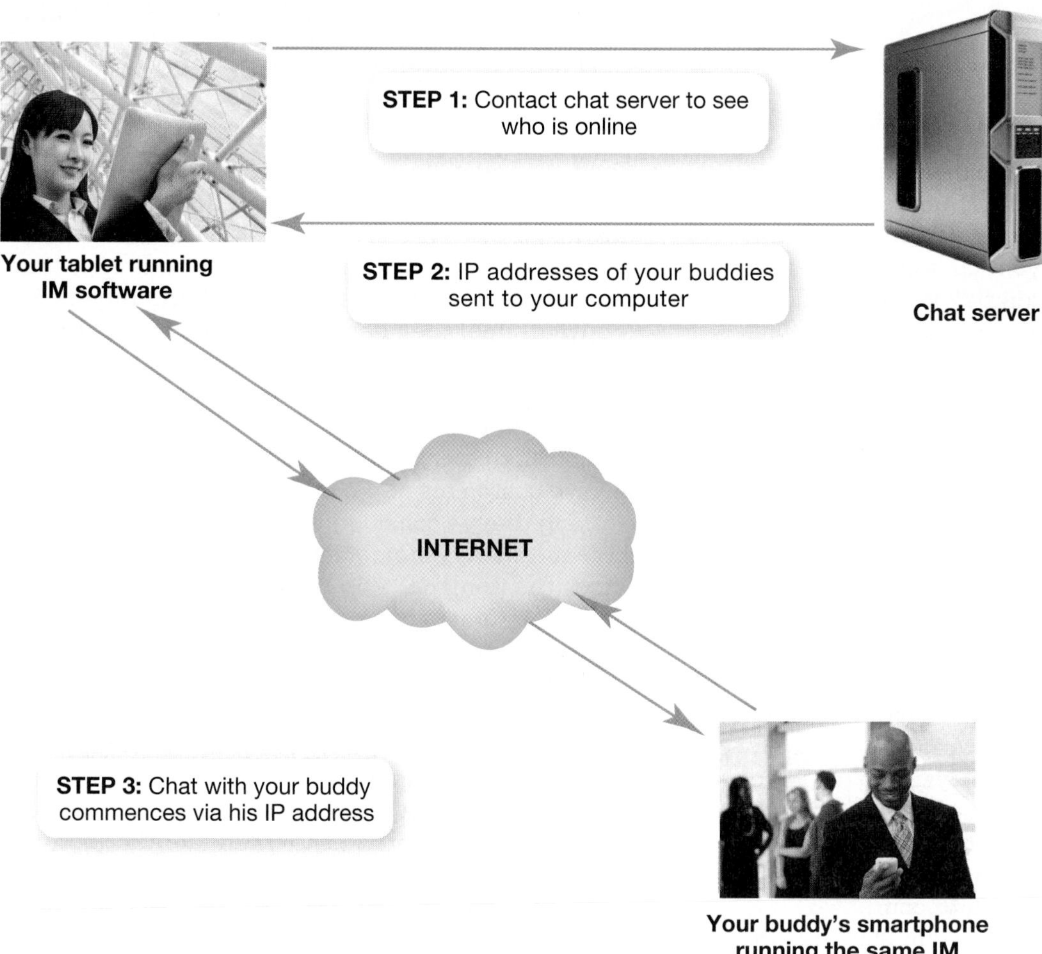
STEP 1: Contact chat server to see who is online
STEP 2: IP addresses of your buddies sent to your computer
Your tablet running IM software
Chat server
INTERNET
STEP 3: Chat with your buddy commences via his IP address
Your buddy's smartphone running the same IM software

**FIGURE 13.20** How an instant messaging program works. *(Tom Wang/Shutterstock; Sashkin/Shutterstock; Tyler Olson/Shutterstock)*

in use today, it would take hundreds of billions of years to crack a 256-bit key.

**Do corporations use special encryption?** Businesses often pay for encryption services that also provide other features such as confirmation of message delivery, message tracking, and overwriting of e-mail messages when they're deleted to ensure that copies don't exist. Companies such as Securus Systems (**safemessage.com**) and ZixCorp (**zixcorp.com**) provide these higher levels of service to businesses.

## Instant Messaging

**What do you need to run instant messaging?** Instant messaging (IM) requires the use of a client program that connects to an IM service. Yahoo! Messenger and GoogleTalk are two popular IM services in use today.

**How does instant messaging work?** The client software running on your device makes a connection with the chat server and provides it with connection information for your device (such as the IP address), as shown in Figure 13.20.

Because both your device and your friend's device have the connection information (the IP addresses) for each other, the server isn't involved in the chat session. Chatting takes place directly between the two devices over the Internet.

**Is sending an IM secure?** Most IM services do not use a high level of encryption for their messages—if they bother to use encryption at all. In addition to viruses, worms, and hacking threats, IM systems are vulnerable to eavesdropping, in which someone using a packet sniffer "listens in" on IM conversations. Although several measures are underway to increase the security of this method of real-time communication, major vulnerabilities still exist. And employers can install monitoring software to record IM sessions. Therefore, it's not a good idea to send sensitive information using IM because it's susceptible to interception and possible misuse by hackers. ■

**Before moving on to the Chapter Review:**
- **Watch Replay Video 13.2** .
- Then check your understanding of what you've learned so far.

# trends in IT

## Crowdsourcing: Harnessing the Power of Social Networks

Starting and running a small business involves risk, especially when you're running a merchandising business. Deciding what products to buy and sell to customers is tricky. Will your customers buy the products you think are wonderful? Will they buy them quickly enough so that you can free up your cash to buy more inventory? What quantities should you stock? If you're an entrepreneur, you usually have to make these decisions yourself. Wouldn't it be better to let your customers tell you what to sell?

Many businesses harness the power of their customers (and potential customers) by using the Internet to take advantage of a technique known as *crowdsourcing*. When you crowdsource, you take a task that an employee or a contractor usually performs and instead outsource that task to a large group of people, usually via the Internet. In this way, you can have many individuals work on a task in order to take advantage of aggregated brainpower. Or you can aggregate and analyze the results of feedback from the crowdsourcers to make informed business decisions. A company that exemplifies the crowdsourcing model of customer-driven merchandise buying is ModCloth (**modcloth.com**).

ModCloth is a company founded in 2002 by two high-school students who were just 17 years old. They started selling only vintage clothing but then expanded to offer vintage-inspired designs by indie designers. When ordering clothing from designers, there's usually a minimum order quantity that often exceeds 100 pieces. Although the buyers for ModCloth feel they have a good eye for what their customers like, it's still risky for a small business to order large quantities of items because they may take a long time to sell.

ModCloth started its Be the Buyer program to involve customers in the buying process. They post clothing they're considering buying on the ModCloth site, and then customers vote to either "Pick It" (stock the item) or "Skip It," as shown in Figure 13.21. Customers can post comments about the items, which range from humorous to constructive. ModCloth also provides links so that voters can easily share items with their friends on social networks like Facebook and Twitter. Constructive ideas from potential customers can be sent back to designers who might make suggested alterations to items before ModCloth orders them. When ModCloth orders a popular item, customers who indicated they liked it can be contacted via e-mail to stimulate sales.

Be part of the businesses you patronize—look for the chance to be heard through crowdsourcing.

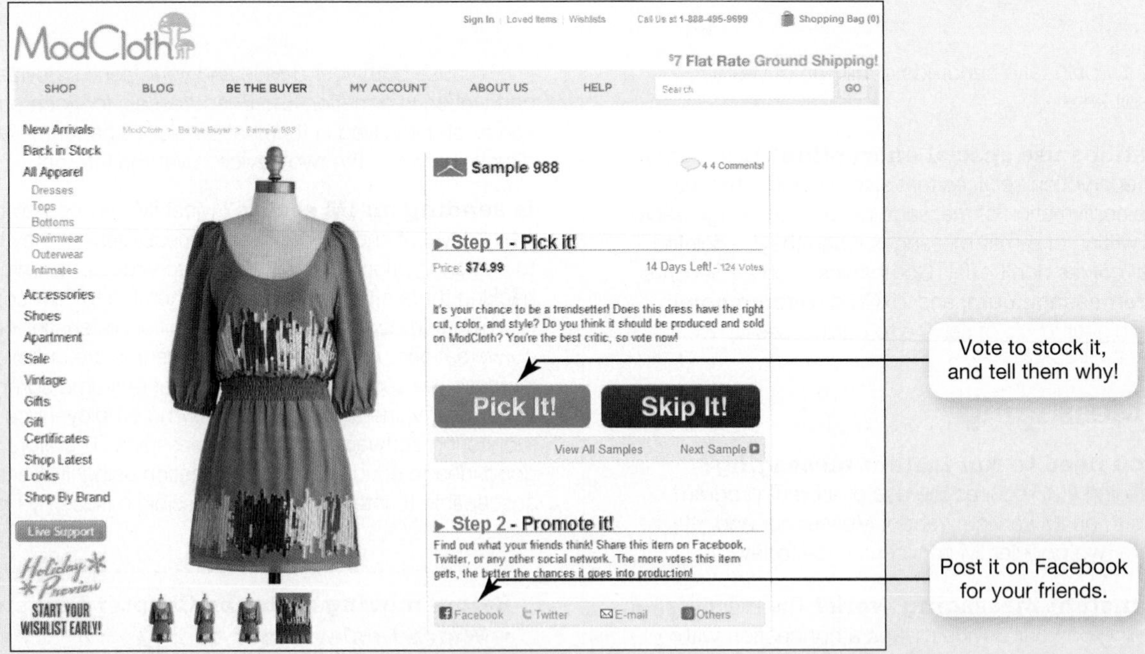


**FIGURE 13.21** Customers vote and comment on products that ModCloth is thinking about stocking. *(Courtesy of ModCloth)*

# check your understanding//

For a quick review to see what you've learned so far, answer the following questions. Visit **pearsonhighered.com/techinaction** to check your answers.

## multiple choice

1. XML and JSON
   - **a.** create a secure connection between client and server.
   - **b.** allow web services to exchange information.
   - **c.** encrypt e-mail messages.
   - **d.** cannot be easily read by humans since they are in binary.
2. The protocol used to send e-mail over the Internet is
   - **a.** HTTP.
   - **b.** DHTML.
   - **c.** DNS.
   - **d.** SMTP.
3. Cascading style sheets allow you to quickly change
   - **a.** from server-side processing to client-side processing.
   - **b.** to a more secure transport protocol.
   - **c.** the rules for applying formatting to an HTML document.
   - **d.** from HTML to XML.
4. A Java applet is
   - **a.** downloaded and run in the client browser software.
   - **b.** executed using JavaScript on the server.
   - **c.** incredibly fast because it has no load time.
   - **d.** software that runs exclusively under Mac OS X.
5. MIME is a protocol that's used when you're
   - **a.** sending a video file to YouTube.
   - **b.** encrypting an e-mail message.
   - **c.** executing a CGI script.
   - **d.** sending an e-mail that has a file attached.

## true-false

_____ **1.** Instant messaging services encrypt with 256-bit keys.

_____ **2.** HTML5 allows you to create your own tags to describe data, like <shoesize>.

## critical thinking

1. **Computer Speak**

   There are two type of communication happening on the Internet at any time: humans to computers and computers to computers. How do these compare? Which do you think represents the largest percentage of Internet traffic? Consider the evolution of the Internet of Things (a term for the growing number of devices that are Internet-enabled). How will that impact the answer in two years?

2. **Breaking Encryption**

   Encryption programs based on 256-bit encryption algorithms are currently considered unbreakable. The U.S. government places restrictions on exports of these encryption products. The government is considering a requirement that all encryption products have a "backdoor" code that would allow government agencies (such as the FBI and CIA) to read encrypted messages. Do you think this backdoor requirement should be implemented?

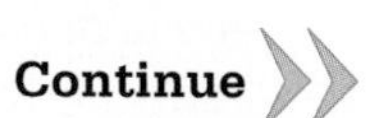

# 13 Chapter Review

## summary//

### The Management of the Internet

**1. Who owns, manages, and pays for the Internet?**

- Management of the Internet is carried out by several nonprofit organizations and user groups such as the Internet Society, the Internet Engineering Task Force (IETF), the Internet Architecture Board (IAB), the Internet Corporation for Assigned Names and Numbers (ICANN), and the World Wide Web Consortium (W3C). Each group has different responsibilities and tasks.
- Currently, the U.S. government funds a majority of the Internet's costs. Other countries also pay for Internet infrastructure and development.

### Internet Networking, Data Transmission, and Protocols

**2. How do the Internet's networking components interact?**

- Computing devices or networks connect to the Internet using Internet service providers (ISPs). These providers vary in size and work like the physical highway system.
- The largest paths of the Internet, along which data travels the most efficiently and quickly, make up the Internet backbone. Homes and all but the largest businesses connect to the Internet through regional or local connections, which then connect to the Internet through the entities that make up the Internet backbone. The largest businesses, educational centers, and some government agencies make up the Internet backbone.
- Optical carrier (OC) lines are high throughput and are used to connect large corporations to their ISPs.
- Service providers use an Internet exchange point (IXP) to connect directly to each other, reducing cost and latency time.
- Individual users enter their ISP through a point of presence (POP), a bank of routers and switches through which many users can connect simultaneously.

**3. What data transmissions and protocols does the Internet use?**

- Data is transmitted along the Internet using packet switching. Data is broken up into discrete units known as *packets*, which can take independent routes to the destination before being reassembled.
- A computer protocol is a set of rules for exchanging electronic information. Although many protocols are available on the Internet, the main suite of protocols used to move information over the Internet is TCP/IP. The suite is named after the original two protocols that were developed for the Internet: the Transmission Control Protocol (TCP) and the Internet Protocol (IP).
- TCP is responsible for preparing data for transmission, but IP actually sends data between computers on the Internet.

### Internet Identity: IP Addresses and Domain Names

**4. Why are IP addresses and domain names important for Internet communications?**

- An IP address is a unique number assigned to all computers connected to the Internet. The IP address is necessary so that packets of data can be sent to a particular location (computer) on the Internet.
- A domain name is merely a name that stands for a certain IP address and that makes it easier for people to remember it.
- DNS servers act as the phone books of the Internet. They enable your computer to find out the IP address of a domain by looking up its corresponding domain name.

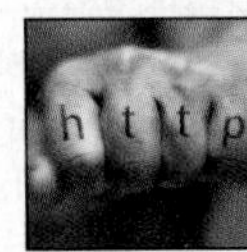


### HTML, XML, and Other Web Building Blocks

**5. What web technologies are used to develop web applications?**

- The Hypertext Transfer Protocol (HTTP) is the protocol used on the Internet to display web pages in your browser.

- The Hypertext Markup Language (HTML) is a set of rules for marking up blocks of text so that a browser knows how to display them. Most web pages are generated with at least some HTML code.
- Blocks of text in HTML documents are surrounded by a pair of tags (such as <b> and </b> to indicate bolding). These tags and the text between them are referred to as ***elements***. By examining the elements, your browser determines how to display the text on your computer screen.
- The HTML standard is being updated to HTML5, which offers much better support for media like audio and video.
- Because HTML wasn't designed for information exchange, eXtensible Markup Language (XML) was created. Instead of locking users into standard tags and formats for data, XML enables users to create their own markup languages to accommodate particular data formats and needs. JSON is another standard supporting the exchange of information between web services.
- Software is developed on both the server and on the client side to make web pages more responsive and interactive. Server-side programming includes CGI and ASP.NET. Client-side programs can run faster because they don't need to wait for information exchanges with the server. Embedded JavaScript and Java applets are two common approaches for writing client-side programs.

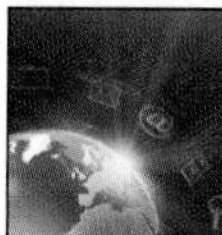

## Communications Over the Internet

**6. How do e-mail and instant messaging work, and how is information using these technologies kept secure?**

- Simple Mail Transfer Protocol (SMTP) is the protocol responsible for sending e-mail over the Internet.
- E-mail is a client/server application. E-mail passes through e-mail servers, whose functions are to store, process, and send e-mail to its ultimate destination. ISPs and portals such as Gmail maintain e-mail servers to provide e-mail functionality to their customers.
- Your ISP's e-mail server uses DNS servers to locate the IP addresses for the recipients of the e-mail you send.
- Encryption software, such as Pretty Good Privacy (PGP), is used to code messages so that they can be decoded only by authorized recipients.
- Instant messaging (IM) software communicates with a chat server to quickly deliver communications to your friends who are online. It's not secure and can be vulnerable to eavesdropping.

Be sure to check out the companion website for additional materials to help you review and learn, including a Tech Bytes Weekly newsletter—**pearsonhighered.com/techinaction**. And don't forget the Replay Videos.

## key terms//

applet **549**
cascading style sheet **546**
CGI script **549**
cgi-bin **549**
circuit switching **535**
classless interdomain routing (CIDR) **540**
client/server model **534**
client-side program **549**
commerce server **534**
Common Gateway Interface (CGI) **548**
computer protocol **535**
connectionless protocol **538**
connection-oriented protocol **538**
Document Object Model (DOM) **550**
domain name system (DNS) server **542**
dotted decimal number (dotted quad) **537**
dynamic addressing **540**
Dynamic Host Configuration Protocol (DHCP) **540**
dynamic HTML (DHTML) **550**
element **546**
e-mail server **551**
encryption **552**
eXtensible Markup Language (XML) **548**
file server **534**
handshaking **538**
hexadecimal digit **540**
HTML embedded scripting language **549**
HTML tag **546**
Hypertext Transfer Protocol (HTTP) **548**
Hypertext Transfer Protocol Secure (HTTPS) **548**
Internet backbone **533**
Internet cache **540**
Internet Corporation for Assigned Names and Numbers (ICANN) **537**
Internet exchange point (IXP) **534**
Internet Protocol (IP) **536**
Internet Protocol version 4 (IPv4) **540**
Internet Protocol version 6 (IPv6) **540**
IP address **537**
JavaScript **550**
JSON **548**
key pair **552**
Multipurpose Internet Mail Extensions (MIME) **552**
negative acknowledgment (NAK) **538**
network prefix **540**
octet **537**
open system **535**
optical carrier (OC) line **533**
packet (data packet) **535**
packet switching **535**
point of presence (POP) **534**
positive acknowledgment (ACK) **538**
Pretty Good Privacy (PGP) **554**
private key **554**
private-key encryption **552**
proprietary system **535**
public key **554**
public-key encryption **552**
root DNS server **542**
second-level domain **541**
Secure Sockets Layer (SSL) **548**
server-side program **548**
Simple Mail Transfer Protocol (SMTP) **551**
static addressing **540**
T line **533**
TCP/IP **536**
three-way handshake **538**
Transmission Control Protocol (TCP) **536**
Transport Layer Security (TLS) **548**
User Datagram Protocol (UDP) **538**
web server **534**

## making the transition to . . . next semester//

1. **Registering a Domain Name**

   A friend of yours wants to launch a company offering a line of T-shirts and other clothing for bicycling enthusiasts. She needs a catchy domain name. Develop five good domain name candidates for the company. Check **networksolutions.com** to see if the domain names are available. Are any of the ones you created available for sale? Check on **sedo.com** and **buydomains.com**.

2. **Code on the Client Side**

   Next semester you are taking a geography course and want to build some applications using maps. Take a look at the Google Maps JavaScript API (Application Programming Interface). What does the JavaScript code look like to render a simple map? What information do you need to provide? What options can you control to customize the map view?

## making the transition to . . . the workplace//

1. **Website Privacy Issues**

   Your employer, a distributor of aftermarket automotive accessories, recently discovered that an employee was using his Facebook account to post disparaging remarks about the company president. The employee was fired. Is this legal in your state? Should an employer have the right to fire a person for expressing an opinion on a social networking site?

2. **Creating an Online Presence for a Business**

   You work at a local coffee shop that offers live music on the weekends. Your boss has asked you to help the coffee shop enhance its web presence to better connect with customers. On which social networking sites would you create a page for the coffee shop? What types of information would you post on the social network pages? What strategies would you use to make customers aware of the coffee shop's social networking sites?

3. **"Googling" Yourself**

   At your company, someone was just fired because sensitive information related to a company product was associated with the person's name on the Internet. Discretion being the better part of valor, you decide to do a search for your name on the web using a search engine such as Google (**google.com**) just to see what is out there. Prepare a report on what you found. Your report should answer the following questions:

   **a.** Did you find any accurate information about yourself (such as your home page URL or résumé)? Did you find any erroneous information that you need to correct?

   **b.** Did you find websites or information about other people with the same name as you? Could any of that information be damaging to your reputation if someone thought the other person was you? If so, provide examples.

   **c.** Is there information that you found about yourself or others that you think should never be available on the Internet? Provide examples and an explanation of why you feel certain information shouldn't be available.

   **d.** Is there any information on social networking sites, such as Google+ or Facebook, that could be damaging to you if an employer or school administrator were to see it?

team time//

# Using Crowdsourcing in a Business

## Background

In today's fast-paced business environment, determining the right merchandise to sell is more critical than ever. Having a website that's designed to use crowdsourcing—either to gather information about products you already carry, such as customer reviews on Amazon, or to determine what merchandise you're going to stock—provides you with a competitive advantage. In this Team Time, you'll consider how best to take advantage of crowdsourcing in starting a new business venture.

## Task

Your teacher has been contacted by the local chamber of commerce. There are three individuals starting new businesses who have requested help in designing their websites and their customer interaction programs. The businesses are (a) a coffee shop that offers live music on nights and weekends; (b) a clothing company for young, urban professionals; and (c) a company that sells iPad, iPod, and iPhone accessories. You need to help these businesses choose appropriate domain names for their companies and suggest a crowdsourcing strategy for the businesses.

## Process

Break the class into small teams of three or four students. Each team should select one of the businesses described previously (or select their own business type). Multiple teams could work on the same type of business. Each team should prepare a report as follows:

1. Determine an appropriate domain name for the company's website. Make sure that the web address you propose is available by using a Whois service such as **whois.net**.
2. Decide on the general types of products that will be sold by the company. For each category of product, decide what product attributes you feel customers will comment on when giving input on products to be sold on the site.
3. Decide if the company will solicit feedback from potential customers on all products to be sold or whether the company will offer a core selection of products without soliciting feedback from customers. Divide the products into two lists: core products and products subject to crowdsourcing.
4. Determine a social networking strategy for the company to promote its products on Facebook, Twitter, and other sites. How will customers be driven to the company website to participate in the crowdsourcing for incentives, discount coupons, contests, and such?
5. Develop a PowerPoint presentation to summarize your findings and present your proposed solution to the class.

## Conclusion

E-commerce websites are relatively cheap and easy to deploy using the vast array of tools available on the Internet today. But substantial risk exists when financing and stocking products to be sold. Gathering crowdsourcing feedback can help businesses minimize the risk of stocking unwanted products.

# Privacy at School

In this exercise, you'll research and then role-play a complicated ethical situation. The role you play might not match your own personal beliefs; regardless, your research and use of logic will enable you to represent the view assigned. An arbitrator will watch and comment on both sides of the arguments, and together, the team will agree on an ethical solution.

## Problem

Many Americans consider privacy to be a fundamental and unalienable right even though privacy isn't specifically spelled out as a right in the U.S. Constitution or the Bill of Rights. Parents are especially concerned about protecting their children's privacy rights. With the widespread use of technology, infringing on personal privacy rights has become easier, even if it's often done innocently or inadvertently.

School administrators are quickly learning that they need to craft policies that set appropriate boundaries and guidelines for monitoring students. Should school districts be allowed to monitor students? Should school districts be required to inform students and parents of any monitoring that takes place?

## Research Areas to Consider

- Lower Merion school district in Pennsylvania using webcams to monitor students in their homes
- Schools using the Geo Listening service to monitor students' social media posts
- The Family Educational Rights and Privacy Act (FERPA)

## Process

1. Divide the class into teams.
2. Research the areas cited above and devise a scenario in which a school district has been monitoring students without their knowledge and has potentially violated their privacy.
3. Team members should write a summary that provides background information for their character—for example, student, parent, school official, or arbitrator—and that details their character's behaviors to set the stage for the role-playing event. Then, team members should create an outline to use during the role-playing event.
4. Team members should arrange a mutually convenient time to meet for the exchange, using a virtual meeting tool or by meeting in person.
5. Team members should present their case to the class or submit a PowerPoint presentation for review by the rest of the class, along with the summary and resolution they developed.

## Conclusion

As technology becomes ever more prevalent and integrated into our lives, ethical dilemmas will present themselves to an increasing extent. Being able to understand and evaluate both sides of the argument, while responding in a personally or socially ethical manner, will be an important skill.

# Glossary

**3-D sound card** An expansion card that enables a computer to produce omnidirectional or three-dimensional sounds.

**4G** The latest mobile communication standard with faster data transfer rates than 3G

## A

**access card reader** A device that reads information from a magnetic strip on the back of a credit card–like access card.

**access method** A method to control which computer is allowed to use transmission media at a certain time.

**access time** The time it takes a storage device to locate its stored data.

**accounting software** An application program that helps business owners manage their finances more efficiently by providing tools for tracking accounting transactions such as sales, accounts receivable, inventory purchases, and accounts payable.

**ActionScript** The programming language used by Adobe Flash; similar to JavaScript.

**Active Server Pages (ASP)** Programming language used to build websites with interactive capabilities; adapts an HTML page to the user's selections.

**active topology** In a network, a type of topology where the nodes participate in moving data through the network.

**Adobe Flash** A software product for developing web-based multimedia.

**adware** A program that downloads on your computer when a user installs a freeware program, game, or utility. Generally, adware enables sponsored advertisements to appear in a section of a browser window or as a pop-up ad.

**affective computing** A type of computing that relates to emotion or that deliberately tries to influence emotion.

**aggregator** A software program that finds and retrieves the latest update of web material (usually podcasts) according to your specifications.

**AJAX (Asynchronous JavaScript and XML)** A collection of technologies that allow the creation of web applications that can update information on a page without requiring the user to refresh or leave the page.

**algorithm** A set of specific, sequential steps that describe exactly what the computer program must do to complete the required work.

**all-in-one computer** A desktop system unit that houses the computer's processor, memory, and monitor in a single unit.

**all-in-one printer** Combines the functions of a printer, scanner, copier, and fax into one machine.

**alphabetic check** In a database, confirms that only textual characters are entered in a field.

**analog** Waves that illustrate the loudness of a sound or the brightness of the colors in an image at a given moment in time.

**analog-to-digital converter chip** Converts analog signals into digital signals.

**antivirus software** Software specifically designed to detect viruses and protect a computer and files from harm.

**app bars** Bars that float above the screen and that contain applications such as the Tabs bar and the Address bar; a new feature of Internet Explorer 10.

**applet** A small application located on a server; when requested, the applet is downloaded to the client.

**application programming interface (API)** A set of software routines that allows one software system to work with another.

**application server** A server that acts as a repository for application software.

**application software** The set of programs on a computer that helps a user carry out tasks such as word processing, sending e-mail, balancing a budget, creating presentations, editing photos, taking an online course, and playing games.

**architecture neutral** A feature of Java whereby code needs to be compiled only once, after which the code can be run on many different CPUs.

**artificial intelligence** The branch of computer science that deals with the attempt to create computers that think like humans.

**aspect ratio** The width-to-height proportion of a monitor.

**assembly language** See *second-generation language (2GL)*.

**audio-editing software** Programs that perform basic editing tasks on audio files such as cutting dead air space from the beginning or end of a song or cutting a portion from the middle.

**audio MIDI interface** Interface technology that allows a user to connect guitars and microphones to their computer.

**augmented reality** A combination of our normal sense of the objects around us with an overlay of information displayed.

**authentication** The process of identifying a computer user, based on a login or username and password. The computer system determines whether the computer user is authorized and what level of access is to be granted on the network.

**authentication server** A server that keeps track of who's logging on to the network and which services on the network are available to each user.

## B

**backdoor program** Program that enables a hacker to take complete control of a computer without the legitimate user's knowledge or permission.

**backup** A copy of a computer file that can be used to replace the original if it's lost or damaged.

**backward compatibility** The accommodation of current devices being able to use previously issued software standards in addition to the current standards.

**bandwidth** The maximum speed at which data can be transmitted between two nodes on a network; usually measured in megabits per second (Mbps). See also *data transfer rate*.

**base class** In object-oriented analysis, the original class.

**base transceiver station** A large communications tower with antennas, amplifiers, and receivers/transmitters.

**basic input/output system (BIOS)** A program that manages the data between a computer's operating system and all the input and output devices attached to the computer; also responsible for loading the operating system (OS) from its permanent location on the hard drive to random access memory (RAM).

**bastion host** A heavily secured server located on a special perimeter network between the company's secure internal network and its firewall.

**batch processing** The accumulation of transaction data until a certain point is reached, at which time several transactions are processed at once.

**beta version** A version of the software that's still under development. Many beta versions are available for a limited trial period and are used to help the developers correct any errors before they launch the software on the market.

**binary decision** A type of decision point in an algorithm that can be answered in one of only two ways: yes (true) or no (false).

**binary digit (bit)** A digit that corresponds to the on and off states of a computer's switches. A bit contains a value of either 0 or 1.

**binary language** The language computers use to process data into information, consisting of only the values 0 and 1.

**biometric authentication device** A device that uses some unique characteristic of human biology to identify authorized users.

**black-hat hacker** A hacker who uses his or her knowledge to destroy information or for illegal gain.

**binary large object (BLOB)** See *unstructured data.*

**blog** A personal log or journal posted on the web; short for *web log*.

**Bluetooth (technology)** A type of wireless technology that uses radio waves to transmit data over short distances (approximately 3–300 feet depending on power); often used to connect peripherals such as printers and keyboards to computers or headsets to cell phones.

**Blu-ray disc (BD)** A method of optical storage for digital data, developed for storing high-definition media. It has the largest storage capacity of all optical storage options.

**bookmarks** Features in some browsers that place markers of websites' Uniform Resource Locators (URLs) in an easily retrievable list.

**Boolean operator** A word used to refine logical searches. For Internet searches, the words AND, NOT, and OR describe the relationships between keywords in the search.

**boot process** The process for loading the operating system (OS) into random access memory (RAM) when the computer is turned on.

**boot-sector virus** A virus that replicates itself into the master boot record of a flash drive or hard drive.

**botnet** A large group of software applications (called *robots* or *bots*) that run without user intervention on a large number of computers.

**breadcrumb trail** A navigation aid that shows users the path they have taken to get to a web page or where the page is located within the website; it usually appears at the top of a page.

**bridge** A device that's used to send data between different collision domains in a network, depending on where the recipient device is located.

**broadband** A high-speed Internet connection such as cable, satellite, or digital subscriber line (DSL).

**brute force attack** An attempt to access an account by repeatedly trying different passwords.

**bus (linear bus) topology** A system of networking connections in which all devices are connected in sequence on a single cable.

**business intelligence systems** Systems used to analyze and interpret data in order to enable managers to make informed decisions about how best to run a business.

**business-to-business (B2B)** E-commerce transactions between businesses.

**business-to-consumer (B2C)** E-commerce transactions between businesses and consumers.

**byte** Eight binary digits (bits).

## C

**C** A programming language originally developed for system programmers.

**C++** A programming language; takes C to an object-oriented level.

**C#** A Microsoft programming language developed to compete with Java.

**cable Internet** A broadband service that transmits data over coaxial cables.

**cache memory** Small blocks of memory, located directly on and next to the central processing unit (CPU) chip, that act as holding places for recently or frequently used instructions or data that the CPU accesses the most. When these instructions or data are stored in cache memory, the CPU can more quickly retrieve them than if it had to access the instructions or data from random access memory (RAM).

**cascading style sheet** A list of rules that defines in one single location how to display HTML elements.

**Cat 6 cable** A UTP cable type that provides more than 1 Gb/s of throughput.

**cellular (cell) phone** A telephone that operates over a mobile network. Cell phones can also offer Internet access, text messaging, personal information management (PIM) features, and more.

**central processing unit (CPU, or processor)** The part of the system unit of a computer that is responsible for data processing; it is the largest and most important chip in the computer. The CPU controls all the functions performed by the computer's other components and processes all the commands issued to it by software instructions.

**centralized** A characteristic of client/server networks where the server, not the individual user, coordinates data security.

**cgi-bin** On a web server, a directory created by the network administrator who configures the web server.

**CGI script** A CGI program file.

**charms** Special shortcuts for performing common tasks, such as searching or sharing information, created for Windows 8.

**circuit switching** Where a dedicated connection is formed between two points (such as two people on telephones) and the connection remains active for the duration of the transmission.

**class** A category of input identified in object-oriented analysis; classes are defined by information and actions.

**classless interdomain routing (CIDR)** An Internet addressing scheme that allows a single Internet protocol (IP) address to represent several unique IP addresses by adding a *network prefix* to the last octet.

**clickstream data** Software used on company websites to capture information about each click that users make as they navigate through the site.

**client** A computer that requests information from a server in a client/server network (such as your computer when you are connected to the Internet).

**client/server model** A model of network communications where a client device such as a computer, tablet, or smartphone uses browsers to request services from networks that make up the Internet.

**client/server network (server-based network)** A type of network that uses servers to deliver services to computers that are requesting them (clients).

**client-side program** A program that runs on the client computer and that requires no interaction with a web server.

**clock speed** The steady and constant pace at which a computer goes through machine cycles, measured in hertz (Hz).

**cloud computing** The process of storing data, files, and applications on the web, which allows access to and manipulation of these files and applications from any Internet-connected device.

**cloud server** A server that is maintained by a hosting company and that is connected to networks via the Internet.

**cluster** The smallest increment in which data is stored on hard disks; hard disks are divided into *tracks*, then *wedges*, then *sectors*, then clusters.

**coaxial cable** A single copper wire surrounded by layers of plastic insulation, metal sheathing, and a plastic jacket; used mainly in cable television and cable Internet service.

**code editing** The step of programming in which a programmer types the code to be executed.

**codec** A rule, implemented in either software or hardware, which squeezes a given amount of audio and video information into less space.

**coding** Translating an algorithm into a programming language.

**cognitive surplus** The combination of leisure time and the tools needed to be creative.

**cold boot** The process of starting a computer from a powered-down or off state.

**collaborative consumption** Joining together as a group to use a specific product more efficiently.

**command-driven interface** Interface between user and computer in which the user enters commands to communicate with the computer system.

**comment** A note left by a programmer in the program code to explain the purpose of a section of code, to indicate the date the program was written, or to include other important information about the code so that other programmers can more easily understand and update it.

**commerce server** Computers that host software that enables users to buy goods and services over the web.

**Common Gateway Interface (CGI)** A method of designing programs that provides a methodology by which a browser can request a program file be executed instead of just being delivered to the browser.

**communications server** A server that handles all communications between the network and other networks, including managing Internet connectivity.

**compact disc (CD)** A method of optical storage for digital data; originally developed for storing digital audio.

**compilation** The process by which code is converted into machine language—the language the central processing unit can understand.

**compiler** A program that understands both the syntax of the programming language and the exact structure of the central processing unit and its machine language.

**completeness check** In a database, ensures that all required fields have been completed.

**computer** A data-processing device that gathers, processes, outputs, and stores data and information.

**computer-aided design (CAD)** A 3-D modeling program used to create automated designs, technical drawings, and model visualizations.

**computer forensics** The application of computer systems and techniques to gather potential legal evidence; a law enforcement specialty used to fight high-tech crime.

**computer literate** Being familiar enough with computers that a user knows how to use them and understands their capabilities and limitations.

**computer protocol** A set of rules for exchanging electronic information.

**connection-oriented protocol** A protocol for exchanging information that requires two computers to exchange control packets, thereby setting up the parameters of the data-exchange session, before sending packets that contain data.

**connectionless protocol** A protocol that a host computer can use to send data over the network without establishing a direct connection with any specific recipient computer.

**connectivity port** A port that enables a computing device to be connected to other devices or systems such as networks, modems, and the Internet.

**consistency check** In a database, compares the values of data in two or more fields to see if those values are reasonable.

**consumer-to-consumer (C2C)** E-commerce transactions between consumers through online sites such as eBay.

**control structure** General term used for a keyword in a programming language that allows the programmer to direct the flow of the program based on a decision.

**cookie** A small text file that some websites automatically store on a client computer's hard drive when a user visits the site.

**copyleft** A simplified licensing scheme that enables copyright holders to grant certain rights to a work while retaining other rights.

**core** A complete processing section from a central processing unit, embedded into one physical chip.

**course management software** A program that provides traditional classroom tools, such as calendars and grade books, over the Internet, as well as areas for students to exchange ideas and information in chat rooms, discussion forums, and e-mail.

**CPU benchmarks** Measurements used to compare performance between processors.

**CPU usage** The percentage of time the central processing unit (CPU) is working.

**CPU usage graph** Records your central processing unit (CPU) usage for the past several seconds.

**crisis-mapping tool** A tool that collects information from e-mails, text messages, blog posts, and Twitter tweets and maps them, making the information instantly publicly available.

**crowdfunding** Asking for small donations from a large number of people, often using the Internet; a style of generating capital to start a business through social media.

**crowdsourcing** The phenomenon of consumers checking in with the voice of the crowd before making purchases.

**CSMA/CD** The method used on Ethernet networks to avoid data collisions; short for *carrier sense multiple access with collision detection*. A node connected to the network uses carrier sense to verify that no other nodes are currently transmitting data signals.

**custom installation** The process of installing only those features of a software program that a user wants on the hard drive.

**cybercrime** Any criminal action perpetrated primarily through the use of a computer.

**cybercriminal** An individual who uses computers, networks, and the Internet to perpetrate crime.

**cyberloafing** Doing anything with a computer that's unrelated to a job (such as playing video games) while one's supposed to be working. Also called *cyberslacking*.

## D

**data** Numbers, words, pictures, or sounds that represent facts, figures, or ideas; the raw input that users have at the start of a job.

**data breach** When sensitive or confidential information is copied, transmitted, or viewed by an individual who is not authorized to handle the data.

**data centralization** When data is maintained in only one file.

**data collision** When two computers send data at the same time and the sets of data collide somewhere in the connection media.

**data dictionary (database schema)** A map of a database that defines the features of the fields in the database.

**data file** A file that contains stored data.

**data-flow diagrams** Diagrams that trace all data in an information system from the point at which data enters the system to its final resting place (storage or output).

**data inconsistency** Data for a record being different in two different lists.

**data integrity** When the data in a database is accurate and reliable.

**data mart** Small slices of a data warehouse grouped together and separated from the main body of data in the data warehouse so that related sets of data can be analyzed.

**data mining** The process by which great amounts of data are analyzed and investigated. The objective is to spot significant patterns or trends within the data that would otherwise not be obvious.

**data plan** A connectivity plan or text messaging plan in which data charges are separate from cell phone calling charges and are provided at rates different from those for voice calls.

**data redundancy** Duplicated data in a list.

**data staging** The act of formatting data from source databases before fitting it into a data warehouse; it consists of three steps: extraction, transformation, and storage.

**data transfer rate** The maximum speed at which data can be transmitted between two nodes on a network; measured in megabits per second (Mbps) or gigabits per second (Gbps).

**data type (field type)** (1) Describes the kind of data being stored at the memory location; each programming language has its own data types (although there is some degree of overlap). (2) In a database, indicates what type of data can be stored in a field and prevents the wrong type of data from being entered into the field.

**data warehouse** A large-scale collection of data that contains and organizes in one place all the data from an organization's multiple databases.

**database** A digital collection of related data that can be stored, sorted, organized, and queried.

**database administrator (database designer)** An information technology professional responsible for designing, constructing, and maintaining databases.

**database management system (DBMS)** A specially designed application software used to create and manage databases.

**database server** A server that provides client computers with access to information stored in databases.

**database software** An electronic filing system best used for larger and more complicated groups of data that require more than one table and the ability to group, sort, and retrieve data and generate reports.

**debugger** A tool in an integrated development environment that helps programmers analyze a program as it runs.

**debugging** The process of running a program over and over to find and repair errors and to make sure the program behaves in the way it should.

**decentralized** A characteristic of peer-to-peer networks where the individual user coordinates data security.

**decision point** A place where a program must choose from a list of actions based on the value of a certain input.

**decision support system (DSS)** A type of business intelligence system designed to help managers develop solutions for specific problems.

**dedicated server** A server used to fulfill one specific function, such as handling e-mail.

**default value** The value a database automatically uses for a field unless the user enters another value.

**denial-of-service (DoS) attack** An attack that occurs when legitimate users are denied access to a computer system because a hacker is repeatedly making requests of that computer system that tie up its resources and deny legitimate users access.

**derived class** In object-oriented analysis, the modified class.

**desktop computer** A computer that's intended for use at a single location. A desktop computer consists of a case that houses the main components of the computer, plus peripheral devices.

**desktop publishing (DTP) software** Programs for incorporating and arranging graphics and text to produce creative documents.

**detail report** A report generated by a management information system that provides a list of the transactions that occurred during a certain time period.

**device driver** Software that facilitates the communication between a device and its operating system or between a network adapter and a server's operating system and the operating system of the computer in which the adapter is installed.

**digital convergence** The use of a single unifying device to handle media, Internet, entertainment, and telephony needs; expressed in the range of devices now on the market.

**digital divide** The discrepancy between those who have access to the opportunities and knowledge that computers and the Internet offer and those who do not.

**digital rights management (DRM)** A system of access control that allows only limited use of material that has been legally purchased.

**digital signal processor** A specialized chip that processes digital information and transmits signals very quickly.

**digital subscriber line (DSL)** A type of connection that uses telephone lines to connect to the Internet and that allows both phone and data transmissions to share the same line.

**digital video (or versatile) disc (DVD)** A method of optical storage for digital data that has greater storage capacity than compact discs.

**digital video–editing software** A program for editing digital video.

**digital video interface (DVI) port** Video interface technology that newer LCD monitors, as well as other multimedia devices such as televisions, DVD players, and projectors, use to connect to a PC.

**directory** A hierarchical structure that include files, folders, and drives used to create a more organized and efficient computer.

**Disk Cleanup** A Windows utility that removes unnecessary files from the hard drive.

**disk defragmenting** A utility that regroups related pieces of files on the hard drive, enabling faster retrieval of the data.

**distributed denial-of-service (DDoS) attack** An automated attack that's launched from more than one zombie computer at the same time.

**Distributions (distros)** Linux download packages.

**Document Object Model (DOM)** Used by JavaScript to organize objects and page elements.

**documentation** Description of the technical details of the software, how the code works, and how the user interacts with the program; in addition, all the necessary user documentation that will be distributed to the program's users.

**domain name** A part of a Uniform Resource Locator (URL). Domain names consist of two parts: the site's host and a suffix that indicates the type of organization (example: popsci.com, where *popsci* is the domain name and *com* is the suffix).

**domain name system (DNS) server** A server that maintains a database of domain names and converts domain names to Internet protocol addresses.

**dotted decimal number (dotted quad)** The form of an Internet protocol address, where sets of numerals are separated by decimals, i.e., 197.169.73.63.

**drawing software (illustration software)** Programs for creating or editing two-dimensional line-based drawings.

**drive bay** A special shelf inside a computer that is designed to hold storage devices.

**drive-by download** The use of malicious software to attack a computer by downloading harmful programs onto a computer, without the user's knowledge, while they are surfing a website.

**dynamic addressing** A way of assigning Internet protocol addresses where a computer is assigned a temporary address from an available pool of addresses.

**dynamic decision making** The ability of a web page to decide how to display itself based on the choices the reader makes.

**Dynamic Host Configuration Protocol (DHCP)** A protocol for assigning dynamic internet protocol addresses.

**Dynamic HTML (DHTML)** A combination of technologies—HTML, cascading style sheets, and JavaScript—used to create lively and interactive websites.

## E

**e-commerce (electronic commerce)** The process of conducting business online for purposes ranging from fund-raising to advertising to selling products.

**editor** A special tool in an integrated development environment (IDE) that helps programmers as they enter code.

**electronic data interchange (EDI)** The exchange of large amounts of data in a standardized electronic format.

**electronic ink (E ink)** A very crisp, sharp grayscale representation of text achieved by using millions of microcapsules with white and black particles in a clear fluid.

**electronic text (e-text)** Textual information stored as digital information so that it can be stored, manipulated, and transmitted by electronic devices.

**element** In HTML, a pair of tags and the text between them.

**e-mail (electronic mail)** Internet-based communication in which senders and recipients correspond.

**e-mail client** A software program that runs on a computer and is used to send and receive e-mail through an Internet service provider's server.

**e-mail server** A server whose sole function is to process and deliver incoming and outgoing e-mail.

**e-mail virus** A virus transmitted by e-mail that often uses the address book in the victim's e-mail system to distribute itself.

**embedded computer** A specially designed computer chip that resides inside another device, such as a car. These self-contained computer devices have their own programming and typically neither receive input from users nor interact with other systems.

**encryption** The process of coding e-mail so that only the person with the key to the code (the intended recipient) can decode the message.

**encryption virus** A malicious program that searches for common data files and compresses them into a file using a complex encryption key, thereby rendering the files unusable.

**End User License Agreement (EULA)** See *software license*.

**enterprise resource planning (ERP) system** A business intelligence system that accumulates in a central location all information relevant to running a business and makes it readily available to whoever needs it to make decisions.

**e-reader** A device that can display e-text and that has supporting tools, like note taking, bookmarks, and integrated dictionaries.

**ergonomics** How a user sets up his or her computer and other equipment to minimize risk of injury or discomfort.

**error-checking** A Windows utility that checks for lost files and fragments as well as physical errors on a hard drive.

**error handling** The part of a problem statement where programmers describe what the program should do if the input data is invalid or just gibberish.

**Ethernet network** A network that uses the Ethernet protocol as the means (or standard) by which the nodes on the network communicate.

**Ethernet port** A port that's slightly larger than a standard phone jack and that transfers data at speeds of up to 10,000 Mbps; used to connect a computer to a DSL or cable modem or to a network.

**event** The result of an action, such as a keystroke, mouse click, or signal to the printer, in the respective device (keyboard, mouse, or printer) to which the operating system responds.

**exception report** A report generated by a management information system that shows conditions that are unusual or that need attention by system users.

**executable program** The binary sequence that instructs the central processing unit to run the programmer's code.

**expansion card (adapter card)** A circuit board with specific functions that augment the computer's basic functions and provide connections to other devices; examples include the sound card and the video card.

**expert system** A system that tries to replicate the decision-making processes of human experts in order to solve specific problems.

**eXtensible Markup Language (XML)** A markup language that enables designers to define their own data-based tags, making it much easier for a website to transfer the key information on its page to another site; it defines what data is being described rather than how it's to be displayed.

**extension (file type)** In a file name, the three letters that follow the user-supplied file name after the dot (.); the extension identifies what kind of family of files the file belongs to, or which application should be used to read the file.

**external hard drive** A hard drive that is enclosed in a protective case to make it portable; the drive is connected to the computer with a data transfer cable and is often used to back up data.

**extranet** An area of an intranet that only certain corporations or individuals can access; the owner of the extranet decides who will be permitted to access it.

## F

**Favorites** A feature in Microsoft Internet Explorer that places a marker of a website's Uniform Resource Locator (URL) in an easily retrievable list in the browser's toolbar. (Called Bookmarks in some browsers.)

**feature phones** Inexpensive cell phones with modest processors, simple interfaces, and, often, no touch screens.

**fiber-optic cable** A cable that transmits data at close to the speed of light along glass or plastic fibers.

**fiber-optic service** Internet access that is enabled by transmitting data at the speed of light through glass or plastic fibers.

**field** The component of a database in which the database stores each category of information.

**field constraint** A property that must be satisfied for an entry to be accepted into the field.

**field properties** In an Access database table, the field name, data type, and other data elements.

**field size** Defines the maximum number of characters that a field can hold in a database.

**fifth-generation language (5GL)** A computer language in which a problem is presented as a series of facts or constraints instead of as a specific algorithm; the system of facts can then be queried; considered the most "natural" of languages.

**file** A collection of related pieces of information stored together for easy reference.

**file allocation table (FAT)** An index of all sector numbers that the hard drive stores in a table to keep track of which sectors hold which files.

**file compression utility** A program that takes out redundancies in a file in order to reduce the file size.

**File Explorer** The main tool for finding, viewing, and managing the contents of your computer by showing the location and contents of every drive, folder, and file; called Windows Explorer prior to Windows 8.

**File History** A Windows utility that automatically creates a duplicate of your libraries, desktop, contacts, and favorites and copies it to another storage device, such as an external hard drive.

**file management** The process by which humans or computer software provide organizational structure to a computer's contents.

**file name** The first part of the label applied to a file; generally the name a user assigns to the file when saving it.

**file path** The exact location of a file, starting with the drive in which the file is located and including all folders, subfolders (if any), the file name, and the extension (example: C:\Users\username\Documents\Illustrations\EBronte.jpg).

**file server** A server that stores and manages files for network users or that acts as a storehouse for files that users can download.

**File Transfer Protocol (FTP)** A protocol used to upload and download files from one computer to another over the Internet.

**filter** In a database, temporarily displays records that match certain criteria.

**financial planning software** Programs for managing finances, such as Intuit's Quicken, which include electronic checkbook registers and automatic bill-payment tools.

**firewall** A software program or hardware device designed to prevent unauthorized access to computers or networks.

**FireWire 800** An interface port that transfers data at 800 Mbps.

**firmware** System software that controls hardware devices.

**first-generation language (1GL)** The machine language of a central processing unit (CPU); the sequence of bits that the CPU understands.

**flash drive** A drive that plugs into a universal serial bus (USB) port on a computer and that stores data digitally. Also called a USB drive, jump drive, or thumb drive.

**flash memory card** A form of portable storage; this removable memory card is often used in digital cameras, smartphones, video cameras, and printers.

**flowchart** Visual diagram of a process, including the decisions that need to be made along the way.

**folder** A collection of files stored on a computer.

**For** In Visual Basic, programmers use the keyword For to implement a loop; after the keyword For, an input or output item is given a starting value, and then the statements in the body of the loop are executed.

**foreign key** In a relational database, the common field between tables that's not the primary key.

**fourth-generation language (4GL)** A computer language type that includes database query languages and report generators.

**frame** Groups of data packets that are sent together in a package.

**freeware** Any copyrighted software that can be used for free.

**full installation** The process of installing all the files and programs from the distribution media to the computer's hard drive.

**fuzzy logic** Enables the interjection of experiential learning into knowledge-based systems by allowing the consideration of probabilities.

## G

**general availability (GA)** The point in the release cycle, where, after release to manufacturers, software is available for purchase by the public.

**geotag** Data attached to a photograph that indicates the latitude and longitude where you were standing when you took the photo.

**gigabit Ethernet** The most commonly used wired Ethernet standard deployed in devices designed for home networks; provides bandwidth of up to 1 Gbps.

**gigabyte (GB)** About a billion bytes.

**gigahertz (GHz)** One billion hertz.

**global positioning system (GPS)** A system of 21 satellites (plus 3 working spares), built and operated by the U.S. military, that constantly orbit the earth. The satellites provide information to GPS–capable devices to pinpoint locations on the earth.

**graphical user interface (GUI)** Unlike the command- and menu-driven interfaces used in earlier software, GUIs display graphics and use the point-and-click technology of the mouse and cursor, making them much more user friendly.

**graphics double data rate 5 (GDDR5)** A standard of video memory.

**graphics processing unit (GPU)** A specialized logic chip that's dedicated to quickly displaying and calculating visual data such as shadows, textures, and luminosity.

**grey-hat hacker** A cross between black and white—a hacker who will often illegally break into systems merely to flaunt his or her expertise to the administrator of the system he or she penetrated or to attempt to sell his or her services in repairing security breaches.

## H

**hacker** Anyone who unlawfully breaks into a computer system (whether an individual computer or a network).

**handshaking** In a connection-oriented protocol, the process of exchanging control packets before exchanging data packets.

**hard disk drive (HDD)** The computer's nonvolatile, primary storage device for permanent storage of software and documents.

**hardware** Any part of a computer or computer system you can physically touch.

**head crash** Impact of the read/write head against the magnetic platter of the hard drive; often results in data loss.

**hexadecimal digit** A digit with 16 possible values: 0–9 and A–F.

**hibernate** A power-management mode that saves the current state of the current system to the computer's hard drive.

**high definition** A standard of digital TV signal that guarantees a specific level of resolution and a specific *aspect ratio*, which is the rectangular shape of the image.

**high-definition multimedia interface (HDMI)** A compact audio–video interface standard that carries both high-definition video and uncompressed digital audio.

**home area network (HAN)** A network located in a home that's used to connect all of its digital devices.

**home network server** A device designed to store media, share media across the network, and back up files on computers connected to a home network.

**honey pot** A computer system that's set up to attract unauthorized users by appearing to be a key part of a network or a system that contains something of great value.

**host** The portion of a domain name that identifies who maintains a given website. For example, berkeley.edu is the domain name for the University of California at Berkeley, which maintains that site.

**HTML embedded scripting language** A programming language that tucks programming code directly within the HTML of a web page; the most popular example is JavaScript.

**HTML tags** Tags that surround and define HTML content (such as <b> and </b>, which indicate bolding).

**hybrid topology** Combining multiple topologies into one network.

**hyperlink** A type of specially coded text that, when clicked, enables a user to jump from one location, or web page, to another within a website or to another website altogether.

**Hypertext Markup Language (HTML)** A series of tags that define how elements on a website should be displayed in a browser.

**Hypertext Transfer Protocol (HTTP)** The protocol that allows files to be transferred from a web server so that you can see them on your computer by using a browser.

**Hypertext Transfer Protocol Secure (HTTPS)** The Internet protocol that ensures data is sent securely over the web.

**hyperthreading** A technology that permits quicker processing of information by enabling a new set of instructions to start executing before the previous set has finished.

## I

**identity theft** The process by which someone uses personal information about someone else (such as the victim's name, address, and Social Security number) to assume the victim's identity for the purpose of defrauding another.

**if else** In C++, a binary decision in the code where the program can follow one of two paths: If the decision is made one way, the program follows one path; if made the other way (else), the program follows another path.

**image backup (system backup)** A copy of an entire computer system, created for restoration purposes.

**image-editing software** Programs for editing photographs and other images.

**impact printer** A printer that has tiny hammer-like keys that strike the paper through an inked ribbon, thus making a mark on the paper. The most common impact printer is the dot-matrix printer.

**incremental backup (partial backup)** A type of backup that only backs up files that have changed since the last time files were backed up.

**information** Data that has been organized or presented in a meaningful fashion; the result, or output that users require at the end of a job.

**information assurance** Ensuring that information systems contain accurate information and are adequately secured against tampering.

**information system** A system that includes data, people, procedures, hardware, and software that help in planning and decision making; a software-based solution used to gather and analyze information.

**information technology (IT)** The set of techniques used in processing and retrieving information.

**inheritance** In object-oriented analysis, the ability of a new class to automatically pick up all the data and methods of an existing class and then extend and customize those to fit its specific needs.

**initial value** A beginning point.

**inkjet printer** A nonimpact printer that sprays tiny drops of ink onto paper.

**inoculation** A process used by antivirus software; compares old and current qualities of files to detect viral activity.

**input device** A hardware device used to enter, or input, data (text, images, and sounds) and instructions (user responses and commands) into a computer. Some input devices are keyboards and mice.

**input form** Used to control how new data is entered into a shared database.

**instant messaging (IM)** A program that enables users to communicate online in real time with others who are also online.

**integrated development environment (IDE)** A developmental tool that helps programmers write and test their programs; one IDE can be configured to support many different languages.

**internal hard drive** A hard drive that resides within the computer's system unit and that usually holds all permanently stored programs and data.

**Internet** A network of networks that's the largest network in the world, connecting billions of computers globally.

**Internet backbone** The main pathway of high-speed communications lines over which all Internet traffic flows.

**Internet cache** A section of the hard drive that stores information that may be needed again, such as Internet protocol addresses and frequently accessed web pages.

**Internet Corporation for Assigned Names and Numbers (ICANN)** The organization that registers Internet protocol addresses to ensure they're unique and haven't been assigned to other users.

**Internet exchange point (IXP)** A way of connecting Internet service providers (ISPs) that's made up of one or more network switches to which the ISPs connect.

**Internet Protocol (IP)** One of the original two protocols developed for the Internet.

**Internet Protocol (IP) address** The means by which all computers connected to the Internet identify each other. It consists of a unique set of four numbers separated by dots, such as 123.45.178.91.

**Internet Protocol version 4 (IPv4)** The original Internet protocol addressing scheme, created in 1981.

**Internet Protocol version 6 (IPv6)** An Internet protocol (IP) addressing scheme that makes IP addresses longer, thereby providing more available addresses.

**Internet service provider (ISP)** A company that specializes in providing Internet access. ISPs may be specialized providers, like Juno, or companies that provide other services in addition to Internet access (such as phone and cable television).

**interpreter** For a programming language, translates the source code into an intermediate form, line by line; each line is then executed as it's translated.

**interrupt** A signal that tells the operating system that it's in need of immediate attention.

**interrupt handler** A special numerical code that prioritizes requests from various devices. These requests then are placed in the interrupt table in the computer's primary memory.

**intranet** A private network set up by a business or an organization that's used exclusively by a select group of employees, customers, suppliers, volunteers, or supporters.

**IP address** See *Internet Protocol (IP) address*.

## J

**jam signal** A special signal sent to network nodes alerting them that a data collision has occurred.

**Java** An object-oriented programming language that has a large set of existing classes.

**Java applet** A small Java-based program.

**JavaScript** A scripting language that's often used to add interactivity to web pages; often used for creating Dynamic HTML effects.

**JavaServer Pages (JSP)** Programming language used to build websites with interactive capabilities; adapts the HTML page to the user's selections.

**join query** A query used to extract data that's in two or more tables in a database.

**JSON** Stands for Javascript Object Notation; a syntax for exchanging text information between computers.

## K

**kernel (supervisor program)** The essential component of the operating system that's responsible for managing the processor and all other components of the computer system. Because it stays in random access memory (RAM) the entire time the computer is powered on, the kernel is called memory resident.

**key pair** The two keys used in public-key encryption.

**keyboard** A hardware device used to enter typed data and commands into a computer.

**keystroke logger (keylogger)** A type of spyware program that monitors keystrokes with the intent of stealing passwords, login IDs, or credit card information.

**keyword** (1) A specific word a user wishes to query (or look for) in an Internet search. (2) A specific word that has a predefined meaning in a particular programming language.

**kilobyte (KB)** A unit of computer storage equal to approximately 1,000 bytes.

**knowledge-based system** A business intelligence system that provides intelligence that supplements the user's own intellect and makes the decision support system more effective.

## L

**laptop (or notebook) computer** A portable computer with a keyboard, a monitor, and other devices integrated into a single compact case.

**laser printer** A nonimpact printer known for quick and quiet production and high-quality printouts.

**latency (rotational delay)** The process that occurs after the read/write head of the hard drive locates the correct track and then waits for the correct sector to spin to the read/write head.

**legacy technology** Comprises computing devices, software, or peripherals that use techniques, parts, and methods from an earlier time that are no longer popular.

**library** Introduced with Windows 7, a folder that's used to display files from different locations as if they were all saved in a single folder, regardless of where they are actually stored in the file hierarchy.

**light-emitting diode (LED)** A newer, more energy-efficient technology used in monitors. It may result in better color accuracy and thinner panels than traditional LCD monitors.

**Linux** An open-source operating system based on UNIX. Because of the stable nature of this operating system, it's often used on web servers.

**liquid crystal display (LCD)** The technology used in flat-panel computer monitors.

**live bookmark** A bookmark that delivers updates as soon as they become available, using Really Simple Syndication (RSS).

**local area network (LAN)** A network in which the nodes are located within a small geographic area.

**logic bomb** A computer virus that runs when a certain set of conditions is met, such as when a program is launched a specific number of times.

**logical error** An error in a program that produces unintended or undesired output, where the syntax is correct but some other human error has occurred.

**logical port** A virtual communications gateway or path that enables a computer to organize requests for information (such as web page downloads and e-mail routing) from other networks or computers.

**logical port blocking** A condition in which a firewall is configured to ignore all incoming packets that request access to a certain port so that no unwanted requests will get through to the computer.

**loop** A type of decision point in an algorithm. In a loop, a question is asked, and if the answer is *yes*, a set of actions is performed.

Once the set of actions has finished, the question is asked again, creating a loop. If the answer to the question is *no*, the algorithm breaks free of the loop and moves on to the first step that follows the loop.

## M

**Mac OS** The first commercially available operating system to incorporate a graphical user interface (GUI) with user-friendly point-and-click technology.

**machine cycle** The series of steps a central processing unit goes through when it performs a program instruction.

**machine language** See *first-generation language (1GL)*.

**macro** A small program that groups a series of commands to run as a single command.

**macro virus** A virus that's distributed by hiding it inside a macro.

**mainframe** A large, expensive computer that supports hundreds or thousands of users simultaneously and executes many different programs at the same time.

**malware** Software that's intended to render a system temporarily or permanently useless or to penetrate a computer system completely for purposes of information gathering. Examples include spyware, viruses, worms, and Trojan horses.

**management information system (MIS)** A type of business intelligence system that provides timely and accurate information that enables managers to make critical business decisions.

**many-to-many relationship** In a relational database, records in one table are related to multiple records in a second table, and vice versa.

**master boot record** A small program that runs whenever a computer boots up.

**media access control (MAC) address** The physical address, similar to a serial number, of each network adapter.

**megabyte (MB)** A unit of computer storage equal to approximately 1 million bytes.

**memory module (memory card)** A small circuit board that holds a series of random access memory (RAM) chips.

**menu-driven interface** A user interface in which the user chooses a command from menus displayed on the screen.

**metadata** Data that describes other data.

**metasearch engine** A search engine, such as Dogpile, that searches other search engines rather than individual websites.

**method** The process of how a program converts inputs into the correct outputs.

**metropolitan area network (MAN)** A wide area network (WAN) that links users in a specific geographic area (such as within a city or county).

**microphone (mic)** A device that allows you to capture sound waves, such as those created by your voice, and to transfer them to digital format on your computer.

**mobile broadband** Connection to the Internet through the same cellular network that cell phones use to get 3G or 4G Internet access.

**mobile switching center** A central location that receives cell phone requests for service from a base station.

**model management system** Software that assists in building management models in decision support systems; an analysis tool that, through the use of internal and external data, provides a view of a particular business situation for the purposes of decision making.

**monitor (display screen)** A common output device that displays text, graphics, and video as soft copies (copies that can be seen only on screen).

**Moore's Law** A prediction, named after Gordon Moore, the co-founder of Intel; states that the number of transistors on a central processing unit chip will double every two years.

**motherboard** A special circuit board in the system unit that contains the central processing unit, the memory (RAM) chips, and the slots available for expansion cards; all of the other boards (video cards, sound cards, and so on) connect to it to receive power and to communicate.

**mouse** A hardware device used to enter user responses and commands into a computer.

**multidimensional database** A database that stores data from different perspectives, called dimensions, and organizes data in cube format.

**multimedia** Anything that involves one or more forms of media plus text.

**multimedia software** Programs that include image-, video-, and audio-editing software, animation software, and other specialty software required to produce computer games, animations, and movies.

**multipartite virus** Literally meaning "multipart" virus; a type of computer virus that attempts to infect computers using more than one method.

**Multipurpose Internet Mail Extensions (MIME)** Specification for sending files as attachments to e-mail.

**multitask** The ability of an operating system to perform more than one process at a time.

**multiuser operating system (network operating system)** An operating system that enables more than one user to access the computer system at one time by efficiently juggling all the requests from multiple users.

## N

**natural language processing (NLP) system** A knowledge-based business intelligence system that enables users to communicate with computer systems using a natural spoken or written language instead of a computer programming language.

**negative acknowledgment (NAK)** In data exchange, the communication sent from one computer or system to another stating that it did not receive a data packet in readable form.

**netbook** A computing device that runs a full-featured operating system but that weighs two pounds or less.

**network** A group of two or more computers (or nodes) that are configured to share information and resources such as printers, files, and databases.

**network adapter** A device that enables the computer (or peripheral) to communicate with the network using a common data communication language, or protocol.

**network address translation (NAT)** A process that firewalls use to assign internal Internet protocol addresses on a network.

**network administration** Involves tasks such as (1) installing new computers and devices, (2) monitoring the network to ensure it's performing efficiently, (3) updating and installing new software on the network, and (4) configuring, or setting up, proper security for a network.

**network administrator** Person who maintains networks for businesses.

**network architecture** The design of a computer network; includes both physical and logical design.

**network-attached storage (NAS) device** A specialized computing device designed to store and manage network data.

**network interface card (NIC)** An expansion card that enables a computer to connect other computers or to a cable modem to facilitate a high-speed Internet connection.

**network navigation device** A device on a network such as a router or switch that moves data signals around the network.

**network operating system (NOS)** Software that handles requests for information, Internet access, and the use of peripherals for the rest of the network node, providing the services necessary for the computers on the network to communicate.

**network prefix** The slash and number added to the end of an internet protocol (IP) address that allows a single IP address to represent several unique IP addresses in *classless interdomain routing*.

**network-ready device** A device (such as a printer or an external hard drive) that can be attached directly to a network instead of needing to attach to a computer on the network.

**network topology** The physical or logical arrangement of computers, transmission media (cable), and other network components.

**Next** In Visual Basic, programmers use the keyword Next to implement a loop; when the Next command is run, the program returns to the For statement and increments the value of the input or output item by 1 and then runs a test cycle.

**node** A device connected to a network such as a computer, a peripheral (such as a printer), or a communications device (such as a modem).

**nonimpact printer** A printer that sprays ink or uses laser beams to make marks on the paper. The most common nonimpact printers are inkjet and laser printers.

**nonvolatile storage** Permanent storage, as in read-only memory (ROM).

**normalization** A process to ensure data is organized most efficiently in a database.

**numeric check** In a database, confirms that only numbers are entered in a field.

## O

**object** An example of a class in object-oriented analysis.

**object-oriented analysis** A type of analysis in which programmers first identify all the categories of inputs that are part of the problem the program is meant to solve.

**object-oriented database** A database that stores data in objects rather than in tables.

**Object Query Language (OQL)** A query language used by many object-oriented databases.

**Objective C** The programming language most often used to program applications to run under OS X.

**octet** A reference to each of the four numbers in a dotted decimal number internet protocol address, so called because each number would have eight numerals in binary form.

**office support system (OSS)** A system designed to improve communications and assist employees in accomplishing their daily tasks.

**one-to-many relationship** In a relational database, a record appears only once in one table while having the capability of appearing many times in a related table.

**one-to-one relationship** In a relational database, for each record in a table there's only one corresponding record in a related table.

**online analytical processing (OLAP)** Software that provides standardized tools for viewing and manipulating data in a data warehouse.

**online transaction processing (OLTP)** The real-time processing of database transactions online.

**open source software** Program code made publicly available for free; it can be copied, distributed, or changed without the stringent copyright protections of proprietary software products.

**open system** A system having the characteristic of being public for access by any interested party; as opposed to a *proprietary system*.

**Open Systems Interconnection (OSI)** A networking protocol established by the Institute of Electrical and Electronics Engineers (IEEE) that provides guidelines for modern networks.

**operating system (OS)** The system software that controls the way in which a computer system functions, including the management of hardware, peripherals, and software.

**operator** A coding symbol that represents a fundamental action of the programming language.

**optical carrier (OC) line** A high-speed fiber-optic line.

**optical drive** A hardware device that uses lasers or light to read from, and even write to, CDs, DVDs, or Blu-ray discs.

**optical media** Portable storage devices, such as CDs, DVDs, and Blu-ray discs, that use a laser to read and write data.

**optical mouse** A mouse that uses an internal sensor or laser to control the mouse's movement. The sensor sends signals to the computer, telling it where to move the pointer on the screen.

**organic light-emitting diode (OLED) displays** Displays that use organic compounds to produce light when exposed to an electric current. Unlike LCDs, OLEDs do not require a backlight to function and therefore draw less power and have a much thinner display, sometimes as thin as 3 mm.

**output device** A device that sends processed data and information out of a computer in the form of text, pictures (graphics), sounds (audio), or video.

**overclocking** Running the central processing unit at a speed faster than the manufacturer recommends.

## P

**packet (data packet)** A small segment of data that's bundled for sending over transmission media. Each packet contains the address of the computer or peripheral device to which it's being sent.

**packet analyzer (sniffer)** A computer hardware device or software program designed to detect and record digital information being transmitted over a network.

**packet screening** Having an external screening router examine incoming data packets to ensure they originated from or are authorized by valid users on the internal network.

**packet switching** A communications methodology that makes computer communication efficient; in packet switching, data is broken into smaller chunks called *packets*.

**paging** The process of swapping data or instructions that have been placed in the swap file for later use back into active random access memory (RAM). The contents of the hard drive's swap file then become less active data or instructions.

**Pascal** A programming language; the only modern language that was specifically designed as a teaching language.

**passive topology** In a network, a type of topology where the nodes do nothing to move data along the network.

**path (subdirectory)** The information after the slash that indicates a particular file or path (or subdirectory) within the website.

**path separator** The backslash mark (\) used by Microsoft Windows and DOS in file names. Mac files use a colon (:), and UNIX and Linux use the forward slash (/) as the path separator.

**peer-to-peer (P2P) network** A network in which each node connected to the network can communicate directly with every other node on the network.

**peer-to-peer (P2P) sharing** The process of users transferring files between computers.

**peripheral device** A device such as a monitor, printer, or keyboard that connects to the system unit through a data port.

**personal area network (PAN)** A network used for communication among devices close to one person, such as smartphones, laptops, and tablets, using wireless technologies such as Bluetooth.

**personal firewall** A firewall specifically designed for home networks.

**personal information manager (PIM) software** Programs such as Microsoft Outlook or Lotus Organizer that strive to replace the various management tools found on a traditional desk such as a calendar, address book, notepad, and to-do lists.

**petabyte (PB)** $10^{15}$ bytes of digital information.

**pharming** Planting malicious code on a computer that alters the browser's ability to find web addresses and that directs users to bogus websites.

**phishing** The process of sending e-mail messages to lure Internet users into revealing personal information such as credit card or Social Security numbers or other sensitive information that could lead to identity theft.

**PHP (Hypertext Preprocessor)** Programming language used to build websites with interactive capabilities; adapts the HTML page to the user's selections.

**physical memory** The amount of random access memory (RAM) that's installed in a computer.

**piggybacking** The process of connecting to a wireless network without the permission of the owner of the network.

**pinning** The process through which you choose which applications are visible on the Windows Start screen.

**pixel** A single point that creates the images on a computer monitor. Pixels are illuminated by an electron beam that passes rapidly back and forth across the back of the screen so that the pixels appear to glow continuously.

**platform** The combination of a computer's operating system and processor. The two most common platform types are the PC and the Apple.

**platter** A thin, round, metallic storage plate stacked onto the hard drive spindle.

**plotter** A large printer that uses a computer-controlled pen to produce oversize pictures that require precise continuous lines to be drawn, such as maps and architectural plans.

**Plug and Play (PnP)** The technology that enables the operating system, once it is booted up, to recognize automatically any new peripherals and to configure them to work with the system.

**plug-in (player)** A small software program that "plugs in" to a web browser to enable a specific function—for example, to view and hear certain multimedia files on the web.

**podcast** A clip of audio or video content that's broadcast over the Internet using compressed audio or video files in formats such as MP3.

**point of presence (POP)** A bank of modems, servers, routers, and switches through which Internet users connect to an Internet service provider.

**polymorphic virus** A virus that changes its virus signature (the binary pattern that makes the virus identifiable) every time it infects a new file. This makes it more difficult for antivirus programs to detect the virus.

**port** An interface through which external devices are connected to the computer.

**portability** The capability to move a completed solution easily from one type of computer to another.

**positive acknowledgement (ACK)** In data exchange, the confirmation sent from one computer or system to another saying that the computer has received a data packet that it can read.

**possessed object** Any object that users carry to identify themselves and that grants them access to a computer system or facility.

**power-on self-test (POST)** The first job the basic input/output system (BIOS) performs, ensuring that essential peripheral devices are attached and operational. This process consists of a test on the video card and video memory, a BIOS identification process (during which the BIOS version, manufacturer, and data are displayed on the monitor), and a memory test to ensure memory chips are working properly.

**power supply** A power supply regulates the wall voltage to the voltages required by computer chips; it's housed inside the system unit.

**preemptive multitasking** When the operating system processes the task assigned a higher priority before processing a task that has been assigned a lower priority.

**presentation software** An application program for creating dynamic slide shows, such as Microsoft PowerPoint or Apple Keynote.

**pretexting** The act of creating an invented scenario (the pretext) to convince someone to divulge information.

**Pretty Good Privacy (PGP)** A public-key package for encryption available for download on the Internet.

**primary key field** In a database, a field that has a value unique to a record.

**print queue** A software holding area for print jobs. Also called a print spooler.

**print server** A server that manages all client-requested printing jobs for all printers on a network.

**printer** A common output device that creates tangible or hard copies of text and graphics.

**private key** The key for decoding retained as private in public-key encryption.

**private-key encryption** A type of encryption where only the two parties involved in sending the message have the code.

**problem statement** The starting point of programming work; a clear description of what tasks the computer program must accomplish and how the program will execute those tasks and respond to unusual situations.

**processing** Manipulating or organizing data into information.

**productivity software** Programs that enable a user to perform various tasks generally required in home, school, and business. Examples include word processing, spreadsheet, presentation, personal information management, and database programs.

**program** A series of instructions to be followed by a computer to accomplish a task.

**program development life cycle (PDLC)** The process of performing a programming project, which consists of five stages: describing the problem, making a plan, coding, debugging, and testing and documentation.

**program files** Files that are used in the running of software programs and that do not store data.

**program specification** A clear statement of the goals and objectives of the project.

**programming** The process of translating a task into a series of commands a computer will use to perform that task.

**programming language** A kind of "code" for the set of instructions the central processing unit knows how to perform.

**projector** A device that can project images from your computer onto a wall or viewing screen.

**proprietary software** Custom software application that's owned and controlled by the company that created it.

**proprietary system** A system having the characteristic of being closed to public access (private), as opposed to an *open system*.

**protocol** A set of rules for exchanging communications.

**prototype** A small model of a program built at the beginning of a large project.

**proxy server** A server that acts as a go-between, connecting computers on the internal network with those on the external network (the Internet).

**pseudocode** A text-based approach to documenting an algorithm.

**public key** The key for coding distributed to the public in public-key encryption.

**public-key encryption** A type of encryption where two keys, known as a *key pair*, are created. One key is used for coding and the other for decoding. The key for coding is distributed as a public key, while the private key is retained for decoding.

## Q

**quarantining** The placement (by antivirus software) of a computer virus in a secure area on the hard drive so that it won't spread infection to other files.

**query** In a database, a way of retrieving information that defines a particular subset of data; can be used to extract data from one or more tables.

**query language** A specially designed computer language used to manipulate data in or extract data from a database.

**QR (quick response) codes** Technology that lets any piece of print in the real world host a live link to online information and video content.

**QWERTY keyboard** A keyboard that gets its name from the first six letters on the top-left row of alphabetic keys on the keyboard.

## R

**RAID 0** The strategy of running two hard drives in one system, cutting in half the time it takes to write a file.

**RAID 1** The strategy of mirroring all the data written on one hard drive to a second hard drive, providing an instant backup of all data.

**random access memory (RAM)** The computer's temporary storage space or short-term memory. It's located in a set of chips on the system unit's motherboard, and its capacity is measured in megabytes or gigabytes.

**range check** Ensures that the data entered into the field of a database falls within a certain range of values.

**rapid application development (RAD)** An alternative program-development method; instead of developing detailed system documents before they produce the system, developers first create a prototype, then generate system documents as they use and remodel the product.

**read-only memory (ROM)** A set of memory chips, located on the motherboard, which stores data and instructions that cannot be changed or erased; it holds all the instructions the computer needs to start up.

**read/write head** The mechanism that retrieves (reads) and records (writes) the magnetic data to and from a data disk.

**real-time operating system (RTOS)** A program with a specific purpose that must guarantee certain response times for particular computing tasks or else the machine's application is useless. Real-time operating systems are found in many types of robotic equipment.

**real-time processing** The processing of database transactions in which the database is updated while the transaction is taking place.

**Really Simple Syndication (RSS)** An XML–based format that allows frequent updates of content on the World Wide Web.

**record** A group of related fields in a database.

**Recycle Bin** A folder on a Windows desktop in which deleted files from the hard drive are held until permanently purged from the system.

**redundant array of independent disks (RAID)** A set of strategies for using more than one drive in a system.

**referential integrity** In a relational database, a condition where, for each value in the foreign key table, there's a corresponding value in the primary key table.

**Refresh your PC** A new utility program in Windows 8 that attempts to diagnose and fix errors in your Windows system files that are causing your computer to behave improperly.

**registry** A portion of the hard drive containing all the different configurations (settings) used by the Windows operating system as well as by other applications.

**relational algebra** The use of English-like expressions that have variables and operations, much like algebraic equations, to extract data from databases using Structured Query Language.

**relational database** A database type that organizes data into related tables based on logical groupings.

**relationship** In a relational database, a link between tables that defines how the data is related.

**release to manufacturers (RTM)** The point in the release cycle, where, after beta testing, a manufacturer makes changes to the software and releases it to other manufacturers, for installation on new machines, for example.

**resolution** The clearness or sharpness of an image, which is controlled by the number of pixels displayed on the screen.

**reusability** In object-oriented analysis, the ability to reuse existing classes from one project for another project.

**ring (loop) topology** A type of network topology where computers and peripherals are laid out in a configuration resembling a circle.

**root directory** The top level of the filing structure in a computer system. In Windows computers, the root directory of the hard drive is represented as C:\.

**root DNS server** A domain name system (DNS) server that contains the master listings for an entire top-level domain.

**rootkits** Programs that allow hackers to gain access to your computer and take almost complete control of it without your knowledge. These programs are designed to subvert normal login procedures to a computer and to hide their operations from normal detection methods.

**router** A device that routes packets of data between two or more networks.

**runtime error** An error in a program that occurs when a programmer accidentally writes code that divides by zero, a mathematical error.

## S

**sampling rate** The number of times per second a signal is measured and converted to a digital value. Sampling rates are measured in kilobits per second.

**satellite Internet** A way to connect to the Internet using a small satellite dish, which is placed outside the home and is connected to a computer with coaxial cable. The satellite company then sends the data to a satellite orbiting the Earth. The satellite, in turn, sends the data back to the satellite dish and to the computer.

**scalability** A characteristic of client/server networks where more users can be easily added without affecting the performance of other network nodes.

**scanner** A type of input device that inputs images into computers.

**scareware** A type of malware that's downloaded onto your computer and that tries to convince you that your computer is infected with a virus or other type of malware.

**scope creep** An ever-changing set of requests from clients for additional features as they wait longer and longer to see a working prototype.

**script** A list of commands (mini-programs or macros) that can be executed on a computer without user interaction.

**scripting language** A simple programming language that's limited to performing a set of specialized tasks.

**search engine** A set of programs that searches the web for specific words (or keywords) you wish to query (or look for) and that then returns a list of the websites on which those keywords are found.

**second-generation language (2GL)** A computer language that allows programmers to write programs using a set of short, English-like commands that speak directly to the central processing unit and that give the programmer direct control of hardware resources; also called *assembly language*.

**second-level domain** A domain that's directly below a top-level domain.

**sector** A section of a hard drive platter, wedge-shaped from the center of the platter to the edge.

**Secure Sockets Layer (SSL)** A network security protocol that provides for the encryption of data transmitted using the Internet. The current versions of all major web browsers support SSL.

**seek time** The time it takes for the hard drive's read/write heads to move over the surface of the disk to the correct track.

**select query** In Structured Query Language, displays a subset of data from a table (or tables) based on the criteria specified.

**semantic web (Web 3.0)** An evolving extension of the World Wide Web in which information is defined in such a way as to make it more easily readable by computers.

**server** A computer that provides resources to other computers on a network.

**server-side program** A type of program that runs on a web server rather than on a computer.

**service pack** A software update.

**service set identifier (SSID)** A network name that wireless routers use to identify themselves.

**shielded twisted-pair (STP) cable** Twisted-pair cable that contains a layer of foil shielded to reduce interference.

**short message service (SMS)** Technology that enables short text messages (up to 160 characters) to be sent over mobile networks.

**Simple Mail Transfer Protocol (SMTP)** The protocol responsible for sending e-mail along the Internet to its destination; part of the Internet Protocol suite.

**simulation program** Software, often used for training purposes, which allows the user to experience or control an event as if it's reality.

**sleep mode** A low-power mode for electronic devices such as computers that saves electric power consumption and saves the last-used settings. When the device is "woken up," work is resumed more quickly than when cold booting the computer.

**social bookmark (tagging)** A keyword or term that Internet users assign to a web resource such as a web page, digital image, or video.

**social commerce** A subset of e-commerce that uses social networks to assist in marketing and purchasing products.

**social engineering** Any technique that uses social skills to generate human interaction for the purpose of enticing individuals to reveal sensitive information.

**social networking** A means by which people use the Internet to communicate and share information among their immediate friends and to meet and connect with others through common interests, experiences, and friends.

**software** The set of computer programs or instructions that tells the computer what to do and that enables it to perform different tasks.

**Software as a Service (SaaS)** Software that's delivered on demand over the Internet.

**software license** An agreement between the user and the software developer that must be accepted before installing the software on a computer.

**software piracy** Violating a software license agreement by copying an application onto more computers than the license agreement permits.

**software suite** A collection of software programs that have been bundled together as a package.

**solid-state drive (SSD)** A storage device that uses the same kind of memory that flash drives use but that can reach data in only a tenth of the time a flash drive requires.

**sound card** An expansion card that attaches to the motherboard inside the system unit and that enables the computer to produce sounds by providing a connection for the speakers and microphone.

**source code** The instructions programmers write in a higher-level language.

**spam** Unwanted or junk e-mail.

**spam filter** An option you can select in your e-mail account that places known or suspected spam messages into a folder other than your inbox.

**speakers** Output devices for sound.

**spear phishing** A targeted phishing attack that sends e-mails to people known to be customers of a company. Such attacks have a much greater chance of successfully getting individuals to reveal sensitive data.

**spooler** A program that helps coordinate all print jobs being sent to the printer at the same time.

**spreadsheet software** An application program such as Microsoft Excel or Lotus 1-2-3 that enables a user to do calculations and numerical analyses easily.

**spyware** An unwanted piggyback program that downloads with the software you want to install from the Internet and then runs in the background of your system.

**star topology** The most widely deployed client/server network topology, where the nodes connect to a central communications device called a switch in a pattern resembling a star.

**Start screen** The first interaction you have with the Windows operating system and the pace where you begin your computing activities.

**statement** A sentence in a code.

**static addressing** A way of assigning internet protocol addresses where the address for a computer never changes and is most likely assigned manually by a network administrator or an Internet service provider.

**stealth virus** A virus that temporarily erases its code from the files where it resides and hides in the active memory of the computer.

**streaming audio** Technology that enables audio files to be fed to a browser continuously. This lets users avoid having to download an entire file before listening.

**streaming video** Technology that enables video files to be fed to a browser continuously. This lets users avoid having to download the entire file before viewing.

**structured (analytical) data** Data such as "Bill" or "345," as opposed to *unstructured data*.

**Structured Query Language (SQL)** A database programming language used to construct queries to extract data from relational databases; one example of a fourth-generation language.

**stylus** A pen-shaped device used to tap or write on touch-sensitive screens.

**subject directory** A structured outline of websites organized by topics and subtopics.

**summary report** A report generated by a management information system that provides a consolidated picture of detailed data; these reports usually include some calculation or visual displays of information.

**supercomputer** A specially designed computer that can perform complex calculations extremely rapidly; used in situations in which complex models requiring intensive mathematical calculations are needed (such as weather forecasting or atomic energy research).

**SuperFetch** A memory-management technique used by Windows 7. Monitors the applications you use the most and preloads them into your system memory so that they'll be ready to go.

**surge protector** A device that protects computers and other electronic devices from power surges.

**surround sound** A type of audio processing that makes the listener experience sound as if it were coming from all directions.

**surround-sound speaker** A system of speakers set up in such a way that it surrounds an entire area (and the people in it) with sound.

**swap file (page file)** A temporary storage area on the hard drive where the operating system "swaps out" or moves the data or instructions from random access memory (RAM) that haven't recently been used. This process takes place when more RAM space is needed.

**switch** A device for transmitting data on a network. A switch makes decisions, based on the media access control address of the data, as to where the data is to be sent.

**synchronizing (or syncing)** The process of updating data on portable devices (such as a cell phone or iPod) and a computer so that they contain the same data.

**syntax** An agreed-on set of rules defining how a language must be structured.

**syntax error** A violation of the strict set of rules that define the programming language.

**system development life cycle (SDLC)** A process used to develop information systems; it consists of the following six steps: problem and opportunity identification, analysis, design, development, testing and installation, and maintenance and evaluation.

**system evaluation** The process of looking at a computer's subsystems, what they do, and how they perform to determine whether the computer system has the right hardware components to do what the user ultimately wants it to do.

**system files** The main files of an operating system.

**system requirements** The set of minimum storage, memory capacity, and processing standards recommended by the software manufacturer to ensure proper operation of a software application.

**System Restore** A utility in Windows that restores system settings to a specific previous date when everything was working properly.

**system restore point** In Windows, a snapshot of your entire system's settings used for restoring your system to a prior point in time.

**system software** The set of programs that enables a computer's hardware devices and application software to work together; it includes the operating system and utility programs.

**system unit** The metal or plastic case that holds all the physical parts of the computer together, including the computer's processor (its brains), its memory, and the many circuit boards that help the computer function.

## T

**T line** A communications line that carries digital data over twisted-pair wires.

**table (file)** A group of related records in a database.

**tablet computer** A mobile computer, such as the Apple iPad or Samsung Galaxy Tab, integrated into a flat multitouch-sensitive screen. It uses an onscreen virtual keyboard, but separate keyboards can be connected via Bluetooth or wires.

**tablet PC** A laptop computer designed specifically to work with handwriting-recognition technology.

**Task Manager** A Windows utility that shows programs currently running and permits you to exit nonresponsive programs when you click End Task.

**taskbar** In later versions of Windows operating systems, a feature that displays open and favorite applications for easy access.

**tax preparation software** An application program, such as Intuit's TurboTax or H&R Block's At Home, for preparing state and federal taxes. Each program offers a complete set of tax forms and instructions as well as expert advice on how to complete each form.

**TCP/IP** The main suite of protocols used for transmitting data over the Internet. Named after Transmission Control Protocol (TCP) and the Internet Protocol (IP).

**telephony** The use of equipment to provide voice communications over a distance.

**template** A form included in many productivity applications that provides the basic structure for a particular kind of document, spreadsheet, or presentation.

**Terabyte (TB)** 1,099,511,627,776 bytes or $2^{40}$ bytes.

**terminator** A device that absorbs a signal so that it's not reflected back onto parts of the network that have already received it.

**test condition** A check to see whether the loop in an algorithm is completed.

**testing plan** The part of the problem statement that lists specific input numbers the programmers would typically expect the user to enter; the plan then lists the precise output values that a perfect program would return for those input values.

**tethering** Approach which makes sure that as long as you have a 3G signal, your computer can access the Internet even when it tells you there are no available wireless networks. Several smartphones offer this capability.

**thermal printer** A printer that works either by melting wax-based ink onto ordinary paper (in a process called *thermal wax transfer printing*) or by burning dots onto specially coated paper (in a process called *direct thermal printing*).

**third-generation language (3GL)** A computer language that uses symbols and commands to help programmers tell the computer what to do, making 3GL languages easier for humans to read and remember; examples of 3GL languages include BASIC, FORTRAN, COBOL, C/C++, and JAVA.

**thrashing** A condition of excessive paging in which the operating system becomes sluggish.

**three-way handshake** In Transmission Control Protocol, the process used to establish a connection between two computers before exchanging data. The steps in a three-way handshake are as follows: One computer establishes a connection to the Internet service provider (ISP) and announces it has e-mail to send, the ISP server responds that it's ready to receive, and the computer acknowledges the ready state of the server and begins to transmit the e-mail.

**throughput** The actual speed of data transfer that's achieved. It's usually less than the data transfer rate and is measured in megabits per second (Mbps).

**Thunderbolt port** A high speed input/output port; Thunderbolt 2 provides two channels of 20 Gbps capacity on one port.

**time bomb** A virus that's triggered by the passage of time or on a certain date.

**time-variant data** Data that doesn't pertain to one period in time.

**token** A special data packet used to pass data in a ring topology network.

**token method** The access method used by ring networks to avoid data collisions.

**top-down design** A systematic approach in which a problem is broken into a series of high-level tasks.

**top-level domain** The suffix, often of three letters (such as .com or .edu), in the domain name that indicates the kind of organization the host is.

**touch pad (trackpad)** A small, touch-sensitive screen at the base of a laptop keyboard that's used to direct the cursor.

**touch screen** A type of monitor (or display in a smartphone or tablet computer) that accepts input from a user touching the screen.

**track** A concentric circle that serves as a storage area on a hard drive platter.

**transaction-processing system (TPS)** A type of business intelligence system for keeping track of everyday business activities.

**Transmission Control Protocol (TCP)** One of the original two protocols developed for the Internet.

**transmission media** The radio waves or the physical system (cable) that transports data on a network.

**Transport Layer Security (TLS)** An updated extension of *Secure Sockets Layer*.

**Trojan horse** A computer program that appears to be something useful or desirable (such as a game or a screen saver), but at the same time does something malicious in the background without the user's knowledge.

**tunneling** The main technology for achieving a virtual private network; the placement of data packets inside other data packets.

**twisted-pair cable** Cables made of copper wires that are twisted around each other and are surrounded by a plastic jacket (such as traditional home phone wire).

## U

**ultrabook** A full-featured but lightweight laptop computer that features a low-power processor and a solid-state drive; it tries to reduce its size and weight to extend battery life without sacrificing performance.

**Uniform Resource Locator (URL)** A website's unique address; an example is microsoft.com.

**uninterruptible power supply (UPS)** A device designed to power a computer from large batteries for a brief period during a loss of electrical power.

**universal serial bus (USB) port** A port that can connect a wide variety of peripheral devices to the computer, including keyboards, printers, mice, smartphones, external hard drives, flash drives, and digital cameras.

**UNIX** An operating system originally conceived in 1969 by Ken Thompson and Dennis Ritchie of AT&T's Bell Labs. In 1974, the UNIX code was rewritten in the standard programming language C. Today there are various commercial versions of UNIX.

**unshielded twisted-pair (UTP) cable** The most popular transmission media option for Ethernet networks. UTP cable is composed of four pairs of wires that are twisted around each other to reduce electrical interference.

**unstructured data** Audio clips, video clips, pictures, and extremely large documents. Also called *binary large object (BLOB)*.

**User Datagram Protocol (UDP)** An Internet Protocol that creates data packets across the Internet.

**user interface** Part of the operating system that enables individuals to interact with the computer.

**utility program** A small program that performs many of the general housekeeping tasks for the computer, such as system maintenance and file compression.

## V

**validation** The process of ensuring that data entered into a field of a database meets specified guidelines.

**validation rule** In a database, generally defined as part of the data dictionary and specified in the field properties for each field; violations result in an error message and a suggested action.

**variable** Each input and output item the program manipulates.

**variable declaration** Tells the operating system that the program needs to allocate storage space in RAM.

**VBScript** A subset of Visual Basic, used to introduce dynamic decision making into web pages.

**vertical market software** Software that's developed for and customized to a specific industry's needs (such as a wood inventory system for a sawmill) as opposed to software that's useful across a range of industries (such as word processing software).

**video card (video adapter)** An expansion card that's installed inside a system unit to translate binary data (the *1*s and *0*s the computer uses) into the images viewed on the monitor.

**video graphics array (VGA) port** A port to which a cathode ray tube monitor connects.

**video log (vlog or video blog)** A personal online journal that uses video as the primary content in addition to text, images, and audio.

**video memory** Random access memory that's included as part of a video card.

**virtual memory** The space on the hard drive where the operating system stores data if there isn't enough random access memory to hold all of the programs you're currently trying to run.

**virtual private network (VPN)** A network that uses the public Internet communications infrastructure to build a secure, private network among various locations.

**virtualization** Using specialized software to make individual physical servers behave as though they are more than one physical device.

**virus** A computer program that attaches itself to another computer program (known as the host program) and attempts to spread itself to other computers when files are exchanged.

**virus signature** A portion of the virus code that's unique to a particular computer virus and that makes it identifiable by antivirus software.

**Visual Basic (VB)** A programming language used to build a wide range of Windows applications.

**visual programming** In programming languages that support Windows programming, programmers can use the mouse to lay out on the screen where the scroll bars and buttons will be in the application; the code needed to explain this to the computer is then written automatically.

**Voice over Internet Protocol (VoIP)** A technology that facilitates making telephone calls across the Internet instead of using conventional telephone lines.

**volatile storage** Temporary storage, such as in random access memory. When the power is off, the data in volatile storage is cleared out.

## W

**warm boot** The process of restarting the system while it's powered on.

**Web 2.0** Tools and web-based services that emphasize online collaboration and sharing among users.

**web-based application** A program that's hosted on a website and that doesn't require installation on the computer.

**web-based e-mail** A type of e-mail system that's managed by a web browser and that allows access to e-mail from the web.

**web browser (browser)** Software installed on a computer system that allows individuals to locate, view, and navigate the web.

**web page–authoring software** Programs you can use to design interactive web pages without knowing any HyperText Markup Language (HTML) code.

**web server** A computer running a specialized operating system that enables it to host web pages (and other information) and to provide requested web pages to clients.

**web services** Part of the Microsoft .NET Framework, programs that a website uses to make information available to other websites.

**webcam** A small camera that sits on top of a computer monitor (connected to the computer by a cable) or that's built into a laptop computer and is usually used to transfer live video.

**webcast** The broadcast of audio or video content over the Internet. Unlike a podcast, a webcast is not updated automatically.

**website** A location on the web.

**white-hat hacker (ethical hacker)** A hacker who breaks into systems just for the challenge of it (and who doesn't wish to steal or wreak havoc on the systems). Such hackers tout themselves as experts who are performing a needed service for society by helping companies realize the vulnerabilities that exist in their systems.

**whole-house surge protector** A surge protector that's installed on (or near) the breaker panel of a home and that protects all electronic devices in the home from power surges.

**wide area network (WAN)** A network made up of local area networks (LANs) connected over long distances.

**wiki** A type of website that allows anyone visiting the site to change its content by adding, removing, or editing the content.

**Windows** An operating system by Microsoft that incorporates a user-friendly, graphical interface.

**Windows 8** Newest release of Microsoft's operating system that provides, a new interface optimized for touch-screen devices.

**Windows 8 apps** Applications specifically designed to run in the Windows 8 interface; these apps are displayed full screen, without borders or controls.

**Windows 8 interface** New interface designed for Windows 8; features large type with clean, readable block images inspired by metropolitan service signs such as those found on bus stations and subways.

**Windows account** A tool for allowing multiple people to share a Windows 8 computer while maintaining individual settings and preferences.

**wireless access point (WAP)** Gives wireless devices a sending and receiving connection point to the network.

**wireless fidelity (WiFi)** The 802.11 standard for wireless data transmissions established by the Institute of Electrical and Electronics Engineers (IEEE).

**wireless Internet service provider (wireless ISP)** An ISP that provides service to wireless devices such as smartphones.

**wireless network interface card (wireless NIC)** A special network adapter card that allows a computing device to connect to a network using wireless access.

**wireless range extender** A device that amplifies your wireless signal to get it out to parts of your home that are experiencing poor connectivity.

**wizard** A step-by-step guide that walks a user through the necessary steps to complete a complicated task.

**word processing software** Programs used to create and edit written documents such as papers, letters, and résumés.

**World Wide Web (WWW or the web)** The part of the Internet used the most. What distinguishes the web from the rest of the Internet are (1) its use of common communication protocols (such as Transmission Control Protocol/Internet Protocol, or TCP/IP) and special languages (such as the HyperText Markup Language, or HTML) that enable different computers to talk to each other and display information in compatible formats and (2) its use of special links (called hyperlinks) that enable users to jump from one place to another in the web.

**worm** A program that attempts to travel between systems through network connections to spread infections. Worms can run independently of host file execution and are active in spreading themselves.

## Z

**zombie** A computer that's controlled by a hacker who uses it to launch attacks on other computer systems.

# Index